AF777289

4

NOW READ THE CHAPTER AGAIN, SLOWLY AND CAREFULLY. Pay particular attention to the key terms, which are printed in bold type and defined again in the margins. Highlight the three or four most important points in each major section, and copy them into your notes. Be sure to include the page number where they appear for reference later. Look for answers to any questions you jotted in the margins. Study the artwork in the chapter, too, because the figures present important data and summarize key points; write your own brief note detailing each figure's main point in the margin. Read the photo captions carefully and test your judgment by tackling the questions posed in each.

5

USE THE EXTRA STUDY FEATURES IN EACH CHAPTER TO MAKE YOUR STUDY AN ACTIVE LEARNING EXPERIENCE.

- Try to answer the boxed "Thinking Critically" questions in the margins; if you can't, review the section you just read and try again before you move on.
- The "Myth-Fact" boxes correct common misconceptions about criminal justice; test the accuracy of your thinking against these myths.
- The "CJ Online" activities direct you to Internet sites to research real-world data and criminal cases. Make notes to help you recall what you learn there.
- Use the "Careers in Criminal Justice" boxes as a study break. These boxes introduce you to real people working in the field of criminal justice and the day-to-day challenges they encounter on the job.

6

AFTER REREADING THE CHAPTER, REREAD THE SUMMARY. Be sure you understand each of the main points and have completely mastered all the concepts listed under each chapter objective. These represent the minimum you need to know after your careful reading of the chapter. If you feel weak in any area, stop, reread, and review. Make sure your notes are complete and that you have not overlooked anything important.

7

STUDY THE KEY TERMS AGAIN. Try writing the definitions on a separate sheet of paper without looking them up first. You can refresh your memory of the key terms by looking at the page number where each first appears (see the list following the summary) or by skimming the chapter again and looking for the definitions in the margins. Make sure you are very familiar with the vocabulary of criminal justice before you go on.

CONTINUED ON INSIDE BACK COVER

IMPORTANT:

HERE IS YOUR REGISTRATION CODE TO ACCESS YOUR PREMIUM McGRAW-HILL ONLINE RESOURCES.

For key premium online resources you need THIS CODE to gain access. Once the code is entered, you will be able to use the Web resources for the length of your course.

If your course is using **WebCT** or **Blackboard**, you'll be able to use this code to access the McGraw-Hill content within your instructor's online course.

Access is provided if you have purchased a new book. If the registration code is missing from this book, the registration screen on our Website, and within your WebCT or Blackboard course, will tell you how to obtain your new code.

Registering for McGraw-Hill Online Resources

To gain access to your McGraw-Hill web resources simply follow the steps below:

1. USE YOUR WEB BROWSER TO GO TO: **www.mhhe.com/bohm4**
2. CLICK ON **FIRST TIME USER**.
3. ENTER THE REGISTRATION CODE* PRINTED ON THE TEAR-OFF BOOKMARK ON THE RIGHT.
4. AFTER YOU HAVE ENTERED YOUR REGISTRATION CODE, CLICK **REGISTER**.
5. FOLLOW THE INSTRUCTIONS TO SET-UP YOUR PERSONAL UserID AND PASSWORD.
6. WRITE YOUR UserID AND PASSWORD DOWN FOR FUTURE REFERENCE. KEEP IT IN A SAFE PLACE.

TO GAIN ACCESS to the McGraw-Hill content in your instructor's **WebCT** or **Blackboard** course simply log in to the course with the UserID and Password provided by your instructor. Enter the registration code exactly as it appears in the box to the right when prompted by the system. You will only need to use the code the first time you click on McGraw-Hill content.

Thank you, and welcome to your McGraw-Hill online resources!

Mc Graw Hill Higher Education

* YOUR REGISTRATION CODE CAN BE USED ONLY ONCE TO ESTABLISH ACCESS. IT IS NOT TRANSFERABLE.

0-07-297526-1 T/A BOHM: INTRODUCTION TO CRIMINAL JUSTICE, 4/E

MCGRAW-HILL

ONLINE RESOURCES

REGISTRATION CODE

DG6Z-1CMX-917N-AEZG-FM7N

Mc Graw Hill Higher Education

INTRODUCTION TO

CRIMINAL JUSTICE

Acknowledgments

This book, like any book, is the product of a collaborative effort. We would like to acknowledge and thank the many people who helped to make this and previous editions possible. First, our thanks go to **Kevin I. Minor** and **H. Preston Elrod,** both at Eastern Kentucky University, for their significant contributions to the chapters on corrections and the juvenile justice system, respectively. We would also like to thank the following colleagues for their substantial help with revisions: **James R. Acker,** State University of New York at Albany (Chapter 4: The Rule of Law); **John O. Smykla,** University of South Alabama (Chapter 12: Community Corrections); and **Donna M. Bishop,** Northeastern University (Chapter 13: Juvenile Justice). In addition, for their insightful reviews, criticism, helpful suggestions, and information, we would like to thank:

Brandon Applegate
University of Central Florida

Richard L. Ashbaugh
Clackamas Community College

Gregg Barak
Eastern Michigan University

David Barlow
Fayetteville State University

Michael Barrett
Ashland University

Denny Bebout
Central Ohio Technical College

Anita Blowers
University of North Carolina at Charlotte

Robert J. Boyer
Luzerne Country Community College

William D. Burrell
Probation Services Division, State of New Jersey

Michael Cain
Coastal Bend Community College

Vincent J. Capozzella
Jefferson Community College

Jonathan Cella
Central Texas Community College

Charles Chastain
University of Arkansas at Little Rock

Daryl Cullison
Columbus State Community College

Hank DiMatteo
New Mexico State University

Vicky Dorworth
Montgomery College

Joyce K. Dozier
Wilmington College

Mary Ann Eastep
University of Central Florida

Randy Eastep
Brevard Community College

Robert R. Eiggins
Cedarville College

John W. Flickinger
Tiffin University

Kenneth A. Frayer
Schoolcraft College at Radcliff

David O. Friedrichs
University of Scranton

Rodney Friery
Jacksonville State University

Alex Greenberg
Niagara County Community College

Bob Hale
Southeastern Louisiana University

David O. Harding
Ohio University at Chillicothe

Stuart Henry
Wayne State University

Joseph Hogan
Central Texas College

Thomas E. Holdren
Muskingum Technical College

James Houston
Grand Valley State University

James L. Hudson
Clark State Community College

W. Richard Janikowski
University of Memphis

Lamar Jordan
Southern Utah University

Don Knueve
Defence College

Peter C. Kratcoski
Kent State University

Gregory C. Leavitt
Green River Community College

Vivian Lord
University of North Carolina at Charlotte

Karol Lucken
University of Central Florida

Richard Lumb
State University of New York at Brockport

Kathleen Maguire
Hindelang Criminal Justice Research Center

Bradley Martin
University of Findlay

Richard M. Martin
Elgin Community College

Alida Merlo
Indiana University of Pennsylvania

Dale Mooso
San Antonio College

James Newman
Rio Hondo College

Sarah Nordin
Solano Community College

Les Obert
Casper College

Nancy Oesch
Florida Metropolitan University

Angela Ondrus
Owens Community College

Mary Carolyn Purtill
San Joaquin Delta College

Jerome Randall
University of Central Florida

Matthew Robinson
Appalachian State University

Joseph B. Sanborn, Jr.
University of Central Florida

Martin D. Schwartz
Ohio University

Lance Selva
Middle Tennessee State University

David Slaughter
University of Central Florida

James E. Smith
West Valley College

Jeffrey B. Spelman
North Central Technical College

Clayton Steenberg
Arkansas State University at Mountain Home

Gene Stephens
University of South Carolina

James Stinchcomb
Miami-Dade Community College

David Streater
Catawba Valley Community College

William L. Tafoya
University of Illinois of Chicago

Henry A. Townsend
Washtenaw Community College

Roger D. Turner
Shelby State Community College

Ronald E. Vogel
California State University at Long Beach

Harold Williamson
Northeastern Louisiana University

Ross Wolf
University of Central Florida

Peter Wood
Mississippi State University

We would also like to thank **Jack Bohm,** Leawood, Kansas; **Richard Bohm,** New York, New York; and **Lorie Klumb,** Denver, Colorado, for their help with this book. Finally, we would like to express our appreciation to our families and friends for their understanding and patience over the several years we have worked on this project.

INTRODUCTION TO

CRIMINAL JUSTICE

FOURTH EDITION

ROBERT M. BOHM
University of Central Florida

KEITH N. HALEY
Tiffin University

McGraw Hill

Boston Burr Ridge, IL Dubuque, IA Madison, WI New York San Francisco St. Louis
Bangkok Bogotá Caracas Kuala Lumpur Lisbon London Madrid Mexico City
Milan Montreal New Delhi Santiago Seoul Singapore Sydney Taipei Toronto

INTRODUCTION TO CRIMINAL JUSTICE

Published by McGraw-Hill, a business unit of The McGraw-Hill Companies, Inc., 1221 Avenue of the Americas, New York, NY, 10020.

This book is printed on acid-free paper.

1 2 3 4 5 6 7 8 9 0 DOW/DOW 0 9 8 7 6 5 4

ISBN 0-07-296116-3

Publisher: *Phillip A. Butcher*
Senior sponsoring editor: *Carolyn Henderson Meier*
Senior marketing manager: *Daniel M. Loch*
Media producer: *Jessica Bodie*
Senior project manager: *Christina Thornton-Villagomez*
Senior production supervisor: *Carol A. Bielski*
Senior designer: *Gino Cieslik*
Lead supplement producer: *Marc Mattson*
Photo research coordinator: *Alexandra Ambrose*
Photo researcher: *Judy Mason*
Art editor: *C. Cristin Yancey*
Permissions editor: *Marty Granahan*
Cover and interior design: *Ellen Pettengell*
Typeface: *9.5/12 New Astor*
Compositor: *The GTS Companies/York, PA Campus*
Printer: *R.R. Donnelley and Sons Inc.*

Library of Congress Cataloging-in-Publication Data

Bohm, Robert M.
Introduction to criminal justice / Robert Bohm, Keith Haley.—4th ed.
p. cm.
Includes index.
ISBN 0-07-296116-3 (alk. paper)
1. Criminal justice, Administration of—United States. 2. Crime—United States 3. Criminal law—United States. I. Haley, Keith N. II. Title.
HV9950.B63 2005
364.973—dc22

2003066001

Dedication

To my wife, Linda Taconis, with love.

Robert M. Bohm

To my wife, Shelby, and daughter, Jill, with love.

Keith N. Haley

About the Authors

Robert M. Bohm is professor of Criminal Justice and Legal Studies at the University of Central Florida in Orlando. He has also been a faculty member in the Departments of Criminal Justice at the University of North Carolina at Charlotte (1989–1995) and at Jacksonville State University in Alabama (1979–1989). From 1973 to 1974, he worked for the Jackson County Department of Corrections in Kansas City, Missouri, first as a corrections officer and later as an instructor/counselor in the Model Inmate Employment Program, a Law Enforcement Assistance Administration sponsored–work-release project. He received his PhD in Criminology from Florida State University in 1980. He has published numerous journal articles and book chapters in the areas of criminal justice and criminology. Besides being the coauthor of *Introduction to Criminal Justice,* 4th ed. (McGraw-Hill, 2005), he is the editor of *The Death Penalty in America: Current Research,* the author of *A Primer on Crime and Delinquency Theory,* 2nd ed., and *Deathquest II: An Introduction to the Theory and Practice of Capital Punishment in the United States,* 2nd ed., and an editor (with James R. Acker and Charles S. Lanier) of *America's Experiment with Capital Punishment: Reflections on the Past, Present, and Future of the Ultimate Sanction,* 2nd ed. He has been active in the American Society of Criminology, the Southern Criminal Justice Association, and especially the Academy of Criminal Justice Sciences, having served as Trustee-at-Large (1987–90), Second Vice-President (1990–91), First Vice-President (1991–92), and President (1992–93). In 1989, he was selected as the *Outstanding Educator of the Year* by the Southern Criminal Justice Association. In 1999, he was elected a Fellow of the Academy of Criminal Justice Sciences and, in 2001, he was presented with the Founder's Award of the Academy of Criminal Justice Sciences.

Keith N. Haley is professor of Criminal Justice, teaching in both graduate and undergraduate degree programs in the School of Criminal Justice, and associate vice president for special projects at Tiffin University. Mr. Haley has also been the dean of the School of Criminal Justice, and the dean of the School of Off-Campus Learning at Tiffin University. He has acted as the primary contact for the TU MBA program in Bucharest, Romania, and the head of the Tiffin University Romania Study team that worked to establish a Master of Community Justice Administration degree program at the University of Bucharest. He has also served as coordinator of the criminal justice programs at Collin County Community College in Texas; executive director of the Ohio Peace Officer Training Commission; chairman of the criminal justice program at the University of Cincinnati; police officer in Dayton, Ohio; community school director in Springfield, Ohio; director of the criminal justice program at Redlands Community College in Oklahoma and electronics repairman and NCO in the U.S. Marine Corps. Haley holds a BS in Education from Wright State University and an MS in Criminal Justice from Michigan State University. He is the author, coauthor, and/or editor of 12 books, several book chapters, and many articles in criminal justice publications. He has served as a consultant to many public service, university, business, and industrial organizations on management, online learning, criminal justice research, and memory skills. Haley is also the secretary of the police section of the Academy of Criminal Justice Sciences. Haley received the 2001 Nikolai N. Khaladjan International Award for Innovation in Higher Education. The Khaladjan Award is given to the higher education program that is the most innovative and has the widest potential for impact on postsecondary education.

Brief Contents

Contents

PART ONE
The Foundations of Criminal Justice 1

CHAPTER ONE
Crime and Justice in the United States 3

CHAPTER TWO
Crime and Its Consequences 28

CHAPTER THREE

Explaining Crime 62

CHAPTER FOUR

The Rule of Law 102

PART TWO

Law Enforcement 143

CHAPTER FIVE

History and Structure of American Law Enforcement 144

HISTORY · OF
1658
Thief
Felon
The Rattle Watch

PART THREE

The Courts 263

CHAPTER EIGHT

The Administration of Justice 264

CHAPTER NINE

Sentencing, Appeals, and the Death Penalty 308

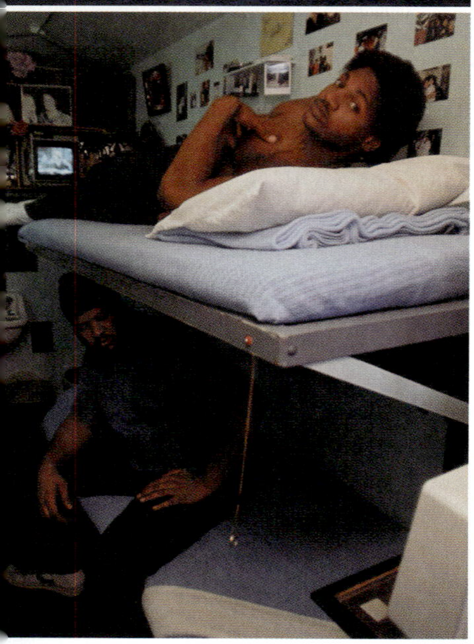

PART FOUR

Corrections 347

CHAPTER TEN

Institutional Corrections 348

CHAPTER ELEVEN

Prison Life, Inmate Rights, Release, and Recidivism 394

CHAPTER TWELVE

Community Corrections 422

PART FIVE

Additional Issues in Criminal Justice 471

CHAPTER THIRTEEN

Juvenile Justice 472

CHAPTER FOURTEEN

The Future of Criminal Justice in the United States 514

Careers in Criminal Justice Boxed Inserts

Preface

We are convinced that a good postsecondary education in criminal justice—and in liberal arts generally—can significantly improve the performance of most criminal justice personnel by equipping them, as this text does, to think critically, act ethically, and solve problems effectively. *Introduction to Criminal Justice,* Fourth Edition is not just for students interested in pursuing a career in criminal justice, however. It is also for students who simply want to learn more about this important social institution, which is vital to a free and democratic society.

All citizens need to know their legal rights and responsibilities. The better informed citizens are, the better able they are to protect themselves. A major theme of this book is that much of what the public "knows" about criminal justice in the United States is myth—that is, either wrong or significantly misunderstood. Consequently, in addition to presenting current, accurate information about criminal justice in the United States and generally accepted interpretations of historical and modern developments, this book "sets the record straight" in areas where, we believe, many people are being misled.

With the help of a quality education in criminal justice, people will feel more comfortable and better equipped to participate in criminal justice policy formulation. They will also be more effective in solving problems in their communities. They will have the critical thinking skills they need if they are to be constructive participants in a democratic nation and to have greater control over their own destinies.

The Fourth Edition

Since 9/11, many people who once had no fear of public transportation, especially air travel, now fear it, afraid that a bomb might explode onboard or that an airplane, for example, will be commandeered by terrorists who turn it into a weapon of mass destruction. People are even more suspicious of strangers, particularly of members of certain ethnic groups who before 9/11 caused little concern. We now live with a color-coded warning system that alerts us to the risk of terrorist attacks. In short, we now live in the Age of Terror.

The most significant change in this fourth edition of *Introduction to Criminal Justice* is the examination of criminal justice's new expanded role in the "war against terrorism." This war has caused the most dramatic transformation of the U.S. government in more than 50 years and has altered criminal justice at all levels of government in many ways. For example, a new Department of Homeland Security has been created. The top priority of the FBI has shifted from being a federal police agency to being an intelligence and counterterrorism agency. New laws have been passed to provide governments with broad new powers to combat terrorism. Those laws have changed many of the traditional rules of criminal justice. In this fourth edition, the criminal justice response to terrorism receives serious treatment in several chapters. A list of those additions and many others is provided below.

In addition to integrating detailed coverage of terrorism and updating the text throughout with the latest available statistics and research, this edition also features coverage of some of today's highest-profile criminal investigations and cases—from MCI/WorldCom to Kobe Bryant to Winona Ryder to Richard Reid (the "Shoe Bomber") to John Geoghan (the "Pedophile Priest")—as well as expanded discussion of some of today's most pressing issues in criminal justice:

- Chapter 4, "The Rule of Law," includes new material on Barry Scheck and Peter Neufeld's Innocence Project as well as on the USA PATRIOT Act and the potential threat it poses to traditional procedural rights.
- Chapter 5, "The History and Structure of American Law Enforcement," has been extensively revised and now features coverage of the Department of Homeland Security, the war on terrorism, the FBI's new role in the war on terrorism, and the role of private security in the fight against terrorism.
- Chapter 6, "Policing: Roles, Styles, and Functions," has also been extensively revised and now includes an extended discussion of terrorism (beyond the basics in Chapter 5), drug enforcement, and crime mapping.

- Chapter 8, "The Administration of Justice," now features a discussion of a recent national survey of prosecutors, as well as material on the Foreign Intelligence Surveillance Act (FISA) court, the nation's first "collections court," indigent defense systems, court caseflow management, the forfeiture of bonds and absconders, and hung juries.
- Chapter 10, "Institutional Corrections," includes new material on private correctional facilities; Camp Delta, the supermaximum security prison that holds suspected terrorists; mentally ill prisoners; and the populations, functions, architecture, and management of jails.
- Chapter 12, "Community Corrections," has new material about special conditions of probation, parole recidivism, home confinement, and electronic monitoring.
- Chapter 14, "The Future of Criminal Justice in the United States," now features extended discussions of identity theft and transnational organized crime as well as a new closing section, "Criminal Justice in the Age of Terror."

Organization

This book is divided into fourteen chapters that are organized into five parts. Part I, "The Foundations of Criminal Justice," introduces students to the concepts of crime and justice as well as how crime impacts society, how it can be explained, and the rule of law. Part II, "Law Enforcement," is dedicated to the law enforcement component of criminal justice—its history, structure, roles, ethical issues, and challenges. Part III, "The Courts," focuses on the administration of justice, sentencing, appeals, and the court process as a whole. Part IV, "Corrections," introduces students to the corrections system, jails, prisons, alternative sanctions, community corrections, and release of prisoners back into the community. And finally, Part V, "Additional Issues in Criminal Justice," touches on some of the most pressing challenges in the system today: juvenile crime/justice, terrorism, transnational organized crime, and more.

Pedagogical Aids

Working together, the authors and editor have developed a learning system designed to help students get the most out of their first criminal justice course. This commitment to student success is evident from the very first pages of the text, which feature a unique roadmap to student success. This roadmap, titled "10 Steps to Success" and printed on the text's inside front and back covers, gives students all the tips and tools they need to excel in their first criminal justice course.

The Bohm/Haley commitment to student success goes well beyond these unique guidelines, however, for the learning system as a whole is without peer in Introduction to Criminal Justice textbooks. In addition to the many changes already mentioned, we have included a wealth of new photographs to make the book even more inviting and relevant for students. To this same end we have added chapter-opening *Crime Story* vignettes to this edition, giving the material a fresh flavor intended to motivate students to read on. Redesigned and carefully updated tables and figures highlight and amplify the text coverage. And chapter outlines, objectives, reviews, marginal definitions, and an end-of-book glossary all help students master the material. Other innovative learning tools include

- *Careers in Criminal Justice.* These mini-biographies highlight some of the most exciting career options available to criminal justice majors and keep the book relevant for students. For a complete list of these boxes, see page xv.
- *CJ Online.* These inserts enable students to explore chapter topics on the Net in a directed fashion.
- *FYI.* These sidebars present eye-opening additional information to retain students' interest and keep them thinking about what they are reading.
- *Myth vs. Fact.* These inserts debunk common misconceptions about the system and alert students to the need to question what they see in the media.
- *Thinking Critically.* These sections throughout the chapter challenge students to think about and apply chapter concepts.

We are especially proud of our comprehensive end-of-chapter review sections. In these sections, we provide every kind of review and study tool students could need:

- *Summary*—a terrific study tool, because it is organized into sections that mirror the chapter-opening objectives exactly.
- *Key Terms*—a comprehensive list of the terms defined in the chapter, complete with page references to make it easy for students to go back and review further.
- *Review Questions*—study questions that allow students to test their knowledge and prepare for exams.
- *In the Field Activities*—unique experiential exercises that enable students to broaden their understanding of chapter material by taking it to the next level.
- *On the Net Exercises*—still more Internet-based exercises for today's Net-oriented learner.
- *Critical Thinking Questions*—unique scenario-based activities that challenge students to apply what they've learned in the chapter.

Supplements Package

As a full-service publisher of quality educational products, McGraw-Hill does much more than just sell textbooks. The company creates and publishes an extensive array of print, video, and digital supplements for students and instructors. This edition of *Introduction to Criminal Justice* is accompanied by a comprehensive supplements package:

FOR THE STUDENT

- *Reel Justice CD-ROM*—this unique interactive movie takes the concept of active learning to a whole new level, enabling students to take on the role of one of the story's characters and influence key plot turns by making choices for that character. The movie, centered on a domestic violence incident that takes place in a college town, allows students to explore course concepts and terminology in a relevant and meaningful context. Movie segments are augmented by a robust array of review and assessment features. With this breakthrough learning tool, students can explore a wide variety of criminal justice issues first-hand—criminal responsibility; theories of crime causation; civil versus criminal law; police roles, functions, and ethics; the courts; and more—and master course concepts more completely than they could by just reading any text.
- *Online Learning Center Website*—an innovative, text-specific website featuring interactive cases and PowerWeb—online access to articles from the popular and scholarly press, weekly updates, daily news-feeds, and a search engine—as well as flashcards that can be used to master vocabulary, quizzes with feedback that students can use to study for exams, downloadable state supplements, and more.
- *CyberJustice Website*—this custom-crafted criminal justice supersite features a large library of URLs for help writing papers, a unique assortment of supplementary readings on terrorism, and much more.

FOR THE INSTRUCTOR

- *Instructor's Resource CD*—a single CD with an easy-to-use interface providing access to a wide array of important ancillaries:
    - *Instructor's Manual/Testbank*—detailed chapter outlines, key terms, overviews, lecture notes, and a complete testbank.
    - *Reel Justice Instructor's Guide*—teaching tips and notes that make it easy to integrate the *Reel Justice* CD into your course.
    - *Computerized Testbank*—easy-to-use computerized testing program for both Windows and Macintosh computers.
    - *PowerPoint Slides*—complete, chapter-by-chapter slide shows featuring text, art, figures, and tables.
- *Online Learning Center Website*—password-protected access to downloadable state supplements and other important instructor support materials and additional resources.
- *Reel Justice Lecture Launcher Videotape*—so even if you can't require students to use the CD, you can use the movie footage to jumpstart lectures in an exciting fashion.
- *NBC News Lecture Launcher Videotape*—unique video featuring brief clips from NBC News programs that can also be used to jumpstart lectures.
- *Full-Length Videotapes*—a wide variety of videotapes from the *Films for the Humanities and Social Sciences* series is available to adopters of the text.
- *Course Management Systems*—whether you use WebCT, Blackboard, e-College, or another course management system, McGraw-Hill will provide you with a cartridge that enables you either to conduct your course entirely online or to supplement your lectures with online material. And if your school does not yet have one of these course management systems, we can provide you with PageOut, an easy-to-use tool that allows you to create your own course Web page and access all material on the Online Learning Center.
- *Primis Online*—a unique database publishing system that allows instructors to create a customized text from material in this text or elsewhere and deliver that text to students electronically as an e-book or in print format via the bookstore.

In closing we would like to acknowledge the help and support we received from the McGraw-Hill staff: our editor Carolyn Henderson Meier, our project manager Christina Thornton-Villagomez, Gino Cieslik for the design, Alexandra Ambrose and Judy Mason for photo research and the rest of the team.

Robert Bohm
Keith Haley

A Guided Tour

COMPLETE COVERAGE OF TERRORISM

Complete coverage of the war on terrorism, the department of Homeland Security, the USA PATRIOT Act, Camp Delta, and more.

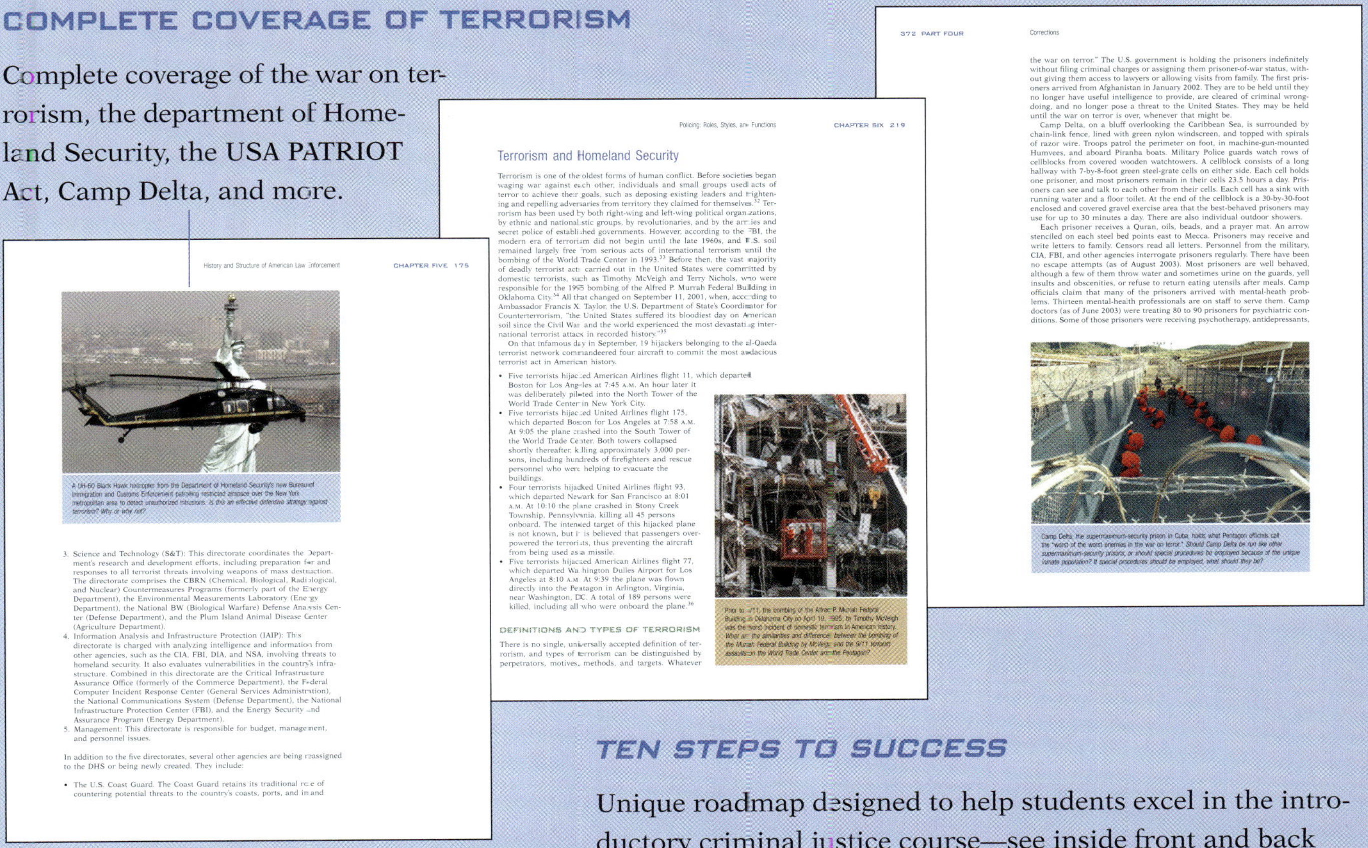

TEN STEPS TO SUCCESS

Unique roadmap designed to help students excel in the introductory criminal justice course—see inside front and back covers of this textbook.

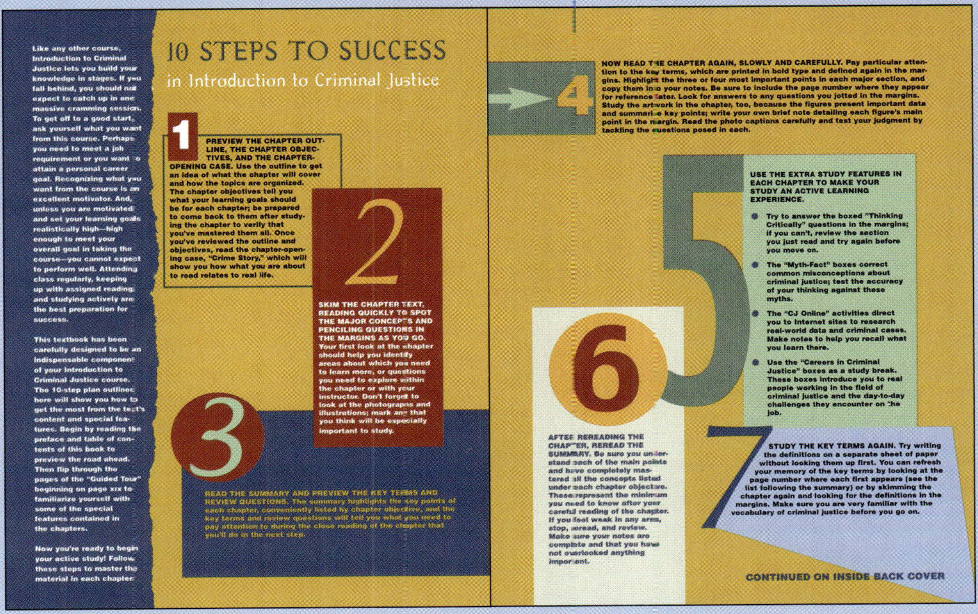

UP-TO-THE-MINUTE COVERAGE

High-profile events and cases taken from today's headlines keep the book current and relevant for today's students.

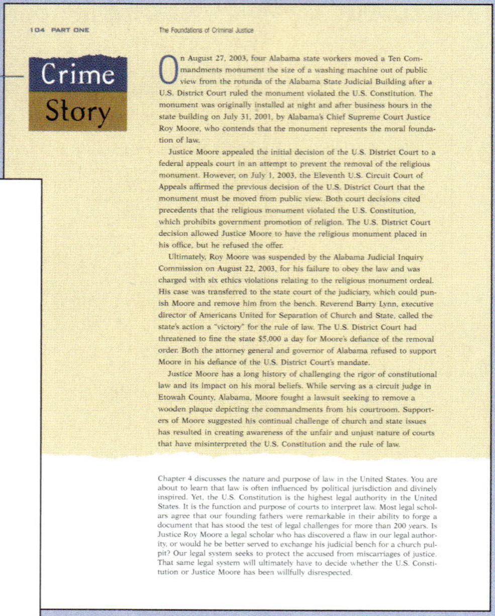
104 PART ONE The Foundations of Criminal Justice

Crime Story

On August 27, 2003, four Alabama state workers moved a Ten Commandments monument the size of a washing machine out of public view from the rotunda of the Alabama State Judicial Building after a U.S. District Court ruled the monument violated the U.S. Constitution. The monument was originally installed at night and after business hours in the state building on July 31, 2001, by Alabama's Chief Supreme Court Justice Roy Moore, who contends that the monument represents the moral foundation of law.

Justice Moore appealed the initial decision of the U.S. District Court to a federal appeals court in an attempt to prevent the removal of the religious monument. However, on July 1, 2003, the Eleventh U.S. Circuit Court of Appeals affirmed the previous decision of the U.S. District Court that the monument must be moved from public view. Both court decisions cited precedents that the religious monument violated the U.S. Constitution, which prohibits government promotion of religion. The U.S. District Court decision allowed Justice Moore to have the religious monument placed in his office, but he refused the offer.

Ultimately, Roy Moore was suspended by the Alabama Judicial Inquiry Commission on August 22, 2003, for his failure to obey the law and was charged with six ethics violations relating to the religious monument ordeal. His case was transferred to the state court of the judiciary, which could punish Moore and remove him from the bench. Reverend Barry Lynn, executive director of Americans United for Separation of Church and State, called the state's action a "victory" for the rule of law. The U.S. District Court had threatened to fine the state $5,000 a day for Moore's defiance of the removal order. Both the attorney general and governor of Alabama refused to support Moore in his defiance of the U.S. District Court's mandate.

Justice Moore has a long history of challenging the rigor of constitutional law and its impact on his moral beliefs. While serving as a circuit judge in Etowah County, Alabama, Moore fought a lawsuit seeking to remove a wooden plaque depicting the commandments from his courtroom. Supporters of Moore suggested his continual challenge of church and state issues has resulted in creating awareness of the unfair and unjust nature of courts that have misinterpreted the U.S. Constitution and the rule of law.

Chapter 4 discusses the nature and purpose of law in the United States. You are about to learn that law is often influenced by political jurisdiction and divinely inspired. Yet, the U.S. Constitution is the highest legal authority in the United States. It is the function and purpose of courts to interpret law. Most legal scholars agree that our founding fathers were remarkable in their ability to forge a document that has stood the test of legal challenges for more than 200 years. Is Justice Roy Moore a legal scholar who has discovered a flaw in our legal authority, or would he be better served to exchange his judicial bench for a church pulpit? Our legal system seeks to protect the accused from miscarriages of justice. That same legal system will ultimately have to decide whether the U.S. Constitution or Justice Moore has been willfully disrespected.

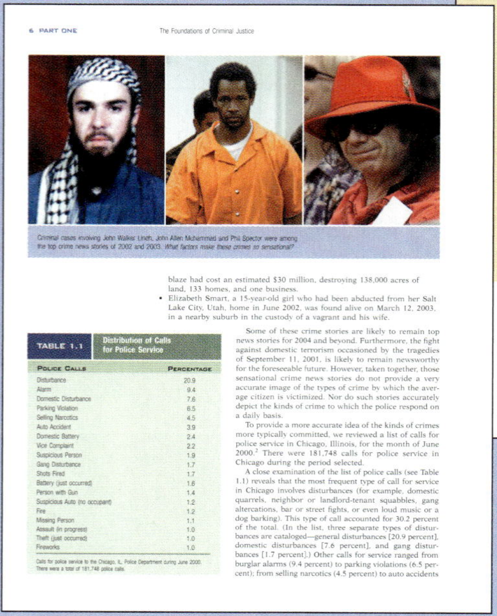
6 PART ONE The Foundations of Criminal Justice

Criminal cases involving John Walker Lindh, John Allen Muhammad and Phil Spector were among the top crime news stories of 2002 and 2003. *What factors make these crimes so sensational?*

blaze had cost an estimated $30 million, destroying 138,000 acres of land, 133 homes, and one business.

- Elizabeth Smart, a 15-year-old girl who had been abducted from her Salt Lake City, Utah, home in June 2002, was found alive on March 12, 2003, in a nearby suburb in the custody of a vagrant and his wife.

TABLE 1.1 Distribution of Calls for Police Service

Police Calls	Percentage
Disturbance	20.9
Alarm	9.4
Domestic Disturbance	7.6
Parking Violation	6.5
Selling Narcotics	4.5
Auto Accident	3.9
Domestic Battery	2.4
Vice Complaint	2.2
Suspicious Person	1.9
Gang Disturbance	1.7
Shots Fired	1.7
Battery (just occurred)	1.6
Person with Gun	1.4
Suspicious Auto (no occupant)	1.2
Fire	1.2
Missing Person	1.1
Assault (in progress)	1.0
Theft (just occurred)	1.0
Fireworks	1.0

Calls for police service to the Chicago, IL, Police Department during June 2000. There were a total of 181,748 police calls.

Some of these crime stories are likely to remain top news stories for 2004 and beyond. Furthermore, the fight against domestic terrorism occasioned by the tragedies of September 11, 2001, is likely to remain newsworthy for the foreseeable future. However, taken together, those sensational crime news stories do not provide a very accurate image of the types of crime by which the average citizen is victimized. Nor do such stories accurately depict the kinds of crime to which the police respond on a daily basis.

To provide a more accurate idea of the kinds of crimes more typically committed, we reviewed a list of calls for police service in Chicago, Illinois, for the month of June 2000.[2] There were 181,748 calls for police service in Chicago during the period selected.

A close examination of the list of police calls (see Table 1.1) reveals that the most frequent type of call for service in Chicago involves disturbances (for example, domestic quarrels, neighbor or landlord-tenant squabbles, gang altercations, bar or street fights, or even loud music or a dog barking). This type of call accounted for 30.2 percent of the total. (In the list, three separate types of disturbances are cataloged—general disturbances [20.9 percent], domestic disturbances [7.6 percent], and gang disturbances [1.7 percent].) Other calls for service ranged from burglar alarms (9.4 percent) to parking violations (6.5 percent); from selling narcotics (4.5 percent) to auto accidents

CHAPTER-OPENING PREVIEWS

Detailed chapter-opening objectives, outlines, and vignettes draw students in and help them focus on the chapter's most critical concepts.

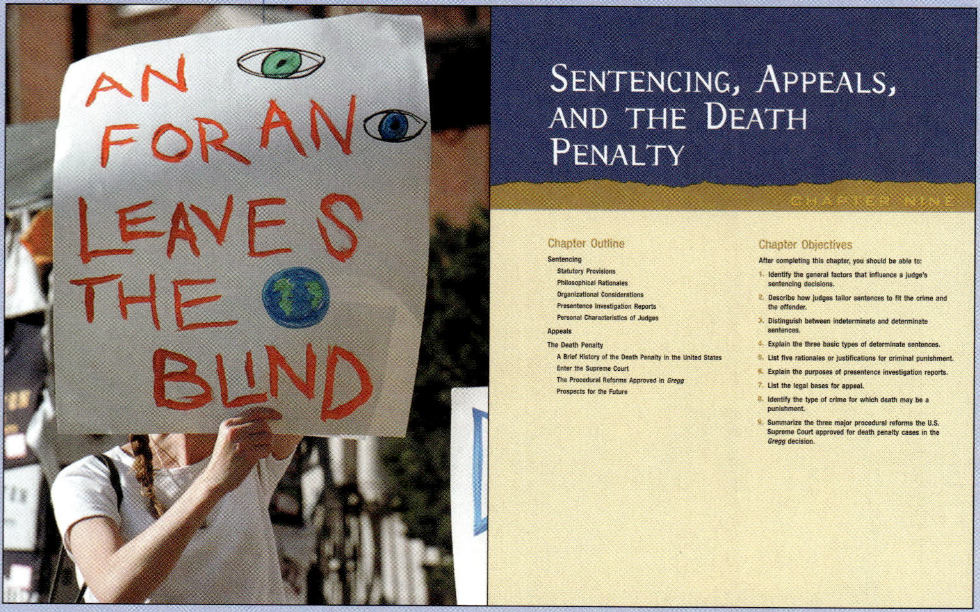

SENTENCING, APPEALS, AND THE DEATH PENALTY

CHAPTER NINE

Chapter Outline

- Sentencing
  - Statutory Provisions
  - Philosophical Rationales
  - Organizational Considerations
  - Presentence Investigation Reports
  - Personal Characteristics of Judges
- Appeals
- The Death Penalty
  - A Brief History of the Death Penalty in the United States
  - Enter the Supreme Court
  - The Procedural Reforms Approved in *Gregg*
  - Prospects for the Future

Chapter Objectives

After completing this chapter, you should be able to:

1. Identify the general factors that influence a judge's sentencing decisions.
2. Describe how judges tailor sentences to fit the crime and the offender.
3. Distinguish between indeterminate and determinate sentences.
4. Explain the three basic types of determinate sentences.
5. List five rationales or justifications for criminal punishment.
6. Explain the purposes of presentence investigation reports.
7. List the legal bases for appeal.
8. Identify the type of crime for which death may be a punishment.
9. Summarize the three major procedural reforms the U.S. Supreme Court approved for death penalty cases in the *Gregg* decision.

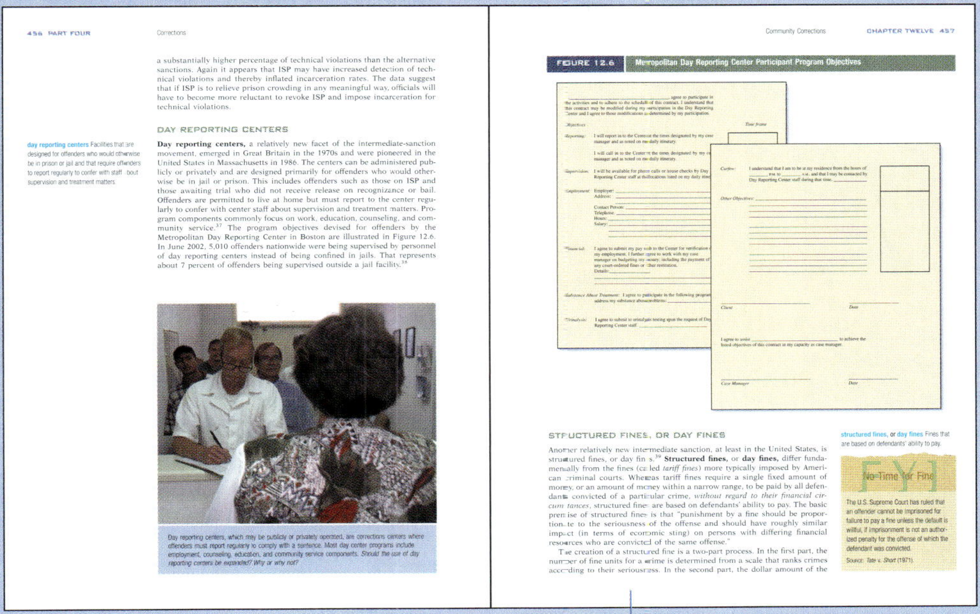

PLENTIFUL VISUALS

Photographs with thought-provoking captions and questions, as well as figures and tables on almost every page of the text bring material to life.

CAREERS IN CRIMINAL JUSTICE BOXES

Boxed inserts highlight the wide array of career options available to the criminal justice major.

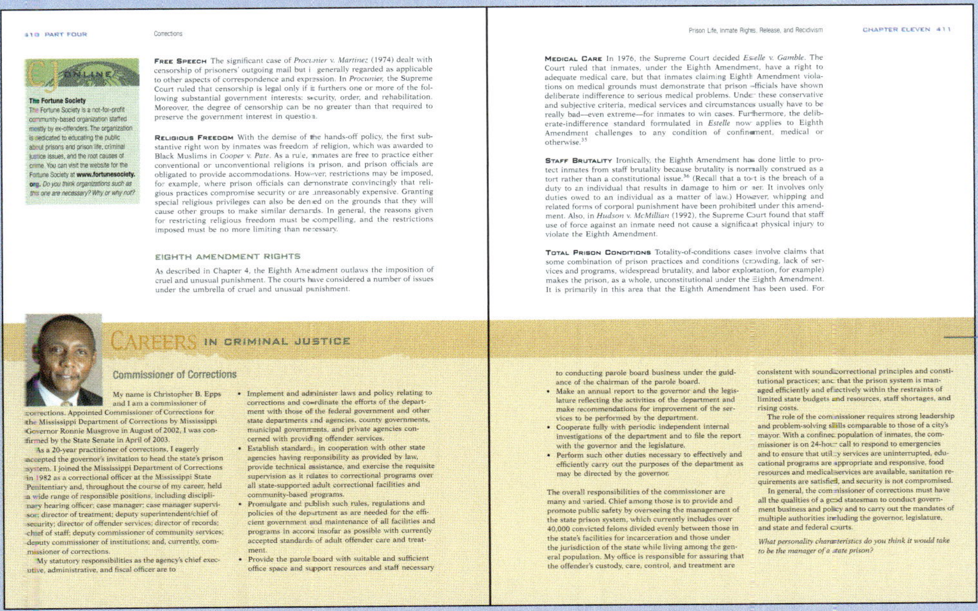

CJ ONLINE INSERTS

Websites that students can visit to explore chapter topics on the Net in greater depth.

MYTH VS. FACT BOXES

Boxed inserts debunk common misconceptions about criminal justice and alerts students to the need to question what they see in the media.

FYI SIDEBARS

Margin notes that present eye-opening information and keep students thinking about what they are reading.

THINKING CRITICALLY SECTIONS

End-of-section critical thinking questions throughout every chapter challenge students to apply chapter concepts.

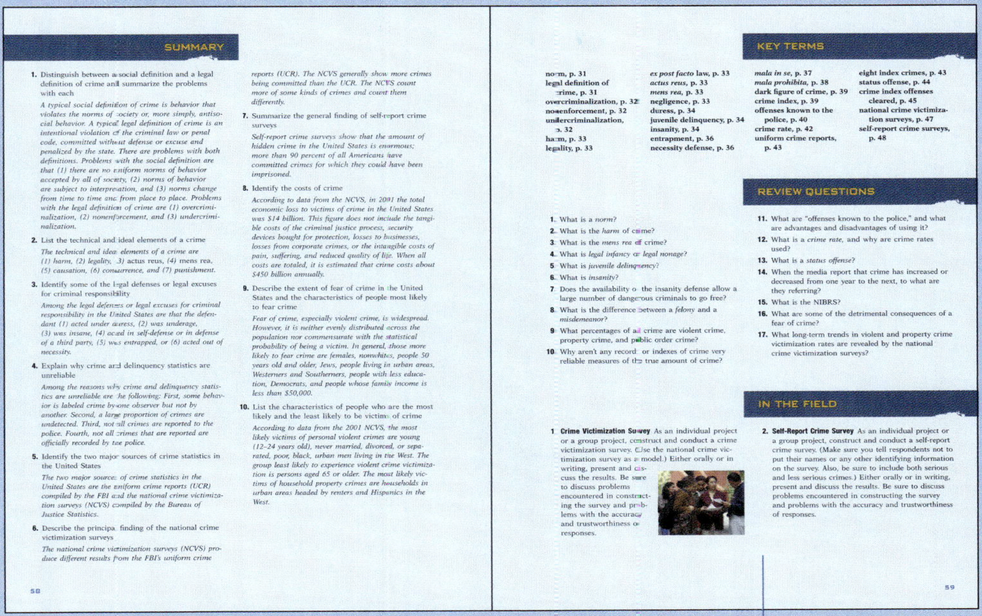

EASY-TO-USE CHAPTER REVIEWS

Clear, concise chapter summaries, key terms lists, and review questions provide students with essential study materials.

UNIQUE END-OF-CHAPTER EXERCISES

End-of-chapter critical thinking, experiential, and Internet activities challenge students to explore and think critically about chapter issues.

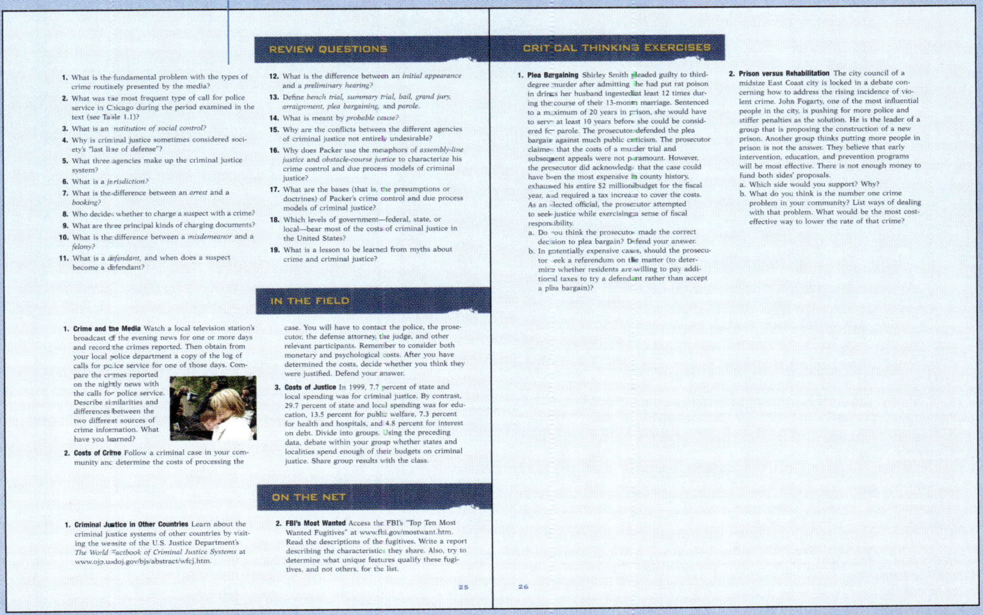

REEL JUSTICE INTERACTIVE MOVIE CD-ROM

A unique interactive movie that takes the concept of active learning to a whole new level, enabling students to take on the role of one of the story's characters and influence key plot turns by making choices for that character.

The movie, centered on a domestic violence incident that takes place in a college town, allows students to explore course concepts and terminology in a relevant and meaningful context. Movie segments are augmented by a robust array of review and assessment features.

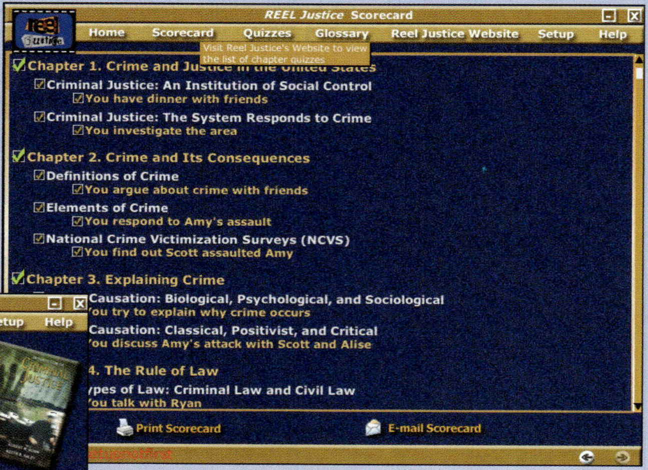

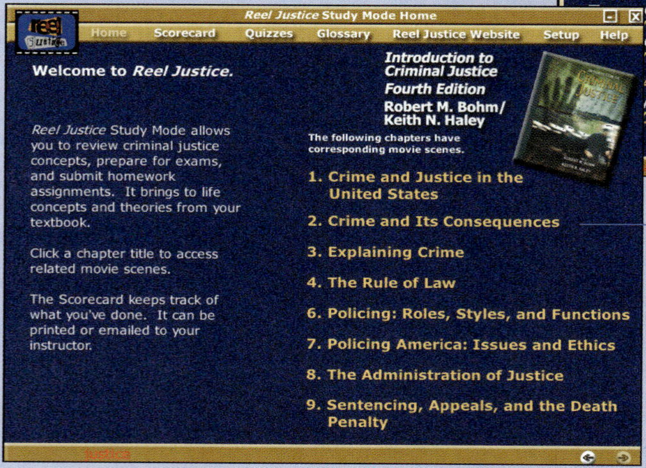

With this breakthrough learning tool, students can explore a wide variety of criminal justice issues firsthand—criminal responsibility, theories of crime causation, civil vs. criminal law, police roles, functions, and ethics, the courts, and more—and master course concepts more completely than they could by just reading any text.

ONLINE LEARNING CENTER WEBSITE

Book-specific website features unique interactive cases as well as chapter quizzes, online access to a wealth of popular press and scholarly articles, flashcards that can be used to master vocabulary, and many other chapter review tools.

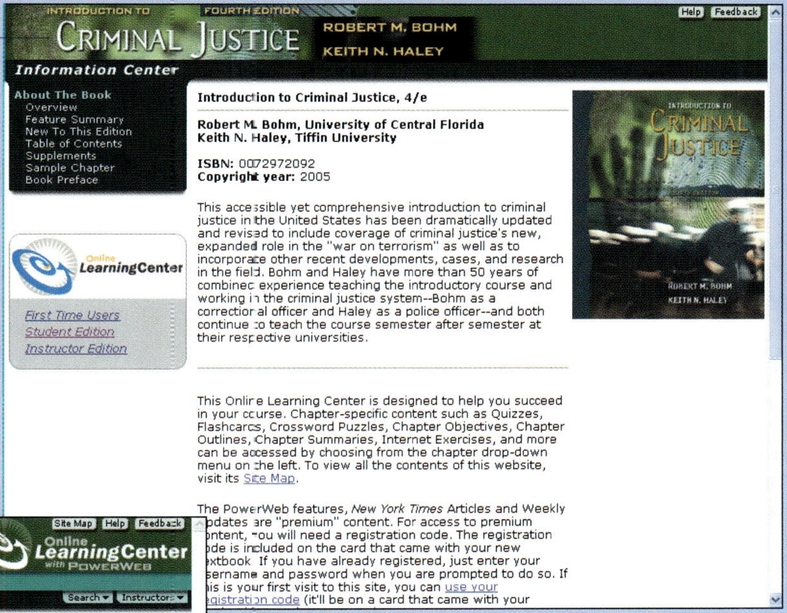

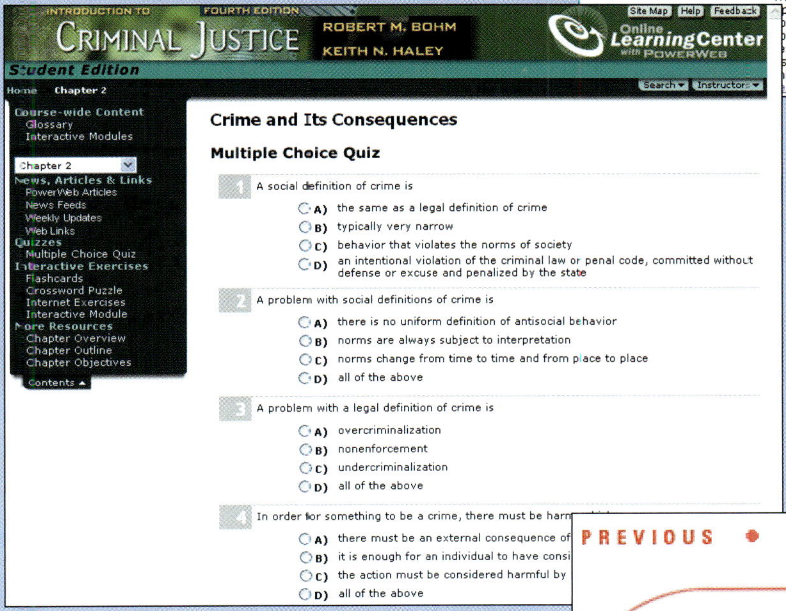

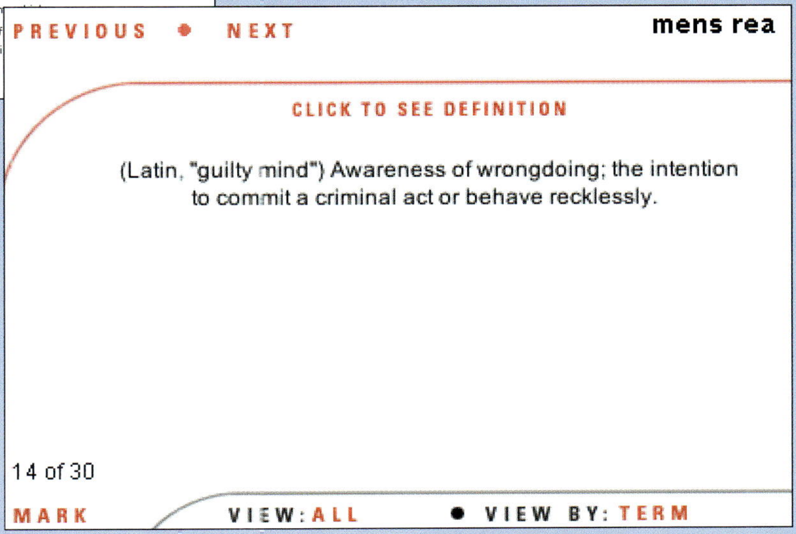

PART ONE

THE FOUNDATIONS OF CRIMINAL JUSTICE

CRIME AND JUSTICE IN THE UNITED STATES

CHAPTER ONE

Chapter Outline

Crime in the United States

Criminal Justice: An Institution of Social Control

Criminal Justice: The System

- Police
- Courts
- Corrections

Criminal Justice: The Nonsystem

Two Models of Criminal Justice

- The Crime Control Model
- The Due Process Model
- Crime Control versus Due Process

Costs of Criminal Justice

Myths About Crime and Criminal Justice

Chapter Objectives

After completing this chapter, you should be able to:

1. Describe how the type of crime routinely presented by the media compares with crime routinely committed.
2. Identify institutions of social control and explain what makes criminal justice an institution of social control.
3. Summarize how the criminal justice system responds to crime.
4. Explain why criminal justice in the United States is sometimes considered a nonsystem.
5. Point out major differences between Packer's crime control and due process models.
6. Describe the costs of criminal justice in the United States and compare those costs among federal, state, and local governments.
7. Explain how myths about crime and criminal justice affect the criminal justice system.

Crime Story

On June 30, 2003, Los Angeles Laker, Kobe Bryant, checked into a luxury resort in Edwards, Colorado. Within days, the nation would learn that the 24-year-old basketball superstar was a suspect in the sexual assault of a teenaged hotel employee during his stay at the prestigious mountain resort. On July 4, Bryant was arrested for raping the young girl. Bryant would later admit in a televised news conference, with his wife at his side, that he did have sexual relations with the young hotel employee, although he adamantly denied raping the girl. The small, close-knit Colorado town of Eagle, where the trial would likely be held, braced itself for an onslaught of media coverage of what some observers suggested would be the trial of the century.

Various news media and sport reporters seemed both shocked and astonished that Bryant, who has been described as having a squeaky-clean image with the National Basketball Association, could be capable of committing such an act. Almost immediately following the news of Bryant's arrest, media reports began to circulate that the alleged victim might have devised a scheme to extort money from Bryant. Reportedly, some Internet websites publicly identified the teenaged victim and circulated photographs of her in an apparent attempt to defame her character and suggest she might not be a victim at all. Some of Kobe Bryant's most loyal fans posted various Web-based articles devoted to proclaiming the innocence of the highly respected basketball star.

The obsession with reporting high-profile criminal cases in the United States and an attempt by various news sources to satisfy the almost insatiable public appetite for information frequently collide with constitutional protections afforded by law, such as the right to a fair trial and due process. England, by contrast, prohibits any detailed news reports of a criminal case before a trial is held. Its law is based on the notion that any pretrial publicity might erode a defendant's presumption of innocence. Only after the trial has ended is England's news media allowed to report the details of particular criminal cases.

Does the criminal justice system in the United States encourage criminal defendants of high status and reputation, such as Kobe Bryant, to be given special treatment? As you are about to learn in Chapter 1, the criminal justice system operates both formally and informally. The social cost of increasing the speed of processing cases through our criminal justice system through plea bargaining often results in the accused giving up the constitutional right of due process normally afforded through criminal trials. If Kobe Bryant pled guilty to a lesser charge in exchange for probation, this would circumvent the trial process and likely bring a quick end to a publicly embarrassing and damaging story. But is this fair if Bryant is innocent? On the other hand, is it fair to deny a teenaged rape victim the opportunity to tell her story before the court? If he is guilty, is it fair that Bryant escape the full measure of the law? Such issues illustrate the tensions that exist in the effort to administer justice in the United States.

Crime in the United States

Every day we are flooded with reports of crime in newspapers, magazines, and radio and television news programs. We also see crime in TV docudramas; on such popular shows as the fictional *NYPD Blue, Law & Order,* and the *CSI* series; and on the reality-based *America's Most Wanted, Cops,* and *Unsolved Mysteries.* There is also Court TV, an entire network devoted to crime and justice issues. Crime is also a favorite subject of movies and novels. Unfortunately, some of us encounter crime more directly, as victims. No wonder crime is a top concern of the American public.

We should keep in mind, however, that the crimes presented by the media are usually more sensational than the crimes routinely committed. Consider some of the top crime news stories in the United States at the end of 2002 and through mid-May 2003:[1]

- On October 4, 2002, John Walker Lindh, a U.S. citizen captured by U.S. forces while he was fighting with Afghanistan's Taliban militia, was sentenced to 20 years in prison.
- Sniper attacks between October 2 and October 22, 2002, killed 10 people and wounded 3 others in the Washington, DC, area. On October 24, police arrested suspects John Allen Muhammad, 41, and John Lee Malvo, 17, who by November 14 were charged or suspected in a total of 23 shooting incidents across the country.
- Richard Reid, the foiled "shoe bomber," who in October 2002 had pleaded guilty to attempting to bomb a trans-Atlantic flight, was sentenced on January 30, 2003, by a judge in the U.S. District Court in Boston to life in prison. Reid was the first admitted al-Qaeda member to be sentenced in the United States since September 11, 2001.
- Betty Loren-Maltese, former town president of Cicero, Illinois, was sentenced on January 9, 2003, to 8 years and 1 month in prison for participating in the theft of $12 million from the town's employee insurance fund. She was also fined $100,000 and ordered to pay more than $8 million in restitution. There were six other defendants in the case including Michael Spano, Sr., the reputed organized crime boss in Cicero, and former Cicero police chief Emil Schullo.
- Andrew Luster, an heir to the Max Factor cosmetics fortune, was sentenced on February 18, 2003, to 124 years in prison for raping three women and drugging two of them at his home between 1996 and 2000. Luster, 39, was also ordered to pay $1 million in restitution.
- On February 3, 2003, police in California arrested record producer Phil Spector and charged him with the murder of television and film actress Lana Clarkson, 41, at his palatial home on the outskirts of Los Angeles.
- On February 28, 2003, a U.S. District Court jury in Jackson, Mississippi, found reputed Ku Klux Klan member Ernest Avants guilty of aiding and abetting the 1966 murder of Ben Chester White, a 67-year-old black farm worker. The slaying had been designed to lure civil rights leader Rev. Martin Luther King, Jr., to the area, where Avants and two accomplices planned to assassinate him.
- Former U.S. Forest Service employee Terry Lynn Barton was given the maximum sentence of 12 years in prison on March 5, 2003, for starting the largest wildfire in Colorado history in June 2002. The sentence would be served concurrently with a six-year federal sentence handed down on February 21, 2003. Barton had admitted that she had started the fire in Pike National Forest by burning a letter from her estranged husband. The

FYI: Crime and the Media

A study conducted jointly by researchers at eight universities (Miami, Columbia, Northwestern, Syracuse, Southern California, Texas, Oregon, and Ball State) found that crime stories dominate local television news shows, confirming the adage, "If it bleeds, it leads." The researchers reported that stories about crime and criminal justice, particularly those involving blood and mayhem, accounted for nearly 30 percent of the broadcasts. Stories about government and politics, once the mainstay of local news, were given the second largest amount of time (about 15 percent). Natural disaster stories were third, with about 10 percent of the time. One of the researchers speculated that excessive crime news "has a numbing effect on the public." He added that "people withdraw from activities because of fear."

SOURCE: "Crime Is Tops on TV News, Study Says," *The Orlando Sentinel,* May 7, 1997, p. A-10.

CJ ONLINE

Crime in the News

You can read more about past and present crime news stories by visiting the CRIMEBLOG website at **www.crimeblog.com/news.** *Does this website provide a balanced picture of crime in the United States or does it primarily provide sensational news coverage?*

Criminal cases involving John Walker Lindh, John Allen Muhammad and Phil Spector were among the top crime news stories of 2002 and 2003. *What factors make these crimes so sensational?*

blaze had cost an estimated $30 million, destroying 138,000 acres of land, 133 homes, and one business.

- Elizabeth Smart, a 15-year-old girl who had been abducted from her Salt Lake City, Utah, home in June 2002, was found alive on March 12, 2003, in a nearby suburb in the custody of a vagrant and his wife.

Some of these crime stories are likely to remain top news stories for 2004 and beyond. Furthermore, the fight against domestic terrorism occasioned by the tragedies of September 11, 2001, is likely to remain newsworthy for the foreseeable future. However, taken together, those sensational crime news stories do not provide a very accurate image of the types of crime by which the average citizen is victimized. Nor do such stories accurately depict the kinds of crime to which the police respond on a daily basis.

To provide a more accurate idea of the kinds of crimes more typically committed, we reviewed a list of calls for police service in Chicago, Illinois, for the month of June 2000.[2] There were 181,748 calls for police service in Chicago during the period selected.

A close examination of the list of police calls (see Table 1.1) reveals that the most frequent type of call for service in Chicago involves disturbances (for example, domestic quarrels, neighbor or landlord-tenant squabbles, gang altercations, bar or street fights, or even loud music or a dog barking). This type of call accounted for 30.2 percent of the total. (In the list, three separate types of disturbances are cataloged—general disturbances [20.9 percent], domestic disturbances [7.6 percent], and gang disturbances [1.7 percent].) Other calls for service ranged from burglar alarms (9.4 percent) to parking violations (6.5 percent); from selling narcotics (4.5 percent) to auto accidents

TABLE 1.1 Distribution of Calls for Police Service

Police Calls	Percentage
Disturbance	20.9
Alarm	9.4
Domestic Disturbance	7.6
Parking Violation	6.5
Selling Narcotics	4.5
Auto Accident	3.9
Domestic Battery	2.4
Vice Complaint	2.2
Suspicious Person	1.9
Gang Disturbance	1.7
Shots Fired	1.7
Battery (just occurred)	1.6
Person with Gun	1.4
Suspicious Auto (no occupant)	1.2
Fire	1.2
Missing Person	1.1
Assault (in progress)	1.0
Theft (just occurred)	1.0
Fireworks	1.0

Calls for police service to the Chicago, IL, Police Department during June 2000. There were a total of 181,748 police calls.

As shown in Table 1.1, Chicago police respond to disturbance calls more often than any other type of call for service, by a wide margin. *To what types of disturbances should the police respond and not respond?*

(3.9 percent); and from domestic battery (2.4 percent) to vice complaints (2.2 percent). The calls for police service listed in Table 1.1 represent only those calls that accounted for at least 1 percent of the total calls. In all, there were 122 categories of calls for police service. There were also serious crimes or potential crimes not included in the list (because they accounted for less than 1 percent of the total calls): 1,241 robbery calls, 111 death investigation calls, 78 kidnapping calls, and 69 arson calls. Police are also called to assist motorists and to provide escorts for funeral processions—to name just two additional services. Police services and responsibilities will be discussed further in Chapter 6.

Here it is important to observe that the calls to which the police routinely respond rarely involve the sensational crimes reported by the media. In many cases, they do not involve crimes at all. Critics argue that the news media have a dual obligation to (1) present news that reflects a more balanced picture of the overall crime problem and (2) reduce their presentation of sensational crimes, especially when such crimes are shown not so much to inform as to pander to the public's curiosity and its simultaneous attraction *and* repulsion to heinous crimes. The more fundamental problem, however, is that the public's conception of crime is to a large extent shaped by the media, and what the media present, for the most part, misleads the public about the nature of crime.

THINKING CRITICALLY

1. Do you think the news media are obligated to present a balanced picture of the overall crime problem and reduce their presentation of sensational crimes? Why or why not?
2. How much do you think the public conception of crime is influenced by the media? How do you think the media select crime stories on which to focus?

Criminal Justice: An Institution of Social Control

In the United States, there are a variety of responses to crime. When a child commits a criminal act, even if that act does not come to the attention of the police, parents or school authorities nevertheless may punish the child for the offense (if they find out about it). Attempts to prevent crime by installing burglar alarms in automobiles and homes are other ways of responding to crime. Throughout this book, we focus on the criminal justice response to crime.

institution of social control An organization that persuades people, through subtle and not-so-subtle means, to abide by the dominant values of society.

Like the family, schools, organized religion, the media, and the law, criminal justice is an **institution of social control** in the United States. A primary role of such institutions is to persuade people, through subtle and not-so-subtle means, to abide by the dominant values of society. Subtle means of persuasion include gossip and peer pressure, whereas expulsion and incarceration are examples of not-so-subtle means.

As an institution of social control, criminal justice differs from the others in two important ways. First, the role of criminal justice is restricted officially to persuading people to abide by a limited range of social values: those whose violation constitutes crime. Thus, although courteous behavior is desired of all citizens, rude behavior is of no official concern to criminal justice, unless it violates the criminal law. Dealing with noncriminal rude behavior is primarily the responsibility of the family. Second, criminal justice is generally society's "last line of defense" against people who refuse to abide by dominant social values and commit crimes. Usually, society turns to criminal justice only after other institutions of social control have failed.

THINKING CRITICALLY

1. Given what you know about crime in the United States, do you think that the criminal justice system is a strong institution of social control? Why?
2. Do you think that other institutions such as the family, schools, and organized religion are better institutions of social control than the criminal justice system? If so, which ones? Why?

Criminal Justice: The System

Criminal justice in the United States is administered by a loose confederation of more than 50,000 agencies of federal, state, and local governments. Those agencies consist of the police, the courts, and corrections. Together they are commonly referred to as the *criminal justice system*. Although there are differences in the ways the criminal justice system operates in different jurisdictions, there are also similarities. The term **jurisdiction,** as used here, means a politically defined geographical area (for example, a city, a county, a state, or a nation).

jurisdiction A politically defined geographical area.

The following paragraphs will provide a brief overview of a typical criminal justice response to criminal behavior. Figure 1.1 is a graphic representation of the process. It includes the variations for petty offenses, misdemeanors, felonies, and juvenile offenses. A more detailed examination of the criminal justice response to crime and delinquency will be provided in later chapters of this book.

POLICE

The criminal justice response to crime begins when a crime is reported to the police or, far less often, when the police themselves discover that a crime has been committed. Sometimes solving the crime is easy—the victim or a witness knows the perpetrator, or where to find him or her. Often, an arrest supported by witness statements and crime scene evidence is sufficient to close a case, especially with a less serious crime. More often, though, the police must conduct an in-depth investigation to determine what happened in a particular crime. Even when the police start with a known crime or a cooperative victim or witness, the investigation can be lengthy and difficult.

If police investigation of the crime is successful, a suspect is arrested. An **arrest** is the seizing and detaining of a person by lawful authority. After an arrest has been made, the suspect is brought to the police station to be booked.

arrest The seizing and detaining of a person by lawful authority.

Booking is the administrative recording of the arrest. It typically involves entering the suspect's name, the charge, and perhaps the suspect's fingerprints or photograph in the police blotter.

booking The administrative recording of an arrest. Typically, the suspect's name, the charge, and perhaps the suspect's fingerprints or photograph are entered in the police blotter.

COURTS

Soon after a suspect has been arrested and booked, a prosecutor reviews the facts of the case and the available evidence. Sometimes a prosecutor reviews the case before arrest. The prosecutor decides whether to charge the suspect with a crime or crimes. If no charges are filed, the suspect must be released.

Charging Documents There are three principal kinds of charging documents:

1. A complaint.
2. An information.
3. A grand jury indictment.

If the offense is a **misdemeanor** (a less serious crime) or an **ordinance violation** (usually the violation of a law of a city or town), then in many jurisdictions the prosecutor prepares a complaint. A **complaint** is a charging document specifying that an offense has been committed by a person or persons named or described. If the offense is a **felony** (a serious offense punishable by confinement in a prison for more than 1 year or by death), an information is used in about half the states. A grand jury indictment is used in the other half. An **information** outlines the formal charge or charges, the law or laws that have been violated, and the evidence to support the charge or charges. A **grand jury indictment** is a written accusation by a grand jury that one or more persons have committed a crime. (Grand juries will be described later in this discussion.) On rare occasions, police may obtain an arrest warrant from a lower-court judge before making an arrest. An **arrest warrant** is a written order directing law enforcement officers to arrest a person. The charge or charges against a suspect are specified on the warrant. Thus, an arrest warrant may also be considered a type of charging document.

misdemeanor A less serious crime generally punishable by a fine or by incarceration in jail for not more than 1 year.

ordinance violation Usually the violation of a law of a city or town.

complaint A charging document specifying that an offense has been committed by a person or persons named or described.

felony A serious offense punishable by confinement in prison for more than 1 year or by death.

information A document that outlines the formal charge(s) against a suspect, the law(s) that have been violated, and the evidence to support the charge(s).

grand jury indictment A written accusation by a grand jury that one or more persons has committed a crime.

arrest warrant A written order directing law enforcement officers to arrest a person.

Pretrial Stages After the charge or charges have been filed, the suspect, who is now the **defendant,** is brought before a lower-court judge for an initial appearance. At the **initial appearance** the defendant is given formal notice of the charge or charges against him or her and advised of his or her constitutional rights (for example, the right to counsel). In the case of a misdemeanor or an ordinance violation, a **summary trial** (an immediate trial without a jury) may be held. In the case of a felony, a hearing is held to determine whether the defendant should be released or whether there is probable cause to hold the defendant for a preliminary hearing. **Probable cause** is a standard of proof that requires trustworthy evidence sufficient to make a reasonable person believe that, more likely than not, the proposed action is justified. If the suspect is to be held for a preliminary hearing, bail is set if the judge believes release on bail is appropriate. **Bail,** usually a monetary guarantee deposited with the court, is meant to ensure that the defendant will appear at a later stage in the criminal justice process.

In about half of all states, the initial appearance is followed by a preliminary hearing. Preliminary hearings are used only in felony cases. The purpose of the **preliminary hearing** is for a judge to determine whether there is

defendant A person against whom a legal action is brought, a warrant is issued, or an indictment is found.

initial appearance A pretrial stage in which a defendant is brought before a lower court to be given notice of the charge(s) and advised of her or his constitutional rights.

summary trial An immediate trial without a jury.

probable cause A standard of proof that requires evidence sufficient to make a reasonable person believe that, more likely than not, the proposed action is justified.

bail Usually a monetary guarantee deposited with the court to ensure that suspects or defendants will appear at a later stage in the criminal justice process.

preliminary hearing In a felony case, a pretrial stage at which a judge determines whether there is probable cause.

FIGURE 1.1 Overview of the Criminal Justice System

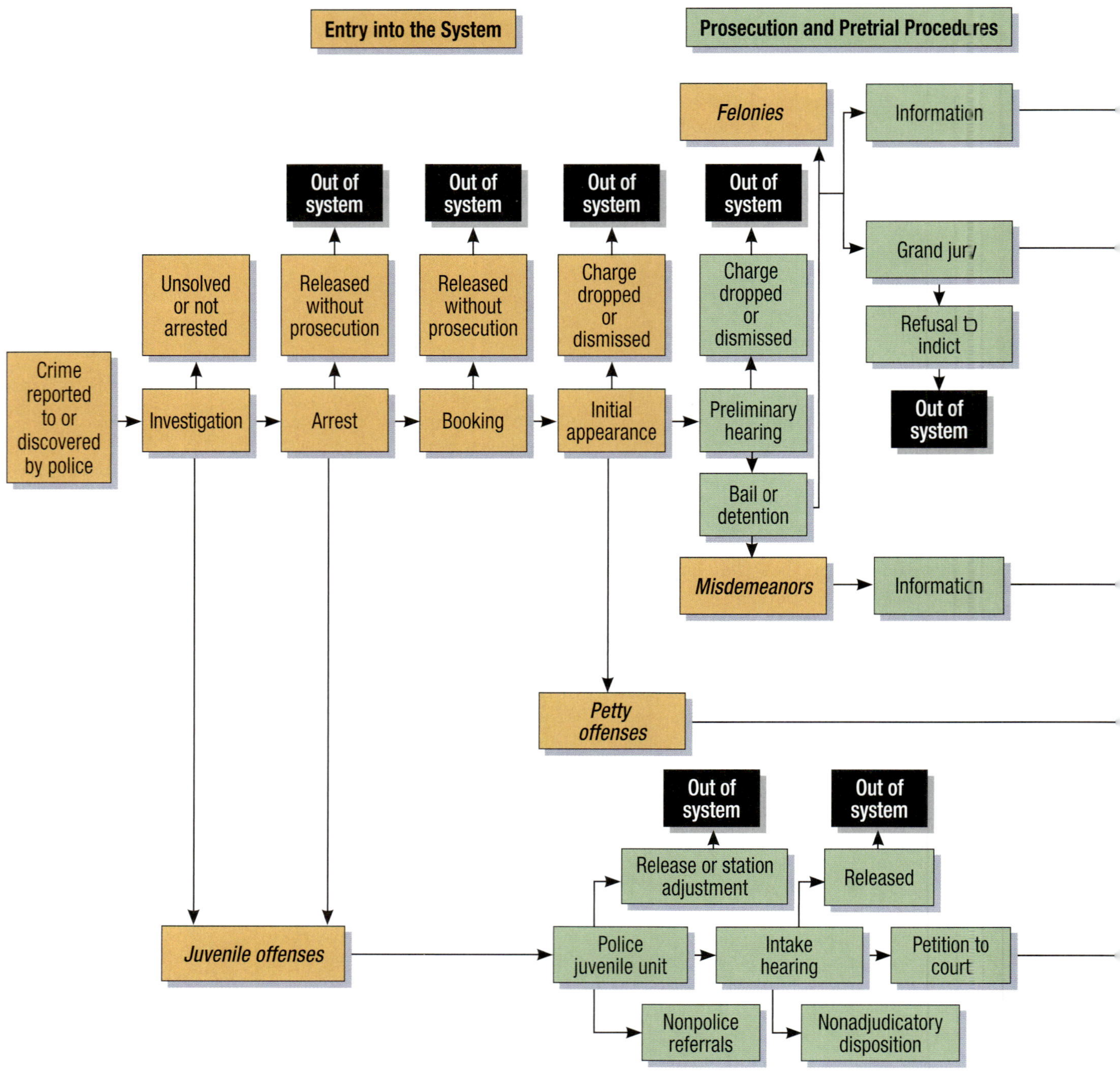

Procedures vary among jurisdictions.

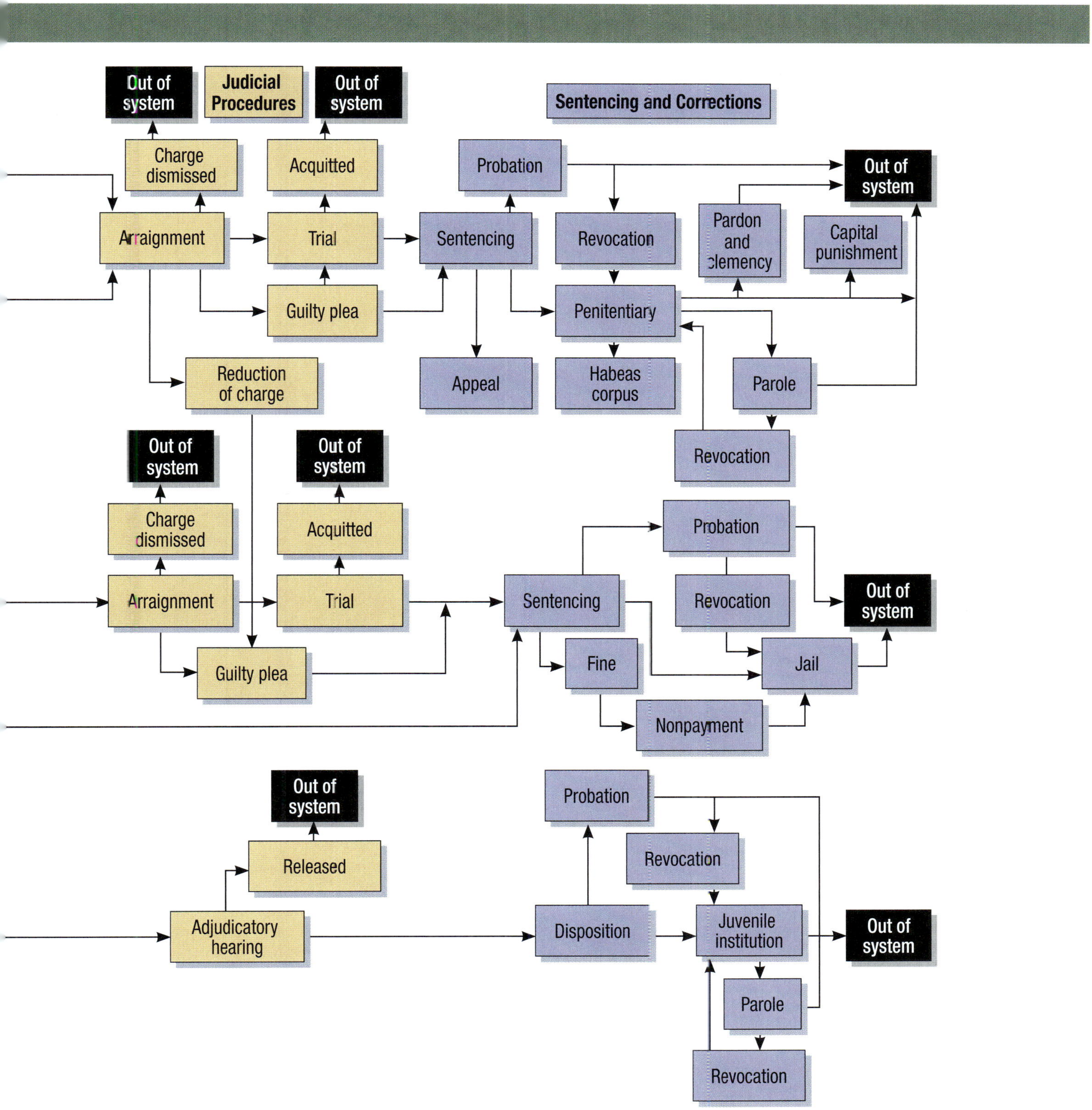

Out of system
Judicial Procedures
Out of system
Sentencing and Corrections
Charge dismissed
Acquitted
Probation
Out of system
Arraignment
Trial
Sentencing
Revocation
Pardon and clemency
Capital punishment
Guilty plea
Penitentiary
Reduction of charge
Appeal
Habeas corpus
Parole
Revocation
Out of system
Out of system
Charge dismissed
Acquitted
Probation
Arraignment
Trial
Sentencing
Revocation
Out of system
Guilty plea
Fine
Jail
Nonpayment
Out of system
Probation
Released
Revocation
Adjudicatory hearing
Disposition
Juvenile institution
Out of system
Parole
Revocation

probable cause to believe that the defendant committed the crime or crimes with which he or she is charged. If the judge finds probable cause, the defendant is bound over for possible indictment in a state with grand juries or for arraignment on an information in a state without grand juries.

grand jury A group of citizens who meet to investigate charges coming from preliminary hearings.

Grand juries are involved in felony prosecutions in about half the states. A **grand jury** is a group of citizens who meet in closed sessions for a specified period to investigate charges coming from preliminary hearings and to fulfill

CAREERS IN CRIMINAL JUSTICE

Law Enforcement/Security

BATF Agent
Border Patrol Agent
Campus Police Officer
Crime Prevention Specialist
Criminal Investigator
Criminal Profiler
Customs Officer
Deputy Sheriff
Deputy U.S. Marshal
Drug Enforcement Officer
Environmental Protection Agent
FBI Special Agent
Federal Agency Investigator
Fingerprint Technician
Forensic Scientist
Highway Patrol Officer
INS Officer
Insurance Fraud Investigator
Laboratory Technician
Loss Prevention Officer
Military Police Officer
Park Ranger
Police Administrator
Police Dispatcher
Police Officer
Polygraph Examiner
Postal Inspector
Private Investigator
Secret Service Agent
State Trooper

Courts/Legal

Arbitrator
Attorney General
Bailiff
Clerk of Court
Court Reporter
District Attorney
Judge
Jury Assignment Commissioner
Jury Coordinator
Juvenile Magistrate
Law Clerk
Law Librarian
Legal Researcher
Mediator
Paralegal
Public Defender
Public Information Officer
Trial Court Administrator
Victim Advocate

Teaching/Research

Agency Researcher
Community College, College, or University Lecturer or Professor

Corrections/Rehabilitation

Activity Therapy Administrator
Business Manager
Case Manager
Chaplain
Chemical Dependency Manager
Child Care Worker
Children's Services Counselor
Classification Officer
Client Service Coordinator
Clinical Social Worker
Community Liaison Officer
Correctional Officer
Dietary Officer
Drug Court Coordinator
Field Administrator
Fugitive Apprehension Officer
Home Detention Supervisor
Human Services Counselor
Job Placement Officer
Juvenile Detention Officer
Juvenile Probation Officer
Mental Health Clinician
Parole/Probation Officer
Presentence Investigator
Prison Industries Superintendent
Program Officer/Specialist
Programmer/Analyst
Psychologist
Recreation Coordinator
Rehabilitation Counselor
Researcher
Residence Supervisor
Sex Offender Therapist
Social Worker
Statistician
Substance Abuse Counselor
Teacher
Vocational Instructor
Warden or Superintendent
Youth Service Worker/Coordinator
Youth Supervisor

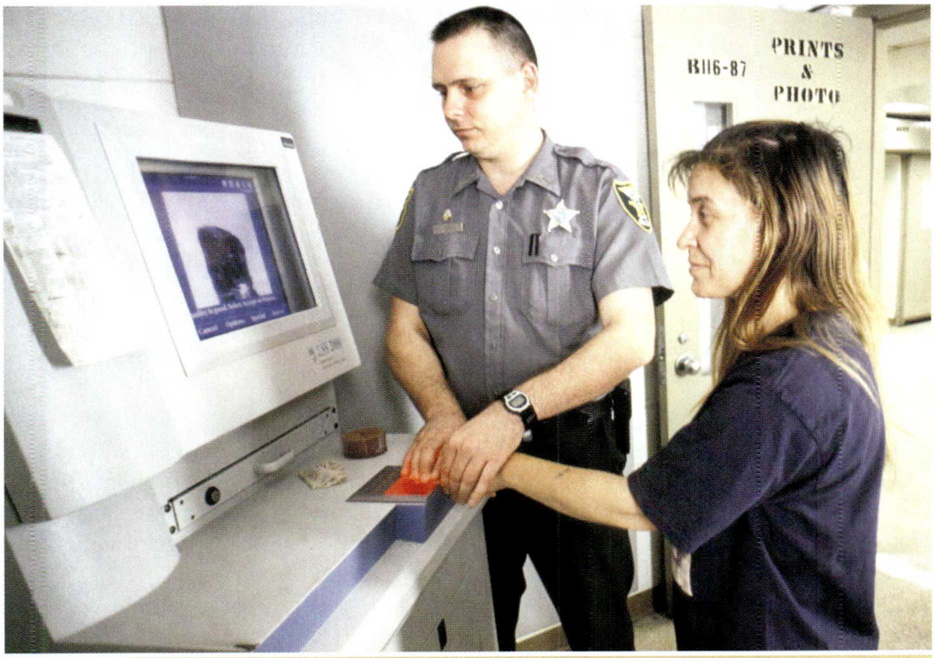

Getting fingerprints is generally a part of the booking into jail process. Pictured here is an inmate being fingerprinted with a technologically advanced "Printrat Livescan Finger Machine." *Why are inmates fingerprinted?*

other responsibilities. Thus, a primary purpose of the grand jury is to determine whether there is probable cause to believe that the accused committed the crime or crimes with which the prosecutor has charged her or him. The grand jury can either indict or fail to indict a suspect. If the grand jury fails to indict, the prosecution must be dropped.

Once an indictment or information is filed with the trial court, the defendant is scheduled for arraignment. The primary purpose of **arraignment** is to hear the formal information or indictment and to allow the defendant to enter a plea. About 90 percent of criminal defendants plead guilty to the charges against them, in an arrangement called *plea bargaining*. **Plea bargaining** is the practice whereby the prosecutor, the defense attorney, the defendant, and, in many jurisdictions, the judge agree on a specific sentence to be imposed if the accused pleads guilty to an agreed-upon charge or charges instead of going to trial.

TRIAL If a defendant pleads not guilty or not guilty by reason of insanity, a trial date is set. Although all criminal defendants have a constitutional right to a trial (when imprisonment for 6 months or more is a possible outcome), only about 10 percent of all criminal cases are disposed of by trial. Approximately 5 percent of criminal cases involve jury trials. The remaining cases that are not resolved through plea bargaining are decided by a judge in a **bench trial** (without a jury). Thus, approximately 90 percent of all criminal cases are resolved through plea bargaining, about 5 percent through jury trials, and about 5 percent through bench trials. (See Figure 1.2.) In most jurisdictions the choice between a jury trial and a bench trial is the defendant's to make.

If the judge or the jury finds the defendant guilty as charged, the judge begins to consider a sentence. In some jurisdictions the jury participates to varying degrees in the sentencing process. The degree of jury participation

arraignment A pretrial stage to hear the information or indictment and to allow a plea.

plea bargaining The practice whereby a specific sentence is imposed if the accused pleads guilty to an agreed-upon charge or charges instead of going to trial.

bench trial A trial before a judge without a jury.

FIGURE 1.2 Criminal Case Dispositions

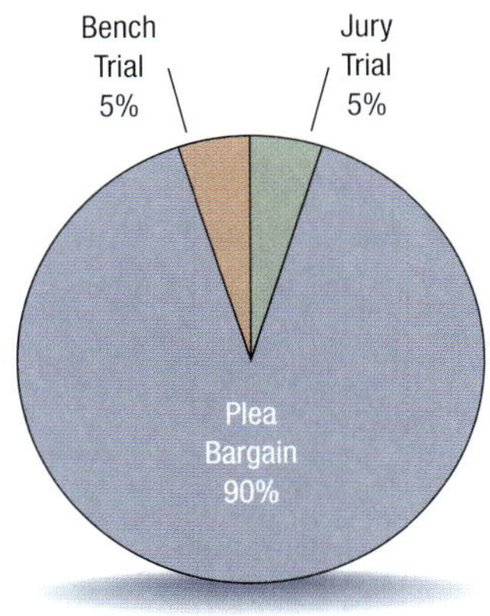

depends on the jurisdiction and the crime. If the judge or jury finds the defendant not guilty, the defendant is released from the jurisdiction of the court and becomes a free person.

CORRECTIONS

Judges cannot impose just any sentence. There are many factors that restrict sentencing decisions. They are limited by statutory provisions. They are guided by prevailing philosophical rationales, by organizational considerations, and by presentence investigation reports. They are also influenced by their own personal characteristics. Presentence investigation reports are used in the federal system and in the majority of states to help judges determine appropriate sentences.

Currently, five general types of punishment are in use in the United States: fines, probation, intermediate punishments (various punishments that are more restrictive than probation but less restrictive and less costly than imprisonment), imprisonment, and death. As long as a judge imposes one or a combination of the five punishments and the sentence length and type are within statutory limits, the judge is free to set any sentence.

Defendants who are found guilty can appeal their convictions either on legal grounds or on constitutional grounds. Examples of legal grounds include defects in jury selection, improper admission of evidence at trial, and mistaken interpretations of law. Constitutional grounds include illegal search and seizure, improper questioning of the defendant by the police, identification of the defendant through a defective police lineup, and incompetent assistance of counsel.

parole The conditional release of prisoners before they have served their full sentences.

The appellate court can either *affirm* the verdict of the lower court and let it stand; modify the verdict of the lower court, without totally reversing it; reverse the verdict of the lower court, which requires no further court action; or reverse the decision and *remand*, or return, the case to the court of original jurisdiction for either a retrial or resentencing.

A defendant sentenced to prison may be eligible for parole (in those jurisdictions that grant parole) after serving a portion of his or her sentence. **Parole** is the conditional release of prisoners before they have served their full sentences. Generally, the decision to grant parole is made by a parole board. Once offenders have served their sentences, they are released from criminal justice authority.

THINKING CRITICALLY

1. Do you think the criminal justice system "works" in the United States? Why or why not?
2. What improvements do you think should be made to the criminal justice system?
3. Do you think judges should be limited in the sentences they are allowed to impose? Why or why not?

Criminal Justice: The Nonsystem

As noted earlier, the many police, court, and corrections agencies of the federal, state, and local governments, taken together, are commonly referred to as the criminal justice system. However, the depiction of criminal justice—or, more specifically, of the interrelationships and inner workings of its various components—as a "system" may be inappropriate and misleading for at least two reasons.

First, there is no single "criminal justice system" in the United States. Rather, as noted earlier, there is a loose confederation of many independent criminal justice agencies at all levels of government. This loose confederation is spread throughout the country with different, sometimes overlapping, jurisdictions. Although there are some similarities among many of those agencies, there are

Arrestees can spend up to 48 hours or more in a jail holding cell before a judge decides whether an arrest was justified. *What problems could occur as a result of this practice?*

also significant differences. The only requirement they all share, a requirement that is the basis for their similarities, is that they follow procedures permitted by the U.S. Constitution.

Second, if a **system** is thought of as a smoothly operating set of arrangements and institutions directed toward the achievement of common goals, one is hard-pressed to call the operation of criminal justice in the United States a system. Instead, because there is considerable conflict and confusion between different agencies of criminal justice, a more accurate representation may be that of a criminal justice *nonsystem*.

system A smoothly operating set of arrangements and institutions directed toward the achievement of common goals.

For example, police commonly complain that criminal offenders who have been arrested after weeks or months of time-consuming and costly investigation are not prosecuted or are not prosecuted vigorously enough. Police often maintain that prosecutors are not working with them or are making their jobs more difficult than necessary. Prosecutors, on the other hand, often gripe about shoddy police work. Sometimes, they say, they are unable to prosecute a crime because of procedural errors committed by the police during the investigation or the arrest.

Even when a criminal offender is prosecuted, convicted, and sentenced to prison, police often argue that the sentence is not severe enough to fit the seriousness of the crime, or they complain when the offender is released from prison after serving only a portion of his or her sentence. In such situations, police frequently argue that the courts or the correctional agencies are undermining their efforts by putting criminals back on the streets too soon.

Myth	Fact
The agencies that administer criminal justice in the United States form a unified system: the criminal justice system.	There is no single "criminal justice system" in the United States. Instead, there is a loose confederation of many independent criminal justice agencies at all levels of government. Moreover, instead of operating together as a system, agencies of criminal justice in the United States interact but generally operate independently of each other, each agency often causing problems for the others.

Conflicts between the courts and corrections sometimes occur when judges continue to impose prison sentences on criminal offenders, especially so-called petty offenders, even though the judges know that the prisons are under court orders to reduce overcrowding.

Additionally, there is a mostly separate process for juvenile offenders. Criminal justice officials frequently complain that their jobs are made more difficult because of the practice, common in many states, of sealing juvenile court records. That practice withholds juvenile court records from the police, prosecutors, and judges even though the records may be relevant and helpful in making arrests, prosecuting criminal cases, and determining appropriate sentences. A rationale for concealing juvenile court records is to prevent, as much as possible, the labeling of juvenile offenders as delinquents, which could make them delinquents. (Labeling theory will be discussed in Chapter 3.)

THINKING CRITICALLY

1. What do you think are some of the positive aspects of having a criminal justice "nonsystem"?
2. What do you think are some of the disadvantages of having a criminal justice "nonsystem"?

In short, rather than operating together as a system, agencies of criminal justice in the United States generally operate independently of each other, each agency often causing problems for the others. Such conflicts may not be entirely undesirable, however, since they occur in a context of checks and balances by which the courts ensure that the law is enforced according to constitutional principles.

Two Models of Criminal Justice

crime control model One of Packer's two models of the criminal justice process. Politically, it reflects traditional conservative values. In this model, the control of criminal behavior is the most important function of criminal justice.

due process model One of Packer's two models of the criminal justice process. Politically, it embodies traditional liberal values. In this model, the principal goal of criminal justice is at least as much to protect the innocent as it is to convict the guilty.

In his influential 1968 book entitled *The Limits of the Criminal Sanction*, legal scholar Herbert Packer describes the criminal justice process in the United States as the outcome of competition between two value systems.[3] Those two value systems, which represent two ends of a value continuum, are the basis for two models of the operation of criminal justice—the crime control model and the due process model. Figure 1.3 depicts this continuum. From a political standpoint, the **crime control model** reflects traditional conservative values, while the **due process model** embodies traditional liberal values.[4] Consequently, when politically conservative values are dominant in society, as they are currently, the principles and policies of the crime control model seem to dominate the operation of criminal justice. During more politically liberal periods, such as the 1960s and 1970s, the principles and policies of the due process model seem to dominate criminal justice activity.

FIGURE 1.3 Two Models of the Criminal Justice Process

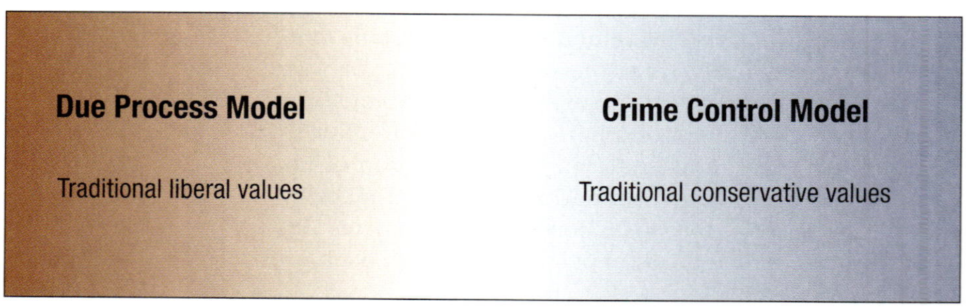

The models are ideal types, neither of which corresponds exactly to the actual day-to-day practice of criminal justice. Rather, they both provide a convenient way to understand and discuss the operation of criminal justice in the United States. In practice, the criminal justice process represents a series of conflicts and compromises between the value systems of the two models. In the following sections, we describe Packer's two models in detail.

THE CRIME CONTROL MODEL

In the crime control model, the control of criminal behavior is by far the most important function of criminal justice. Although the means by which crime is controlled are important in this view (illegal means are not advocated), they are less important than the ultimate goal of control. Consequently, the primary focus of this model is on efficiency in the operation of the criminal justice process. Advocates of the crime control model want to make the process more efficient—to move cases through the process as quickly as possible and to bring them to a close. Packer characterizes the crime control model as "assembly-line justice." To achieve "quick closure" in the processing of cases, a premium is placed on speed and finality. Speed requires that cases be handled informally and uniformly; finality depends on minimizing occasions for challenge, that is, appeals.

To appreciate the assembly-line metaphor used by Packer and to understand how treating cases uniformly speeds up the process and makes it more efficient, consider the way that McDonald's sells billions of hamburgers. When you order a Big Mac from McDonald's, you know exactly what you are going to get. All Big Macs are the same, because they are made uniformly. Moreover, you can get a Big Mac in a matter of seconds most of the time. However, what happens when you order something different, or something not already prepared, such as a hamburger with ketchup only? Your order is taken, and you are asked to stand to the side because your special order will take a few minutes. Your special order has slowed down the assembly line and reduced efficiency. This happens in criminal justice, too! If defendants ask for something special, such as a trial, the assembly line is slowed and efficiency is reduced.

As described in Chapter 8 ("The Administration of Justice"), even when criminal justice is operating at its best, it is a slow process. The time from arrest to final case disposition can typically be measured in weeks or months. If defendants opt for a jury trial, as is their right in most felony cases, the cases are handled formally and are treated as unique; no two cases are the same in their circumstances or in the way they are handled. If defendants are not satisfied with the outcome of their trials, then they have the right to appeal. Appeals may delay by years the final resolution of cases.

To increase efficiency—meaning speed and finality—crime control advocates prefer plea bargaining. As described in Chapter 8, plea bargaining is an informal process that is used instead of trial. Plea bargains can be offered and accepted in a relatively short time. Also, cases are handled uniformly because the mechanics of a plea bargain are basically the same; only the substance of the deals differs. Additionally, with successful plea bargains, there is no opportunity for challenge; there are no appeals. Thus, plea bargaining is the perfect mechanism for achieving the primary focus of the crime control model—efficiency.

The key to the operation of the crime control model is "a presumption of guilt." In other words, advocates of this model assume that if the police have expended the time and effort to arrest a suspect and the prosecutor has

Gary Ridgway, the so-called Green River Killer, was allowed to plead guilty to 48 counts of murder in exchange for helping authorities find some of his victims' remains. The plea bargain allowed him to escape the death penalty. He was sentenced to 48 consecutive life sentences without parole instead. *Was the plea bargain in this case justified? Why or why not?*

formally charged the suspect with a crime, then the suspect must be guilty. Why else would police arrest and prosecutors charge? Although the answers to that question are many (see the discussions in Chapters 7 and 8 of the extralegal factors that influence police and prosecutorial behavior), the fact remains that a presumption of guilt is accurate most of the time. That is, most people who are arrested and charged with a crime or crimes are, in fact, guilty. A problem—but not a significant one for crime control advocates—is that a presumption of guilt is not accurate all of the time; miscarriages of justice do occur (see the discussion in Chapter 4, "The Rule of Law"). An equally important problem is that a presumption of guilt goes against one of the oldest and most cherished principles of American criminal justice—that a person is considered innocent until proven guilty.

Reduced to its barest essentials and operating at its highest level of efficiency, the crime control model consists of an administrative fact-finding process with two possible outcomes: a suspect's exoneration or the suspect's guilty plea.

THE DUE PROCESS MODEL

Advocates of the due process model, by contrast, reject the informal fact-finding process as definitive of factual guilt. They insist, instead, on formal, adjudicative fact-finding processes in which cases against suspects are heard publicly by impartial trial courts. In the due process model, moreover, the factual guilt of suspects is not determined until the suspects have had a full opportunity to discredit the charges against them. For those reasons, Packer characterizes the due process model as "obstacle-course justice."

What motivates this careful and deliberate approach to the administration of justice is the realization that human beings sometimes make mistakes. The police sometimes arrest the wrong person, and prosecutors sometimes charge the wrong person. Thus, contrary to the crime control model, the demand for finality is low in the due process model, and the goal is at least as much to protect the innocent as it is to convict the guilty. Indeed, for due process model advocates, it is better to let a guilty person go free than it is to wrongly convict and punish an innocent person.

doctrine of legal guilt The principle that people are not to be held guilty of crimes merely on a showing, based on reliable evidence, that in all probability they did in fact do what they are accused of doing. Legal guilt results only when factual guilt is determined in a procedurally regular fashion, as in a criminal trial, and when the procedural rules designed to protect suspects and defendants and to safeguard the integrity of the process are employed.

The due process model is based on the doctrine of legal guilt and the presumption of innocence. According to the **doctrine of legal guilt,** people are not to be held guilty of crimes merely on a showing, based on reliable evidence, that in all probability they did in fact do what they are accused of doing. In other words, it is not enough that people are factually guilty in the due process model; they must also be legally guilty. Legal guilt results only when factual guilt is determined in a procedurally regular fashion, as in a criminal trial, and when the procedural rules, or due process rights, designed to protect suspects and defendants and to safeguard the integrity of the process are employed. Many of the conditions of legal guilt—that is, procedural, or due process, rights—are described in Chapter 4. They include:

- Freedom from unreasonable searches and seizures.
- Protection against double jeopardy.

- Protection against compelled self-incrimination.
- A speedy and public trial.
- An impartial jury of the state and district where the crime occurred.
- Notice of the nature and cause of the accusation.
- The right to confront opposing witnesses.
- Compulsory process for obtaining favorable witnesses.
- The right to counsel.
- The prohibition of cruel and unusual punishment.

In short, in the due process model, factual guilt is not enough. For people to be found guilty of crimes, they must be found *both* factually and legally guilty.

This obstacle-course model of justice is championed by due process advocates because they are skeptical about the ideal of equality on which American criminal justice is supposedly based. They recognize that there can be no equal justice where the kind of trial a person gets, or whether he or she gets a trial at all, depends substantially on how much money that person has. It is assumed that in an adversarial system of justice (as described in Chapter 8 and employed in the United States), an effective defense is largely a function of the resources that can be mustered on behalf of the accused. It is also assumed that there are gross inequalities in the financial means of criminal defendants. Most criminal defendants are indigent or poor, and because of their indigence, they are frequently denied an effective defense. Although procedural safeguards, or conditions of legal guilt, cannot by themselves correct the inequity in resources, they do provide indigent defendants, at least theoretically, with a better chance for justice than they would receive without them.

Fundamentally, the due process model defends the ideal of personal freedom and its protection. The model rests on the assumption that preventing tyranny by the government and its agents is the most important function of the criminal justice process.

CRIME CONTROL VERSUS DUE PROCESS

As noted earlier, which of the models dominates criminal justice policy in the United States at any particular time depends on the political climate. Currently, the United States is in the midst of a prolonged period—beginning in the mid-1970s—in which traditional politically conservative values have dominated the practice of criminal and juvenile justice. Thus, it should come as no surprise that the crime control model of criminal justice more closely resembles the actual practice of criminal and juvenile justice in the United States today. At the time Packer wrote and published his book, however, politically liberal values and, thus, the principles and policies of the due process model dominated the operation of criminal and juvenile justice.

In any event, neither model is likely to completely control criminal justice. Even though the current operation of criminal and juvenile justice reflects the dominance of the crime control model, elements of the due process model remain evident. How long this trend will continue is anybody's guess. Many suspect that the American people will eventually get tired of seeing their tax dollars spent on programs and a process that is not providing them with the safety from criminal behavior that they so desperately desire. However, if Packer's model of criminal justice is correct, a shift in criminal justice practice will come only after a shift in the values held by American political leaders and, of course, American citizens.

THINKING CRITICALLY

1. What do you think are some of the fundamental problems with the crime control model? What are the benefits of this model?
2. What do you think are some of the fundamental problems with the due process model? What are the benefits of this model?

Costs of Criminal Justice

Each year in the United States, an enormous amount of money is spent on criminal justice at the federal, state, and local levels. In 1999 (the latest year for which figures are available), a total of $146 billion was spent on civil and criminal justice. That represents approximately $525 for every resident of the United States. Table 1.2 shows the breakdown of spending among the three main segments of the criminal justice system and among the federal, state, and local levels. The $146 billion was an increase of about 8 percent from 1998 and 309 percent from 1982.[5]

Criminal justice is primarily a state and local function; state and local governments spent about 85 percent of the 1999 total. Note that state and local governments share the costs of criminal justice by making police protection primarily a local function and corrections primarily a state function. In 1999, local governments spent 70 percent of the total spent on police protection, while state governments spent nearly 63 percent of the total spent on corrections. The expense of judicial and legal services was more evenly divided between state and local governments; still, local governments (primarily counties) spent more than state governments on those services (43 percent versus 35 percent).

It is important to note that although the bulk of government spending on criminal justice is at the state and local levels, the federal government uses its expenditures strategically to influence criminal justice policy at the other levels of government. For example, the federal government develops and tests new approaches to criminal justice and crime control. It then encourages state and local criminal justice agencies to duplicate effective programs and practices by awarding monetary grants to interested and willing agencies. Grants are also awarded to state and local criminal justice agencies to implement programs that address the federal government's crime control priorities, such as its current emphasis on violent and drug-related crimes. In 1999, the federal government spent 15 percent of the total expenditures on criminal and civil justice.

TABLE 1.2 Costs of Criminal Justice

In 1999, federal, state, and local governments spent $146 billion in direct expenditures for the criminal and civil justice systems.

Police Protection	$ Millions
70% Local	$45,590
12% States	7,810
18% Federal	11,964
100%	65,364
Judicial/Legal Services	
43% Local	$13,914
35% States	11,385
21% Federal	6,885
100%	32,184
Corrections	
30% Local	$14,938
63% States	30,770
7% Federal	3,299
100%	49,007

Detail may not add to 100% because of rounding.

SOURCE: Sidra Lea Gifford, "Justice Expenditure and Employment in the United States, 1999," *Bureau of Justice Statistics Bulletin*, U.S. Department of Justice (Washington, DC: GPO, February 2002).

It is also noteworthy that despite the billions of dollars spent on criminal and civil justice at the state and local levels, as a percentage of all government expenditures, the amount spent on criminal justice represents only a tiny fraction—about 8 percent (3.3 percent for police protection, 2.8 percent for corrections, and 1.6 percent for judicial and legal services). In other words, only about 8 cents of every state and local tax dollar is spent on criminal justice. Include federal tax dollars and only about 4 cents of every tax dollar is spent on criminal justice—an amount that has stayed about the same for nearly 20 years. Thus, compared with expenditures on other government services, such as social insurance, national defense, international relations, interest on debt at the federal level, public welfare, education, health and hospitals, and interest on debt at the state and local levels, spending on criminal justice remains a relatively low priority—a point apparently not missed by the American public.[6]

For almost three decades, public opinion polls have shown that about two-thirds of all Americans believe that too little money is spent on crime control. Very few people think that too much is being spent.[7] In a 2000 public opinion poll, for example, 59 percent of people surveyed believed that too

The state of Florida reportedly spent $10 million to administer justice to serial murderer Ted Bundy in 1989, and the federal government spent more than $100 million to execute mass murderer Timothy McVeigh in 2001. *Were the executions worth the expense? Why or why not?*

little was being spent to halt the rising crime rate (down from 75 percent in 1994). What is not clear, however, because no data are available, is whether those people who believe more money should be spent to fight crime are willing to pay higher taxes to provide that money.

The data presented so far in this section provide a general overview of the aggregate costs of criminal justice in the United States. They do not, however, reveal the expenses of individual-level justice, which vary greatly. On one hand, administering justice to people who commit capital or death-eligible crimes costs, on average, between $2.5 and $5 million per case (the cost of the entire process); extraordinary cases can cost much more. For example, the state of Florida reportedly spent $10 million to administer justice to serial murderer Ted Bundy in 1989, and the federal government spent more than $100 million to execute mass murderer Timothy McVeigh in 2001.[8]

On the other hand, the routine crimes processed daily cost much less. A better idea of the costs of justice in more typical cases comes from an examination of the costs of each stage of the local criminal justice process. The results of such a study are presented below.[9] A 39-year-old male burglar was arrested in Orange County, Florida, in 1995. The state of Florida and Orange County spent $46,106 to administer justice to that offender, who had stolen approximately $5,100 of merchandise and caused about $1,000 in damages to the store. Of course, the costs of the crime include more than just the stolen merchandise and damaged property. They also include the psychological costs of victimization (for example, the loss of a sense of security, a greater fear of crime), which are difficult to place a dollar figure on. Figure 1.4 displays the total cost of the case and the costs for each of the specific criminal justice functions. As shown, corrections costs accounted for the bulk of expenditures (98 percent). Law enforcement, prosecution, and court costs were

FYI Money and Crime

Americans have definite opinions about crime and the money spent to fight it. To lower the crime rate, most Americans (54 percent) think that the money available should be spent on social and economic problems; 31 percent think it should be spent on criminal justice (police, prisons, and judges); 13 percent think money should be spent on both social and economic problems and criminal justice; and, finally, 2 percent think money should not be spent on either one.

SOURCE: Jurg Gerber and Simone Engelhardt Greer, "Just and Painful: Attitudes Toward Sentencing Criminals," pp. 62–74 in T. J. Flanagan and D. R. Longmire (eds.), *Americans View Crime and Justice: A National Public Opinion Survey* (Thousand Oaks, CA: Sage, 1996), p. 71, Table 5.3.

FIGURE 1.4 Total Costs of the Orange County, Florida, Burglary Case by Specific Criminal Justice Functions

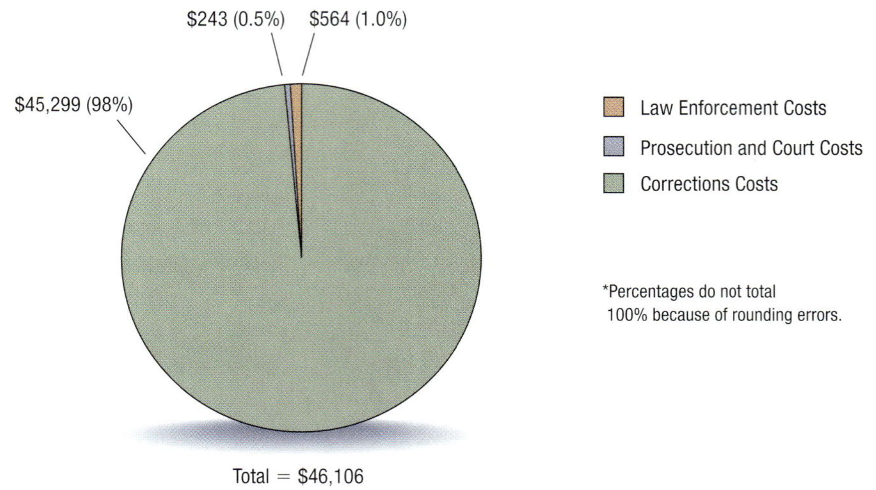

- Law enforcement costs include the time spent capturing and arresting the offender, writing reports, and conducting the investigation.
- Prosecution costs include the time spent reviewing the case and filing charges, negotiating a plea with the public defender, and attending the sentencing hearing and the support staff who performed various tasks such as filing and forwarding documents.
- Defense costs include the time spent reviewing the case, talking to the defendant, negotiating a plea, and attending the sentencing hearing.
- Judicial costs include time spent at the initial appearance and arraignment and completing required paperwork.
- Court support staff costs include time spent filing the charges, entering the file into the computer, assigning the case number, scheduling the arraignment, preparing subpoenas, and recording minutes of the formal proceedings.
- Corrections costs include the costs of booking the offender, detaining him in jail while awaiting adjudication of the case, and incarcerating him in prison as a result of the sentence imposed.

minimal in comparison. An interesting postscript is that in 2002, the offender was adjudicated guilty on several charges stemming from separate incidents in 1999 and 2000. The charges included battery on a law enforcement officer, resisting arrest with violence, burglary of a conveyance, possession of burglary tools, and grand theft. His combined sentence for all charges was 20 years with credit for 3 years' time served. Florida law mandates that offenders serve at least 85 percent of their initial sentence. Therefore, this offender is not scheduled for release until 2017. Given the severity of the offenses and the duration of his prison sentence, it now appears that this offender is anything but typical.

THINKING CRITICALLY

Do you think more money needs to be spent on criminal justice? Why or why not?

Myths About Crime and Criminal Justice

myths Beliefs based on emotion rather than analysis.

A major theme of this book is to expose and correct misconceptions the American public has about crime and criminal justice. Much of the public's understanding of crime and criminal justice is wrong; it is based on myths. **Myths** are "simplistic and distorted beliefs based upon emotion rather than rigorous analysis" or "at worst . . . dangerous falsifications."[10] More specifically, myths are "credible, dramatic, socially constructed representation[s] of perceived realities that people accept as permanent, fixed knowledge of reality while forgetting (if they were ever aware of it) [their] tentative, imaginative, creative, and perhaps fictional qualities."[11] For example, during the Middle Ages in Europe, people commonly believed that guilt or innocence could be determined through *trial by ordeal*. The accused might be required to walk barefoot over hot coals, hold a piece of red-hot iron, or walk through fire. The absence of any injury was believed to be a sign from God that the person was innocent. Although we may now wonder how such a distorted and simplistic belief could have been taken as fact and used to determine a person's guilt or innocence, people did not consider the belief a myth during the time that it was official practice. The lesson to be learned from this example is that a belief that is taken as fact at one time may in retrospect be viewed as a myth. In this book, we attempt to place such myths about crime and criminal justice in perspective.[12]

Throughout this text, we present generally accepted beliefs about crime or the justice system that can be considered myths because they can be contradicted with facts. In some instances it can be demonstrated that the perpetuation and acceptance of certain myths by the public, politicians, and criminal justice practitioners has contributed to the failure to significantly reduce predatory criminal behavior and to increase peace. It is also possible that acceptance of these myths as accurate representations of reality or as facts results in the waste of billions of dollars in the battle against crime.

During the Middle Ages, Holy Roman Emperor Otto III married the King of Aragon's daughter, who fell in love with a count of the court. When the count refused her advances, the emperor's wife accused him of making an attempt on her honor. The scene shows the count's wife attempting to prove his innocence by trial by fire (a red-hot rod in her hand). When she was not burned, the count's innocence was proved and the emperor's wife was burned alive for making the false accusation. *How could people believe that guilt or innocence could be proven in this way?*

SUMMARY

1. Describe how the type of crime routinely presented by the media compares with crime routinely committed

   Crime presented by the media is usually more sensational than crime routinely committed.

2. Identify institutions of social control and explain what makes criminal justice an institution of social control

   Institutions of social control include the family, schools, organized religion, the media, the law, and criminal justice. Such institutions attempt to persuade people to abide by the dominant values of society. Criminal justice is restricted to persuading people to abide by a limited range of social values, the violation of which constitutes crime.

3. Summarize how the criminal justice system responds to crime

   The typical criminal justice response to the commission of a crime involves the following: investigation; arrest (if the investigation is successful); booking; the formal charging of the suspect; an initial appearance; a preliminary hearing (for a felony); either indictment by a grand jury followed by arraignment, or arraignment on an information; either a plea bargain or a trial; sentencing; possible appeal; and punishment (if the defendant is found guilty).

4. Explain why criminal justice in the United States is sometimes considered a nonsystem

   Criminal justice in the United States is sometimes considered a nonsystem for two major reasons. First, there is no single system, but instead a loose confederation of more than 50,000 agencies on federal, state, and local levels. Second, rather than being a smoothly operating set of arrangements and institutions, the agencies of the criminal justice system interact with one another, but generally operate independently, often causing problems for one another.

5. Point out major differences between packer's crime control and due process models

   From a political standpoint, the crime control model of criminal justice reflects traditional conservative values, while the due process model embodies traditional liberal values. In the crime control model, the control of criminal behavior is by far the most important function of criminal justice. Consequently, the primary focus of this model is on efficiency in the operation of the criminal justice process. The goal of the due process model, on the other hand, is at least as much to protect the innocent as it is to convict the guilty. Fundamentally, the due process model defends the ideal of personal freedom and its protection, and rests on the assumption that the prevention of tyranny on the part of government and its agents is the most important function of the criminal justice process.

6. Describe the costs of criminal justice in the United States and compare those costs among federal, state, and local governments

   An enormous amount of money is spent each year on criminal justice in the United States. In 1999, federal, state, and local governments spent a total of $146 billion on police protection ($65 billion), judicial/legal services ($32 billion), and corrections ($49 billion). The bulk of government spending on criminal justice is at the state and local levels, but the federal government spends money strategically to influence criminal justice policy at the other levels of government.

7. Explain how myths about crime and criminal justice affect the criminal justice system

   The acceptance and perpetuation of myths, or simplistic beliefs based on emotion rather than rigorous analysis, can harm the criminal justice system by contributing to the failure to reduce crime and to the waste of money in the battle against crime.

KEY TERMS

institution of social control, p. 8
jurisdiction, p. 8
arrest, p. 8
booking, p. 9
misdemeanor, p. 9
ordinance violation, p. 9
complaint, p. 9
felony, p. 9
information, p. 9
grand jury indictment, p. 9
arrest warrant, p. 9
defendant, p. 9
initial appearance, p. 9
summary trial, p. 9
probable cause, p. 9
bail, p. 9
preliminary hearing, p. 9
grand jury, p. 12
arraignment, p. 13
plea bargaining, p. 13
bench trial, p. 13
parole, p. 14
system, p. 15
crime control model, p. 16
due process model, p. 16
doctrine of legal guilt, p. 18
myths, p. 22

REVIEW QUESTIONS

1. What is the fundamental problem with the types of crime routinely presented by the media?
2. What was the most frequent type of call for police service in Chicago during the period examined in the text (see Table 1.1)?
3. What is an *institution of social control?*
4. Why is criminal justice sometimes considered society's "last line of defense"?
5. What three agencies make up the criminal justice system?
6. What is a *jurisdiction?*
7. What is the difference between an *arrest* and a *booking?*
8. Who decides whether to charge a suspect with a crime?
9. What are three principal kinds of charging documents?
10. What is the difference between a *misdemeanor* and a *felony?*
11. What is a *defendant,* and when does a suspect become a defendant?
12. What is the difference between an *initial appearance* and a *preliminary hearing?*
13. Define *bench trial, summary trial, bail, grand jury, arraignment, plea bargaining,* and *parole.*
14. What is meant by *probable cause?*
15. Why are the conflicts between the different agencies of criminal justice not entirely undesirable?
16. Why does Packer use the metaphors of *assembly-line justice* and *obstacle-course justice* to characterize his crime control and due process models of criminal justice?
17. What are the bases (that is, the presumptions or doctrines) of Packer's crime control and due process models of criminal justice?
18. Which levels of government—federal, state, or local—bear most of the costs of criminal justice in the United States?
19. What is a lesson to be learned from myths about crime and criminal justice?

IN THE FIELD

1. **Crime and the Media** Watch a local television station's broadcast of the evening news for one or more days and record the crimes reported. Then obtain from your local police department a copy of the log of calls for police service for one of those days. Compare the crimes reported on the nightly news with the calls for police service. Describe similarities and differences between the two different sources of crime information. What have you learned?

2. **Costs of Crime** Follow a criminal case in your community and determine the costs of processing the case. You will have to contact the police, the prosecutor, the defense attorney, the judge, and other relevant participants. Remember to consider both monetary and psychological costs. After you have determined the costs, decide whether you think they were justified. Defend your answer.
3. **Costs of Justice** In 1999, 7.7 percent of state and local spending was for criminal justice. By contrast, 29.7 percent of state and local spending was for education, 13.5 percent for public welfare, 7.3 percent for health and hospitals, and 4.8 percent for interest on debt. Divide into groups. Using the preceding data, debate within your group whether states and localities spend enough of their budgets on criminal justice. Share group results with the class.

ON THE NET

1. **Criminal Justice in Other Countries** Learn about the criminal justice systems of other countries by visiting the website of the U.S. Justice Department's *The World Factbook of Criminal Justice Systems* at www.ojp.usdoj.gov/bjs/abstract/wfcj.htm.
2. **FBI's Most Wanted** Access the FBI's "Top Ten Most Wanted Fugitives" at www.fbi.gov/mostwant.htm. Read the descriptions of the fugitives. Write a report describing the characteristics they share. Also, try to determine what unique features qualify these fugitives, and not others, for the list.

CRITICAL THINKING EXERCISES

1. **Plea Bargaining** Shirley Smith pleaded guilty to third-degree murder after admitting she had put rat poison in drinks her husband ingested at least 12 times during the course of their 13-month marriage. Sentenced to a maximum of 20 years in prison, she would have to serve at least 10 years before she could be considered for parole. The prosecutor defended the plea bargain against much public criticism. The prosecutor claimed that the costs of a murder trial and subsequent appeals were not paramount. However, the prosecutor did acknowledge that the case could have been the most expensive in county history, exhausted his entire $2 million budget for the fiscal year, and required a tax increase to cover the costs. As an elected official, the prosecutor attempted to seek justice while exercising a sense of fiscal responsibility.
   a. Do you think the prosecutor made the correct decision to plea bargain? Defend your answer.
   b. In potentially expensive cases, should the prosecutor seek a referendum on the matter (to determine whether residents are willing to pay additional taxes to try a defendant rather than accept a plea bargain)?

2. **Prison versus Rehabilitation** The city council of a midsize East Coast city is locked in a debate concerning how to address the rising incidence of violent crime. John Fogarty, one of the most influential people in the city, is pushing for more police and stiffer penalties as the solution. He is the leader of a group that is proposing the construction of a new prison. Another group thinks putting more people in prison is not the answer. They believe that early intervention, education, and prevention programs will be most effective. There is not enough money to fund both sides' proposals.
   a. Which side would you support? Why?
   b. What do you think is the number one crime problem in your community? List ways of dealing with that problem. What would be the most cost-effective way to lower the rate of that crime?

POLICE
KOOL

CRIME AND ITS CONSEQUENCES

CHAPTER TWO

Chapter Outline

Definitions of Crime

- Social Definitions
- A Legal Definition
- Elements of Crime
- Degrees or Categories of Crime

Measurement of Crime

- Crime Statistics
- Crime Rates
- Uniform Crime Reports (UCR)
- National Incident-Based Reporting System (NIBRS)
- National Crime Victimization Surveys (NCVS)
- Self-Report Crime Surveys

Costs of Crime

Fear of Crime

- What People Fear
- When and Where People Fear
- Who Fears Crime

Victims of Crime

- Victimization Trends
- Who the Victims Are

Chapter Objectives

After completing this chapter, you should be able to:

1. Distinguish between a social definition and a legal definition of crime and summarize the problems with each.
2. List the technical and ideal elements of a crime.
3. Identify some of the legal defenses or legal excuses for criminal responsibility.
4. Explain why crime and delinquency statistics are unreliable.
5. Identify the two major sources of crime statistics in the United States.
6. Describe the principal finding of the national crime victimization surveys.
7. Summarize the general finding of self-report crime surveys.
8. Identify the costs of crime.
9. Describe the extent of fear of crime in the United States and the characteristics of people most likely to fear crime.
10. List the characteristics of people who are the most likely and the least likely to be victims of crime.

Crime Story

On August 27, 2003, Oklahoma's attorney general filed criminal charges against bankrupt telecom firm MCI WorldCom, its former CEO Bernard Ebbers, and five other former WorldCom officials for violating the Oklahoma Securities Act. The defendants were charged with a total of 15 counts of security violations and are likely to face additional federal criminal charges associated with an accounting fraud that was disclosed in June of 2002. Reportedly, U.S. Attorney General John Ashcroft had appealed to Oklahoma's officials to hold off on filing the charges to avoid potential interference with an ongoing federal investigation. However, Oklahoma officials felt compelled to seek justice for its people.

The charges stem from an accounting scam that resulted in losses of more than $11 billion for investors and various associates of WorldCom. WorldCom is now doing business as MCI, following its filing of Chapter 11 bankruptcy to protect its remaining financial assets. WorldCom was alleged to have artificially inflated corporate profits to avoid detection by regulatory auditors. The accounting slight-of-hand resulted in the loss of more than 17,000 jobs and the value of former WorldCom stock plummeting from $64 a share to 21 cents per share. In May of 2003, MCI WorldCom agreed to pay a record fine of $500 million to the Securities and Exchange Commission for the accounting debacle.

MCI no longer provides mobile phone services in the United States. However, it does serve as the largest communications supplier for the U.S. Department of Defense. The company supplied telecommunications to the U.S. military and federal agencies in Afghanistan during and after the 2001 war. In May of 2003, MCI was awarded a U.S. government contract to begin rebuilding Iraq's shattered communication network resulting from the 2003 war with Iraq. MCI's government contract is estimated to be worth between $30 million and $90 million. MCI will supply mobile phone services to about 10,000 military and aid workers in Baghdad.

Chapter 2 describes the traditional methods of measuring the costs of crime, which include property losses, cash losses, medical expenses, and income lost from work. The costs of corporate crime are frequently not factored into traditional measuring methods. How do the costs of corporate crime, such as the MCI WorldCom scandal, figure into the economic and social costs of crime? The reduction in the quality of life for former employees and investors of MCI WorldCom is difficult to assess in tangible measures. Because the criminal justice system has typically focused on street crime, it is difficult for people to fully appreciate the harms of corporate criminal acts. By all estimates, the costs of corporate crime are much higher when compared to street crimes.

Equally frustrating for some observers of the criminal justice system is the continual business association between U.S. government officials and known criminal elements. Convicted street criminals often find it difficult to resume their lives and begin new careers after having been convicted of criminal acts. Yet corporate criminals may be awarded huge government contracts—an enviable second chance. Why do you suppose street criminals and corporate criminals are treated so differently?

Definitions of Crime

The object of criminal justice in the United States is to prevent and control crime. Thus, to understand criminal justice, it is necessary to understand crime. An appropriate definition of crime, however, remains one of the most critical unresolved issues in criminal justice today. One problem is that many dangerous and harmful behaviors are not defined as crimes, while many less dangerous and less harmful behaviors are. We begin, then, by examining how crime is defined and the problems with defining what is a crime.

> **FYI: Crime**
>
> Crime is from the Latin *crimen*, meaning "accusation" or "fault."
>
> SOURCE: *Webster's New Twentieth Century Dictionary of the English Language Unabridged* (Williams Collins, 1980.)

SOCIAL DEFINITIONS

The broadest definitions of crime are social definitions. A typical social definition of crime is behavior that violates the norms of society—or, more simply, antisocial behavior. A **norm** is any standard or rule regarding what human beings should or should not think, say, or do under given circumstances. Because social definitions of crime are broad, they are less likely than narrower definitions to exclude behaviors that ought to be included. Nevertheless, there are several problems with social definitions of crime.

norm Any standard or rule regarding what human beings should or should not think, say, or do under given circumstances.

First, norms vary from group to group within a single society. There is no uniform definition of antisocial behavior. Take, for example, the acts involved in gambling, prostitution, abortion, and homosexual behavior. As current public debates indicate, there is much controversy in the United States over whether those acts should be crimes. Even with acts about which there seems to be a consensus, like murder and rape, there is no agreement on what constitutes such acts. For example, if a patient dies from a disease contracted from a doctor who did not wash his or her hands before examining the patient, has the doctor committed murder? Or, if a man has forcible sexual intercourse with a woman against her will but, before the act, at the woman's request, puts on a condom so that the woman will not get a sexually transmitted disease, has the man committed rape? Those examples illustrate the difficulty of determining what, in fact, constitutes antisocial behavior, let alone crime.

Second, norms are always subject to interpretation. Each norm's meaning has a history. Consider abortion, for example. For some people, abortion is the killing of a fetus or a human being. For other people, abortion is not killing because, for them, human life begins at birth and not at conception. For the latter group, the abortion issue concerns women's freedom to control their own bodies. For the former group, abortion constitutes an injustice to the helpless.

Third, norms change from time to time and from place to place. For example, the consumption of alcohol was prohibited in the United States during the 1920s and early 1930s but is only regulated today. Until the passage of the Harrison Act in 1914, it was legal in the United States to use opiates such as opium, heroin, and morphine without a doctor's prescription. Such use is prohibited today. Casino gambling is allowed in some states but forbidden in other states. Prostitution is legal in a few counties in Nevada, but illegal in the rest of the United States. Prior to the mid-1970s, a husband could rape his wife with impunity in all but a handful of states. Today, laws in every state prohibit a husband from raping or assaulting his wife.

> **FYI: Illegal Behaviors**
>
> Examples of behaviors that were prohibited in the early 1990s by criminal law (and may still be):
>
> - Securing a giraffe to a telephone pole in Atlanta.
> - Gargling in public in Louisiana.
> - Sneezing in public in Nebraska.
> - Serving ice cream on cherry pie in Kansas.
> - Entering a theater within 4 hours of eating garlic in Gary, Indiana.
> - Fishing in your pajamas in Chicago.
> - Shooting open a can of food in Indiana.
> - Setting a fire under a mule in Ohio.
> - Breaking more than three dishes a day in Florida.
>
> SOURCE: Sheryl Lindsell-Roberts, *Loony Laws and Silly Statutes* (New York: Sterling, 1994).

A LEGAL DEFINITION

In an attempt to avoid the problems with social definitions of crime, a legal definition of crime is used in criminal justice in the United States. A typical **legal definition of crime** is an intentional violation of the criminal law or penal code, committed without defense or excuse and penalized by the state.

legal definition of crime An intentional violation of the criminal law or penal code, committed without defense or excuse and penalized by the state.

More and more states are legalizing casino gambling as a means of generating income. *Is this a desirable trend? Why or why not?*

The major advantage of a legal definition of crime, at least on the surface, is that it is narrower and less ambiguous than a social definition of crime. If a behavior violates the criminal law, then by definition it is a crime. However, although a legal definition eliminates some of the problems with social definitions of crime, a legal definition of crime has problems of its own.

First, some behaviors prohibited by the criminal law arguably should not be. This problem of **overcriminalization** arises primarily in the area of so-called victimless crimes. Lists of victimless crimes typically include gambling, prostitution involving consenting adults, homosexual acts between consenting adults, and the use of some illegal drugs, such as marijuana. Ultimately, whether those acts should or should not be prohibited by criminal law depends on whether they are truly victimless—an issue we will not debate here.

A second problem with a legal definition of crime is that for some behaviors prohibited by the criminal law, the law is not routinely enforced. **Nonenforcement** is common for many white-collar and government crimes. It is also common for blue laws, which require stores and other commercial establishments to be closed on Sundays. Many jurisdictions in the United States have blue laws, or they did until recently. The principal problem with the nonenforcement of prohibitions is that it causes disrespect for the law. People come to believe that because criminal laws are not routinely enforced, there is no need to routinely obey them.

A third problem with a legal definition of crime is the problem of **undercriminalization.** That is, some behaviors that arguably should be prohibited by the criminal law are not. Have you ever said to yourself that there ought to be a law against whatever it is you are upset about? Of course, most of the daily frustrations that people claim ought to be crimes probably should not be. Some people argue, however, that some very harmful and destructive actions or inactions that are not criminal should be. Examples include the government allowing employers (generally through the nonenforcement of laws) to maintain unsafe working conditions that cause employee deaths and injuries, and corporations' intentional production of potentially hazardous products to maximize profits.[1]

overcriminalization The prohibition by the criminal law of some behaviors that arguably should not be prohibited.

nonenforcement The failure to routinely enforce prohibitions against certain behaviors.

undercriminalization The failure to prohibit some behaviors that arguably should be prohibited.

ELEMENTS OF CRIME

A legal definition of crime is the basis of criminal justice in the United States. The legal definition of crime provided earlier in this chapter, however, is only a general definition. It does not specify all the elements necessary to make a behavior a crime. Technically and ideally, a crime has not been committed unless all seven of the following elements are present:[2]

1. Harm
2. Legality
3. *Actus reus*
4. *Mens rea*
5. Causation
6. Concurrence
7. Punishment

It is only in a technical and ideal sense that all seven elements must be present. In practice, a behavior is often considered a crime when one or more of the elements of crime is absent. We will examine each of the seven elements in turn, indicating exceptions to the technical and ideal where relevant.

HARM For crime to occur, there must be an external consequence, or **harm.** A mental or emotional state is not enough. Thus, thinking about committing a crime or being angry enough to commit a crime, without acting on the thought or the anger, is not a crime.

The harm may be physical or verbal. Physically striking another person without legal justification is an example of an act that does physical harm. An example of an act that does verbal harm is a threat to strike another person, whether or not the threat is carried out. Writing something false about another person that dishonors or injures that person is a physical harm called *libel*. The spoken equivalent of libel is called *slander*.

Whether the legal element of harm is present in all crimes is sometimes questioned. Some crimes, such as gambling, prostitution, marijuana consumption, and certain consensually committed sexual acts such as sodomy, have come to be called "victimless crimes" by those who argue that only those people involved in these behaviors are harmed, if at all. Other people maintain that the participants, their families, and the moral fabric of society are jeopardized by such behavior. In short, there is considerable debate as to whether so-called victimless crimes really are harmless.

Ever since criminal sanctions were established for illegal drug use, some have argued for decriminalization by elimination or reduction of criminal penalties for possession or distribution of certain drugs. *Do you agree with this argument? Why or why not?*

harm The external consequence required to make an action a crime.

LEGALITY The element of **legality** has two aspects. First, the harm must be legally forbidden for a behavior to be a crime. Thus, violations of union rules, school rules, religious rules, or any rules other than those of a political jurisdiction may be "wrong," but they are not crimes unless they are also prohibited by criminal law. Furthermore, rude behavior may be frowned upon, but it is not criminal.

Second, a criminal law must not be retroactive, or *ex post facto*. An ***ex post facto* law** (1) declares criminal an act that was not illegal when it was committed, (2) increases the punishment for a crime after it is committed, or (3) alters the rules of evidence in a particular case after the crime is committed. The first meaning is the most common. The U.S. Constitution (Article I, Section 10.1) forbids *ex post facto* laws.

legality The requirement (1) that a harm must be legally forbidden for the behavior to be a crime and (2) that the law must not be retroactive.

***ex post facto* law** A law that (1) declares criminal an act that was not illegal when it was committed, (2) increases the punishment for a crime after it is committed, or (3) alters the rules of evidence in a particular case after the crime is committed.

ACTUS REUS The Latin term ***actus reus*** refers to criminal conduct—specifically, intentional or criminally negligent (reckless) action or inaction that causes harm. Crime involves not only things people do but also things they do not do. If people do not act in situations where the law requires them to act, they are committing crimes. For example, parents are legally required to provide their children with adequate food, clothing, and shelter. If parents fail to provide those necessities—that is, if they fail to act when the law requires them to—they are committing a crime.

actus reus Criminal conduct—specifically, intentional or criminally negligent (reckless) action or inaction that causes harm.

MENS REA The Latin term ***mens rea*** refers to criminal intent or a guilty state of mind. It is the mental aspect of a crime. Ideally, criminal conduct is limited to intentional or purposeful action or inaction and not to accidents. In practice, however, reckless actions or *negligence* may be criminal. **Negligence** is the failure to take reasonable precautions to prevent harm.

mens rea Criminal intent; a guilty state of mind.

negligence The failure to take reasonable precautions to prevent harm.

In some cases, offenders lack the capacity (sometimes called competence) to form *mens rea*. If they do not have that capacity, they are not to be held responsible for their criminal conduct. If they have a diminished capacity to form *mens rea,* they are to be held less than fully responsible. In other cases, offenders who have the capacity to form *mens rea* are not held responsible for their crimes, or are held less responsible for them, either because they did not have *mens rea* when they acted or because there were extenuating circumstances when they did act with *mens rea.*

Legal Defenses for Criminal Responsibility. In the United States, an offender is not considered responsible or is considered less responsible for an offense if he or she, for example, (1) acted under duress, (2) was underage, (3) was insane, (4) acted in self-defense or in defense of a third party, (5) was entrapped, or (6) acted out of necessity. Those conditions are legal defenses or legal excuses for criminal responsibility.

duress Force or coercion as an excuse for committing a crime.

If a person did not want to commit a crime but was forced or coerced to do so against his or her will, he or she committed the crime under **duress** and is generally excluded from criminal liability. Suppose that an intruder held a gun to the head of a loved one and threatened to kill that person if you did not rob a local convenience store and return immediately to give the intruder the money. If you committed the robbery to save the life of your loved one, you would probably not be held legally responsible for the crime, because you committed it under duress. There were extenuating circumstances when you acted with *mens rea.* To prevent all offenders from claiming duress, the burden of proof is placed on the defendant.

Another legal excuse or legal defense against criminal responsibility is being underage. Although the age at which a person is considered legally responsible for his or her actions varies by jurisdiction, in most American jurisdictions a child under the age of 7 is not held responsible for a crime. It is assumed that a child under 7 years of age does not have the capacity to form *mens rea.* A child under 7 years of age is considered a *legal infant* or of *legal nonage.* Such a child is protected by the criminal law but not subject to it. Thus, if a 6-year-old child picks up a shotgun and shoots his or her parent, the child is unlikely to be charged with a crime. On the other hand, if a parent abuses a child, the criminal law protects the child by holding the abusive parent responsible for his or her actions.

FYI Legal Infancy

On February 29, 2000, a Mount Morris Township, Michigan, 6-year-old first grader pulled a gun from his pants and shot and killed a 6-year-old classmate in front of his teacher and classmates. He had quarreled with her on the playground the day before. Because of his age, he was neither charged nor held criminally responsible because, legally, he could not form *mens rea* or the intent to kill.

SOURCE: "A 1st-grader turns killer," *The Orlando Sentinel* (March 1, 2000), p. A-1; "6-year-old boy who killed girl lived in 'flophouse'," *The Orlando Sentinel* (March 2, 2000), p. A-1.

juvenile delinquency A special category of offense created for young offenders, usually those between 7 and 18 years of age.

In most developed countries children under 18 years of age are not considered entirely responsible for their criminal acts. It is assumed that their capacity to form *mens rea* is not fully developed. A special category of offense called **juvenile delinquency** has been created for those children. In most American jurisdictions, the upper age limit for juvenile delinquency is 18. The lower limit is usually 7. The criminal law generally treats anyone who is 18 or older as an adult. However, the upper age limit of juvenile delinquency is lower in some jurisdictions and sometimes varies with the sex of the offender. In some jurisdictions there is a legal borderland between the ages of 16 and 18. An offender in that age range may be treated as a juvenile or as an adult, depending on the severity of the offense. In some cases, an offense is considered heinous enough for a court to certify a juvenile, regardless of age, as an adult and to treat him or her accordingly. The subject of juvenile delinquency will be discussed more fully in Chapter 13.

insanity Mental or psychological impairment or retardation as a defense against a criminal charge.

A third legal defense or legal excuse from criminal responsibility is insanity. **Insanity** is a legal term, not a medical one. It refers to mental or psychological impairment or retardation. Like many of the other legal defenses or excuses, an insanity defense rests on the assumption that someone who is insane at the time of a crime lacks the capacity, or has diminished capacity, to form *mens rea.* Thus, that person either should not be held responsible or should be held less responsible for a given crime.

In most western European nations, legal insanity is determined solely by the judgment and testimony of medical experts. British and American law, by contrast, provide guidelines for judges, juries, and medical experts to follow in determining whether a defendant is legally insane. The oldest—and, until recently, the most popular—of those guidelines is the M'Naghten rule, which was first used in an English trial in 1843.

Under the M'Naghten rule:

> [E]very man is to be presumed to be sane, and . . . to establish a defense on the ground of insanity, it must be clearly proved that, at the time of the committing of the act, the party accused was laboring under such a defect of reason, from disease of the mind, as not to know the nature and quality of the act he was doing; or if he did know it, that he did not know he was doing what was wrong.[3]

In short, according to the M'Naghten rule, a person is legally insane if, at the time of the commission of the act, he or she (1) did not know the nature and quality of the act or (2) did not know that the act was wrong. The burden of proof is on the defendant.

One problem with the M'Naghten rule is the difficulty of determining what a person's state of mind was at the time of the commission of the criminal act. The rule has also been criticized for its ambiguity. What is a "defect of reason," and by whose standards is the act a product of defective reason? Does "disease of the mind" refer to organic diseases, nonorganic diseases, or both? What does it mean to "know" the nature and quality of the act? Does it mean an intellectual awareness, an emotional appreciation, or both? Does "wrong" mean legally wrong, morally wrong, or both?

Perhaps the most serious problem with the M'Naghten rule is that it does not address the situation of a defendant who knew the difference between right and wrong but was unable to control his or her actions. To remedy that problem, some states have adopted the *irresistible-impulse* or *control test* and use it in conjunction with the M'Naghten rule. In those states a defense against conviction on grounds of insanity is first made by using the M'Naghten rule.

CJ ONLINE

Daniel M'Naghten

Daniel M'Naghten was acquitted of the murder of a person he had mistaken for his real target, Sir Robert Peel, then the Prime Minister of Great Britain. M'Naghten claimed that he was delusional at the time of the killing. Go to **http://wings.buffalo.edu/law/bclc/web/mnaghten.htm** and research the M'Naghten case. *Explain the insanity defense in that case and give your opinion about the court's ruling.*

In a 1994 trial in Virginia, attorneys for Lorena Bobbitt, who had sliced off her husband's penis with a kitchen knife while he was sleeping, successfully used the *irresistible-impulse* defense against charges of malicious wounding. She was acquitted of the crime. *Was Bobbitt's act of slicing off her husband's penis uncontrollable or uncontrolled? Defend your answer.*

Myth

The availability of an insanity defense allows dangerous offenders to escape conviction and go free.

Fact

Defendants found not guilty by reason of insanity rarely go free. Generally, they are confined to a mental institution until they are deemed by the committing court or some other judicial body to be sane or no longer dangerous. Also, there are only about 300 insanity pleas per year in the entire United States, approximately 0.1 percent of all felony complaints in a year.

SOURCE: Herbert Modlin, "Crime and Insanity," *Firing Line,* May 25, 1984; Samuel Walker, *Sense and Nonsense about Crime and Drugs: A Policy Guide,* 3rd ed. (Belmont, CA: Wadsworth, 1994), p. 151.

If the conditions of M'Naghten are met, the irresistible-impulse or control test is applied. If it is determined that the defendant knew that he or she was doing wrong at the time of the commission of the criminal act but nevertheless could not control his or her behavior, the defendant is entitled to an acquittal on the grounds of insanity. The major problem with the irresistible-impulse or control test is distinguishing between behavior that is uncontrollable and behavior that is simply uncontrolled.

Since 1980, the test for insanity used by most states has been the *substantial-capacity test* of the American Law Institute's Model Penal Code. Under that test, a defendant is not to be found guilty of a crime "if at the time of such conduct as a result of mental disease or defect he lacks substantial capacity either to appreciate the criminality of his conduct or to conform his conduct to the requirements of law." By using the term *substantial capacity,* the test does not require that a defendant be completely unable to distinguish right from wrong. The test has been criticized for its use of the ambiguous terms *substantial capacity* and *appreciate.* It also does not resolve the problem of determining whether behavior is uncontrollable or uncontrolled.

Following the public uproar over the 1982 acquittal of John Hinckley, the would-be assassin of President Ronald Reagan, on the grounds that he was legally insane, several states enacted "guilty but insane" or "guilty but mentally ill" laws. Defendants who are found guilty but insane generally receive sentences that include psychiatric treatment until they are cured. Then they are placed in the general prison population to serve the remainder of their sentences.

FYI: Insanity Defense

States are free to abolish insanity as a defense. The first state to do so was Montana, in 1979. Idaho and Utah are the only other states that have eliminated any possibility of a criminal defendant's being found not guilty by reason of insanity.

SOURCE: Joan Biskupic, "Court: Insanity Defense Not a Right," *The Washington Post* (March 29, 1994), p. A-3.

A fourth legal defense or legal excuse from criminal responsibility is self-defense or the defense of a third party. Generally, people are relieved of criminal responsibility if they use only the amount of force reasonably necessary to defend themselves or others against an apparent threat of unlawful and immediate violence. When it comes to the protection of property, however, the use of force is much more limited. Deadly force is not allowed, but nondeadly force may be used to protect one's property. The reason people are not held legally responsible for acting in self-defense or in defense of a third party is that due to extenuating circumstances, they do not act with *mens rea.*

entrapment A legal defense against criminal responsibility when a person, who was not already predisposed to it, is induced into committing a crime by a law enforcement officer or by his or her agent.

Entrapment is a fifth legal defense or legal excuse from criminal responsibility. People are generally considered either not responsible or less responsible for their crimes if they were entrapped, or induced into committing them, by a law enforcement officer or by someone acting as an agent for a law enforcement officer, such as an informer or an undercover agent. A successful entrapment defense, however, requires proof that the law enforcement officer or his or her agent instigated the crime or created the intent to commit the crime in the mind of a person who was not already predisposed to committing it. Thus, it is not entrapment if a law enforcement officer merely affords someone an opportunity to commit a crime, as, for example, when an undercover agent poses as a drug addict and purchases drugs from a drug dealer.

necessity defense A legal defense against criminal responsibility used when a crime has been committed to prevent a more serious crime.

The final legal defense or legal excuse from criminal responsibility to be discussed here is necessity. A **necessity defense** can be used when a crime has been committed to prevent a greater or more serious crime. In such a situation, there are extenuating circumstances, even though the act was committed with *mens rea.* Although it is rarely used, the necessity defense has been invoked occasionally, especially in cases of "political" crimes. The necessity defense was used successfully by Amy Carter (daughter of former President Jimmy Carter), Jerry Rubin, and other activists who were charged with trespassing for protesting apartheid on the property of the South African embassy in Washington, DC. The court agreed with the protesters that apartheid was a greater crime than trespassing. Interestingly, the law does not recognize economic necessity as a defense against or an excuse from criminal responsibility Therefore, the unemployed and hungry thief who steals groceries cannot successfully employ the necessity defense.

Causation A fifth ideal legal element of crime is causation, or a causal relationship between the legally forbidden harm and the *actus reus*. In other words, the criminal act must lead directly to the harm without a long delay. In a recent case in Georgia, for example, a father was accused of murdering his baby daughter. The murder charges were dropped, however, because too much time had passed between the night the 3½-month-old girl was shaken into a coma and her death 18 months later. Because of Georgia's year-and-a-day rule, the father was not charged with murder, but he still faced a charge of cruelty to children, which in Georgia carries a maximum sentence of 20 years. The purpose of the requirement of causation is to prevent people from facing the threat of criminal charges the rest of their lives.

> **FYI — The Year-And-A-Day Rule**
>
> The rule that a person cannot be prosecuted for murder if the victim dies more than a year and a day after the injury is based on thirteenth-century English common law.
>
> Source: *Tennessee v. Rogers,* 992 S.W.2d 393 (1999); *United States v. Jackson,* 528 A.2d 1211, 1214 (D.C.1987).

Concurrence Ideally, for any behavior to be considered a crime, there must be concurrence between the *actus reus* and the *mens rea*. In other words, the criminal conduct and the criminal intent must occur together. For example, suppose you call someone to repair your broken washing machine, and that person comes to your home, fixes your washing machine, and on the way out takes your television set. The repair person cannot be found guilty of entering your home illegally (trespass) because that was not his or her initial intent. However, the repair person can be found guilty of stealing your television set.

Punishment The last of the ideal legal elements of a crime is punishment. For a behavior to be considered a crime, there must be a statutory provision for punishment or at least the threat of punishment. Without the threat of punishment, a law is unenforceable and is therefore not a criminal law.

DEGREES OR CATEGORIES OF CRIME

Crimes can be classified according to the degree or severity of the offense, according to the nature of the acts prohibited, or on some other basis, such as a statistical reporting scheme. One way crimes are distinguished by degree or severity of the offense is by dividing them into *felonies* and *misdemeanors*. The only way to determine whether a crime is a felony or misdemeanor is by knowing the legislated punishment. Consequently, a felony in one jurisdiction might be a misdemeanor in another jurisdiction, and vice versa. Generally, a felony, as noted in Chapter 1, is a relatively serious offense punishable by death, a fine, or confinement in a state or federal prison for more than 1 year. A misdemeanor, on the other hand, is any lesser crime that is not a felony. Misdemeanors are usually punishable by no more than a $1,000 fine and 1 year of incarceration, generally in a county or city jail.

Another way of categorizing crimes is to distinguish between offenses that are *mala in se* and offenses that are *mala prohibita*. Crimes ***mala in se*** are "wrong in themselves." They are characterized by universality and timelessness. That is, they are crimes everywhere and have been crimes at all times.

mala in se Wrong in themselves. A description applied to crimes that are characterized by universality and timelessness.

mala prohibita Offenses that are illegal because laws define them as such. They lack universality and timelessness.

Examples are murder and rape. Crimes ***mala prohibita*** are offenses that are illegal because laws define them as such. They lack universality and timelessness. Examples are trespassing, gambling, and prostitution.

For statistical reporting purposes, crimes are frequently classified as *crimes against the person* or *violent crimes* (for example, murder, rape, assault), *crimes against property* or *property crime* (for instance, burglary, larceny, auto theft), and *crimes against public decency, public order, and public justice* or *public order crimes* (for example, drunkenness, disorderly conduct, vagrancy).

Table 2.1 is a list of selected crimes and their definitions, grouped by type. The selection, placement, and definition of the crimes are somewhat arbitrary.

TABLE 2.1 Types and Definitions of Selected Crimes

Violent Crimes	Crimes that involve force or threat of force.
Murder	The unlawful killing of another human being with malice aforethought.
Manslaughter	The unlawful killing of another human being without malice aforethought.
Aggravated assault	An assault committed (1) with the intention of committing some additional crime, (2) with peculiar outrage or atrocity, or (3) with a dangerous or deadly weapon.
Forcible rape	The act of having sexual intercourse with a woman, by force and against her will.
Robbery	Theft from a person, accompanied by violence, threat of violence, or putting the person in fear.
Kidnapping	The unlawful taking and carrying away of a human being by force and against his or her will.
Property Crimes	Crimes that involve taking money or property, but usually without force or threat of force.
Larceny	The unlawful taking and carrying away of another person's property with the intent of depriving the owner of that property.
Burglary	Entering a building or occupied structure to commit a crime therein.
Embezzlement	The willful taking or converting to one's own use another person's money or property, which was lawfully acquired by the wrongdoer by reason of some office, employment, or position of trust.
Arson	Purposely setting fire to a house or other building.
Extortion/blackmail	The obtaining of property from another by wrongful use of actual or threatened force, violence, or fear, or under color of official right.
Receiving stolen property	Knowingly accepting, buying, or concealing goods that were illegally obtained by another person.
Fraud	The false representation of a matter of fact, whether by words or by conduct, by false or misleading allegations, or by concealment of that which should have been disclosed, which deceives and is intended to deceive, and causes legal harm.
Forgery	The fraudulent making of a false writing having apparent legal significance.
Counterfeiting	Under federal law, falsely making, forging, or altering any obligation or other security of the United States, with intent to defraud.
"Morals" Offenses	Violations of virtue in sexual conduct (for example, fornication, seduction, prostitution, adultery, illicit cohabitation, sodomy, bigamy, and incest).
Public Order Offenses	Violations that constitute a threat to public safety or peace (for example, disorderly conduct, loitering, unlawful assembly, drug offenses, driving while intoxicated).
Offenses Against the Government	Crimes motivated by the desire to effect social change or to rebel against perceived unfair laws and governments (for example, treason, sedition, hindering apprehension or prosecution of a felon, perjury, and bribery).
Offenses by Government	Harms inflicted upon people by their own governments or the governments of others (for example, genocide and torture, police brutality, civil rights violations, and political bribe taking).
Hate Crimes	Criminal offenses committed against a person, property, or society and motivated, in whole or in part, by the offender's bias against a race, a religion, an ethnic/national origin group, or a sexual-orientation group.
Organized Crimes	Unlawful acts of members of highly organized and disciplined associations engaged in supplying illegal goods and services, such as gambling, prostitution, loansharking, narcotics, and labor racketeering.
White-Collar and Corporate Crimes	Generally nonviolent offenses committed for financial gain by means of deception by entrepreneurs and other professionals who utilize their special occupational skills and opportunities (for example, environmental pollution, manufacture and sale of unsafe products, price fixing, price gouging, and deceptive advertising).
Occupational Crimes	Offenses committed through opportunities created in the course of a legal business or profession and crimes committed by professionals, such as lawyers and doctors, acting in their professional capacities.
"Victimless" Crimes	Offenses involving a willing and private exchange of goods or services that are in strong demand but are illegal (for example, gambling, prostitution, drug law violations, and homosexual acts between consenting adults).

There are many different types of crime, and some crimes can be placed in more than one category. Legal definitions of crime vary among jurisdictions and frequently list numerous degrees, conditions, and qualifications. A good source of legal crime definitions is *Black's Law Dictionary*.

THINKING CRITICALLY

1. Are there any acts that are currently legal that you think should be illegal? If so, what?
2. Do you think there should be other elements of crime besides the seven listed in this section? If so, what other elements should there be?

Measurement of Crime

Many people who read the daily newspaper or watch the nightly news on television believe that crime is the most pressing problem in the United States. But is it? How do you know how much crime is committed? How do you know whether crime is, in fact, increasing or decreasing? Besides what you learn from the media, perhaps you have been the victim of crime or know someone who has been. Although that information is important, it does not indicate whether your experience with crime or the experience of someone you know is typical. The fact is that what we and the media know about crime, by and large, is based on statistics supplied by government agencies.

FYI — The Distribution of Crime

Although social concern about crime is directed primarily at violent crimes, only 5–15 percent of all crime committed annually, according to official statistics, is violent crime. The remaining 85–95 percent is property crime and public order crime.

SOURCE: See, for example, Federal Bureau of Investigation, *Crime in the United States 2002*, U.S. Department of Justice (Washington, DC: GPO, 2003).

CRIME STATISTICS

The difficulty in relying on crime statistics to measure the prevalence of crime is that "statistics about crime and delinquency are probably the most unreliable and most difficult of all social statistics."[4] In other words, "it is impossible to determine with accuracy the amount of crime [or delinquency] in any given jurisdiction at any particular time."[5] Why? There are several reasons. First, "some behavior is labeled . . . 'crime' by one observer but not by another."[6] If a behavior is not labeled a crime, it is not counted. On the other hand, if a behavior is wrongly labeled a crime, then it may be wrongly counted as a crime. Both situations contribute to the inaccuracy of crime statistics. Second, a large proportion of crimes are undetected. Crimes that are not detected obviously cannot be counted. Third, some crimes may not be reported to the police. If they are not reported to the police, they are unlikely to be counted. Fourth, crimes that are reported to the police may not be officially recorded by them, for various reasons (to be discussed later), or may be inaccurately recorded. Crimes that are not officially recorded by the police are called the **dark figure of crime** (see Figure 2.1).

dark figure of crime The number of crimes not officially recorded by the police.

crime index An estimate of crimes committed.

For all of the foregoing reasons, any record of crimes—such as "offenses known to the police," arrests, convictions, or commitments to prison—can be considered at most a **crime index,** or an estimate of crimes committed. Unfortunately, no index or estimate of crimes is a reliable indicator of the actual amount of crime. The indexes or estimates vary independently of the true amount of crime, whatever that may be. Figure 2.1 portrays one possible relationship of a crime index to the dark figure of crime and the true amount of crime. It shows how great a discrepancy there can be between the index and the actual amount of crime.

Many people learn about crime from the media. *How does the media determine which crimes to report?*

FIGURE 2.1 Dark Figure of Crime

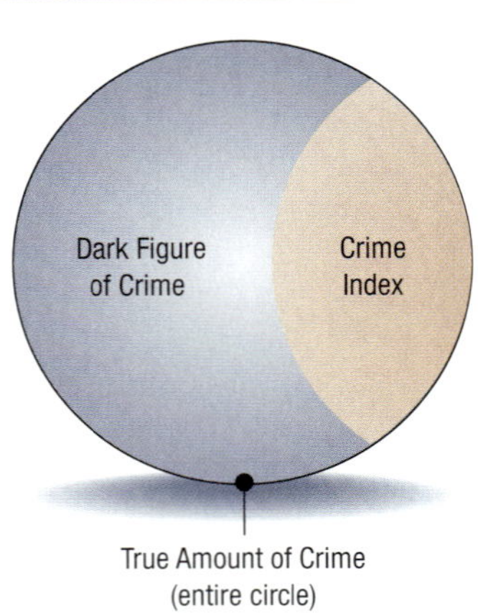

Adding to the confusion is the reality that any index of crime varies with changes in police practices, court policies, and public opinion—to name just three factors. Suppose, for example, that a large city is hosting a major convention and city leaders want to make a good impression on visitors. The mayor asks the police chief to order officers to "sweep" the streets of prostitutes. As a result of that police policy, there is a dramatic increase in arrests for prostitution and in the index measuring prostitution. Does the increase in the index mean that the true amount of prostitution increased in the city? The answer is that we do not know and, for that matter, can never know. All we do know is that the index measuring prostitution increased as a result of police practices.

Thus, despite what some government agencies or the media may suggest, we do not know, nor can we ever know, the true amount of crime. For the same reasons, we can never know for sure whether crime is increasing, decreasing, or remaining at the same level. The sophisticated student of crime knows only that indexes of crime are imperfect estimates that vary widely. Those variations, which are independent of variations in the true amount of crime, depend on such things as police practices, court policies, and public opinion. Therefore, comparisons of crime measures are an especially dubious exercise. Criminal justice officials and professors routinely compare crime measures in different jurisdictions and at different times. What they are doing, though they rarely acknowledge it, even when they are aware of it, is comparing indexes or estimates of crime. Although such comparisons tell us nothing about differences in true amounts of crime, they do provide insights into police practices, court policies, and public opinion.

offenses known to the police A crime index, reported in the FBI's uniform crime reports, composed of crimes that are both reported to and recorded by the police.

Probably the best index of crime—that is, the least inaccurate!—is **offenses known to the police.** That index, which is reported in the FBI's uniform crime reports (to be discussed later), is composed of crimes that are both reported to and recorded by the police. The reason it is an inaccurate measure of the true amount of crime is that the number of offenses known to the police is always much smaller than the number of crimes actually committed. One reason is that victims do not report all crimes to the police. There are many reasons for the nonreporting of crimes:[7]

1. Victims may consider the crime insignificant and not worth reporting.
2. They may hope to avoid embarrassing the offender, who may be a relative, school friend, or fellow employee.
3. They may wish to avoid the publicity that might result if the crime were reported.
4. They might have agreed to the crime, as in gambling offenses and some sexual offenses.
5. They may wish to avoid the inconvenience of calling the police, [filling out a report, appearing in court, and so on].
6. They may be intimidated by [or afraid of] the offender.
7. They may [dislike] the police or [be] opposed to the punitive policies of the legal system.
8. They may feel that the police are so inefficient that they will be unable to catch the offender even if the offense is reported.

Another reason the number of offenses known to the police is necessarily much smaller than the number of crimes actually committed is that the police do not always officially record the crimes that are reported to them. In practice, police officers often use their discretion to handle informally an incident reported to them; that is, they do not make an official report of the incident. Or they may exercise discretion in enforcing the law (for instance, by not arresting the customer in a case of prostitution). The law is often vague, and

CJ ONLINE

Crime on Campus

Go to the U.S. Department of Education's Office of Post Secondary Education Campus Security Statistics website at **www.ed.gov/offices/OPE/PPI/security.html** for information and statistics on reported criminal offenses at colleges and universities across the United States. *What do the statistics say about crime at schools in your area?*

Los Angeles police officers respond to a bungled bank robbery. The heavily armed, masked robbers fired hundreds of shots in a gun battle getaway that left 2 dead and at least 11 hurt. *In this crime event, what crimes would be officially recorded for purposes of the FBI's uniform crime reports?*

officers may not know the law or how to enforce it. Still another reason is that some police officers feel they are too busy to fill out and file police reports. Also, some officers, feeling an obligation to protect the reputations of their cities or being pressured by politicians to "get the crime rate down," may manipulate statistics to show a decrease in crime.[8]

Additionally, the number of offenses included in the index is much smaller than the actual number of crimes because of the way crimes are counted. For the FBI's uniform crime reports, when more than one crime is committed during a crime event, only the most serious is counted for statistical purposes. The seriousness of the crime is determined by the maximum legal penalty associated with it. Thus, for example, if a robber holds up 10 people in a tavern, takes their money, shoots and kills the bartender, and makes a getaway in a stolen car, only one crime, the murder, is counted for statistical purposes. However, the offender could legally be charged with several different crimes. (The practice of counting only the most serious offense in a multiple-crime event is being changed with the implementation of the National Incident-Based Reporting System, which will be discussed later in this chapter.)

Despite the problems in recording crime events, *offenses known to the police* is a more accurate index of crime than arrest statistics, charging statistics, trial statistics, conviction statistics, sentencing statistics, or imprisonment statistics. As shown in Figure 2.2, the further a crime index is from the initial commission of crime, the more inaccurate it is as a measure of the true amount of crime.

FYI Underreporting Crime

In 1998, Philadelphia police failed to report 13,000 to 37,000 major crimes including robberies, aggravated assaults, and thefts. The review of city crime statistics by the city controller's office also revealed that other crimes were wrongly classified as less serious crimes.

SOURCE: "Philly underreports crime," *The Orlando Sentinel* (September 15, 2000), p. A-11.

FIGURE 2.2 Indexes of Crime

Most Accurate → Least Accurate

Crimes committed (true amount of crime) ▶ Crimes discovered ▶ Crimes reported to the police ▶ Crimes recorded by the police ▶ Arrests ▶ Criminal charges ▶ Trials ▶ Convictions ▶ Imprisonments

The further away from the initial commission of a crime, the more inaccurate crime indexes are as measures of the true amount of crime.

CRIME RATES

crime rate A measure of the incidence of crime expressed as the number of crimes per unit of population or some other base.

FYI: Age and Crime Rates

It has been estimated that changes in the age structure of the population account for approximately 40 percent of the changes in the crime rate.

SOURCE: Darrell Steffensmeir, "Is the Crime Rate Really Falling? An 'Aging' U.S. Population and Its Effect on the Nation's Crime Rate, 1980–1984," *Journal of Research in Crime and Delinquency* 24 (1987), pp. 23–48.

When crime indexes are compared, rarely are total numbers of crimes used. Instead, crime is typically reported as rates. A **crime rate** is expressed as the number of crimes per unit of population or some other base. Crime rates are used instead of total numbers because they are more comparable. For example, suppose you wanted to compare the crime of murder in the United States for the years 1960 and 2000. There were 9,110 murders and nonnegligent manslaughters reported to and recorded by the police in 1960; there were 15,517 murders and nonnegligent manslaughters reported to and recorded by the police in 2000. According to those data, the total number of murders and nonnegligent manslaughters reported to and recorded by the police in 2000 increased about 70 percent from the number reported and recorded by the police in 1960. Although this information may be helpful, it ignores the substantial increase in the population of the United States—and thus in the number of potential murderers and potential murder victims—between 1960 and 2000.

A better comparison—though, of course, not an accurate one—would be a comparison that takes into account the different population sizes. To enable such a comparison, a population base, such as "per 100,000 people" is arbitrarily chosen. Then the total number of murders and nonnegligent manslaughters for a particular year is divided by the total population of the United States for the same year. The result is multiplied by 100,000. When those calculations are made for the years 1960 and 2000, the rate of murders and nonnegligent manslaughters is 5.1 per 100,000 people for 1960 and 5.5 per 100,000 people for 2000 (see Figure 2.3). According to those figures, the rate of murder and nonnegligent manslaughter in 2000 was about 8 percent higher than it was in 1960. Thus, although both sets of data show that murders and nonnegligent manslaughters reported to and recorded by the police increased between 1960 and 2000, the increase is not nearly as great when the increase in the size of the population (which was 57 percent) is taken into account. Crime rates provide a more accurate indication of increases or decreases in crime indexes than do total numbers of crimes. Remember, however, that what are being compared are indexes and not true amounts.

FIGURE 2.3 Calculating Crime Rates

1960

$$\frac{\text{9,110 murders \& nonnegligent manslaughters}}{\text{179,323,175 (1960 U.S. population)}} \times 100{,}000 = 5.1 \text{ per 100,000 people}$$

2000

$$\frac{\text{15,517 murders \& nonnegligent manslaughters}}{\text{281,421,906 (2000 U.S. population)}} \times 100{,}000 = 5.5 \text{ per 100,000 people}$$

A variety of factors indirectly related to crime can affect crime rates. For example, burglary rates might increase, not because there are more burglaries, but because more things are insured, and insurance companies require police reports before they will reimburse their policyholders. Changing demographic characteristics of the population can also have an effect. For example, because of the post–World War II baby boom (1945–1964), between 1963 and 1988 there were more people in the age group most prone to committing recorded crime (18- to 24-year-olds). All other things being equal, higher crime rates would be expected between 1963 and 1988 simply because there were more people in the age group that commits the most recorded crime. By the same token, a decrease in crime rates might be expected after 1988, all other things being equal, because the baby boom generation is no longer at those crime-prone ages. However, an increase in crime might be expected when their children reach the age range 18 to 24.

Urbanization is another factor, especially with regard to violent crime. Violent crime is primarily a big-city phenomenon. Thus, violent crime rates might increase as more of the population moves from rural to urban areas or as what were once rural areas become more urban.

FYI: Florida Crime Rate

Florida's crime rate dropped 1.7 percent from 1995 to 1996, according to the Florida Department of Law Enforcement (FDLE). Using that statistic, state officials claimed success for the state's emphases on imprisonment and juvenile crime. However, the FDLE report failed to mention that 20 Florida police agencies had not submitted crime reports for 1996. Rather than exclude those 20 agencies from the analysis, the FDLE instead recorded no crimes for the 348,231 residents of those 20 jurisdictions. If the FDLE had used numbers only from those agencies that reported, its calculation of the Florida crime rate would have been 0.2 percent higher in 1996 than it was in 1995, not 1.7 percent lower.

SOURCE: "Crime Drop: More Fiction Than Fact?" *The Orlando Sentinel* (May 11, 1997), p. B-1.

UNIFORM CRIME REPORTS (UCR)

A primary source of crime statistics in the United States is the **uniform crime reports** (UCR), which are a collection of crime statistics and other law enforcement information published annually under the title *Crime in the United States*. They are the result of a voluntary national program begun in the 1920s by the International Association of Chiefs of Police.[9] The program was turned over to the FBI in 1930 by the attorney general, whose office Congress had authorized to serve as the national clearinghouse for crime-related statistics. Today more than 17,000 city, county, and state law enforcement agencies are active in the program; they represent more than 95 percent of the U.S. population.[10]

uniform crime reports A collection of crime statistics and other law enforcement information gathered under a voluntary national program administered by the FBI.

The uniform crime reports include two major indexes: (1) offenses known to the police, discussed earlier, and (2) statistics about persons arrested. The section on offenses known to the police, or offenses reported to the police, provides information about the **eight index crimes,** or Part I offenses:

eight index crimes The Part I offenses in the FBI's uniform crime reports. They are (1) murder and nonnegligent manslaughter, (2) forcible rape, (3) robbery, (4) aggravated assault, (5) burglary, (6) larceny-theft, (7) motor vehicle theft, and (8) arson, which was added in 1979.

1. Murder and nonnegligent manslaughter.
2. Forcible rape.
3. Robbery.
4. Aggravated assault.
5. Burglary.
6. Larceny-theft.
7. Motor vehicle theft.
8. Arson (added in 1979).

The first four offenses are considered violent offenses; the last four are considered property offenses. According to the UCR, in 2001 more than 11.8 million index offenses, excluding arson, were reported to the police, up 2.1 percent from the previous year. This was the first increase in the index since 1991. Note that the terrorist crimes committed on September 11, 2001, are not included in these data.

The 1996 edition of the uniform crime reports included for the first time data reported on crimes motivated by bias against individuals on account of race, religion, disability, sexual orientation, or ethnicity/national origin. The UCR designated these as hate crimes or bias crimes. In 2001, crimes against persons made up 64.6 percent of the 11,447 hate crime offenses reported; crimes against property accounted for 34.7 percent, and less than 1 percent to crimes against society.[11] Intimidation was the single most frequently reported offense, accounting for 37.9 percent of the total, followed by damage, destruction, or vandalism of property, 26.4 percent; simple assault, 18.8 percent; and aggravated assault, 10.9 percent.[12] Of all the hate crimes reported,

Myth | Fact

Myth	Fact
When the media report that crime has increased or decreased from one year to the next, they are generally referring to increases or decreases in the true amount of crime.	What the media are usually referring to when they report that "crime" has increased or decreased from one year to the next is an increase or decrease in the aggregate rate of the eight index crimes (that is, the "crime index total"), not the rates of other crimes or the true amount of crime.

46.2 percent were motivated by racial bias, 17.5 percent by religious bias, 13.9 percent by sexual-orientation bias, 21.9 percent by ethnic bias, and 0.3 percent by disability bias.[13]

The other major crime index in the uniform crime reports is based on arrest statistics. Arrest data are provided for the eight index crimes, as well as 21 other crimes and status offenses. The 21 other crimes and status offenses are referred to as Part II offenses. A **status offense** is an act that is illegal for a juvenile but would not be a crime if committed by an adult (such as truancy or running away from home). Table 2.2 lists the Part I and Part II offenses in the FBI's uniform crime reports.

status offense An act that is illegal for a juvenile but would not be a crime if committed by an adult.

According to the UCR, law enforcement agencies made about 14 million arrests for violations of Part I and Part II offenses nationwide in 2001, down 2 percent from the previous year.[14] The offenses for which the most arrests were made in 2001 (approximately 1.6 million and 1.4 million arrests, respectively) were drug abuse violations and driving under the influence.[15] The third largest number of arrests (about 1.3 million) was for simple assault.[16] Arrestees generally were young (46 percent were under 25 years of age), male (77.5 percent), and white (69.5 percent).[17] The index crime for which women were most frequently arrested was larceny-theft, which accounted for 71 percent of all female arrests for index offenses and 14 percent of all female arrests.[18]

In addition to statistics on offenses known to the police and persons arrested, the UCR include statistics on crime index offenses cleared by the

FYI: Decline in Violent Crime Rates

According to the FBI's 2001 uniform crime report, the rate of violent crimes reported to the police increased slightly for the first time since 1992. Among the factors that police chiefs and academics cite for the preceding 9-year decline are (1) aging-out of the crime-prone years by the postwar baby boom generation; (2) fewer turf battles over crack cocaine distribution because of market maturation and consolidation; (3) police efforts to disarm criminals and juveniles; (4) more police officers on the beat; (5) smarter policing; (6) tougher criminal justice legislation, such as the federal law that ties financial aid for prison building to a requirement that states keep violent offenders incarcerated for at least 85 percent of their sentences; (7) increased interest in "grass-roots" crime prevention; and (8) a better economy that has provided jobs and given cities more to invest in crime control.

SOURCE: "Serious Crimes Decline for 8th Consecutive Year," *The Orlando Sentinel,* May 8, 2000, p. A-7; "Violent Crimes Plummet 7%—Drop Biggest in 35 Years," *The Orlando Sentinel,* June 2, 1997, p. A-4; "FBI Report: Crime Rate Still Falling," *The Orlando Sentinel,* October 5, 1997, p. A-3.

TABLE 2.2 Part I and Part II Offenses of the FBI's Uniform Crime Reports

Part I Offenses—Index Crimes	Part II Offenses
Violent Crime	1. Other assaults (simple)
1. Murder and nonnegligent manslaughter	2. Forgery and counterfeiting
2. Forcible rape	3. Fraud
3. Robbery	4. Embezzlement
4. Aggravated assault	5. Stolen property: buying, receiving, possessing
Property Crime	6. Vandalism
5. Burglary—breaking or entering	7. Weapons: carrying, possessing, etc.
6. Larceny-theft	8. Prostitution and commercialized vice
7. Motor vehicle theft	9. Sex offenses
8. Arson	10. Drug abuse violations
	11. Gambling
	12. Offenses against the family and children
	13. Driving under the influence
	14. Liquor laws
	15. Drunkenness
	16. Disorderly conduct
	17. Vagrancy
	18. All other offenses
	19. Suspicion
	20. Curfew and loitering laws
	21. Runaway

police. **Crime index offenses cleared** (also called *clearance rates* or *percent cleared by arrest*) is a rough index of police performance in solving crimes. According to the UCR, an offense that is cleared is one for which "at least one person is arrested, charged with the commission of the offense, and turned over to the court for prosecution."[19] The arrest of one person may clear several crimes, or one offense may be cleared by the arrest of several people. Clearances recorded in one year may be for offenses committed in previous years. Clearance rates remain remarkably stable from year to year. Generally, the police are able to clear about 70 percent of murders and nonnegligent manslaughters, 50 percent of forcible rapes, 25 percent of robberies, 60 percent of aggravated assaults, 15 percent of burglaries, 20 percent of larceny-thefts, 15 percent of motor vehicle thefts, and 15 percent of acts of arson.[20] Annually, the police are able to clear about 20 percent of all index offenses (19.6 percent in 2001).[21]

crime index offenses cleared The number of offenses for which at least one person has been arrested, charged with the commission of the offense, and turned over to the court for prosecution.

The UCR also provide statistics about law enforcement personnel, such as the number of full-time sworn officers in a particular jurisdiction and the number of law enforcement officers killed in the line of duty.

Finally, in recent editions of the UCR, special sections have been devoted to topical studies. For example, the 1996 special section, entitled "Drugs in America: 1980–1995," presented a relatively detailed examination of the national drug arrest trends during that period. In the 1999 edition of the UCR the special section is entitled "The Chances of Lifetime Murder Victimization, 1997." Among data presented are comparisons of age-specific murder rates, by race and sex, for the years 1978 and 1997. The 2001 UCR has two special sections: "The Terrorist Attacks of September 11, 2001: A Compilation of Data" and "Injuries from Violent Crime, 2000: A Study Using NIBRS Data" (the NIBRS is discussed in the next section).[22]

NATIONAL INCIDENT-BASED REPORTING SYSTEM (NIBRS)

In 1982, a joint task force of the Bureau of Justice Statistics (BJS) and the Federal Bureau of Investigation (FBI) was created to study and recommend ways to improve the quality of information contained in the uniform crime reports.[23] The result is the National Incident-Based Reporting System (NIBRS), which collected its first data in 1991. Under NIBRS, participating law enforcement authorities provide offense and arrest data on 22 broad categories of crime, covering 46 offenses (as compared to the 8 UCR index offenses), and provide only arrest information on 11 other offenses (as compared to the 21 Part II UCR offenses) (see Table 2.3).

Perhaps the greatest and most important difference between the NIBRS and the UCR is that the NIBRS contains more data on each crime, making it possible to examine crimes in much more detail. The NIBRS contains more than 50 different pieces of information about a crime, divided into six segments, or categories. It is hoped that the increased amount of information in the NIBRS will provide the basis for a much greater understanding of crime and its causes (or at least of crime reporting and recording behavior) than is possible with the data from the UCR. Table 2.4 lists the NIBRS data elements.

TABLE 2.3 The National Incident-Based Reporting System

GROUP A OFFENSES	GROUP B OFFENSES
Arson	Bad checks
Assault offenses	Curfew/loitering/vagrancy
Bribery	Disorderly conduct
Burglary/breaking and entering	Driving under the influence
Counterfeiting/forgery	Drunkenness
Destruction/damage/vandalism	Liquor law violations
Drug/narcotic offenses	Nonviolent family offenses
Embezzlement	Peeping Tom
Extortion/blackmail	Runaways
Fraud offenses	Trespassing
Gambling offenses	All other offenses
Homicide offenses	
Kidnapping/abduction	
Larceny/theft offenses	
Motor vehicle theft	
Pornography/obscene material	
Prostitution offenses	
Robbery	
Sex offenses, forcible	
Sex offenses, nonforcible	
Stolen property offenses	
Weapons law violations	

TABLE 2.4 NIBRS Data Reporting Elements

Administrative Segment	Victim Segment
1. ORI (originating agency identifier) number	24. Victim number (ID)
2. Incident number	25. Victim UCR offense code
3. Incident date/hour	26. Type of victim
4. Exceptional clearance indicator	27. Age of victim
5. Exceptional clearance date	28. Sex of victim
Offense Segment	29. Race of victim
6. UCR offense code	30. Ethnicity of victim
7. Attempted/completed code	31. Resident status of victim
8. Alcohol/drug use by offender	32. Homicide/assault circumstances
9. Type of location	33. Justifiable homicide circumstances
10. Number of premises entered	34. Type of injury
11. Method of entry	35. Related offender murder
12. Type of criminal activity	36. Relationship of victim to offender
13. Type of weapon/force used	**Offender Segment**
14. Bias crime code	37. Offender number (ID)
Property Segment	38. Age of offender
15. Type of property loss	39. Sex of offender
16. Property description	40. Race of offender
17. Property value	**Arrestee Segment**
18. Recovery date	41. Arrestee number (ID)
19. Number of stolen motor vehicles	42. Transaction number
20. Number of recovered motor vehicles	43. Arrest date
21. Suspected drug type	44. Type of arrest
22. Estimated drug quantity	45. Multiple clearance indicator
23. Drug measurement unit	46. UCR arrest offense code
	47. Arrestee armed indicator
	48. Age of arrestee
	49. Sex of arrestee
	50. Race of arrestee
	51. Ethnicity of arrestee
	52. Resident status of arrestee
	53. Disposition of arrestee under 18

The BJS and the FBI hope that eventually the NIBRS will replace the UCR as the source of official FBI crime counts. As of December 2002, 21 states have been NIBRS certified, that is, have shown that they are capable of meeting NIBRS's data submission requirements, 15 states are in the process of testing NIBRS, and an additional 8 states are developing NIBRS with plans to test in the future. Only 6 states (Alaska, Florida, Georgia, Mississippi, Nevada, and Wyoming) have no formal plans or no current interest in participating in NIBRS.[24] So far, the biggest impediment to implementation of the NIBRS is that it is a "paperless" reporting system and, thus, requires the use of a computerized records management system. Many larger law enforcement agencies have older computer systems that require extensive and costly modifications. Many smaller agencies do not have computer systems. Although some agencies have received federal and state grants to upgrade or buy computer systems for the NIBRS, the amounts allocated have covered only a small part of the need.[25]

Adding to the implementation problem are benefit and policy concerns. Some law enforcement agencies question who, other than researchers, will benefit from their reporting NIBRS data. Others fear that, because NIBRS reports

FYI

Switching Reporting Systems

In 1997, the state of Florida decided to abandon incident-based reporting after using it for nearly 8 years. The Florida Department of Law Enforcement expects to save $1 million a year by switching to summary-based reporting, which requires less information.

Source: "Crime Drop: More Fiction Than Fact?" *The Orlando Sentinel*, May 11, 1997, p. B-1.

The National Incident-Based Reporting System provides the FBI more data on crime. *How will the new data help the FBI more effectively combat crime?*

multiple offenses within an incident, crime will appear to increase, causing a public relations nightmare for law enforcement officials. Some law enforcement administrators are concerned that the detailed incident reporting required for NIBRS will tie up patrol officers, keeping them from responding to the needs of the community.

NATIONAL CRIME VICTIMIZATION SURVEYS (NCVS)

The **national crime victimization surveys (NCVS)** are the other major source of crime statistics in the United States. The surveys provide a detailed picture of crime incidents, victims, and trends from the victim's perspective. Formerly called the national crime surveys (NCS), they have been conducted annually since 1972 by the Bureau of the Census for the U.S. Department of Justice's Bureau of Justice Statistics.[26] The NCVS, published under the title *Criminal Victimization in the United States,* were created not only as a basis for learning more about crime and its victims, but also as a means of complementing and assessing what is known about crime from the FBI's uniform crime reports. (From 1996 on, the NCVS are available only in electronic formats, see www.ojp.usdoj.gov.)

national crime victimization surveys
A source of crime statistics based on interviews in which respondents are asked whether they have been victims of any of the FBI's index offenses (except murder, nonnegligent manslaughter, and arson) or other crimes during the past 6 months. If they have, they are asked to provide information about the experience.

From a nationally representative sample of about 50,000 households, respondents aged 12 or older are asked in interviews whether they have been victims of any of the FBI's index offenses (except murder, nonnegligent manslaughter, and arson) or any other crimes during the past 6 months. If they have, they are asked to provide information about the experience. Because major changes were made in the format and methodology of the NCVS in 1992, adjustments have been made to the data before 1993 to make them comparable with data collected since the changes. Like the UCR, the NCVS are merely an index of crime and not an accurate measure of the true amount of crime that is committed.

Generally, the national crime victimization surveys produce different results from the FBI's uniform crime reports. For nearly all offenses, the NCVS show more crimes being committed than the UCR. This underestimation by the UCR may result from victims' failure to report crimes to the police or from failure by the police to report to the FBI all the crimes they know about. The UCR count more of some kinds of offenses (such as assault) and count them differently. For example, the UCR count each report of a domestic assault at the same address separately; the NCVS count the repeated assaults as one victimization. The UCR count crimes reported by people and businesses that the NCVS don't reach. Unlike the UCR, the NCVS rely on random samplings of victims and their memories of things that may have happened months ago, both of which are subject to some degree of error. Other problems with the NCVS are interviewers who may be biased or who may cheat, and respondents who may lie or exaggerate, or may respond without understanding the questions.

Differences in the data sources help explain the differences in the trends indicated by the NCVS and the UCR. For example, in one year (1990), NCVS respondents indicated that they had experienced about 50 percent more crimes, on average, than were recorded by the FBI. However, the differences varied by offense. The smallest difference between the two indexes for that year was for motor vehicle theft (20 percent). The largest difference was for burglary (67 percent). The smaller difference for motor vehicle theft was probably due to insurance companies requiring a police report before reimbursing policyholders for their losses.

Sometimes overall changes in the two indexes differ. For example, between 1984 and 1985, the total number of crimes in the UCR increased 4.6 percent, while the total number of crimes in the NCVS decreased 1.9 percent. The difference probably stems from the difference in what the two indexes measure. Thus, between 1984 and 1985, there was an apparent increase in the number of crimes reported to and recorded by the police, but an apparent decrease in the number of crimes to which people said they had been subjected. Figure 2.4 displays the trends in four measures or indexes of serious violent crime. Remember that serious violent crimes include murder, rape, robbery, and aggravated assault.

CJ ONLINE

Gallup Crime Polls

The Gallup Organization conducts public opinion polls on a variety of topics that affect Americans. You can learn more about the public's view of crime issues by visiting the Gallup website at **www.gallup.com.** *What connection, if any, is there between public opinion toward crime and crime statistics?*

self-report crime surveys Surveys in which subjects are asked whether they have committed crimes.

FYI

Common Offenses

The most commonly reported offenses in self-report crime surveys are larceny, indecency, and tax evasion.

SOURCE: Thomas Gabor, *Everybody Does It! Crimes by the Public* (Toronto: University of Toronto Press, 1994).

Self-report crime surveys ask selected subjects whether they have committed crimes. *What are some problems with getting accurate information about crime from these surveys?*

SELF-REPORT CRIME SURVEYS

Whereas other tallies of crime rely on summary police reports, incident-based reports, or victim interviews, **self-report crime surveys** ask selected subjects whether they have committed crimes. Self-report crime surveys, like all crime measures, are indexes of crime; they are not accurate measures of the true amount of crime. To date, most self-report crime surveys conducted in the United States have been administered to schoolchildren, especially high school students. Some examples of such nationwide self-report crime survey efforts are the National Youth Survey, begun in 1975, and the effort to ascertain and to gauge fluctuations in the levels of smoking, drinking, and illicit drug use among secondary school students, begun by the National Institute on Drug Abuse in 1975.

Earlier self-report crime surveys of adults interestingly enough found an enormous amount of hidden crime in the United States. Those self-report crime surveys indicated that more than 90 percent of all Americans had committed crimes for which they could have been found guilty and imprisoned.[27] This is not to say that all Americans are murderers, thieves, or rapists, for they are not, but only that crime serious enough to warrant an individual's imprisonment is more widespread among the U.S. population than many people might think or imagine. Moreover, it is unlikely that the pervasiveness of crime in the population has lessened significantly since the earlier self-report crime surveys were conducted.

FIGURE 2.4 **Four Measures of Serious Violent Crime**

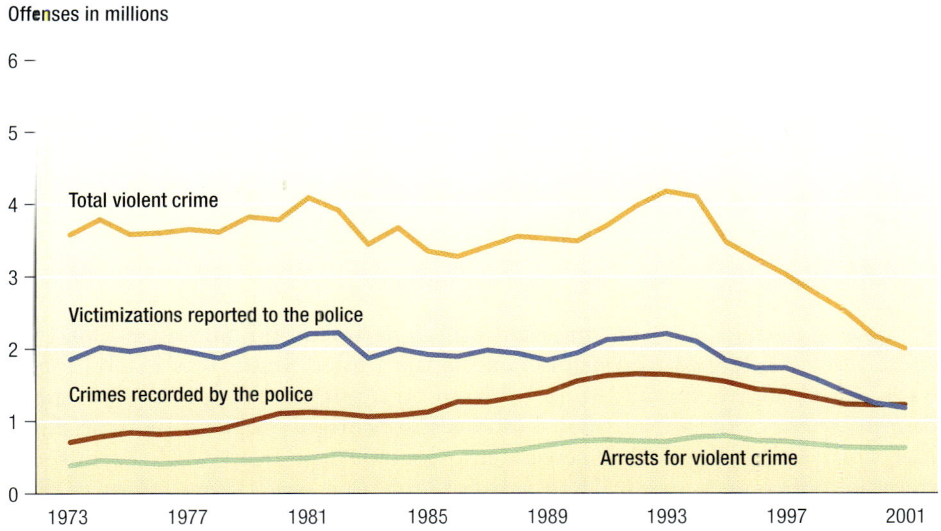

Notes:

1. The serious violent crimes included are rape, robbery, aggravated assault, and homicide. Because of changes made to the victimization survey, data prior to 1993 are adjusted to make them comparable to data collected under the redesigned methodology. Estimates for 1993 and beyond are based on collection year while earlier estimates are based on data year.
2. The measures of violent crime came from two sources of data: The National Crime Victimization Surveys (NCVS), household surveys ongoing since 1972, which interview about 80,000 persons age 12 and older in 43,000 households twice each year about their victimizations from crime; and The Uniform Crime Reports (UCR), which collect information on crimes and arrests reported by law enforcement authorities to the FBI.
3. Definitions:

   Total violent crime: The number of homicides recorded by police plus the number of rapes, robberies, and aggravated assaults from the victimization survey whether or not they were reported to the police. From the NCVS + homicide from the UCR.

   Victimizations reported to the police: The number of homicides recorded by police plus the number of rapes, robberies, and aggravated assaults from the victimization survey that victims said were reported to the police. From the NCVS + homicide from the UCR.

   Crimes recorded by the police: The number of homicides, forcible rapes, robberies, and aggravated assaults included in the Uniform Crime Reports of the FBI excluding commercial robbery and those that involved victims under age 12. From the UCR.

   Arrests for violent crimes: The number of persons arrested for homicide, forcible rape, robbery, or aggravated assault as reported by law enforcement agencies to the FBI. From the UCR.

SOURCE: Bureau of Justice Statistics, www.ojp.usdoj.gov/bjs/.

One lesson that can be learned from the aforementioned survey findings is that most people are better described as representing a continuum, that is, as having committed more crime or less crime, rather than simply being described as criminal or noncriminal. In society, there are probably few "angels," that is, people who have never committed a crime. Likewise, there are probably few criminals whose whole lives are totally oriented toward the commission of crimes. Most people have committed a crime at some point in their lives and some have committed crimes repeatedly. It probably makes more sense for us, then, to talk about relative degrees of criminality, rather than to talk about all-encompassing criminality or its absence.

One of the criticisms of the National Youth Survey, and a problem with many self-report crime surveys, is

Myth

Criminal activity is concentrated among certain groups of people.

Fact

Early self-report crime surveys of adults found an enormous amount of hidden crime in the United States. They found that more than 90 percent of all Americans had committed crimes for which they could have been imprisoned.

THINKING CRITICALLY

1. Of the various methods of measuring crime presented in this section, which one do you think is the most accurate? Why? Which one do you think is the least accurate? Why?
2. Do you think there are ways to get more victims of crime to report criminal incidents? If so, what would you suggest?

that it asks about less serious offenses, such as cutting classes, disobeying parents, and stealing items worth less than $5, while omitting questions about serious crimes, such as robbery, burglary, and sexual assault. Self-report crime surveys also suffer from all the problems of other surveys, problems that were described in the last subsection—they produce different results from other surveys, and they are not an accurate measure of crime.

FYI: Costs of Corporate Crime

The $14 billion cost to victims of crimes reported in the 2001 national crime victimization survey is less than one-tenth as great as the annual losses of victims of corporate crimes, estimated at $200 billion. The crime of price-fixing, in which competing companies explicitly agree to keep prices artificially high to maximize profits, is estimated by itself to cost consumers about $60 billion a year.

SOURCE: David R. Simon, *Elite Deviance*, 7th ed. (Boston: Allyn and Bacon, 2002) pp. 93, 104.

Costs of Crime

According to data from the national crime victimization survey, in 2001 the total economic loss to victims of crime in the United States was $14 billion.[28] Table 2.5 shows the breakdown of this amount among categories of personal and property crimes. The total includes losses from property theft or damage, cash losses, medical expenses, and income lost from work because of injuries, police and court-related activities, or time spent repairing or replacing property.[29] It does not include the cost of the criminal justice process (described in Chapter 1), increased insurance premiums, security devices bought for protection, losses to businesses (which are substantial), or corporate crime.[30]

Until recently, the NCVS provided the best estimates of the costs of crime. Those cost estimates, however, are deficient in two ways. First, they include only a limited number of personal and property crimes. And, as noted previously, they do not include the cost of the criminal justice process, increased insurance premiums, security devices bought for protection, losses to businesses, or corporate crime. Second, they report estimates only of relatively short-term and tangible costs. They do not include long-term and intangible costs associated with pain, suffering, and reduced quality of life.

To compensate for the deficiencies of the NCVS, a 1996 study was sponsored by the National Institute of Justice.[31] In addition to the more standard cost estimates in the NCVS, the new study estimated long-term costs as well as the intangible costs of pain, suffering, and reduced quality of life. Intangible costs were calculated in a number of ways. For example, the costs of pain, suffering, and reduced quality of life for nonfatal injuries were estimated by analyzing jury awards to crime and burn victims. Only the portion of the jury award intended to compensate the victim for pain, suffering, and reduced quality of life was used; punitive damages were excluded from the estimates.

Furthermore, although the new study includes only "street crimes" and "domestic crime," it expands on the crime categories and information included in the NCVS by (1) including crimes committed against people under the age of 12, (2) using better information on domestic violence and sexual assault, (3) more fully accounting for repeat victimizations, and (4) including child abuse and drunk driving. Excluded from the new study are crimes committed against business and government, personal fraud, white-collar crime, child neglect, and most "victimless" crimes, including drug offenses.

The study estimates that the annual tangible cost of personal and property crime—including medical costs,

TABLE 2.5 Total Economic Loss to Victims of Personal and Property Crimes, 2001

Type of Crime	Gross Loss (in millions of dollars)
All crimes	14,013
Personal Crimes	**1,320**
Crimes of violence	1,269
Rape/sexual assault	61
Robbery	695
Assault	514
Purse snatching	5
Pocket picking	45
Property Crimes	**12,693**
Household burglary	2,877
Motor vehicle theft	5,403
Thefts	4,413

Note: Detail may not add to total shown because of rounding.

SOURCE: *Criminal Victimization in the United States 2001 Statistical Tables*, Table 82, www.ojp.usdoj.gov/bjs/pub/pdf/cvus0104pdf.

FIGURE 2.5 Annual Cost of Crime in the United States

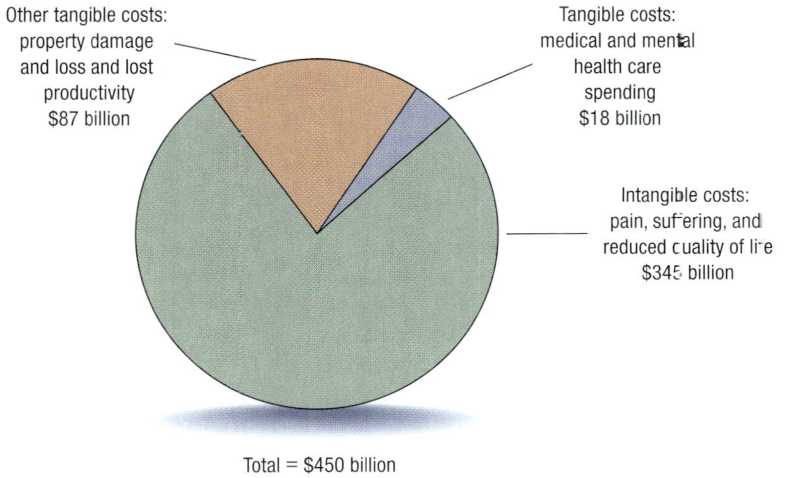

SOURCE: Ted R. Miller, Mark A. Cohen, and Brian Wiersema, *Victim Costs and Consequences: A New Look,* U.S. Department of Justice, National Institute of Justice Research Report (Washington, DC: GPO, February 1996), p. 17.

lost earnings, and public program costs related to victim assistance—are $105 billion, or more than $400 per U.S. resident. When the intangible costs of pain, suffering, and reduced quality of life are added, the annual cost increases to an estimated $450 billion, or about $1,800 per U.S. resident. Figure 2.5 shows how the $450 billion is divided into specific costs of crime.

Violent crime (including drunk driving and arson) accounts for $426 billion of the total, while property crime accounts for the remaining $24 billion. The study found that violence against children accounts for more than 20 percent of all tangible costs and more than 35 percent of all costs (including pain, suffering, and reduced quality of life).

Of the crimes included in the study, rape has the highest annual victim costs, at $127 billion a year (excluding child sexual abuse). Second is assault, with victim costs of $93 billion a year, followed by murder (excluding arson and drunk driving deaths), at $71 billion annually. Drunk driving (including fatalities) is next at $61 billion a year, and child abuse is estimated to cost $56 billion annually.

Among the tangible costs of crime excluded from the study are the costs of the criminal justice process and private security expenditures. Omitted also are the intangible costs of fear of crime, a fear that makes people prisoners in their own homes, divides people, and destroys communities.

FYI: War on Drugs

Between 1980 and 2003, the United States spent more than $300 billion on federal, state, and local antidrug efforts. That is more than the federal government spent on medical research into cancer, heart disease, or AIDS. In 2002, the federal government alone spent an estimated $18.8 billion to combat illegal drugs. About one-third of the 2002 federal expenditures was designated for demand reduction (programs and research related to drug abuse treatment and prevention) and about two-thirds was designated for supply reduction (a wide scope of law enforcement-related activities). Of the two-thirds devoted to supply reduction, about half was for domestic law enforcement, about 6 percent for international law enforcement, and about 11 percent for interdiction.

SOURCE: Michael Griffin, "Drug War Strategies Are Not Poles Apart," *The Orlando Sentinel,* October 29, 1996, p. A-1; Ann L. Pastore and Kathleen Maguire (eds.), *Sourcebook of Criminal Justice Statistics 2001,* U.S. Department of Justice, Bureau of Justice Statistics (Washington, DC: GPO, 2002), p. 16, Table 1.12.

THINKING CRITICALLY

1. What would you estimate is the cost of crimes that go unreported?
2. Why are the highest costs of crimes the intangible costs?

Fear of Crime

A by-product of crime, beyond actual physical or material loss, is fear. For many crime victims, it is the most burdensome and lasting consequence of their victimizations. However, fear of crime is also contagious. One does not have to be a victim of violent crime to be fearful of violent crime. In fact, research shows that people who have heard about other people's victimizations are nearly as fearful as the people who have been victimized themselves.[32]

Many people take extraordinary measures to protect themselves from crime. *Why are people so fearful of crime? Should they be? Why or why not?*

WHAT PEOPLE FEAR

Fear of crime, especially violent crime, is widespread. For example, a public opinion poll found that 80 percent of Americans are "concerned . . . about becoming a victim of crime"; 29.4 percent are "somewhat concerned"; and 50.6 percent are "very concerned."[33] When Americans are asked specifically what they fear, surveys show the following categories:[34]

- 40 percent worry about sexual assault, either against themselves or against a family member.
- 40 percent are concerned about burglaries when they are not home.
- 30 percent worry about being attacked while driving their cars.
- 30 percent worry about being mugged.
- 25 percent worry about being beaten up, knifed, or shot.
- 25 percent worry about burglaries when they are home.
- 20 percent worry about being murdered.

It is interesting to note that no more than 40 percent of Americans are fearful of any specific type of crime, though 80 percent of Americans are fearful of crime in general. Those survey results suggest that there is a greater fear of being a crime victim in general—that is, a greater abstract fear of crime—than there is of being the victim of a specific crime.

FYI Fear of Crime

According to a 1998 survey, the percentage of residents in each of 12 cities surveyed who said that they were fearful of crime in their neighborhood ranged from 20 percent to 48 percent: Chicago, IL (48 percent), Kansas City, MO (33 percent), Knoxville, TN (30 percent), Los Angeles, CA (44 percent), Madison, WI (20 percent), New York, NY (42 percent), San Diego, CA (30 percent), Savannah, GA (33 percent), Spokane, WA (32 percent), Springfield, MA (45 percent), Tucson, AZ (40 percent), and Washington, DC (48 percent). Ten percent or less in each city said they were "very fearful" of neighborhood crime. In 11 of the cities, a third or more of the residents said they were fearful of becoming a victim of street crime, especially being assaulted with a gun or being robbed.

SOURCE: Steven K. Smith, Greg W. Steadman, and Todd D. Minton, *Criminal Victimization and Perceptions of Community Safety in 12 Cities, 1998.* U.S. Department of Justice, Bureau of Justice Statistics, www.ojp.usdoj.gov/bjs/pub/ascii/cvpcs98.txt.

WHEN AND WHERE PEOPLE FEAR

Fear of violent crime is greatest at night when a person is alone and away from home. Although fewer than 10 percent of Americans feel unsafe and insecure in their own homes at night, 30 percent of them are afraid to walk alone at night in some areas within a mile of their homes.[35] The latter fear has been declining over the past decade.[36]

WHO FEARS CRIME

Fear of criminal victimization is neither evenly distributed across the population nor commensurate with the statistical probability of being the victim of crime. Surveys reveal some of the differences in the public's fear of crime.[37] Among those differences are the following:

- **Gender** Females are more fearful than males.
- **Race/Ethnicity** Nonwhites, especially Hispanics and blacks, are more fearful than whites.
- **Age** People 30 to 49 years old are slightly less fearful than people in other age categories. Historically, people 50 years old and older have been the most fearful.
- **Religion** Historically, Jews have been more fearful than either Protestants or Catholics, although in 2000, Catholics were slightly more fearful than members of the other two religious groups.
- **Community** People living in urban areas are more fearful than people living in suburban or rural areas.
- **Region** People living in the South and West have been more fearful than people living in the Northeast and Midwest. (Overall, concern about crime does not differ greatly by region of the country.)
- **Education** A person's fear of crime is slightly lower the higher the level of education. Adults who did not attain a high school diploma tend to be the most fearful.
- **Politics** Democrats are more fearful of crime than either Republicans or Independents.

- **Income** Fear of crime victimization declines with increasing family income. (People whose family income is $50,000 or more are less fearful of crime than people whose family income is less than $50,000.)

It is important to stress that the preceding descriptions of the kinds of people who are most and least fearful of crime in general do not address the specific types of crimes that people fear. Also, the descriptions are generalizations. As with all generalizations, there are exceptions or qualifications. In a study of fear of seven types of criminal victimization, four exceptions to or qualifications of the preceding general descriptions were revealed.[38]

First, although females are generally more fearful of crime than are males, their greater fear applies only to sexual assault and other personal violent crimes. Females are no more fearful than males of having their homes burglarized. Second, although people 50 years old and older are slightly more fearful in general than people less than 50 years old, younger people are more fearful than older people of sexual assault and burglary. For nonsexual violent offenses, there are no age differences. Third, Hispanics and blacks are more fearful than whites only of sexual assault of themselves or someone in their household and of being murdered. Fourth, only fear of being beaten, knifed, or shot and fear of getting mugged increase with the level of urbanization of the community in which people live.

As noted previously, the groups that are the most fearful of crime are not necessarily those with the highest rates of victimization. For example, elderly women, the demographic group most afraid of crime, are the least likely to be victimized.[39] More generally, women and older people are more fearful of crime than are men and younger people, even though women and older persons are less likely to be victims of crime.[40]

Fear of crime has many detrimental consequences. It makes people feel vulnerable and isolated, it reduces a person's general sense of well-being, it motivates people to buy safety devices with money that otherwise could be used to improve their quality of life, and it also contributes to neighborhood decline and the crime problem. As criminologist Wesley Skogan explains:

> Fear . . . can work in conjunction with other factors to stimulate more rapid neighborhood decline. Together, the spread of fear and other local problems provide a form of positive feedback that can further increase levels of crime. These feedback processes include (1) physical and psychological withdrawal from community life; (2) a weakening of the informal social control processes that inhibit crime and disorder; (3) a decline in the organizational life and mobilization capacity of the neighborhood; (4) deteriorating business conditions; (5) the importation and domestic production of delinquency and deviance; and (6) further dramatic changes in the composition of the population. At the end lies a stage characterized by demographic collapse.[41]

Myth	Fact
The people most fearful of crime are the people most vulnerable to crime.	The people most fearful of crime are not necessarily members of groups with the highest rates of victimization. For example, the demographic group most afraid of crime, elderly women, is the least likely to be victimized.

THINKING CRITICALLY

1. What steps could be taken, if any, to reduce people's overall fear of crime?
2. Why do you think there is no correlation between those who fear crime the most and the most likely victims of crime?
3. What factors contribute to people's fear of crime?
4. What are the costs, if any, of a fear of crime?

Victims of Crime

Findings from the 2001 NCVS reveal that in 2001 a total of 24.2 million crimes were attempted or completed against U.S. residents aged 12 or older—approximately 5.9 million personal crimes (rape and sexual assault, robbery,

FYI: National Crime Victims' Fund

In 1984, during the Reagan administration, a national crime victims' fund was created to help crime victims and the nonprofit organizations that serve them, such as shelters for battered women, rape crisis centers, and children's advocacy centers. Money for the fund comes from federal fines, penalties, and forfeitures collected from convicted criminals. Between 1985 and 2001, more than $3 billion was deposited in the fund. In 1996 alone, the fund was increased $440 million by fines paid by just two federal defendants. With money from the fund, states can aid crime victims with unpaid medical bills, lost wages, health counseling, emergency transportation to court, and funeral costs.

SOURCE: National Crime Victims Fund and Federal Service Awards 2002, www.ojp.usdoj.gov/ovc/ncvrw/cvfa/2002/cvfa2002.pdf; Office for Victims of Crime, OVC Fact Sheet, U.S. Department of Justice, www.ojp.usdoj.gov/ovc/factshts/cvfvca.htm; Bruce M. Taylor, "Changes in Criminal Victimization, 1994–95," U.S. Department of Justice, Bureau of Justice Statistics (Washington, DC: GPO, April 1997), p. 2, Table 1; Michael R. Rand, James P. Lynch, and David Cantor, "Criminal Victimization, 1973–95," U.S. Department of Justice, Office of Justice Programs, Bureau of Justice Statistics (Washington, DC: GPO, April 1997), p. 1.

aggravated and simple assault, pocket picking, purse snatching, and attempted purse snatching) and about 18.3 million property crimes (household burglary, motor vehicle theft, and other thefts).[42] Of the approximately 5.9 million personal crimes, 5.7 million were violent.[43] However, in 68 percent of all violent crimes, the crime was attempted or threatened but not completed.[44] Still, in about 32 percent of the violent crimes, a victim was injured.[45]

VICTIMIZATION TRENDS

According to 2001 NCVS data, the violent and property crime victimization rates were 25 and 167 per 1,000 persons age 12 or older, respectively. The violent crime rate was 10 percent lower than the 2000 rate, a decline that continued a trend that began in 1994 (see Figure 2.6, top graph).[46] The 2001 property crime rate decreased 6 percent from the 2000 rate, a decline that continued a trend that began in 1974 (see Figure 2.6, bottom graph).[47] Combined, the 2001 violent and property crime rates were the lowest recorded since the survey was first administered in 1973.[48] Figure 2.6 shows that the decline in the violent crime rate is primarily a result of a decline in simple assaults, while the decrease in the property crime rate is almost entirely attributable to a decrease in thefts.

WHO THE VICTIMS ARE

Although each year millions of people are victimized by crime, victimization—like the fear of crime—is not spread evenly throughout the population. Certain types of people are much more likely to be crime victims. The types of

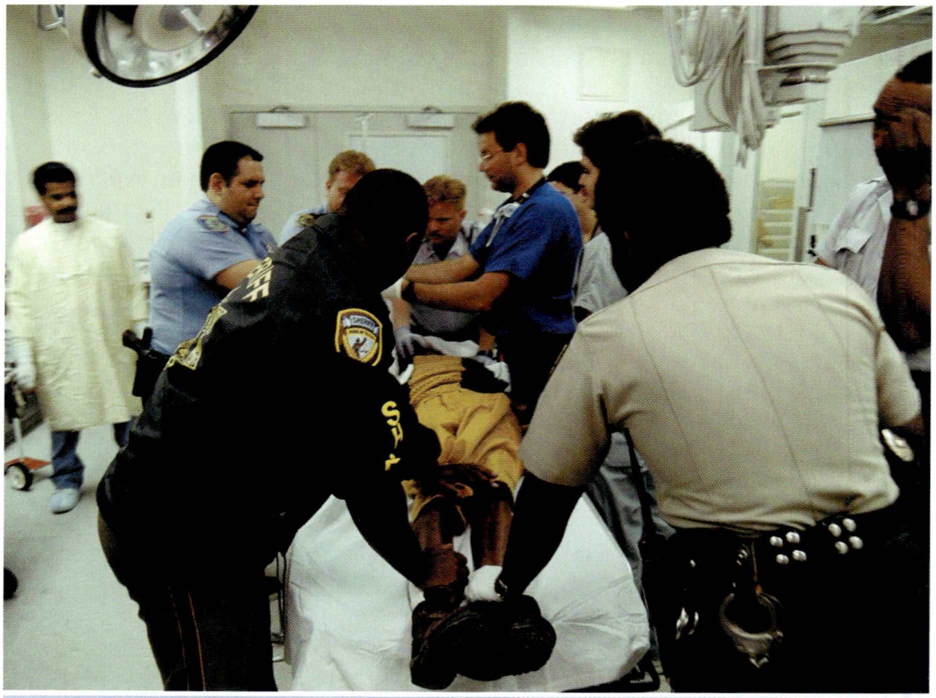

Young, economically disadvantaged black males are the most likely victims of personal violent crime. *Why and what can be done about it?*

FIGURE 2.6 **Trends in Violent and Property Crime Rates**

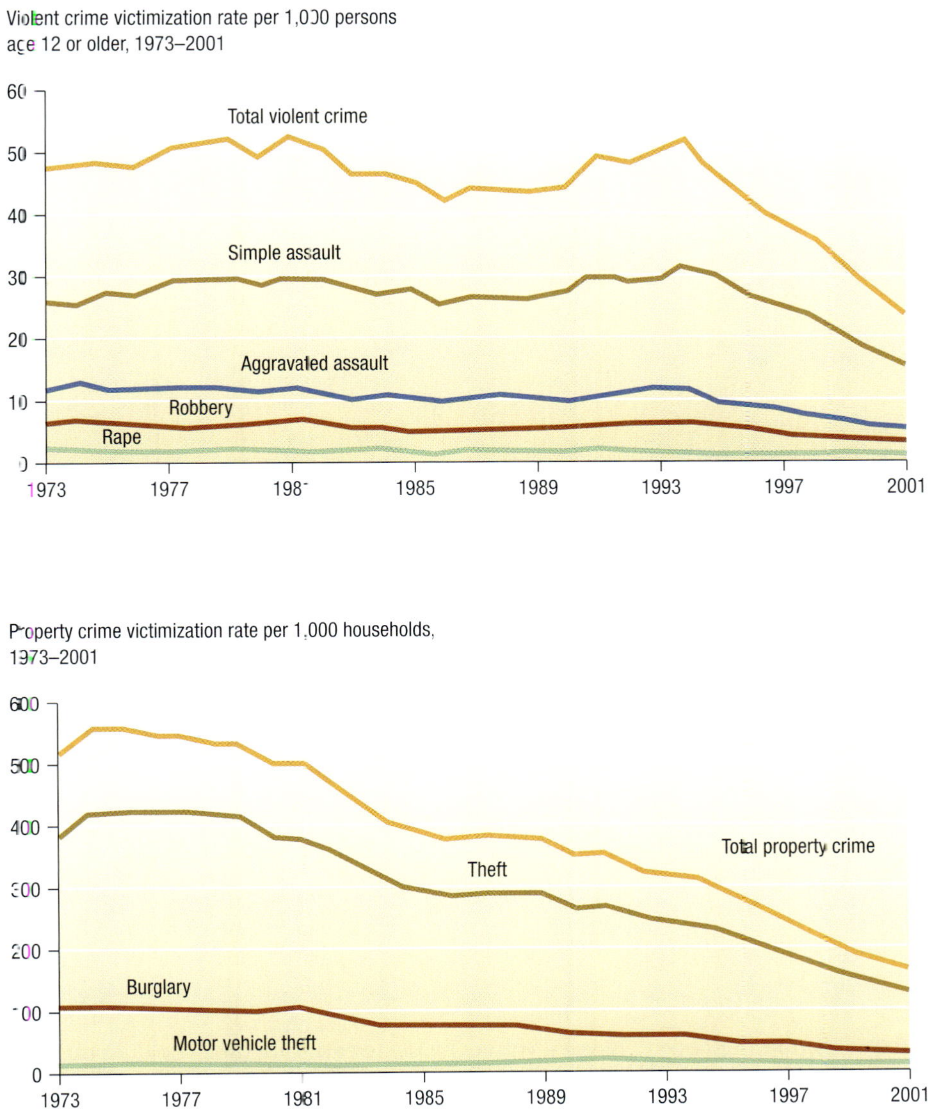

Note: From 1973 through June 1992 data were collected under the National Crime Survey (NCS) and made comparable to data collected under the redesigned methods of the NCVS that began in July 1992.

SOURCE: Callie Marie Rennison, *Criminal Victimization 2001: Changes 2000–01, Trends 1993–2001,* U.S. Department of Justice, Bureau of Justice Statistics, National Crime Victimization Survey (Washington, DC: GPO, September 2002), p. 2.

people that were most vulnerable to , victimization in the past continue to be the most vulnerable.

Based on 2001 NCVS data the demographic groups with the highest rates of violent crime victimization per 1,000 persons age 12 or older (from highest to lowest overall rate) were:[49]

- **Younger persons** Persons 12–24 had about double the violent crime victimization rates of persons 25 or older and about 15 times the rate of persons 65 or older. Persons 16–19 had the highest rate, 55.8, and persons 65 and older had the lowest rate, 3.2.

- **Never married, divorced, or separated persons** Never married, divorced, or separated persons were nearly four times more likely than married persons and nearly six times more likely than widowed persons to be violent crime victims. The rates for never married and divorced or separated persons were 44.7 and 42, respectively, compared to the rate of 11.4 for married persons and 7.7 for widowers.
- **Poorer persons** Persons with annual household incomes of less than $7,500 had violent victimization rates 2.5 times higher than victims with annual household incomes of $75,000 or more. The rate for the lower income category was 46.6; the rate for the highest income category was 18.5.

CAREERS IN CRIMINAL JUSTICE

Dori DeJong, Victim Advocate

My name is Dori DeJong and I am a victim advocate with the Denver District Attorney's Office in Denver, Colorado. I have a Bachelor's Degree in education from the University of Northern Colorado, a Master's Degree in social work and a Juris Doctor from the University of Denver. Prior to working in the district attorney's office, I worked as a counselor at a children's psychiatric hospital, as a children's counselor at a battered women's shelter, and as a legal advocate for a community agency that provided assistance to victims of domestic violence. I decided to become a victim advocate because it was a great way to combine my educational background in both social work and law.

A typical day as a victim advocate includes contacting the victims of crimes (domestic violence, stranger assault, sex assault, child abuse, etc.) and explaining the criminal justice system to them; providing details about their specific case; giving notification of their rights as a victim; referring victims to various outside assistance agencies; and obtaining their input as to the best possible outcome of the case in which they are involved. Additionally, I coordinate and participate in the meetings between the victims and the assistant district attorneys to assist in the preparation of the victims for trial, and to answer any questions they have about the process. I accompany the victims in the courthouse on the day of the trial to provide encouragement, support, and understanding of the process in order for them to get through a very difficult experience. I also send update letters and victim impact statements to victims, notify other agencies and jurisdictions of active cases, run criminal background checks on defendants to identify habitual offenders, and maintain statistics on domestic violence cases. I have regular contact and communication with police officers, detectives, district attorneys, investigators, and other victim advocates. I also communicate with staff from outside assistance agencies to help sustain continuing support for the victim.

The most positive aspect of the job is the ability to help people and feel that you are really making a difference in someone's life. It is so encouraging when you have a client call you months or even years after you've assisted them, to thank you and tell you what a difference you've made in their lives and their children's lives. It is also rewarding to be a part of the prosecution team that holds criminals responsible and accountable for their behavior.

Being a victim advocate can sometimes be difficult and frustrating because you work with people that are in crisis, and often are not appreciative of your involvement in their lives. Sometimes their anger about the incident is misdirected at the victim advocate and the system, which is trying to provide justice.

The job of a victim advocate is interesting, challenging, often fast paced, and can be very rewarding. However, the job can also be overwhelming since it frequently involves dealing with offensive criminal defendants and their actions, and the sometimes inequitable system of justice. If you are considering a job as a victim advocate, I would encourage you to volunteer or do an internship in an agency that works with victims. This invaluable experience will provide you with the knowledge to determine if this career suits you.

Do you have any characteristics and/or abilities that you think would make you particularly suited to be a victim's advocate? If so, what?

- **Blacks** The rate of violent crime victimization for blacks was 31.2; for whites, 24.5; and for others, 18.2. The rate for Hispanics was 29.5.
- **Urban residents** The violent crime victimization rates for urban, suburban, and rural residents were 33.2, 22.3, and 21.1, respectively.
- **Men** The violent crime victimization rate for men was 27.3; the rate for women was 23.
- **Persons living in the West** Persons living in the West had a violent crime victimization rate of 32.3, while persons living in the Midwest, South, and Northeast had rates of 24.4, 23.8, and 20.2, respectively.

Whereas violent crime victimization rates are measures of the characteristics of victims age 12 and older, property crime victimization rates are measures of the characteristics of victimized households or heads of households. Consequently, there are no property crime victimization rates by gender, age, or marital status, but there is the category of home ownership. The characteristics of households or heads of households with the highest 2001 rates of property crime victimization per 1,000 households (from highest to lowest overall rate) were:[50]

- **Urban residences** The property crime victimization rates for urban, suburban, and rural residences were 212.8, 156.7, and 131.9, respectively.
- **Renters** The rate of property crime victimization of renters was 209.6; the rate for homeowners was 146.3.
- **Hispanic households** The property crime victimization rate of black households was 179.7; for white households, 165.1; and for the households of other races, 163.6. The rate for Hispanics was 224.1.
- **Western households** The rate of property crime victimization for households in the West was 216.4; in the Midwest, 172.3; in the South, 157.5; and in the Northeast, 123.9.

There was not much difference in the property crime victimization rates for households of different incomes. For example, the rate for households with incomes of less than $7,500 was 184.6, while the rate for households with incomes of $75,000 or more was 180.

There were two other interesting findings in the 2001 NCVS. The first deals with the victim-offender relationship. While strangers victimized a majority of men (55 percent), a majority of women (66 percent) were victimized by someone they knew.[51] The second finding was that in two-thirds of violent victimizations no weapon was used. A weapon was known to be used in 55 percent of robberies, 24 percent of assaults, and only 7 percent of rapes or sexual assaults.[52]

FYI: Violence on Television

The relationship between the viewing of violence on television and the violence in society is a hotly debated topic. However, television violence may have more to do with fear of crime than it does with actual violent behavior. George Gerbner, a professor and dean emeritus at the Annenberg School for Communication at the University of Pennsylvania, has studied the subject for more than 20 years. He says, "The contribution of television to the committing of violence is relatively minor, maybe five percent. Whereas the contribution of television to the perception of violence is much higher. People are almost paralyzed by fear." From his research, Gerbner has concluded that heavy television viewers tend to suffer from what he calls the "mean world syndrome." Heavy viewers are more likely than light viewers to overestimate their chances of encountering violence, to believe that their neighborhoods are unsafe, and to assume that crime is rising, whether or not it actually is. They are also more likely to buy guns for protection.

SOURCE: Elizabeth Kolbert, "Aggression in Kids Linked to TV Violence: Experts Say Connection Isn't Cause," *The Charlotte (NC) Observer,* December 18, 1994, p. 18A.

THINKING CRITICALLY

Why do you think that certain types of people are more likely to become crime victims than others?

SUMMARY

1. Distinguish between a social definition and a legal definition of crime and summarize the problems with each

A typical social definition of crime is behavior that violates the norms of society or, more simply, antisocial behavior. A typical legal definition of crime is an intentional violation of the criminal law or penal code, committed without defense or excuse and penalized by the state. There are problems with both definitions. Problems with the social definition are that (1) there are no uniform norms of behavior accepted by all of society, (2) norms of behavior are subject to interpretation, and (3) norms change from time to time and from place to place. Problems with the legal definition of crime are (1) overcriminalization, (2) nonenforcement, and (3) undercriminalization.

2. List the technical and ideal elements of a crime

The technical and ideal elements of a crime are (1) harm, (2) legality, (3) actus reus, *(4)* mens rea, *(5) causation, (6) concurrence, and (7) punishment.*

3. Identify some of the legal defenses or legal excuses for criminal responsibility

Among the legal defenses or legal excuses for criminal responsibility in the United States are that the defendant (1) acted under duress, (2) was underage, (3) was insane, (4) acted in self-defense or in defense of a third party, (5) was entrapped, or (6) acted out of necessity.

4. Explain why crime and delinquency statistics are unreliable

Among the reasons why crime and delinquency statistics are unreliable are the following: First, some behavior is labeled crime by one observer but not by another. Second, a large proportion of crimes are undetected. Third, not all crimes are reported to the police. Fourth, not all crimes that are reported are officially recorded by the police.

5. Identify the two major sources of crime statistics in the United States

The two major sources of crime statistics in the United States are the uniform crime reports (UCR) compiled by the FBI and the national crime victimization surveys (NCVS) compiled by the Bureau of Justice Statistics.

6. Describe the principal finding of the national crime victimization surveys

The national crime victimization surveys (NCVS) produce different results from the FBI's uniform crime reports (UCR). The NCVS generally show more crimes being committed than the UCR. The NCVS count more of some kinds of crimes and count them differently.

7. Summarize the general finding of self-report crime surveys

Self-report crime surveys show that the amount of hidden crime in the United States is enormous; more than 90 percent of all Americans have committed crimes for which they could have been imprisoned.

8. Identify the costs of crime

According to data from the NCVS, in 2001 the total economic loss to victims of crime in the United States was $14 billion. This figure does not include the tangible costs of the criminal justice process, security devices bought for protection, losses to businesses, losses from corporate crimes, or the intangible costs of pain, suffering, and reduced quality of life. When all costs are totaled, it is estimated that crime costs about $450 billion annually.

9. Describe the extent of fear of crime in the United States and the characteristics of people most likely to fear crime

Fear of crime, especially violent crime, is widespread. However, it is neither evenly distributed across the population nor commensurate with the statistical probability of being a victim. In general, those more likely to fear crime are females, nonwhites, people 50 years old and older, Jews, people living in urban areas, Westerners and Southerners, people with less education, Democrats, and people whose family income is less than $50,000.

10. List the characteristics of people who are the most likely and the least likely to be victims of crime

According to data from the 2001 NCVS, the most likely victims of personal violent crimes are young (12–24 years old), never married, divorced, or separated, poor, black, urban men living in the West. The group least likely to experience violent crime victimization is persons aged 65 or older. The most likely victims of household property crimes are households in urban areas headed by renters and Hispanics in the West.

KEY TERMS

norm, p. 31
legal definition of crime, p. 31
overcriminalization, p. 32
nonenforcement, p. 32
undercriminalization, p. 32
harm, p. 33
legality, p. 33
ex post facto law, p. 33
actus reus, p. 33
mens rea, p. 33
negligence, p. 33
duress, p. 34
juvenile delinquency, p. 34
insanity, p. 34
entrapment, p. 36
necessity defense, p. 36
mala in se, p. 37
mala prohibita, p. 38
dark figure of crime, p. 39
crime index, p. 39
offenses known to the police, p. 40
crime rate, p. 42
uniform crime reports, p. 43
eight index crimes, p. 43
status offense, p. 44
crime index offenses cleared, p. 45
national crime victimization surveys, p. 47
self-report crime surveys, p. 48

REVIEW QUESTIONS

1. What is a *norm?*
2. What is the *harm* of crime?
3. What is the *mens rea* of crime?
4. What is *legal infancy* or *legal nonage?*
5. What is *juvenile delinquency?*
6. What is *insanity?*
7. Does the availability of the insanity defense allow a large number of dangerous criminals to go free?
8. What is the difference between a *felony* and a *misdemeanor?*
9. What percentages of all crime are violent crime, property crime, and public order crime?
10. Why aren't any records or indexes of crime very reliable measures of the true amount of crime?
11. What are "offenses known to the police," and what are advantages and disadvantages of using it?
12. What is a *crime rate,* and why are crime rates used?
13. What is a *status offense?*
14. When the media report that crime has increased or decreased from one year to the next, to what are they referring?
15. What is the NIBRS?
16. What are some of the detrimental consequences of a fear of crime?
17. What long-term trends in violent and property crime victimization rates are revealed by the national crime victimization surveys?

IN THE FIELD

1. **Crime Victimization Survey** As an individual project or a group project, construct and conduct a crime victimization survey. (Use the national crime victimization survey as a model.) Either orally or in writing, present and discuss the results. Be sure to discuss problems encountered in constructing the survey and problems with the accuracy and trustworthiness of responses.

2. **Self-Report Crime Survey** As an individual project or a group project, construct and conduct a self-report crime survey. (Make sure you tell respondents not to put their names or any other identifying information on the survey. Also, be sure to include both serious and less serious crimes.) Either orally or in writing, present and discuss the results. Be sure to discuss problems encountered in constructing the survey and problems with the accuracy and trustworthiness of responses.

ON THE NET

3. Crime Statistics Examine the latest edition of the FBI's uniform crime reports at www.fbi.gov/ucr/ucr.htm. Then choose one of the eight index crimes listed in Table 2.2, and search the site for statistics about that crime. Write a brief report summarizing the results of your research. As an alternative, examine the printed version, *Crime in the United States,* at an area library.

4. Victimization Data Examine the latest edition of the NCVS at the Bureau of Justice Statistics site at www.ojp.usdoj.gov/bjs. Click on "criminal victimization" and scroll to the newest edition (hardcopies of the NCVS are no longer available). Compare the latest victimization data with the data presented in your textbook. Write a brief report summarizing any changes.

CRITICAL THINKING EXERCISES

1. The Twinkie Defense Dan White had been elected as city supervisor of San Francisco. White resigned on November 10, 1978. Four days later, he changed his mind and asked Mayor George Moscone to reappoint him to his former position. The mayor refused and appointed Harvey Milk, a leader in San Francisco's gay community. On the morning of November 27, White confronted the mayor and demanded to be reappointed. When the mayor refused, White shot the mayor five times. White reloaded the gun, walked across the hall to Milk's office, and shot him four times. White fled, but shortly thereafter went to the police and confessed. He was charged with first-degree murder. During his trial, several psychologists called by the defense testified that White's behavior was the result of long-term depression exacerbated by a craving for junk food. They testified that White's judgment and ability to control his behavior were altered by the huge amount of sugar he had consumed the night before the killings. The so-called "Twinkie defense" worked. White was convicted of voluntary manslaughter instead of first-degree murder, and on May 21, 1979, he was sentenced to a prison term of 5 years to 7 years 8 months.

a. What is the legal rationale for accepted legal defenses against or excuses from criminal responsibility? Do you agree with the rationale?

b. Should all legal defenses or excuses be abolished? Why or why not?

2. Fighting Illegal Drugs Activists are advocating a different strategy in the fight against illegal drugs. In agreement with the American Medical Association, they maintain that drug addiction is a disease. They believe it should be treated as a public health problem, not as a law enforcement problem. They propose a change in strategy from prohibition to decriminalization or legalization. According to these activists, decriminalization or legalization would do the following:

- Reduce profits from drug trafficking, crime caused by the need to support drug habits, and the prison population.
- Allow money used for incarceration to fund new models of drug control.
- Allow drugs such as marijuana to be regulated and taxed.
- Reduce the negative health consequences from using drugs of unknown potency and purity.
- Improve pain control options for certain medical conditions.
- Free physicians from fear of entrapment for prescribing certain drugs.
- Shift the focus of criminal justice to more serious crime problems.

a. One of the seven elements of a crime is harm. Do you think that illegal drug use is harmful? Explain.

b. If the use of addictive drugs is illegal, should addictive substances such as nicotine (in cigarettes) or caffeine (in coffee) also be made illegal? Explain.

EXPLAINING CRIME

CHAPTER THREE

Chapter Outline

Introduction to Criminological Theory

Classical and Neoclassical Approaches to Explaining Crime

- Classical Theory
- Neoclassical Theory

Positivist Approaches to Explaining Crime

- Biological Theories
- Psychological Theories
- Sociological Theories

Critical Approaches to Explaining Crime

- Labeling Theory
- Conflict Theory
- Radical Theory
- Other Critical Theories

Chapter Objectives

After completing this chapter, you should be able to:

1. Define criminological theory.
2. State the causes of crime according to classical and neoclassical criminologists.
3. Describe the biological theories of crime causation and their policy implications.
4. Describe the different psychological theories of crime causation.
5. Explain sociological theories of crime causation.
6. Distinguish major differences among classical, positivist, and critical theories of crime causation.
7. Describe how critical theorists would explain the causes of crime.

Crime Story

On August 27, 2003, Salvador Tapia, a disgruntled former auto parts worker, opened fire on seven of his former coworkers at a Chicago Illinois, auto supply warehouse. Four of the warehouse workers died at the scene of the shooting and two others died at hospitals. Tapia was shot and killed by police after the only survivor of the shooting incident managed to escape from the warehouse and alert police. The lone survivor described Tapia as being completely covered in blood and looking like some kind of devil. Police, friends, and relatives described Tapia as having a violent temper with a history of making threats, including calls to the owners of the businesses who fired him. Tapia's family members later told police that he had previously been arrested 12 times for a variety of assault and weapon offenses.

Similar workplace incidents have recently occurred across the nation. On July 8, 2003, Doug Williams, an employee of a Lockheed Martin aircraft plant in Meridian, Mississippi, was attending a training session with coworkers on ethics and sensitivity when he abruptly left and returned armed with an arsenal of weapons. Williams shot five workers to death and wounded nine others before killing himself. Williams was described by work associates as being a gun enthusiast.

On July 2, 2003, in Jefferson City, Missouri, Jonathon Russell shot and killed three coworkers at a manufacturing plant where he worked. Russell also wounded five others before shooting and killing himself. Russell was described as a quiet man with no prior criminal record. The night of the shootings Russell clocked in for work, reported to his work post, pulled out a semiautomatic 40-caliber handgun, and began firing. Authorities were unable to establish a motive for the shootings.

Violence in the workplace is considered as one of the most extreme forms of homicide. According to the Bureau of Labor, workplace violence is the third-leading cause of fatal occupational death for men, and the first-leading cause of fatal occupational death for women in the United States. The term "going postal" has gained wide acceptance in the United States when referring to violent acts connected to the workplace. This term was first used to describe some of the early and most widely reported cases of workplace violence, which were associated with the United States Postal Service.

Chapter 3 discusses an assortment of criminological theories used by criminal justice scholars to make sense of criminal behavior. Would an understanding of why people kill other people they work with help reduce workplace violence? You will readily discover that many criminological theories can be used to explain the same criminal behavior. Unfortunately, no single criminological theory likely explains all forms of workplace violence to everyone's total satisfaction.

Introduction to Criminological Theory

A **theory** is an assumption (or set of assumptions) that attempts to explain why or how things are related to each other. A theory of crime attempts to explain why or how a certain thing or certain things are related to criminal behavior. For example, some theories assume that crime is part of human nature, that some human beings are born evil. In those theories, human nature is examined in relation to crime. Other theories assume that crime is caused by biological things (for example, chromosome abnormalities, hormone imbalances), psychological things (for example, below-normal intelligence, satisfaction of basic needs), sociological things (for example, social disorganization, inadequate socialization), economic things (for example, unemployment, economic inequality), or some combination of all four kinds of things. In this chapter, we will examine a variety of crime theories and discuss the policy implications of each. (Unless indicated otherwise, the term *crime* includes delinquency.)

theory An assumption (or set of assumptions) that attempts to explain why or how things are related to each other.

Criminological theory is important because most of what is done in criminal justice is based on criminological theory, whether we or the people who propose and implement policies based on the theory know it or not. The failure to understand the theoretical basis of criminal justice policies leads to at least two undesirable consequences. First, if criminal justice policy makers do not know the theory or theories on which their proposed policies are based, then they will be unaware of the problems that are likely to undermine the success of the policies. Much time and money could be saved if criminal justice policies were based on a thorough theoretical understanding. Second, criminal justice policies invariably intrude on people's lives (for example, people are arrested and imprisoned). If people's lives are going to be disrupted by criminal justice policies, it seems only fair that there be very good reasons for the disruption.

criminological theory The explanation of criminal behavior, as well as the behavior of police, attorneys, prosecutors, judges, correctional personnel, victims, and other actors in the criminal justice process.

Technically, criminological theory refers not only to explanations of criminal behavior but also to explanations of police behavior and the behavior of attorneys, prosecutors, judges, correctional personnel, victims, and other actors in the criminal justice system. However, in this chapter, our focus is on theories of crime causation. Table 3.1 outlines the crime causation theories presented in this chapter.

THINKING CRITICALLY

What is a theory? Why is it important to understand the various theories of criminal behavior?

Classical and Neoclassical Approaches to Explaining Crime

The causes of crime have long been the subject of much speculation, theorizing, research, and debate among scholars and the public. Each theory of crime has been influenced by the religious, philosophical, political, economic, social, and scientific trends of the time. One of the earliest secular approaches to explaining the causes of crime was the classical theory, developed in Europe at the time of profound social and intellectual change. Before classical theory, crime was generally equated with sin and was considered the work of demons or the devil.

classical theory A product of the Enlightenment, based on the assumption that people exercise free will and are thus completely responsible for their actions. In classical theory, human behavior, including criminal behavior, is motivated by a hedonistic rationality, in which actors weigh the potential pleasure of an action against the possible pain associated with it.

CLASSICAL THEORY

Classical theory is a product of the Enlightenment period, or the Age of Reason, a period of history that began in the late 1500s and lasted until the

TABLE 3.1 Theories of Crime Causation

	Theorists	Causes	Policy Implications
Classical and Neoclassical Theories			
	Beccaria	Free-willed individuals commit crime because they rationally calculate that crime will give them more pleasure than pain.	Deterrence: Establish social contract. Enact laws that are clear, simple, unbiased, and reflect the consensus of the population. Impose punishments that are proportionate to the crime, prompt certain, public, necessary, the least possible in the given circumstances, and dictated by law, not judges' discretion. Educate the public. Eliminate corruption from the administration of justice. Reward virtue.
Positivist Theories			
Biological			
	Lombroso, Sheldon	Biological inferiority or biochemical processes cause people to commit crimes.	Isolate, sterilize, or execute offenders. For specific problems, brain surgery, chemical treatment, improved diets, and better mother and child health care.
Psychological			
Intelligence	Goddard	Mental inferiority (low IQ) causes people to commit crimes.	Isolate, sterilize, or execute offenders.
Psychoanalytic	Freud	Crime is a symptom of more deep-seated problems.	Provide psychotherapy or psychoanalysis.
Humanistic	Maslow	Crime is a means by which individuals can satisfy their basic human needs.	Help people satisfy their basic needs legally.
	Halleck	Crime is an adaptation to helplessness caused by oppression.	Eliminate sources of oppression. Provide legal ways of coping with feelings of helplessness caused by oppression; psychotherapy.
Sociological			
Durkheim	Durkheim	Crime is a social fact. It is a "normal" aspect of society, although different types of societies should have greater or lesser degrees of it. Crime is also functional for society.	Contain crime within reasonable boundaries.
Chicago School	Park, Burgess, Shaw, McKay	Delinquency is caused by detachment from conventional groups, which is caused by social disorganization.	Organize and empower neighborhood residents.
Anomie or strain	Merton, Cohen	For Merton, crime is caused by anomie or strain, which is the contradiction between cultural goals and the social structure's capacity to provide the institutionalized means to achieve those goals. For Cohen, gang delinquency is caused by anomie or strain, which is the inability to conform to middle-class values or to achieve status among peers legally.	Reduce aspirations. Increase legitimate opportunities. Do both.
Learning	Tarde, Sutherland, Burgess, Akers, Jeffery	Crime is committed because it is positively reinforced, negatively reinforced, or imitated.	Provide law-abiding models. Regulate associations. Eliminate crime's rewards. Reward law-abiding behavior. Punish criminal behavior effectively.
Control	Reiss, Toby, Nye, Reckless, Hirschi	Crime is a result of improper socialization.	Properly socialize children so that they develop self-control and a strong moral bond to society.

(continued)

TABLE 3.1 Theories of Crime Causation (concluded)

Critical Theories			
	Theorists	**Causes**	**Policy Implications**
Labeling	Becker, Lemert	Does not explain the initial cause of crime and delinquency (primary deviance); explains only secondary deviance, which is the commission of crime after the first criminal act with the acceptance of a criminal label.	Do not label. Employ radical nonintervention. Employ reintegrative shaming.
Conflict	Vold, Turk	Crime is caused by relative powerlessness.	Dominant groups give up power to subordinate groups. Dominant groups become more effective rulers and subordinate groups better subjects.
Radical	Quinney, Chambliss, Platt	Competition among wealthy people and among poor people as well as between rich and poor (the class struggle) and the practice of taking advantage of other people cause crime.	Define crime as a violation of basic human rights. Replace the criminal justice system with "popular" or "socialist" justice. Create a socialist society appreciative of human diversity.
British or Left Realism	Young	Relative deprivation is a potent, though not exclusive, cause of crime.	Employ police power to protect people living in working-class communities.
Peacemaking	Quinney, Pepinsky	Same as radical (different prescription for change).	Transform human beings so that they are able to experience empathy with those less fortunate and respond to other people's needs. Reduce hierarchical structures. Create communities of caring people. Champion universal social justice.
Feminist theory	Daly, Chesney-Lind, Simpson	Patriarchy (men's control over women's labor and sexuality) is the cause of crime.	Abolish patriarchal structures and relationships. Champion greater equality for women in all areas.
Postmodernism	Henry, Milovanovic	Crime is caused by processes that result in the denial of responsibility for other people and to other people.	Similar to peacemaking criminological theory.

late 1700s. The Enlightenment thinkers, including members of the classical school of criminology, promoted a new, scientific view of the world. In so doing, they rejected the then-dominant religious view of the world, which was based on revelation and the authority of the Church. The Enlightenment thinkers assumed that human beings could understand the world through science—the human capacity to observe and to reason. Moreover, they believed that if people could understand the world and its functioning, they could change it. The Enlightenment thinkers rejected the belief that either the nature of the world or the behavior of the people in it was divinely ordained or predetermined.

Instead, the Enlightenment thinkers believed that people exercise *free will,* or the ability to choose any course of action, for which they are completely responsible. Human behavior was considered motivated by a *hedonistic rationality,* in which a person weighs the potential pleasure of an action against the possible pain associated with it. In that view, human beings commit crime because they rationally calculate that the crime will give them more pleasure than pain.

Classical criminologists, as Enlightenment thinkers, were concerned with protecting the rights of humankind from the corruption and excesses of the existing legal institutions. Horrible and severe punishments were common both before and during the Enlightenment. For example, in England during the eighteenth century, almost 150 offenses carried the death penalty

Classical criminologist Cesare Beccaria believed that the only justified rationale for laws and punishments is the principle of utility, that is, "the greatest happiness shared by the greatest number." *Do you agree with him? Why or why not?*

including stealing turnips, associating with gypsies, cutting down a tree, and picking pockets. Barbarous punishments were not the only problem. At the time, crime was rampant, yet types of crime were poorly defined. What we today call *due process of law* was either absent or ignored. Torture was employed routinely to extract confessions. Judgeships were typically sold to wealthy persons by the sovereign, and judges had almost total discretion. Consequently, there was little consistency in the application of the law or in the punishments imposed.

It was within that historical context that Cesare Beccaria, perhaps the best known of the classical criminologists, wrote and published anonymously in 1764 his truly revolutionary work, *An Essay on Crimes and Punishments* (*Dei Delitti e delle Pene*). His book is generally acknowledged to have had an enormous practical influence on the establishment of a more humane system of criminal law and procedure.[1] In the book, Beccaria sets forth most of what we now call classical criminological theory.

According to Beccaria, the only justified rationale for laws and punishments is the principle of **utility,** that is, "the greatest happiness shared by the greatest number."[2] The basis of society, as well as the origin of punishments and the right to punish, is the **social contract.** The social contract is an imaginary agreement entered into by persons who sacrifice the minimum amount of their liberty necessary to prevent anarchy and chaos.

Beccaria believed that the only legitimate purpose of punishment is deterrence, both special and general.[3] **Special** or **specific deterrence** is the prevention of the punished persons from committing crime again. **General deterrence** is the use of the punishment of specific individuals to prevent people in general or society at large from engaging in crime. To be both effective and just, Beccaria argued, punishments must be "public, prompt, necessary, the least possible in the given circumstances, proportionate to the crime, dictated by the laws."[4] It is important to emphasize, however, that Beccaria promoted crime prevention over punishment.

utility The principle that a policy should provide "the greatest happiness shared by the greatest number."

social contract An imaginary agreement to sacrifice the minimum amount of liberty necessary to prevent anarchy and chaos.

special or **specific deterrence** The prevention of individuals from committing crime again by punishing them.

general deterrence The prevention of people in general or society at large from engaging in crime by punishing specific individuals and making examples of them.

In addition to the establishment of a social contract and the punishment of people who violate it, Beccaria recommended four other ways to prevent or to deter crime.[5] The first was to enact laws that are clear, simple, and unbiased and that reflect the consensus of the population. The second was to educate the public. Beccaria assumed that the more educated people are, the less likely they are to commit crimes. The third was to eliminate corruption from the administration of justice. Beccaria believed that if the people who dispense justice are themselves corrupt, people lose respect for the justice system and become more likely to commit crimes. The fourth was to reward virtue. Beccaria asserted that punishing crime is not enough; it is also important to reward law-abiding behavior. Such rewards might include public recognition of especially meritorious behavior or, perhaps, an annual tax deduction for people who have not been convicted of a crime.

The application of classical theory was supposed to make criminal law fairer and easier to administer. To those ends, judges would not select sentences. They could only impose the sentences dictated by legislatures for specific crimes. All offenders would be treated alike, and similar crimes would be treated similarly. Individual differences among offenders and unique or mitigating circumstances about the crime would be ignored. A problem is that all offenders are not alike and similar crimes are not always as similar as they might appear on the surface. Should first offenders be treated the same as those who commit crime repeatedly? Should juveniles be treated the same as adults? Should the insane be treated the same as the sane? Should a crime of passion be treated the same as the intentional commission of a crime? The classical school's answer to all of those difficult questions would be a simple yes.

Despite those problems, Beccaria's ideas were very influential. France, for example, adopted many of Beccaria's principles in its Code of 1791—in particular, the principle of equal punishments for the same crimes. However, because classical theory ignored both individual differences among offenders and mitigating circumstances, it was difficult to apply the law in practice. Because of that difficulty, as well as new developments in the emerging behavioral sciences, modifications of classical theory and its application were introduced in the early 1800s.

FYI: Cesare Beccaria

Cesare Beccaria, the best known of the classical criminologists, opposed the death penalty. In *An Essay on Crimes and Punishments,* he wrote: "The death penalty cannot be useful, because of the example of barbarity it gives. . . . It seems to me absurd that the laws, which are an expression of the public will, which detest and punish homicide, should themselves commit it, and that to deter citizens from murder, they order a public one."

NEOCLASSICAL THEORY

Several modifications of classical theory are collectively referred to as **neoclassical theory.** The principal difference between the two theories has to do with classical theory's assumption about free will. In the neoclassical revision, it was conceded that certain factors, such as insanity, might inhibit the exercise of free will. Thus, the idea of premeditation was introduced as a measure of the degree of free will exercised. Also, mitigating circumstances were considered legitimate grounds for an argument of diminished responsibility.

neoclassical theory A modification of classical theory in which it was conceded that certain factors, such as insanity, might inhibit the exercise of free will.

Those modifications of classical theory had two practical effects on criminal justice policy. First, they provided a reason for nonlegal experts such as medical doctors to testify in court as to the degree of diminished responsibility of an offender. Second, offenders began to be sentenced to punishments that were considered rehabilitative. The idea was that certain environments, for example, environments free of vice and crime, were more conducive than others to the exercise of rational choice.

The reason we have placed so much emphasis on the classical school of criminology and its neoclassical revisions is that, together, they are essentially the model on which criminal justice in the United States is based today. During the past 30 years or so, at least in part because the public frequently perceived as too lenient the sentences imposed by judges for certain crimes, such measures as legislatively imposed sentencing guidelines have limited the sentencing authority of judges in many jurisdictions. Public outrage over the decisions of other criminal justice officials has led to similar measures. For example, parole has been abolished in the federal jurisdiction and in some states because many people believe that parole boards release dangerous criminals from prison too soon.

Historians of criminal law credit Beccaria's arguments in his book, *An Essay on Crimes and Punishments,* with ending legal torture throughout Christendom. However, in 1999, Haitian immigrant Abner Louima was brutally tortured by New York City police officers. *How could this have happened?*

THINKING CRITICALLY

1. Name four of the ways that classical criminologist Cesare Beccaria thought were best to prevent or deter crime. Do you agree with Beccaria? Why or why not?
2. What are the main differences between classical and neoclassical theories?

The revival of classical and neoclassical theories during the past three decades, and the introduction of a more modern version called *rational choice theory,* are also probably a reaction to the allegation of some criminologists and public officials that criminologists have failed to discover the causes of crime. As a result of that belief, there has been a renewed effort to deter crimes by sentencing more offenders to prison for longer periods of time and, in many jurisdictions, by imposing capital punishment for heinous crimes. Ironically, one reason the theory of the classical school lost favor in the nineteenth century was the belief that punishment was not a particularly effective method of preventing or controlling crime.

FYI: Americans Behind Bars

At midyear 2002, there were more than 2 million people incarcerated in the United States. More than 1.2 million were in state prisons, nearly 149,000 were in federal prisons, and about 665,000 were in local jails. Between 1990 and midyear 2002, the state prison population increased 75 percent, the federal prison population 153 percent, and jail populations 64 percent. Between 1995 and midyear 2002, the population grew on average 3.8% annually. On June 30, 2002, one in every 142 U.S. residents was incarcerated.

SOURCE: Paige M. Harrison and Jennifer C. Karbeg, "Prison and Jail Inmates at Midyear 2002," U.S. Department of Justice, *Bureau of Justice Statistics Bulletin* (Washington, DC: GPO, April 2003).

Positivist Approaches to Explaining Crime

The theory of the positivist school of criminology grew out of positive philosophy and the logic and basic methodology of empirical or experimental science. Positive philosophy was an explicit rejection of the critical and "negative" philosophy of the Enlightenment thinkers. Among the founders of positivism was Auguste Comte, who also has been credited with founding sociology. Comte acknowledged that the Enlightenment thinkers had contributed to progress by helping to break up the old system and by paving the way for a new one.[6] However, Comte argued that the ideas of the Enlightenment period had outlived their usefulness and had become obstructive.

At about the same time that positivist philosophy was developing, experimentation with animals was becoming an increasingly accepted way of learning about human beings in physiology, medicine, psychology, and psychiatry. Human beings were beginning to appear to science as one of many creatures, with no special connection to God. Human beings were beginning to be understood, not as free-willed, self-determining creatures who could do anything that they wanted to do, but rather as beings whose action was determined by biological and cultural factors.

Positivism was a major break with the classical and neoclassical theories that had preceded it. The following are key assumptions of the positivist school of thought:

1. Human behavior is determined and not a matter of free will. Consequently, positivists focus on cause-and-effect relationships.
2. Criminals are fundamentally different from noncriminals. Positivists search for such differences by scientific methods.
3. Social scientists (including criminologists) can be objective, or value-neutral, in their work.
4. Crime is frequently caused by multiple factors.
5. Society is based on consensus but not on a social contract.

As the social sciences developed and social scientists directed their attention to the problem of crime, they adopted, for the most part, positivist assumptions. For example, theories of crime were (and continue to be) based on biological positivism, psychological positivism, sociological positivism, and so on. However, as theories based on positivist assumptions were developed, it became apparent to close observers that there were problems, not only with the theories, but with the positivist assumptions as well. We will briefly discuss five of those problems.[7] In subsequent subsections, we will also describe problems peculiar to specific positivist theories of crime causation.

The first problem with positivism is overprediction: positivist theories generally account for too much crime. They also do not explain exceptions very well. For example, a positivist theory that suggests crime is caused by poverty overpredicts because not all poor people commit crime.

Second, positivist theories generally ignore the criminalization process, the process by which certain behaviors are made illegal. They separate the study of crime from a theory of the law and the state and take the legal definition of crime for granted. Ignored is the question of why certain behaviors are defined as criminal while other, similar behaviors are not.

A third problem with positivism is its consensual worldview, the belief that most people agree about most things most of the time. Such a view ignores a multitude of fundamental conflicts of value and interest in society. It also tends to lead to a blind acceptance of the status quo.

A fourth problem is positivism's belief in determinism, the idea that choice of action is not free, but is determined by causes independent of a person's will. Positivists generally assume that humans only adapt or react, but humans also create. How else could we explain new social arrangements or ways of

FYI: Charles Darwin

In *The Descent of Man* (1871), British naturalist Charles Darwin suggested that some people were "less highly evolved or developed than others," that some people "were nearer their apelike ancestors than others in traits, abilities, and dispositions."

SOURCE: George B. Vold, *Theoretical Criminology,* 2nd ed. (New York: Oxford, 1979).

CAREERS IN CRIMINAL JUSTICE

Criminologist

My name is Alida Merlo, and I am a professor of criminology at Indiana University of Pennsylvania. I have taught criminal justice and criminology for more than 25 years. I have a PhD in sociology from Fordham University, a master's degree in criminal justice from Northeastern University, and a bachelor's degree from Youngstown State University. As an undergraduate, I majored in sociology and corrections.

I became interested in criminology while taking an undergraduate course in juvenile delinquency. That course inspired me to pursue a career in criminal justice as a probation officer and then as an intake supervisor for the Mahoning County Juvenile Court in Youngstown, Ohio. These experiences led me to enroll in graduate school to learn more about crime causation and the criminal justice process.

During graduate school, I realized I would like to teach criminology and criminal justice. I was attracted to the profession for a variety of reasons: It would enable me to do research, teach, develop programs, and pursue professional activities and community service. Teaching and studying criminal justice and criminology seemed a wonderful opportunity.

Being a criminologist involves developing and teaching courses, reading and contributing to the literature in the field, serving on departmental and university committees, advising students about courses, research, career options, and graduate education, meeting prospective students and their families, applying for research funding, conducting research, sharing research findings with colleagues at state, regional, national, and international meetings, being involved in professional organizations, and serving on community boards or assisting in community programs.

One great joy of teaching criminology and criminal justice is assisting students as they develop and blossom in the discipline. Many of my students work in the field. Former students have been awarded doctoral degrees and teach criminal justice. It is exciting to have played a part in their professional development.

One disadvantage of being a criminologist is the inability to communicate to the public and to policy makers the realities of criminal justice and the implications of one's research. Confronting the fact that policies are often developed and enforced with little enlightenment is frustrating, but I am confident that criminologists will play a greater role in the future.

What qualities does a criminologist need to succeed? Why?

thinking? A belief in determinism allows positivists to present an absolute situation uncomplicated by the ability to choose.

Finally, a fifth problem with positivist theories is the belief in the ability of social scientists (criminologists) to be objective, or value-neutral, in their work. Positivists fail to recognize that to describe and evaluate such human actions as criminal behavior is fundamentally a moral endeavor and, therefore, subject to bias.

BIOLOGICAL THEORIES

Biological theories of crime causation (biological positivism) are based on the belief that criminals are physiologically different from noncriminals. Early biological theories assumed that structure determined function. In other words, criminals behave differently because, structurally, they are different. Today's biocriminologists are more likely to assume that biochemistry determines function or, more precisely, the difference between criminals and noncriminals is the result of a complex interaction between biochemical and environmental factors. To test biological theories, efforts are made to demonstrate, through measurement and statistical analysis, that there are or are not significant structural or biochemical differences between criminals and noncriminals.

biological inferiority According to biological theories, a criminal's innate physiological makeup produces certain physical or genetic characteristics that distinguish criminals from noncriminals.

Historically, the cause of crime, from this perspective, was **biological inferiority.** Biological inferiority in criminals was assumed to produce certain physical or genetic characteristics that distinguished criminals from noncriminals. It is important to emphasize that in these theories, the physical or genetic characteristics themselves did not cause crime; they were only the symptoms, or *stigmata,* of the more fundamental inferiority. The concept of biological inferiority has lost favor among today's biocriminologists who generally prefer to emphasize the biological differences between criminals and noncriminals without adding the value judgment. In any event, several different methodologies have been employed to detect physical differences between criminals and noncriminals. They are criminal anthropology; study of body types; heredity studies, including family trees, statistical comparisons, twin studies, and adoption studies; and, in the last 15 to 20 years or so, studies based on new scientific technologies that allow, for example, the examination of brain chemistry processes.

criminal anthropology The study of "criminal" human beings.

Criminal Anthropology **Criminal anthropology** is the study of "criminal" human beings. It is associated with the work of an Italian army doctor and later, university professor, Cesare Lombroso. Lombroso first published his theory of a physical criminal type in 1876.

Lombroso's theory consisted of the following propositions:[8]

1. Criminals are, by birth, a distinct type.
2. That type can be recognized by physical characteristics, or *stigmata,* such as enormous jaws, high cheekbones, and insensitivity to pain.
3. The criminal type is clearly distinguished in a person with more than five stigmata, perhaps exists in a person with three to five stigmata, and does not necessarily exist in a person with fewer than three stigmata.
4. Physical stigmata do not cause crime; they only indicate an individual who is predisposed to crime. Such a person is either an **atavist**—that is, a reversion to a savage type—or a result of degeneration.
5. Because of their personal natures, such persons cannot desist from crime unless they experience very favorable lives.

atavist A person who reverts to a savage type.

Lombroso's theory was popular in the United States until about 1915, although variations of his theory are still being taught today. The major problem with Lombroso's criminal anthropology is the assumption that certain physical characteristics are indicative of biological inferiority. Unless there is independent evidence to support that assumption, other than the association of the physical characteristics with criminality, then the result is circular reasoning. In other words, crime is caused by biological inferiority, which is itself indicated by the physical characteristics associated with criminality.

Body-Type Theory Body-type theory is an extension of Lombroso's criminal anthropology. William Sheldon, whose work in the 1940s was based on earlier work by Ernst Kretchmer in the 1920s, is perhaps the best known of the body-type theorists. According to Sheldon, human beings can be divided into three basic body types, or *somatotypes*, which correspond to three basic temperaments.[9] The three body types are the endomorphic (soft, fat), the mesomorphic (athletically built), and the ectomorphic (tall, skinny).

Sheldon argued that everyone has elements of all three types but that one type usually predominates. In a study of 200 Boston delinquents between 1939 and 1949, Sheldon found that delinquents were more mesomorphic than nondelinquents and that serious delinquents were more mesomorphic than less serious delinquents. Subsequent studies by the Gluecks in the 1950s and by Cortes in the 1970s also found an association between mesomorphy and delinquency.

The major criticism of the body-type theory is that differences in behavior are indicative of the social selection process and not biological inferiority. In other words, delinquents are more likely to be mesomorphic than nondelinquents because, for example, mesomorphs are more likely to be selected for gang membership. Also, the finding that delinquents are more likely than nondelinquents to be mesomorphic contradicts, at least with regard to physique, the theory's general assumption that criminals (or delinquents) are biologically inferior.

In any event, if one believes that crime is the product of biological inferiority, then the policy implications are limited. Either criminals are isolated from the rest of the population by imprisoning them, for example, or they are

CJ ONLINE

Biological Causes of Crime

Learn more about the biological causes of criminal, violent, and psychopathic behavior. Go to **www.crime-times.org** for the Crime Times website. Review the issue and/or subject index and read a few articles related to biology and criminal behavior. *Do you think that biological theories of crime causation adequately explain criminal behavior?*

William Sheldon, a well-known body-type theorist, divided humans into three basic body types. Left: endomorphic (soft fat); center: mesomorphic (athletically built); right: ectomorphic (tall, skinny). *Why would delinquents more likely have a mesomorphic body type rather than an endomorphic or ectomorphic body type?*

executed. If they are isolated, they may also need to be sterilized to ensure that they do not reproduce.

HEREDITY STUDIES A variety of methods has been employed to test the proposition that criminals are genetically different from noncriminals.

Family Tree Studies Perhaps the earliest method was the use of family trees, in which a family known to have many "criminals" was compared with a family tree of "noncriminals." (See FYI.) However, a finding that criminality appears in successive generations does not prove that criminality is inherited or is the product of a hereditary defect. For example, the use of a fork in eating has been a trait of many families for generations, but that does not prove that the use of a fork is inherited. In short, the family tree method cannot adequately separate hereditary influences from environmental influences.

FYI: The Family Tree Method

The family tree method was used by Dugdale (1877) and Estabrook (1916), who both compared the Jukes family with the Jonathan Edwards family. The Jukes family presumably had 7 murderers, 60 thieves, 50 prostitutes, and assorted other criminals. The Edwards family, on the other hand, presumably had no criminals but, instead, had presidents of the United States, governors, Supreme Court justices, federal court justices, and assorted writers, preachers, and teachers. As it turns out, the Edwards family was not as crime-free as originally believed. Apparently, Jonathan Edwards's maternal grandmother had been divorced on grounds of adultery, a grandaunt had murdered her son, and a granduncle had murdered his sister.

SOURCE: Richard L. Dugdale, *The Jukes: A Study in Crime, Pauperism, Disease and Heredity* (New York: Putnam, 1877); Arthur H. Estabrook, *The Jukes in 1915* (Washington, DC: Carnegie Institute of Washington, 1916).

Statistical Comparisons A second method used to test the proposition that crime is inherited or is the product of a hereditary defect is statistical comparison. The rationale is that if criminality exhibits the same degree of family resemblance as other physical traits, such as eye or hair color, then criminality, like those other traits, must be inherited. Although there is some evidence to support the notion, statistical comparisons also fail to separate adequately hereditary influences from environmental influences.

Twin Studies A third, more sophisticated method of testing the proposition that crime is inherited or is the result of a hereditary defect is the use of twin studies. Heredity is assumed to be the same in identical twins because they are the product of a single egg. Heredity is assumed to be different in fraternal twins because they are the product of two eggs fertilized by two sperm. The logic of the method is that if there is greater similarity in behavior between identical twins than between fraternal twins, the behavior must be due to heredity, since environments are much the same. More than a half century of this methodology has revealed that identical twins are more likely to demonstrate concordance (both twins having criminal records) than are fraternal twins, thus supporting the hereditary link. A problem with the twin studies, however, is the potential confounding of genetic and environmental influences. Identical twins tend to be treated more alike by others, spend much more time together, and have a greater sense of shared identity than do fraternal twins.

Adoption Studies A fourth method, the most recent and most sophisticated method of examining the inheritability of criminality, is the adoption study. The first such study was conducted in the 1970s. In this method, the criminal records of adopted children (almost always boys) who were adopted at a relatively early age are compared with the criminal records of both their biological parents and their adoptive parents (almost always fathers). The rationale is that if the criminal records of adopted boys are more like those of their biological fathers than like those of their adoptive fathers, the criminality of the adopted boys can be assumed to be the result of heredity.

The findings of the adoption studies reveal that the percentage of adoptees who are criminal is greater when the biological father has a criminal record than when the adoptive father has one. However, there also is an interactive effect. A greater percentage of adoptees have criminal records when both fathers have criminal records than when only one of them does. Like the twin studies, the adoption studies presumably demonstrate the influence of heredity but cannot adequately separate it from the influence of the environment.

A problem with the adoption studies is the difficulty of interpreting the relative influences of heredity and environment, especially when the adoption does not take place shortly after birth or when, as is commonly the case, the adoption agency attempts to find an adoptive home that matches the biological home in family income and socioeconomic status.

If criminals are genetically different from noncriminals or the product of genetic defect, then the policy implications are the same as for other theories that propose that criminals are biologically inferior: isolate, sterilize, or execute. However, in the future, new technologies may make possible genetic engineering—that is, the removal or alteration of defective genes.

FYI: Genetic Unity (DNA)

Based on the analysis of thousands of DNA samples, preliminary findings of the Human Genome Diversity Project—the first worldwide survey of humankind—demonstrate the "genetic unity that binds our diverse, polyglot species." The data show that "any two people, regardless of geography or ethnicity, share at least 99.99 percent of their genetic makeups." As for the 0.01 percent of the genome that makes people different, "it doesn't shake out along racial lines. . . . Instead, some 85 percent of human genetic diversity occurs within ethnic groups, not between them."

SOURCE: Paul Salopek, "What's Next for Mankind?" *The Orlando Sentinel* (from the *Chicago Tribune*), June 1, 1997, p. G-1.

MODERN BIOCRIMINOLOGY Ongoing research has revealed numerous biological factors associated either directly or indirectly with criminal or delinquent behavior. Among such factors are certain chemical, mineral, and vitamin deficiencies in the diet, diets high in sugar and carbohydrates, hypoglycemia (low blood sugar level), certain allergies, ingestion of food dyes and lead, exposure to radiation from fluorescent tubes and television sets, and all sorts of brain dysfunctions such as attention deficit/hyperactivity disorder.[10] This section focuses on a few more of the biological factors linked to criminality and delinquency: disorders of the limbic system and other parts of the brain, brain chemical dysfunctions, minimal brain damage, and endocrine abnormalities.

Limbic System Disorders At least some unprovoked violent criminal behavior is believed to be caused by tumors and other destructive or inflammatory processes of the limbic system.[11]

The **limbic system** (see Figure 3.1) is a structure surrounding the brain stem that, in part, controls the life functions of heartbeat, breathing, and sleep. It also is believed to moderate expressions of violence; such emotions as anger, rage, and fear; and sexual response. Violent criminal behavior has also been linked to disorders in other parts of the brain. Recent evidence suggests that chronic violent offenders have much higher levels of brain disorder when compared to the general population. Surgical removal of the affected area sometimes eliminates expressions of violence. A problem with that type of intervention, however, is that it can cause unpredictable and undesirable

limbic system A structure surrounding the brain stem that, in part, controls the life functions of heartbeat, breathing, and sleep. It also is believed to moderate expressions of violence; such emotions as anger, rage, and fear; and sexual response.

FIGURE 3.1 The Limbic System

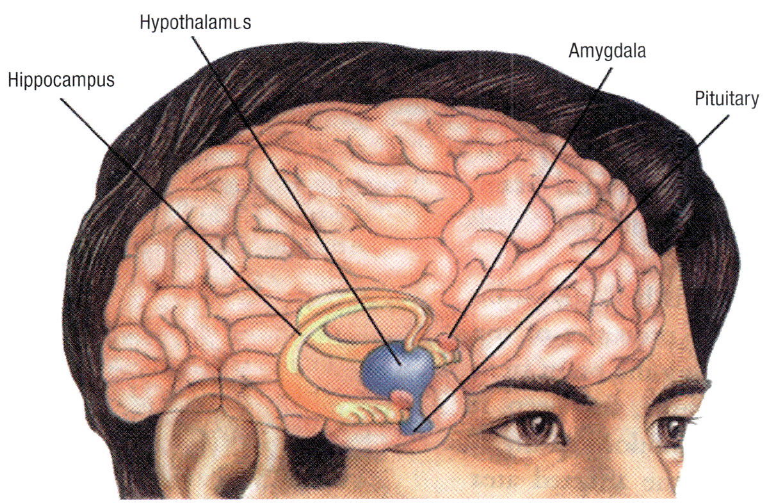

behavior changes and, of course, is irreversible. Irreversibility is less a problem with newer chemical interventions, but the problem of unpredictable and undesirable behavior changes remains.

Chemical Dysfunctions Some criminal behaviors are believed to be influenced by low levels of brain neurotransmitters (substances brain cells use to communicate).[12] For example, low levels of the brain neurotransmitter *serotonin* have been found in impulsive murderers and arsonists. Research is currently being conducted to determine whether low levels of another neurotransmitter, *norepinephrine,* are associated with compulsive gambling. Another interesting discovery in this area may help explain cocaine use. Apparently cocaine increases the level of the neurotransmitter *dopamine,* which activates the limbic system to produce pleasure. If such chemical deficiencies are linked to those behaviors, chemical treatment or improved diets might help. Neurotransmitters are products of the foods people eat.

Minimal Brain Damage Research on minimal brain damage has found that it increases an individual's chances of being identified as delinquent.[13] Minimal brain damage is believed to be most commonly caused by nutritional or oxygen deficiencies during pregnancy, or during or shortly after birth, or by insufficient protein and sensory stimulation during a child's formative years. Because minimal brain damage is also strongly associated with lower socioeconomic status, social deprivation must be considered a crucial element in its occurrence.

To reduce minimal brain damage in the population, adequate prenatal medical care and nutrition must be provided to all expectant mothers. To minimize complications during birth, adequate medical assistance must be provided. Further reductions in minimal brain damage would require providing adequate protein and social and intellectual stimulation to developing infants and young children.

FYI

Chemical Castration

In 1996, California became the first state to require chemical castration of repeat child molesters. Under the law, molesters who commit a second crime against a child under 13 must receive weekly injections of Depo-Provera. In 1997, Florida and Georgia passed similar legislation requiring repeat offenders to be chemically castrated, and Texas approved voluntary castration for repeat molesters. In all four states, offenders may choose surgical castration instead.

Endocrine Abnormalities Criminal behaviors have also been associated with endocrine, or hormone, abnormalities, especially those involving *testosterone* (a male sex hormone) and *progesterone* and *estrogen* (the female sex hormones).[14] For example, administering estrogen to male sex offenders has been found to reduce their sexual drives. A similar effect has been achieved by administering the drug Depo-Provera®, which reduces testosterone levels. However, a problem with Depo-Provera is that it is successful only for male sex offenders who cannot control their sexual urges. The drug does not seem to work on offenders whose sex crimes are premeditated. Studies have also found that a large number of crimes committed by females are committed during the menstrual or premenstrual periods of the female hormonal cycle. Those periods are characterized by a change in the estrogen-progesterone ratio.

In sum, there are probably no positivist criminologists today who would argue that biology or genetics makes people criminals. Nor, for that matter, are there many criminologists today who would deny that biology has some influence on criminal behavior. The position held by most criminologists today is that criminal behavior is the product of a complex interaction between biology and environmental or social conditions. What is inherited is not criminal behavior, but rather the way in which the person responds to his or her environment. In short, biology or genetics gives an individual a predisposition, or a tendency, to behave in a certain way. Whether a person actually behaves in that way and whether that behavior is defined as a crime depend primarily on environmental or social conditions.

PSYCHOLOGICAL THEORIES

This section examines psychological theories of crime causation, namely, the relationship between intelligence, criminality, and delinquency and discusses psychoanalytic and humanistic psychological theories. Learning or behavioral theories will be discussed along with sociological theories.

INTELLIGENCE AND CRIME The idea that crime is the product primarily of people of low intelligence was popular in the United States from about 1914 until around 1930. It received some attention again during the mid-1970s and in the mid-1990s. The belief requires only a slight shift in thinking from the idea that criminals are biologically inferior to the idea that they are mentally inferior.

In 1931, Edwin Sutherland reviewed approximately 350 studies on the relationship between intelligence and delinquency and criminality.[15] The studies reported the results of intelligence tests of about 175,000 criminals and delinquents. Sutherland concluded from the review that although intelligence may play a role in individual cases, given the selection that takes place in arrest, conviction, and imprisonment, the distribution of the intelligence scores of criminals and delinquents is very similar to the distribution of the intelligence scores of the general population.

For the next 40 years or so, the issue of the relationship between intelligence and crime and delinquency appeared resolved. However, in the mid-1970s, two studies were published that resurrected the debate.[16] Those studies found that IQ was an important predictor of both official and self-reported juvenile delinquency, as important as social class or race. Both studies acknowledged the findings of Sutherland's earlier review. Both also noted that a decreasing number of delinquents had been reported as being of below-normal intelligence over the years. However, in both studies, it was maintained that the difference in intelligence between delinquents and nondelinquents had never disappeared and had stabilized at about eight IQ points. The studies failed to note, however, that the eight-point IQ difference found between delinquents and nondelinquents was generally within the normal range. The authors of the studies surmised that IQ influenced delinquency through its effect on school performance.

At this time, we cannot conclude with any degree of confidence that delinquents, as a group, are less intelligent than nondelinquents. We do know that most adult criminals are not of below-normal intelligence. Obviously, low-level intelligence cannot account for the dramatic increase in the crime rate over the last couple of decades, until recently, unless one is prepared to conclude that the population of offenders is getting less intelligent. Low-level intelligence certainly cannot account for complex white-collar and political crimes.

Nevertheless, to the degree, if any, that crime is caused by low-level intelligence, the policy implications are the same as for theories of biological inferiority: isolate, sterilize, or execute. Intelligence is believed to have a large genetic component.

PSYCHOANALYTIC THEORIES Psychoanalytic theories of crime causation are associated with the work of Sigmund Freud and his followers.[17] Freud did not theorize much about criminal behavior itself, but a theory of crime causation can be deduced from his more general theory of human behavior and its disorders. Had he contemplated the issue, Freud probably would have argued that crime, like other disorders, was a symptom of more deep-seated problems and that if the deep-seated problems could be resolved, the symptom of crime would go away.

FYI: IQ and Crime

One of the earliest promoters in the United States of the relationship between low IQ and crime was H.H. Goddard. In 1914, he published *Feeblemindedness: Its Causes and Consequences.* In the book, Goddard argued that criminals are feebleminded, an old-fashioned term that means below-normal intelligence.

SOURCE: George B. Vold and Thomas J. Bernard, *Theoretical Criminology,* 3rd ed. (New York: Oxford, 1986) p. 72.

In "Criminality from a Sense of Guilt" (1915), Sigmund Freud, founder of psychoanalysis, suggested that some people commit crimes in order to be caught and punished—not for the crime for which they had been caught, but for something that they had done in the past about which they felt guilty and for which they were not caught or punished. *Do you think Freud was right? Why or why not?*

psychopaths, sociopaths, or **antisocial personalities** Persons characterized by no sense of guilt, no subjective conscience, and no sense of right and wrong. They have difficulty in forming relationships with other people; they cannot empathize with other people.

CJ ONLINE

Serial Killers

Serial killers are characterized as psychopaths or sociopaths. Go to **www.crimelibrary.com/serialkillers.htm** to read more about serial killers that are under investigation and some of the most well-known cases involving serial killers in the U.S. *Were you able to note any of the characteristics of a psychopath listed in Table 3.2 in these articles?*

Freud believed that some people who had unresolved deep-seated problems were psychopaths (sociologists call them *sociopaths*). **Psychopaths, sociopaths,** or **antisocial personalities** are characterized by no sense of guilt, no subjective conscience, and no sense of right and wrong. They have difficulty in forming relationships with other people; they cannot empathize with other people. Table 3.2 provides an extended list of the characteristics of psychopaths.

The principal policy implication of considering crime symptomatic of deep-seated problems is to provide psychotherapy or psychoanalysis. *Psychoanalysis* is a procedure first developed by Freud that, among other things, attempts to make patients conscious or aware of unconscious and deep-seated problems in order to resolve the symptoms associated with them. Methods used include a variety of projective tests (such as the interpretation of Rorschach inkblots), dream interpretation, and free association. Another policy implication that derives logically from Freudian theory is to provide people with legal outlets to sublimate or redirect their sexual and aggressive drives. (Freud believed that all human beings are born with those two drives and that those drives are the primary sources of human motivation.)

Psychoanalysis, and the psychoanalytic theory on which it is based, are components of a medical model of crime causation that has, to varying degrees, informed criminal justice policy in the United States for a century. The general conception of this medical model is that criminals are biologically or, especially, psychologically "sick" and in need of treatment.

Jeffery Dahmer was accused by the prosecutor in his case of being "an evil psychopath who lured his victims and murdered them in cold blood." He was convicted of 15 counts of murder and sentenced to serve 15 consecutive life sentences or a total of 957 years in prison. Dahmer was killed in prison in 1994. *Was Dahmer a psychopath? Why or why not?*

Despite the enduring popularity of this theory, a number of problems have been identified with it. First, the bulk of the research on the issue suggests that most criminals are not psychologically disturbed or, at least, are no more disturbed than the rest of the population.[18]

Second, if a person who commits a crime has a psychological disturbance, that does not mean that the psychological disturbance causes the crime. Many people with psychological disturbances do not commit crimes, and many people without psychological disturbances do commit crimes.

Third, psychoanalytic theory generally ignores the environmental circumstances in which the problematic behavior occurs. The problem is considered a personal problem and not a social one.

Fourth, there are problems with psychoanalysis and other forms of psychotherapy. Psychotherapy rests on faith. Much of its theoretical structure is scientifically untestable. The emphasis of psychotherapy as an approach to rehabilitation is on the individual offender and not on the offender in interaction with the environment in which the criminal behavior occurs. The behaviors that are treated in psychotherapy are not criminal; they are the deep-seated problems. It is assumed that criminal behavior is symptomatic of those problems. That assumption may not be true. Many people who do not engage in crime have deep-seated problems, and many people who do not have those problems do engage in crime.

Humanistic Psychological Theory Humanistic psychological theory, as described here, refers primarily to the work of Abraham Maslow and Seymour Halleck. The theories of Maslow and Halleck are fundamentally psychoanalytic, but they are called humanistic because they assume that human beings are basically good even though they are sometimes influenced by society to act badly. By contrast, Freudian theory assumes that human beings are inherently bad, motivated by sexual and aggressive drives.

Maslow did not apply his theory to crime itself, so we must infer from Maslow's work what we think he would have said about the causes of crime had he addressed the subject. Abraham Maslow believed that human beings are motivated by a hierarchy of basic needs. (See Figure 3.2.)

1. Physiological (food, water, and procreational sex).
2. Safety (security; stability; freedom from fear, anxiety, chaos, etc.).
3. Belongingness and love (friendship, love, affection, acceptance).
4. Esteem (self-esteem and the esteem of others).
5. Self-actualization (being true to one's nature, becoming everything that one is capable of becoming).[19]

According to Maslow, during a given period, a person's life is dominated by a particular need. It remains dominated by that need until the need has been relatively satisfied, at which time a new need emerges to dominate that person's life. From this view, crime may be understood as a means by which individuals satisfy their basic human needs. They choose crime because they cannot satisfy their needs legally or, for whatever reason, choose not to satisfy their needs legally. An obvious policy implication of the theory is to help people satisfy their basic human needs in legitimate ways.

TABLE 3.2 Characteristics of the Psychopath

1. Superficial charm and good "intelligence."
2. Absence of delusions and other signs of irrational "thinking."
3. Absence of "nervousness" or psychoneurotic manifestations.
4. Unreliability.
5. Untruthfulness and insincerity.
6. Lack of remorse or shame.
7. Inadequately motivated antisocial behavior.
8. Poor judgment and failure to learn by experience.
9. Pathologic egocentricity and incapacity for love.
10. General poverty in major affective reactions.
11. Specific loss of insight.
12. Unresponsiveness in general interpersonal relations.
13. Fantastic and uninviting behavior, with drink and sometimes without.
14. Suicide rarely carried out.
15. Sex life impersonal, trivial, and poorly integrated.
16. Failure to follow any life plan.

SOURCE: From Hervey Cleckley's "The Mask of Sanity," *Institutions, Etc.: A Journal of Progressive Human Services* 8, no. 9 (September 1985), p. 21. Reprinted by permission of Dolan, Pollak & Schram.

FIGURE 3.2 Maslow's Hierarchy of Needs

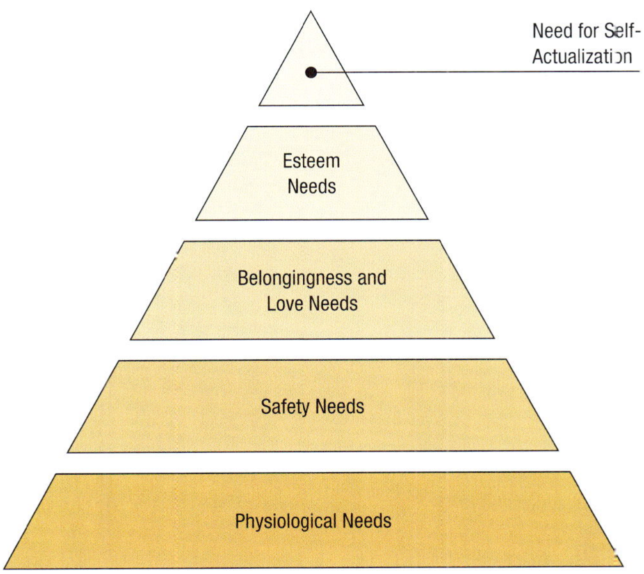

SOURCE: From Abraham Maslow, *Toward a Psychology of Being,* Van Nostrand 1968. This material is used by permission of John Wiley & Sons, Inc.

That may require governments to ensure adequate food, shelter, and medical care for those in need or to provide educational or vocational opportunities for those who are unable to obtain them. Those strategies are implied by several sociological theories as well. On a basic, interpersonal level, Maslow's theory might imply the need to make sympathetic listeners available to people who would benefit from sharing their problems.

Seymour L. Halleck views crime as one of several adaptations to the helplessness caused by oppression.[20] For Halleck, there are two general types of oppression, *objective* and *subjective*. Each has two subtypes. The subtypes of objective oppression are (a) social oppression (for example, oppression resulting from racial discrimination) and (b) the oppression that occurs in two-person interactions (for example, a parent's unfair restriction of the activities of a child). The subtypes of subjective oppression are (a) oppression from within (guilt) and (b) projected or misunderstood oppression (a person's feeling of being oppressed when, in fact, he or she is not).

For Halleck, the emotional experience of either type of oppression is helplessness, to which the person sometimes adapts by resorting to criminal behavior. Halleck suggests that the criminal adaptation is more likely when alternative adaptations, such as conformity, activism, or mental illness, are not possible or are blocked by other people. He also maintains that criminal behavior is sometimes chosen as an adaptation over other possible alternatives because it offers gratifications or psychological advantages that could not be achieved otherwise. Halleck's psychological advantages of crime are listed in Table 3.3.

There are at least three crime policy implications of Halleck's theory. First, sources of social oppression should be eliminated wherever possible. Affirmative action programs, which attempt to rectify historic patterns of discrimination in such areas as employment, are an example of such efforts. Second, alternative, legal ways of coping with oppression must be provided. An example is the opportunity to file claims with the Equal Employment

TABLE 3.3 Halleck's 14 Psychological Advantages of Crime

1. The adaptational advantages of crime in changing one's environment are more desirable than illness or conformity.
2. Crime involves activity, and when man is engaged in motoric behavior, he feels less helpless.
3. However petty a criminal act may be, it carries with it a promise of change in a favorable direction.
4. During the planning and execution of a criminal act, the offender is a free man. (He is immune from the oppressive dictates of others.)
5. Crime offers the possibility of excitement.
6. Crime calls for the individual to maximize his faculties and talents which might otherwise lie dormant.
7. Crime can relieve feelings of inner oppression and stress.
8. Crime increases external stresses, which allows the individual to concentrate upon these threats to his equilibrium and temporarily allows him to abandon his chronic intrapsychic problems.
9. Once a person has convinced himself that the major pressures in his life come from without, there is less tendency to blame himself for this failure.
10. Adopting the criminal role provides an excellent rationalization for inadequacy.
11. Crime has a more esteemed social status than mental illness.
12. America has an ambivalent attitude toward crime. Although crime is regularly condemned, it is also glamorized.
13. Deviant behavior sometimes helps the criminal to form close and relatively nonoppressive relations with other criminals.
14. Crime can provide pleasure or gratify needs.

SOURCE: Seymour L. Halleck, *Psychiatry and the Dilemmas of Crime* (New York: Harper and Row, 1967), pp. 76–80.

Opportunity Commission (EEOC) in individual cases of employment discrimination. Third, psychotherapy should be provided for subjective oppressions. Psychotherapy could make the individual aware of oppressive sources of guilt or sources of misunderstood oppression so that the individual could better cope with them.

A major problem with the theories of Maslow and Halleck is that they do not go far enough. Neither Maslow nor Halleck asks the basic questions: Why can't people satisfy their basic needs legally, or why do they choose not to? Why don't societies ensure that basic needs can be satisfied legally so that the choice to satisfy them illegally makes no sense? Similarly, why does society so oppress many people, and why aren't more effective measures taken to greatly reduce that oppression?

SOCIOLOGICAL THEORIES

Sociologists emphasize that human beings live in social groups and that those groups and the social structure they create (for example, political and economic systems) influence behavior. Most sociological theories of crime causation assume that a criminal's behavior is determined by his or her social environment, which includes families, friends, neighborhoods, and so on. Most sociological theories of crime explicitly reject the notion of the born criminal.

The Contributions of Durkheim Many of the sociological theories of crime (actually delinquency) causation have their roots in the work of the French sociologist Émile Durkheim. Durkheim rejected the idea that the world is simply the product of individual actions. His basic premise is that society is more than a simple aggregate of individuals; it is a reality *sui generis* (unique).[21] Rejecting the idea that social phenomena, such as crime, can be explained solely by the biology or psychology of individuals, Durkheim argued that society is not the direct reflection of the characteristics of its individual members, because individuals cannot always choose. For Durkheim, social laws and institutions are "social facts" that dominate individuals, and all people can do is submit to them. The coercion may be formal (by means of law) or informal (by means of peer pressure). Durkheim maintained that with the aid of positive science, all people can expect is to discover the direction or course of social laws so that they can adapt to them with the least amount of pain.

anomie For Durkheim, the dissociation of the individual from the collective conscience.

collective conscience The general sense of morality of the times.

Émile Durkheim wrote in his volume, *Moral Education*, that, "The more detached from any collectivity man is, the more vulnerable to self-destruction he becomes." *Do you agree? Why? Why not?*

For Durkheim, crime, too, is a social fact. It is a normal aspect of society, because it is found in all societies. Nevertheless, different types of societies should have greater or lesser degrees of it. The cause of crime for Durkheim is **anomie,** that is, the dissociation of the individual from the **collective conscience,** or the general sense of morality of the times. He also believed that crime is functional for society by marking the boundaries of morality. In other words, people would not know what acceptable behavior is if crime did not exist. Crime is also functional because it provides a means of achieving necessary social change through, for example, civil disobedience and, under certain circumstances, directly contributes to social change, as in the repeal of prohibition. Durkheim advocated containing crime within reasonable boundaries. He warned, however, that too much crime could destroy society.

Chicago School A group of sociologists at the University of Chicago who assumed in their research that delinquent behavior was a product of social disorganization.

social disorganization The condition in which the usual controls over delinquents are largely absent, delinquent behavior is often approved of by parents and neighbors, there are many opportunities for delinquent behavior, and there is little encouragement, training, or opportunity for legitimate employment.

THE THEORY OF THE CHICAGO SCHOOL In the 1920s, members of the Department of Sociology at the University of Chicago tried to identify environmental factors associated with crime. Specifically, they attempted to uncover the relationship between a neighborhood's crime rate and the characteristics of the neighborhood. It was the first large-scale study of crime in the United States and was to serve as the basis for many future investigations into the causes of crime and delinquency.

The research of the **Chicago School** was based on a model taken from ecology, and as a result, that school is sometimes called the Chicago School of Human Ecology.[22] Ecology is a branch of biology in which the interrelationship of plants and animals is studied in their natural environment. Robert Park was the first of the Chicago theorists to propose this organic or biological analogy—that is, the similarity between the organization of plant and animal life in nature and the organization of human beings in societies.

Park and his colleagues described the growth of American cities like Chicago in ecological terms, saying growth occurs through a process of invasion, dominance, and succession.[23] That is, a cultural or ethnic group *invades* a territory occupied by another group and *dominates* that new territory until it is displaced, or *succeeded,* by another group and the cycle repeats itself.

This model of human ecology was used by other Chicago theorists, most notably Clifford R. Shaw and Henry D. McKay in their studies of juvenile delinquency in Chicago.[24] From the life histories of delinquents, Shaw and McKay confirmed that most of the delinquents were not much different from nondelinquents in their personality traits, physical condition, and intelligence.[25] However, Shaw and McKay did find that the areas of high delinquency were "socially disorganized." For the Chicago theorists, **social disorganization** is the condition in which the usual controls over delinquents are largely absent, delinquent behavior is often approved of by parents and neighbors, there are many opportunities for delinquent behavior, and there is little encouragement, training, or opportunity for legitimate employment.

In 1932, Shaw and his colleagues established the Chicago Area Project (CAP), which was designed to prevent delinquency through the organization and empowerment of neighborhood residents. Neighborhood centers, staffed

From his analysis of the life histories of individual delinquents, Chicago sociologist Clifford Shaw discovered that many delinquent activities began as play activities at an early age. *What kind of play activities do you think are delinquent activities?*

and controlled by local residents, were established in six areas of Chicago. The centers had two primary functions. One was to coordinate community resources, such as schools, churches, labor unions, and industries, to solve community problems. The other function was to sponsor activity programs, such as scouting, summer camps, and sports leagues, to develop a positive interest by individuals in their own welfare and to unite citizens to solve their own problems. CAP operated continuously for 25 years, until Shaw's death in 1957. Evaluations of the project suggest that it had a negligible effect on delinquency.

One of the problems with the theory of the Chicago School is the presumption that social disorganization is a cause of delinquency. Both social disorganization and delinquency may be the product of other, more basic factors. For example, one factor that contributes to the decline of city neighborhoods is the decades-old practice of *redlining,* in which banks refuse to lend money in an area because of the race or ethnicity of the inhabitants. Though illegal today, the practice continues. What usually happens in redlined areas is that neighborhood property values decline dramatically. Then land speculators and developers, typically in conjunction with political leaders, buy the land for urban renewal or gentrification and make fortunes in the process. In other words, political and economic elites may cause both social disorganization and delinquency—perhaps not intentionally, but by the conscious decisions they make about how a city will grow—making social disorganization appear to be the basic cause of delinquency.

Anomie or Strain Theory In an article published in 1938, Robert K. Merton observed that a major contradiction existed in the United States between cultural goals and the social structure.[26] He called the contradiction **anomie,** a concept first introduced by Durkheim. Specifically, Merton argued that in the United States the cultural goal of achieving wealth is deemed possible for all citizens, even though the social structure limits the legitimate "institutionalized means" available for obtaining the goal. For Merton, legitimate institutionalized means are the Protestant work ethic (hard work, education, and deferred gratification); illegitimate means are force and fraud. Because the social structure effectively limits the availability of legitimate institutionalized means, a *strain* is placed on people (hence the other name of the theory). Merton believed that strain could affect people in all social classes, but he acknowledged that it would most likely affect members of the lower class.

anomie For Merton, the contradiction between the cultural goal of achieving wealth and the social structure's inability to provide legitimate institutional means for achieving the goal. For Cohen, it is caused by the inability of juveniles to achieve status among peers by socially acceptable means.

Merton proposed that individuals adapt to the problem of anomie or strain in one of several different ways: (1) conformity, (2) innovation, (3) ritualism, (4) retreatism, and (5) rebellion. Table 3.4 displays these different adaptations. According to Merton, most people adapt by conforming; they "play the game."

TABLE 3.4 Merton's Typology of Modes of Individual Adaptation

Modes of Adaptation	Culture Goals	Institutional Means
I. Conformity	+	+
II. Innovation	+	−
III. Ritualism	−	+
IV. Retreatism	−	−
V. Rebellion	±	±

Key: + signifies "acceptance," − signifies "rejection," and ± signifies "rejection of prevailing values and substitution of new values."

Source: Reprinted with permission of The Free Press, a Division of Simon & Schuster Adult Publishing Group from *Social Theory and Social Structure* by Robert K. Merton.

FYI Youth Gangs

The 2000 National Youth Gang Survey sponsored by the Office of Juvenile Justice and Delinquency Prevention estimated that 24,500 youth gangs with a total of 772,500 members were active in the United States in 2000. A youth gang is defined as "a group of youths or young adults in [the respondent's] jurisdiction that [the respondent] or other responsible persons in [the respondent's] agency or community are willing to identify or classify as a 'gang.' Motorcycle gangs, hate or ideology groups, prison gangs, and exclusively adult gangs were excluded from the survey."

SOURCE: Arlen Egley, Jr., and Mehala Arjunan, "Highlights of the 2000 National Youth Gang Survey," U.S. Department of Justice, Office of Juvenile Justice and Delinquency Prevention Fact Sheet (Washington, DC: GPO, February 2002).

Conformers pursue the cultural goal of wealth only through legitimate institutional means. Innovation is the adaptation at the root of most crime. After rejecting legitimate institutional means, innovators pursue the cultural goal of wealth through illegitimate means. Ritualism is the adaptation of the individual who "takes no chances," usually a member of the lower middle class. Ritualists do not actively pursue the cultural goal of wealth (they are willing to settle for less) but follow the legitimate institutional means anyway. Retreatists include alcoholics, drug addicts, psychotics, and other outcasts of society. Retreatists "drop out"; they do not pursue the cultural goal of wealth, so they do not employ legitimate institutional means. Last is the adaptation of rebellion. Rebels reject both the cultural goal of wealth and the legitimate institutional means of achieving it. They substitute both different goals and different means. Rebellion can also be a source of crime.

In summary, Merton believed that a source of some, but not all, crime and delinquency was anomie or strain, a disjunction or contradiction between the cultural goal of achieving wealth and the social structure's ability to provide legitimate institutional means of achieving the goal.

Beginning in the mid-1950s, concern developed over the problem of juvenile gangs. Albert K. Cohen adapted Merton's anomie or strain theory to his attempt to explain gang delinquency.[27] In attempting to explain such behavior, Cohen surmised that it was to gain status among peers. Thus, Cohen substituted the goal of status among peers for Merton's goal of achieving wealth.

For Cohen, anomie or strain is experienced by juveniles who are unable to achieve status among peers by socially acceptable means, such as family name and position in the community or academic or athletic achievement. In response to the strain, either they can conform to middle-class values (generated primarily through the public school) and resign themselves to their inferior status among their peers, or they can rebel and establish their own value

According to Albert K. Cohen's version of anomie theory, juveniles who are unable to achieve status among their peers by socially acceptable means sometimes turn to gangs for social recognition. *What are some other reasons why juveniles join gangs?*

structures by turning middle-class values on their head. Juveniles who rebel in this way tend to find each other and to form groups or gangs to validate and reinforce their new values. Like Merton, Cohen believed that anomie can affect juveniles of any social class but that it disproportionately affects juveniles from the lower class.

Richard Cloward and Lloyd Ohlin extended Merton's and Cohen's formulations of anomie theory by suggesting that not all gang delinquents adapt to anomie in the same way. Cloward and Ohlin argue that the type of adaptation made by juvenile gang members depends on the *illegitimate opportunity structure* available to them.[28] They identified three delinquent subcultures: the criminal, the violent, and the retreatist. According to Cloward and Ohlin, if illegitimate opportunity is available to them, most delinquents will form *criminal* gangs to make money. However, if neither illegitimate nor legitimate opportunities to make money are available, delinquents often become frustrated and dissatisfied and form *violent* gangs to vent their anger. Finally, there are delinquents who, for whatever reason, are unable to adapt by joining either criminal or violent gangs. They *retreat* from society, as in Merton's retreatist adaptation, and become alcoholics and drug addicts.

The policy implications of anomie or strain theory are straightforward: reduce aspirations or increase legitimate opportunities or do both. Increasing legitimate opportunities, already a cornerstone of the black civil rights movement, struck a responsive chord as the 1960s began. Examples of this strategy are affirmative action employment programs, expansion of vocational education programs, and government grants that enable low-income students to attend college. Reducing aspirations (that is, desires to be wealthy) received little attention, however, because to attempt it would be to reject the "American dream," a principal source of motivation in a capitalist society.

Among the problems with the anomie theories of Merton, Cohen, and Cloward and Ohlin is their reliance on official statistics (police and court records) as measures of crime. Because these theorists relied on official statistics, their theories focus on lower-class crime and delinquency and ignore white-collar and government crimes.

FYI: Juvenile Delinquency Prevention and Control

When Robert Kennedy was Attorney General of the United States under his brother, President John F. Kennedy, he read Cloward and Ohlin's book *Delinquency and Opportunity: A Theory of Delinquent Gangs* (1960). Kennedy asked Lloyd Ohlin to help shape a new federal policy on juvenile delinquency. That effort, based on anomie theory, produced the Juvenile Delinquency Prevention and Control Act of 1961. The act included a comprehensive action program to provide employment opportunities and work training, in combination with community organization and improved social services, to disadvantaged youths and their families.

SOURCE: George B. Vold and Thomas J. Bernard, *Theoretical Criminology,* 3rd ed. (New York: Oxford, 1986), p. 201.

Learning Theories Gabriel Tarde was one of the first theorists to believe that crime was something learned by normal people as they adapted to other people and the conditions of their environment. His theory was a product of his experience as a French lawyer and magistrate and was described in his book *Penal Philosophy,* published in 1890. Reflecting the state of knowledge about the learning process in his day, Tarde viewed all social phenomena as the product of imitation. Through **imitation** or **modeling,** a person can learn new responses, such as criminal behavior, by observing others, without performing any overt act or receiving direct reinforcement or reward.[29]

imitation or **modeling** A means by which a person can learn new responses by observing others without performing any overt act or receiving direct reinforcement or reward.

The first twentieth-century criminologist to forcefully argue that criminal behavior was learned was Edwin H. Sutherland. His theory of **differential association,** developed between 1934 and 1947, was that persons who become criminal do so because of contacts with criminal patterns and isolation from noncriminal patterns. Together with its more recent modifications, his theory remains one of the most influential theories of crime causation.[30] The nine propositions of Sutherland's theory are presented in Table 3.5.

differential association Sutherland's theory that persons who become criminal do so because of contacts with criminal patterns and isolation from anticriminal patterns.

Borrowing a premise from the theory of the Chicago School, Sutherland maintained that differential associations would not produce criminality if it were not for *differential social organization*. In other words, the degree to which communities promote or inhibit criminal associations varies with the way or the degree to which they are organized (that is, the extent of *culture conflict*).

TABLE 3.5 Sutherland's Propositions of Differential Association

1. Criminal behavior is learned.
2. Criminal behavior is learned in interaction with other persons in a process of communication.
3. The principal part of the learning of criminal behavior occurs within intimate personal groups.
4. When criminal behavior is learned, the learning includes (a) techniques of committing the crime, which are sometimes very complicated, sometimes very simple; and (b) the specific direction of motives, drives, rationalizations, and attitudes.
5. The specific direction of motives and drives is learned from definitions of the legal codes as favorable and unfavorable.
6. A person becomes delinquent because of an excess of definitions favorable to violation of law over definitions unfavorable to violation of law. This is the principle of differential association.
7. Differential associations may vary in frequency, duration, priority, and intensity.
8. The process of learning criminal behavior by association with criminal and anticriminal patterns involves all of the mechanisms that are involved in any other learning.
9. While criminal behavior is an expression of general needs and values, it is not explained by those general needs and values, since noncriminal behavior is an expression of the same needs and values.

SOURCE: Edwin H. Sutherland and Donald R. Cressey, *Criminology,* 9th ed. (Philadelphia: J. B. Lippincott, 1974), pp. 75–77. Reprinted by permission.

Since its final formulation in 1947, modifications and additions have been made to Sutherland's theory as new developments in learning theory have emerged. For example, Daniel Glaser modified Sutherland's theory by introducing *role theory* and by arguing that criminal behavior could be learned by identifying with criminal roles and not just by associating with criminals.[31] Thus, a person could imitate the behavior of a drug dealer without actually having met one. Glaser obviously believed that the media had a greater influence on the learning of criminal behavior than Sutherland believed they had.

Robert L. Burgess and Ronald L. Akers, as well as C. Ray Jeffery, adapted the principles of *operant conditioning* and *behavior modification,* developed by the psychologist B. F. Skinner, and the principles of *modeling,* as developed by Albert Bandura, to the explanation of criminal behavior. Burgess, Akers, and Jeffery integrated psychological concepts with sociological ones. Although they referred to their theories by different names, we will use the more general term *learning theory.*

learning theory A theory that explains criminal behavior and its prevention with the concepts of positive reinforcement, negative reinforcement, extinction, punishment, and modeling or imitation.

Learning theory explains criminal behavior and its prevention with the concepts of *positive reinforcement, negative reinforcement, extinction, punishment,* and *modeling* or *imitation.* In this view, crime is committed because it is positively reinforced, negatively reinforced, or imitated. We described the imitation or modeling of criminal behavior in our earlier discussion of Tarde. Here we will focus on the other concepts.[32]

positive reinforcement The presentation of a stimulus that increases or maintains a response.

Positive reinforcement is the presentation of a stimulus that increases or maintains a response. The stimulus, or *reward,* can be either material, like money, or psychological, like pleasure. People steal (a response) because of the rewards—for example, the objects or money—that they receive. They use drugs (at least at first) because of the rewards, the pleasure, that the drugs give them.

negative reinforcement The removal or reduction of a stimulus whose removal or reduction increases or maintains a response.

Negative reinforcement is the removal or reduction of a stimulus whose removal or reduction increases or maintains a response. The stimulus in negative reinforcement is referred to as an *aversive stimulus.* Aversive stimuli, for most people, include pain and fear. Stealing may be negatively reinforced by removing or reducing the aversive stimuli of the fear and pain of poverty. For drug addicts, the use of addictive drugs is negatively reinforced because the drugs remove or reduce the aversive stimulus of the pain of drug withdrawal.

In short, both positive and negative reinforcement explain why a behavior, such as crime, is maintained or increases. Both types of reinforcement can simultaneously affect the same behavior. In other words, people may commit crime, in this view, both because the crime is rewarded and because it removes an aversive stimulus.

According to learning theory, criminal behavior is reduced, but not necessarily eliminated, through *extinction* or *punishment*. **Extinction** is a process in which behavior that previously was positively reinforced is no longer reinforced. In other words, the rewards have been removed. Thus, if burglars were to continually come up empty-handed in their quests—not to receive rewards for their efforts—they would no longer continue to commit burglary. **Punishment** is the presentation of an aversive stimulus to reduce a response. It is the principle method used in the United States, and in other countries, to prevent crime or, at least, reduce it. For example, one of the reasons offenders are imprisoned is to punish them for their crimes.

extinction A process in which behavior that previously was positively reinforced is no longer reinforced.

punishment The presentation of an aversive stimulus to reduce a response.

Among the policy implications of learning theory is to punish criminal behavior effectively, that is, according to learning theory principles. For a variety of reasons, punishment is not used effectively in criminal justice in the United States. For example, to employ punishment effectively, one must prevent escape. Escape is a natural reaction to the presentation of an aversive stimulus like imprisonment. In the United States, the chances of an offender's escaping punishment are great. Probation probably does not function as an aversive stimulus, and most offenders, especially first-time offenders, are not incarcerated.

To be effective, punishment must be applied consistently and immediately. As for immediacy, the process of criminal justice in the United States generally precludes punishment immediately after a criminal act is committed. The process is a slow and methodical one. Consistent application of punishment is rare because most criminal offenders are not caught.

In addition, extended periods of punishment should be avoided, or the effectiveness of the punishment will be reduced. The United States currently imprisons more of its offenders for longer periods than any other country in the world, except perhaps Russia, though in many cases inmates actually serve only a fraction of their original sentences. A related issue is that punishment is far less effective when the intensity with which the aversive stimulus is presented is increased gradually than when the stimulus is introduced at full intensity. Prolonged imprisonment is a gradual process of punishment that lacks the full intensity and immediacy of corporal punishment, for example.

In 1994, then 18-year-old American student Michael Fay pled guilty to vandalism charges in Singapore and was sentenced to 3 months in jail, a $2,200 fine, and 6 strokes of the cane. *Should the flogging of convicted offenders be allowed in the United States? Why or why not?*

To be effective, punishment must also be combined with extinction. That is, the rewards that maintain the behavior must be removed. In the United States, after imprisonment, offenders are generally returned to the environments in which their crimes originally were committed and rewarded.

Finally, for punishment to be effective, it must be combined with the positive reinforcement of alternative, prosocial behaviors.

We must emphasize that for learning theorists, positive reinforcement is a much more effective and preferred method of manipulating behavior than is punishment, because positive reinforcement does not suffer the disadvantages associated with punishment. That point is often overlooked by criminal justice decision makers. Among the disadvantages of punishment are the effort to escape punishment by means other than law-abiding behavior; the development of negative self-concepts by offenders, who come to view

FIGURE 3.2 How Caning Is Done in Singapore

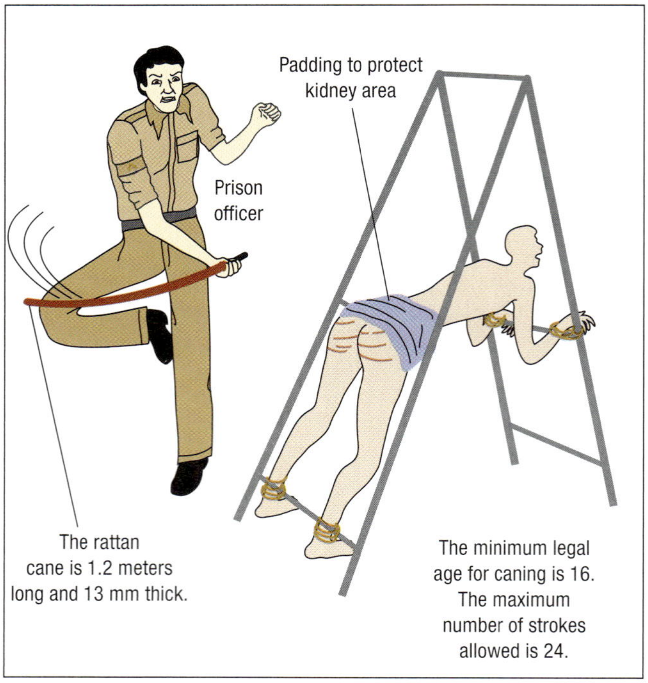

themselves (instead of their criminal behaviors) as bad, making rehabilitation difficult; and the causing of aggression.

Among the problems with a learning theory of crime causation is that it ignores the criminalization process. It fails to consider why the normal learned behaviors of some groups are criminalized while the normal learned behaviors of other groups are not. For example, why is marijuana consumption illegal, while cigarette or alcohol consumption is not? Learning theory ignores the effect that political and economic power has on the definition of criminal behavior.

Social Control Theories The key question for social control theorists is not why people commit crime and delinquency, but rather why do they not. Why do people conform? From the perspective of **social control theory,** people are expected to commit crime and delinquency unless they are prevented from doing so. They will commit crime, that is, unless they are properly socialized.

social control theory A view in which people are expected to commit crime and delinquency unless they are prevented from doing so.

Like many of the other sociological theories of crime causation, social control theories have their origins in the work of Durkheim. It was not until the 1950s, however, that social control theories began to emerge to challenge other, more dominant theories, such as strain and differential association. Among the early social control theorists were Albert J. Reiss, Jackson Toby, F. Ivan Nye, and Walter C. Reckless. Despite the important contributions of those early theorists, modern social control theory in its most detailed elaboration is attributed to the work of Travis Hirschi. Hirschi's 1969 book, *Causes of Delinquency,* has had a great influence on current criminological thinking.

As did proponents of earlier social control theories, Hirschi argued that delinquency (his was not a theory of adult criminality) should be expected if a juvenile is not properly socialized. For Hirschi, proper socialization involves the establishment of a strong moral bond between the juvenile and society. This *bond to society* consists of (1) *attachment* to others, (2) *commitment* to conventional lines of action, (3) *involvement* in conventional activities, and (4) *belief* in the moral order and law. Thus, delinquent behavior is likely to occur if there is (1) inadequate attachment, particularly to parents and school, (2) inadequate commitment, particularly to educational and occupational success, (3) inadequate involvement in such conventional activities as scouting and sports, and (4) inadequate belief, particularly in the legitimacy and morality of the law. For Hirschi, the units of social control most important in the establishment of the bond are the family, the school, and the law.

In a more recent book, Michael Gottfredson and Travis Hirschi argue that the principal cause of many deviant behaviors, including crime and delinquency, is ineffective child-rearing, which produces people with low self-control.[33] Low self-control impairs a person's ability to accurately calculate the consequences of his or her actions and is characterized by impulsivity, insensitivity, physical risk taking, shortsightedness, and lack of verbal skills. This theory posits that everyone has a predisposition toward criminality; therefore, low self-control makes it difficult to resist.

One of the appealing aspects of Hirschi's social control theory—and Gottfredson and Hirschi's theory, too—is their seemingly commonsense policy implications. To prevent delinquency, juveniles must be properly socialized;

they must develop a strong moral bond to society. As part of that strategy, children must be reared properly so that they develop a high level of self-control.

Although social control theory is currently very influential in the thinking of many criminologists, it has not escaped extensive criticism. Perhaps the major problem, at least for some criminologists, is the theory's assumption that delinquency will occur if not prevented. Some criminologists find it troublesome that the theory rejects altogether the idea of delinquent motivation. Another problem with social control theory is that it does not explain how juveniles are socialized. For example, how are attachments to others produced and changed? Finally, Hirschi's argument, as stated, does not allow for delinquency by juveniles who are properly socialized, nor does it allow for conformity by juveniles who are not properly socialized.

THINKING CRITICALLY

1. What are the five key assumptions of the positivist school of thought?
2. How much crime do you think is related to biological factors? Which factors are most important?
3. Explain psychoanalytic and humanistic psychological theory. What are some of the problems associated with those theories?
4. Which one of the sociological theories do you think explains the most crime? Defend your choice.

Critical Approaches to Explaining Crime

Critical theories are, in part, a product of a different conception of American society that began to emerge toward the end of the 1950s. Concepts like racism, sexism, capitalism, imperialism, monopoly, exploitation, and oppression were beginning to be employed with greater frequency to describe the social landscape. In the 1960s, the period of naive acceptance of the status quo and the belief in the purely benevolent actions of government ended for many social scientists, and the seeds of critical theory began to sprout.

Not surprisingly, the basic assumptions of critical theories differ both from those of classical and neoclassical theories and from those of positivist theories. First, unlike classical and neoclassical theories, which assume that human beings have free will, and positivist theories, which assume that human beings are determined, critical theories assume that human beings are both determined *and* determining. In other words, critical theories assume that human beings are the creators of the institutions and structures that ultimately dominate and constrain them. Second, in contrast to both classical and neoclassical theories and positivist theories, critical theories assume that conflict is the norm, that society is characterized primarily by conflict over moral values. Finally, unlike positivist theorists, many critical theorists assume that everything they do is value-laden by virtue of their being human; that is, they believe it is impossible to be objective or value-neutral in anything a person does.

LABELING THEORY

The focus of **labeling theory** is the **criminalization process**—the way people and actions are defined as criminal—rather than the positivist concern with the peculiarities of the criminal actor. From this perspective, the distinguishing feature of all "criminals" is that they have been the object of a *negative social reaction.* In other words, they have been designated by the state and its agents as different and "bad."

labeling theory A theory that emphasizes the criminalization process as the cause of some crime.

criminalization process The way people and actions are defined as criminal.

It is important to note that labeling theorists attempt to explain only what Edwin Lemert called *secondary deviance.*[34] For our purposes, *secondary deviance* is the commission of crime subsequent to the first criminal act and the acceptance of a criminal label. Secondary deviance begins with an initial criminal act, or what Lemert called *primary deviance.* The causes of initial criminal acts are unspecified. Nevertheless, if society reacts negatively to an initial criminal act, especially through official agents of the state, the offender is likely to be *stigmatized,* or negatively labeled. It is possible, even likely, that there will be no reaction at all to an initial criminal act or that the offender will not accept or internalize the negative label. However, if the negative label is successfully applied to the offender, the label may become a *self-fulfilling prophecy,* in which the offender's self-image is defined by the label. Secondary deviance is the prophecy fulfilled.

As is well known, once a person is labeled and stereotyped as a "criminal," he or she probably will be shunned by law-abiding society, have difficulty finding a good job, lose some civil rights (if convicted of a felony), and suffer a variety of other disabilities. The "criminal" (or "delinquent") label is conferred by all of the agencies of criminal justice—the police, the courts, and the correctional apparatus—as well as by the media, the schools, churches, and other social institutions. The irony is that in its attempt to reduce crime and delinquency, society may inadvertently be increasing it by labeling people and producing secondary deviance.

FYI: Shaming as a Crime Prevention Strategy

Current crime prevention programs based on the theoretical proposition that shame will prevent crime include programs that publicize the names and faces of people arrested for trying to buy or sell sex or require convicted DUI offenders to put bumper stickers on their cars identifying them as such. For the most part, these strategies ignore reintegration.

A policy implication of labeling theory is simply not to label or to employ *radical nonintervention.*[35] This might be accomplished through decriminalization (the elimination of many behaviors from the scope of the criminal law), diversion (removing offenders from involvement in the criminal justice process), greater due-process protections (replacing discretion with the rule of law), and deinstitutionalization (a policy of reducing jail and prison populations and construction).[36]

An alternative to the nonintervention strategy is John Braithwaite's *reintegrative shaming.*[37] In this strategy, disappointment is expressed for the offender's actions, and the offender is shamed and punished. What is more important, however, is that following the expression of disappointment and shame is a concerted effort on the part of the community to forgive the offender and reintegrate him or her back into society. Braithwaite contends that the practice of reintegrative shaming is one of the principal reasons for Japan's relatively low crime rate.

A problem with labeling theory is that it tends to overemphasize the importance of the official labeling process.[38] On one hand, the impression is given that innocent people are arbitrarily stigmatized by an oppressive society and that as a result, they begin a life of crime. That probably does not happen very much. On the other hand, the impression is given that offenders resist the criminal label and accept it only when they are no longer capable of fighting it. However, in some communities, the criminal label, or some variation of it, is actively sought. Perhaps the most telling problem with labeling theory is the question of whether stigmatizing someone as criminal or delinquent causes more crime and delinquency than it prevents. To date, the answer is unknown.

Myth	Fact
Most offenders resist being labeled criminal and accept the label only when they are no longer capable of fighting it.	In some communities the label *criminal,* or some variation of it, is actively sought.

CONFLICT THEORY

conflict theory A theory that assumes that society is based primarily on conflict between competing interest groups and that criminal law and the criminal justice system are used to control subordinate groups. Crime is caused by relative powerlessness.

Unlike classical and neoclassical and positivist theories, which assume that society is characterized primarily by consensus, **conflict theory** assumes that society is based primarily on conflict between competing interest groups—for instance, the rich against the poor, management against labor, whites against minorities, men against women, adults against children. In many cases, competing interest groups are not equal in power and resources. Consequently, one group is dominant and the other is subordinate.

For conflict theorists, conflict between competing interest groups can sometimes lead to crime. *What kinds of group conflicts are more likely to lead to crime?*

One of the earliest theorists in the United States to apply conflict theory to the study of crime was George B. Vold. For Vold and other conflict theorists, such as Austin T. Turk, many behaviors are defined as crimes because it is in the interest of dominant groups to do so.[39]

According to conflict theorists, criminal law and the criminal justice system are used by dominant groups to control subordinate ones. However, the public image is quite different. The public image of the criminal law and the criminal justice system is that they are value-neutral institutions—that is, that neither institution has a vested interest in who "wins" a dispute. The public image is that the only concern of the criminal law and the criminal justice system is resolving disputes between competing interest groups justly and—more importantly—peacefully. According to conflict theorists, this public image legitimizes the authority and practices of dominant groups and allows them to achieve their own interests at the expense of less powerful groups. In this view, crime also serves the interest of dominant groups. It deflects the attention of subordinate group members from the many problems that dominant groups create for them and turns that attention to subordinate group members who are defined as criminal.

All behavior, including criminal behavior, in this view, occurs because people act in ways consistent with their social positions. Whether white-collar crime or ordinary street crime, crime is a response to a person's social situation. The reason members of subordinate groups appear in official criminal statistics more frequently than members of dominant groups is that the dominant groups have more control over the definition of criminality. Thus they are better able to ensure that the responses of subordinate group members to their social situations will be defined and reacted to as criminal. For conflict theorists, the amount of crime in a society is a function of the extent of conflict generated by **power differentials,** or the ability of some groups to dominate other groups in that society. Crime, in short, is caused by **relative powerlessness,** the inability to dominate other groups.

power differentials The ability of some groups to dominate other groups in a society.

relative powerlessness In conflict theory, the inability to dominate other groups in society.

There are two principal policy implications of conflict theory. One is for dominant groups to give up some of their power to subordinate groups, making the weaker more powerful and reducing conflict. Increasing equality in that way might be accomplished by redistributing wealth through a more progressive tax system, for example. Another way to increase equality, at least in the political arena, would be to strictly limit or eliminate altogether the contributions of wealthy people and corporations to political candidates. The other policy implication is for dominant group members to become more effective rulers and subordinate group members better subjects. To do so, dominant group members would have to do a better job of convincing subordinate group members that the current unfair distribution of power in society is in their mutual interests.

A problem with conflict theory is that it generally fails to specify the sources of power in society. When those sources are identified, they are usually attributed to the personal characteristics of elites; that is, people with power are said to be smarter, better educated, luckier, and better able to defer gratification. Conflict theorists seem to ignore that power in society comes primarily from the ownership of private property.

Another criticism of conflict theory is that it is basically reformist in its policy implications. Conflict theorists generally assume that crime, as well as other social problems, can be corrected by existing social institutions. For example, if only the agencies of criminal justice were more effective, a conflict theorist might argue, crime would be reduced greatly. Historical evidence suggests that this assumption may not be true.

RADICAL THEORY

The social and political turmoil in the United States during the 1960s and 1970s created a renewed interest in Marxist theory. Although Karl Marx wrote very little about crime and criminal justice, **radical theories** of crime causation are generally based on Marx's ideas. Among the first criminologists in the United States to employ Marxist theory to explain crime and justice were Richard Quinney, William J. Chambliss, and Anthony M. Platt.

radical theories Theories of crime causation that are generally based on a Marxist theory of class struggle.

Radical criminologists argue that *capitalism* is an economic system that requires people to compete against each other in the individualistic pursuit of material wealth. A defining characteristic of a capitalist society is that a very small percentage of people are the big winners in the competitive struggle for material wealth. Table 3.6 shows the distribution of income (a proxy for wealth) in the United States in 2001.

FYI: Karl Marx

In an article entitled "Population, Crime and Pauperism," which appeared in the *New York Daily News* on September 16, 1859, Karl Marx observed that "there must be something rotten in the very core of a social system which increases its wealth without decreasing its misery; and increases in crimes even more than in numbers."

The winners do everything in their considerable power to keep from becoming losers, including taking advantage of other people, preying on them. Their power is considerable, by virtue of their ownership of material wealth. (The really big winners are members of the *ruling class.*) Losers—relatively speaking, members of the *working class* and the *nonworking class*—in an effort to become winners, usually do what the winners do: prey on weaker people. Radical criminologists believe that the more unevenly wealth is distributed in a society, the more likely people are to be able to find persons weaker than themselves.

It is important to understand that for radical criminologists, the destructive effects of capitalism, such as crime, are not caused by income or property inequality or by poverty. Rather, the competition among wealthy people and among poor people and between rich and poor people—the **class struggle**—and the practice of taking advantage of other people cause crime. They also cause income or property inequality, poverty, and many of the other problems that are characteristic of a capitalist society. Crime in capitalist societies is a rational response to the circumstances in which people find themselves in the

class struggle For radical criminologists, the competition among wealthy people and among poor people and between rich people and poor people, which causes crime.

TABLE 3.6 Distribution of 2001 Income in the United States Received by Each Fifth of Families (Households)

Families (Households) by Fifths	Percentage of Total Income	Average Household Income[a]
Poorest fifth	3.5%	$10,136
Second fifth	8.7%	$25,468
Third fifth	14.6%	$42,269
Fourth fifth	23.0%	$66,839
Richest fifth[b]	50.2%	$145,970

a. Average income of all families (households) in 2001 = $58,208.

b. The table fails to accurately convey the inequitable distribution of income/wealth in the highest category. In 2001, there were 490 billionaires in the United States (compared to 267 billionaires in 1999 and 71 billionaires in 1991). The richest individual (not household) in 2001 was William Henry Gates, III (Microsoft), whose net worth was conservatively estimated to be $59 billion ($85 billion in 1998). The second and third richest individuals were Warren Edward Buffett (Berkshire Hathaway), worth about $32 billion, and Paul Gardner Allen (Microsoft), worth approximately $30 billion.

Source: Carmen DeNaras-Walt and Robert W. Cleveland, U.S. Census Bureau, Current Population Reports. P60-218, *Money Income in the United States: 2001* (Washington, DC: GPO, 2002), pp. 19–20, Tables A-2 and A-3.

Forbes.com

www.forbes.com/people/2001/06/21/billionairesindex.html

competitive class struggle to acquire material wealth. "Senseless" violent crime, which is most often committed by poor people against each other, is frequently a product of the demoralizing and brutalizing conditions under which many people are forced to live.

Radical criminologists argue that noncapitalist societies should have different types of crime and much lower rates of crime, as traditionally defined, "because the less intense class struggle should reduce the forces leading to and the functions of crime."[40]

Radical criminologists define crime as a violation of politically defined human rights, such as the right to shelter. *Do you think that Americans should have a right to shelter? Why or why not?*

Radical criminologists also define crime as a violation of human rights. As Tony Platt explains:

> A radical perspective defines crime as a violation of politically defined human rights: the truly egalitarian rights to decent food and shelter, to human dignity and self-determination, rather than the so-called right to compete for an unequal share of wealth and power.[41]

A radical definition of crime includes "imperialism, racism, capitalism, sexism and other systems of exploitation which contribute to human misery and deprive people of their human potentiality."[42] Although many behaviors currently proscribed by criminal law would be included in this radical definition, other behaviors now considered crimes would be excluded, such as prostitution, gambling, and drug use, and some behaviors not now considered crimes would be added, such as racism, sexism, and imperialism.

Consequently, the policy implications of radical theory include demonstrating that the current legal definition of crime supports the ruling class in a capitalist system and redefining crime as the violation of human rights. For nearly all radical criminologists—anarchists are exceptions—the solution to the crime problem is a benevolent socialist society governed by democratically elected representatives of the population. Arguably the biggest difference between the envisioned socialist society and the current capitalist society in the United States is that governments in the socialist society would regulate the economy to promote public welfare. Governments in capitalist America regulate the economy to promote the accumulation of material wealth by individuals. Radical criminologists stress that the difference is primarily a matter of priorities. Some accumulation of private material wealth would probably exist in the socialist society, and even capitalist America provides for the public welfare through such socialistic programs as Social Security, Medicare, and Medicaid. Another important difference between the two societies is that in the socialist society, human diversity in all areas of life would be not only tolerated but also appreciated by government agents (and, one would hope, by the rest of society). In the socialist society, the criminal law would be based on a slightly modified version of the positive sanction of the classical school: that every member of society has a right to do anything that is not prohibited by law without fearing anything but natural consequences. Acts prohibited by law would be those that violate basic human rights or the public welfare, interpreted as liberally as possible. The recognition of "hate crimes" by federal legislation in the United States is an example of an attempt to protect human diversity.

Radical criminologists maintain that creating such a socialist society would first require the development of political awareness among all people disadvantaged by the capitalist system. Such people must be made aware that they are in a class struggle. Once enough people are aware, according to radical criminologists, then only through *praxis* (human action based on theoretical understanding) will the new socialist society be achieved.

One objection to radical theory is that the radical definition of crime as the violation of human rights is itself too broad and vague. Although radical criminologists concede that it may be difficult to determine what a human right is, they generally assume that most people know when a human right has been violated.

Other criticisms of radical theory are that its adherents are pursuing a political agenda and thus are not objective in their work; that its causal model is wrong, that is, that social arrangements do not cause people to commit crime, as radical theorists argue, but rather that crime is committed by people who are born evil and remain evil; that it has not been tested satisfactorily; that it cannot be tested satisfactorily; and that it is utopian in its policy implications.

FYI Utopians

Early socialists criticized the rise of industry as the cause of great hardship among working people. During the early 1800s, socialists, who were sometimes called *utopians*, tried to foster communities with ideal social and economic conditions. Their name came from Sir Thomas More's *Utopia*, published in England in 1516. More's book describes an ideal society, with justice and equality for all citizens.

OTHER CRITICAL THEORIES

The law-and-order climate of the 1980s and 1990s was not a period in which critical theories of crime causation received much attention from government bureaucrats and criminal justice practitioners. Nevertheless, critical scholars continued to produce and to refine critical analyses of government efforts to understand and to address the crime problem. In this subsection we will briefly describe some of the new directions taken by critical theorists. These descriptions will show the diversity of current critical thought.

British or Left Realism The focus of many critical criminologists has been on crimes committed by the powerful. While pursuing that area of study, however, they have tended either to ignore or to romanticize working-class crime and criminals. By the mid-1980s, a group of social scientists in Great Britain had begun to criticize that tendency and to argue that critical criminologists needed to redirect their attention to the fear and the very real victimization experienced by working-class people.[43] These **left realists** correctly observed that crimes against the working class were being perpetrated not only by the powerful but also by members of their own class. They admonished their critical colleagues to take crime seriously, especially "street crime" and domestic violence.

left realists A group of social scientists who argue that critical criminologists need to redirect their attention to the fear and the very real victimization experienced by working-class people.

Recently, one of the leading exponents of left realism, Jock Young, has identified relative deprivation as a potent, though not exclusive cause of crime.[44] **Relative deprivation** refers to inequalities (in resources, opportunities, material goods, etc.) that are defined by a person as unfair or unjust. Left realists have argued that police power must be employed to protect people living in working-class communities. Certain versions of community policing are examples of such policy.

relative deprivation refers to inequalities (in resources, opportunities, material goods, etc.) that are defined by a person as unfair or unjust.

Left realism has been criticized for holding a contradictory position regarding the police (and other agencies of criminal justice).[45] On one hand, left realists want to give the police more power to combat crime, especially crime committed against the working class. On the other hand, they want to reduce the power of the police to intervene in people's lives and want to make the police more accountable for their actions. Another criticism of left realism is that its emphasis on the reform of criminal justice practice, rather than on radical change, makes it little different in that regard from conflict theory, classical and neoclassical theories, and many positivist theories.[46]

Peacemaking Criminology This perspective rejects the idea that predatory criminal violence can be reduced by repressive state violence. In this view, "wars" on crime only make matters worse. Consisting of a mixture of anarchism, humanism, socialism, and Native American and Eastern philosophies, **peacemaking criminology** suggests that the solutions to all social problems, including crime, are the transformation of human beings, mutual dependence, reduction of class structures, the creation of communities of caring people, and universal social justice. For peacemaking criminologists, crime is suffering, and, therefore, to reduce crime, suffering must be reduced.[47] Policy emphasis is placed on the transformation of human beings through an inner rebirth or spiritual rejuvenation (inner peace) that enables individuals to experience empathy with those less fortunate and a desire to respond to the needs of other people.

peacemaking criminology An approach that suggests that the solutions to all social problems, including crime, are the transformation of human beings, mutual dependence, reduction of class structures, the creation of communities of caring people, and universal social justice.

Peacemaking criminology has been criticized for its extreme idealism and its emphasis on the transformation of individuals as a way of transforming society rather than on the transformation of society as a way of transforming individuals.

Feminist Theory Although feminism is not new, the application of feminist theory to the study of crime is.[48] Recognizing that the study of crime has

Peacemaking criminologists advocate restorative justice, compassion, and community action. *Should these principles replace the punitive justice that currently guides criminal justice in the United States? Why or why not?*

feminist theory A perspective on criminality that focuses on women's experiences and seeks to abolish men's control over women's labor and sexuality.

patriarchy Men's control over women's labor and sexuality.

always been male-centered, feminist criminologists seek a feminine perspective. Specifically, the focus of **feminist theory** is on women's experiences and ways of knowing because, in the past, men's experiences have been taken as the norm and generalized to the population. As a result, women and girls have been omitted almost entirely from theories of crime and delinquency.

Three areas of crime and justice have commanded most of the attention of feminist theorists: (1) the victimization of women, (2) gender differences in crime, and (3) *gendered justice,* that is, differing treatment of female and male offenders and victims by the agencies and agents of criminal justice. Regarding gender differences in crime, two questions seem to dominate: (1) Do explanations of male criminality apply to women? (2) Why are women less likely than men to engage in crime?

Not all feminists share the same perspective on the issues noted. At least four different types of feminist thought have been identified: liberal, radical, Marxist, and socialist. (Conspicuously omitted from this typology are women of color, whose gender and race place them in a uniquely disadvantaged position.) Radical, Marxist, and socialist feminist thought share, to varying degrees, a belief that the problems of women, including female victimization, lie in the institution of **patriarchy,** men's control over women's labor and sexuality. The principal goal of most feminist theory is to abolish patriarchal relationships.

Liberal feminists are the exception. They do not generally view discrimination against women as the product of patriarchy. For them, the solution to women's subordinate position in society is the removal of obstacles to their full participation in social life. Liberal feminists seek equal opportunity, equal rights, and freedom of choice. As for crime, liberal feminists point to gender socialization (that is, the creation of masculine and feminine identities) as the primary culprit.

One of the principal criticisms of feminist criminology is the focus on gender as a central organizing theme. Such a focus fails to appreciate differences among women—for example, differences between the experiences of black women and white women.[49] Another problem similar to the one associated with left realism is many feminists' contradictory position regarding the police (and the criminal justice system in general). On one hand, several feminists call for greater use of the police to better protect women from abuse; on the other hand, some feminists concede that giving more power to the police, under present circumstances, will only lead to further discrimination and harassment of minority males and females.[50] A similar contradictory position is held by many feminists toward using the law to improve gender relations. The law, after all, is almost entirely the product of white males.

Postmodernism **Postmodernism** originated in the late 1960s as a rejection of the "modern" or Enlightenment belief in scientific rationality as the route to knowledge and progress. Among the goals of this area of critical thought are to understand the creation of knowledge, and how knowledge and language create hierarchy and domination. Postmodernist ideas began to be introduced in law and criminology during the late 1980s.[51] As applied to the area of crime and criminal justice, the major foci have been critical analyses of the privileged position of "the Law" and the construction of crime theories.

With regard to "the Law," postmodernist criminologists reject the idea "that there is only one true interpretation of a law or for that matter the U.S. Constitution."[52] They argue, instead, that there is a plurality of interpretations that are dependent, in part, on the particular social context in which they arise. As in other critical criminologies, the law, from a postmodernist view, always has a human author and a political agenda.[53] As for crime theories, postmodernist criminologists typically abandon the usual notion of causation. From the postmodernist perspective:

> Crime is seen to be the culmination of certain processes that allow persons to believe that they are somehow not connected to other humans and society. These processes place others into categories or stereotypes and make them different or alien, denying them their humanity. These processes result in the denial of responsibility for other people and to other people.[54]

Postmodernist criminologists would, among other things, replace the prevailing description of the world with new conceptions, words, and phrases that convey alternative meanings, as Sutherland did when he introduced the concept of "white-collar crime." These new descriptions would tell different stories about the world as experienced by historically subjugated people.[55] Postmodernist criminologists would also replace the formal criminal justice apparatus with informal social controls so that the current functions of criminal justice are handled by local groups and local communities.[56] This strategy is consistent with the one advocated by peacemaking criminologists. Postmodernist criminology has been criticized for its relativism and subjectivism or for being an "anarchy of knowledge": "If truth is not possible, how can we decide anything?"[57]

FYI: NVAW Rape Survey

In a victimization survey informed by feminist ideas—The National Violence Against Women survey (NVAW)—researchers found, among other things, that in 1995 and 1996, there were more rapes committed in the United States than were reported by the Bureau of Justice Statistics in the National Crime Victimization Survey (NCVS). Among the findings of the NVAW was that 1 of every 6 U.S. women and 1 of every 33 U.S. men has experienced an attempted or completed rape as a child and/or an adult. Put differently, 18 percent of surveyed women and 3 percent of surveyed men said they experienced a completed or attempted rape at some time in their life. Rape was defined as forced vaginal, oral, and anal sex.

Source: Patricia Tjaden and Nancy Thoennes, "Prevalence, Incidence, and Consequences of Violence Against Women: Findings from the National Violence Against Women Survey," *National Institute of Justice, Centers for Disease Control and Prevention, Research in Brief* (Washington, DC: GPO, November 1998).

postmodernism An area of critical thought that, among other things, attempts to understand the creation of knowledge, and how knowledge and language create hierarchy and domination.

THINKING CRITICALLY

1. How would you explain labeling theory?
2. What is peacemaking criminology? Is this theory realistic?
3. Explain feminist theory and its key criticisms.
4. How might postmodernists explain acts of domestic terrorism?

SUMMARY

1. Define criminological theory

Criminological theory is the explanation of the behavior of criminal offenders, as well as the behavior of police, attorneys, prosecutors, judges, correctional personnel, victims, and other actors in the criminal justice process. It helps us understand criminal behavior and the basis of policies proposed and implemented to prevent and control crime.

2. State the causes of crime according to classical and neoclassical criminologists and their policy implications

Classical and neoclassical criminologists theorize that human beings are free-willed individuals who commit crime when they rationally calculate that the crime will give them more pleasure than pain. In an effort to deter crime, classical criminologists advocate the following policies: (1) establish a social contract, (2) enact laws that are clear, simple, unbiased, and reflect the consensus of the population, (3) impose punishments that are proportionate to the crime, prompt, certain, public, necessary, the least possible in the given circumstances, and dictated by law rather than by judges' discretion, (4) educate the public, (5) eliminate corruption from the administration of justice, and (6) reward virtue. Neoclassical criminologists introduced the concepts that mitigating circumstances might inhibit the exercises of free will and that punishment should be rehabilitative.

3. Describe the biological theories of crime causation and their policy implications

The basic cause of crime for biological positivists has been biological inferiority, which is indicated by physical or genetic characteristics that distinguish criminals from noncriminals. The policy implications of biological theories of crime causation include a choice of isolation, sterilization, or execution. Biological theorists also advocate brain surgery, chemical treatment, improved diets, and better mother and child care.

4. Describe the different psychological theories of crime causation and their policy implications

According to psychological theories, crime results from individuals' mental or emotional disturbances, inability to empathize with others, inability to legally satisfy their basic needs, or oppressive circumstances of life. To combat crime, psychological positivists would isolate, sterilize, or execute offenders not amenable to treatment. For treatable offenders, psychotherapy or psychoanalysis may prove effective. Other policy implications are to help people satisfy their basic needs legally, to eliminate sources of oppression, and to provide legal ways of coping with oppression.

5. Explain sociological theories of crime causation and their policy implications

Sociological theories propose that crime is caused by anomie, *or the dissociation of the individual from the* collective conscience; *by* social disorganization; *by* anomie *resulting from a lack of opportunity to achieve aspirations; by the learning of criminal values and behaviors; and by the failure to properly socialize individuals. Among the policy implications of sociological theories of crime causation are containing crime within reasonable boundaries; organizing and empowering neighborhood residents; reducing aspirations, increasing legitimate opportunities; providing law-abiding models, regulating associations, eliminating crime's rewards, rewarding law-abiding behavior, punishing criminal behavior effectively; and properly socializing children so that they develop self-control and a strong moral bond to society.*

6. Distinguish major differences among classical, positivist, and critical theories of crime causation

Unlike classical theories, which assume that human beings have free will, and positivist theories, which assume that human beings are determined, critical theories assume that human beings are both determined and determining. In contrast to both classical and positivist theories, which assume that society is characterized primarily by consensus over moral values, critical theories assume that society is characterized primarily by conflict over moral values. Finally, unlike positivist theorists, who assume that social scientists can be objective or value-neutral in their work, many critical theorists assume that everything they do is value-laden by virtue of their being human, that it is impossible to be objective.

7. Describe how critical theorists would explain the causes of crime and their policy implications

Depending on their perspective, critical theorists explain crime as the result of labeling and stigmatization; of relative powerlessness, the class struggle, and the practice of taking advantage of other people; or of patriarchy. Those who support labeling theory would address crime by avoiding labeling people as criminals or by employing radical nonintervention or reintegrative shaming. Conflict theorists would address crime by having dominant groups give up some of their power to subordinate groups or having dominant group members become more effective rulers and subordinate group members better subjects. Radical theorists would define crime as a violation of basic human rights, replace the criminal justice system with popular or socialist justice, and (except for anarchists) would create a socialist society appreciative of human diversity. Left realists would use police power to protect people living in working-class communities. Peacemaking criminologists would transform human beings so that they were able to empathize with those less fortunate and respond to other people's needs, would reduce hierarchical structures, would create communities of caring people, and would champion universal social justice. Feminist theorists would address crime by eliminating patriarchal structures and relationships and promoting greater equality for women. Postmodernist criminologists would replace the prevailing description of the world with new conceptions, words, and phrases, that convey alternative meanings, as experienced by historically subjugated people. They would also replace the formal criminal justice system with informal social controls handled by local groups and local communities.

KEY TERMS

theory, p. 65
criminological theory, p. 65
classical theory, p. 65
utility, p. 68
social contract, p. 68
special or specific deterrence, p. 68
general deterrence, p. 68
neoclassical theory, p. 69
biological inferiority, p. 72
criminal anthropology, p. 72
atavist, p. 72
limbic system, p. 75
psychopaths, p. 78
sociopaths, p. 78
antisocial personalities, p. 78
anomie (Durkheim), p. 81
collective conscience, p. 81
Chicago School, p. 82
social disorganization, p. 82
anomie (Merton and Cohen), p. 83
imitation or modeling, p. 85
differential association, p. 85
learning theory, p. 86
positive reinforcement, p. 86
negative reinforcement, p. 86
extinction, p. 87
punishment, p. 87
social control theory, p. 88
labeling theory, p. 89
criminalization process, p. 89
conflict theory, p. 90
power differentials, p. 91
relative powerlessness, p. 91
radical theories, p. 92
class struggle, p. 92
left realists, p. 95
relative deprivation, p. 95
peacemaking criminology, p. 95
feminist theory, p. 96
patriarchy, p. 96
postmodernism, p. 97

REVIEW QUESTIONS

1. What are two undesirable consequences of the failure to understand the theoretical basis of criminal justice policies?
2. Before the Enlightenment and classical theory, what was generally believed to be the cause of crime?
3. Who was arguably the best known and most influential of the classical criminologists, and how did his ideas become known?
4. What is the difference between *special* or *specific deterrence* and *general deterrence?*
5. What are five problems with positivist theories?
6. What is the position held by most criminologists today regarding the relationship between biology and crime?
7. What does research indicate about the relationship between intelligence and both juvenile delinquency and adult criminality?
8. What are problems with psychological or psychoanalytic theories of crime and their policy implications?
9. In what ways did Durkheim believe that crime was functional for society?
10. What is a potential problem with the theory of the Chicago School?
11. What is a criticism of most anomie theories?
12. Who was the first twentieth-century criminologist to argue forcefully that crime was learned, and what is his theory called?
13. What is arguably the major problem with social control theory?
14. What is *secondary deviance,* and how does it occur, according to labeling theorists?
15. What are major criticisms of conflict theory? Radical theory?
16. What contributions to criminological theory have been made by British or left realism, peacemaking criminology, feminist theory, and postmodernism?

IN THE FIELD

1. **Professional Perspectives on Crime** Interview representatives of the criminal justice process—a police officer, a prosecutor, a defense attorney, a judge, a correctional officer, and a probation or parole officer. Ask each to explain why crimes are committed. Ask them how they would prevent or reduce crime. After completing the interviews, identify the theories and policy implications described in the textbook that best correspond to their responses. Explain any differences in responses that emerged. Present your findings in a brief written report.

2. **Literary Perspectives on Crime** Read a nonfiction book about crime. Explain the criminal behavior, orally or in writing, using the theories in this chapter. Some good books are Truman Capote's *In Cold Blood,* Vincent Bugliosi's *Helter Skelter,* and Norman Mailer's *The Executioner's Song.*

3. **Explaining Crimes** Select several crimes from Table 2.1 and explain them by using the theories in Chapter 3.

ON THE NET

4. **Comparing Crime Rates** Use the Internet to research crime rates of several capitalist and noncapitalist countries. (Remember that crime rates, as discussed in Chapter 2, are not accurate measures of the true amount of crime.) Then write a paragraph in which you support or oppose the proposition that capitalist countries have higher crime rates than noncapitalist countries.

5. **Criminologists** Go to www.asc4l.com to learn more about professional, mostly academic criminologists. Read about the history of the American Society of Criminology. Examine the annual meeting information to see the topics on which criminologists are currently working. Explore specialty areas in criminology. Scan employment information to discover the types of jobs available.

CRITICAL THINKING EXERCISES

1. **The Dahmer Case** Jeffrey Dahmer, a white male, was sentenced to 957 years in prison (Wisconsin had no death penalty) for the murder and dismemberment of 15 young males—mostly black and homosexual—in Milwaukee, Wisconsin.

   Dahmer was arrested without a struggle at his apartment on Milwaukee's crime-infested west side in August 1991, after one of his victims had escaped and notified the police. Dahmer was 31 years old and had recently been fired from his job at a chocolate factory. He immediately confessed to 11 murders. He told the police that he lured men from bars and shopping malls by promising them money to pose for pictures. He would then take them to his apartment, drug them, strangle them, and dismember their bodies. He boiled the heads of some of his victims to remove the flesh and had sex with the cadaver of at least one of them. Police found rotting body parts lying around his apartment, along with bottles of acid and chemical preservatives. Photographs of mutilated men were on a freezer that contained two severed heads. Another severed head was in the refrigerator. Dahmer told the police that he had saved a heart to eat later.

   Dahmer's stepmother told the press that as a child, he liked to use acid to scrape the meat off dead animals. When he was 18, his parents divorced. He lived with his mother until, one day, she took his little brother and disappeared, leaving him alone. He went to live with his grandmother, where he started to abuse alcohol. During the 6 years he lived with his grandmother, mysterious things were occurring in the basement and garage. Dahmer's father, a chemist, discovered bones and other body parts in containers. Dahmer told his father that he had been stripping the flesh from animals he found.

In 1988, Dahmer spent 10 months in prison for fondling a 13-year-old Laotian boy. On his release from prison, he was placed on probation, but his probation officer never visited him.

Dahmer's defense attorney claimed that his client was insane at the time of the murders. The jury rejected the insanity defense.

a. Which theory or theories of crime causation described in this chapter best explains Jeffrey Dahmer's criminal behavior?
b. What crime prevention and correctional policies described in this chapter should be employed with criminal offenders like Jeffrey Dahmer?

2. **Breaking the Law** Stacey Raines drives from Indianapolis to Fort Wayne, Indiana, twice a month as part of her job as a sales representative for a pharmaceutical company. Although the posted speed limit is 65 miles per hour, Stacey generally cruises at 80 to 85 intentionally exceeding the speed limit.
    a. Which theory or theories of crime causation described in this chapter best explains the behavior of intentional speeders?
    b. What crime prevention and correctional policies described in this chapter should be used with intentional speeders?

CONTRACTS
Third Edition

THE RULE OF LAW

CHAPTER FOUR

Chapter Outline

Two Types of Law: Criminal Law and Civil Law

- Substantive versus Procedural Law
- Ideal Characteristics of the Criminal Law
- Criminal Law as a Political Phenomenon
- Creating Criminal Laws in the United States

Procedural Law: Rights of the Accused

- The Bill of Rights
- The Fourteenth Amendment and the Selective Incorporation of the Bill of Rights
- The Fourth Amendment
- The Fifth Amendment
- The Sixth Amendment
- The Eighth Amendment

Protecting the Accused from Miscarriages of Justice

Chapter Objectives

After completing this chapter, you should be able to:

1. Distinguish between criminal law and civil law.
2. Distinguish between substantive law and procedural law.
3. List five features of "good" criminal laws.
4. Explain why criminal law is a political phenomenon.
5. Summarize the origins of American criminal law.
6. Describe the procedural rights in the Fourth Amendment.
7. Describe the procedural rights in the Fifth Amendment.
8. Describe the procedural rights in the Sixth Amendment.
9. Describe the procedural rights in the Eighth Amendment.
10. Explain why procedural rights are important to those accused of crimes.

Crime Story

On August 27, 2003, four Alabama state workers moved a Ten Commandments monument the size of a washing machine out of public view from the rotunda of the Alabama State Judicial Building after a U.S. District Court ruled the monument violated the U.S. Constitution. The monument was originally installed at night and after business hours in the state building on July 31, 2001, by Alabama's Chief Supreme Court Justice Roy Moore, who contends that the monument represents the moral foundation of law.

Justice Moore appealed the initial decision of the U.S. District Court to a federal appeals court in an attempt to prevent the removal of the religious monument. However, on July 1, 2003, the Eleventh U.S. Circuit Court of Appeals affirmed the previous decision of the U.S. District Court that the monument must be moved from public view. Both court decisions cited precedents that the religious monument violated the U.S. Constitution, which prohibits government promotion of religion. The U.S. District Court decision allowed Justice Moore to have the religious monument placed in his office, but he refused the offer.

Ultimately, Roy Moore was suspended by the Alabama Judicial Inquiry Commission on August 22, 2003, for his failure to obey the law and was charged with six ethics violations relating to the religious monument ordeal. His case was transferred to the state court of the judiciary, which could punish Moore and remove him from the bench. Reverend Barry Lynn, executive director of Americans United for Separation of Church and State, called the state's action a "victory" for the rule of law. The U.S. District Court had threatened to fine the state $5,000 a day for Moore's defiance of the removal order. Both the attorney general and governor of Alabama refused to support Moore in his defiance of the U.S. District Court's mandate.

Justice Moore has a long history of challenging the rigor of constitutional law and its impact on his moral beliefs. While serving as a circuit judge in Etowah County, Alabama, Moore fought a lawsuit seeking to remove a wooden plaque depicting the commandments from his courtroom. Supporters of Moore suggested his continual challenge of church and state issues has resulted in creating awareness of the unfair and unjust nature of courts that have misinterpreted the U.S. Constitution and the rule of law.

Chapter 4 discusses the nature and purpose of law in the United States. You are about to learn that law is often influenced by political jurisdiction and divinely inspired. Yet, the U.S. Constitution is the highest legal authority in the United States. It is the function and purpose of courts to interpret law. Most legal scholars agree that our founding fathers were remarkable in their ability to forge a document that has stood the test of legal challenges for more than 200 years. Is Justice Roy Moore a legal scholar who has discovered a flaw in our legal authority, or would he be better served to exchange his judicial bench for a church pulpit? Our legal system seeks to protect the accused from miscarriages of justice. That same legal system will ultimately have to decide whether the U.S. Constitution or Justice Moore has been willfully disrespected.

Two Types of Law: Criminal Law and Civil Law

As discussed in Chapter 2, the conventional, though not necessarily the best, definition of *crime* is "a violation of the criminal law." **Criminal law** is one of two general types of law practiced in the United States; the other is civil law. Criminal law is:

> a formal means of social control [that] involves the use of rules that are interpreted, and are enforceable, by the courts of a political community. . . . The function of the rules is to set limits to the conduct of the citizens, to guide the officials (police and other administrators), and to define conditions of deviance or unacceptable behavior.[1]

criminal law One of two general types of law practiced in the United States (the other is civil law); "a formal means of social control [that uses] rules . . . interpreted [and enforced] by the courts . . . to set limits to the conduct of the citizens, to guide the officials, and to define . . . unacceptable behavior."

The purpose of criminal justice is to enforce the criminal law.

A crime, as noted, is a violation of the criminal law, or of the **penal code** of a political jurisdiction. Although crime is committed against individuals, it is considered an offense against the state, that is, the political jurisdiction that enacted the law.[2] A **tort,** on the other hand, is a violation of the **civil law** and is considered a private matter. Civil law includes the law of contracts and property as well as subjects such as administrative law (which deals with the rules and regulations created by government agencies) and the regulation of public utilities.

penal code The criminal law of a political jurisdiction.

tort A violation of the civil law.

civil law One of two general types of law practiced in the United States (the other is criminal law); a means of resolving conflicts between individuals. It includes personal injury claims (torts), the law of contracts and property, and subjects such as administrative law and the regulation of public utilities.

For legal purposes, a particular act may be considered an offense against an individual or the state or both. It is either a tort or a crime or both, depending on how it is handled. For example, a person who has committed an act of assault may be charged with a crime. If that person is convicted of the crime, the criminal court may order the offender to be imprisoned in the county jail for 6 months and to pay a fine of $2,000. Both the jail sentence and the fine are punishments, with the fine going to the state or local treasury (in federal court to the national treasury). The criminal court could also order the offender to pay restitution to the victim. In that case, the offender would pay the victim a sum of money either directly or indirectly, through an intermediary. In addition, the victim may sue the offender in civil court for damages, such as medical expenses or wages lost because of injury. If the offender is found liable (responsible) for the damages because he or she has committed a tort (civil courts do not "convict"), the civil court may also order the offender to compensate the victim in the amount of $2,000 for damage to the victim's interests. The payment of compensation in the civil case is not punishment; it is for the purpose of "making the victim whole again."

SUBSTANTIVE VERSUS PROCEDURAL LAW

There are two types of criminal law: substantive and procedural. **Substantive law** is the body of law that defines criminal offenses and their penalties. Substantive laws, which are found in the various penal codes, govern what people legally may and may not do. Examples of substantive laws are those that prohibit and penalize murder, rape, robbery, and other crimes. **Procedural law,** sometimes called *adjective* or *remedial* law, governs the ways in which the substantive laws are to be administered. It covers such subjects as the way suspects can legally be arrested, searched, interrogated, tried, and punished. In other words, procedural law is concerned with **due process of law,** or the rights of people suspected of or charged with crimes. The last part of this chapter is devoted to a detailed description of procedural law.

substantive law The body of law that defines criminal offenses and their penalties.

procedural law The body of law that governs the ways substantive laws are administered; sometimes called *adjective* or *remedial* law.

due process of law The rights of people suspected of or charged with crimes.

IDEAL CHARACTERISTICS OF THE CRIMINAL LAW

Legal scholars identify five features that all "good" criminal laws ideally ought to possess. To the extent that those features are absent in criminal laws, the laws can be considered "bad" laws, and bad laws do exist. The five ideal

FIGURE 4.1 Ideal Characteristics of Criminal Law

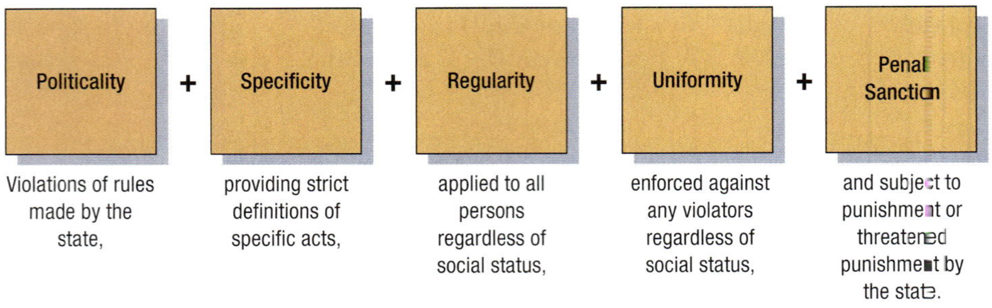

features of good criminal laws are (1) politicality, (2) specificity, (3) regularity, (4) uniformity, and (5) penal sanction (see Figure 4.1).

politicality An ideal characteristic of criminal law, referring to its legitimate source. Only violations of rules made by the state, the political jurisdiction that enacted the laws, are crimes.

POLITICALITY **Politicality** refers to the legitimate source of criminal law. Only violations of rules made by the state (that is, the political jurisdiction that enacted the laws) are crimes. Violations of rules made by other institutions, such as families, churches, schools, and employers, may be "bad," "sinful," or "socially unacceptable," but they are not crimes because they are not prohibited by the state.

specificity An ideal characteristic of criminal law, referring to its scope. Although civil law may be general in scope, criminal law should provide strict definitions of specific acts.

SPECIFICITY **Specificity** refers to the scope of criminal law. Although civil law may be general in scope, criminal law should provide strict definitions of specific acts. The point is illustrated by an old case in which a person stole an airplane but was found not guilty of violating a criminal law that prohibited the taking of "self-propelled vehicles." The judge ruled that at the time the law was enacted, *vehicles* did not include airplanes. Ideally, as the Supreme Court ruled in *Papachristou* v. *City of Jacksonville* (1972), a statute or ordinance "is void for vagueness . . . [if] it fails to give a person of ordinary intelligence fair notice that his contemplated conduct is forbidden."

regularity An ideal characteristic of criminal law: the applicability of the law to all persons, regardless of social status.

REGULARITY **Regularity** is the applicability of the criminal law to all persons. Ideally, anyone who commits a crime is answerable for it, regardless of the person's social status. Thus, ideally, when criminal laws are created, they should apply not only to the women who violate them, but also to the men; not only to the poor, but also to the rich. In practice, however, this ideal feature of law has been violated. Georgia's pre–Civil War criminal laws, for example, provided for a dual system of crime and punishment, with one set of laws for "slaves and free persons of color" and another for all other persons. Another example of the violation of this principle is illustrated by the case of *Michael M.* v. *Superior Court of Sonoma County* (1981). In this case, the U.S. Supreme Court upheld California's statutory rape law that made men alone criminally responsible for the act of illicit sexual intercourse with a minor female.

uniformity An ideal characteristic of criminal law: the enforcement of the laws against anyone who violates them, regardless of social status.

UNIFORMITY **Uniformity** refers to the way in which the criminal law should be enforced. Ideally, the law should be administered without regard for the social status of the persons who have committed crimes or are accused of committing crimes. Thus, when violated, criminal laws should be enforced against both young and old, both rich and poor, and so on. However, as is the case with regularity, the principle of uniformity is often violated because some people consider the strict enforcement of the law unjust in some cases. For

TABLE 4.1 Five General Types of Penal Sanctions

Type	Purpose	Focus
Punishment	Prevent undesired conduct. Provide retribution ("an eye for an eye").	Offending conduct
Restitution	Make the victim "whole again" by having the offender directly or indirectly pay the victim.	Crime victim
Compensation	Make the victim "whole again" by having the state pay for damages to the victim.	Crime victim
Regulation	Control future conduct toward the best interests of the community (e.g., making it a crime or traffic violation to operate a motor vehicle with a blood alcohol content higher than a specified level).	The entire community
Treatment or rehabilitation	Change the offender's behavior and, perhaps, personality.	Criminal offender

example, juveniles who are caught misbehaving in violation of the criminal law are sometimes ignored or treated leniently through the exercise of police or judicial discretion.

Penal Sanction The last ideal feature of criminal law is **penal sanction,** the principle that violators will be punished, or at least threatened with punishment, by the state. Conventional wisdom suggests that there would be no point in enacting criminal laws if their violation were not responded to with punishment or threat of punishment. Most people assume that sanctionless criminal laws would be ignored. Because all criminal laws carry sanctions, the power of sanctionless laws can be left to philosophers to debate. Table 4.1 shows the five general types of penal sanctions currently used in the United States, as well as the purpose and focus of each sanction. Combining different penal sanctions in the administration of justice is not uncommon.

penal sanction An ideal characteristic of criminal law: the principle that violators will be punished or at least threatened with punishment by the state.

CRIMINAL LAW AS A POLITICAL PHENOMENON

People sometimes forget that criminal law is a political phenomenon, that it is created by human beings to regulate the behavior of other human beings. Some people, for example, view the criminal law as divinely inspired, something that should not be questioned or challenged. That viewpoint probably comes from a belief in the biblical story of Moses receiving the Ten Commandments from God on Mount Sinai. However, as critical theorists are quick to point out, criminal law frequently promotes the interests of some groups over the interests of other groups. Thus, regardless of the law's source of inspiration, it is important to understand that what gets defined as criminal or delinquent behavior is the result of a political process in which rules are created to prohibit or to require certain behaviors. Nothing is criminal or delinquent in and of itself; only the response of the state makes it so.

Myth	Fact
Law makes people behave.	The existence of a law prohibiting a particular behavior does not necessarily prevent an individual from engaging in that behavior. Common sense suggests the implausibility of the notion. Ask yourself, if it were not for laws prohibiting murder, prostitution, or heroin use, for example, would you murder, engage in prostitution, or use heroin? How effective are speed limits in preventing you from exceeding them?

Origins of Laws Formal, written laws are a relatively recent phenomenon in human existence. The first were

Bas relief depicting King Hammurabi with his code of laws. *Why do people believe that criminal laws come from God?*

created about 5,000 years ago. They emerged with the institutions of property, marriage, and government. "Stateless" societies apparently managed without them for two primary reasons.[3] First, most stateless societies were governed by rigid customs to which citizens strictly adhered. Second, crimes of violence were considered private matters and were usually resolved through bloody personal revenge. Formal, written laws partially replaced customs when nation-states appeared, although customs often remained the force behind the laws. Formal laws also replaced customs with the advent of writing, which allowed recorded legislation to replace the recollections of elders and priests.

The first known written laws (approximately 3000 B.C.) have been found on clay tablets among the ruins of Ur, one of the city-states of Sumeria. Attributed to King Urukagina of Lagash, the laws were truly enlightened for their time and attempted to free poor people from abuse by the rich and everybody from abuse by the priests. For example, one law forbade the high priest from coming into the garden of a poor mother and taking wood or fruit from her to pay taxes. Laws also cut burial fees to one-fifth of what they had been and forbade the clergy and high officials from sharing among themselves the cattle that were sacrificed to the gods. By 2800 B.C. the growth of trade had forced the city-states of Sumeria to merge into an empire governed by a single, all-powerful king.

Around 2200 B.C., a war settlement between the Sumerians and the Akkadians produced the Babylonian civilization. Babylonia's best-known king was Hammurabi (1792–1750 B.C.), who ruled for 43 years. Hammurabi is famous for the first great code of laws. The Code of Hammurabi, like the laws of Moses later, presumably was a gift from God. Hammurabi was said to have received it from the sun god, Shamash, about 1780 B.C. There was a total of 285 laws in the code, arranged under the headings of personal property, real estate, trade and business, the family, injuries, and labor. The Code of Hammurabi combined very enlightened aims, such as "to prevent the strong from oppressing the weak, . . . to enlighten the land and to further the welfare of the people," with very barbaric punishments.

All the ancient nation-states or civilizations had formal legal codes. In addition to the laws of King Urukagina of Lagash (Sumeria) and the Code of Hammurabi (Babylonia), legal codes were established by the Egyptians, the Assyrians, the Hebrews, the Persians, the Indians, the Chinese, the Greeks (especially the codes of Lycurgus, Draco, Solon, and Plato), and the Romans (for example, the Twelve Tables, the Justinian Code, and the Law of the Nations). The development and the content of those legal codes are of mostly historical interest. The criminal law of the United States, for the most part, is derived from the laws of England.

England's Contribution to American Criminal Law Before the Norman Conquest in 1066, England was populated by Anglo-Saxon tribes that regulated themselves through custom.[4] Wars between those tribes resulted in the taking of the tribal lands of the losers by the leader of the victorious tribe, who, by force, made the newly acquired land his own private property and himself the feudal lord. By the time of the Norman Conquest, there were about eight large and relatively independent feudal landholdings. In an effort to increase their power, the feudal lords took it on themselves to dispense justice among their subjects and began to require that disputes between subjects be settled in local courts rather than by relatives, as had previously been the custom.

When William I of Normandy conquered England in 1066 and proclaimed himself king, he declared that all land, and all land-based rights, including the administration of justice, were now vested in the king. King William also rewarded the Norman noblemen who had fought with him with large grants of formerly Anglo-Saxon land.

To make the dispensing of justice a profitable enterprise for the king and to make sure the local courts remained under his control, the institution of the *eyre* was created early in the twelfth century. The eyre was composed of traveling judges who represented the king and examined the activities of the local courts.

Of particular interest to the eyre was the resolution of cases of sufficient seriousness as to warrant the forfeiture of the offender's property as punishment. The notion of forfeiture was based on the feudal doctrine that the right to own private property rested on a relationship of good faith between the landowner and his lord. The Norman kings expanded the notion of forfeiture to include any violation of the "king's peace," which enabled the king to claim forfeited property for a variety of offenses, including such minor ones as trespassing. It was the responsibility of the judges in eyre to make sure the king received his portion of forfeited property.

A secondary responsibility of the eyre was to hear common pleas, which consisted primarily of disputes between ordinary citizens. Although common pleas could be handled in the local courts, which in many instances were still influenced by Anglo-Saxon customs, the Norman settlers frequently felt more comfortable having their cases heard in the king's courts, of which the eyre was one. It was the common-plea decisions made by judges in eyre that formed the body of legal precedent that became known as the *common law,* that is, the rules used to settle disputes throughout England. Thus, as the judges of eyre resolved common-plea disputes, they created precedents to be followed in similar cases. Because the common law was built case by case, it is sometimes also called *case law.* Many of the precedents that were created in medieval England became the basis of statutory law in modern England, as well as in the United States. In both countries, some of the early precedents are still used as the basis for settling disputes not covered by statutes.

The efforts of the Norman kings to centralize their power over all of England were only partially successful. In 1215, powerful landholding nobles rebelled against the heavy taxation and autocratic rule of King John and forced him to sign the Magna Carta (the Great Charter). The primary purpose of the Magna Carta was to settle the dispute between the king and his nobles by placing checks on royal power. (It did little for the common person.) From that time forward, kings and queens of England were supposed to be governed by

FYI

Felony

The term *felony* originally meant an offense serious enough "to break the relationship between [the landowner and his lord] and to cause the [land] holding to be forfeited to the lord."

SOURCE: S. Francis Milson, *The Historical Foundations of the Common Law* (London: Butterworths, 1969), p. 355.

The Magna Carta, signed by England's King John in 1215, placed limits on royal power and established the principle of the rule of law. *Which is preferable: unregulated royal power or the rule of law? Why?*

FYI Common Law

Many states have provisions in their statutes like Florida's: "The common law of England in relation to crimes . . . shall be of full force in this state where there is no existing provision by statute on the subject."

SOURCE: § 775.01, Fla. Stat.

laws and customs rather than by their own wills, and the laws were supposed to be applied in a regular and fair way by the king or queen and his or her judges. Thus, the Magna Carta not only created the idea of the rule of law, but also formed the basis of what would later be called *due process of law*.

CREATING CRIMINAL LAWS IN THE UNITED STATES

In the United States, criminal laws (or criminal statutes) are almost entirely a product of constitutional authority and the legislative bodies that enact them. They are also effected by common law or case law interpretation and by administrative or regulatory agency decisions.

CONSTITUTIONS AND LEGISLATIVE BODIES Constitutions generally provide for the creation of legislative bodies empowered to enact criminal and other laws. The U.S. Constitution, for example, created Congress and gave it lawmaking power. The Bill of Rights of the Constitution (the first 10 amendments), as well as similar amendments to state constitutions, also describe procedural laws that dictate how substantive laws are to be administered. Constitutions are important to the substantive criminal law because they set limits on what can be defined as a crime.

As noted, criminal laws are products of the lawmaking bodies created by constitutional authority. Thus, federal statutes are enacted by Congress, and state statutes are enacted by state legislatures. Laws created by municipalities, such as by city councils, are generally called *ordinances*. Both the federal criminal statutes and the criminal statutes of particular states, including the definitions of crimes and the penalties associated with them, can be found in penal codes, one for each jurisdiction.

Generally, statutes and ordinances apply only in the particular jurisdiction in which they were enacted. A crime must be prosecuted in the jurisdiction in which it was committed, and it is generally held to have been committed

Federal statutes are enacted by Congress? *How does Congress create statutes?*

in the jurisdiction in which it was completed or achieved its goal. Federal crimes violate federal statutes, and state crimes violate state statutes. A crime in one state may not be a crime in another state, but a violation of a federal statute is a crime if committed anywhere in the United States. When a certain behavior violates both federal and state statutes, and possibly local ordinances, as is the case with many drug law violations, there is overlapping jurisdiction. In such cases, there is frequently confusion over which jurisdiction should assume responsibility for the enforcement of the law and the prosecution of the crime.

Common Law Common law, also called *case law,* is a by-product of decisions made by trial and appellate court judges, who produce case law whenever they render a decision in a particular case. The decision becomes a potential basis, or **precedent,** for deciding the outcomes of similar cases in the future. Although it is possible for the decision of any trial court judge to become a precedent, it is primarily the written decisions of appellate court judges that do. The reasons on which the decisions of appellate court judges are based are the only ones required to be in writing. This body of recorded decisions has become known as *common law.* Generally, whether a precedent is binding is determined by the court's location. (The different levels of courts in the United States will be described in detail in Chapter 8.)

precedent A decision that forms a potential basis for deciding the outcomes of similar cases in the future; a by-product of decisions made by trial and appellate court judges, who produce case law whenever they render a decision in a particular case.

The principle of using precedents to guide future decisions in court cases is called ***stare decisis*** (Latin for "to stand by decided cases"). Much of the time spent by criminal lawyers in preparing for a case is devoted to finding legal precedents that support their arguments. The successful outcome of a case depends largely on the success of lawyers in that endeavor.

stare decisis The principle of using precedents to guide future decisions in court cases; Latin for "to stand by decided cases."

Ordinances are the laws of municipalities and are created by city councils, for example, often with more citizen input than laws created at the state or federal levels of government. *How much input should citizens have in the creation of criminal laws? Defend your answer.*

Although common law was an important source of criminal law in colonial America, it is less so today. Currently, what were originally common law crimes, as well as many new crimes, have been defined by statutes created by legislatures in nearly all states. There is no federal criminal common law. Nevertheless, as noted previously, common law or case law remains important for purposes of statutory interpretation.

ADMINISTRATIVE OR REGULATORY AGENCY DECISIONS Administrative or regulatory agencies are the products of statutes enacted by the lawmaking bodies of different jurisdictions. Those agencies create rules, regulate and supervise activities in their areas of responsibility, and render decisions that have the force of law. Examples of federal administrative or regulatory agencies are the Federal Trade Commission (FTC), the Federal Communications Commission (FCC), the Nuclear Regulatory Commission (NRC), the Drug Enforcement Administration (DEA), and the Occupational Safety and Health Administration (OSHA). There are administrative or regulatory agencies at the state and local levels as well. Although violations of the rules and regulations of such agencies are generally handled through civil law proceedings, some violations—especially habitual violations—may be addressed through criminal proceedings if provided for by statute. Additionally, legislatures often enact criminal statutes based on the recommendations of regulatory agencies.

CJ ONLINE

DEA

You can learn more about the programs, major operations, statistics, etc., of the Drug Enforcement Administration by visiting their website at **www.usdoj.gov/dea/agency/agency.htm.** *How much power should the recommendations of regulatory agencies like the DEA have in shaping criminal laws?*

THE INTERDEPENDENCY AMONG SOURCES OF LEGAL AUTHORITY Although federal and state criminal statutes are essentially independent of one another, and although almost all of the action in the enforcement of criminal laws is at the state level, there is an important interdependency among sources of legal authority. For example, during the 1984 Republican National Convention in Dallas, Texas, Gregory Lee Johnson was part of a political protest of Reagan administration policies. As part of the protest, Johnson burned an American flag. Johnson was arrested and convicted of violating a Texas statute prohibiting the desecration of a venerated object. Several witnesses testified that the flag burning seriously offended them. A state court of appeals affirmed the conviction, but the Texas Court of Criminal Appeals reversed it, holding that to punish Johnson for burning the flag in this situation was inconsistent with the First Amendment. The U.S. Supreme Court agreed (*see Texas* v. *Johnson*, 1989). Provisions of the Constitution always take precedence over state statutes. However, if the state statute were not challenged, it would remain in effect in the particular state that enacted it.

THINKING CRITICALLY

1. Which of the five features of "good" criminal laws do you think are most important? Why?
2. Are there any other features that could/should be added to "good" criminal laws?

Procedural Law: Rights of the Accused

Most of the procedural, or due process rights, given to criminal suspects or defendants in the United States are found in the Bill of Rights. The Bill of Rights went into effect on December 15, 1791. Other procedural rights are found in state constitutions and federal and state statutes. Probably the best systematic collection of due process rights is the *Federal Rules of Criminal Procedure*. Those rules apply only to federal crimes prosecuted in federal courts. Most states also have collections of rules regarding criminal procedures in state courts. Ohio, for example, has 60 such rules in its *Ohio Rules of Criminal Procedure*.

TABLE 4.2 The 12 Provisions in the Bill of Rights Applicable to the Criminal Justice Process

Procedural Right	Amendment
1. Freedom from unreasonable searches and seizures	Fourth
2. Grand jury indictment in felony cases*	Fifth
3. No double jeopardy	Fifth
4. No compelled self-incrimination	Fifth
5. Speedy and public trial	Sixth
6. Impartial jury of the state and district where crime occurred	Sixth
7. Notice of nature and cause of accusation	Sixth
8. Confront opposing witnesses	Sixth
9. Compulsory process for obtaining favorable witnesses	Sixth
10. Counsel	Sixth
11. No excessive bail and fines*	Eighth
12. No cruel and unusual punishment	Eighth

**This right has not been incorporated by and made applicable to the states.*

THE BILL OF RIGHTS

The ink was barely dry on the new Constitution before critics attacked it for not protecting the rights of the people. The First Congress quickly proposed a set of 12 amendments and sent them to the states for ratification. By 1791, the states had ratified 10 of the amendments, which became known as the Bill of Rights (the first 10 amendments of the Constitution). Although the Bill of Rights originally applied only to the national government, almost all of its provisions have also been applied to the states through a series of U.S. Supreme Court decisions. Table 4.2 lists the 12 provisions in the Bill of Rights that are applicable to the criminal justice process. Note that only two of the provisions—the prohibition against excessive bail and fines and the right to a grand jury indictment—are not yet applicable to the states.

> **CJ ONLINE**
>
> **ACLU**
>
> The American Civil Liberties Union is a nonprofit, nonpartisan, advocacy group devoted to the protection of civil liberties for all Americans. You can learn more about the organization and its defense of the Constitution—especially the Bill of Rights—by going to **www.aclu.org.** Review "The Issues" section, and look at issues such as criminal justice, cyber-liberties, and drug policy. *Do you think that organizations like the ACLU are necessary? Why or why not?*

THE FOURTEENTH AMENDMENT AND THE SELECTIVE INCORPORATION OF THE BILL OF RIGHTS

The Fourteenth Amendment was finally ratified by the required three-fourths of all states in 1868, shortly after the conclusion of the Civil War. In part, the amendment reads as follows:

> No State shall make or enforce any law which shall abridge the privileges or immunities of citizens of the United States, nor shall any State deprive any person of life, liberty, or property, without due process of law; nor deny to any person within its jurisdiction the equal protection of the laws.

One of the interesting and long-debated questions about the Fourteenth Amendment was whether its original purpose was to extend the procedural safeguards described in the Bill of Rights to people charged with crimes at the state level. Before the passage of the Fourteenth Amendment, the Bill of Rights applied only to people charged with federal crimes; individual states were not bound by its requirements. Some justices of the Supreme Court—for example, William Douglas (justice from 1939 to 1975), Hugo Black (justice from 1937 to 1971), and Frank Murphy (justice from 1940 to 1949)—believed that the Fourteenth Amendment was supposed to *incorporate* the Bill of Rights and make it applicable to the states. However, other justices, perhaps even a majority of them, did not. Thus, until the 1960s the Supreme

From left to right: Chief Justices William Rehnquist, Warren Burger, and Earl Warren. Whereas the politically liberal Warren Court of the 1960s championed the rights of criminal suspects by extending procedural safeguards, the politically conservative Burger and Rehnquist courts of the 1970s, 1980s, 1990s, and the first few years of the twenty-first century have actively reversed or altered in other ways the work of the Warren Court. *How can the different direction in criminal procedure taken by the Burger and Rehnquist courts be explained?*

Court did not interpret the Fourteenth Amendment as incorporating the Bill of Rights.

There are at least three different explanations for the actions or, in this case, inactions of the Supreme Court.[5] First, there is little evidence that supporters of the Fourteenth Amendment intended it to incorporate the Bill of Rights. Second, by 1937, a series of court decisions had established the precedent that the due-process clause of the Fourteenth Amendment did not require states to follow trial procedures mandated at the federal level by provisions in the Bill of Rights. The Supreme Court had held that due process was not violated if procedures followed in state courts were otherwise fair. Third, there was the states' rights issue. Because the administration of justice is primarily a state and local responsibility, many people resented what appeared to be unwarranted interference by the federal government in state and local matters. Indeed, the Constitution, for the most part, leaves questions about policing and administering justice to the states, unless a state's procedure violates a fundamental principle of justice.

Regardless of the reason, it was not until the early 1960s that the Supreme Court, then headed by Chief Justice Earl Warren, began to selectively incorporate most of the procedural safeguards contained in the Bill of Rights, making them applicable to the states.

Thus, it took nearly 100 years after the ratification of the Fourteenth Amendment for suspects charged with crimes at the state level to be afforded most of the same due process protections as people charged with crimes at the federal level. During the past 35 years, however, the composition of the Supreme Court has changed dramatically, and with the change in personnel, the Court's views of due process rights have changed as well. Whereas the politically liberal Warren Court of the 1960s championed the rights of criminal suspects by extending procedural safeguards, the politically conservative

FYI

"Evolving Standards of Decency"

In *Trop* v. *Dulles* (1958) Chief Justice Warren wrote that the protections of the Bill of Rights "must draw [their] meaning from evolving standards of decency that mark the progress of a maturing society."

Burger and Rehnquist Courts of the 1970s, 1980s, 1990s, and the first few years of the twenty-first century have actively reversed or altered in other ways the work of the Warren Court.[6]

In the rest of this section, we will consider the procedural rights in the Bill of Rights, which are found in the Fourth, Fifth, Sixth, and Eighth Amendments to the Constitution.[7] Before we do, however, it is important to emphasize that the specific interpretation of each of the procedural or due process rights has evolved over time through dozens of Supreme Court and lower-court decisions, or precedents. In this introductory examination, we will limit our consideration of the legal development of those rights to what we believe are the most consequential cases, the landmark cases.

searches Explorations or inspections, by law enforcement officers, of homes, premises, vehicles, or persons, for the purpose of discovering evidence of crimes or persons who are accused of crimes.

seizures The taking of persons or property into custody in response to violations of the criminal law.

warrant A written order from a court directing law enforcement officers to conduct a search or to arrest a person.

arrest The seizure of a person or the taking of a person into custody, either actual physical custody, as when a suspect is handcuffed by a police officer, or constructive custody, as when a person peacefully submits to a police officer's control.

THE FOURTH AMENDMENT

The Fourth Amendment reads as follows:

> The right of the people to be secure in their persons, houses, papers, and effects, against unreasonable searches and seizures, shall not be violated, and no warrants shall issue, but upon probable cause, supported by Oath or affirmation, and particularly describing the place to be searched, and the person or things to be seized.

The Fourth Amendment (as well as other provisions of the Constitution) protects individual privacy against certain types of governmental interference. However, it does not provide a general constitutional "right to privacy," as many people wrongly believe. Nearly every governmental action interferes with personal privacy to some extent. Thus, the question in Fourth Amendment cases is limited to whether a governmental intrusion violates the Constitution.[8]

The procedural rights in the Fourth Amendment influence the operation of criminal justice in the United States nearly every day. They concern the legality of searches and seizures and the question of what to do with evidence that is illegally obtained. **Searches** are explorations or inspections, by law enforcement officers, of homes, premises, vehicles, or persons, for the purpose of discovering evidence of crimes or persons who are accused of crimes. A search occurs "when an expectation of privacy that society is prepared to consider reasonable is infringed [by the government]."[9] **Seizures** are the taking of persons or property into custody in response to violations of the criminal law. A seizure of property occurs "when there is some meaningful interference [by the government] with an individual's possessory interests in that property."[10] For the seizure of a person, see *United States* v. *Mendenhall* (FYI on p. 116) and *California* v. *Hodari D.* (FYI on p. 119).

According to the Supreme Court, the Fourth Amendment allows two kinds of searches and seizures: those made with a warrant and those made without a warrant. A **warrant** is a written order from a court directing law enforcement officers to conduct a search or to arrest a person. An **arrest** is the seizure of a person or the taking of a person into custody. An arrest can be either taking actual physical custody, as when a suspect is handcuffed by a police officer, or constructive custody, as when a

Samar Kaukab sued the Illinois National Guard and O'Hare International Airport security officers for strip-searching her at the Chicago airport before a flight simply because she was wearing a hijab—a Muslim head scarf. *Were the security officers justified in conducting the strip-search? Why or why not?*

FYI

United States v. Mendenhall

In *United States* v. *Mendenhall* (1980), the Supreme Court created the following test for determining whether an encounter constitutes a Fourth Amendment seizure: "A person has been 'seized' within the meaning of the Fourth Amendment only if, in view of all the circumstances surrounding the incident, a reasonable person would have believed that he was not free to leave." The Court provided these examples of situations that might be construed as seizures, even if the person did not attempt to leave: (1) the threatening presence of several officers, (2) the display of a weapon by an officer, (3) some physical touching of the person, or (4) the use of language or a tone of voice that indicated that compliance with the officer's request might be compelled.

person peacefully submits to a police officer's control. An arrest can occur without an officer's physically touching a suspect.

The Fourth Amendment requires only that searches and seizures not be "unreasonable." Searches and seizures conducted with a legal warrant are generally considered reasonable. However, what is "reasonable" in warrantless searches remained vague for more than 100 years after the ratification of the amendment. It was not until a series of cases beginning in the 1960s that the Supreme Court began to provide a more precise definition of the term. Because the law concerning warrantless searches and seizures is complex, only a relatively brief and simplified overview will be provided in that section.

Searches and Seizures With a Warrant First, law enforcement officers must have *probable cause* before a judicial officer can legally issue a search or arrest warrant. Probable cause for a search warrant requires substantial and trustworthy evidence to support two conclusions: (1) that the specific objects to be searched for are connected with criminal activity and (2) that the objects will be found in the place to be searched. In nearly all jurisdictions, law enforcement officers seeking a search warrant must specify in a signed *affidavit,* a written and sworn declaration, the facts that establish probable cause. The facts in the affidavit are the basis for determining later whether there was probable cause to issue the warrant in the first place. Some jurisdictions allow sworn oral testimony to establish probable cause.

The Fourth Amendment requires that a search warrant contain a particular description of the place to be searched and the person or things to be seized. Thus, the warrant must be specific enough that a law enforcement officer executing it would know where to search and what objects to seize, even if the officer was not originally involved in the case. However, absolute technical accuracy in the description of the place to be searched is not necessary. It is required only that an officer executing a warrant can find, perhaps by asking questions of neighborhood residents, the place to be searched.

A warrant may also be issued for the search of a person or an automobile, rather than a place. A warrant to search a person should provide the person's name or at least a detailed description. A warrant to search an automobile should include either the car's license number or its make and the name of its owner.

Search warrants are required to be executed in a reasonable amount of time. For example, federal law requires that a search be conducted within 10 days after the warrant is issued. The federal government and nearly half of the states also have laws limiting the time of day during which search warrants may be executed. In those jurisdictions, searches may be conducted only during daytime hours unless there are special circumstances.

Generally, before law enforcement officers may enter a place to conduct a search, they must first announce that they are law enforcement officers, that they possess a warrant, and that they are there to execute it. The major exceptions to this requirement are situations in which it is likely that the evidence would be destroyed immediately on notification or in which notification would pose a threat to officers. However, if officers are refused entry after identifying themselves, they may then use force to gain entry, but only after they have given the occupant time to respond. In short, they cannot legally yell "police officers," and immediately kick down the door. Finally, if in the course of conducting a legal search, law enforcement officers discover **contraband** (an illegal substance or object) or evidence of a crime not covered by the warrant, they may seize that contraband or evidence under the plain-view exception (discussed later) without getting a new warrant specifically covering it. Figure 4.2 shows a sample search and arrest warrant and the supporting affidavit.

contraband An illegal substance or object.

FIGURE 4.2 Sample Search and Arrest Warrant

SEARCH AND ARREST WARRANT

THE STATE OF TEXAS § 155 E. Main Street
§ Dallas, Dallas County, Texas
COUNTY OF DALLAS §

THE STATE OF TEXAS to the Sheriff or any Peace Officer of Dallas County, Texas, or any Peace Officer of the State of Texas,

GREETINGS:

WHEREAS, the Affiant whose signature is affixed to the Affidavit appearing on the reverse hereof is a Peace Officer under the laws of Texas and did heretofore this day subscribed and swear to said Affidavit before me (which said affidavit is by this reference incorporated herein for all purposes), and whereas I find that the verified facts by Affiant in said Affidavit show that Affiant has probable cause for the belief he expresses therein and establishes the existence of proper grounds for the issuance of this Warrant:

NOW, THEREFORE, you are commanded to enter the suspecte
described in said Affidavit and to there search for the per
described in said Affidavit and to seize the same and brin
And, you are commanded to arrest and bring before me ea
and accused in said Affidavit. Herein fail not, but have yo
this Warrant executed within three days, exclusive of the
issuance and exclusive of the day of its execution with yo
thereon, showing how you have executed the same.

ISSUED AT 11:35 o'clock A M., on this the 23
of March, 1999 to certify which witness
day.

Sarah H. Solano
MAGISTRATE, DALLAS COUNTY, TE

RETURN AND INVENTORY

THE STATE OF TEXAS §
§
COUNTY OF DALLAS §

The undersigned Affiant, being a Peace Officer under the
and being duly sworn, on oath certifies that the foregoing Wa
hand on the day it was issued and that it was executed on th
of ____________, 19____, by making the search d
therein and seizing during such search the following describe
property:

AFFIANT

SUBSCRIBED AND SWORN to before me, the undersigned
the______day of ________________, 19______

Notary Public in and for Dallas County, Te

AFFIDAVIT FOR SEARCH WARRANT AND ARREST WARRANT

THE STATE OF TEXAS § 155 E. Main Street
§ City of Dallas, Dallas County, Texas
COUNTY OF DALLAS §

The undersigned Affiant being a Peace Officer under the laws of Texas and being duly sworn, on oath makes the following statements and accusations:

1. There is in Dallas County, Texas, a suspected place and premises described and located as follows: A one story family dwelling, which is white in color, with a grey composition roof. The location of this residence is 155 E. Main Street, located in the City of Dallas, Dallas County, Texas.

2. There is at said suspected place and premises personal property concealed and kept in violation of the laws of Texas and described as follows: A CONTROLLED SUBSTANCE: TO WIT: Cocaine

3. Said suspected place and premises are in charge of and controlled by each of the following persons: A white male approximately 25 years of age, 5'10 in height, 160 pounds, with a mustache, black hair and brown eyes and other person or persons whose names, ages, and descriptions are unknown to the affiant.

4. It is the belief of Affiant, and he hereby charges and accuses, that: The above listed white male described in paragraph number 3 was in possession of an amount of cocaine located in the residence at 155 E. Main Street, located in the City of Dallas, Dallas County, Texas.

5. Affiant has probable cause for said belief by reason of the following facts: Affiant, Officer Smith, is employed by the City of Dallas Police Department and is currently assigned to the Narcotics Bureau.

I, the affiant, personally purchased an amount of cocaine from the suspect described in paragraph number 3 out of the aforementioned address at 155 E. Main Street, and that the affiant has been inside the above described residence within the last 24 hours, and personally observed the above described white male and other person, persons, whose names, ages, and identities, and descriptions are unknown to the affiant, in possession of and selling cocaine. Detective Jones purchased 0.3g of cocaine from the above described suspect for twenty dollars U.S. Currency. The cocaine was field tested by the affiant who knows due to his experience as a narcotics officer, what cocaine looks like and how it is packaged for resale.

I, the affiant, observed this on March 22, 1999.

Wherefore, Affiant asks for issuance of a warrant that will authorize him to search said suspected place and premises for said personal property and seize the same and to arrest each said described and accused person.

James C. Smith
AFFIANT

Subscribed and sworn to before me by said Affiant on this the 23rd day of March, 1999.

Sarah H. Solano
MAGISTRATE, DALLAS COUNTY, TEXAS

FYI

E-mail and Privacy

E-mail does not have the same privacy protections as does "regular mail." Depending on where the e-mail is sent from and where it is sent to, privacy rights vary greatly. However, under no circumstances can e-mail messages ever be considered confidential. Both government employees (federal, state, and local) and employees in the private sector have few, if any, privacy rights in the e-mail messages they send or receive. Employers are free to examine all electronic communications stored on their systems. The e-mail messages of government employees may also be available to the public through a freedom of information request. In addition, commercial service providers (such as *America Online*) are permitted to disclose messages to law enforcement officials when they "inadvertently" come across messages containing references to illegal activity. Finally, regardless of the setting (work or home), e-mail can be subpoenaed, discovered, and intercepted under existing wiretap laws.

SOURCE: Erik C. Garcia, "E-mail and Privacy Rights," www.wings.buffalo.edu.

ARRESTS WITH A WARRANT Most arrests are made without a warrant. Generally, an arrest warrant is legally required when law enforcement officers want to enter private premises to make an arrest unless there is consent or exigent circumstances (discussed later). An arrest warrant is issued only if substantial and trustworthy evidence supports these two conclusions: (1) a violation of the law has been committed and (2) the person to be arrested committed the violation.

SEARCHES AND SEIZURES WITHOUT A WARRANT In guaranteeing freedom from illegal searches and seizures, the Fourth Amendment protects a person's privacy. Under most circumstances, the amendment requires a warrant signed by a judge to authorize a search for and seizure of evidence of criminal activity. However, Supreme Court interpretations of the Fourth Amendment have permitted warrantless searches and seizures in some circumstances. A person is generally protected from searches and seizures without a warrant in places, such as home or office, where he or she has a legitimate right to privacy. That same protection, however, does not extend to all places where a person has a legitimate right to be. For example, the Supreme Court has permitted the stopping and searching of automobiles under certain circumstances and with probable cause. Several doctrines concerning search and seizure without a warrant have developed over time.

Before 1969, when law enforcement officers arrested a suspect, they could legally search, without a warrant, the entire premises surrounding the arrest. That kind of search is called a *search incident to arrest,* and like a search with a warrant, it required probable cause. Evidence obtained through a search incident to arrest was admissible as long as the arrest was legal.

In 1969, in the case of *Chimel* v. *California,* the Supreme Court limited the scope of *searches incident to an arrest.* The Court restricted the physical area in which officers could conduct a search to the area within the suspect's immediate control. The Court interpreted the area within the suspect's immediate control as an area near enough to the suspect to enable him or her to obtain a weapon or destroy evidence. The Court also ruled that it is permissible for officers, incident to an arrest, to protect themselves, to prevent a suspect's escape by searching the suspect for weapons, and to preserve evidence within the suspect's grabbing area.

The Supreme Court has continued to refine the scope of warrantless searches and seizures incident to an arrest. For example, in 1981, in *New York* v. *Belton,* the Court ruled that after police have made a lawful arrest of the occupant of an automobile, they may, incident to an arrest, search the automobile's entire passenger compartment, and the contents of any opened or closed containers found in the compartment. The police had long been able to legally search the automobile's trunk, providing there was probable cause (see *Carroll* v. *United States,* 1925). In *United States* v. *Ross* (1982) the Court held that when police "have probable cause to search an entire vehicle, they may conduct a warrantless search of every part of the vehicle [including the trunk] and its contents, including all containers and packages, that may conceal the object of the search." Then, in 1991, in the case of *California* v. *Acevedo,* the Court ruled that the police, "in a search extending only to a container within an automobile, may search the container without a warrant where they have probable cause to believe that it holds contraband or evidence." The Court will also allow the police, with probable cause, to search an automobile passenger's belongings, if he or she is capable of concealing the object of the search (see *Wyoming* v. *Houghton,* 1999).

Other Supreme Court decisions have established principles governing when private areas may be searched incident to an arrest. In 1968, for instance, in the case of *Harris* v. *United States,* the Court established the *plain-view doctrine.* Under this doctrine, the police may seize an item—evidence or contraband—without a warrant if they are lawfully in a position to view the item and if it is immediately apparent that the item is evidence or contraband. In 1990, the Court clarified its ruling in *Harris* by adding that the discovery of the item in plain view need not be "inadvertent." That is, the plain-view doctrine applies even when the police expect in advance to find the item in plain view (*Horton* v. *California*). Also, in 1990, in the case of *Maryland* v. *Buie,* the Court addressed the issue of *protective sweeps.* The Court held that when a warrantless arrest takes place in a suspect's home, officers, with reasonable suspicion, may make only a "cursory visual inspection" of areas that could harbor an accomplice or a person posing danger to them.

Even a warrantless search not incident to an arrest may be justified under the Supreme Court's *exigent circumstances* doctrine. It permits police to make warrantless searches in exigent, or emergency, situations. Such situations could include a need to prevent the imminent destruction of evidence a need to prevent harm to individuals, or the hot pursuit of suspects.

Frequently, law enforcement officers are not hampered by the warrant requirement, because suspects often consent to a search. In other words, law enforcement officers who do not have enough evidence to obtain a search warrant, or who either cannot or do not want to take the time and trouble to obtain one, may simply ask a suspect whether they may conduct a search. If the suspect consents voluntarily, the search can be made legally. Law enforcement officers call this strategy "knock and talk." In 1973, in the case of *Schenckloth* v. *Bustamonte,* the Supreme Court upheld the legality of *consent searches.* The Court also ruled that officers do not have to tell suspects that they have a right to withhold consent unless they ask.

It is not surprising that consent searches have become the most common type of searches performed by law enforcement officers. They are used frequently in traffic stops and drug interdiction efforts at airports and bus terminals. In the 1980s, as a new tool in the war on drugs, several police departments adopted programs in which officers boarded buses and asked passengers to consent to searches. The practice was challenged in a 1985 Florida case in which a bus passenger had consented to having his luggage searched. When the police found cocaine, the passenger was arrested and subsequently convicted. The Florida Supreme Court ruled that the search was unconstitutional. In 1991, the U.S. Supreme Court reversed the Florida Supreme Court (in *Florida* v. *Bostick*) and held that the search was not unconstitutional and that law enforcement officers may make such a search without a warrant or suspicion of a crime—as long as the passenger feels free to refuse the search.

Critics argue that, in most cases, consent searches cannot be truly voluntary, even when permission is granted, because most people are intimidated by the police and would have a hard time telling them no. Moreover, most people probably do not know that they may refuse a warrantless search except under the conditions described earlier.

Arrests without a Warrant Officers may not enter a private home to make a warrantless arrest unless there is consent or the offense is a serious one and there are exigent circumstances, such as the likely destruction of evidence or the hot pursuit of a felony suspect. This is the same *exigent circumstances* doctrine that applies to warrantless searches and seizures.

A suspect who is arrested without a warrant and remains confined is entitled to have a judge determine whether there was probable cause for the

> **FYI**
> **Meaning of Seizure**
>
> Supreme Court rulings often modify previous decisions. In *California* v. *Hodari D.* (1991), for example, the Court modified the plurality holding in *Mendenhall* (1980). In *Hodari D.,* the suspect ran from the police, and an officer pursued, thereby creating a circumstance in which a "reasonable person would have believed that she or he was not free to leave" or to disobey the officer's command to halt. There was no physical touching of the suspect. The Court held that in cases involving a "show of authority," as distinguished from physical touching, no "seizure" occurs unless and until the suspect yields or submits to the assertion of authority.

arrest. Ordinarily, judges must make such a determination within 48 hours of arrest. The purpose of this proceeding is to ensure that the suspect's continuing custody is based on a judicial determination of probable cause and not merely on the police officer's judgment that probable cause supported an arrest.

Standards of Proof As mentioned previously and as specified in the Fourth Amendment, neither search nor arrest warrants can be issued legally unless law enforcement officers convince a judge or a magistrate that there is probable cause to believe either that the specific items to be searched for are related to criminal activity and the items will be found in the place to be searched or that a violation of the law has been committed and the person to be arrested committed the violation. Probable cause is one among a number of standards of proof for various criminal justice activities. The amount of proof necessary depends on the activity in question. Figure 4.3 shows various standards of proof, along a continuum of certainty, and the criminal justice activities that correspond to them.

mere suspicion The standard of proof with the least certainty; a "gut feeling." With mere suspicion, a law enforcement officer cannot legally even stop a suspect.

Toward one end of the continuum is the standard of proof with the least certainty: *mere suspicion.* **Mere suspicion** is equivalent to a "gut feeling." In other words, a law enforcement officer may have a feeling that something is wrong—an uncanny knack that some experienced law enforcement officers possess—but be unable to state exactly what it is. With only mere suspicion, law enforcement officers cannot legally even stop a suspect.

reasonable suspicion A standard of proof that is more than a gut feeling. It includes the ability to articulate reasons for the suspicion. With reasonable suspicion, a law enforcement officer is legally permitted to stop and frisk a suspect.

frisking Conducting a search for weapons by patting the outside of a suspect's clothing, feeling for hard objects that might be weapons.

A standard of proof with greater certainty is *reasonable suspicion.* **Reasonable suspicion** is more than a gut feeling. It includes the ability to articulate reasons for the suspicion. For example, if a law enforcement officer observes a person in front of a bank wearing a heavy trench coat on a hot summer day, the officer might have a reasonable suspicion that something is wrong. The officer could state that idling in front of a bank while wearing a heavy trench coat on a hot summer day is suspect behavior. Until recently, an anonymous tip, as long as there were other reliable indicators, could be the basis for reasonable suspicion. However, in *Florida* v. *J.L.* (2000), the Supreme Court ruled that an uncorroborated anonymous tip was unconstitutional.[11] On the other hand, the Court, in *Illinois* v. *Wardlow* (2000), recently confirmed that running from the police when they enter a high-crime area is reasonably suspicious behavior.[12] With reasonable suspicion, a law enforcement officer is legally permitted to stop and frisk a suspect (*Terry* v. *Ohio,* 1968). **Frisking** a

FIGURE 4.3 Standards of Proof and Criminal Justice Activities

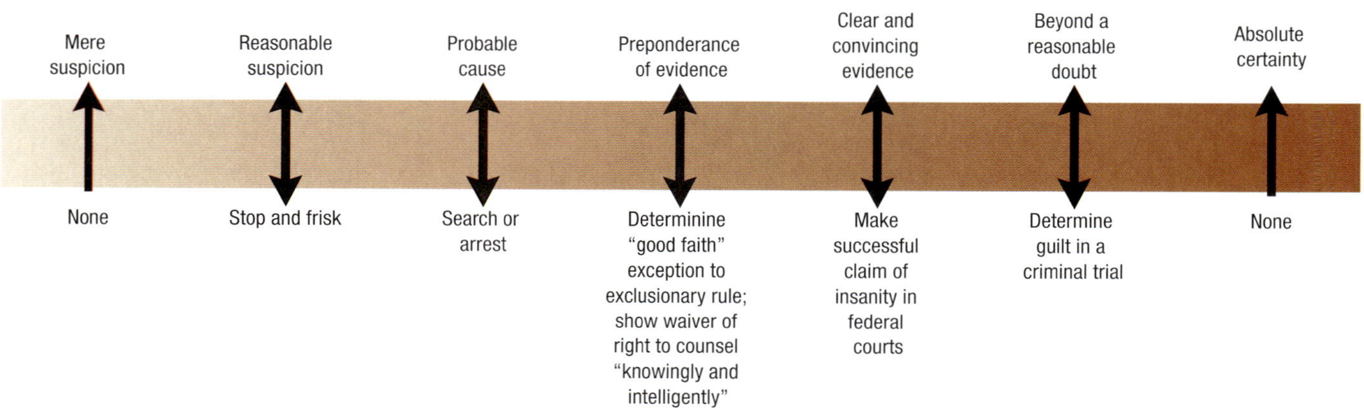

suspect means conducting a search for weapons by patting the outside of a suspect's clothing, feeling for hard objects that might be weapons. Only if an officer feels something that may be a weapon may he or she search inside a pocket or an article of clothing. If evidence of a crime is discovered, the officer is permitted to make an arrest.

The standard of proof needed to conduct a search or to make an arrest is *probable cause*. The conventional definition of **probable cause** is the amount of proof necessary for a reasonably intelligent person to suspect that a crime has been committed or that items connected with criminal activity can be found in a particular place. Although its meaning is not entirely clear—what is "reasonably intelligent"?—probable cause has a greater degree of certainty than reasonable suspicion. For probable cause, law enforcement officers must have some tangible evidence that a crime has been committed, but that evidence does not have to be admissible at trial. Such evidence might include a tip from a reliable informant or the pungent aroma of marijuana in the air.

probable cause The amount of proof necessary for a reasonably intelligent person to suspect that a crime has been committed or that items connected with criminal activity can be found in a particular place. It is the standard of proof needed to conduct a search or to make an arrest.

The line between probable cause and reasonable suspicion, or even mere suspicion, is a fine one and a matter of interpretation. In practice, there are many gray areas. Consequently, criminal courts and the judicial officers who are authorized to approve search warrants have been given the responsibility of determining whether a standard of proof has been met in a particular situation. As noted, search warrants, for example, must generally be approved by a judicial officer before they can be executed. The way courts and judicial officers determine whether a standard of proof has been met will be discussed in detail in Chapter 8. Here we simply observe that, for much of the public, one of the frustrating aspects of criminal justice is that offenders who are factually guilty of their crimes sometimes escape punishment because a judicial officer did not have probable cause to issue a warrant, or a police officer did not have probable cause to make an arrest or have reasonable suspicion to stop and frisk the suspect.

The next standard of proof along the continuum of legal certainty is *preponderance of evidence*. **Preponderance of evidence** is evidence that more likely than not outweighs the opposing evidence, or sufficient evidence to overcome doubt or speculation. It is the standard of proof necessary to find a defendant liable in a civil lawsuit. This standard is also used in determining whether the *inevitable-discovery rule* applies. That is, the prosecution must prove by a preponderance of the evidence that evidence actually uncovered as a result of a constitutional violation would inevitably have been discovered through lawful means, independent of the action constituting the violation. Finally, preponderance of evidence is the standard of proof in criminal proceedings by which the state must show that the right to counsel has been waived "knowingly and intelligently."

preponderance of evidence Evidence that more likely than not outweighs the opposing evidence, or sufficient evidence to overcome doubt or speculation.

Next along the continuum of certainty is **clear and convincing evidence.** It is the standard of proof required in some civil cases and, in federal courts, the standard of proof necessary for a defendant to make a successful claim of insanity.

clear and convincing evidence The standard of proof required in some civil cases and, in federal courts, the standard of proof necessary for a defendant to make a successful claim of insanity.

Of greater certainty still is proof **beyond a reasonable doubt,** the standard of proof necessary to find a defendant guilty in a criminal trial. Reasonable doubt is the amount of doubt about a defendant's guilt that a reasonable person might have after carefully examining all the evidence. In the case of *Sandoval* v. *California* (1994), the Court upheld the following definition of *reasonable doubt*:

beyond a reasonable doubt The standard of proof necessary to find a defendant guilty in a criminal trial.

> It is *not a mere possible doubt;* because everything relating to human affairs, and *depending on moral evidence,* is open to some possible or imaginary doubt. It is that state of the case which, after the entire comparison and consideration of all the evidence, leaves the minds of the jurors in that they cannot say they feel an abiding conviction, *to a moral certainty,* of the truth of the charge. [Emphasis in original.]

The theoretical rationale behind the protection against double jeopardy is that the state should have one and only one chance to convict a defendant charged with a crime. Otherwise, the state could endlessly harass its citizens, as sometimes happens in countries without this protection.

Protection Against Compelled Self-Incrimination Arguably, the most important procedural safeguard in the Fifth Amendment is the protection against compelled **self-incrimination.** The protection guarantees that in criminal cases, suspects or defendants cannot be forced to be witnesses against themselves. The protection is based on the belief that confessions may not be truthful if they are not made voluntarily. It also expresses an intolerance for certain methods used to extract confessions, even if the confessions ultimately prove to be reliable. A **confession** is an admission by a person accused of a crime that he or she committed the offense as charged. According to the Supreme Court's **doctrine of fundamental fairness,** confessions are inadmissible in criminal trials if they were obtained by means of either psychological manipulation or "third-degree" methods—for example, beatings, subjection to unreasonably long periods of questioning, or other physical tactics.

self-incrimination Being a witness against oneself. If forced, it is a violation of the Fifth Amendment.

confession An admission by a person accused of a crime that he or she committed the offense charged.

doctrine of fundamental fairness The rule that makes confessions inadmissible in criminal trials if they were obtained by means of either psychological manipulation or "third-degree" methods.

Although the Fifth Amendment protection against compelled self-incrimination has long been observed in federal trials, it was not until the 1960s, in the case of *Malloy* v. *Hogan* (1964), that the Fifth Amendment protection against compelled self-incrimination was extended to trials in state courts. In *Miranda* v. *Arizona* (1966), the Court broadened the protection against compelled self-incrimination to cover nearly all custodial police interrogations. (Custodial police interrogations essentially mean questionings that take place after an arrest or the functional equivalent of an arrest; they may or may not take place at the police station.) In *Miranda,* the Court added that confessions obtained without suspects' being notified of their specific rights could not be admitted as evidence. Perhaps even more important, it established specific procedural safeguards that had to be followed to avoid violation of the protection against compelled self-incrimination. The court said:

> [P]rocedural safeguards must be employed to protect the privilege [against self-incrimination], and unless other fully effective means are adopted to notify the person of his right of silence and to assure that the exercise of the right will be scrupulously honored, the following measures are required. [The suspect] must be warned prior to any questioning (1) that he has the right to remain silent, (2) that anything he says can be used against him in a court of law, (3) that he has the right to the presence of an attorney, and (4) that if he cannot afford an attorney one will be appointed for him prior to any questioning if he so desires.

FYI: Interrogation

In the case of *Rhode Island* v. *Innis* (1980), the Supreme Court stated: [T]he term "interrogation" under *Miranda* refers not only to express questioning, but also to any words or actions on the part of the police (other than those normally attendant to arrest and custody) that the police should know are reasonably likely to elicit an incriminating response from the suspect.

If suspects indicate, prior to or during questioning, that they wish to remain silent, the interrogation must cease; if they state that they want an attorney, the questioning must cease until an attorney is present. Where an interrogation is conducted without the presence of an attorney and a statement is taken, a heavy burden rests on the government to demonstrate that a suspect knowingly and intelligently waived his or her right to counsel. However, if an individual being questioned is not yet in custody, the *Miranda* warnings do not have to be given. Also, volunteered confessions do not violate *Miranda* or the Fifth Amendment.

The Fifth Amendment protection against compelled self-incrimination has been weakened recently by the Supreme Court. For example, in *New York* v. *Quarles* (1984), the Supreme Court created a public-safety exception to the Fifth Amendment protection. Also, in *Arizona* v. *Fulminante* (1991),

Former Enron Corporation CEO Kenneth Lay is sworn in before the Senate Committee on Commerce, Science and Transportation. He exercised his Fifth Amendment right and did not testify. *Should Mr. Lay have been compelled to testify before the Committee? Why or why not?*

the Court ruled that improper use of a coerced confession is a harmless trial error if other evidence is strong enough to convict the defendant. The burden of proof is on the state to show that a coerced confession is harmless error. The case involved a defendant who had been sentenced to death for killing his 11-year-old stepdaughter. While in prison, the defendant confessed to an FBI informant after the informant promised to protect the defendant from other inmates. Prior to *Fulminante,* such a conviction would most likely have been reversed on appeal because of the use of the coerced confession.

However, in *Dickerson* v. *United States* (2000), the Court reaffirmed the importance of *Miranda,* even when it inconveniences law enforcement officers. In *Dickerson,* a bank robbery suspect asked the Court to throw out incriminating statements he made to FBI agents because he was not given *Miranda* warnings prior to questioning. Prosecutors argued that the suspect made voluntary statements, which were admissible under a law approved by Congress in 1968. The law gives federal judges authority to admit statements from suspects if the judges believe that the statements are voluntary. The Court disagreed and held that Congress did not have the authority to supersede the Supreme Court's interpretation of the Constitution. Therefore, the incriminating statements made by the bank robbery suspect were inadmissible.[15]

The Fifth Amendment protection against compelled self-incrimination also applies to trial procedures. If defendants do not voluntarily take the stand to testify, not only do they have a right to refuse to answer any questions put to them by the prosecution during a trial (by "pleading the fifth"), but they also have the right not to take the witness stand in the first place. Moreover, the prosecution is forbidden to comment on the defendant's silence or refusal to take the witness stand. This protection rests on a basic legal principle: the government bears the burden of proof. Defendants are not obligated to help the government prove they committed a crime. In 1964 and 1965, those Fifth Amendment rights were extended to defendants being tried in state courts in the cases of *Malloy* v. *Hogan* and *Griffin* v. *California,* respectively.

THE SIXTH AMENDMENT

The Sixth Amendment reads as follows:

> In all criminal prosecutions, the accused shall enjoy the right to a speedy and public trial, by an impartial jury of the State and district wherein the crime shall have been committed; which district shall have been previously ascertained by law, and to be informed of the nature and cause of the accusation; to be confronted with the witnesses against him; to have compulsory process for obtaining witnesses in his favor, and to have the assistance of counsel for his defence.

RIGHT TO A SPEEDY AND PUBLIC TRIAL The Sixth Amendment right to a speedy and public trial applies directly to trials in federal courts. It was extended to trials in state courts in 1967, in the case of *Klopfer* v. *North Carolina* (right to a speedy trial), and in 1948, in the case of *In re Oliver* (right to a public trial). Delays in a trial can severely hamper a defendant's

FYI Jury Trials

The fundamental right to a jury trial, itself, is provided in Article 3, Section 2.3, of the U.S. Constitution: "The Trial of all Crimes, except in Cases of impeachment, shall be by Jury, and such Trial shall be held in the State where the said crimes shall have been committed; but when not committed within any State, the Trial shall be at such Place or Places as the Congress may by Law have directed."

FYI: The Speedy Trial Act

Federal courts are now regulated by the Speedy Trial Act of 1974, which specifies two separate time limits: one for the period between arrest and charging, and the other for the period between charging and trial. The act stipulates that, generally, a delay between arrest and charging (that is, the filing of an indictment or information) may be no more than 30 days, and a delay between charging and trial may be no more than 70 days. The act also specifies periods of delay that do not count—for example, delay due to the unavailability of an essential witness or continuances (that is, postponements) that serve "the ends of justice." If the delay, excluding periods of delay that do not count, is longer than the number of days allowed, the court must dismiss the charges. A dismissal with prejudice, which is given when there are no good reasons for the delay, prevents the re-prosecution of the case. A dismissal without prejudice gives the prosecutor the option of prosecuting the case again.

case if favorable witnesses have died, have moved and cannot be found, or have forgotten what they saw. Delays can also adversely affect defendants by forcing them to remain in jail for long periods of time while awaiting trial. A long wait in jail can be a very stressful and sometimes dangerous experience.

In *United States* v. *Marion* (1971), the Supreme Court held that the right to a speedy trial "is activated only when a criminal prosecution has begun and extends only to those persons who have been 'accused' in the course of that prosecution." It added that "invocation of the right need not await indictment, information, or other formal charge but begins with the actual restraints imposed by arrest if those restraints precede the formal preferring of charges." In determining what constitutes a speedy trial, the Supreme Court has created a balancing test that weighs both the defendant's and the prosecution's behavior (see *Barker* v. *Wingo,* 1972). Thus, the reason for the delay in a trial is critical. For example, a search for a missing witness would probably be considered an acceptable reason for delay. Court congestion, on the other hand, typically would not.

The acceptable length of delay in a trial also depends partly on the nature of the charge. In *Barker,* the Court held that "the delay that can be tolerated for an ordinary street crime is considerably less than for a serious, complex conspiracy charge." There has been great variation in the length of delay tolerated by specific courts.

The Sixth Amendment right to a public trial means that a trial must be open to the public, but it need not be open to all who want to attend. Obviously, the number of people who can attend a trial depends on the size of the courtroom. The right would be violated only if the trial were held, for example, in a prison or in a closed judge's chambers against a defendant's wishes. Defendants have no right to a private trial.

A trial may be closed to the public if the defendant's right to a public trial is outweighed by "a compelling state interest." However, before a trial is closed, "the party seeking to close the hearing must advance an overriding interest that is likely to be prejudiced, the closure must be no broader than necessary to protect that interest, the trial court must consider reasonable alternatives to closing the proceeding, and it must make findings adequate to support the closure" (*Waller* v. *Georgia,* 1984). In some cases, parts of a trial may be closed—for example, to protect the identity of an undercover informant during his or her testimony.

Right to Impartial Jury of the State and District Wherein the Crime Shall Have Been Committed The right to an impartial jury promises not only that a jury will be unbiased but also that there will be a jury trial. As interpreted by the Supreme Court, this right means that defendants charged with felonies or with misdemeanors punishable by more than 6 months' imprisonment are entitled to be tried before a jury. The right was extended to the states in 1968, in the case of *Duncan* v. *Louisiana.* Most states also allow defendants to be tried by a jury for less serious misdemeanors but states are not constitutionally required to do so.

For practical purposes, the right to an impartial jury is achieved by providing a representative jury, that is, a jury randomly selected from a fair cross section of the community. However, whether members of such a jury will be impartial in a particular case is a question that defies an easy answer. Juries will be discussed more extensively in Chapter 8.

venue The place of the trial. It must be geographically appropriate.

Finally, the Sixth Amendment guarantees the specific **venue,** or the place of trial. (Venue is also mentioned in the Constitution in Article 3, Section 2: "Trial shall be held in the State where the said Crimes shall have been committed. . . . ") The venue of a trial must be geographically appropriate.

Generally, a crime must be tried in the jurisdiction—the politically defined geographical area—in which it was committed. However, if a defense attorney believes that a client cannot get a fair trial in the appropriate venue because of adverse publicity or for some other reason, the attorney can ask the court for a change of venue. If the change of venue is granted, the trial will be moved to another location (within the state in cases of state law violations), where, presumably, the adverse publicity or other factors are not as great.

Right to Be Informed of the Nature and Cause of the Accusation
The right to notice and a hearing is the very core of what is meant by due

FYI

Jury Flexibility

In 1994, the state of Florida passed a law allowing a jury selected in one county to hear a trial in another county. Before the law, trials—not juries—were moved, often causing hardship to victims' families.

Careers in Criminal Justice

Public Defender

My name is Junior A. Barrett and I am an assistant public defender in the Major Crimes Unit of the Public Defender Office in the Ninth Judicial Circuit (Orange and Osceola Counties in Florida). I have a Bachelor of Science degree in Criminal Justice Administration and Planning from John Jay College of Criminal Justice, City University of New York. I also have a Juris Doctor from Union University, Albany Law School, Albany, New York.

My decision to represent indigent clients was made before I even started college. I wanted to do something that was not only challenging, but where I felt I could help the poor. Growing up on the island of Jamaica and in Brooklyn, New York, I saw what can happen to people who don't receive proper legal representation. I knew people who were railroaded by the criminal justice system and by lawyers who did not really care, but instead saw what they did as just a job.

I started working for the Public Defender's Office in July of 1991 doing misdemeanor and traffic-related offenses. About six years ago, I was promoted to the Major Crimes Unit where I represent clients charged with capital sexual battery and first-degree murder.

My days are never typical. Sometimes they start with a trip to the Orange County Jail to talk to a client about his case and what we will need to do to prepare for court. Another day might begin with me sitting down with an investigator to talk about locating witnesses.

A large portion of my day is spent trying to reconstruct my client's life and reviewing evidence. Reconstructing my client's life involves contacting family and friends of my client. It also involves my spending a lot of time contacting different agencies in order to get copies of my client's school records, medical records, mental health records, military records, job records, and even records of time the client spent in jail or prison. This information is then used to try and convince a jury that my client should not be executed.

Ultimately, every thing I do is in preparation for trying the case. A first-degree murder trial usually takes about a week to try. If the death penalty is involved, it can take two weeks. Often, the case does not end at a trial. There are appeals, rehearings, and sometimes even retrials.

It is hard to say what I like best and least about my job. Sometimes it is seeing the tears of joy running down the cheeks of my client as a jury says not guilty. Sometimes it is knowing that the State of Florida will not be able to execute my client. Other times it is the camaraderie that I find in the Public Defender's Office. On the flip side, one of the things I enjoy least about my job is a verdict of guilty in spite of the evidence. I also dislike the fact that even after a verdict of not guilty, my client's life is ruined forever. I have had clients who have lost many months of their lives because they were in jail awaiting a final disposition of their case. There is no way to give back to an innocent client the months he sat in jail waiting to be tried by a jury.

The job of an Assistant Public Defender is a morally rewarding one. You deal with real-life situations that are often interesting, challenging and fast-paced. You put in long hours for little pay. You have to deal with Assistant State Attorneys who think your clients are scum, judges who care little for your clients' rights, and clients who sometimes verbally abuse you. If you can handle all that, at the end of the day you will feel that you have truly helped another human being. You have to be prepared to fight the good fight.

Would you choose to defend indigent clients? Why or why not?

FYI: Stun Belts

In about 30 states, potentially disruptive defendants may have a stun belt strapped to their waist instead of being shackled. If they become violent or try to escape during court proceedings, a deputy can push a remote-control button that will deliver an 8-second charge of 50,000 volts and 4 milliamps of electricity to the defendants' kidneys. The jolt of electricity will likely knock them to the floor, incapacitate them, and cause them to writhe in pain. They may also lose control of their bladders and bowels. Apparently, the fear of being shocked is enough to keep defendants in line. Nationally, between about 1991 and 2002, the belt has been strapped on 62,000 defendants and has been activated only 34 times.

SOURCE: Susan Clary, "Stunning: Remote-Control Belts Keep Peace in Courts," *The Orlando Sentinel,* December 1, 2001, p. H6.

subpoena A written order issued by a court that requires a person to appear at a certain time and place to give testimony. It can also require that documents and objects be made available for examination by the court.

process. In *Twining* v. *New Jersey* (1908), for example, the Supreme Court held that "due process requires . . . that there shall be notice and opportunity for hearing given the parties. . . . [T]hese two fundamental conditions . . . seem to be universally prescribed in all systems of law established by civilized countries." The reason for the right is to prevent the practice, common in some countries, of holding suspects indefinitely without telling them why they are being held.

RIGHT TO CONFRONT OPPOSING WITNESSES The Sixth Amendment right to confront opposing witnesses was extended to trials in state courts in 1965, in the case of *Pointer* v. *Texas.* In essence, it means that defendants have a right to be present during their trials (otherwise, they could not confront opposing witnesses) and to cross-examine witnesses against them. However, the right to be present during the trial may be forfeited by a defendant's disruptive behavior. Thus, if a defendant continues to scream, use profanity, or refuse to sit quietly after being warned by the judge, the judge may have the defendant removed from the trial (see *Illinois* v. *Allen,* 1970).

RIGHT TO COMPULSORY PROCESS FOR OBTAINING FAVORABLE WITNESSES This right ensures a defendant the use of the subpoena power of the court to compel the testimony of any witnesses who may have information useful to the defense. A **subpoena** is a written order issued by a court that requires a person to appear at a certain time and place to give testimony. It can also require that documents and objects be made available for examination by the court. Even though the right to compulsory process for obtaining favorable witnesses was already applicable in many states because of its inclusion in state constitutions and laws, the Supreme Court officially extended it to state trials in 1967, in the case of *Washington* v. *Texas.*

RIGHT TO COUNSEL The Sixth Amendment right to privately retained and paid-for counsel has existed in federal courts since the ratification of the Bill of Rights. Criminal defendants in state courts did not gain the right until 1954. In the case of *Chandler* v. *Fretag,* the Supreme Court held that the right to a privately retained lawyer is "unqualified," that is, as long as a criminal defendant (or suspect) can afford to hire an attorney, he or she has the right to be represented by that attorney, not only at trial, but at any stage of the criminal justice process. But what if a criminal defendant were indigent, lacking the funds to hire an attorney? It was not until 1938, in the case of *Johnson* v. *Zerbst,* that the Supreme Court first extended the Sixth Amendment right to court-appointed counsel to indigent defendants facing felony charges in federal trials. Another 25 years passed before the right to court-appointed counsel was extended to indigent defendants facing felony charges in state courts. That right was granted in the famous case of *Gideon* v. *Wainwright* (1963). In 1972, in the case of *Argersinger* v. *Hamlin,* the Court extended the Sixth Amendment right to court-appointed counsel to defendants in misdemeanor trials in which a sentence to jail might result. Thus, as a result of those decisions, no person may be imprisoned for any offense, whether classified as petty, misdemeanor, or felony, unless he or she is represented by counsel. If the person cannot afford to hire an attorney, then the court is required to appoint one. However, if there is no possibility of incarceration, then a defendant has no right to state-furnished counsel (see *Scott* v. *Illinois,* 1979). Later, in *Alabama* v. *Shelton* (2002), the Court added that indigents have a right to court-appointed counsel even when a defendant is given "a suspended sentence that may 'end up in the actual deprivation of a person's liberty'."

In other Supreme Court decisions, the Sixth Amendment right to counsel has been extended to indigents at additional *critical stages* (described in Chapter 8 and elsewhere in this book) and other circumstances in the administration of justice. Those include (by date of Supreme Court decision):

1. Arraignment, under most circumstances (*Hamilton* v. *Alabama,* 1961).
2. The plea bargaining process (*Carnley* v. *Cochran,* 1962).
3. Initial appearances where defendants may be compelled to make decisions that may later be formally used against them (*White* v. *Maryland,* 1963).
4. Interrogations after formal charges (*Massiah* v. *United States,* 1964).
5. Post-charge police lineups (*Gilbert* v. *California,* 1967).
6. Sentencing (*Mempa* v. *Rhay,* 1967).
7. Preliminary hearings (*Coleman* v. *Alabama,* 1970).
8. A psychiatric examination used by the prosecution to show that a murder defendant remains dangerous and should receive the death penalty (*Estelle* v. *Smith,* 1981).

To date, the Court has not extended the Sixth Amendment right to counsel to preindictment lineups, booking, grand jury investigations, or appeals after the first one.

The Sixth Amendment not only guarantees the right to counsel in the areas to which it has been extended, it also guarantees the right to the effective "assistance of counsel." However, it was not until 1984, in the case of *Strickland* v. *Washington,* that the Supreme Court first established standards to define "ineffective assistance of counsel." The Court ruled that two facts must be proved to show that counsel was ineffective: (1) that counsel's performance was "deficient," meaning that counsel was not a "reasonably competent attorney" or that his or her performance was below the standard commonly expected, and (2) that the deficiencies in the attorney's performance were prejudicial to the defense, meaning that there is a "reasonable probability that, but for the counsel's unprofessional errors, the result of the proceeding would have been different." In other words, not only must it be shown that an attorney was incompetent, it must also be shown that there is a reasonable probability that the incompetence led to the final result. Thus, if the defendant were clearly guilty of the crime with which he or she was charged, it would most likely be impossible to win a claim of "ineffective assistance of counsel."

Finally, the right to counsel may be waived, but only if the waiver is made knowingly, intelligently, and voluntarily. Thus, the Sixth Amendment has also been interpreted to mean that defendants have the right to represent themselves, that is, to conduct the defense *pro se* (see *Faretta* v. *California,* 1975). However, if defendants choose to represent themselves, they cannot claim later, on appeal, that their defense suffered from ineffective assistance of counsel.

FYI — Right to Counsel

The Supreme Court extended the right to court-appointed counsel to indigents in death penalty cases in *Powell* v. *Alabama* (1932). The right, however, was extended only to indigents who were "incapable adequately of making [their] own defense because of ignorance, feeble-mindedness, illiteracy or the like." Moreover, the Court's decision in *Powell* was based on the Fourteenth Amendment right to due process and not on the Sixth Amendment right to counsel.

THE EIGHTH AMENDMENT

The Eighth Amendment reads as follows:

> Excessive bail shall not be required, nor excessive fines imposed, nor cruel and unusual punishments inflicted.

Protection Against Excessive Bail and Fines The Eighth Amendment protection against excessive bail and fines is the second Bill of Rights guarantee dealing directly with criminal justice that has not been extended to the states. (The first is the right to a grand jury indictment in felony cases.) However, there is a good possibility that the protection against excessive bail will be incorporated and made applicable to state-level criminal cases when the issue is finally brought before the Supreme Court.

In any event, it is important to note that the Eighth Amendment to the Constitution does not require that bail be granted to all suspects or defendants, only that the amount of bail not be excessive. What constitutes excessive bail is determined by several factors, including the nature and circumstances of the offense, the weight of evidence against the suspect or defendant, the character of the suspect or defendant, the suspect or defendant's ties to the community, and the ability of the suspect or defendant to pay bail. The subject of bail will be discussed more fully in Chapter 8.

The Eighth Amendment also prohibits excessive fines. What is excessive depends on the seriousness of the crime. For example, in a conviction for illegal possession of a small amount of marijuana, a defendant's having to forfeit his or her home might be considered an excessive fine.

Protection Against Cruel and Unusual Punishments The final prohibition of the Eighth Amendment is against "cruel and unusual punishments." That prohibition was extended to trials in state courts in 1962, in *Robinson* v. *California*. Generally, discussions of this issue involve the practice of capital punishment, or the death penalty, which will be discussed in detail in Chapter 9. Here we will provide only a brief history of the definition of cruel and unusual punishments.

FYI

Bills of Attainder

The Constitution—in Article 1, Sections 9.3 and 10.1— prohibits bills of attainder. Under English common law, these legal documents stripped convicted offenders of their citizenship and allowed the Crown to confiscate all of their property. They also extended to offenders' families, who were judged "attainted" and could not inherit the offender's property. Recent civil forfeitures of property in drug violations seem to circumvent the constitutional prohibition. In some cases, property has been confiscated even though the suspect was never arrested or convicted of a crime.

For approximately 120 years after the adoption of the Bill of Rights, the Supreme Court employed a fixed, historical meaning for "cruel and unusual punishments." In other words, the Court interpreted the concept's meaning in light of the practices that were authorized and were in use at the time the Eighth Amendment was adopted (1791). Thus, only the most barbarous punishments and tortures were prohibited. Capital punishment itself was not prohibited, because there was explicit reference to it in the Fifth Amendment and it was in use when the Eighth Amendment was adopted.

The Court, in *Wilkerson* v. *Utah* (1878), provided examples of punishments that were prohibited by the Eighth Amendment because they involved "torture" or "unnecessary cruelty." They included punishments in which the criminal "was emboweled alive, beheaded, and quartered." In another case, *In re Kemmler* (1890), the Court expanded the meaning of cruel and unusual punishments to include punishments that "involve torture or lingering death . . . something more than the mere extinguishment of life." The Court also provided some examples of punishments that would be prohibited under that standard: "burning at the stake, crucifixion, breaking on the wheel, or the like."

In 1910, in the noncapital case of *Weems* v. *United States*, the Supreme Court abandoned its fixed, historical definition of cruel and unusual punishments and created a new one. Weems was a U.S. government official in the Philippines who was convicted of making two false accounting entries, amounting to 616 pesos.[16] He was sentenced to 15 years of hard labor and was forced to wear chains on his ankles and wrists. After completing his sentence, he was to be under surveillance for life, and he was to lose his voting rights as well. Weems argued that his punishment was disproportionate to his crime, and, therefore, cruel and unusual.

The Court agreed with Weems and, breaking with tradition, held "(1) that the meaning of the Eighth Amendment is not restricted to the intent of the Framers, (2) that the Eighth Amendment bars punishments that are excessive, and (3) that what is excessive is not fixed in time but changes with evolving social conditions." Thus, the Court no longer interpreted the concept of cruel

During the Inquisition, heretics were subjected to fire torture on the wheel. *Do you consider this cruel and unusual punishment in violation of the Eighth Amendment? Why or why not?*

and unusual punishments in the context of punishments in use when the Eighth Amendment was adopted. Instead, it chose to interpret the concept in the context of "evolving social conditions."

The Court further clarified its position nearly 50 years later, in another noncapital case, *Trop* v. *Dulles* (1958). As punishment for desertion during World War II, Trop was stripped of his U.S. citizenship. In reviewing the case on appeal, the Court ruled that the punishment was cruel and unusual because it was an affront to basic human dignity. Noting that the "dignity of man" was "the basic concept underlying the Eighth Amendment," the Court held that Trop's punishment exceeded "the limits of civilized standards." Referring to the earlier *Weems* case, the Court emphasized that "the limits of civilized standards . . . draws its meaning from the evolving standards of decency that mark the progress of a maturing society." Those "evolving standards of decency" are, in turn, determined by "objective indicators, such as the enactments of legislatures as expressions of 'the will of the people,' the decisions of juries, and the subjective moral judgments of members of the Supreme Court itself." In short, it appears that a punishment enacted by a legislature and imposed by a judge or jury will *not* be considered cruel and unusual, as long as the U.S. Supreme Court determines that (1) it is not grossly disproportionate to the magnitude of the crime, (2) it has been imposed for the same offense in other jurisdictions, and (3) it has been imposed for other offenses in the same jurisdiction (see *Solem* v. *Helm,* 1983; *Harmelin* v. *Michigan,* 1991; *Ewing* v. *California,* 2003; *Lockyer* v. *Andrade,* 2003).

THINKING CRITICALLY

1. Which of the amendments within the Bill of Rights do you think are the most protective of the rights of the accused? Why?
2. Why is the Bill of Rights subject to interpretation by the Supreme Court?

Protecting the Accused From Miscarriages of Justice

The legal system of the United States is unique in the world in the number of procedural rights that it provides people suspected or accused of crimes. The primary reason for procedural rights is to protect innocent people, as much as possible, from being arrested, charged, convicted, or punished for crimes they did not commit. One of the basic tenets of our legal system is that a person is considered innocent until proven guilty. However, even with arguably the most highly developed system of due-process rights in the world, people

CAREERS IN CRIMINAL JUSTICE

Paralegal

My name is Renée Daniel and I have an Associate of Applied Science Degree in Paralegal Studies from State Technical Institute at Memphis now called Southwest Tennessee Community College. Currently I am a senior pursuing a Bachelor of Arts Degree in Criminology and Criminal Justice from the University of Memphis. After graduating from State Tech, I was chosen by the chairperson and associate professors of the Paralegal Studies Department to be the recipient of a scholarship to pursue my Bachelors Degree and also work as a paralegal in the Shelby County Jail Law Library.

Prior to graduating from State Tech, I interned as a paralegal for the Shelby County Division of Corrections. As a paralegal intern I had the opportunity to learn the various duties and responsibilities a paralegal encounters. During my internship I was able to review and answer inmate disciplinary appeals, draft documents, review discovery for litigation, and research case law and brief cases.

As a paralegal in the County Jail I assist inmates/pretrial detainees with legal research. Inmates are scheduled to report to the law library through program services in groups. My job involves assisting them in locating case law, statutes, sentencing guidelines, information pertaining to criminal procedure, pretrial motions and petitions. I act as a liaison between the inmates and the courts by verifying all outgoing legal calls. I have contacted attorneys, probation officers, parole officers, court clerks, and on some occasions, Immigration and Naturalization Services. My duties as a paralegal not only involve assisting inmates with preparation for trial/appeal but also managing and organizing the law library. I log and inventory all legal material that comes to the library and supervise the placement and rotation of books and supplements. In order to adequately assist the inmates with significant research, the legal material must be monitored at all times. I consult frequently with practicing attorneys regarding relevant substantive and procedural legal material that would help those who are preparing for trial or filing motions. If we do not already have the material, I submit a request to the director of programs to order necessary items.

The aspect I like most about my job is the opportunity I have to utilize the skills I have learned in the Paralegal Studies and Criminology and Criminal Justice programs. I enjoy legal research and applying legal principles to substantive criminal law. My job allows me to see firsthand how the criminal justice system works from arrest to sentencing and appeal. What I like least about my job are the imperfections that exist in the criminal justice system. I often see several inmates who have been detained in the jail for a year or more before they are indicted. There have been cases where inmates have served their entire sentences in the jail by the time they go to trial. Another aspect about my job that I like least is the destructive behavior that some inmates display by destroying legal books. Once these books are destroyed it is difficult to have them replaced.

Paralegals work in several areas of the legal system with knowledge of substantive and procedural law. A paralegal has the opportunity to work in numerous areas of the law. I would advise paralegal students to intern first to gain insight and experience in the area of law in which they wish to work.

What type of growth opportunities would you expect as a paralegal?

continue to be victims of miscarriages of justice. For example, attorney Barry Scheck and his colleagues report, "Of the first eighteen thousand results [of DNA tests] at the FBI and other crime laboratories, at least five thousand prime suspects were excluded *before* their cases were tried." In other words, more than 25 percent of the prime suspects were wrongly accused. Scheck is a co-founder of the Innocence Project at the Cardoza School of Law in New York City.[17]

Unfortunately, there is no official record of miscarriages of justice, so it is impossible to determine precisely how many actually occur each year. Nevertheless, in an effort to provide some idea of the extent of the problem, a study was conducted of wrongful convictions—miscarriages of justice at just one of the stages in the administration of justice.[18] In the study, *wrongful convictions* were defined as

> cases in which a person [is] convicted of a felony but later . . . found innocent beyond a reasonable doubt, generally due to a confession by the actual offender, evidence that had been available but was not sufficiently used at the time of conviction, new evidence that was not previously available, and other factors.

The conclusions of the study were based on the findings of a survey. All attorneys general in the United States and its territories were surveyed, and in Ohio, all presiding judges of common pleas courts, all county prosecutors, all county public defenders, all county sheriffs, and the chiefs of police of seven major cities were also surveyed. The authors of the study conservatively estimated that approximately 0.5 percent of all felony convictions are in error. In other words, of every 1,000 persons convicted of felonies in the United States, about 5 are probably innocent. The authors believe that the frequency of error is probably higher in less serious felony and misdemeanor cases.

Although an error rate of 0.5 percent may not seem high, consider that in 2001, a typical year, approximately 13.7 million people were arrested in the United States.[19] Assuming conservatively that 50 percent of all people arrested are convicted[20]—about 6.85 million convictions in 2001—then approximately 34,250 people were probably wrongfully convicted!

Eyewitness misidentification is the most important factor contributing to wrongful convictions. For example, a study of DNA exonerations by the Innocence Project found that more than 80 percent of wrongful convictions could be attributed, at least in part, to eyewitness or victim misidentification.[21] The second and third most important contributing factors are police and prosecutorial errors, respectively. They accounted for nearly 65 percent of the DNA exonerations in the Innocence Project study.[22] Overzealous police officers and prosecutors, convinced that a suspect or defendant is guilty, may prompt witnesses, suggest to witnesses what may have occurred at the time of the crime, conceal or fabricate evidence, or even commit perjury. Another factor contributing to wrongful convictions is guilty pleas made "voluntarily" by innocent defendants. Innocent defendants are more likely to plead guilty to crimes they did not commit when they are faced with multiple charges and when the probability of severe punishment is great. They are also more likely to plead guilty to crimes they did not commit when they are mentally incompetent.

When the charge is a less serious one, innocent people who are unable to post bail sometimes admit guilt to be released from jail immediately. For many people, release from jail is more important than a minor criminal record. Besides, it is often difficult to prove one's innocence. (Remember that in the United States the prosecution is required to prove, beyond a reasonable doubt, that defendants are guilty. Defendants are not required to prove their innocence.)

FYI: Death Row Reversals

From 1973 through April 2003, 107 inmates have been freed from death row because of problems or errors in the legal process. Common reasons for reversals include (1) key witnesses lied or recanted their testimony, (2) police overlooked or withheld important evidence, (3) DNA testing showed someone else committed the crime, (4) the defense lawyer was incompetent or negligent, and (5) prosecutors withheld exculpatory evidence from the defense.

SOURCE: The Death Penalty Information Center, www.deathpenaltyinfo.org; Jonathan Alter, "The Death Penalty on Trial," *Newsweek*, June 12, 2000.

Problems faced by innocent people wrongly accused of crimes include inability to establish an alibi; misidentification by witnesses who swear they saw the defendant commit the crime; a lawyer who lacks the skill, time, or resources to mount a good defense; and a lawyer who is unconvinced of the defendant's innocence. Inadequate legal representation is one of the most important factors in wrongful convictions in death penalty cases.[23] It accounted for nearly a third of the wrongful convictions discovered in the Innocence Project study.[24]

Other factors contributing to wrongful convictions are community pressures, especially in interracial and rape cases; false accusations; knowledge of a defendant's prior criminal record; judicial errors, bias, or neglect of duty; errors made by medical examiners and forensic experts; and errors in criminal record keeping and computerized information systems.[25] In short, numerous factors can cause wrongful convictions. And remember, the foregoing discussion addresses only wrongful convictions; it does not consider wrongful arrests or other miscarriages of justice.

Despite such miscarriages of justice, many people still resent the provision of procedural safeguards to criminal suspects. The accusation is frequently made that procedural rights protect criminals and penalize victims—that many criminals escape conviction and punishment because of procedural technicalities. For example, a driving force behind the good faith and inevitable-discovery exceptions was the belief that a substantial number of criminal offenders escaped punishment because of the exclusionary rule. The available evidence, however, does not support the belief. One of the most thorough studies of the effect of the exclusionary rule was conducted by the National Institute of Justice (NIJ).[26] The NIJ study examined felony cases in California between 1976 and 1979—a period during which the American public was becoming increasingly alarmed about the problem of crime and especially about what was perceived as the practice of allowing a substantial number of criminals to escape punishment because of legal

CJ ONLINE

NIJ

Learn more about the National Institute of Justice and its various research findings by accessing their website at **www.ojp.usdoj.gov/nij.** *Why is it important to have research organizations like the NIJ?*

Roberto Miranda is one of more than 100 inmates since 1973 who has been released from death row because of evidence of his innocence. Mr. Miranda spent 14 years on Nevada's death row. *What, if anything, does the state of Nevada owe Mr. Miranda?*

technicalities. The study found that only a tiny fraction (fewer than 0.5 percent) of the felony cases reaching the courts were dismissed because of the exclusionary rule. It is important to emphasize that the study examined only the cases that reached the courts. It excluded cases that prosecutors elected not to pursue to trial because they assumed that the exclusionary rule would make the cases impossible to win. However, studies show that although there is some variation between jurisdictions, fewer than 1 percent of cases overall are dropped by prosecutors before trial because of search and seizure problems.[27] Interestingly, 71.5 percent of the California cases affected by the exclusionary rule involved drug charges. The problem in most of the drug cases was that in the absence of complaining witnesses, overaggressive law enforcement officers had to engage in illegal behavior to obtain evidence.

A study of the effect of the exclusionary rule at the federal level was conducted by the General Accounting Office (GAO).[28] The GAO examined 2,804 cases handled by 38 different U.S. attorneys in July and August of 1978. The GAO found results similar to those found by the NIJ in California. In only 1.3 percent of the nearly 3,000 cases was evidence excluded in the federal courts. Again, it is important to emphasize that the study included only cases that went to trial. However, as noted earlier, evidence shows that, overall, fewer than 1 percent of cases are dropped by prosecutors before trial because of search and seizure problems. It is important to understand, moreover, that having evidence excluded from trial does not necessarily mean that a case is impossible to win and that the defendant will escape punishment. A defendant may still be convicted on the basis of evidence that was not illegally obtained.

The *Miranda* mandates, like the exclusionary rule, are also viewed by many people as legal technicalities that allow guilty criminals to escape punishment. That view is fortified by Supreme Court Justice Byron White's dissent in *Miranda:* "In some unknown number of cases the rule will return a killer, a rapist or other criminal to the streets." No doubt, Justice White's warning is true, but the evidence suggests that only a very small percentage of cases are lost as a result of illegal confessions. In one large survey, for example, fewer than 1 percent of all cases were thrown out because of confessions illegally obtained.[29]

In another study of decisions made by the Indiana Court of Appeals or the Indiana Supreme Court from November 6, 1980, through August 1, 1986, the researchers found that in only 12 of 2,354 cases (0.51 percent) was a conviction overturned because of the failure of the police to correctly implement the *Miranda* safeguards.[30] In only 213 of the 2,354 cases (9 percent) was a claim even made about improper interrogation procedures by the police, and in 201 of those 213 cases, the conviction was affirmed by the appellate court, resulting in a reversal rate of 5.6 percent for the cases raising a *Miranda* question.

The authors of that study speculated on possible reasons for the low rate of successful appeals. One was that the police routinely comply with the *Miranda* decision. In fact, most police support *Miranda* and the other reforms because it makes them appear more professional. The second possible reason was that the police are able to solve most cases without having to question suspects. Studies show that the *Miranda* warnings rarely stop suspects from confessing anyway. Nearly 80 percent of suspects waive their Miranda rights. As many as 75 percent of suspects attempt to clear themselves in the eyes of the police and end up incriminating themselves instead; other suspects simply do not understand that they have a right to remain silent.[31] Third, the police are able to evade *Miranda* by using more-sophisticated strategies,

FYI: Reforming the Criminal Justice System

The authors of *Actual Innocence* suggest the following reforms: *DNA testing:* Allow postconviction DNA testing nationwide. Test DNA on unsolved crimes where evidence exists. *Witness IDs:* Independent, trained examiner who does not know the suspect should conduct lineups and photo IDs to ensure investigators don't influence witnesses. Videotape lineups, photo spreads, and other identification processes to ensure neutrality. *Confessions:* Videotape all interrogations. *Informants:* Committee of prosecutors should screen all informant testimony before permission to use at trial. All deals between prosecutors and informants must be in writing. *Forensics:* Crime labs should function and be funded separately from police, prosecution, or defense. Strengthen accreditation programs for labs, establish postgraduate forensic programs at universities. *Police, prosecutors:* Establish disciplinary committees to deal with legal misconduct by police and prosecution. *Defense attorneys:* Increase fees to attract competent lawyers. Public defenders' pay should equal prosecutors' pay. *Wrongful convictions:* Establish innocence commissions to investigate wrongful convictions. Create and fund innocence projects at law schools to represent clients. Provide compensation to those who were clearly wrongly convicted. Moratorium on death penalty.

SOURCE: Jim Dwyer, Peter Neufeld, and Barry Scheck, *Actual Innocence: Five Days to Execution and Other Dispatches from the Wrongly Convicted* (New York: Doubleday, 2000).

Myth	Fact
Many criminals escape punishment because of the Supreme Court's decision in *Miranda* v. *Arizona.*	Very few criminals escape punishment because of that decision.

such as skillfully suggesting that suspects volunteer confessions or casually talking with suspects in the back of squad cars.[32] And, fourth, prosecutors, knowing that they cannot win cases involving illegal interrogations, screen them out before trial or settle them through alternative means, such as plea bargaining. However, as with the exclusionary rule, fewer than 1 percent of cases overall are dismissed or handled in other ways by prosecutors because of *Miranda*.[33] In short, the available evidence suggests that the effects of both *Miranda* and the exclusionary rule in Fourth and Fifth Amendment contexts have been minor.[34]

THINKING CRITICALLY

1. Do you think miscarriages of justice are on the increase? Decrease? Why or why not?
2. Do you think that anything can be done to combat miscarriages of justice?

SUMMARY

1. Distinguish between criminal law and civil law

There are two general types of law practiced in the United States—criminal and civil. Criminal law is a formal means of social control that involves the use of rules that are interpreted, and are enforceable, by the courts of a political community. The violation of a criminal law is a crime and is considered an offense against the state. Civil law is a means of resolving conflicts between individuals. The violation of a civil law is a tort—an injury, damage, or wrongful act—and is considered a private matter between individuals.

2. Distinguish between substantive law and procedural law

There are two types of criminal law—substantive and procedural. Substantive law defines criminal offenses and their penalties. Procedural law specifies the ways in which substantive laws are administered. Procedural law is concerned with due process of law—the rights of people suspected of or charged with crimes.

3. List five features of "good" criminal laws

Ideally, "good" criminal laws should possess five features: (1) politicality, (2) specificity, (3) regularity, (4) uniformity, and (5) penal sanction.

4. Explain why criminal law is a political phenomenon

Criminal law is the result of a political process in which rules are created by human beings to prohibit or regulate the behavior of other human beings. Nothing is criminal in and of itself; only the response of the state makes it so.

5. Summarize the origins of American Criminal Law

The criminal law of the United States is, for the most part, derived from the laws of England and is the product of constitutions and legislative bodies, common law, and, if provided for by statute, some administrative or regulatory agency rules and decisions.

6. Describe the procedural rights in the Fourth Amendment

The Fourth Amendment protects persons from unreasonable searches and seizures (including arrests). Under most circumstances, it requires that a judge issue a search warrant authorizing law officers to search for and seize evidence of criminal activity, but the warrant can be issued only when there is probable cause. *In 1914, the Supreme Court adopted the* exclusionary rule, *which barred evidence seized illegally from being used in a criminal trial; in 1961, the rule was made applicable to the states. Subsequent Supreme Court decisions have narrowed the application of the exclusionary rule. The Fourth Amendment also protects persons from warrantless searches and seizures in places where they have a legitimate right to expect privacy. The protection, however, does not extend to every place where a person has a legitimate right to be. The Court has permitted stopping and searching an automobile when there is probable cause to believe the car is carrying something illegal.*

7. Describe the procedural rights in the Fifth Amendment

The Fifth Amendment provides many procedural protections, the most important of which is the protection against compelled self-incrimination. This protection was extended to most police custodial interrogations in the 1966 case of Miranda *v.* Arizona. *According to* Miranda, *police custody is threatening and confessions obtained during custody can be admitted into evidence only if suspects have been (1) advised of their constitutional right to remain silent, (2) warned that what they say can be used against them in a trial, (3) informed of the right to have an attorney, and (4) told that if they cannot afford an attorney, one will be appointed for them prior to questioning, if they so desire. Suspects may waive their* Miranda *rights, but only if the waiver is made knowingly, intelligently, and voluntarily. Other due process rights in the Fifth Amendment are the right to a grand jury indictment in felony cases (in federal court) and protection against double jeopardy.*

8. Describe the procedural rights in the Sixth Amendment

Many due process rights are provided by the Sixth Amendment: the right to a speedy and public trial, the right to an impartial jury of the state and district where the crime occurred, the right to be informed of the nature and cause of the accusation, the right to confront opposing witnesses, the right to compulsory process for obtaining favorable witnesses, and the right to counsel. In the 1963 case of Gideon *v.* Wainwright, *the Supreme Court extended the right to court-appointed counsel to any poor state defendant charged with a felony.*

9. Describe the procedural rights in the Eighth Amendment

The Eighth Amendment protects against "cruel and unusual punishments." The Supreme Court has rarely ruled on this provision, generally approving a punishment as long as it has been enacted by a legislature, it has been imposed by a judge or jury, and the Court determines that (1) it is not grossly disproportionate to the magnitude of the crime, (2) it has been imposed for the same offense in other jurisdictions, and (3) it has been imposed for other offenses in the same jurisdiction. The Eighth Amendment also protects against excessive bail and fines, but those protections have not been made binding on state courts.

10. Explain why procedural rights are important to those accused of crimes

The primary reason for procedural rights is to protect innocent people, as much as possible, from being arrested, charged, convicted, or punished for crimes they did not commit. However, even with the most highly developed system of procedural, or due process, rights in the world, criminal defendants in the United States still face miscarriages of justice.

KEY TERMS

criminal law, p. 105
penal code, p. 105
tort, p. 105
civil law, p. 105
substantive law, p. 105
procedural law, p. 105
due process of law, p. 105
politicality, p. 106
specificity, p. 106
regularity, p. 106
uniformity, p. 106
penal sanction, p. 107
precedent, p. 111
***stare decisis*, p. 111**
searches, p. 115
seizures, p. 115
warrant, p. 115
arrest, p. 115
contraband, p. 116
mere suspicion, p. 120
reasonable suspicion, p. 120
frisking, p. 120
probable cause, p. 121
preponderance of evidence, p. 121
clear and convincing evidence, p. 121
beyond a reasonable doubt, p. 121
exclusionary rule, p. 122
double jeopardy, p. 125
self-incrimination, p. 126
confession, p. 126
doctrine of fundamental fairness, p. 126
venue, p. 128
subpoena, p. 130

REVIEW QUESTIONS

1. How does one know whether a particular offense is a *crime* or a *tort*?
2. How did the institution of the *eyre* contribute to the development of American criminal law?
3. What is the importance of the Magna Carta for American criminal law?
4. To what jurisdiction do federal and state criminal statutes (and local ordinances) apply?
5. What is *stare decisis*?
6. Why did it take nearly 100 years after the ratification of the Fourteenth Amendment before suspects charged with crimes at the state level were afforded most of the same due process protections as people charged with crimes at the federal level?
7. What are *searches* and *seizures*?
8. What is an *arrest*?
9. What two conclusions must be supported by substantial and trustworthy evidence before either a search warrant or an arrest warrant is issued? (The two conclusions are different for each type of warrant.)
10. In *Chimel* v. *California* (1969), what limitations did the U.S. Supreme Court place on searches incident to an arrest?
11. What is *probable cause*?
12. Today, what is the principal purpose of the exclusionary rule?
13. What are the major provisions of the PATRIOT Act?
14. To what critical stages in the administration of justice has the Sixth Amendment right to counsel been extended, and to what critical stages has it not been extended?
15. What two conditions must be met to show that counsel was ineffective?
16. What are some of the factors that contribute to wrongful convictions?
17. Do many criminals escape conviction and punishment because of procedural technicalities, such as the exclusionary rule or the *Miranda* mandates?

IN THE FIELD

1. **Make a Law** By yourself or as part of a group, create a law. Choose a behavior that is currently not against the law in your community, and write a statute to prohibit it. Make sure that all five features of "good" criminal laws are included. (If this is a group exercise, decide by majority vote any issue for which there is not a consensus.) Critique the outcome.

2. **Exclusionary Rule** Make an oral or written evaluation of the good faith and inevitable-discovery exceptions to the exclusionary rule. Has the Supreme Court gone too far in modifying the exclusionary rule? Defend your answer.

ON THE NET

1. **Historical Perspectives** "The Timetable of World Legal History" found at www.wwlia.org/hist.htm provides brief descriptions of important historical legal developments. (This website also provides links to other sources of legal information.) Choose among the available topics (for instance, the actual text of the Magna Carta), and write a summary of the information you find.

2. **Supreme Court Decisions** Access the Supreme Court website at www.supremecourtus.gov. Then select subjects of interest (especially Fourth, Fifth, Sixth, and Eighth Amendment cases), and read the Supreme Court's most recent decisions.

CRITICAL THINKING EXERCISES

1. **Megan's Law** The sexual assault and murder of 7-year-old Megan Kanka in New Jersey on October 31, 1994, struck a national nerve. Megan was assaulted and killed by a neighbor, Jesse Timmendequas, who had twice been convicted of similar sex offenses and was on parole. In response to the crime and public uproar, the state of New Jersey enacted "Megan's Law." The law, as originally passed, required sex offenders, upon their release from prison, to register with New Jersey law enforcement authorities, who are to notify the public about their release. The public was to be provided with the offender's name; a recent photograph; a physical description; a list of the offenses for which he or she was convicted; the offender's current address and place of employment or school; and the offender's automobile license plate number. The Supreme Court recently upheld Megan's Law.

   Currently, all 50 states and the federal government have Megan's laws that require sex offenders released from prison to register with local law enforcement authorities. Many of those laws, like New Jersey's, require that law enforcement officials use the information to notify schools and day-care centers and, in some cases, the sex offender's neighbors. In 1997, California enacted a law allowing citizens access to a CD-ROM with detailed information on 64,000 sex offenders living in California who had committed a broad range of sex crimes since 1944. Megan's laws are not uniform across states. For example, not all states require active community notification; many of them (including the U.S. government) only make the information available to the public.

   In 1996, President Clinton signed into law the Pam Lyncher Sexual Offender Tracking and Identification Act, which called for a national registry of sex offenders, to be completed by the end of 1998. The national registry allows state officials to submit queries, such as the name of a job applicant at a day-care center, and to determine whether the applicant is a registered sex offender in any of the participating states.

a. Is Megan's Law a good law? (Consider the ideal characteristics of the criminal law.)
b. Is Megan's Law fair to sex offenders who have served their prison sentences (that is, "paid their debt to society")?
c. What rights does a sex offender have after being released from prison?
d. What rights does a community have to protect itself from known sex offenders who have been released from prison?
e. When the rights of an individual and the rights of a community conflict, whose rights should take precedence? Why?

2. **Surveillance Cameras** In January 1998, police in Cincinnati, Ohio, began using a special video camera to monitor activity on a "crime-ridden street corner." The camera, which cost $11,000, rotates, enabling it to observe activity in a 1,000-foot radius. It records 24 hours a day, and it can read a license plate number from more than a block away. To protect privacy, policy requires that all tapes be erased after 96 hours if they show no criminal activity. Residents of the area claim that the camera's presence has cleaned up the area by, among other things, scaring away drug dealers. Critics worry about government spying on residents. The city council is considering putting cameras in other parts of the city.
a. Should the city council have surveillance cameras installed in other parts of the city? Why or why not?
b. What legal or procedural issues should be considered before making a decision?

PART TWO

LAW ENFORCEMENT

CHAPTER FIVE

History and Structure of American Law Enforcement

CHAPTER SIX

Policing: Roles, Styles, and Functions

CHAPTER SEVEN

Policing America: Issues and Ethics

HISTORY · OF
CIVIC · SERVICES
IN THE · CITY · OF · NEW · YORK
POLICE
No. I
Stadt Huys
1658
On October 4, 1658 a paid Rattle Watch of eight men, to do the duty from 9 o'clock at night until morning drum beat, was established, the duty being imposed upon each of the citizens by turns, and each householder was taxed 15 stivers for its support.
Thief
Felon
USA
WORK
WPA
The Rattle Watch

History and Structure of American Law Enforcement

CHAPTER FIVE

Chapter Outline

Chapter Objectives

After completing this chapter, you should be able to:

1. Briefly describe the jurisdictional limitations of American law enforcement.
2. Trace the English origins of American law enforcement.
3. Discuss the early development of American law enforcement.
4. Describe the major developments that have occurred in policing in America.
5. Describe the structure of American law enforcement.
6. Explain the relationship between the FBI and the Department of Homeland Security.
7. Discuss the development and growth of private security in the United States.

Crime Story

On January 30, 2003, Richard Reid, commonly known as the "shoe bomber," was sentenced to life in prison on three counts: one for attempted use of a weapon of mass destruction against U.S. nationals outside the United States, and two for interference with a flight crew by using a dangerous weapon. He was also ordered to pay a $2 million fine sentenced to consecutive 20-year terms on four other counts, and given a 30-year term on an eighth count. After learning his fate, Reid was dragged from the courtroom yelling at the judge and proclaiming his allegiance to Osama bin Laden.

The harsh sentences levied against Reid resulted from his actions on December 22, 2001, when he tried to detonate explosive material concealed in his shoes while onboard an American Airlines Boeing 767 airliner carrying 185 passengers from Paris to Miami. The incident began around 11 A.M. EST when a passenger onboard the plane alerted a flight attendant that Reid was trying to set fire to his shoes. Flight attendants and passengers managed to subdue Reid, who was later strapped to a chair with belts after being sedated by two doctors who were onboard the plane. One flight attendant was later taken to the hospital for treatment after being bitten by Reid during the melee.

The airliner landed safely at Boston's Logan Airport after being escorted to the ground by two F-15 fighter jets, which had intercepted the aircraft after being alerted to the emergency by the North American Aerospace Defense Command (NORAD). The tactical response by NORAD to secure the commercial airliner was a result of heightened security measures to prevent additional terrorist attacks in the aftermath of September 11, 2001.

The hijacking of commercial airliners by terrorists is not a new phenomenon. What is new is the demonstrated ability of terrorists to convert a passenger-filled airliner into a guided missile and weapon of mass destruction. Also new is the capability of terrorists to use such a weapon on American soil. Unfortunately, there are likely to be more people like Richard Reid, and the United States is preparing to deal with them.

Prior to 9/11, the prevention of terrorism was primarily the job of the FBI. That has changed. Preventing terrorism, now the number one priority of the FBI, has also become a major focus of law enforcement agencies at all levels of government. Chapter 5 discusses the history and structure of American law enforcement, including the new Department of Homeland Security. Questions abound. At the federal level, will the FBI be able to work effectively with Department of Homeland Security agencies? Can the different levels of law enforcement effectively coordinate their efforts to prevent terrorism? Are local law enforcement agencies capable of dealing effectively with terrorist threats? Will the new focus on terrorism divert law enforcement's attention and resources form traditional criminal activity? Can our safety be increased without violating our freedoms? Answers to those questions and others are likely to define the role of law enforcement during the early part of the twenty-first century.

The Limited Authority of American Law Enforcement

The United States has almost 18,000 public law enforcement agencies at the federal, state, and local levels of government. The vast majority of those agencies, however, are local, serving municipalities, townships, villages, and counties. The authority of each agency—whether it is the FBI, a state highway patrol, or a county sheriff's department—is carefully limited by law. The territory within which an agency may operate is also restricted. The city police, for example, may not patrol or answer calls for service outside the city's boundaries unless cooperative pacts have been developed. **Jurisdiction,** which is defined as a specific geographical area, also means the right or authority of a justice agency to act in regard to a particular subject matter, territory, or person. It includes the laws a particular police agency is permitted to enforce and the duties it is allowed to perform. The Oklahoma Highway Patrol, for example, has investigative and enforcement responsibilities only in traffic matters, while the Kentucky State Police have a broader jurisdiction that includes the authority to conduct criminal investigations throughout the state. Each of the 69 federal law enforcement agencies, large and small, has a specific jurisdiction, although one criminal event may involve crimes that give several federal agencies concurrent jurisdiction. For example, in a bank robbery, if mail of any sort is taken, both the Postal Inspection Service and the FBI are likely to investigate the case.

jurisdiction The right or authority of a justice agency to act in regard to a particular subject matter, territory, or person.

Beyond the statutes that create and direct law enforcement agencies, the procedural law derived from U.S. Supreme Court decisions also imposes limitations on the authority of those agencies. Giving arrested suspects the familiar *Miranda* warnings before questioning is a good example of the Court's role in limiting the authority of the police. In addition, police civilian review boards, departmental policies and procedures, and civil liability suits against officers who have abused their authority curtail the power of the police in the United States.

The only police contact most citizens have is in a traffic situation in a local or state jurisdiction. *Should citizens have more contact with the police in non–law enforcement situations? Why or why not?*

Thus, there is a great difference between law enforcement with limited authority, operating under the rule of law in a democratic nation, and law enforcement in countries where the law is by decree and the police are simply a tool of those in power. Even in comparison with other democratic nations of the world, however, the United States has remarkably more police agencies that operate under far more restrictions on their authority. To understand the origin of those unique qualities of law enforcement in the United States, it is necessary to look first at the history of law enforcement in England, the nation that provided the model for most of American criminal justice.

THINKING CRITICALLY

Why do you think it is important that law enforcement agencies have limited authority?

English Roots

If you are the victim of a crime, you might expect that a uniformed patrol officer will respond quickly to your call and that a plainclothes detective will soon follow up on the investigation. Because there are thousands of police departments in local communities across the nation, you might also take for granted that the police handling your case are paid public servants employed by your city or county. Such was not always the case in the United States—nor in England, where the basic concepts of American law enforcement and criminal justice originated. The criminal justice system in England took hundreds of years to develop, but eventually the idea arose of a locally controlled uniformed police force with follow-up plainclothes investigators.

THE TITHING SYSTEM

Before the twelfth century in England, justice was primarily a private matter based on revenge and retribution.[1] Victims of a crime had to pursue perpetrators without assistance from the king or his agents. Disputes were often settled by blood feuds, in which families would wage war on each other.

By the twelfth century, a system of group protection had begun to develop. Often referred to as the **tithing system** or the frankpledge system, it afforded some improvements over past practices. Ten families, or a *tithing,* were required to become a group and agree to follow the law, keep the peace in their areas, and bring law violators to justice. Over even larger areas, 10 tithings were grouped together to form a *hundred,* and one or several hundreds constituted a *shire,* which was similar to a modern American county. The shire was under the direction of the **shire reeve** (later called the *sheriff*), the forerunner of the American sheriff. The shire reeve received some assistance from elected constables at the town and village levels, who organized able-bodied citizens into **posses** to chase and apprehend offenders.[2] County law enforcement agencies in the United States still sometimes use posses to apprehend law violators.

tithing system A private self-help protection system in early medieval England, in which a group of 10 families, or a *tithing,* agreed to follow the law, keep the peace in their areas, and bring law violators to justice.

shire reeve In medieval England, the chief law enforcement officer in a territorial area called a *shire;* later called the *sheriff.*

posses Groups of able-bodied citizens of a community, called into service by a sheriff or constable to chase and apprehend offenders.

constable-watch system A system of protection in early England in which citizens, under the direction of a constable, or chief peacekeeper, were required to guard the city and to pursue criminals.

constable The peacekeeper in charge of protection in early English towns.

THE CONSTABLE-WATCH SYSTEM

The Statute of Winchester, passed in 1285, formalized the **constable-watch system** of protection. The statute provided for one man from each parish to be selected as **constable,** or chief peacekeeper. The statute further granted constables the power to draft citizens as watchmen and require them to guard the city at night. Watchmen were not paid for their efforts and, as a result, were often found sleeping or sitting in a pub rather than performing their duties. In addition, the statute required all male citizens between the ages of 15 and 60 to maintain weapons and to join in the *hue and cry,* meaning to come to the aid of the constable or the watchman when either called for help. If they did not come when called, the male citizens were subject to criminal penalties for aiding the offender. This system of community law enforcement lasted well into the 1700s.

Two features of this system are worthy of note. First, the people were the police, and second, the organization of the protection system was local. These two ideas were transported to the American colonies centuries later.

THE BOW STREET RUNNERS

In 1748, Henry Fielding, a London magistrate, founded a group of professional law enforcement agents to apprehend criminals and recover stolen property in the entertainment district of London, known as Bow Street Covent Garden. This publicly funded detective force, named the Bow Street Runners, was by far the most effective official law enforcement organization of its day. Efforts to duplicate it in other parts of London proved unsuccessful, but Fielding's work in organizing the first British detective force, and his writing addressing the shortcomings of the criminal justice system, had a great deal of influence. They helped pave the way for a more professional and better-organized response to the crime problems that were dramatically increasing in London by the end of the eighteenth century.[3]

FYI Henry Fielding

Henry Fielding, founder of the Bow Street Runners, is perhaps better known for his literary accomplishments. His most famous novel is *Tom Jones.*

THE LONDON METROPOLITAN POLICE

Because of the Industrial Revolution, urban populations in cities like London swelled with an influx of people from the countryside looking for work in factories. A major result of this social transformation was that England began experiencing increasing poverty, public disorder, and crime. There was no clear consensus about what to do. Several efforts to establish a central police

The London Metropolitan Police discover another victim of Jack the Ripper. *What do you suppose were some of the unique problems encountered by the first "bobbies" or "peelers"?*

TABLE 5.1 Robert Peel's Principles of Policing

1. The police must be stable, efficient, and organized along military lines.
2. The police must be under governmental control.
3. The absence of crime will best prove the efficiency of police.
4. The distribution of crime news is essential.
5. The deployment of police strength both by time and area is essential.
6. No quality is more indispensable to a policeman than a perfect command of temper; a quiet, determined manner has more effect than violent action.
7. Good appearance commands respect.
8. The securing and training of proper persons is at the root of efficiency.
9. Public security demands that every police officer be given a number.
10. Police headquarters should be centrally located and easily accessible to the people.
11. Policemen should be hired on a probationary basis.
12. Police records are necessary to the correct distribution of police strength.

force for London had been opposed by people who believed that police of any kind were a throwback to the absolute power formerly wielded by English kings. Parliament eventually responded, in 1829, with the London Metropolitan Police Act. It created a 1,000-officer police force with professional standards to replace the patchwork of community law enforcement systems then in use. Members of the London Police became known as *bobbies* or *peelers,* after Robert Peel, the British Home Secretary who had prodded Parliament to create the police force.

Peel's Principles of Policing A dozen standards proposed by Robert Peel, the author of the legislation resulting in the formation of the London Metropolitan Police Department. The standards are still applicable to today's law enforcement.

To ensure discipline, the London Police were organized according to military rank and structure and were under the command of two magistrates, who were later called commissioners. According to Peel, the main function of the police was to prevent crime, not by force but by preventive patrol of the community. Londoners, who resented such close scrutiny, did not at first welcome this police presence in the community. Eventually, though, the bobbies (the term was originally derogatory) showed that the police could have a positive effect on the quality of life in the community. Peel's military approach to policing, as well as some of his other principles, remain in effect today throughout the world. **Peel's Principles of Policing** are outlined in Table 5.1.[4]

THINKING CRITICALLY

Do you think any of the early English systems of law enforcement (e.g., tithing) could work today? Why or why not?

The Development of American Law Enforcement

The United States has more police departments than any other nation in the world. The major reason for this is that local control is highly regarded in the United States. Thus, like many other services, even small communities that can barely afford police service provide it locally. This practice is primarily responsible for the disparity in the quality of American police personnel and service. The struggle to improve American law enforcement began even before formal police departments came into existence.

EARLY AMERICAN LAW ENFORCEMENT

The chance for a better life, free of government intervention, was key in the decision of many colonists to cross the Atlantic and settle in the New World.

American colonists from England brought with them the constable-watch system with which they were familiar, if not completely satisfied. Boston established a night watch as early as 1634. Except for the military's intervention in major disturbances, the watch system, at least in the cities, was the means of preventing crime and apprehending criminals for the next two centuries. As in England, the people were the police. Citizens could pay for watch replacements, and often the worst of the lot ended up protecting the community. In fact, Boston and other cities frequently deployed the most elderly citizens and occasionally sentenced minor offenders to serve on the watch.[5] Later, in rural and southern areas of the country, the office of sheriff was established and the power of the posse was used to maintain order and apprehend offenders. In essence, two forms of protection began to evolve—the watch in the villages, towns, and cities and the sheriff in the rural areas, unincorporated areas, and counties. Communities in the North often had both systems.

LAW ENFORCEMENT IN THE CITIES

As had happened in England, the growth of the Industrial Revolution lured people away from the farms to cities. Large groups of newcomers, sometimes immigrants from other countries, settled near factories. Factory workers put in long days, often in unsafe and unhealthy working conditions. Some workers organized strikes, seeking better working conditions, but the strikes were quickly suppressed. As the populations of cities swelled, living conditions in some areas became overcrowded and unhealthy.

Major episodes of urban violence occurred in the first half of the nineteenth century because of the social and economic changes transforming American cities. Racial and ethnic tensions often reached a boiling point, resulting in mob disturbances that lasted for days. A particular source of trouble were the drinking establishments located throughout working-class districts of cities. Regular heavy drinking led to fights, brawls, and even full-scale riots

Unlike London, which organized its police force in 1829, American citizens resisted the formation of police departments, relying instead on the constable-watch system, whose members lit streetlights, patrolled the streets to maintain order, and arrested some suspicious people. Constables often had daytime duties, which included investigating health hazards, carrying out orders of the court, clearing the streets of debris, and apprehending criminals against whom complaints had been filed. Neither the night watch nor the constables tried to prevent or discover crime, nor did they wear any kind of uniform. This weak protection system was unable to contain the increasing level of lawlessness.

> **FYI — The "Leatherheads"**
>
> In Dutch-influenced New York in the seventeenth century, the first paid officers on the night watch were known as *leatherheads* because they wore leather helmets similar in appearance to the helmets worn by today's firefighters. The leatherheads were not known for their attention to duty and often spent entirely too much of their watch schedule inside.
>
> SOURCE: Carl Sifakis, "Leatherheads: First New York Police," *The Encyclopedia of American Crimes* (New York: Smithmark Publishers, Inc., 1992).

MUNICIPAL POLICE FORCES In 1844, New York City combined its day and night watches to form the first paid, unified police force in the United States. Close ties developed between the police and local political leaders. As with the first police in London, citizens were suspicious of the constant presence of police officers in their neighborhoods. Also, citizens had little respect for the New York police because they thought they were political hacks, appointed by local officials who wanted to control the police for their own gain. During the next several years, the struggle to control the police in New York built to a fever pitch.[6]

In 1853, the New York state legislature formed the Municipal Police Department, but within 4 years that force was so corrupt from taking bribes to overlook crime that the legislature decided to abolish it. It was replaced by the Metropolitan Police, which was administered by five commissioners appointed by the governor. The commissioners then selected one superintendent. Each

A street arrest in 1878 Manhattan, New York. *What problems did the police of this era encounter?*

commissioner was to oversee the others, as well as the superintendent, and keep them all honest. The new structure was an improvement, in the minds of the legislature, that would prevent corruption in the top level of the department. But when the Metropolitan Police Board called on Mayor Fernando Wood to abolish the Municipal Police, he refused. Even after New York's highest court upheld a decision to disband the Municipals, the mayor refused. The Metropolitans even tried to arrest Mayor Wood, but that failed attempt resulted in a pitched battle between the two police forces. When the National Guard was called in, Mayor Wood submitted to arrest but was immediately released on bail.

During the summer of 1857, the two police forces often fought over whether to arrest certain criminals. A particularly troubling practice was one police force's releasing from custody the criminals arrested by the other force. Lawbreakers operated freely during the dispute between the two police forces. Criminal gangs had a free hand to commit robberies and burglaries during most of that summer. The public became enraged over this neglect of duty and the increased danger on the streets of New York City. Only when another court order upheld the decision to disband the Municipal Police did Mayor Wood finally comply.

Following the course charted by New York City, other large cities in the United States soon established their own police departments. In 1855, Boston combined its day and night watches to form a city police department. By the end of the decade, police departments had been formed in many major cities east of the Mississippi. The duties of the officers did not vary substantially from the duties of those who had served on the watch. After the Civil War, however, peace officers began to take on the trappings of today's police. They began to wear uniforms, carry nightsticks, and even carry firearms, although many citizens resisted giving this much authority to the police.

Tangle of Politics and Policing Until the 1920s in most American cities, party politics prevented the development of professional police departments. Local political leaders understood that controlling the police was a means of maintaining their own political power and of allowing criminal friends and political allies to violate the law with impunity. In fact, in some cities, the police were clearly extensions of the local party machine, which attempted to dominate all activity in a community. If local politicians gave police applicants a job, it became the hired officers' job to get out the vote so that the politicians could keep their positions. The system was so corrupt in some cities that police officers bought their jobs, their promotions, and their special assignments. In collaboration with local politicians, but often on their own, the police were more than willing to ignore violations of the law if the lawbreakers gave them money, valuables, or privileges.

A Brief History of Blacks in Policing For most of American history blacks who have wanted to be police officers have faced blatant discrimination and have generally been denied the opportunity.[7] The first black police officers in the United States were "free men of color." They were hired around

By the early 1900s, most American cities had organized, uniformed police forces similar to the police force of Newport, Rhode Island, pictured circa 1910. *How do current police officers differ from those depicted in the photo?*

1805 to serve as members of the New Orleans city watch system. They were hired primarily because other people did not want the job. In addition to serving on the watch, they were responsible for catching runaway slaves and generally policing black slaves in New Orleans.

By 1830, policing had become more important in New Orleans, and the "free men of color" lost their jobs on the city police force to others who wanted them. Not until after the Civil War were black Americans allowed to be police officers again. During Reconstruction, black Americans were elected to political office and hired as police officers throughout the South. This did not last long. By 1877, the backlash to Reconstruction drove black Americans and their white Republican allies from elective offices, and black police officers throughout the South lost their jobs. By 1890, most southern cities had all-white police departments. The few black police officers in the southern cities that retained them generally could not arrest white people and were limited to patrolling only areas and communities where other black Americans lived. By 1910, there were fewer than 600 black police officers in the entire United States, and most of them were employed in northern cities.

It was not until the 1940s and 1950s that black police officers began to be hired again in most southern cities. They were hired primarily to patrol black communities, to prevent crime, and to improve race relations. Still, few black Americans ever rose to command positions in their departments. Indeed, prior to the 1950s, only two black Americans had ever been promoted to the command position of captain: Octave Rey of New Orleans and John Scott of Chicago. Both served relatively short tenures in the position: Rey from 1868 to 1877 and Scott from 1940 to 1946.

The plantation slave patrols have been called "the first distinctively American police system." *Have any elements of the slave patrols influenced contemporary American policing? If yes, what are they?*

LAW ENFORCEMENT IN THE STATES AND ON THE FRONTIER

The development of law enforcement on the state level and in the frontier territories was often peculiar to the individual location. Without large population centers that required the control of disorderly crowds, law enforcement was more likely to respond to specific situations—for example, by rounding up cattle rustlers or capturing escaped slaves. Still, out of this kind of limited law enforcement activity, the basic organizational structure of police units with broader responsibilities was born.

Southern Slave Patrols In the South, the earliest form of policing was the plantation **slave patrols.**[8] They have been called "the first distinctively American police system."[9] The slave patrols were created to enforce the infamous slave codes, the first of which was enacted by the South Carolina legislature in 1712. Eventually all the Southern colonies enacted slave codes. The slave codes protected the slaveholders' property rights in human beings, while holding slaves responsible for their crimes and other acts that were not crimes if committed by free persons. Under some slave codes, enslaved people could not hold meetings, leave the plantation without permission from the master, travel without a pass, learn to read and write, carry a firearm, trade, or gamble. Both the slave codes and the slave patrols were created in part because of a fear of bloody slave revolts, such as had already occurred in Virginia and other parts of the South.

slave patrols The earliest form of policing in the South. They were a product of the slave codes.

Generally consisting of three men on horseback who covered a beat of 15 square miles, a slave patrol was responsible for catching runaway slaves, preventing slave uprisings, and maintaining discipline among the slaves. To maintain discipline, the patrols often whipped and terrorized black slaves who were caught after dark without passes. The slave patrols also helped enforce the laws prohibiting literacy, trade, and gambling among slaves. Although the law required that all white males perform patrol services, the large plantation owners usually hired poor, landless whites to substitute for them. The slave patrols lasted until the end of the Civil War, in 1865. After the Civil War, the Ku Klux Klan served the purpose of controlling blacks just as the slave patrols had before the Civil War.

FYI Nat Turner Rebellion

Perhaps the most publicized slave revolt was the Nat Turner Rebellion of 1831 in Virginia. Turner and five other slaves killed Joseph Travis, Turner's owner, and his family. Approximately 70 more rebels joined Turner, whose immediate plan was to capture the county seat, where munitions were stored. Turner was unsuccessful in his plan, but during the siege, he and his rebels killed 57 whites. Turner was tried, convicted, and hanged, along with 16 other rebels. In response to the revolt, white mobs lynched nearly 200 blacks, most of whom were innocent.

SOURCE: John Duff and Peter Mitchell, *The Nat Turner Rebellion: The Historical Event and the Modern Controversy* (New York: Harper & Row, 1971).

Frontier Law Enforcement In the remote and unpopulated areas of the nation, and particularly on the expanding frontier, justice was often in the hands of the people in a more direct way. Vigilantism was often the only way that people could maintain order and defend themselves against renegades and thugs.[10] Even when formal law enforcement procedures were provided by the sheriff or a marshal, courts in many communities were held only once or twice a year, leaving many cases unresolved. This idea of self-protection remains very popular in the South and the West, where firearms laws in many states permit people to carry loaded weapons in a vehicle, or even on their persons if they have completed a qualification and licensing procedure.

State Police Agencies Self-protection did not prove sufficient as populations and their accompanying problems increased. As early as 1823, mounted militia units in Texas protected American settlers throughout that territory.

The Texas Rangers, organized in the early 1800s to fight Native Americans, patrol the Mexican border, and track down rustlers, were the first form of state police. *Why and how do you think the Rangers have endured for so long?*

Called *rangers,* these mounted militia fought Native Americans and Mexican bandits. The Texas Rangers were officially formed in 1835, and the organization remains in existence today as an elite and effective unit of the Texas Department of Public Safety.[11]

The inefficiency and unwillingness of some sheriffs and constables to control crime, along with an emerging crime problem that exceeded the local community's ability to deal with it, prompted other states to form state law enforcement agencies. In 1905, Pennsylvania established the first modern state law enforcement organization with the authority to enforce the law statewide, an authority that made it unpopular in some communities where enforcement of state laws had been decidedly lax.[12] The advent of the automobile and the addition of miles of state highways extended the authority of state police agencies. Some form of state law enforcement agency existed in every state by the 1930s.

CJ ONLINE

Texas Rangers

To learn more about the history of the Texas Rangers, visit the Texas Ranger Hall of Fame and Museum website at **www.texasranger.org/Index.htm.** *Why do you think the Texas Rangers have elite status?*

PROFESSIONALISM AND REFORM

You will recall that the people themselves were once the police, as they served on the watch. Being an adult citizen was about the only qualification. No training was required, and it was common practice for citizens who did not want to serve to hire replacements, sometimes hiring sentenced offenders. Because of the few services and the little order the watch provided, not much else seems to have been required. Even when organized police forces were developed in the 1840s and 1850s in the United States, qualifications for the job mattered little beyond the right political connections or the ability to purchase one's position outright.

Not until the latter part of the nineteenth century did qualifications for the position of police officer begin to evolve. In the 1880s, Cincinnati posted two qualifications to be a police officer.[13] First, an applicant had to be a person of high moral character—an improvement over earlier times. Three citizens had to vouch for the applicant's character at a city council meeting. If deemed acceptable by the council, the applicant was immediately taken to a gymnasium and tested for the second qualification, foot speed.

Both Cincinnati and New York began police academies in the 1880s, but the curriculum was meager and recruits were not required to pass any examinations to prove their competence. The lack of adequate standards and training for police officers was recognized as a major stumbling block to improved policing. A group of reformers within policing allied themselves with the Progressives, a movement for political, social, and economic change. Among the reformers was August Vollmer, who became chief of police of Berkeley, California, in 1909. During his tenure as chief from 1909 to 1932, Vollmer attempted to create a professional model of policing. With Vollmer and a succession of internal reformers who followed, a new era of professional policing began.

Vollmer and his followers advocated training and education as two of the key ingredients of professionalism in policing. He also believed strongly that the police should stay out of politics and that politics should stay out of policing. Vollmer believed that the major function of the police was fighting crime, and he saw great promise in professionalizing law enforcement by emphasizing that role.[14] He began to hire college graduates for the Berkeley Police Department, and he held college classes on police administration.

Within a few decades, this professional model, sometimes called the reform model, had taken root in police departments across the country. To eliminate political influences, gain control of officers, and establish crime-fighting priorities, departments made major changes in organization and operation. Those changes included the following:

- Narrowing of the police function from social service and the maintenance of order to law enforcement only.
- Centralization of authority, with the power of precinct captains and commanders checked.
- Creation of specialized, centrally based crime-fighting units, as for burglary.
- A shift from neighborhood foot patrol to motorized patrol.
- Implementation of patrol allocation systems based on such variables as crime rates, calls for service, and response times.
- Reliance on technology, such as police radios, to both control and aid the policing function.
- Recruitment of police officers through psychological screening and civil service testing.
- Specific training in law enforcement techniques.

CONFLICTING ROLES

Throughout their history, Americans have never been sure precisely what role they want their police officers to play. Much of the ambivalence has to do with American heritage, which makes many Americans suspicious of government authority. At one time or another, local police have acted as peacekeepers, social workers, crime fighters, and public servants, completing any task that was requested. Often, the police have been asked to take on all those roles simultaneously.

For most of the nineteenth century, distrust of government was so strong and the need to maintain order in the cities so critical that the police operated almost exclusively as peacekeepers and social service agents, with little or no concern for enforcing the law beyond what was absolutely necessary to maintain tranquility.[15] In this role, the police in many American cities administered the laws that provided for public relief and support of the poor. They

Brutal tactics by some police officers to suppress civil rights protests during the 1960s led to calls for improved standards of police conduct and training. *Have new standards of conduct and training ended brutal police tactics?*

fed the hungry and housed the homeless at the request of the politicians who controlled them. Later, other social service agents, such as social workers, began to replace them, and a reform effort developed to remove policing from the direct control of corrupt politicians. As a result, the police began to focus on crime-fighting as early as the 1920s. Having the police enforce the law fairly and objectively was thought to be a major way of professionalizing law enforcement. This approach also fit the professional model of policing advocated by Vollmer and other reformers.

By the end of the 1960s, strong doubts about the role of the police emerged again. The role they had been playing encouraged them to ferret out crime and criminals through such practices as aggressive patrol, undercover operations, and electronic surveillance. In some neighborhoods, the police came to be viewed as armies of occupation. Some confrontations between police and citizens resulted in violence. The civil rights movement produced a series of demonstrations and civil disorders in more than 100 cities across America, beginning in 1964. As in the labor struggles of the late nineteenth and early twentieth centuries, the police were called in to restore order. Some police officers suppressed the demonstrations with brutal tactics. The anti–Vietnam War movement during the 1960s sparked protests all over the country, especially on college campuses. Again, police officers were called upon to maintain and sometimes to restore order. Thousands of students were sprayed with tear gas, and some were beaten and even killed by police.

By the end of the 1960s, it was clear that police standards and training had to be improved. To many observers, fast response and proactive patrols did not seem effective in reducing crime, and officers increasingly were seeing their work world through the windshield of a cruiser. The likelihood of establishing rapport with the people they served was remote as officers dashed from one crime scene to another.

Four blue-ribbon commissions studied the police in the United States. The names of the four commissions and the years in which they released their reports are as follows:

- 1967 National Advisory Commission on Civil Disorders
- 1967 President's Commission on Law Enforcement and the Administration of Justice
- 1973 National Advisory Commission on Criminal Justice Standards and Goals
- 1973 American Bar Association's Standards Relating to Urban Police Function

All four reports made the same major recommendations: They pointed out the critical role police officers play in American society, called for careful selection of law enforcement officers, and recommended extensive and continuous training. The reports also recommended better police management and supervision, as well as internal and external methods of maintaining integrity in police departments.

In an attempt to follow many of the specific recommendations of the reform commissions' reports, police selection became an expensive and elaborate process. It was designed to identify candidates who had the qualities to be effective law enforcement officers: integrity, intelligence, interpersonal skills, mental stability, adequate physical strength, and agility. Attempts were also made to eliminate discriminatory employment practices that had prevented minorities and women from entering and advancing in law enforcement. Finally, it became more common for police officers to attend college, and some police agencies began to set a minimum number of college credit hours as an employment qualification.

Myth

Random patrol, as opposed to directed patrol, reduces crime. It is important to have police out in patrol cars, scouting neighborhoods and business districts.

Fact

There is not much value to such random patrols other than perhaps helping people feel safe. They would probably feel even safer if the police were walking a beat. However, little research supports the idea that officers who ride around for 3 to 5 hours of their shifts are repressing crime. Even being available to respond to calls from the public is not a strong argument for such patrols. Only a small percentage of reported crimes and other incidents require a rapid response.

COMMUNITY POLICING

By the 1970s, research began to show that a rapid response to crime does not necessarily lead to more arrests and that having more police officers using methods made popular under the professional or reform model does not significantly reduce crime.[16] What was emerging was the view that unattended disorderly behavior in neighborhoods—such as unruly groups of youths, prostitution, vandalism, drunk and disorderly vagrants, and aggressive street people—is a signal to more serious criminals that residents do not care what goes on in their community and that the criminals can move in and operate with impunity.

The 1970s and 1980s saw some experimentation with community- and neighborhood-based policing projects.[17] Those projects got mixed results, and many were abandoned because of high costs, administrative neglect, and citizen apathy. However, higher crime rates, continued community deterioration, and recognition of the failure to control crime caused law enforcement to again question the role it was playing. The enforcer role still was not working well enough. It appeared senseless simply to respond to calls for service and arrive at scenes of crime and disorder time and time again without resolving the problems or having any lasting effect on the lives of the residents of the community. Out of this failure and frustration came the contemporary concept of **community policing.**

community policing A contemporary approach to policing that actively involves the community in a working partnership to control and reduce crime.

Under a community policing philosophy, the people of a community and the police form a lasting partnership, in which they jointly approach the problems of maintaining order, providing services, and fighting crime.[18] If the police show they care about the minor problems associated with community disorder, two positive changes are likely to occur: citizens will develop better relations with the police as they turn to them for solutions to the disorder, and criminals will see that residents and the police have a commitment to keeping all crime out of the neighborhood. Once again, the emphasis has shifted from fighting crime to keeping peace and delivering social services. The goal is eradicating the causes of crime in a community, not simply responding to symptoms.

In the early 1990s, many communities across the nation began implementing community policing strategies. Community policing called for a shift from incident-based crime fighting to a problem-oriented approach, in which police would be prepared to handle a broad range of troublesome situations in a city's neighborhoods. There was greater emphasis on foot patrol so that officers could come to know and be known by the residents of a neighborhood. Those citizens would then be more willing to help the police identify and solve problems in the neighborhood. Many other aspects of community policing will be discussed more fully in Chapter 6.

THINKING CRITICALLY

1. Which of the major changes in the organization and operation of police departments listed on page 156 do you think brought about the most significant change? Why?
2. What do you think are the key benefits of community policing? Why?

The Structure of American Law Enforcement

Describing American law enforcement and its structure is especially difficult today because of its ongoing restructuring and transformation, from community policing at the local level to the new Department of Homeland Security at the federal level and increasing privatization at all levels. It is also difficult to describe because law enforcement agencies are so diverse. To begin with, you must decide which law enforcement agency you are talking about. For example, Oklahoma Highway Patrol officers cruise the highways and back roads, enforcing traffic laws, investigating accidents, and assisting motorists over seemingly endless miles of paved and unpaved routes. They do not ordinarily investigate criminal violations unless the violations are on state property. In contrast, a sheriff and three deputies in rural Warren County, Georgia, conduct criminal investigations, serve subpoenas, and investigate accidents. In the towns of Astoria, Homer, and Newman, Illinois, only one employee, the chief of police, works in each department, and that person is responsible for all law enforcement, public order, and service duties. The 60 sworn law enforcement officers at the University of Texas in Austin are also a part of American law enforcement.[19]

Altogether, tens of thousands of law enforcement officers at the federal, state, county, and municipal levels protect life and property and serve their respective publics. They are employed by government, private enterprise, and quasi-governmental entities. Their responsibilities are specific and sometimes unique to the kind of organization that employs them. Examples of these organizations are airports, transit authorities, hospitals, and parks.

At the state level, there are highway patrols, bureaus of investigation, park rangers, watercraft officers, and other law enforcement agencies and personnel with limited jurisdictions. Colleges and universities employ police officers, and some of those forces are comparable to many medium-sized police departments in the United States.

At the federal level, there are about 69 law enforcement agencies if all of the small agencies with very specific jurisdictions are included. The Federal Bureau of Investigation (FBI), the U.S. Secret Service, and the Drug Enforcement Admin-

CJ ONLINE

Secret Service
To learn more about the U.S. Secret Service, visit their website at **www.treas.gov/usss.** *Based on what you have learned from the website, do you think that you would be interested in a career with the Secret Service? Why or why not?*

Before entering some schools, students have their bags checked every day by special law enforcement officers with limited jurisdiction. *Is this practice necessary? Why or why not?*

istration (DEA) are three of the better-known agencies. The U.S. Marshals Service, the Bureau of Alcohol, Tobacco, and Firearms (ATF), and the Customs Service are other federal law enforcement agencies, as are the Internal Revenue Service's Criminal Investigation Division, the United States Postal Inspection Service, the Border Patrol, and several dozen other agencies. As of June 2000, federal law enforcement agencies employed more than 88,000 full-time personnel authorized to make arrests and carry firearms.[20]

As the aforementioned list of law enforcement agencies suggests, explaining the law enforcement mandate and its execution in the United States is difficult. The structure of American police services is different from those of other countries. Japan and many other nations have only one police department. The United States has almost 18,000 public law enforcement agencies, and probably more when all the special police jurisdictions in the public sector are counted—including game protection agencies, water conservancies, and mental health institutions. Figure 5.1 summarizes the various law enforcement agencies in the United States.

You have already learned that law enforcement in America is fragmented, locally controlled, and limited in authority; to that, you can also add the terms *structurally* and *functionally different*. Virtually no two police agencies in America are structured alike or function in the same way. Police officers themselves are young and old; well-trained and ill-prepared; educated and uninformed; full-time and part-time; rural, urban, and suburban; generalists and specialists; paid and volunteer; and public and private. These differences lead to the following generalizations about law enforcement in the United States:

FIGURE 5.1 Public Law Enforcement Agencies in the United States

The United States has almost 18,000 public law enforcement agencies.

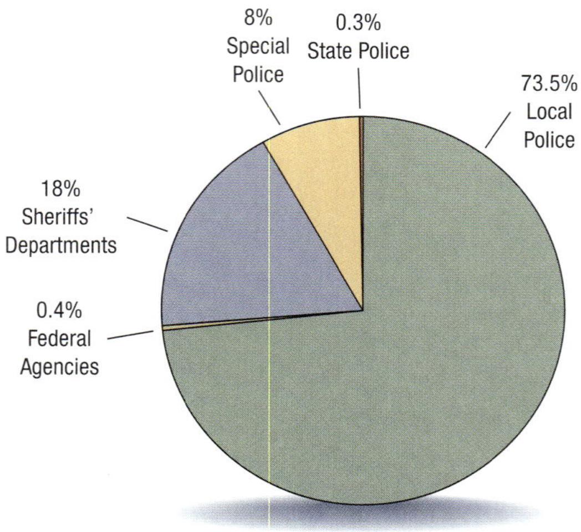

Does not include 623 county constable offices in Texas.

SOURCE: Calculated from material in Brian A. Reaves and Matthew J. Hickman, *Census of State and Local Law Enforcement Agencies, 2000,* U.S. Department of Justice, *Bureau of Justice Statistics Bulletin* (Washington DC: GPO, October 2002) and Brian A. Reaves and Timothy C. Hart, *Federal Law Enforcement Officers, 2000,* U.S. Department of Justice, *Bureau of Justice Statistics Bulletin* (Washington DC: GPO, July 2001).

1. The quality of police services varies greatly among states and localities across the nation.
2. There is no consensus on professional standards for police personnel, equipment, and practices.
3. Expenditures for police services vary greatly among communities.
4. Obtaining police services from the appropriate agency is often confusing for crime victims and other clients.

LOCAL POLICING AND ITS DUTIES

If a person knows a law enforcement agent at all, it is probably a local police officer. The officer may have given the person a traffic ticket or investigated an automobile accident. The officer may have conducted a crime prevention survey. Children meet local police officers through Drug Abuse Resistance Education (D.A.R.E.) in public or private schools. Almost everyone has seen the beat cop drive by in a patrol car. Some people have reported thefts or burglaries, but it is doubtful that even they understand what local police officers in America really do, besides what they see on television and in movies.

Municipal Police Departments Municipal police departments come in all sizes, but most of them are small in the number of officers employed. The overwhelming majority of police departments in America employ fewer than 50 sworn officers. Figure 5.2 shows the number of sworn officers in local

> **FYI: Drug Enforcement**
>
> In 2000, 15 percent of local police departments had officers assigned full-time to a special unit for drug enforcement, with 13,600 officers so assigned nationwide. Approximately 20 percent of departments had officers assigned to a multiagency drug task force, with a total of 5,800 officers assigned full-time nationwide.
>
> Source: Matthew J. Hickman and Brian A. Reaves, *Local Police Departments, 2000* (Washington, DC: Bureau of Justice Statistics, 2003), p. iii.

FIGURE 5.2 Number of Sworn Personnel in Local Departments, 2000

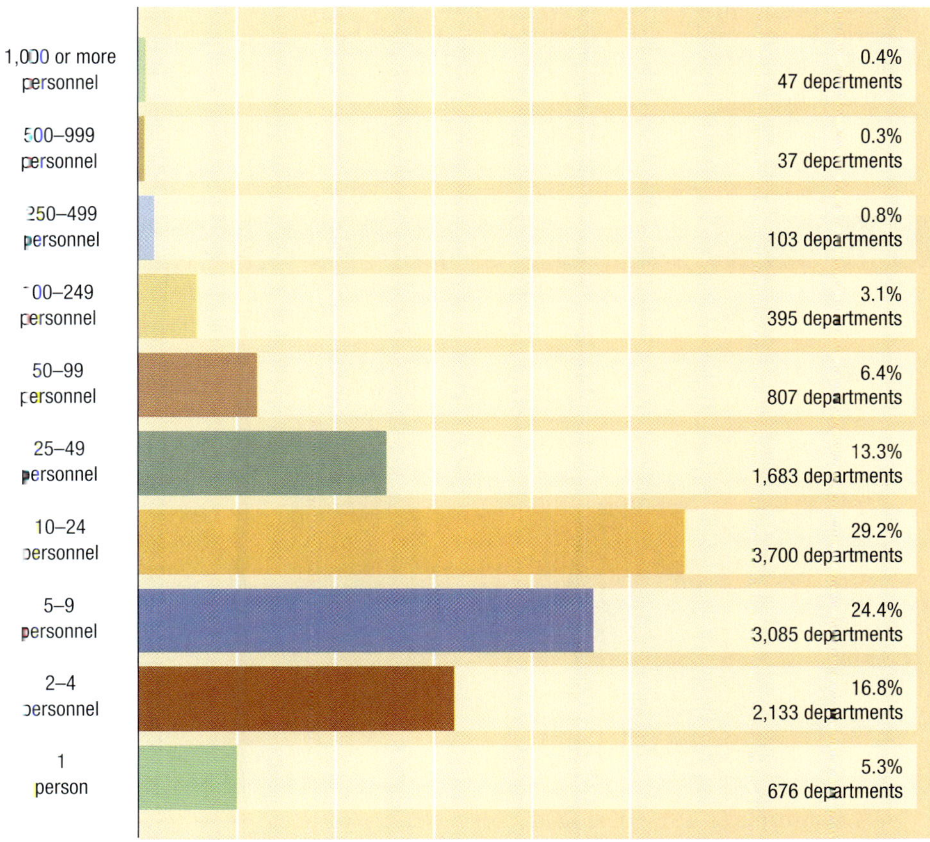

Source: Matthew J. Hickman and Brian A. Reaves, *Local Police Departments, 2000,* U.S. Department of Justice, Bureau of Justice Statistics (Washington, DC: GPO, January, 2003).

FYI First Policewomen

The first woman to have full police power (1905) was Lola Baldwin of Portland, Oregon. The first uniformed policewoman was Alice Stebbins Wells, who was hired by the Los Angeles Police Department in 1910. By 1916, 16 other police departments had hired policewomen as a result of the success in Los Angeles.

SOURCE: Roy Robert, John Crank, and Jack Kuykendall, *Police and Society* (Los Angeles, CA: Roxbury Publishing Company, 1999), pp. 432–33.

police agencies in the United States. As shown in Figure 5.2, nearly one-half of all local police departments in the United States employ fewer than 10 officers, and fewer than 1 percent employ more than 1,000 sworn personnel.

What are some of the characteristics of the sworn personnel who occupy the ranks of municipal police agencies in the United States? Most police officers are white males. In 2000, 70.9 percent of full-time sworn officers were white men, down from 78.4 percent in 1997. The larger the police agency the more likely it is to employ minority officers. Women represented about 10 percent of all sworn officers in the nation's local police departments in 2000. Figure 5.3 provides a breakdown of police employment in local agencies by gender, race, and ethnicity.

A high school diploma or higher educational achievement was required by 83 percent of the local police departments of the nation in 2000. Fifteen percent of local police departments in 2000 required some college courses (up from 6 percent in 1990), but only 8 percent of the agencies required recruits to have a minimum of two years of college. Just 1 percent required new recruits to have a 4-year college degree.[21]

LOCAL POLICE DUTIES The local police are the workhorses of the law enforcement system in America. They have many duties and tasks that will never be included in police detective novels or in movies about law enforcement. Their duties have been categorized in several different ways. One general grouping lists these four categories of local police duties:

1. **Law enforcement**—examples are investigating a burglary, arresting a car thief, serving a warrant, or testifying in court.
2. **Order maintenance or peacekeeping**—examples are breaking up a fight, holding back a crowd at a sporting event, or intervening in a domestic dispute before it gets violent.
3. **Service**—examples are taking people to the hospital, escorting funeral processions, delivering mail for city officials, or chasing bats out of a caller's house.

FYI Policewomen

It took a long time for policewomen to gain the opportunity to perform the same roles and duties as their male counterparts. From the early 1900s until 1972, when the Equal Employment Opportunity Commission began to assist women police officers in obtaining equal employment status with male officers, policewomen were responsible for protection and crime prevention work with women and juveniles, particularly with girls. The Los Angeles Police Department created the City Mother's Bureau in 1914 and hired policewomen to work with delinquent and predelinquent children whose mothers did not want formal intervention by a law enforcement agency. Policewomen were also used to monitor, investigate, and punish young girls whose behavior flouted social and sexual conventions of the times.

FIGURE 5.3 Characteristics of Local Full-Time Police Officers

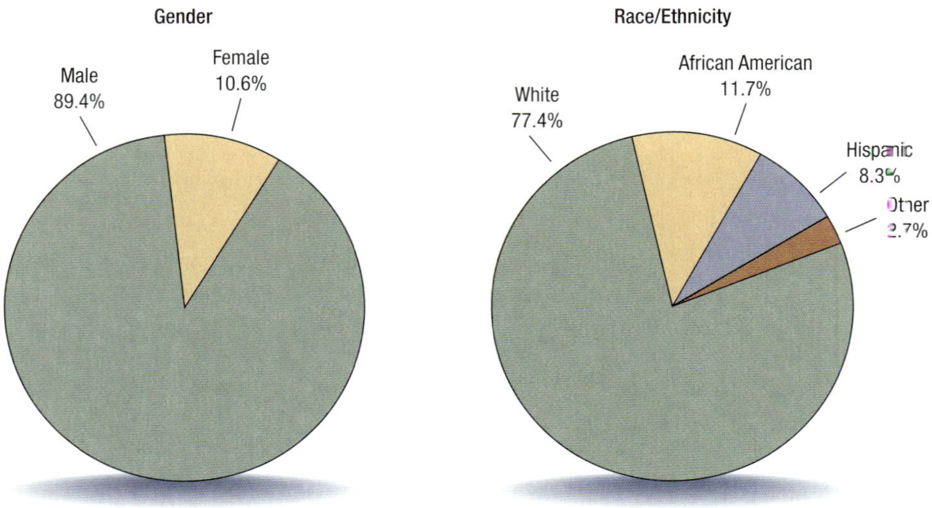

SOURCE: Matthew J. Hickman and Brian A. Reaves *Local Police Departments, 2000,* U.S. Department of Justice, Bureau of Justice Statistics (Washington, DC: GPO, January 2003).

4. **Information gathering**—examples are determining neighborhood reactions to a proposed liquor license in the community, investigating a missing child case, or investigating and reporting on a dangerous road condition.

Some police academies teach recruits the duties of a police officer through the use of the acronym *PEPPAS:*

P—Protect life and property (patrol a business district at night, keep citizens from a fire scene, or recover and return lost property).
E—Enforce the law (ensure traffic laws are obeyed, warn jaywalkers of the inherent danger, make out criminal complaints, or seize illegal weapons).
P—Prevent crime (give home security advice, patrol high crime areas, or work as a D.A.R.E. officer in schools).
P—Preserve the peace (disband disorderly groups, have a visible presence at sporting events, or intervene in neighbor conflicts).
A—Arrest violators (apprehend fleeing suspects, give citations to alcohol permit holders who sell to minors, or conduct drug raids).
S—Serve the public (give directions to travelers, deliver emergency messages, or administer first aid).

Myth	Fact
The police spend most of their time and resources apprehending law violators and combating crime.	Only about 10 percent of police time and resources are devoted to apprehending law violators and combating crime. Most of their time and resources are spent "keeping the peace," which means maintaining a police presence in the community, for example, by routine patrolling.

There are literally dozens of other duties that the police of a city, town, or village carry out, and much of the work falls into the category of helping out when

Local police departments, which make up the bulk of law enforcement agencies in America, are responsible for law enforcement, order maintenance, service, and information gathering. *How important is public relations for local police departments? Why?*

no one else seems to be available. Because the police are on duty 24 hours a day in nearly every community, they are often called on to perform services that have nothing to do with law enforcement. That round-the-clock availability also significantly affects the structure, work life, and activity of a police agency.

Organizational Structure How a police agency is structured depends on the size of the agency, the degree of specialization, the philosophy the leadership has chosen (such as community policing), the political context of the department (the form of municipal government), and the history and preferences of a particular community. Most medium- to large-staffed police agencies are subdivided into patrol, criminal investigation, traffic, juvenile, and technical and support services. Subspecialties include robbery, gangs, training, bombs, property, victims' services, jail, and mounted patrol.

The Dallas (Texas) Police Department, with 2,977 sworn officers and 556 nonsworn employees, is large, sophisticated, and very specialized. For example, it has a separate detective unit for each major category of crime. Evidence technicians collect and preserve evidence during the preliminary investigation of a crime. An entire contingent of officers is assigned to traffic regulation and enforcement duties. Bicycle patrol officers work the popular West End entertainment and restaurant section downtown. The Dallas police even have sworn officers who serve as crime analysts and collect, analyze, map, and report crime data to enable better prevention and repression of crime by means of scientific deployment of officers and other strategies. Figure 5.4 presents the organizational structure of the Dallas Police Department.

Most police agencies in the United States do not have or need elaborate organizational structures. Police officers on the beat are generalists, and when special circumstances arise, such as a homicide or a complex financial investigation, they can usually rely on state bureaus of investigation to assist them. Moreover, local cooperation pacts among departments in a particular region often provide for sharing resources and specialized assistance when needed.

The infrequent need for homicide investigation skills in communities under 30,000 people, for example, makes it impractical to train one or more officers in the methods of conducting a thorough death investigation. An officer so trained might have to wait an entire career to put into practice the acquired skills, and it is most likely that by the time they were needed, the officer would have forgotten them. The lack of a trained specialist for the infrequent complex investigation, however, is one of the major reasons criminal investigation services in small communities are not equal to those in larger police departments.

The question has been raised whether larger, regional police departments would be more efficient providers of police services, but as you have already discovered, policing in America is a local concern, and that is not likely to change.

The police are organized militarily with regard to accountability, discipline, rank, dress, and decorum. Many people believe that the military structure of a chain of command may be dysfunctional because police work is so varied. Some people believe that a military structure is best suited for situations where the objectives are simple and few, which is not the case in municipal policing. Some commentators think the military structure impedes the flow of communication and the development of good community relations because people are suspicious of the police or even fear them in some neighborhoods. Despite these criticisms, most police departments retain this organizational structure, which originated in the hiring of military leaders as the first police chiefs. Attempts to change the military structure of policing have generally failed. One reason is that police officers have often resisted any type of reorganization.

FIGURE 5.4 Dallas Police Department Organization Chart

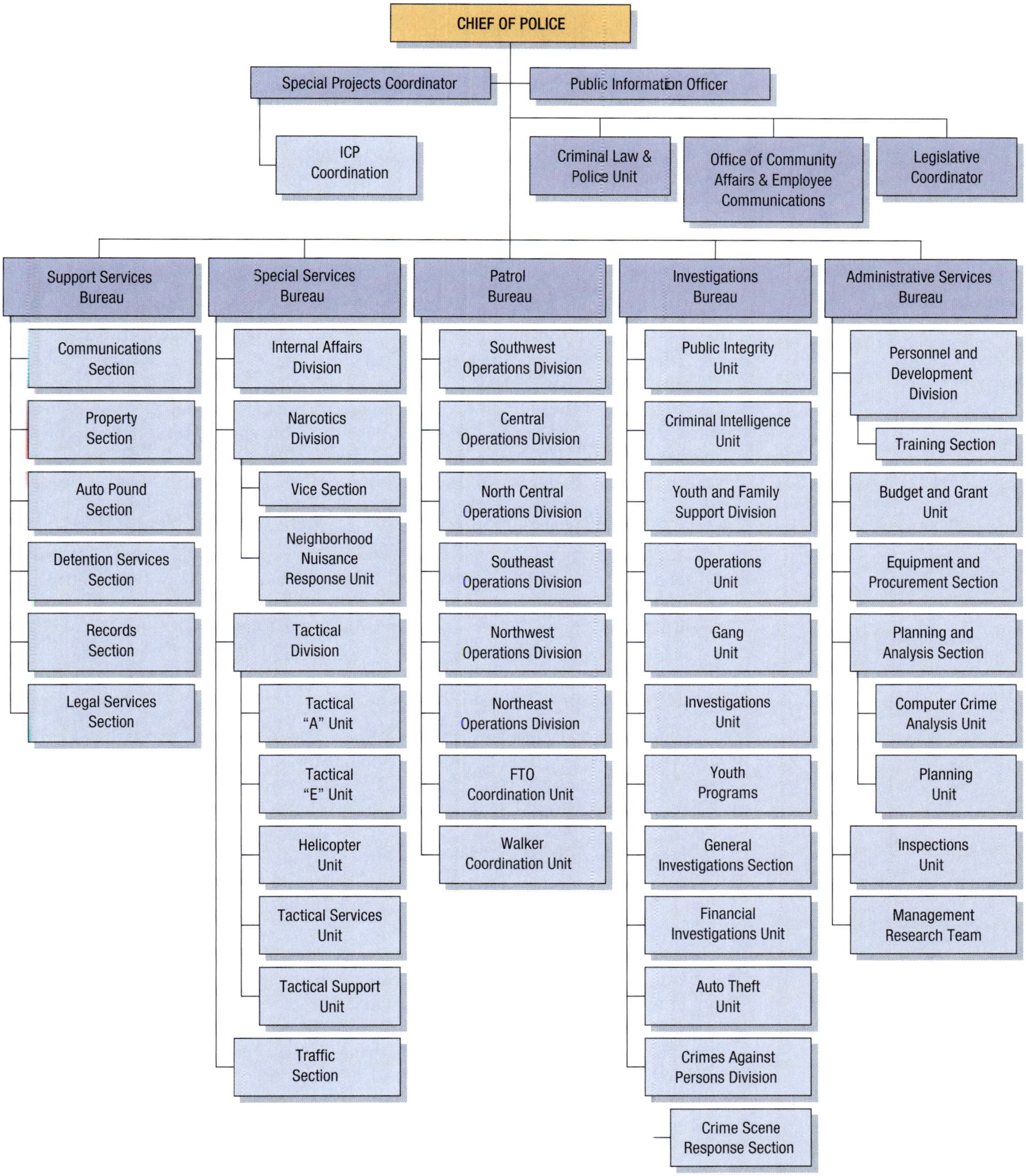

The Political Context of Policing A police department of any size is part of a larger government entity. Municipalities generally operate under one of four forms of municipal government:[22]

Strong Mayor-Council—Voters elect the mayor and the city council; the mayor appoints heads of departments.

Weak Mayor-Council—Voters elect the mayor and the city council; the city council appoints heads of departments.

City Manager—Voters elect the city council and, in some cities, a mayor; the city council selects the city manager, who appoints heads of departments.

Commission—Voters elect a board of commissioners, who become the heads of departments; the commission or the voters may choose one commissioner to be mayor.

As you can see, the forms of municipal government vary in the amount of control citizens have over the municipality's leaders, the source of the executive authority of the chief of police, and the degree of insulation a chief of police has from interference by the executive head of the city (mayor or city manager) or the city council. Each form has advantages and disadvantages. At one time it was thought that city manager government was the system under which the police were most likely to develop professionally, be free of political meddling from city lawmakers, and be insulated from local corruption. Although many progressive and effective police departments operate under a city manager form of government, other municipal forms of government have records of both success and failure in local police effectiveness and integrity.

You have probably noticed from reading newspapers and listening to radio and television that chief executives of local police agencies have different titles, depending on the locale. Popular titles are chief of police (Kansas City), director of police (Dayton, Ohio), and commissioner (New York City).

COUNTY LAW ENFORCEMENT

A substantial portion of law enforcement work in the United States is carried out by sheriffs' departments. In 2000, the nation had 3,070 sheriffs' departments, employing 293,823 full-time personnel. About 56 percent of the personnel were sworn peace officers. Sheriffs frequently employ part-time personnel who work as special deputies, assisting with posses, disasters, county fairs, traffic control, and other duties. Sheriffs' departments represent about 18 percent of all the law enforcement departments in the United States. In 2000, the cost to provide county law enforcement was $17.7 billion, 45 percent more than in 1990 after adjusting for inflation.[23]

> **FYI — Female Sheriffs**
>
> Before 1992, no woman had ever been elected to the position of sheriff in the United States. The first two were elected in 1992: The first was Jackie Barrett in Fulton County, Georgia, and the second was Judy Pridgen in Saline County, Arkansas.

Sheriffs' personnel are 82.9 percent white, 9.4 percent black, 6.1 percent Hispanic, and 1.6 percent other. Women make up 12.5 percent of the sworn personnel working for sheriffs' departments.[24] (See Figure 5.5.)

As are most municipal police departments, most sheriffs' departments in America are small. Figure 5.6 shows the number of departments and their respective sizes. More than one-half of all sheriffs' departments employ fewer than 25 sworn personnel.

Sheriffs' departments often have employment qualifications similar to those of municipal police agencies. Eighty-six percent of sheriffs' departments require new officers to have a high school diploma; 11 percent require some college, usually a 2-year degree, up from 4 percent in 1990.

County Law Enforcement Functions The sheriff and department personnel perform functions that range from investigation to supervision of

FIGURE 5.5 Characteristics of Sheriffs' Personnel, 2000

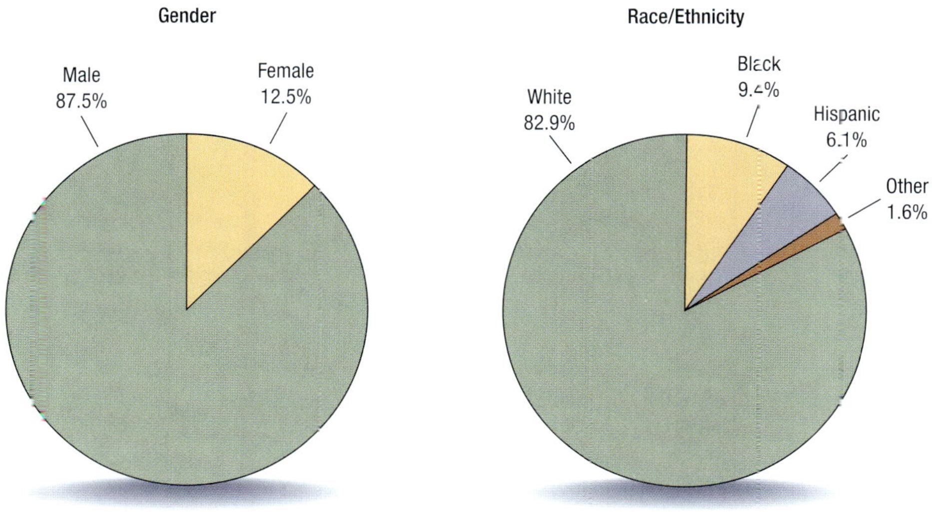

SOURCE: Matthew J. Hickman and Brian A. Reaves, *Sheriffs' Offices, 2000* (Washington, DC: Bureau of Justice Statistics, 2003).

sentenced offenders. Even in the smallest departments, sheriffs are responsible for investigating crimes and enforcing the criminal and traffic laws of the state. They also perform many civil process services for the court, such as serving summonses, warrants, and various writs. In addition, they provide courtroom security and confine and transport prisoners. The larger the sheriff's department, the more confinement and corrections responsibilities it has. Sheriffs' departments frequently operate the county jail, which houses hundreds and even thousands of prisoners, depending on the particular county. In some counties, the sheriff's department shares law enforcement duties with a separate police department.

Politics and County Law Enforcement Most sheriffs are directly elected and depend on an elected board of county commissioners or supervisors for their funding and some oversight of their operations. Sheriffs generally have a freer hand in running their agencies than do police chiefs. In many counties, local politics govern the operation of the sheriff's department, and the sheriff must operate as a partisan politician to remain in office. The authority to appoint special deputies and to award patronage jobs contributes to the sheriff's power and influence in a county.

STATE LAW ENFORCEMENT

Filling the complement of law enforcement agencies in a particular state are one or more state law enforcement agencies, which provide criminal and traffic law enforcement, as well as other services peculiar to the needs of that state government. In 2000, the 49 primary state law enforcement agencies (Hawaii has no state police agency) had 87,028 employees, of which 56,348 or 65 percent were full-time sworn officers. Seventeen state agencies employ more than 1,000 personnel. The California Highway Patrol is the largest state law enforcement agency, with nearly 10,000 personnel, of which about two-thirds are sworn officers.[25]

FIGURE 5.6 Number of Sworn Personnel in Sheriffs' Departments, 2000

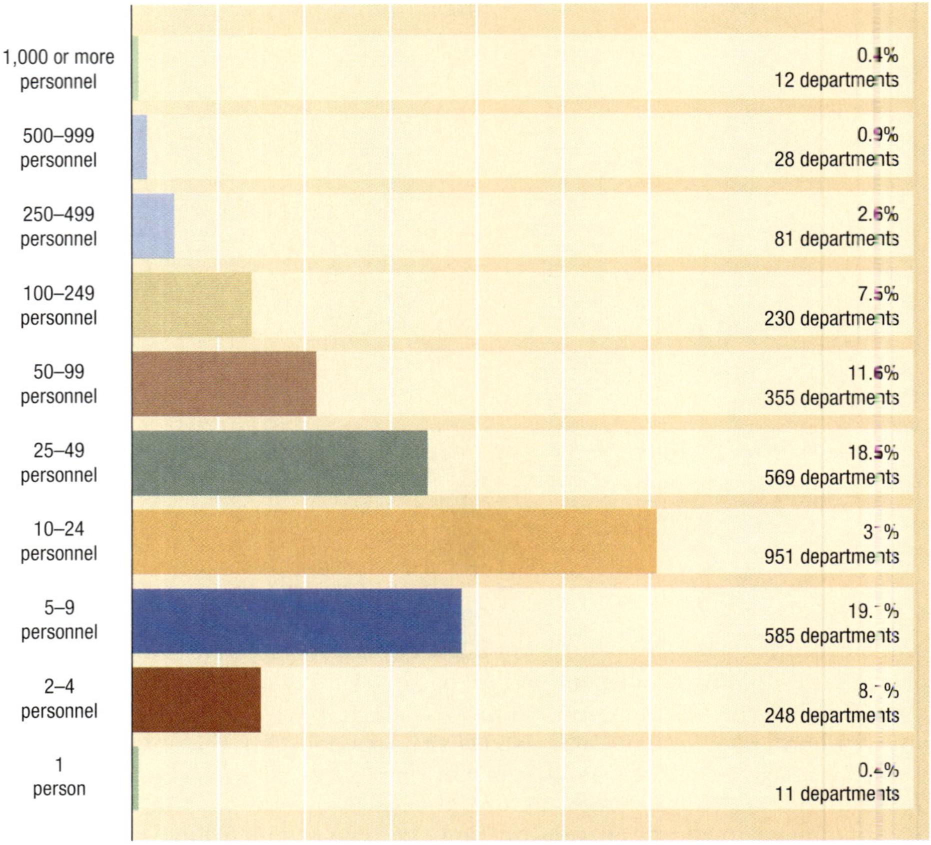

SOURCE: Matthew J. Hickman and Brian A. Reaves, *Sheriffs' Offices, 2000* (Washington, DC: Bureau of Justice Statistics, 2003).

state police model A model of state law enforcement services in which the agency and its officers have the same law enforcement powers as local police but can exercise them anywhere within the state.

highway patrol model A model of state law enforcement services in which officers focus on highway traffic safety, enforcement of the state's traffic laws, and the investigation of accidents on the state's roads, highways, and property.

For the most part, each state has chosen one of two models for providing law enforcement services at the state level. The first model is the **state police model,** in which the agency and its officers have essentially the same enforcement powers as local police in the state and can work cases and enforce the law anywhere within the state's boundaries. One of the best known state police agencies is the Texas Rangers, part of the Texas Department of Public Safety, which also employs state troopers to enforce criminal and traffic laws. The Rangers usually focus on special and complex investigations, such as the Branch Davidian case in Waco in 1993. A number of states have placed some restrictions on state police activities to avoid clashes with local politicians and local police agencies.

The second model for state law enforcement services is the **highway patrol model,** in which officers focus almost exclusively on highway traffic safety, enforcement of the state's traffic laws, and investigation of accidents on the state's roads and highways. Even highway patrols, however, may retain responsibility for investigating criminal violations on state property and in state institutions or for conducting drug interdictions.

States that employ the highway patrol model often have other state law enforcement agencies with narrow service mandates, such as the following:

- Bureaus of criminal investigation (to investigate white-collar and organized crime, narcotics, etc.).

State police agencies in every state except Hawaii have statewide jurisdiction and may be set up according to state police or highway patrol models. *Are state police agencies necessary? Why or why not?*

- State criminal identification services.
- Forest, game, and watercraft protection services.
- Alcoholic beverage control and enforcement.
- Crime laboratory and criminalistics services.
- Driver's license examinations.
- Drug interdiction activities.
- Peace officer training and certification.

Both state police and highway patrol agencies help regulate commercial traffic, conduct bomb investigations, protect the governor and the capitol grounds and buildings, and administer computerized information networks for the state, which link up with the National Crime Information Center (NCIC) run by the FBI.

Some tension always seems to exist between state police agencies and local law enforcement over legal jurisdiction and recognition for conducting investigations and making arrests. Recall that policing in America and the political system that governs it are local. Much of the resentment by locals over state interference is similar to the suspicions and doubts concerning federal involvement at the local level.

A significant function performed by a special category of state law enforcement officers is university or campus policing. Some of the large state and private universities and colleges have full-blown police agencies with many special subdivisions. They are very much like municipal police departments—and rightly so, because a community's problems with crime and public order do not end at the university gate.

FEDERAL LAW ENFORCEMENT

Everyone has heard of a few of the better-known federal law enforcement agencies. The FBI, the U.S. Secret Service, and even the T-men and T-women of the Treasury Department have had their own television shows, creating wider public recognition of those agencies. The unrelenting war on drugs has brought to the attention of the American public the activities of the Drug Enforcement Administration (DEA). There are also other, lesser-known federal police agencies. Their law enforcement jurisdictions are narrowly defined by specific statutes, and their work is unlikely to come to the attention of most American citizens.

Three major differences exist between federal law enforcement and the local and state police agencies with which we are likely to be more familiar. First, federal agencies such as the FBI operate across the entire nation and even have agents serving abroad. Second, federal police agencies do not, as a rule, have the peacekeeping or order maintenance duties typical in local policing. Finally, some federal law enforcement agencies have extremely narrow jurisdictions. (The U.S. Supreme Court Police, for example, provide protective and investigative services for the Supreme Court only.)

Federal Law Enforcement Personnel As of June 2002, federal agencies employed nationwide about 93,000 full-time personnel authorized to make arrests and carry firearms—an increase of about 6 percent since June 2000 and 26 percent since June 1996.[26] Another 1,300 federal officers worked in U.S. territories, and some were employed in foreign countries. (Officer counts were conducted prior to enactment of legislation creating the Department of Homeland Security.) Approximately 60 percent of federal officers were employed by the four largest agencies: the Immigration and Naturalization Service, the Federal Bureau of Prisons, the U.S. Customs Service, and the Federal Bureau of Investigation.[27] (Note that on March 1, 2003, the former Immigration and Naturalization Service, the border and agency functions of the U.S. Customs Service, and the Federal Protective Service were reorganized into the Bureau of Immigration and Customs Enforcement in the new

Federal law enforcement agencies investigate violations of federal law, enforce laws that involve interstate crimes, and conduct activities to prevent and control domestic and international terrorism. *How do the jobs of federal law enforcement agents differ from the jobs of other law enforcement officers?*

TABLE 5.2 Major Employers of Federal Officers Authorized to Make Arrests and Carry Firearms, by Officers, Gender, and Race/Ethnicity

Agency	Number of Officers[a]	Gender		Race/Ethnicity				
		Male	Female	White	American Indian	Black or African American	Asian or Pacific Islander	Hispanic or Latino of Any Race
Immigration and Naturalization Service	17,973	88.7%	11.3%	58.2%	0.5%	5.3%	2.2%	33.2%
Federal Bureau of Prisons	13,714	86.9	13.1	60.8	1.4	24.5	1.1	12.1
Federal Bureau of Investigation	11,712	82.9	17.1	83.6	0.5	6.2	2.7	7.1
U.S. Customs Service	10,820	80.9	19.1	64.5	0.8	7.4	3.5	23.8
Drug Enforcement Administration	4,201	91.6	8.4	82.[illegible]	0.0	8.0	1.9	7.3
U.S. Secret Service	4,039	90.9	9.1	79.5	0.8	12.4	1.8	5.6
U.S. Postal Inspection Service	3,456	84.1	15.9	64.3	0.4	23.6	3.6	8.2
Internal Revenue Service	2,742	72.7	27.3	79.0	1.1	9.6	3.5	6.8
U.S. Marshals Service	2,777	88.0	12.0	82.1	0.6	7.9	1.9	7.5
National Park Service	2,195	86.5	13.5	86.9	2.0	5.2	2.2	3.7
Ranger Activities Division	1,551	84.7	15.3	89.4	2.7	2.5	2.0	3.4
U.S. Park Police	644	90.8	9.2	80.9	0.3	11.6	2.6	4.5
Bureau of Alcohol, Tobacco and Firearms	1,983	88.0	12.0	80.3	1.2	9.9	1.6	7.0
U.S. Capitol Police	1,199	82.2	17.8	67.4	0.3	28.8	1.1	2.5
U.S. Fish and Wildlife Service	895	86.6	13.4	86.3	3.9	2.1	1.5	5.7
GSA–Federal Protective Service	809	91.1	8.9	55.6	0.4	32.4	1.5	10.1
Bureau of Diplomatic Security	617	90.3	9.7	92.9	0.2	3.7	1.6	1.6
USDA Forest Service	586	83.1	16.9	81.7	3.0	3.1	1.0	6.1

Notes: Officer counts were conducted prior to the enactment of legislation creating the Department of Homeland Security. Data on gender and race or ethnicity of officers were not provided by the Administrative Office of the U.S. Courts. Detail may not add to total because of rounding.

[a]Includes employees in U.S. Territories.

SOURCE: Brian A. Reaves and Lynn M. Bauer, *Federal Law Enforcement Officers, 2002,* U.S. Department of Justice, *Bureau of Justice Statistics Bulletin* (Washington, DC: GPO, August 2003), p. 7, Table 5.

Department of Homeland Security, which is described in detail in the next section.) Table 5.2 shows the major employers of federal officers authorized to make arrests and carry firearms (prior to the reorganization). In addition to those federal officers, the 69 federal agencies employed about 72,000 full-time support personnel. Combined, the federal law enforcement agencies had an annual budget of approximately $18 billion in 2000 (the latest year for which data were available).[28]

Of the federal officers with arrest and firearm authority in 2002, about 85 percent were men and 15 percent were women—an increase in women of about 1 percent since 1996. The Internal Revenue Service employed the largest percentage of women (28 percent), while the Drug Enforcement Agency employed the fewest women (less than 9 percent).[29] Nearly one-third of federal officers were members of a racial or ethnic minority—an increase from 28 percent in 1996. Approximately 17 percent of them were Hispanic or Latino, almost 12 percent were non-Hispanic blacks, 2.5 percent were Asians or Pacific Islanders, and 1.2 percent were American Indians. The former Immigration and Naturalization Service had the largest minority percentage (nearly 47 percent, of which about 38 percent were Hispanic or Latino.) The agency with the fewest minorities was the National Park Service, Ranger Activities Division (with fewer than 10 percent). The largest percentage of black officers (about 30 percent) were employed by the Federal Protective Service, the Forest Service employed the largest percentage of

FYI

Offices of Inspector General

Offices of inspector general (IG) investigate criminal violations and prevent and detect fraud, waste, and abuse related to federal programs, operations, and employees. In June of 2002, there were 57 statutory federal IG offices, half of which employed criminal investigators with arrest and firearm authority. Overall, these agencies employed nearly 3,000 officers. The largest IG employer of federal officers authorized to arrest and carry firearms in 2002 was the Department of Health and Human Services (with 436 officers).

SOURCE: Brian A. Reaves and Lynn M. Bauer, *Federal Law Enforcement, 2000,* U.S. Department of Justice, *Bureau of Justice Statistics Bulletin* (Washington, DC: GPO, August 2003), p. 6.

American Indians (about 7 percent), and the Internal Revenue Service employed the largest percentage of Asians and Pacific Islanders (4.4 percent).[30] Table 5.2 also shows the gender and race or ethnicity of federal officers with arrest and firearm authority that were working for agencies that employed 500 or more full-time officers in 2002.

Training Federal Law Enforcement Officers The Federal Law Enforcement Training Center (FLETC) is the largest law enforcement-training establishment in the United States.[31] It provides some or all of the training for a majority of federal law enforcement agencies, as well as for many state, local, and international law enforcement agencies. Notable exceptions are the FBI and DEA, which train their special agents at their respective academies in Quantico, Virginia. Until 2003, when it became a part of the Department of Homeland Security, FLETC was a bureau of the Treasury Department with an annual budget of about $200 million.

The FLETC got its start in the late 1960s, when a federal government study disclosed that the training of most federal law enforcement personnel was inadequate at worst and substandard at best. With only a few exceptions, part-time instructors, on an irregular basis, conducted most training in inferior facilities. Much of the training duplicated the training of other federal agencies or was inconsistent with it. A government task force recommended that a federal law enforcement training center be established to provide the training for most federal law enforcement personnel. The center would have a professionally trained, full-time staff that offered consistent and high-quality programs in state-of-the-art facilities.

FLETC first opened in Washington, DC, in 1970. That year it graduated 848 students. In 1975, its first full year of operation at its current headquarters location on a 1,500-acre campus in Glenn County ("Glynco"), Georgia (near Brunswick, Georgia), it graduated more than 5,000 students. At year-end 2002, more than 32,000 students graduated from the FLETC at Glynco, including about 2,600 state and local officers. Another 6,000 students graduated from the FLETC Office of Artesia Operations (OAO) in New Mexico. OAO was opened in 1990 to provide training for agencies with a large number of officers in the western United States. OAO also provides training for federal air marshals. Before the tragedy of September 11, 2001, OAO trained about four air marshals a year. In the year after September 11, it trained about 5,000 air marshals. A temporary satellite training campus was opened in Charleston, South Carolina, in 1995 to train an increasing number of INS and border patrol agents. In 2002, the facility graduated nearly 1,000 officers. A fourth training facility that was being developed in 2002 in Cheltenham, Maryland, will be used primarily for in-service and requalification training for officers and agents in the Washington, DC, area. It will also serve as the new home for the U.S. Capitol Police Training Academy. FLETC also provides training at other temporary sites in the United States and in foreign countries.

Because basic training requirements for federal officers vary by agency and by position within agencies, FLETC provides more than 100 different agency-specific training programs. About half of the instructors are permanent employees, while the other half are federal officers on short-term assignment from their respective agencies. Depending on the agency, classroom instruction ranges from about 8 to 22 weeks for criminal investigators and from 4 to 26 weeks for patrol officers. Field training requirements range from 2 weeks to 6 months for patrol officers and up to 2 years for investigators.

CJ ONLINE

Federal Law Enforcement Training Center

To learn more about the FLETC, visit its website at **www.fletc.gov.** Access its Catalog of Training Programs. *Which programs, if any, would be of interest to you? Why?*

THINKING CRITICALLY

1. What do you think are the pros and cons of working at the local, state, and federal levels of law enforcement?
2. Do you think that any one of the three major areas of law enforcement (local, state, federal) is more prestigious? Why?

THE DEPARTMENT OF HOMELAND SECURITY

The U.S. Congress responded to the terrorist attacks of September 11, 2001 (described in Chapter 6), by enacting the Homeland Security Act of 2002.[32] Among other provisions, such as allowing commercial pilots to carry guns in cockpits, the act established the Department of Homeland Security (DHS). According to the legislation, this new executive department was created to

1. Prevent terrorist attacks within the United States.
2. Reduce the vulnerability of the United States to terrorism.
3. Minimize the damage, and assist in the recovery, from terrorist attacks that do occur within the United States.

CAREERS IN CRIMINAL JUSTICE

FBI Special Agent

My name is Michelle L. Rankin and I am an FBI special agent in the Washington, DC (PCU) field office, Public Corruption Unit. The Washington, DC, Field Office is the second largest field office in the FBI. I thoroughly enjoy my career with the FBI.

The PCU investigates allegations of bribery involving public officials, including extortion or using the mail to defraud the public. Examples include the issuance of licenses, permits, contracts, or zoning variances; judicial case fixing; and law enforcement corruption.

The PCU's responsibilities are divided into two squads. My squad focuses on the District of Columbia government. The other squad concentrates on the executive branch of the federal government in the Washington, DC, area. Twelve agents are assigned to my squad, along with non-agent support specialists.

Prior to transferring to the PCU, I worked on a special inquiry squad, conducting background investigations for White House staff and presidential appointees. It was in this capacity that I had the opportunity to interview Attorney General Janet Reno as well as other prominent politicians.

People often ask about training at the FBI Academy. The program is 16 weeks of rigorous and intellectually challenging work. You have to study 12–15 major subject areas and you often have 3 hours of homework for the next day's classes and you may also have an exam in another course the next day. Some agents realize that the FBI is not what they thought it was. Others find it difficult to be away from family and friends.

I have a B.A. in Criminal Justice from California State University at San Bernardino. While working on a Certificate in Crime and Intelligence Analysis through the California State University system and the California Department of Justice, I began to volunteer with the Riverside County Sheriff's Department. I eventually obtained a full-time position as an analyst there. Later I went to the Santa Clara Police Department as a Certified Crime and Intelligence Analyst. I designed and directed their crime analysis unit for 4 years. I left Santa Clara in 1999 to become an FBI agent.

To become an FBI Special Agent, applicants must be between the ages of 23 and 37. The FBI prefers to hire people who are already successful in some other field. Prior work experience need not be in law enforcement. The FBI hires agents from four career categories: law; accounting; foreign languages; and "diversified"—which includes criminal justice. You need to have a minimum of 3 years of work experience in your chosen field before applying to be an agent. When hired, new FBI Special Agents start at a GS-10, step 1 pay grade, which is now approximately $40,000 per year before overtime.

My advice to someone who wants to become an FBI agent is to maintain the highest standards of conduct in your life. Your first job out of college does not have to be in criminal justice, but be sure to be successful in whatever you do.

After reading this account, what do you think is a key quality of a good FBI agent?

4. Carry out all functions of entities transferred to the department, including by acting as a focal point regarding natural and manmade crises and emergency planning.
5. Ensure that the functions of the agencies and subdivisions within the department that are not related directly to securing the homeland are not diminished or neglected except by an explicit act of Congress.
6. Ensure that the overall economic security of the United States is not diminished by efforts, activities, and programs aimed at securing the homeland.
7. Monitor connections between illegal drug trafficking and terrorism, coordinate efforts to sever such connections, and otherwise contribute to efforts to interdict illegal drug trafficking.

The act also stipulates that "primary responsibility for investigating and prosecuting acts of terrorism shall be vested not in the Department, but rather in Federal, State, and local law enforcement agencies with jurisdiction over the acts in question."

The creation of the Department of Homeland Security represents the most dramatic transformation of the U.S. government since 1947, when President Harry S Truman combined the various branches of the U.S. military into the Department of Defense. On an even grander scale, President Bush has combined 22 previously separate domestic agencies into the new department to protect the country from future threats. To head the new department, President Bush selected former Pennsylvania Governor Tom Ridge. He will work with more than 180,000 employees from the combined agencies.

The new department, whose development is ongoing, has five major divisions, or "directorates":

1. Border and Transportation Security (BTS): This is the largest of the directorates and is responsible for maintaining the security of U.S. borders and transportation systems. To carry out its mission, BTS integrates the U.S. Customs Service (formerly part of the Treasury Department), the enforcement division of the Immigration and Naturalization Service, which includes the Border Patrol (Justice Department), the Animal and Plant Health Inspection Service (Agriculture Department), the Federal Law Enforcement Training Center (Treasury Department), and the Transportation Security Administration (Transportation Department). BTS also includes the Federal Protective Service (General Services Administration) to perform the additional function of protecting government buildings, and the Office for Domestic Preparedness (Justice Department), which is charged with enhancing the ability of state and local first responders to react to incidents of terrorism involving weapons of mass destruction. On March 1, 2003, the border and agency functions of the U.S. Customs Service, the Federal Protective Service, and the former Immigration and Naturalization Service were reorganized into the Bureau of Immigration and Customs Enforcement.
2. Emergency Preparedness and Response (EPR): This directorate is responsible for preparing the nation and enabling it to recover from terrorist attacks and natural disasters. Agencies in this directorate are the Federal Emergency Management Agency, the Strategic National Stockpile and the National Disaster Medical System, the Nuclear Incident Response Team (formerly part of the Energy Department), the Domestic Emergency Support Teams (Justice Department), and the National Domestic Preparedness Office (FBI).

A UH-60 Black Hawk helicopter from the Department of Homeland Security's new Bureau of Immigration and Customs Enforcement patrolling restricted airspace over the New York metropolitan area to detect unauthorized intrusions. *Is this an effective defensive strategy against terrorism? Why or why not?*

3. Science and Technology (S&T): This directorate coordinates the Department's research and development efforts, including preparation for and responses to all terrorist threats involving weapons of mass destruction. The directorate comprises the CBRN (Chemical, Biological, Radiological, and Nuclear) Countermeasures Programs (formerly part of the Energy Department), the Environmental Measurements Laboratory (Energy Department), the National BW (Biological Warfare) Defense Analysis Center (Defense Department), and the Plum Island Animal Disease Center (Agriculture Department).
4. Information Analysis and Infrastructure Protection (IAIP): This directorate is charged with analyzing intelligence and information from other agencies, such as the CIA, FBI, DIA, and NSA, involving threats to homeland security. It also evaluates vulnerabilities in the country's infrastructure. Combined in this directorate are the Critical Infrastructure Assurance Office (formerly of the Commerce Department), the Federal Computer Incident Response Center (General Services Administration), the National Communications System (Defense Department), the National Infrastructure Protection Center (FBI), and the Energy Security and Assurance Program (Energy Department).
5. Management: This directorate is responsible for budget, management, and personnel issues.

In addition to the five directorates, several other agencies are being reassigned to the DHS or being newly created. They include:

- The U.S. Coast Guard. The Coast Guard retains its traditional role of countering potential threats to the country's coasts, ports, and inland

CJ ONLINE

Department of Homeland Security
To learn more about the Department of Homeland Security, visit its website at **www.dhs.gov/dhspublic.** *Based on what you have learned, do you think the DHS will be effective in preventing terrorism on American soil?*

waterways. It will also enforce increased security measures of commercial, tanker, passenger, and merchant vessels.

- The U.S. Secret Service. The Secret Service also retains its traditional role of protecting the president and other government leaders, providing security for designated national events, and safeguarding U.S. currency from counterfeiters and Americans from credit card fraud. However, it now has at its disposal access to DHS intelligence analysis and the ability to coordinate its activities more efficiently with other key agencies.
- The Bureau of Citizenship and Immigration Services (BCIS). While the BTS is responsible for the enforcement of the country's immigration laws, the BCIS provides efficient immigration services to ease the transition to American citizenship. Examples of services provided by the BCIS are immigrant and nonimmigrant sponsorship; adjustment of status; work authorization and other permits; naturalization of qualified applicants for U.S. citizenship; and asylum or refugee processing.
- The Office of State and Local Government Coordination. This office coordinates state and local first responders, emergency services, and governments.
- The Office of Private Sector Liaison. This office works directly with individual businesses and through trade associations and other nongovernmental organizations to address the post-9/11 concerns of the country's business sector.
- The Office of Inspector General. This office serves as an independent and objective inspection, audit, and investigative body to promote effectiveness, efficiency, and economy in the DHS's programs and operations by preventing and detecting fraud, abuse, mismanagement, and waste.

It is important to note that not all of the responsibilities of existing agencies have been transferred to the DHS. Some responsibilities remain with the original agency or have been transferred to agencies outside of the new department. The organization chart of the Department of Homeland Security is shown in Figure 5.7.

The 2004 annual budget for the Department of Homeland Security was $36.2 billion. That was 7.4 percent more than the 2003 annual budget and nearly 65 percent more than the 2002 annual budget. It was also more than twice the 2000 annual budget for all federal law enforcement agencies combined. Figure 5.8 shows how the DHS's 2004 annual budget was distributed. Note that half of it went to increase border and transportation security.

HOMELAND SECURITY AND THE FBI Before the creation of the Department of Homeland Security, the FBI had primary responsibility for locating terrorist groups and preventing terrorist acts in the United States. It had many successes. According to FBI data, for example, the agency prevented 130 terrorist acts between 1980 and 1999.[33] However, following the al-Qaeda attacks on New York and Washington, the FBI was heavily criticized for missing clues and intelligence failures.[34] For example, Senator John Edwards of North Carolina, who had oversight responsibility for the FBI as a member of both the Intelligence and Judiciary committees, remarked, "The FBI is clearly broken, and we can accept no further delay in the effort to fix it." He added, "The FBI should do what it does best: law enforcement [rather than] collecting information, fitting it into a bigger picture and sharing that information with people who can act on it." To root out terrorists within the United States, legislators on Capitol Hill called for the creation of a new domestic intelligence-gathering agency similar to the MI-5 in Great Britain.

FIGURE 5.7 Department of Homeland Security

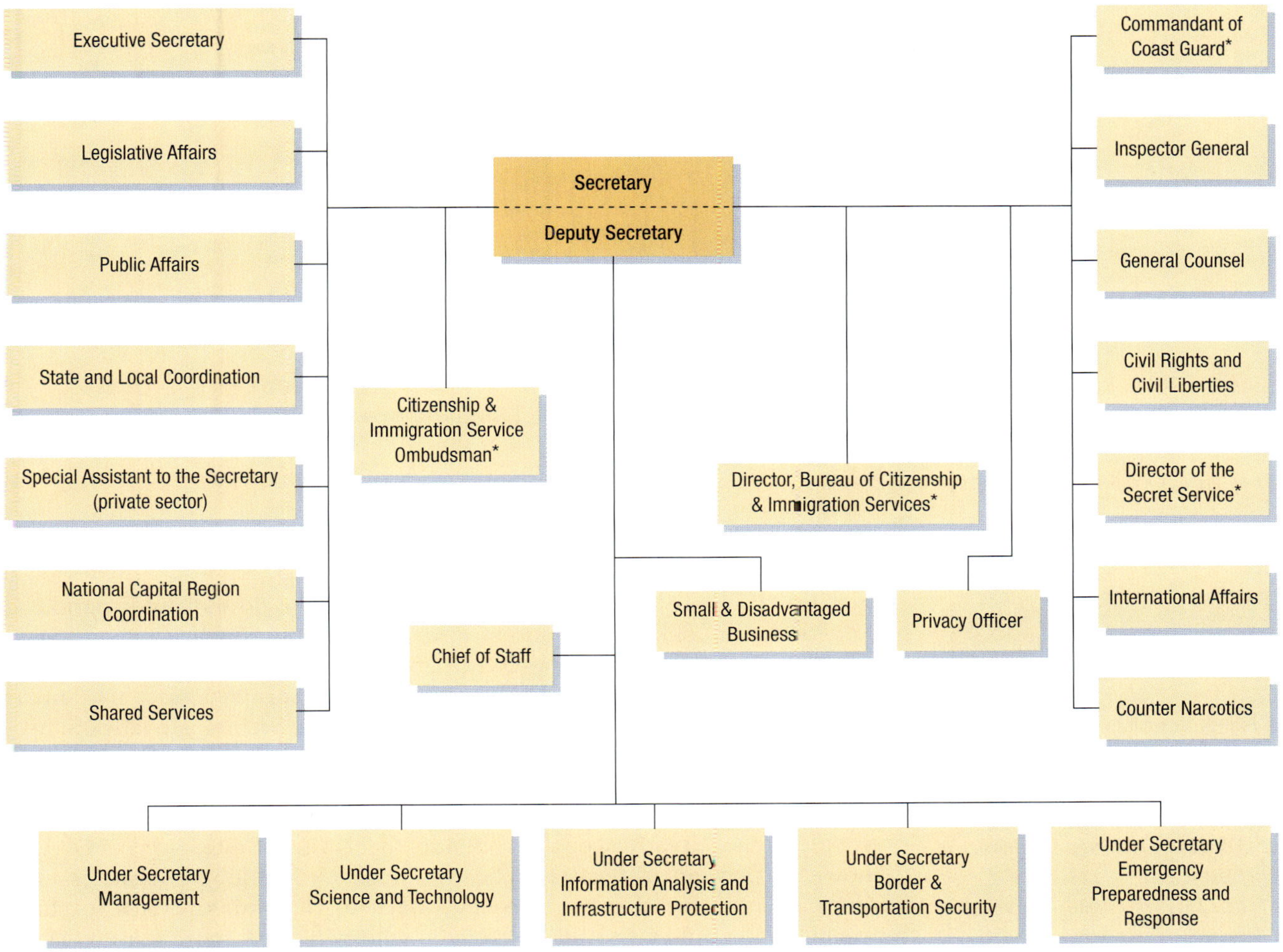

*Effective March 1st, 2003.

SOURCE: Department of Homeland Security at www.dhs.gov/dhspublic.

FBI Director Robert Mueller defended his agency. He responded, "Establishing a new domestic intelligence agency would constitute a step backward in the war on terror, not a step forward." He maintained that rather than "create a new agency from whole cloth, the public would be better served by improving what the FBI is already doing."

Director Mueller won a reprieve for the FBI and quickly began implementing fundamental changes. First, he shifted the top priority of the FBI from being a federal police agency to being an intelligence and counterterrorism agency. In doing so, he no longer allows local field offices to establish their own distinct agendas. Second, he restructured the management hierarchy at FBI headquarters in Washington to support counterterrorism efforts. Third, he reassigned about one-quarter of the FBI's 11,000 agents to work on counterterrorism. That represents a doubling of the number of agents handling terrorism cases and a quadrupling of the number of strategic analysts at FBI headquarters. Fourth, he established a National Joint Terrorism Task Force at FBI headquarters that includes staffers from federal, state, and local

FIGURE 5.8 Department of Homeland Security 2004 Budget (in $ billions)

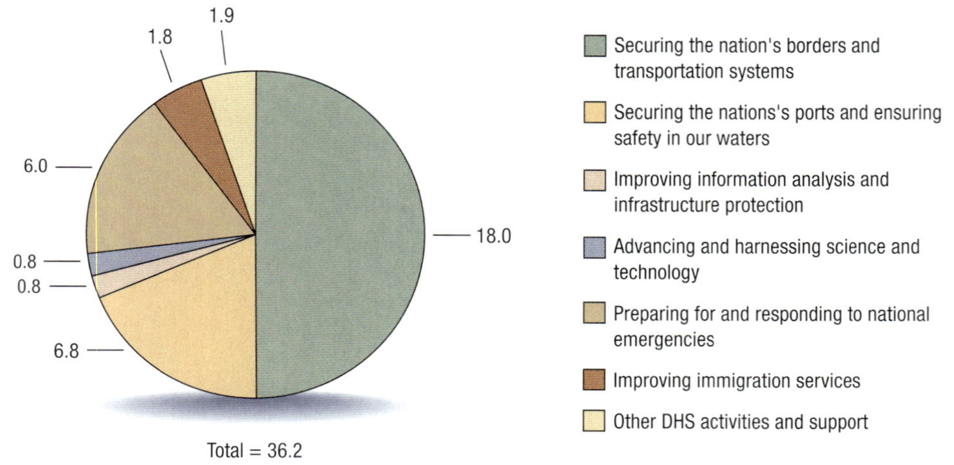

SOURCE: Department of Homeland Security, "Budget in Brief," p.1, at www.dhs.gov/dhspublic.

> **CJ ONLINE**
>
> **FBI Fights Terrorism**
>
> To learn more about the FBI's efforts to combat terrorism, visit its website at **www.fbi.gov.** Click on "Terrorism" and then click on "Counterterrorism Website." *From what you have learned, do you think the FBI will be effective in combating terrorism?*

agencies. They are responsible for coordinating the flow of information with task forces in each of the bureau's 56 field offices. Fifth, to more directly address the global threat of al-Qaeda and other terrorist groups, he plans on opening FBI offices in Kabul, Afghanistan; Sarajevo, Bosnia; Jakarta, Indonesia; Tashkent, Uzbekistan; and Belgrade, Serbia. He also plans on expanding FBI offices in Ottawa, Canada; Seoul, South Korea; London, Berlin, and Moscow. Since the tragic events of 9/11, about 500 FBI agents and 200 support personnel have been working outside the United States on terrorism investigation. Already working outside the United States were FBI agents known as permanent legal attaches, or "legats." The job of legats is to feed information gathered from interviews back to the United States for further investigation. Unlike CIA agents, legats, who will work more closely with the CIA, do not operate covertly and are involved more with investigations than with gathering intelligence. In sum, through the efforts of Director Mueller, the FBI will remain an independent agency, albeit with a new top priority, and retain its traditional responsibility of intelligence gathering and analysis. However, it will now closely coordinate its antiterrorism activities with the CIA and the new Department of Homeland Security.

THE WAR ON TERRORISM: A PRELIMINARY EVALUATION

Advocates of the new Department of Homeland Security are confident that the DHS will have the financial, intelligence, and tactical resources necessary to prevent and control domestic terrorism. At this writing, the DHS had just begun to assess the threats against the United States and coordinate the resources of law enforcement and other kinds of agencies that are necessary to defeat terrorism at home. One of its first efforts was the creation of a color-coded warning system to alert citizens to the likelihood of a terrorist attack. The hope is that as the warning level is raised, the vigilance of Americans will increase and information will be discovered that will prevent a terrorist act.

The war on terrorism is an ongoing battle with no end in sight. Nevertheless, there already have been some successes. For example, between September 11,

2001, and the end of 2002, as a result of cooperation among law enforcement agencies, more than 3,000 members of al-Qaeda or their associates had been captured and detained in more than 100 countries.[35] In addition, more than one-third of al-Qaeda's top leadership had been killed or captured.[36] The financial resources of terrorist groups have also been successfully attacked. Leaders of more than 166 countries have ordered the freezing of more than $121 million in terrorist-related financial assets.[37] In the United States, under the authority of Executive Order 13224, which was issued by President Bush on September 23, 2001, more than 250 terrorist groups and entities have been listed as possible targets for the freezing of their U.S.-based assets.[38] Further, any American citizen who contributes money or other aid to any of the 250 organizations and entities automatically becomes suspect. Most importantly, the United States, as of July 2003, has not experienced a repeat of the 9/11 tragedy. On the other hand, Osama bin Laden (probably) and other key al-Qaeda leaders were still at large (as of July 2003) despite the best efforts of the United States and its coalition partners and a reward of up to $25 million authorized by Secretary of State Colin Powell for information leading to their capture.[39]

A major problem in the war on terrorism is lax and poorly enforced immigration policies. Both the United States and Canada have some of the most lenient immigration policies in the world, and the result has been that terrorists and their supporters have found safe haven in both nations. A recent study found that 15 out of 80 identified international terrorist groups have members or significant supporters in Canada.[40] Another study of both legal and illegal immigration in the United States discovered that the 19 terrorist hijackers of September 11, 2001, could not have accomplished their mission without the failures of U.S. immigration agencies. It is widely believed that "we unlocked our doors, spread out the welcome mat, and allowed these foreign visitors to plot death and destruction in the comfort of our home. And they can do it again in a heartbeat."[41] Hopefully, through the efforts of the Department of Homeland Security, law enforcement agencies at all levels of government, and vigilant American citizens, acts of terrorism can be prevented in the future.

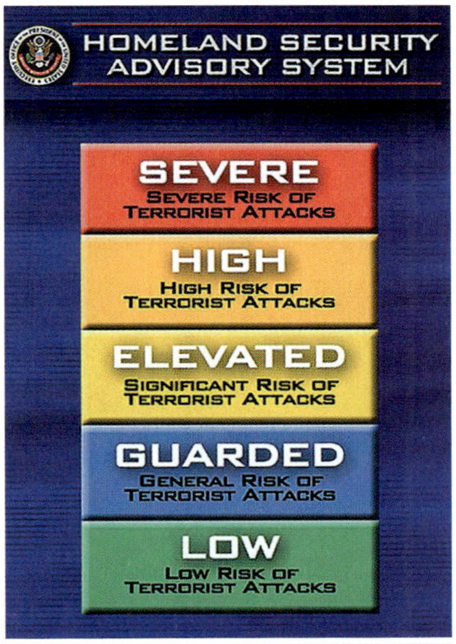

The Homeland Security Department's color-coded national threat alert system is intended to help citizens better prepare for potential terrorist attacks. *Do you believe the system will be effective? Why or why not?*

FYI

Rewards for Justice

Rewards of up to $5 million are available through the Rewards for Justice program for information that prevents or favorably resolves acts of international terrorism against U.S. citizens or property anywhere in the world.

SOURCE: U.S. State Department, *Patterns of Global Terrorism 2002*, April 2003, p. xi, at www.state.gov/s/ct/rls/pgtrpt/2002.

American Private Security

Private security is a huge enterprise that complements public law enforcement in the United States. The Department of Labor's Bureau of Labor Statistics projects the continued growth of private security employment well into this century.[42] It has been estimated that twice as many people work in private security as in public law enforcement. Until recently, substantially more money was being spent on private security than on public policing, but that gap has been narrowing somewhat because of the increases in spending on public law enforcement during the 1990s and the federalizing of airport security (through the Transportation Security Administration) in the wake of the 9/11 terrorist assault.

A common way to categorize private security employment is to classify the agencies and personnel as either contract or proprietary. **Contract security** companies offer protective services for a fee to people, agencies, and companies that do not employ their own security personnel or that need extra protection. A state university, for example, may employ private security officers to work at a football game. Contract security employees are not peace officers. **Proprietary security** agents and personnel provide protective services

contract security Protective services that a private security firm provides to people, agencies, and companies that do not employ their own security personnel or that need extra protection.

proprietary security In-house protective services that a security staff provides for the entity that employs it.

for the entity that employs them. They are also not classified as sworn peace officers. For example, the Ford Motor Company employs its own security forces at its large manufacturing plants. Primarily for cost reasons, the number of contract security jobs is likely to increase faster than the number of proprietary security jobs.

PRIVATE SECURITY OFFICERS

Private security officers, or "guards," are hired to provide protection.[43] They typically work 8-hour shifts, 5 days a week. In 2000, they were paid between about $13,000 and $29,000 annually. The average salary for a private security officer in 2000 was $17,570. Managers and corporate officers made more. About 60 percent of private security officers in 2000 worked for industrial security firms or guard agencies.

Because of relatively low wages, private security officers frequently work part-time or have another "primary" job and use their security job wages to supplement their incomes. In 2000, there were more than one million private security officers. A private security officer's duties vary and depend on the employers' particular needs. Private security officers generally specialize in one of the following areas:

- Protecting people, records, merchandise, money, and equipment in department stores; also working with undercover store detectives to prevent theft by customers or store employees and helping in the apprehension of shoplifting suspects before the police arrive.
- Patrolling the parking lots of shopping centers and theaters, sometimes on horseback or bicycles, to deter car theft and robberies.
- Maintaining order and protecting property, staff, and customers in office buildings, banks, and hospitals.
- Protecting people, freight, property, and equipment at air, sea, and rail terminals as well as other transportation facilities; also screening passengers and visitors for weapons and explosives using metal detectors and high-tech equipment, ensuring that nothing is stolen while being loaded or unloaded, and watching for fires and criminals.
- Protecting paintings and exhibits by inspecting people and packages entering and leaving public buildings such as museums or art galleries.
- Protecting information, products, computer codes, and defense secrets and checking the credentials of people and vehicles entering or leaving the premises of factories, laboratories, government buildings, data-processing centers, and military bases.
- Performing crowd control, supervising parking and seating, and directing traffic at universities, parks, and sports stadiums.
- Preventing access by minors, collecting cover charges at the door, maintaining order among customers, and protecting property and patrons while stationed at the entrance to bars and places of adult entertainment such as night clubs.

Private security is assuming an increasing role in maintaining order, investigating crime, and apprehending criminals. *Is this a positive trend? Why or why not?*

- Protecting money and valuables during transit in armored cars; also protecting individuals responsible for making commercial bank deposits from theft or bodily injuries.
- Observing casino operations for irregular activities, such as cheating or theft, by employees or patrons.

REASONS FOR GROWTH

A number of factors have stimulated the phenomenal growth of private security since the 1970s.

Declining Revenues for Public Policing In virtually all major cities and in state governments in the United States, the competition for limited funds to operate public services is fierce. Public police agencies have experienced their share of across-the-board government belt-tightening, and that has caused limitations and even freezes on the hiring of additional police officers. (That trend has been decreasing recently.) As a result, police departments have curtailed services no longer deemed critical. Often, businesses have filled the service gap by employing private security personnel.

The Private Nature of Crimes in the Workplace A business depends on a positive reputation to remain competitive. Widespread employee theft, embezzlement scandals, and substance abuse harm an organization's public image and may cause potential customers to question the quality of a company's products and services. By employing private security personnel to prevent and repress crime in their facilities, businesses can either hide the crimes that occur or minimize the negative publicity.

Better Control and Attention to the Problem By employing in-house security personnel or by contracting with an outside firm, the management of a business can direct security personnel to do precisely what is needed to prevent crime, minimize substance abuse, and discipline wayward employees. Public police would have to combine the concerns of a business with the priorities of the citizens of the community.

Fewer Constitutional Limitations Some of the constitutional restrictions that would limit the actions of public police officers working undercover to curtail drug trafficking in an industrial plant, for example, would not restrict private security personnel employed directly by that industry. U.S. Supreme Court prohibitions that restrict a public police officer's right to search and seize property, for instance, would not limit the actions of a private security agent.

ISSUES INVOLVING PRIVATE SECURITY

A number of unresolved problems and issues impinge on the potential for development of the private security industry. Some of them put the industry at odds with public law enforcement.

Legal Status and Authority Private security officers' legal status and authority derive from the rights of the owner who employs them to protect property on the premises. These rights are essentially the same ones you have to protect your life and property at home.

If this view prevails, private security personnel face few constitutional limitations in investigating crime, obtaining evidence, employing reasonable force, searching personal property stored in corporate spaces, and interrogating suspects. Although this is not a unanimous view among courts, it is the most prevalent one. However, private security officers and their employers face the possibility of being held civilly or criminally liable for violating an individual's civil rights or for false arrest.

Public Policing in a Private Capacity Although some police departments prohibit moonlighting, thousands of police officers still work in a private capacity during their off-duty hours. Some police agencies even cooperate with private agencies in scheduling their officers for off-duty assignments. With regard to their legal status and authority, are these officers considered public police or private security personnel? The private organization that employs them believes that off-duty police officers are better qualified, have more authority to arrest, and will have a greater deterrent effect on the crimes and disturbances of the peace the employer is trying to prevent.

An equally important question is, Who is liable should moonlighting officers abuse their authority or make a mistake? At present, it seems police agencies that take an active role in scheduling off-duty assignments accept greater liability than the police departments that do not. Many agencies limit the assignments officers are allowed to accept and the number of hours they are permitted to work.

Careers in Criminal Justice

U.S. Customs Special Agent

My name is Jose Pagan and I became a U.S. Customs Special Agent/Criminal Investigator in 1987. During my career, I have served as a federal law enforcement officer in the U.S. Virgin Islands, Puerto Rico, and Orlando, Florida, where I have been assigned since December 2000.

I have had the opportunity to conduct and participate in numerous narcotic interdiction investigations, as well as become a liaison officer between U.S. Customs and other federal and international law enforcement agencies.

As a U.S. Customs special agent, I have learned the value of organization and sound criminal investigation procedures as the primordial law enforcement tools. The investigation of crimes, regardless of type (passion, violence, financial, fraud, narcotic smuggling, counterfeiting, etc.), depends on sound standardized investigatory procedures. I have also mastered many investigative techniques. Among these techniques are interviewing skills such as detecting and utilizing flaws in elicited responses from a suspect, as well as observing behavior that could assist me in assessing the subject's veracity.

By utilizing proven criminal investigation procedures, in conjunction with the officer's experience, crime investigation becomes a scientific, measurable, and reliable method of protecting the public. Even in the investigation of the most heinous crimes, a reliable investigation, based on facts properly discovered and presented in an orderly, organized, and logical fashion, will always portray a fair, just, and clear case for the jury.

I have participated in operations such as the marine interdiction of narcotics and illegal aliens, as well as serving dozens of search warrants, all of which have demanded a great deal of physical exertion (added to the emotional stress that an assertive law enforcement action creates on the officers). Cases such as joint international investigations of narcotic smuggling have given me the opportunity to learn other countries' law enforcement techniques, customs, and points of view. At the same time, counterfeiting cases offer the opportunity to learn about the U.S. and international trade systems, as well as teaching the true impact that unfair trade practices have on the U.S. economy.

There are no typical days at the office in this career. On any given day, I could be on a vessel, sailing to prevent narcotic smuggling into the U.S., or interviewing the operation manager of a large company whose product has been counterfeited.

What parts of the U.S. Customs Special Agent's role do you find most and least appealing? Why?

Qualifications and Training Many superbly qualified people work in private security at all levels throughout the United States, but those people are not the norm. Although the minimum qualifications for private security personnel at all levels of employment are increasing, they lag far behind those of the public police. Few states enforce any educational, physical, or background integrity qualifications for private security personnel. In most states, the training required to become a private security officer is less than a week long. However, private security officers at nuclear power plants, for example, receive months of training before they are placed on the job under close supervision. In some states, armed security officers must attend a firearms course, including a section on the laws applicable to the use of deadly force, and must successfully complete a practical firearms qualification test. In nearly all states, public police officers who work off duty in a private policing capacity are exempt from any private security training, even if the nature of their private police work is substantially different from their police department functions.

The qualifications of proprietary security officers are generally higher than those of contract security officers, demonstrating corporate demand for high-quality security services even when they cost more.

FYI: Laws Governing Private Security

There are no federal laws governing the private security industry. No training is required for unarmed guards in 29 states and the District of Columbia. Private security officers do not have to be licensed in 22 states. In 16 states, background checks are not required.

Source: Mimi Hall, "Private Security Guards: Homeland Defense's Weak Link," *USA Today*, January 23, 2003, p. 1A.

Diminished Public Responsibility The current mixture of public and private protection is a matter of concern to many. What does it say about a government's ability to govern and provide for the general welfare—let alone what it says about American society—that ever more frequently it is shifting responsibility for protecting life and property to private security enterprises? To some, it seems to mean that public police officers and the governments that employ them have defaulted on a major portion of the social contract.

Private Security's Role in the Fight against Terrorism Private security officers are often the first line of defense against terrorism in the United States and other nations. They guard government buildings, utilities, schools, courts, corporate headquarters, office complexes, laboratories, and transportation facilities, to name only a few. Unfortunately, with relatively few exceptions, most of the nation's more than one million security officers are unlicensed, untrained, and do not undergo background checks (see the FYI above).

The private security industry and its officers have been given more protection responsibilities as the threat of domestic terrorism in the United States has increased. Public law enforcement alone cannot begin to meet the protection responsibilities necessary to prevent terrorism. This means that the private security industry, comprising 11,000 companies throughout America, will have to begin improving its selection standards and training if the nation's people, visitors, and assets are to be protected. As unbelievable as it is, hundreds of security guards employed to protect the Statue of Liberty were found in 2002 to have no licenses and their ranks included ex-convicts.

Because it is so difficult to find enough capable private security officers, the proprietary security firms, motivated by large profits, have been employing hundreds if not thousands of unqualified and unmotivated applicants. For many of the guards, the position is a second or low-paying job that they can easily quit if they find a better-paying job or simply choose to do so. More troublesome is that foreign and domestic terrorists could easily obtain a private security position and inflict physical and emotional havoc on the nation by initiating some terrorist activity inside a vulnerable site.

Seldom is throwing money at a problem a solution in and of itself; yet, if the private security industry is to fulfill its obligation to protect the homeland, it is going to need more financial resources. It may be necessary, for example, to provide government subsidies for training and background checks and a significant increase in the amount of cooperation between the public police and the private security industry. That sort of investment and training can bring positive results. Following the 1993 World Trade Center bombing, the security officers at the World Trade Center were provided in-depth and regular follow-up training on such topics as emergency evacuation procedures and building layout. On September 11, 2001, security officers helped thousands of building workers safely out of the World Trade Center before the twin towers fell.

THINKING CRITICALLY

1. What do you think are some of the benefits and drawbacks of being a private security officer?
2. Do you think that stricter qualification standards should be established for private security personnel? Why or why not?

SUMMARY

1. Briefly describe the jurisdictional limitations of American law enforcement

The authority of public law enforcement agencies in the United States, whether they are local, state, or federal agencies, is carefully limited by law. The territory within which each may operate is also restricted.

2. Trace the english origins of American law enforcement

Many institutions of American law enforcement evolved from the English tradition. The medieval tithing system and the constable-watch system were early methods of community protection that led to the development of the positions of sheriff and constable. The Bow Street Runners in the city of London in the 1750s were an early group of crime fighters who patrolled neighborhoods and pursued lawbreakers. The London Metropolitan Police, founded in 1829, became the model for municipal police departments in the United States.

3. Discuss the early development of American law enforcement

Americans at first adopted the British system of community protection. When the constable-watch system proved inadequate in meeting the peacekeeping needs of the nation's major cities, municipal police forces were established in the mid-1800s. They soon became entangled with local politics. In the states and on the frontier, law enforcement reflected regional differences. In the South, the earliest policing was the plantation slave patrols. On the frontier, vigilantism and later, local sheriffs or U.S. marshals dealt with lawbreakers. In some states, state police agencies, such as the Texas Rangers, were established to enforce laws statewide.

4. Describe the major developments that have occurred in policing in America

During the period of professionalism and reform that lasted from about 1920 to 1970, the police became professional crime fighters, relying on the centralization of authority, motorized patrols, specialization, and technological aids. In the 1960s, the crime-fighting role of the police came into conflict with the social and political upheavals of the time, causing critics to call for improved standards and training. By the early 1990s, some police agencies began to turn to community policing, attempting to eliminate crime problems in neighborhoods and return to their role as peacekeepers. At the start of the twenty-first century, the prevention and repression of domestic terrorism has also become a major priority of police in America.

5. Describe the structure of American law enforcement

Law enforcement agencies are found at all levels of government in the United States. Most law enforcement officers work for local governments and are responsible for enforcing laws, maintaining order, providing service, and gathering information. In rural areas, the county sheriffs' department is responsible for law enforcement. Every state, except Hawaii, has a state law enforcement agency. The law enforcement agencies of the federal government are concerned primarily with violations of federal laws, especially violations that cross state boundaries; maintaining homeland security; and preventing domestic terrorism.

6. Explain the relationship between the FBI and the Department of Homeland Security

Since 9/11, the FBI has undergone fundamental changes. The biggest change is that it has shifted its top priority from being a federal police agency to being an intelligence and counterterrorism agency. Although it remains an independent agency in the Justice Department, it will now closely coordinate its antiterrorism activities with the CIA and the Department of Homeland Security.

7. Discuss the development and growth of private security in the United States

The private security industry has grown rapidly over the past 30 years for a number of reasons: revenues for public policing have declined (until recently); crimes in the workplace are often private, costly, and embarrassing; employers have better control of private security officers; and fewer constitutional limits restrict private security officers.

KEY TERMS

jurisdiction, p. 147
tithing system, p. 148
shire reeve, p. 148
posses, p. 148
constable-watch system, p. 148
constable, p. 148
Peel's Principles of Policing, p. 150
slave patrols, p. 154
community policing, p. 158
state police model, p. 169
highway patrol model, p. 169
contract security, p. 179
proprietary security, p. 179

REVIEW QUESTIONS

1. What is meant by *jurisdiction*?
2. What was the *tithing system*?
3. Who were the Bow Street Runners?
4. In what year was the London Metropolitan Police founded?
5. Who was Robert Peel? What name is given to his 12 standards for policing?
6. What system of English policing did the colonists bring to America?
7. What were the *slave codes*?
8. What group is considered to be the first state police agency?
9. How did August Vollmer change policing?
10. How did police response to the demonstrations and civil disorders of the 1960s affect policing?
11. What is *community policing*?
12. What are the four main functions of local police?
13. Why do county sheriffs have more political clout than police chiefs?
14. What is the difference between a *state police model* and a *highway patrol model* of state law enforcement?
15. Name some federal law enforcement agencies.
16. Distinguish between *contract* and *proprietary private security services*.
17. What are some successes and problems in the war on terrorism?
18. How do the employment qualifications for private security personnel in the United States compare and contrast with the qualifications to be a police officer, deputy sheriff, state police, or federal agent?

IN THE FIELD

1. **Your Local Law Enforcement** Identify all the local law enforcement agencies in your area. Divide up the list among your classmates and arrange to visit your assigned agency. On the day that you visit, find out how many calls the department received and/or how many crimes the agency personnel investigated in the 24-hour period prior to your visit, what types of calls were received or crimes were investigated, and how the agency handled the situation. Categorize the actions of the agency personnel into law enforcement, order maintenance, service, or information gathering. Identify the category with the most action. Share your findings with others in the class. What conclusions can you draw about the operation of the local law enforcement agencies in your area?

2. **Local and Private Police** Describe the possibilities you see for local police departments and private security agencies to work together more closely. To prepare for this activity, interview a local police official and a private security manager, either by telephone or in person, asking them what obstacles prevent closer cooperation between local policing and private security.

ON THE NET

1. **Local Police Jobs** Go to the following links for sites dedicated to law enforcement careers and select two municipal police departments, one large and one small, and one county sheriffs' department that list the agency's employment qualifications on their Web page:

   http://copspotweb.hypermart.net/employment
   http://govtjobs.com/safe/index.html
   http://www.jawp.org/jobs.htm
   http://www.jobs4police.com
   http://www.lawenforcementjobs.com
   http://www.cops2be.com/jobs/new_jobs_database.htm
   http://www.onpatrol.com/employ.html
   http://www.policecareer.com
   http://www.policeemployment.com
   http://www.wpoaca.com/job.html
   http://www.lawenforcementjobs.com

Then find the qualifications for a private security officer through other applicable career sites provided at www.securityjobs.net or www.bls.gov/oco/ocos159.htm. Make a list of the similarities and differences between police and deputy sheriff qualifications and private security officer qualifications. Given your background and abilities, for which type of work would you be best suited? Why? Compile your findings in a two-page report and present it to the class.

2. **Federal Law Enforcement** To learn about the responsibilities of some of the lesser-known federal law enforcement agencies, access their websites: (1) *Food and Drug Administration, Office of Criminal Investigations,* http://www.fda.gov/ora/inspect_ref/iom/ChapterText/980.html; (2) *National Park Service, U.S. Park Police,* http://www.nps.gov/usparkpolice; (3) *U.S. Fish and Wildlife Service, Division of Law Enforcement,* http://www.le.fws.gov; and (4) *U.S. Capitol Police.* http://www.fedquest.com/opmrefs/tei51.htm. Which agency seems the most interesting? Why?

CRITICAL THINKING EXERCISES

1. **Neighborhood Watch** You live in a middle-class community of single-family homes close to the center of a midsize city. Over the past 5 years, everyone in your neighborhood has noted the rise in burglaries and many people feel that it is not safe to walk around the neighborhood after dark. You think that setting up a neighborhood watch would help lower the burglary rate and make people feel safer. Prepare an oral presentation of your ideas for a community meeting. Use the following questions as a guide.
   a. How would you go about organizing a night watch?
   b. How would you select volunteers?
   c. What training, if any, would volunteers have to have?
   d. How would you maintain interest and participation in the watch?

2. **Public Officer or Private Citizen?** An off-duty police officer was seated in a restaurant when two men entered, drew guns, and robbed the cashier. The officer made no attempt to prevent the robbery or apprehend the robbers. Later the officer justified the conduct by stating that an officer, when off duty, is a private citizen with the same duties and rights as all private citizens. Do you agree? Explain.

POLICING: ROLES, STYLES, AND FUNCTIONS

CHAPTER SIX

Chapter Outline

Chapter Objectives

After completing this chapter, you should be able to:

1. Identify characteristics of police work.
2. Distinguish among James Q. Wilson's three operational styles in policing.
3. List the four major functions of police departments.
4. List the drug enforcement strategies of local police agencies.
5. Explain the main components of community policing.
6. Identify the four steps in a community policing approach to problem solving.
7. Define terrorism and identify different types of terrorism.

Crime Story

On June 5, 2002, 14-year-old Elizabeth Smart was abducted from her Salt Lake City home by a gunman who entered after cutting a window screen near the back door of the home. She was taken from a bedroom that she shared with her 9-year-old sister, Mary Katharine. The younger girl told authorities she heard the gunman threaten to hurt Elizabeth if the teenager did not keep quiet.

Police initially focused their investigation on Richard Albert Ricci, a handyman who previously had worked for the Smart family. Ricci denied any involvement in the kidnapping case and later died on August 30, 2002, after suffering a brain hemorrhage while in the Utah State Prison on charges related to an earlier burglary incident of the Smart family home.

On March 12, 2003, Elizabeth Smart was found in Sandy, Utah, within 15 miles of her Salt Lake City home. The teen's blonde hair had been concealed with a veil and wig in an attempt to elude detection by authorities. Elizabeth was in the company of 45-year-old Brian David Mitchell and a woman believed to be his wife, 57-year-old Wanda Eileen Barzee. Mitchell was described as a self-proclaimed prophet, who ironically had also been a former handyman of the Smart family. Both Mitchell and Barzee were subsequently charged with aggravated kidnapping, aggravated sexual assault, and aggravated burglary in connection with Smart's abduction.

Elizabeth's father, Ed Smart, while tearfully speaking at a news conference, challenged Congress to pass the AMBER legislation that was being considered by national lawmakers at the time. Smart believed that if a communitywide early warning system had been available, then his daughter's abductors would likely have been detected sooner.

The so-called AMBER Plan was first created in 1996 as a legacy to 9-year-old Amber Hagerman who was kidnapped while riding her bicycle in Arlington, Texas, and later murdered. Dallas area residents suggested that radio stations broadcast special-alert messages that would allow the community to assist police in detecting and apprehending child abductors. Time is of the essence in locating abducted children, and this innovative early warning system has proven effective in some abduction cases.

Chapter 6 discusses the philosophy and various components of community policing. Implementation of community policing requires police agencies to provide an assessment of their overall effectiveness in preventing crime within a given area or community. Determining the true crime-reducing power of community policing is difficult to accurately assess, because the amount of crime that has already occurred is easier to measure than the amount of crime that has been successfully deterred. Would effective community policing and the availability of an AMBER alert system have resulted in Elizabeth Smart returning home sooner? The answer to this question is not readily apparent. However, if community policing strategies such as AMBER alert increase public awareness about crime, and encourage interactions between police and citizenry, then community policing may become an effective tool for combating crime.

Policing in America

The police are at the forefront of the criminal justice process and, for most people, the only personal experience they have with that process is contact with a local police officer. Most people have never been in a courthouse for a criminal matter or in a jail or prison for any reason. This chapter examines what the police do, and the qualities they need to do it.

THE ROLES OF THE POLICE

Our expectations of police behavior depend on where we live and when we consider the question. For example, we saw in the last chapter that Cincinnati wanted its police officers in the 1880s to be fleet-footed and honest. In Dallas, Miami, and New York City, citizens may expect police officers to have a working knowledge of Spanish. In Alaska, we would expect police officers to be self-reliant, enjoy the outdoors, and not mind working by themselves in lonely surroundings. In essence, what we expect from the police depends on how we view their role in society.

A **role** consists of the rights and responsibilities associated with a particular position in society. A related concept is **role expectation,** the behavior and actions that people expect from a person in a particular role. Suppose, for example, that teenagers living in a wealthy neighborhood have been caught drinking alcohol. Their parents probably expect police officers to warn the young people and bring them home. In a less affluent neighborhood, on the other hand, the expectation of community residents might be that the police will arrest the teenagers and bring them into juvenile court. This example illustrates a problem that often arises in our attempt to understand the police role in America. When the public's expectations differ from the official police role, the public may become disenchanted and sometimes hostile toward law enforcement officers. Such negative feelings

role The rights and responsibilities associated with a particular position in society.

role expectation The behavior and actions that people expect from a person in a particular role.

Police officers are expected to respond to traffic accidents. *How might such experiences affect them?*

role conflict The psychological stress and frustration that results from trying to perform two or more incompatible responsibilities.

cause officers personal frustration and role conflict. **Role conflict** is the psychological strain and stress that results from trying to perform two or more incompatible responsibilities. A common source of role conflict for the police is the expectation that they should be social or helping agents at the same time they are expected to be control agents by arresting law violators.

What we expect from police officers, then, depends on how we view the police role—a role that has been described as complex, ambiguous, changing, and repressive. Obviously, not everyone views the role of the police in the same way, but a definition that includes the majority of perspectives is possible. The police:

1. Are community leaders in public safety. (By nature, this makes the work potentially dangerous.)
2. Possess broad discretion.
3. Solve sociological and technological problems for people on a short-term basis.
4. Occasionally serve in a hostile or dangerous environment.[1]

Think about some of the common situations in which police officers find themselves when people call and want something "fixed." One example would be an officer's response to freeway accidents where vehicles are overturned and burning and people are trapped inside. Such situations require leadership, informed and quick decisions, the solving of numerous immediate problems, and the use of extreme caution to prevent further injury to citizens or the police officer. Another example would be intervention in a long-running family dispute that has suddenly turned violent. Such a situation requires caution, quick thinking, and the solving of a number of problems in an effort to ensure the safety of all parties. Still another typical role of a police officer is to provide protection at protests and strikes. Those potentially volatile circumstances clearly illustrate the key elements of the police role. Of course, sometimes an officer's role may be simply to solve problems in the course of providing service, as when retrieving a citizen's dropped keys from below a sewer grate.

CHARACTERISTICS OF POLICE WORK

Police work requires a combination of special characteristics. Personnel with the following qualities are best able to carry out the difficult service role mandated for law enforcement officers.

Quick Decision Making Sometimes police officers must make on-the-spot decisions about whether to use force, how to maneuver a patrol car, or whether to stop a suspect. Making the wrong decision can be fatal for the officer or the other person. All of the work in a lengthy investigation can be ruined by a single procedural law violation if an officer unintentionally makes a wrong decision.

The Independent Nature of Police Work The position of peace officer in all states in the United States is a position of honor and trust. After patrol officers attend roll call, stand inspection, check out their equipment, and depart into the streets in their patrol cars, they work virtually unsupervised until the end of their tour of duty.

Figure 6.1 shows the Law Enforcement Officer's Code of Ethics, which was written as a guide for working police officers. It offers some professional

FIGURE 6.1 **Law Enforcement Officer Code of Ethics**

The purpose of the Code of Ethics is to ensure that all peace officers are fully aware of their individual responsibility to maintain their own integrity and that of their agency. Every peace officer, during basic training, or at the time of appointment, shall be administered the [following] Code of Ethics.

As a law enforcement officer, my fundamental duty is to serve mankind; to safeguard lives and property; to protect the innocent against deception, the weak against oppression or intimidation, and the peaceful against violence or disorder; and to respect the constitutional rights of all men to liberty, equality, and justice.

I will keep my private life unsullied as an example to all; maintain courageous calm in the face of danger, scorn, or ridicule; develop self-restraint; and be constantly mindful of the welfare of others. Honest in thought and deed in both my personal and official life, I will be exemplary in obeying the laws of the land and the regulations of my department. Whatever I see or hear of a confidential nature or that is confided to me in my official capacity will be kept ever secret unless revelation is necessary in the performance of my duty. I will never act officiously or permit personal feelings, prejudices, animosities, or friendships to influence my decisions. With no compromise for crime and with relentless prosecution of criminals, I will enforce the law courteously and appropriately without fear or favor, malice or ill will, never employing unnecessary force or violence, and never accepting gratuities.

I recognize the badge of my office as a symbol of public faith, and I accept it as a public trust to be held so long as I am true to the ethics of the police service. I will constantly strive to achieve these objectives and ideals, dedicating myself to my chosen profession—law enforcement.

Canons

1. The primary responsibility of police officers and organizations is the protection of citizens by upholding the law and respecting the legally expressed will of the whole community and not a particular party or clique.

2. Police officers should be aware of the legal limits on their authority and the "genius of the American system," which limits the power of individuals, groups, and institutions.

3. Police officers are responsible for being familiar with the law and not only their responsibilities but also those of other public officials.

4. Police officers should be mindful of the importance of using the proper means to gain proper ends. Officers should not employ illegal means, nor should they disregard public safety or property to accomplish a goal.

5. Police officers will cooperate with other public officials in carrying out their duties. However, the officer shall be careful not to use his or her position in an improper or illegal manner when cooperating with other officials.

6. In their private lives, police officers will behave in such a manner that the public will "regard (the officer) as an example of stability, fidelity, and morality." It is necessary that police officers conduct themselves in a "decent and honorable" manner.

7. In their behavior toward members of the public, officers will provide service when possible, require compliance with the law, respond in a manner that inspires confidence and trust, and will be neither overbearing nor subservient.

8. When dealing with violators or making arrests, officers will follow the law; officers have no right to persecute individuals or punish them. And officers should behave in such a manner so the likelihood of the use of force is minimized.

9. Police officers should refuse to accept any gifts, favors, or gratuities that, from a public perspective, could influence the manner in which the officer discharges his or her duties.

10. Officers will present evidence in criminal cases impartially because the officer should be equally concerned with both the prosecution of criminals and the defense of innocent persons.

SOURCE: Commission on Peace Officer Standards and Training, *Administrative Manual* (State of California POST, 1990), p. c.-5.

TABLE 6.1 Law Enforcement Officers Assaulted in the United States, 2001

Circumstances at Scene of Incident	Total
Total	56,666
Percent of Total	100%
Disturbance calls (family quarrel, man with gun, etc.)	17,809
	31.4%
Burglaries in progress or pursuit of burglary suspects	778
	1.4%
Robberies in progress or pursuit of robbery suspects	549
	1.0%
Other arrest attempts	9,107
	16.1%
Civil disorders (mass disobedience, riot, etc.)	579
	1.0%
Handling, transporting, custody of prisoners	7,343
	13.0%
Investigation of suspicious persons and circumstances	5,862
	10.3%
Ambush (no warning)	179
	0.3%
Mentally deranged	914
	1.6%
Traffic pursuits and stops	6,345
	11.2%
All other	7,201
	12.7%

Source: United States Department of Justice, Federal Bureau of Investigation, *Uniform Crime Reports*, www.fbi.gov/ucr/ucr.htm, May 10, 2003, p. 93, Table 38.

direction in a line of work with many opportunities to go astray. The independent nature of police work increases the chances of malfeasance and corruption—topics to be discussed in the next chapter.

"Dirty Work" Most people agree that police work needs to be done, but police work is sometimes distasteful—for example, dealing with people who have committed horrible acts and viewing mangled, broken, and decomposed bodies. Oftentimes, the police must deal with people at their worst—angry, drunk, in trouble, victimized, violent, and so forth. The distasteful part of policing has been referred to as "dirty work."[2]

Danger Police officers in the United States spend a substantial amount of their time trying to resolve conflicts, frequently in hostile environments.[3] Table 6.1 identifies dangerous circumstances in which officers find themselves. Contrary to the media image, police officers are often afraid on the job, and far too many are injured or killed. The data reveal that disturbance calls (for example, a family quarrel or a man with a gun) and arrests of suspects are the most dangerous circumstances for police officers. Because of the danger they face, many departments require their field officers to wear body armor

TABLE 6.2 **Body Armor Requirements for Field Officers in Local Police Departments, by Size of Population Served, 2000**

Population Served	Percent of Agencies Requiring Field Officers to Wear Armor While on Duty		
	Total	All Officers	Some Officers
All Sizes	64%	56%	8%
1,000,000 or more	67%	53%	14%
500,000–999,999	75	44	31
250,000–499,999	57	42	15
100,000–249,999	56	50	6
50,000–99,999	66	50	16
25,000–49,999	66	54	12
10,000–24,999	71	61	10
2,500–9,999	68	60	8
Under 2,500	59	52	7

SOURCE: Matthew J. Hickman and Brian A. Reaves, *Local Police Departments, 2000,* U.S. Department of Justice, Bureau of Justice Statistics (Washington, DC: GPO, January 2003), p. 18, Table 38.

while on duty. Table 6.2 shows the percentage of local police departments, by size of population served, that required field officers to wear body armor while on duty in 2000.

Despite the use of body armor and other precautions, each year police officers are killed while on duty. In 2002, for example, 56 officers were feloniously killed in the line of duty, many fewer than the 142 officers killed feloniously in 2001 and a few more than the 51 officers killed feloniously in 2000. However, 2001 was an unusual year. Among the 142 officers feloniously killed were the 72 federal, state, and local officers killed during the tragedy of September 11—the most officers killed in the United States on a single day. In 1999, only 42 officers were feloniously killed in the line of duty, which was the lowest recorded figure in more than 35 years.[4]

Of the 56 officers feloniously killed in the line of duty in 2002, 14 lost their lives during ambush situations, 10 officers were murdered answering disturbance calls, 10 were killed during traffic pursuits and stops, another 10 during arrest situations, 8 while investigating suspicious persons or circumstances, and 4 by mentally deranged assailants.[5] Accidents, such as automobile accidents, during the performance of official duties claimed the lives of an additional 76 officers in 2002, 78 in 2001, 84 in 2000, and 65 in 1999.[6]

From 1972 through 2002, 4,512 law enforcement officers were killed in the line of duty: 2,623 were feloniously killed and 1,889 were accidentally killed. The most officers killed in any one year were 220 in 2001, while the least in any year was 107 in 1999. In general, and with the exception of 2001, the number of law enforcement officers killed while on duty has declined since the early 1970s.[7]

FYI

Killed in the Line-of-duty

Today, more than 800,000 sworn officers put their lives on the line for our protection each day. The first known line-of-duty death was that of U.S. Marshal Robert Forsyth, who was shot and killed on January 11, 1794, while serving court papers in a civil suit. Wilmington, Delaware, police matron Mary T. Davis was the first female officer killed on duty. She was beaten to death in 1924 while guarding a prisoner in the city jail.

OPERATIONAL STYLES

After police officers are trained and begin to gain experience and wisdom from their encounters with veteran police officers and citizens on the street,

operational styles The different overall approaches to the police job.

it is believed that they develop **operational styles** that characterize their overall approach to the police job. If these styles actually exist, it means that the effort of the police department to systematically train and deploy officers with the same philosophy and practical approach to policing in the community has not been entirely successful. The research on operational styles shows that they vary both between departments and among officers of the same department.

One of the earliest scholars to report on the existence of policing styles was James Q. Wilson, who found the following three styles in a study of eight police departments:

1. Legalistic style. The emphasis is on violations of law and the use of threats or actual arrests to solve disputes in the community. In theory, the more arrests that are made, the safer a community will be. This style is often found in large metropolitan areas.
2. Watchman style. The emphasis is on informal means of resolving disputes and problems in a community. Keeping the peace is the paramount concern, and arrest is used only as a last resort to resolve any kind of disturbance of the peace. This style of policing is most commonly found in economically poorer communities.
3. Service style. The emphasis is on helping in the community, as opposed to enforcing the law. Referrals and diversion to community treatment agencies are more common than arrest and formal court action. The service style is most likely to be found in wealthy communities.[8]

John Broderick, another scholar who studied operational styles among the police, classified police officers by their degree of commitment to maintaining order and their respect for due process:

1. Enforcers. The emphasis is on order, with little respect for due process.
2. Idealists. The emphasis is on both social order and due process.
3. Optimists. The emphasis is on due process, with little priority given to social order.
4. Realists. Little emphasis is given to due process or social order.[9]

Another classification is based on the way officers use their authority and power in street police work. The two key ingredients of this scheme are passion and perspective. Passion is the ability to use force or the recognition that force is a legitimate means of resolving conflict; perspective is the ability to understand human suffering and to use force ethically and morally. According to William Muir's styles of policing, police officers may be:

1. Professionals. Officers have the necessary passion and perspective to be valuable police officers.
2. Enforcers. Officers have passion for the job, for enforcing the law, for taking decisive action; their inner drive or value system allows them to be comfortable using force to solve problems.
3. Reciprocators. Officers lack the passion to do the job; they have a difficult time taking action, making arrests, enforcing the law; their values make it difficult for them to use force to solve problems.
4. Avoiders. Officers have neither passion nor perspective, resulting in no recognition of people's problems and no action to resolve them.[10]

Are there identifiable styles of policing? What value do these styles hold for us? In any area of human endeavor, classifications have been constructed. We have developed classifications for leaders, prisoners, quarterbacks, and teachers. These classifications give us a framework of analysis, a basis for discussion. But can they be substantiated when we go into a police agency to see if they actually exist?

Ellen Hochstedler examined the issue of policing styles with 1,134 Dallas, Texas, police officers and was not able to confirm the officer styles identified in the literature by Broderick, Muir, and others. Her conclusion was that it is not possible to "pigeonhole" officers into one style or another because the way officers think and react to street situations varies, depending on the particular situation, the time, and the officers themselves.[11]

THINKING CRITICALLY

1. Which characteristics do you think are the most important for police officers to have? Why?
2. Is there an operational style of policing that you think is the most effective? If so, which one?
3. Do you think it is possible to identify styles of policing? If so, how can it be done? If not, what obstacles prevent identification?

Police Functions

The list of functions that police are expected to carry out is long and varies from place to place. In the following sections, we will look at the major operations of police departments and the services they provide.

PATROL

Police administrators have long referred to patrol as the backbone of the department. It is unquestionably the most time-consuming and resource-intensive task of any police agency. More than half of the sworn personnel in any police department are assigned to patrol. In Houston, Chicago, and New York, for example, patrol officers make up more than 65 percent of the sworn personnel in each department.

Patrol officers respond to burglar alarms, investigate traffic accidents, care for injured people, try to resolve domestic disputes, and engage in a host of other duties that keep them chasing radio calls across their own beats and the entire city and county when no other cars are available to respond. Precisely how to conduct patrol activities, however, is a matter of much debate in the nation today. Indeed, it seems that there are many ways to police a city.

preventive patrol Patrolling the streets with little direction; between responses to radio calls, officers are "systematically unsystematic" and observant in an attempt to both prevent and ferret out crime. Also known as random patrol.

PREVENTIVE PATROL For decades, police officers patrolled the streets with little direction. Between their responses to radio calls, they were told to be "systematically unsystematic" and observant in an attempt to both prevent and ferret out crime on their beats. In many police departments, as much as 50 percent of an officer's time is uncommitted and available for patrolling the beats that make up a political jurisdiction. The simultaneous increases in the official crime rate and the size of police forces beginning in the 1960s caused police managers and academics to question the usefulness of what has come to be known as **preventive patrol** or random patrol. To test the usefulness of preventive patrol, the now famous Kansas City (Missouri) Preventive Patrol Experiment was conducted in 1972.

Street patrol is the most resource-intensive task of any police agency. *Are there acceptable alternatives to street patrol? If yes, what are they?*

The Kansas City, Missouri, Police Department and the Police Foundation set up an experiment in which 15 patrol districts were divided into three matched groups according to size, record of calls for service, and demographic characteristics. In the first group, the "control beats," the police department operated the same level of patrol used previously in those beats. In the second group of districts, the "proactive beats," the police

Myth	Fact
Adding more police officers will reduce crime.	Short of having a police officer on every corner, evidence indicates no relationship between the number of police officers and the crime rate.

department doubled or even tripled the number of patrol officers normally deployed in the area. In the third group of districts, the "reactive beats," the police department deployed no officers at all on preventive patrol. Officers only responded to calls for service and did no patrolling on their own. At the end of the 1-year study, the results showed no significant differences in crime rates among the three groups of patrol districts. In other words, a group of districts that had no officers on preventive patrol had the same crime rates as groups that had several times the normal level of staffing engaged in patrol activity. The number of officers made no difference in the number of burglaries, robberies, vehicle thefts, and other serious crimes experienced in the three groups of police districts. Perhaps even more important is that the citizens of Kansas City did not even notice that the levels of patrol in two of the three districts had been changed.[12]

The law enforcement community was astounded by the results of the study, which showed that it made no difference whether patrol officers conducted preventive, or random, patrol. The research was immediately attacked on both philosophical and methodological grounds. How could anyone say that having patrol officers on the street made no difference?

One of the criticisms of the study was that no one in the community was told that there were no officers on patrol in reactive districts. What might have happened to the crime rates had the community known no officers were on patrol? Moreover, during the course of the study, marked police cars from other departments and districts crossed the reactive districts to answer calls but then left when the work was completed. Thus, there appeared to be a police presence even in the so-called reactive districts.

This study has forced police executives and academics to reconsider the whole issue of how patrol is conducted, once considered a closed issue. Police administrators have begun to entertain the possibility of reducing the number of officers on patrol. Innovations in patrol methods have also been proposed.

directed patrol Patrolling under guidance or orders on how to use patrol time.

Directed Patrol In **directed patrol,** officers are given guidance or orders on how to use their patrol time. The guidance is often based on the results of crime analyses that identify problem areas. Evidence shows that directed patrol can reduce the incidence of targeted crimes such as thefts from autos and robberies.[13]

GIS crime mapping A technique that involves the charting of crime patterns within a geographic area.

Crime Mapping One technological innovation in crime analysis that has aided directed patrol is Geographic Information Systems (GIS) crime mapping. **GIS crime mapping** is a technique that involves the charting of crime patterns within a geographic area. Crime mapping makes it possible to keep a closer watch on crime and criminals through the generation of crime maps capable of displaying numerous fields of information. If, for example, a series of armed robberies of dry cleaning stores had been committed over a period of several weeks in three adjacent police beats, police crime analysts would be able to record, analyze, determine a definite pattern to these robberies, and make a reasonable prediction as to when and where the next robbery in the series is likely to occur. The patrol and investigation forces could be deployed at a prescribed time to conduct surveillance of the prospective target dry cleaning store or stores with a good chance the robber can be arrested. This use of crime mapping is referred to as "resource reallocation" and is probably the most widely used crime-mapping application. Figure 6.2 is an example of a crime map.

FIGURE 6.2 **Crime Map of Portland Metro Area 1997 Number of Violent Crimes**

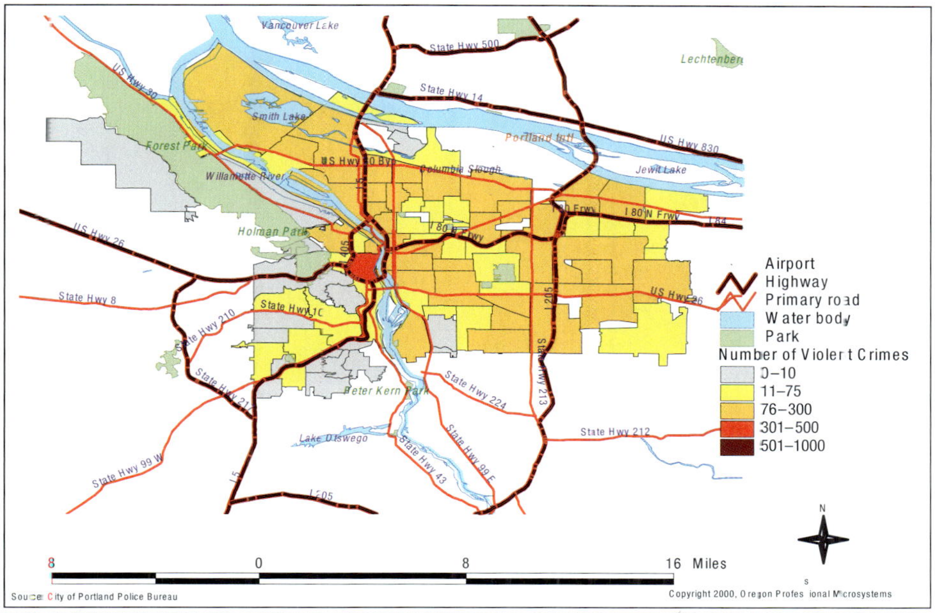

This crime map shows the number of violent crimes in areas of Portland, Oregon. *What can be learned about the causes of crime from crime mapping?*

Crime mapping is also used as a tool to help evaluate the ability of police departments to resolve the problems in their communities. This is the primary purpose of the New York City Police Department's CompStat process, for example.[14] Begun in 1994, CompStat is a divisional unit responsible for statistical analysis of daily precinct crime reports frequently using crime mapping. The information produced by CompStat is used by the chief of police to judge the performance of precinct commanders and by precinct commanders to hold their officers accountable.

Crime mapping is likely to be used increasingly in crime scene investigations and the forensic sciences. For example, a GIS-based system has been created that can determine the origin of gunshots through sound triangulation. Crime mapping will also be combined with other technologies such as aerial photography so that geocoded data can be superimposed on aerial photographs rather than computer-generated maps. This should aid community-policing efforts by making census data, liquor license locations, drug-market data, and probationer addresses, for example, readily available in a more useful form. Another technology that will be combined with crime mapping is Global Positioning Systems (GPS) technology. Such technology would allow beat officers to track and monitor probationers and parolees in the area, for example. It is currently used in some departments to help manage the department's fleet of vehicles.[15]

CJ ONLINE

GIS Crime Mapping

To learn more about GIS crime mapping and how it works, visit the GIS Lounge at **http://gislounge.com/features/aa101100.shtml.** *Why is crime mapping important?*

Aggressive Patrol In nearly all police departments, some patrol officers have used aggressive patrol tactics and have been rewarded as high performers because they made many arrests for both minor and serious offenses. When the entire patrol section is instructed to make numerous traffic stops

Field interrogation has been found to reduce crime in targeted areas. *What are some of the problems with field interrogations?*

aggressive patrol The practice of having an entire patrol section make numerous traffic stops and field interrogations.

field interrogation A temporary detention in which officers stop and question pedestrians and motorists they find in suspicious circumstances.

and field interrogations, the practice is referred to as **aggressive patrol.** A **field interrogation** is a temporary detention in which officers stop and question pedestrians and motorists they find in suspicious circumstances. Such procedures have been found to reduce crime in targeted areas.[16]

At least two problems can occur as a result of aggressive patrol. First, random traffic stops and field interrogations inconvenience innocent citizens. To avoid conflict, the police must be certain that those tactics are necessary, and they must explain the necessity to the public. Second, it is often difficult to get all officers on each work shift and in each patrol division motivated to use aggressive patrol tactics. Many officers are reluctant to carry out their duties in an aggressive way. Nevertheless, with crime rates high and research confirming that aggressive patrol can reduce crime, aggressive patrol tactics are likely to continue.

FYI

Patrolling

In 2000, 62 percent of local police departments, including 86 percent of those serving 250,000 or more residents, routinely used foot patrol. All local police departments used automobiles for routine patrol. In addition, approximately 40 percent of departments, including more than 90 percent of those serving 100,000 or more residents, used bicycle patrol on a regular basis.

SOURCE: Matthew J. Hicks and Brian A. Reaves, *Local Police Departments, 2000* (Washington, DC: Bureau of Justice Statistics, 2003), p. iii.

FOOT PATROL For sometime, there has been renewed interest in having police officers patrol their beats on foot. Is there value in this practice, or is it just nostalgia for a more romantic period in law enforcement? The use of motorized patrols has allowed the police to respond rapidly to citizen calls and to cover large geographical areas. Yet, officers working a busy shift, perhaps responding to more than two dozen calls, come to feel as if they are seeing the world through a windshield. Moreover, it is now generally accepted that rapid response time is useful in only a small portion of the incidents and crimes to which the police are asked to respond.

Challenging conventional wisdom about rapid response, two cities—Flint, Michigan, and Newark, New Jersey—launched substantial programs in foot patrol. In Newark, the results of the foot patrol experiment showed that foot patrol had little or no effect on the level of crime. However, positive effects were identified:

1. Newark residents noticed whether foot patrol officers were present.
2. They were more satisfied with police service when foot patrol officers delivered it.
3. They were less afraid than citizens being served by motorized patrol.[17]

TABLE 6.3 Types of Patrol Used on a Routine Basis by Local Police Departments, by Size of Population Served, 2000

Population Served	Percent of Agencies Using Each Type of Patrol on a Routine Basis					
	Automobile	Foot	Bicycle	Motorcycle	Marine	Horse
All sizes	100%	62%	43%	12%	3%	2%
1,000,000 or more	100%	87%	93%	87%	53%	67%
500,000–999,999	100	78	97	91	56	53
250,000–499,999	100	93	98	88	30	63
100,000–249,999	100	65	91	88	13	26
50,000–99,999	100	65	84	65	11	9
25,000–49,999	100	58	79	48	6	3
10,000–24,999	100	59	71	18	5	1
2,500–9,999	100	64	51	6	2	1
Under 2,500	100	61	17	1	2	—

—Less than 0.5%.

Source: Matthew J. Hickman and Brian A. Reaves, *Local Police Departments, 2000,* U.S. Department of Justice, Bureau of Justice Statistics (Washington, DC: GPO, January 2003), p. 10, Table 18.

In Flint, Michigan, the extensive neighborhood foot patrol experiment also had positive results:

1. Flint residents had a decreased fear of crime.
2. Their satisfaction with police service increased.
3. There were moderate decreases in crime.
4. There were decreased numbers of calls for police service.

Citizens would wait to talk to their neighborhood foot patrol officer about a problem instead of calling the police department through 911 and speaking with an officer they were not likely to know. One astounding result of the Flint program was that the foot patrol officers became so popular that citizens saw them as real community leaders. They often became more influential than some elected officials. Evidence of the degree of satisfaction with the foot patrol program in Flint was that the community voted three times to continue and expand foot patrol at a time when the city was experiencing one of the nation's highest unemployment rates.[18] Perhaps even more important, the findings of foot patrol research provided the seeds of a much broader concept for law enforcement: community policing, which we will discuss later in this chapter. Table 6.3 shows the percentage of agencies, by size of population served, that used various types of patrol on a routine basis in 2000.

INVESTIGATION

The role of the detective has generally been glorified by media sources in both fiction and nonfiction accounts. Homicide investigation, in particular, has captured the imagination of fiction readers worldwide. Most police officers aspire to be investigative specialists by attaining the position of detective. But it should be noted that detectives represent only one unit in a police department that conducts investigations. Investigators work in a variety of capacities in a police agency:

1. Traffic homicide and hit-and-run accident investigators in the traffic section.
2. Undercover investigators in narcotics, vice, and violent gang cases.
3. Internal affairs investigators conducting investigations of alleged crimes by police personnel.
4. Investigators conducting background checks of applicants to the police department.
5. Uniformed patrol officers investigating the crimes they have been dispatched to or have encountered on their own while on patrol.
6. Detectives of Criminal Investigation Divisions who conduct investigations into reports of criminal activity made by patrol officers.

What Is Criminal Investigation? Criminal investigation has been defined as a lawful search for people and things to reconstruct the circumstances of an illegal act, apprehend or determine the guilty party, and aid in the state's prosecution of the offender.[19] The criminal investigation process is generally divided into two parts: the preliminary, or initial, investigation and the continuing, or follow-up, investigation. Most of the time the preliminary investigation in both felony and misdemeanor cases is conducted by patrol officers, although for homicides and other complex, time-consuming investigations, trained investigators are dispatched to the crime scene immediately. The continuing investigation in serious crimes is ordinarily conducted by plainclothes detectives, although small and medium-sized agencies may require patrol officers or a patrol supervisor to follow up on serious criminal offenses.

Investigative Functions In any type of investigation in a police agency, all investigators share responsibility for a number of critical functions. They must:

1. Locate witnesses and suspects.
2. Arrest criminals.
3. Collect, preserve, and analyze evidence.
4. Interview witnesses.
5. Interrogate suspects.
6. Write reports.
7. Recover stolen property.
8. Seize contraband.
9. Prepare cases and testify in court.

The specific application and context of those functions vary considerably, depending on whether the investigation is of the theft of expensive paintings, for example, or the rape of an elderly widow living alone.

The Role of the Detective At first glance, the role of the detective seems highly desirable. To a patrol officer who has been rotating work shifts for several years, seldom getting a weekend off, detectives in the police department seem to have a number of advantages:

1. They do not have to wear uniforms.
2. They have anonymity during work hours if they choose it.
3. They have steady work hours, often daytime hours with weekends off.
4. They have offices and desks.
5. They enjoy the prestige associated with the position.
6. In many agencies, detectives receive higher compensation and hold a higher rank.
7. Perhaps most important, they enjoy more freedom than patrol officers from the police radio, geographical boundaries, and close supervision.

FYI — Crime Assessment

For less serious crimes, many police departments use solvability-factor score sheets or software programs to assess information collected at crime scenes. The assessment, which is done by the responding officer, a case-screening officer, or a felony-review unit, determines which cases are likely to be solved, given the initial information obtained. Promising cases are turned over to detectives for follow-up investigation. The rest are often closed on the basis of the preliminary investigation and are reopened only if additional information is uncovered.

Source: Alfred Blumstein and Joan Petersilia, "NIJ and Its Research Program," *25 Years of Criminal Justice Research* (Washington, DC: The National Institute of Justice, 1994), p. 13.

Criminal investigation is a time-consuming task that requires much attention to detail. *What aspects of criminal investigations are the most time-consuming and why?*

All these advantages add up to a high-status position, both within the police department and in the eyes of the public.

Productivity Despite all the advantages of being a detective, investigators are often faced with insurmountable obstacles and stressful work conditions. Notifying the next of kin in a homicide is one of the worst tasks:

> Of all the dirty tasks that go with the dirty work of chasing a killer, notifying the next of kin is the job that homicide detectives hate most. It's worse than getting up at 3 a.m. on a February night to slog through a field of freezing mud toward a body that needed burying two days ago. Worse than staring into the flat cold eyes of a teenager who bragged about dragging a man through the streets to his death. Worse than visiting every sleazy dive in town until you finally find the one person who can put the murderer away and having that person say as cool as a debutante with a full dance card, "I don't want to get involved."[20]

Detectives have the cards stacked against them most of the time. Unless they discover, during the preliminary investigation, a named suspect or a description or other information that leads to a named suspect, the chances of solving the crime are low. Property crimes with no witnesses are particularly hard to solve. In 2001, for example, the clearance rates for crimes against persons were 62.4 percent for murder, 56.1 percent for aggravated assault, 44.3 percent for forcible rape, and 24.9 percent for robbery. In crimes against property, the clearance rates were 12.7 percent for burglary, 17.6 percent for larceny-theft, and 13.6 percent for motor vehicle theft. Clearances for crimes against persons are generally higher than

Myth	Fact
Improvements in detective work and criminal investigation will significantly raise clearance rates or lower the crime rate.	"Cleared" crimes generally solve themselves. The offender either is discovered at the scene or can be identified by the victim or a witness. Investigation rarely solves "cold" or "stranger" crimes.

for property crimes because crimes against persons receive more intensive investigative effort and because victims and witnesses frequently identify the perpetrators. Overall, the national clearance rate in 2001 was 19.6 percent.[21] Studies have found that much of what a detective does is not needed and that an investigator's technical knowledge often does little to help solve cases.[22] In one study, for example, fewer than 10 percent of all arrests for robbery were the result of investigative work by detectives.[23] Nevertheless, police agencies retain detectives and plainclothes investigators for a number of reasons:

1. Detectives have interrogation and case presentation skills that assist in prosecution.
2. Technical knowledge, such as knowing about burglary tools, does help in some investigations and prosecutions.
3. Law enforcement executives can assign detectives to a major, high-profile case to demonstrate to the public that they are committing resources to the matter.

The major studies of investigative effectiveness emphasize the value of improving the suspect-identification process. Once a suspect is identified by name or some other clearly distinguishing characteristic, the chances of making an arrest are increased substantially.

FYI

DNA

In approximately one-third of DNA examinations, the suspect's DNA cannot be matched with biological evidence from the crime scene. Thus, potential suspects can be eliminated from consideration early in the investigative process, allowing investigators to focus their efforts more effectively on other suspects or cases.

Recent Identification Developments in Criminal Investigation Two of the most significant advances in criminal investigation have been the development of fingerprinting and DNA profiling. Fingerprinting has resulted in the arrest and conviction of millions of criminal suspects who otherwise might never have been brought to justice. DNA profiling holds even greater promise.

CJ ONLINE

DNA Evidence

The National Commission on the Future of DNA Evidence is a program sponsored by the National Institute of Justice. Visit the program's website at **www.ojp.usdoj.gov/nij/dna.** *How big a role should DNA play in criminal investigations?*

DNA profiling DNA (deoxyribonucleic acid) is a molecule present in all forms of life. A unique genetic profile can be derived from blood, hair, semen, or other bodily substances found at the scene of a crime or on a victim. Not only can bodily substances found at a crime scene be matched with DNA samples from a suspect to give an extremely high probability of identifying the perpetrator, but it is believed that soon DNA from a sample as small as a flake of dandruff will yield a positive, unique identification, with no need to consider mathematical probabilities.

DNA profiling has three distinct functions: linking or eliminating identified suspects to a crime; identifying "cold hits" where a sample from a crime scene is matched against numerous cases in a DNA database and a positive match is made; and clearing convicted rapists and murderers years after they began serving their sentences. DNA profiling would be very useful, for example, in cases where a murderer's blood was found at the scene of a crime after a deadly struggle or in a rape case where seminal fluid could be obtained from the victim.

A serious issue at present is whether DNA databases ought to be assembled and from whom the samples should be taken. Many states permit the taking of DNA samples from arrested and convicted subjects. Some enthusiasts believe that DNA samples should be taken from all suspects in crimes, while a smaller number believe the samples should be collected from all people at birth. Currently, the most complete DNA database is the Combined DNA Index System (CODIS), which is managed by the Federal Bureau of Investigation. CODIS comprises DNA profiles that have been entered into local, state, and other national databases. The profiles are from either biological evidence left at crime scenes or individuals convicted of violent crimes and other felonies. Undoubtedly the more collected samples in a database, the more likely a match is going to be found. But privacy concerns and the potential for misuse of DNA samples are likely to hinder any more intrusive measures on the part of agents of the justice system.

Myth	Fact
Fingerprints are crucial in solving crimes.	Although fingerprints are useful in cases involving known suspects, they are rarely helpful in solving crimes where the suspect is unknown (the vast majority of criminal cases) because of the difficulty of obtaining usable prints at the crime scene.

Automated Fingerprint Identification System An expensive but invaluable tool in criminal investigation is the Automated Fingerprint Identification System (AFIS). This relatively new technology allows investigators to sort through thousands of sets of stored fingerprints for a match with those of a suspect in a crime. In fact, many of the current attempts to match prints would not have been made without AFIS, because the old process would have taken thousands of hours. Large metropolitan police agencies use it to identify 200–500 suspects a year who would have escaped apprehension before the implementation of AFIS. The initial and maintenance costs for an AFIS, however, are expensive. The FBI's AFIS is the world's largest, with more than 44 million prints on file. The Florida Department of Law Enforcement's system, by contrast, has only about 2.6 million prints on file.[24]

CYBERCRIME The use of computer technology to commit crime is of increasing concern to law enforcement officials. The FBI reports that the losses from **cybercrime** each year total $10 billion even though two-thirds of computer crime victims fail to notify the authorities. Some of the reasons for not reporting computer crime are the fear of loss of the public's confidence in the organization, the attention to vulnerability that a crime report would attract, and the shame of not providing adequate security to protect trusted assets.

cybercrime The use of computer technology to commit crime.

Since so little hardware and expense is involved, any person with a computer and modem connection to the Internet has the potential to attack computer systems and people online. The knowledge to carry out these attacks is often available online at hacker websites, message boards, and chat rooms. The cybercriminal can be as unsophisticated as a teenage amateur hacker just out for some fun or a talented computer specialist possessing skills on par with technical experts employed by the nation's top security organizations. Each of these types of computer criminal can wreak destructive havoc on a computer system, invade the privacy of thousands of citizens, and engage in the theft of millions of dollars' worth of trade secrets or steal large sums of money. At present, unfortunately, most law enforcement agencies in America are ill prepared to detect, investigate, and prosecute cybercriminals.[25]

CJ ONLINE

Combating Cybercrime

To learn more about what the U.S. government is doing to combat cybercrime, visit the U.S. Department of Justice cybercrime website at **www.usdoj.gov/criminal/cybercrime.** *Do you think that there is anything more the government can do to prevent cybercrime?*

A variety of offenses can be committed using computer and Internet technology.

1. Sex Crimes—Predators search the Internet looking for sexually explicit content as well as child pornography. Much of the sexually explicit and pornographic content is in JPEG and MPEG formats, which allow it to be downloaded to a person's hard drive easily.[26] Downloading much of this material is illegal in a number of states. The origin of some of this content is often from other nations of the world, thus complicating investigation and prosecution.

2. Illegal Access, Destruction, and Manipulation of Data—Cybercriminals break into computer systems and obtain data that is illegal for them to have,

FYI The Sniffer

Hundreds of police agencies nationwide use the P.A.S. III Sniffer to detect alcohol on motorists' breath. The Sniffer, on the market since 1993, is a tiny, battery-powered device on the end of a flashlight that when placed 6 inches from a driver's face sucks in breath and analyzes it for traces of alcohol. For daytime use when the flashlight isn't appropriate, a clip-board containing the alcohol sensor can be substituted. The constitutionality of the Sniffer has never been tested in court—it presumably falls under the "plain-view doctrine"—and nobody is arrested based solely on a positive reading by the Sniffer. If the device indicates alcohol in the air sample, the driver is held for further tests.

SOURCE: "Tricky flashlight worries ACLU," *The Orlando Sentinel*, August 13, 2000, p. A-4.

such as credit card numbers, bank records, and software codes. In October of 2000, someone illegally entered Microsoft's computer system and stole software codes for some of its future products. Hackers often illegally enter computer systems and introduce viruses or worms that infect that computer system and any other storage device that interacts with it. Computer data can also be illegally manipulated in a variety of ways. Computer records can be altered at financial, business, and educational institutions. Millions of dollars have been illegally transferred to the accounts of cybercriminals since the inception of electronic data storage. (The crime of identity theft, which can involve cybercrime, is discussed at length in Chapter 14.)

In a survey involving 114 state and local law enforcement agencies, it was revealed that these agencies lacked the adequate training, equipment, and staff to confront present and future incidents of cybercrime.[27] Cooperative efforts are now underway among law enforcement, business, high-tech, and national security organizations to better prepare the nation's police agencies to combat cybercrime.

TRAFFIC

When loss of life, serious injury, suffering, and property damage are all considered, the regulation and control of vehicle and pedestrian traffic are important, if not the most important, police responsibilities. Each year, nearly twice as many people are killed in automobile accidents on the streets and highways of the nation as are murdered.

A large percentage of this highway death and suffering is attributable to alcohol. Enforcement of DUI (driving under the influence) laws is critical to the safety of a community. In addition, automobile insurance rates are based to some degree on a community's level of traffic enforcement. Thus, if the police neglect traffic regulation and enforcement, they are likely to hear about it from both insurance companies and premium payers.

traffic accident investigation crews In some agencies, the special units assigned to all traffic accident investigations.

Some of the debate about traffic enforcement concerns whether the major enforcers of traffic regulations should be specialized personnel or uniformed patrol officers. Some traffic responsibilities are already delegated to specialized personnel, such as enforcement of parking regulations and investigations of hit-and-run accidents and traffic fatalities. In some agencies, special **traffic accident investigation crews** are assigned to all traffic accident investigations. Otherwise, patrol officers investigate accidents and attend to other traffic-related duties as a normal part of their everyday workload.

Scientific traffic accident investigation requires technical expertise. *Should all patrol officers be trained to conduct traffic investigations? Why or why not?*

Traffic units exist in nearly all medium-to-large police agencies. Some of their more important functions are:

- To educate motorists in a community about traffic safety and proper driving procedures.
- To enforce traffic laws, particularly when violations of those laws cause traffic accidents.
- To recommend traffic engineering changes that will enhance the flow of traffic and promote safety.

Enforcing traffic laws may also reduce criminal activity because stopping vehicles for traffic violations both day and night is likely to put police officers in contact with criminals.

Many veteran officers consider working in the traffic division "clean" police work because it does not normally involve responding to radio calls that take them to the scene of fights, domestic disturbances, or other distasteful incidents, such as those involving drunks. Traffic officers in large police agencies are usually well schooled in scientific accident investigation, a skill that makes them employable in the private sector, usually doing traffic reconstruction for insurance companies. The Traffic Institute at Northwestern University is one of the major schools that prepare officers for sophisticated accident investigation, although many state peace officer and highway patrol academies now have comparable training programs.

DRUG ENFORCEMENT

Over the last several decades, drug enforcement has become an increasingly important responsibility of police departments across the nation. Although the war on drugs is a priority of state and federal law enforcement agencies as well, it has been at the local level that many of the battles have been fought. Approximately 90 percent of local police departments regularly engaged in drug enforcement in 2000 (the latest year for which data were available), and all police departments that served 100,000 or more residents did so.[28]

Fifteen percent of local police departments in 2000 had a special drug enforcement unit with one or more officers assigned to it full time. Larger departments were much more likely than smaller departments to have special drug enforcement units and more full-time officers assigned to them. For example, all departments serving one million or more residents had such units, and a majority of departments serving at least 50,000 residents had them. The average number of full-time officers assigned to drug enforcement units was 7, but departments serving one million or more residents averaged 335 full-time officers. In departments serving less than 10,000 residents, only an average of one full-time officer was assigned to the special drug enforcement unit in those departments that had one.

In 2000, approximately one in five local police departments had one or more officers assigned full time to a multiagency drug enforcement task force. Again, larger departments were more likely than smaller departments to participate in these task forces and assign full-time officers to them. Nearly 90 percent of local police departments serving 250,000 or more residents participated in a multiagency drug enforcement task force in 2000, and nearly two-thirds of the departments serving 25,000 or more residents participated in them. About 6,000 local police officers were assigned full time to a task force in 2000. The average number of officers assigned ranged from 35 in departments serving one million or more residents to about 2 in departments serving fewer than 100,000 residents.

Although all levels of government are waging the war on drugs, the focus of the remainder of this section is the drug enforcement strategies of local police (and sheriffs') agencies. The particular strategies employed by individual agencies vary widely, but the most common strategies are street-level enforcement, midlevel investigations, major investigations, crop eradication, smuggling interdiction, problem-oriented and community policing strategies, drug demand reduction, and asset forfeiture. It is important to note at the outset that none of these strategies has had much of a long-term effect on the U.S. drug problem.

Street-Level Enforcement Patrol officers, officers assigned to special drug enforcement units, and plainclothes officers do most of the street-level enforcement. Their tactics include surveillance, interruption of suspected transactions, raids of "shooting galleries" and "crack houses," buy-and-bust operations, and "reverse stings," in which plainclothes officers offer to sell

FYI: Extent of Drug Use

According to the Substance Abuse and Mental Health Services Administration's *2001 National Household Survey on Drug Abuse*, 15.9 million Americans ages 12 and older (7.1 percent) reported using an illegal drug in the month before the survey was conducted. More than 12 percent reported illegal drug use during the past year and 41.7 percent reported use of an illegal drug at least once during their lifetime. The most common illegal drugs used by current users over the age of 12 were marijuana (12.1 million users, or 5.4 percent of the population), cocaine (1.7 million users, or 0.7 percent of the population), and hallucinogens, which include LSD, PCP, and MDMA (1.3 million users, or 0.6 percent of the population). Approximately 37 percent of those over the age of 12 reported lifetime use of marijuana, 12.3 percent reported lifetime use of cocaine, and 12.5 percent reported lifetime use of hallucinogens.

Source: "Drug Data Summary," Office of National Drug Control Policy, Drug Policy Information Clearinghouse, March 2003, at www.whitehousedrugpolicy.gov.

FYI: Drug Arrests

In 2001, 11.6 percent of all state and local arrests reported to the FBI were drug arrests (nearly 1.6 million). According to the National Institute of Justice's Arrestee Drug Abuse Monitoring (ADAM) program, approximately 64 percent of both male and female arrestees tested positive for at least one of the following drugs: cocaine, opiates, marijuana, methamphetamine, and PCP. Marijuana was the drug most commonly used by male arrestees, followed by cocaine, opiates, methamphetamine, and PCP. Cocaine was the drug most commonly used by female arrestees, followed by marijuana, methamphetamine, opiates, and PCP.

SOURCE: "Drug Data Summary," Office of National Drug Control Policy, Drug Policy Information Clearinghouse, March 2003, at www.whitehousedrugpolicy.gov.

drugs to willing customers. Street-level enforcement is responsible for most drug arrests and seizures. However, typically, the people arrested are either drug users or small-time dealers, and the seizures are for small amounts of drugs.

MID-LEVEL INVESTIGATIONS Informants or undercover police officers are frequently employed in mid-level investigations. The primary purpose of these investigations is to identify and make cases against mid-level dealers. Although mid-level dealers generally occupy relatively low-level positions in a drug distribution network and are easily replaced, they often are the highest-ranking drug traffickers that local police agencies can catch. The basic tactic used in these investigations is for undercover officers to gain the confidence of street-level dealers and work their way up to mid-level dealers by requesting to buy larger quantities of drugs than the street-level dealer can provide. Another tactic is for an informant to simply introduce an undercover officer to a mid-level dealer. Street-level dealers often become informants when they are arrested and agree to inform on their suppliers in return for some consideration in prosecution.

MAJOR INVESTIGATIONS The goal of major investigations is to arrest drug kingpins and shut down the organizations responsible for producing, importing, and distributing large quantities of illegal drugs. Major investigations are conducted primarily by federal and state law enforcement agencies, but sometimes the largest local police agencies are involved as well. Most local police agencies do not have the resources to engage in major investigations, which often require long-term commitments, extensive travel, and specialized expertise. In some cases, however, local police agencies participate in major investigations as part of a multiagency task force.

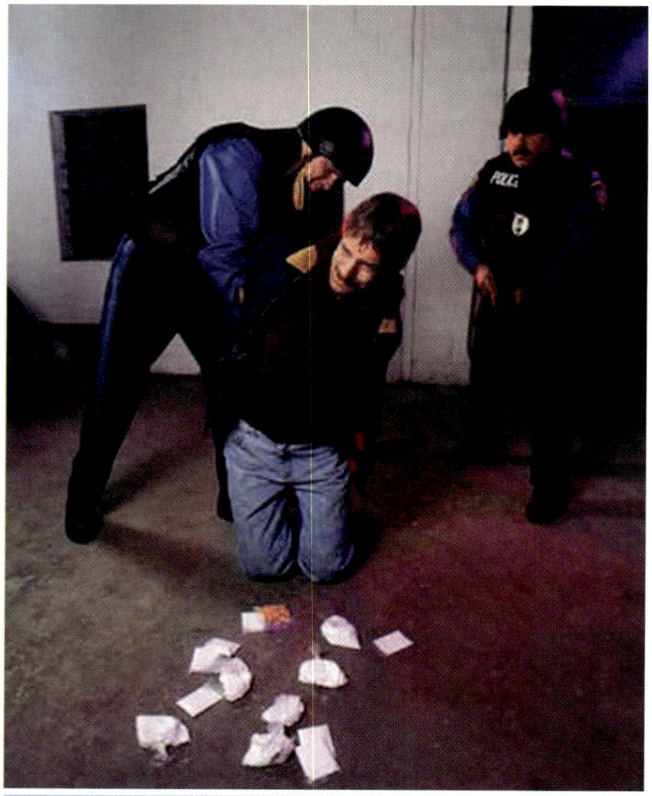

Drug busts can be dangerous. *As a law enforcement officer, would you be willing to participate in drug busts? Why or why not?*

CROP ERADICATION Crop eradication is a tactic employed by federal, state, and local law enforcement agencies. However, the only crop targeted by local police agencies is cannabis (marijuana) because it is the only major illegal drug grown in the United States. Because cannabis eradication intervenes at the beginning of the trafficking process, in theory it should have the greatest potential for eliminating or at least significantly reducing marijuana availability and use. In practice, however, a number of problems reduce the effectiveness of the eradication strategy. First, large quantities of marijuana are generally grown in remote, largely inaccessible areas. This makes locating and destroying crops by hand difficult, time-consuming, labor-intensive, and dangerous. Second, spraying crops with chemicals can be hazardous to people, water supplies, animals, and other vegetation. Third, even when crop eradication is successful in one area, a new crop can easily be grown in another area. The huge profits that can be made from a marijuana crop create a powerful incentive not to be deterred by eradication efforts.

SMUGGLING INTERDICTION Federal law enforcement agencies have the primary responsibility for smuggling interdiction, but local police agencies can play a role.

Local police officers in jurisdictions near the U.S. borders or those in jurisdictions with international airports or even small airports and airfields can be on the lookout for drug smugglers.

Problem-Oriented and Community Policing Strategies Problem-oriented policing is a strategy that focuses on the underlying problems that cause crime rather than focusing on each specific criminal event. The strategy involves identifying the underlying problems, analyzing them in detail, applying solutions to them, and then evaluating the effectiveness of the solutions. The problem-oriented approach to drug enforcement has been adopted by many local police agencies to address drug problems in public housing projects, drug abuse among teenagers, and drug abuse in abandoned buildings. The strategy makes sense because it promotes careful analysis of a community's unique drug problem before action is taken, advocates customizing responses and targeting resources, and recommends working with other public and private agencies in the problem-solving process.

Community policing, which is addressed in more detail later in the chapter, is both a philosophy and a set of methods. The philosophy is that citizens and the police must form a partnership and work collectively to identify problems, propose solutions, implement action, and evaluate results in the community. Methods include foot patrol, storefronts and other mini-stations in the community, door-to-door contact with citizens, community organizing, ombudsperson-like activities, provision of social services, and problem-oriented policing. Community policing can contribute to drug enforcement in several ways. For example, foot patrol and problem-oriented policing can reduce street-level dealing. Successful community policing may increase public support for drug enforcement efforts by encouraging citizens to report drug crimes and identify drug dealers. Community organizing may empower citizens to resist drug dealers and drug abusers who invade their communities. The provision of enhanced social services, whether provided by police officers or through police ombudspersons, may help individuals resist the temptation of illegal drugs.

Drug Demand Reduction Local police agencies can play a role in drug demand reduction strategies in at least four ways. First, through visible drug enforcement efforts, the police may discourage some people from using drugs in the first place because of a fear of arrest. Second, the police may stop some people from continuing to use drugs by arresting them so that they can get court-ordered treatment or by diverting them to drug treatment programs. Third, through public education programs, especially in the schools, the police may get young people to resist the temptations of drugs or the peer pressure to use them. Fourth, the police can lend their stature and credibility to efforts to increase funding for drug treatment, prevention, and education programs.

Asset Forfeiture A huge incentive for local police departments to participate in drug enforcement activities is *asset forfeiture*. Nearly two of every five local police departments in 1999 (the latest year for which data were available) received money, property, or goods from a drug asset forfeiture program. At least 60 percent of local police departments serving 10,000 or more

Myth	Fact
Drug interdiction and eradication are effective strategies.	Despite the regular seizure of huge quantities of illegal drugs, federal, state, and local law enforcement efforts net only about 10 to 15 percent of the total supply. As for drug interdiction, if correctional officials cannot keep illegal drugs out of maximum security prisons, how effective is the government going to be in keeping illegal drugs from entering the country?

FYI

Money Spent on Drugs

In 2000, Americans spent an estimated $36 billion on cocaine, $11 billion on marijuana, $10 billion on heroin, $5.4 billion on methamphetamine, and $2.4 billion on other illegal substances.

Source: "Drug Data Summary," Office of National Drug Control Policy, Drug Policy Information Clearinghouse, March 2003, at www.whitehousedrugpolicy.gov.

D.A.R.E. programs are taught in more than 80 percent of the nation's school districts. *Why haven't these programs been more effective in reducing illegal drug use among the nation's youth?*

residents and more than 80 percent of departments serving 25,000 or more residents had such a program.

Asset forfeiture for crimes is an ancient practice that is referred to in the Bible. It was part of English common law and helped instigate the American Revolution. Partly because of asset forfeiture abuses, the due process clause of the Fifth Amendment was included in the U.S. Constitution to guarantee that property could not be taken from citizens without a judicial hearing.

Congress enacted the first drug-related civil asset forfeiture law in 1970, as part of the Comprehensive Drug Abuse and Prevention Act. The law authorized the government to seize and forfeit illegal drugs, manufacturing and storage equipment, and vehicles used to transport drugs. A major rationale for the law was the belief that drug traffickers should not benefit financially from their illegal activities or be able to use property or money obtained illegally in future drug crimes. In 1978 and throughout the 1980s, Congress passed several more antidrug laws that enhanced the government's power to seize and forfeit property.

It is important to note that the government can seize a person's property under both criminal and civil law. A reason why civil asset forfeiture is the preferred tool in drug enforcement is that property can only be forfeited under criminal law, if the property owner has been convicted of a crime (beyond a reasonable doubt). Under civil forfeiture law, on the other hand, the government is only required to have probable cause to seize a person's property. Furthermore, under civil forfeiture law, an owner must be proactive to get his or her property back: An owner must prove in a civil proceeding by a preponderance of the evidence that the property was not used in a crime.

Assets can be forfeited under either federal or state law. When federal agencies are involved in a successful drug enforcement operation, they can return up to 80 percent of forfeited assets to other participating state or local law enforcement agencies. The amount of money or property returned depends on the particular agency's level of involvement in the case. Federal law requires that all funds returned to state and local law enforcement agencies

FYI

D.A.R.E. Programs

D.A.R.E. (Drug Abuse Resistance Education) is the nation's largest and best-known substance abuse prevention program. It was developed in 1983 by Los Angeles Police Chief Daryl Gates and is now taught in more than 80 percent of the school districts nationwide. It is a school-based collaborative effort among police departments, schools, parents, and community leaders to teach children how to recognize and resist the direct and subtle pressures that influence them to experiment with alcohol, tobacco, marijuana, and other drugs. Usually addressing children in the fifth or sixth grade, a specially trained uniformed police officer comes to the school 1 day a week for 17 weeks and teaches the children for about an hour. The D.A.R.E. curriculum is integrated with other regular subjects. Although D.A.R.E. programs are hugely popular, no scientific study, among the many evaluations that have been conducted, has discovered any statistically significant difference in drug-usage rates between students who had taken D.A.R.E. and those who had not.

SOURCE: Drug Abuse Resistance Education at www.dare.com; The Drug Reform Coordination Network, "A Different Look at D.A.R.E." at www.drcnet.org/DARE.

be used for law enforcement activities. Each state has its own formula for how forfeited assets are to be distributed and used. For example, some states, such as Montana, Oklahoma, Oregon, and Pennsylvania, require all forfeitures to be used for drug enforcement activities. Some states, such as Indiana and Missouri, require forfeited assets to be given to the state educational system. Other states, such as Iowa and Vermont, require the proceeds from forfeitures to be deposited in the state treasury to be used at the legislature's discretion.

Local police departments in 1999 (the latest year for which data were available) received an estimated $320 million in forfeited money, goods, and property. The average amount received across all participating departments was about $5,000. The largest departments serving one million or more residents averaged about $1.9 million per department in 1999; those serving fewer than 2,500 residents received about $2,000 per department. Including departments with and without receipts, the $320 million received in 1999 amounted to $703 per sworn officer employed.

Critics point to many problems with civil asset forfeiture laws. First, as noted previously, civil asset forfeiture laws place the burden of proof on the owner of the property seized to show that the property was not used in a drug-related crime. Not only is it difficult to prove a negative—that the property was *not* used in a drug-related crime—the government has to prove almost nothing.

Second, the costs involved in a civil asset forfeiture proceeding can be prohibitively high. For example, to contest a federal forfeiture, a property owner must post a bond equal to 10 percent of the seized property's value. This requirement places a burden on the poor. The poor are further handicapped in civil asset forfeiture proceedings because the government is not obligated to provide counsel, as the Sixth Amendment requires in criminal trials. In many cases, property owners simply forfeit the seized property because of the high costs of getting it back. In some cases, the costs of getting property back are higher than the value of the seized property itself.

Third, innocent owners can lose their property when someone else uses it without their permission or knowledge to commit a drug crime. In the case of *Calero-Toledo* v. *Pearson Yacht Leasing Company* (1974), for example, law enforcement officers found a marijuana cigarette onboard a yacht rented by the Pearson Yacht Leasing Company. The yacht was forfeited to the government because it was used to transport a controlled substance. The U.S. Supreme Court upheld the forfeiture, establishing the principle that the government can seize an innocent owner's property in a civil proceeding. This seeming injustice was corrected somewhat in 1988, when Congress passed the Asset Forfeiture Amendments Act. The act created forfeiture exceptions for some, but not all, innocent owners and for violations involving the possession of personal-use quantities of drugs. However, innocent owners were not fully protected by the exception. For example, in 1999, a Wichita, Kansas, couple had their motel forfeited and sold because drugs had been sold on the property. The couple had tried to keep drug dealers off the property by installing floodlights and fences and calling the police, but their property was forfeited anyway.

Fourth, critics argue that the standard of proof in civil forfeiture cases is too low. Because probable cause is the standard of proof necessary to seize property that was used to facilitate a drug crime, little more than hearsay evidence is required. Potential informants have a real incentive to lie to the police about property owners because the law allows them to receive part of the forfeited property. Moreover, in civil asset forfeiture proceedings, property owners are not allowed to question their accusers, making it more difficult to refute any lies. Another problem with probable cause as the standard of proof

FYI: Civil Forfeiture

Civil forfeiture is based on the legal fiction that the property that facilitates or is connected to a crime has itself committed a wrong and can be seized and tried in civil court. Such judicial hearings are referred to as *in rem* proceedings, meaning "against the thing."

SOURCE: Scott Ehlers, *Policy Briefing: Asset Forfeiture,* The Drug Policy Foundation (Washington, DC: GPO, 1999), p. 4.

in civil asset forfeiture proceedings is exemplified by the sheriff of Volusia County, Florida (near Daytona Beach), who defined probable cause for purposes of asset forfeiture as having more than $100 in cash.

Fifth, civil asset forfeiture policy undermines the integrity of the police and the criminal justice system. The proceeds that can be had from civil asset forfeitures are a corrupting influence for many law enforcement officers. Sometimes officers are more concerned with seizing assets than they are with getting drugs off the streets. In some cases, law enforcement officers simply extort money and property from innocent people. Civil asset forfeiture laws sometimes promote other illegal practices such as racial profiling (which is described in Chapter 7). Sometimes resources are diverted from more serious crimes to drug cases that promise asset forfeitures. In short, although civil asset forfeiture helps fuel the war on drugs and can reduce the profits from the illegal drug trade, there are many reasons to question its fairness and utility. Its harshest critics contend that civil asset forfeiture should be eliminated altogether because criminal asset forfeiture is available and has procedures that better protect the innocent.

Myth	Fact
Illegal drug use causes crime.	Illegal drug use is not a significant cause of crime. Although the effects of some illegal drugs may cause a very small number of violent crimes, the vast majority of drug-related crimes are caused by the drug laws, which make the possession, distribution, cultivation, or manufacture of certain drugs a crime. The drug laws also cause crime by creating an illegal market in which drug prices are artificially and dramatically increased. This makes it necessary for some drug users, especially addicts, to steal or deal to get money to buy drugs. It also contributes to the violence of rival drug dealers seeking to monopolize a market. The illegality of desired drugs also puts otherwise law-abiding people in contact with members of the criminal underworld from whom they can learn criminal skills. Ironically, alcohol is the only drug that has been found to cause a significant amount of crime, and alcohol is legal for adults.

Criticisms of the War on Drugs In addition to the already mentioned problems with specific aspects of drug enforcement, the war on drugs, itself, has been severely criticized. First, critics contend that the government has exaggerated the dangers of illegal drug use to gain public support for the war on drugs and has generally ignored the harms caused by the drug laws themselves. For example, it has been estimated that about 3,600 people die each year from the consumption of all illegal drugs combined. While any death from illegal drug consumption is regrettable, the 3,600 deaths attributed to illegal drugs pale in comparison to the approximately 200,000 alcohol-related and 400,000 tobacco-related deaths each year. Moreover, rarely are drug-related deaths the result of abuse or misuse of the drugs. Instead, most of the drug-related deaths are directly attributable to the drug laws that prohibit their use. For example, most heroin overdoses occur because the heroin is adulterated (that is, the drug is "cut" or mixed with dangerous substances to increase the quantity of the drug available to sell or to produce a more readily ingestible form of the drug). The reason why the heroin is adulterated is because it is illegal and unregulated; there is no quality control in its production and distribution. Also, because it is illegal, heroin addicts share needles, which spreads disease and illness. It has been estimated that 25 percent of all AIDS cases in the United States are a direct result of the unsafe and unsanitary conditions in which illegal drugs are consumed. The same is true of cocaine. Because of the drug laws, the price of using powder cocaine is too high for many people so they substitute the more affordable and more dangerous crack cocaine. A person is more likely to die or suffer injury from smoking the drug than he or she is from snorting it. As for marijuana, no one has ever died from using marijuana. The greatest danger to marijuana smokers is in smoking the drug after it has been adulterated by government control programs, such as the spraying of herbicides on marijuana crops.

Another way the government has tried to rally support for the drug war has been to try to persuade the public of a direct connection between illegal drug use and crime. However, as described in the nearby myth/fact box, it is not drugs that cause crime, but rather the drug laws that cause crime.

About 60 percent of people arrested for possession of powder cocaine are white, while about 90 percent of people arrested for possession of crack cocaine are black. *Should law enforcement authorities distinguish between powder cocaine and crack cocaine when making arrests for possession? Why or why not?*

Second, critics have argued that the drug war is racist. Of the approximately 1.6 million people arrested in 2001 for drug abuse violations, 64.2 percent were white and 34.5 percent were black. Yet, blacks are only about 14 percent of all drug users, and a National Institute on Drug Abuse (NIDA) survey showed that the prevalence of drug use is nearly the same among whites and blacks. Furthermore, in many jurisdictions the penalties are much more severe for possession of crack cocaine than they are for the possession of powder cocaine, although pharmacologically they are identical drugs. About 60 percent of people arrested for possession of powder cocaine are white, while about 90 percent of the people arrested for possession of crack cocaine are black. Ironically, relatively low-level crack cocaine dealers have received longer prison sentences than wholesale-level powder cocaine dealers from whom the crack dealer originally bought the powder to make the crack.

Third, as noted previously, critics point out that the war on drugs and the huge amount of money involved in the drug trade have corrupted many law enforcement personnel, who have been found guilty of drug dealing providing protection for drug dealers, conspiracy, extortion, bribery, robbery, theft, and murder. Unfortunately, examples abound. A *New York Times* report disclosed that each year more than 100 law enforcement officers are prosecuted in state and federal courts on drug corruption charges.

Fourth, critics maintain that the war on drugs is hugely expensive, diverts resources from arguably more important projects, and has had little lasting effect on illegal drug use. Between 1980 and 2003, the United States spent more than $300 billion on federal, state, and local antidrug efforts. That was more than was spent on medical research into cancer, heart disease, or AIDS—to name just three worthwhile projects. Furthermore, despite the huge amount of money and effort spent on the drug war, the prices of many illegal drugs have not increased and in many cases have fallen, and the purity of illegal drugs and their availability have not decreased but in many cases have increased. If the drug war were successfully reducing supply or demand, one would expect prices to increase, and the purity and availability of illegal drugs to decline.

Although the measurement of illegal drug use is fraught with all sorts of reliability problems, according to the Substance Abuse and Mental Health Services Administration's annual *National Household Survey on Drug Abuse*, there was a significant decline in illegal drug use among both youths and adults between 1979 and 1992 (from 25 million past-month illegal drug users to 12 million past-month illegal drug users). However, the number of past-month illegal drug users has increased unevenly between 1992 and 2002. The estimated number of past-month illegal drug users in the United States in 2001 was 16 million. The higher number is attributed to a much

FYI Drug Offenders in Prison

In 2001, 55 percent of federal prisoners and 20 percent of state prisoners were incarcerated for drug offenses. That compares with 58 percent of federal prisoners and 21 percent of state prisoners who were incarcerated for drug offenses in 1998.

SOURCE: Paige M. Harrison and Allen J. Beck, "Prisoners in 2002," U.S. Department of Justice, *Bureau of Justice Statistics Bulletin* (Washington, DC: GPO, July 2003), p. 10, Table 15, and p. 11, Table 18; Allen J. Beck, "Prisoners in 1999," U.S. Department of Justice, *Bureau of Justice Statistics Bulletin* (Washington, DC: GPO, August 2000), p. 10, Table 15, and p. 12, Table 21.

THINKING CRITICALLY

1. What do you think are the pros and cons of being an investigator/detective? Does this type of work sound attractive to you?
2. Do you think there are any ways to protect individuals and businesses from becoming victims of cybercrime? If so, what do you propose?

higher rate of use among youths, a small increase in the rate of use among adults, and a 10 percent increase in the size of the U.S. population. Critics are calling for an end to the drug war. Some critics want illegal drugs to be decriminalized or legalized. Other critics want the drug problem treated as a public health problem and not as a criminal justice problem. Perhaps it is time to seriously rethink America's strategy for dealing with illegal drug use.

Community Policing

For decades, police followed the professional model, which rested on three foundations: preventive patrol, quick response time, and follow-up investigation. Sensing that the professional model did not always operate as efficiently and effectively as it could, criminal justice researchers set out to review current procedures and evaluate alternative programs. One of the first and best-known of these studies was the Kansas City, Missouri, Preventive Patrol Experiment, discussed earlier in this chapter. That study's conclusion was that preventive patrol did not necessarily prevent crime or reassure citizens. Following the study, some police departments assigned police units to proactive patrol, giving them specific assignments rather than having them randomly cruise the streets.

Another study, again with the Kansas City Police Department, examined the effects of police response time. The study found that police response time was unrelated to the probability of making an arrest. Researchers discovered that the time it takes a citizen to report a crime—not the speed with which police respond—was the major determinant of whether an on-scene arrest took place or witnesses could be located. In 90 percent of crimes, citizens wait 5 to 10 minutes to call the police, precluding catching the criminal at the scene.

As preventive patrol and fast response time were being questioned, so too was follow-up investigation. A study by the Rand Corporation reviewed the criminal investigation process for effectiveness. The researchers concluded that

Community police officers visit with a citizen. *How does such activity contribute to crime fighting?*

the work of a criminal investigator alone rarely leads to an arrest and that the probability of arrest is determined largely by information that patrol officers obtain at the crime scene in their preliminary investigation.[29]

Criminal justice researchers continued their review of accepted police functions with the aim of making policing more effective by initiating new techniques and procedures. One of the interesting findings of the foot patrol research was that foot patrol officers were better able to deal with minor annoyances—such as rowdy youths, panhandlers, and abandoned cars—that irritate citizens.

In a theory called "broken windows," James Q. Wilson and George Kelling proposed that those minor annoyances are "signs of crime" and cause a fear of crime and that if they are not dealt with early, more serious and more costly problems are likely to occur.[30] Wilson and Kelling concluded that to help solve both minor and major problems in a neighborhood and to reduce crime and fear of crime, police officers must be in close, regular contact with citizens. That is, police and citizens should work cooperatively to build a strong sense of community and should share responsibility in the neighborhood to improve the overall quality of life within the community.

Myth	**Fact**
Shorter police response time contributes to more arrests.	For most crimes, police response time is irrelevant. Approximately two-thirds of crimes are "cold"; the offender is gone long before the crime is discovered. In cases where time counts, the critical delay often occurs in the time it takes the victim to call the police.

THE PHILOSOPHY AND COMPONENTS OF COMMUNITY POLICING

With community policing, citizens share responsibility for their community's safety. Citizens and the police work collectively to identify problems, propose solutions, implement action, and evaluate the results in the community. A community policing perspective differs in a number of ways from a traditional policing perspective. For example, in community policing, the police must share power with residents of a community, and critical decisions need to be made at the neighborhood level, not at a downtown police headquarters. Such decentralization of authority means that credit for bringing about a safer and more secure community must be shared with the people of the community, a tall order for any group of professionals to accept. Achieving the goals of community policing requires successful implementation of three essential and complementary components or operational strategies: community partnership, problem solving, and change management.[31]

Community Partnership Establishing and maintaining mutual trust between citizens of a community and the police is the main goal of the first component of community policing. Police have always recognized the need for cooperation with the community and have encouraged members of the community to come forward with crime-fighting information. In addition, police have spoken to neighborhood groups, worked with local organizations, and provided special-unit services. How are those cooperative efforts different from the community partnership of community policing?

In community policing, the police become an integral part of the community culture, and the community, in turn, helps the police define future crime prevention strategies and allocate community protection services. Establishing a community partnership means adopting a policing perspective that exceeds the standard law enforcement emphasis. The police no longer view the community as a passive presence connected to the police by an isolated incident or series of incidents. The community's concerns with crime and disorder become the target of efforts by the police and the community working together.

FYI

The Crime Act and COPS

The Violent Crime Control and Law Enforcement Act of 1994—popularly known as the Crime Act—authorized $8.8 billion over 6 years for grants to local policing agencies to add 100,000 officers and promote community policing in innovative ways. To implement the law, the Office of Community Oriented Policing Services (COPS) was created in the U.S. Department of Justice. COPS cuts red tape to make it easier for local police agencies to apply for and receive federal community policing grants.

A community police officer talks to a boy at the Puerto Rico Day Parade. *What, if anything, is the police officer trying to accomplish?*

For patrol officers, building police-community partnerships entails such activities as talking to local business owners to identify their concerns, visiting residents in their homes to offer advice on security, and helping to organize and support neighborhood watch groups and regular community meetings. It also involves ongoing communication with residents. For example, a patrol officer might canvass a neighborhood for information about a string of burglaries and then revisit those residents to inform them when the burglar is caught.

FYI

School Resource Officers

School resource officers use a community policing approach to provide a safe environment for students and staff. They respond to calls for service within the school and work with school administrators and staff to prevent crime and disorder by monitoring crime trends, problem areas, cultural conflicts, and other concerns. As of June 2000, local police departments had nearly 14,000 full-time sworn personnel serving as school resource officers.

SOURCE: Matthew J. Hickman and Brian A. Reaves, *Local Police Departments, 2000*, U.S. Department of Justice, Bureau of Justice Statistics (Washington, DC: GPO, January 2003), p. 15.

PROBLEM SOLVING Problem solving requires a lot more thought, energy, and action than traditional incident-based police responses to crime and disorder. In full partnership, the police and a community's residents and business owners identify core problems, propose solutions, and implement a solution. Thus, community members identify the concerns that they feel are most threatening to their safety and well-being. Those areas of concern then become priorities for joint police-community interventions.

For this problem-solving process to operate effectively, the police need to devote time and attention to discovering a community's concerns, and they need to recognize the validity of those concerns. Police and neighborhood groups may not always agree on the specific problems that deserve attention first. For example, the police may regard robberies as the biggest problem in a particular neighborhood, while residents find derelicts who sleep in doorways, break bottles on sidewalks, and pick through garbage cans the number-one problem. In community policing, both problems should receive early attention from the police, other government agencies, and the community.

Some community policing advocates recommend a four-step problem-solving process referred to as SARA: *S*canning—identifying problems; *A*nalysis—understanding underlying conditions; *R*esponse—developing and implementing solutions; *A*ssessment—determining the solutions' effect. One useful tool in working toward a solution is known as the *crime triangle*. The crime triangle is a view of crime and disorder as an interaction among three variables: a victim, an offender, and a location. Solutions can be developed that affect one or more of the three elements of the crime triangle. For example, suppose elderly residents are being jeopardized by speeding teenagers in automobiles as they walk across the streets of a suburban residential neighborhood. Using a crime triangle analysis might

Community police officers discussing neighborhood problems with residents. *In what ways can elderly citizens contribute to crime fighting?*

result in the following police-community solutions: using the juvenile court to alter the probation period of offending drivers (focus on the offender), installing speed bumps in the pavement or changing the cycles of traffic signals on opposite ends of the street so that motorists cannot build up speed (focus on the location), holding safety education classes at the senior center to educate elderly residents to use marked crosswalks (focus on the victim). More than likely, in community policing, a combination of those solutions would be used. Such a response to a community problem is much more thorough than merely having a squad car drive by the location when a citizen calls in a complaint.

Change Management Forging community policing partnerships and implementing problem-solving strategies necessitate assigning new responsibilities and adopting a flexible style of management. Traditionally, patrol officers have been accorded lower status in police organizations and have been dominated by the agency's command structure. Community policing, in contrast, emphasizes the value of the patrol function and the patrol officer as an individual. It requires the shifting of initiative, decision making, and responsibility downward within the police organization. The neighborhood police officer or deputy sheriff becomes responsible for managing the delivery of police services to the community or area to which he or she is permanently assigned. Patrol officers are the most familiar with the needs and concerns of their communities and are in the best position to forge the close ties with the community that lead to effective solutions to local problems.

Under community policing, police management must guide, rather than dominate, the actions of the patrol officer and must ensure that patrol officers have the necessary resources to solve the problems in their communities. Management must determine the guiding principles to convert the philosophy of the agency to community policing and then to evaluate the effectiveness of the strategies implemented.

> **FYI**
>
> **Community Policing**
>
> According to a recent survey, 68 percent of local police departments, employing 90 percent of all officers, had a community policing plan of some type in 2000. Eighteen percent of departments, employing 50 percent of officers, had a formal, written plan. Two-thirds of all departments, employing 86 percent of all officers, used full-time community policing officers in 2000, 103,000 local police officers were designated community policing officers in 2000.
>
> Source: Matthew J. Hickman and Brian A. Reaves, *Local Police Departments, 2000*, U.S. Department of Justice, Bureau of Justice Statistics (Washington, DC: GPO, January 2003), p. iii.

IMPLEMENTING COMMUNITY POLICING

Implementation plans for community policing vary from agency to agency and from community to community. The appropriate implementation

THINKING CRITICALLY

1. Can you think of ways to make community policing even more effective?
2. Do you think there is a certain operational style that is most appropriate for community policing? If so, which one?

strategy depends on conditions within the law enforcement agency and the community embarking on community policing. Successful implementation requires that the police and the members of the community understand the underlying philosophy of community policing and have a true commitment to the community policing strategy. Communication, cooperation, coordination, collaboration, and change are the keys to putting community policing into action. The community policing philosophy has become so popular and broadly implemented that it exists as the operating method of police departments in colleges and universities, transit systems, and even airports. At Dallas Love Field, City of Dallas police officers maintain a community police substation in the airport as part of the regular security force and receive specially marked federal funds and airport community police training.

CAREERS IN CRIMINAL JUSTICE

Ohio State Highway Patrol Officer

My name is Lieutenant Brenda Sue Collins. I have had an exciting career with the Ohio State Highway Patrol and have worked in a variety of assignments since 1985. Currently I am the post commander for the Fremont post of the State Highway Patrol, responsible for the leadership of all operational and staff personnel serving at the Fremont post. I have also served as a cadet dispatcher (my first job with the patrol), a highway trooper, an academy instructor, an officer in the Traffic and Drug Interdiction Unit, a supervisor in the recruiting section, and a public information officer. I am married to Captain Richard Collins, a district commander of the patrol stationed in Findlay.

An Ohio State Highway Patrol Officer's major responsibility is to patrol the roadways and keep them safe. That responsibility includes investigating vehicle crashes, gaining obedience to the traffic laws by enforcement and other means, giving assistance to motorists 24 hours a day, keeping the roadway free of obstructions, enforcing the extensive commercial vehicle laws, and checking for signs of criminal activity during vehicle stops. One of the toughest parts of the patrol officer's job is to make death notifications to family members of loved ones who have been killed in a fatal crash.

I graduated in the 116th Academy class and was assigned to the Portsmouth post as a trooper where I was somewhat of a novelty with the citizens since there were not that many female highway patrol officers. But when people see that you do your job effectively and professionally just like your male counterparts, the novelty soon wears off. Now we have about 130 female troopers out of a total of approximately 1,400 troopers.

I attended Ohio University where I studied forensic chemistry and law enforcement and Ohio State University in Marion. The OSHP provides tuition assistance that varies depending on the grades you receive in courses.

Being married to another highway patrol officer really has its advantages. First, you can learn from each other because you have worked in different assignments and have experienced common things at different times in your career. Richard and I also know the language and values of the highway patrol, therefore allowing us to communicate a lot more clearly than a married couple working at entirely different jobs. The only disadvantage that I can see is that when both of you are senior officers in the patrol, you have to deal with the issue of promotions. As a married couple we are not allowed to serve in the same posts of the patrol, but can be in adjacent districts if there are openings for our rank. Consequently when promotional opportunities come up for one or the other of us, we have to think of what kind of disruption that will cause in our home life.

The advice I would offer to somebody that wants to be a highway patrol officer is to work in a job you really want until the highway patrol officer's job becomes available. The selection process is long and difficult. I would suggest that you investigate and really find out what a highway patrol officer's job is like. The job entails round-the-clock duty in all sorts of weather, including the worst weather. In fact, you may be the only one out on the highways during bad weather. You are more likely to stick with it when you know these things up front.

What characteristics of your personality do you think would make you best suited to be a highway patrol officer?

Terrorism and Homeland Security

Terrorism is one of the oldest forms of human conflict. Before societies began waging war against each other, individuals and small groups used acts of terror to achieve their goals, such as deposing existing leaders and frightening and repelling adversaries from territory they claimed for themselves.[32] Terrorism has been used by both right-wing and left-wing political organizations, by ethnic and nationalistic groups, by revolutionaries, and by the armies and secret police of established governments. However, according to the FBI, the modern era of terrorism did not begin until the late 1960s, and U.S. soil remained largely free from serious acts of international terrorism until the bombing of the World Trade Center in 1993.[33] Before then, the vast majority of deadly terrorist acts carried out in the United States were committed by domestic terrorists, such as Timothy McVeigh and Terry Nichols, who were responsible for the 1995 bombing of the Alfred P. Murrah Federal Building in Oklahoma City.[34] All that changed on September 11, 2001, when, according to Ambassador Francis X. Taylor, the U.S. Department of State's Coordinator for Counterterrorism, "the United States suffered its bloodiest day on American soil since the Civil War, and the world experienced the most devastating international terrorist attack in recorded history."[35]

On that infamous day in September, 19 hijackers belonging to the al-Qaeda terrorist network commandeered four aircraft to commit the most audacious terrorist act in American history.

- Five terrorists hijacked American Airlines flight 11, which departed Boston for Los Angeles at 7:45 A.M. An hour later it was deliberately piloted into the North Tower of the World Trade Center in New York City.
- Five terrorists hijacked United Airlines flight 175, which departed Boston for Los Angeles at 7:58 A.M. At 9:05 the plane crashed into the South Tower of the World Trade Center. Both towers collapsed shortly thereafter, killing approximately 3,000 persons, including hundreds of firefighters and rescue personnel who were helping to evacuate the buildings.
- Four terrorists hijacked United Airlines flight 93, which departed Newark for San Francisco at 8:01 A.M. At 10:10 the plane crashed in Stony Creek Township, Pennsylvania, killing all 45 persons onboard. The intended target of this hijacked plane is not known, but it is believed that passengers overpowered the terrorists, thus preventing the aircraft from being used as a missile.
- Five terrorists hijacked American Airlines flight 77, which departed Washington Dulles Airport for Los Angeles at 8:10 A.M. At 9:39 the plane was flown directly into the Pentagon in Arlington, Virginia, near Washington, DC. A total of 189 persons were killed, including all who were onboard the plane.[36]

Prior to 9/11, the bombing of the Alfred P. Murrah Federal Building in Oklahoma City on April 19, 1995, by Timothy McVeigh was the worst incident of domestic terrorism in American history. *What are the similarities and differences between the bombing of the Murrah Federal Building by McVeigh and the 9/11 terrorist assaults on the World Trade Center and the Pentagon?*

DEFINITIONS AND TYPES OF TERRORISM

There is no single, universally accepted definition of terrorism, and types of terrorism can be distinguished by perpetrators, motives, methods, and targets. Whatever

terrorism The systematic use of terror or unpredictable violence against governments, publics, or individuals to attain a political objective; the unlawful use of force and violence against persons or property to intimidate or coerce a government, the civilian population, or any segment thereof, in furtherance of political or social objectives; or premeditated, politically motivated violence perpetrated against noncombatant targets by subnational groups or clandestine agents, usually intended to influence an audience.

domestic terrorism The unlawful use, or threatened use, of force or violence by a group or individual based and operating entirely within the United States or its territories without foreign direction committed against persons or property to intimidate or coerce a government, the civilian population, or any segment thereof, in furtherance of political or social objectives.

international terrorism Violent acts dangerous to human life that are a violation of the criminal laws of the United States or any state, or that would be a criminal violation if committed within the jurisdiction of the United States or any state. These acts appear to be intended to intimidate or coerce a civilian population, influence the policy of a government by intimidation or coercion, or affect the conduct of a government by assassination or kidnapping. International terrorist acts occur outside the United States or transcend national boundaries in terms of the means by which they are accomplished, the persons they appear intended to coerce or intimidate, or the locale in which the perpetrators operate or seek asylum.

the definition, the key elements of terrorism are fear, panic, violence, and disruption.[37] The FBI defines **terrorism** as "the systematic use of terror or unpredictable violence against governments, publics, or individuals to attain a political objective."[38] In the U.S. Code of Federal Regulations (28 C.F.R. Section 0.85), terrorism is defined as "the unlawful use of force and violence against persons or property to intimidate or coerce a government, the civilian population, or any segment thereof, in furtherance of political or social objectives."[39] Title 22 of the U.S. Code, Section 2656f(d), defines terrorism as "premeditated, politically motivated violence perpetrated against noncombatant targets by subnational groups or clandestine agents, usually intended to influence an audience."[40]

The FBI divides terrorism into two broad categories: *domestic terrorism* and *international terrorism.*

Domestic terrorism is the unlawful use, or threatened use, of force or violence by a group or individual based and operating entirely within the United States or its territories without foreign direction committed against persons or property to intimidate or coerce a government, the civilian population, or any segment thereof, in furtherance of political or social objectives.[41]

International terrorism involves violent acts dangerous to human life that are a violation of the criminal laws of the United States or any state, or that would be a criminal violation if committed within the jurisdiction of the United States or any state. These acts appear to be intended to intimidate or coerce a civilian population, influence the policy of a government by intimidation or coercion, or affect the conduct of a government by assassination or kidnapping. International terrorist acts occur outside the United States or transcend national boundaries in terms of the means by which they are accomplished, the persons they appear intended to coerce or intimidate, or the locale in which the perpetrators operate or seek asylum.[42]

The FBI further divides domestic terrorism into "right-wing terrorism," "left-wing terrorism," "special interest terrorism," and "individual terrorism." *Right-wing terrorist groups,* such as the Aryan Nations and the World Church of the Creator, generally oppose government in general and government regulation in particular. Members typically are virulent racists who believe in racial supremacy and conspiracy theories.[43] *Left-wing terrorist groups* generally believe in revolutionary socialist doctrine and seek radical change outside the established political process. They want to liberate people from the dehumanizing effects of capitalism and imperialism. With the collapse of the Soviet Union and the fall of communism in Eastern Europe in the 1980s, left-wing terrorist groups no longer pose much of a threat to the United States.[44] The goal of *special interest terrorist groups* is to change the attitudes of the public about specific issues that are important to the group rather than to bring about fundamental political change. These groups generally are fringe elements of antinuclear, environmental, pro-life, animal rights, and other movements.[45] As of this writing, the FBI considers the Animal Liberation Front (ALF) and the Earth Liberation Front (ELF) as two of the most active special interest terrorist groups. *Individual terrorist acts* are committed by "lone wolf" extremists who operate alone or in small groups and defy detection both as to their identities and their plans for destruction. Timothy McVeigh and Eric Robert Rudolph are examples of this category of terrorist.[46] Figure 6.3 classifies the type of perpetrators responsible for terrorist acts in the United States from 1980 through 1999.

The FBI estimates that about 20 to 30 percent of international terrorist incidents that occur annually in the United States and abroad are directed at U.S.

FIGURE 6.3 Terrorism by Group Class, 1980–1999

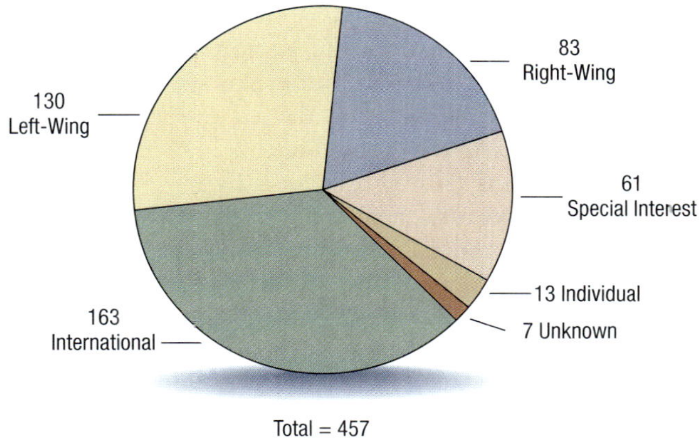

Figure includes terrorist incidents, suspected terrorist incidents, and preventions.

SOURCE: Federal Bureau of Investigation, *Terrorism in the United States, 1999,* p. 33, at www.fbi.gov/publications/terror/terroris.htm.

interests.[47] These threats to U.S. interests are divided into three categories: state sponsors of international terrorism, formalized terrorist organizations, and loosely affiliated extremists and rogue international terrorists.[48] The principal *state sponsors of terrorism* are Cuba, Iran, Iraq (until recently), Libya, North Korea, Sudan, and Syria. For these countries, terrorism is a tool of foreign policy.[49] *Formal terrorist organizations* are autonomous, generally transnational, and have their own personnel, infrastructures, financial arrangements, and training facilities. Examples are the Irish Republican Army, Palestinian Hamas, the Egyptian Al-Gama al-Islamiyya (IG), Lebanese Hizballah, 17 November (based in Greece), and the Revolutionary Armed Forces of Columbia (FARC).[50] *Loosely affiliated extremists and rogue international terrorists* include the World Trade Center bombers and rogue terrorists such as Ramzi Yousef, Osama bin Laden, and members of al-Qaeda.[51]

Another way of characterizing terrorism is by the methods used by terrorists. The traditional method has involved a conventional bomb. However, today, the most feared method involves weapons of mass destruction (WMDs), such as nuclear, radiological, and biological devices. Agroterrorism is another method and is an attack on a food source or the distribution of food supplies. Cyberterrorism, dubbed "information warfare," may take various forms including the hacking into or destroying of the nation's electronic infrastructure rendering mass communications via the Internet inoperable. High-energy radio frequency (HERF) and electromagnetic pulse weapons (EMPs) can shut down mass communication systems almost instantly.[52]

For purposes of this textbook, it is important to note that terrorists are criminals, according to the FBI's counterterrorism policy.[53] However, it is also important to remember that one person's terrorist is another person's freedom fighter. The British, for example, accused the American revolutionaries of being terrorists.[54]

THE EXTENT OF TERRORISM IN THE UNITED STATES AND THE LAW ENFORCEMENT RESPONSE

Most Americans know little about terrorism, except for the spectacular terrorist events that kill and injure large numbers of innocent victims. Terrorism, however, is much more prevalent than most people think it is. Figure 6.4 identifies terrorist incidents in the United States from 1980 through 1999. The data show that the United States was a frequent victim of both domestic and international terrorism during the last two decades of the twentieth century. Those terrorist acts resulted in loss of life, serious injury, and the destruction of property. Figure 6.4 also provides a numerical breakdown of domestic and international terrorist acts in which the United States was victimized. From 1981 to 2001, 670 U.S. citizens were killed and 2,269 were wounded as a result of international terrorist acts (not shown in a figure).[55] Figure 6.5 shows the number of casualties of domestic terrorism from 1980 to 1999. The total for the period was 205 deaths and 2,037 injured.

Terrorists' acts are often perpetrated by disaffected and angry individuals and groups who are far removed from the everyday American scene. Yet, through the media, American citizens are learning more about terrorism than ever before. Still, terrorism is a complex phenomenon. American law enforcement officers have no choice anymore. They must learn all they can to protect the nation and its people.

Since the tragedy of September 11, 2001, terrorism has been at the top of the national agenda. People are frightened without knowing exactly what to do about it. Local, state, and federal law enforcement agencies have new responsibilities for the prevention of both domestic and international terrorism and for reducing America's fear. To guide them, especially at the national level, President Bush has laid out four general policy principles:

1. Make no concessions to terrorists and strike no deals (even if U.S. citizens are held hostage).

FYI

9/11 and Terrorism

According to Ambassador Francis X. Taylor, U.S. Department of State's Coordinator for Counterterrorism, "History will record 2001 as a watershed year in the international fight against terrorism."

SOURCE: U.S. State Department, *Patterns of Global Terrorism, 2001,* May 2002, p. v, at www.state.gov/s/ct/rls/pgtrpt/2000/pdf.

FIGURE 6.4 Terrorist Activity by Classification, 1980–1999

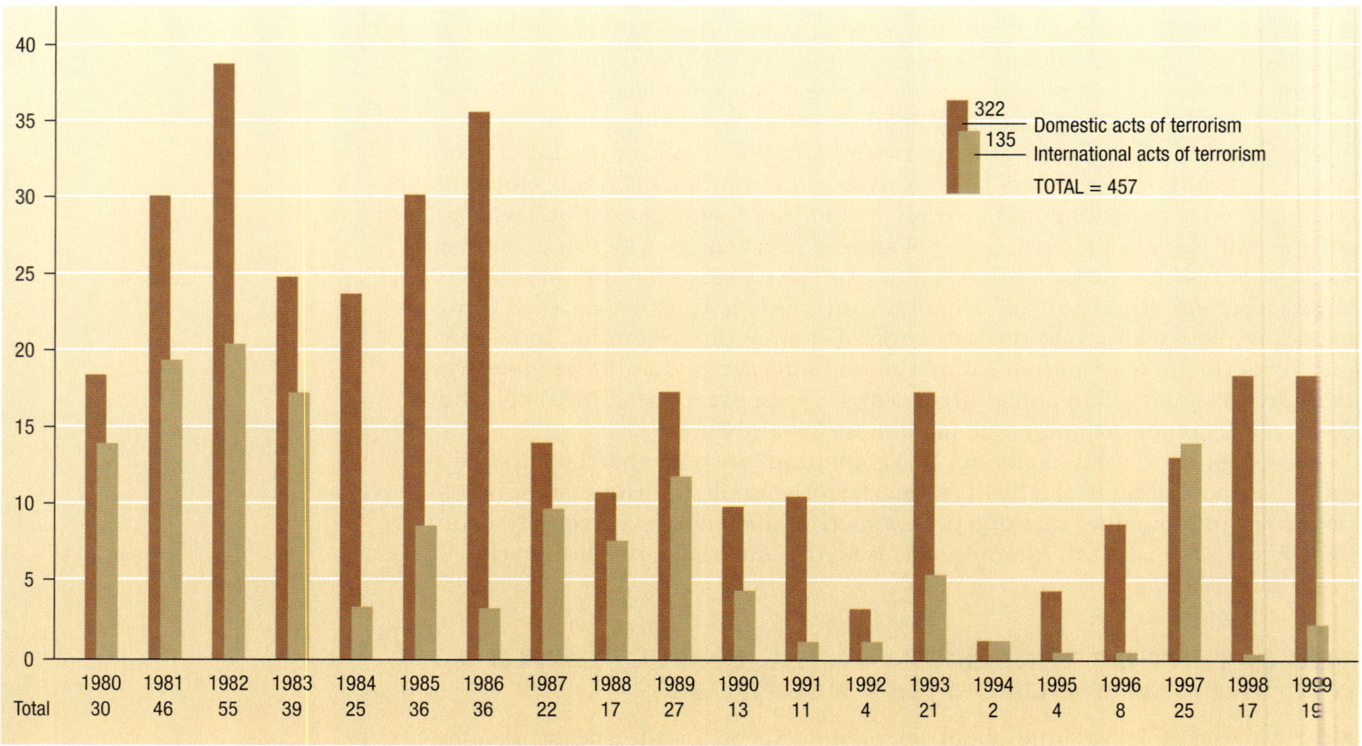

Figures include terrorist incidents, suspected terrorist incidents, and preventions.

SOURCE: Federal Bureau of Investigation, *Terrorism in the United States, 1999,* p. 37, at www.fbi.gov/publications/terror/terroris.htm.

FIGURE 6.5 Casualties of Domestic Terrorism, 1980–1999

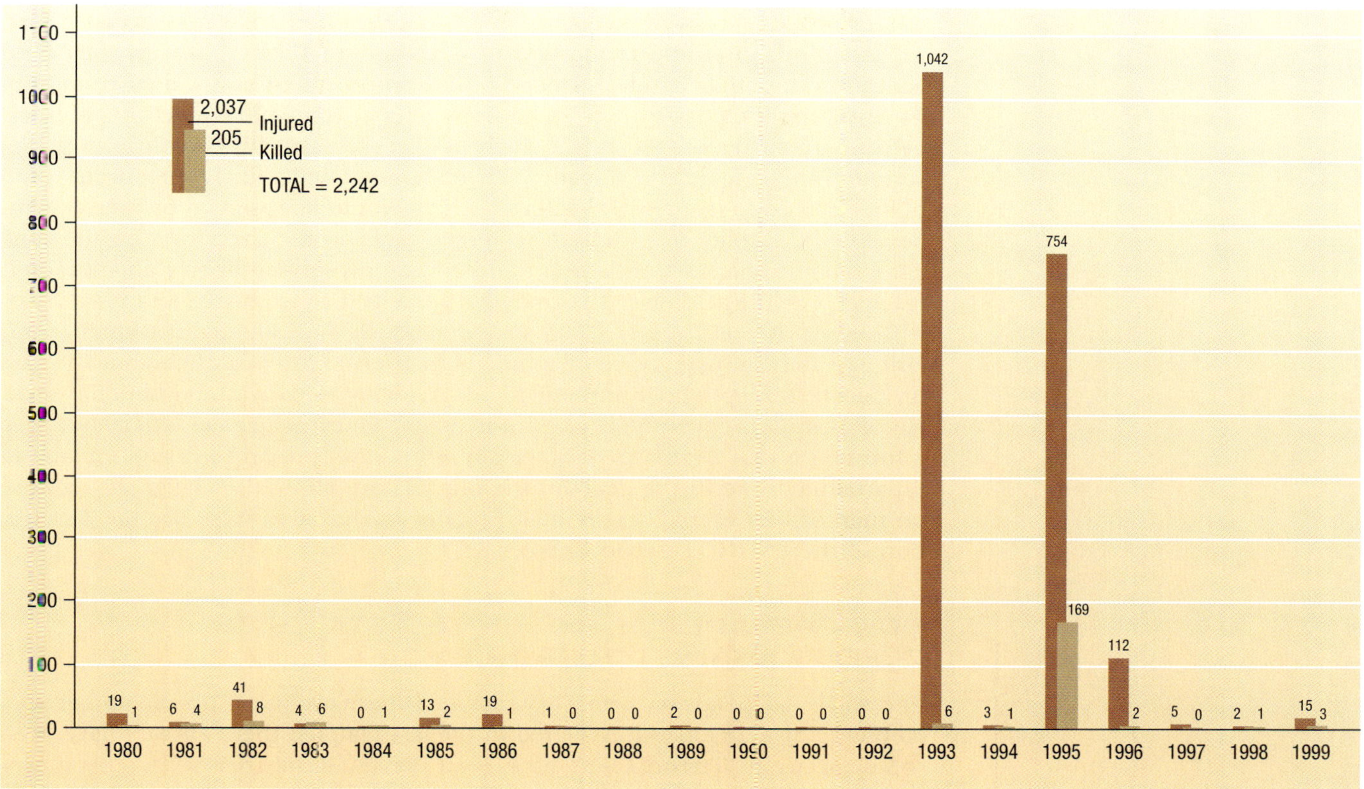

SOURCE: Federal Bureau of Investigation, *Terrorism in the United States, 1999,* p. 53, at www.fbi.gov/publications/terror/terroris.htm.

2. Bring terrorists to justice for their crimes (no matter how long it takes).
3. Isolate and apply pressure on states that sponsor terrorism to force them to change their behavior.
4. Bolster the counterterrorist capabilities of those countries that work with the United States and require assistance.[56]

To prevent terrorism, billions of dollars are being committed and spent, and some civil liberties have been curtailed or severely restricted. The typical business or pleasure trip by airplane, for example, has become an even more taxing and intrusive experience. Even a simple trip to the library can make a person suspect should he or she select literary works that trigger the suspicion of a federal law enforcement agency. In a nation that was founded on the principles of freedom, openness, and anonymity for the most part, the new security, surveillance, and intelligence initiatives implemented since 9/11 have created concerns for many Americans.

Attempting to prevent terrorism is a daunting task. How can law enforcement officers protect every soft and hard target in America: all schools, all local water supplies, all food supply lines, all religious institutions, every public building in large and small communities, and all sources of energy? While Herculean does not adequately describe the charge, the protection of the American people and the nation's physical assets, as well as the reduction of fear from the threat of terrorism, is precisely what American law enforcement aims to do.

American law enforcement is now engaged in both defensive and offensive strategies to combat terrorism. However, in a free, open, and largely anonymous society, terrorists and potential terrorists know that the United States is

FYI: Terror Drill

Beginning on May 12, 2003, and lasting more than 5 days, the new DHS and 8,000 federal, state, and local police officers participated in the largest terror drill ever carried out in the United States at a cost of about $16 million. Two coordinated attacks occurred in the simulation. A radiological dirty bomb went off in downtown Seattle, and hospitals in Chicago were suddenly flooded with people who experienced flulike symptoms as a result of a bioterrorist attack. Although the results of the law enforcement and other agencies' responses were not perfect in all respects in this first-of-its-kind simulation, the drill was considered a success because of the unprecedented cooperation and learning that occurred.

SOURCE: Brian Blomquist, "Terror Test Run," *New York Post Online Edition,* May 12, 2003, at www.nypost.com.

fertile ground for terrorism. The police are faced with a dilemma. If the police are too aggressive trying to find and capture terrorists, American citizens are likely to become more fearful, anxious, and either resistant to or overly enthusiastic about repressive measures. If that occurs, terrorists win because fear, intimidation, disruption, and media attention to their cause are principal goals. On the other hand, if American law enforcement is not firm enough in its resolve and tactics to repress terrorism, terrorists will be able to again perpetrate a disaster on the public such as the events of 9/11, with loss of life, serious injury, fear, and anger. Such an event would likely encourage even tighter domestic security procedures, which would be resented by many members of the public, and the entire terror cycle would start over again. Law enforcement officers walk a fine line between preserving liberty and tranquility and providing security that may be perceived as excessive and repressive.

To illustrate, on June 17, 2003, President Bush issued guidelines barring federal agents from using race or ethnicity in routine investigations, but the policy permits exceptions in investigations involving terrorism and national security issues. Consequently, if law enforcement and intelligence officials receive information that terrorists of a certain ethnic group plan to hijack a plane in a particular state in the near future, officials are allowed to heighten security on men of that ethnicity that board planes in that area (also see the description of the PATRIOT Act in Chapter 4).[57]

HOW PREPARED IS THE UNITED STATES TO DEFEND AGAINST TERRORISM?

The answer depends on whom you ask and there are many people and groups willing to give an answer. As noted in the last chapter, there already have been some successes. Terrorist acts have been prevented; terrorists have been captured and brought to justice; and the nation, as of July 2003, has avoided another tragedy of 9/11 proportions. Nevertheless, U.S. borders remain porous, and U.S. assets are still vulnerable.

In 2003, two reports critical of the nation's preparedness to respond to terrorist attacks were released. The independent and bipartisan Council on Foreign Relations concluded that the United States was "drastically underfunding local emergency responders and remains dangerously unprepared to handle another September 11 event."[58] The nonprofit Partnership for Public Service determined that the United States is likely to be overwhelmed in the event of a bioterrorism attack because of serious shortages in skilled medical and scientific personnel.[59] The conclusion, it seems, is that the United States has much more to do in its preparation to fight terrorism.

THINKING CRITICALLY

1. What type of terrorism do you think poses the greatest threat to the United States and why?
2. Which of America's assets do you think are most vulnerable to terrorist attacks, and what do you think can be done to better defend them?

SUMMARY

1. Identify characteristics of police work

   The role of the police officer is complex and requires a combination of special characteristics, which involve quick decision making, invisible work, "dirty work," and danger.

2. Distinguish among James Q. Wilson's three operational styles in policing

   Wilson's three operational styles in policing are legalistic, which emphasizes violations of the law and the use of arrests to resolve community disputes; watchman, emphasizing informal means of resolving disputes and using arrest only as a last resort; and service, which emphasizes helping in the community over enforcing the law.

3. List the four major functions of police departments

   The four major functions of police departments in the United States are patrol, investigation, traffic, and drug enforcement.

4. List the drug enforcement strategies of local police agencies

   Although the particular drug enforcement strategies employed by individual agencies vary widely, the most common strategies are street-level enforcement, mid-level investigations, major investigations, crop eradication, smuggling interdiction, problem-oriented and community policing strategies, drug demand reduction, and asset forfeiture.

5. Explain the main components of community policing

   The three main components of community policing are community partnership, problem solving, and change management.

6. Identify four steps in a community policing approach to problem solving

   Community policing relies heavily on problem solving. The four steps in a community policing approach to problem solving are often referred to as SARA: Scanning—identifying problems, Analysis—understanding underlying conditions, Response—developing and implementing solutions, Assessment—determining the solutions' effect.

7. Define terrorism and identify different types of terrorism

   Terrorism has been defined as the systematic use of terror or unpredictable violence against governments, publics, or individuals to attain a political objective; the unlawful use of force and violence against persons or property to intimidate or coerce a government, the civilian population, or any segment thereof, in furtherance of political or social objectives; or premeditated, politically motivated violence perpetrated against noncombatant targets by subnational groups or clandestine agents, usually intended to influence an audience. Two broad categories of terrorism are domestic terrorism and international terrorism. Specific types of domestic terrorism are right-wing terrorism, left-wing terrorism, special interest terrorism, and individual terrorism. International terrorism is divided into state-sponsored terrorism, formalized terrorist organizations, and loosely affiliated extremists and rogue international terrorists.

KEY TERMS

role, p. 191
role expectation, p. 191
role conflict, p. 192
operational styles, p. 196
preventive patrol, p. 197
directed patrol, p. 198
GIS crime mapping, p. 198
aggressive patrol, p. 200
field interrogation, p. 200
cybercrime, p. 205
traffic accident investigation crews, p. 206
terrorism, p. 220
domestic terrorism, p. 220
international terrorism, p. 220

REVIEW QUESTIONS

1. What is a common source of role conflict for the police?
2. Distinguish among the three sets of operational styles identified by criminal justice scholars.
3. How are preventive patrol, directed patrol, and aggressive patrol different?
4. What are the major uses of GIS crime mapping in law enforcement?
5. What are some of the functions of a criminal investigator?
6. What are three distinct functions of DNA profiling?
7. What are two broad categories of cybercrime?
8. What are some of the more important functions of traffic units?
9. What are some of the problems with the use of civil asset forfeiture in drug enforcement?
10. What is the philosophy of community policing?
11. What are the three complementary operational strategies of community policing?
12. How frequently has the United States been victimized by domestic and international terrorism?

IN THE FIELD

1. **SARA Approach** In groups of three or four, select a local crime or disorder problem. Using the first three components of the SARA approach to problem solving (scanning, analysis, and response) and considering the elements of the crime triangle, formulate some options to deal with the problem. Present your options to the class, and let the whole class vote to determine which option is the best to solve the problem. Do you agree with the class vote? Why or why not? What do the results of this vote say about attitudes toward crime-related problem solving?

2. **Law Enforcement Resources** Look through several police periodicals, such as *Law and Order, Police Chief,* or other professional police magazines. What do the advertised products tell you about law enforcement? What law enforcement issues are addressed in the articles? Write a brief summary of your findings.

ON THE NET

1. **Cybercrime** Ask a local police officer what the needs of the police in combating cybercrime in your area are. Make a list of the types of cybercrimes that have actually occurred in your area. Compare and contrast that list with what experts on CNET (go to their Web page at www.CNET.com) and the material in your text describe as the important concerns in addressing cybercrime. Is there cause for concern? Why or why not?
2. **Drug Enforcement** To learn more about illegal drugs and drug control policy, visit the website of the Office of National Drug Control Policy at www.whitehousedrugpolicy.gov. Based on what you have learned, write an essay or prepare an oral presentation on whether national drug control policy has been or will be effective in reducing drug use and abuse among the American public.

CRITICAL THINKING EXERCISES

1. **Police Patrol** Assume that you are the patrol commander in a southern city that has large numbers of African American and Hispanic residents. All shifts of your patrol division have embraced and supported a "broken windows" and "zero-tolerance" approach to patrol work. Your patrol division's style could clearly be called aggressive, but for the past 5 years the city's violent, property, and minor offense rates have been dropping steadily. Some citizens have complained each month about the aggressive and sometimes intrusive vehicle stops. Most of the complainants have been African Americans who live in neighborhoods where the recorded crime rate has dropped the most dramatically since the implementation of the aggressive patrol style. They accuse officers of racial profiling. Racial profiling is illegal and occurs when minority citizens are stopped in their cars and on the street for little or nothing more than their race as the cause. (Racial profiling is discussed in greater detail in the next chapter.) When applied to motorists, racial profiling has even acquired a popular name, "Driving While Black" or DWB or DWBB, "Driving While Black or Brown."
   a. What steps would you take as patrol commander to assure the chief of police, the city's leaders, and the public at large that neither racial profiling is occurring in your patrol division nor are infringements on citizens' liberties beyond what are legal and necessary?
   b. What impact would validated cases of "Driving While Black or Brown" (or racial profiling) in other cities have on your plan?

2. **Community Policing** You are a new community police officer assigned with seven other officers to a low-income, heterogeneous, high-turnover, high-crime neighborhood. How should you and your fellow officers address the following problems?
   a. Neighborhood residents, neighborhood business owners, and community leaders disagree about the most important problems of the neighborhood and what to do about them. What should you and your fellow officers do?
   b. You organize and heavily publicize a meeting to discuss neighborhood problems and their solutions. However, only about 10 to 20 percent of neighborhood residents attend and most of them are white and more affluent homeowners who live in the better parts of the neighborhood. Few minorities or renters attend. What should you and your fellow officers do?
   c. Your precinct captain disagrees with neighborhood residents about the most important problems in the neighborhood. Your precinct captain's top priority is abandoned cars used for drug dealing. The top priority of neighborhood residents is the overall appearance of the neighborhood. What should you and your fellow officers do?

JOHN'S
91

Policing America: Issues and Ethics

CHAPTER SEVEN

Chapter Outline

Chapter Objectives

After completing this chapter, you should be able to:

1. Describe the general attitude of the public toward the police.
2. Summarize the steps in an effective police officer selection process.
3. Identify factors that affect the exercise of police discretion and methods of limiting discretion.
4. Describe two general ways that law enforcement agencies can reduce stress on the job.
5. Explain the circumstances under which police officers may be justified in using deadly force.
6. List some of the ways to control and reduce police corruption.

Crime Story

On July 6, 2002, 16-year-old Donavan Jackson was with his father, Coby Chavis, buying gas for their car at an Inglewood, California, gas station. After Jackson went inside the station to pay for the gas and buy a bag of potato chips, he returned to the car and found four Inglewood police officers questioning his father about an expired license plate on the car. Within moments the officers turned their attention to the teenaged youth and placed him in handcuffs for allegedly becoming disorderly after learning that his father was about to be arrested. While attempting to restrain Jackson, the youth was slammed against a police car and punched in the face by Inglewood police officer Jeremy Morse. Morse later defended his actions by contending that Jackson grabbed the officer's groin while in handcuffs.

The nation would soon learn that the incident was captured on videotape by amateur photographer Mitchell Crooks. Crooks taped the confrontation from a hotel across the street from the gas station. The video received widespread attention by both local and national television and provoked public debate about the alleged abusive nature of the police officer's conduct. Various protesters and political figures demanded that the officers be fired, especially 3-year police veteran, Jeremy Morse.

Inglewood Mayor Roosevelt F. Dorn ordered the immediate suspension of Jeremy Morse, who would later be terminated and charged with one count of assault under the color of authority. The crime carries a maximum penalty of 3 years in state prison and a $10,000 fine. Morse's partner, Bijan Darvish, was charged with filing a false report in conjunction with the investigation of the incident. No action was taken against the other two Inglewood officers who were present at the gas station when Jackson was arrested.

In July of 2003, joint trials were held for Jeremy Morse and Bijan Darvish concerning the allegations of excessive force and misconduct. After 4 days of jury deliberations, Bijan Darvish was acquitted of filing a false report. Both Darvish and his attorney were observed in the courtroom pounding their fists on the table in jubilation following the reading of the verdict. However, the jury was not as successful in deciding the case of former officer Jeremy Morse. Judge William Hollingsworth declared a hung jury on July 29, 2003. The jury foreman told the court that 7 of the 12 jurors wanted to find Morse guilty and 5 held out for a not-guilty verdict. A retrial of the Morse case was then scheduled for October of 2003.

Chapter 7 discusses various issues surrounding policing in America such as racial profiling, use of force, and ethics. The Donavan Jackson incident brings the debate over police use of excessive force to the forefront. Were the officers responding appropriately while making an arrest, or is this incident a clear-cut case of police abuse? Professionalization of law enforcement through education and training seeks to avoid and reduce the number of mistakes made by police officers. Once again, it will be the task of the courts to determine if former police officer Jeremy Morse acted appropriately and justifiably in the performance of his duties.

The Police and the Public

To carry out the duties of law enforcement, order maintenance, service, and information gathering successfully, the police must have the trust and cooperation of the public. The manner in which they carry out those functions, especially law enforcement and order maintenance, determines the community's respect for and trust in the police. Citizens who trust and respect the police are much more likely to help them carry out their duties; citizens who lack that trust and respect may rebel against the police in particular and government in general.

PUBLIC ATTITUDES TOWARD THE POLICE

What do people think of the police? The answer depends on what and whom you ask. It also depends on people's prior experience with the police. Research shows that citizens who have experienced positive contacts with the police generally have positive attitudes toward the police.[1] Figure 7.1 reveals that, overall, 59 percent of the public have "a great deal" or "quite a lot" of confidence in the police, 31 percent have "some" confidence, and 10 percent have "very little" or "none." However, among blacks, only 31 percent have "a great deal" or "quite a lot" of confidence in the police, another 39 percent have "some" confidence, and 30 percent have "very little" or "none." What is it about the police that the public has or does not have confidence?

To begin with, a majority of the public rate the police "excellent" or "very good" at responding quickly to calls for help and assistance, preventing crime, solving crime, being helpful and friendly, treating people fairly, and not using excessive force. As shown in Figure 7.2, between 60 and 70 percent of the public (18 years of age and older) rate the police "excellent" or "very good" on the six aforementioned issues. Between 16 and 24 percent rate the police "only fair," and between 7 and 10 percent rate them "poor" (3 to 9 percent were "not

The level of respect and confidence the public has for the police is not particulary high, especially among minorities. *Why is this the case?*

FIGURE 7.1 Views of the Public Toward the Police in the United States

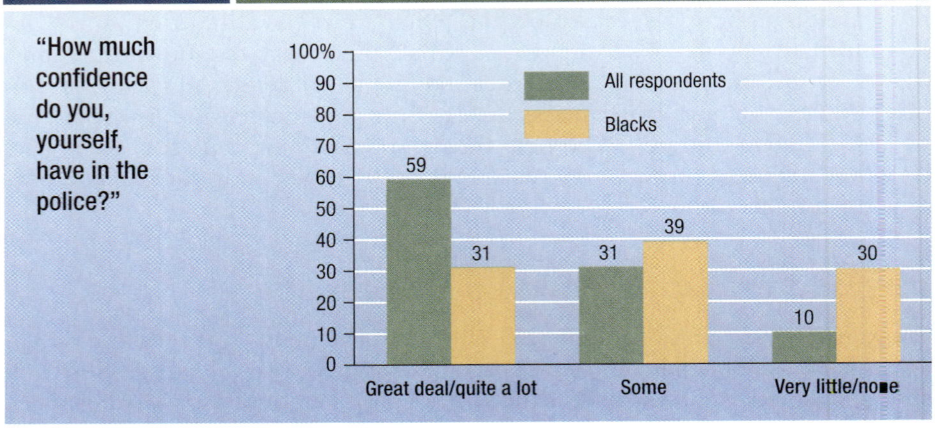

SOURCE: Ann L. Pastore and Kathleen Maguire, eds., *Sourcebook of Criminal Justice Statistics, 2002,* at www.albany.edu/sourcebook, p. 108, Table 2.16.

About 60 percent of Americans rate the police as either pretty good or excellent at solving crimes. *Why isn't the percentage higher?*

sure" or refused to answer). A different poll shows that 58 percent of the public have "a great deal" or "quite a lot" of confidence in the police's ability to protect it from violent crime; 39 percent do "not [have] very much confidence"; 9 percent have "none at all"; and 2 percent have "no opinion." The only significant change in any of the measures since 1999 was an increase in the public's confidence in the police's ability to prevent crime (from 58 percent to 65 percent). The public's confidence in the police's ability to protect it from violent crime has not changed much in more than two decades. In short, a majority of the public has at least some confidence in the ability of the police to do its job in a professional manner.

Among minorities, however, confidence in the police is much lower. Minorities differ from whites primarily in their beliefs about how the police carry out their duties:

- Only 43 percent of blacks and 41 percent of Hispanics, compared to 61 percent of whites, believe that "the police treat all races fairly."
- Eighty percent of blacks and 66 percent of Hispanics are much more likely to believe that "police brutality against minorities happens 'occasionally' (or more often) in their communities." Fifty-one percent of whites also agree with the statement.
- Thirty-two percent of blacks and 24 percent of Hispanics, compared to 6 percent of whites, believe that "police brutality against minorities in their communities happens 'often'."
- Forty-two percent of blacks and 39 percent of Hispanics, compared to 16 percent of whites, are sometimes "afraid that they will be arrested when they are completely innocent."[2]

When asked to rate the honesty and ethical standards of the police, 23 percent of the general public rate the police as "very high" on this measure, 45 percent rate them as "high," 26 percent rate them as "average," 5 percent rate them as "low," and 1 percent rate them as "very low." Blacks rate the honesty and ethical standards of police lower: Only 18 percent rate the police as "very high," 28 percent rate them as "high," 42 percent rate them as "average," 10 percent rate them as "low," and 2 percent rate them as "very low." (See Figure 7.3.)

FIGURE 7.2 Respondents' Ratings of Performance of Police in Own Community, United States, 2000 and 2002[a]

"How would you rate the police in your community on the following—excellent, pretty good, only fair or poor?"

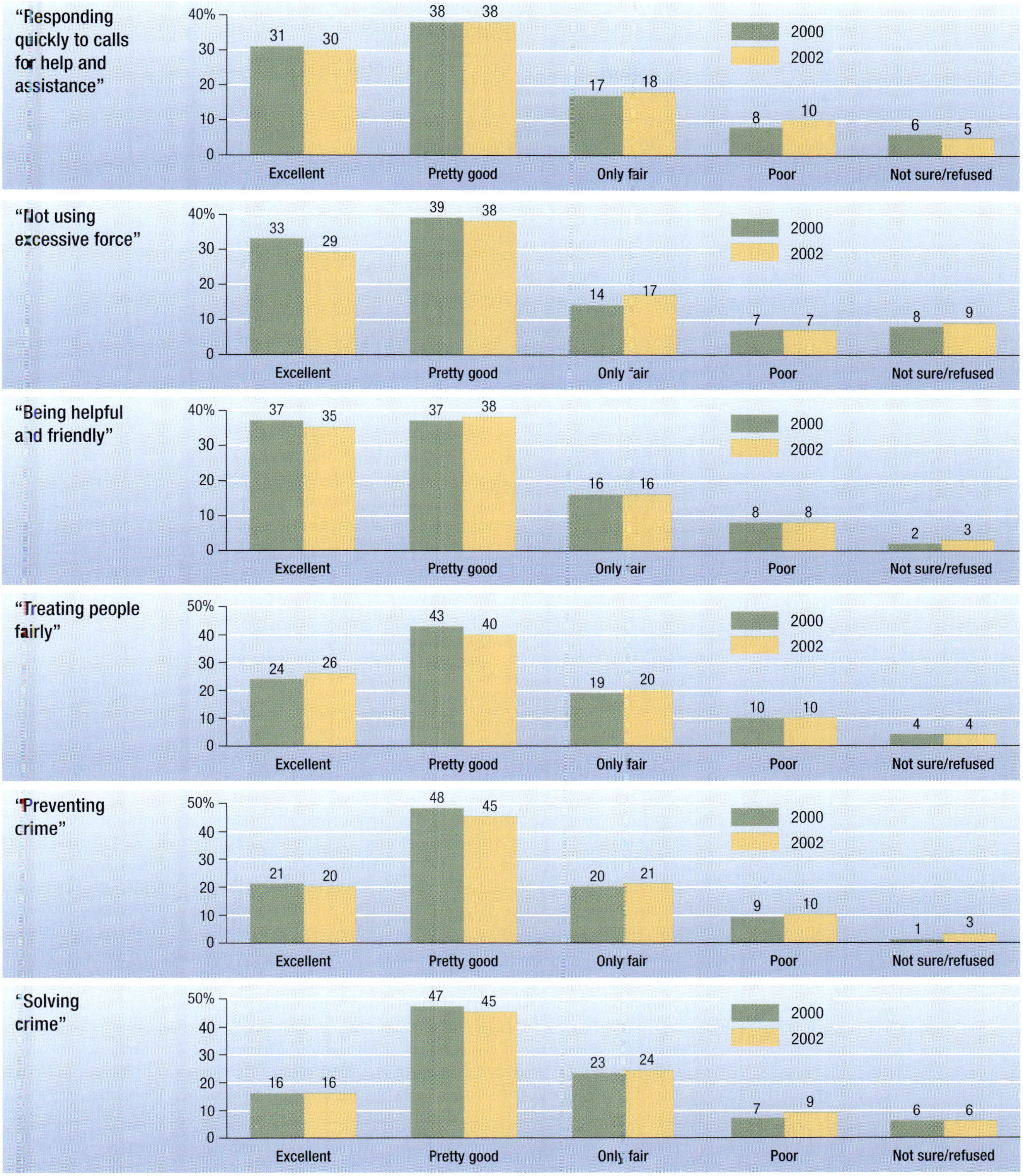

Note: Sample sizes vary from year to year; the data for 2002 are based on telephone interviews with a randomly selected national sample of 1,021 adults, 18 years of age and older, conducted Feb. 13–19, 2002.

[a]Percents may not add to 100 because of rounding.

SOURCE: Harris Interactive, Inc., *The Harris Poll,* March 1, 2000, p. 3; March 20, 2002, p. 3 (Los Angeles: Creators Syndicate, Inc.). Reprinted by permission of The Harris Poll and Creators Syndicate, Inc.

FIGURE 7.3 Views of the Public Toward the Police in the United States

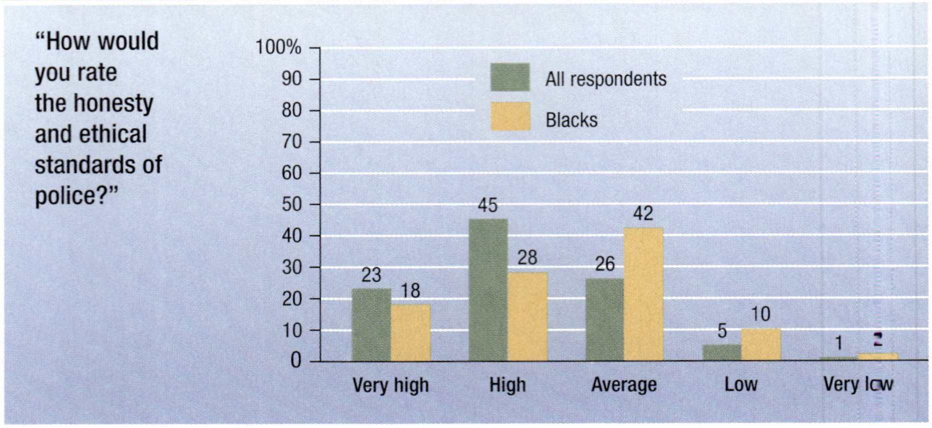

SOURCE: Ann L. Pastore and Kathleen Maguire, eds. *Sourcebook of Criminal Justice Statistics, 2001*, www.albany.edu/sourcebook, p. 114, Table 2.25.

THINKING CRITICALLY

1. Why do you think that racial groups differ so greatly in their attitudes toward the police?
2. What do you think could be done to improve public attitudes toward the police?
3. How accurate do you think the public's perceptions of the police are?
4. How do the perceptions presented in this section compare with your own?

In sum, these data clearly show that the public as a whole has more respect for the police and their honesty and ethical standards than it does for a variety of other occupations.[3] Yet, the level of respect and confidence is not particularly high, nor is it uniform across races. While most of the public believes that the police do a pretty good job, it also believes there is much room for improvement. One way to improve the police is to employ better police officers.

Police Recruitment and Selection

Deciding whom to employ should be simple: hire the type of police officer that the citizens of the community want. Of course, that approach assumes that the citizens of a community have some idea of what it takes to be a police officer. Then, there is the matter of which people to consult. Who should decide? The wealthy? The middle class? The poor? The politically conservative? The politically liberal? The young? The old? The business community? Community leaders? Crime victims? Those people most likely to be policed? Some consensus is needed on the type of police officer desired. Seeking that consensus in metropolitan communities is filled with conflict. Police administrators need to be very careful in choosing police officers, who may well be with the agency for 20 years or more. A police department will never reach its full potential without selecting the best available personnel. Selection decisions have momentous long-term implications for a police department.[4]

QUALITIES OF A SUCCESSFUL POLICE OFFICER

Given the complexity of the role of the police officer, it comes as no surprise that deciding what qualities the successful police officer needs is not easy. Indeed, police officers require a combination of qualities and abilities that is rare in any pool of applicants. Robert B. Mills, a pioneer in the psychological testing of police officers, believes that police applicants should possess the following psychological qualities:

- Motivation for a police career.
- Normal self-assertiveness.
- Emotional stability under stress.
- Sensitivity toward minority groups and social deviates.
- Collaborative leadership skills.
- A mature relationship with social authority.
- Flexibility.
- Integrity and honesty.
- An active and outgoing nature.[5]

The Berkeley, California, Police Department lists these qualities:

- Initiative.
- Ability to carry heavy responsibilities and handle emergencies alone.
- Social skills and ability to communicate effectively with persons of various cultural, economic, and ethnic backgrounds.
- Mental capacity to learn a wide variety of subjects quickly and correctly.

CAREERS IN CRIMINAL JUSTICE

Police Officer

My name is Robert Bour. I really enjoy being a police officer in Tiffin, Ohio, a small city of about 20,000 people. My assignment is in the patrol section, but I also work as a bike patrol officer, a field training officer, and a member of the SWAT team. As a SWAT officer, I go out mainly on search warrant and drug raids and in cases where someone has barricaded him- or herself in and a life is in danger. In a small police department, you have the opportunity to be involved in a number of specialized assignments.

As a patrol officer, I have the opportunity to interact with the public a great deal. We have always done community policing here in one form or another. Small communities have to. You stop people on the street and say hello, chat with business owners, and meet as many residents as you can. People always have questions for you; often they are about traffic laws and enforcement.

I also have to respond to calls for services and these calls take precedence over everything else. I get one to three calls per hour on the evening and early morning shift, but there are rare times when I don't get any calls during the entire 10 hours of work.

My third area of activity involves self-initiated patrol activity. That includes traffic enforcement, of course, but also patrolling the alleys and streets around bars when they are closing in order to protect inebriates who may have passed out outside the establishment. The patrol also includes guarding against people who may be driving under the influence of alcohol. Tiffin has two universities, so sometimes college students may get a little more disorderly than they should and we have to respond.

I graduated in 1992 from a police academy that was hosted by a local community college. Before becoming a police officer in Tiffin, I worked as a sheriff's deputy and a village police officer, both full- and part-time. The Tiffin police department now requires a 2-year college degree as the minimum to become employed. At the time I came on, it was not necessary, but I intend to go back to college and finish my degree anyway.

I can offer a few suggestions for anyone who wants to be a police officer. First, you should have a desire to work with people from diverse backgrounds because that is what police work is. Second, you must genuinely want to help people, keeping in mind that you are not always able to help everybody; sometimes that is frustrating. Finally, you must think about your family. They must support you in being a cop because there is some danger involved in the job. Still, police work is one of the best jobs a person can have.

What are the pros and cons of being a police officer?

Police officers must have a variety of qualities to be successful on the job. *What qualities would you bring to the position?*

- Ability to adapt thinking to technological and social changes.
- Understanding of other human beings and the desire to help those in need.
- Emotional maturity to remain calm and objective and provide leadership in emotionally charged situations.
- Physical strength and endurance to perform these exacting duties.[6]

three I's of police selection Three qualities of the American police officer that seem to be of paramount importance: intelligence, integrity, and interaction skills.

Three qualities seem to be of paramount importance. One commentator refers to them as the **three I's of police selection:** intelligence, integrity, and interaction skills. In short, police officers need to be bright enough to complete rigorous training. They should be honest enough to resist—and have a lifestyle that allows them to resist—the temptation of corrupting influences in law enforcement. They should also be able to communicate clearly and get along with people of diverse backgrounds.

Nearly as important as the three I's, however, are common sense and compassion. In resolving conflicts and solving problems they encounter, police officers must often choose a course of action without much time to think about it. Common sense is a key quality, for example, in locating a suspect who has just fled a crime scene on foot, or in deciding when to call off a high-speed vehicle pursuit that suddenly endangers innocent citizens and other police officers.

Police agencies also seek to employ officers with the core value of compassion. Without a genuine concern for serving one's fellow human beings, a police officer is not likely to sustain a high level of motivation over a long period of time. Many people the police meet on a daily basis simply need help, sometimes required by law, but more often these officers are spurred by a compassion for helping people no matter what their need.

Other qualities, such as physical strength, endurance, and appearance, seem less important. If you were the one who needed to be dragged from a burning automobile, however, the physical strength of the police officer might be important to you.

THE POLICE RECRUITMENT PROCESS

Few occupations have selection processes as elaborate as the ones used in choosing police officers in most departments of the nation. Before choices are made, a wide net must be cast in the recruiting effort to come up with enough potential applicants to fill the vacancies for an academy class. Police departments, often working with city personnel agencies, are generally guided in their selection decisions by civil service regulations. Those regulations are developed either locally or at the state level. They guarantee a merit employment system with equal opportunity for all.

Because employment qualifications are supposed to be based on perceived needs in policing, law enforcement agencies must be careful not to set unnecessary restrictions that have no bearing on an officer's ability to complete training and perform successfully on the job. The addition of just one seemingly minor qualification, such as requiring four pull-ups instead of three during physical ability testing, or making the eyesight requirement slightly more stringent, may eliminate thousands of men and women from the selection process in a large metropolitan area. It is difficult enough to find capable police candidates without needlessly eliminating them from the selection process.

Recruitment Most police agencies have finally realized that the kind of officers they desire will not gravitate naturally to the doors of the department. The search for top-notch applicants is very competitive, and many chiefs and sheriffs believe that they have to look at larger pools of applicants than in the past to find the same number of qualified officers. The reasons for the increased difficulty in finding good police candidates involve social maturity and lifestyle issues. Problems with drugs and alcohol, sexually transmitted diseases, personal debt, and dependability have reduced the number of qualified police applicants.

FYI Police Salaries

In 2001, the average (mean) beginning salary for police officers in cities of 10,000 or more persons was $32,502. In 2000, the average beginning salary for police officers was about $8,000 higher in departments that authorized collective bargaining than in those that did not authorize it. Nationwide, 40 percent of all local police departments, employing 72 percent of all officers, authorized collective bargaining for sworn personnel. The average maximum salary for police officers (who held no promotional rank) in 2001 was $45,209. On average, it took 7 years to reach the maximum salary.

Source: Ann L. Pastore and Kathleen Maguire, eds. *Sourcebook of Criminal Justice Statistics, 2001*, www.albany.edu/sourcebook, p. 51, Table 1.47; Matthew J. Hickman and Brian A. Reaves, *Local Police Departments, 2000*, U.S. Department of Justice, Bureau of Justice Statistics (Washington, DC: GPO, January 2003), p. 9.

In recruiting new police officers, efforts are made to cast police work as an attractive and sustaining career. *What should people interested in becoming police officers be told about the job?*

TABLE 7.1 Average Base Annual Salary for Selected Positions in Local Police Departments, by Size of Population Served, 2000

Population Served	Entry-Level Officer		Sergeant or Equivalent		Chief	
	Minimum	Maximum	Minimum	Maximum	Minimum	Maximum
All sizes	$25,500	$30,300	$35,100	$39,600	$43,700	$49,200
1,000,000 or more	$33,900	$51,300	$53,700	$65,300	$104,400	$136,400
500,000–999,999	33,400	47,500	50,000	59,000	99,600	116,000
250,000–499,999	34,200	48,400	49,000	59,400	85,000	111,600
100,000–249,999	34,700	46,800	49,100	58,900	84,400	104,300
50,000–99,999	34,100	44,300	49,800	57,300	78,300	92,700
25,000–49,999	32,800	42,500	46,700	54,000	70,100	82,200
10,000–24,999	29,700	36,600	41,800	46,700	58,000	65,800
2,500–9,999	25,900	30,900	34,200	38,200	43,300	48,700
Under 2,500	20,900	22,900	26,000	29,200	30,200	32,600

Note: Salary figures have been rounded to the nearest $100. Computation of average salary excludes departments with no full-time employee in that position.

SOURCE: Matthew J. Hickman and Brian A. Reaves, *Local Police Departments, 2000,* U.S. Department of Justice, Bureau of Justice Statistics (Washington, DC: GPO, January 2003), p. 8, Table 14.

The major goal of the recruiting effort is to cast police work as an attractive and sustaining career, even to those who might initially be turned off by it. Research supports the allure of policing for many people who view a career in law enforcement as financially rewarding and status enhancing. In addition, the work itself is intrinsically satisfying because it is nonroutine, exciting, generally outdoors, and people oriented.[7] Table 7.1 shows the average base annual salary for selected positions in local police departments, by size of population served in 2000. Many departments also offer the opportunity to earn special pay. Table 7.2 shows the percentage of local police departments, by size of population served, that authorize various types of special pay.

TABLE 7.2 Local Police Departments Authorizing Special Pay for Full-Time Sworn Personnel by Size of Population Served, 2000

Population Served	Percent of Agencies Authorizing Pay for—					
	Tuition Reimbursement	Education Incentive	Merit	Shift Differential	Special Skills	Hazardous Duty
All sizes	38%	30%	21%	19%	12%	4%
1,000,000 or more	73%	60%	40%	73%	67%	53%
500,000–999,999	66	39	30	60	40	48
250,000–499,999	83	63	43	72	43	40
100,000–249,999	78	70	37	45	40	32
50,000–99,999	75	67	32	42	37	16
25,000–49,999	67	65	37	36	33	8
10,000–24,999	58	58	24	36	24	8
2,500–9,999	40	33	23	20	11	2
Under 2,500	19	8	13	5	2	0

SOURCE: Matthew J. Hickman and Brian A. Reaves, *Local Police Departments, 2000,* U.S. Department of Justice, Bureau of Justice Statistics (Washington, DC: GPO, January 2003), p. 9, Table 15.

Affirmative Action Since the passage of the Civil Rights Act of 1964 and the threat of court challenges to the fairness of the police selection process, police agencies have struggled to find the best-qualified applicants and yet achieve satisfactory race and gender representation within the ranks of the department. Failure to seriously pursue equitable representation has led to expensive lawsuits, consent decrees, and court-ordered quotas to achieve the desired diversity. Consequently, affirmative action has become a major concern in police selection and employment. Now affirmative action programs are being questioned on several legal grounds. That questioning may lead to more difficulty in trying to achieve race and gender balance in police departments.

How successful has affirmative action been in accomplishing the desired goal of race and gender balance in police departments? Affirmative action *has* been relatively successful in increasing the percentage of minority members in policing. It has been less successful in increasing the percentage of women. As noted previously, more than 70 percent of the sworn officers in the nation's police departments are white males. However, as shown in Table 7.3, the percentage of black and Hispanic officers in local departments is 11.7 and 8.3, respectively. Those figures closely approximate the percentage of blacks and Hispanics in the general population of the United States (12.7 percent for blacks and 10.9 percent for Hispanics). However, women, who compose over 50 percent of the United States population, represent only 10.6 percent of the police officers in local police departments.[8]

TABLE 7.3 Minority Representation in Local Police Departments in the United States, 2000

Race/Ethnicity	Police	Population
Black	11.7%	12.7%
Hispanic	8.3	10.9
White	77.4	82.7
Other	2.7	4.8

Source: Matthew J. Hickman and Brian A. Reaves, *Local Police Departments, 2000,* U.S. Department of Justice, Bureau of Justice Statistics (Washington, DC: GPO, 2003), and U.S. Census Bureau.

FYI: Increase in Minority and Female Police Officers

From 1990 to 2000, the number of African American local police officers increased by 13,300, or 35 percent; Hispanic officers by 17,600, or 93 percent; and female officers by 17,300, or 59 percent.

Source: Matthew J. Hickman and Brian A. Reaves, *Local Police Departments, 2000,* U.S. Department of Justice, Bureau of Justice Statistics (Washington, DC: GPO, 2003), p. iii.

Education Given the amount of discretion that law enforcement officers have and the kinds of sociological problems with which they deal, selecting reasonably intelligent, college-educated officers seems a wise practice. Many police agencies in the country currently require some college background. As a result, the average level of education in policing today is nearly 2 years of college. Table 7.4 shows the minimum educational requirement for new officers in local departments, by size of population served. Among the advantages of hiring college-educated officers are the following:

1. Better written reports.
2. Enhanced communication with the public.
3. More effective job performance.
4. Fewer citizen complaints.
5. Wiser use of discretion.
6. Heightened sensitivity to racial and ethnic issues.
7. Fewer disciplinary actions.[9]

CJ ONLINE

Women and Policing

The National Center for Women & Policing is a nationwide resource that seeks to increase the number of women in policing. You can visit its website at **www.womenandpolicing.org/default.asp.** *What are some of the best ways to increase the number of women in policing?*

This list of advantages should impress police administrators and the public. Satisfied citizens, the savings of substantial amounts of money by avoiding lawsuits, and fewer disciplinary actions against officers are good reasons for law enforcement executives to search for police applicants with college backgrounds.

Recognition that college-educated police officers are generally better performers than officers without that level of education is long overdue. And the idea is catching on. Minnesota's Peace Officer Licensing Commission now requires a 4-year college degree for licensing. The Peace Officer Council in Ohio now has more than one dozen **college academies,** where students pursue a program that integrates an associate's degree curriculum in law enforcement

college academies Schools where students pursue a program that integrates an associate's degree curriculum in law enforcement or criminal justice with the state's required peace officer training.

TABLE 7.4 **Minimum Educational Requirement for New Officers in Local Police Departments, by Size of Population Served, 2000**

		Percent of Agencies Requiring a Minimum of:			
Population Served	Total with Requirement	High School Diploma	Some College*	2-Year College Degree	4-Year College Degree
All sizes	98%	83%	6%	8%	1%
1,000,000 or more	100%	67%	33%	0%	0%
500,000–999,999	100	71	18	6	6
250,000–499,999	98	65	18	10	5
100,000–249,999	99	71	18	9	2
50,000–99,999	99	65	17	16	1
25,000–49,999	99	73	11	13	2
10,000–24,999	99	78	8	12	1
2,500–9,999	99	85	4	9	1
Under 2,500	97	86	4	6	—

Note: Detail may not add to total because of rounding.

*Nondegree requirements.

— Less than 0.5 percent.

Source: Matthew J. Hickman and Brian A. Reaves, *Local Police Departments, 2000,* U.S. Department of Justice, Bureau of Justice Statistics (Washington, DC: GPO, January 2003), p. 6, Table 10.

or criminal justice with the state's required peace officer training. Upon receipt of the associate's degree, students sit for the peace officer certification exam. If they receive a passing score on the exam, they are eligible to be hired by any police agency and to go to work without any additional academy training.

Increasing the number of female officers is a major concern in police selection and employment. *What are some of the advantages of having a greater number of female police officers?*

SUCCESSFUL RECRUITING PRACTICES

Where do you find the best-qualified police applicants? Some of the more successful recruiting practices have included going to colleges, neighborhood centers, and schools in minority communities; using television, radio, and newspaper advertisements; and working with local employment offices. Demystifying the nature of police work and the selection process and shortening the time from application to final selection have also helped to attract and retain qualified candidates.

PUBLIC SAFETY OFFICERS Another promising recruitment strategy has been the employment of 18-year-olds as **public safety officers** (sometimes called community service officers or public service aides), who perform many police service functions but do not have arrest powers. By the time they are 21, the department has had an excellent opportunity to assess their qualifications and potential to be sworn officers.

public safety officers Police department employees who perform many police services but do not have arrest powers.

POLICE CADETS **Police cadet programs** have been around since the 1960s (Cincinnati Police), and as recently as the 1990s, the New York City Police launched a cadet program combining a college education with academy training and work experience in the police department. Upon graduation from the university, a cadet is promoted to police officer.

police cadet program A program that combines a college education with agency work experience and academy training. Upon graduation, a cadet is promoted to police officer.

HIGH SCHOOL TECH PREP PROGRAMS A new idea is beginning to take hold that will attract capable police officers at an even earlier age. The program is known as **tech prep** or **technical preparation** for a criminal justice career. Area community colleges and high schools team up to offer 6 to 9 hours of college law enforcement courses in the eleventh and twelfth grades, as well as one or two training certifications, such as police dispatcher or local corrections officer. Students who graduate are eligible for employment at age 18. They become interested in law enforcement work early and are ideal police applicants when they become old enough to apply. Accurate law enforcement career information can be passed on to high school students through a tech

tech prep (technical preparation) A program in which area community colleges and high schools team up to offer 6 to 9 hours of college law enforcement courses in the eleventh and twelfth grades, as well as one or two training certifications, such as police dispatcher or local corrections officer. Students who graduate are eligible for police employment at age 18.

Pictured here are police cadets searching a parking lot, where a woman was shot and killed by a sniper. *What are some of the advantages of police cadet programs?*

prep program because the teachers are required to either currently work in law enforcement or have police experience in their backgrounds.

Police Corps The federal Police Corps program was created as part of the Violent Crime Control and Law Enforcement Act of 1994.[10] Its purposes are to (1) address violent crime by increasing the number of police with advanced education and training on community patrol and (2) provide educational assistance to law enforcement personnel and students who possess a sincere interest in public service in the form of law enforcement. Through its state-level affiliates, the program provides federal scholarships on a competitive basis to college students who agree to serve where needed on community patrol as police officers or sheriffs' deputies for at least 4 years. Students who are accepted into the Police Corps programs receive up to $7,500 a year to pay the expenses toward a bachelor's or graduate degree. A student may receive up to $30,000 under the program, including reasonable room and board. Undergraduate participants must be full-time students at an accredited public or nonprofit 4-year college or university. They may pursue a degree in any relevant field of study, including criminal justice or law enforcement. Shortly after graduation, participants begin their work as officers. Those who pursue a graduate degree complete their service in advance.

In addition to their college education, all Police Corps participants must satisfactorily complete a rigorous 16- to 24-week residential Police Corps basic law enforcement training program paid for by the federal government. The law enforcement agency with which the participant serves provides additional training as appropriate. If a Police Corps participant fails to complete his or her bachelor's degree, Police Corps training, and 4 years of required service with the assigned agency, he or she must repay all scholarships and reimbursements received through the program, plus 10 percent interest.

Police Corps participants are expected to work as community patrol officers in geographic areas that have a great need for additional officers and to be assigned to challenging beats where they can be most effective. The program encourages states, where feasible, to place participants in areas where they have community or family ties. Participants receive the same pay and benefits and have the same responsibilities as any other officer of similar rank and tenure.

THE POLICE SELECTION PROCESS

merit system A system of employment whereby an independent civil service commission, in cooperation with the city personnel section and the police department, sets employment qualifications, performance standards, and discipline procedures.

In many communities, selection of police officers takes place through a merit system. A **merit system** of employment is established when an independent civil service commission, in cooperation with the city personnel section and the police department, sets employment qualifications, performance standards, and discipline procedures. Officers employed under such a system are hired and tenured, in theory, only if they meet and maintain the employment qualifications and performance standards set by the civil service commission. Officers in such a system cannot be fired without cause.

To find the best possible recruits to fill department vacancies, police agencies use a selection process that includes some or all of the following steps:

Short Application This brief form registers the interest of the applicant and allows the agency to screen for such things as minimum age, level of education, residency, and other easily discernible qualifications.

Detailed Application This document is a major source of information for the department and background investigators. The applicant is asked for complete education and work histories, military status, medical profile, references, a record of residence over many years, and other detailed information.

Physical ability tests are common in police selection. *Why are they important?*

Applicants are also asked to submit copies of credentials, military papers, and other certificates.

MEDICAL EXAMINATION This exam determines if applicants are free of disease, abnormalities, and any other medical problems that would disqualify them for police work. This information is critical because retiring a young officer on a medical disability shortly after employment could cost the public hundreds of thousands of dollars. Table 7.5 shows the percentage of local police departments by population served that use medical exams, as well as various interviews, tests, and other exams, in the selection of new officer recruits.

PHYSICAL ABILITY TEST Physical ability tests are common in police selection despite having been challenged in the courts as having an adverse effect

TABLE 7.5 Interviews, Tests, and Examinations Used in Selection of New Officer Recruits in Local Police Departments, by Size of Population Served, 2000

Population Served	Personal Interview	Medical Exam	Drug Test	Psychological Evaluation	Physical Agility Test	Written Aptitude Test	Personality Inventory	Polygraph Exam
All sizes	96%	81%	67%	61%	44%	43%	31%	21%
1,000,000 or more	100%	100%	100%	93%	87%	73%	47%	73%
500,000–999,999	94	94	85	94	88	91	71	61
250,000–499,999	95	100	90	93	90	80	60	80
100,000–249,999	95	96	89	94	83	84	62	72
50,000–99,999	99	98	87	97	81	78	60	53
25,000–49,999	98	99	87	95	81	79	54	50
10,000–24,999	98	98	78	86	69	68	45	32
2,500–9,999	96	87	74	65	43	48	29	23
Under 2,500	94	65	52	41	24	21	20	7

Note: List of selection methods is not intended to be exhaustive.

SOURCE: Matthew J. Hickman and Brian A. Reaves, *Local Police Departments, 2000,* U.S. Department of Justice, Bureau of Justice Statistics (Washington, DC: GPO, January 2003), p. 5, Table 8.

FYI Screening New Police Recruits

In 2000, local police departments used the following methods to screen new recruits: criminal record checks (99 percent), background investigations (98 percent), personal interviews (97 percent), medical exams (96 percent), drug tests (88 percent), and psychological evaluations (88 percent).

SOURCE: Matthew J. Hickman and Brian A. Reaves, *Local Police Departments, 2000,* U.S. Department of Justice, Bureau of Justice Statistics (Washington, DC: GPO, 2003), p. iii.

on the hiring of female applicants. Physical ability tests were initially a direct response to the elimination of height and weight standards, which were also discriminatory against female applicants. The first tests required exceptional speed and strength, such as going over walls that were taller than any of the walls in the cities that had such tests. Those tests were struck down by the courts as not being job-related. Today, any physical ability tests must be based on a thorough analysis of the actual work of police officers. See Table 7.5 for the percentage of local police departments that use physical agility tests in the selection of new officer recruits.

WRITTEN EXAMINATION Police agencies once used intelligence tests in their selection process. Most agencies now use some type of aptitude, personality, general knowledge, reading comprehension, writing, or police skill exam. The courts have held that those tests must be true measures of the knowledge and abilities needed to perform police work successfully. Preemployment tests have been the subject of much controversy in the courts.

BACKGROUND INVESTIGATION Investigators in this process look for any factors in the backgrounds of applicants that would prevent them from performing successfully as police officers. Past drug use or excessive alcohol use, a poor driving record, employer problems, a bad credit history, criminal activity, and social immaturity are areas of concern in the background investigation. The investigator relies heavily on the detailed application, verifies its contents, explores any discrepancies, and develops additional leads to follow. Table 7.6 shows the percentage of local police departments by population served that use various types of background checks in the selection of new officer recruits.

PSYCHOLOGICAL TESTING Emotional stability and good mental health are critical to the ability to perform police work, which can be very stressful. Departments have been held liable for not screening their applicants for those psychological traits.[11]

TABLE 7.6 Background Checks Used in Selection of New Officer Recruits In Local Police Departments, by Size of Population Served, 2000

Population Served	Background Investigation	Criminal Record Check	Driving Record Check	Credit History Check	Volunteer Service Check
All sizes	96%	96%	93%	48%	6%
1,000,000 or more	100%	100%	100%	87%	20%
500,000–999,999	94	97	94	85	12
250,000–499,999	98	100	100	93	13
100,000–249,999	99	99	98	79	7
50,000–99,999	99	100	100	80	9
25,000–49,999	99	99	99	76	7
10,000–24,999	98	99	96	73	10
2,500–9,999	97	98	96	52	5
Under 2,500	95	93	89	28	5

Note: List of selection methods is not intended to be exhaustive.

SOURCE: Matthew J. Hickman and Brian A. Reaves, *Local Police Departments, 2000,* U.S. Department of Justice, Bureau of Justice Statistics (Washington, DC: GPO, January 2003), p. 5, Table 9.

Systematic psychological testing of police officers began in the 1950s. At first, the typical approach was to have the psychological evaluators look for disqualifying factors. The process included a pencil-and-paper test and a one-on-one interview with a psychologist. Today, the testing focus has generally shifted to a search for the positive psychological qualities required in police work. Current tests include multiple versions of both written and clinical evaluations.

The validity of psychological tests has been an issue for decades. Psychologists are often reluctant to rate with any specificity the police candidates they evaluate. Candidates considered "unacceptable" are sometimes classified as "uncertain" to avoid lawsuits. It is important to remember that understanding and predicting human behavior is an inexact art. So it is easy to appreciate the reluctance of psychologists to be more specific. See Table 7.5 for the percentage of local police departments by population served that use psychological tests and evaluation in the selection of new officer recruits.

At the end of many police academy training programs, there is a state licensing or certification examination. *Do you believe those examinations are necessary? Why or why not?*

Oral Interview/Oral Board This step is frequently the final one in the selection process. Members of the interview team have the results of the previous selection procedures, and they now have an opportunity to clear up inconsistencies and uncertainties that have been identified. The board normally restricts itself to evaluating the following qualities:

1. Appearance, poise, and bearing.
2. Ability to communicate orally and organize thoughts.
3. Attitude toward law enforcement and the job required of police officers.
4. Speech and the ability to articulate.
5. Attitude toward drug, narcotic, and alcohol use.
6. Sensitivity to racial and ethnic issues.[12]

See Table 7.5 for the percentage of local police departments by population served that use personal interviews in the selection of new officer recruits.

Academy Training The police academy is part of the selection process. Virtually every academy class in any sophisticated police department loses up to 10 percent of its students. Thus, to survive academy training, students must be committed to the process. Students undergo from 400 to more than 1,000 hours of academic, skill, and physical training and are tested virtually every week of the process. In 2000, for example, state-mandated field and academy training requirements for new officers averaged about 750 hours combined. Additional training beyond state requirements averaged about 300 hours (see Table 7.7). At the end of many academy training programs, students must take a state licensing or certification examination.

Probation Under local or state civil service requirements, employers may keep a new police officer on probation for 6 months to a year. The probation period gives the new police officer a chance to learn policing under the guidance of a well-qualified field training officer. Formal field training is a wise investment, and it ensures that new officers get as much knowledge and experience as possible before an agency commits to them for their careers.

A problem is that with police academy training now often extending 5 or 6 months, a 6-month probation period no longer seems logical. The agency is, in effect, offering the police officer tenure in a matter of weeks after graduation

TABLE 7.7 Training Requirements for New Officer Recruits in Local Police Departments, by Size of Population Served, 2000

	Average Number of Hours Required					
	Academy			Field		
Population Served	Total	State-Mandated	Other Required	Total	State-Mandated	Other Required
All sizes	637	514	123	417	228	189
1,000,000 or more	1,051	564	487	534	189	345
500,000–999,999	950	586	364	784	425	359
250,000–499,999	991	577	414	659	336	323
100,000–249,999	853	601	252	757	425	322
50,000–99,999	790	604	186	689	414	275
25,000–49,999	763	586	177	680	334	346
10,000–24,999	751	574	177	537	297	240
2,500–9,999	611	514	97	389	235	154
Under 2,500	532	469	63	244	153	91

Note: Average number of training hours excludes departments not requiring training.

SOURCE: Matthew J. Hickman and Brian A. Reaves, *Local Police Departments, 2000,* U.S. Department of Justice, Bureau of Justice Statistics (Washington, DC: GPO, January 2003), p. 6, Table 11.

FYI

Executive Salaries

As of July–November 2001, the average (mean) salary of police chiefs was $65,041, up from $58,055 in 1999. However, salaries varied greatly depending on the city population size. For cities with populations of one million or more, the average salary of police chiefs was $139,321, down from $144,788 in 1999. On the other hand, in cities of fewer than 2,500 the average salary of police chiefs was $43,267, up from $39,480 in 1999. The same is true of county sheriffs. As of July–November 2001, the average (mean) salary of county sheriffs was $57,822, up from $52,067 in 1999. In counties with a population of one million or more, the average salary was $120,183, up from $108,054 in 1999. In counties with populations of fewer than 2,500 the average salary was $34,198, up from $32,490 in 1999.

SOURCE: Ann L. Pastore and Kathleen Maguire, eds. *Sourcebook of Criminal Justice Statistics, 2001,* www.albany.edu/sourcebook, pp. 52–55, Tables 1.48 and 1.49

from the academy. This practice defeats the purpose of probation, which was designed to allow the employer to see whether the newly trained officer can successfully perform the job.

THE SELECTION OF A LAW ENFORCEMENT EXECUTIVE

No less important than the selection of operations-level officers is the choice of the chief executive of a police agency. This executive might be a chief of police, a sheriff, or the head of a state law enforcement organization. A crucial decision in the selection process is whether to allow people from outside the agency to apply. In some police agencies in the United States, civil service regulations prohibit the selection of outside candidates. The rationale for this rule is that there must be qualified internal candidates. In addition, it is discouraging to hard-working and talented police administrators to be denied a chance to lead the agency they have spent many years serving.

Actual hiring decisions are usually shared by members of a selection committee. Frequently, an executive search firm is also employed. The selection committee usually consists of representatives of the local government, the police department, the search firm, and the community. Applicants are put through a rigorous process that includes several visits to the city, written exams, interviews, and assessment center testing, in which candidates try to resolve real-world management problems. Once the interviews and testing have been completed, applicants are normally ranked, and the list is presented to the city manager, the mayor, or others so that a final selection can be made.

The pursuit of a police chief's job is very competitive. Often several hundred candidates contend for a position even in a small suburban community. A typical police chief rarely serves longer than 10 years, and life in the chief's seat may not be very comfortable, particularly if a new chief intends to change things. Much of the political controversy and many of the social problems in major cities and counties end up at the door of the police department, so police chiefs must be politically savvy to survive. Many chiefs discover that they cannot please everybody, particularly if they are trying to change the department. Should police chiefs have protection under civil service? Most commentators say no, arguing that mayors and city managers ought to have the authority to pick the management teams that work immediately under their direction. A small number of cities give their police chiefs civil service protection to insulate them from unnecessary political interference.

The selection of a sheriff of one of the nation's counties is just as important as choosing a police chief. The difference in the two processes has to do with who does the selecting. In all but a few of the nation's counties, sheriffs are elected by the county's eligible voters. Not all sheriffs have a law enforcement background. In most states, they are not required to be licensed or certified peace officers as their deputies or municipal officers are. As a result, people from various occupations often succeed in being elected sheriff. To be elected, sheriffs must be good politicians. They often have a much better idea of the priorities of a community and wield more influence with prosecutors and in the legislature than chiefs of police. Sheriffs who do not exhibit this political acumen are not likely to be reelected.

THINKING CRITICALLY

1. What do you think are the most important qualities for police officers to have? Why?
2. How much formal education do you think police officers should have? Why?

Issues in Policing

The discussion of law enforcement thus far has made it clear that not all matters of policing in America are settled. In this final section of the chapter, some of the issues that continue to be major topics of debate in law enforcement and have significant impact on the quality of life in neighborhoods and communities across the nation will be highlighted.

DISCRETION

discretion The exercise of individual judgment, instead of formal rules, in making decisions.

Discretion is the exercise of individual judgment, instead of formal rules, in making decisions. No list of policies and procedures could possibly guide police officers in all of the situations in which they find themselves. Even the police officer writing a ticket for a parking meter violation exercises a considerable amount of discretion in deciding precisely what to do.[13] Police even have the discretion to ignore violations of the law when they deem it appropriate in the context of other priorities.

The issue of police discretion is very controversial. Some believe that the discretion of police officers should be reduced. The movement to limit the discretion of police officers is the result of abuses of that discretion, such as physical abuse of citizens or unequal application of the law in making arrests. Other people argue that we should acknowledge that officers operate with great discretion and not attempt to limit it. Advocates of this view believe that better education and training would help officers exercise their judgment more wisely.

Patrol Officer Discretion Patrol officers frequently find it necessary to exercise their discretion. Within the geographical limits of their beats, they have the discretion to decide precisely where they will patrol when they are not answering radio calls. They decide whom to stop and question. For example, they may tell some children playing ball in the street to move, while they ignore others. Patrol officers decide for themselves which traffic violators are worth chasing through busy traffic and which ones are not. They even have the right not to arrest for a minor violation when, for example, they are on the way to investigate a more serious matter.

Some of the more critical situations involve decisions about stopping, searching, and arresting criminal suspects. Many citizens have been inconvenienced and some have been abused because of a police officer's poor use of discretion in those areas.

full enforcement A practice in which the police make an arrest for every violation of law that comes to their attention.

Police officers cannot make an arrest for every violation of law that comes to their attention—that is, they cannot provide **full enforcement.** The police do not have the resources to enforce the law fully, nor can they be everywhere at once. And even if full enforcement were possible, it may not be desirable. For example, persons intoxicated in front of their own homes may not need to be arrested, but only to be told to go inside. Motorists slightly exceeding the speed limit need not be arrested if they are moving with the flow of traffic. Prostitution may be widely practiced in large metropolitan areas, but police officers have little to gain by searching hotels and motels to stamp it out, particularly when judges will turn the prostitutes right back out on the street. Generally, only when such an activity becomes a clear nuisance, is the subject of a public outcry, or threatens health and safety do the police department and its officers choose to take formal action.

selective enforcement The practice of relying on the judgment of the police leadership and rank-and-file officers to decide which laws to enforce.

The practice of relying on the judgment of the police leadership and rank-and-file officers to decide which laws to enforce is referred to as **selective enforcement.** The practice allows street police officers to decide important matters about peacekeeping and enforcement of the law. For most violations of the law, but not all felonies, a police officer can usually exercise a number of options:

1. Taking no action at all if the officer deems that appropriate for the situation.
2. Giving a verbal warning to stop the illegal action.
3. Issuing a written warning for the violation.
4. Issuing a citation to the perpetrator to appear in court.
5. Making a physical arrest in serious matters or in situations with repeat offenders.

Police officers can exercise discretion in arrest situations. *Should police officers be allowed to use discretion in arrest situations? Why or why not?*

Factors Affecting Discretion Dozens of studies have been conducted on the exercise of discretion by police patrol officers. A number of significant factors affect discretion:

- **The Nature of the Crime** The more serious the crime, the more likely it is that police officers will formally report it. In cases involving lesser felonies, misdemeanors, and petty offenses, police officers are more likely to handle the offenses informally. A minor squabble between over-the-fence neighbors is an example of a matter that would probably be handled informally.
- **Departmental Policies** If the leadership of a police department gives an order or issues a policy demanding that particular incidents be handled in a prescribed way, then an officer is not supposed to exercise discretion but is to do as the order or policy directs. Thus, if a city has had many complaints about dangerous jaywalking in a certain downtown area, the chief of police may insist that citations be issued to those found jaywalking, even though, in the past, citations had not been issued.
- **The Relationship Between the Victim and the Offender** Particularly for minor offenses, the closer the relationship between the victim of an alleged offense and the suspected perpetrator, the more discretion the officer is able to exercise. For example, police officers are not likely to deal formally with a petty theft between two lovers if they believe that the victim will not prosecute his or her partner.
- **The Amount of Evidence** If officers do not have enough evidence to substantiate an arrest or to gain a conviction in court, they are likely to handle the case in some way other than making an arrest.
- **The Preference of the Victim** Sometimes the victim of a crime may simply want to talk the matter over with someone, and the police are available on a 24-hour basis. Also, if the officer senses that the victim of a minor assault does not wish to prosecute the perpetrator of the offense, the patrol officer will not make a formal complaint, and the complainant will most likely never know that a report was not made.
- **The Demeanor of the Suspect** Suspects who are disrespectful and uncooperative may very well feel the full brunt of the law. Patrol officers often choose the most severe option possible in dealing with such suspects.
- **The Legitimacy of the Victim** Patrol officers are bound to pass some kind of judgment on the legitimacy of the victim. An assault victim who is belligerent and intoxicated, for instance, will not be viewed favorably by the investigating officer. Criminals victimized by other criminals are also seen as less than fully authentic victims, no matter what the offense.
- **Socioeconomic Status** The more affluent the complainant, the more likely a patrol officer is to use formal procedures to report and investigate a crime. Contrary to popular belief, the personal characteristics of an officer (such as race, gender, and education) do not seem to influence the exercise of discretion.

Discretion and Domestic Violence Police officers have intervened in domestic violence cases and other kinds of family disputes, sometimes off-duty, since the inception of public policing. For the longest period of time, these interventions were viewed as peacekeeping activities when, in fact, they should have been treated as criminal matters. Many women and some men were hurt, and some killed, as a result of the restrictions on the police in making arrests for assault misdemeanors not made in their presence and a view among the police that these calls were the private business of the family instead of real police matters. Traditionally, law enforcement has been less interested in arresting perpetrators of crimes when the victim and the perpetrator have a close relationship.

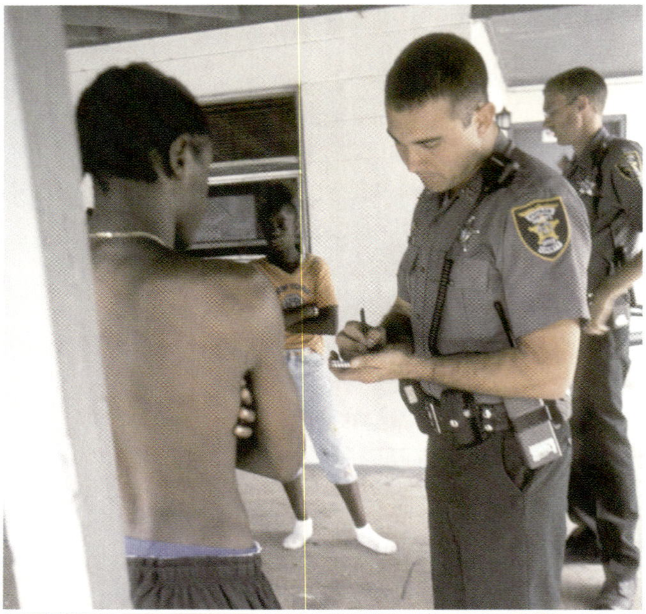

Many states have mandatory arrest laws that require police officers to arrest any suspect that has battered a spouse or domestic partner. *Do you support mandatory arrest laws in domestic violence cases? Why or why not?*

Approximately one million women are victims of domestic violence each year. Even today, with every state requiring the police to have domestic violence intervention training, some commentators believe that the police are not the best qualified of available community helpers to intervene. On the other hand, if crimes are committed in the form of physical abuse, the police are not only the best qualified to intervene but are also required by law to do so. Certainly, the availability of 24-hour service has always made the police the major responder to domestic violence calls.

The police in general do not relish the task of responding to domestic violence calls for several reasons. First, the calls can be dangerous, although generally no more dangerous than other disturbance calls. Nevertheless, officers are hurt each year by responding to domestic violence complaints. Second, police officers know from experience that many of the tense and hostile dynamics that exist between quarreling spouses, couples, and other family members have a way of dissipating over time or at least subsiding for awhile. Third, the police know that they have often conducted investigations, even arrested the suspected batterer, and the victim has later chosen to drop charges. Finally, the police know that responding to the minor assault cases in domestic violence calls is not always the best thing for the family because the arrest creates its own complications that may, in fact, exacerbate the family crisis to a state of irreparable harm.

Police have responded to domestic violence in three distinct ways: mediate the dispute, separate domestic partners in minor disputes, and arrest the perpetrator of the assault. Which of these ways is the most effective? This question was put to the test in a 3-year study in the city of Minneapolis. In minor domestic dispute cases, Minneapolis police officers gave up their discretion in handling domestic violence calls. Instead of deciding for themselves the appropriate disposition for each call, they randomly chose either arrest, separation, or mediation. The results of the study showed that the arrested perpetrators were about half as likely to repeat their violence against the original victim.[14] This study may have been the impetus for many states to implement a mandatory arrest domestic violence law. Subsequent studies, however, have not been able to clearly support the mandatory arrest disposition as the most effective way to handle the problem of domestic violence. Yet today nearly half of the states have a mandatory arrest law requiring the arrest of any suspect that has battered a spouse or domestic partner. While victim safety and welfare are indeed the major reasons for police intervention, more research is clearly needed to determine the best approaches to handling domestic violence calls.

CJ ONLINE

ACLU

To learn more about what is being done to combat racial profiling, visit the American Civil Liberties Union (ACLU) website on racial profiling at **www.aclu.org/profiling.** *What can police departments do to prevent racial profiling?*

racial profiling The stopping and/or detaining of individuals by law enforcement officers based solely on race.

Discretion and Racial Profiling **Racial profiling** is of growing concern to law enforcement officials and the public. Just how frequently this illegal practice occurs is difficult to discern, particularly since the term racial profiling is seldom defined in the discussions found in the national media. Racial profiling is a law enforcement infringement on a citizen's liberty based solely on race. On freeways, highways, and streets throughout the nation blacks and other minorities are stopped for traffic violations and field interrogations in numbers disproportionate to their representation in the population. Many of these stops are pretext stops where the stop is justified by a minor equipment or moving traffic violation that might otherwise be ignored. Where the practice is widely experienced, it has been called "driving while black or brown" (DWBB). At the root of such a practice is racial stereotyping and prejudice.

Racial profiling is a hot topic in the U.S. Congress, state legislatures, county commissions, and city councils, as well as in the meeting rooms of civil rights and professional police organizations. The American Civil Liberties Union, for example, has started a national project to eliminate racial profiling and even provides citizens with a "Bust Card" that tells them how to respectfully interact with the police (acknowledging the difficulty of their job) even when falling victim to racial profiling.

Racial profiling to any degree is a blight on the record of professional law enforcement and democracy. Some of the methods that have been prescribed to stop racial profiling include racial and cultural diversity training for police personnel, strong discipline for errant officers, videotaping all traffic stops, collecting data on the race of stopped motorists and pedestrians and the disposition of the encounter, and having police officers distribute business cards to all motorists and pedestrians they stop.

The business card may reduce race-based stops because it would allow an officer to be easily identified at a later time. But city leaders throughout the United States are in a quandary as to precisely what to do to stop racial profiling. Thirty-six members of the National League of Cities' public safety committees met in Oklahoma City and determined that they oppose police profiling of suspects when it violates a person's civil rights, but they could not agree whether all profiling should be banned.[15]

FYI

Racial Profiling

According to a recent national survey, 59 percent of Americans believe that racial profiling by the police is widespread. Among blacks, 77 percent believe the practice is widespread. Only 14 percent of Americans approve of the use of racial profiling by the police; only 9 percent of blacks approve of it.

SOURCE: Ann L. Pastore and Kathleen Maguire, eds., *Sourcebook of Criminal Justice Statistics, 2000,* www.albany.edu/sourcebook, December 16, 2000, p. 111, Table 2.33.

FACTORS LIMITING DISCRETION Several methods are employed to control the amount of discretion exercised by police officers. One method is close supervision by a police agency's management. For example, a department may require that officers consult a sergeant before engaging in a particular kind of action. Department directives or policies also limit the options police officers have in particular situations. Decisions of the U.S. Supreme Court, such as one restricting the use of deadly force to stop a fleeing felon, limit the options available to officers on the street. Finally, the threat of civil liability suits has reduced the discretion an officer has, for example, in the use of deadly force or in the pursuit of fleeing suspects in an automobile.

The debate over how much control should be placed on the exercise of police discretion is ongoing. Few other professionals have experienced a comparable attack on their authority to make decisions for the good of the clients they serve. The continuing attempt to limit discretion also seems out of place at a time when community policing is being widely advocated. Remember that community policing decentralizes authority and places it in the hands of the local beat officers and their supervisors. Community policing is bound to fail if citizens see that the police they work with every day do not have the authority and discretion to make the decisions that will ultimately improve the quality of life in a community.

JOB STRESS

Stress in the workplace is common today. A recent survey revealed that 80 percent of responding workers reported at least some degree of stress.[16] Given the nature of police work, no one is surprised to discover that a law enforcement officer's job is stressful. Police officers intervene in life's personal emergencies and great tragedies. Working extended shifts, for example, at the scene of the bombing of the federal building in Oklahoma City or the World Trade Center disaster would tax the resources of even the most resourceful police officer. Who would deny the stress involved in working deep undercover on a

Police officers sometimes manage stress by seeking counseling. *Are there ways that you handle stress that you think would work particularly well in policing?*

narcotics investigation over a period of several months? Some officers are able to manage stress on the job better than others.

Job stress is defined as the harmful physical and emotional outcomes that occur when the requirements of a job do not match the capabilities, resources, or needs of the worker. Poor health and injury are possible results of prolonged job stress. Police work has long been identified as one of the most stressful of all occupations, and many police officers suffer each year from the deleterious effects of a job that tests their physical and emotional limits.

job stress The harmful physical and emotional outcomes that occur when the requirements of a job do not match the capabilities, resources, or needs of the worker.

copicide A form of suicide in which a person gets fatally shot after intentionally provoking police officers.

Sources and Effects of Stress A number of conditions can lead to stress: (1) Design of tasks—heavy lifting, long hours without breaks, and monotonous repetition of dangerous maneuvers; (2) Management style—lack of participation by workers in decision making, poor communication, lack of family-friendly policies; (3) Interpersonal relationships—poor social environment and lack of support from co-workers and supervisors; (4) Work roles—conflicting or uncertain job expectations, wearing too many hats, too much responsibility.[17] The signs that stress is becoming a problem with an officer are frequent headaches, difficulty in concentrating, short temper, upset stomach, job dissatisfaction, abuse of alcohol and drugs, and low morale. Individually and collectively these symptoms can have other origins, but job stress is often the source.

Copicide As if the work of confronting dangerous suspects and preserving the peace were not stressful enough, "copicide" or "death by cop" has entered the worklife of some police officers. **Copicide** is a form of suicide in which a person gets fatally shot after intentionally provoking police officers.[18] A recent study of police shootings resulting in the death of a citizen in Los Angeles found that 10 percent could be attributed to copicide.[19] One commentator believes that "dozens of times each year during jittery hostage dramas and routine traffic stops, desperate people lure police officers into shooting them in a phenomenon known in law enforcement circles as 'suicide by cop'."[20] The truth is that no one knows exactly how many times copicide incidents occur each year. Most police officers require a lot of time to emotionally recover from a fatal shooting in circumstances where they were fully authorized to use deadly force. To later discover that they were provoked into killing people who simply used police as a tool in a suicide scheme creates an extra emotional burden to bear.

Stress Management and Reduction Fortunately, there are ways to manage and reduce stress without leaving police work. The "fixes" for stress come in two general categories. Stress management now encompasses a variety of programs and procedures that include discussing stressful events with colleagues and mental health professionals, regular exercise, relaxation techniques such as structured visualization, a healthy diet that also eliminates caffeine and nicotine, enriched family support, religious support, prayer, meditation, and stress management classes that often involve spouses.

Organizational change can also reduce the potential for stress in the police work environment. Officers, for example, may be given more discretion in determining their work hours and shifts as long as the police agency is able to respond effectively to the workload requirements of the community. Flattening the organizational structure can help reduce stress by giving officers more discretion in carrying out the responsibilities of their job. Community policing is an effective paradigm for increasing officers' ability to control their work and perhaps minimize stress. Job redesign can assist assigning the right number and type of tasks to a police position when one job requires too much of an officer to maintain emotional stability and good health. Finally, excellent public safety equipment can minimize stress. Proper police weaponry, dependable vehicles, and the best of protective equipment such as high-grade body armor can not only protect officers but can also put their minds a little more at ease on those important concerns.[21]

USE OF FORCE

No issue in policing has caused as much controversy in recent decades as the use of force. In New York, Los Angeles, Detroit, Miami, and many other cities, excessive-force charges against police officers have been made and documented and have resulted in the loss of public confidence in the police. Although the vast majority of police officers of this country go to work every day with no intention of using excessive force, far too many instances of brutality still occur.

A precise definition of brutality is not possible. However, the use of excessive physical force is undoubtedly a factor in everyone's definition. For many people, particularly members of racial and ethnic minorities, brutality also includes verbal abuse, profanity, harassment, threats of force, and unnecessary stopping, questioning, and searching of pedestrians or those in vehicles.

EXCESSIVE FORCE Why do the police have to use force as frequently as they do? A major responsibility of police officers is to arrest suspects so that they can answer criminal charges. No criminal suspect wants his or her liberty taken away, so some of them resist arrest. Invariably, a few suspects are armed with some kind of weapon, and some are prepared to use that weapon against the police to foil the arrest. The police need to establish their authority to control such conflicts. They have a variety of nonlethal weapons at their disposal to accomplish that task (see Table 7.8). The disrespect and physical resistance that are frequently the result of encounters with suspects have caused the police on occasion to use **excessive force,** which is a measure of coercion beyond that necessary to control participants in a conflict.

excessive force A measure of coercion beyond that necessary to control participants in a conflict.

Not only is the persistent use of excessive force by the police against citizens unethical, civilly wrong, and criminally illegal, but it also creates a situation where nobody wins. Police may face criminal and civil prosecution in such cases, citizens build up layers of resentment against the police, and law enforcement agencies pay out millions of dollars in damages while losing respect in the eyes of the community. Disturbing events like the brutal beating and sexual assault of Abner Louima in 1997, and the shooting death of Amadou Diallo in 1999, by New York City police officers received nationwide media attention while causing great concern by citizens and law enforcement over the use of excessive force. There were also charges of racism by the police because both incidents involved the use of excessive force by white police officers against black men.

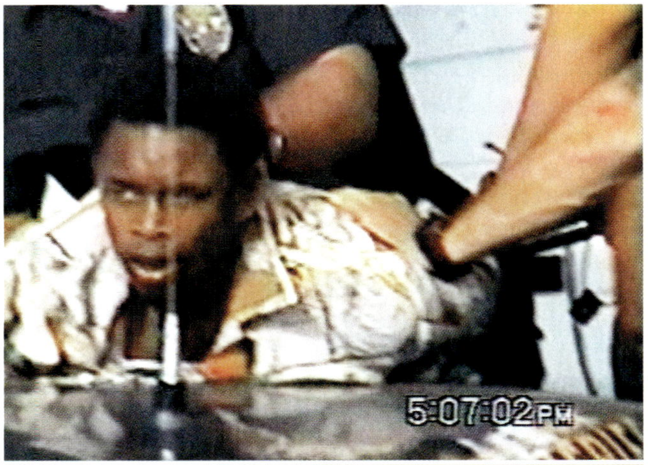

There is much debate on how much control should be placed on the decisions of police officers in arrest situations. *How much control should be placed on them and why?*

Abner Louima, a 30-year-old Haitian immigrant, was accused of assaulting a police officer outside a nightclub in the city. Louima claimed that following his arrest and

TABLE 7.8 Types of Nonlethal Weapons Authorized for Personal Use by Sworn Personnel in Local Police Departments, by Size of Population Served, 2000

	Percent of Agencies Authorizing							
	Chemical Agents—Personal Use				Batons			
Population Served	Any Type Listed in Survey	Pepper Spray	CS	Tear Gas	Any Type Listed in Survey	Collapsible	PR-24	Traditional
All sizes	91%	91%	4%	3%	88%	73%	40%	38%
1,000,000 or more	87%	87%	0%	0%	100%	80%	53%	67%
500,000–999,999	88	88	9	0	91	77	41	59
250,000–499,999	88	85	5	0	100	78	45	55
100,000–249,999	96	95	2	1	98	84	42	53
50,000–99,999	97	96	4	3	97	83	42	50
25,000–49,999	95	94	4	3	99	82	51	39
10,000–24,999	98	97	3	2	95	76	42	33
2,500–9,999	92	92	3	2	91	79	41	41
Under 2,500	87	86	5	5	82	65	36	36

— Less than 0.5 percent.

[a]Includes hand-held direct contact devices (such as stun gun) and hand-held stand-off devices (such as taser).

[b]Includes neck restraints.

SOURCE: Matthew J. Hickman and Brian A. Reaves, *Local Police Departments, 2000,* U.S. Department of Justice, Bureau of Justice Statistics (Washington, DC: GPO, January 2003), p. 19, Table 39.

arrival at the station house, a white officer, Justin Volpe, savagely beat and sodomized him with a toilet plunger. In 1999, Volpe plead guilty to charges stemming from the beating. Charles Schwarz, another police officer accused of holding Louima down while Volpe attacked him, was convicted separately in a federal trial of violating Louima's rights. Three other NYPD officers said to be involved in the event were acquitted of all charges.

Amadou Diallo, a 22-year-old West African immigrant, was hit by 19 of the 41 bullets shot by police officers from the NYPD street crimes unit. Diallo died at the scene. The officers claimed that Diallo fit the description of a rape suspect for whom they had been searching. When the officers tried to stop Diallo, he reached for what police officers thought was a weapon; they then began to shoot. Apparently Diallo, who spoke little English, was reaching for his wallet. The officers involved in the shooting were charged with second-degree murder; however, a state jury found the officers innocent.

Although past and recent incidents of excessive force have been disturbing, research reveals that police brutality does not occur as often as some people might think. For example, in a study conducted in the state of Washington, only 4 percent of brutality complaints against the police could be substantiated, and most of the charges were of verbal abuse or insults.[22] Widespread media coverage of high-profile cases, such as the Los Angeles police officers' assault on Rodney King, can lead the public to believe that brutality is much more common than it really is. The Los Angeles police, however, had a higher rate of wounding and killing suspects than any other police department in the nation, according to the Christopher Commission, which investigated the assault on Rodney King.

FYI Sidearms

In 2000, 98 percent of local police departments, employing 99 percent of all local police officers, authorized the use of some type of semiautomatic sidearm. This was up from 73 percent of departments and 91 percent of all officers in 1990. Among the semiautomatic firearms authorized in 2000 were: the .40-caliber semiautomatic (authorized by 75 percent of departments), the 9 mm (67 percent), the .45-caliber (54 percent), the .380-caliber, (38 percent), and the 10 mm (30 percent). Sixty percent of local departments, employing 71 percent of all officers, supplied regular field officers with their primary sidearm.

SOURCE: Matthew J. Hickman and Brian A. Reaves, *Local Police Departments, 2000,* U.S. Department of Justice, Bureau of Justice Statistics (Washington, DC: GPO, 2003), p. 18.

DEADLY FORCE The greatest concern over the use of force by the police has to do with the infliction of death or serious injury on citizens and criminal

TABLE 7.8 Types of Nonlethal Weapons Authorized for Personal Use by Sworn Personnel in Local Police Departments, by Size of Population Served, 2000 (concluded)

	Percent of Agencies Authorizing						
	Other Weapons/Actions						
Population Served	Flash/Bang Grenade	Soft Projectile	Electrical Devices[a]	Choke/Carotid Hold[b]	Rubber Bullet	Blackjack	Capture Net
All sizes	13%	9%	7%	7%	3%	3%	1%
1,000,000 or more	40%	33%	40%	40%	7%	0%	0%
500,000–999,999	41	23	15	18	6	0	3
250,000–499,999	58	25	28	33	13	5	3
100,000–249,999	63	41	21	28	12	2	3
50,000–99,999	58	33	17	19	10	1	2
25,000–49,999	41	23	12	13	9	1	3
10,000–24,999	23	14	8	5	4	2	—
2,500–9,999	8	5	5	7	3	2	0
Under 2,500	3	4	6	4	2	3	1

suspects. Since the U.S. Supreme Court's 1985 decision in *Tennessee* v. *Garner*, the use of deadly force has been severely restricted, and police shootings of suspects and citizens have been reduced. In the *Garner* case, an unarmed teenage boy was shot as he fled a house burglary, failing to heed the warning to stop given by a Memphis police officer. The boy later died of a gunshot wound to the head. He was found with $10 in his pocket that he had stolen from the home. The Memphis officer was acting in compliance with his department's policy on the use of deadly force and with the law in Tennessee and in most other states in the nation.

Giving law enforcement officers the authority to use deadly force to stop a fleeing felon, even when they know the suspect is unarmed and not likely to be a danger to another person, derives from the common law in England and the United States, which permitted such a practice. At the time the rule developed, however, unlike today, dozens of crimes were capital offenses, and the fleeing suspect, if apprehended and convicted, would have been executed. The *Garner* decision, no doubt, was long overdue, and it included a rule that many police agencies in the nation had adopted years earlier. The perspective that professional law enforcement agencies had already begun to adopt on deadly force was from the Model Penal Code, Section 307(2)(B).

It reads:

The use of deadly force is not justifiable under this section unless:

1. The arrest is for a felony.
2. The person effecting the arrest is authorized to act as a peace officer or is assisting a person whom he believes to be authorized to act as a peace officer.
3. The actor believes that the force employed creates no substantial risk of injury to innocent persons.

FYI

Use of Force Policies

In 2000, 93 percent of local police departments, employing 99 percent of all officers, had a written policy on the use of deadly force. Eighty-seven percent of departments, employing 95 percent of all officers, had a written policy on the use of nonlethal force.

SOURCE: Matthew J. Hickman and Brian A. Reaves, *Local Police Departments, 2000*, U.S. Department of Justice, Bureau of Justice Statistics (Washington, DC: GPO, 2003), p. 19.

4. The actor believes that: (a) The crime for which the arrest is made involved conduct including the use or threatened use of deadly force. (b) There is substantial risk that the person to be arrested will cause death or serious bodily harm if his on her apprehension is delayed.

Even with explicit guidelines, the decision to use deadly force is seldom clear-cut for police officers, because of the violent and occasionally ambiguous situations in which they find themselves. For example, consider the confrontation a Dallas, Texas, police officer had in the summer of 1993. As a plainclothes officer, he responded to a call at an apartment complex where it was reported that a man had fired shots. It was nighttime, and when he arrived at the parking lot of the complex, he saw a man perhaps 50 feet from him with the butt end of a pistol sticking out of the waistband of his trousers. The police officer told him to stop and put his hands in the air. Instead of doing what he was ordered to do, the man pulled the gun from his waistband and moved it toward the officer. The officer responded by firing his weapon several times at the man and killing him. Later, it was discovered that the man was a Mexican citizen who spoke no English.

Some members of the Hispanic community were enraged that the officer did not offer commands in Spanish, because Dallas officers were required to study 20 hours of the language in the police academy. After several months of investigation and the grand jury's ignoring the case, the officer was exonerated. However, the chief of police assured the community that new police recruits would study three times the previously required amount of Spanish and that annual in-service training would also require the study of Spanish. In addition, the chief stated that in situations such as the one in question, undercover and plainclothes officers would be required, if possible, to put on jackets that would readily identify them as police officers. Some people argue that the man with the gun in this situation not only did not understand English but also had no idea that the officer with drawn gun was a police officer.

It should not be forgotten that citizens and criminal suspects also attack the police. Mentally ill persons, parties to a family dispute, and suspects trying to avoid arrest feloniously assault between 50 and 100 officers each year. About two-thirds of those assaults are shootings. In response, police officers exercise caution by wearing protective vests, they proactively use what they learn in courses on self-defense (unarmed and armed), and they attempt to defuse hostile situations through peaceful techniques they learn in training.

POLICE CORRUPTION

Almost from the beginning of formal policing in the United States, corruption of law enforcement officers has been a fact of life. Nothing is more distasteful to the public than a police officer or a whole department gone bad. Throughout history, police officers have bought their positions and promotions, sold protection, and ignored violations of the law for money.

Why is policing so susceptible to bribery and other forms of corruption? Perhaps it has to do with the combination of two critical features of the police role in society. On the one hand, the police have authority to enforce laws and to use power to make sure that those laws are obeyed. On the other hand, they also have the discretion *not* to enforce the law. The combination of those two features makes the police vulnerable to bribes and other forms of corruption. Other features of police work add to the potential for corruption: low pay in relation to important responsibilities, cynicism about the courts' soft handling of criminals that the police spend so much time trying to apprehend, society's ambivalence about vice (most citizens want the laws on the books, but many of them are willing participants), and the practice of recruiting officers from working-class and lower-class backgrounds, where skepticism about obeying the law might be more prevalent.

TYPES OF CORRUPTION In 1972, the Knapp Commission issued a report on corruption in the New York City Police Department. Two types of corrupt officers were identified: "grass eaters" and "meat eaters." **"Grass eaters"** were officers who occasionally engaged in illegal or unethical activities, such as accepting small favors, gifts, or money for ignoring violations of the law during the course of their duties. **"Meat eaters,"** on the other hand, actively sought ways to make money illegally while on duty. For example, they would solicit bribes, commit burglaries, or manufacture false evidence for a prosecution.[23]

"grass eaters" Officers who occasionally engage in illegal and unethical activities, such as accepting small favors, gifts, or money for ignoring violations of the law during the course of their duties.

"meat eaters" Officers who actively seek ways to make money illegally while on duty.

More than 30 years ago, Ellwyn Stoddard identified a more complete list of types of police misconduct, with examples, in what he described as the "blue-coat code":

1. Bribery: accepting cash or gifts in exchange for nonenforcement of the law.
2. Chiseling: demanding discounts, free admission, and free food.
3. Extortion: the threat of enforcement and arrest if a bribe is not given.
4. Favoritism: giving breaks on law enforcement, such as for traffic violations committed by families and friends of the police.
5. Mooching: accepting free food, drinks, and admission to entertainment.
6. Perjury: lying for other officers apprehended in illegal activity.
7. Prejudice: unequal enforcement of the law with respect to racial and ethnic minorities.
8. Premeditated theft: planned burglaries and thefts.
9. Shakedown: taking items from the scene of a theft or a burglary the officer is investigating.
10. Shopping: taking small, inexpensive items from a crime scene or an unsecured business or home.[24]

CONTROLLING CORRUPTION Corruption in law enforcement strikes at the core of the profession and takes a heavy toll. All peace officer positions are positions of honor and trust, and agencies invest money and time in selecting officers with integrity. To see this investment lost is disheartening. But more than anything else, public confidence and trust plummet after a widely publicized corruption case, such as the police drug-trafficking episode in Miami. In the following list, some ways to control and reduce corruption in policing are described.

- **High Moral Standards** Selecting and maintaining officers with high moral standards is a step in the right direction. Some police agencies in the United States still hire convicted felons to do police work. In-depth academy and in-service training on ethical issues that officers are likely to face would prepare officers for the compromises they may be asked to make later in their careers.
- **Police Policies and Discipline** A police department should develop rigid policies that cover the wide range of activities that corruption comprises. Drug testing of officers, particularly those in narcotics-sensitive positions, may be necessary, although unpopular. Policies mean nothing unless

Policing is susceptible to bribery and other forms of corruption. *Who is policing the police? Are controls adequate?*

they are enforced. Discipline should be imposed and prosecutions should go forward when officers are found guilty of violating established policies and laws.

internal affairs investigations unit The police unit that ferrets out illegal and unethical activity engaged in by the police.

- **Proactive Internal Affairs Unit** The **internal affairs investigations unit** of a police department should ferret out illegal and unethical activity. Any internal affairs unit that waits for complaints probably is not going to receive many of them. First-line supervisors should know whether their subordinates are engaging in unethical and illegal violations of department rules and state laws. They should also be held responsible for the actions of their subordinates.
- **Uniform Enforcement of the Law** If a police agency makes it clear that no group of citizens, no matter what their affiliation with the police department, is going to receive special treatment from the police department, the incentive for offering bribes and other forms of corruption will be minimized. This process starts with clear policies and procedures and must be backed up with discipline, when necessary.
- **Outside Review and Special Prosecutors** Heavily resisted by police leadership and police labor associations is any kind of outside review of their actions. However, both the Christopher Commission and the Knapp Commission are examples of outside reviews that brought about improvements in the agencies they investigated. Special prosecutors are recommended in serious cases to relieve the police and the government of any accusations of a whitewash.
- **Court Review and Oversight** Criminal prosecutions or civil liability suits deriving from police corruption cases can be very costly to a police agency. Such visible forms of oversight often result in adverse media coverage, civil liability awards, and higher insurance rates—all of which should encourage police agencies to control corruption.[25]

FYI

"Collars for Dollars"

An 8-month investigation by the *Miami Herald* in 1997 documented a police scam involving hundreds of officers in thousands of cases in Dade County. Dubbed "collars for dollars," the scam works like this. Police officers list one another as witnesses in drunken-driving and misdemeanor cases even if they do little or no police work on the cases. They then go to court on overtime and receive pay they don't deserve. According to the newspaper report, "collars for dollars" happens often and costs Dade County taxpayers millions of dollars.

SOURCE: Jeff Leen, Gail Epstein, and Lisa Getter, "Dade Cops Like to Plan Collars for Dollars," *The Orlando Sentinel,* July 20, 1997, p. B-1.

PROFESSIONALIZING LAW ENFORCEMENT

Many people would argue that policing in America has already reached professional status. Law enforcement is a valued service. Its agents make important decisions daily that substantially affect the lives of people and the quality of life in a community. The police officer's position is one of honor and trust. There are academy programs consisting of hundreds of hours of instruction, as well as law enforcement degree programs. Now there are even signs that law enforcement is attempting to police its own profession. Professional accreditation for police agencies is a rite of passage that is needed if law enforcement is to join the list of the most respected professions. Nevertheless, resistance to it and the other developments is still widespread.

Not everyone has the qualities to be a police officer. To allow into law enforcement those people with no desire to serve, low intelligence, a shady past, poor work habits, and no ability to communicate effectively is to court disaster for every department that does so—and for the entire profession.

Some police officers and their leaders resist 600 hours of initial training and do all they can to avoid continuing education and training. Real professionals seek advanced training.

Professionals in any field make mistakes, and a caring public should forgive most of them. In police work, there are incomplete interviews, evidence left at crime scenes, and bad reports written. In the long run, the consequences of such mistakes are generally insignificant as long as corrections are made. Mistakes can also be technological, such as the failure of a radar gun. No one should blame the police for technological mishaps that are not the result of negligence.

FYI

Accreditation

By March 2003, 562 police agencies in the United States, Canada, and Barbados were accredited or recognized (for smaller law enforcement agencies) by the Commission on Accreditation for Law Enforcement Agencies (CALEA).

SOURCE: "CALEA, Commission on Accreditation for Law Enforcement Agencies," www.calea.org.

One kind of mistake, however, stands out more than any other: the condoning of racist and brutal tactics like the Los Angeles police officers' beating of Rodney King. The findings of the Christopher Commission confirmed that such tactics were generally condoned and even encouraged. The videotaped replay of that performance will be an embarrassment to professional policing for years to come. Police departments need to remove from the profession officers who would participate in or overlook such violence.

Many police officers go to work each day with a negative attitude, and some may take out their frustrations on the citizens they meet. Police officers need to treat their on-duty time as a professional performance and render the best service possible on any given day. If they treat the citizens they serve with respect and concern, officers will make great progress in improving the public's perception of law enforcement as a profession worthy of trust and admiration.

THINKING CRITICALLY

1. What do you think are the best ways for police officers to handle stress on the job?
2. What do you think are the best ways to recruit new police officers?

SUMMARY

1. Describe the general attitude of the public toward the police

    According to surveys, the American public is generally satisfied with the quality of the service the police provide. The level of confidence varies across racial and ethnic groups. As with most services, the public believes there is room for improvement.

2. Summarize the steps in an effective police officer selection process

    Police applicants go through several different kinds of testing to become law enforcement officers. Steps in an effective police officer selection process include: recruitment, short application, detailed application, medical examination, physical ability test, written examination, background investigation, psychological testing, oral interview/oral board, academy training, and a probationary employment period.

3. Identify factors that affect the exercise of police discretion and methods of limiting discretion

    Factors that affect the exercise of police discretion include the nature of the crime, departmental policies, the relationship between the victim and the offender, the amount of evidence, the preference of the victim, the demeanor of the suspect, the legitimacy of the victim, and the suspect's socioeconomic status. Methods of limiting police discretion are close supervision by a police agency's management, department directives and policies, U.S. Supreme Court decisions, and the threat of civil liability suits.

4. Describe two general ways that law enforcement agencies can reduce stress on the job

    Two general ways that law enforcement agencies can reduce job stress for police officers are (1) to employ stress management *strategies, such as discussing stressful events with colleagues and mental health professionals, regular exercise, relaxation techniques, healthy diet, religious support, enriched family support, prayer, meditation, and stress management classes that often involve spouses, and (2) to implement* organizational change, *such as allowing officers more discretion in determining work hours and shifts, flattening the organizational structure and giving officers more discretion in carrying out their responsibilities, job redesign that assigns unwanted or unnecessary tasks for a police officer to another position, and having excellent public safety equipment such as weaponry, vehicles, and body armor.*

5. Explain the circumstances under which police officers may be justified in using deadly force

    The use of deadly force by a police officer may be justifiable if (1) the arrest is for a felony; (2) the person effecting the arrest is authorized to act as a peace officer or is assisting a person whom he believes to be authorized to act as a peace officer; (3) the officer believes that the force employed creates no substantial risk of injury to innocent persons; (4) the officer believes that the crime for which the arrest is made involved conduct including the use or threatened use of deadly force; and (5) the officer believes there is substantial risk that the person to be arrested will cause death or serious bodily harm if his or her apprehension is delayed.

6. List some of the ways to control and reduce police corruption

    Ways to control and reduce police corruption include selecting and maintaining officers with high moral standards, developing rigid departmental policies that cover the wide range of activities that corruption comprises, disciplining and prosecuting officers who are guilty of violating established policies and laws, utilizing a proactive internal affairs investigations unit, holding first-line supervisors responsible for the actions of their subordinates, employing outside review and special prosecutors, and emphasizing to officers the costs to police agencies of criminal prosecutions and civil liability suits.

KEY TERMS

three I's of police selection, p. 236
college academies, p. 239
public safety officers, p. 241
police cadet program, p. 241
tech prep (technical preparation), p. 241
merit system, p. 242
discretion, p. 247
full enforcement, p. 248
selective enforcement, p. 248
racial profiling, p. 250
job stress, p. 252
copicide, p. 252
excessive force, p. 253
"grass eaters," p. 257
"meat eaters," p. 257
internal affairs investigations unit, p. 258

REVIEW QUESTIONS

1. In general, what is the attitude of the American public toward the police?
2. Explain how the three I's of police selection (intelligence, integrity, and interaction skills) relate to the success of a police officer.
3. What are some advantages of hiring college-educated police officers?
4. What are some arguments in favor of and opposing the reduction of police discretion?
5. Why do police generally not like to respond to domestic violence calls?
6. What is *racial profiling* in law enforcement, and what are some of the methods that have been prescribed to stop it?
7. What are some of the conditions that can lead to police job stress?
8. What is meant by *copicide?*
9. What is meant by *excessive force?*
10. What are some types of police misconduct?

IN THE FIELD

1. **Neighborhood Survey** Conduct a survey about the police in your neighborhood. Use the same survey questions and categories as in Figures 7.1, 7.2, and 7.3. Try to get respondents from as many races, genders, and age groups as possible. Compare the results of your survey with the results in Figures 7.1, 7.2, and 7.3. Note any gender, race, or age differences in responses.
2. **Police Recruiting** Contact your local police department, and find out what it does to recruit police candidates. Does it run a police academy? Does it generally recruit officers from other jurisdictions? Compare your findings with those of others in the class and what you have learned from your textbook.

ON THE NET

1. **Racial Profiling** Go to the website of the American Civil Liberties Union at http://archive.aclu.org/profiling/report/index.html and look at its report on "Driving While Black: Racial Profiling on Our Nation's Highways," by Professor David A. Harris from the University of Toledo College of Law. Read Professor Harris's report and his five recommendations for ending racial profiling. Which of the five recommendations do you agree with and why? Which do you disagree with and why? Discuss these findings in class and see if other students share your views.
2. **Job Qualifications** Go the websites of four large police departments (New York City at www.ci.nyc.ny.us/html/nypd/home.html; Los Angeles at www.lapdonline.org; Philadelphia at www.ppdonline.org; and Houston at www.ci.houston.tx.us/departme/police) and identify the major qualifications to be a police officer that are listed there. What qualifications are the same or similar among the agencies you examined? What qualifications are unique among those listed by the four agencies? Which employment qualifications are the most difficult to meet? Do you agree that all of the qualifications most difficult to meet are necessary? Would you add any qualifications? If so, what would they be? What would be the impact of your new qualifications on the recruitment and selection of police officers?

CRITICAL THINKING EXERCISES

1. **Police Academy** Recently, "Police Corps," a new military-style police academy, has opened in cities such as Jacksonville and Tampa, Florida. The cadets of the mentally exhausting 6-month program eat, sleep, and live together in rooms near the academy with no televisions and with the constant threat of surprise inspections. Their days involve marching in military formation with a platoon leader barking out cadences, weightlifting, and classes on self-defense as well as law and criminal procedure. Afternoons are spent at the firing range, where they train with pistols, MP-5 submachine guns, and AR-15 assault rifles. After ending their days at 10 P.M. with little or no time for themselves to relax or study, they are occasionally awakened at 2 A.M. as instructors push them for practice in high-speed driving and patrolling tactics. At some point in the course, the cadets are put through 24 to 72 hours of sleep deprivation to teach them the effects of stress and lack of sleep on their bodies. The punishment for not following orders correctly is pushups.

   Supporters of the new academy maintain that the Navy SEAL–type training will help officers become more disciplined and community-oriented. Critics contend that the program is too extreme and isn't necessary for a community police force, that it "isn't needed in our society unless we're in a warfare environment."

   a. What are the pros and cons of this new military-style police academy training?
   b. What effects, if any, are such training methods likely to have on police recruitment?
   c. Is such training needed in our society?

2. **Stress** You are the commander of the operations division of a medium-sized police department, in charge of the patrol, criminal investigation, and traffic sections.

   a. What would you do if several officers from each of the sections came to you and said that they believed that job stress was hindering officer performance and endangering the health of several officers in each of the units?
   b. How would you go about validating their claims of job stress in the work environment?
   c. If it were determined that stressors such as too frequent shift changes, poor communication among the various ranks, and a lack of sufficient safety equipment were present, what would be your plan to improve working conditions and reduce job stress?
   d. Provide a step-by-step summary of what you would do.

PART THREE

THE COURTS

CHAPTER EIGHT

The Administration of Justice

CHAPTER NINE

Sentencing, Appeals, and the Death Penalty

The Administration of Justice

CHAPTER EIGHT

Chapter Outline

The American Court Structure
- The Federal Courts
- The State Courts

Purposes of Courts

Key Actors in the Court Process
- The Prosecutor
- The Defense Attorney
- The Judge

Pretrial Stages
- Caseflow Management
- From Arrest Through Initial Appearance
- Bail and Other Methods of Pretrial Release
- Information
- Preliminary Hearing
- Grand Jury
- Arraignment

Plea Bargaining

The Criminal Trial
- The Jury
- The Trial Process

Chapter Objectives

After completing this chapter, you should be able to:

1. Identify the type of court structure in the United States and describe its various components.
2. Summarize the purposes of courts.
3. Identify the most powerful actors in the administration of justice and explain what makes them so powerful.
4. Summarize the types of attorneys available to a person charged with a crime.
5. Describe the responsibilities of a judge.
6. Describe the purposes of an initial appearance.
7. Explain what bail is and describe the different methods of pretrial release.
8. Define grand jury and explain its purposes.
9. Describe the purposes of the arraignment and the plea options of defendants.
10. Describe the interests served and not served by plea bargaining.
11. List and define the stages in a criminal trial.

Crime Story

On April 18, 2002, police arrested Hollywood actor Robert Blake for the murder of his 44-year-old wife, Bonny Lee Bakley. Blake's arrest ended an 11-month police investigation, which led authorities to believe that the aging actor fatally shot his wife on May 4, 2001, outside a North Hollywood restaurant where the couple had finished dining for the evening. Reportedly, Blake and his wife were in their car preparing to leave the restaurant when Blake went back inside the restaurant to retrieve his gun that he had inadvertently left inside. Upon returning to the car he discovered his wife had been shot in the head.

Harland Braun, a highly esteemed criminal defense attorney, was retained to represent Blake. Braun was unable to secure bail for Blake immediately following his arrest. The distinguished defense attorney appeared on numerous television newscasts and talk shows to proclaim Blake's innocence. Additionally, Braun argued unsuccessfully against a pretrial motion to allow news cameras into the courtroom proceedings and ultimately resigned from representing Blake on October 22, 2002, after his celebrity client wanted to speak with ABC News journalist Diane Sawyer about the details of his case. Authorities denied Sawyer access to Blake despite his wish to speak about his impending trial. However, Blake was successful on February 26, 2003, in telling his story to ABC's *20/20* news journalist Barbara Walters. Many observers described the interview as a setback to Blake's legal defense due to the seemingly angry and staged incoherent ramblings of the actor.

Following the resignation of Braun, Blake retained Thomas Mesereau, Jr., as his new defense attorney to represent him in a lengthy preliminary hearing in February and March of 2003. During the televised hearing various prosecution witnesses testified that Blake attempted to solicit them to murder Bakley on several occasions. On May 13, 2003, Superior Court Judge Lloyd Nash concluded that evidence indicated Blake should stand trial for the murder of his wife. Nash also ruled that Blake could be released on a $1.5 million bond, which seemed to stun the 69-year-old actor who had been in jail for almost 1 year. Blake was released pending his court trial the next day on March 14, 2003, after posting the bond. He currently awaits his trial.

Chapter 8 discusses the administration of justice in America. The various legal processes encountered by Robert Blake illustrate some of the problems defense attorneys can encounter when representing clients in criminal matters. Attorneys almost always demand their clients not speak of their guilt or innocence preceding a trial. Not all criminal defendants are allowed bail or bond for crimes of murder or have the ability to post huge bail amounts such as in the case of Robert Blake. Furthermore, preliminary hearings are often cost prohibitive for most criminal defendants. Will the celebrity status of Robert Blake propel him to an acquittal for murder? The nation will watch with great interest the final outcome of the saga of defendant Robert Blake which may well be more dramatic than those of Hollywood movies or television shows.

The American Court Structure

The United States has a **dual court system**—a separate judicial system for each of the states and a separate federal system. Figure 8.1 displays this dual court system and routes of appeal from the various courts. The only place where the two systems connect is in the U.S. Supreme Court.

The authority of a court to hear and decide cases is called the court's **jurisdiction.** It is set by law and is limited by territory and type of case. A court of **original jurisdiction** has the authority to hear a case when it is first brought to court. Courts having the power to review a case for errors of law are courts of **appellate jurisdiction.** Courts having the power to hear any type of case are said to exercise **general jurisdiction.** Those with the power to hear only certain types of cases have **special jurisdiction. Subject matter jurisdiction** is the court's power to hear a particular type of case. **Personal jurisdiction** is the court's authority over the parties to a lawsuit.

dual court system The court system in the United States, consisting of one system of state and local courts and another system of federal courts.

jurisdiction The authority of a court to hear and decide cases.

original jurisdiction The authority of a court to hear a case when it is first brought to court.

appellate jurisdiction The power of a court to review a case for errors of law.

general jurisdiction The power of a court to hear any type of case.

special jurisdiction The power of a court to hear only certain kinds of cases.

subject matter jurisdiction The power of a court to hear a particular type of case.

personal jurisdiction A court's authority over the parties to a lawsuit.

THE FEDERAL COURTS

The authority for the federal court system is the U.S. Constitution, Article III, Section 1, which states, "The judicial Power of the United States, shall be vested in one supreme Court, and in such inferior Courts as the Congress may from time to time ordain and establish." The federal court system includes the Supreme Court, the federal courts of appeals, and the federal district courts. The federal court system is shown in Figure 8.2.

U.S. District Courts Forming the base of the federal court structure are the U.S. district courts. These are courts of original jurisdiction, or courts where most violations of federal criminal and civil law are first adjudicated. Today, there are 94 district courts divided into 13 circuits, with at least one federal district court in each state, one each in the District of Columbia and the commonwealths of Puerto Rico and the Northern Mariana Islands, and

FIGURE 8.1 Dual Court System of the United States

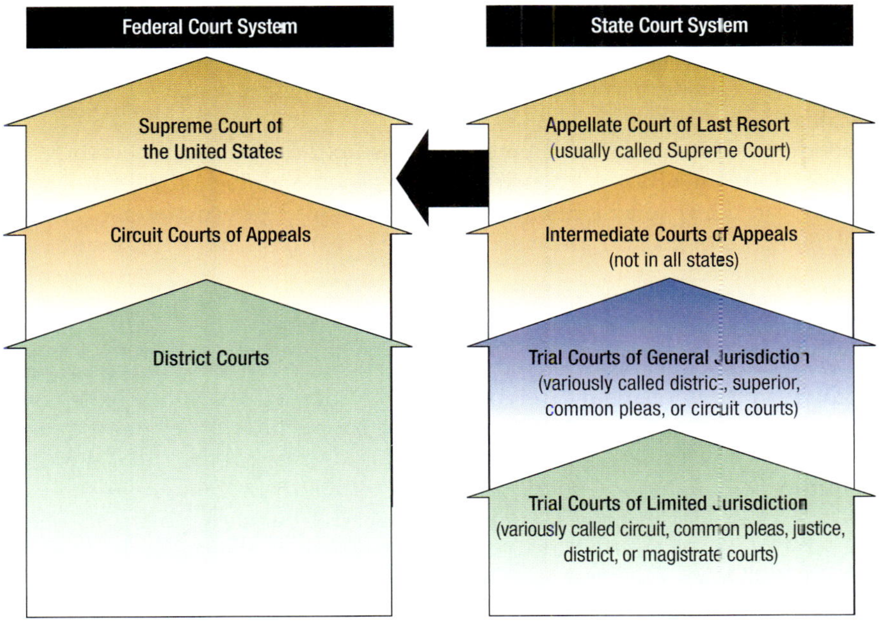

FIGURE 8.2 The Federal Court Structure

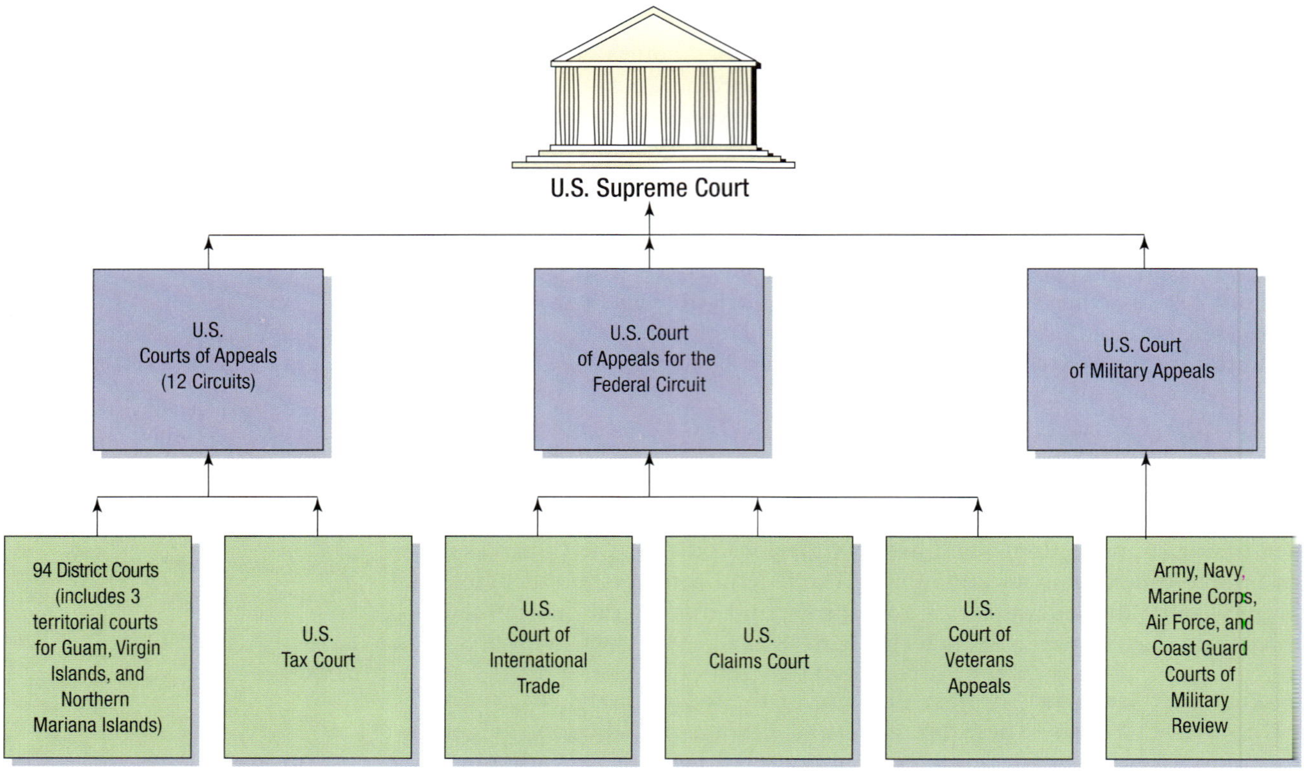

one each in the U.S. territories of the Virgin Islands and Guam. In some states, the courts are divided into districts geographically. New York, for example, has northern, eastern, southern, and western district courts.

Two factors determine the jurisdiction of federal district courts: the subject matter of a case and the parties to a case. Federal district courts have subject matter jurisdiction over cases that involve federal laws, treaties with foreign nations, or interpretations of the Constitution. Cases involving admiralty or maritime law—the law of the sea, including ships, their crews, and disputes over actions and rights at sea—also come under federal district court jurisdiction.

Federal district courts have personal jurisdiction in cases if certain parties or persons are involved. These include (1) ambassadors and other representatives of foreign governments, (2) two or more state governments, (3) the U.S. government or one of its offices or agencies, (4) citizens of different states, (5) a state and a citizen of a different state, (6) citizens of the same state claiming lands under grants of different states, and (7) a state or its citizens and a foreign country or its citizens.

U.S. district courts are presided over by district court judges who are appointed by the President, are confirmed by the Senate, and, except for the territorial judges who serve 10-year terms, serve for life (if they choose, do not resign, or are not impeached and convicted by Congress). In 2003, there were 680 authorized federal district judgeships (including 13 temporary judgeships). Several district courts, such as the district court of North Dakota had only two judges, while the southern-district court of New York in New York City had the most with 28.[1] The annual salary of a U.S. district court judge is $154,700 (as of January 1, 2003).

In 1989, the Exxon *Valdez* supertanker struck a reef in Alaska's Prince William Sound and spilled 11 million gallons of oil. It was the largest oil spill and greatest environmental disaster in American history. The subsequent civil jury trial between Exxon Corporation and Alaska commercial fishermen, Natives, property owners, and others affected by the spill was conducted in a U.S. district court in Alaska in 1994. *Why was the case tried in a U.S. district court?*

Usually a single federal judge presides over a trial, and trial by jury is allowed if requested by a defendant. Some complex civil cases are heard by a special panel of three judges. The bulk of the workload of the U.S. district courts is devoted to civil cases, the number of which has risen dramatically in recent years, to more than 265,000 in 2002. Federal criminal cases involve such crimes as bank robbery, counterfeiting, mail fraud, kidnapping, and civil rights abuses. Until 1980, the number of criminal cases in federal district courts remained relatively stable at about 30,000 a year. However, as a result of the federal government's War on Drugs and an increase in illegal immigration cases, the number of criminal cases had doubled to more than 63,000 by the end of 2002. Thirty percent of the criminal cases filed in U.S district courts in 2002 were drug cases and 18 percent were immigration cases.[2]

To ease the caseload of U.S. district court judges, Congress created the judicial office of federal magistrate in 1968. The title changed to magistrate judge in 1990. As their caseloads require and as funding from Congress permits, district judges may appoint magistrate judges to part-time or full-time positions. Magistrate judges handle civil consent cases, misdemeanor trials, preliminary hearings, pretrial motions and motion hearings, and conferences in felony cases.[3]

Circuit Courts of Appeals A person or group that loses a case in district court may appeal to a federal circuit court of appeals or, in some instances, directly to the Supreme Court. Congress created the U.S. circuit courts of appeals in 1891 to reduce the case burden of the Supreme Court. The U.S. circuit courts of appeals have only appellate jurisdiction and review a case for errors of law, not of fact. Most appeals arise from the decisions of district courts, the U.S. Tax Court, and various territorial courts (see Figure 8.2).

FYI: FISA Court

Since its creation in 1978, a secretive federal court known as the Foreign Intelligence Surveillance Act Court, or FISA court, has approved thousands of Justice Department requests to conduct secret searches and surveillance of people in the United States who are suspected of having links to foreign agents or powers, often involving terrorism and espionage. The legislation that created the now 11-member FISA court also established a three-member Foreign Intelligence Surveillance Court of Review, which has never been used because the FISA court almost always grants the government's requests, and suspects are never notified that they are the target of a search or surveillance. The U.S. Supreme Court has the final authority to review cases from the Court of Review. The Supreme Court's chief justice appoints all members of both courts. The 11 FISA court judges are selected from among U.S. district court judges, and the three judges of the Court of Review are selected from the U.S. district courts or courts of appeals. Judges serve for a maximum of 7 years.

Source: Legal Information Institute, U.S. Code Collection, www4.law.cornell.edu/uscode/50/1803.html.

The 9th U.S. Circuit Court of Appeals in San Francisco, California (pictured here), has the most judges (28) of all the circuit courts of appeals. *What determines how many judges are selected to serve on a U.S. circuit court of appeals?*

FYI Circuit Courts

The circuit courts are so named because early in the nation's history, federal judges traveled by horseback to each of the courts in a specified region, or "circuit," in a particular sequence. In short, they rode the circuit.

SOURCE: Howard Ball, "The Federal Court System," in R.J. Janosik (ed.), *Encyclopedia of the American Judicial System: Studies of the Principal Institutions and Processes of Law* (New York: Charles Scribner's Sons, 1987), p. 556.

Federal courts of appeals also hear appeals of the rulings of regulatory agencies, such as the Federal Trade Commission. An appeal to the U.S. circuit court of appeals is a matter of right—the court cannot refuse to hear the case. However, unless appealed to the Supreme Court, decisions of the courts of appeals are final. U.S. courts of appeals hear more than 50,000 cases annually (57,555 in 2002); less than 30 percent (about 20 percent in 2002) of those cases are criminal.[4]

There are currently 13 U.S. circuit courts of appeals (see Figure 8.3). Twelve of them have jurisdiction over cases from particular geographic areas. The Court of Appeals for the Federal Circuit, created in 1982, has national jurisdiction over specific types of cases, such as appeals from the U.S. Court of International Trade.[5] Like U.S. district judges, federal appellate judges are nominated by the President, are confirmed by the Senate, and may serve for life. Currently, 179 judges serve on the 13 U.S. circuit courts (167 on the 12 regional courts and 12 on the federal circuit).[6] The yearly salary of a U.S. circuit court of appeals judge is $164,000 (as of January 1, 2003). The number of judges assigned to each court of appeals ranges from 6 (the First Circuit) to 28 (the Ninth Circuit) and, normally, 3 judges sit as a panel. Jury trials are not allowed in these courts. In highly controversial cases, all of the judges in a circuit may sit together and hear a case. Those *en banc* hearings are rare; there probably are no more than 100 of them in all of the circuits in 1 year.

THE U.S. SUPREME COURT The U.S. Supreme Court is the court of last resort in all questions of federal law (see Figure 8.2). It has the final word in any case involving the Constitution, acts of Congress, and treaties with other nations. Under the Supreme Court's appellate jurisdiction, the Court hears cases appealed from federal courts of appeals, or it may hear appeals from federal district courts in certain circumstances in which an act of Congress has been held unconstitutional.

FIGURE 8.3 The 13 U.S. Circuits

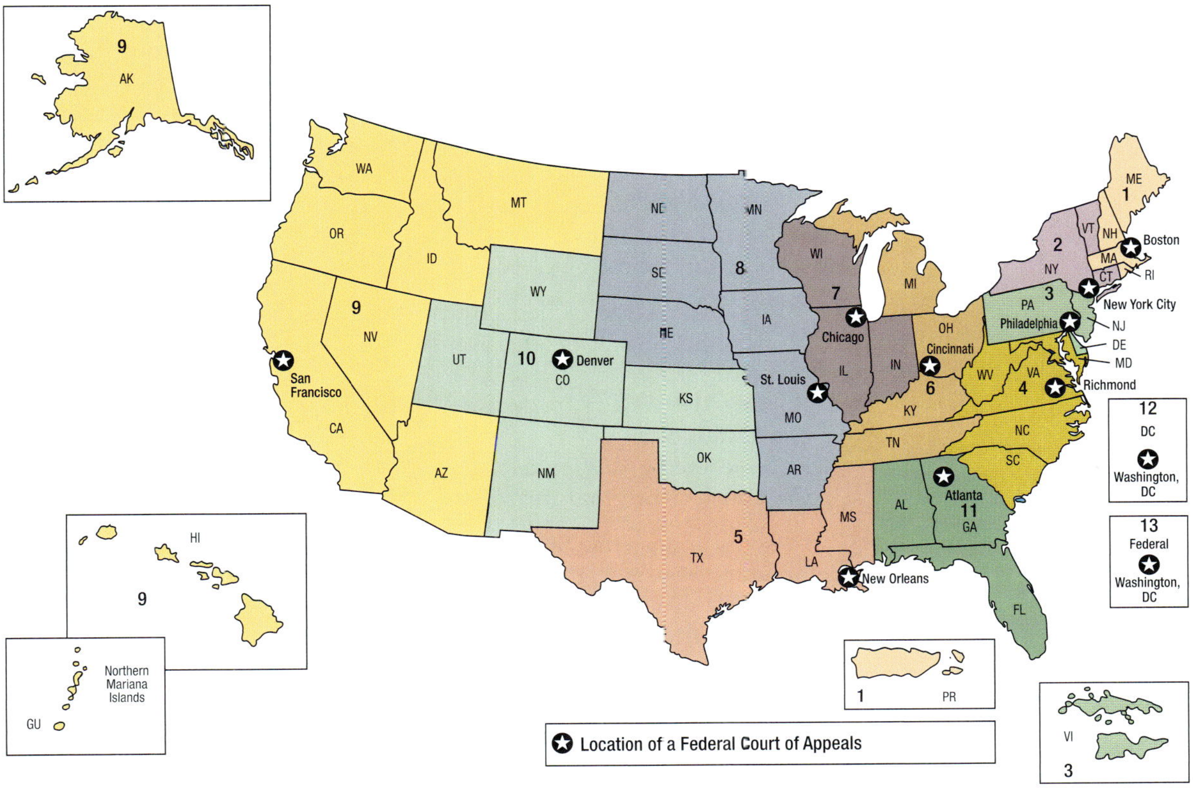

The Supreme Court may also hear cases that are appealed from the high court of a state, if claims under federal law or the Constitution are involved. In such cases, however, the Court has the authority to rule only on the federal issue involved, not on any issues of state law. For example, suppose a state tries a person charged with violating a state law. During the trial, the accused claims that the police violated Fourth Amendment rights with an illegal search at the time of the arrest. The defendant may appeal to the Supreme Court on the constitutional issue only. The Supreme Court generally has no jurisdiction to rule on the state issue (whether the accused actually violated state law). The Court would decide only whether Fourth Amendment rights were violated. Decisions of the Supreme Court are binding on all lower courts.

The Supreme Court is composed of a chief justice, officially known as the Chief Justice of the United States, and eight associate justices. They are appointed for life by the President with the consent of the Senate and, like other federal judges, can be removed from office against their will only by "impeachment for, and Conviction of, Treason, Bribery, or other high Crimes and Misdemeanors." The Chief Justice, who is specifically nominated by the President for the position, presides over the Court's public sessions and private conferences, assigns justices to write opinions (when the Chief Justice has voted with the majority), and supervises the entire federal judiciary. (When the Chief Justice has voted with the minority, the Associate Justice who has the greatest seniority, that is, has been on the Court the longest, assigns who writes the opinion.) The salary of the Chief Justice is $198,600; the salaries of the Associate Justices are $190,100 (as of January 1, 2003).

FYI

The Judicial Conference of the United States

The Judicial Conference of the United States governs the federal court system. The conference is composed of 27 federal judges and is presided over by the Chief Justice of the U.S. Supreme Court. The conference meets twice a year to consider policies affecting the federal courts, to make recommendations to Congress on legislation affecting the judicial system, to propose amendments to the federal rules of practice and procedure, and to address administrative problems of the courts.

SOURCES: Administrative Office of the U.S. Courts, Federal Judiciary website at www.uscourts.gov/taq.html.

writ of *certiorari* A written order, from the U.S. Supreme Court to a lower court whose decision is being appealed, to send the records of the case forward for review.

For a case to be heard by the Supreme Court, at least four of the nine justices must vote to hear the case (the "rule of four"). When the required number of votes has been achieved, the Court issues a **writ of *certiorari*** to the lower court whose decision is being appealed, ordering it to send the records of the case forward for review. The Court is limited by law and custom in the types of cases for which it issues writs of *certiorari*. The Court will issue a "writ" only if the defendant in the case has exhausted all other avenues of appeal and the case involves a substantial federal question as defined by the appellate court. A substantial federal question, as noted, is one in which there is an alleged violation of either the U.S. Constitution or federal law.

When the Supreme Court decides a case it has accepted on appeal, it can do one of the following:

1. Affirm the verdict or decision of the lower court and "let it stand."
2. Modify the verdict or decision of the lower court, without totally reversing it.
3. Reverse the verdict or decision of the lower court, requiring no further court action.
4. Reverse the verdict or decision of the lower court and remand the case to the court of original jurisdiction, for either retrial or resentencing.

In some cases, the Supreme Court has ordered trial courts to resentence defendants whose original sentences violated the Eighth Amendment prohibition against cruel and unusual punishment. In other cases, prison authorities have been ordered to remedy unconstitutional conditions of imprisonment.

Appeals to the Supreme Court are heard at the discretion of the Court, in contrast to appeals to the U.S. circuit courts, which review cases as a matter of right. Generally, the Supreme Court's refusal to hear a case ends the process of direct appeal. In fiscal year 2001, for example, the Supreme Court denied

FYI Court Fees

The fee for filing an appeal with the U.S. Supreme Court is $300. Fees are waived for indigent defendants. Approximately 90 percent of the criminal proceedings appealed to the Supreme Court involve indigent defendants. The fees do not include the costs of printing various documents required under other court rules.

SOURCE: Clerk of the Supreme Court; 28 U.S.C. § 1911.

CJ ONLINE

Supreme Court Justices

The Supreme Court Justices of the United States have varied biographical, legal, and educational backgrounds. Learn more about the current justices by going to the following website: **http://supct.law.cornell.edu/supct/justices/fullcourt.html.** *What do the justices have in common? How do their backgrounds differ?*

Current U.S. Supreme Court Justices. Top row (L-R): Associate Justices Ruth Bader Ginsburg, David Souter, Clarence Thomas, and Stephen Breyer. Bottom row (L-R): Associate Justices Antonin Scalia and John Paul Stevens, Chief Justice William Rehnquist, Associate Justices Sandra Day O'Connor and Anthony Kennedy. *How well does the Supreme Court reflect the demographic distribution of the U.S. population?*

nearly 81 percent of the petitions filed in 2001 for review on writ of *certiorari* in criminal proceedings.[7] Writs of *certiorari* in criminal proceedings accounted for 36 percent of such writs filed with the Court; the rest were either civil appeals or administrative appeals.[8] In certain circumstances, an imprisoned defendant whose appeal has been denied may still try to have the Supreme Court review his or her case on constitutional grounds by filing a writ of *habeas corpus*. A **writ of *habeas corpus*,** which is guaranteed by Article I, Section 9, of the Constitution, the Federal Habeas Corpus Act, and state *habeas corpus* laws, is a court order directing a law officer to produce a prisoner in court to determine if the prisoner is being legally detained or imprisoned. The *habeas corpus* proceeding does not test whether the prisoner is guilty or innocent.

writ of *habeas corpus* An order from a court to an officer of the law to produce a prisoner in court to determine if the prisoner is being legally detained or imprisoned.

The Supreme Court also has original jurisdiction. However, Article III, Section 2.2, of the Constitution limits the Court's original jurisdiction to two types of cases: (1) cases involving representatives of foreign governments; and (2) certain cases in which a state is a party. Many cases have involved two states and the federal government. When Maryland and Virginia argued over oyster fishing rights, and when a dispute broke out between California and Arizona over the control of water from the Colorado River, the Supreme Court had original jurisdiction in the matters. Original jurisdiction cases are a very small part of the Court's yearly workload. Most of the cases the Court decides fall under its appellate jurisdiction.

THE STATE COURTS

The state courts have general power to decide nearly every type of case, subject only to the limitations of the U.S. Constitution, their own state constitutions, and state law. State and local courts are the courts with which citizens most often have contact. These courts handle most criminal matters and the majority of day-to-day legal matters. The laws of each state determine the organization, function, and even the names of its courts. Thus, no two state court systems are exactly alike. For discussion purposes, it is useful to distinguish four levels of state courts: trial courts of limited jurisdiction, trial courts of general jurisdiction, intermediate appellate courts, and state courts of last resort.[9]

CJ ONLINE

Court TV

Over the past several years, there has been a growing interest in the inner workings of the American court system. This is evident in the popularity of the television network Court TV. Go to the Court TV website at **www.courttv.com.** Review the list of featured cases and the programming schedule for the network. *Why do you think that shows on Court TV are so popular?*

TRIAL COURTS OF LIMITED JURISDICTION At the base of the state court structure (see Figure 8.1) are the approximately 13,000 trial courts of limited jurisdiction, sometimes referred to generally as "inferior trial courts" or simply as "lower courts." Depending on the jurisdiction, those courts are called city courts, municipal courts, county courts, circuit courts, courts of common pleas, justice-of-the-peace courts, district courts, or magistrate courts. (Technically, most of the lower courts are not really part of the state judicial structure because they are the creation of, and funded by, either city or county governments.) In several states, judges of the lower courts are not required to have any formal legal training.

The lower courts typically deal with minor cases, such as ordinance and traffic violations, some misdemeanors, and—in many jurisdictions—civil cases involving less than $1,000. For those types of offenses, the lower courts in many states are allowed to conduct **summary** or **bench trials,** or trials without a jury. Typically, the greatest penalty that can be imposed is a fine of $1,000 and a maximum of 12 months in jail. Unlike trial courts of general jurisdiction, the lower courts are not courts of record, where detailed transcripts of the proceedings are made. Because they are not courts of record, an appeal from such a lower court requires a **trial *de novo*,** in which the entire case must be reheard by a trial court of general jurisdiction.

summary or **bench trials** Trials without a jury.

trial *de novo* A trial in which an entire case is reheard by a trial court of general jurisdiction because there is an appeal and there is no written transcript of the earlier proceeding.

In addition to handling minor cases, the lower courts in most states hear the formal charges against persons accused of felonies, set bail, appoint counsel for indigent defendants, and conduct preliminary hearings for crimes that must be adjudicated at a higher level. The legal proceedings in these courts are typically less formal, and many cases are resolved without defense attorneys. Lower courts process and quickly dispose of large numbers of cases, approximately 90 million a year.

TRIAL COURTS OF GENERAL JURISDICTION Variously called district courts, superior courts, and circuit courts, depending on the jurisdiction, the more than 3,000 trial courts of general jurisdiction have the authority to try all civil and criminal cases and to hear appeals from lower courts. They are courts of record (formal transcripts of the proceedings are made), and judges and lawyers in those courts have formal legal training. Trial courts of general jurisdiction are funded by the state.

Some states have created specialty courts to deal with increases in certain types of crimes or chronic social problems. In 1989, for instance, Dade County, Florida, became the first jurisdiction to establish a drug court. Within a decade, all but 10 states had at least one such court. Drug courts have been established to (1) help handle the dramatic increase in drug cases

CAREERS IN CRIMINAL JUSTICE

Trial Court Administrator

My name is Todd Nuccio. I am the trial court administrator for the 26th Judicial District in North Carolina. The district encompasses Charlotte and greater Mecklenburg County. It is the largest jurisdiction in the state serving approximately 700,000 people.

I have a BA in political science from Northern Illinois University and an MS in judicial administration from the University of Denver, College of Law. I recently received another BA in psychology from the University of North Carolina at Charlotte because I have come to learn that 90 percent of successfully managing an organization depends upon one's ability to understand and motivate people.

During my final undergraduate semester, a constitutional law professor told me about a program that combined aspects of public administration and law.

Since graduation, I have held the position of assistant court administrator in the 7th Judicial District of Iowa, the trial court administrator position in the 12th Judicial District in North Carolina, and my current position here in Charlotte.

The responsibilities of a trial court administrator are similar to the more commonly known position of hospital administrator. The only difference is that the hospital administrator manages operations for doctors, whereas the trial court administrator manages operations for lawyers serving in the capacity of judges.

Court administration involves everything that goes into making a court system good or bad. The court manager's mission is to improve the administration of justice by: (1) working with other court officials to facilitate change, (2) initiating and coordinating discussions that form the basis of consensus, and (3) identifying problems and recommending solutions that lead to a more accessible, accountable, effective, and efficient court system.

My primary responsibilities include developing local rules and administrative policies to facilitate calendaring and administrative activities, research, strategic planning, case-flow and jury management, budgeting, personnel oversight, facilities management, grant procurement, program development, project management, coordination of alternative dispute-resolution programs, and oversight of the drug treatment and family court operations and collections department.

What I like best about my job is the variety. There are always new programs to develop and projects to manage.

What do you think are the pros and cons of being a trial court administrator?

resulting from the War on Drugs that have been overwhelming the trial courts of general jurisdiction, and (2) use the court's authority to reduce crime by changing defendants' drug-using behavior. In exchange for the possibility of dismissed charges or reduced sentences, defendants accept diversion to drug treatment programs during the judicial process. Drug court judges preside over drug court proceedings, monitor the progress of defendants by means of frequent status hearings, and prescribe sanctions and rewards as appropriate, in collaboration with prosecutors, defense attorneys, treatment providers, and others.[10]

Noelle Bush, daughter of Florida Governor Jeb Bush, is shown with her brother George P. Bush in Orange County, Florida drug court during her status hearing. Noelle was charged with contempt of court and spent 43 hours in jail for violating her court-ordered drug treatment plan. She was ordered to continue in the drug program. *Are drug courts a good idea? Why or why not?*

In 1997, Broward County in south Florida instituted the first mental-health court in the nation. This court is charged with ensuring treatment for mentally ill or developmentally disabled individuals who have been charged with nonviolent misdemeanors and, at the same time, the court is charged with protecting the public. Before the court was created, mentally disabled people often sat in jail for weeks or months for crimes that typically warranted no more than several days of confinement for other offenders. Mentally disabled arrestees often remained in jail for such long periods because they were unable to make a telephone call or post bond. The specialty court speeds up first appearances for those defendants and generally orders them to be hospitalized for evaluation.[11]

In 1999, Orange County (Orlando), Florida, established the nation's first "collections court." This specialty court was created in response to the problem of collecting court costs and restitution from offenders, particularly probationers. Prior to the introduction of the court, probation officers were responsible for collecting court costs and restitution from their clients. They were not very good at it. For example, in 1999, before the court took over collections, only 7 percent of offenders were making payments on their court costs. By December 2000, 87 percent of offenders were making payments. The court accepts payments as small as $1 and returns nearly a half-million dollars each month to victims and a similar amount to the criminal justice system. Collecting restitution has been a challenge for both state governments and the federal government. According to a U.S. government study, the amount of outstanding criminal debt more than doubled from $5.6 billion in 1995 to about $13 billion toward the end of 1999.[12]

The state of New York has recently begun developing "community courts" that aim to restore distressed New York neighborhoods by making low-level, nonviolent offenders clean streets and remove graffiti as punishment for their crimes. Also being developed are "domestic-violence courts" that emphasize victim safety and defendant accountability.[13]

FYI: Drug Courts

As of December 2000, there were nearly 600 drug court programs in operation in all 50 states, the District of Columbia, Puerto Rico, Guam, 2 Federal Districts, and a number of Native American Tribal Courts. Another 456 drug courts were being planned. Since 1989, the programs have admitted more than 140,000 offenders. Recidivism among all drug court participants has ranged from 5 to 28 percent and less than 4 percent for drug court graduates.

SOURCES: "Drug Court Resources—Facts and Figures" at www.ncjrs.org/drug_courts/facts.html; "Looking at a Decade of Drug Courts" at www.american.edu/academic.depts/spa/justice/publications/decadel.htm.

INTERMEDIATE APPELLATE COURTS In some of the geographically smaller and less-populous states, there is only one appellate court, the state court of last resort, usually called the state supreme court. Many states, however, have created intermediate appellate courts to reduce the overwhelming case burden of the state supreme court. As of January 1, 2003, 40 states had intermediate courts of appeal.[14]

The intermediate appellate courts have no trial jurisdiction. They hear only appeals in both civil and criminal cases from the trial courts of general jurisdiction. An appeals court is charged with reviewing a case for errors of law and ensuring that legal procedures were followed. The decision rendered by the appeals court is based on a review of the trial court's official transcript and any other legally relevant information that may be submitted. Brief oral arguments by the attorneys for both sides are also allowed.

Like their federal counterparts, the intermediate appellate courts cannot refuse to hear any legally appealed case. The number of judges assigned to intermediate appellate courts ranges from 3 in some states to 93 in California.[15] Normally, three judges sit as a panel to decide cases.

State Courts of Last Resort In most states, the state court of last resort is referred to as the state supreme court, although, as noted above, some states use different names. In Massachusetts and Maine, for example, the state court of last resort is called the Supreme Judicial Court; in Maryland and New York, it is called the Court of Appeals. Oklahoma and Texas have two courts of last resort: the Court of Criminal Appeals (for criminal appeals) and the Supreme Court (for civil cases). The Court of Last Resort in 13 states or the Chief Justice of the Court of Last Resort in 36 states is the designated head of a state's judicial branch. In one state, Utah, the Judicial Council is the designated head of the judicial branch.

As previously noted, the primary responsibility of state courts of last resort is to hear appeals from either trial courts of general jurisdiction (in those states without intermediate appellate courts) or intermediate appellate courts. In states with intermediate courts of appeal, the state court of last resort, like the U.S. Supreme Court, has discretion in which cases it will hear. And, like the U.S. Supreme Court, most state courts of last resort have original jurisdiction over a few types of cases.

Depending on the state, the number of judges that serve on the state court of last resort ranges from five to nine, though more than half the states have seven.[16] However, unlike judges of intermediate courts of appeal, judges of the state court of last resort are not divided into panels to hear cases. Instead, all of the judges hear all of the cases; that is, they sit *en banc*. State courts of last resort have the final word on matters involving interpretation of state law. Although defendants dissatisfied with a verdict rendered in a state court of last resort may appeal the decision to the Supreme Court, the Supreme Court will hear the appeal only if it involves an alleged violation of the Constitution or federal law. In deciding cases, most state courts of last resort follow procedures similar to those employed by the Supreme Court.

THINKING CRITICALLY

1. What are some of the benefits of a dual court system?
2. Why is it difficult for a case to make it all the way to the Supreme Court? Should it be that difficult? Why or why not?

Purposes of Courts

Ted Rubin, former juvenile court judge and noted expert on juvenile justice, court, and rehabilitation issues, outlines 10 purposes of courts.[17] The first is to "do justice." However, whether justice is done usually depends on the interests and viewpoints of the parties involved in a dispute. Typically, the "winning" party believes that justice has been done, while the "loser" thinks otherwise.

A second purpose of courts is "to appear to do justice." Even when a decision rendered by a court seems unjust to some people, it is still important that the court appear to "do justice." The appearance of justice is accomplished primarily by providing due process of law. **Due process of law,** as noted in Chapter 4, refers to the procedures followed by courts to ensure that a defendant's constitutional rights are not violated.

due process of law The procedures followed by courts to ensure that a defendant's constitutional rights are not violated.

A third purpose of courts is "to provide a forum where disputes between people can be resolved justly and peacefully." Until the creation of courts of

A purpose of courts is to provide a forum where disputes between people, such as the legendary feud between the Hatfields and McCoys (pictured here), can be resolved justly and peacefully. *How successful have the courts been in achieving this purpose? Defend your answer.*

law, disputes were often settled violently, through blood feuds and other acts of revenge. Aggrieved parties would gather their extended families and friends and make war against the families and friends of the person or persons who had presumably violated their rights. Sometimes those feuds would span generations, as did the legendary battles between the Hatfields and the McCoys. Courts were instituted, at least in part, to prevent those calamities. Thus, regardless of which side in a dispute "wins," what is important, from the standpoint of the court, is that the dispute be resolved justly and, perhaps more important, peacefully.

A fourth purpose of courts is "to censure wrongdoing." To *censure* means to condemn or to blame. In this context, it refers to condemning or blaming people who have violated the law.

Purposes five through eight involve specific outcomes that courts hope to achieve by their actions. They are **incapacitation,** or the removal or restriction of the freedom of those found to have violated criminal laws; **punishment,** or the imposition of a penalty for criminal wrongdoing; **rehabilitation,** or the attempt to "correct" the personality and behavior of convicted offenders through educational, vocational, or therapeutic treatment and to return them to society as law-abiding citizens; and **general deterrence,** or the attempt to prevent people in general from engaging in crime by punishing specific individuals and making examples of them. (Omitted from Rubin's list is special or specific deterrence.) These purposes are discussed at greater length in the next chapter under the goals of sentencing.

A ninth purpose of courts is to determine legal status. For example, courts determine marital status by dissolving marriages and granting divorces. Similarly, parental status is determined by approving adoptions.

A tenth and critically important purpose of courts is to protect individual citizens against arbitrary government action. Recourse through the courts is

FYI: Public Opinion and the Courts

Although the public generally has trust and confidence in the courts in its communities, there is a fair amount of dissatisfaction with certain aspects of the court system, especially among racial and ethnic minorities. While 85 percent of the public agree at least somewhat that the courts protect defendants' constitutional rights, only about half the public rate the courts good or excellent in handling criminal cases. Nearly 70 percent of the public believe that it is too expensive to bring a case to court, 80 percent agree at least somewhat that cases are not resolved in a timely manner, and almost 60 percent agree at least somewhat that the courts do not make sure their orders are enforced. The public generally believes that the wealthy receive preferential treatment from the courts. However, most Americans feel that people like themselves are treated either better or the same as others. African Americans are an exception. Two-thirds of African Americans feel that people like them are treated somewhat or far worse than other people. Also, more than half of the public feel that non-English-speaking people get somewhat worse or far worse treatment from the courts.

SOURCE: National Center for State Courts, *How the Public Views the State Courts: A 1999 National Survey,* at www.ncsconline.org/D_Research/descriptions.html#publicview.

incapacitation The removal or restriction of the freedom of those found to have violated criminal laws.

punishment The imposition of a penalty for criminal wrongdoing.

rehabilitation The attempt to "correct" the personality and behavior of convicted offenders through educational, vocational, or therapeutic treatment and to return them to society as law-abiding citizens.

general deterrence The attempt to prevent people in general from engaging in crime by punishing specific individuals and making examples of them.

> **THINKING CRITICALLY**
>
> 1. The first purpose of the court is to "do justice." Given what you know about the American court system, do you think that justice is done? Why or why not?
> 2. Of the remaining nine purposes of the courts, which ones do you think can be most easily achieved? Why?

available to citizens who have been abused by government agencies and agents. Examples of such abuses include illegal invasion of a person's privacy; interference with a person's First Amendment rights of religious choice, speech, press, and assembly; and denial of public employment because of race, gender, or age. In summary, by custom and law, courts have become an integral and seemingly indispensable part of modern life.

Key Actors in the Court Process

The three key actors in the court process are the prosecutor, the defense attorney, and the judge. In this section, we will examine the roles those three officers of the court play in the administration of justice.[18]

THE PROSECUTOR

> **FYI U.S. Attorneys**
>
> Violations of federal laws are prosecuted by the U.S. Justice Department. The Justice Department is headed by the U.S. Attorney General and staffed by 93 U.S. attorneys (Guam and the Northern Mariana Islands share 1), each of whom is nominated to office by the President and confirmed by the Senate. One U.S. attorney is assigned to each of the federal district court jurisdictions. There were approximately 5,000 assistant U.S. attorneys in 2000.
>
> SOURCE: United States Attorneys at www.usdoj.gov/usao/index.html and Executive Office for United States Attorneys, personal correspondence, August 10, 2000.

nolle prosequi (nol. pros.) The notation placed on the official record of a case when prosecutors elect not to prosecute.

Because most crimes violate state laws, they fall under the authority, or jurisdiction, of the state court system and its prosecutors. The prosecutor is a community's chief law enforcement official and is responsible primarily for the protection of society.[19] Depending on the state, the prosecutor may be referred to as the district attorney, the prosecuting attorney, the county attorney, the state's attorney, the commonwealth's attorney, or the solicitor. In large cities, the day-to-day work of the prosecutor's office is performed by assistant district attorneys. Whatever the name, the prosecutor is the most powerful actor in the administration of justice. Not only do prosecutors conduct the final screening of each person arrested for a criminal offense, deciding whether there is enough evidence to support a conviction, but in most jurisdictions they also have unreviewable discretion in deciding whether to charge a person with a crime and whether to prosecute the case. In other words, regardless of the amount (or lack) of incriminating evidence, and without having to provide any reasons to anyone, prosecutors have the authority to charge or not charge a person with a crime and to prosecute or not prosecute the case. If they decide to prosecute, they also determine what the charge or charges will be. (The charge or charges may or may not be the same as the one or ones for which the person was arrested.) Prosecutors are not required to prosecute a person for all the charges that the evidence will support. However, the more charges they bring against a suspect, the more leverage prosecutors have in plea bargaining, which will be discussed later in this section.

Regardless of the reason, when prosecutors elect not to prosecute, they enter a notation of ***nolle prosequi (nol. pros.)*** on the official record of the case and formally announce in court the decision to dismiss the charge or charges.

THE DECISION TO CHARGE AND PROSECUTE The exercise of prosecutorial discretion in charging contrasts sharply with the way prosecutors are supposed to behave in their professional capacities. Ideally, prosecutors are supposed to charge an offender with a crime and to prosecute the case if after full investigation three, and only three, conditions are met:

1. They find that a crime has been committed.
2. A perpetrator can be identified.
3. There is sufficient evidence to support a guilty verdict.

On the other hand, prosecutors are not supposed to charge suspects with more criminal charges or for more serious crimes than can be reasonably supported by the evidence. They are not supposed to be deterred from prosecution because juries in their jurisdiction have frequently refused to convict persons of particular kinds of crimes. Conversely, they are not supposed to prosecute simply because an aroused public demands it. Prosecutors are not supposed to be influenced by the personal or political advantages or disadvantages that might be involved in prosecuting or not prosecuting a case. Nor, for that matter, are they supposed to be swayed by their desire to enhance their records of successful convictions. It would be naive, however, to believe that those factors do not have at least some influence on prosecutors' decisions to pursue or to drop criminal cases.

Prosecutors sometimes choose not to charge or prosecute criminal cases for any of the following nine additional reasons. The first is their belief that an offense did not cause sufficient harm. This decision is usually a practical one. Given limited time and resources, overworked and understaffed prosecutors often have to choose which cases go forward and which do not.

A second reason involves the relationship between the statutory punishment and the offender or the offense. In today's legal climate of increasingly harsh sentencing laws, a prosecutor may feel that the statutory punishment for a crime is too severe for a particular offender (for example, a first-time offender) or for a particular offense. In an effort to be fair, at least in their own minds, prosecutors in such cases impose their own sense of justice.

CAREERS IN CRIMINAL JUSTICE

Assistant State Attorney

My name is Wilson Green and I am an Assistant State Attorney (prosecutor) in Orlando. I received a BA from Vanderbilt, an **MDiv** from Reformed Theological Seminary, and my JD from the University of Mississippi, with some Navy time along the way. I interviewed for and began my current job about 20 years ago here at the State Attorney's Office.

I am in the homicide unit. Most of us deal either with misdemeanor or felony cases that are set for trial. Most cases are resolved by defendants pleading guilty (or no contest) and being sentenced by a judge, while others proceed to a jury trial. The prosecutor is assigned cases as they come to our office from law enforcement agencies and after the defendants have been formally charged by other attorneys in our office.

The first step is to "work-up" each case—to review the entire file (police reports, witness statements, photos, tape recordings, lab reports, etc.) and to send out appropriate "discovery" to the defendant's attorney. Witnesses must be listed and subpoenaed for trial. Requests for further investigation may be needed as the prosecutor anticipates what the defense will probably be. Often the defense attorney will take depositions of state witnesses before trial, which we attend. There may also be pretrial hearings on legal issues, as well as plea negotiations.

Jury trials generally may last a day or so or up to a week or more. A prosecutor may have as many as a hundred cases pending at one time (spread over a few month period), with new ones coming in as fast as others are resolved. The stress level can be high at times, due to the caseload, problem cases, witness problems, cases being postponed at the last minute, not knowing which case will actually go to trial until the last minute, and having to make appropriate plea offers. On the plus side, prosecutors (who are to be "ministers of justice," not just "win" cases) have a beneficial role in society, have much discretion in handling their cases, are in the courtroom on a regular basis, and are in touch with the "real world" through their contact with police agencies, witnesses, victims, families of victims, judges, and juries. They can use both common sense and legal training. Each case seems to have something new.

Those considering becoming prosecutors might think about sampling criminal justice and prelaw undergraduate courses, taking advantage of internships with law enforcement agencies or prosecutors' offices, or simply observing court proceedings as a citizen. Use any employment opportunities as a way to gain commonsense experience that will help in a later career. Take advantage of any group or public speaking opportunities as well.

What do you think is the most challenging part of a prosecutor's job? Explain.

District Attorney Mark Hulbert, right, responds to questions about the arrest of Los Angeles Lakers' star Kobe Bryant during a news conference at the Eagle county Justice Center in Eagle, Colorado. Listening on the left is Sheriff Joseph Hoy. *Was it appropriate for DA Hulbert to hold a press conference about the case? Why or why not?*

A third reason for not prosecuting, even when the three ideal conditions are met, is an improper motive on the part of a complainant. The prosecutor may feel that a criminal charge has been made for the wrong reasons. For example, if a prosecutor were convinced that a woman who caught her husband cheating had lied when charging her husband with beating her, the prosecutor might elect not to charge the husband with assault or some other crime.

A fourth reason prosecutors sometimes choose not to prosecute a case is that the particular law has been violated with impunity for a long time with few complaints by the public. In the case of "blue laws," for example, which may require stores to be closed on Sundays, prosecutors would occasionally get complaints from outraged churchgoers. In some cases, prosecutors simply ignored the complaints because the law, although on the books for decades, had not been enforced for years and few complaints had been received. In most states, incidentally, blue laws have been declared unconstitutional.

A fifth reason prosecutors often choose not to prosecute a case, even though, ideally, prosecution is required, is that a victim may refuse to testify. In rape cases, for example, prosecutors realize that it is nearly impossible to secure a conviction without the testimony of the victim. Thus, if the victim refuses to testify, the prosecutor may decide to drop the case, knowing that the chances of obtaining a conviction are reduced dramatically without the cooperation of the victim.

A sixth reason for not prosecuting has to do with humanitarian concerns for the welfare of the victim or the offender. In child sexual molestation cases, for example, conviction depends on the victim's testimony. Prosecutors may decline to prosecute because of the possible psychological injury to a child who is forced to testify. When offenders are suffering from mental illness, prosecutors may decide that diverting the offender to a mental health facility rather than prosecuting for a crime is in the best interests of all concerned.

Seventh, prosecutors sometimes do not prosecute a case otherwise worthy of prosecution because the accused person cooperates in the apprehension or conviction of other criminal offenders. In drug cases, for example, prosecutors often "cut deals" (make promises not to prosecute) with users or low-level dealers in order to identify "higher-ups" in the drug distribution network. Prosecutors make similar deals with low-level operatives in organized crime.

An eighth reason prosecutors sometimes choose not to prosecute is that the accused is wanted for prosecution of a more serious crime in another jurisdiction. Thus, there is little reason to expend resources prosecuting a case if an offender is likely to receive greater punishment for a crime committed elsewhere. It is easier and cheaper simply to extradite, or to deliver, the offender to the other jurisdiction.

Finally, if an offender is on parole when he or she commits a new crime, prosecutors may not prosecute the new crime because they consider it more cost-effective to simply have the parole revoked and send the offender back to prison.

FYI

Not Prosecuting Cases

Insufficient evidence is the most frequent reason given by prosecutors for not prosecuting cases. In most cities, prosecutors refuse to formally charge a person in about one-half of all felony arrests.

The Decision to Plea-Bargain Unreviewable discretion in deciding whether to charge and prosecute citizens for their crimes is the principal reason the prosecutor is considered the most powerful figure in the administration of justice, but it is by no means the prosecutor's only source of power. Probably the most strategic source of power available to prosecutors is their authority to decide which cases to "plea bargain." **Plea bargaining** or **plea negotiating**

plea bargaining or **plea negotiating** The practice whereby the prosecutor, the defense attorney, the defendant, and—in many jurisdictions—the judge agree on a specific sentence to be imposed if the accused pleads guilty to an agreed-upon charge or charges instead of going to trial.

Actor Robert Downey Jr. departs Riverside County Superior Court after pleading no contest to a felony count for cocaine possession and a misdemeanor count for being under the influence of the drug in a plea bargain that allowed him to continue live-in drug treatment, rather than face jail time. *What factors might influence a prosecutor's plea-bargaining decision? Are all of those factors legitimate?*

refers to the practice whereby the prosecutor, the defense attorney, the defendant, and—in many jurisdictions—the judge agree to a negotiated plea. For example, they may agree on a specific sentence to be imposed if the accused pleads guilty to an agreed-upon charge or charges instead of going to trial. It is the prosecutor alone, however, who chooses what lesser plea, if any, will be accepted instead of going to trial. Contrary to popular belief, justice in the United States is dispensed mostly through plea bargaining. Criminal trials are relatively rare events; plea bargaining is routine. Plea bargaining and the different types of plea bargains will be discussed in more detail later in this chapter.

Recommending the Amount of Bail In addition to control over charging, prosecuting, and plea bargaining, another source of power for the prosecutor in many jurisdictions is the responsibility of recommending the amount of bail. Although the final decision on the amount or even the opportunity for bail rests with the judge, the prosecutor makes the initial recommendation. By recommending a very high bail amount, an amount that a suspect is unlikely to be able to raise, a prosecutor can pressure a suspect to accept a plea bargain. Bail will be discussed later in this chapter.

Rules of Discovery Perhaps the only weakness in a prosecutor's arsenal of weapons is the legal rules of discovery. The **rules of discovery** mandate that a prosecutor provide defense counsel with any exculpatory evidence in the prosecutor's possession. Exculpatory evidence is evidence favorable to the accused that has an effect on guilt or punishment. Examples of possible exculpatory evidence are physical evidence, evidentiary documents (such as a defendant's recorded statements to police, or reports of medical examinations or scientific tests), and lists of witnesses. A prosecutor's concealment or misrepresentation of evidence is grounds for an appellate court's reversal of a conviction. Defense attorneys, on the other hand, are under no constitutional obligation to provide prosecutors with incriminating evidence. However, most states and the federal

FYI: Guilty Pleas

About 95 percent of all convictions in felony cases are the result of guilty pleas. Guilty pleas account for an even higher percentage of convictions in misdemeanor cases.

Source: See, for example, Matthew R. Durose and Patrick A. Langan "Felony Sentences in State Courts, 2000," U.S. Department of Justice, *Bureau of Justice Statistics Bulletin* (Washington, DC: GPO, June 2003), p. 9, Table 10.

rules of discovery Rules that mandate that a prosecutor provide defense counsel with any exculpatory evidence (evidence favorable to the accused that has an effect on guilt or punishment) in the prosecutor's possession.

system have by statute or by court rules given the prosecution some discovery rights (for example, the right to notice of the defense's intent to use an alibi or an insanity defense). The rationale for the rules of discovery is that, ideally, the prosecutor's job is to see that justice is done and not necessarily to win cases.

Selection and Career Prospects of Prosecutors Given the power of prosecutors in the administration of justice, the public can only hope that prosecutors wield their power wisely and justly. We believe that many of them do. Unfortunately, political considerations and aspirations may be too enticing to some prosecutors, causing them to violate the canons of their position. The partisan political process through which the typical prosecutor is elected increases the chances that political influence will affect the prosecutor's decisions.

The potential for political influence is increased even further by prosecutors' frequent use of the position as a stepping-stone to higher political office (several mayors, governors, and presidents have been former prosecutors). There are very few career prosecutors. Those who are not elected to higher political office and those who choose not to seek it typically go into private law practice.

> **FYI — Running for Office**
>
> In most jurisdictions, prosecutors run for office on either the Democratic or Republican ticket, although in some jurisdictions, they are elected in nonpartisan races—that is, without party affiliation. Although prosecutors can be removed from office for criminal acts or for incompetence, removal is rare.

Assistant District Attorneys The workhorses of the big-city prosecutor's office, as already noted, are the assistant district attorneys (or deputy district attorneys), who are hired by the prosecutor. Generally, assistant district attorneys are hired right out of law school or after a brief and usually unsuccessful stint in private practice. Most of them remain in the prosecutor's office for only 2 to 4 years and then go into, or back into, private law practice. Reasons for leaving the prosecutor's office include low pay, little chance for advancement, physical and psychological pressures, boredom, and disillusionment with the criminal adjudication process. Assistant district attorneys provide an important social service, and the job is a good way of gaining legal experience. Lawyers who occupy the position, however, usually do not consider it anything more than temporary employment before they go into private practice.

National Survey of Prosecutors According to a recent government survey of prosecutors, 2,341 prosecutors' offices handled felony cases in 2001.[20] More than 79,000 attorneys, investigators, victim advocates, and support staff worked in those offices. The average number of employees across all prosecutor offices was nine, including the chief prosecutor. Full-time offices in large districts averaged staffs of 456, with an average of 151 assistant prosecutors, 21 supervisory attorneys (attorneys who also have managerial responsibilities), and 145 support staff. A prosecutorial district consists of one or more counties.

The total amount spent for prosecutorial services nationwide in 2001 was approximately $4.6 billion. The average budget was $2 million. Annual budgets ranged between $6,000 and $373 million. About one-third of the offices did not include in their budgets the costs of expert services, nearly half of the offices excluded investigators' services, about 60 percent of offices excluded DNA testing, and 85 percent of the budgets did not include the costs of social services. Most of the funding for prosecutors' offices came from county governments, although funding in some offices was also received from state governments, city governments, and grant funds.

State law determines the number of chief prosecutors and whether they are elected or appointed. In 2001, all chief prosecutors were elected, except for those in Alaska, Connecticut, the District of Columbia, and New Jersey, where they were appointed. Nearly 90 percent of chief prosecutors were elected or appointed to 4 year terms. States with the largest number of chief prosecutors were Texas (155), Virginia (120), and Missouri (115).

Chief prosecutors served for an average of about 7 years. Nearly a third of the chief prosecutors had served 4 years or less, while one in five had served 15 years or more. The longest term of service reported in the survey was 40 years.

A chief prosecutor's annual salary depended primarily on whether the job was part-time or full-time and the size of the prosecutorial district. In 2001, 75 percent of chief prosecutors worked in districts with fewer than 100,000 residents, while only 5 percent served in districts with populations of 500,000 or more. Annual salaries of chief prosecutors in 2001 ranged from $10,500 to $189,000. Half of chief prosecutors earned $85,000 or more annually.

Nearly 27,000 assistant prosecutors, including supervisory attorneys, were employed in 2001. Entry-level annual salaries for half of the beginning assistant prosecutors were $35,000 or more. Full-time assistants with 5 years' experience earned $45,000 or more a year, and half of the supervisory attorneys made $60,000 or more a year. About a third of the offices had difficulties in recruiting or retaining staff attorneys. The primary reason for the problems was low salaries.

In 2000, prosecutors' offices closed more than 2.3 million felony cases and nearly seven million misdemeanor cases. That amounted to about 857 felony cases per 100,000 residents and approximately 87 felony cases per assistant prosecutor. As an indication of the importance of plea bargaining, the average number of felony jury trial verdicts per office was eight, while the average conviction rate for felony cases was about 90 percent.

The survey found an element of danger in the work of prosecutors. About 40 percent of prosecutors' offices reported a work-related threat or assault against a staff member in 2001. Approximately one-third of chief prosecutors and one-quarter of assistant prosecutors nationwide received a work-related threat or were assaulted. Consequently, various security measures were used for protection, such as electronic security systems, building guards, metal detectors, electronic surveillance, and police protection. About one in five chief prosecutors carried a firearm for personal security. Generally, the smaller the prosecutor's office, the more likely the chief prosecutor carried a firearm for protection.

THE DEFENSE ATTORNEY

The Sixth Amendment to the U.S. Constitution and several modern Supreme Court decisions, discussed in Chapter 4, guarantee the right to the "effective assistance" of counsel to people charged with crimes.[21] (The terms *counsel, attorney,* and *lawyer* are interchangeable.)

The right to counsel extends not only to representation at trial but also to other critical stages in the criminal justice process, "where substantial rights of the accused may be affected." Thus, defendants have a right to counsel during custodial interrogations, preliminary hearings, and police lineups. They also have a right to counsel at certain posttrial proceedings, such as their first (and only the first) appeal that is a matter of right, and probation and parole revocation hearings. The Supreme Court has also extended the right to counsel to juveniles in juvenile court proceedings.

A defendant may waive the right to counsel and appear on his or her own behalf. However, given the technical nature of criminal cases and the stakes involved (an individual's freedom!), anyone arrested for a crime is well advised to secure the assistance of counsel at the earliest opportunity. The phone call routinely given to arrested suspects at the police station is for the specific purpose of obtaining counsel. If a suspect cannot afford an attorney and is accused of either a felony or a misdemeanor for which imprisonment could be the result of conviction, the state is required to provide an attorney at the state's expense.

Lawyers are sometimes vilified by the media and the public for defending people unquestionably guilty of crimes. That lawyers sometimes succeed in getting guilty persons "off" by the skillful use of "legal technicalities" only

FYI: Public Opinion and Lawyers

In 2002, only 18 percent of Americans rated the honesty and ethical standards of lawyers "high" (16 percent) or "very high" (2 percent), 45 percent rated lawyers' honesty and ethical standards "average," 35 percent rated them "low" (25 percent) or "very low" (10 percent).

SOURCE: *Sourcebook of Criminal Justice Statistics,* www.albany.edu/sourcebook/ Table 2.22.

makes matters worse. However, what some people fail to understand is that in the American system of justice, it is not the role of defense lawyers to decide their clients' guilt or innocence. Rather, the role of defense lawyers is to provide the best possible legal counsel and advocacy within the legal and ethical limits of the profession. Legal and ethical codes forbid lawyers, for example, to mislead the court by providing false information or by using perjured testimony (false testimony under oath). The American system of justice is based on the premise that a person is innocent until proven guilty. In the attempt to ensure, as far as possible, that innocent people are not found guilty of crimes, all persons charged with crimes are entitled to a rigorous defense. The constitutional right to counsel and our adversarial system of justice would be meaningless if lawyers refused to defend clients that they "knew" were guilty.

Not all lawyers are adequately trained to practice in the specialized field of criminal law. Law schools generally require only a one-semester course in criminal law and a one-semester course in criminal procedure, though additional courses may be taken as electives in a typical 6-semester or 3-year program. Many lawyers prefer to practice other, often more lucrative, areas of law, such as corporate, tax, or tort law. Compared with those other areas of legal practice, the practice of criminal law generally provides its practitioner less income, prestige, and status in the community.

For those reasons, criminal defendants in search of counsel are limited by practical considerations. They can choose a privately retained lawyer who specializes in criminal law, if they can afford one. Or, if they are indigent and cannot afford one, they will receive a court-appointed attorney (who may or may not be skilled in the practice of criminal law), a public defender, or a "contract" lawyer. In large cities, there is little problem in locating a criminal lawyer. They are listed in the Yellow Pages of the local telephone book. In rural areas, however, finding a lawyer who specializes in criminal law may be more difficult. Because of the lower volume of criminal cases in rural areas, attorneys who practice in those areas generally must practice all kinds of law to make a living; they cannot afford to specialize. Outside of large cities, then, a criminal defendant may have no better option than to rely on the services of a court-appointed attorney, a public defender, or a contract lawyer, whichever is provided in that particular jurisdiction. Court-appointed attorneys, public defenders, and contract lawyers will be discussed further later in this section.

> **FYI — Determining Indigency**
>
> In some jurisdictions, indigency is determined by the examination of tax returns or the filing of affidavits documenting resources. Generally, defendants are deemed indigent if their resources place them below the government's official poverty level. In other jurisdictions, indigency is determined simply by defendants' response to the judge's question whether they can afford an attorney.
>
> Source: See, for example, Steven K. Smith and Carol J. DeFrances, "Indigent Defense," U.S. Department of Justice, *Bureau of Justice Statistics Selected Findings* (Washington, DC: GPO, February 1996).

Criminal Lawyers In discussing privately retained criminal lawyers, it is useful to think of a continuum. At one end are a very few nationally known, highly paid, and successful criminal lawyers, such as Gerry Spence, Johnnie Cochran, Jr., and Alan Dershowitz. Those criminal lawyers generally take only three kinds of cases: (1) those that are sensational or highly publicized, (2) those that promise to make new law, or (3) those that involve large fees. A little further along the continuum is another small group of criminal lawyers, those who make a very comfortable living in the large cities of this country by defending professional criminals, such as organized crime members, gamblers, pornographers, and drug dealers. Toward the other end of the continuum are the vast majority of criminal lawyers who practice in the large cities of this country.

Most criminal lawyers must struggle to earn a decent living. They have to handle a large volume of cases to make even a reasonable salary. To attract clients, some criminal lawyers engage in the unethical practice of paying kickbacks to ambulance drivers, police officers, jailers, and bail bonds people for client referrals. Some criminal lawyers also engage in the unethical practice of soliciting new clients in courthouse hallways.

Although a few criminal lawyers are known for their criminal trial expertise, most relatively successful criminal lawyers gain their reputations from

From left to right, Johnnie Cochran, Jr., Gerry Spence, and Alan Dershowitz are among the very few nationally known, highly paid, and successful criminal lawyers. *What do you think distinguishes these lawyers from all other lawyers?*

their ability to "fix" cases, that is, their ability to produce the best possible outcome for a client, given the circumstances of the case. Fixing cases usually involves plea bargaining but may also include the strategic use of motions for continuances and for changes in the judge assigned to the case. *Who* a lawyer knows is often more important than *what* the lawyer knows. In other words, a close personal relationship with the prosecutor or a hearing before the "right" judge is often far more important to the case's outcome (for example, a favorable plea bargain) than is an attorney's legal ability.

Besides legal expertise and good relationships with other actors in the adjudication process, the only other commodity criminal lawyers have to sell is their time. Thus, for the typical criminal lawyer, time is valuable. As a result, criminal lawyers try to avoid time-consuming court battles and are motivated to get their clients to plead guilty to reduced charges.

Another reason most criminal lawyers prefer plea bargaining to trials is that they are more likely to receive a fee, however small, from their typically poor clients for arranging the plea. When cases go to trial and the legal fee has not been paid in advance, there is the possibility that the lawyer will receive no compensation or inadequate compensation from his or her client, especially if the case is lost.

To prevent nonpayment for services, criminal lawyers sometimes engage in unethical, if not illegal, behavior. Sometimes criminal lawyers plea-bargain cases that they know they can win at trial. They do this because they know that their clients do not have the money to compensate them for the time they would put into a trial. If clients have only a few hundred dollars, some unscrupulous criminal lawyers reason that those clients can afford only "bargain" justice. Another unethical tactic employed by some criminal lawyers to secure a fee from their clients is to seek delays in a case and allow their clients to remain in jail until they have been paid for services yet to be performed. Getting a client to pay a legal fee is not a legitimate basis for seeking a court delay.

Criminal lawyers often spend more time at the county jail and the courthouse, where their clients are, than in their offices, which generally are spartan compared with the plush offices of their corporate counterparts. They are sometimes told by their clients about grisly crimes that have been committed or will be committed in the future. Because of attorney-client privilege, the lawyer in possession of this information cannot reveal it, under penalty of disbarment (the revocation of his or her license to practice law). In short, many criminal lawyers are considered somewhat less than respectable by their professional colleagues and much of the general public because their clients are "criminals," they deal with some of the more unsavory aspects of human existence, and a few may engage in unethical behavior to earn a living.

> **CJ ONLINE**
>
> **Rules of Conduct**
>
> As noted previously, the American public generally does not rate the honesty and ethical standards of lawyers very high. Go to the American Bar Association's website at **www.abanet.org** and review the Model Rules of Professional Conduct. Although individual states have their own rules, most states modeled their rules after these. *From what you have read and heard, which of the rules do you think are most commonly violated?*

The Court-Appointed Lawyer In some jurisdictions, criminal suspects or defendants who cannot afford to hire an attorney are provided with court-appointed lawyers. The court-appointed lawyer is usually selected in one of two ways. In some jurisdictions, lawyers volunteer to represent indigent offenders and are appointed by judges on a rotating basis from a list or from lawyers present in the courtroom. In other jurisdictions, lawyers are appointed by a judge from a list of attorneys who are members of the county bar association.

In the past, appointed lawyers frequently represented indigent clients *pro bono* (without pay). Today, however, the vast majority of appointed lawyers are paid by the jurisdiction. Hourly fees are usually much less than would be charged by privately retained counsel. Seldom is money available to hire investigators or to secure the services of expert witnesses, the lack of which weakens the defense that can be provided a client.

> | Myth | Fact |
> |---|---|
> | Crafty defense attorneys help criminals escape conviction. | Although this may be true in a very small fraction of cases, most felony cases are handled by conscientious but overworked public defenders. |

In addition, although appointed attorneys may be experts in some areas of law, they may not be familiar with the intricacies of a criminal defense. They may have never before represented a client charged with a crime. Nevertheless, many lawyers view their appointments as a public service and do their best to represent their clients in a professional manner. Some, however, take cases grudgingly (they can refuse an appointment only for very good reasons) and regard an appointment as a financially unrewarding and unpleasant experience. They perform well enough only to escape charges of malpractice. In many cases, an appointed attorney first meets his or her client in the courtroom, where they have a brief conference before a guilty plea is arranged.

> **FYI — Wrongful Convictions**
>
> An estimated 34,250 people are convicted wrongfully in American courts every year.
>
> Source: Based on figures provided in C. Ronald Huff, Arye Rattner, and Edward Sagarin, "Guilty Until Proven Innocent: Wrongful Conviction and Public Policy," *Crime and Delinquency* 32 (1986), pp. 518–44, and U.S. Department of Justice, Federal Bureau of Investigation, *Crime in the United States, 2001* (Washington, DC: GPO, 2002) p. 233.

The Public Defender In many jurisdictions today, people who are charged with crimes and cannot afford an attorney are provided with public defenders. Public defenders are paid a fixed salary by a jurisdiction (city, county, state, or federal) to defend indigents charged with crimes. Frequently, public defenders are assigned to courtrooms instead of to specific clients. They defend all of the indigent clients who appear in their courtrooms. As a result, a defendant may have a different public defender at different stages in the process (for example, preliminary hearing, arraignment, and trial). Public defenders commonly spend only 5 to 10 minutes with their clients. In addition, this bureaucratic arrangement makes the public defender a part of a courtroom work group that includes the judge, the prosecutor, and the other courtroom actors with whom the public defender interacts daily. This work group, in turn, may be more interested in processing cases efficiently and maintaining cooperative relationships with each other than in pursuing adversarial justice. Nevertheless, despite the method of assignment, the impersonal nature of the defense, and the potential conflict of interest, most indigent

Defense lawyers spend much of their time at the local jail. *Do you think that the jail setting influences a lawyer's opinion of his or her client?*

clients in criminal cases prefer public defenders to court-appointed attorneys because public defenders practice criminal law full-time.

Like prosecutors, many public defenders regard their position not as a career, but as a valuable learning experience that will eventually lead to private law practice.

The Contract Lawyer A relatively new and increasingly popular way of providing for indigent defense is the contract system. In this system, private attorneys, law firms, and bar associations bid for the right to represent a jurisdiction's indigent defendants. Terms of contracts differ, but in the typical contract, counsel agrees to represent either all or a specified number of indigent defendants in a jurisdiction during a certain period of time, in exchange for a fixed dollar amount. Contracts are awarded on the basis of costs to the jurisdiction, qualifications of bidders, and other factors.

In certain situations, some jurisdictions employ a combination of indigent defense systems. For example, jurisdictions that regularly use public defenders sometimes contract out the defense of cases where there is a conflict of interest (for example, multiple-defendant cases) or cases that require special expertise (such as some death penalty cases).

Comparing Indigent Defense Systems At the end of the twentieth century, 90 percent of the nation's 100 most populous counties had public defender programs, 89 percent had assigned counsel programs, and 42 percent had contract programs.[22] More than $1 billion were spent on indigent defense in the most populous counties in 1999: approximately 73 percent on public defender programs, 21 percent on assigned counsel programs, and 6 percent on awarded contracts. County governments provided 60 percent of the funding, and state governments provided 25 percent of the funding.

The 100 most populous counties provided indigent defense in more than four million cases in 1999. More than 80 percent of the cases were handled by public defenders, 15 percent were handled by court-appointed private attorneys, and

FYI — Female Lawyers

In 1971, just 3 percent of all lawyers in the United States were women. By 1980, the percentage of female lawyers had increased to 8 percent, and by 2000, nearly 30 percent of all lawyers were women. In 1961, only 4 percent of the 16,489 first-year law students were women. In 2000, nearly half of the 43,518 first-year law students were women. Still, women comprise less than 16 percent of the partners in the nation's approximately 50,000 major law firms. The percentage of associates is much higher (nearly 42 percent). In 1981, Sandra Day O'Connor became the first female justice of the U.S. Supreme Court. Ruth Bader Ginsburg became the second in 1993. Also in 1993, Janet Reno became the first female Attorney General of the United States.

Source: American Bar Association, Commission on Women in the Profession at www.abanet.org/women/articles.html; "Despite Gains, Women Lawyers Still Face Bias," *The Orlando Sentinel*, August 18, 1996, p. A20; "Where My Girls At? Women Are Finally Catching Up to Men in Law School Enrollment," *The Princeton Review* at www.princetonreview.com/law/research/articles/decide/gender.asp.

3 percent by contract attorneys. Conviction rates for indigent defendants in federal and state courts were about the same as they were for defendants with privately retained counsel. However, incarceration rates were higher for defendants with publicly financed attorneys than for those with privately retained counsel: in the federal courts, 88 percent to 77 percent, and in the state courts, 71 percent to 54 percent. Ironically, the length of jail or prison sentence was shorter for defendants with publicly financed attorneys. Those defendants with publicly financed attorneys received sentences in federal courts that averaged just less than 5 years; those with privately retained counsel averaged sentences of a little more than 5 years. In the state courts, defendants with publicly financed attorneys received sentences that averaged about 2.5 years, while those with privately retained counsel received sentences that averaged about 3 years.

Nearly 70 percent of state prison inmates had attorneys appointed by the court. However, among minorities the percentage was higher: 77 percent of black inmates and 73 percent of Hispanic inmates. Among federal prison inmates, 65 percent of blacks, 57 percent of whites, and 56 percent of Hispanics had publicly financed attorneys.

THE JUDGE

For most people, black-robed judges are the embodiment of justice, and although they are generally associated with trials, judges actually have a variety of responsibilities in the criminal justice process.[23] Among their nontrial duties are determining probable cause, signing warrants, informing suspects of their rights, setting and revoking bail, arraigning defendants, and accepting guilty pleas. Judges spend much of the workday in their chambers (offices), negotiating procedures and dispositions with prosecutors and defense attorneys. The principal responsibility of judges in all their duties is to ensure that suspects and defendants are treated fairly and in accordance with due process of law.

Furthermore, in jurisdictions without professional court administrators, judges are responsible for the management of their own courtrooms and staff. Judges in some jurisdictions are also responsible for the entire courthouse and its personnel, with the added duties of supervising building maintenance, budgeting, and labor relations.

In jury trials, judges are responsible for allowing the jury a fair chance to reach a verdict on the evidence presented. Judges must ensure that their behavior does not improperly affect the outcome of the case. Before juries retire to deliberate and reach a verdict, judges instruct them on the relevant law. This involves interpreting legal precedents and applying them to the unique circumstances of the case. Those jury instructions are reviewable by an appellate court.

Characteristics of Judges In the United States, judges are overwhelmingly white and male. They generally come from upper-middle-class backgrounds, are Protestant, are better educated than most citizens, and average over 50 years of age. A majority of them were in private legal practice before becoming judges. Most were born in the communities in which they preside and attended college and law school in that state.

Selection of Judges States vary in the ways they select judges. The two most common selection methods are election and merit selection. Other, less common, ways of selecting judges are gubernatorial appointment and legislative election.

Like prosecutors, many state judges are elected to their positions in either partisan (with political party designation) or nonpartisan elections. This selection process exposes judges, like prosecutors, to potential charges of political influence. It may also discourage some of the best lawyers from becoming judges. Successful lawyers with lucrative practices may not want to interrupt

FYI Judicial History

According to the Bible, the idea of judges was first suggested to Moses by his father-in-law, Jethro. Following their exodus from Egypt, the Hebrews, having been slaves, had no formal government. Because Moses was the only one among them with evident authority, he served as arbiter of domestic controversies—a time-consuming and exhausting job. Jethro recognized the problem with this arrangement and suggested to Moses that he create a kind of theocracy. Moses would be the supreme judge and would represent the people before God. He would also teach the people laws governing everyday behavior. The actual administration of the laws, which came from God through Moses, was to be handled "by able men, . . . such as fear God, men who are trustworthy and who hate a bribe." These "judges" were to be established in a hierarchical order, so that the highest would be rulers over thousands of people; beneath them would be, successively, rulers of hundreds, fifties, and tens.

Source: Elisha P. Douglass, "Judges were suggested by Jethro," *The Anniston* (Alabama) *Star,* June 9, 1983.

Judges spend much of their workday in their chambers (offices). *How does this differ from what the public generally believes about judges?*

their careers to take the chance of becoming a judge, only to lose the position in the next election. Besides, successful lawyers generally earn much more money than judges.

In an attempt to reduce the appearance of possible political influence, several states have adopted merit selection, sometimes referred to as the "Missouri Plan," as their method of selecting judges. First used in Missouri in 1940, merit selection is a process in which the governor appoints judges from a list of qualified lawyers compiled by a nonpartisan nominating commission composed of both lawyers and other citizens. After serving a short term on the bench, usually 1 year, the appointed judges face the voters in an uncontested election. Voters are instructed to vote yes or no on whether the judge should be retained in office. If a majority vote yes, the judge remains in office for a full term (usually 6 years; the range is 4 years to life). In Illinois, a judge must receive at least 60 percent of the votes. Toward the end of the term, the judge must face the voters again in the same kind of election. The merit plan does not entirely eliminate political influence from the selection process, but it seems to have less potential for influence than the direct popular election of judges.

- As of April 2002, states used the following methods for initially selecting their highest *appellate court judges:*
  Merit selection—24 states (and the District of Columbia)
  Nonpartisan election—12 states
  Partisan election—9 states
  Appointment by the governor—4 states
  Election by the legislature—1 state
  Judicial selection committee—1 state
- As of the same date, states used the following methods for initially selecting their *general-jurisdiction court judges:*
  Nonpartisan election—18 states
  Merit selection—18 states (and the District of Columbia)
  Partisan election—14 states
  Appointment by the governor—3 states

FYI: Judicial Elections

According to U.S. Supreme Court Justice John Paul Stevens, "electing judges is like allowing football fans to select their referees—an unwise practice." Stevens noted that "a campaign promise to 'be tough on crime' or to 'enforce the death penalty' is evidence of bias that should disqualify a candidate from sitting in criminal cases." He concluded that "making the retention of judicial office dependent on the popularity of the judge inevitably affects the decisional process in high-visibility cases, no matter how conscientious the judge may be."

SOURCE: Debbie Salamone and Gerald Shields, "Justice to ABA: Races Not Popularity Contests," *The Orlando Sentinel,* August 4, 1996, p. A-23.

Election by the legislature—1 state
In California, local voters can choose either nonpartisan elections or gubernatorial appointment of general-jurisdiction court judges. In Kansas, in 17 of 31 districts, merit selection is used; the remaining 14 employ partisan elections.[24]

Qualifications and Training Although in most jurisdictions lower-court judges are not required to be lawyers or to possess any special educational or professional training, nearly all states require judges who sit on the benches of appellate courts and trial courts of general jurisdiction to be licensed attorneys and members of the state bar association. However, being a lawyer is not the same as being a judge. Many judges come to the bench without any practical experience with criminal law or procedure. Consequently, many states now require new appellate court and trial court judges to attend state-sponsored judicial training seminars. In addition, more than 1,500 judges a year take 1- to 4-week summer courses offered by the National Judicial College, founded in 1963 and located at the University of Nevada, Reno. Despite those efforts, most judges still learn the intricacies of their profession "on the job."

THINKING CRITICALLY

1. Do you think prosecutors have too much power? Why or why not?
2. Of the different types of attorneys a defendant might have, which one do you think will do the best job of defending the accused? Why?

Pretrial Stages

As described in Chapter 2, probably fewer than one-half of the crimes committed each year are reported to the police and, of those, only a fraction are officially recorded. Of the crimes that are recorded by the police, only about 20 percent are "cleared by arrest." Still, an arrest by no means guarantees prosecution and conviction. As a result of initial prosecutorial screening, for example, about 25 percent of all arrests are rejected, diverted, or referred to other jurisdictions. Another 20 percent or so of all people arrested are released later for various reasons during one of the pretrial stages. Thus a powerful "funneling" or screening process in the administration of justice eliminates about one-half of all persons arrested. Figures 8.4 and 8.5 illustrate this funneling or screening process.

FIGURE 8.4 Funneling Effect

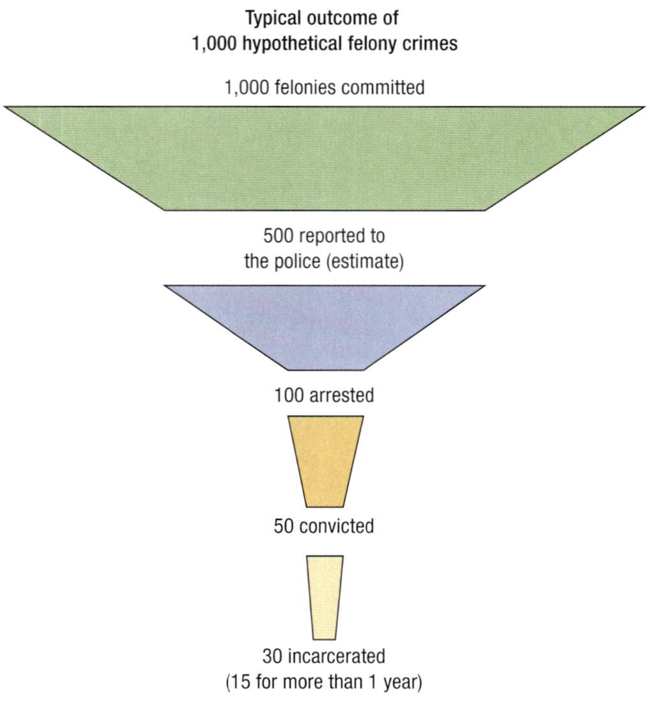

The pretrial stages do not have the same names or order in every jurisdiction. So what follows should be considered only a general overview. States are required to provide only a prompt, neutral review of the evidence to determine whether there is probable cause that the suspect/defendant committed the crime or crimes with which he or she is charged. *Probable cause,* which was described in more detail in Chapter 4, is an abstract term that basically means that a law enforcement officer or a judge has trustworthy evidence that would make a reasonable person believe that, more likely than not, the proposed action, such as an arrest, is justified. Figure 1.2 in Chapter 1 provides a simplified view of the case flow through the criminal justice process, highlighting pretrial stages.[25] We will describe the pretrial stages typical of many jurisdictions following a brief consideration of caseflow management.

FIGURE 8.5 Typical Outcome of 100 Hypothetical Arrests Brought by the Police for Prosecution

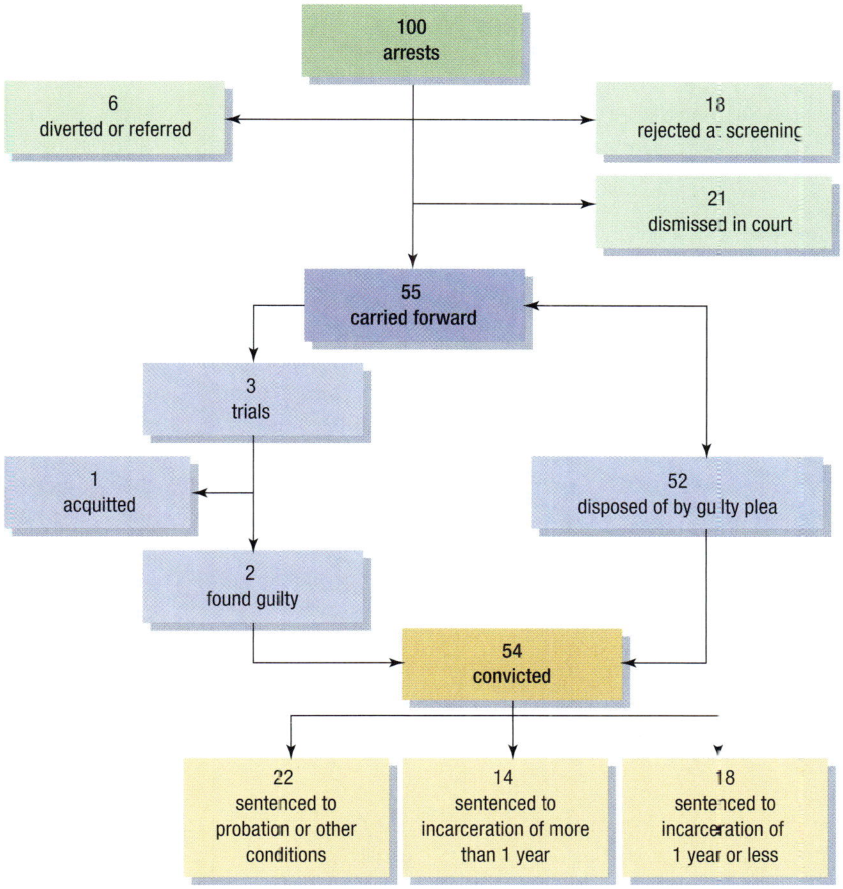

SOURCE: U.S. Department of Justice, Bureau of Justice Statistics, *The Prosecution of Felony Arrests, 1988* (Washington, DC: GPO, 1992), p. 3.

CASEFLOW MANAGEMENT

Increasingly large caseloads in the state and federal courts are requiring new management skills that enable the courts to process a huge volume of civil and criminal cases as efficiently as possible. In a recent book on the subject, caseflow management was called "the conceptual heart of judicial administration in the new millennium."[26] Today's court administrators (see the nearby Careers in Criminal Justice box) are being influenced by basic business principles. Among the subjects being learned about managing jury trials, for example, are "How to Relieve Juror Boredom," "Routine Use of Anonymous Juries," "Juror Questions to Witnesses," and "Post-verdict Debriefings with the Trial Judge."[27] There is even *A Manual for Managing Notorious Cases.*[28]

FROM ARREST THROUGH INITIAL APPEARANCE

Soon after most suspects are arrested, they are taken to the police station to be "booked." **Booking** is the process in which suspects' names, the charges for which they were arrested, and perhaps their fingerprints or photographs are entered on the police blotter. Following booking, a prosecutor is asked to review the facts of the case and, considering the available evidence, to decide whether a suspect should be charged with a crime or crimes (sometimes

booking The process in which suspects' names, the charges for which they were arrested, and perhaps their fingerprints or photographs are entered on the police blotter.

prosecutors review a case prior to the arrest). As a result of the review, the prosecutor may tell the police that they do not have a case or that the case is weak, requiring further investigation and additional evidence.

However, if the prosecutor decides that a suspect is "chargeable," the prosecutor prepares a charging document. The crime or crimes with which the suspect is charged may or may not be the same crime or crimes for which the suspect was originally arrested.

There are three primary kinds of charging documents: (1) a complaint, (2) an information, and (3) a grand jury indictment. If the offense is either a misdemeanor or an ordinance violation, then the prosecutor in many jurisdictions prepares a complaint. A **complaint** is a charge that an offense has been committed by a person or persons named or described. Complaints must be supported by the oath or affirmation of either the arresting officer or the victim. If the offense is a felony, an information is used in those states that do not rely on a grand jury indictment. An **information** outlines the formal charge or charges, the law or laws that have been violated, and the evidence to support the charge or charges. A **grand jury indictment,** on the other hand, is a written accusation by a grand jury charging that one or more persons have committed a crime. Informations and grand juries are described later in this section.

complaint A charging document specifying that an offense has been committed by a person or persons named or described; usually used for misdemeanors and ordinance violations.

information A document that outlines the formal charge or charges, the law or laws that have been violated, and the evidence to support the charge or charges.

grand jury indictment A written accusation by a grand jury charging that one or more persons have committed a crime.

arrest warrant A written order directing law enforcement officers to arrest a person. The charge or charges against a suspect are specified on the warrant.

On rare occasions, the police obtain an arrest warrant from a lower-court judge prior to making an arrest. An **arrest warrant** is a written order directing law enforcement officers to arrest a person. The charge or charges against a suspect are specified on the warrant. An example of an arrest warrant is provided in Chapter 4, Figure 4.2. Police officers more frequently make an arrest and then apply for an arrest warrant. Some jurisdictions have created joint police-prosecution teams so that decisions about arrest and chargeability can be coordinated and can be made early on. If no charges are filed, the suspect must be released.

After the charge or charges have been filed, suspects, who are now *defendants,* are brought before a lower-court judge for an initial appearance, where they are given formal notice of the charges against them and advised of their constitutional rights (for example, the right to counsel). For misdemeanors or ordinance violations, a summary trial may be held. About 75 percent of misdemeanants and ordinance violators plead guilty at the initial appearance and are sentenced on the spot. For felonies, a hearing is held to determine whether the suspect should be released or whether there is probable cause to hold the suspect for a preliminary hearing. If the suspect is to be held for a preliminary hearing, bail may be set if the judge believes release on bail is appropriate.

One of the critical questions about the initial appearance is how long suspects may be held in jail before being brought before a judge. In some countries the answer to the question is "indefinitely," but in the United States there is a limit so that innocent persons are not left in jail too long. If suspects are freed after having posted station-house bail (based on a bail fee schedule for minor offenses posted at the police station), then the initial appearance may be several days after the arrest. However, if suspects remain in custody (the usual scenario), they must be brought for an initial appearance "without unnecessary delay." In 1975, in *Gerstein* v. *Pugh,* the Supreme Court held that a "prompt" judicial hearing is required in a warrantless arrest to determine whether the officer had probable cause to make the arrest. The vast majority of arrests are warrantless. If suspects are not brought before a judge promptly, then they are to be released. The one exception to this requirement is suspects arrested on a Friday night and not brought before a judge until Monday morning.

FYI: Bail

The granting of bail and pretrial release to criminal suspects was common practice in England by the twelfth century. It was officially recognized and legally regulated by the Statute of Westminster in 1275.

SOURCE: No author, "Bail: An Ancient Practice Reexamined," *Yale Law Journal* 70 (1961), pp. 966–77.

A problem with the Supreme Court's promptness requirement is that the Court did not define *prompt.* The norm in most jurisdictions was between 24 and 72 hours. Even after the ruling, however, some jurisdictions held suspects much longer than that. For example, in 1975, a district court judge in

Birmingham, Alabama, ruled that because of abusive holding practices in that city, suspects arrested on a felony charge could not be held longer than 24 hours. In 1984, the same judge set a new limit of 8 hours for holding suspects, because his previous order had been ignored. The judge added, however, that in certain cases a limited time extension could be obtained. In 1991, in *County of Riverside* v. *McLaughlin,* the Supreme Court finally clarified the situation by ruling that anyone arrested without a warrant may be held no longer than 48 hours before a judge decides whether the arrest was justified.

BAIL AND OTHER METHODS OF PRETRIAL RELEASE

A **bail bond** or **bail** is usually a monetary guarantee deposited with the court that is supposed to ensure that the suspect or defendant will appear at a later stage in the criminal justice process. In other words, it allows suspects or defendants to remain free while awaiting the next stage in the adjudication process. It is *not* a fine or a penalty; it is only an incentive to appear. Opportunities for bail follow arrest, initial appearance, preliminary hearing, arraignment, and conviction.

bail bond/bail Usually a monetary guarantee deposited with the court that is supposed to ensure that the suspect or defendant will appear at a later stage in the criminal justice process.

CJ ONLINE

Bail Agents

You can learn more about how bail agents work by going to the website of The Professional Bail Agents of the United States at **www.pbus.com.** Once at the site, review the code of ethics for bail agents. *What does the code of ethics tell you about the different responsibilities of a bail agent?*

Although bail-setting practices vary widely by jurisdiction, the amount of bail, assuming that bail is granted, generally depends on the likelihood that the suspect or defendant will appear in court as required. If the suspect or defendant has strong ties to the community—for example, a house, a family, or a job—then the amount of bail will be relatively low (depending on the seriousness of the offense and other factors). However, if the suspect or defendant has few or no ties to the community, the amount of bail will be relatively high, or the judge may refuse to grant bail.

Next to likelihood of appearance, the most important factor in a judge's determination of the amount of bail—and, perhaps, whether bail is granted at all—is the seriousness of the crime. Generally, the more serious the crime, the higher the bail amount. A third influence on the amount of bail is prior criminal record. A prior criminal record usually increases the amount of bail. Jail conditions are a fourth influencing factor—at least on whether bail is set. If the jail is overcrowded, as are many of the jails in the United States, judges are more likely to grant bail, particularly in borderline cases.

In rare cases, when a judge believes that a suspect or defendant would pose a threat to the community if released, the judge can refuse to set bail. Holding suspects or defendants in jail without giving them an opportunity to post bail, because of the threat they pose to society, is called **preventive detention.** Preventive detention is used most often in cases involving violent crimes, drug crimes, and immigration offenses. However, in *U.S.* v. *Salerno* (1987), the Supreme Court made clear that before a judge can legally deny bail for reasons of preventive detention, a suspect or defendant must have the opportunity for a hearing on the decision. At the hearing, the individual circumstances of the suspect or defendant (such as community ties, convictions, and past dangerous tendencies) must be considered. About 60 percent of all states and the federal jurisdiction have enacted laws that provide for some form of preventive detention, although the laws, at least at the state level, are rarely implemented. The reason is that they are unnecessary. Judges have traditionally imposed high bail amounts on dangerous suspects or defendants. Preventive detention has been employed more frequently at the federal level.

preventive detention Holding suspects or defendants in jail without giving them an opportunity to post bail, because of the threat they pose to society.

Myth	Fact
Preventive detention will reduce violent crime.	Preventive detention is not new and has always been used by judges in the United States, even though it was not referred to by that name. Judges simply set bail at a level beyond the financial means of a person suspected of violent crime.

For suspects or defendants who cannot afford to post bail, professional bonds people, who are private

Without the cooperation of the bail bond industry, jail populations would be unmanageable. *Is that reason enough to allow the bail bond industry to exist?*

entrepreneurs, are available to post it for them for a nonrefundable fee. The fee is typically 10 percent of the required amount. Thus, a bonds person would collect $500 for posting a $5,000 bond. If a suspect or a defendant is considered a greater than average risk, then the bonds person can require collateral—something of value like money or property—in addition to the fee.

Bail bonds people are under no obligation to post a surety bond if they believe that a suspect or a defendant is a bad risk. If bonds people believe that a client might flee and not appear as required, they have the right to revoke the bond without refunding the fee. Bail bonds people or their agents (modern-day bounty hunters known as "skip tracers") are also allowed, without a warrant, to track down clients who fail to appear and to return them forcibly, if necessary, to the jurisdiction from which they fled. If the client crosses state lines, the bonds person does not have to seek extradition, as would a law enforcement official, to bring the client back. Clients sign extradition waivers as a condition of receiving bail.

In practice, most bail bonds people assume little risk. Many of them use part of their fee (generally 30 percent) to secure a surety bond from a major insurance company, which then assumes financial liability if the bail is forfeited. However, even this practice is unnecessary in many jurisdictions because the courts do not collect forfeited bonds. Judges are able to use their discretion to simply vacate outstanding bonds and, by doing so, relieve the bail bonds person or the insurance company of any financial obligation. Judges vacate bonds because they realize that without the cooperation of bail bonds people, the courts would be faced with an unmanageably large jail population and prohibitively high pretrial detention costs. If the bond is not vacated, the bonds person will generally stop looking for the fugitive after 2 years because, by then, there is little chance that the bonds person will get his or her money back.[29]

Suspects or defendants who post their own bail ("full cash bond," 100 percent of the amount required), or have family members or friends do it for them, get it all back after they appear. Sometimes the court will accept property instead of cash. If the suspect or defendant does not appear, the bail is forfeited and the judge issues a **bench warrant** or ***capias*** authorizing the suspect's or defendant's arrest. Orange County (Orlando), Florida, for example, has netted an average of $1.4 million a year from bonds that were forfeited. It has been estimated that about 18 percent of Orange County's felony defendants in 1996 did not appear after they were released. A year later, more than 10 percent of the absconders were still fugitives. However, not all bail skippers flee. Some are just irresponsible and do not come to court until someone drags them in. Others change their address so often they do not receive the notices to appear. Still others do not appear because they are in jail or prison in other counties or states.[30] Once arrested, the absconder must be brought before the judge who issued the warrant and cannot be released on bail again. Failure to appear also constitutes a new offense, "bond jumping," that carries criminal penalties.

bench warrant or ***capias*** A document that authorizes a suspect's or defendant's arrest for not appearing in court as required.

FYI
Release on Bail

About 85 percent of all suspects or defendants are released prior to the final disposition of their cases but, in some jurisdictions, as many as 90 percent of them are held in jail because they are unable to afford bail.

Courts in Illinois, Kentucky, and Pennsylvania, as well as the federal courts, allow defendants to post 10 percent of the required bond (*deposit bond*) directly with the court, thereby circumventing the need for bail bonds people. When a defendant makes all required court appearances, 90 percent of the amount posted is refunded (the remaining 10 percent covers administrative costs). Defendants who fail to appear are still liable for the entire bail amount.

Myth	Fact
The most dangerous defendants released on bail are the ones least likely to appear as required.	Defendants accused of minor offenses and released on bail have the highest rates of failure to appear.

As noted in Chapter 4, the Eighth Amendment to the Constitution does not require that bail be granted to all suspects or defendants. It requires only that the amount of bail, when granted, not be excessive. What constitutes excessive bail is determined by several factors, including the nature and circumstances of the offense, the weight of evidence against the suspect/defendant, the character of the suspect/defendant, and the ability of the suspect/defendant to provide bail.

The bail system has been criticized for unfairly discriminating against the poor, who are the least likely to have the assets for their own bail and are least able to pay the fee to a bail bonds person. In most jurisdictions, defendants held in jail because they are unable to post bail (about one-half of the jail population nationwide) are mixed with the rest of the jail population, that is, convicted offenders. They are also treated in the same way as the rest of the jail population. One of the tragedies of this practice is the occasional brutalization (for example, rape) of the jailed indigent defendant whose case is later dismissed for lack of evidence or who is found not guilty at trial. Although brutalization of any prisoner is horrible and reprehensible, it is particularly so when the prisoner is an innocent person.

Jailed indigent defendants are also likely to lose their jobs and have their personal lives disrupted in other ways as a result of their detention. Studies consistently show that jailed defendants, who are frequently brought into court in jail clothes and handcuffs, are more likely to be indicted and convicted and are sentenced more severely than defendants who have been released pending the next stage in the process. However, it is not clear whether those disparities are the result of pretrial detention or of the selection process in which suspects or defendants charged with more serious crimes and with prior criminal records are more likely to be denied bail.

When the crime is minor and suspects or defendants have ties to the community, they are generally released on their own recognizance. **Release on own recognizance (ROR)** is simply a release secured by a suspect's written promise to appear in court. Another nonfinancial means of release, more restrictive than ROR, is **conditional release.** This form of release (sometimes called *supervised release*) usually requires that a suspect/defendant maintain contact with a pretrial release program or undergo regular drug monitoring or treatment. Some conditional release programs also require a third-party custody agreement (that is, a promise by a reputable person to monitor the person released). Another way that suspects or defendants are released without a financial requirement is by **unsecured bond.** Under this arrangement, bail is set, but no money is paid to the court. Suspects or defendants are liable for the full amount of bail if they do not appear as required.

release on own recognizance (ROR) A release secured by a suspect's written promise to appear in court.

conditional release A form of release that requires that a suspect/defendant maintain contact with a pretrial release program or undergo regular drug monitoring or treatment.

unsecured bond An arrangement in which bail is set but no money is paid to the court.

INFORMATION

If the decision is made to prosecute a defendant, in states that do not use grand juries, the prosecutor drafts a document called an *information.* The information outlines the formal charge or charges, the law or laws that have been violated, and the evidence to support the charge or charges. The information is generally filed with the court at the preliminary hearing or, if the preliminary hearing is waived, at the arraignment.

PRELIMINARY HEARING

The purpose of the **preliminary hearing,** used in about one-half of all states, is for a judge to determine whether there is probable cause to support the charge or charges imposed by the prosecutor. Preliminary hearings are used

preliminary hearing A pretrial stage used in about one-half of all states and only in felony cases. Its purpose is for a judge to determine whether there is probable cause to support the charge or charges imposed by the prosecutor.

only in felony cases, and defendants may waive the right to the hearing. A preliminary hearing is similar to a criminal trial in two ways but also differs from a criminal trial in two ways. It is similar in that defendants can be represented by legal counsel and can call witnesses on their behalf. It differs in that the judge must determine only that there is probable cause that the defendant committed the crime or crimes with which he or she is charged. At criminal trials, guilt must be determined "beyond a reasonable doubt." Also, at preliminary hearings, unlike criminal trials, defendants have no right to be heard by a jury.

If the judge determines that there is probable cause that a defendant committed the crime or crimes with which he or she is charged, then the defendant is bound over for possible indictment in states with grand juries or for arraignment on an information in states without grand juries. In grand jury states, even if the judge at the preliminary hearing rules that there is insufficient evidence to proceed, the case is not necessarily dropped. The prosecutor could take the case directly to the grand jury. If the case is not dropped for lack of evidence, then the judge may set bail again or may continue the previous bail to ensure that the defendant appears at the next stage in the process.

Although judges at preliminary hearings are supposed to examine the facts of the case before making a probable cause determination, in practice they seldom do. In big cities, judges do not generally have the time to inquire into the facts of a case. Consequently, at most preliminary hearings, judges simply assume that if a police officer made an arrest and a prosecutor charged the defendant with a crime or crimes, then there must be probable cause that the defendant, in fact, committed the crime or crimes. Few cases are dismissed for lack of probable cause at preliminary hearings.

FYI: Preliminary Hearings

In some jurisdictions, preliminary hearings are frequently waived by defendants. Perhaps the best example is the federal courts, where the majority of criminal cases begin with a grand jury indictment rather than with an arrest.

grand jury Generally a group of 12 to 23 citizens who meet in closed sessions to investigate charges coming from preliminary hearings or to engage in other responsibilities. A primary purpose of the grand jury is to determine whether there is probable cause to believe that the accused committed the crime or crimes.

indictment A document that outlines the charge or charges against a defendant.

subpoena A written order to testify issued by a court officer.

GRAND JURY

A **grand jury** is generally a group of 12 to 23 citizens who, for a specific period of time (generally 3 months), meet in closed sessions to investigate charges coming from preliminary hearings or to engage in other responsibilities. Thus a primary purpose of the grand jury is to determine whether there is probable cause to believe that the accused is guilty of the charge or charges brought by the prosecutor. Grand juries do not convene every day. Many federal grand juries meet only once a week, and some may meet only twice a month. State practice varies, but a state grand jury may meet only twice a month, or even only once a month. Sometimes a grand jury does not convene unless it is asked to do so by a prosecutor with cases to hear. Grand juries are involved in felony prosecutions in about half the states and in the federal system. The alternative to the grand jury is the filing of an information.

Before appearing before a grand jury, the prosecutor drafts an **indictment,** a document that outlines the charge or charges against a defendant. Because the grand jury has to determine only whether there is probable cause that a defendant committed the crime or crimes with which he or she is charged, only the prosecution's evidence and witnesses are heard. In most jurisdictions, neither the defendant nor the defendant's counsel has a right to be present during the proceedings. Furthermore, in grand jury proceedings, unlike criminal trials, prosecutors are allowed to present *hearsay* evidence (information learned from someone other than the witness who is testifying). They may also use illegally obtained evidence because the exclusionary rule does not apply to grand jury proceedings. Prosecutors can subpoena witnesses to testify. A **subpoena** is a written order to testify issued by a court officer. A witness who refuses to testify can be held in contempt and can be jailed until he or she provides the requested information. In practice, however, a witness jailed for contempt is generally held only as long as the grand jury is in session and no longer than 18 months in the federal jurisdiction.

FYI: Grand Jury Indictments

All but two states and the District of Columbia use grand juries to indict. Twenty-three states plus the District of Columbia require that indictments be used to charge certain crimes, generally serious crimes. Twenty-five states make the use of indictments optional. Connecticut and Pennsylvania have abolished the use of grand juries to return indictments, but they have retained them to investigate crimes and the conduct of public affairs. The most common civil matter they investigate is the operation and condition of local jails and other confinement facilities. In the federal system, a grand jury indictment is required in all felony prosecutions, unless the defendant waives that right.

SOURCE: "Federal Grand Jury" at www.udayton.edu/~grandjur/index.htm.

After hearing the prosecutor's evidence and witnesses, the grand jury makes its probable cause determination and, usually on a majority vote, either indicts (issues a *true bill*) or fails to indict (issues *no bill*). If the grand jury fails to indict, then in most jurisdictions, the prosecution must be dropped. However, in some jurisdictions, the case can be brought before another grand jury.

In practice, the grand jury system is criticized for merely providing a rubber stamp for whatever the prosecutor wants to do. In other words, in cases where the prosecutor wants an indictment, the grand jury is likely to indict. Likewise, in cases where the prosecutor does not want to indict, the grand jury tends to fail to indict. The reason that prosecutors are so successful with grand juries is that they manage the entire proceedings (remember, only the prosecution's evidence and witnesses are heard). So it should not be surprising that suspects waive the right to a grand jury hearing in about 80 percent of cases. Defendants may also waive the right to a grand jury hearing to speed up their trial date.

You might be wondering why prosecutors would want a grand jury to fail to indict after they have gone to the trouble of bringing a case to the grand jury in the first place. The reason is political. To avoid losing marginal cases or looking cowardly by dropping charges, prosecutors can bring a case to the grand jury, have the grand jury fail to indict, and then blame the grand jury for its failure. The strategy deflects criticism from the prosecutor to the anonymous members of the grand jury. Sometimes prosecutors delay preliminary hearings to await a grand jury action to avoid disclosing evidence in open court that might help defense attorneys at trial. Because of the way the grand jury is used today, some critics of the system suggest that it ought to be abolished.

ARRAIGNMENT

The primary purpose of an **arraignment** is to hear the formal information or indictment and to allow the defendant to enter a plea. The two most common pleas are "guilty" and "not guilty." "Not guilty" is the most common plea at arraignments. However, some states and the federal courts allow defendants to plead *nolo contendere* to the charges against them. ***Nolo contendere*** is Latin for "no contest." When defendants plead *"nolo,"* they do not admit guilt but are willing to accept punishment anyway. The *nolo* plea is used for strategic purposes. If a defendant does not admit guilt in a criminal trial, admission of guilt cannot be the basis for a subsequent civil lawsuit. If there is a subsequent civil lawsuit, the lack of an admission of guilt in a criminal trial may allow the defendant to avoid a penalty of treble, or triple, damages. Furthermore, in some states, defendants can stand mute or can plead "not guilty by reason of insanity." Standing mute at arraignment is interpreted as pleading "not guilty." In states that do not accept a plea of "not guilty by reason of insanity," defendants plead "not guilty" and assume the burden of proving insanity at trial.

arraignment A pretrial stage; its primary purpose is to hear the formal information or indictment and to allow the defendant to enter a plea.

nolo contendere Latin for "no contest." When defendants plead *nolo*, they do not admit guilt but are willing to accept punishment.

FYI: An Alford Plea

In an Alford plea, a defendant pleads guilty but asserts factual innocence. An Alford plea is used by a defendant who says that he or she is innocent but nevertheless will plead guilty to a lesser charge to avoid the possibility of a death sentence.

If a defendant pleads guilty, the judge must determine whether the plea was made voluntarily and whether the defendant is fully aware of the consequences of his or her action. If the judge doubts either of those conditions, then the judge can refuse to accept the guilty plea and can enter in the record a plea of "not guilty" for the defendant.

At arraignment, the judge also determines whether a defendant is competent to stand trial. Defendants can seek a delay before trial to consult further with their attorneys. A defendant who does not already have an attorney can ask for one to be appointed. Finally, defendants sometimes attempt to have their cases dismissed at arraignment. For example, they may assert that the state lacks sufficient evidence or that improper arrest procedures were used.

THINKING CRITICALLY

Do you agree with the criticism that the poor are unfairly discriminated against because they are the least able to pay their own bail and the least able to pay the fee to a bail bonds person? Why or why not?

Plea Bargaining

As noted earlier in this chapter, justice in the United States is dispensed mostly through plea bargaining.[31] About 90 percent of all convictions in felony cases are the result of guilty pleas; criminal trials are relatively rare. We already saw in Figure 8.5 the typical outcome of 100 felony arrests and the prevalence of plea bargaining.

There are three basic types of plea bargains. First, the defendant may be allowed to plead guilty to a lesser offense. For example, a defendant may be allowed to plead guilty to manslaughter rather than to first-degree murder. Second, at the request of the prosecutor, a defendant who pleads guilty may receive a lighter sentence than would typically be given for the crime. Note, however, that the prosecutor can only recommend the sentence; the judge does not have to grant it. Third, a defendant may plead guilty to one charge in return for the prosecutor's promise to drop other charges that could be brought.

Myth

All guilty pleas are the result of plea bargaining.

Fact

Although the vast majority of guilty pleas probably are a product of plea bargaining—we do not know for sure—some defendants simply plead guilty to the original charges and do not bargain.

The bargain a prosecutor will strike generally depends on three factors. The most important factor is the seriousness of the offense. Generally, the more serious the crime, the more difficult it is to win concessions from the prosecutor. A second factor is the defendant's criminal record. Defendants with criminal records usually receive fewer concessions from prosecutors. The final factor is the strength of the prosecutor's case. The stronger the case, the stronger is the position of the prosecutor in plea negotiations.

Surprisingly, there is neither a constitutional basis nor a statutory basis for plea bargaining. It is a custom that developed because of the mutual interests it serves. The custom received formal recognition from the Supreme Court in 1970 in the case of *Brady* v. *United States*. In that case, the Court upheld the use of plea bargaining because of the "mutuality of advantage" it provided the defendant and the state. In two later cases, the Court provided safeguards for the bargaining process. In the 1971 case of *Santobello* v. *New York*, the Court held that the "deal" offered by a prosecutor in a plea negotiation must be kept. In 1976, in the case of *Henderson* v. *Morgan*, the Court held that to be valid, a guilty plea must be based on full knowledge of its implications and must be made voluntarily. However, prosecutors are under no obligation to plea-bargain. Once defendants plead guilty and are sentenced, they are almost always stuck with the bargain, even if they have a change of heart. Nevertheless, in most jurisdictions, defendants are allowed to withdraw their guilty pleas before sentencing.

FYI: Plea Bargaining

Plea bargaining became a common practice in state courts shortly after the Civil War. The practice was instituted at the federal level during Prohibition, in the 1930s, as a result of the tremendous number of liquor law violations.

SOURCES: Albert W. Alschuler, "Plea Bargaining and Its History," *Law and Society Review* 13 (1979), pp. 211–45; John F. Padgett, "Plea Bargaining and Prohibition in the Federal Courts, 1908–1934," *Law and Society Review* 24 (1990), pp. 413–50.

As just noted, the reason justice in the United States is administered primarily through plea bargaining is that the process seemingly serves the interests of all the court participants by, among other things, reducing uncertainty. Uncertainty is a characteristic of all criminal trials because neither the duration of the trial, which may be a matter of minutes or of months, nor the outcome of the trial can ever be predicted with any degree of accuracy. Plea bargaining eliminates those two areas of uncertainty by eliminating the need for a trial.

Plea bargaining also serves the interests of the individual participants in the administration of justice. Prosecutors, for example, are guaranteed high conviction rates. For prosecutors and, apparently, the general public, a conviction is a conviction, whether it is obtained through plea bargaining or as the result of a trial. A prosecutor's conviction rate is one of the principal indicators of job performance, and job performance certainly helps determine whether the prosecutor will fulfill his or her aspirations for higher political office.

Plea bargaining also serves the interests of judges by reducing their court caseloads, allowing more time to be spent on more difficult cases. In addition, if a large proportion of the approximately 90 percent of felony cases that are handled each year by plea bargaining were to go to trial instead, the administration of justice in the United States would be even slower than it already is.

Federal judges and the judges in seven states are legally prohibited from participating in plea negotiations. In other states, their role in the process is limited by law.

Plea bargaining serves the interests of criminal defense attorneys by allowing them to spend less time on each case. It also allows them to avoid trials. Trials are relatively expensive events. Because most criminal defendants are poor, they are usually unable to pay a large legal fee. Thus, when criminal defense attorneys go to trial, they are frequently unable to recoup all of their expenses. Plea bargaining provides many criminal defense attorneys with the more profitable option of charging smaller fees for lesser services and handling a larger volume of cases.

Myth / Fact

Myth	Fact
Abolishing plea bargaining would reduce the level of serious crime.	Despite the administrative nightmare it would cause, the abolition of plea bargaining would probably only shift discretion to another area. It would be unlikely to have any effect on crime.

FYI: Three Strikes Law

Although habitual-offender statutes have existed in many jurisdictions for decades, the first state to enact a "three strikes and you're out" law was Washington, in 1993. The Washington law, called the Persistent Offender Accountability Act, allows three-time felons to be imprisoned for life without parole. In August 1996, the Washington Supreme Court upheld the law as constitutional. Currently, 26 states and the federal government have three-strike laws on their books.

SOURCE: "Washington Court Deems '3 Strikes' Constitutional," *The Orlando Sentinel*, August 9, 1996, p. A-12; William Hughes, "Three Strikes Laws: Only the Poor Need Apply," *CounterPunch*, November 12, 2002, at www.counterpunch.org/hughes1112.html.

Even most criminal defendants are served by plea bargaining. A guilty plea generally results in either no prison sentence or a lesser prison sentence than the defendant might receive if found guilty at trial. Plea bargaining also often allows defendants to escape conviction of socially stigmatizing crimes, such as child abuse. By "copping" a plea to assault rather than to statutory rape, for example, a defendant can avoid the embarrassing publicity of a trial and the wrath of fellow inmates or of society in general.

Two types of criminal defendants are not served by the practice of plea bargaining. The first are innocent, indigent, highly visible defendants who fear being found guilty of crimes they did not commit and receiving harsh sentences. Such defendants are sometimes pressured by unscrupulous defense attorneys into waiving their constitutional right to trial.

The second type is the habitual offender. In this context, a habitual offender is a person who has been convicted under a state's habitual-offender statute (sometimes called a "three strikes and you're out" law). Most such statutes provide that upon conviction of a third felony, a defendant must receive life imprisonment. Although habitual-offender statutes would seem to imprison offenders for life, they actually are used mostly as bargaining chips by prosecutors in plea negotiations and not as they were intended.

A problem with those statutes is illustrated by the Supreme Court case of *Bordenkircher* v. *Hayes* (1978). The defendant, who had previously been convicted of two minor felonies, was arrested and charged with forging an $88 check. The prosecutor in the case told the defendant that if he did not plead guilty to the charge and accept a 5-year prison sentence, which on its face seemed very harsh, then the prosecutor would invoke the state's habitual-offender statute. The statute required the judge to impose a sentence of life imprisonment if the defendant were found guilty at trial. The defendant elected to play "you bet your life" and turned down the prosecutor's plea offer. At trial, the defendant was found guilty of forging the check and was sentenced to life imprisonment. Clearly, the defendant in this case was not served by plea bargaining or, perhaps, was not served by refusing the prosecutor's offer. In either case, with the possible exception of habitual offenders and innocent people, plea bargaining serves the interests of all the actors in the administration of justice. It does so by allowing cases to be disposed of predictably, quickly, and with little of the adversarial conflict associated with criminal trials.

THINKING CRITICALLY

1. Do you think that the plea-bargaining process is beneficial? Why or why not?
2. Why is murder the crime least likely by far to be resolved through a guilty plea (see Table 8.1)?
3. How could the plea-bargaining process be improved?

The Criminal Trial

One of the distinctive features of criminal justice in the United States is trial by a jury of one's peers.[32] The principal purpose of jury trials—and of criminal trials without juries—is to discover the truth of whether defendants are guilty or innocent of the crimes with which they are charged. The process by which truth is sought is an adversarial one regulated by very specific procedures and rules. The adversaries in a criminal trial are the state (represented by the prosecutor) and the defendant (usually represented by defense counsel). The burden of proof is on the prosecution to show, beyond a reasonable doubt, that the defendant is guilty. The goal of defense counsel is to discredit the prosecution's case and to create reasonable doubt about the defendant's guilt. It is the responsibility of the jury (in jury trials) or the judge (in trials without juries) to determine and assign guilt.

Myth	Fact
Criminal justice in the United States is dispensed primarily through jury trials.	Jury trials are relatively rare. Approximately 90 percent of all criminal cases are resolved through guilty pleas. Only about 10 percent are decided by bench or jury trials.

Although all criminal defendants have a constitutional right to a jury trial (when imprisonment for 6 months or more is a possible outcome), only about 5 percent of all criminal cases are disposed of in this way. Approximately 90 percent of cases are resolved through a guilty plea, and the remaining cases are decided by a judge in a **bench trial** (without a jury). In most jurisdictions, defendants may choose whether they want to exercise their right to a jury trial or whether they prefer a bench trial. Table 8.1 shows the type of conviction of felony defendants in 2000, by type of offense. The principal reason that so few criminal cases are decided by criminal trials is undoubtedly the advantages associated with plea bargaining.

bench trial A trial before a judge without a jury.

THE JURY

Trial by a jury of one's peers is an exalted American tradition.[33] Its principal purposes are:

1. To protect citizens against arbitrary law enforcement.
2. To prevent government oppression.
3. To protect citizens from overzealous or corrupt prosecutors and from eccentric or biased judges.

But jury trials in the United States are relatively rare. So on those rare occasions when defendants are tried by a jury, seldom is the jury composed of their peers. Until the mid-twentieth century, many states excluded women and people of color from jury service. Even today, class, gender, and racial biases enter into the jury selection process.

In many jurisdictions, jury pools are selected from voter registration lists. About 30 percent of eligible voters do not register; in some jurisdictions, the rate is as high as 60 percent. People not registered to vote are excluded from jury service. Studies show that the poor, the poorly educated, the young, and people of color are least likely to register to vote and, as a result, are least likely to be called for jury service. To remedy this problem, some jurisdictions now use multiple-source lists for obtaining jurors. In addition to voter registration lists, their sources include lists of licensed drivers, lists of utility users, and names listed in the telephone directory. Appellate courts have ruled that master jury lists must reflect an impartial and representative cross-section of the population. People of color and women cannot be excluded systematically from juries solely because of race, ethnicity, or gender. But this does not mean that people of color and women must be included on all juries, only that they cannot be denied the opportunity of being chosen for jury service.

FYI: Trial By Jury

Trial by a jury of one's peers originated in England as a way of limiting the power of the king. When the Magna Carta was signed in 1215, it contained the following provision: No freeman shall be seized or imprisoned, or stripped of his rights or possessions, or outlawed or exiled, or deprived of his standing in any other way, nor will we proceed with force against him, or send others to do so, except by the lawful judgment of his equals or by the law of the land.

SOURCE: www.wwlia.org/uk-magna.htm.

TABLE 8.1 Offenses of Felons Convicted in State Courts, by Type of Conviction, 2000

Most Serious Conviction Offense	Percent of Felons Convicted by— Jury Trial	Bench Trial	Guilty Plea
All Offenses[a]	3%	2%	95%
Violent Offenses	9	2	89
Murder[b]	38	4	58
Sexual assault[c]	10	2	88
Robbery	8	3	89
Aggravated assault	6	3	91
Other violent[d]	7	2	91
Property Offenses	2	1	97
Burglary	2	1	97
Larceny[e]	2	1	97
Fraud[f]	1	1	98
Drug Offenses	2	2	96
Possession	1	2	97
Trafficking	2	2	96
Weapons Offenses	3	4	93
Other Offenses[g]	2	1	97

[a]Data on conviction type were available for 558,871 cases.
[b]Includes nonnegligent manslaughter.
[c]Includes rape.
[d]Includes offenses such as negligent manslaughter and kidnapping.
[e]Includes motor vehicle theft.
[f]Includes forgery and embezzlement.
[g]Composed of nonviolent offenses such as receiving stolen property and vandalism.

Source: Matthew R. Durose and Patrick A. Langan, "Felony Sentences in State Courts, 2000" U.S. Department of Justice, *Bureau of Justice Statistics Bulletin* (Washington, DC: GPO, June 2003), p. 9, Table 10.

From the master list of all eligible jurors (sometimes called the *master wheel* or the *jury wheel*), a sufficient number of people are randomly chosen to make up the jury pool, or **venire.** Those chosen are summoned for service by the sheriff. However, not all those summoned will actually serve on the venire. Potential jurors must generally be U.S. citizens, residents of the locality of the trial, of a certain minimum age, and able to understand English. Convicted felons and insane persons are almost always excluded. Most jurisdictions also require that jurors be of "good character" and be "well-informed," which eliminates other potential jurors.

venire The pool from which jurors are selected.

In addition, members of other groups often escape jury service. Professionals such as doctors, lawyers, and teachers; some elected officials; military personnel on active duty; and law enforcement personnel frequently are not called for jury duty because their professional services are considered indispensable or because they are connected to the criminal justice process. Many jurisdictions allow citizens to be excused from jury service if it would cause them physical or economic difficulties. Compensation for jury service is minimal, currently averaging $15 a day nationwide. The most generous state in 2002 was West Virginia, which paid its jurors $40.00 a day. The federal government also paid $40.00 a day. Other states, as well as the federal government, raised their pay to a maximum of $50.00 a day after a certain number of days of service. Some states do not pay jurors for the first day or first 3 days of jury service.[34] Not all employers pay for time lost from work. Consequently, only about 15 percent of adult Americans have ever served on juries. The result is that juries are composed disproportionately of retired persons, the unemployed, and homemakers with grown children—those people least likely to be inconvenienced by the requirement of many states for jurors to serve for 30 days.

From the venire, as many as 30 people (in felony prosecutions that mandate 12 jurors) are randomly selected by the court clerk for the jury panel from which the actual trial jury is selected. To ensure a fair trial, potential trial jurors go through ***voir dire,*** a process in which persons who might be biased or unable to render a fair verdict are screened out. During *voir dire,* which means "to speak the truth," the defense, the prosecution, and the judge question jurors about their backgrounds and knowledge of the case and the defendant. If it appears that a juror might be biased or unable to render a fair verdict, the juror can be challenged "for cause" by either the defense or the prosecution. If the judge agrees, the juror is dismissed from jury service. In death penalty trials, for example, death penalty opponents can be excluded from juries for cause if they are opposed to the death penalty under any circumstances (*Lockhart* v. *McCree,* 1986). Generally, there is no limit to the number of jurors that can be eliminated for cause. In practice, however, few potential jurors are eliminated for cause, except in high-profile trials, such as the O.J. Simpson murder trial in 1995.

voir dire The process in which potential jurors who might be biased or unable to render a fair verdict are screened out.

Another way that either the defense or the prosecution can eliminate potential jurors from jury service is by the use of *peremptory challenges,* which allow either prosecutors or defense attorneys to excuse jurors without having to provide a reason. Peremptory challenges are frequently used to eliminate jurors whose characteristics place them in a group likely to be unfavorable to the case of either the prosecution or the defense. For example, in death penalty cases, prosecutors often use their peremptory challenges to eliminate people of color and women from the juries because, statistically, people of color and women are less likely to favor capital punishment. However, prosecutors must be careful in their use of peremptory challenges for such purposes because the Supreme Court has forbidden the use of peremptory challenges to exclude potential jurors solely on account of their race (*Batson* v. *Kentucky,* 1989) or gender (*J.E.B.* v. *Alabama,* 1994). The number of peremptory challenges is limited by statute. In most jurisdictions, the prosecution is allowed from 6 to 8 peremptory challenges and the defense from 8 to 10. *Voir dire* continues until the required number of jurors have been selected. The *voir dire* process may take an hour or two or, in rare cases, months.

FYI

SmartJURY

Software, called SmartJURY, has been developed that can evaluate the demographic profile and verbal and nonverbal clues given by potential jurors to calculate with precision whether they will acquit or convict a criminal defendant. The cost of the software is $995 a year.

SOURCE: Amie K. Streater, "High-Tech, Cheap Way Found to Pick a Jury," *The Orlando Sentinel,* January 5, 2003, p. B5.

Traditionally, a jury in a criminal trial, sometimes called a *petit jury* to distinguish it from a grand jury, consists of 12 citizens plus one or two alternates, who will replace any jurors unable to continue because of illness, accident, or personal emergency. Recently, however, primarily to reduce expenses, some states have gone to six-, seven-, and eight-member juries in noncapital criminal cases. The Supreme Court will not allow criminal trial juries with five or fewer members, and 12-member juries are still required in all states in capital (death penalty) cases.

Recently, attempts have been made to reduce the burden of jury service. In many jurisdictions, jurors can now call a number to find out whether they will be needed on a particular day during their term of service. Some jurisdictions have instituted "1 day/1 trial" jury systems, which require jurors to serve either for 1 day or for the duration of one trial. Once they have served, they are exempt from jury service for 1 or 2 years. Each year in the United States, approximately 2 million jurors serve in about 200,000 criminal and civil trials.

THE TRIAL PROCESS

Before a criminal trial formally begins, attorneys in about 10 percent of felony cases file pretrial motions. A motion is an application to a court, requesting a judge to order a particular action. Motions can also be made during and after a trial. Common pretrial motions are to obtain discovery of the prosecution's evidence and to have some of the prosecution's evidence suppressed (for example, to have a confession ruled inadmissible because of *Miranda* violations).

The following is a general description of the stages in a criminal trial.[35] Figure 8.6 shows that process and includes some pretrial stages as well (not all stages occur in every trial). After the jury has been sworn in (if the case is tried before a jury) and the court clerk has read the criminal complaint, the prosecution begins the trial with an opening statement, outlining its case. Next is the opening statement by the defense. However, the defense is not required to make an opening statement. In some jurisdictions, the defense is allowed to defer its opening statement until after the prosecution has presented its case. Opening statements are rarely made in bench trials.

The prosecution then submits its evidence and questions its witnesses. The prosecution must establish beyond a reasonable doubt each element of the crime. The elements of a crime vary by offense and jurisdiction. In other words, two jurisdictions (for example, two states) may have different elements for the same crime. The specific elements of each crime are provided in state and federal statutes. Some of the elements common to most crimes were described in Chapter 2 and include *actus reus, mens rea,* and concurrence.

If the defense believes that the prosecution has failed to make its case, then the defense may choose to *rest,* that is, not to defend against the charge or charges. At this point, the defense in most states is allowed to request a *directed verdict* or to make a motion for dismissal. If the judge agrees with the defense that the prosecution's evidence is insufficient for conviction, then the judge can either direct the jury to acquit the defendant or "take the case from the jury" and grant the motion for dismissal.

If the defense does not seek a dismissal or a dismissal is not granted, the defense follows the prosecution with its witnesses and any contrary evidence. Then the prosecution and the defense take turns offering rebuttals to the other side's evidence, cross-examining witnesses, and reexamining their own witnesses. Following the rebuttal period, the prosecution summarizes its case. The defense then summarizes its case and makes its closing statement. The closing statement by the prosecution ends the adversarial portion of the trial.

FYI: McVeigh's Jury Pool

The jury pool in Timothy McVeigh's trial for the Oklahoma City bombing favored the prosecution. Most members of the jury pool were white and well educated, had close ties to the military, and believed in God, family, and the justice system. All of them had vivid memories of the Oklahoma City bombing, and nearly every one of them said they could look McVeigh in the eye and sentence him to death. According to a former U.S. attorney for Colorado, Bob Miller, "As a prosecutor, I would feel pretty comfortable. And I wouldn't feel so comfortable if I was a defense attorney."

SOURCE: "McVeigh's Jury Pool: Educated, Patriotic," *The Orlando Sentinel,* April 20, 1997, p. A-5.

Attorneys from opposing sides in a trial sometimes confer with the judge. *Why does this happen and what do you think is discussed?*

FIGURE 8.6 Stages in a Criminal Trial

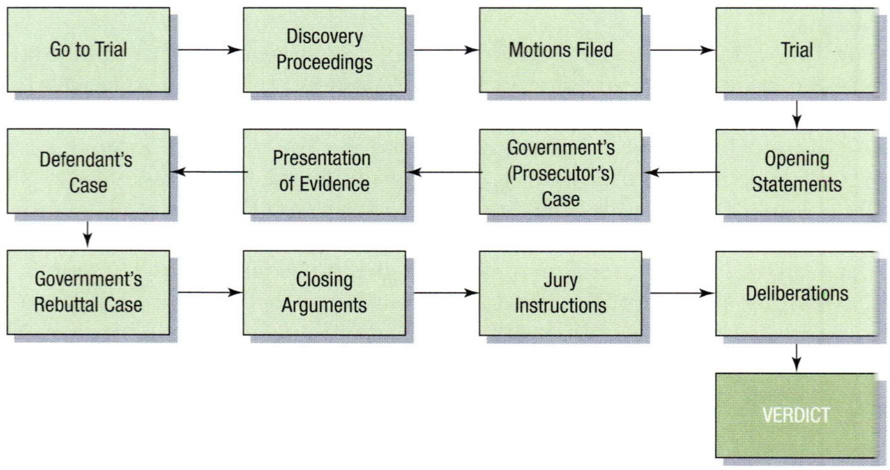

FYI: A Coin Toss

A Louisville, Kentucky, circuit court judge recently declared a mistrial when he learned from the jury foreman that a coin was flipped to decide whether the defendant was guilty of murder or manslaughter.

Source: "Judge Mad After Hearing Jurors Just Flipped a Coin," *The Orlando Sentinel*, April 26, 2000, p. A-10.

Normally, after the closing statement by the prosecution, the judge instructs, or *charges*, the jury concerning the principles of law the jurors are to utilize in determining guilt or innocence. The judge also explains to the jury the charges, the rules of evidence, and the possible verdicts. In some jurisdictions, the judge summarizes the evidence presented from notes taken during the trial. The jury then retires to deliberate until it reaches a verdict. In a room where it has complete privacy, the jury elects from its members a foreperson to preside over the subsequent deliberations. Jurors are not allowed to discuss the case with anyone other than another juror. In some cases, a jury is sequestered at night in a hotel or motel to prevent any chance of outside influence.

To find a defendant guilty as charged, the jury must be convinced "beyond a reasonable doubt" that the defendant has committed the crime. Some juries reach a verdict in a matter of minutes; some juries have taken weeks or more. If the jury finds the defendant guilty as charged, as it does in two-thirds of criminal cases, the judge begins to consider a sentence. In some jurisdictions, the jury participates to varying degrees in the sentencing process. If the jury finds the defendant not guilty, the defendant is released from the jurisdiction of the court and is a free person. After the verdict has been read in the courtroom, either the defense or the prosecution may ask that the jury be polled individually, with each juror stating publicly how he or she voted.

hung jury The result when jurors cannot agree on a verdict. The judge declares a mistrial. The prosecutor must decide whether to retry the case.

In the federal courts and in nearly every state, a unanimous verdict is required. If, after serious deliberation, even one juror cannot agree with the others on a verdict, the result is a **hung jury.** In that case, the judge declares a mistrial, and the prosecutor must decide whether to retry the case. Recent data show that in the small number of jury trials (less than 3 percent of all criminal case dispositions), hung juries occur infrequently: only in about 6 percent of state court criminal jury trials and in fewer than 3 percent of federal court criminal jury trials. The percentage of hung juries in the state courts ranged from 0 percent to nearly 19 percent. In state court criminal trials that end in hung juries, possible outcomes include case dismissal, guilty plea, another jury trial, or a bench trial. The average percentage of hung juries in criminal trials has not varied much in the past 40 years.[36]

THINKING CRITICALLY

1. What are some of the benefits of having a trial by jury?
2. How could the jury system be improved so that there is a more diverse mix of people?

SUMMARY

1. Identify the type of court structure in the United States and describe its various components

The United States has a dual court system—a separate judicial system for each of the states and a separate federal system. The only place where the two systems "connect" is in the U.S. Supreme Court. The federal court system is composed of U.S. district courts, U.S. circuit courts of appeals, and the U.S. Supreme Court. The state court system consists of trial courts of limited jurisdiction, trial courts of general jurisdiction, intermediate appellate courts (in most states), and state courts of last resort.

2. Summarize the purposes of courts

The purposes of courts are (1) to do justice, (2) to appear to do justice, (3) to provide a forum where disputes between people can be resolved justly and peacefully, (4) to censure wrongdoing, (5) to incapacitate criminal offenders, (6) to punish offenders, (7) to rehabilitate offenders, (8) to deter people from committing crimes, (9) to determine legal status, and (10) to protect individual citizens against arbitrary government action.

3. Identify the most powerful actors in the administration of justice and explain what makes them so powerful

Prosecutors are the most powerful actors in the administration of justice because they conduct the final screening of all persons arrested for criminal offenses, deciding whether there is enough evidence to support a conviction, and because, in most jurisdictions, they have unreviewable discretion in deciding whether to charge a person with a crime and prosecute the case.

4. Summarize the types of attorneys a person charged with a crime might have

People charged with crimes may have privately retained counsel, or if indigent, they may have court-appointed attorneys, public defenders, or "contract" lawyers, depending on which is provided by the jurisdiction.

5. Describe the responsibilities of a judge

Judges have a variety of responsibilities in the criminal justice process. Among their nontrial duties are determining probable cause, signing warrants, informing suspects of their rights, setting and revoking bail, arraigning defendants, and accepting guilty pleas. Judges spend much of the workday in their chambers, negotiating procedures and dispositions with prosecutors and defense attorneys. The principal responsibility of judges in all of those duties is to ensure that suspects and defendants are treated fairly and in accordance with due process of law. In jury trials, judges are responsible for allowing the jury a fair chance to reach a verdict on the evidence presented. A judge must ensure that his or her behavior does not improperly affect the outcome of the case. Before juries retire to deliberate and reach a verdict, judges instruct them on the relevant law. Additionally, in jurisdictions without professional court administrators, each judge is responsible for the management of his or her own courthouse and its personnel, with the added duties of supervising building maintenance, budgets, and labor relations.

6. Describe the purposes of an initial appearance

At the initial appearance—the first pretrial stage—defendants are given formal notice of the charges against them and are advised of their constitutional rights. For a misdemeanor or an ordinance violation, a summary trial may be held. For a felony, a hearing is held to determine whether the suspect should be released or whether the suspect should be held for a preliminary hearing.

7. Explain what bail is and describe the different methods of pretrial release

Bail is usually a monetary guarantee deposited with the court that is supposed to ensure that the suspect or defendant will appear at a subsequent stage in the criminal justice process. Different pretrial release options include station-house bail, surety bonds, full cash bonds, deposit bonds, release on own recognizance (ROR), conditional release, and unsecured bonds.

8. Define what a grand jury is and explain its purposes

A grand jury is a group of generally 12 to 23 citizens who, for a specific period of time, meet in closed sessions to investigate charges coming from preliminary hearings or to engage in other responsibilities. A primary purpose of the grand jury is to determine whether there is probable cause to believe that the accused committed the crime or crimes with which he or she is charged by the prosecutor. Other purposes of a grand jury are to protect citizens from unfounded charges and to consider the misconduct of government officials.

9. Describe the purposes of the arraignment and the plea options of defendants

The primary purpose of arraignment is to hear the formal information or grand jury indictment and to allow defendants to enter a plea. Plea options include "guilty," "not guilty," and in some states and the federal courts, "nolo contendere." In some states, defendants can also stand mute or can plead "not guilty by reason of insanity."

10. Describe the interests served and not served by plea bargaining

Plea bargaining seemingly serves the interests of all the court participants by, among other things, reducing uncertainty about the length or outcome of trials. Plea bargains serve prosecutors by guaranteeing them high conviction rates; judges by reducing court caseloads; defense attorneys by allowing them to avoid trials and spend less time on each case; and even some criminal offenders by enabling them to escape a prison sentence altogether, to receive a lesser sentence than they might have received if convicted at trial, or to escape conviction of socially stigmatizing crimes. Two types of criminal offenders are not served by plea bargaining: (1) innocent, indigent defendants who fear being found guilty of crimes they did not commit and receiving harsh sentences, and (2) habitual offenders.

11. List and define the stages in a criminal trial

The stages in a criminal trial are as follows: (1) selection and swearing in of the jury, in jury trials; (2) opening statements by the prosecution and the defense; (3) presentation of the prosecution's case; (4) presentation of the defense's case; (5) rebuttals, cross-examination, and reexamination of witnesses; (6) closing arguments by the defense and the prosecution; (7) the judge's instructing, or charging, the jury; and (8) deliberation and verdict.

KEY TERMS

dual court system, p. 267
jurisdiction, p. 267
original jurisdiction, p. 267
appellate jurisdiction, p. 267
general jurisdiction, p. 267
special jurisdiction, p. 267
subject matter jurisdiction, p. 267
personal jurisdiction, p. 267
writ of *certiorari*, p. 272
writ of *habeas corpus*, p. 273
summary or bench trials, p. 273
trial *de novo*, p. 273
due process of law, p. 276
incapacitation, p. 277
punishment, p. 277
rehabilitation, p. 277
general deterrence, p. 277
***nolle prosequi (nol. pros.)*, p. 278**
plea bargaining or plea negotiating, p. 280
rules of discovery, p. 281
booking, p. 291
complaint, p. 292
information, p. 292
grand jury indictment, p. 292
arrest warrant, p. 292
bail bond/bail, p. 293
preventive detention, p. 293
bench warrant or *capias*, p. 294
release on own recognizance (ROR), p. 295
conditional release, p. 295
unsecured bond, p. 295
preliminary hearing, p. 295
grand jury, p. 296
indictment, p. 296
subpoena, p. 296
arraignment, p. 297
***nolo contendere*, p. 297**
bench trial, p. 300
venire, p. 301
***voir dire*, p. 302**
hung jury, p. 304

REVIEW QUESTIONS

1. What is the difference between *original* and *appellate jurisdiction*? Between *general* and *special jurisdiction*? Between *subject matter* and *personal jurisdiction?*
2. Under what circumstances will the U.S. Supreme Court issue a writ of *certiorari?*
3. Ideally, what are the three conditions that must be met before a prosecutor charges a person with a crime and prosecutes the case?
4. Why do prosecutors sometimes choose not to prosecute criminal cases?
5. In general, when does an individual accused of a crime have the right to counsel?
6. By what methods are judges selected?
7. Describe the "funneling" or screening process in the administration of justice.
8. When do suspects officially become defendants?
9. How long may suspects arrested without a warrant be held in jail before being brought before a judge for an initial appearance?
10. In what two ways are preliminary hearings similar to criminal trials, and in what two ways do preliminary hearings differ from criminal trials?
11. What is the primary purpose of a grand jury?
12. What are three basic types of plea bargains?
13. What are three principal purposes of jury trials?
14. What is *voir dire,* and what is its purpose?
15. What are the stages of a criminal trial?

IN THE FIELD

1. **Bail Bonds** Visit the office of a local bail bonds person. It is generally near the courthouse and well marked. Ask the bonds person to describe the job. Ask about major problems with the business and satisfactions of the job. Specific questions could be: (1) For what type of offender is it most risky to provide bail? (2) How does a bail transaction work? (3) Do bonds people actually have to give money to the court when they put up bail?

2. **Court Proceedings** Visit several different types of courts, such as a lower court, a trial court, an appellate court, state courts, and federal courts. Observe the proceedings and describe how they differ from or are similar to those described in this chapter and to each other.
3. **Report on a Criminal Trial** Scan a local newspaper for a story of a criminal trial. Write a report that includes information about (1) the type of court in which the trial is being held and why it has jurisdiction, (2) the type of case being tried (misdemeanor or felony), (3) the outcome of the case.

ON THE NET

1. **District Courts** Go to the Federal Judiciary website at www.uscourts.gov and find the directory of district courts. Look up the number of districts your state is divided into, where the courts for the districts are located, and how many judgeships are authorized for each district. Report the results to your class or instructor.
2. **State Courts** Go to the U.S. Department of Justice, Bureau of Justice Statistics *State Court Organization 1998* document at www.ojp.usdoj.gov/bjs/abstract/sco98.htm. Examine the material in each table for your state. Write a report about your state court system.

CRITICAL THINKING EXERCISES

1. **What Would You Do?** As a defense attorney, what would you do under the following circumstances?
   a. Your client tells you that he committed the crime or crimes for which he is being prosecuted.
   b. Your client tells you about a serious crime that will be committed sometime next week.
   c. Your client tells you that if you lose the case, his friends will harm your family.
   d. You learn that your client, who has paid you nothing so far for your services, will not be able to pay your fee.
   e. Your client insists on testifying, even though you believe that it is not in his best interests to do so.
2. **Jury Nullification** In John Grisham's 1992 novel, *A Time To Kill,* the defendant, a black man whose young daughter was viciously raped by two white men, is on trial for gunning down the two men on the courthouse steps in full view of many bystanders. Even though it was obvious to all that the defendant had killed the two men, the jury in the case returned a not-guilty verdict, and the defendant was allowed to walk free. This is an example of *jury nullification,* the power of a jury in a criminal case to acquit a defendant despite overwhelming evidence. The jury can acquit for any reason or for no reason at all, and the decision of the jury cannot be appealed. Jury nullification is one of the problems cited by critics who call for the abolition of the present American jury system. Another complaint about the jury system is the inability of some jurors in some trials to understand legal arguments, the evidence presented, or the instructions of the judge. Critics of the jury system suggest replacing jury trials with bench trials or with trials before a panel of judges or substituting professionally trained jurors for the current "amateur" jurors.
   a. Should the American jury system be abolished? Why or why not?
   b. Do you believe that any of the alternatives suggested by jury critics would produce a better or more just system? Defend your answer.

AN
FOR AN
LEAVES
THE
BLIND

Sentencing, Appeals, and the Death Penalty

CHAPTER NINE

Chapter Outline

Chapter Objectives

After completing this chapter, you should be able to:

1. Identify the general factors that influence a judge's sentencing decisions.
2. Describe how judges tailor sentences to fit the crime and the offender.
3. Distinguish between indeterminate and determinate sentences.
4. Explain the three basic types of determinate sentences.
5. List five rationales or justifications for criminal punishment.
6. Explain the purposes of presentence investigation reports.
7. List the legal bases for appeal.
8. Identify the type of crime for which death may be a punishment.
9. Summarize the three major procedural reforms the U.S. Supreme Court approved for death penalty cases in the *Gregg* decision.

Crime Story

On September 2, 2003, the Ninth Circuit Court of Appeals in San Francisco, California, overturned 111 death sentences that had previously been imposed by judges in Arizona, Idaho, and Montana. The 8-3 vote of the federal appeals court commuted the death sentences of the inmates to life in prison. Judge Sidney Thomas of the Ninth Circuit based his ruling on the recent 2002 *Ring* v. *Arizona* case in which the U.S. Supreme Court altered the practice of judges handing down death sentences. The legal question before the federal appeals court was whether *Ring* v. *Arizona* applied retroactively to death sentences that judges previously imposed within their jurisdictional territory.

The U.S. Supreme Court decision in *Ring* v. *Arizona* held that only juries have the constitutional right to impose death sentences in capital cases. The retroactive application of the Supreme Court's ruling was considered when the Ninth Circuit Court of Appeals reviewed the death penalty sentence of Warren Summerlin, which ironically is an Arizona case as well. Warren Summerlin was convicted of murdering a finance administrator who had come to his house in 1981 to discuss money owed on a loan. After a jury had convicted Summerlin, a judge sentenced him to death citing aggravating factors. Legal scholars have suggested that the federal appeals court in having to decide the constitutionality of Summerlin's death sentence was challenged by the bizarre events that occurred during Summerlin's trial. During the death sentence appeal, Summerlin's attorneys noted the following events: an incriminating police tip from the defendant's mother-in-law based on extrasensory perception, an alleged romantic encounter between one of Summerlin's defense attorneys and the prosecutor during a possible plea negotiation, and the sentencing judge being under the influence of marijuana, which later led to the judge's disbarment.

The recent court decisions have helped to refocus public awareness on the issue of imposing death sentences. On January 11, 2003, outgoing Illinois Governor George Ryan commuted the sentences of all the state's 156 death row inmates. The governor's unprecedented decision was based on his belief that our capital system is subject to error and inequality associated with race and poverty in determining who deserves to die.

Chapter 9 discusses sentencing, appeals, and the death penalty. The decisions of the Supreme Court and former Governor George Ryan are fuel for debate over the utility of the death penalty. Does the fear of being put to death deter anyone from committing a crime such as murder? Most scientific studies indicate that the death penalty does not have a unique deterrent effect. Even if it did, would that justify imposing the death penalty in error or selectively against minorities and the poor? When we learn the facts surrounding the application of the death penalty, we are ultimately forced to rethink our stance on this highly controversial topic.

Sentencing

If a criminal defendant pleads guilty or is found guilty by a judge or jury, then the judge must impose a sentence.[1] In a few jurisdictions, sentencing is the responsibility of the jury for certain types of offenses (for example, capital crimes). Table 9.1 displays, by the most serious offense, the amount of time from conviction to sentencing for defendants in the 75 largest U.S. counties in 1998. As Table 9.1 shows, for most offenses a majority of defendants are sentenced either on the day of conviction or the next day.

Sentencing is arguably a judge's most difficult responsibility. Judges cannot impose just any sentence. They are limited by statutory provisions and guided by prevailing philosophical rationales, organizational considerations, and presentence investigation reports. They are also influenced by their own personal characteristics.

STATUTORY PROVISIONS

As described in Chapter 4, state and federal legislative bodies enact penal codes that specify appropriate punishments for each statutory offense or class of offense, such as a class B felony or class C felony. Currently, five general

TABLE 9.1 Time from Conviction to Sentencing for Convicted Defendants, by Most Serious Conviction Offense, 1998

Most Serious Conviction Offense	Number of Defendants	Total	Percent of Convicted Defendants in the 75 Largest Counties Who Were Sentenced within: 0–1 Day	2–30 Days	31–60 Days	61 Days or More
All offenses	30,485	100%	61%	15%	13%	11%
All felonies	25,026	100%	57%	18%	14%	11%
Violent offenses	4,276	100%	50%	17%	19%	13%
Murder	73	100	33	25	21	21
Rape	207	100	50	12	19	19
Robbery	1,204	100	49	16	19	15
Assault	1,867	100	52	18	19	11
Other violent	924	100	49	18	21	12
Property offenses	7,642	100%	61%	17%	13%	9%
Burglary	1,909	100	62	17	14	8
Larceny/theft	2,707	100	65	14	12	8
Motor vehicle theft	769	100	62	23	8	7
Forgery	764	100	57	17	17	9
Fraud	547	100	57	17	17	9
Other property	947	100	54	18	15	13
Drug offenses	10,341	100%	56%	19%	13%	13%
Trafficking	4,832	100	48	20	16	16
Other drug	5,509	100	63	17	10	10
Public-order offenses	2,629	100%	60%	16%	15%	9%
Weapons	900	100	59	17	15	9
Driving-related	1,056	100	61	16	13	11
Other public-order	673	100	58	16	18	8
Misdemeanors	5,459	100%	80%	5%	7%	8%

Note: Data on time from conviction to sentencing were available for 90% of convicted defendants. Total for all felonies includes cases that could not be classified into 1 of the 4 major offense categories. Detail may not add to total because of rounding.

SOURCE: Brian A. Reaves, *Felony Defendants in Large Urban Counties, 1998*, U.S. Department of Justice, Bureau of Justice Statistics (Washington, DC: GPO, 2001), p. 29, Table 29.

FYI
The Longest Sentences

The longest prison sentence in the United States is believed to be a 10,000-year sentence imposed on Dudley Wayne Kyzer, 40, on December 4, 1981, in Tuscaloosa, Alabama, for a triple murder committed in 1976. The longest federal prison sentence is presumably the 845-year sentence imposed on Sholam Weiss, 47, in absentia, on February 15, 2000, in Orlando, Florida, for his role in the largest insurance company fraud in American history.

SOURCE: George E. Rush, *The Dictionary of Criminal Justice*, 5th Ed. (Sluice Dock, Guilford, CT: Dushkin/McGraw-Hill, 2000), p. 295; Susan Clary, "Almost 3 Years Later, Weiss Shows in Court," *The Orlando Sentinel*, June 11, 2002, p. C1.

restitution Money paid or services provided by a convicted offender to victims, their survivors, or the community to make up for the injury inflicted.

types of punishment are in use in the United States: fines, probation, intermediate punishments (various punishments that are more restrictive than probation but less restrictive and costly than imprisonment), imprisonment, and death. As long as judges impose one or a combination of those five punishments, and the sentence type and length are within statutory limits, judges are free to set any sentence they want.

Thus, within limits, judges are free to tailor the punishment to fit the crime and the offender. As noted, judges can impose a combination sentence of, for example, imprisonment, probation, and a fine. They can suspend the imprisonment portion of a combination sentence, or they can suspend the entire sentence if the offender stays out of trouble, makes **restitution** (pays money or provides services to victims, their survivors, or the community to make up for the injury inflicted), or seeks medical treatment. If the offender has already spent weeks, months, or sometimes even years in jail awaiting trial, judges can give the offender credit for jail time and deduct that time from any prison sentence. When jail time is not deducted from the sentence, it is called "dead time." In some cases, the sentence that a judge intends to impose closely matches the time an offender has already spent in jail awaiting trial. In such cases, the judge may impose a sentence of "time served" and release the offender. When an offender is convicted of two or more crimes, judges can order the prison sentences to run concurrently (together) or consecutively (one after the other). Judges can also delay sentencing and retain the right to impose a sentence at a later date if conditions warrant. Table 9.2 shows, by offense, the types of felony sentences imposed by state courts in 2000. Note that two-thirds of all offenders were incarcerated; only one-third received probation. The largest percentage of offenders incarcerated were violent offenders (78 percent).

The sentence of death is generally limited to offenders convicted of "aggravated" murder, and because most criminal offenders are poor, fines are seldom

"Three strikes and you're out" laws have been used against offenders whose third felony was a relatively minor offense. *Are "three strikes" laws good laws? Why or why not?*

TABLE 9.2 Distribution of Types of Felony Sentences Imposed by State Courts, by Offense, 2000

Most Serious Conviction Offense	Percent of Felons Sentenced to—				
		Incarceration			
	Total	Total	Prison	Jail	Probation
All offenses	100%	68%	40%	28%	32%
Violent offenses	100%	78%	54%	24%	22%
Murder[a]	100	95	93	2	5
Sexual assault[b]	100	84	64	20	16
Rape	100	90	70	20	10
Other sexual assault	100	80	60	20	20
Robbery	100	89	74	15	11
Aggravated assault	100	71	40	31	29
Other violent[c]	100	71	42	29	29
Property offenses	100%	64%	37%	27%	36%
Burglary	100	76	52	24	24
Larceny[d]	100	63	33	30	37
Motor vehicle theft	100	73	41	32	27
Fraud[e]	100	54	29	25	46
Drug offenses	100%	67%	38%	29%	33%
Possession	100	64	33	31	36
Trafficking	100	69	41	28	31
Weapon offenses	100%	70%	41%	29%	30%
Other offenses[f]	100%	66%	32%	34%	34%

Note: For persons receiving a combination of sentences, the sentence designation came from the most severe penalty imposed—prison being the most severe, followed by jail, then probation. Prison includes death sentences. Felons receiving a sentence other than incarceration or probation are classified under "probation." This table is based on an estimated 919,387 cases.

[a]Includes nonnegligent manslaughter.

[b]Includes rape.

[c]Includes offenses such as negligent manslaughter and kidnaping.

[d]Includes motor vehicle theft.

[e]Includes forgery and embezzlement.

[f]Composed of nonviolent offenses such as receiving stolen property and vandalism.

Source: Matthew R. Durose and Patrick A. Langan, *Felony Sentences in State Courts, 2000*, U.S. Department of Justice, *Bureau of Justice Statistics Bulletin* (Washington, DC: GPO, 2003), p. 2, Table 2.

imposed for serious crimes. (When they are, it is generally for symbolic reasons.) Thus, in practice, judges have three sentencing options—probation, intermediate punishments, and imprisonment. Later chapters in this text will cover those options. The death penalty will be discussed at the end of this chapter.

The type of sentence imposed on an offender can be a highly volatile issue. Also controversial is the length of the sentence imposed. Judges in states that have indeterminate sentencing statutes generally have more discretion in sentencing than do judges in states with determinate sentencing laws. An **indeterminate sentence** has a fixed minimum and maximum term of incarceration, rather than a set period. Sentences of 10 to 20 years in prison or of not less than 5 years and not more than 25 years in prison are examples of indeterminate sentences. The amount of the term that is actually served is determined by a parole board. In 2000, about 25 percent of prison releases were determined by a parole board decision.[2]

Indeterminate sentences have been a principal tool in the effort to rehabilitate offenders for much of the past 75 years. They are based on the idea that correctional personnel must be given the flexibility necessary to successfully treat offenders and return them to society as law-abiding members. The

indeterminate sentence A sentence with a fixed minimum and maximum term of incarceration, rather than a set period.

FYI Sentencing

In 1975, Maine became the first state to replace indeterminate sentencing with determinate sentencing. It abolished parole at the same time.

Source: Robert Carter, "Determinate Sentences," pp. 147–49, in M.D. McShane and F.P. Williams III (eds.), *Encyclopedia of American Prisons* (New York: Garland, 1996), p. 148.

Myth Determinate sentencing, especially mandatory sentencing, has a significant impact on serious crime.

Fact In practice, this myth has at least two problems. First, "mandatory" aspects of the laws are easy to evade. Second, the basic assumption on which the myth rests is wrong: that "soft" judges release too many dangerous offenders on probation. A recent study shows that two-thirds of all offenders convicted in the 75 largest counties were sentenced to either prison or jail; only one-third received probation and/or a fine. Even 54 percent of misdemeanants were incarcerated, 52 percent in jail. Seventy-eight percent of violent offenders and 71 percent of drug offenders were incarcerated.

SOURCE: Brian Reaves, *Felony Defendants in Large Urban Counties, 1998,* U.S. Department of Justice, Bureau of Justice Statistics (Washington, DC: GPO, 2001), p. 30, Table 30.

rationale underlying indeterminate sentencing is that the time needed for "correcting" different offenders varies so greatly that a range in sentence length provides a better opportunity to achieve successful rehabilitation.

Beginning in the early 1970s, social scientists and politicians began to question whether the rehabilitation of most criminal offenders was even possible. Skepticism about rehabilitation of offenders, a public outcry to do something about crime, and a general distrust of decisions made by parole boards continued to grow. By the mid-1970s, several state legislatures had abandoned or at least deemphasized the goal of rehabilitation and had begun to replace indeterminate sentencing with determinate sentencing.

A **determinate sentence** has a fixed period of incarceration, which eliminates the decision-making responsibility of parole boards. The hope of determinate sentencing is that it will at least get criminals off the street for longer periods of time. Some people also consider a determinate sentence more humane because prisoners know exactly when they will be released, something that they do not know with an indeterminate sentence. Several states and the federal government have developed guidelines for determinate sentencing; other states have established sentencing commissions to do so.

There are three basic types of determinate sentences: flat-time, mandatory, and presumptive. With **flat-time sentencing,** judges may choose between probation and imprisonment but have little discretion in setting the length of a prison sentence. Once an offender is imprisoned, there is no possibility of a reduction in the length of the sentence. Thus, parole and **good time** (the number of days deducted from a sentence by prison authorities for good behavior or for other reasons) are not options under flat-time sentencing. Before New York imposed the first indeterminate sentence in the United States in 1924, nearly all sentences to prison in the United States were flat-time sentences. Flat-time sentences are rarely imposed today.

determinate sentence A sentence with a fixed period of incarceration, which eliminates the decision-making responsibility of parole boards.

flat-time sentencing Sentencing in which judges may choose between probation and imprisonment but have little discretion in setting the length of a prison sentence. Once an offender is imprisoned, there is no possibility of reduction in the length of the sentence.

good time The number of days deducted from a sentence by prison authorities for good behavior or for other reasons.

mandatory sentencing Sentencing in which a specified number of years of imprisonment (usually within a range) is provided for particular crimes.

With **mandatory sentencing,** the second type of determinate sentencing, a specified number of years of imprisonment, usually within a range, is provided for particular crimes. Mandatory sentencing usually allows credit for good time but does not allow release on parole. Beginning in the 1980s, two principal variations of mandatory sentencing emerged. The first was *mandatory minimum* sentences, which require that offenders serve a specified amount of prison time. Mandatory minimum sentences are most frequently imposed on offenders who commit certain types of offenses such as drug offenses, offenses committed with weapons, and offenses committed by repeat or habitual ("three strikes and you're out") offenders. All states and the federal government have one or more mandatory minimum sentencing laws.

Similar to mandatory minimum sentences are sentences based on *truth-in-sentencing* laws. First enacted in the state of Washington in 1984, truth-in-sentencing laws require offenders to serve a substantial portion of their prison sentence, usually 85 percent of it. Most truth-in-sentencing laws target violent offenders and restrict or eliminate parole eligibility and good-time credits. Probably because of incentive grants authorized by Congress in 1994 to build or expand correctional facilities, nearly all states and the District of Columbia have enacted truth-in-sentencing laws modeled after the federal government's, which requires that for certain offenses 85 percent of a prison sentence must be served.

The third type of determinate sentencing is presumptive sentencing. **Presumptive sentencing** allows a judge to retain some sentencing discretion, subject to appellate review. In presumptive sentencing, the legislature determines a sentence range for each crime usually based on the seriousness of the crime and the criminal history of the offender. The judge is expected to impose the typical sentence, specified by statute, unless mitigating or aggravating circumstances justify a sentence below or above the range set by the legislature. Any sentence that deviates from the norm, however, must be explained in writing and is subject to appellate review. Generally, with presumptive sentencing, credit is given for good time, but there is no opportunity for parole. Presumptive sentencing is a compromise between legislatively mandated determinate sentences and their indeterminate counterparts. Figure 9.1 displays Minnesota's presumptive sentencing guidelines grid.

presumptive sentencing Sentencing that allows a judge to retain some sentencing discretion, subject to appellate review. The legislature determines a sentence range for each crime.

Presumptive sentences may also be based on *sentencing guidelines* developed, not by legislatures, but by *sentencing commissions* comprised of both criminal justice professionals and private citizens. Sentencing guidelines are a different way of restricting the sentencing discretion of judges. In 1984, Congress created the nine-member U.S. Sentencing Commission, which is charged with creating and amending federal sentencing guidelines.

In today's "law and order" climate, state legislatures, as noted, are increasingly replacing indeterminate sentences with determinate ones. This trend, however, has not escaped criticism. For example, it has been argued that the consequences of determinate sentencing include longer prison sentences and overcrowded prisons. Whether it is the result of a shift in sentencing philosophy or some other factor or factors, there is no question that the United States has been experiencing a dramatic increase in the number of people sentenced to prison and in the length of terms of incarceration. A result has been a crisis of prison overcrowding. In recent years, the United States has had one of the highest imprisonment rates in the world. Furthermore, as of September 30, 2002, the entire adult correctional departments of 10 states (Alabama, Arizona, California, Connecticut, Illinois, Michigan, Minnesota, Mississippi, Texas, and Washington) were under court orders to reduce overcrowding or improve other conditions of confinement.[3] In another 12 states (Arizona, California, Delaware, Georgia, Indiana, Iowa, Massachusetts, Michigan, Nevada, Pennsylvania, Texas, and Washington) and the District of Columbia, one or more institutions were under court orders to reduce overcrowding or improve other conditions of confinement.

A related criticism of determinate sentencing is that it produces an unusually harsh prison system. For example, because of prison overcrowding, many states have all but abandoned even the pretense of rehabilitating offenders. Prisons are increasingly becoming places where offenders are simply "warehoused." In addition, because of the abolition of good time and parole under some determinate sentencing schemes, prison authorities are having a more difficult time maintaining discipline and control of their institutions. Eliminating good time and parole removed two of the most important incentives that prison authorities use to get inmates to behave and to follow prison rules. Also, because of the perceived harshness of some of the determinate sentencing schemes, some judges simply ignore the guidelines. Other judges have ignored sentencing guidelines because they believe they are too lenient. In short, many judges resent sentencing guidelines and refer to their use as "justice by computer."

FYI

Truth-in-Sentencing

Violent offenders released from prison in 1996 were sentenced to serve an average of 85 months in prison. Prior to release they served about half of their prison sentences or 45 months. Under a truth-in-sentencing law requiring 85 percent of the sentence to be served, violent offenders would be expected to serve an estimated 15 months longer.

SOURCE: Paula M. Ditton and Doris Jane Wilson, "Truth in Sentencing in State Prisons" (U.S. Department of Justice, *Bureau of Justice Special Report*, 1999).

A third criticism of determinate sentencing is that it merely shifts sentencing discretion from judges to legislatures and prosecutors (through plea bargaining). Whether this shift in sentencing responsibility is desirable is a matter of debate. On one hand, prosecutors generally exercise their discretion in secret, whereas

FIGURE 9.1 Sample Sentencing Guidelines

MINNESOTA SENTENCING GUIDELINES GRID

Presumptive Prison Sentence Lengths in Months

LESS SERIOUS ⟵⟶ MORE SERIOUS

LESS SERIOUS ↕ MORE SERIOUS

SEVERITY OF OFFENSE (Illustrative Offenses)	CRIMINAL HISTORY SCORE 0	1	2	3	4	5	6 or more
Sale of simulated controlled substance	12*	12*	12*	13	15	17	19 *18–20*
Theft Related Crimes ($2500 or less) Check Forgery ($200–$2500)	12*	12*	13	15	17	19	21 *20–22*
Theft Crimes ($2500 or less)	12*	13	15	17	19 *18–20*	22 *21–23*	25 *24–26*
Nonresidential Burglary Theft Crimes (over $2500)	12*	15	18	21	25 *24–26*	32 *30–34*	41 *37–45*
Residential Burglary Simple Robbery	18	23	27	30 *29–31*	38 *36–40*	46 *43–49*	54 *50–58*
Criminal Sexual Conduct 2nd Degree	21	26	30	34 *33–35*	44 *42–46*	54 *50–58*	65 *60–70*
Aggravated Robbery	48 *44–52*	58 *54–62*	68 *64–72*	78 *74–82*	88 *84–92*	98 *94–102*	108 *104–112*
Criminal Sexual Conduct, 1st Degree Assault, 1st Degree	86 *81–91*	98 *93–103*	110 *105–115*	122 *117–127*	134 *129–139*	146 *141–151*	158 *153–163*
Murder, 3rd Degree Murder, 2nd Degree (felony murder)	150 *144–156*	165 *159–171*	180 *174–186*	195 *189–201*	210 *204–216*	225 *219–231*	240 *234–246*
Murder, 2nd Degree (with intent)	306 *299–313*	326 *319–333*	346 *339–353*	366 *359–373*	386 *379–393*	406 *399–413*	426 *419–433*

[shaded box] At the discretion of the judge, up to a year in jail and/or other non-jail sanctions can be imposed instead of prison sentences as conditions of probation for most of these offenses. If prison is imposed, the presumptive sentence is the number of months shown.

[empty box] Presumptive commitment to state prison for all offenses.

Notes: 1. Criminal history score is based on offender's prior record and seriousness of prior offenses. 2. Numbers in italics represent the range of months within which a judge may sentence without the sentence being deemed a departure from the guidelines. 3. First degree murder is excluded from the guidelines by law and carries a mandatory life sentence.

*One year and one day

SOURCE: Minnesota Sentencing Guidelines Commission. Effective August 1, 1994; reprinted in *Seeking Justice: Crime and Punishment in America* (New York: The Edna McConnell Clark Foundation, 1995), p. 24.

judges exercise discretion in the open. Also, prosecutors and legislators are generally subject to more political influence than are judges.

Yet, on the other hand, one of the major criticisms of indeterminate sentencing and a principal reason for the adoption of determinate sentencing schemes by some states is judicial disparity in sentencing. Judges vary widely in the sentences they impose for similar crimes and offenders. For example, in one study, 41 New York state judges were asked to review files of actual cases and to indicate the sentences they would impose. Sentences for the same crime were quite different. In one case, a heroin addict robbed an elderly man at gunpoint. The assailant was unemployed, lived with his pregnant wife, and had a minor criminal record. He was convicted of first-degree robbery, and under New York's indeterminate sentencing statute, the actual sentence was between 0 and 5 years. When the 41 judges were asked what sentence they would impose in the case, 22 percent of them chose the actual sentence (between 0 and 5 years), 29 percent chose a sentence of 5 to 10 years, another 29 percent selected a sentence of 10 to 15 years, 12 percent opted for a sentence of 15 to 20 years, and 7 percent of them chose a sentence of 20 to 25 years.[4] Figure 9.2 displays the

Myth	Fact
Judges are "soft" on crime, allowing many dangerous criminals to escape imprisonment.	Whether an offender is imprisoned usually depends on the facts of the case. In cases of robbery and burglary, for example, judges are generally "hard" on robberies involving strangers and relatively "soft" on prior-relationship burglaries. According to a 2000 public opinion poll, 68 percent of Americans think that the courts are not harsh enough with criminals. In general, however, the "softness" or "hardness" of a judge's sentence depends on the seriousness of the offense, and only about 10 percent of all felonies reported to the police are violent.

FIGURE 9.2 **Sentencing Choices of 41 New York State Judges**

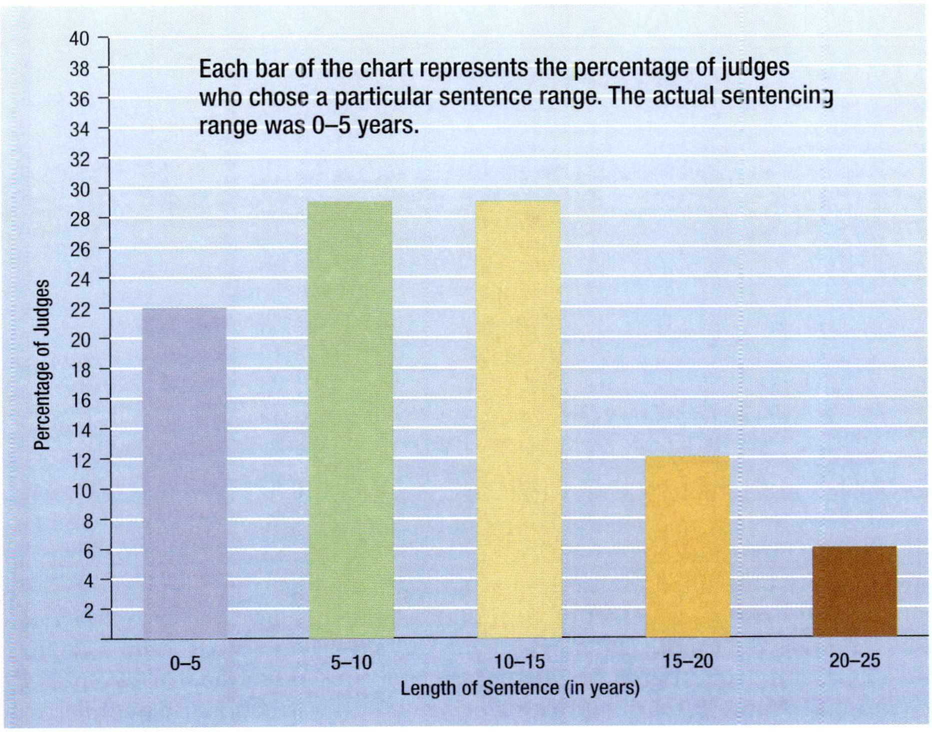

SOURCE: Adapted from "Sentence Disparity in New York: The Response of Forty-One Judges," *The New York Times* March 30, 1979, p. B3.

FYI: Public Opinion and Sentencing

Most Americans (55 percent) think mandatory sentences are a good idea; only 38 percent think judges should decide sentences.

SOURCE: Jurg Gerber and Simone Engelhardt-Greer, "Just and Painful: Attitudes Toward Sentencing Criminals," in Timothy J. Flanagan and Dennis R. Longmire (eds.), *Americans View Crime and Justice: A National Public Opinion Survey* (Thousand Oaks, CA: Sage, 1996), p. 70, Table 5.2.

TABLE 9.3 Comparison of the Outcomes of Felony Convictions in State and Federal Courts, 2000

Most Serious Conviction Offense	Felony Convictions			Federal Felony Convictions as Percent of Total	Percent of Felons Sentenced to Incarceration (Prison or Jail)		Mean Maximum Sentence Length (in Months) for Felons Sentenced to Incarceration (Prison or Jail)	
	Total	State	Federal		State	Federal	State	Federal
All Offenses	983,823	924,700	59,123	6.0%	68%	83%	36 mo	58 mo
Violent Offenses	175,756	173,200	2,556	1.5%	78%	92%	66 mo	86 mo
Murder	8,883	8,600	283	3.2	95	88	242	94
Sexual assault	31,811	31,500	311	1.0	84	89	87	85
Rape	10,686	10,600	86	0.8	90	92	110	134
Other sexual assault	21,125	20,900	225	1.1	80	88	73	65
Robbery	38,379	36,800	1,579	4.1	89	97	82	93
Aggravated assault	79,653	79,400	253	0.3	71	74	37	33
Other violent	17,130	17,000	130	0.8	71	86	33	77
Property Offenses	273,986	262,000	11,986	4.4%	64%	59%	27 mo	23 mo
Burglary	79,357	79,300	57	0.1	76	79	39	33
Larceny	101,533	100,000	1,533	1.5	63	52	21	27
Motor vehicle theft	12,039	11,900	139	1.2	73	74	18	28
Other theft	89,494	88,100	1,394	1.6	61	49	21	27
Fraud	93,096	82,700	10,396	11.2	54	60	21	23
Fraud	49,594	40,500	9,094	18.3	50	61	20	23
Forgery	43,502	42,200	1,302	3.0	57	58	22	20
Drug Offenses	343,906	319,700	24,206	7.0%	67%	92%	30 mo	76 mo
Possession	118,231	116,300	1,931	1.6	64	89	20	81
Trafficking	225,675	203,400	22,275	9.9	69	93	35	75
Weapon Offenses	32,396	28,200	4,196	13.0%	70%	91%	25 mo	91 mo
Other Offenses	157,779	141,600	16,179	10.3%	66%	83%	22 mo	33 mo

The vast majority of all felony convictions in the United States occur in State courts. Overall, Federal courts account for a relatively small number.

- In 2000 Federal courts convicted 59,123 persons of a violent, property, drug, or other felony. State courts convicted an estimated 924,700 bringing the combined U.S. total to 983 823 felons convicted. Federal courts accounted for 6 percent of the national total.
- Violent offenses comprised 4 percent of felony convictions in Federal courts but 19 percent of those in State courts.
- In 2000, 83 percent of felons convicted in Federal courts were sentenced to incarceration. The remaining 17 percent received probation. State courts sentenced 68 percent of felons to incarceration (prison or jail) and 32 percent to straight probation.
- The average Federal incarceration sentence was just under 5 years in 2000. By contrast, State incarceration sentences (prison or jail) had an average of 3 years.
- Federal drug offenders received incarceration terms that were about twice the length of drug offenders in State courts (6 years and 4 months versus 2 years and 6 months).
- In 2000 Federal offenders released from prison served an average of 91 percent of their prison term before release. Felons convicted in State courts served a significantly smaller proportion of their total incarceration sentence. For instance, State prisoners (not including felons sentenced to jail) served about 55 percent of their total prison sentence in 2000.

SOURCE: Matthew R. Durose and Patrick A. Langan, *Felony Sentences in State Courts, 2000,* U.S. Department of Justice, *Bureau of Justice Statistics Bulletin* (Washington, DC: GPO, 2003 p. 3).

CJ ONLINE

U.S. Sentencing Commission
To learn more about the U.S. Sentencing Commission, visit its website at **www.ussc.gov.** *Why do you think sentencing commissions are necessary?*

judges' choices. Table 9.3 provides a comparison of the outcomes of felony convictions in state and federal courts in 2000. Obviously, different judges view the same circumstances very differently. Critics have charged that disparity in sentencing has resulted in discrimination against people of color and the poor.

A fourth, related criticism of determinate sentencing in those jurisdictions that retain good time is that sentencing discretion, at least to some degree, actually shifts from legislators and prosecutors to correctional personnel. By charging inmates with violations of prison rules, correctional personnel can reduce (if the charges are upheld) the amount of good time earned by inmates and, by doing so, increase an inmate's time served.

In response to overcrowding, some states erected tents on prison grounds, as in this Huntsville, Texas, facility. *Do you think that the use of tents to deal with prison overcrowding is acceptable? Why or why not?*

A fifth criticism of determinate sentencing is that it is virtually impossible for legislatures or sentencing commissions to define in advance all of the factors that ought to be considered in determining a criminal sentence. You may recall from the discussion in Chapter 3 that this was a problem with one of the crime prevention implications of the classical school (equal punishment for equal crime) and the major reason for neoclassical reforms.

FYI

Appropriate Sentencing

Most Americans (76 percent) think that the courts do not sentence offenders appropriately. Nearly all of those people (68 percent) feel that criminals are not treated harshly enough.

SOURCE: Kathleen Maguire and Ann L. Pastore (eds.), *Sourcebook of Criminal Justice Statistics 2001 (Online)*, p. 137, Table 2.54 at www.albany.edu/sourcebook.

PHILOSOPHICAL RATIONALES

At the beginning of Chapter 2, the goals of criminal justice in the United States were identified as the prevention and the control of crime. Those are also the goals of **criminal sanctions** or **criminal punishment**—the penalties that are imposed for violating the criminal law. What has always been at issue, however, is how best to achieve those goals. This decision is the main problem faced by legislators who determine what the criminal sanctions will be in general and by judges who make sentencing decisions in individual cases. Historically, four major rationales or justifications have been given for the punishment imposed by the criminal courts: retribution, incapacitation, deterrence, and rehabilitation. A fifth rationale, restoration, has also been receiving greater attention.

criminal sanctions or **criminal punishment** Penalties that are imposed for violating the criminal law.

Frequently, judges impose sentences for all five reasons, but at certain times in history, one or more of the reasons have been seen as less important than the others. Today, for example, punishment is imposed less for rehabilitative purposes than it once was because of the prevalent view that we do not know how to change the behavior of criminal offenders. We will now examine each of the rationales for criminal punishment.

retribution A justification for punishment that implies repayment for an offense committed.

RETRIBUTION From biblical times through the eighteenth century, **retribution** was the dominant justification for punishment. It implies repayment for an offense committed. Although it has probably always played some role in sentencing decisions, it is now increasingly popular with the public as a rationale for punishment. However, *retribution* is an imprecise term that has been defined in many ways.[5] Nevertheless, when people say that criminal punishment should be imposed for retribution, what most of them want is probably either *revenge* or *just deserts*. **Revenge** is the justification for punishment expressed by the biblical phrase, "An eye for an eye, and a tooth for a tooth." People who seek revenge want to pay back offenders by making them suffer for what they have done. The concept of **just deserts** is another justification in which punishment is seen as a payback, one that is based on something more than vindictive revenge. It supposedly does not contain the emotional element of vengeance. *Just deserts* draws part of its meaning from the idea, attributed to the German philosopher Immanuel Kant (1724–1804), that offenders should be punished automatically, simply because they have committed a crime—they "deserve" it. Another aspect of *just deserts* is proportionality of punishment. That is, a punishment should fit the crime and should not be more nor less than the offender deserves.

revenge The punishment rationale expressed by the biblical phrase, "An eye for an eye, and a tooth for a tooth." People who seek revenge want to pay back offenders by making them suffer for what they have done.

just deserts The punishment rationale based on the idea that offenders should be punished automatically, simply because they have committed a crime—they "deserve" it—and the idea that the punishment should fit the crime.

Based on the assumption that the desire for revenge is a basic human emotion, retributivists generally believe that state-authorized punishment greatly reduces the likelihood that individual citizens will take it upon themselves to pay back offenders for what they have done. Vigilante justice is thereby avoided. Retributivists also believe that if offenders are not punished for their crimes, then other people will lose respect for the criminal law and will not obey it.

Finally, retribution is the only rationale for criminal punishment that specifically addresses what has happened in the past; that is, to pay back offenders for their crimes. All of the other rationales focus on the future and seek to influence it; for example, to restrain or prevent an offender from committing future crimes.

incapacitation The removal or restriction of the freedom of those found to have violated criminal laws.

INCAPACITATION **Incapacitation** is the removal or restriction of the freedom of those found to have violated criminal laws. Incapacitation makes it virtually impossible for offenders to commit crimes during the period of restraint. Banishment or exile was once used to achieve incapacitation. Even today, foreign nationals are deported after conviction of certain crimes. Currently, incapacitation is achieved primarily through imprisonment, which keeps inmates from committing further crimes (at least outside the prison). Some states, as noted previously, have habitual-offender statutes or "three strikes and you're out" laws that are intended to incapacitate repeat felons for life. Capital punishment is the ultimate means of incapacitation. An executed offender can never commit a crime again.

DETERRENCE As described in Chapter 3, in keeping with their goal of achieving the "greatest happiness for the greatest number," Beccaria and other classical theorists believed that the only legitimate purpose for punishment is the prevention or deterrence of crime. They generally viewed punishment for purely retributive reasons as a pointless exercise.

special or **specific deterrence** The prevention of individuals from committing crimes again by punishing them.

general deterrence The prevention of people in general from engaging in crime by punishing specific individuals and making examples of them.

There are two forms of deterrence. **Special** or **specific deterrence** is the prevention of individuals from committing crime again by punishing them. **General deterrence** is the prevention of people in general from engaging in crime by punishing specific individuals and making examples of them.

One of the problems with general deterrence as a rationale for punishment is that even though it makes intuitive sense, social science is unable to measure its effects. Only those people who have not been deterred come to the attention of social scientists and criminal justice personnel.

Historically, many people have believed that public executions have a general deterrent effect. *Do you agree? Why or why not?*

rehabilitation The attempt to "correct" the personality and behavior of convicted offenders through educational, vocational, or therapeutic treatment and to return them to society as law-abiding citizens.

Rehabilitation For much of the twentieth century, the primary rationale for punishing criminal offenders has been **rehabilitation,** which is the attempt to "correct" the personality and behavior of convicted offenders through educational, vocational, or therapeutic treatment. The goal has been to return them to society as law-abiding citizens. However, the goal of rehabilitating offenders has been challenged on the grounds that we simply do not know how to correct or cure criminal offenders because the causes of crime are not fully understood. Beginning in the mid-1970s, the goal of rehabilitation was abandoned altogether in some states, or at least deemphasized in favor of the goals of retribution and incapacitation. In other states, attempts at rehabilitation continue in an institutional context that seems to favor retribution and incapacitation (as it probably always has). Some critics have suggested that punishment and rehabilitation are incompatible ways of preventing and controlling crime and that rehabilitation generally cannot be achieved in a prison setting. This criticism, however, has apparently not influenced judges, who continue to send criminal offenders to prison to rehabilitate them.

Restoration and Victims' Rights Until recently, victims of crime and their survivors have generally been forgotten or neglected in criminal justice. They have not been important or respected participants in the adjudication process except, perhaps, as witnesses to their own or their loved ones' victimization. Beginning in the 1980s, however, because of increased scholarly attention to their plight and a fledgling victims' rights movement, attempts have been made to change the situation. Today, at least in some jurisdictions, a greater effort is being made to do something for victims and their survivors—to restore them, as much as possible, to their previous state and to make them "whole" again.

FYI

Purpose of Sentencing

Most Americans (53 percent) think the most important purpose in sentencing should be retribution, 21 percent think it should be rehabilitation, and 13 percent each choose deterrence or incapacitation. Retribution is chosen more frequently than rehabilitation even though three-fifths (61 percent) of Americans think that most or some offenders could be rehabilitated "given early intervention with the right program." Only 9 percent of Americans think that no offenders can be rehabilitated.

Source: Timothy J. Flanagan, "Reform or Punish: Americans' Views of the Correctional System," in Timothy J. Flanagan and Dennis R. Longmire (eds.), *Americans View Crime and Justice: A National Public Opinion Survey* (Thousand Oaks, CA: Sage, 1996), p. 69, Table 5.1, and p. 78.

CJ ONLINE

Victim Assistance

The U.S. Department of Justice established the Office for Victims of Crime (OVC) in 1983. OVC provides federal funding for victim assistance and compensation programs throughout the country. It also develops policies and works with criminal justice professionals in order to support crime victims. Visit the OVC website at www.ojp.usdoj.gov/ovc. *Do you think that enough is being done to support crime victims?*

In the early 1980s, only four states had laws that protected the basic rights of crime victims in the criminal justice system. Now, every state has such laws. In fact, there has been an explosion of activity in this area over the last 25 years. States have enacted more than 27,000 crime-victim-related statutes, at least 32 state victims' rights constitutional amendments have been passed, and the federal government has passed legislation providing basic rights and services to federal crime victims, such as victim assistance and victim compensation programs.[6]

The federal government, through its Crime Victims Fund, has also made millions of dollars available for state crime victim compensation, local victim assistance programs, and national training and technical assistance. The Crime Victims Fund is derived from fines and penalties paid by federal criminal offenders. Since the fund was established in 1984 and through 2000, nearly $4 billion have been collected, and more than 2 million victims have been helped each year.[7]

Among the rights now granted crime victims in at least some jurisdictions are:

- The right to notice of victims' rights.
- The right to be treated with fairness, dignity, and respect.
- The right to be informed, present, and heard at important criminal justice proceedings.
- The right to confer with the prosecutor.
- The right of sexual assault victims to be paid for forensic exams.
- The right to HIV testing of sex offenders and notification of the results.
- The right to reasonable protection from the accused.
- The right to privacy (including a prohibition against compelling testimony about personal information in open court, exclusion or limited disclosure of victim-identifying information in criminal justice records, and protection from release of addresses and phone numbers provided for notice purposes).
- The right to a speedy resolution of the case.
- The right to a prompt return of the victim's property.
- The right to notice of the offender's release.
- The right to restitution from the offender or compensation from the state.[8]

victim-impact statements Descriptions of the harm and suffering that a crime has caused victims and their survivors.

In the sentencing process, the U.S. Supreme Court ruled in 1991 in *Payne v. Tennessee* that judges and juries may consider *victim-impact statements* in their sentencing decisions. **Victim-impact statements** are descriptions of the harm and suffering that a crime has caused victims and their survivors. Before the Court's 1991 decision, victim-impact statements were considered irrelevant and potentially inflammatory and were not allowed.

Despite the many rights that have been granted crime victims in the United States, there are many problems with the victims' rights laws and their implementation. Victims' rights vary greatly among states and at the federal level. Even in states that have constitutional rights for victims, those rights often are ignored, suffer from arbitrary implementation, or depend on the whims of criminal justice officials. Victims from other cultures and those with disabilities frequently are not informed of their rights or given the opportunity to participate in criminal and juvenile justice proceedings. There are also gaps in the laws. For example, many states do not provide comprehensive rights for the victims of crimes committed by juveniles. Victims' rights in tribal, military, and administrative proceedings are generally nonexistent.[9]

Another effort at restoration places equal emphasis on victims' rights and needs and the successful reintegration (and, in some cases, initial integration) of offenders into the community. Unlike retribution, which focuses almost entirely on offenders and their punishments, restorative justice seeks to restore

Brendan Costin, the 14-year-old son of hockey dad victim Michael Costin, becomes emotional as he delivers a victim impact statement about his deceased father while sitting next to a framed memorial the family set up on the witness stand at the sentencing hearing of hockey dad Thomas Junta. *Should victim impact statements be allowed at sentencing hearings? Why or why not?*

the health of the community, repair the harm done, meet victims' needs, and require the offender to contribute to those repairs. Following Braithwaite's theory of reintegrative shaming, described in Chapter 3, in restorative justice the criminal act is condemned, offenders are held accountable, participants are involved, and repentant offenders are encouraged to earn their way back into society.[10]

Restitution and community service are two examples of restorative practices (they are used for other purposes as well). Restitution is a court requirement that a victims' convicted offender pay money or provide services to victims, survivors, or the community that has been victimized. Typically, laws specify that restitution may be ordered to cover medical expenses, lost wages, counseling expenses, lost or damaged property, funeral expenses, and other direct out-of-pocket expenses. In more than one-third of all states, courts are required by law to order restitution unless there are compelling or extraordinary circumstances.[11] Unfortunately, a problem with restitution is that most offenders have neither the financial means nor the abilities to provide adequate restitution.

FYI — 1984 Crime Control Act

The 1984 Federal Comprehensive Crime Control Act requires that when offenders convicted of federal violations are sentenced to probation, they must pay a fine, make restitution, perform community service, or do all three.

ORGANIZATIONAL CONSIDERATIONS

A judge's sentence is also guided by organizational considerations. We have already discussed at some length the practice of plea bargaining and have shown that without it, the judicial process could not function. For practical reasons, judges almost always impose the sentence agreed upon during plea negotiations. If they did not, plea bargaining would not work. That is, if defendants could not be sure that judges would impose the agreed-upon sentence, there would be no reason for them to plead guilty. They might as well take their chances at trial.

Another organizational consideration is the capacity of the system. As we already have noted, many of the prisons in this country and some entire state prison systems are overcrowded and are under federal court order to reduce the problem. Judges in jurisdictions with overcrowded prisons are generally less inclined to sentence offenders to prison.

A third organizational consideration is the cost-benefit question. Every sentence involves some monetary and social cost. Judges must be sensitive to this issue and must balance the costs of the sentence they impose with the benefits that might be derived from it.

PRESENTENCE INVESTIGATION REPORTS

presentence investigation reports Reports, often called PSIs or PSIRs, that are used in the federal system and the majority of states to help judges determine the appropriate sentence. They are also used in classifying probationers, parolees, and prisoners according to their treatment needs and security risk.

A purpose of **presentence investigation reports** (PSIs or PSIRs), used in the federal system and by the majority of states, is to help judges determine the appropriate sentence for particular defendants. They are also used in classifying probationers, parolees, and prisoners according to their treatment needs and security risk. Generally, a PSI is prepared by a probation officer, who conducts as thorough a background check as possible on a defendant. In some jurisdictions, probation officers recommend a sentence based on the information in the PSI. In other jurisdictions, they simply write the report and do not make a sentencing recommendation. Studies show that judges follow the sentencing recommendations in PSIs most of the time, although they are not required to do so.

allocution The procedure at a sentencing hearing in which the convicted defendant has the right to address the court before the sentence is imposed. During allocution, a defendant is identified as the person found guilty and has a right to deny or explain information contained in the PSI if his or her sentence is based on it.

pardon A "forgiveness" for the crime committed that stops further criminal processing.

In most jurisdictions, after the PSI has been submitted to the judge, a sentencing hearing is held at which the convicted defendant has the right to address the court before the sentence is imposed. This procedure is called **allocution.** During allocution, a defendant is identified as the person found guilty and has a right to deny or explain information contained in the PSI if his or her sentence is based on it. The defendant also has the opportunity to plead for a **pardon** (a "forgiveness" for the crime committed that stops further criminal processing). He or she may also attempt to have the sentencing process stopped or may explain why a sentence should not be pronounced. However, defendants are not entitled to argue during allocution about whether they are guilty. Among the claims that a convicted offender can make at allocution are the following:

1. That he or she is not the person who was found guilty at trial.
2. That a pardon has been granted for the crime in question.
3. That he or she has gone insane since the verdict was rendered. Rules of due process prohibit the sentencing of convicted offenders if they do not understand why they are being punished. Punishment must be deferred until they are no longer insane.
4. That she is pregnant. The sentence of a pregnant offender must be deferred or adjusted, especially in a capital case.

A judge's sentencing is the result of a complex set of factors. *Which factors do you consider to be the most important and the least important? Why?*

PERSONAL CHARACTERISTICS OF JUDGES

Although extralegal factors are not supposed to influence a judge's sentencing decision, studies show that they invariably do. Judges, after all, are human beings with all of the human frailties and prejudices of other human beings. Among the personal characteristics of judges that have been found to affect their sentencing decisions are the following:

1. Their socioeconomic backgrounds.
2. The law schools they attended.

3. Their prior experiences both in and out of the courtroom.
4. The number of offenders they defended earlier in their careers.
5. Their biases concerning various crimes.
6. Their emotional reactions and prejudices toward the defendants.
7. Their own personalities.
8. Their marital and sexual relations.

In summary, a judge's sentencing decision is the result of the complex interplay of several different factors. Those factors include statutory provisions, philosophical rationales, organizational considerations, presentence investigation reports, results of the allocution, and personal characteristics of the judge.

THINKING CRITICALLY

1. What do you think are some of the most important issues to consider when sentencing a convicted criminal?
2. Do you think that victims should play more or less of a role in sentencing?

Appeals

As described previously, defendants can appeal their convictions either on legal grounds (for example, defects in jury selection, improper admission of evidence at trial, mistaken interpretations of law) or on constitutional grounds

CAREERS IN CRIMINAL JUSTICE

Court Reporter

My name is Debora Randolph, and I am an official court reporter with the Johnson County, Kansas District Court. I have an associate of applied science degree in court reporting and also an associate's degree in specialized business.

I began thinking about a career in court reporting when I was in high school. At the time, Kansas City Business College was the only school that had a court reporting program but it was being phased out. I then enrolled in another program and received my specialized business degree. I worked as a secretary at first. Still having a desire to be a court reporter, I opened the phonebook hoping to find a school that offered such a program and came across Brown Mackie College. I enrolled in the evening program and attended school for 2 years while working a full-time job as an administrative assistant. I successfully completed the program and received an A.A. degree. I then took and passed the required state certification test and was hired by the state of Kansas. I subsequently received my national certification. I have also taught court reporting courses.

As an official court reporter for the state of Kansas, my job entails recording verbatim reports of judicial trials, conferences, and hearings. Notes are taken at a high rate of speed through the use of a stenotype machine. As an officer of the court, it is my responsibility to prepare a complete and accurate report of proceedings which may involve highly technical terminology used in a number of different fields. Although the proceedings may not be transcribed until some time later, I also provide "realtime" or instant-text translation feed to the attorneys and judges. Text is displayed on computer monitors for attorneys and judges to view during the proceedings. Additionally, I provide input to the judge and administrative assistant regarding docket management.

One of the things I like best about my job is I am constantly learning because of the varied cases I take. I also get to listen to some very interesting life experiences. Court reporting is an interesting, challenging, and rewarding career; however, because of the long hours involved, it can be overwhelming. I often work evenings and weekends producing transcripts. I would advise anyone who is thinking of court reporting as a career to be prepared to dedicate a considerable amount of time to the profession. Many aspiring court reporters do not make it past the first year of school. Training requires much practice time to learn to "write" up to 25 words per minute in addition to the other core requirements.

Which aspect of this job would you find the most rewarding?

(for instance, illegal search and seizure, improper questioning of the defendant by the police, identification of the defendant through a defective police lineup, incompetent assistance of counsel). However, they are not entitled to present new evidence or testimony on appeal if that evidence or testimony could have been presented at trial. If new evidence is discovered that was unknown or unknowable to the defense at trial, then an appeal can sometimes be made on the basis of that new evidence. Still, in *Herrera* v. *Collins,* 1993, a death penalty case, the Supreme Court ruled that, absent constitutional grounds, new evidence of innocence is no reason for a federal court to order a new state trial. In any event, because the defendant has already been found guilty, the presumption of innocence no longer applies during the appellate process, and the burden of showing why the conviction should be overturned shifts to the defendant.

Generally, notice of intent to appeal must be filed within 30 to 90 days after conviction. Also, within a specified period of time, an *affidavit of errors* specifying the alleged defects in the trial or pretrial proceedings must be submitted. If those two steps are followed, the appellate court must review the case. Nevertheless, very few appeals are successful. Nearly 80 percent of state trial court decisions are affirmed on appeal. (See Chapter 8 for more on the appellate courts.)

THINKING CRITICALLY

Why do you think so few appeals are successful? Do you think the appeals process works effectively? Why or why not?

The Death Penalty

For a century after the ratification of the Eighth Amendment, hanging was the only legally authorized method of execution in the United States. The one exception was that spies, traitors, and deserters convicted under federal statutes could be shot. Hanging is no longer authorized as the sole or principal method of execution in any executing jurisdiction. *Why was hanging as a method of execution abandoned?*

Before concluding this chapter, we will examine in some detail the death penalty in the United States, because, as the Supreme Court has acknowledged, "death is different."[12] Other sentencing options are discussed in later chapters of this book. As a punishment for the most heinous of crimes, the death penalty, or capital punishment, differs from all other criminal sanctions, not only in the nature of the penalty itself (the termination of life), but also in the legal procedures that lead to it. However, before describing the unique way in which capital punishment is administered in the United States, we will provide some background about the penalty.

A BRIEF HISTORY OF THE DEATH PENALTY IN THE UNITED STATES

When the first European settlers arrived in America, they brought with them the legal systems from their native countries, which included the penalty of death for a variety of offenses. For example, the English Penal Code at the time, which was adopted by the British colonies, listed more than 50 capital offenses, but actual practice varied from colony to colony. In the Massachusetts Bay Colony, 12 crimes carried the death penalty:

- Idolatry.
- Witchcraft.
- Blasphemy.
- Rape.
- Statutory rape.
- Perjury in a trial involving a possible death sentence.
- Rebellion.
- Murder.
- Assault in sudden anger.
- Adultery.
- Buggery (sodomy).
- Kidnapping.

In the statute, each crime was accompanied by an appropriate biblical quotation justifying the capital punishment. Later the colony added arson, treason, and grand larceny to the list of capital offenses. In contrast, the Quakers adopted much milder laws. The Royal Charter for South Jersey (1646), for example, did not permit capital punishment for any crime, and in Pennsylvania, William Penn's Great Act of 1682 limited the death penalty to treason and murder. Most colonies, however, followed the much harsher British Code.

The earliest recorded lawful execution in America was in 1608 in the colony of Virginia. Captain George Kendall, a councillor for the colony, was executed for being a spy for Spain. Since Kendall, nearly 19,000 legal executions have been performed in the United States under civil authority. However, only about 3 percent of those people executed since 1608 have been women. Ninety percent of the women executed were executed under local, as opposed to state, authority, and the majority (87 percent) were executed before 1866. The first woman executed was Jane Champion in the Virginia colony in 1632. She was hanged for murdering and concealing the death of her child, who was fathered by a man other than her husband.

In addition, about 2 percent of those executed in the United States since 1608 have been juveniles, those whose offenses were committed prior to their eighteenth birthdays. The first juvenile executed in America was Thomas Graunger in the Plymouth Colony in 1642, for the crime of bestiality. Since 1990, the United States is one of only 7 countries that has executed anyone under 18 years of age at the time of the crime; the others are the Democratic Republic of Congo, Iran, Nigeria, Pakistan, Saudi Arabia, and Yemen. Pakistan and Yemen no longer execute juveniles. The United States has executed 22 juveniles since 1976 (as of April 3, 2003). About 2 percent of current death row inmates are juveniles.[13]

FYI: Women Executed

Of the 3,525 people on death rows in the United States, as of April 1, 2003, only about 1.5 percent were women. As of April 1, 2003, only 10 women have been executed in the United States since 1962. The first was Velma Barfield, who was executed in North Carolina on October 2, 1984.

SOURCE: Death Penalty Information Center at www.deathpenaltyinfo.org.

ENTER THE SUPREME COURT

Before 1968, the only issues the Supreme Court considered in relation to capital punishment concerned the means of administering the death penalty. The one exception was the case of *Powell* v. *Alabama* (1932), in which the Court held that failure to provide counsel in a capital case violates due process as required under the Fourteenth Amendment. In the other pre-1968 cases, the Court upheld the constitutionality of the following methods of execution: shooting (*Wilkerson* v. *Utah*, 1878), electrocution (*In re Kemmler*, 1890), a second electrocution after the first attempt has failed to kill the offender (*Louisiana ex rel. Francis* v. *Resweber*, 1947), and hanging (*Andres* v. *United States*, 1948). Currently, there are 5 methods of execution in use: lethal injection, electrocution, lethal gas, hanging, and firing squad. Lethal injection is used by the most states. Table 9.4 lists the states that employ each method of execution.

FYI: *Heckler* v. *Chaney*

In the 1985 case of *Heckler* v. *Chaney*, the Supreme Court upheld the constitutionality of lethal injection as an execution method.

Between 1968 and 1972, a series of lawsuits challenged various aspects of capital punishment as well as the constitutionality of the punishment itself. During this period, an informal moratorium on executions was observed, pending the outcome of the litigation, and no death row inmates were executed. Some of the suits were successful, and some of them were not. Finally, on June 29, 1972, the Supreme Court set aside death sentences for the first time in its history. In its decisions in *Furman* v. *Georgia*, *Jackson* v. *Georgia*, and *Branch* v. *Texas* (hereafter referred to as the *Furman* decision), the Court held that the capital punishment statutes in those 3 cases were unconstitutional because they gave the jury complete discretion to decide whether to impose the death penalty or a lesser punishment in capital cases. Although 9 separate opinions were written—a very rare occurrence—the majority of

TABLE 9.4 Method of Execution, by Jurisdiction, June 2003

Lethal Injection	Lethal Injection (continued)	Electrocution	Lethal Gas	Hanging	Firing Squad
Alabama [1, 2]	New Hampshire [11]	Alabama [1, 2]	Arizona [1, 3]	Delaware [1, 6]	Idaho [8]
Arizona [1, 3]	New Jersey	Arkansas [1, 4]	California [1, 5]	New Hampshire [11]	Oklahoma [12]
Arkansas [1, 4]	New Mexico	Florida [1, 7]	Maryland [10]	Washington [1]	Utah [1]
California [1, 5]	New York	Kentucky [1, 9]	Missouri [1]		
Colorado	North Carolina	Nebraska	Wyoming [14]		
Connecticut	Ohio	Oklahoma [12]			
Delaware [1, 6]	Oklahoma [12]	South Carolina [1]			
Florida [1, 7]	Oregon	Tennessee [13]			
Georgia	Pennsylvania	Virginia [1]			
Idaho [1, 8]	South Carolina [1]				
Illinois	South Dakota				
Indiana	Tennessee [13]				
Kansas	Texas				
Kentucky [1, 9]	Utah [1]				
Louisiana	Virginia [1]				
Maryland [10]	Washington [1]				
Mississippi	Wyoming [14]				
Missouri [1]	U.S. Government				
Montana	U.S. Military				
Nevada					

1. Authorizes two methods of execution.
2. Effective July 1, 2002, Alabama authorizes lethal injection unless the inmate requests electrocution.
3. Arizona authorizes lethal injection for persons sentenced after November 15, 1992; those sentenced before that date may select lethal injection or lethal gas.
4. Arkansas authorizes lethal injection for persons committing a capital offense after July 4, 1983; those who committed the offense before that date may select lethal injection or electrocution.
5. California authorizes lethal injection unless the inmate requests lethal gas.
6. Delaware authorizes lethal injection for those whose capital offense occurred after June 13, 1986; those who committed the offense before that date may select lethal injection or hanging.
7. Florida allows inmates to choose either lethal injection or electrocution.
8. Idaho authorizes firing squad only if lethal injection is "impractical."
9. Kentucky authorizes lethal injection for those convicted after March 31, 1998; those who committed the offense before that date may select lethal injection or electrocution.
10. Maryland authorizes lethal injection for those whose capital offenses occurred on or after March 25, 1994; those who committed the offense before that date may select lethal injection or lethal gas.
11. New Hampshire authorizes hanging only if lethal injection cannot be given.
12. Oklahoma authorizes electrocution if lethal injection is ever held to be unconstitutional and firing squad if both lethal injection and electrocution are held unconstitutional.
13. Tennessee authorizes lethal injection for those sentenced after January 1, 1999, and those currently on death row will choose between the electric chair and lethal injection.
14. Wyoming authorizes lethal gas if lethal injection is ever held to be unconstitutional.

The method of execution of federal prisoners for offenses under the Violent Crime Control and Law Enforcement Act of 1994 is that of the state in which the conviction took place. If the state has no death penalty, the judge may choose the method of another state. For offenses under the 1988 Drug Kingpin law, the method of executions is lethal injection.

SOURCE: The Death Penalty Information Center, www.deathpenaltyinfo.org, June 9, 2003.

5 justices (Douglas, Brennan, Stewart, White, and Marshall) pointed out that the death penalty had been imposed arbitrarily, infrequently, and often selectively against people of color. According to the majority, those statutes constituted "cruel and unusual punishment" under the Eighth and Fourteenth Amendments. (The 4 dissenters were Chief Justice Burger and justices Blackmun, Powell, and Rehnquist.) It is important to emphasize that the Supreme Court did not rule that the death penalty itself was unconstitutional, only the way in which it was being administered.

The practical effect of the *Furman* decision was that the Supreme Court voided the death penalty laws of some 35 states, and more than 600 men and women had their death sentences vacated and commuted to a term of imprisonment. Although opponents of capital punishment were elated that the United States had finally joined all the other Western industrialized nations in abolishing capital punishment either in fact or in practice, the joy was short-lived. By the fall of 1974, 30 states had enacted new death penalty statutes that were designed to meet the Court's objections.

The new death penalty laws took two forms. Some states removed all discretion from the process by mandating capital punishment upon conviction for certain crimes (mandatory statutes). Other states provided specific guidelines that judges and juries were to use in deciding if death was the appropriate sentence in a particular case (guided-discretion statutes).

The constitutionality of the new death penalty statutes was quickly challenged, and on July 2, 1976, the Supreme Court announced its rulings in five test cases. In *Woodson* v. *North Carolina* and *Roberts* v. *Louisiana,* the Court rejected "mandatory" statutes that automatically imposed death sentences for defined capital offenses. However, in *Gregg* v. *Georgia, Jurek* v. *Texas,* and *Proffitt* v. *Florida* (hereafter referred to together as the *Gregg* decision), the Court approved several different forms of guided-discretion statutes. Those statutes, the Court wrote, struck a reasonable balance between giving the jury some guidance and allowing it to consider the background and character of the defendant and the circumstances of the crime.

During the 20th century, more people were executed by electrocution than by any other method. Today, Nebraska is the only state that still uses electrocution as the sole method of execution. *Why have states abandoned electrocution as an execution method?*

The most dramatic effect of the *Gregg* decision was the resumption of executions on January 17, 1977, when the state of Utah executed Gary Gilmore (at his own request) by firing squad. Since then, 856 people have been executed in 32 states and by the federal government, which has executed three (as of June 5, 2003).[14] More than half of the 856 executions have taken place in just three states—Texas (304), Virginia (88), and Oklahoma (64). Figure 9.3 shows the states in which executions have taken place. Note that Texas alone accounts for more than one-third of all post-*Furman* executions. Texas has executed more than three times as many offenders as any other state.

Table 9.5 shows the race or ethnicity and gender of both the defendants executed and their victims, as well as defendant-victim racial or ethnic combinations. As shown, nearly all of the people executed since Gilmore's execution in 1977 have been male, while the gender of the victims is divided nearly evenly between males and females. As for race, nearly 57 percent of all people executed under post-*Furman* statutes have been white; about 34 percent have been black. Thus, the percentage of blacks who have been executed far exceeds their proportion of the general population (about 13 percent). Particularly interesting is that more than 80 percent of the victims of those executed have been white. What makes this finding interesting is that murders, including capital murders (all post-*Furman* executions have been for capital murders; see the following discussion), tend to be intraracial crimes. However, the death penalty is imposed primarily on the killers of white people, regardless of the race or ethnicity of the

Myth	Fact
There is no gender discrimination in the administration of capital punishment.	Although women commit approximately 20 percent of all criminal homicides, only 10 women—about 1 percent of all executions since 1977—have been executed since executions resumed in 1977.

FIGURE 9.3 State-by-State Count of Inmates Executed in 32 States Since Executions Resumed in 1977

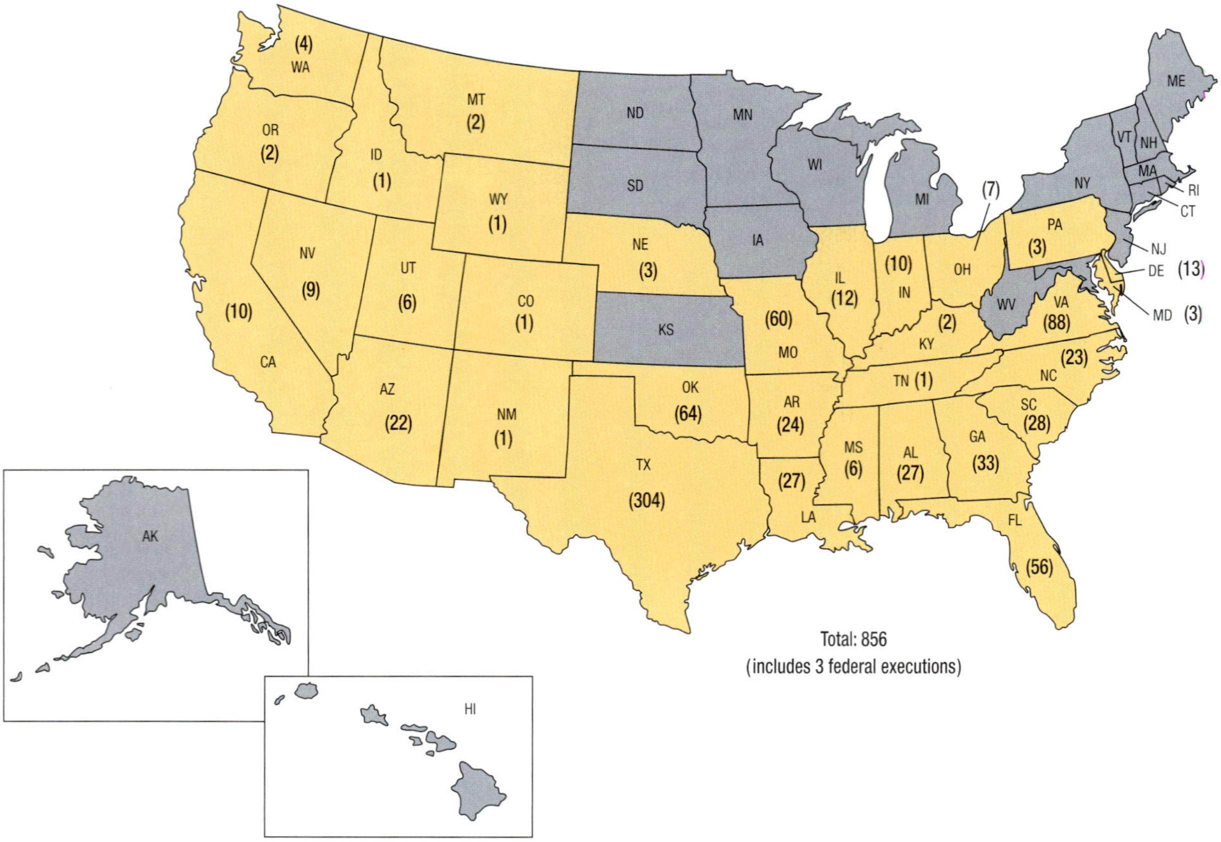

Source: Adapted from Death Penalty Information Center at www.deathpenaltyinfo.org, June 2003.

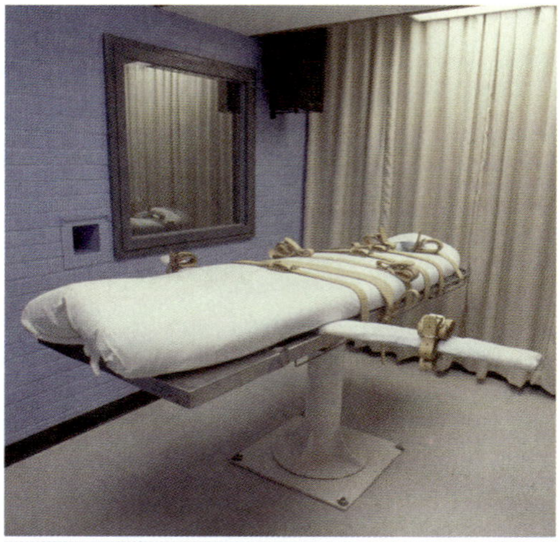

Lethal injection has become the sole or principal method of execution in all but one executing jurisdiction in the United States (the exception is Nebraska). *Why?*

offender. The figures on defendant-victim racial or ethnic combinations (see Table 9.5) further support this conclusion. Note that about 52 percent of executions have involved white killers of white victims, and about 22 percent of executions have involved black killers of white victims. On the other hand, only about 10 percent of executions have been of black killers of black victims, and there have been only 12 executions of white killers of black persons (less than 2 percent).

Currently (as of April 1, 2003), 40 jurisdictions have capital punishment statutes, although New Hampshire has no death sentences imposed. Thirteen jurisdictions do not have capital punishment statutes. Figure 9.4 shows the jurisdictions with and without capital punishment statutes.

In decisions since *Gregg,* the Supreme Court has limited the crimes for which death is considered appropriate and has further refined death penalty jurisprudence. In 1977, in the cases of *Coker* v. *Georgia* and *Eberheart* v. *Georgia,* the Court held that rape of an adult female (in *Coker*) and kidnapping (in *Eberheart*), where the victim was not killed, do not warrant death. Those two decisions effectively limited the death penalty to those offenders convicted of capital, or aggravated, murder.

TABLE 9.5 Race or Ethnicity and Sex of Defendants Executed and Their Victims and Defendant-Victim Racial or Ethnic Combinations

Gender of Defendants Executed			Gender of Victims		
Total Number 842			Total Number 1271		
Female	10	(1.19%)	Female	623	(49.02%)
Male	832	(98.81%)	Male	648	(50.20%)
Race of Defendants Executed			**Race of Victims**		
White	477	(56.65%)	White	1022	(80.41%)
Black	290	(34.44%)	Black	174	(13.69%)
Latino/a	56	(6.65%)	Latino/a	50	(3.93%)
Native American	13	(1.54%)	Native American	3	(0.24%)
Asian	6	(0.71%)	Asian	22	(1.73%)
Defendant-Victim Racial or Ethnic Combinations					
White Defendant and			Asian Defendant and		
White Victim	448	(52.02%)	White Victim	2	(0.24%)
Black Victim	12	(1.43%)	Black Victim	0	(0.00%)
Latino/a Victim	6	(0.71%)	Latino/a Victim	0	(0.00%)
Asian Victim	3	(0.36%)	Asian Victim	4	(0.48%)
Native American Victim	0	(0.00%)	Native American Victim	0	(0.00%)
Black Defendant and			Native American and		
White Victim	182	(21.62%)	White Victim	12	(1.43%)
Black Victim	87	(10.33%)	Black Victim	0	(0.00%)
Latino/a Victim	10	(1.19%)	Latino/a Victim	0	(0.00%)
Asian Victim	7	(0.83%)	Asian Victim	0	(0.00%)
Native American Victim	0	(0.00%)	Native American Victim	1	(0.12%)
Latino/a Defendant and			TOTAL		
White Victim	28	(3.33%)	White Victim	672	(79.81%)
Black Victim	2	(0.24%)	Black Victim	101	(12.00%)
Latino/a Victim	22	(2.61%)	Latino/a Victim	38	(4.51.%)
Asian Victim	1	(0.12%)	Asian Victim	15	(1.78%)
Native American Victim	0	(0.00%)	Native American Victim	1	(0.12%)

Note: *In addition, there were 15 defendants executed for the murders of multiple victims of different races. Of those, 8 defendants were white, 4 black, and 3 Latino. (1.78%)*

Source: *Death Row, U.S.A.*, NAACP Legal Defense and Educational Fund (April 1, 2003).

The most celebrated recent execution by firing squad was the January 17, 1977, execution of Gary Gilmore in Utah. It no longer is authorized as the sole or principal method of execution in any executing jurisdiction. *Does execution by firing squad have any advantages over other methods of execution? If so, what are they?*

In 1986, in *Ford* v. *Wainwright,* the Court barred states from executing inmates who have developed mental illness while on death row, and, in 2002, in *Atkins* v. *Virginia,* the Court held that it is cruel and unusual punishment to execute the mentally retarded. In the 1988 case of *Thompson* v. *Oklahoma* and the 1989 cases of *Stanford* v. *Kentucky* and *Wilkins* v. *Missouri,* the Court effectively limited capital punishment to offenders who are 16 years of age or older at the time of their offenses. Another death penalty decision of the Supreme Court is the 1987 case of *McCleskey* v. *Kemp,* in which the Court held that state death penalty statutes are constitutional even when statistics indicate that they have been applied in racially biased ways. The Court ruled that racial discrimination must be shown in individual cases. The *McCleskey* decision was particularly disheartening to opponents of capital punishment because, for them, the case was the last best chance of having the Supreme Court declare the death penalty unconstitutional once and for all.

FIGURE 9.4 Jurisdictions With and Without Capital Punishment Statutes

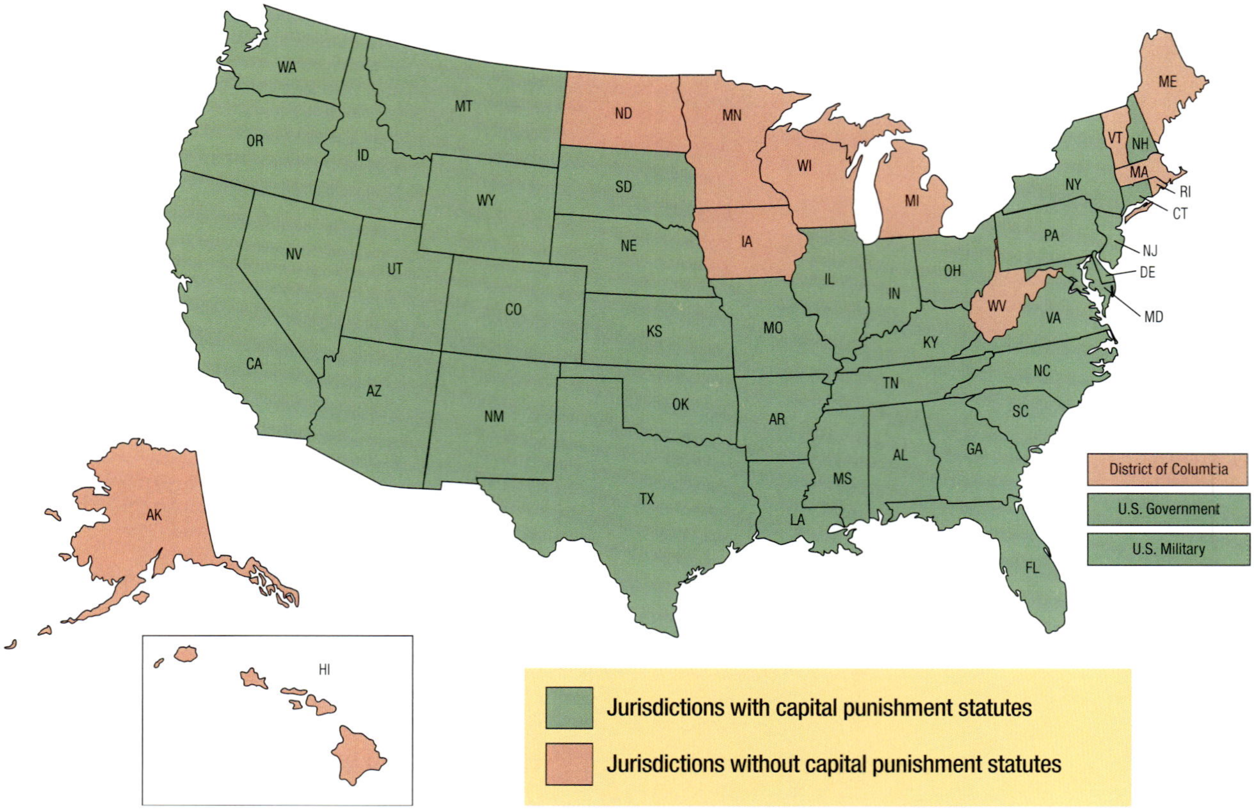

SOURCE: Adapted from *Death Row, U.S.A.*, NAACP Legal Defense and Educational Fund (April 1, 2003).

Myth

Capital punishment is no longer administered in a way that is racially discriminatory and legally impermissible.

Fact

Dozens of scientific studies clearly show that the death penalty continues to be administered in a legally impermissible and discriminatory fashion against blacks and the killers of whites.

SOURCE: For a summary of those studies, see United States General Accounting Office, *Death Penalty Sentencing: Research Indicates Pattern of Racial Disparities, Report to the Senate and House Committees on the Judiciary* (Washington: GPO, 1990). For the view that the evidence does not show racial discrimination, see William Wilbanks, *The Myth of a Racist Criminal Justice System* (Monterey, CA: Brooks/Cole, 1987).

The 1994 federal crime bill (the Violent Crime Control and Law Enforcement Act) expanded the number of federal crimes punishable by death to about 50. (Estimates vary depending on whether statutes or offenses are counted, and how offenses are counted.) All but four of the federal crimes involve murder. The four exceptions are treason; espionage; drug trafficking in large quantities; and attempting, authorizing, or advising the killing of any public officer, juror, or witness in a case involving a continuing criminal enterprise—regardless of whether such a killing actually occurs. In addition, the bill reinstated the death penalty for federal crimes for which previous death penalty provisions could not pass constitutional muster. The new law brought the earlier statutes into compliance with guidelines established by the Supreme Court. The U.S. government executed Timothy McVeigh and Juan Raul Garza in 2001, and Louis Jones, Jr., in 2003. They were the first federal executions in nearly 40 years. Prior to those three, the last execution by the U.S. government was on March 15, 1963, when Victor H. Feguer was hanged at Iowa State Penitentiary.

THE PROCEDURAL REFORMS APPROVED IN *GREGG*

It is important to emphasize that the Supreme Court approved the new death penalty statutes in *Gregg* "on their face." That is, the Court assumed, without any evidence, that the new guided-discretion statutes would eliminate the arbitrariness and discrimination that the Court found objectionable in its *Furman* decision. The Court was particularly optimistic about the following procedural reforms: bifurcated trials, guidelines for judges and juries, and automatic appellate review.

Bifurcated Trials A **bifurcated trial** is a two-stage trial—unlike the one-stage trial in other felony cases—consisting of a guilt phase and a separate penalty phase. If, in the guilt phase, the defendant is found guilty as charged, then at the penalty phase, the jury must determine whether the sentence will be death or life in prison (there are no other choices except, in some states, life imprisonment without opportunity for parole).

bifurcated trial A two-stage trial (unlike the one-stage trial in other felony cases) consisting of a guilt phase and a separate penalty phase.

Some states require the selection of two separate juries in capital trials, one for the guilt phase and one for the penalty phase. During *voir dire* in capital cases, each side is generally allowed more peremptory challenges, necessitating a larger panel from which to select the jury. California, for example, allows 26 peremptory challenges in capital cases and only 10 in noncapital cases. During both phases of a bifurcated capital trial, evidence may be introduced and witnesses may be called to testify. In short, all of the procedures of due process apply to both phases of the bifurcated trial.

Guidelines for Judges and Juries What the Court found especially appealing about the guided-discretion statutes approved in *Gregg* is that judges and juries are provided with standards that presumably restrict, but do not eliminate, their sentencing discretion. Specifically, judges and juries, in most states, are provided with lists of aggravating and, at least in some states, mitigating factors. **Aggravating factors** are circumstances that make a crime worse than usual. **Mitigating factors** make a crime less severe than usual. The Court has since ruled (in *Lockett* v. *Ohio*, 1978; *Bell* v. *Ohio*, 1978; and *Hitchcock* v. *Dugger*, 1987) that judges and juries must consider any mitigating circumstance offered by the defense, whether it is listed in the statute or not. Table 9.6 lists the aggravating and mitigating factors in Florida's current death penalty statute. The factors are typical of most states that provide them.

aggravating factors In death sentencing, circumstances that make a crime worse than usual.

mitigating factors In death sentencing, circumstances that make a crime less severe than usual.

Under Florida's death penalty statute, which is an "aggravating-versus-mitigating" type, at least one aggravating factor must be found before death may be considered as a penalty. If one or more aggravating factors is found, it is weighed against any mitigating factors. If the aggravating factors outweigh the mitigating factors, the sentence is death. However, if the mitigating factors outweigh the aggravating factors, the sentence is life imprisonment without opportunity for parole. Currently, in Florida (and Alabama) the jury's recommendation is only advisory to the judge. That is, in those states, the judge may impose death even if the jury recommends life, or may impose life even if the jury recommends death. This override provision may not survive constitutional challenge because in *Ring* v. *Arizona* (2002) the U.S. Supreme Court ruled that juries and not judges must determine whether death is the appropriate penalty in a capital case.

Another type of guided-discretion statute is Georgia's "aggravating-only" statute. In Georgia, if a jury finds at least one statutory aggravating factor, then it may, but need not, recommend death. The jury may also consider any mitigating factors, although mitigating factors are not listed in the

- Only 16 "executing" states (48 percent) have conducted 10 or more executions.

KEY TERMS

restitution, p. 312
indeterminate sentence, p. 313
determinate sentence, p. 314
flat-time sentencing, p. 314
good time, p. 314
mandatory sentencing, p. 314
presumptive sentencing, p. 315
criminal sanctions or criminal punishment, p. 319
retribution, p. 319
revenge, p. 320
just deserts, p. 320
incapacitation, p. 320
special or specific deterrence, p. 320
general deterrence, p. 320
rehabilitation, p. 321
victim-impact statements, p. 322
presentence investigation reports, p. 324
allocution, p. 324
pardon, p. 324
bifurcated trial, p. 333
aggravating factors, p. 333
mitigating factors, p. 333
proportionality review, p. 335
commutations, p. 337

REVIEW QUESTIONS

1. What are five general types of punishment currently being used in the United States?
2. What are some criticisms of determinate sentencing?
3. Which rationale for criminal punishment is the only one that specifically addresses what has happened in the past, and what are its two major forms?
4. What are three organizational considerations that may influence a judge's sentencing decision?
5. What is *allocution?*
6. What two steps must be taken before an appellate court will hear an appeal?
7. What was the landmark 1972 decision in which the Supreme Court set aside death sentences for the first (and only) time in its history?
8. What are the five methods of execution currently used in the United States?

IN THE FIELD

1. **Sentencing** Select a criminal case that is currently receiving publicity in your community. Conduct an informal survey, asking respondents what sentence they believe would be appropriate in the case. Ask them why they chose the sentence. Determine whether respondents tended to agree with each other. If they did not tend to agree, speculate on the reasons for the disagreement.

2. **Death Penalty Opinion** With family members or friends, discuss the death penalty. Ask them why they hold their particular positions (in favor, opposed, undecided). Also, ask them under what circumstances they would change their positions. Would any of the mitigating circumstances listed in the second Critical Thinking exercise that follows cause any of them to change their positions?

ON THE NET

1. **Death Penalty** Access the Death Penalty Information Center website at www.deathpenaltyinfo.org and the "Pro Death Penalty pages" at www.prodeathpenalty.com. Choose the same topic included in both sources, and review the information provided. Write a brief summary of the information you discovered and how it affected your view of capital punishment.
2. **Mandatory Minimums** Access the website of Families Against Mandatory Minimums at www.famm.org. After studying information provided at the site, write an essay or prepare an oral presentation critiquing mandatory minimum sentences.

CRITICAL THINKING EXERCISES

1. **The Three Strikes Law** In March 1995, a 27-year-old man who had stolen a slice of pizza from a group of children sitting outside a pizza parlor became the first person to be sentenced to 25 years to life in prison under California's "three strikes and you're out" law. Enacted March 7, 1995, the law was reinforced November 8, 1995, by a constitutional amendment supported by 72 percent of California voters. The "three strikes" law is triggered by two past felony convictions. In this case, the defendant was convicted of "petty theft with a prior felony conviction." He had already been convicted of robbery, attempted robbery, drug possession, and riding a stolen motorcycle.
   a. It will cost the taxpayers of California about $26,000 a year to incarcerate the man. Is it worth it? Is it a wise expenditure of tax dollars?
   b. Is the punishment proportional to the crime or crimes? Should it be?
   c. Do you think "petty theft with a prior conviction" is a legitimate trigger of a "three strikes" law?
   d. There is no question that the offender was a criminal. He had a reputation for being a bully. Nevertheless, are "three strikes and you're out" laws an ethically defensible way of dealing with such criminals? Why or why not?

2. **Sentencing** You are a juror in a death penalty case. The defendant in the case has already been found guilty of capital murder during the guilt phase of the trial. During the penalty phase, you have to determine whether the defendant is to be sentenced to death or to life imprisonment without opportunity for parole (LWOP). The judge has instructed you (and the rest of the jury) to consider the aggravating and mitigating circumstances of the case. If the aggravating circumstances outweigh the mitigating circumstances, you are expected to vote for death. On the other hand, if the mitigating circumstances outweigh the aggravating circumstances, you are expected to vote for LWOP. The lone aggravating circumstance in the case is that the defendant committed the capital murder during the commission of a robbery. Though they are not aggravating circumstances, the defendant also has two prior convictions for robbery and one prior conviction for the sale of illegal drugs. Under which of the following mitigating circumstances would you vote for LWOP or death in this case? Explain the reasons for your decision.
   a. The defendant was 14 years old at the time the crime was committed.
   b. The defendant is a female with children.
   c. The defendant is mentally retarded (that is, has an IQ of 60).
   d. The defendant was seriously abused, both mentally and physically, as a child.
   e. The defendant is legally insane.

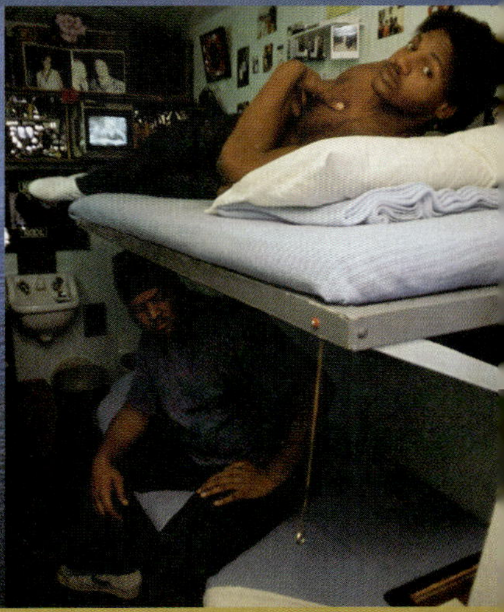

PART FOUR

CORRECTIONS

CHAPTER TEN
Institutional Corrections

CHAPTER ELEVEN
Prison Life, Inmate Rights, Release, and Recidivism

CHAPTER TWELVE
Community Corrections

INSTITUTIONAL CORRECTIONS

CHAPTER TEN

Chapter Outline

Chapter Objectives

After completing this chapter, you should be able to:

1. Summarize the purposes of confinement in Europe before it became a major way of punishing criminals.
2. Describe how offenders were punished before the large-scale use of confinement.
3. Explain why confinement began to be used as a major way of punishing offenders in Europe.
4. Describe the recent trends in the use of incarceration in the United States.
5. List some of the characteristics of the incarcerated population in the United States.
6. Describe how incarceration facilities are structured, organized, and administered by the government in the United States.
7. Name some of the common types of correctional facilities in the United States.
8. Identify some of the procedures that institutions employ to maintain security and order.
9. List the services and programs that are commonly available to inmates.

Crime Story

On October 10, 2003, Warden Gene Fischi of the Luzeren County Correctional Facility in Wilkes-Barre, Pennsylvania, called for an inspection of the facility's windows after an inmate charged with two murders escaped. The escape occurred during an exercise period when cells are unlocked and inmates in the overcrowded maximum-security unit are permitted to socialize with each other.

Inmates Hugo Selenski, 30, and Scott Bolton, 39, walked into another inmate's cell about 9:30 P.M. and removed a 12-inch-by-18-inch window on the seventh floor of the facility. The inmates climbed down a rope that had been fashioned from 12 bed sheets. Inmate Bolton suffered critical injuries after falling onto a rooftop below and was subsequently captured by prison officials on the rooftop. Bolton later claimed that Selenski pushed him during their escape, but he was unsure whether it was intentional or an accident. At the time of the escape, Selenski was being held in the correctional facility after being charged with two counts of murder following the exhumation of the remains of two persons from the yard of his home outside Wilkes-Barre. Selenski is also suspected of killing three other persons whose bodies were recovered from his property.

Warden Fischi ordered all the correctional facility windows to be tested following Selenski's escape and called for an immediate investigation into the incident. Ironically, the same window removed by Selenski and Bolton had been taken out in an earlier failed escape attempt in 1990, which prompted correctional officials to weld the windows shut, install bolts, and add a layer of wire mesh to the interior. Officials were left to wonder why the window modifications did not prevent Selenski's escape.

Pennsylvania prison officials criticized correctional workers for allowing Selenski access to other inmates, access to a broom handle that might have been used to pry open the window, and for inmates being allowed to wear civilian clothes. Normally, inmates are required to wear green jumpsuits, however, Selenski was not required to on the night of his escape. Following the escape, Warden Fischi added perimeter building checks and more regular inspections of the facility's windows.

Chapter 10 discusses the various types of correctional institutions in the United States including jails. For decades, critics have maintained that jail conditions and correctional management practices need reform. Was the escape of Hugo Selenski related to poor facility design, or the failure of management and supervision strategies? The investigation of the Pennsylvania facility may not reveal a clear-cut answer to that question. However, the escape and its consequences are yet another reminder of the important function that correctional facilities provide in keeping society safe from criminal offenders.

Historical Overview of Institutional Corrections

Students often wonder why they must learn about the history of institutional corrections. One reason is that it is impossible to fully understand (and improve) the present state of affairs without knowledge of the past; the present developed out of the past. People who fail to remember the past are destined to repeat its mistakes. Another reason is that nothing helps us see how institutional corrections is linked to our larger society and culture better than the study of history. Try to keep those two points in mind when studying history.

EUROPEAN BACKGROUND

In Europe, institutional confinement did not become a major punishment for criminals until the 1600s and 1700s. (In the United States, institutional confinement was not used extensively as a punishment until the 1800s.) As a practice, though, institutional confinement has existed since ancient times. Before the 1600s, however, it usually served functions other than punishment for criminal behavior. For example, confinement was used to:

1. Detain people before trial.
2. Hold prisoners awaiting other sanctions, such as death and corporal punishment.
3. Coerce payment of debts and fines.
4. Hold and punish slaves.
5. Achieve religious indoctrination and spiritual reformation (as during the Inquisition).
6. Quarantine disease (as during the bubonic plague).[1]

Myth	Fact
Throughout history, imprisonment has been the primary sentence for lawbreakers, and it still is today.	Viewed historically, imprisonment is a relatively recent sentence for lawbreaking. Even today in the United States, the number of people in prison is small compared with the number on probation or under other types of supervision in the community.

Forerunners of Modern Incarceration Unlike modern incarceration, which strives to change the offender's character and is carried out away from public view, popular early punishments for crime, which predated the large-scale use of imprisonment, were directed more at the offender's body and property; one basic goal was to inflict pain.[2] Furthermore, those punishments were commonly carried out in public to humiliate the offender and to deter onlookers from crime. Examples of such early punishments are fines, confiscation of property, and diverse methods of corporal and capital punishment. Some popular methods of corporal and capital punishment were beheading, stoning, hanging, crucifixion, boiling and burning, flogging, branding, or placement in the stocks or pillory.[3] As this brief list illustrates, the eventual shift to incarceration reduced the severity and violence of punishment.

Two additional forerunners of modern incarceration were banishment and transportation. In essence, they were alternatives to the more severe corporal punishments or capital punishment. Originating in ancient times, **banishment** required offenders to leave the community and live elsewhere, commonly in the wilderness. The modern version of banishment is long-term incarceration (for example, life imprisonment without opportunity for parole). As population and urban growth displaced frontiers across Europe and as demands for cheap labor increased with the rise of Western capitalism, **transportation** of offenders from their home nation to one of that nation's colonies gradually replaced banishment. England, for instance, was transporting hundreds of

FYI: Mamertine Prison

Although it surely did not resemble today's prisons, one of the earliest known prisons was the Mamertine Prison, built around 64 B.C. under the sewers of Rome.

Source: Robert Johnson, *Hard Time: Understanding and Reforming the Prison* (Monterey, CA: Brooks/Cole, 1987).

banishment A punishment, originating in ancient times, that required offenders to leave the community and live elsewhere, commonly in the wilderness.

transportation A punishment in which offenders were transported from their home nation to one of that nation's colonies to work.

Besides being painful, placement in the stocks or pillory was intended to humiliate and shame offenders. *Is a greater emphasis on the shame of punishment needed today? If so, how should it be accomplished?*

convicts a year to North America by the early 1600s.[4] Transportation fell into disuse as European colonies gained independence.

workhouses European forerunners of the modern U.S. prison, where offenders were sent to learn discipline and regular work habits.

The closest European forerunners of the modern U.S. prison were known as **workhouses** or *houses of correction.* Offenders were sent to them to learn discipline and regular work habits. The fruits of inmate labor were also expected to pay for facility upkeep and even to yield a profit. One of the first and most famous workhouses, the London Bridewell, opened in the 1550s, and workhouses spread through other parts of Europe thereafter. Such facilities were used extensively throughout the next three centuries, coexisting with such responses to crime as transportation, corporal punishment, and capital punishment. In fact, crowding in workhouses was a major impetus for the development of transportation as a punishment.

Reform Initiatives As described in Chapter 3, the Enlightenment was a time of faith in science and reason as well as a period of humanistic reform. The Enlightenment thinkers and reformers of the 1700s and 1800s described the penal system of their day with such terms as *excessive, disorderly, inefficient, arbitrary, capricious, discriminatory* (against the poor), and *unjust.* Three reformers who were important to initiatives in corrections were Cesare Beccaria (1738–1794), John Howard (1726–1790), and Jeremy Bentham (1748–1832).

Criminologists Graeme Newman and Pietro Marongiu contend that Beccaria's famous book, *On Crimes and Punishments* (1764), though often acclaimed for its originality, actually brought together the reformist principles espoused by other thinkers of the era, such as Montesquieu and Voltaire.[5] One of those principles concerned replacing the discretionary and arbitrary administration of justice with a system of detailed written laws describing the behaviors that constitute crime and the associated punishments. People need to know, Beccaria believed, exactly what punishments are prescribed for various offenses if the law is to deter criminal behavior. As part of his quest to deter crime, Beccaria declared that the punishment should fit the crime in two senses. First, the severity of punishment should parallel the severity of harm resulting from the crime. Second, the punishment should be severe enough to outweigh the pleasure obtainable from the crime. Furthermore, to deter crime, he believed, punishment needed to be certain and swift. Certainty implies that the likelihood of getting caught and punished is perceived as high. Swiftness implies that punishment will not be delayed after commission of the crime.

Beccaria did not ground his thinking firmly in empirical observations and did little to actively campaign for the reforms he advocated.[6] The work of John Howard, an English sheriff and social activist, presents an interesting contrast in that regard. Howard's 1777 book, *The State of the Prisons in England and Wales,* was based on his visits to penal institutions in various parts of Europe. Howard was appalled by the crowding, overall poor living conditions, and disorderly and abusive practices he observed in those facilities. He advocated that penal environments be made safe, humane, and orderly. Howard's opinion was that incarceration should do more than punish—that it should also instill discipline and reform inmates. Toward that end, he proposed an orderly institutional routine of religious teaching, hard work, and solitary confinement to promote introspection and penance.[7] Howard's work inspired the growing popularity of the term *penitentiary* to refer to penal confinement facilities.

Myth	Fact
The reason punishment fails to adequately deter crime in the United States is that it is not severe enough.	The United States has a higher rate of imprisonment and longer sentences than virtually any other nation. It is also one of the few advanced, industrialized nations to have retained the death penalty. It is hard indeed to support the argument that our punishment is not severe enough. Certainty and swiftness, however, are lacking, and that is the failure to which Beccaria would probably point.

In **penology,** the study of prison management and the treatment of offenders, Jeremy Bentham is perhaps best remembered for his idea that order and reform could be achieved in a prison through architectural design. His **panopticon** ("all-seeing" or "inspection-house") prison design consisted of a round building with tiers of cells lining the circumference and facing a central inspection tower so that prisoners could be watched by staff from the tower. Although no facilities completely true to Bentham's panopticon plan were ever constructed, structures similar in design were erected at Illinois's Stateville Penitentiary (now Stateville Correctional Center), which opened in 1925.

penology The study of prison management and the treatment of offenders.

panopticon A prison design consisting of a round building with tiers of cells lining the inner circumference and facing a central inspection tower.

In sum, the historical roots of the modern prison lie in Europe. It was in America, however, that the penitentiary concept was first put into wide practice.

DEVELOPMENTS IN THE UNITED STATES

In colonial America, penal practice was loose, decentralized, and unsystematic, combining private retaliation against wrongdoing with fines, banishment, harsh corporal punishments, and capital punishment. Local jails were scattered about the colonies, but they were used primarily for temporary holding rather than for punishment.[8] Some people, such as William Penn, promoted incarceration as a humane alternative to the physically brutal punishments that were common. However, that idea was largely ignored because there was no stable central governmental authority to coordinate and finance (through tax revenue) the large-scale confinement of offenders.

Stateville Correctional Center in Illinois is similar in design to Bentham's panopticon plan. *Why wasn't this prison design used more widely in the United States?*

The Penitentiary Movement In the aftermath of the American Revolution, it rapidly became apparent that the colonial system of justice would not suffice. Economic chaos and civil disorder followed the war. Combined with population growth and the transition from an agricultural society to an industrial one, they created the need for a strong, centralized government to achieve political and economic stability. The rise of the penitentiary occurred in that context.[9] Philosophically, it was guided by Enlightenment principles. In 1790, the Walnut Street Jail in Philadelphia was converted from a simple holding facility to a prison to which offenders could be sentenced for their crimes. It is commonly regarded as the nation's first state prison. In a system consistent with Howard's plan, its inmates labored in solitary cells and received large doses of religious teaching. Later in the 1790s, New York opened Newgate Prison. Other states quickly followed suit, and the penitentiary movement was born. By 1830, Pennsylvania and New York had constructed additional prisons to supplement their original ones.

Pennsylvania and New York pioneered the penitentiary movement by developing two competing systems of confinement.[10] The **Pennsylvania system,** sometimes called the *separate system,* required that inmates be kept in solitary cells so that they could study religious writings, reflect on their misdeeds, and perform handicraft work. In the New York system, or the **Auburn system** (named after Auburn Penitentiary and also referred to as the *congregate* or *silent system*), inmates worked and ate together in silence during the day and were returned to solitary cells for the evening. Ultimately, the Auburn system prevailed over the Pennsylvania system as the model followed by other states. It avoided the harmful psychological effects of total solitary confinement and allowed more inmates to be housed in less space because cells could be smaller. In addition, the Auburn system's congregate work principle was more congruent with the system of factory production emerging in wider society than was the outdated craft principle of the separate system. If prison labor was to be profitable, it seemed that the Auburn plan was the one to use.

Pennsylvania system An early system of U.S. penology in which inmates were kept in solitary cells so that they could study religious writings, reflect on their misdeeds, and perform handicraft work.

Auburn system An early system of penology, originating at Auburn Penitentiary in New York, in which inmates worked and ate together in silence during the day and were placed in solitary cells for the evening.

It is interesting that although penitentiary construction flourished and the United States became the model nation in penology during the first half of the nineteenth century, there was serious discontent with the penitentiary by the end of the Civil War. There were few signs penitentiaries were deterring crime, reforming offenders, or turning great profits from inmate labor. In fact, prisons were becoming increasingly expensive to run, and opposition was growing to selling prisoner-made goods on the open market. With faith in the penitentiary declining, the stage was set for a new movement—a movement that, rather than challenging the fundamental value of incarceration as a punishment, sought to improve the method of incarceration.

The Elmira Reformatory, which opened in 1876 in Elmira, New York, was the first institution for men that was based on reformatory principles. *What caused the change in penal philosophy?*

THE REFORMATORY MOVEMENT The reformatory movement got its start at the 1870 meeting of the National Prison Association, in Cincinnati. The principles adopted there were championed by such leaders in the field as Enoch Wines (1806–1879) and Zebulon Brockway (1827–1920).[11] A new type of institution, the reformatory, was designed for younger, less hardened offenders, between 16 and 30 years of age. Based on a military model of regimentation, it emphasized academic and vocational training in addition to work. A classification system was introduced, in which inmates' progress toward reformation was rated. The sentences for determinate periods of time (for example, 5 years) were replaced with indeterminate terms, in which inmates served sentences within given ranges (for example, between 2 and 8 years). Parole or early release could be granted for favorable progress in reformation.

It has been observed that indeterminate sentences and the possibility of parole facilitate greater control over inmates than do determinate sentences. Many inmates are interested, above all else, in gaining their freedom. The message conveyed by indeterminate sentences and the possibility of parole is this: "Conform to institutional expectations or do more time."

INSTITUTIONS FOR WOMEN Until the reformatory era, there was little effort to establish separate facilities for women. Women prisoners were usually confined in segregated areas of male prisons and generally received inferior treatment. The reformatory movement, reflecting its assumptions about differences between categories of inmates and its emphasis on classification, helped feminize punishment.[12] The first women's prison organized according to the reformatory model opened in Indiana in 1873. By the 1930s, several other women's reformatories were in operation, mainly in the Northeast and the Midwest. Most employed cottages or a campus and a family-style living plan, not the cell-block plan of men's prisons. Most concentrated on molding inmates to fulfill stereotypical domestic roles, such as cleaning and cooking, upon release.

TWENTIETH CENTURY PRISONS Criminologist John Irwin has provided a useful typology for summarizing imprisonment in the last century.[13] According to Irwin, three types of institutions have been dominant. Each has dominated

Big-house prisons, which consisted of large cell blocks containing stacks of cells, were the dominant prison design of the early twentieth century. *What are some problems with the big-house prison design?*

a different part of the century. The dominant type for about the first three decades was the "big house." In Irwin's words:

> The Big House was a walled prison with large cell blocks that contained stacks of three or more tiers of one- or two-man cells. On the average, it held 2,500 men. Sometimes a single cell block housed over 1,000 prisoners in six tiers of cells. Most of these prisons were built over many decades and had a mixture of old and new cell blocks. Some of the older cell blocks were quite primitive.[14]

It is important to realize that big houses were not new prisons, distinct from earlier penitentiaries and reformatories. They were the old penitentiaries and reformatories, expanded in size to accommodate larger inmate populations. Originally, big-house prisons exploited inmate labor through various links to the free market. Industrial prisons predominated in the North, while plantation prisons characterized much of the South. With the rise of organized labor and the coming of the Great Depression, free-market inmate labor systems fell into demise during the 1920s and 1930s. Big houses became warehouses oriented toward custody and repression of inmates.

medical model A theory of institutional corrections, popular during the 1940s and 1950s, in which crime was seen as symptomatic of personal illness in need of treatment.

What Irwin calls the "correctional institution" arose during the 1940s and became the dominant type of prison in the 1950s. Correctional institutions generally were smaller and more modern in appearance than big houses. However, correctional institutions did not replace big houses; they simply supplemented them, though correctional-institution principles spread to many big houses. Correctional institutions emerged as penologists turned to the field of medicine as a model for their work. During that phase of corrections, a so-called **medical model** came to be used, as crime was seen as symptomatic of personal illness in need of treatment. Under the medical model, shortly after being sentenced to prison, inmates were subjected to psychological assessment and diagnosis during classification processes. Assessment and diagnosis were followed by treatment designed to address the offender's supposed illness. The main kinds of treatment, according to Irwin, were academic and vocational education and therapeutic counseling. After institutional treatment came parole, which amounted to follow-up treatment in the community. Importantly, the ways of achieving control over inmate behavior shifted from the custodial repression typical of the big house to more subtle methods of indirect coercion: inmates knew that failure to participate in treatment and exhibit "progress" in prison meant that parole would be delayed.

During the 1960s and 1970s, both the effectiveness and the fairness of coerced prison rehabilitation programming began to be challenged,[15] and the correctional institution's dominance began to wane. In Irwin's view, the third type of prison, the "contemporary violent prison," arose by default as the correctional institution faded. Gone were many of the treatment-program control mechanisms of the correctional institution. Further, many of the repressive measures used to control inmates in the big house became illegal after the rise of the inmates' rights movement during the 1960s (to be discussed later). In essence, what emerged in many prisons was a power vacuum that was filled with inmate gang violence and interracial hatred.

Privatization and Shock Incarceration As will be readily apparent in the next section of this chapter, the last three decades are likely to be remembered for the largest incarceration boom to date and for desperate attempts to deal with prison crowding by developing alternatives to traditional incarceration.

One alternative to traditional confinement is the move toward **privatization,** the involvement of the private sector in the construction and operation of confinement facilities. The private sector has a long tradition in institutional corrections. For instance, such diverse services as food, legal aid, medical and psychiatric care, and education have long been provided through private vendors. There is a rich history of private labor contracting in the operation of prisons, and it is now witnessing something of a revival in certain jurisdictions. Also, the private sector has operated juvenile institutions for many years. But mounting prison populations, combined with space and budget limitations, have helped give privatization new twists. One of those twists entails having the private sector finance construction of institutions under what amounts to a lease-purchase agreement. The Potosi Correctional Center in Missouri was constructed under such a strategy. In another twist, the state contracts with private companies like U.S. Corrections Corporation to have them operate prisons. One of the earliest privately operated state prisons for adult felons, Kentucky's minimum-security Marion Adjustment Center, was opened in January 1986.

privatization The involvement of the private sector in the construction and the operation of confinement facilities.

At the end of 2001, 27 states, the District of Columbia, Puerto Rico, the Federal Bureau of Prisons, the Immigration and Naturalization Service, and the U.S. Marshals Service had contracts in force with one or more of 13 private companies to house prisoners in 154 privately managed, secure adult correctional facilities (jails or prisons).[16] About 40 percent of those facilities were located in Texas (with 42) and California (with 22). No other jurisdiction had more than eight private adult correctional institutions; most jurisdictions had only one facility.[17] Together, those institutions had the capacity to hold approximately 6 percent of all local, state, and federal inmates.[18] Two companies—Corrections Corporation of America (with a 52 percent market share) and Wackenhut Corrections Corporation (with a 22 percent market share)—dominate the industry.[19]

FYI: The Convict Lease System

One of the darkest chapters in the history of American corrections involves the convict lease system that was adopted by many southern states following the Civil War. It perpetuated slavery in the states that embraced it. Counties and states leased thousands of prisoners (mostly black) to private individuals and companies to work (and die) in cotton fields, mines, and forests of the Deep South. Governments made millions of dollars in lease payments, and those who leased prisoners and brutally exploited them made millions more. The practice did not end until the 1920s.

SOURCE: www.crim.ufl.edu/pcp, "Frequently Asked Questions."

Proponents of states' contracting to have the private sector finance construction and operate prisons often point to efficiency, flexibility, and cost-effectiveness. Opponents frequently worry about liability issues, about creating a profit motive for incarcerating people, and about the incentive to trim inmate services and programs to maximize profits.

Research shows the following about private correctional facilities:

- Private facilities can be constructed and opened more quickly. Following contract awards, private facilities can be constructed within 12 to 18 months; similar facilities constructed by governments usually take 36 to 48 months to be brought "on line."
- Construction cost savings of 25 percent or more and operating cost savings of 10 to 15 percent are common for private facilities.
- The quality of services and programs in private facilities is frequently superior to that in publicly operated facilities.
- Private contractors can frequently deliver correctional services more cost-effectively than public employees.

The incarceration boom of the past three decades has required the construction of dozens of new prisons. *Was this construction boom necessary? Why or why not?*

- Privatization can substantially reduce legal liability costs of operating prisons and jails.
- Necessary changes in the nature and scope of prisoner programs can be made quicker and easier in private facilities.
- The existence of private facilities in a jurisdiction sometimes encourages improvements in the public facilities in that jurisdiction.
- Prisoners in private facilities have a broader array of legal remedies when challenging conditions of confinement than prisoners in public facilities.[20]

In sum, based on the available evidence, privately operated correctional facilities seem to be a viable alternative.

shock incarceration The placement of offenders in facilities patterned after military boot camps.

A second confinement alternative to traditional incarceration is **shock incarceration,** the placement of offenders in facilities patterned after military boot camps. Such facilities are ordinarily designed for young, nonviolent offenders without extensive criminal records. Instead of being given traditional prison sentences, those offenders are sentenced to shock incarceration facilities for relatively short periods (for instance, 90 days). There, they are subjected to a strict, military-style program of work, physical conditioning, and discipline. Boot camps vary considerably in their emphasis on treatment. After completing the program, inmates are released into the community on probation or parole. Shock incarceration is appealing to those who wish to convey a "tough on crime" message to the general public. However, as criminologists Doris Layton MacKenzie and James Shaw observe, the "studies examining the recidivism of boot camp releasees have been disappointing for those who expect the programs to affect offenders' activities after release."[21]

FYI

Prison Growth

Several states in the United States now have as many prisons in operation as some entire Western nations—or more. As of January 1, 2001, the states, the District of Columbia, and the federal government, combined, operated a total of 1,384 adult prisons.

SOURCE: Camille Graham Camp and George M. Camp, *The 2001 Corrections Yearbook: Adult Systems* (Middletown, CT: Criminal Justice Institute, 2002), p. 80.

The popularity of boot-camp programs has probably peaked. In 1997, the California state legislature ended the state's boot-camp program after 5 years of operation. A California Department of Corrections evaluation found that the program reduced neither recidivism nor costs to the state.[22] Boot-camp prisons are considered an intermediate sanction, which will be discussed in Chapter 12 ("Community Corrections").

CYCLES IN HISTORY The history of institutional corrections has evolved in cycles of accumulation. Developments viewed as innovative replacements for old practices almost always contain vestiges of the old practices, and the old practices seldom disappear when "new" ones are introduced. The new is implemented alongside the old and contains elements of the old. Penitentiaries were not torn down when reformatories were introduced, nor were big houses abolished when correctional institutions arose. Similarly, many jurisdictions have recently moved away from indeterminate sentences toward determinate ones. Those determinate sentences, although often seen as innovative, are hard to distinguish from the fixed sentences that preceded the move to indeterminate sentencing. Likewise, the modern trend toward boot camps revives the quasi-military organization that was present at Elmira Reformatory. An interesting question is whether penological history represents progress or the coming back around of what went around before.

Chain gangs are another recent example of the "what goes around comes around" phenomenon. In 1995, Alabama became the first state to reintroduce the chain gang. Arizona became the second state to do so the same year. Arizona is also the first state to allow female prisoners to work on chain gangs. Both states put shackled prisoners to work along the roadside, cutting high weeds, picking up trash, and clearing muddy ditches. Arizona's female chain gang members also dig graves and bury indigents who have died, paint curbs, and remove graffiti. Prisoners are supervised by gun-toting guards. Alabama's experiment with chain gangs lasted less than 4 years. Among problems blamed for its demise were escape attempts, inmate fights, lack of productivity (people chained together move slowly), and the need for more guards inside prisons. As of this writing, Arizona was still using chain gangs but participation was voluntary. In addition, unlike in Alabama where inmates were chained together, in Arizona, inmates are chained individually. In Florida in 1997, legislation was proposed to put chain gangs on state highways as a crime deterrent. The legislation failed because lawmakers felt the plan was too risky. Widespread use of chain gangs ended between the Depression and World War II, though it was not until the early 1960s that Georgia abolished the practice.

THINKING CRITICALLY

1. Do you think any of the early forerunners to modern corrections (such as banishment, etc.) could be used today? Why or why not?
2. Do you think that shock incarceration has any merit? Why or why not?

The Incarceration Boom

For most of the past 65 years, the incarceration rate was fairly steady. Only since 1973 has there been a continuing increase, with each year showing a new high.

RECENT TRENDS

There were 329,821 inmates in state and federal prisons at the end of 1980 (305,458 state prison inmates and 24,363 federal prison inmates). By mid-decade, the total number of prison inmates had increased 52 percent, to 502,752 inmates, and by the end of the 1980s, there were a total of 712,967 inmates, an increase of 116 percent over 1980.[23] That represents an average increase of about 9 percent per year.

A little more than a decade later, at year-end 2002, the adult prison population stood at 1,440,665 (1,277,127 state prison inmates and 163,528 federal prison inmates), an increase of 102 percent over the beginning of 1990 and an increase of 337 percent over 1980. The total number of prison inmates at year-end 2002 was 2.6 percent more than the record high of 1,404,032 inmates at year-end 2001. (Between 1980 and year-end 2002, the state prison population increased 318 percent and the federal prison population increased 571 percent.) In other words, between 1980 and year-end 2002, the adult prison population (both state and federal) had more than quadrupled.[24]

However, the growth of the prison population slowed somewhat in the 1990s to an average of about 6.5 percent per year (from approximately 9 percent per year during the 1980s). In 1999, the prison population grew 3.4 percent—the smallest yearly increase since 1988. Between year-end 2001 and year-end 2002, the prison population grew 2.6 percent (the state prison population increased only 2.4 percent, while the federal prison population increased 4.8 percent). The level of growth (1.1 percent) in the state and federal prison population in 2001 was the lowest annual rate recorded since 1972 and is entirely attributable to the slower growth in the state prison population. The overall growth of the state (but not federal) prison population has been slowing since 1995.[25] Table 10.1 shows the jurisdictions with the largest and smallest numbers of prison inmates and the highest and lowest incarceration rates per 100,000 residents at year-end 2002. (We will discuss incarceration rates later in this section.)

FYI: Federal vs. State Prisons

Only about 10 percent of all inmates at midyear 2002 were in federal prisons. The remaining 90 percent were in state and D.C. prisons.

SOURCE: Paige M. Harrison and Jennifer C. Karberg, "Prison and Jail Inmates at Midyear 2002." U.S. Department of Justice, *Bureau of Justice Statistics Bulletin* (April 2003).

TABLE 10.1 Jurisdictions With the Largest and Smallest Numbers of Prison Inmates and Incarceration Rates per 100,000 Residents at Year-End 2002

Prison Population	Number of Inmates	Incarceration Rates, 2002	Rate per 100,000 State Residents[a]
5 largest:			
Federal	163,528	Louisiana	794
California	162,317	Mississippi	743
Texas	162,003	Texas	692
Florida	75,210	Oklahoma	667
New York	67,065	Alabama	612
5 smallest:			
North Dakota	1,112	Maine	141
Wyoming	1,737	Minnesota	141
Vermont	1,863	North Dakota	167
Maine	1,900	Rhode Island	191
New Hampshire	2,451	New Hampshire	192

[a]The number of prisoners with a sentence of more than 1 year per 100,000 residents in the state population.

SOURCE: Paige M. Harrison and Allen J. Beck, "Prisoners in 2002," U.S. Department of Justice, *Bureau of Justice Statistics Bulletin* (Washington, DC: GPO, July 2003), p. 1.

It is important to emphasize that the approximately 1.45 million state and federal prison inmates did not include all persons incarcerated in the United States and its territories at yearend 2002 (or the end of 2001). For example, not included in that number were 93,771 prisoners held in privately operated facilities; 71,256 state and federal prisoners held in local jails or other facilities operated by county or local authorities; the 665,475 local jail inmates (more about the jail population later); the 16,206 inmates held in territorial and commonwealth prisons; the 8,748 inmates held in facilities operated by or exclusively for the Bureau of Immigration and Customs Enforcement (formerly the U.S. Immigration and Naturalization Service); the 2,377 inmates in military facilities; the 1,912 inmates in jails in Indian country (as of midyear 2001); or the 110,284 inmates (as of October 2000) in juvenile facilities (discussed in Chapter 13). Overall, the United States had more than two million people incarcerated at year-end 2002.[26]

TABLE 10.2 The 10 Largest Local Jail Jurisdictions with Their Average Daily Populations at Midyear 2002

Jurisdiction	Average Daily Population
Los Angeles County, CA	19,258
New York City, NY	13,952
Cook County, IL	10,888
Maricopa County, AZ	8,008
Philadelphia City, PA	7,221
Dade County, FL	6,680
Harris County, TX	6,641
Dallas County, TX	6,567
Orleans Parish, LA	5,875
Broward County, FL	5,116

SOURCE: Adapted from Paige M. Harrison and Jennifer C. Karberg, "Prison and Jail Inmates at Midyear 2002," U.S. Department of Justice, *Bureau of Justice Statistics Bulletin*, April 2003.

Similar, though somewhat less drastic, trends are evident when local jails are examined. Between 1982 and 1990, the number of jail inmates increased nearly 89 percent, from 209,582 to 395,553. On June 30, 2002, the local jail population stood at a record high of 655,475 inmates, an increase of about 66 percent over the beginning of 1990 and 213 percent over 1982.[27] If the additional 72,437 persons being supervised outside a jail facility (in community service programs, weekender programs, by electronic monitoring, etc.) at midyear 2002 are added to the 655,475 confined inmates, the total number of people under the supervision of local jails increases to 737,912, an increase of about 5 percent over the previous year.[28] Table 10.2 lists the

10 largest local jail jurisdictions in the United States, along with their average daily populations at midyear 2002 (the latest year for which data were available).

We must be cautious about looking exclusively at changes in the sheer number of people incarcerated, because such changes do not take into consideration changes in the size of the general population. We might wonder whether big increases in the number of people incarcerated simply reflect growth in the U.S. population. Researchers typically convert a raw figure to an **incarceration rate** to deal with that problem. The incarceration rate is calculated by dividing the number of people incarcerated by the population of the area and multiplying the result by 100,000:

$$\text{Incarceration rate} = \frac{\text{number incarcerated}}{\text{population}} \times 100{,}000$$

Figure 10.1 is a display of the incarceration boom of recent years with shifts in the size of the general population taken into account. As shown in the figure, the U.S. adult prison incarceration rate was comparatively stable from the period before 1930 until the mid-1970s, at which time the dramatic upward climb began. Between 1980 and year-end 2002, the prison incarceration rate rose approximately 242 percent, from 139 to 476 prisoners per 100,000 residents.[29] Likewise, between 1982 and midyear 2002, the jail incarceration rate rose from 90 to 231 per 100,000 residents, or approximately 157 percent.[30]

Incarceration rates also differ significantly among nations. The data in Figure 10.2 show the prison population rates for 20 selected nations as of January 1, 2003. Note that the United States has the highest rate of incarceration in the world.

Annual incarceration rates such as those depicted in Figure 10.2 and discussed earlier reflect the numbers of people admitted to institutions, the

incarceration rate A figure derived by dividing the number of people incarcerated by the population of the area and multiplying the result by 100,000; used to compare incarceration levels of units with different population sizes.

FYI: Incarceration Rates

Males are far more prone to crime and incarceration than females. At year-end 2002, the rate for men was 906 per 100,000, compared with 60 per 100,000 for women.

SOURCE: Paige M. Harrison and Allen J. Beck, "Prisoners in 2002," U.S. Department of Justice, *Bureau of Justice Statistics Bulletin*, July 2003, p. 4.

FIGURE 10.1 Sentenced Prisoners in State and Federal Institutions

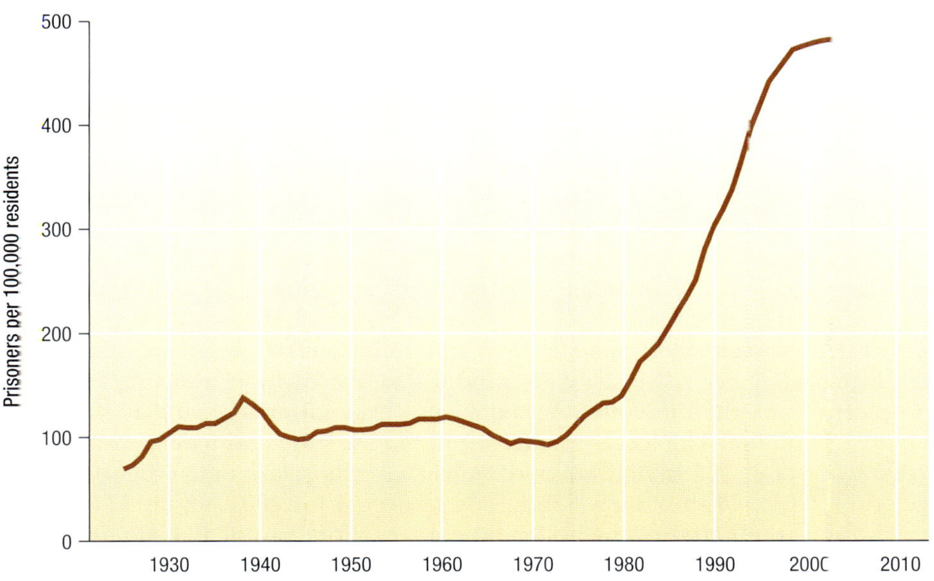

SOURCES: Kathleen Maguire and Ann L. Pastore (eds.), *Sourcebook of Criminal Justice Statistics 1996*, U.S. Department of Justice, Bureau of Justice Statistics (Washington, DC: GPO, 1997), p. 517, Table 6.4 and p. 518, Table 6.21; Paige M. Harrison and Allen J. Beck, "Prisoners in 2002," U.S. Department of Justice, *Bureau of Justice Statistics Bulletin* (Washington, DC: GPO, July 2003).

FIGURE 10.2 Incarceration Rates for Selected Nations

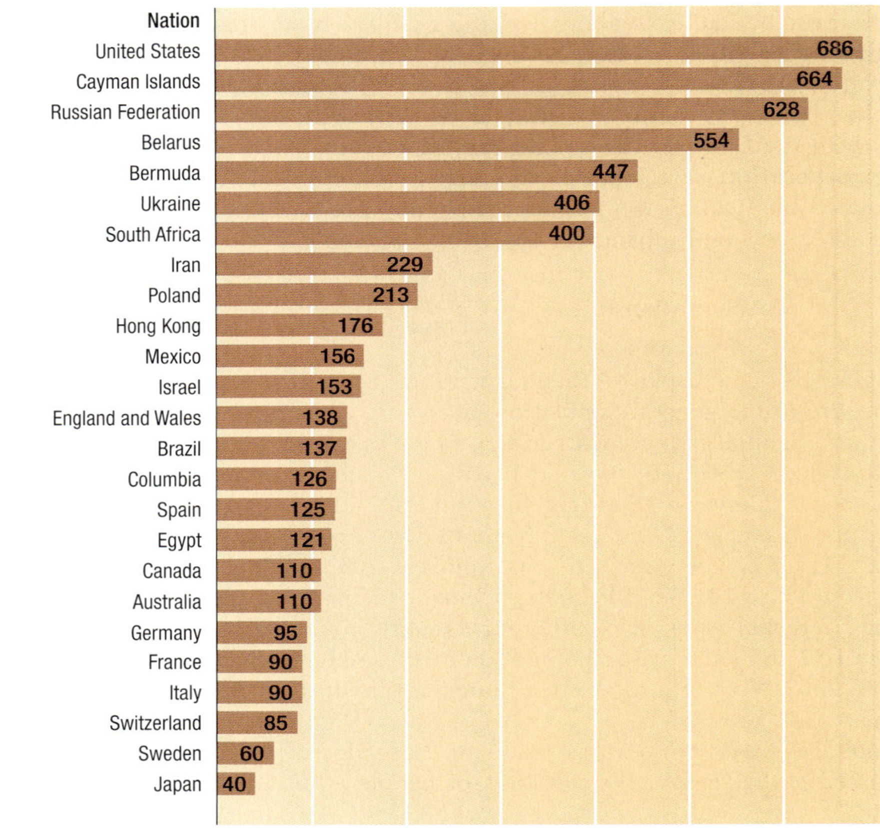

SOURCE: The first 17 nations are from Kings College London: International Centre for Prison Studies, World Prison Brief—Highest Prison Population Rates at www.kcl.ac.uk/depsta/rel/icps/worldbrief/highest_rates(manual).html, January 1, 2003; the bottom 8 nations are from The Sentencing Project at www.sentencingproject.org, 1997–1999.

lengths of time those people serve, and (for purposes of international comparisons) the nations' levels of crime. Nations with higher levels of crime, with more people admitted to prison, and with prisoners serving longer terms can be expected to have higher annual rates of incarceration. Thus, James Lynch argues that the type of international comparisons depicted in Figure 10.2 may be misleading because the United States has a more serious crime problem than most other nations.[31] Lynch contends that if the analysis is controlled for nations' levels of crime, the differences between the United States and other nations in the use of imprisonment are smaller.

CJ ONLINE

Incarceration Rates
For the incarceration rates of 99 nations, including the top 17 in Figure 10.2, access the International Centre for Prison Studies website at **www.kcl.ac.uk/depsta/rel/icps/worldbrief/world_brief.html.** *Why do you think incarceration rates vary so greatly among different nations?*

COST ESTIMATES Total spending on state and federal prisons in fiscal year 2001 was budgeted at nearly $36 billion (45 percent more than in 1995 and 4 percent more than in 2000). Actual agency expenditures during 2000 totaled about $32 billion. The total amount requested for state and federal prisons for 2002 was about $35 billion (approximately $1 billion less than what was budgeted in 2001). Of the nearly $36 billion budgeted for 2001, about $3.8 billion were for capital improvements (new construction, physical plant improvements, and equipment), about $1.4 billion for food, and nearly $3.5 billion for medical care. California budgeted the most of any state (slightly more than $5 billion); North Dakota, the least ($26.4 million).[32]

The average daily cost of incarceration per inmate in 2000 was $61.04 ($22,279.60 per inmate per year). Alaska had the highest daily cost ($111.89, or $40,839.85 per year), and Alabama had the lowest ($25.19, or $9,194.35 per year). The average daily cost per inmate for food was $3.62; the highest daily food cost was in Hawaii ($13.00), and the lowest in Alabama ($0.75). (Food costs include the costs of food, food supplies, and food staff and inmate salaries.) The average daily cost per inmate for medical care was $7.39; the highest daily cost was $16.69 (Alaska), and the lowest was $1.02 (California). Medical costs do not include the costs of mental health services.[33]

For local jails for which data are available, the average amount budgeted in fiscal year 2000 was approximately $36 million per jail. The range was from a high of about $834 million in New York City to a low of about $2.3 million in Dorchester County, Maryland. The overall average 2000 cost per jail inmate was $58.64 per day (or $21,403.60 per year). New York City had the highest daily cost, $201.00 per inmate ($73,365 per year), and Sullivan County, Tennessee, had the lowest daily cost, $18.93 per inmate ($6,909.45 per year).[34]

FYI: Prison Costs

In 1995, for the first time ever, more money was spent building new prisons than new university structures in the United States—$2.5 billion for construction in higher education and $2.6 billion for prison construction. From 1987 to 1995, state prison expenditures rose 30 percent while higher-education funding fell 18 percent.

SOURCE: "More Spent on Prisons Than Universities in 1995," *The Orlando Sentinel*, February 25, 1997, p. A-6.

THE CROWDING ISSUE Crowding has always been a problem in American prisons, but it has become especially troublesome over the past two decades. The increase in prison construction across the nation of late, while staggering, has failed to keep pace with the increase in prison populations, produced partly by the War on Drugs. Far more than half the states now have at least one institution under court order to rectify crowded conditions, and many state prisoners are being held in local jails because of insufficient prison space. Furthermore, crowded prisons are often volatile prisons, and efforts to address problems related to crowding frequently end up diverting resources from inmate services and programs. How did we arrive at this state of affairs?

The most obvious explanation is that a massive outbreak of crime in the United States has fueled the growth of the prison population. But as criminologist Nils Christie and a number of other observers have pointed out, that explanation is simply not supported by the data, which show relatively stable, and in some cases even declining, rates of crime for much of the period of the incarceration boom.[35] Likewise, there has not been an increase in the proportion of young adults, who constitute the most prison-prone age group, in the general population.

Law professor Franklin Zimring offers an interesting public opinion explanation.[36] Zimring claims that members of the public will think punishment for crime is too soft and will demand more imprisonment as long as they think crime is too high. The problem is that prisons generally do an unsatisfactory job of controlling crime, so the public continues to perceive crime as high, despite increases in the prison population. The inability of prisons to control crime fuels the public demand for still more punishment (such as more imprisonment). Zimring uses the analogy of a person who finds that the medicine he or she has been taking for a headache is not helping and decides to increase the dose of the same medication.

Myth	Fact
Six percent of America's criminals commit 70 percent of all violent crimes. Thus crime control could be improved dramatically if only those 6 percent were imprisoned.	This well-publicized statistic comes from a misinterpretation of two studies focusing on criminal activity by boys born in Philadelphia. Dr. Marvin Wolfgang of the University of Pennsylvania discovered that 6 percent of the boys born in Philadelphia in 1945 were responsible for more than half of the serious crimes committed by the entire group. Of those born in 1958, 7.5 percent committed 69 percent of the serious crimes. Those who cite these outdated studies focus erroneously on 6 percent of "criminals"—as if future high-rate offenders could be predicted—instead of 6 percent of all male children born in a given year, whose future criminal behavior is also not predictable. SOURCE: *Seeking Justice: Crime and Punishment in America*, Edna McConnell Clark Foundation (New York: 1997), p. 12.

We can expand a bit on Zimring's perspective. Over the last 200 years, Americans have developed a tradition of strong reliance on the prison to control crime. It has never done very well. As Zimring observes, the typical response to high crime and high recidivism is to conclude that criminals are not being punished enough and to gradually increase the use of imprisonment. In pursuing that strategy, we get caught in a loop. We are continually forced to direct the greatest portions of our overall correctional budgets toward imprisonment. Relatively few resources are left to develop effective programs in community corrections and crime prevention programs that might reduce reliance on imprisonment. The lack of resources devoted to community corrections and crime prevention helps ensure that programs in those areas will fail to control crime. So there will always be an abundant supply of offenders to feed the prison population and escalate the cost of maintaining that population. The irony is clear and substantial. While crowding in correctional institutions suggests the need for effective alternatives in community corrections and crime prevention, that same crowding and the resources it consumes preclude such alternatives. Ineffectiveness in community corrections and crime prevention simply makes the crowding worse, thereby consuming even more resources.

FYI

Prison Resources

About two-thirds of all money spent on corrections is used to finance institutions. Roughly a quarter of all persons under correctional supervision are incarcerated. Therefore, about three-quarters of the correctional population must be accommodated with one-third of the resources.

PRISON INMATE CHARACTERISTICS

Who are the people in prison, and why are they there? First, we must distinguish between federal and state prisoners. At year-end 2002, 89 percent of all prisoners in the United States were state prisoners, while only 11 percent were federal prisoners.[37] Because most prisoners are state prisoners, we will focus on them. At the end of this section, however, we will indicate some important differences between state and federal prisoners. One last point before we begin: The characteristics of both state and federal prisoners are remarkably stable over time, that is, they do not change much from one year to the next.

From Figure 10.3 it is evident that the largest proportion of state prisoners are male and black. In addition, a large proportion had not completed high school or did not have a GED, were under 35 years of age and never married, were employed full-time prior to arrest, and had relatively low monthly incomes. Three things about these data bear mention. First, even though there is actually a greater percentage of females than males in the U.S. population, males make up about 93 percent of the state and federal prison population; that is what is meant by saying that men are disproportionately represented in prison. Second, although 68 percent of the prisoners were employed in the month preceding their arrests, the monthly income figures reveal the low-paying jobs they held. More than half of all inmates had monthly incomes under $1,000 in the month prior to their current arrest. (However, only about 10 percent of state inmates were homeless—living on the street or in a shelter—in the year prior to their incarceration.) Third, blacks are disproportionately represented in state prisons. While blacks make up approximately 13 percent of the general U.S. population, they account for nearly half

Myth

Prisons have a revolving door, and inmates are now serving far shorter prison terms than in the past.

Fact

Since 1923, the average prison term served by inmates in the United States has remained constant at about 2 years. State prisoners are still serving sentences that average 2 years. Federal inmates, however, have been serving slightly longer sentences since the passage of the Sentencing Reform Act of 1984 and the adoption of mandatory sentencing laws. The act introduced truth in sentencing in federal courts, which mandates that offenders serve a minimum of 85 percent of their sentences.

SOURCE: *Seeking Justice: Crime and Punishment in America,* Edna McConnell Clark Foundation (New York: 1997), p. 16; *Sourcebook of Criminal Justice Statistics 2001* (Online), p. 505, Table 6.40 and p. 513, Table 6.52.

FIGURE 10.3 Characteristics of State Prison Inmates

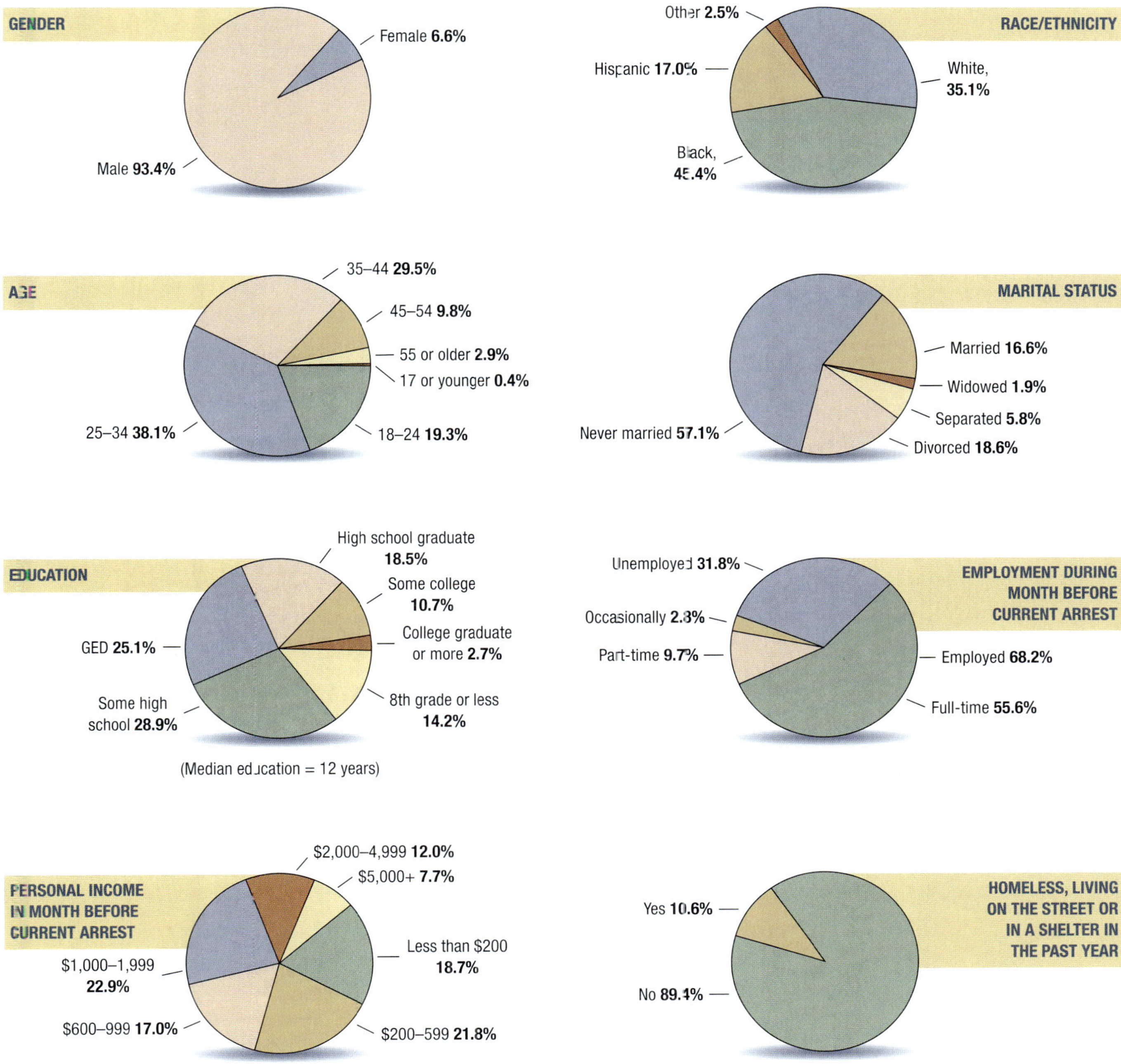

SOURCE: Disaggregated estimates for gender, race/ethnicity, and age graciously provided by Allen Beck from "Prison and Jail Inmates at Midyear 2002," U.S. Department of Justice, Bureau of Justice Statistics; data for the other characteristics are from published and unpublished data from 1997 surveys of state and federal inmates that were graciously provided by Allen Beck and Christopher Mumola, U.S. Department of Justice, Bureau of Justice Statistics (November 9, 2000).

of the state prison population. Further, the vast majority of blacks in prison are male, and black males constitute somewhere around half of all black persons in the United States. The overrepresentation of blacks in prison is a very heated issue in criminal justice today, and research has not established a consensus on the reasons for that overrepresentation. Currently, however, the weight of the evidence suggests that offense seriousness and prior criminal record generally

The largest proportion of state prisoners are male and black. Why, and what can be done about it?

FYI Incarcerated Parents

In 1999, nearly 1.5 million children had at least one parent in state or federal prison (up from less than 1 million in 1991).

SOURCE: Ellis Close, "The Prison Paradox," *Newsweek,* November 13, 2000, p. 45; Christopher J. Mumola, "Incarcerated Parents and Their Children," U.S. Department of Justice, *Bureau of Justice Special Report* (Washington, DC: GPO, August 2000).

exert a stronger impact on decisions to imprison than do extralegal factors such as race.[38]

In 2001, about half of state prison inmates were serving sentences for violent offenses, about 20 percent were serving sentences for property offenses, approximately 20 percent were serving terms for drug offenses, and most of the remainder were doing time for public order offenses. A more detailed breakdown for the violent and property offense categories is shown in Table 10.3.

The overall profile of inmate characteristics does not change drastically when we shift our attention to the federal prison population. However, there are some noteworthy differences. For example, in 2001, about 26 percent of

TABLE 10.3 Most Serious Offenses for Which State Inmates Were Serving Sentences in 2001

Offense	Percentage of Inmates	Offense	Percentage of Inmates	Offense	Percentage of Inmates
Violent Offenses	49.3	**Property Offenses**	19.3	**Drug Offenses**	20.4
Murder[a]	13.2	Burglary	8.7	**Public Order Offenses[b]**	10.7
Manslaughter	1.4	Larceny	3.8	**Other/Unspecified Offenses[c]**	0.3
Rape	2.6	Motor vehicle theft	1.5		
Other sexual assault	7.2	Fraud	2.8		
Robbery	12.8	Other property offenses	2.6		
Assault	9.8				
Other violent offenses	2.3				

Note: Data are for inmates with a sentence of more than 1 year under the jurisdiction of state correctional authorities. The number of inmates by offense were estimated using 1997 Survey of Inmates in State Correctional Facilities and rounded to the nearest 100.

[a]Includes nonnegligent manslaughter.

[b]Includes weapons, drunk driving, court offenses, commercialized vice, morals and decency charges, liquor law violations, and other public-order offenses.

[c]Includes juvenile offenses and unspecified felonies.

SOURCE: Paige M. Harrison and Allen J. Beck, "Prisoners in 2002," U.S. Department of Justice, *Bureau of Justice Statistics Bulletin* (Washington, DC: GPO, July 2003), p. 10, Table 15.

the federal prison population were white, about 28 percent were Hispanic, and about 43 percent were black. Federal inmates are, on average, somewhat older and possess higher education levels than state inmates. Also, about 55 percent of federal inmates were serving time for drug offenses.[39]

THINKING CRITICALLY

What do the characteristics of prison inmates say about American society as a whole?

Incarceration Facilities

In the United States, the organizational and administrative structure of institutional corrections is diffuse and decentralized. Primary administrative responsibility for facilities lies with the executive branch of government, but the legislative and judicial branches are also involved. For example, the legislative branch appropriates resources and passes statutes that affect sentence length. The judicial branch sentences offenders to facilities and oversees the legality of institutional practices.

CJ ONLINE

U.S. Corrections

To learn more about a variety of issues that affect corrections in the United States, go to **www.corrections.com.** *What does this website tell you about the state of corrections in the U.S.?*

ORGANIZATION AND ADMINISTRATION BY GOVERNMENT

Incarceration facilities exist at all three levels of government (federal, state, and local), and power and decision-making responsibility are widely distributed both among and within levels. Within broad guidelines, the federal level and the various state and local (county and city) jurisdictions have much autonomy to organize and carry out incarceration practices. As a general rule, the federal government operates its own prison system, each state operates its own prison system, and local jurisdictions operate their own jail systems. Decentralization and autonomy notwithstanding, there are interrelationships between levels. For example, federal requirements affect the operation of state prisons, and local jails are affected by both federal and state regulations.

Federal institutions are administered by the Federal Bureau of Prisons (BOP), which was established within the U.S. Justice Department in 1930 under the Hoover Administration. Before the BOP was created, there were seven federal prisons, each separately funded and each operated under policies and procedures established by its warden. The BOP's mission is "to protect society by confining offenders in the controlled environments of prison and community-based facilities that are safe, humane, and appropriately secure, and that provide work and other self-improvement opportunities to assist offenders in becoming law-abiding citizens."[40] The bureau's central office is in Washington, DC, and there are six regional offices, in Philadelphia; Annapolis Junction, Maryland (near Baltimore); Atlanta; Dallas; Kansas City, Kansas; and Dublin, California (near San Francisco). The bureau also has two staff training centers and 29 community corrections offices. As of May 2003, the BOP operated 102 institutions (see Figure 10.4), with more in various stages of construction. The bureau's facilities hold inmates convicted of violating the U.S. Penal Code. In 2001, the BOP assumed the added responsibility of incarcerating the

Harley G. Lappin, Director, Federal Bureau of Prisons. *What do you suppose are the major challenges for the director of the BOP?*

FIGURE 10.4 Locations of Institutions in Federal Bureau of Prisons

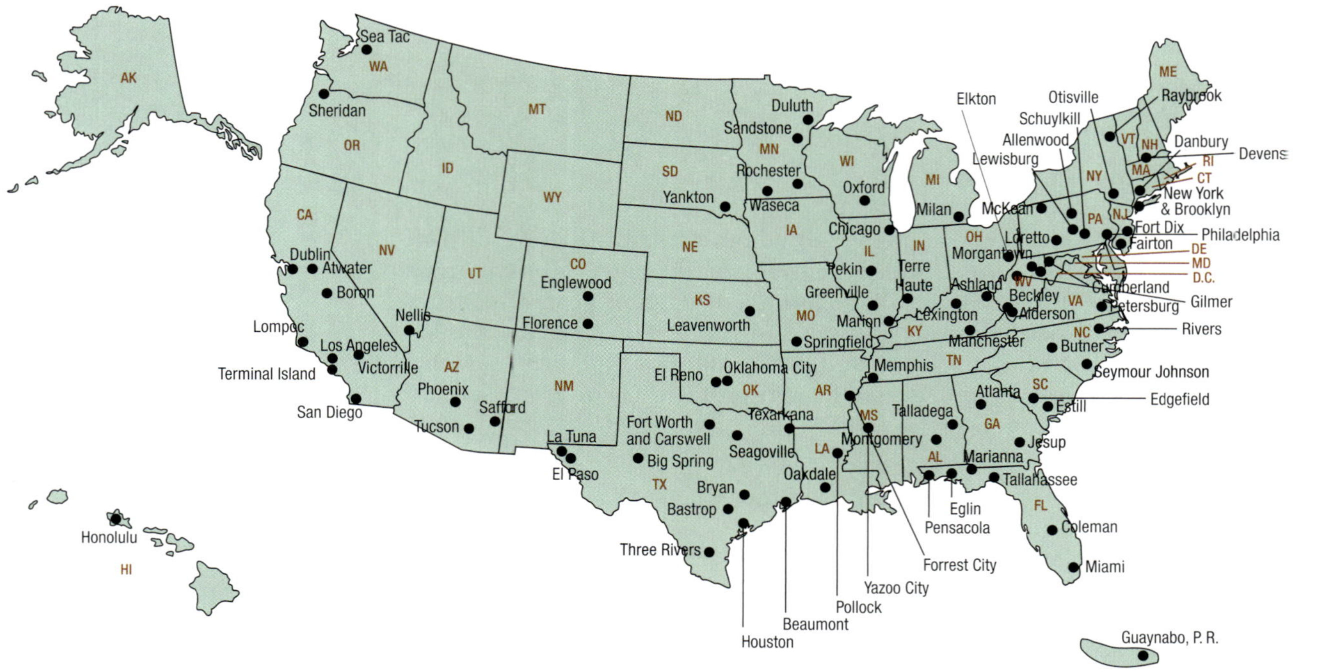

SOURCE: Federal Bureau of Prisons at www.bop.gov, May 2003. Some locations have more than one institution.

FYI

The Largest Prison System

By midyear 2002, the federal prison system, with 161,681 inmates, for the first time in U.S. history had more inmates than any state system. By year-end 2002, the federal prison population stood at 163,528 inmates.

SOURCE: Paige M. Harrison and Jennifer C. Karberg, "Prison and Jail Inmates at Midyear 2002," U.S. Department of Justice, *Bureau of Justice Statistics Bulletin*, April 2003; Paige M. Harrison and Allen J. Beck, "Prisoners in 2002," U.S. Department of Justice, *Bureau of Justice Statistics Bulletin*, July 2003.

classification facility A facility to which newly sentenced offenders are taken so that their security risks and needs can be assessed and they can be assigned to a permanent institution.

District of Columbia's sentenced felons because of federal legislation passed in 1997.[41] The administrative organization of the bureau is shown in Figure 10.5. The bureau has come to serve as a source of innovation and professionalization in the field of institutional corrections.

Although states vary in the way they organize institutional corrections, each state has a department of corrections or a similar administrative body to coordinate the various adult prisons in the state. Whether federal or state, correctional institutions are formal, bureaucratic organizations characterized by agency goals, rules and regulations, a staff chain of command, a staff division of labor, and similar features. Most adult prisons employ a quasi-military model of administration and management. Figure 10.6 displays the organizational chart for the California Department of Corrections.

CLASSIFICATION AND OTHER SPECIAL FACILITIES

When offenders are sentenced to the custody of the department of corrections in most states, they are transported initially to a **classification facility** (sometimes referred to as an assessment, reception, or diagnostic center). Stays at classification facilities are ordinarily short (for example, 60 days). The process of classification entails assessing an offender's security risk and determining which program services (for instance, counseling and education) the offender needs. Assessment information is used in deciding to which institution in the jurisdiction an offender will go to begin his or her term and which problems (such as alcohol dependency) the offender must address while imprisoned. A variety of other factors influence those decisions, including the nature of the offense; the offender's prior record (if any), propensity toward violence and escape, and vulnerability to victimization by other inmates; and the programs offered at the state's various institutions, as well as the levels of

FIGURE 10.5 Organization of Federal Bureau of Prisons

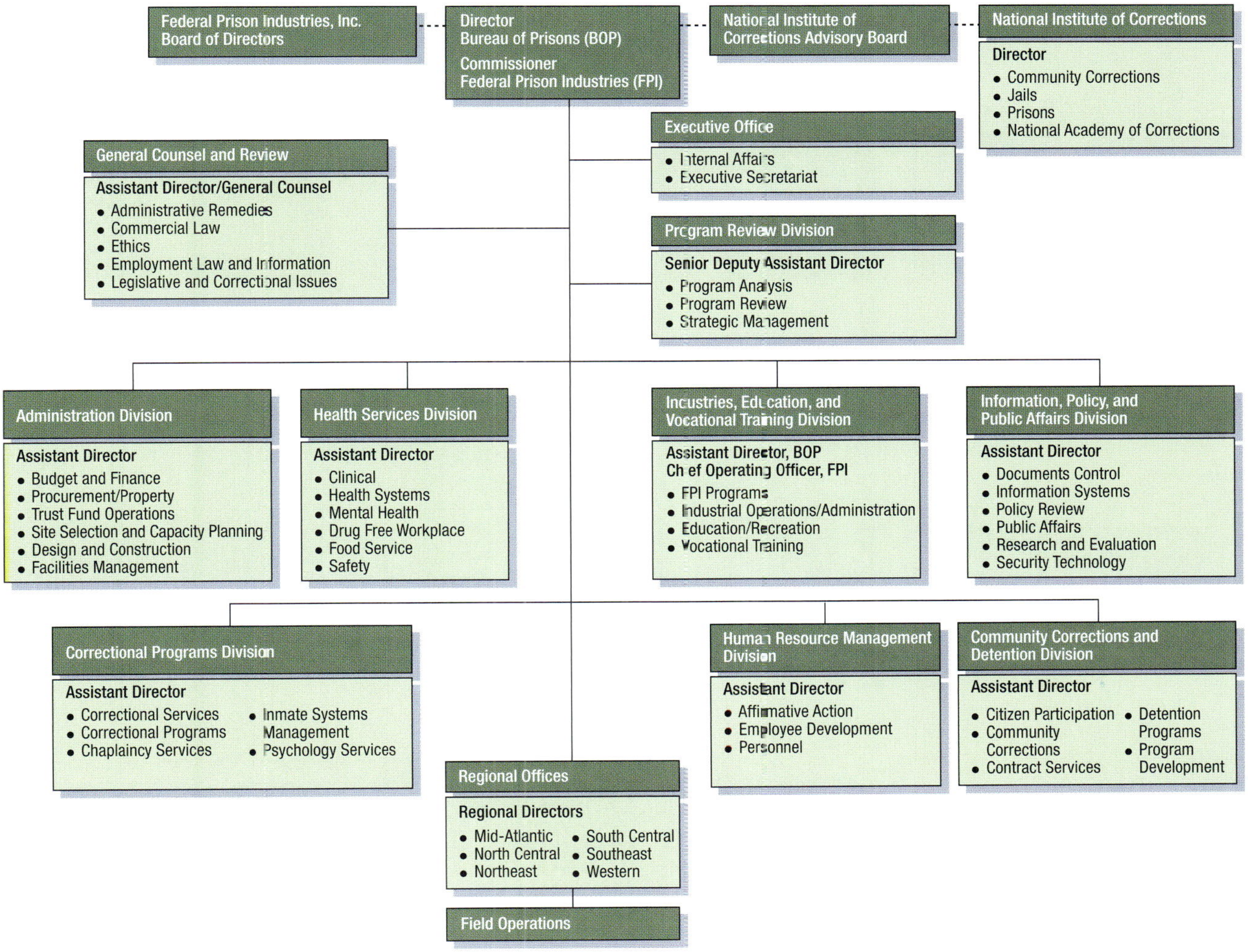

crowding at those institutions. The idea is to place inmates in facilities that can accommodate their risk-and-needs profiles.

Classification is not a one-time process; it occurs periodically throughout an inmate's sentence. Inmates are routinely monitored and reclassified to preserve institutional security and for purposes of transfer, programming, and release decisions.

Classification centers are not the only short-term-stay facilities. For example, the Federal Bureau of Prisons administers a number of medical institutions that receive inmates with health problems and provide them with health care services. If an inmate's condition improves, he or she is returned to the institution of origin or sent to another institution to complete the sentence. Other short-term facilities in various jurisdictions provide services for offenders with mental disorders.

MEN'S PRISONS

Men's prisons, the most common general type of prison in the nation, are often distinguished from one another by **security level.** An institution's security level is determined by two related factors: (1) the degree of external or perimeter

security level A designation applied to a facility to describe the measures taken, both inside and outside, to preserve security and custody.

FIGURE 10.6 Organization of the California Department of Corrections

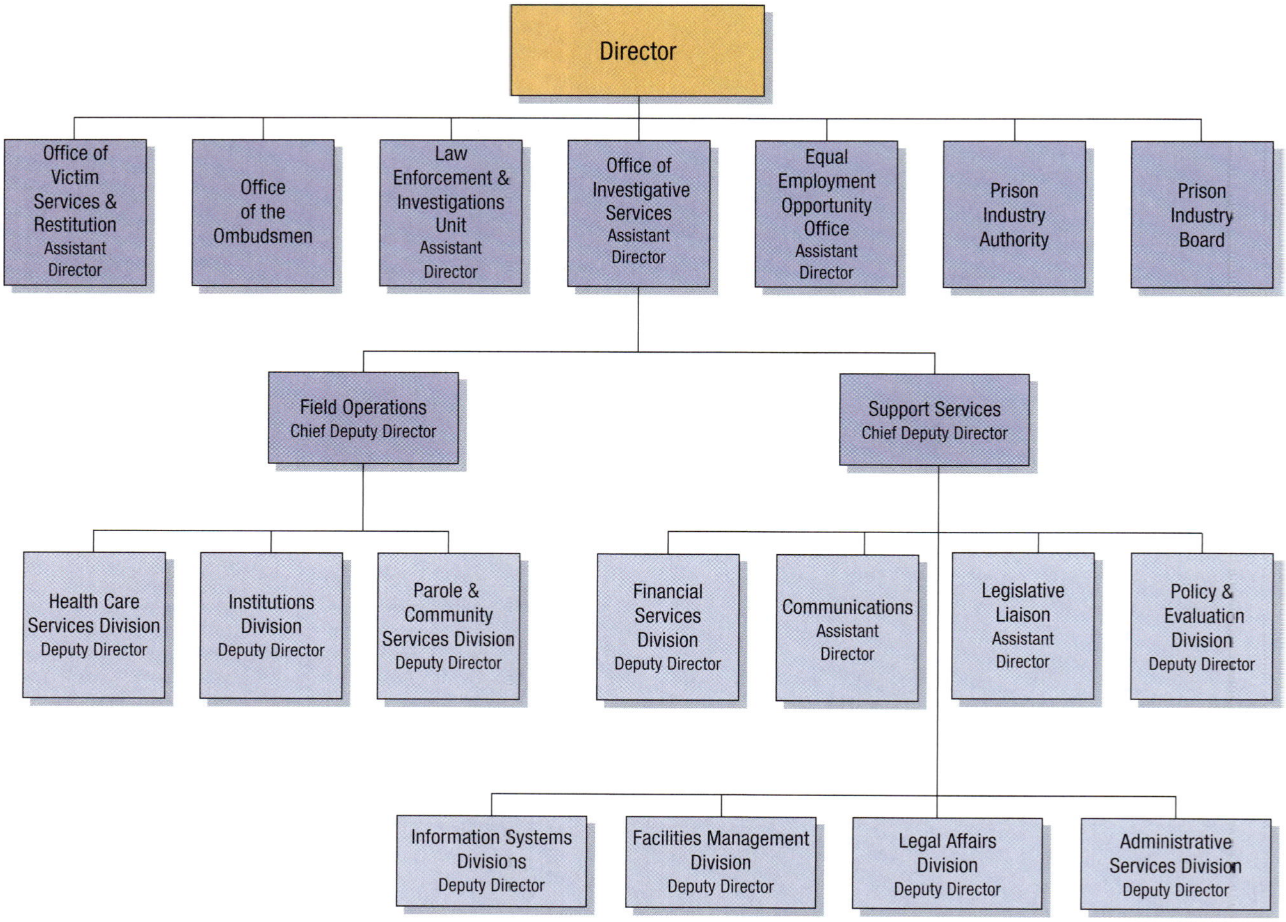

For full content go to http://www.cdc.state.ca.us/CDC/div_prog.asp.

security surrounding the prison and (2) the measures taken to preserve internal security within the institution. The simplest security level categorization is maximum, medium, and minimum. Of the 1,384 adult correctional facilities in operation on January 1, 2001, 6.9 percent were maximum-security facilities, 23.6 percent were medium-security facilities, 23.5 percent were minimum-security facilities, and 21.8 percent were multilevel-security facilities. In addition, 6.6 percent of the correctional facilities were designated "high/close," a security level between maximum and medium, 3.5 percent were intake facilities, which include reception and diagnostic facilities and admissions and orientation facilities, and 14 percent were community (low) security facilities, such as prerelease facilities.[42] Jurisdictions vary in the security categorizations they use.

Maximum-Security Facilities Maximum-security facilities are characterized by very tight external and internal security. A high wall or razor-wire fencing, with armed-guard towers, electronic detectors, or both, usually surrounds the prison. External armed patrol is also common. Some maximum-security institutions have a wide, open buffer zone between the outer wall or fence and the free community. Most maximum-security prison designs follow the radial plan or the telephone pole plan. Pottsville Prison is based on the racial plan, and the Oregon State Correctional Institution displays the telephone pole design. Internal security consists of such features as cell-block living, restrictions on inmate movement, and the capability of closing off areas of the institution to contain riots and disruptions.

"Supermax" Facilities A recent development is the construction of "ultramaximum-" or "supermaximum-security" prisons intended to house notorious offenders and problem inmates from other institutions. These prisons utilize total isolation of inmates and constant lockdowns, during which inmates are not permitted to leave their cells. The Federal Bureau of Prisons opened one of the first of these types of prisons in November 1994 in Florence, Colorado. The $60 million state-of-the-art prison (a modern-day Alcatraz) was custom-built to hold the 400 most predatory convicts in the federal system. The new prison is divided into nine units. Security is controlled by means of 1,400 electronically controlled gates and doors and 168 television monitors. Each unit is self-contained and includes separate sick-call rooms, law libraries, and barber chairs. Inmates do not leave their cells for more than an hour a day. When they must leave their cells, they do so only with leg irons, handcuffs, and an escort of two or three guards per inmate. Each cell has a double-entry door, with the classic barred cage door backed up by a windowed steel door that minimizes voice contact among prisoners, and cells are staggered so that inmates cannot make eye contact with each other. After 3 years of this type of confinement, a successful inmate can gradually regain social contact by being allowed to go to the recreation yard or the cafeteria.[43] Currently, more than 30 states and the federal government are operating either one or more "supermax" units within existing maximum-security facilities or entire "supermax" facilities.[44] Pelican Bay Prison in northern California is another example of the ultramaximum- or supermaximum-security prison.

Camp Delta: A Special Supermaximum Facility The war on terrorism has given rise to a new, special kind of supermaximum-security prison, Camp Delta, at the Guantanamo Bay Naval Base in Cuba.[45] The prison holds more than 600 of what Pentagon officials call the "worst of the worst enemies in

[FYI] Prison Misconduct

Ten federal prison guards at the supermaximum-security prison at Florence were indicted for 52 acts of abuse against at least 20 inmates from 1995 to 1997. The renegade group of guards, called "The Cowboys," was charged with kicking inmates, smashing their heads into walls, and mixing human waste into their food. In some cases, the guards injured themselves so they could claim the inmates had attacked them first. Some of the guards told prosecutors that they had a "green light" from prison authorities to "take care of business."

Source: "Guards charged with abusing prisoners," *The Orlando Sentinel*, November 4, 2000, p. A10.

Pottsville Prison in Pennsylvania (left) is an example of the radial prison design, and the Oregon State Correctional Institution (right) is an example of the telephone pole prison design. *What are advantages and disadvantages of each of these prison designs?*

the war on terror." The U.S. government is holding the prisoners indefinitely without filing criminal charges or assigning them prisoner-of-war status, without giving them access to lawyers or allowing visits from family. The first prisoners arrived from Afghanistan in January 2002. They are to be held until they no longer have useful intelligence to provide, are cleared of criminal wrongdoing, and no longer pose a threat to the United States. They may be held until the war on terror is over, whenever that might be.

Camp Delta, on a bluff overlooking the Caribbean Sea, is surrounded by chain-link fence, lined with green nylon windscreen, and topped with spirals of razor wire. Troops patrol the perimeter on foot, in machine-gun-mounted Humvees, and aboard Piranha boats. Military Police guards watch rows of cellblocks from covered wooden watchtowers. A cellblock consists of a long hallway with 7-by-8-foot green steel-grate cells on either side. Each cell holds one prisoner, and most prisoners remain in their cells 23.5 hours a day. Prisoners can see and talk to each other from their cells. Each cell has a sink with running water and a floor toilet. At the end of the cellblock is a 30-by-30-foot enclosed and covered gravel exercise area that the best-behaved prisoners may use for up to 30 minutes a day. There are also individual outdoor showers.

Each prisoner receives a Quran, oils, beads, and a prayer mat. An arrow stenciled on each steel bed points east to Mecca. Prisoners may receive and write letters to family. Censors read all letters. Personnel from the military, CIA, FBI, and other agencies interrogate prisoners regularly. There have been no escape attempts (as of August 2003). Most prisoners are well behaved, although a few of them throw water and sometimes urine on the guards, yell insults and obscenities, or refuse to return eating utensils after meals. Camp officials claim that many of the prisoners arrived with mental-heath problems. Thirteen mental-health professionals are on staff to serve them. Camp doctors (as of June 2003) were treating 80 to 90 prisoners for psychiatric conditions. Some of those prisoners were receiving psychotherapy, antidepressants,

Camp Delta, the supermaximum-security prison in Cuba, holds what Pentagon officials call the "worst of the worst enemies in the war on terror." *Should Camp Delta be run like other supermaximum-security prisons, or should special procedures be employed because of the unique inmate population? It special procedures should be employed, what should they be?*

and antipsychotic drugs. Since Camp Delta opened (through June 2003), 18 prisoners have attempted suicide a total of 29 times. Most have tried to hang themselves during an exercise period. Troublemakers are moved to solid-steel-walled cells that impede communication with other prisoners and are allowed to shower only twice a week. Cooperative prisoners may be moved to Camp Four, a medium-security section of Camp Delta. In Camp Four, prisoners live in open bays of 10 bunks and may gather and eat in open common areas.

Critics contend that not all of the prisoners are terrorists or have meaningful connections to the Taliban or al-Qaeda. Prisoners are from 42 countries. Most of them are from the Middle East and Central Asia, but some of them are citizens of Great Britain, Canada, Australia, China, and Russia. Unfortunately, for them, there is no way to challenge their detention. The Pentagon will not hold the Geneva Convention hearings that would officially classify them as either prisoners of war or terror suspects, and the federal courts have determined that they do not have jurisdiction over the prisoners.

Medium-Security Facilities Compared with maximum-security prisons, medium-security institutions place fewer restrictions on inmate movement inside the facility. Cell blocks often coexist with dormitory- or barracks-type living quarters, and in some medium-security prisons, cells are relatively few. Typically, there is no wall for external security. Fences and towers exist but are less forbidding in appearance; razor wire may be replaced with less expensive barbed wire.

Minimum-Security Facilities Compared with prisons at the other security levels, minimum-security prisons are smaller and more open. Inmates are frequently transferred to such prisons from more secure facilities after they have established records of good behavior or when they are nearing release. Dorm or barracks living quarters predominate, and often there are no fences. Some inmates may be permitted to leave the institution during the day to work (under *work release*) or study (under *study release*) in the community. Likewise, some inmates may be granted furloughs so that they can reestablish ties with family members, make living arrangements for their upcoming release, or establish employment contacts.

Custody Level vs. Security Level *Custody level* should be distinguished from *security level*. Whereas institutions are classified by security level, individual inmates are classified by custody level. An inmate's **custody level** indicates the degree of precaution that needs to be taken when working with that inmate. Confusion arises because custody levels are sometimes designated by the same terms used to designate institutional security levels (maximum, medium, and minimum). However, the two levels are independent of one another. For example, some inmates with medium or minimum custody levels may be housed in maximum-security prisons.

custody level The classification assigned to an inmate to indicate the degree of precaution that needs to be taken when working with that inmate.

WOMEN'S PRISONS AND COCORRECTIONAL FACILITIES

As pointed out earlier, women make up about 7 percent of the population of both state and federal prisons. In recent years, however, incarceration rates for females in the United States have grown faster than incarceration rates for males. For example, between 1995 and 2003 the annual rate of growth of the female inmate population has averaged 5.2 percent, compared to a 3.5 percent average increase in the male inmate population. While the total number of male inmates has grown 27 percent between 1995 and 2003, the number of female inmates has increased 42 percent. Nevertheless, at year-end 2002 there were 60 sentenced female inmates per 100,000 women

FIGURE 10.7 Percentage of Adult State Prison Inmate Population by Security Level and Gender, September 2001

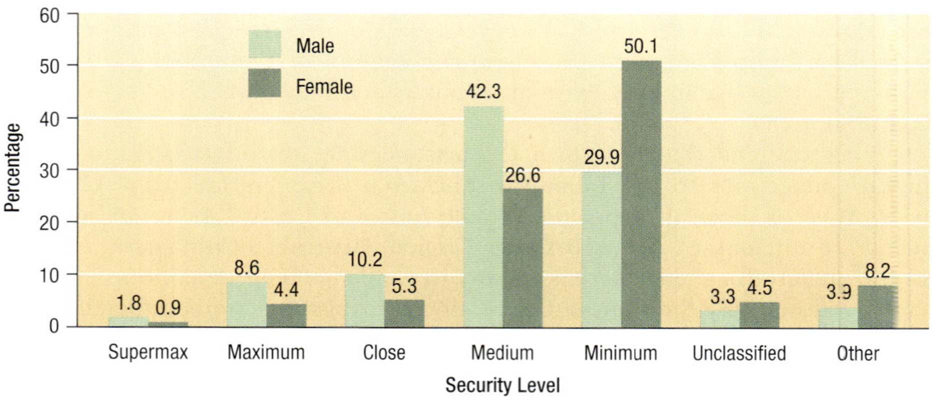

SOURCE: American Correctional Accociation, *2002 Directory: Juvenile and Adult Correctional Departments, Institutions, Agencies and Paroling Authorities.* (Lanham, MD: American Correctional Association, 2002).

in the United States, compared to 906 sentenced male inmates per 100,000 men.[46] One difference between male and female state prisoners is that a somewhat greater proportion of women than men are serving sentences for property offenses (26 percent female vs. 19 percent male) and drug offenses (30 percent female vs. 20 percent male), while a greater proportion of men are serving time for violent crimes (50 percent male vs. 32 percent female).[47] Other differences are that female inmates are more likely than male inmates to have dependent children and to be serving their first prison term. Figure 10.7 shows the percentage of the adult state prison population by security level and gender.

In 2002, 84 percent of all state adult prisons in the nation were for men only, 9 percent were for women only, and 6 percent were for both men and women.[48] Many states operate only one major prison for women. In general, prisons exclusively for women are smaller and house fewer inmates than institutions exclusively for men. Dorm and cottage plans are much more common than cell-block plans in institutions for women.

cocorrectional facilities Usually small, minimum-security institutions that house both men and women with the goal of normalizing the prison environment by integrating the daytime activities of the sexes.

Cocorrectional facilities, which house both male and female inmates, have been in operation (in contemporary form) since the 1970s. The goal of cocorrections is to normalize the prison environment by integrating the daytime activities of the sexes. In 2002, 54 cocorrectional facilities were in operation in the United States (down from 97 in 1997 but up from 36 in 2000).[49] Cocorrectional prisons are usually small, and security is typically minimum. A comprehensive review of the effect of cocorrections on women prisoners paints a bleak picture: "[C]ocorrections offers women prisoners few, if any, economic, educational, vocational, and social advantages. Cocorrections benefits male prisoners and system maintenance."[50]

JAILS AND LOCKUPS

lockup A very short-term holding facility that is frequently located in or very near an urban police agency so that suspects can be held pending further inquiry.

jail A facility, usually operated at the local level, that holds convicted offenders and unconvicted persons for relatively short periods.

A **lockup** is a very short-term (for instance, 24- to 48-hours) holding facility that is frequently located in or very near an urban police agency so that suspects can be held pending further inquiry into their cases by the police or the court. If there is cause, a suspect may be transferred from the lockup to the jail.

A **jail** is a facility that holds convicted offenders and unconvicted persons for relatively short periods. The modern term "jail" comes from the English term "gaol" (the pronunciation is identical), and English gaols have a history that dates to the 1100s. In contrast to prisons, most jails are administered at the county or city level of government. Excluding lockups, there are more jails (between 3,000 and 4,000) than any other kind of confinement facility in the United States. Although most jails in the United States are small (about half of them hold fewer than 50 people), some, such as those in Los Angeles and New York City, are very large (refer to Table 10.2).

Jail Functions Most people think of jails primarily as short-term holding facilities where suspects or defendants are detained pending further court processing, such as arraignment, trial, conviction, or sentencing. In practice, though, jails serve a catchall function in criminal justice and corrections. For example, jails also

- Readmit probation, parole, and bail-bond violators and absconders.
- Temporarily detain juveniles pending transfer to juvenile authorities.
- Hold mentally ill persons pending their movement to appropriate health facilities.
- Hold individuals for the military.
- Hold individuals for protective custody.
- Hold individuals for contempt (*contempt* refers to conduct that defies the authority or dignity of a court or legislature).
- Hold witnesses for the courts (witnesses are sometimes held in jails for their safety or if they are unlikely to appear in court when requested).
- Release convicted inmates to the community upon completion of sentence.
- Transfer inmates to federal, state, or other authorities.
- House inmates for federal, state, or other authorities because of crowding of their facilities.
- Sometimes operate community-based programs as alternatives to incarceration (those programs are described in Chapter 12).
- Hold inmates sentenced to short terms (generally under 1 year).[51]

Because jails must be able to hold all types of people, including those who pose grave threats to the security and safety of others, the limited funds available through local taxes are directed primarily toward custody and security. Accommodations, services, and programs for inmates often suffer as a consequence.

Jail Populations The number of people being held in local jails has risen dramatically in recent years. The U.S. local jail population increased from 209,582 in 1982 to 665,475 at midyear 2002, an increase of about 218 percent (see Figure 10.8). The jail incarceration rate was 96 inmates per 100,000 U.S. residents in 1983; by June 28, 2002, that number had climbed to 231 per 100,000, an increase of 141 percent.[52] Although just 1 percent of the jail population consisted of juveniles, that percentage amounts to 7,248 juveniles. The practice of holding juveniles in adult jails, where they are vulnerable to influence and victimization by adult criminals, is most common in rural areas, where there are no separate juvenile detention centers. That practice has been the target of much criticism and many policy initiatives for more than two decades. Nevertheless, the number of juveniles held in adult jails had been on the rise in recent years until lately; the number increased by 69 percent between midyear 1993 and midyear 2002 (from 4,300 to 7,248).[53] Table 10.4, which displays selected characteristics of the jail population, also shows that the greatest proportions of jail inmates were male and racial or ethnic minorities in 2002. Less than half of the jail population had been convicted of

CJ ONLINE

Jail Statistics
To obtain the most recent jail statistics, go to the Bureau of Justice Statistics website at **www.ojp.usdoj/bjs/jails.htm.** *How has the jail population changed since midyear 2002?*

FIGURE 10.8 Growth in Local Jail Population, 1982–Midyear 2002

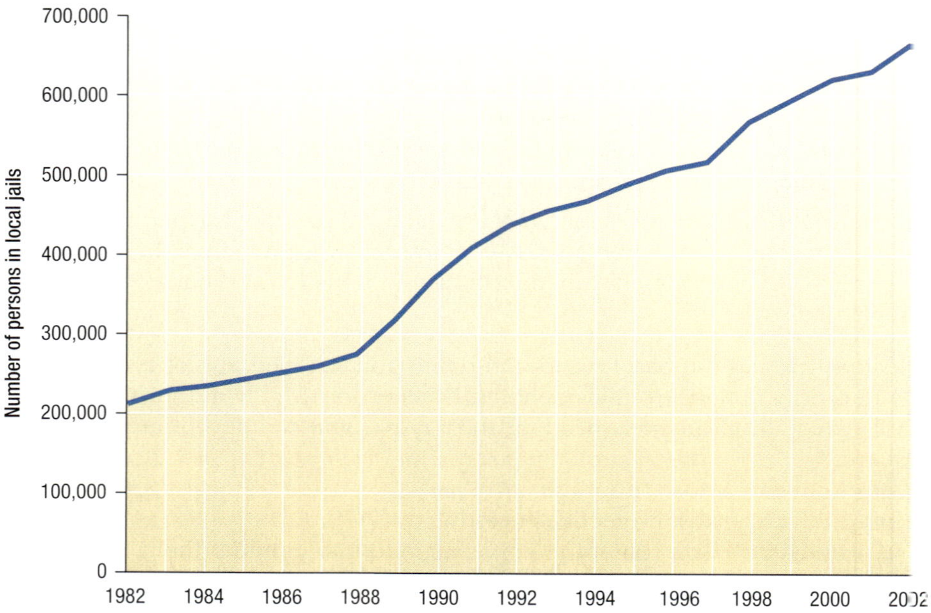

SOURCES: Adapted from Darrell K. Gilliard and Allen J. Beck, "Prison and Jail Inmates at Midyear 1997," U.S. Department of Justice, *Bureau of Justice Statistics Bulletin*, January 1998; Craig A. Perkins, James J. Stephan, and Allen J. Beck, "Jails and Jail Inmates 1993–1994," U.S. Department of Justice, *Bureau of Justice Statistics Bulletin*, April 1995; Allen J. Beck, "Prison and Jail Inmates at Midyear 1999," U.S. Department of Justice, *Bureau of Justice Statistics Bulletin*, April 2000; Paige M. Harrison and Jennifer C. Karberg, "Prison and Jail Inmates at Midyear 2002, "U.S. Department of Justice, *Bureau of Justice Statistics Bulletin*, April 2003.

FYI

Largest Jail Population

During 2002, the average daily population of the nine jails in Los Angeles County, California, the largest jail system in the nation, was 19,258 inmates.

SOURCE: Paige M. Harrison and Jennifer C. Karberg, "Prison and Jail Inmates at Midyear 2002," U.S. Department of Justice, *Bureau of Justice Statistics Bulletin*, April 2003.

criminal activity. The remainder were unconvicted persons (usually awaiting trial or other case disposition).

In a classic study of jails,[54] criminologist John Irwin found that, although members of the public tend to believe that jails are heavily populated with dangerous criminals, jails actually hold few such people. Jails are populated disproportionately with members of what Irwin calls the "rabble" class. The rabble class consists of people who are poor, undereducated, alienated from mainstream society, disreputable, and more likely than the general population to belong to an ethnic minority. Most of them have not committed serious offenses. In short, Irwin argues that the main function of the jail is to manage

TABLE 10.4 Selected Characteristics of Jail Inmates, Midyear 2002

Inmate Characteristic	Percent of Inmates (Total = 665,475)	Inmate Characteristic	Percent of Inmates (Total = 665,475)	Incarceration Rate per 100,000 Residents in Each Group	
Age		**Race/Hispanic Origin**		White, Non-Hispanic	147
Juvenile	1.0	White, non-Hispanic	43.8	Black, Non-Hispanic	740
Adult	99.0	Black, non-Hispanic	39.8	Hispanic	256
Gender (adults only)		Hispanic	14.7	Other	72
Male	88.3	Other	1.6		
Female	11.7	**Legal Status (adults only)**			
		Convicted	40.0		
		Unconvicted	60.0		

SOURCE: Paige M. Harrison and Jennifer C. Karberg, "Prison and Jail Inmates at Midyear 2002," U.S. Department of Justice, *Bureau of Justice Statistics Bulletin*, April 2003.

or control marginal members of our society and that as an unintended result of that process, the degradation those people experience in jail makes them even more marginal.

However, another study of jail bookings challenges Irwin's conclusion that jails tend to house mostly "rabble." By analyzing the characteristics of persons booked into two jails (one urban, one rural), researchers found that nearly 47 percent had been charged with felonies, and more than 90 percent had been booked for a felony or a class A misdemeanor. Moreover, in 1-day counts of those jails, the researchers discovered that 82.5 percent of those held had been either charged with or convicted of a felony offense. As the authors of the study observe, "These data do not appear to support Irwin's claims about detached and disreputable persons whose real problem is offensiveness, not serious criminality."[55]

Jail Architecture and Management Philosophies Jails have traditionally represented, and continue to represent, one of the most problematic aspects of criminal justice. Many jails in the nation are old buildings plagued by overcrowding, a lack of services and programs for inmates, inadequate staffing, and unsanitary and hazardous living conditions. Some of the interrelated reasons for those problems are (1) the limited and unstable nature of local taxes to fund and staff jails, (2) a general lack of public support for jail reform, (3) rapid rates of inmate turnover, which make it difficult to coordinate programs, and (4) the sheer diversity of the risks and needs of the inmates. Also, in many areas, the chief jail administrator is the local sheriff, an elected or appointed political official. Because jails are usually under local administration, they are sometimes affected by the erratic and corrupt elements that often characterize local politics.

With increasing pressure from the courts to reform jail conditions and management practices,[56] efforts at jail reform continue. Historically, jails have progressed through three general overlapping stages of architectural design. Each design reflects a different philosophy about how to operate a jail.[57] The earliest jails, which date back to the eighteenth century, were built in a linear design. These *first-generation jails* have inmates live together in cells, dormitories, or "tanks." The cells line corridors, which make the supervision of inmates difficult (see Figure 10.9). Guards (they did not become "correctional officers" until the late 1960s or early 1970s, see the nearby FYI) at regular intervals walk up and down the corridors and observe inmates in their cells. To observe the inmates in the dormitories or tanks, guards periodically walk through the dormitories or along a perimeter catwalk, which separates them from the inmates by bars. (This type of supervision is referred to as "intermittent surveillance.") A "48-man tank," for example, is a large cage that might have six inner cells, each with eight bunks, that open into a "dayroom" or "bullpen" equipped with two long metal picniclike tables attached to the floor and, perhaps, one television for the entire tank. In the cells, beds, sinks, and toilets are made of reinforced metal and are bolted to the floor or wall. There is little direct contact between the guards and inmates, unless the guards have to respond to an incident, such as a fight or medical emergency. The first-generation jail is often a separate building or set of buildings surrounded by walls of reinforced concrete topped with razor wire (but see the nearby FYI). Many first-generation jails resemble early prisons.

Second-generation jails began to emerge in the 1960s. In these jails, correctional officers constantly supervise inmates from secure control booths that overlook inmate living areas, called "pods" or "modules." (This type of supervision is referred to as "indirect supervision" or "remote surveillance.") Cells become rooms and are clustered around dayrooms or common living areas, where inmates can congregate for activities (see Figure 10.10). Inmate rooms

> **FYI**
> **First Generation Jails**
>
> The first-generation jail in which Robert Bohm (an author of this textbook) worked in the early 1970s was located on the eleventh to fifteenth floors of the Jackson County Courthouse in Kansas City, Missouri. When Bohm was hired as a guard, the official title of the jail was the Jackson County Jail. During the time he worked there, the official title of the jail was changed to the Jackson County Department of Corrections, and Bohm became a "correctional officer." Physically, the jail remained the same, and Bohm's work duties did not change.
>
> Source: Personal experience.

FIGURE 10.9 A Typical First-Generation Jail Design

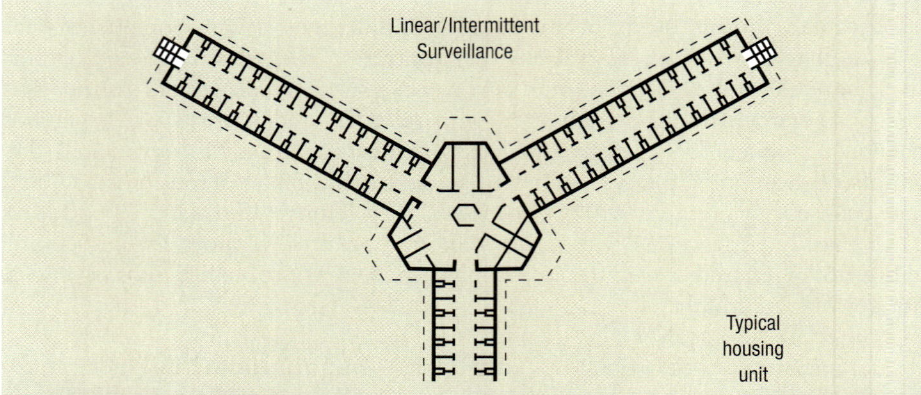

In first-generation jails, correctional officers cannot observe all inmate housing areas from one location, so they can only provide intermittent surveilance. *What are the advantages and disadvantages of working in this type of jail?*

SOURCE (of diagram): *Podular, Direct Supervision Jails: Information Packet,* U.S. Department of Justice, National Institute of Corrections, Jails Division, January 1993, at www.nicic.org/resources/topics/DirectSupervisionJails.aspx.

have reinforced metal doors with unbreakable windows instead of bars and generally house only one or two inmates. Beds, sinks, toilets, desks, and tables (in the dayrooms) are made of concrete or reinforced metal bolted to the floor or wall. There is very little direct interaction between inmates and correctional officers. Officers generally communicate with inmates by using a public address or intercom system. When trouble occurs inside the living area, a response team is called to intervene. The facility's perimeter walls continue to be made of reinforced concrete topped with razor wire or, in some cases, fences secured by razor wire.

Third-generation, new-generation, or *direct-supervision jails* emerged in the late 1970s. They use a "podular" or "modular" design similar to the one employed in second-generation jails in which inmates' rooms are arranged around a common area or dayroom. A third-generation jail may have one or more pods, with a pod typically containing 48 to 60 beds. However, in third-generation jails, there is no secure control booth for correctional officers, and

FIGURE 10.10 A Typical Second-Generation Jail Design

In second-generation jails, correctional officers continuously observe inmates from a secure control booth that overlooks inmate living areas, called "pods" or "modules." They provide indirect or remote supervision. *What are the advantages and disadvantages of working in this type of jail?*

SOURCE (of diagram): *Podular, Direct Supervision Jails: Information Packet,* U.S. Department of Justice, National Institute of Corrections, Jails Division, January 1993, at www.nicic.org/resources/topics/DirectSupervisionJails.aspx.

there are no physical barriers between correctional officers and inmates (see Figure 10.11). Officers may have a desk or table for paperwork, but it is in the open dayroom area. Many new-generation jails have added amenities in inmate living areas, such as carpeting, upholstered furnishings, individual shower stalls, several television sets and viewing areas, collect-call telephones, game tables, and exercise equipment. Third-generation jails generally have strong perimeter security.

FIGURE 10.11 A Typical Third-Generation Jail Design

Third-generation jails employ a "podular" or "modular" design, but unlike in second-generation jails, correctional officers are stationed inside the housing unit where they directly supervise and interact with inmates. *What are the advantages and disadvantages of working in this type of jail?*

SOURCE (of diagram): *Podular, Direct Supervision Jails: Information Packet,* U.S. Department of Justice, National Institute of Corrections, Jails Division, January 1993, at www.nicic.org/resources/topics/DirectSupervisionJails.aspx.

[FYI] Video Visitation

To reduce costly and potentially dangerous inmate transport and to stop contraband from entering the institution, some new-generation jails are employing new technology for visitation. They are installing state-of-the-art video screens and phones in cubicles or carrels in inmate living areas and in remote video visitation centers for family members and friends. Attorneys, chaplains, or others visiting inmates for professional reasons, however, still are allowed to visit in person.

SOURCE: Doris Bloodsworth, "Jail Ready to Debut Visitation by Video," *The Orlando Sentinel,* January 5, 2003, p. B1.

The pods in third-generation jails are self-contained to reduce costly and potentially dangerous inmate transport. Consider visitation, for example. In older jails, including many second-generation jails, inmates are moved from secure housing units to a visitation area. In many new-generation jails, visitors are taken to the housing unit by way of a nonsecure corridor and visit through a high-security glass barrier. The inmate stays securely in the housing unit and the visitor stays in the nonsecure corridor. This arrangement also stops contraband from entering the institution by way of visitors. To reduce inmate transport, many new-generation jails also have their own courtroom, which is used primarily for arraignments and other pretrial proceedings.

The major difference between second- and third-generation jails is that third-generation jails are based on a different philosophy or management strategy called *direct supervision*. In this strategy, correctional officers continue to constantly supervise inmates, but rather than isolate themselves from the

FIGURE 10.12 American Jail Association's Code of Ethics for Jail Officers

As an officer employed in a detention/correctional capacity, I swear (or affirm) to be a good citizen and a credit to my community, state, and nation at all times. I will abstain from questionable behavior which might bring disrepute to the agency for which I work, my family, my community, and my associates. My lifestyle will be above and beyond reproach and I will constantly strive to set an example of a professional who performs his/her duties according to the laws of our country, state, and community and the policies, procedures, written and verbal orders, and regulations of the agency for which I work.

On the Job I promise to:

KEEP	The institution secure so as to safeguard my community and the lives of the staff, inmates, and visitors on the premises
WORK	With each individual firmly and fairly without regard to rank, status, or condition.
MAINTAIN	A positive demeanor when confronted with stressful situations of scorn, ridicule, danger, and/or chaos.
REPORT	Either in writing or by word of mouth to the proper authorities those things which should be reported, and keep silent about matters which are to remain confidential according to the laws and rules of the agency and government.
MANAGE	And supervise the inmates in an evenhanded and courteous manner.
REFRAIN	At all times from becoming personally involved in the lives of the inmates and their families.
TREAT	All visitors to the jail with politeness and respect and do my utmost to ensure that they observe the jail regulations.
TAKE	Advantage of all education and training opportunities designed to assist me to become a more competent officer.
COMMUNICATE	With people in or outside of the jail, whether by phone, written word, or word of mouth, in such a way so as not to reflect in a negative manner upon my agency.
CONTRIBUTE	To a jail environment which will keep the inmate involved in activities designed to improve his/her attitude and character.
SUPPORT	All activities of a professional nature through membership and participation that will continue to elevate the status of those who operate our nation's jails. Do my best through word and deed to present an image to the public at large of a jail professional, committed to progress for an improved and enlightened criminal justice system.

The American Jail Association's Board of Directors has approved the AJA Code of Ethics as part of an integral program to achieve a high standard of professional conduct among those officers employed in our nation's jails. Adopted by the American Jail Association Board of Directors on November 10, 1991. Revised May 19, 1993.

SOURCE: American Jail Association at http://www.corrections.com/aja/about/code.shtml. The American Jail Association, 1135 Professional Court, Hagerstown, MD 21740-5853.

inmates, they are stationed inside the pod to give the inmates the opportunity to directly and regularly interact with them. (Direct supervision is also employed in some prisons.) In the new-generation jail, each congregate living area is a staff post, usually with one correctional officer in direct control of 40 to 50 inmates.

Correctional officers in direct-supervision jails are more than just "turnkeys"; they are professionals that need skills in interpersonal communication, crisis intervention, and counseling. Perhaps that is why research has found that female officers do at least as well as male officers while working in male units. Officers are taught to view the pods as space that they control, to be leaders and mentors in their pods, and to encourage inmates to change their destructive behaviors and ways of thinking. Correctional officers are more independent in direct-supervision jails and have the primary responsibility for daily decision making in the pods. Supervisors evaluate officer performance based on some of the following objectives:

- Being in daily contact with inmates in pods.
- Refraining from doing or saying anything that would belittle or degrade an inmate.
- Reporting promptly critical information to superior officers (for example, inmate escape plans).
- Engaging in continual visual observation of inmates.
- Investigating activity appearing out of the ordinary.[58]

THINKING CRITICALLY

1. What, if any, impact does a jail's architectural design have on inmates?
2. Do you agree that one of a jail's functions is to manage marginal members of society? Why or why not?

Research suggests that direct-supervision jails provide a less-stressful, more positive, and safer environment for inmates and staff, may enhance supervision by reducing the number of unsupervised areas, and reduce inmate violations for contraband possession, destruction of property, escapes, disrespecting officers and staff, suicides, and violence, including sexual assaults.[59] In 2001, there were approximately 180 direct-supervision jails in 48 states and Puerto Rico.[60] Figure 10.12 shows the American Jail Association's Code of Ethics for Jail Officers. It reflects the professionalism expected of correctional officers that work in today's jails.

FYI: Prison Watchtowers Being Replaced

In a recent national trend, prison watchtowers staffed with prison guards are being replaced with electronic security systems. Under the new system, the interior fence is outfitted with one device that detects movements such as the fence being shaken or cut and then sounds an alarm. Razor wire is then unrolled between the interior and exterior fences. Motion detectors that sound alarms when triggered also monitor that space. Once an alarm sounds, officers in the main control room can radio officers inside the prison and those circling the prison in vehicles. The electronic system is cheaper, too. It costs $175,000 to install the system, which should last 8 to 10 years. It costs about $800,000 to staff the watchtowers.

SOURCE: "Prisons Favoring Electronic Security," *The Orlando Sentinel*, February 4, 2002, p. C3.

Institutional Security, Services, and Programs

In many ways, an incarceration facility is like a miniature society within the larger society. Institutions have many of the same features as the wider society, such as security procedures for maintaining order and preserving the safety of inhabitants, as well as a variety of services and programs meant to provide for inmate needs and encourage inmates to better themselves.

SECURITY AND INMATE DISCIPLINE

An orderly and safe environment is the foundation for all else that happens in an institution. When the environment is not stable, everything else tends to become secondary. For that reason, security procedures strongly affect the daily activities of both staff and inmates.

In any prison or jail, special security precautions are directed toward certain locations because of the importance of those locations to the institution's capacity for maintaining order. Examples of such locations include:

1. The front entry to the facility, through which all persons coming and going must pass.
2. The control room, which is usually located close to the front entry and is the heart of the institution's communication system.

3. The cell blocks or other quarters where the inmates live.
4. The dining area.
5. The area where the institution's confidential records and documents are maintained.
6. The indoor recreation areas and the outdoor recreation area or yard.
7. The sites where inmates work.

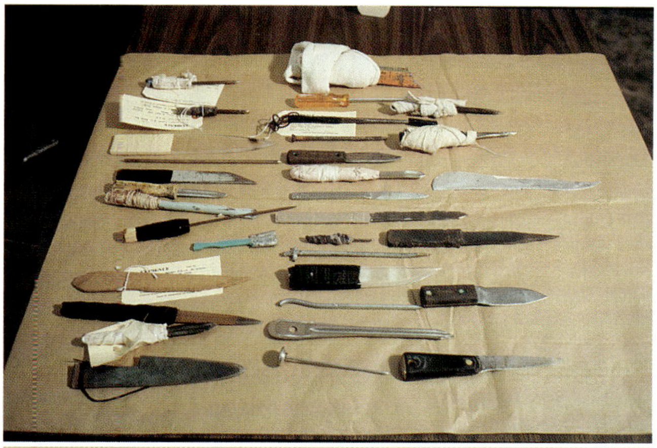

Handmade weapons such as those shown here are contraband and make prisons and jails dangerous places. *Where do inmates get the materials for these weapons?*

All institutions routinely employ a range of security procedures to maintain control over inmates. The classification of inmates by custody levels, mentioned earlier, is one such method. An inmate's custody level indicates the degree of precaution to be used when working with that inmate. In some facilities, certain inmates are given special custody designations that distinguish them from members of the general inmate population. Those inmates are not permitted to live among the general population of the facility. For example, inmates who are vulnerable to assault by other inmates may be designated for **protective custody,** meaning that they are to be kept segregated for their own safety. In contrast, inmates who represent a danger to other inmates or staff may be designated for **administrative segregation,** indicating that they must be kept in secure isolation so that they cannot harm others. Inmates who display signs of serious mental disorders may be segregated in a similar fashion.

protective custody The segregation of inmates for their own safety.

administrative segregation The keeping of inmates in secure isolation so that they cannot harm others.

CAREERS IN CRIMINAL JUSTICE

Visitation Coordinator

My name is Pat Bryant and I am an administrative coordinator with the Central Visitation Center (CVC) for the South Carolina Department of Corrections (SCDC), Charleston, South Carolina. I have a bachelor of science degree in criminal justice from Benedict College, Columbia, South Carolina. I have held several positions with the South Carolina Department of Corrections during the course of my career including administrative assistant, project developer, and business manager, to name a few. I have found these positions to be very rewarding.

The inmate visitation program is recognized by SCDC as an integral component of the rehabilitation process as it encourages inmates to have the opportunity to visit with family members and friends. The Central Visitation Center became operational in the fall of 1996 at which time I became the administrative coordinator.

A typical day as administrative coordinator for CVC involves communicating directly with family and friends of inmates in person, by telephone, or written correspondence and explaining to the prospective visitor the reason he/she may have been disapproved as a visitor, and providing guidance and technical assistance as it relates to inmate visitation to the 31 correctional institutions within the SCDC and other law enforcement agencies as requested. One of the most significant aspects of this job is ensuring that all Requests for Visiting Privileges forms are reviewed and approved (if deemed appropriate) and an automated record is created for the prospective visitor. The CVC processes approximately 500–600 visitation applications per day. Some other aspects of this job include coordinating and conducting training for employees involved in the inmate visitation process and conducting semiannual visits to each institution to ensure visitation procedures are being implemented according to policy.

While the job of administrative coordinator is certainly an interesting one, it can also be a challenge. The reward is knowing that you have assisted someone who may not have had a clear understanding of the visitation process and being a part of the solution.

What do you think are the greatest challenges for a visitation coordinator?

Family visitation is extremely important to inmate morale. *What are other advantages and disadvantages of family visitation?*

As a basis for security procedures, institutions publish written rules that regulate the daily activities of inmates and staff alike. During the course of daily activities, staff routinely count inmates to detect escapes, and inmate whereabouts are constantly monitored within the facility. There are standard procedures for staff to follow when transporting certain inmates within the facility or from the facility to an outside location, such as to another prison, to court, or to a hospital in the community. Much effort goes into controlling the property of the institution—for example, firearms, medicine, keys, tools, and basic commodities like clothes and food. In many prisons and jails, searches of inmates' clothing and bodies and shakedowns (usually random and warrantless searches) of their cells are commonplace in an effort to control the flow of contraband, especially handmade knives and other weapons. There are special procedures and even special staff units for responding to riots, escapes, and other disturbances.

The mail and phone conversations of inmates may be monitored if there is sufficient security justification. Inmates may visit with relatives and friends only at designated times and may visit only those people the institution has approved. Although a small number of prisons permit **conjugal visits**—in which an inmate and his or her spouse or significant other visit in private to maintain their personal relationship—routine visits usually occur in large, open rooms with other inmates, their visitors, and staff present. Visits are supervised closely because of the potential for contraband to enter the prison (but see the discussion of visitation in new-generation jails in the previous section).

conjugal visits An arrangement whereby inmates are permitted to visit in private with their spouses or significant others to maintain their personal relationship.

It is important to emphasize that written rules and regulations are not the exclusive basis for institutional security. Written rules and regulations are part of an institution's formal bureaucratic structure, which was discussed earlier in this chapter. Within that formal structure, there develops an unwritten, informal structure of norms and relations that is vital to the operation of the facility. For example, most institutions have an elaborate **snitch system** in which staff learn from inmate informants about the presence of contraband, the potential for disruptions, and other threats to security. Informants often receive special concessions and protection in exchange for snitching on other inmates. Such arrangements can be very elaborate, as illustrated by the research of criminologists James Marquart and Ben Crouch. In their study of a Texas prison, Marquart and Crouch found that certain elite inmates, known as building tenders, actually functioned as extensions of the uniformed guard force to achieve control of the institution.[61] The use of inmates (building tenders or trustees) to discipline other inmates was formally outlawed in 1984.

snitch system A system in which staff learn from inmate informants about the presence of contraband, the potential for disruptions, and other threats to security.

FYI: Conjugal Visits

As of January 1, 2001, only six agencies permitted conjugal visiting: in California, Connecticut, Mississippi, New Mexico, New York, and Washington.

SOURCE: Camille Graham Camp and George M. Camp, *The Corrections Yearbook 2001: Adult Systems* (Middletown, CT: Criminal Justice Institute, 2002), p. 147.

Inmates who violate formal institutional regulations may be subjected to disciplinary measures. Staff members typically have broad discretion when they detect rule violations. They may simply overlook the infraction or may issue an informal warning. Alternatively, they may file a disciplinary report so that formal sanctions can be considered. The report usually leads to a disciplinary hearing, during which the charges and supporting evidence are presented to the institution's disciplinary committee or hearing officer. If the report is found to be valid, a number of sanctions are possible. For example, the inmate may have some of his or her privileges temporarily restricted (for instance, no commissary or store privileges for 30 days), may be placed in solitary confinement or "the hole" for a specified number of days, may forfeit some of the time that has been deducted from his or her sentence for good behavior, or may even be transferred to another facility. Because institutions have many rules governing the behavior of inmates, it should come as no surprise that rule infractions and disciplinary measures occur frequently.[62]

SERVICES AND PROGRAMS

Many of the human services and programs found in the free society are duplicated within institutions. At a minimum, inmates must be fed, clothed, and provided with such basic shelter requirements as warmth, electricity, and plumbing, and their health care needs must be addressed.

Food services are an important part of an institution's operation. Waste and inefficiency must be avoided to control expense, but inmate demand and dietary standards must be met.

Prisons and jails are buildings that, like all buildings, require maintenance and repair. A large portion of the maintenance and repair work is performed by inmates as part of their job assignments.

Courts have held that inmates are entitled to medical and dental services. Prisons normally have an infirmary where less serious ailments can be treated. More serious problems necessitate transfer to either a prison with more extensive medical services or a hospital in the local community.

Institutions make an array of services available to inmates for their leisure time. We have already mentioned mail, phone, and visitation services. In addition, institutions operate commissaries where inmates can purchase such items as food, tobacco, radios, reading materials, and arts and crafts supplies. A number of recreational facilities are also provided, such as weight-lifting equipment, softball fields, basketball courts, game tables, and television viewing areas. In addition, legal resources and religious services are available. They will be discussed in more detail in the next chapter. Although most prisons still offer a substantial number of services to prisoners, there has been a movement to reduce services over the past two decades.

INMATES WITH SPECIAL NEEDS All institutions have special-needs populations. Although those populations generally consist of far fewer inmates than the general prison population, it is still necessary to provide services for them. For example, elderly inmates frequently need more medical attention than younger inmates. The number of elderly prison inmates is increasing. In 1990, 4.9 percent (or about 35,000) of state and federal prisoners were 50 or older. In 2001, 7.9 percent (or about 113,400) were 50 or older—an increase of 61 percent in the percentage of inmates 50 or older and an increase of 224 percent in the number of inmates 50 or older. In the federal prison system, each inmate 55 or older costs the government about $69,000 a year in maintenance costs, two or three times as much as is spent on inmates younger than 55. Most of the added expense is related to health costs. One health-related problem that has not been adequately addressed is the decreased mobility of older inmates—a problem that current prisons are rarely designed to accommodate.[63]

Another special-needs population is the mentally ill.[64] Since the deinstitutionalization of the mentally ill in the 1960s, in favor of treating them in the community, prisons and especially jails have become surrogate public mental hospitals. According to a 1999 Justice Department report, at least 16 percent of the total jail and prison population, or approximately 300,000 inmates, have

FYI Prison Security

A recent national survey revealed that 67 percent of the American public think that prisons do an excellent (18 percent) or good (49 percent) job of "maintaining high security to keep prisoners from escaping"; 23 percent think that they do only a fair job, and 8 percent think they do a poor job (2 percent had no opinion). As for "maintaining a safe environment for inmates in prison," 30 percent of the public think that the prisons are excellent (5 percent) or good (25 percent), 37 percent think they are only fair, and 26 percent think they are poor (7 percent had no opinion).

SOURCE: *Sourcebook of Criminal Justice Statistics 2001,* p. 112, Table 2.20, at www.albany.edu/sourcebook.

FYI Aging Inmates

Correctional officials generally consider 50-year-old inmates geriatrics because their lives have probably been filled with violence, drug, alcohol and tobacco abuse, poor diets, and inadequate medical care.

SOURCE: "Virginia Opens Special Prison for Aging Inmates," *The Dallas Morning News,* July 3, 1999, www.dallasnews.com/national/0703nat4prison.html, December 21, 2000.

Myth

The high cost of incarceration is a product of amenities provided to inmates, such as cable television, law libraries, and weight-lifting equipment. Eliminating these "country club" add-ons will make prison costs more reasonable.

Fact

Actually, 4 out of every 5 dollars of prison operating costs are for employee salaries and facility maintenance. In addition, debt service to finance prison construction triples the original cost of construction. A maximum security prison in New York State, for example, costs about $100,000 per bed to build, but financing costs add another $200,000 per bed. Finally, costs have grown substantially as a result of the health care needs of an increasingly older and AIDS-afflicted inmate population.

SOURCE: *Seeking Justice: Crime and Punishment in America,* Edna McConnell Clark Foundation (New York: 1997), p. 9.

a serious mental illness. The costs of incarcerating the mentally ill are huge. The Justice Department estimates that it costs at least $15 billion a year to house inmates with psychiatric disorders (about $50,000 per inmate per year). Such inmates may require segregated housing for their own protection and the protection of other inmates, frequent consultation with psychologists and psychiatrists, efforts to ensure that they take prescribed medication, and special safety precautions (for example, for a suicidal inmate, the use of paper sheets rather than cloth to prevent hanging).

The problem is particularly acute in jails. Mentally ill people are frequently held in jails even though they have not been charged with a crime. Many of them are held under state laws that permit emergency detentions of people suspected of being mentally ill. They are typically incarcerated pending a psychiatric evaluation or until they can be transported to a psychiatric hospital.

Most mentally ill inmates who are arrested are charged with misdemeanors such as trespassing or disorderly conduct. They are also frequently charged with drug- or alcohol-related offenses. Inmates with more serious psychiatric problems, such as paranoid schizophrenia, are sometimes arrested for assault because they mistakenly believe that someone was following them or trying to hurt them. Police also arrest people with severe psychiatric problems (so-called mercy bookings) to protect them from harm. This is especially true of women on the streets who are easily victimized, including being raped. Family members sometimes have mentally ill relatives arrested because it is the easiest and most effective way to get the mentally ill relative needed treatment. Sometimes being incarcerated is the only way for mentally ill people to get needed treatment.

Unfortunately, for the mentally ill, most jails do not provide adequate mental health services. More than 20 percent of jails provide no mental health services at all. Correctional officers in the vast majority of jails receive either no training or less than 3 hours of training in dealing with the special needs of inmates with severe mental illness. Prisons generally do a better job of accommodating the needs of mentally ill inmates. For example, at midyear 2000, nearly 90 percent of state public and private adult prisons provided mental health services to their inmates. About 12.5 percent of state prisoners were receiving some mental health therapy or counseling. About 10 percent of state prisoners were receiving psychotropic medications.[65] Still, jails and prisons are often brutal places for mentally ill inmates, where they are vulnerable to assault, rape, and exposure to infectious diseases. Because many of them are unable to describe their symptoms to correctional officers, their needs, even in facilities equipped to deal with them, are often ignored.

Much controversy surrounds the presence of the human immunodeficiency virus (HIV) and acquired immune deficiency syndrome (AIDS) among institutional populations. As of year-end 2000, 2.2 percent of state prison inmates (24,074) and 0.8 percent of federal prison inmates (1,014) were reported by prison officials to be HIV-positive.[66] About 25 percent of the HIV-infected inmates were held in New York prisons. Of the HIV-positive inmates, 22 percent (5,528) had confirmed cases of AIDS. This was down from the 6,642 confirmed cases of AIDS in 1999, and the first decrease in confirmed AIDS cases since data were first collected in 1991. In 2000, 174 state prison inmates and 21 federal prison inmates died from AIDS-related causes. This was the fewest state prison inmates to die from AIDS-related causes in 10 years and less than a fifth of the number (1,010) recorded in 1995—the peak year. In 2000, 6 percent of state prison inmate deaths were attributed to AIDS, down from 32 percent in 1995. At the end of 2000, the rate of confirmed AIDS cases in state and federal prisons was 4 times the rate in the total U.S. population. Intravenous drug use is the key risk factor for AIDS among inmates.

At year-end 2000, 20 states and the federal government tested all inmates for HIV at some point during their sentences, a controversial practice known as *mass screening*. New York, Oregon, Virginia, and the Federal Bureau of Prisons (BOP) test inmates chosen randomly. Most jurisdictions test inmates if they have HIV-related symptoms, or if inmates request a test. The BOP and 41 states test inmates if they have been involved in an incident, and 15 states test "high-risk" inmates. Alabama, Missouri, Nevada, and the BOP test inmates before their release. The testing policies of each jurisdiction have not changed much since 1991. In addition to mass mandatory screening, other debated issues are whether HIV-positive inmates should be segregated and the degree to which HIV-positive test results should be kept confidential by attending medical staff. At present, the trend seems to be away from blanket segregation and toward confidentiality.

INMATE REHABILITATION PROGRAMS Inmates hoping to better themselves during their incarceration normally have the opportunity to participate in a number of rehabilitation programs. The particular programs offered vary across jurisdictions and institutions. Examples are:

1. Self-improvement programs offered by religious and civic groups (Alcoholics Anonymous, the Jaycees, a Bible club).
2. Work programs.
3. Education and vocational training.
4. Counseling and therapy.

Work Programs Since the creation of the first houses of correction in Europe, there has been one constant: the belief that the imprisonment experience should improve inmates' work habits. Today, however, there is tremendous variation among institutions regarding work programs. In some institutions, all inmates who are physically able are required to work. In other institutions, the inmates who work are those who choose to do so. Likewise, there is great variation in the types of work inmates perform. Some inmates are employed to help the daily running of the institution and work in such areas as food services, maintenance and repair, laundry, health care, and clerical services. Other inmates work in factories at industrial tasks, such as wood or metal manufacturing. Still other inmates perform agricultural work.

As of January 1, 2001, the average daily wage earned by prison inmates working in agency-operated industries ranged from $3.03 to $8.14, compared to $2.17 to $8.94 in 1999. The average workday was slightly down to 6.78 hours per day from 7 hours. The average daily wage earned by prison inmates working in nonindustry jobs ranged from $0.93 to $4.73, down from $1.42 to $5.09 in 1999. The average workday was about the same as in 1999. Some states, such as Georgia and Texas, do not pay inmates for their work. The state of Nevada pays its inmates the most, $31.41 a day, for work in agency-operated industries (Hawaii paid its inmates $49.88 in 1999); the state of Washington pays

Myth	Fact
The services and programs available to inmates make prisons seem like country clubs. Therefore, services and programs should be severely cut back or eliminated so that inmates receive punishment while incarcerated.	First, the services and programs available to inmates are sometimes of inferior quality when compared with those available in the free community. Second, programs and services perform a vital time management function. Institutions would be much more volatile and disorderly than they currently are without programs and services to fill time.

its inmates the most, $30.45 a day, for work in nonindustry jobs (it paid its inmates $29.75 in 1999). Inmates who work in privately operated industries generally earn more.[67]

Institutions also vary in the degree to which the private sector is involved in work programming. Although the early history of the prison in the United States was characterized by extensive ties between inmate labor and the free market, those ties diminished during the first half of the 1900s. That change was due to concern by organized labor about unemployment among free citizens, concern by businesses that did not employ convict labor about their ability to compete on the open market, and concern by prison reformers about exploitation of inmates. Because of a series of laws restricting the private use of inmate labor, the *state-use system* became—and still is—the predominant way of arranging inmate work programs. Under that system, inmates are allowed to produce goods and services for the government. For example in the main work program operated by the Federal Bureau of Prisons, known as UNICOR, inmates make a variety of products used by agencies of the federal government. Recently, however, legal restrictions on the private use of prison labor have been loosened, and the practice is witnessing somewhat of a resurgence in certain jurisdictions.

Education and Vocational Training It has long been assumed that rehabilitation can be facilitated by improving inmates' academic skills and providing them with job skills. Many offenders enter prison with deficits in their education. It is not at all uncommon to encounter adult inmates who are reading, writing, and performing math operations at an elementary school level. Therefore, much prison education amounts to remedial schooling designed to prepare inmates to obtain their GEDs. College courses are made available in some prisons through correspondence or study release arrangements or by bringing college instructors to the prison to offer courses. However, low educational levels render college courses inappropriate for many inmates.

Research shows that inmates exposed to education programs have lower recidivism rates than nonparticipants. *Why do only 25–50 percent of inmates take part in some form of education?*

A recent study found that two-thirds of prison inmates have such poor reading and arithmetic skills that they are unable to write a brief letter explaining a billing error or to interpret a bar graph. Only about half of all prisoners have completed high school or its equivalent, but even inmates who have a high school diploma demonstrate lower basic skills than do members of the general public with a high school diploma. Yet, over the past few years, while the prison population has expanded dramatically, more than half the states have cut back their educational and training budgets. The percentage of inmates enrolled in educational programs ranges from a high of 86 percent in Kentucky to a low of 7 percent in Nebraska. In most states, only 25–50 percent of inmates take part in some form of education, even though several studies show that inmates exposed to education programs have lower recidivism rates than nonparticipants.[68]

Some prison vocational programs operate as part of job assignments (on-the-job training), and others are separate from job assignments. Either way, the goal is to provide inmates with job skills that will improve their marketability upon release. Most prison vocational training is geared toward traditional blue-collar employment, such as welding and auto mechanics. Vocational programs offered in women's prisons have often been criticized for concentrating excessively on stereotypical women's jobs, such as cosmetology.

Counseling and Therapy A wide range of counseling techniques and therapy modalities are used in prisons across the nation. The description of specific techniques and modalities, however, is beyond the scope of this chapter.[69] Suffice it to say that the techniques and modalities used at a given institution ordinarily reflect the training and professional orientation of the treatment staff—caseworkers, religious counselors, social workers, psychologists, and psychiatrists.

A distinction is usually drawn between individual counseling, which involves one-on-one interaction between the counselor and the inmate, and group counseling, which involves the interaction of the counselor with a small group of inmates. Those categories of treatment may overlap, because an inmate receiving individual counseling may also be in group counseling, and many of the techniques and principles used in individual counseling are also applied to group settings. Still, the distinction has merit, because individual counseling is more appropriate for some inmates (for example, those with deep-seated problems who will require long-term help), and group counseling is more appropriate for other inmates (for example, those who are defensive, manipulative, and prone to denying their problems).

Group counseling is more popular than individual counseling in institutional settings, primarily because it is more economical and because there are large numbers of inmates who share similar backgrounds and problems. In fact, the members of a group are frequently selected on the basis of their common backgrounds and problem behavior patterns. For example, a group may consist of persons who have substance abuse problems or those who are sex offenders. Some institutions employ a variant of group therapy known as **milieu therapy** (also called a *therapeutic community*). Rather than having inmates attend periodic group sessions (one or two hourly sessions per week), milieu therapy encompasses the total living environment of inmates so that the environment continually encourages positive behavioral change. In effect, the entire inmate population becomes the group, and inmates have active roles in helping other inmates change.

milieu therapy A variant of group therapy that encompasses the total living environment so that the environment continually encourages positive behavioral change.

Most counselors and therapists who work in prison spend a considerable portion of their time performing **crisis intervention.** Crisis intervention consists of a counselor's efforts to address some crisis that has erupted in an inmate's life (for example, suicidal thoughts, rejection by the spouse, a mental

crisis intervention A counselor's efforts to address some crisis in an inmate's life and to calm the inmate.

breakdown, or a conflict between inmates). Institutions are stressful living environments, so inmate crises are common. The counselor's task is to assist inmates in restoring a state of emotional calm and greater stability so that problems can be addressed rationally before inmates harm themselves or others.

FYI: Rehabilitating Inmates

A recent national survey shows that only 14 percent of the American public think that prisons are doing an excellent (2 percent) or good (12 percent) job "rehabilitating inmates so they are less likely to commit crimes in the future"; 34 percent think they do only a fair job, and 48 percent think they do a poor job. The rest had no opinion.

SOURCE: *Sourcebook of Criminal Justice Statistics 2001* (online), p. 112, Table 2.20.

Programs in Perspective We usually think of rehabilitation programs as serving one main objective: to help inmates better themselves. In practice, however, programs serve other, more subtle functions as well. Programs give inmates a way to occupy themselves; they help inmates manage time. They also help the institution achieve control over inmates. For example, inmates who are in counseling for displaying too much aggression toward other inmates may realize that unless they demonstrate "progress" in reducing their aggression, the counselor will not recommend them to the parole board for early release (in states where parole is available). Although such progress may be achieved quickly in prison, it may be short-lived upon release. Similarly, from the standpoint of inmates, the most desirable work assignments are those that give inmates access to valued resources (for instance, a kitchen job provides greater access to food). More desirable work assignments are routinely held out by the staff as privileges to be earned through good behavior.

Institutional programs are also plagued by a variety of problems that hinder their ability to effect rehabilitation. For example, prison work assignments frequently do not parallel work in the free world. In prison, workdays are often short and interrupted. In many cases, there is little concern for the quantity and quality of work. Furthermore, some of the jobs lack any real counterpart in the free world. The classic example is license plate manufacturing. In many prisons, educational programs suffer from a lack of funding. Vocational training focuses primarily on traditional blue-collar jobs and thus prepares inmates to enter jobs for which there is already abundant competition. A dilemma is created by the argument that inmates should not receive highly technical or professional training (such as training in computer programming) because many members of the free, law-abiding community cannot afford such training. That argument is based on the **less-eligibility principle,** the position that prisoners should receive no service or program superior to the services and programs available to free citizens without charge. Moreover, prison education and vocational programs can do little to create jobs. If an inmate returns to a community with a poor economy and high unemployment, the education and training received in prison may do little more than raise the inmate's expectations to unrealistic levels.

less-eligibility principle The position that prisoners should receive no service or program superior to the services and programs available to free citizens without charge.

For their part, counseling and therapy programs must operate against the harsh realities of the prison environment, where custody and security ordinarily take priority over rehabilitation. Despite those obstacles, some programs are able to bring about positive changes in offenders' attitudes and behavior. Psychologist Ted Palmer has observed that although no single type of treatment can be identified as the most effective, one feature that seems to characterize programs that consistently reduce offender recidivism is the quality of the program's implementation. Thus, when the integrity of treatment efforts is allowed to take priority over institutional concerns for security and custody, offending can be reduced.[70] Also, as criminologist Robert Johnson points out, many counseling programs place nearly exclusive emphasis on inmates' pasts and futures, with insufficient attention given to present coping patterns. Johnson recommends that programs begin teaching inmates to cope maturely and constructively with their present environment so that they will be better able to cope with life after release.[71]

THINKING CRITICALLY

1. Do you think inmate rehabilitation programs can truly make a difference? Why or why not?
2. Do you think inmates should earn money for the work they do while in prison? Why or why not?

SUMMARY

1. Summarize the purposes of confinement in Europe before it became a major way of punishing criminals

Confinement became a major way of punishing criminals in Europe in the 1600s and 1700s. Before that, it was used to (1) detain people before trial, (2) hold prisoners awaiting other sanctions, such as death and corporal punishment, (3) coerce payment of debts and fines, (4) hold and punish slaves, (5) achieve religious indoctrination and spiritual reformation (as during the Inquisition), and (6) quarantine disease (as during the bubonic plague).

2. Describe how offenders were punished before the large-scale use of confinement

Before the large-scale use of confinement, punishments were directed more at the offender's body and property. One basic goal was to inflict pain. Those punishments were commonly carried out in public to humiliate the offender and to deter onlookers from crime. Examples of such punishments are fines, confiscation of property, and diverse methods of corporal and capital punishment.

3. Explain why confinement began to be used as a major way of punishing offenders in Europe

Enlightenment-era reforms led to an emphasis on deterring and reforming criminals through confinement. Confinement was also advocated as a humane alternative to older punishments. In addition, during the 1500s and 1600s, workhouses were established as places where offenders could be sent to learn discipline and productive work habits.

4. Describe the recent trends in the use of incarceration in the United States

There has been a dramatic increase since the mid-1970s in the number of people incarcerated in the United States, partly due to the War on Drugs. That increase has been accompanied by much concern over rising costs and institutional crowding. In response to those problems, confinement alternatives to traditional incarceration have been developed. Two of those alternatives are contracts with the private sector for the construction or operation of some confinement facilities and the use of shock incarceration, or "boot camp" prisons, for young, nonviolent offenders without extensive prior criminal records.

5. List some of the characteristics of the incarcerated population in the United States

The incarcerated population in the United States is disproportionately male, black, young, single, undereducated, and poor. Nearly half of state prison inmates are serving time for violent offenses, whereas approximately 55 percent of federal prison inmates are serving sentences for drug offenses. More than half of jail inmates are unconvicted, usually awaiting trial or other case disposition.

6. Describe how incarceration facilities are structured, organized, and administered by the government in the United States

Incarceration facilities in the United States are administered primarily by the executive branch of government. They exist at all three levels of government. Prisons are administered at the federal level and state levels, while jails tend to be locally administered. Despite this diversification, all the institutions have somewhat similar administrative structures, ranging from the warden or superintendent at the top to the correctional (line) officers at the bottom.

7. Name some of the common types of correctional facilities in the United States

Common types of adult correctional facilities in the United States include (1) classification and special facilities, (2) "supermaximum-," maximum-, medium-, and minimum-security men's prisons, (3) women's and co-correctional facilities, and (4) jails and lockups.

8. Identify some of the procedures that institutions employ to maintain security and order

To maintain security and order, correctional institutions employ a number of procedures. Among them are the use of custody designations for inmates, inmate counts, property control, searches of inmates and their living quarters, and restrictions on inmate communication (mail, phone calls, and visits) with outsiders. Also, institutions commonly rely on inmate-informant, or snitch, systems to maintain security. Inmates found guilty of violating institutional rules may be subjected to a variety of disciplinary sanctions (such as loss of good time, restriction of privileges, and solitary confinement) to deter future rule infractions.

9. List the services and programs that are commonly available to inmates

Some of the services and programs available to inmates are subsistence services (food, clothing, and shelter), health care services, legal services, recreation, and religious services. There are also a number of programs designed to improve inmates' lives. They include low-paying work, education and vocational training, and group and individual counseling.

KEY TERMS

banishment, p. 351
transportation, p. 351
workhouses, p. 352
penology, p. 353
panopticon, p. 353
Pennsylvania system, p. 354
Auburn system, p. 354
medical model, p. 356
privatization, p. 357
shock incarceration, p. 358
incarceration rate, p. 361
classification facility, p. 368
security level, p. 369
custody level, p. 373
cocorrectional facilities, p. 374
lockup, p. 374
jail, p. 374
protective custody, p. 383
administrative segregation, p. 383
conjugal visits, p. 384
snitch system, p. 384
milieu therapy, p. 389
crisis intervention, p. 389
less-eligibility principle, p. 390

REVIEW QUESTIONS

1. What did Cesare Beccaria, the Enlightenment thinker, mean when he said that a punishment should fit the crime?
2. What reforms in penal institutions did John Howard advocate in his book *The State of the Prisons in England and Wales* (1777)?
3. What is generally considered the first state prison in the United States, and of what did the daily routine of inmates in this prison consist?
4. How did the Pennsylvania system of confinement differ from the Auburn system of confinement, and which system became the model followed by other states?
5. What were the main features of the reformatory?
6. According to John Irwin, what three types of penal institutions dominated different parts of the last century?
7. What is an incarceration rate, and why is it used?
8. How does the incarceration rate of the United States compare with the incarceration rates of other countries?
9. How do the authors of this textbook explain the prison overcrowding crisis in the United States?
10. What are some major differences between the federal prison and state prison populations?
11. What is the official mission of the Federal Bureau of Prisons?
12. What are the purposes of inmate classification?
13. What are prison security and custody levels, and how do they differ?
14. What are the purposes of a jail?
15. Why do jails represent one of the most problematic aspects of criminal justice?
16. What are some objectives of inmate rehabilitation programs?
17. What is the less-eligibility principle, as applied to corrections?

IN THE FIELD

1. **Prison Tour** Many prisons and jails conduct tours for students in criminal justice courses. Arrange to visit one or more prisons and jails in your area. Compare and contrast what you see during your visit(s) with the material in this chapter. Also, if you tour both a prison and a jail, describe similarities and differences between the two institutions. Either present your findings orally in class or put them in writing for your instructor.

2. **Create a Prison** Design a prison conceptually and, perhaps, three-dimensionally. Decide what type of inmates the prison is to hold (men, women, or both; prisoners requiring maximum security, minimum security, etc.) and what the security level will be. Consider location, architectural design, bureaucratic structure, security and discipline procedures, and inmate services and programs.

ON THE NET

1. **Federal Bureau of Prisons** Go to the Federal Bureau of Prisons website at www.bop.gov. Access "Public Info" and then "Quick Facts and Statistics" from the topic list. Use the data provided to construct a current profile of inmates. Then access the "Weekly Population Report," and search for data about any federal prisons in your state. Write a brief report on what you find.

2. **Incarceration Worldwide** Review the document, "Comparative International Rates of Incarceration: An Examination of Causes and Trends," at The Sentencing Project website at www.sentencingproject.org/june/usccr-incarceration.pdf. Write a brief essay explaining why rates of incarceration vary so greatly among countries of the world.

CRITICAL THINKING EXERCISES

1. **Prison Research** A Florida prison has recently been transformed into a combination hospital and prison where most inmates have HIV. They participate in tests of some of the newest HIV drugs being developed and have access to some of the nation's leading AIDS researchers. Only about 120 of the 3,000 or so state inmates who are known to be HIV positive are able to participate. Some inmates are due to be released in a few weeks or months; others are serving life sentences. On the street, the treatment would cost about $1,400 a month; participating inmates get it for free.

   The program is controversial. Although it has been praised as a model for the rest of the country's prisons to copy, it has also been criticized for conducting drug trials or medical studies on inmates. Because inmates are a captive audience, a major question is whether they can truly give informed consent to participate in the voluntary program. Before they are allowed to participate, inmates must sign a 5-page consent form that lists the possible benefits and side effects of the drugs. The state also has no relationship with the drug companies and accepts no money from them.

   a. Should the program continue and be spread to other prisons? Why or why not?
   b. Address these questions: Can inmates give informed consent? Does it matter? If inmates are allowed to participate, how should they be chosen from among all those who volunteer?

2. **The Ex-Convict** To the average citizen, the ex-convict is an individual of questionable character. This image is reinforced by the fact that the only thing that is usually newsworthy about ex-convicts is bad news, such as when they are rearrested. Few citizens know a rehabilitated offender for obvious reasons. Yet, the rehabilitated ex-convict faces a variety of civil disabilities. Not the least among those is the difficulty of getting a "good" job. On virtually every job application, there is the question: "Have you ever been convicted of a felony or misdemeanor or denied bond in any state? In addition, prospective employers generally ask applicants to reveal their former substance abuse, which is a problem that most former offenders had. An affirmative answer to either question almost always eliminates a person's chance for employment.

   a. How can ex-offenders shed the ex-convict status? Should they be allowed to shed it? Why or why not?
   b. Does your answer to (a) change depending upon the ex-convict's conviction offense?

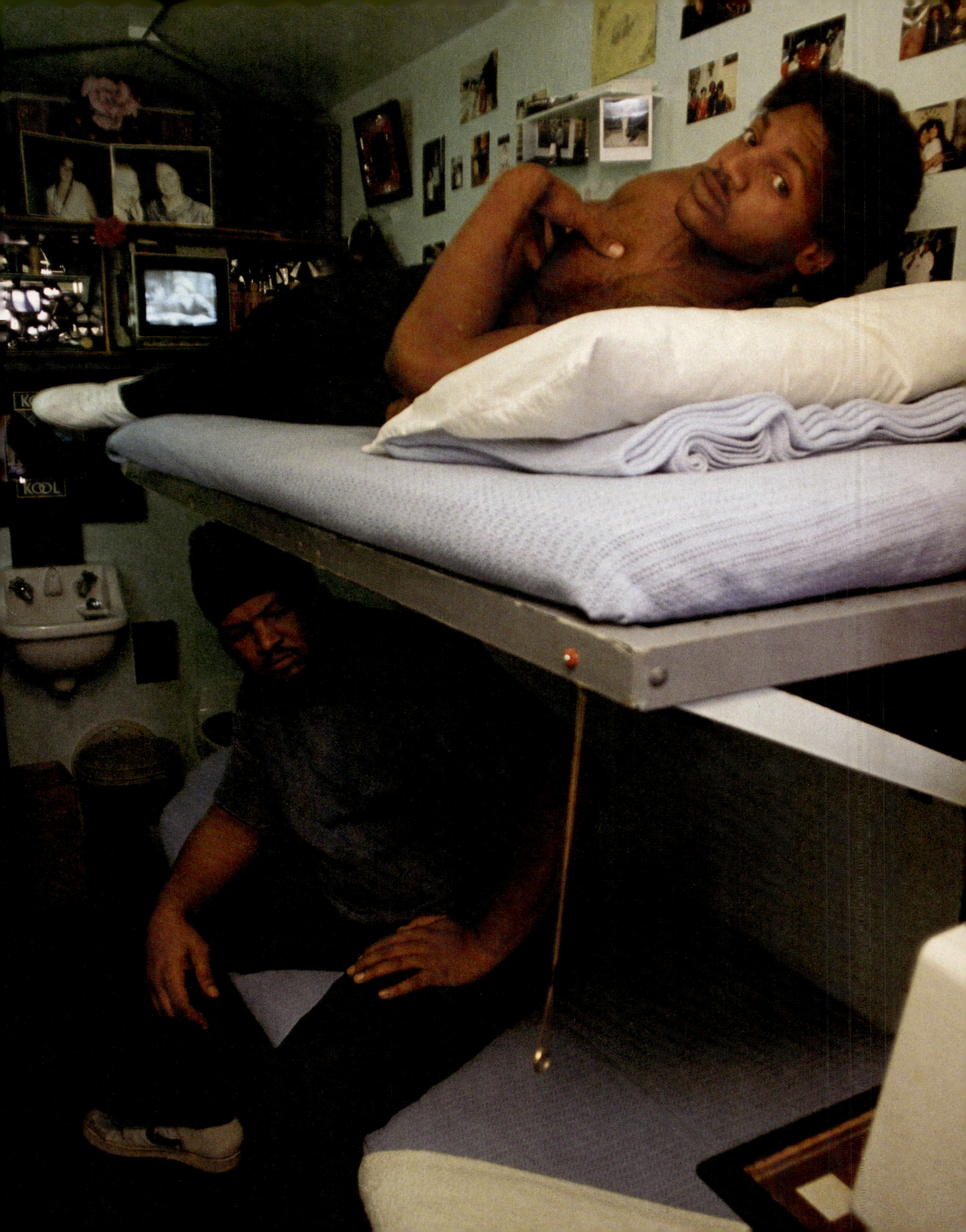
KOOL

PRISON LIFE, INMATE RIGHTS, RELEASE, AND RECIDIVISM

CHAPTER ELEVEN

Chapter Outline

Chapter Objectives

After completing this chapter, you should be able to:

1. **Distinguish between the deprivation and importation models of inmate society.**
2. **Explain how today's inmate society differs from those of the past.**
3. **Identify some of the special features of life in women's prisons.**
4. **Describe the profile of correctional officers and explain some of the issues that they face.**
5. **Identify prisoners' rights and relate how they were achieved.**
6. **List the two most common ways that inmates are released from prison and compare those two ways in frequency of use.**
7. **Summarize what recidivism research reveals about the success of the prison in achieving deterrence and rehabilitation.**

Crime Story

On August 23, 2003, defrocked Catholic priest John Geoghan was murdered by a fellow inmate at a Massachusetts prison. Geoghan, who has been described as an unrepentant pedophile, was serving a 9-to-10-year sentence for groping a 10-year-old boy. The case unleashed a massive sex abuse scandal within the Catholic Church that captured both national and worldwide attention. As the scandal swept across the nation more than 300 priests were eventually stripped of their duties for similar allegations of sex abuse. Geoghan was ordained into the priesthood in 1962 and ousted in 1998 after the details of the sex abuse surfaced. At the time of his death, he still faced two more criminal trials and 147 lawsuits.

The 68-year-old Geoghan was attacked and strangled by convicted murderer and neo-Nazi Joseph Druce around noon at the Souza-Baranowski Correctional Center in Shirley, Massachusetts. Reportedly, Druce had been planning the murder undetected for more than a month. Massachusetts District Attorney John Conte stated that Druce utilized a t-shirt, a pair of socks, a book, a toothbrush, and nail clippers in the strangulation death of Geoghan. According to Conte, Druce used the t-shirt to tie Geoghan's hands behind his back and used the socks as a ligature device to strangle him. The book, toothbrush, and nail clippers were used to jam the electric cell door to avoid any interruption of Druce's scheme by correctional officers. Following the attack, Geoghan was pronounced dead at 1:17 P.M. after being rushed to a nearby Boston hospital.

The 37-year-old Druce is serving a life sentence for strangling and mutilating a 51-year-old gay bus driver in 1989. Conte suggested in media reports that Druce has a longstanding phobia toward homosexuals. Druce has been treated in various mental hospitals for a history of bizarre behaviors. In 2002, Druce pleaded guilty to sending a federal prosecutor a swastika-emblazoned letter that he falsely claimed contained anthrax. Druce has also been suspected of sending letters containing his own fecal waste to federal judges and the state attorney general within the past 2 years. The deadly attack on the defrocked priest raised questions about why Geoghan, who was in protective custody at his own request, was housed only a few cells away from Druce who has a known contempt for homosexuals. State officials indicated that an investigation into prison procedures would be conducted.

Chapter 11 discusses the characteristics of prison environments and how inmates adjust to prison life. Most people can only imagine what life inside a prison is really like. Was the violence directed at John Geoghan attributable to inmates from very different worlds being unable to adjust to the prison environment? Or was it a reflection of improper correctional management? The search for the answers to questions such as these is frequently elusive to both correctional scholars and practitioners.

Living in Prison

When people think of prisons, they usually imagine the big-house, maximum-security prison for men. Indeed, the majority of scholarly research on prison life has focused on this type of institution. In this chapter, we survey some of that research. However, we caution the reader to be careful about generalizing findings from studies of the big house to all institutions. As we have already seen, institutions are quite diverse.

INMATE SOCIETY

In his classic book *Asylums*, sociologist Erving Goffman described prisons as total institutions. Goffman defined a **total institution** as "a place of residence and work where a large number of like-situated individuals, cut off from the wider society for an appreciable period of time, together lead an enclosed, formally administered round of life."[1] As already pointed out and as further implied by Goffman's definition, a prison represents a miniature, self-contained society.

total institution An institutional setting in which persons sharing some characteristics are cut off from the wider society and expected to live according to institutional rules and procedures.

Although prisons are certainly influenced by the outside world,[2] they are also separated and closed off from that world. A society of prisoners, like any society, possesses distinctive cultural features (values, norms, and roles), and because prisoners do not serve their time completely isolated from other inmates, the features of the inmate society influence the way prisoners adjust to prison life.

Central to the inmate society of traditional men's prisons in the United States is the convict code. The **convict code** is a constellation of values, norms, and roles that regulate the way inmates interact with one another and with prison staff. For example, a principle of the convict code is that individual inmates should mind their own affairs and do their own time. Other principles are that inmates should not inform the staff about the illicit activities of other prisoners and that inmates' overall attitude and behavior should be indifferent to the staff and loyal to other convicts. "Conning" and manipulation skills are highly valued under the code, as is the ability to show strength, courage, and toughness.

convict code A constellation of values, norms, and roles that regulate the way inmates interact with one another and with prison staff.

Two major theories of the origins of the inmate society have been advanced: the deprivation model and the importation model. Advocates of the **deprivation model** (sometimes called the "indigenous origins model") contend that the inmate society arises in response to the prison environment and the painful conditions of confinement.[3] Specifically, imprisonment deprives inmates of such things as material possessions, social acceptance, heterosexual relations, personal security, and liberty. This environment of shared deprivation gives inmates a basis for solidarity. The inmate society and its convict code represent a functional, collective adaptation of inmates to this environment. When an inmate enters prison for the first time, the inmate is socialized into the customs and principles of the inmate society, a process author Donald Clemmer termed **prisonization.**[4] Clemmer believed that the longer inmates stayed in prison, the more "prisonized" they became and the more likely they were to return to crime after their release from prison.

deprivation model A theory that the inmate society arises as a response to the prison environment and the painful conditions of confinement.

prisonization The process by which an inmate becomes socialized into the customs and principles of the inmate society.

An alternative to the deprivation model is the **importation model,** which holds that the inmate society is shaped by factors external to the prison environment—specifically, the preprison experiences and socialization patterns that inmates bring with them when they enter prison.[5] For example, inmates who were thieves and persistently associated with other thieves before going to prison bring the norms and values of thieves into the prison. They will remain more loyal to those norms and values than to the staff while incarcerated. On the other hand, if an inmate primarily conformed to the law before entering prison, the inmate will probably exhibit greater loyalty to staff norms once in prison. In short, the deprivation model assumes that new inmates are socialized

importation model A theory that the inmate society is shaped by the attributes inmates bring with them when they enter prison.

Conflict builds when inmates form competing gangs along ethnic, racial, and geographic lines. *Why do inmates form gangs in prison?*

into the existing inmate society, which arises in response to the prison environment; the importation model suggests that the inmate society is the product of the socialization inmates experience before entering prison.

The deprivation and importation models were developed from studies of prisons of the pre-1960s era. Some scholars believe that the image of a fairly unified inmate society with an overarching convict code fails to characterize many of today's crowded and violent prisons. According to those scholars, several factors have rendered the inmate society fragmented, disorganized, and unstable:

1. Increasing racial heterogeneity.
2. The racial polarization of modern prisoners.
3. Court litigation.
4. The rise and fall of rehabilitation.
5. The increased politicalization of inmates.

The order and stability provided by the old inmate subculture has been replaced by an atmosphere of conflict and tension, in which inmates align themselves into competing gangs (such as the Aryan Brotherhood, the Mexican Mafia, and the Black Guerrilla Family) and other inmate organizations (such as the Lifer's Club and the Muslims).[6]

Violence and Victimization It is generally agreed that there is more physical violence by inmates in today's men's prisons than there was in earlier periods. In recent years, thousands of inmates and staff have been assaulted. In 2000, for example, 55 inmates but no staff members were killed by inmates in state prisons.[7] There is also consensus that staff violence against inmates is less common today. However, the number of inmates killed by staff in the last few years is unknown.

Commonly cited reasons for high rates of prison violence include improper management and classification practices by staff, high levels of crowding and competition over resources, the young age of most inmates in many prisons,

Prison violence and disorder generally result spontaneously from particular circumstances. *What are some of those circumstances?*

and increases in racial tensions and prison gang activity. Although gang and racial conflicts surely play a role, it seems unlikely that the bulk of prison violence is extensively planned or gang-orchestrated. One reason is that many prisons across the United States lack well-developed gang structures and serious gang problems, but they are still plagued by violence. Furthermore, what we know about violent crime in general suggests that much prison violence is probably spontaneous, motivated by particular circumstances. Some common perpetrator motives for physical violence in prison are to (1) demonstrate power and dominance over others; (2) retaliate against a perceived wrong, such as the failure of another inmate to pay a gambling debt; and (3) prevent the perpetrator from being victimized (for example, raped) in the future.

A good deal of prison violence—but not all—has sexual overtones. It is important to realize that not all instances of sex in prison are violent, that not all instances are homosexual in nature, and that sexual encounters can involve both inmates and staff. Instances of prison sex can be further divided into three basic categories: (1) consensual sex for gratification, (2) prostitution, and (3) sexual assault. The third category obviously involves violence, and the first two sometimes have indirect links to violence. For example, a consensual sexual relationship between two inmates may have started out as a forced one. Likewise, an inmate who is vulnerable to sexual assault may perform sexual favors for an aggressive, well-respected prisoner in exchange for protection from other inmates. In the language of the prison, such vulnerable inmates are known as "punks." Prison sexual encounters can be intraracial or interracial; however, sexual assaults are more often interracial than intraracial.

Physical victimization is not the only or even the most frequent kind of victimization that takes place in prison. Lee Bowker identifies three other kinds: economic, psychological, and social.[8] As with physical victimization, these three kinds may be perpetrated by inmates against other inmates, by inmates against staff, or by staff against inmates. In addition, the four kinds of victimization are interrelated: combinations can occur, and one can lead to another.

[FYI] Attica Prison Riot

The deadliest prison riot in the nation's history occurred at the Attica Correctional Facility in upstate New York in September 1971. The uprising began when inmates took over one of the prison yards, and held 49 guards hostage, demanding better living conditions within the facility. It ended 4 days later after state troopers, under orders from then-Governor Nelson Rockefeller, raided the prison, sparking violence that left 11 guards and 32 prisoners dead and more than 80 others wounded. On February 15, 2000, a U.S. District Court judge approved a settlement under which New York State, without admitting wrongdoing or liability, would pay $8 million to 1,280 inmates who were abused by law enforcement officials during the riot. The agreement concluded a long-stalled $2.8 billion class action lawsuit originally filed against prison and state officials in 1974.

Source: "$8 Million Award Ends Attica Prison Suit," *Facts on File: World News Digest with Index,* No. 3097 (April 13, 2000), p. 248.

Prostitution is part of prison culture in many institutions. *Why do some prisoners prostitute themselves?*

sub-rosa economy The secret exchange of goods and services among inmates; the black market of the prison.

All societies have an economy, and most have a black-market component. The inmate society is no exception. The **sub-rosa** (secret or underground) **economy** of an institution consists of the exchange of goods and services that, though often illicit, are in high demand among inmates. Examples of such goods and services include food, clothes, alcohol and other drugs, pornography, weapons, loan services, protection, sex, and gambling. Engaging in illicit economic exchanges is commonly referred to as "playing the rackets" or "hustling." Cigarettes often serve as the medium of exchange because currency is typically contraband. The money inmates earn from prison work is usually maintained in accounts from which they may deduct only specified amounts for specified purposes. Hence, packs and cartons of cigarettes assume the symbolic value of money in the sub-rosa economy. However, currency may also be used. Like any kind of contraband (drugs, for example), currency can enter the institution via mail, visits, or staff. The sub-rosa economy sets the stage for various types of economic victimization, including theft, robbery, fraud, extortion, loansharking, and price-fixing by gangs and cliques.

Psychological victimization consists of subtle manipulation tactics and mind games that occur frequently in prison. For example, a staff member may obtain sensitive confidential information from an inmate's file and proceed to "mess" with the inmate's mind by threatening to convey the information to other inmates. Likewise, an inmate may threaten to convey to superiors some instance of a staff member's corruption or failure to follow procedure. Examples of psychological victimization are numerous. Combined with the crowded and noisy living conditions, separation from the outside world, and the threats to physical safety, psychological victimization contributes significantly to the stress of the prison environment. It is small wonder that many prisoners suffer from a host of psychological maladaptations, such as fear, paranoia, excess anxiety, depression, anger, and lack of trust in others.

Social victimization involves prejudice or discrimination against a person because of some social characteristic that person has. The social characteristic may be race, age, class background, religious preference, political position, or another factor. For example, racial segregation and discrimination against minorities was official policy in many prisons until the 1960s. Following the desegregation movement in the wider society, prisons, too, have become more racially integrated. Today, the segregation that remains is typically voluntary on the part of inmates.

INMATE COPING AND ADJUSTMENT Living in prison is fundamentally different from living in the free community. In prison, for example, deprivation of personal freedom and material goods is much more pronounced. There is less privacy, there is more competition for scarce resources, and life is typified by greater insecurity, stress, and unpredictability. Moreover, prison life may encourage qualities counter to those required for functioning effectively in the free community. Criminologist Ann Cordilia, expanding on the work of Erving Goffman, argues that prisons "desocialize" and alienate inmates by discouraging personal responsibility and independence, creating excessive dependency on authority, and diminishing personal control over life events.[9] One

Inmates develop a variety of coping mechanisms in prison. *If you were in prison, how would you cope?*

result is what Goffman called "self-mortification," a subduing or deadening of self-identity and self-determination.[10]

Therefore, a person coming from the free community into prison must learn to cope with and adjust to the institutional environment. Building on the ideas of criminologist Hans Toch,[11] criminologist Robert Johnson identifies two broad ways that inmates cope with imprisonment.[12] Some inmates enter what Johnson describes as the public domain of prison culture. Predatory, violent convicts, many of whom have lengthy prior records of incarceration (that is, are "state-raised youths") dominate this domain. Those convicts seek power and status in the prison world by dominating and victimizing others. Johnson claims that most inmates do not enter the public domain and live by its norms. Instead, most enter the prison's private culture. To understand this method of coping and adjustment, we must realize that each inmate brings a unique combination of personal needs into prison. That is, inmates vary in their needs for such things as privacy, environmental stimulation, safety, and emotional feedback. Entering the private culture of the prison means finding in the diverse environment of the institution a niche that will accommodate the inmate's unique combination of needs. For example, an inmate who has strong needs for privacy, safety, and intellectual stimulation may arrange to have a job in the prison library. The library becomes the inmate's niche. The private domain of prison culture consists of many diverse niches.

From another perspective, criminologist John Irwin suggests that in coping and adjusting to prison, an inmate will develop a prison career or lifestyle.[13] Three such lifestyles are "doing time," "jailing," and "gleaning." Inmates who adopt the "doing time" lifestyle are primarily concerned with getting out of prison as soon as possible and avoiding hard time in the process. Avoiding hard time means maximizing comfort and minimizing discomfort in a way that does not threaten to extend the sentence or place the inmate in danger. The "jailing" lifestyle is often embraced by people with lengthy prior records of incarceration, who are more accustomed to life *in* an institution than life

FYI: Drug Use in Federal Prisons

The Justice Department's Inspector General reported on January 22, 2003, that more than 2,800 federal inmates (about 2 percent of the federal prison population) had tested positive for illegal drugs each year from 1997 to 2001. Fifty inmates had died of drug overdoses since 1997, and drugs had been confiscated in more than 1,100 separate incidents since 2000. Narcotics typically entered the prison system through visitors, prison staff, and the mail.

SOURCE: *Facts on File World Digest* 63, no. 3245 (February 20, 2003), p. 108.

outside one. Those inmates are concerned with achieving positions of influence in the inmate society; prison is their world. "Gleaning" entails trying to take advantage of the resources available for personal betterment, such as obtaining marketable vocational skills. The idea is to prepare for life after release. Relatively few inmates adopt the gleaning lifestyle.

LIFE IN WOMEN'S PRISONS

Life in women's prisons is similar to life in men's prisons in some respects, but there are also important differences. For example, both female and male inmates must cope with the deprivations, stress, depersonalization, and authoritarian atmosphere of prison life. However, women's prisons are usually not characterized by the levels of violence, interpersonal conflict, and interracial tension found in men's institutions. Nor is the antistaff mentality of male prisoners as common among female inmates. Consequently, the environments of women's institutions are often less oppressive.

Those observations should not be taken to mean that female inmates generally do easier time than male inmates. Indeed, it has been suggested that women experience imprisonment more negatively than men.[14] A major reason for this is separation from friends and family.[15] Female inmates are more likely than male inmates to have children and to have been living with those children immediately before incarceration. In recent years, for example, about 65 percent of female state prisoners had children under 18 years old, and about the same percentage of those women lived with their children before incarceration.[16]

Procedures for determining the custodial relationship between a female inmate and her child vary widely. In some cases, very young children of incarcerated women may live with their mothers in prison for a temporary period. In other cases, maternal custody might be terminated. The procedure depends on the jurisdiction and the particular circumstances. A common arrangement is for children to reside with their fathers, grandparents, or other relatives or friends during the period of incarceration. Visitation is often irregular or nonexistent, and the amount of visitation is dictated by institutional rules and the geographic distance between children and their mothers.[17]

Female inmates are an increasing part of the nation's prison population. *Why?*

PSEUDOFAMILIES AND HOMOSEXUALITY A distinguishing feature of the inmate society in many women's prisons is the presence of make-believe families, known as pseudofamilies. Studies have discovered that some female inmates adopt family roles, such as mother, daughter, sister, husband, and father to form kinship networks.[18] The number of inmates who adopt masculine roles, known as "butches," appears to be small in comparison with the number who take on feminine roles.[19] Furthermore, kinship ties may cut across racial lines, reflecting that race is not the divisive factor in women's prisons that it is in men's institutions. Pseudofamily structures are central to inmate society in women's prisons, providing social interaction and emotional support. Sociologist Rose Giallombardo suggests that pseudofamilies provide imprisoned women with the family affiliation and bonding that they have been socialized to desire but have been deprived of by incarceration.[20]

Myth	Fact
Virtually all female prisoners are lesbians.	Although there are no totally reliable data on the proportion of female inmates who engage in homosexuality while incarcerated, a reasonable estimate (based on the literature) is approximately half. This proportion is comparable to the proportion of male prisoners who do so.

Family activity and homosexual activity appear to be relatively independent of one another. A female prisoner who is involved in homosexuality may or may not be part of a family. Likewise, a female prisoner who is part of a make-believe family may or may not be involved in homosexuality. If she is, she may be having homosexual relations with someone who is part of the family or with someone who is not. The number of female prisoners who take part in family activities probably exceeds the number who participate in homosexuality. In addition, the majority of female inmates who participate in homosexuality are what sociologists David Ward and Gene Kassebaum call "turnouts," those who were heterosexual before incarceration and will return to heterosexuality upon release.[21] As in men's prisons, interracial homosexuality

Many women in prison are mothers or mothers-to-be, and the restrictions imprisonment imposes on them as they try to maintain relationships with their children affect their physical and emotional well-being. *How could the stress of a prison mother's parent/child relationship be reduced?*

is quite common, but in contrast to men's prisons, the overwhelming majority of homosexual activity in women's institutions is consensual and is rooted in affection and attachment instead of dominance motives.

Inmate Roles Social scientist Esther Heffernan identified three roles that women commonly adopt when adjusting to prison. Heffernan's roles are very similar to roles identified by sociologist Schrag in his work on male inmates.[22] The "square" role is adopted by women who were primarily noncriminals before coming to prison, and those women tend toward conventional behavior in prison. The square role discussed by Heffernan corresponds to the "square john" role identified by Schrag. Heffernan's "life" role is analogous to Schrag's "right guy" role. Inmates who assume the life role were habitual offenders before coming to prison, and they continue to adhere to antisocial and antiauthority norms in prison. The "cool" role, or what Schrag referred to as the "con politician," is occupied by sophisticated professional criminals. They try to do easy time by manipulating other inmates and the staff to their own advantage.

THINKING CRITICALLY

1. In comparison to male prisons, why do you think that there is less violence, interpersonal conflict, and interracial tension in women's prisons?
2. Should very young children of incarcerated women be allowed to temporarily live with their mothers in prison? Why or why not?

Correctional Officers

In 1976, criminologist Gordon Hawkins wrote, "It is in fact remarkable how little serious attention has been paid to prison officers in the quite extensive literature on prisons and imprisonment."[23] Although it has increased steadily since, research on prison staff remains sparse compared with research on inmates. Most studies of prison staff have concentrated on guards or correctional officers, and there is good reason for this. Correctional officers represent the majority of staff members in a prison, are responsible for the security of the institution, and have the most frequent and closest contact with inmates. Yet correctional officers should not be thought of as existing in isolation from the larger structure of the prison bureaucracy discussed in the last chapter.

As of January 1, 2001, there were 439,788 employees of adult correctional agencies in the United States, an increase of about 4.2 percent over the beginning of 1999.[24] Of those more than 400,000 employees, 259,934 (about 60 percent) were uniformed staff, an increase of 3.7 percent over 1999. Uniformed staff consists of all correctional security staff, including majors, captains, lieutenants, sergeants, and officers. Of the uniformed staff, 218,382 (84 percent of all uniformed staff and nearly half of all employees) were correctional officers. There were 37,426 new correctional officers hired in 2000 (17 percent of all correctional officers). Nearly 93 percent of both uniformed staff and correctional officers were employed by state agencies. About 77 percent of uniformed staff, including correctional officers, were male (though 35.5 percent of correctional officers hired in 2000 were female), and about 66 percent were white. The average ratio of correctional officers to inmates across the states in 2001 was one officer for every 5.4 inmates, and the average ratio in federal prisons was one correctional officer for every 9.7 inmates.

FYI: Correctional Officer Salaries

Starting salaries for entry-level state correctional officers ranged from a low of $15,324 in Louisiana to a high of $36,850 in New Jersey as of January 1, 2001. They averaged $23,627 (an increase of about 22 percent since 1994). The starting salary for entry-level federal correctional officers was $26,354. Salaries were subject to increases after completion of preservice training and a probationary period.

Source: Camille Graham Camp and George M. Camp, *The Corrections Yearbook 2001: Adult Systems* (Middletown, CT: Criminal Justice Institute, 2002), pp. 168–69.

Correctional officers face a number of conflicts in their work. Criminologists Richard Hawkins and Geoffrey Alpert observe that the job is characterized by both boredom and stimulus overload; officers assigned to the towers may experience the former, whereas officers assigned to work the cell blocks may experience the latter.[25] Much also has been written about the role ambiguity and role strain resulting from conflict between custody and treatment objectives. How does an officer supervise and discipline inmates and at the same time

A correctional officer's custodial role is of primary importance. *Why?*

attempt to counsel and help them? Traditionally, the role of guards was clearer and less ambiguous; they were responsible for custody. With the advent of rehabilitation, guards became correctional officers, and the custodial role grew clouded with treatment considerations. In addition, a series of court decisions has given many officers the perception that they have lost power while inmates have gained it.[26] Officers generally have considerable discretion in discharging their duties within the constraints of rules, regulations, and policies. Yet, because they lack clear and specific guidelines on how to exercise their discretion, they feel vulnerable to second-guessing by their superiors and the courts.

A popular misconception has been that officers manage inmates with an iron fist and are therefore corrupted by the power they have over inmates. However, as Sykes realized, the limits on an officer's power may be the real source of corruption.[27] Although their formal role places them in a superior position over inmates, officers must still obtain a measure of voluntary compliance from inmates. In the modern prison, it is impossible to rely exclusively on force to gain compliance if bureaucratic inefficiency, mass inmate rebellion, and court litigation are to be avoided. Moreover, because of the nature of the

FYI

Inmate Assaults

Although rates of inmate assaults on prison staff have been increasing, the likelihood of an individual staff member's being the victim of an inmate assault, especially a lethal assault, remains fairly low. The assault of staff by inmates is a serious problem and is always a threat in prison, but the risks should not be exaggerated.

FYI: Turnover Rates

In 2000, the average turnover rate for correctional officers in state and federal prisons was 16.1 percent, up 25 percent from 1996. Louisiana had the highest turnover rate (41%), while New York had the lowest (3.8%). The turnover rate for correctional officers in the federal system was 6.1 percent, down about 5 percent from 1998.

SOURCE: Camille Graham Camp and George M. Camp, *The Corrections Yearbook 2001: Adult Systems* (Middletown, CT: Criminal Justice Institute, 2002), pp. 170–71.

prison environment, officers do not have many incentives they can use to solicit compliance, and they do not directly control many of the main rewards, such as release date. Still, officers' performance is often judged by how smoothly the officers interact with inmates and get inmates to go along with their wishes. Consequently, many officers seek inmate compliance through informal negotiation and exchange, and this practice can promote corruption. For example, an officer may gain compliance by becoming friendly with particular inmates, by granting inmates concessions in exchange for their cooperation, and by overlooking certain rule infractions in exchange for compliance with other rules. A study of a federal prison by criminologist John Hewitt and his colleagues found that inmates reported committing, and officers reported observing, far more prison rule infractions than were documented in the institution's official disciplinary files.[28]

How do correctional officers respond to their roles and their work conditions? According to Hawkins and Alpert, some officers become alienated and cynical and withdraw from their work. Withdrawal can be figurative: an officer may minimize his or her commitment to the job and may establish a safe and comfortable niche in the prison, such as prolonged tower duty. Withdrawal can also be literal: turnover and absenteeism are high in many prison systems. Other officers become overly authoritarian and confrontational in a quest to control inmates by intimidation. Those officers put up a tough facade similar to that displayed by some inmates. Still other officers respond by becoming corrupt (for example, selling drugs to inmates in response to a low salary).[29] Finally, a number of officers respond by adopting a human-services orientation toward their work.[30] Those officers seek to make prison a constructive place for themselves and for inmates. They try to deliver goods and services to inmates in a regular and responsive manner, to advocate and make

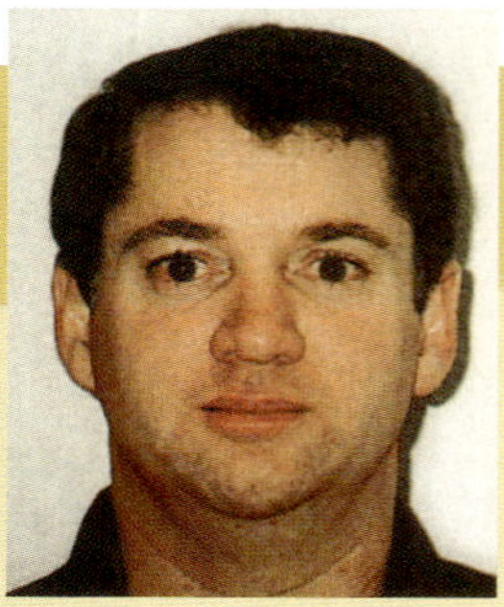

CAREERS IN CRIMINAL JUSTICE

Correctional Sergeant

My name is Pietro DeSantis II and I am a Correctional Sergeant employed by the California Department of Corrections, assigned to the California Correctional Center (CCC) in Susanville, California. I have an Associate of Science Degree from Lassen Community College in Susanville. I began my career as a correctional officer with the department in November of 1986, and was promoted to sergeant in February of 1996. During my tenure with corrections I have also been chapter president and board member of the California Correctional Peace Officer Association and commissioner and curriculum review committee chair of the Correctional Peace Officer Standards and Training (CPOST) Commission.

A normal workday starts as soon as you arrive on grounds and start talking to staff that are either beginning or ending their shift. Normal shifts at CCC are first watch (2200–0600 hours), second watch (0600–1400 hours), and third watch (1400–2200 hours). A normal day on all three watches starts with a security check of our safety equipment and security locks. First watch staff normally read the incoming and outgoing mail, count the inmate population three times, and ensure workers for the culinary service are awakened and report to work. Second watch staff normally feed breakfast and lunch to the inmates and supervise the inmate workers who clean the living quarters inner perimeter yard areas, and the outside grounds. Third watch staff normally deliver the mail, count the inmates twice, feed them dinner, and house new arrivals from the transportation buses. As a sergeant, I could be assigned to supervise an office or unit with between zero and forty correctional officers.

Before entering into a career within corrections, I strongly suggest you do everything possible to become an effective communicator.

Why do you think it is important for a correctional officer to be an effective communicator?

referrals on behalf of inmates when appropriate, and to assist inmates in coping with prison by providing protection and counseling.

Efforts are underway to transform prison work from a mere job into a profession, but a number of problems and issues surround those efforts. First, factors such as low pay, the nature and prestige of the work, and the remote location of many prisons make recruitment of new officers difficult in some jurisdictions. Some people take prison work simply because they believe that nothing better is currently available, with the intent of leaving as soon as a better job opens. Second, the general lack of competition for prison jobs in many jurisdictions makes it difficult to impose restrictive criteria for choosing among applicants. Most states require that applicants be of a certain age (18 or 21) and have completed high school or the GED. Some states have additional requirements, such as no prior felony convictions, related work experience, and the passing of certain tests. Third, in some jurisdictions, a backlash against affirmative action—which has increased female and minority representation among correctional officers—has resulted in tensions between the genders and races[31] and resentment by some white male officers. In jurisdictions where this backlash has occurred, efforts toward professionalization have been hampered. Fourth, once officers have been recruited and hired, they need to be trained, and the move toward professionalization has been accompanied by increased attention to training. Officers are usually trained at the outset of their jobs and then receive annual training thereafter. At present, however, training standards are not uniform across or even within jurisdictions. For example, more than 60 percent of agencies require at least 200 hours of coursework during initial training sessions; Florida, New Hampshire, and Utah require more than 500 hours; and California and Michigan require 640 hours.[32] (See Table 11.1 for the program components of correctional training programs.) Still, when turnover rates are high, training costs are high, and training may start to be viewed as a waste of money and time. Fifth, professionalization has been accompanied by increased unionism among officers. At the end of 2002, only Arkansas, Georgia, Missouri, Nevada, New Mexico, North Carolina, North

FYI: Female Correctional Officers

In 1978, Linda Allen became the first female correctional officer to work at a high-security institution (the U.S. penitentiary at McNeil Island, Washington, now a Washington state correctional facility). Today it is commonplace for female correctional officers to work in federal and state high-security institutions.

SOURCE: Harry E. Allen and Clifford E. Simonsen, *Corrections in America: An Introduction*, 8th ed. (Upper Saddle River, NJ: Prentice Hall, 1998), p. 539.

TABLE 11.1 Percentage of Correctional Training Programs with Particular Program Components

Component	%	Component	%
Administration	78%	Inmate manipulation	100%
Chemical agents	87	Inmate mental health	83
Communicable diseases	93	Inmate programs	85
Communications	98	Race relations	91
CPR	96	Report writing	100
Crisis management	98	Security devices	96
Ethics	98	Self-defense	100
Firearms	87	Spanish	15
Fire/safety	96	Special populations	89
First aid	98	Stress reduction	91
Hostages	93	Substance abuse	89
Inmate classification	98	Suicide prevention	93
Inmate gangs	91	Transportation	89
Inmate health care	78	Use of force	98
Inmate management	89	Workplace violence	63

SOURCE: American Correctional Association, *Corrections Compendium*, (Lanham, MD: American Correctional Association, February 2003), p. 11.

THINKING CRITICALLY

1. What do you think could be done to further professionalize corrections work?
2. What are some ways you can think of to add selectivity to correctional worker recruitment?

Dakota, South Dakota, Tennessee, Texas, Vermont and Wyoming reported that unions were not part of their correctional systems.[33] Although guard unions can help improve pay levels, job benefits, and work conditions, unions can also divide the superior and subordinate ranks. In addition, most guard unions have a very limited ability to engage in collective bargaining because strikes are commonly illegal.

Inmate Rights and Prison Reform

hands-off philosophy A philosophy under which courts are reluctant to hear prisoners' claims regarding their rights while incarcerated.

Over the past four decades, the major means of reforming prisons has been court intervention. Until the middle of the twentieth century, the courts followed a **hands-off philosophy** toward prison matters. Under this hands-off philosophy, court officials were reluctant to hear prisoners' claims regarding their rights while they were incarcerated. Among other considerations, court officials questioned whether they had the necessary expertise in evaluating prison administration, and judges did not want to undermine the power of prison authorities. As a consequence of this inaction, prisoners, for all practical purposes, had no civil rights. (Remember that civil rights are those rights an individual possesses as a member of the state, especially those guaranteed against encroachment by the government.) This situation began to change as progress was made in civil rights in the wider society. Inmates were first granted rights of access to the courts, and the courts subsequently turned their attention to other rights.

ACCESS TO THE COURTS AND LEGAL SERVICES

Ordinarily, prisoners want to get their cases into the federal courts because they perceive those courts as more receptive to their claims than state courts. In its 1941 landmark ruling in *Ex parte Hull,* the U.S. Supreme Court granted inmates the right of unrestricted access to the federal courts. Just 3 years later (in *Coffin* v. *Reichard*, 6th Cir., 1944), a federal circuit court held that prisoners may challenge in federal court not only the fact of their confinement but also the conditions under which they are confined. But the most important U.S. Supreme Court ruling in this area (*Cooper* v. *Pate*) did not occur until 1964, when Thomas Cooper, a Stateville inmate, first successfully used Section 1983 of the Federal Civil Rights Act of 1871 to challenge the conditions of confinement. Prior to the ruling in *Cooper*, inmates had relied primarily on *habeas corpus* petitions to obtain access to the federal courts. ***Habeas corpus*** is a court order requiring that a confined person be brought to court so that his or her claims can be heard. For various technical reasons, it has normally been easier for prisoners to win federal cases under Section 1983 than under *habeas corpus*. In effect, then, the *Cooper* decision launched the prisoners' rights movement by opening the door to a flood of Section 1983 claims from prisoners. Calling *Cooper* v. *Pate* "the Supreme Court's first modern prisoners' rights case," law professor James Jacobs writes:

habeas corpus A court order requiring that a confined person be brought to court so that his or her claims can be heard.

> But for the prisoners' movement it was not the breadth of the decision that mattered but the Supreme Court's determination that prisoners have constitutional rights; prison officials were not free to do with prisoners as they pleased. And the federal courts were permitted, indeed obligated, to provide a forum where prisoners could challenge and confront prison officials. Whatever the outcome of such confrontations, they spelled the end of the authoritarian regime in America penology.[34]

FYI: Petitions Filed by Prison Inmates

In 2001, state and federal prison inmates filed 58,805 petitions in federal district courts seeking release from prison (*habeas corpus;* 51 percent) alleging civil rights violations (27 percent), or complaining of prison conditions (22 percent).

SOURCE: *Sourcebook of Criminal Justice Statistics, 2001* (Online), p. 457, Table 5.63.

To get their cases to court, prisoners need access to legal materials, and many of them need legal assistance from persons skilled in law. The U.S. Supreme Court has recognized those facts. In *Johnson* v. *Avery* (1969), the

Inmates are entitled to adequate law library facilities. *Why do inmates have this right and should they?*

Court held that inmates skilled in legal matters (so-called **jailhouse lawyers**) must be permitted to assist other inmates in preparing cases unless the government provides a reasonable alternative. Furthermore, in *Bounds* v. *Smith* (1977), the U.S. Supreme Court ruled that inmates are entitled to either an adequate law library or adequate legal assistance. So if a correctional institution does not wish to allow a jailhouse-lawyer system and does not wish to provide adequate library facilities for inmates, the implication is that the correctional institution should allow inmates to consult with licensed attorneys to obtain legal assistance.

jailhouse lawyer An inmate skilled in legal matters.

PROCEDURAL DUE PROCESS IN PRISON

In the last chapter, we noted that inmates can face disciplinary action for breaking prison rules. The U.S. Supreme Court has moved to ensure that inmates receive minimal elements of due process during the disciplinary process. Probably the most important case in this area is *Wolff* v. *McDonnell* (1974). In *Wolff,* the Court held that although inmates facing a loss of good time for a rule infraction are not entitled to the same due process protections as in a criminal trial, such inmates are entitled to (1) a disciplinary hearing by an impartial body, (2) 24 hours' written notice of the charges, (3) a written statement of the evidence relied on and the reasons for the disciplinary action, and (4) an opportunity to call witnesses and present documentary evidence, provided that this does not jeopardize institutional security. The Court ruled that inmates are not entitled to confront and cross-examine people who testify against them or to have legal counsel.

FIRST AMENDMENT RIGHTS

The First Amendment to the Constitution guarantees freedom of speech, press, assembly, petition, and religion. The U.S. Supreme Court has rendered numerous decisions affecting prisoners' rights to freedom of speech and expression and freedom of religion.

As a rule, inmates are free to practice their religion in prison. Religious symbols and practices that interfere with institutional security can be restricted. *Should religious practices be allowed in prisons? Why or why not?*

> **FYI — *Brubaker***
>
> In *Holt* v. *Sarver* (1971), the Supreme Court ordered the reform of the Arkansas prison system. The movie *Brubaker,* starring Robert Redford, is a fictionalized account of the real story of Tom Murton, warden of Arkansas's Tucker & Cummins prison in 1967–68. Murton's evidence was instrumental in the Supreme Court's decision. The U.S. District Court characterized the Arkansas prison as "a dark and evil world completely alien to the free world."

example, in the famous case of *Holt* v. *Sarver* (1971), the entire Arkansas prison system was declared unconstitutional on grounds of totality of conditions and was ordered to implement a variety of changes. Totality-of-conditions rulings were later handed down against prisons in Alabama (*Pugh* v. *Locke,* 1976) and Texas (*Ruiz* v. *Estelle,* 1982).

Prisons have long had the right to provide only the minimal conditions necessary for human survival. Such conditions include the necessary food, shelter, clothing, and medical care to sustain life. Whether institutional crowding violates the Eighth Amendment is typically determined in relation to total prison conditions. Instead of being treated as a separate issue, crowding is viewed as part of the totality of conditions. The Supreme Court has been reluctant to side with inmates in their challenges to crowding. In both *Bell* v. *Wolfish* (1979) and *Rhodes* v. *Chapman* (1981), the Court refused to prohibit the placing of two inmates in cells designed for one person ("double-bunking") as a response to crowding. Those rulings are frequently taken to mean that the more conservative Court is drawing the line on inmates' rights and is returning, at least partially, to a hands-off policy.

FOURTEENTH AMENDMENT RIGHTS

As described in Chapter 4, the Fourteenth Amendment guarantees U.S. citizens due process of law and equal protection under law. The due process clause inspired the Supreme Court's decision in the previously discussed case of *Wolff* v. *McDonnell,* for example. Likewise, the equal-protection clause has led the Supreme Court to forbid racial discrimination (*Lee* v. *Washington,* 1968) and has led state courts to target gender discrimination (*Glover* v. *Johnson,* ED Mich., 1979). Compared with the rights of male inmates, however, the rights of female prisoners remain underdeveloped. The inmates' rights movement has been primarily a male phenomenon, and the rights of female prisoners deserve more attention from the courts in the future.

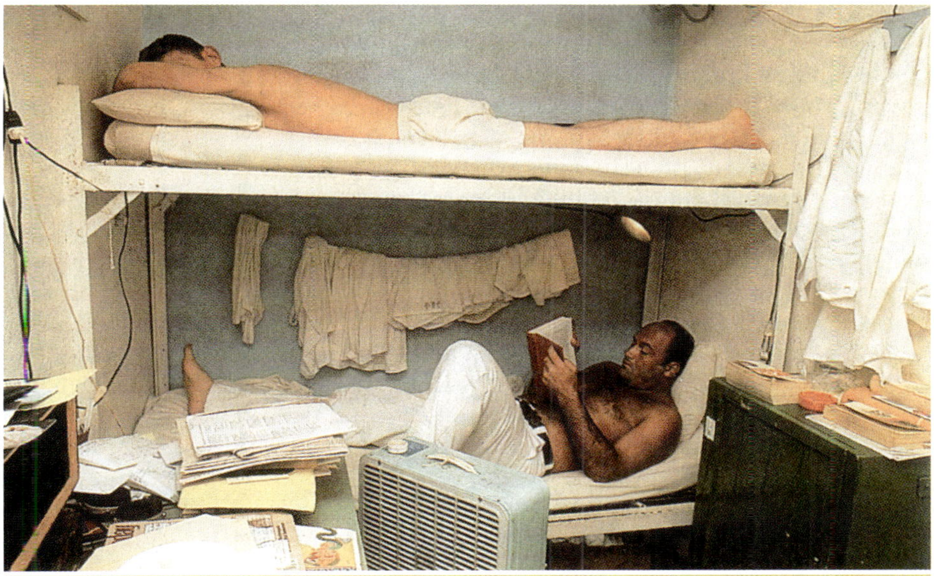

In 1981, the U.S. Supreme Court refused to hold that double-bunking in prison cells was cruel and unusual punishment. *Should double-bunking be allowed in prisons? Why or why not?*

THE LIMITS OF LITIGATION

The progress toward prison reform resulting from the inmates' rights movement should not be underestimated. Nevertheless, one can question on a number of grounds the almost exclusive reliance, during the past four decades, on court intervention to reform the nation's prisons. Perhaps the most basic and compelling argument is that the monies being spent by prison systems to defend against inmate lawsuits and to comply with court orders (when inmate suits are successful) could have been spent better to reform the unacceptable practices that sparked the suits in the first place. Meanwhile, those prison systems are unable to address problems that help generate further inmate lawsuits precisely because they are defending against new suits and trying to comply with past court orders. The result is that even more money must be spent for legal defense and compliance with court orders. This cycle is difficult to break.

Court litigation is not just an expensive way to reform prisons; it is also a very slow and piecemeal way. A high percentage of lawsuits filed by inmates are judged frivolous and are therefore dismissed. If an inmate's suit is not judged frivolous, the inmate must still win the case in court, and many lose in the process. Even when inmates win a case, their success usually does not lead to wide-scale reforms. Successful, large-scale, class-action suits that have far-reaching impact on the prison system are relatively uncommon. Moreover, winning a case and then getting the desired changes implemented can take many years. Prison systems do not comply automatically with court decrees. Achieving compliance with court orders often requires sustained monitoring by court-appointed officials as well as considerable negotiation and compromise by all parties involved to agree on a timetable and the specific nature of reforms. Finally, the transformation of traditional, ingrained practices in a prison system can render the prison environment chaotic and unstable, at least in the short run.

FYI: Sexually Violent Predator Laws

By a 5–4 decision, in *Kansas* v. *Hendricks* (1997), the Supreme Court ruled that sexual predators judged to be dangerous may be confined indefinitely even after they finish serving their sentences. The decision allowed the state of Kansas to continue to hold an admitted pedophile, Leroy Hendricks, under the provisions of the state's Sexually Violent Predator Act. The Court's majority noted that such confinement, intended to protect society, does not violate the constitutional right to due process and is not double punishment for the same crime. At least 16 states, including Arizona, California, Minnesota, Washington, and Wisconsin, have laws similar to the Kansas Sexually Violent Predator Act.

SOURCE: *Kansas* v. *Hendricks,* 117 S.Ct. 2072 (1997); "Court: Sex Predators Can Be Kept in Prison," *The Orlando Sentinel*, June 24, 1997, p. A-1; Thomas L. Hafemeister, "Sexual Predator Laws: Is an Irresistible Impulse Required to Involuntarily Commit Offenders," *Monitor on Psychology* 32, no. 8 (September 2001), at www.apa.org/monitor/sep01/jn.html.

THINKING CRITICALLY

1. What do you think are legitimate complaints from prisoners?
2. What constitutional rights do you think should be extended to prisoners? Or do you think prisoners already have too many rights? Why?

Release and Recidivism

Most inmates (approximately 93 percent) will eventually be released from prison. The 7 percent of inmates who will not be released are serving death or life sentences and likely will die in prison. Figure 11.1 shows the causes of death of the nearly 3,000 inmates who died in prison in 2001.

Depending on the jurisdiction and the specific case, inmates may be released from prison in a number of ways. Examples include expiration of the maximum sentence allowed by law (known as "maxing out"); **commutation,** or reduction of the original sentence by executive authority; release at the discretion of a parole authority; and mandatory release. Of those ways, the two most common are release at the discretion of a parole authority and mandatory release.

commutation Reduction of the original sentence given by executive authority, usually a state's governor.

parole The conditional release of prisoners before they have served their full sentences.

The term **parole** has two basic meanings. It can refer to a way of being released from prison before the entire sentence has been served, or it can refer to a period of community supervision following early release. We are concerned here with the former meaning. In jurisdictions that permit parole release, inmates must establish eligibility for parole. Eligibility normally requires that inmates have served a given portion of their terms minus time served in jail prior to imprisonment and minus good time. **Good time** is time subtracted from the sentence for good behavior and other meritorious activity in prison. Once eligible, an inmate submits a parole plan stipulating such things as where he or she plans to live and work upon release. The parole authority, which may consist of a board, members of the board, or a representative of the board, then considers the inmate's plan. The parole authority also considers reports from institutional staff who have worked with the inmate. The decision to grant or deny parole is announced at a parole-grant hearing. Parole will be discussed more fully in the next chapter.

good time Time subtracted from an inmate's sentence for good behavior and other meritorious activities in prison.

Mandatory release is release under the provisions of law, not at the discretion of a parole board. The inmate is released after serving his or her sentence or a legally required portion of the sentence, minus good-time credits. Mandatory release is similar to parole in that persons let out under either arrangement ordinarily receive a period of community supervision by a parole officer or the equivalent. Their freedom from prison is conditioned on following the rules of their community supervision (for example, obeying curfew, abstaining from drug use, and maintaining gainful employment) and on avoiding criminal activity.

mandatory release A method of prison release under which an inmate is released after serving a legally required portion of his or her sentence, minus good-time credits.

FIGURE 11.1 Causes of Inmate Deaths, 2001 (Total = 2,759)

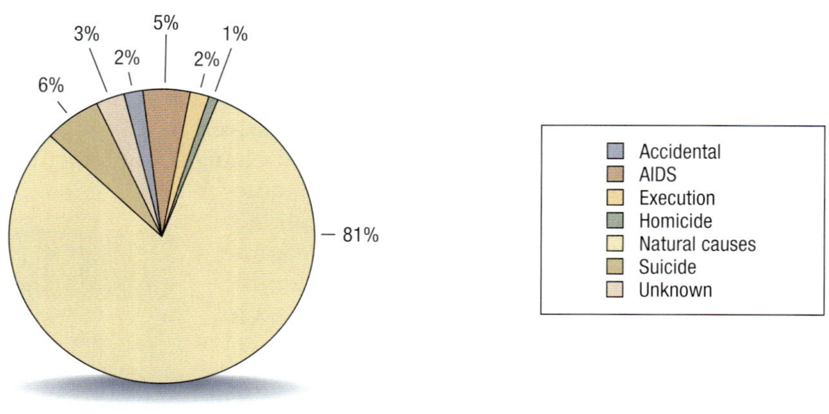

SOURCE: American Correctional Association, *2002 Directory: Juvenile and Adult Correctional Departments, Institutions, Agencies and Paroling Authorities* (Lanham, MD: American Correctional Association, 2002). Reprinted with permission.

Most parole decisions are made by administrative boards whose members are appointed by state governors. An inmate's eligibility for release on parole depends on requirements set by law and on the sentence imposed by the court. *Should parole be abolished? Why or why not? If not, how could the decision-making process be improved?*

In 1977, approximately 72 percent of inmates released from state prisons were released at the discretion of parole boards; only about 6 percent left prison under mandatory release that year. By contrast, in 2001, 36 percent were released by parole boards, compared with approximately 55 percent who received mandatory release.[37] This shifting pattern indicates the strong emphasis placed on determinate sentencing during the 1980s and 1990s and the use of statistical guidelines to structure early-release decisions.

When inmates are released from correctional institutions, the hope is that as a result of deterrence or rehabilitation (discussed in Chapter 9), they will not return to criminal activity. Hence, we will conclude this chapter by considering **recidivism**—the return to illegal activity after release. Measuring recidivism and attributing the lack of recidivism to the influence of correctional programs are complicated by scientific methodological problems. Nevertheless, numerous studies conducted during the past couple of decades in several different jurisdictions reveal that recidivism rates, when recidivism is defined in a similar way, have remained remarkably stable.

recidivism The return to illegal activity after release from incarceration.

At this writing, the most recent national study of recidivism among state prisoners found that 67.5 percent of nearly 300,000 former inmates released from prisons in 1994 were rearrested for a new offense within 3 years of their release.[38] A similar study of inmates released in 1983 showed that 62.5 percent of them were rearrested within 3 years of their release.[39] Inmates in the more recent study were from Arizona, California, Delaware, Florida, Illinois, Maryland, Michigan, Minnesota, New Jersey, New York, North Carolina, Ohio, Oregon, Texas, and Virginia. The average prison sentence was about 5 years. On average, the inmates were released after serving 35 percent of their sentences, or about 20 months.

The study used four measures of recidivism: rearrest, reconviction, resentence to prison, and return to prison with or without a new sentence. In addition to the 67.5 percent of prisoners rearrested for a new offense (almost exclusively a felony or a serious misdemeanor), 46.9 percent were reconvicted

FIGURE 11.2 Recidivism Rates of Prisoners Released in 1994 from Prisons in 15 States, by Time After Release

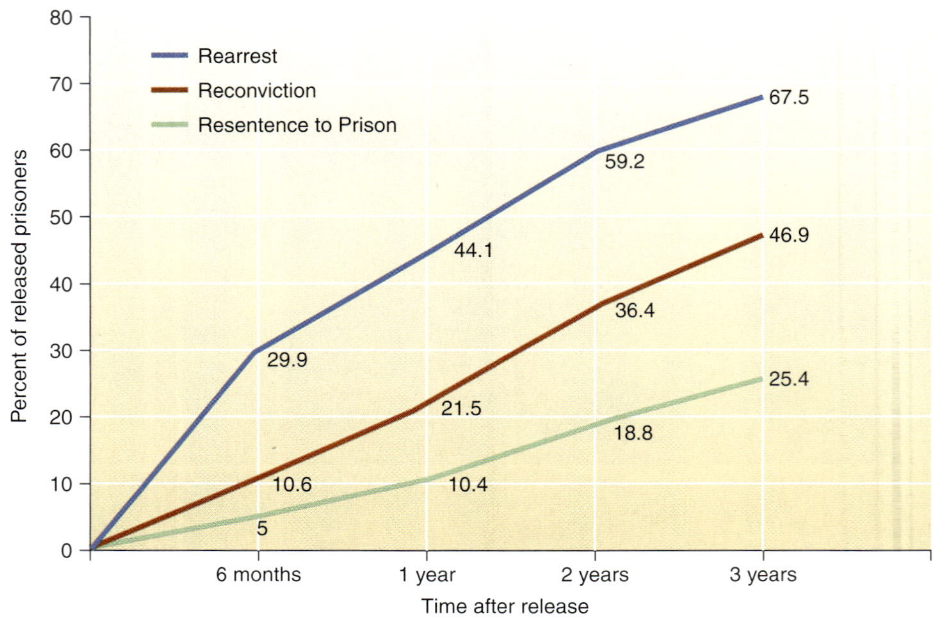

SOURCE: Patrick A. Langan and David J. Levin, "Recidivism of Prisoners Released in 1994," U.S. Department of Justice, *Bureau of Justice Statistics Special Report* (Washington, DC: GPO, June 2002), p. 3.

for a new crime, 25.4 percent were resentenced to prison for a new crime, and 51.8 percent were returned to prison for a new crime (25.4 percent) or for a technical violation of release conditions (26.4 percent), such as failing a drug test or missing an appointment with their parole officer (see Figure 11.2). Not all reconvicted prisoners were sentenced to another prison term for their new offenses. Some were sentenced to confinement in a local jail or probation.

Released prisoners with the highest rearrest rates were motor vehicle thieves (78.8 percent), those in prison for possessing or selling stolen property (77.4 percent), larcenists (74.6 percent), burglars (74 percent), robbers (70.2 percent), and those in prison for possessing, using, or selling illegal weapons (70.2 percent). Released prisoners with the lowest rearrest rates were those in prison for homicide (40.7 percent), nonrape sexual assault (41.4 percent), rape (46 percent), and driving under the influence (51.5 percent). Rearrests of the released prisoners accounted for about 5 percent of all arrests for serious crime from 1994 to 1997. Among other notable findings:

- Men were more likely than women to be rearrested (68.4 percent vs. 57.6 percent), reconvicted (47.6 percent vs. 39.9 percent), resentenced to prison for a new crime (26.2 percent vs. 17.3 percent), and returned to prison with or without a new prison sentence (53 percent vs. 39.4 percent).
- Blacks were more likely than whites to be rearrested (72.9 percent vs. 62.7 percent), reconvicted (51.1 percent vs. 43.3 percent), resentenced to prison for a new crime (28.5 percent vs. 22.6 percent), and returned to prison with or without a new prison sentence (54.2 percent vs. 49.9 percent).
- Non-Hispanics were more likely than Hispanics to be rearrested (71.4 percent vs. 64.6 percent), reconvicted (50.7 percent vs. 43.9 percent), and

FYI: Early Release

Most offenders who receive lengthy prison terms (for example, 25 years) do not serve the entire term, and many do not even come close to doing so. The reason is the availability of parole, good time, and other mechanisms for reducing time served. Some opponents of those reductions in terms fail to understand that the mechanisms are essential to the operation of many current prison systems. Without them, many systems would be rendered dysfunctional by crowding. Additionally, without early release incentives for inmates, it would be extremely difficult to maintain order in prisons.

returned to prison with or without a new prison sentence (57.3 percent vs. 51.9 percent). The difference between non-Hispanics and Hispanics in being resentenced to prison for a new crime was not significant.
- Younger persons were more likely to be rearrested than older persons. For example, more than 80 percent of those under age 18 were rearrested, while only 45.3 percent of those 45 or older were rearrested.

Nearly 70 percent of the inmates released in 1994 had a record of violence. Seventy percent of the released inmates had five or more prior arrests (not counting the arrest that brought them to prison). Half of the inmates had two or more prior convictions (not including the conviction that resulted in their prison sentence). For 56 percent of the released inmates, the prison sentence they were serving when released was their first-ever sentence to prison; the other 44 percent had previously served time in prison.

The nearly 300,000 inmates released in 1994 had amassed 4.1 million arrest charges before their most recent imprisonment and an additional 744,000 charges within 3 years of release. A small percentage of offenders was responsible for a large number of the arrests. An estimated 6.4 percent of the inmates were each charged with 45 or more crimes before and after their release in 1994. About 7.6 percent of all released prisoners were rearrested for a new crime in a state other than the one that released them. They were charged with committing 55,760 such crimes. There was no evidence that spending more time in prison raised the recidivism rate. The evidence was mixed with regard to whether serving more time reduced recidivism. A good predictor of whether an inmate will continue to commit crimes following release is the number of times the inmate has been arrested in the past. Prisoners with longer prior records were more likely to be rearrested than prisoners with shorter prior records. As other recidivism research has shown, the first year of release is the most critical one. Nearly two-thirds of all the recidivism of the first 3 years occurred in the first year (see Figure 11.2).

Obviously, those research findings are not good news for people who believe that imprisonment can achieve large-scale deterrence of crime and rehabilitation of criminals. More bad news for deterrence advocates comes from the research of sociologist Ben Crouch, who found that newly incarcerated offenders frequently express a preference for prison over probation sentences. Crouch explains:

> A fundamental irony emerges in our justice system. That is, the lawbreakers whom middle-class citizens are most likely to fear and want most to be locked away . . . tend to be the very offenders who view prison terms of even two or three years as easier than probation and as preferable. To the extent that these views among offenders are widespread, the contemporary demand for extensive incarceration (but often for limited terms) may foster two unwanted outcomes: less deterrence and more prisoners.[40]

Similar research by criminologist Kenneth Tunnell shows that most repeat property offenders are not threatened by the prospects of imprisonment.[41]

Unfavorable news for advocates of rehabilitation began trickling in even before the release, in 1974, of the famous Martinson report, which cast grave doubts on the ability of prisons to reform offenders.[42] In a later study, criminologist Lynne Goodstein demonstrated that the inmates who adjusted most successfully to prison had the most difficulty adjusting to life in the free community upon release. About her research, Goodstein writes:

> These findings provide a picture of the correctional institution as a place which reinforces the wrong kinds of behaviors if its goal is the successful future adjustment of its inmates. In the process of rewarding acquiescent and compliant behavior, the prison may, in fact, be reinforcing institutional dependence.[43]

FYI

Civil Disabilities of Convicted Felons

Depending on the jurisdiction, convicted felons lose a variety of civil rights. Among the most common rights forfeited are the rights to vote, hold public office, serve on a grand or petit jury, practice a profession that requires an occupational or professional license, be a parent (termination of parental rights), and carry or possess firearms. In many states, women convicted of drug offenses may be denied welfare benefits. If convicted of a federal felony, a person is ineligible for enlistment in any of the armed services, may have public housing benefits restricted under certain circumstances, and, depending on the crime, may lose veteran benefits, including pensions and disability. A majority of jurisdictions provide a means for restoring lost rights. Some rights are restored automatically. Other rights are restored by executive or judicial proceedings that are often based on the ex-offender's demonstration that he or she has been rehabilitated. Some rights are lost permanently.

SOURCE: "Civil Disabilities of Convicted Felons: A State-by-State Survey," U.S. Department of Justice, Office of the Pardon Attorney, October 1996, at www.usdoj.gov/pardon/readingroom.htm; Kevin G. Buckler and Lawrence F. Travis III, "Reanalyzing the Prevalence and Social Context of Collateral Consequence Statutes," *Journal of Criminal Justice* 31 (2003), pp. 435–453.

Of course, some people are deterred from crime by the threat of imprisonment, and the prison experience does benefit some inmates in the way rehabilitation advocates envision. Criminologists Frank Cullen and Paul Gendreau recently completed a comprehensive review of research that evaluated the effects of correctional interventions on recidivism rates.[44] They found that across studies, the correctional interventions reduced recidivism rates, on average, 10 percent. The most successful interventions reduced recidivism 25 percent. They used cognitive-behavioral treatments, targeted known predictors of crime for change, and intervened mainly with high-risk offenders. Cognitive-behavioral treatments emphasize the important role of thinking in how people feel and behave. Therapists help offenders identify the thinking that is causing their problematic feelings and behavior and then teach them how to replace those thoughts with thoughts that will lead to more desirable feelings and actions. Cullen and Gendreau also reported that punishment-oriented, correctional interventions generally had no effect on offender criminality.

We must be careful not to hold unrealistic expectations about what imprisonment can accomplish in our society. Traditionally, we have placed undue confidence in the ability of imprisonment to control crime. But imprisonment is a reactive (versus proactive) response to the social problem of crime, and crime is interwoven with other social problems, such as poverty, inequality, and racism, in our wider society. We should not expect imprisonment to resolve or control those problems.

THINKING CRITICALLY

1. Do you think anything could be done to lower recidivism rates among offenders? If so, what?
2. In your opinion, should prisoners be allowed to reduce their time in prison through parole or good time? Why or why not?

SUMMARY

1. Distinguish between the deprivation and importation models of inmate society

   The deprivation model of inmate society emphasizes the role of the prison environment in shaping the inmate society. The importation model of inmate society emphasizes attributes inmates bring with them when they enter prison.

2. Explain how today's inmate society differs from those of the past

   Compared with prisons of the past, the inmate society in today's prisons is much more fragmented and conflict-ridden. Physical, psychological, economic, and social victimization are facts of life in many contemporary institutions. Inmates must learn to cope with this state of affairs. Some do so by becoming part of the prison's violent public culture. Others carve out niches and meet their needs in the prison's private culture.

3. Identify some of the special features of life in women's prisons

   Life in women's prisons is somewhat different from life in men's prisons. In particular, women's prisons often have less stringent security measures, are less violent, and are characterized by pseudofamily structures that help the inmates cope.

4. Describe the profile of correctional officers and explain some of the issues that they face

   The growing number of correctional officers who staff prisons are predominantly white and male. Correctional officers face a number of problems in their work, including low pay, work-related conflicts, and a potential for corruption. They are also subject to role conflict because of their dual objectives of custody and treatment. Some officers respond to those problems more constructively than others. Efforts are ongoing to transform prison work into a profession, and issues surrounding those efforts include recruitment and selection, the backlash against affirmative action and other hiring practices, training, and unionism.

5. Identify prisoners' rights and relate how they were achieved

   The main way that prisoners have gained rights during the past four decades is through intervention by the courts. Until the 1960s, inmates had minimal rights. As the hands-off policy was lifted, prisoners gained a number of important rights: greater access to the courts, easier access to legal services in prison, and improved prison disciplinary procedures. They also gained certain rights under the First, Eighth, and Fourteenth Amendments.

6. List the two most common ways that inmates are released from prison and compare those two ways in frequency of use

   Most inmates are released from prison at the discretion of a parole authority or under mandatory release laws. Mandatory release, a method of prison release under which an inmate is released after serving a legally required portion of his or her sentence minus good-time credits, has begun to rival parole release in frequency of use.

7. Summarize what recidivism research reveals about the success of the prison in achieving deterrence and rehabilitation

   When inmates are released from prison, it is hoped that they will not return to crime. Studies show, however, that the rate of return to crime, or recidivism, is high. Studies also show that recidivism rates have remained fairly constant for a long time. Those studies call the deterrence and rehabilitation rationales into question. As a society, our expectations of what incarceration can accomplish are probably unrealistic.

KEY TERMS

total institution, p. 397
convict code, p. 397
deprivation model, p. 397
prisonization, p. 397
importation model, p. 397
sub-rosa economy, p. 400
hands-off philosophy, p. 408
***habeas corpus*, p. 408**
jailhouse lawyer, p. 409
commutation, p. 414
parole, p. 414
good time, p. 414
mandatory release, p. 414
recidivism, p. 415

REVIEW QUESTIONS

1. What did Erving Goffman mean when he wrote that prisons are *total institutions*?
2. What is the *convict code*, and why is it central to inmate society in traditional men's prisons?
3. What is *prisonization*?
4. What factors have rendered contemporary inmate society fragmented, disorganized, and unstable?
5. What are some of the reasons for high rates of prison violence?
6. What are four types of victimization that take place in prisons?
7. What are some of the general ways that inmates cope and adjust to the institutional environment, according to Johnson, Irwin, and Heffernan?
8. According to Hawkins and Alpert, what are four ways that correctional officers respond to their roles and their work conditions?
9. In *Wolff* v. *McDonnell* (1974), what rights were given to inmates facing disciplinary actions, and what rights were not extended?
10. How has court intervention limited prison reform?

IN THE FIELD

1. **Rehabilitation Programs** Contact a local prison or jail, and arrange to investigate one or more rehabilitation programs. Obtain pertinent written material, and observe the program in operation as much as possible. Assess how successful the program is in achieving its goals. Consider these specific issues:
   (1) What are the goals of the program?
   (2) Are the goals of the program clearly defined in some document?
   (3) Is the program administered in an effective way?
   (4) Is instruction adequate?
   (5) Is there adequate equipment (if applicable)?
   (6) Will the skills learned in the program be important to inmates upon release?
   (7) How likely are inmates to successfully complete the program?
   (8) Does the program have an evaluation component that would allow officials to determine the program's success or failure?
   (9) On what basis is the program's success or failure judged? After assessing the program, explain what changes, if any, you would recommend.
2. **Prison Films** Watch a video or movie about prison life. Good choices are *Murder in the First* with Kevin Bacon and Christian Slater, *The Shawshank Redemption* with Tim Robbins and Morgan Freeman, *Birdman of Alcatraz* with Burt Lancaster, *Brubaker* with Robert Redford, and *Cool Hand Luke* with Paul Newman. From what you have learned in this chapter, determine how realistic the portrayals are. Note common themes.

ON THE NET

1. **Life in Prison** Visit the website of the North Carolina Department of Corrections at www.doc.state.nc.us/dop/CPtour/index.htm. Access "A Tour of Central Prison." Pretend you are an inmate and write an essay describing your experiences in the prison.
2. **Virtual Prison Tour** Access the Florida Department of Corrections website at www.dc.state.fl.us and take the virtual prison tour through Florida prisons. In either an oral or written presentation describe your impressions of the prison. What surprised you? What, if anything, disturbed you? What changes, if any, should be made? As an option include North Carolina's Central Prison in your description—see On the Net exercise 1.

CRITICAL THINKING EXERCISES

1. **Right to Vote** As of July 2002, 48 states denied incarcerated felons the right to vote (only Maine and Vermont permitted prison inmates to vote); 37 states disenfranchised felony probationers or parolees (or both); and 13 states additionally disenfranchised some or all ex-felons who completed their sentences. Regarding the latter category, Alabama, Florida, Iowa, Kentucky, Mississippi, Nevada, Virginia, and Wyoming denied the right to vote to all ex-offenders who completed their sentences; Arizona and Maryland disenfranchised recidivists; Tennessee disenfranchised ex-felons convicted prior to 1986; Washington disenfranchised ex-felons convicted prior to 1984; and Delaware disenfranchised some ex-offenders for 5 years following their release from prison.

   Each state has developed its own process of restoring voting rights to ex-offenders, but most of those processes are so cumbersome that few ex-offenders are able to take advantage of them. As a result, in the 2000 presidential election, for example, an estimated 4.7 million people (2.3 percent of the voting-age population) were disenfranchised by virtue of having a felony conviction on their record. Of those people disenfranchised, 13 percent are black men. In seven states, 25 percent of the black men are disenfranchised.

   A recent national opinion poll found that 80 percent of the public favors restoring voting rights to ex-felons, generally, while a low of 52 percent even favors restoring voting rights to sex offenders. Sixty percent support enfranchising felony parolees, and 66 percent favor enfranchising ex-felons convicted of a violent crime who have served their entire sentence.

   a. Should incarcerated felons have the right to vote? What about felony probationers or parolees? What about ex-felons who have completed their sentences? What about sex offenders who have completed their sentences? What about felons who were convicted of a violent crime and have completed their sentences? Justify your answers.
   b. If you believe that voting rights should be restored, should there be conditions? If so, what should they be?
   c. Currently, some states restore voting rights automatically; other states do so by executive or judicial action. If you believe that voting rights should be restored, what should the process entail?

2. **Inmate Organ Transplants** On January 3, 2003, a California prison inmate received a donor heart. He had suffered congestive heart failure the month before. The inmate was serving a 14-year sentence for robbery, and the transplant and treatment for his illness may cost California taxpayers as much as $1 million. Critics point out that, among other things, at the time of the surgery, more than 4,000 Americans were on a waiting list for heart transplants, and 700 would die that year waiting for one. At this writing, the prison inmate was recovering nicely.

   a. Should prison inmates be eligible for organ transplants?
   b. Does it matter whether they can pay for them?
   c. What does the law require prison officials to do about organ transplants?
   d. Should the "less eligibility" principle apply to organ transplants? Why or why not?
   e. Should there be limits to the medical services provided to prison inmates and, if so, what should the limits be?

COMMUNITY CORRECTIONS

CHAPTER TWELVE

Chapter Outline

Community Corrections: Definition and Scope
- Goals and Staff Roles
- The Importance of Community Corrections

Probation
- Historical Context
- Administration
- Process and Procedures
- Issues in Probation

Parole
- Historical Context
- Administration
- Process and Procedures
- Parole Issues

Intermediate Sanctions
- Intensive-Supervision Probation and Parole (ISP)
- Day Reporting Centers
- Structured Fines, or Day Fines
- Home Confinement and Electronic Monitoring
- Halfway Houses

Temporary-Release Programs

Chapter Objectives

After completing this chapter, you should be able to:

1. Define community corrections and identify the goals and responsibilities of community corrections agencies and their staffs.
2. Define probation and summarize the research findings on recidivism rates.
3. Distinguish parole from probation.
4. Explain the functions of a parole board.
5. Describe how intermediate sanctions differ from traditional community corrections programs.
6. Explain two major concerns about intensive-supervision probation and parole (ISP).
7. Explain what day reporting centers and structured fines are.
8. Explain what home confinement and electronic monitoring are.
9. Identify the goal of halfway houses and compare them with other community corrections programs.
10. Summarize the purposes and outcomes of temporary-release programs.

Crime Story

In April of 2003, actress Winona Ryder successfully completed a criminal sentence of 480 hours of community service for shoplifting at a Beverly Hills, California, Saks Fifth Avenue store. Ryder was sentenced on December 6, 2002, by California Superior Court Judge Elden Fox, to 3 years probation and ordered to perform community service for stealing merchandise from the upscale department store. Additionally, Ryder was ordered to undergo psychological and drug counseling and to pay more than $10,000 in fines and restitution following her conviction.

The two-time Academy Award nominee reportedly stole more than $5,500 worth of clothing merchandise from the Beverly Hills store. At trial Ryder was represented by esteemed California attorney Mark Geragos, who contended that the actress believed she had an account at the store. Jurors were shown videotapes of then 31-year-old Ryder wandering through the store's designer boutiques and taking a large number of clothing items into dressing rooms. Ryder was accused during the trial of cutting off the sensor tags from the merchandise, while in the dressing rooms, to avoid detection by the store's electronic security scanners.

Ryder's sentencing hearing brought a litany of angry exchanges between attorneys and looks of amazement from Ryder during the disposition process. Before pronouncing the sentence, the judge heard testimony from an attorney representing Saks Fifth Avenue, Ken Metzner, who criticized Ryder for portraying *herself* as the victim. Metzner suggested employees of Saks had been subjected to intense and malicious scrutiny following the shoplifting incident simply because they had the misfortune of apprehending a "movie star thief." Immediately, defense attorney Mark Geragos took issue with Metzner's depiction of his client. Geragos suggested, to the contrary, that Saks had even profited from the publicity surrounding the case and cited recent quarterly reports from Saks to substantiate his claim.

Winona Ryder joins a long list of Hollywood celebrities who have completed community-based correctional treatment. Halle Berry, Kelsey Grammar, rocker Tommy Lee, Rebecca Gayheart, Shannen Doherty, Kiefer Sutherland, and Zsa Zsa Gabor all received probation sentences with a component of community service for a wide variety of crimes including driving under the influence, possession of drugs, assault, and the accidental running over and killing of a 9-year-old boy.

Chapter 12 discusses the definition and scope of community corrections. Community corrections is a diverse regiment of programs. Some critics say that community corrections are soft on crime. Others note that upper-class or high-status criminal offenders seem to be awarded community-based sentences in higher proportion than lower-class offenders. How successful is community corrections in providing a rehabilitative function for criminal offenders? Some criminal offenders actually report they prefer jail-time to probation sentences due to the intense conditional mandates often established by courts and probation officers.

Community Corrections: Definition and Scope

Community corrections can be broadly defined as the subfield of corrections consisting of programs in which offenders are supervised and provided services outside jail or prison. For this reason, community corrections is sometimes referred to as noninstitutional corrections. Community corrections includes such programs as diversion, restitution, probation, parole, halfway houses, and various provisions for temporary release from prison or jail. Those programs are the subject of this chapter.

community corrections The subfield of corrections in which offenders are supervised and provided services outside jail or prison.

It is important to realize that community corrections is a generic term. Federal, state, and local jurisdictions differ widely in the way they organize and administer community corrections and in the specific procedures they use. Criminologist David Duffee's delineation of three varieties of community corrections illustrates this diversity.[1] Community-run correctional programs are controlled by local governments, with minimal connection to state and federal authorities. In effect, local officials determine how such programs will be run within the broad guidelines of state and federal laws. In community-placed programs, as in community-run ones, offenders are handled by agencies within the local district, but agencies in community-placed programs are connected to central state or federal authorities, or both. Consequently, central authority affects program operation, and community-placed programs tend to be more isolated from local affairs than are community-run programs. Community-based correctional programs are a combination of the other two types. Connection to central authority for resources and other support services (a feature of community-placed programs) is combined with strong links between the program and the surrounding locality (a feature of community-run programs).

Myth	Fact
Modern community correctional programs are invariably "soft on crime." They focus too much on rehabilitation, to the exclusion of punishment, deterrence, and incapacitation.	Major prison crowding in the past 15 years or so has made it necessary to channel into the community, under supervision, many felons who formerly would have gone to (or stayed in) prison. The priorities and operations of community agencies have shifted to meet this challenge. Many community programs—especially the newer "intermediate sanctions," such as electronic monitoring—emphasize punishment, deterrence, and incapacitation as much as, if not more than, rehabilitation.

GOALS AND STAFF ROLES

As described in Chapter 9, the goals of sentencing, which also are the goals of corrections, include punishment, deterrence, incapacitation, and rehabilitation. Yet, as a subfield of corrections, community corrections has traditionally emphasized rehabilitation. Although community programs are concerned with supervising and controlling offenders and ensuring that they follow the rules of their sentences, there is frequently great emphasis on assisting offenders with personal problems and needs. Another emphasis is establishing stronger ties between the offender and the community, by helping the offender get and keep a job, for example. However, the traditional preoccupation of community corrections with rehabilitation has given way in recent years to concern with the other goals.

The staff of community correctional programs have two potentially competing roles that reflect different goals. The first amounts to a law enforcement role: seeing that offenders comply with the orders of community sentences. This means that staff must supervise offenders, investigate possible rule infractions, and take action to address any serious or repeated rule violations.

The other role of staff is to help offenders identify and address their problems and needs. This role has three aspects. The first is the direct provision

FYI

Reform vs. Punishment

According to a public opinion poll, 90 percent of Americans support the development of local programs to keep more nonviolent and first-time offenders active and working in the community. Yet, only 8 percent of Americans favor shortening sentences.

SOURCE: Timothy J. Flanagan, "Reform or Punish: Americans' Views of the Correctional System," in T. J. Flanagan and D. R. Longmire (eds.), *Americans View Crime and Justice: A National Public Opinion Survey* (Thousand Oaks, CA: Sage, 1996), p. 87.

One aspect of probation and parole is client counseling. *What kinds of counseling problems are probation or parole officers likely to encounter?*

of services, such as counseling, to offenders. The second is commonly described as the "resource broker" role. In this role, staff identify particular problems and needs and refer offenders to various community agencies for help. An important advantage of community corrections is that correctional agencies can draw on the services of other agencies in the locality. For example, a probation officer may refer a client to a local mental health center for counseling. The third aspect of the helping role is advocacy. A community may not offer services that a significant number of offenders require, for example, opportunities for vocational training. It is the responsibility of staff to advocate greater availability for services that are lacking and to work with community leaders to develop those services.

Many people believe that community correctional staff *should* occupy the dual roles of enforcing the law and helping clients. Those people maintain that supervision and control are necessary to facilitate rehabilitation and that rehabilitation enhances supervision and control. Opponents of that position point to the potential for conflict between roles. They argue that such conflict creates undue stress for staff and makes it difficult to accomplish anything of value.

A recent study of the attitudes of community correctional staff toward their work found that staff attitudes have been shifting away from the helping role and toward the law enforcement role. The findings of this study indicate the declining emphasis on rehabilitation in community corrections and suggest that the potential for role conflict may lessen as well.[2]

FYI — Funding Corrections

Of all adults under some type of correctional supervision in the United States, approximately 30 percent are confined in prisons or jails. Approximately 70 percent are serving community sentences. Approximately 80 percent of all funds allocated to corrections in the United States are spent to build and run institutions, and about 20 percent are spent on community corrections. Thus, 80 percent of the funds are spent on 30 percent of the correctional population, and 20 percent of the funds are left to accommodate 70 percent of that population.

SOURCE: Thomas P. Bonczar and Lauren E. Glaze, "Probation and Parole in the United States, 1998." U.S. Department of Justice, *Bureau of Justice Statistics Bulletin* (Washington, DC: GPO, August 1999), p. 2; Ann L. Pastore and Kathleen Maguire (eds.) *Sourcebook of Criminal Justice Statistics 1999,* U.S. Department of Justice, Bureau of Justice Statistics (Washington, DC: GPO, 2000), p. 11, Table 1.8.

THE IMPORTANCE OF COMMUNITY CORRECTIONS

A discussion of the definition and scope of community corrections would not be complete without stressing how other components of criminal justice depend on community programs. It is not feasible to send all convicted persons—or even all felons—to jail or prison; resources are simply too limited. Were it not for the availability of community programs, the courts and institutional corrections would be overwhelmed by the sheer number of cases.

To illustrate, examine Figure 12.1, which presents data on the number of adults under the supervision of state and federal corrections agencies at the end of 1980, compared with the end of 2002. Note that at the end of 2002, the number of offenders in jail and prison combined is considerably smaller than the number serving community sentences on probation and parole. Approximately 4.75 million adults were on probation or parole at the end of 2002, compared with about 2 million in jail or prison.

CAREERS IN CRIMINAL JUSTICE

U.S. Probation Officer

My name is Steve E. Whisenant and I am an officer with the Federal Corrections and Supervision Division of the U.S. Courts, better known as the U.S. Pretrial and Probation Office. I supervise the Hickory and Statesville, North Carolina, offices, two of the five U.S. Pretrial and Probation Offices that serve the Western District of North Carolina.

My interest in criminal justice was initiated because law enforcement offered a challenging and exciting work environment. At age 20, I began employment with the Burke County, North Carolina, Sheriff's Office. While working as a deputy sheriff, I enrolled in a criminal justice program at Western Piedmont Community College in Morgantown, North Carolina. After receiving a police science associate degree, I transferred to an evening program to earn a Bachelor of Science degree in Social Science/Criminal Justice from Gardner-Webb University in Boiling Springs, North Carolina.

During my service with the sheriff's office as a patrol officer, detective, and captain of law enforcement operations, I met the U.S. probation officer who worked in Burke County. After 9 rewarding years as a sheriff's deputy, the lure of a more stable work schedule and the absence of an election every 4 years made a position with the U.S. Probation Office appealing.

My career as a U.S. probation officer began in 1986. I worked in all three of our major units including (1) pretrial; (2) presentence writing; and (3) supervision. Each of these units offers unique and rewarding challenges. The pretrial unit completes background investigations, prepares written reports, and recommends release conditions for the magistrate's court. This unit also supervises defendants released under various bond conditions including electronic monitoring. Following a defendant's plea or verdict of guilty, the presentence unit conducts investigations and prepares detailed reports with sentencing recommendations for the district court. Its duties include contact with offenders, various law enforcement officers, U.S. attorneys, defense attorneys, and judges. The supervision unit supervises offenders who receive probation or who are released from imprisonment on parole or supervised release. They have contact with a number of persons including local law enforcement agencies, treatment providers, and offenders' employers, families, and acquaintances.

Some challenges faced by probation and pretrial staff include having little control over their workload numbers. Cases are generated by other federal agencies' arrests, releases from prison, and violations generated by the supervised offenders. Additionally, changes in the types of offenders and crimes committed, coupled with society's changing needs and expectations for supervising offenders require a successful organization to be flexible and innovative.

Our district's leadership solicits input from every employee in how to best accomplish the organization's mission. Opportunities to work on various committees and projects abound. Employees are encouraged to promote our organization's national vision statement to exemplify the highest standards in community corrections.

As a supervisor, I support a very competent and highly professional organization. My recommendation for anyone seeking a career within this organization is to excel in fields like criminal justice, psychology, sociology, or human relations.

What do you think are the most important abilities that one must have to be a successful probation officer?

FYI: Increases in the Criminal Justice System

The percentage of adult citizens under control of the criminal justice system increased substantially over the last two decades of the twentieth century. It increased from a little more than 1 percent of the adult population in 1980 to more than 3 percent of all adults in 2000.

SOURCE: Justice department statistician Allen J. Beck, quoted in "Parolees, probationers hit record 4.5 million," *The Orlando Sentinel,* July 24, 2000, p. A10.

FIGURE 12.1 Corrections Populations in the United States

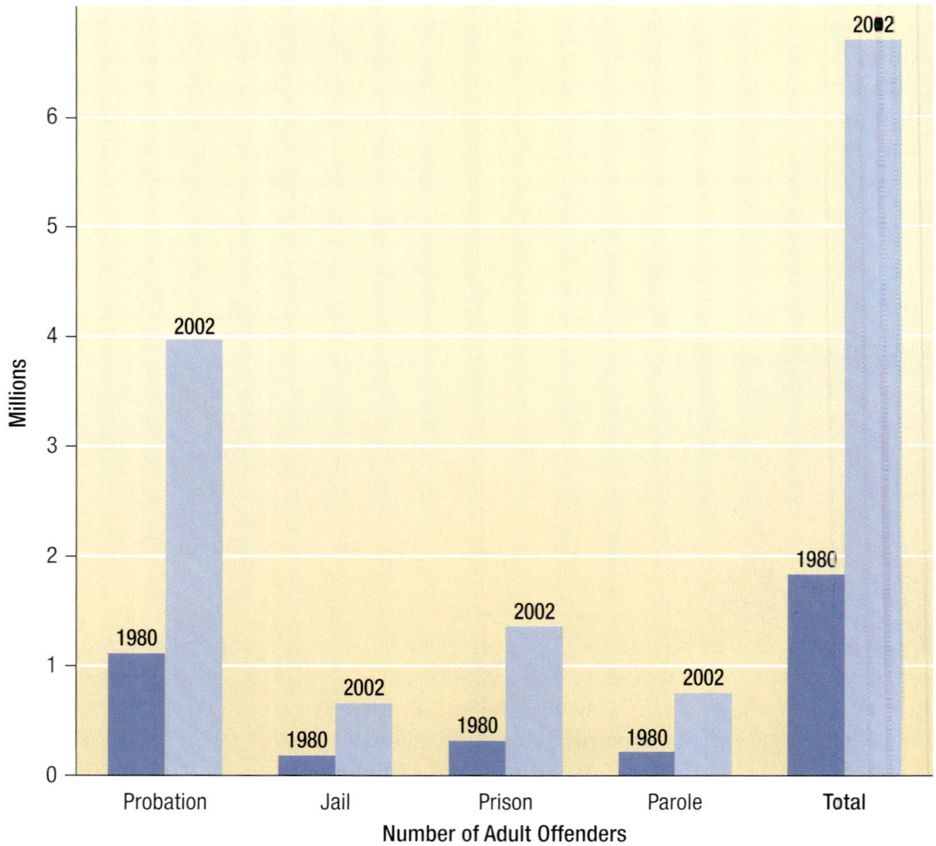

SOURCE: Lauren E. Glaze, "Probation and Parole in the United States, 2002," U.S. Department of Justice, *Bureau of Justice Statistics Bulletin* (Washington, DC: GPO, August 2003), p. 1. Figures for 1980 are from Ann L. Pastore and Kathleen Maguire (eds.) *Sourcebook of Criminal Justice Statistics 1999,* U.S. Department of Justice, Bureau of Justice Statistics (Washington, DC: GPO, 2000), p. 484, Table 6. 1.

THINKING CRITICALLY

Which do you think is more beneficial to society: community corrections or prison? *Why?*

Figure 12.1 also shows that large increases in the prison and jail populations have been accompanied by large increases in the probation and parole populations. Between 1980 and 2003, the probation population increased by 257 percent, and the parole population by 242 percent. The comparable increases in the prison and jail populations were 328 percent and 262 percent, respectively.

Probation

probation A sentence in which the offender, rather than being incarcerated, is retained in the community under the supervision of a probation agency and required to abide by certain rules and conditions to avoid incarceration.

Probation can be defined as a sentence imposed by the courts on offenders who have either pleaded guilty or been found guilty. Instead of being incarcerated, an offender placed on probation is retained in the community under the supervision of a probation agency. The offender is provided with supervision and services. Continuation of probation (that is, avoidance of incarceration) depends on the offender's compliance with the rules and conditions of the probation sentence. Probation is the most frequently imposed criminal sentence in the United States. Table 12.1 shows the states

TABLE 12.1 States with the Largest Probation Populations and the Highest and Lowest Rates of Persons Under Probation Supervision per 100,000 Adult U.S. Residents at Year-End 2002

States with the Largest Probation Populations	Number Supervised	States with the Highest Rates of Supervision, 2002	Persons Supervised per 100,000 Adult U.S. Residents*	States with the Lowest Rates of Supervision, 2002	Persons Supervised per 100,000 Adult U.S. Residents*
Texas	434,493	Washington	3,819	New Hampshire	387
California	358,121	Delaware	3,328	West Virginia	446
Florida	294,281	Idaho	3,263	North Dakota	669
Ohio	211,237	Minnesota	3,237	Utah	671
New York	198,042	Rhode Island	3,168	Virginia	730
Michigan	173,940	Texas	2,758	Kansas	758
Washington	173,198	Ohio	2,469	Nevada	762
Illinois	141,544	Michigan	2,330	Mississippi	794
New Jersey	134,290	Indiana	2,325	Kentucky	804
Pennsylvania	130,786	Florida	2,283	New Mexico	865

Note: This table excludes the District of Columbia, a wholly urban jurisdiction, and Georgia probation courts, which included case-based counts for private agencies.
*Rates are based on the estimated number of adult state residents on December 31, 2002.

SOURCE: Lauren E. Glaze, "Probation and Parole in the United States, 2002," U.S. Department of Justice, *Bureau of Justice Statistics Bulletin* (Washington, DC: GPO, August 2003), p. 2, Table 1.

with the largest probation populations and the highest and lowest rates of persons under probation supervision per 100,000 adult U.S. residents at year-end 2002.

Probation should be distinguished from diversion, although, in broad terms, probation can be thought of as a type of posttrial diversion from

Alcoholics Anonymous and Al-Anon are frequently used as diversion programs for offenders who otherwise would be incarcerated. *Should some offenders be diverted from jail or prison? Why or why not?*

diversion Organized, systematic efforts to remove individuals from further processing in criminal justice by placing them in alternative programs; diversion may be pretrial or posttrial.

incarceration. **Diversion** refers to organized and systematic efforts to remove people from the criminal justice process by placing them in programs that offer alternatives to the next, more restrictive stage of processing. Although diversion is commonly associated with juvenile justice, it is also used in adult criminal justice. Diversion can occur at any point from the initial police contact up to, and even in conjunction with, formal sentencing. For example, the police may divert a domestic violence case by making a referral to a family-in-crisis center instead of making an arrest. Instead of filing charges against an arrestee who is an alcoholic, a prosecutor may divert the case to a detoxification and counseling agency. Those are examples of *pretrial* diversion. *Posttrial* diversion—for example, probation—occurs when an offender who has pleaded guilty or been found guilty is placed in a program that is an alternative to a more restrictive sentence, such as incarceration.

There are five types of probation:

1. *Straight probation* occurs when an offender is sentenced only to probation, with no incarceration or other form of residential placement.
2. In *suspended-sentence probation,* the judge pronounces a jail or prison sentence but suspends the sentence on the condition that the offender performs well on probation.
3. With a *split sentence,* the judge divides a single sentence into a relatively short jail term followed by probation supervision (for example, a 5-year probation sentence with the first 6 months to be served in jail).
4. *Shock probation* usually involves two sentences. The offender is initially sentenced to prison but is soon (perhaps after 120 days) recalled to court and placed on probation.
5. *Residential probation* involves placement of the probationer in a structured, but generally open, living environment, such as a halfway house. When residential probation is used, it is common for the probationer to spend the early part of the sentence in the residential facility and then, upon successful discharge, to complete the probation sentence living in the free community.

At year-end 2002, 60 percent of adults on probation in the United States were sentenced to straight probation, 22 percent were sentenced to suspended-sentence probation, 9 percent were sentenced to split-sentence probation, and the remainder were sentenced to other types of probation.[3]

A probation agency has three fundamental objectives. The first is to assist the court in matters pertaining to sentencing. This is accomplished by conducting inquiries and furnishing the court with information about offenders' backgrounds and current situations. The second objective is to promote community protection by supervising and monitoring the activities of persons sentenced to probation. The third objective is to promote the betterment of offenders by ensuring that they receive appropriate rehabilitation services. Thus, probation agencies work closely with the courts to assist offenders and, when possible, help them avoid incarceration without compromising the safety and security of the community.

FYI John Augustus

John Augustus, the prosperous Boston shoemaker who initiated the concept of probation, received no pay for his 18 years of court work. He used his own money and voluntary contributions from others to finance his efforts.

SOURCE: John Augustus, *A Report of the Labors of John Augustus, For the Last Ten Years, In Aid of the Unfortunate* (Boston: Wright and Hasty, 1852); reprinted as John Augustus, *First Probation Officer* (New York: National Probation Association, 1939).

HISTORICAL CONTEXT

Probation developed out of various practices used under English common law. One such practice, known as benefit of clergy, allowed certain accused individuals to appeal to the court for leniency in sentencing by reading from the Bible. Another practice was judicial reprieve, whereby a convicted offender could ask the judge to suspend the sentence on the condition that the offender display good future behavior. Those and other practices were important forerunners of modern probation.

The more immediate origins of modern probation lie in the efforts of John Augustus (1785–1859), a Boston shoemaker, who is considered the "father" of probation. Starting in the early 1840s, Augustus volunteered to stand bail and assume custody for select, less serious offenders in exchange for the judge's deferring the sentence. Augustus was responsible for monitoring offenders' activities and later reporting to the judge on their performance in the community. If the judge was satisfied with community performance, charges were dropped; if not, sentencing proceeded.

Influenced by the efforts of Augustus, Massachusetts passed the first formal probation law in 1878. By 1920, a majority of the states allowed probation. However, it was not until 1957 that all states had probation statutes. The federal probation system was established in 1925.[4] In more than 160 years, probation has grown from the efforts of a volunteer in Boston into the most frequently used sentence in criminal justice.

ADMINISTRATION

As mentioned earlier in the chapter, probation is administered in many different ways across the nation. The federal government administers its own probation system under the Administrative Office of the Courts, and each state has responsibility for determining how to administer probation. In some states, such as Kentucky, probation is administered at the state level as part of a department of corrections or other state agency. In other states, such as California and Indiana, probation administration is a local function. Still other states combine state and local administration. Under *probation subsidy*, which became popular in the 1960s, states agree to financially support locally administered probation services in exchange for the localities' not sentencing all their offenders to the state prison system. The goal is to give localities a financial incentive to retain offenders in their communities when possible.

There are other variations in the way probation is administered. Depending on the jurisdiction, administrative responsibility may lie with the executive branch, the judicial branch, or both. Adult and juvenile probation services can be administered separately or jointly, as can misdemeanor and felony services. Finally, probation administration can be combined with parole administration, or the two may be separate.

[FYI] Federal Probation Officers

As of June 2002, the Administrative Office of the U.S. Courts employed 4,516 probation officers. They supervise offenders placed on probation and supervised release and conduct presentence investigations to assess the risk to the community of future criminal behavior, the harm caused by the offense, the need for restitution, and the defendant's ability to pay restitution.

SOURCE: Brian A. Reaves and Lynn M. Bauer, "Federal Law Enforcement Officers, 2002," U.S. Department of Justice, *Bureau of Justice Statistics Bulletin* (Washington, DC: GPO, August 2003), p. 3.

PROCESS AND PROCEDURES

A probation sentence can be viewed as a process with an identifiable beginning and end. The process consists of three basic stages:

1. Placement of an offender on probation by a judge.
2. Supervision and service delivery for the probationer by probation officers.
3. Termination of the probation.

Before and during the process, probation agency staff employ a number of important procedures, which will be examined in the following subsections.

PLACEMENT ON PROBATION In deciding whether an offender should be sentenced to probation, a judge usually considers a host of factors, such as statutes outlining eligibility for probation, structured sentencing guidelines (in jurisdictions where they are used), recommendations from the prosecuting and defense attorneys, the offender's freedom or detention in jail before and during trial, the presentence investigation report prepared by the probation agency, and characteristics of the offender and offense. Judges ordinarily give great consideration to the seriousness of the current offense and the prior legal record of the offender. Cases involving more serious offenses or offenders with more extensive prior records are less likely to receive probation.

presentence investigation (PSI) An investigation conducted by a probation agency or other designated authority at the request of a court into the past behavior, family circumstances, and personality of an adult who has been convicted of a crime, to assist the court in determining the most appropriate sentence.

The Presentence Investigation The **presentence investigation (PSI)** is conducted by the probation agency at the request of the judge, usually during the period between the finding or plea of guilt and sentencing. In performing a PSI, a probation officer conducts an inquiry into the offender's past and current social and psychological functioning as well as the offender's prior criminal record. The main task of the inquiry is to estimate the risk the offender presents to the community and to determine the offender's treatment needs. The probation officer obtains the necessary information by interviewing the offender and others who know the offender, such as an employer, family members, and victims. The officer also reviews relevant documents and reports. The information is assembled into a PSI report, which is submitted to the court.

A sample PSI checklist appears in Table 12.2. There are no universally accepted standards for PSI report format and content. However, reports typically contain the following basic elements:

1. A face sheet of identifying demographic data.
2. A discussion of the instant or current offense as perceived by the police, the victim, and the offender.
3. A summary of the offender's prior legal record.
4. An overview of the offender's past and present social and psychological functioning.
5. The probation officer's evaluation of the offender and the officer's recommendation for an appropriate sentence.

FYI

Presentence Investigation Reports

Probation personnel wrote about 460,000 presentence investigation reports during 2000. Personnel in more than 70 percent of the agencies also supervised probationers. In 2000, probation staff in New York wrote the most PSIs (118,446), while staff in Maine wrote the fewest (92).

SOURCE: Camille Graham Camp and George M. Camp, *The 2001 Corrections Yearbook: Adult Systems* (Middletown, CT: Criminal Justice Institute, 2002), p. 221.

As part of a presentence investigation, a probation officer interviews an offender to obtain background information for the court. *What kinds of background information, if any, should influence the length and type of sentence? Why?*

The probation officer must convey the essential information in a concise and objective manner that supports the sentencing recommendation being offered.

Once prepared, the PSI report serves a variety of functions. It is useful in formulating supervision and treatment plans for persons who are given probation sentences. It also serves as the baseline for progress reports on probationers. When an offender is sent to prison, the report helps prison officials learn about and make decisions about the offender. However, the most well-known and immediate function of the PSI report is to assist judges in arriving at a proper sentence.

In most cases, there is a high degree of consistency between the sentencing recommendation in the PSI report and the actual sentence handed down by the judge. As shown in the accompanying Myth/Fact box, however, this does not mean that judges are always strongly influenced by probation officers' sentencing recommendations. In some cases, probation officers recommend sentences that they believe are consistent with judicial expectations.

In addition to questions about the actual effect of PSI reports on sentencing decisions, another issue is whether courts should use PSIs conducted by private individuals and agencies rather than by probation agencies. Private PSIs became popular in the 1960s. Private individuals and agencies may conduct PSIs under contract with the defense or the court. Advocates of privately prepared PSIs argue that privatization reduces probation agency workloads and saves tax dollars (when such PSIs are commissioned by the defendant). Opponents argue that improper sentences may be recommended, that private PSIs can discriminate against the poor, and that the PSIs can reduce the credibility and funding of probation agencies.

The PSI report is usually the property of the court for which it is prepared. Once the report is submitted to the court, a copy is often provided to the defendant, defense counsel, and the prosecuting attorney. Both parties have the opportunity to review the report for accuracy and to bring any concerns to the court's attention. This process is known as "disclosure," and there has been controversy about it. Those who oppose the practice of disclosure maintain that people with important information may not make it available if the offender will see it and know who provided it. Those who support disclosure, on the other hand, argue that it is a matter of fairness that the offender be able to see the information on which the sentence is based, to ensure that it is accurate.

TABLE 12.2 Checklist for Completing a Presentence Investigation Report

Face sheet of identifying demographic information:
- Name, aliases, and address
- Physical description
- Social security number
- Date and place of birth
- School history, occupation, marital status, family members

Instant offense:
- Offense and docket number
- Name(s) of codefendants, if any
- Prosecutor and defense attorney (names and addresses)
- Means of conviction (trial, plea agreement, etc.)
- Sentencing date

Presentence investigation:
- Defendant's version of events relating to offense
- Victim impact, restitution needs
- Jail time served in connection with offense
- Previous record
- Social history (family, friends, self-image)
- Educational history
- Marital history
- Employment history
- Economic situation
- Religious association
- Outside interests
- Health (including drug and alcohol use)
- Present attitudes of defendant
- Plea agreement (if any)
- Fiscal impact of sentencing option(s) to victim and state
- Psychiatric insights
- Statement of probation officer

Sentencing recommendation:

Probation plan:
- Length of probationary period
- Probationer reporting requirements
- Job placement
- Postemployment education training needs
- Community service requirements
- Other probation requirements

The Probation Order When an offender is sentenced to probation, the court files the appropriate documents indicating the length and conditions of the probation sentence (see Figure 12.2).

Although the length of probation sentences varies between jurisdictions and between cases, it is common for adults placed on probation for misdemeanor offenses to receive 1- to 2-year terms. Those convicted of felonies and sentenced to probation generally receive longer terms (for example, 5 years).

FIGURE 12.2 Sample Probation Order

State of New Jersey STANDARD CONDITIONS of ADULT PROBATION	PROBATIONER:
	CASE FILE # /DOCKET #
	COUNTY

The Court, believing that you are capable of living a useful and law-abiding life in the community, has sentenced you to probation for a period of ______________________________ , beginning ______ ______________________ . While on probation, you will be under the supervision of a probation officer. You are required to comply with the conditions of probation listed below.

If there is probable cause to believ
probation, the Court may commit you t
probation, it may impose on you any se
nally convicted, up to and including the

1. You shall obey all federal, state, and
officer if you are arrested or issued a
2. You shall report to your probation of
3. You shall answer truthfully all inquir
4. You shall permit your officer to visit
5. You shall submit at any time to a sea
person, place of residence, vehicle, o
6. You shall promptly report any chang
obtain permission from your probati
may not leave the state of New Jersey
tion officer.
7. You shall cooperate in any medical a
probation officer recommends.
8. You shall submit to drug or alcohol t
9. You shall support your dependents a
10. You shall seek and maintain gainful
your place of employment or find yo
11. You shall not have in your possessior
2C: 39 et seq. If you possess a firearr
bation officer. In addition, if you pre
your local police department or to a
officer.

12. You shall make payments on any fine, penalty assessment, restitution or other financial obligation as provided by Court order. Failure to comply may result in further Court action, pursuant to *N.J.S.A.* 2C:46-2b; including attachment of your wages, filing of a civil judgment, and/or extension of your probation term.

VCCB	$ ________	DEDR	$ ________	Fine	$ ________
FLF	$ ________	Restitution	$ ________	Other	$ ________

Total Amount Ordered $____________. This will be paid at the rate of $____________ per ____________ . If no payment schedule is established, the total is due forthwith. If the offense occurred on or after February 1, 1993, a transaction fee of up to $1.00 is to be paid on each occasion when a payment or installment payment is made (*N.J.S.A.* 2C:46-1d.).

Special Conditions

You must also comply with the following special conditions of probation imposed by the Court in accordance with *N.J.S.A.* 2C: 45-1 et seq.:

- ☐ ___ Hours of Community Service
- ☐ ___ Days in the County Jail
- ☐ Driver's License Suspended for ________
- ☐ Obtain a General Equivalency Diploma (GED)
- ☐ Complete Court Ordered Treatment Program

____
Specify Program

- ☐ ______________________
- ☐ ______________________
- ☐ ______________________
- ☐ ______________________
- ☐ ______________________

I have received a copy of the rules and conditions of probation which have been read and explained to me. I understand the above rules and conditions of probation and that they apply to me, and I further understand that failure to comply on my part constitutes a violation of probation and will cause my return to Court. If I am arrested or detained in any other state or jurisdiction within the United States while I am on this term of probation, my signature below shall be deemed to be a waiver of extradition.

PROBATIONER DATE	ADDRESS: ______________________
PROBATION OFFICER DATE	Telephone: ______________________ DOB: ____/____/____ SS#: ____________ Driver's License #: ______________

Some states allow sentences of lifetime probation. In some cases, the court has the authority to grant early discharge from probation for commendable performance or to extend the term of probation.

Probation conditions are rules that specify what an offender is and is not to do during the course of a probation sentence. They are of crucial significance because the success or failure of the probationer is evaluated with respect to those rules. There are two types of conditions. *Standard* or *general conditions* apply to all persons placed on probation and pertain primarily to control and supervision of the offender. *Special conditions* are imposed at the discretion of the judge and probation officials and are designed to address the offender's particular situation. Special conditions frequently deal with treatment matters. For example, an offender may be ordered to participate in drug abuse counseling. Special conditions can be creative. For example, in Massachusetts, Connecticut, Texas, and a few other states, a special condition of probation for some offenders is participation in a reading program called "Changing Lives Through Literature." Eligible offenders agree to attend a class on a college campus each week for 10 or 12 weeks. They read and discuss such books as *The Old Man and the Sea*, *Deliverance*, *The Sea Wolf*, *Of Mice and Men*, and *One Flew Over the Cuckoo's Nest*. If they complete the program, their probation is reduced, usually by 3 months. An evaluation of the first four classes in Massachusetts found that only 18 percent of the men who completed the class committed crimes again, compared with 43 percent in a comparable group of offenders.[5]

Myth

An essential function of the PSI report is to individualize justice by helping judges structure their sentencing decisions around the offender's unique circumstances.

Fact

In an important study, criminologist John Rosecrance found that experienced probation officers try to recommend sentences that are consistent with judicial expectations, given the seriousness of the offense and the offender's prior criminal record. Rosecrance found that officers selectively structure information in the report to support the recommendations they have already decided on. Information that is inconsistent with those recommendations is minimized in the report. Rosecrance's research implies that the PSI report merely gives the sentencing process a guise of individualized justice.

SOURCE: John Rosecrance, "Maintaining the Myth of Individualized Justice: Probation Presentence Reports," *Justice Quarterly* 5 (1988), pp. 235–56.

In recent years it has become increasingly common for jurisdictions to include restitution orders as part of probation, as either a standard condition or a special condition. (See standard condition 12 in Figure 12.2.) **Restitution,** you may recall, usually means that the offender provides either the victim or the community with money or work service.

probation conditions Rules that specify what an offender is and is not to do during the course of a probation sentence.

restitution Money paid or services provided to victims, their survivors, or the community by a convicted offender to make up for the injury inflicted.

In some areas, the court may later amend or modify conditions outlined in the initial probation order. The conditions can be made more or less restrictive, depending on the probationer's behavior. However, to be legal, it is necessary for all conditions, regardless of when they are imposed, to be clear, reasonable, permitted by the Constitution, and related to the rehabilitation of the offender or the protection of society, or both.[6]

SUPERVISION AND SERVICE DELIVERY Once offenders have been placed on probation, the probation agency must shift attention to supervision and service delivery. At this point, probationers must be assigned to probation officers. In making assignments, it is important to match officer and probationer characteristics. For example, a manipulative probationer who poses a risk to community security might be assigned to an officer with a law enforcement orientation. An offender who poses little risk but has pressing treatment needs might be assigned to an officer with more of a helping background.

Because not all persons placed on probation require the same amounts and types of supervision and services, an important task is to determine what is appropriate for each client. In recent years, this task has been facilitated by the development of risk-and-needs-assessment instruments such as the one shown in Figure 12.3. The probation agency can more objectively determine the amount and type of supervision a probationer requires by examining the risk score. For instance, a probationer with a risk score in the maximum range might receive weekly contacts from the probation officer, whereas a probationer with a minimum-range risk score might receive monthly contacts. Likewise, the amount and kind of services are directed by the needs score. The point is to ensure that the highest levels of supervision are reserved for probationers who present the greatest risk to the community and that the highest levels of treatment services are reserved for those who present the greatest needs.

Once risk-and-needs assessment has been completed, the probation agency can formulate supervision and treatment plans for its clients. In effect, those plans further specify the conditions of probation and describe what is expected of probationers. Some of the requirements might include weekly contacts with the probation officer, random drug tests, weekly Alcoholics Anonymous meetings, or obtainment of a GED. Once supervision and treatment plans are set, the monitoring of probationers and the periodic filing of progress reports for the court can begin.

Termination of Probation Ultimately, the probation agency must make recommendations to the court about how probation is to be terminated. Clients who have generally fulfilled the conditions of their sentences and have served their terms are recommended for successful discharges. If a client has violated the conditions of probation, the probation agency may recommend **revocation,** which entails repealing the probation sentence and substituting a more restrictive sentence, such as a jail or prison term.

revocation The repeal of a probation sentence or parole, and substitution of a more restrictive sentence, because of violation of probation or parole conditions.

technical violations Failure to abide by the technical rules or conditions of probation or parole (for example, not reporting regularly to the probation officer), as distinct from commission of a new criminal act.

Revocation can be recommended for two general categories of violations. One category involves commission of new offenses. The second category, known as **technical violations,** involves failure to abide by the technical rules of the sentence. For example, a probationer might fail to report regularly to the probation officer or might leave the jurisdiction without the officer's consent. A recommendation of revocation is not automatic in the event of a violation, even if the violation is a new crime. Probation agents have considerable discretion on this matter. If the violation is a serious crime, a recommendation of revocation is very likely. On the other hand, a less serious offense or a technical violation may result in a warning, a tightening of probation conditions (perhaps the addition of a nightly curfew), or a brief jail term. Many probation agencies tend to let technical violations and petty offenses accumulate, with warnings and condition modifications along the way. However, repeated and excessive violations of this nature usually result in revocation recommendations.

If the probation agency asks the court to consider revocation of probation, the court must work within the guidelines of case law established by the U.S. Supreme Court. Two landmark cases are *Morrissey* v. *Brewer* and *Gagnon* v. *Scarpelli*. The Court's 1972 ruling in *Morrissey* v. *Brewer* dealt with parole revocation, but by virtue of the 1973 ruling in *Gagnon* v. *Scarpelli*, it also applies to probation revocation. *Morrissey* established that revocation is to be a two-stage process. In the first stage, there must be an informal, preliminary inquiry to establish probable cause that a violation has occurred. If probable cause is established, then in the second stage, there must be a formal court hearing to determine whether the violation warrants revocation. Offenders have certain rights at both stages. They include the right to notice of the hearing and charges, the right to be present at the hearing and to present evidence and witnesses, and the right to a detached and neutral hearing body.

FYI

Revocation

If probation is revoked, the judge can impose any sentence, including incarceration that was authorized for the offense for which the offender was originally placed on probation. Furthermore, the time already spent on probation, even though it may be several years, does not count as credit against the new sentence.

Source: www.defgen.state.vt.us/lawbook/ch38.html.

FIGURE 12.3 Sample Risk and Needs Assessment Instrument

DEPARTMENT OF CORRECTIONS
DIVISION OF PROBATION & PAROLE

Client No. ______ Client Name: ______ Officer No. ______

CLIENT RISK ASSESSMENT

Instructions: Enter numerical rating in box at right.

1. TOTAL NUMBER OF PRIOR FELONY CONVICTIONS: (include juvenile adjudications, if known)
   a. None . . . . Enter 0
   b. One . . . . Enter 2 ☐
   c. Two or more . . . . Enter 4
2. PRIOR NUMBER OF PROBATION/PAROLE SUPERVISION PERIODS: (include juvenile, if known)
   a. None . . . . Enter 0 ☐
   b. One or more . . . . Enter 4
3. PRIOR PROBATION/PAROLE REVOCATIONS: (adult only)
   a. None . . . . Enter 0 ☐
   b. One or more . . . . Enter 4
4. AGE AT FIRST KNOWN CONVICTION OR ADJUDICATION: (include juvenile, if known)
   a. 24 years or older . . . . Enter 0
   b. 20 through 23 years . . . . Enter 2 ☐
   c. 19 years or younger . . . . Enter 4
5. HISTORY OF ALCOHOL ABUSE:
   a. No history of abuse . . . . Enter 0
   b. Occasional or prior abuse . . . . Enter 2 ☐
   c. Frequent current abuse . . . . Enter 4
6. HISTORY OF OTHER SUBSTANCE ABUSE: (prior to incarceration for parolees)
   a. No history of abuse . . . . Enter 0
   b. Occasional or prior abuse . . . . Enter 1 ☐
   c. Frequent current abuse . . . . Enter 2
7. AMOUNT OF TIME EMPLOYED IN LAST 12 MONTHS: (prior to incarceration for parolees, based on 35 hr. week)
   a. 7 months or more . . . . Enter 0
   b. 4 months through 6 months . . . . Enter 1
   c. Less than 4 months . . . . Enter 2 ☐
   d. Not applicable . . . . Enter 0
8. AGENT IMPRESSION OF OFFENDER'S ATTITUDE:
   a. Motivated to change, receptive to assistance . . . . Enter 0
   b. Dependent or unwilling to accept responsibility . . . . Enter 3 ☐
   c. Rationalizes behavior, negative, not motivated to change . . . . . Enter 5
9. RECORD OF CONVICTION FOR SELECTED OFFENSES: (include current offense, add categories and enter total)
   a. None of the following . . . . Enter 0
   b. Burglary, Theft, Auto Theft, Robbery . . . . Add 2 ☐
   c. Forgery, Deceptive Practices (Fraud, Bad Check, Drugs) . . . . . . Add 3
10. ASSAULTIVE OFFENSES:
    a. Crimes against persons which include use of weapon, physical force, threat of force, all sex crimes, and vehicular homicide
    ☐ Yes ☐ No

Total Score ☐☐
(Range 0-34)

CLIENT NEED ASSESSMENT

Instructions: Enter numerical rating in box at right.

1. ACADEMIC/VOCATIONAL SKILLS:
   a. High school or above skill level . . . . Enter 0
   b. Has vocational training, additional not needed/desired . . . . . . Enter 1
   c. Has some skills; additional needed/desired . . . . Enter 3 ☐
   d. No skills, training needed . . . . Enter 5
2. EMPLOYMENT:
   a. Satisfactory employment for 1 year or longer . . . . Enter 0
   b. Employed, no difficulties reported, or homemaker, student, retired, or disabled and unable to work . . . . Enter 1
   c. Part-time, seasonal, unstable employment or needs additional employment unemployed, but has a skill . . . . Enter 4 ☐
   d. Unemployed & virtually unemployable; needs training . . . . Enter 7
3. FINANCIAL STATUS:
   a. Longstanding pattern of self-sufficiency . . . . Enter 0
   b. No current difficulties . . . . Enter 1
   c. Situational or minor difficulties . . . . Enter 4 ☐
   d. Severe difficulties . . . . Enter 6
4. LIVING ARRANGEMENTS (Within last six months):
   a. Stable and supportive relationships with family or others in living group . . . . Enter 0
   b. Client lives alone or independently within another household . . Enter 1
   c. Client experiencing occasional, moderate interpersonal problems within living group . . . . Enter 4
   d. Client experiencing frequent and serious interpersonal problems within living group . . . . Enter 6 ☐
5. EMOTIONAL STABILITY:
   a. No symptoms of instability . . . . Enter 1
   b. Symptoms limit, but do not prohibit adequate functioning . . . Enter 5 ☐
   c. Symptoms prohibit adequate functioning . . . . Enter 8
6. ALCOHOL USAGE (Current):
   a. No interference with functioning . . . . Enter 1
   b. Occasional abuse, some disruption of functioning, may need treatment . . . . Enter 4 ☐
   c. Frequent abuse, serious disruption, needs treatment . . . . Enter 7
7. OTHER SUBSTANCE USAGE (Current):
   a. No interference with functioning . . . . Enter 1
   b. Occasional substance abuse, some disruption of functioning, may need treatment . . . . Enter 4 ☐
   c. Frequent substance abuse, serious disruption, needs treatment . Enter 6
8. REASONING/INTELLECTUAL ABILITY:
   a. Able to function independently . . . . Enter 1
   b. Some need for assistance, potential for adequate adjustment . . . Enter 4 ☐
   c. Deficiencies suggest limited ability to function independently . . Enter 7
9. HEALTH:
   a. Sound physical health, seldom ill . . . . Enter 1
   b. Handicap or illness interferes with functioning on a recurring basis . . . . Enter 2
   c. Serious handicap or chronic illness, needs frequent medical care . . . . Enter 3 ☐
10. AGENT'S IMPRESSION OF CLIENT'S NEEDS:
    a. None . . . . Enter 0
    b. Low . . . . Enter 1
    c. Moderate . . . . Enter 4 ☐
    d. High . . . . Enter 6

Total Score ☐☐
(Range 5-61)

SCORING AND OVERRIDE

Instruction: Check appropriate block

SCORE BASED SUPERVISION LEVEL ☐ Maximum ☐ Medium ☐ Minimum

Check if there is an override ☐ Override Explanation ______

FINAL CATEGORY OF SUPERVISION ☐ Maximum ☐ Medium ☐ Minimum

Date Supervision Level Assigned
MONTH DAY YEAR
☐☐☐☐☐☐

APPROVED (Supervisor Signature and Date) Agent

SOURCE: Anthony Walsh, *Understanding, Assessing, and Counseling the Criminal Justice Client* (Pacific Grove, CA: Brooks/Cole, 1988), p. 110. Reprinted with permission of Anthony Walsh.

Committing a new crime or violating the conditions of probation may lead to revocation of probation. *How serious should a new crime or violation of probation conditions be before probation is revoked?*

The *Gagnon* decision extended the requirements of *Morrissey* to include probationers and also addressed the issue of right to counsel, which the *Morrissey* decision did not address. In *Gagnon*, the Court ruled that there is no absolute right to counsel at revocation proceedings. Whether the offender is provided with counsel is determined on a case-by-case basis, and if there is no compelling reason for providing counsel, counsel is unnecessary. However, the Court added that in probation revocation hearings, counsel should be provided when probationers present a timely claim that (1) they did not commit the violation, or (2) there are mitigating circumstances making revocation inappropriate. In other situations, attorneys are allowed at revocation hearings as long as defendants provide their own at no cost to the state.

ISSUES IN PROBATION

Probation is an evolving, changing field with many controversial issues. Several such issues have already been considered in this chapter. We now turn our attention to some additional issues.

Probation Fees Increases in the probation population have been accompanied by increases in the financial costs of probation. Consequently, a trend has emerged toward having probationers pay fees (for example, $30 per month) to help offset the cost of their supervision and treatment. Probation fees—or supervision fees, as they are sometimes called—are distinct from fines, court costs, and restitution.

Advocates of probation fees argue that fees can help contain the increasingly high costs of probation. Advocates further contend that because the majority of probationers can afford reasonable monthly fees, it is only fair that those probationers be held responsible for supporting at least part of the services they receive. On the other hand, critics charge that fees are unfair for indigent offenders and that offenders should not have to pay for services they are mandated to receive. Critics also claim that the administrative costs associated with collecting fees can exceed the amount of money collected. Given the skyrocketing number of persons on probation and the high cost of supervision and treatment, it seems unlikely that the trend toward probation fees will decrease in the near future.

FYI Probation Fees

In 1929, Michigan became the first jurisdiction in the United States to impose probation supervision fees.

Source: www.appa-net.org.

Legal Issues: Confidentiality and Privacy Counseling is often an aspect of probation. It can be argued that to protect the counseling relationship, the information a probationer shares with a counselor should not be divulged to outside parties. However, it can also be argued that the counselor, who could be the offender's probation officer or a counselor to whom the probation officer has referred the offender, has a duty to divulge information about certain activities, particularly new crimes and technical violations, to appropriate authorities, such as police officers and judges. To what degree, then, should confidentiality govern the relationship between probation officer and probationer? In *Minnesota* v. *Murphy* (1984), the U.S. Supreme Court held that this relationship is not governed by the same degree of confidentiality as that between attorney and client or between physician and patient. Counselors taking probationer referrals can reveal information about a probationer's illegal activities to the probation officer, and the probation officer can notify the police.

Another issue is the conditions under which a probation officer may search a probationer's home for evidence. In its decision in *Griffin v. Wisconsin* (1987), the Supreme Court held that a search warrant based on probable cause is unnecessary for a probation officer to search a probationer's home; reasonable grounds is a sufficient basis for the search. This decision and the *Murphy* decision show that probationers are generally entitled to fewer due process protections than free citizens who are not on probation. Whether this is just and fair is open to debate.

CASELOAD AND RECIDIVISM With the probation population growing each year, it is not unusual for probation officers in larger urban jurisdictions to have as many as 200 offenders in their caseloads. Large caseloads, in turn, have been criticized for contributing to **recidivism** (the return of probationers to crime during or after probation). Clearly, it is difficult for probation officers with large caseloads to give each case individual attention and to provide proper supervision and services for all their clients.

recidivism The return of probationers to crime during or after probation.

Interestingly, however, research has generally failed to confirm that smaller caseloads, such as 25 cases per officer, are associated with decreased recidivism. In the words of criminologist Jay S. Albanese and his colleagues, "It appears from many studies that the simple expedient of reducing caseloads will not of itself assure a reduction of recidivism."[7] In fact, it is reasonable to suppose that caseload reduction may sometimes be associated with an *increase* in recidivism detected by probation officers, because officers with smaller caseloads are able to scrutinize each probationer's activities more closely. There is some support for this supposition.[8] However, to the extent that (1) large caseloads promote recidivism because of the inability of probation officers to provide sufficient supervision and services and (2) smaller caseloads inflate recidivism numbers because of greater scrutiny of probationers' activities, probation agencies are in a no-win situation with respect to the issue of optimal caseload.

How effective is probation in controlling recidivism? First, it should be noted that researchers attempting to address this question confront a variety of difficulties. One difficulty is deciding whether to define probationer recidivism in terms of technical violations, arrests for new crimes, new convictions, or revocations. The definition employed affects the amount of recidivism uncovered. Another important difficulty lies in accurately determining whether it is the probation experience or some additional factor that is responsible for the recidivism observed among a group of probationers. A simple finding that recidivism is low among a group of probationers does not necessarily mean that probation is containing recidivism. Other factors, such as improvements in the local economy or the selection of low-risk offenders for probation, may be responsible. To date, many studies of probation effectiveness have not been designed well enough to rule out the role of factors other than the probation experience. Difficulties like these must be kept in mind when reviewing studies on probation recidivism.

Research suggests that probation is less effective than many people would like in curtailing rearrests of felony offenders. In a well-known California study by criminologist Joan Petersilia and her colleagues, approximately 1,700 felony offenders placed on probation were tracked for a period of 40 months. During this period, about two-thirds of the probationers were rearrested, more than half were reconvicted, and about one-third were sent to jail or prison.[9] In a similar but larger-scale study by the U.S. Justice Department, 79,000 felons sentenced to probation in 1986 by state courts in 17 states were followed for 3 years. By 1989, 43 percent of those felons had been arrested for

FYI

Probation Failures

During 2002, 14 percent of probationers who were discharged from supervision were incarcerated because of a rule violation or new offense. Another 3 percent of those discharged had absconded, and 13 percent were unsuccessful for other reasons.

SOURCE: Lauren E. Glaze, "Probation and Parole in the United States, 2002," U.S. Department of Justice, *Bureau of Justice Statistics Bulletin* (Washington, DC: GPO, August 2003), p. 4, Table 4.

new felonies: 8.5 percent were rearrested for violent offenses, 14.8 percent for property crimes, 14.1 percent for drug offenses, and the remainder for other crimes.[10]

In general, the recidivism figures associated with probation do not seem substantially higher or lower than those associated with incarceration. (See Chapter 11 for data on recidivism following incarceration.) Accordingly, it can be argued that when feasible, probation should be the preferred sentence because probation costs less than imprisonment. Of course, this logic holds true only if probation does not culminate in revocation followed by incarceration. If revocation and subsequent incarceration do occur, the combined costs of probation followed by incarceration may well exceed the cost of incarceration alone.

THINKING CRITICALLY

1. What do you think makes an offender an ideal candidate for probation?
2. What are the benefits and drawbacks of probation vs. traditional jail time?

Parole

parole A method of prison release whereby inmates are released at the discretion of a board or other authority before having completed their entire sentences; can also refer to the community supervision received upon release.

Recall that probation refers to the court-imposed sentence in which the offender, rather than being imprisoned, stays in the local community under the supervision of a probation officer. Two basic differences between probation and **parole** are that (1) parole is not a court-imposed sentence, and (2) parole is used with persons leaving prison. For purposes of definition, parole can be divided into two components. *Parole release* is one mechanism for releasing persons from prison. It involves releasing the inmate from prison, at the discretion of a parole board or similar paroling authority, before his or her sentence expires. *Parole supervision,* the aspect of parole that is often confused with probation, occurs after parole release. Essentially, parole supervision is a community-based continuation of the prison sentence. It involves supervision of the released offender in the community, often for a period roughly equal to the time remaining in the prison sentence.

Probation and parole supervision have similar features, which is why the two are sometimes confused. For example, both involve specific rules and conditions that offenders must follow to avoid revocation, and both entail providing offenders with supervision and services. In some instances, one officer may supervise both probationers and parolees. However, *probationer* and *parolee* are two distinct legal statuses. It is not uncommon for parole rules and conditions to be somewhat stricter and for officers to be less tolerant of violations committed by parolees; revocation of parole may be sought quickly, even for a technical parole violation. In addition, parolees often face greater adjustment problems because of the stigma attached to their prison records and because of the time they have spent away from the free community.

Just as there are different types of probation (suspended-sentence probation, split-sentence probation, etc.), there are two general types of parole. In *straight parole,* offenders are released from prison directly into the community under the supervision of the parole agency. In *residential parole,* offenders serve part of the parole term in a community residential facility or halfway house. There are two variants of residential parole. In the first variant, offenders are released from prison into the residential facility, where they spend a temporary, transitional period before returning home. The idea is to make the release process a gradual one. In the second variant, a person who violates the conditions of parole is kept on parole and is placed in the residential facility for a period of structured living, rather than having parole revoked and being returned to prison.

There are four fundamental objectives of parole. Two of these are also objectives of probation and were discussed earlier in this chapter. As with probation, parole is meant to provide community safety and to promote offender betterment and reintegration into society. The other two objectives of parole are more subtle, often unstated, but no less important. They are to (1) relieve and contain prison crowding and (2) control the behavior of prison inmates.

Since its inception, parole has functioned as a "safety valve" for institutional corrections; crowding levels can be better contained if more inmates are granted early release. One of the clearest manifestations of this objective is the growing popularity of emergency release laws that permit executive authorities (usually governors) to accelerate parole eligibility for selected inmates when prison crowding reaches a particular level. Parole also gives prison officials some control over the behavior of inmates. The prospect of

CAREERS IN CRIMINAL JUSTICE

Parole Agent

My name is Arthur J. Ramirez and I am a Parole Agent III (PA III) for the California State Department of Corrections (CDC) Parole and Community Services Division (P&CSD). Since 1983, I have also taught undergraduate and graduate criminal justice courses at California State University, Long Beach. I hold a bachelor of science degree in Criminal Justice, two master's degrees (Community Clinical Psychology and Criminal Justice), as well as a doctorate degree in Criminology. I chose to work with ex-felons in order to be in a unique position to improve the quality of life in our society.

As a PA III, I provide supervisory direction with respect to the philosophies, policies, and procedures of the CDC for the Long Beach I Parole Unit. I also complete a number of adjunct assignments for the department. A typical day includes reviewing my management formation system to ensure that the operations of the parole unit run smoothly. I hold case conferences with parole agents and/or review reports, written by them, related to the progress of parolees or parole violations committed by them. I review each case in order to determine the appropriate action. The actions may include: reviewing cases for discharge from parole; referring parolees to community programs that are in-line with their needs; approving funds to assist parolees; and reviewing activity reports to continue parolees on parole as a disposition after a parole violation. This allows the parolee to remain in the community and is often accompanied with a referral to a social program. I also make decisions to return parolees back into custody for parole violations. This includes reviewing the violation reports prior to submitting them to the Board of Prison Terms. Additionally, I review reports to initiate warrants for the arrest of parolees when they abscond from parole Another typical day may also include traveling to Sacramento to attend a Commission on Correctional Peace Officer Standards and Training (CPOST) Curriculum Review Committee meeting. In this capacity, I review lesson plans submitted by youth and adult corrections agencies statewide and health care services to ensure that they are in-line with the professional training standards established and approved by CPOST.

It is very rewarding to see parolees making a positive adjustment in their reintegration into society from imprisonment. It is also frustrating to see them being returned to prison for parole violations despite effective casework by a parole agent. Our society is currently faced with the challenge to provide the highest quality criminal justice services in order to respond to our criminal justice problems. I enjoy being a part of this process at the local and state levels. The field of criminal justice provides many career position opportunities for students. I fully believe that students today need to plan for their future careers systematically. Students interested in working in the field of criminal justice need to contact practicing professionals in the community in order to find out more about the position opportunities available in the field. I also recommend that students interested in working in parole should volunteer or enroll in an internship program with an agency that works with parolees or offenders. This will assist them in deciding whether a career in parole is for them.

Compare the information above with the career box on probation officers. Which position would you be more attracted to? Why?

Some offenders are released on parole before the end of their sentences, on the condition that they remain law-abiding and follow the rules designed to control their movement and to help them adjust to society. *Should parole be abolished? Why or why not?*

early release gives inmates an incentive to cooperate with prison officials and to avoid infractions of prison rules.

HISTORICAL CONTEXT

As with probation, parole emerged from earlier practices. One of those is the *tickets-of-leave* concept pioneered around the mid-1800s by Captain Alexander Machonochie off the coast of Australia and by Sir Walter Crofton in Ireland. Under this concept, inmates, after serving a portion of their sentences and exhibiting good performance in prison, could be granted tickets of leave, whereby they were released into the community under supervision. Release was made conditional on continuation of good behavior, so the practice was also known as conditional pardon.

The idea of releasing some prisoners early to community supervision and making release contingent on good conduct found its way to the United States. The idea was initially implemented, along with indeterminate sentencing, in the 1870s by Zebulon Brockway at Elmira Reformatory in New York. Brockway's system allowed prison officials to grant parole release to inmates they perceived as ready for release. Parole spread rapidly after its inception at Elmira. By the turn of the century, 20 states had provisions for parole, and by 1920, the majority of states had adopted such provisions.[11]

ADMINISTRATION

It is helpful to divide parole administration into two areas. The first area is the parole board, or a similar paroling authority, which makes parole release decisions. The second is the parole field service agency, which provides parole supervision in the community after release.

Parole administration, like probation administration, exhibits much variation across the nation. At the federal level, the paroling authority is the United States Parole Commission, and field services are administered by the Administrative Office of the Courts. Each state is responsible for administering its own parole system. Parole at the state level is generally an executive branch function, and each state has its own paroling authority. In most states, parole boards and field service agencies are administratively separate, although in some states, the board administers field services.[12] Whether probation and parole field services are jointly administered by the same government agency varies among the states. It has become quite common, however, for states to combine probation and parole administration. In Kentucky, for example, the same unit of the department of corrections administers both.

Another area of difference between states is whether the paroling authority or board is (1) administratively autonomous and independent of prison officials or (2) administratively consolidated with the department of corrections. Most parole boards are autonomous.[13]

In many ways the parole board is the centerpiece of parole administration; the board is very influential in establishing a jurisdiction's parole policies. A

FYI: Federal Parole

Anyone who has committed a federal crime after November 1, 1987, is no longer eligible for federal parole. (It has been abolished.) Such persons now must serve their entire sentences, less a maximum of 54 days a year good time, if granted. Those people sentenced or under supervision before November 1, 1987, are still eligible for federal parole supervision.

SOURCE: United States Parole Commission at www.usdoj.gov/uspc/mission.html.

national survey of parole boards found that in most states, the governor, subject to legislative confirmation, appoints parole board members. Appointment terms in most states are 4 to 6 years, and the vast majority of states use renewable appointments. The professional qualifications required for appointment differ across states. Interestingly, law in many jurisdictions requires no minimum professional qualifications. The number of parole board members also varies by state, with five and seven members being common. A minority of states employ part-time parole board members. Most of the nations' board members are white, approximately one-quarter are female, and the average age of board members is about 50.[14]

PROCESS AND PROCEDURES

Besides helping establish the jurisdiction's parole policies, the parole board is generally responsible for managing parole release processes and making decisions to terminate parole supervision.

THE PAROLE BOARD—RELEASE AND TERMINATION Prior to appearing before the parole authority for a parole-grant hearing, a prisoner must first become eligible for parole and complete a parole plan describing such things as where he or she plans to live and work after release. In addition, prison staff usually prepare a preparole report for the parole board. The report summarizes the characteristics of the inmate and his or her offense, reviews the inmate's adjustment to prison and his or her progress toward rehabilitation, and presents the inmate's parole plan. Reports sometimes contain a recommendation about whether the inmate should be paroled.

Depending on the jurisdiction and the particular case, the actual parole-grant hearing can be conducted by the full parole board, a partial board, or representatives of the board known as examiners or hearing officers. Roughly half of the states rely on hearing officers.[15] Other concerned parties, such as prison staff, prosecuting attorneys, and victims, may also be present. Parole hearings are typically quite short and routine. Parole authorities review relevant documents, such as the inmate's parole plan, the preparole report, and victim statements, and often interview the inmate. Authorities then vote on whether to grant or to deny parole release. In more than half of the states, the inmate is notified of the outcome of voting at the hearing or immediately thereafter. In the remaining states, notification time frames range from 1 week to more than 30 days.[16] If parole is denied, the inmate is automatically eligible for a future hearing.

parole guidelines Structured instruments used to estimate the probability of parole recidivism and to direct the release decisions of parole boards.

Increasingly, parole authorities are using structured instruments called **parole guidelines** to estimate the probability of recidivism and to direct their release decisions. Those guidelines are similar to the sentencing guidelines used by judges and the risk-and-needs-assessment instruments used in probation work. Only about half the jurisdictions employ parole guidelines, and even in those jurisdictions, parole authorities often have the discretion to override guideline recommendations.[17] A sample parole guideline instrument, developed by the United States Parole Commission, is presented in Figure 12.4.

Parole authorities consider a variety of factors in determining whether to grant or to deny an inmate parole. Furthermore, those factors tend to be assigned different levels of importance. A recent analysis of national data found that the four most important factors, in order, are:

1. Seriousness of the current offense.
2. History of prior violent behavior.
3. Prior felony convictions.
4. Use of a firearm in committing the current offense.

FYI — Charles Manson

In April 2002, Charles Manson, then 67, was denied parole for the tenth time. He was sentenced to death in 1970 for his role in the 1969 Tate-LaBianca murders. When the Supreme Court declared capital punishment unconstitutional in 1972, his death sentence was automatically commuted to life imprisonment with opportunity for parole. His next parole hearing is scheduled for 2007.

SOURCE: "Charles Manson Denied 10th Parole Bid," CBSNEWS.com at www.cbsnews.com/stories/2002/04/25/national/main507237.shtml.

FIGURE 12.4 Parole Guideline Instrument

Item A. PRIOR CONVICTIONS/ADJUDICATIONS (ADULT OR JUVENILE) ....❑
- None ....= 3
- One ....= 2
- Two or three ....= 1
- Four or more ....= 0

Item B. PRIOR COMMITMENT(S) OF MORE THAN THIRTY DAYS (ADULT OR JUVENILE) ....❑
- None ....= 3
- One ....= 2
- Three or more ....= 0

Item C. AGE AT CURRENT OFFENSE/PRIOR COMMITMENTS ....❑
- Age at commencement of the current offense:
  - 26 years of age or more ....= 2*
  - 20–25 years of age ....= 1*
  - 19 years of age or less ....= 0

*EXCEPTION: If five or more prior commitments of more than thirty days (adult or juvenile), place an "x" here___ and score this item ....= 0

Item D. RECENT COMMITMENT-FREE PERIOD (THREE YEARS) ....❑
- No prior commitment of more than thirty days (adult or juvenile) or released to the community from last such commitment at least three years prior to the commencement of the current offense ....= 1
- Otherwise ....= 0

Item E. PROBATION/PAROLE/CONFINEMENT/ESCAPE STATUS VIOLATOR THIS TIME ....❑
- Neither on probation, parole, confinement, or escape status at the time of the current offense, nor committed as a probation, parole, confinement, or escape status violator this time ....= 1
- Otherwise ....= 0

Item F. HEROIN/OPIATE DEPENDENCE ....❑
- No history of heroin/opiate dependency ...= 1
- Otherwise ....= 0

TOTAL SCORE ....❑

SOURCE: Paul F. Cromwell and George C. Hellinger, *Community-Based Corrections,* 3rd ed. (St. Paul, MN: West, 1994), p. 232

Other relevant factors include the number of prior incarcerations, prior adjustment on parole, prison disciplinary record, psychological reports, and victim input.[18]

Due process in parole release decisions was addressed by the U.S. Supreme Court in *Greenholtz* v. *Inmates of the Nebraska Penal and Correctional Complex* (1979). Noting that parole release is an act of grace, the Court held that release on parole is distinct from parole revocation. Thus, the Court declined to apply the provisions outlined in *Morrissey* v. *Brewer*, discussed earlier in this chapter, to parole release. Consequently, what constitutes acceptable due process in release decision making is largely case-specific. Jurisdictions vary considerably in their due process provisions for parole hearings. Most of the jurisdictions allow inmates to be represented by attorneys.[19]

Once inmates receive parole release, they begin the period of parole supervision, discussed later, which continues until it is terminated. In addition to its responsibility for release decisions, the parole board is responsible for parole termination decisions. In most jurisdictions, the board can discharge individuals from parole supervision; this is commonly done upon the recommendation of the parole supervision agency. Alternatively, if no board action is taken, the individual is discharged from parole upon expiration of the legal sentence.

Parole revocation is also the responsibility of the parole board and can occur in response to new crimes or technical violations. Parole revocation is quite similar to probation revocation and is governed by the same case law (*Morrissey* v. *Brewer* and *Gagnon* v. *Scarpelli*). As is true in the field of probation, parole officers enjoy considerable discretion when deciding whether to recommend revocation for violations. If revocation is sought, the two-stage hearing process required under *Morrissey* becomes applicable. Although parole authorities consider various factors in determining whether to revoke parole, a recent study suggests that the two most important factors are the seriousness of the violation and the recommendation of the supervising parole officer.[20]

Myth	Fact
If parole is revoked, return to prison is automatic.	Though reincarceration is common, other options are usually possible, such as placement in a halfway house or reinstatement of parole. Much discretion is involved.

FIELD SERVICES—SUPERVISION AND SERVICE DELIVERY Traditionally, most parole supervision or field service agencies were administered by parole boards. This situation has changed dramatically since the 1960s. Currently, most field service agencies are administratively separate from the parole board.[21] In most of those jurisdictions, parole supervision is administered by the department of corrections. Nevertheless, the basic task of field service agencies has remained constant through the years—to provide control and assistance for persons reentering the community from prison.

Virtually everything that was stated earlier in this chapter about probation supervision and service delivery applies to parole supervision and service delivery. The subtle differences between the two are overshadowed by the many similarities. However, one difference warrants mention. Specialization is more common in parole than in probation supervision. Under specialization, offenders who pose a similar threat to public safety or those who share similar treatment needs are grouped together and assigned to the same officers. Specialization by parole officers is used in slightly more than half the jurisdictions. The two most common areas for specialization are with sex offenders and substance-abusing offenders.[22]

Social scientist Richard McCleary conducted what is considered a classic sociological study of a parole supervision agency.[23] In his book *Dangerous Men*,

Parole officers frequently meet their clients at the clients' workplaces. *What problems, if any, might be created by this practice?*

McCleary observes that parole officers are very concerned with avoiding "trouble" from parolees. Trouble is defined broadly as anything that runs counter to the status quo of the parole agency. Trouble can threaten the agency's public image, thus bringing the agency pressure—and possibly increased structure—from political officials. The likelihood of trouble is reduced to the extent that officers can anticipate what clients might do in response to threats of various punishments and rewards from officers. "Dangerous men" are parolees who do not respond predictably to officers' threats and promises. Dangerous men are not necessarily prone to violent behavior; they are merely unpredictable. Because unpredictability implies possible trouble, officers try to identify dangerous men as soon as possible in the supervision process. The dangerous-man label is used sparingly because it means greater supervision and more documentation and paperwork for officers. However, the label can protect the supervising officer and the agency from subsequent criticism because, early on, it conveys that problems may be expected from a particular parolee. Concerned parties in the parole bureaucracy are alerted to what might happen, and the potential for "surprises" is reduced. Once parolees have acquired the dangerous-man label, the agency is quick to seek reasons to revoke their paroles. McCleary's research underscores the crucial significance of agency bureaucratic dynamics in shaping supervision practices.

PAROLE ISSUES

Since the 1970s, discretionary parole release has been among the most controversial issues in criminal justice. Proponents of parole release argue, for example, that early release provisions are essential for controlling prisoners' behavior and for containing institutional crowding. However, several criticisms have been directed at parole release. Some critics claim that parole undermines both retribution and deterrence because offenders are permitted to leave prison early, sometimes many years before finishing their maximum sentences. Similarly, critics argue that because prisons generally fail to reform offenders and it is impossible for parole boards to accurately predict which offenders will commit new crimes, parole does not sufficiently guarantee public safety. Other critics believe that parole is unfair to offenders. Those opponents charge that parole leads to significant disparities in time served in prison for offenders who should be serving equal amounts of time. For example, two offenders in the same jurisdiction with very similar prior legal backgrounds may be convicted of committing armed robbery under very similar circumstances. One offender may serve 5 years in prison and receive parole, whereas the other may serve twice as long before release. Another contention of critics is that linking the degree of participation in prison treatment programs to the possibility of early parole amounts to subtly coercing inmates into programs that are often of questionable effectiveness.

Those and other criticisms helped persuade a number of jurisdictions to curtail discretionary parole release. Instead, they moved from indeterminate sentencing to determinate sentencing, decreased reliance on parole release and increased reliance on mandatory release, and devised both sentencing and parole guidelines. There were even forceful calls and some initiatives undertaken to completely abolish parole release, although the movement to abolish parole seems to have peaked.[24] Currently, 16 states (Arizona, 1994; California, 1976 (but see below); Delaware, 1990; Florida, 1983; Illinois, 1978; Indiana, 1977; Kansas, 1993; Maine, 1975; Minnesota, 1980; Mississippi, 1995; North Carolina, 1994; Ohio, 1996; Oregon, 1989; Virginia, 1995; Washington, 1984; and Wisconsin, 1999) and the federal government have abolished early release by discretion of a parole board for all offenders. However, parole boards still have discretion over inmates who were sentenced for crimes committed prior to the effective date of the law that eliminated parole board release. A few other states have abolished parole release for certain violent or felony offenders (Alaska, Louisiana, New York, and Tennessee). California allows discretionary release by a parole board only for offenders with indeterminate life sentences.[25] It is important to note that while discretionary release from prison by a parole board has been eliminated by some states, postrelease supervision still exists and is generally referred to as community or supervised release. Parole boards, in various forms, have the responsibility to set conditions of release for offenders under community or supervised release, the authority to return an offender to prison for violating the conditions of supervised release, and the power to grant parole for medical reasons.[26]

Besides the issue of whether parole release should exist, there are a number of other pressing concerns surrounding parole. They include legal issues, strained parole resources, and parolee adjustment and recidivism.

FYI: Public Opinion

According to a public opinion poll, nearly two-thirds of all Americans support allowing prisoners to earn early release through good behavior and participation in educational and work programs. However, only 21 percent of Americans are willing to give parole boards more authority to release offenders early, and 75 percent of Americans do not want to parole prisoners who have been paroled before for a serious crime.

SOURCE: Timothy J. Flanagan, "Reform or Punish: Americans' Views of the Correctional System," in T. J. Flanagan and D. R. Longmire (eds.), *Americans View Crime and Justice: A National Public Opinion Survey* (Thousand Oaks, CA: Sage, 1996), p. 87.

LEGAL ISSUES There are two general categories of legal issues that relate to parole: (1) parolees' civil rights and (2) the liabilities of parole officials.

Individuals forfeit a variety of civil rights when they are convicted of a felony. Some of those include the right to hold public office and certain other jobs, the right to jury service, and the right to obtain some types of licenses and insurance. Although the specific rights forfeited vary by jurisdiction, in many instances parolees must seek court action to restore their rights following release from incarceration. Only a few jurisdictions grant their parole boards authority to restore ex-offenders' rights.[27]

People who support denying released inmates certain rights argue that the practice is necessary to preserve public safety and maintain high moral standards in society. Opponents argue that it is unfair to continue penalizing individuals who have "paid their debts." They point out that denial of civil liberties contributes to poor adjustment on parole. Given the current posture of the nation toward felons and ex-felons, it seems unlikely, at least in the foreseeable future, that the majority of persons coming out of prison will have their rights fully restored.

Can parole board officials and field service agents be held legally liable if a parolee's actions cause harm to a victim or victims? The answer is a qualified yes. Even though the vast majority of paroling authorities enjoy some type of immunity from liability (through constitution, statute, or case law), such immunity has been eroding in recent years.

According to attorney and criminal justice professor John Watkins, Jr., three central elements must be proven to establish liability on the part of parole and probation officials.

1. The existence of a legal duty owed the public.
2. Evidence of a breach of the required standard of duty.
3. An injury or damage to a person or group proximately caused by the breach of duty.

Watkins further observes that as a general rule, tort liability applies to injuries, or damages, caused by the negligent or improper performance of ministerial functions, but not to injuries caused by unsatisfactory performance of discretionary functions. A *discretionary* function is one "that may involve a series of possible choices from a wide array of alternatives, none of which may be absolutely called for in a particular situation." A *ministerial* function is "one regarding which nothing is left to discretion—a simple and definite duty imposed by law, and arising under conditions admitted or proved to exist."[28] An example of a breach of a ministerial function would be if a parole board were to completely disregard parole guidelines that the board is legally bound to consider before releasing inmates. Thus, if parole and probation officials wish to minimize the likelihood of being held liable, those officials should determine what is legally required of them in their jurisdiction and make good faith efforts to abide by those requirements.

FYI: Parole Officer Caseloads

The average parole officer caseload for 18 jurisdictions with separate probation and parole agencies during 2000 was 73. The range was from a low of 25 in Nebraska to a high of 253 in Hawaii. The average caseload in the 20 jurisdictions with combined probation and parole agencies was 94. The range was from 50 in the federal system to 176 in Alabama. In jurisdictions with separate probation and parole agencies, probation caseloads are nearly always larger than parole caseloads–frequently much larger.

SOURCE: Camille Graham Camp and George M. Camp, *The 2001 Corrections Yearbook: Adult Systems* (Middletown, CT: Criminal Justice Institute, 2002), p. 195.

STRAINED PAROLE RESOURCES Parole supervision agencies across the nation are currently attempting to manage record numbers of parolees. On December 31, 2002, for example, 753,141 adults were under active parole supervision. This represents an increase of about 42 percent over the total number of parolees on December 31, 1990.[29] Table 12.3 shows the states with the largest parole populations and the highest and lowest rates of persons under parole supervision per 100,000 adult U.S. residents at year-end 2002. Moreover, an increasingly large proportion of parolees has been released from prison early because of pressures to relieve institutional crowding, rather than because those persons have been judged good candidates for parole. Such parolees often require above-average levels of supervision and services. Because most jurisdictions are facing pressure to expand prison space, it is not surprising that parole resources, such as budgets and staffing, have failed to keep pace with those developments.

The long-term implications of this predicament are often unappreciated. Parolee recidivism is normally quite high, partly because of the strained

TABLE 12.3 States with the Largest Parole Populations and the Highest and Lowest Rates of Persons Under Parole Supervision per 100,000 Adult U.S. Residents at Year-End 2002

States with the Largest Parole Populations		States with the Highest Rates of Supervision, 2002	Persons Supervised per 100,000 Adult U.S. Residents*	States with the Lowest Rates of Supervision, 2002	Persons Supervised per 100,000 Adult U.S. Residents*
California	113,185	Pennsylvania	1,037	Washington	2
Texas	103,068	Oregon	727	Maine	3
Pennsylvania	97,712	Louisiana	715	North Dakota	31
New York	55,990	Texas	654	Florida	40
Illinois	35,458	Arkansas	577	North Carolina	44
Louisiana	23,417	California	439	Nebraska	45
Georgia	20,912	New York	384	Rhode Island	52
Oregon	19,307	Illinois	377	West Virginia	71
Ohio	17,853	Maryland	325	Virginia	82
Michigan	17,648	Missouri	320	Connecticut	86

Note: This table excludes the District of Columbia.
*Rates are based on the estimated number of adult state residents on December 31, 2002.

SOURCE: Lauren E. Glaze, "Probation and Parole Populations in the United States, 2002," U.S. Department of Justice, *Bureau of Justice Statistics Bulletin* (Washington, DC: GPO, August 2003), p. 2, Table 1.

resources of parole agencies. The typical public and political response to high parolee recidivism is to demand a "get-tough" stance that culminates in the return of large numbers of parolees to prison. This exacerbates both prison crowding and the tendency to rely on parole release to relieve crowding. The result is further strain on parole resources and, consequently, further recidivism.

Parolee Adjustment and Recidivism A key to successful community adjustment for inmates leaving prison is **reintegration,** which means rebuilding former prosocial ties to the community and establishing new ties. An important part of reintegration is finding a satisfactory job and obtaining adequate subsistence funds through legal means.

reintegration The process of rebuilding former ties to the community and establishing new ties after release from prison.

The stigma of a prison record can result in grim employment prospects, especially without the assistance of the parole agency. Yet, research suggests that obtaining employment improves adjustment to community life. In a study of the effects of postrelease employment on the emotional well-being of a sample of ex-felons in Texas and Georgia, it was found that employment enhanced emotional well-being by providing wages and improving perceptions of self-worth. The research discovered that sustained unemployment caused emotional distress. This distress reduced the motivation of releasees to search for jobs. In the words of the study's author, "Unemployment fed on itself by creating psychological stress which in turn reduced effectiveness in finding work."[30] Related evidence suggests that providing newly released ex-inmates with temporary unemployment benefits can decrease the recidivism rate, although it is important that such benefits not create a work disincentive.[31]

Research spanning three decades shows that fewer than half of all state prison inmates released on parole successfully complete their term of supervision.[32] For example, during the 1990s, the percentage of successful parole discharges ranged from about 42 percent to about 49 percent. In 2002 (the latest year for which data were available), 45 percent of state parolees successfully completed their term of supervision, 41 percent were returned to prison or jail, 9 percent absconded, and the remainder failed to successfully meet the conditions of supervision but were discharged without incarceration.

States vary widely in their rates of success (see Table 12.4). For example, in 1999, both Massachusetts and Mississippi reported 83 percent success rates, while Utah (18.5 percent) and California (21 percent) had the lowest rates. Differences in success rates can be attributed to a number of factors such as variations in the parole populations (for example, age at release, criminal history, and most serious offense), the level of supervision, and parole agency policies on the revocation of technical violators.

The research shows that inmates released from prison on parole for the first time are more likely to succeed than re-releases. Re-releases are inmates who are being discharged from prison on parole who have served time for a previous violation of parole or conditional release or a new offense committed while under previous parole supervision. In 1999, for example, 63.5 percent of first releases were successful, compared to 21 percent of re-releases (see Table 12.5). However, the success rate for first-time releases declined the longer the inmate had been in prison. In 1999, 74 percent of first-time releases who had been in prison less than 12 months succeeded on parole, compared to 62 percent of first-time releases who had been in prison for 5 years or more (see Table 12.5).

Success rates also vary by method of release. State inmates released by a parole board ("discretionary parole") almost always have a higher rate of success than inmates released through "mandatory parole" (that is, inmates who

FYI Parole Violations

A 37 percent increase in the number of offenders returned to prison for parole violations is one of the reasons for the growth in the state prison population between 1990 and 2003. In 2002, 183,680 of the offenders entering state prison had violated the conditions of their parole, up from 133,870 in 1990. In 2002, 41 percent of the inmates had their paroles revoked because either of a rule violation or new offense. An additional 9 percent had absconded and the remainder had failed to successfully meet the conditions of supervision but were discharged without incarceration.

Source: Lauren E. Glaze, "Probation and Parole in the United States, 2002," U.S. Department of Justice, *Bureau of Justice Statistics Bulletin* (August 2003), p. 6.

TABLE 12.4 Percent Successful Among State Parole Discharges, by State, 1990, 1995, and 1999

Region and Jurisdiction	Percent Successful of All Parole Discharges		
	1990	1995	1999
All States	44.6%	44.3%	41.9%
Northeast			
Connecticut	55.0%	55.3%	57.7%
Maine	/	/	/
Massachusetts	75.8	71.3	82.9
New Hampshire	60.1	67.3	—
New Jersey	61.3	43.1	55.1
New York	48.9	51.9	54.9
Pennsylvania	79.2	70.3	/
Rhode Island	62.6	64.8	65.9
Vermont	38.2	48.6	65.8
Midwest			
Illinois	47.0%	66.3%	62.9%
Indiana	73.0	74.6	63.0
Iowa	69.8	68.0	60.9
Kansas	11.5	37.4	32.3
Michigan	52.7	60.0	51.9
Minnesota	73.3	66.6	55.7
Missouri	52.5	66.4	40.4
Nebraska	68.2	57.3	62.9
North Dakota	76.6	75.7	79.1
Ohio	52.4	50.0	43.6
South Dakota	66.8	70.6	62.6
Wisconsin	72.6	59.1	63.4
South			
Alabama	28.8%	/	72.1%
Arkansas	68.1	40.1%	39.6
Delaware	82.8	—	/
Dist. of Columbia	40.1	48.8	—
Florida	61.2	40.9	56.5
Georgia	62.2	60.2	63.4
Kentucky	22.6	31.6	33.7
Louisiana	61.5	47.8	46.9
Maryland	67.2	64.6	47.0
Mississippi	62.6	78.2	82.7
North Carolina	78.8	68.4	79.8
Oklahoma	69.2	67.0	75.4
South Carolina	54.7	55.9	65.3
Tennessee	35.9	25.8	42.3
Texas	35.1	41.0	54.9
Virginia	68.0	57.8	63.2
West Virginia	48.2	46.0	65.2
West			
Alaska	44.0%	39.5%	33.7%
Arizona	62.3	48.9	61.9
California	19.4	20.9	21.3
Colorado	58.2	48.9	36.3
Hawaii	13.1	40.5	32.4
Idaho	61.5	26.0	46.4
Montana	55.3	—	59.9
Nevada	70.4	74.6	66.8
New Mexico	37.8	28.9	28.5
Oregon	27.9	39.6	50.6
Utah	21.8	23.7	18.5
Washington	47.9	29.4	/
Wyoming	66.1	48.5	59.6

Note: Based on the *Annual Parole Survey.* Counts are for discharges between January 1 and December 31 of each year.

— Not reported. / Not calculated.

SOURCE: Timothy A. Hughes, Doris James Wilson, and Allen J. Beck, "Trends in State Parole, 1990–2000." U.S. Department of Justice, *Bureau of Justice Statistics Special Report* (Washington, DC: GPO, October 2001), p. 11, Table 15.

TABLE 12.5	Percent Successful Among State Parole Discharges, by Selected Characteristics, 1990 and 1999	
	Percent Successful	
Characteristic	**1990**	**1999**
Gender		
Male	35.9%	39.3%
Female	37.1	47.7
Race/Hispanic origin		
White non-Hispanic	44.1%	40.9%
Black non-Hispanic	33.2	39.0
Hispanic	31.0	50.6
Other	33.6	42.2
Age at parole discharge		
17 or younger	26.2%	42.9%
18–24	33.4	36.3
25–29	34.8	42.5
30–34	34.1	39.0
35–39	36.8	38.3
40–44	38.4	39.5
45–54	46.2	43.1
55 or older	56.6	54.5
Method of release		
Discretionary parole	51.6%	54.1%
Mandatory parole	23.8	33.1
Type of release		
First release	56.4%	63.5%
Re-release	14.6	21.1
Most serious offense		
Violent	39.1%	41.0%
Property	33.8	36.5
Drug	33.7	40.9
Public-order	46.1	47.1
Time served in prison*		
Less than 12 months	74.6%	74.0%
12–23 months	67.7	68.7
24–59 months	59.1	62.7
60 months or more	49.5	62.0

Note: Based on prisoners with a sentence of more than 1 year who were released from state prison. Data are from the *National Corrections Reporting Program.*

*First releases only.

Source: Timothy A. Hughes, Doris James Wilson, and Allen J. Beck, "Trends in State Parole, 1990–2000," U.S. Department of Justice, *Bureau of Justice Statistics Special Report* (Washington, DC: GPO, October 2001), p. 12, Table 18.

generally are sentenced under determinate sentencing statutes and are released from prison after serving a portion of their original sentence minus any good time earned). In 1999, for example, 54 percent of inmates released through discretionary parole were successful, while only 33 percent of inmates receiving mandatory parole were successful (see Table 12.5). However, there was an interesting interactive effect in 1999. Inmates released from prison for the first time were more likely to succeed on mandatory release than on discretionary release (79 percent vs. 61 percent), while re-releases were more likely to succeed on discretionary release than on mandatory release (37 percent vs. 17 percent).

There is also a temporal element to parole success or failure. The chances of failure are generally highest during the early stages of parole. The first year appears to be the most critical if a successful discharge from parole is going to occur. In 1999, parolees who succeeded served an average of 27 months under parole supervision, while parolees who failed served an average of 24 months under supervision. Among inmates released from prison for the first time, those who were released by a parole board and succeeded served, on average, 34 months under supervision. Those who failed served an average of 26 months under supervision. Inmates who were released from prison for the first time on mandatory parole and succeeded served, on average, 21 months under supervision, while those who failed served an average of 19 months under supervision.

Parole success and failure also vary by parolee gender, race or ethnicity, age, and most serious offense for which he or she was incarcerated. In 1999, 48 percent of female parolees were successfully discharged from supervision, while only 39 percent of males were successfully discharged. Between 1990 and 1999, the rate of success for female parolees increased about 11 percent; the rate of success for male parolees increased about 3 percent. As for race or ethnicity, in 1999, 51 percent of Hispanic parolees were successfully discharged (up from 31 percent in 1990); 41 percent of white, non-Hispanics were successfully discharged (down from 44 percent in 1990); 39 percent of black, non-Hispanics were successfully discharged (up from 33 percent in 1990); and 42 percent of parolees of other races or ethnicities were successfully discharged (up from 34 percent in 1990). Older parolees (those 45 or older) had the highest rates of successful parole completion in both 1990 and 1999. More than half of the parolees age 55 or older were successfully discharged in both years. Among parolees in other age groups, success rates varied between about 33 percent and 43 percent. Finally, in 1999, 47 percent of parolees whose most serious offense was a public order crime were successfully discharged from supervision (up from 46 percent in 1990), followed by 41 percent of violent and drug offenders (up from 39 percent and 34 percent in 1999, respectively), and 36.5 percent of property offenders (up from 34 percent in 1990). (See Table 12.5.)

THINKING CRITICALLY

1. How much weight do victim impact statements get in the decision to grant parole?
2. Given what you have read, do you think there are ways to improve the parole process? If so, what can be done?

Intermediate Sanctions

Recent dramatic increases in prison, parole, and probation populations have fundamentally altered the field of community corrections. Community corrections has been forced to accommodate (1) growing numbers of the types of offenders the field has traditionally accommodated, plus (2) offenders who would have been sent to—or remained in—prison had sufficient space been available. At the same time, the field has witnessed a general decline in philosophical support for rehabilitation, coupled with a growing emphasis on punishing and controlling offenders. Since the 1980s, the intermediate-sanction trend has grown within this context.

intermediate sanctions Sanctions that, in restrictiveness and punitiveness, lie between traditional probation and traditional imprisonment or, alternatively, between imprisonment and traditional parole.

In restrictiveness and punitiveness, **intermediate sanctions** lie somewhere between traditional probation and traditional imprisonment or, alternatively, between imprisonment and traditional parole supervision (see Figure 12.5). Intermediate sanctions are designed to widen the range of incarceration alternatives and to calibrate that range according to the differential risks and needs of offenders.

FIGURE 12.5 Relationship of Intermediate Sanctions to Traditional Sanctions

No Sanction	Traditional Probation	Intermediate Sanctions	Traditional Imprisonment	Intermediate Sanctions	Traditional Parole Supervision

As a rule, the newer intermediate sanctions are oriented less toward rehabilitation and more toward retribution, deterrence, and incapacitation than older community correctional programs. However, the distinction between intermediate sanctions and older, more traditional programs has become somewhat blurred because some traditional programs, such as restitution and halfway houses, have been incorporated into the intermediate-sanction category. The specific intermediate sanctions to be discussed in this section include intensive-supervision probation and parole, day reporting centers, structured fines (or day fines), home confinement and electronic monitoring, and halfway houses.

INTENSIVE-SUPERVISION PROBATION AND PAROLE (ISP)

Intensive-supervision probation and parole (ISP) provides stricter conditions, closer supervision, and more treatment services than do traditional probation and parole. Offenders are often selected for ISP on the basis of their scores on risk-and-needs-assessment instruments. Alternatively, they may be placed on ISP after violating regular probation or parole. Most ISP programs are for nonviolent felons.

intensive-supervision probation and parole (ISP) An alternative to incarceration that provides stricter conditions, closer supervision, and more treatment services than do traditional probation and parole.

The ISP programs in existence across the nation are diverse, and some programs come much closer than others to providing supervision and services that are genuinely intensive. In theory, ISP programs have the following features:

1. Specially trained intensive-supervision officers with small caseloads (for example, 25 cases per officer).
2. Inescapable supervision, such as multiple weekly contacts between officers and clients and frequent testing for drug use.
3. Mandatory curfews.
4. Mandatory employment or restitution requirements, or both.
5. Mandatory or voluntary participation in treatment.
6. Supervision fees to be paid by clients.

ISP usually lasts 6 months to 2 years. Typically, offenders must pass through a series of phases that become progressively less restrictive during the period of intensive supervision.

The majority of states have implemented ISP programs for adult probationers and parolees.[33] However, out of all persons placed on probation or parole, relatively few are placed under intensive supervision because of resource limitations and the small caseloads required by ISP. Although it is commonly argued that ISP costs less money than incarceration, provided it is not followed by incarceration due to revocation, ISP generally costs more than traditional probation or parole. For this reason, it is used rather sparingly.

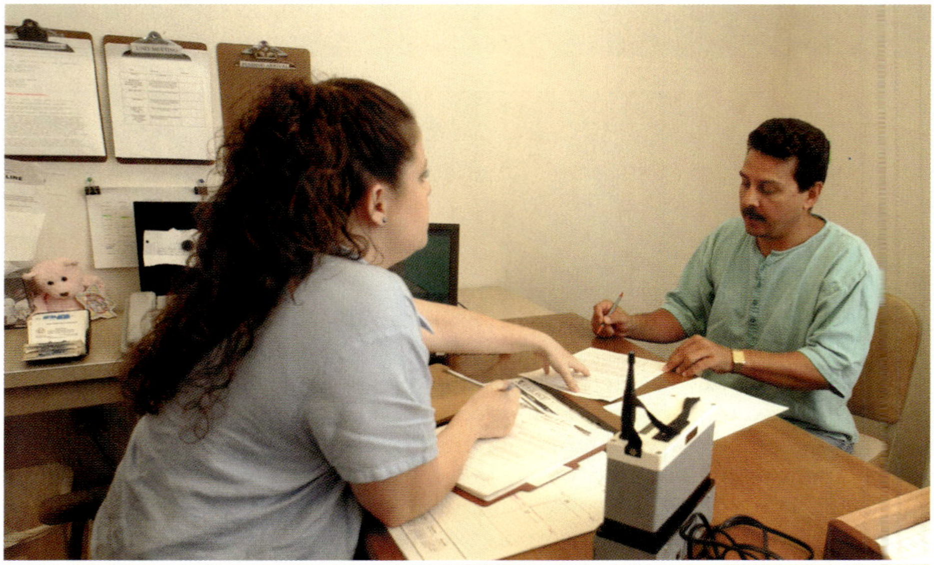

Intensive-supervision probation and parole (ISP) provides stricter conditions, closer supervision, and more treatment services than do traditional probation and parole. *Is ISP worth the extra expense? Why or why not?*

Although a number of concerns have been raised about ISP, two of the most important are (1) the potential for net widening and (2) the lack of demonstrated reduction of recidivism.

net widening A phenomenon that occurs when the offenders placed in a novel program are not the offenders for whom the program was designed. The consequence is that those in the program receive more severe sanctions than they would have received had the new program remained unavailable.

Net widening takes various forms and can plague virtually any type of community correctional program. Net widening occurs when the offenders placed in a novel program like ISP are not the offenders for whom the program was intended. The consequence is that those in the program receive more severe sanctions than they would have received had the new program remained unavailable. Suppose, for example, that a jurisdiction facing a prison crowding crisis establishes a new intensive probation program so that a substantial number of nonviolent offenders can be sentenced to ISP rather than prison. That is, the ISP target group consists of nonviolent felons who would have gone to prison had ISP not become available. If only persons who would formerly have gone to prison are placed on ISP, net widening has not taken place. However, if persons who would formerly have been placed on regular probation are now placed on ISP, net widening has occurred. To the degree that such net widening is the result, ISP becomes a costly addition to ordinary probation, instead of serving its intended function of providing a cost-efficient alternative to imprisonment.

Again, it is important to realize that almost all community correctional programs, especially those specifically designed to divert offenders from more severe sanctions, are vulnerable to net widening. Net widening can be avoided or minimized by establishing and following standard criteria for assigning offenders to programs. If the goal of an intensive probation program is to divert offenders from prison, then only prison-bound offenders should be placed in the program. Offenders who would have been placed on regular probation had the intensive program been unavailable should continue to be placed on regular probation. When modern ISP programs were introduced in the early 1980s, there was much optimism that a cost-efficient means of diverting offenders from prison and controlling their

CJ ONLINE

American Probation and Parole Association

The American Probation and Parole Association explores issues relevant to the field of community corrections. You can visit its website at **www.appa-net.org/** *Would a career in probation or parole be of interest to you? Why or why not?*

recidivism had been found. Writing about the Georgia ISP program, social scientists Billie Erwin and Lawrence Bennett stated that "the recidivism rates are considerably better . . . than for groups under regular probation and for those released from prison. [ISP] offenders commit fewer and less serious crimes."[34] Erwin and Bennett also estimated that Georgia saved $6,775 for each case diverted from prison into ISP.

Unfortunately, the initial optimism surrounding ISP has not been sustained according to subsequent, well-designed research by Joan Petersilia and her colleagues. In one study, criminologists Petersilia and Turner compared offenders who had been randomly assigned to either intensive or regular probation in three California counties. Efforts were made to ensure that only high-risk, serious offenders were included in the study, and offenders were followed for 6 months after program placement. Across counties, an average of 30 percent of the ISP cases had technical violations, and about 20 percent had new arrests. In two counties, ISP clients were significantly more likely than regular probationers to incur technical violations, but neither more nor less likely to incur new arrests. In the other county, ISP cases and regular probationers did not differ significantly in technical violations or new arrests. Petersilia and Turner observe that in the first two counties, the increased supervision of ISP may simply have increased awareness of clients' technical violations. That is, regular probationers may have committed just as many technical violations, but more of the violations may have escaped detection because of less supervision. More important, Petersilia and Turner point out that if ISP simply increases awareness of technical violations and if the official response to such violations is swift revocation of ISP followed by incarceration, two things may occur. First, because offenders are no longer at risk of recidivism in the community once they are incarcerated, the artificial impression may be created that ISP is associated with low arrest rates. Second, ISP will fuel the prison crowding problem it is intended to relieve.[35]

In another study, Petersilia and Turner evaluated a national ISP demonstration project in 14 jurisdictions across nine states.[36] The 14 programs were implemented between 1986 and 1991 and involved approximately 2,000 offenders. In each program, offenders were assigned randomly to either ISP or an alternative sanction, such as regular probation, prison, or regular parole. They were then followed for 1 year. The average results across jurisdictions are summarized in Table 12.6. ISP was associated with

Myth | **Fact**

Myth: Incarceration for technical violations prevents crime.

Fact: In the largest controlled experiment ever conducted nationwide on intensive-supervision probation and parole, researchers found that offenders who committed technical violations were no more likely to be arrested for new crimes than those who did not commit technical violations.

SOURCE: Joan Petersilia and Susan Turner, *Evaluating Intensive Supervision Probation/Parole: Results of a Nationwide Experiment,* U.S. Department of Justice, National Institute of Justice, Research in Brief (Washington, DC: GPO, 1993).

FYI

Intensive Probation and Parole

In 2000, the average caseloads for regular probation and parole supervision were 133 and 73, respectively. By contrast, the 2000 average caseloads for intensive probation and parole supervision were 28 and 25, respectively. The 2000 average costs per day for regular probation and parole supervision were $2.16 and $4.76, respectively, while the 2000 average costs per day for intensive probation and parole supervision were $9.94 and $12.42, respectively. It is important to note, however, that caseloads and amounts spent on the two types of probation and parole supervision varied greatly across the nation. The average daily cost per prison inmate in 2000 was $61.04.

SOURCE: Camille Graham Camp and George M. Camp, *The 2001 Corrections Yearbook: Adult Systems* (Middletown, CT: Criminal Justice Institute, 2002), pp. 106, 195, and 206.

TABLE 12.6 Offender Recidivism Averages in Petersilia and Turner's Study of ISP in 14 Jurisdictions

Sanction	Percentage Arrested	Percentage with Technical Violations	Percentage Returned to Prison
ISP	37	65	24
Alternative	33	38	15

SOURCE: Joan Petersilia and Susan Turner, *Evaluating Intensive Supervision Probation/Parole: Results of a Nationwide Experiment,* U.S. Department of Justice, National Institute of Justice, Research in Brief (Washington, DC: GPO, 1993).

a substantially higher percentage of technical violations than the alternative sanctions. Again it appears that ISP may have increased detection of technical violations and thereby inflated incarceration rates. The data suggest that if ISP is to relieve prison crowding in any meaningful way, officials will have to become more reluctant to revoke ISP and impose incarceration for technical violations.

DAY REPORTING CENTERS

day reporting centers Facilities that are designed for offenders who would otherwise be in prison or jail and that require offenders to report regularly to confer with staff about supervision and treatment matters.

Day reporting centers, a relatively new facet of the intermediate-sanction movement, emerged in Great Britain in the 1970s and were pioneered in the United States in Massachusetts in 1986. The centers can be administered publicly or privately and are designed primarily for offenders who would otherwise be in jail or prison. This includes offenders such as those on ISP and those awaiting trial who did not receive release on recognizance or bail. Offenders are permitted to live at home but must report to the center regularly to confer with center staff about supervision and treatment matters. Program components commonly focus on work, education, counseling, and community service.[37] The program objectives devised for offenders by the Metropolitan Day Reporting Center in Boston are illustrated in Figure 12.6. In June 2002, 5,010 offenders nationwide were being supervised by personnel of day reporting centers instead of being confined in jails. That represents about 7 percent of offenders being supervised outside a jail facility.[38]

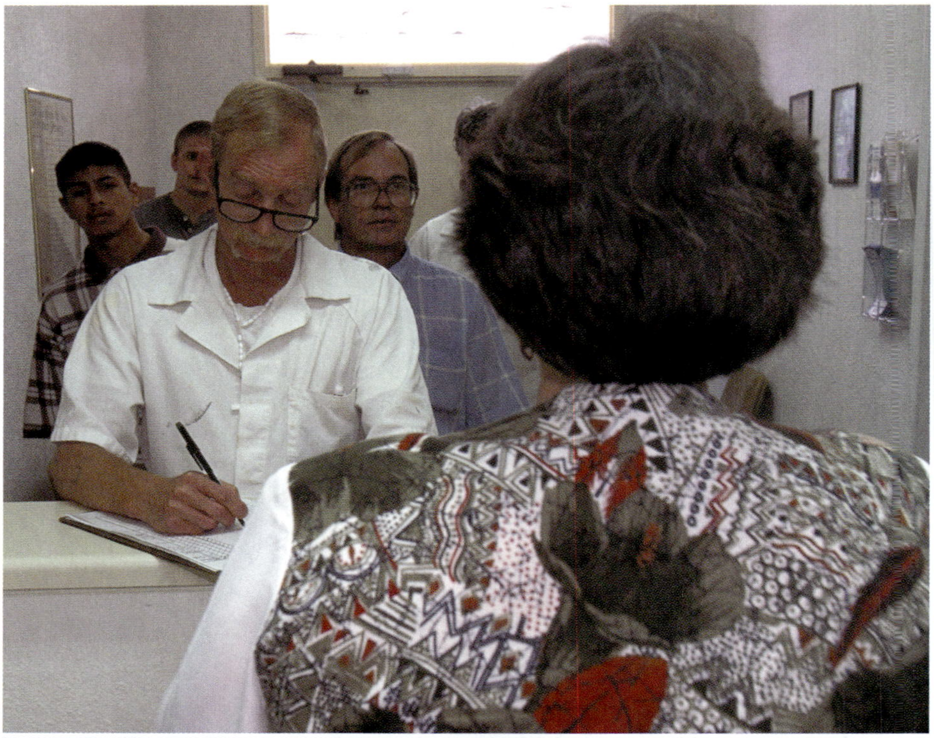

Day reporting centers, which may be publicly or privately operated, are corrections centers where offenders must report regularly to comply with a sentence. Most day center programs include employment, counseling, education, and community service components. *Should the use of day reporting centers be expanded? Why or why not?*

FIGURE 12.6 Metropolitan Day Reporting Center Participant Program Objectives

I, ________________________________, agree to participate in the activities and to adhere to the schedule of this contract. I understand that this contract may be modified during my participation in the Day Reporting Center and I agree to those modifications as determined by my participation.

Objectives *Time frame*

Reporting: I will report in to the Center at the times designated by my case manager and as noted on my daily itinerary.

I will call in to the Center at the times designated by my ca manager and as noted on my daily itinerary.

Supervision: I will be available for phone calls or house checks by Day Reporting Center staff at the locations listed on my daily itine

Employment: Employer: ______
Address: ______
______
Contact Person: ______
Telephone: ______
Hours: ______
Salary: ______
______
______

Financial: I agree to submit my pay stub to the Center for verification c my employment. I further agree to work with my case manager on budgeting my money; including the payment of any court-ordered fines or other restitution.
Details: ______
______
______

Substance Abuse Treatment: I agree to participate in the following program address my substance abuse problems: ______

Urinalysis: I agree to submit to urinalysis testing upon the request of Day Reporting Center staff. ______

Curfew: I understand that I am to be at my residence from the hours of ______ P.M. to ______ A.M., and that I may be contacted by Day Reporting Center staff during that time. ______

Other Objectives: ______

______ ______
Client *Date*

I agree to assist ______________________ to achieve the listed objectives of this contract in my capacity as case manager.

______ ______
Case Manager *Date*

STRUCTURED FINES, OR DAY FINES

structured fines, or **day fines** Fines that are based on defendants' ability to pay.

Another relatively new intermediate sanction, at least in the United States, is structured fines, or day fines.[39] **Structured fines,** or **day fines,** differ fundamentally from the fines (called *tariff fines*) more typically imposed by American criminal courts. Whereas tariff fines require a single fixed amount of money, or an amount of money within a narrow range, to be paid by all defendants convicted of a particular crime, *without regard to their financial circumstances,* structured fines are based on defendants' ability to pay. The basic premise of structured fines is that "punishment by a fine should be proportionate to the seriousness of the offense and should have roughly similar impact (in terms of economic sting) on persons with differing financial resources who are convicted of the same offense."

The creation of a structured fine is a two-part process. In the first part, the number of fine units for a crime is determined from a scale that ranks crimes according to their seriousness. In the second part, the dollar amount of the

FYI: No Time for Fine

The U.S. Supreme Court has ruled that an offender cannot be imprisoned for failure to pay a fine unless the default is willful, if imprisonment is not an authorized penalty for the offense of which the defendant was convicted.

SOURCE: *Tate* v. *Short* (1971).

FYI: Structured Fines

Regarding the use of structured fines, or day fines, in the United States, criminologists Norval Morris and Michael Tonry make this interesting observation: "It is paradoxical that a society that relies so heavily on the financial incentive in its social philosophy and economic practice should be so reluctant to use the financial disincentive as a punishment of crime."

SOURCE: Norval Morris and Michael Tonry (eds.), *Between Prisons and Probation: Intermediate Punishments in a Rational Sentencing System* (New York: Oxford University Press, 1990), p. 111.

fine is determined by multiplying the number of fine units by a proportion of the defendant's net daily income (hence the term *day fine*), adjusted to account for dependents and special circumstances.

Structured fines were first introduced in the 1920s in Sweden and soon thereafter were adopted by other Scandinavian countries. West Germany began employing them in the early 1970s. The western European nations have made day fines the sanction of choice in a large proportion of criminal cases, including many involving serious offenses. For example, in Germany, day fines are used as the only sanction for three-fourths of all offenders convicted of property crimes and for two-thirds of all offenders convicted of assaults.

The first structured-fine program in the United States began in 1988 in Richmond County (Staten Island), New York, as a demonstration project. Other structured-fine demonstration projects have been established in Maricopa County (Phoenix), Arizona; Bridgeport, Connecticut; Polk County (Des Moines), Iowa; and four counties in Oregon (Marion, Malheur, Josephine, and Coos). An evaluation of the Richmond County project, sponsored by the National Institute of Justice, showed very promising results.

Among the presumed advantages of structured-fine or day-fine programs are

1. Offender accountability—"The offender is, quite literally, made to pay his or her debt to society."
2. Deterrence—"Structured fines provide an economic disincentive for criminal behavior."
3. Fairness—Structured fines are fairer than tariff fines because tariff fines frequently are too low to be meaningful to wealthier offenders and too high for poorer offenders to pay.
4. Effective and efficient use of limited system resources—"Structured fines are relatively inexpensive to administer compared with most other types of intermediate sanctions."
5. Revenue—"Structured fines can be more effective than tariff fines in generating revenue."
6. Credibility for the court—Because offenders pay in full in a very large proportion of cases, the sanction has credibility with the offender and the community.

Among the problems with structured fines are

1. Collection problems—"If judges are not convinced that such fines will be paid in a high proportion of cases, or if offenders assume that the fines need not be paid, the usefulness of the structured fine as a criminal sanction is seriously eroded."
2. The effect of other monetary penalties—In most U.S. jurisdictions, defendants convicted of crimes have a variety of monetary penalties to pay, for example, penalty assessment fees, crime victim compensation fees, indigent defense fees, and probation fees. Those monetary sanctions create a high cost to a defendant, even before a fine is imposed. A fine added to those costs may exceed the ability of poorer defendants to pay.

HOME CONFINEMENT AND ELECTRONIC MONITORING

home confinement A program that requires offenders to remain in their homes except for approved periods of absence; commonly used in combination with electronic monitoring.

In **home confinement** programs (also known as home incarceration, home detention, and house arrest), offenders are required by the court to remain in their homes except for preapproved periods of absence. For example, offenders may be permitted to leave home to go to work, school, or church or to run errands. Home confinement is usually considered more punitive than ISP but is often used in conjunction with ISP. For example, home confinement may be required during the initial phase of intensive probation or may be ordered if an offender violates probation or parole. Home confinement can also serve as an alternative to pretrial detention in jail.

House arrest has traditionally been employed in the military and has a long history of limited use in criminal justice. However, home confinement programs did not gain wide popularity until **electronic monitoring** equipment became readily available during the 1980s. Electronic monitoring allows an offender's whereabouts to be gauged through the use of computer technology. Before the use of electronic monitoring, it was time-consuming and expensive for officials to ensure that offenders were complying with home confinement orders. Electronic monitoring rendered home confinement more practical and cost-effective because officials did not have to rely on personal phone calls and home visits to assess compliance with home detention orders. Today, it is very common for home confinement programs to have electronic monitoring components. In June 2002, for example, 10,743 offenders nationwide who otherwise would have been confined in a jail facility were being supervised in a home detention program. That represents about 15 percent of offenders being supervised outside a jail facility. Of those offenders participating in a home detention program, 90 percent were being electronically monitored.[40]

electronic monitoring An arrangement that allows an offender's whereabouts to be gauged through the use of computer technology.

Electronic monitoring devices are used to verify, either through phone lines or radio signals, that offenders are at their designated locations at particular times. The two most popular electronic monitoring devices are the continuously signaling and programmed contact systems. In the continuously signaling system, an offender wears a small transmitter, usually on the ankle, that sends encoded signals to a nearby receiver at regular intervals. In essence, the receiver communicates with the monitoring agency's computer, which contains the offender's schedule, so staff can determine whether the offender is in the designated location at the required time. Under the programmed contact arrangement, the agency's computer generates either random or scheduled phone calls to the designated location, and the offender must respond to the calls. The type of response required from the offender depends on the specific device. For example, some devices require the offender to insert a wristlet into a verifier box hooked on the phone. Others require the offender to speak for purposes of voice verification.

Home confinement and electronic monitoring have not yet been evaluated extensively. However, a national survey found that electronic monitoring has expanded rapidly since its inception. Furthermore, there appears to be a trend toward using electronic monitoring with offenders who have committed more serious crimes.

As might be expected, home confinement and electronic monitoring are controversial practices. This is particularly true of monitoring. Supporters argue that home confinement and monitoring are cost-effective alternatives to incarceration in jail or prison that allow offenders to receive more supervision and punishment than they would receive on traditional probation or parole. Another argument is that offenders are spared the potentially harmful effects of institutionalization, one of the most important of which is the breaking of family ties.

Critics counter with a variety of claims. One important criticism is that home confinement and monitoring encroach on the constitutional rights to privacy, protection

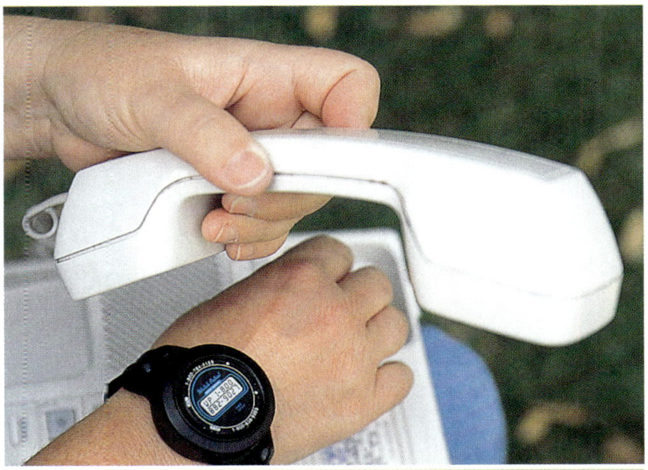

Home confinement requires offenders to remain in their homes except for preapproved periods of absence. Most programs use electronic monitoring equipment to verify that offenders are at their designated locations at particular times. *For what type of offenders are home confinement and electronic monitoring appropriate, and for what type of offenders are they not?*

FYI Electronic Monitoring

Electronic monitoring has rapidly become one of the most widespread and controversial innovations in community corrections since the idea was first introduced, in the 1960s. The first statewide home confinement program without electronic monitoring was implemented in Florida in the early 1980s. St. Louis was one of the cities to pioneer such programming in the early 1970s. Among the first jurisdictions to implement an electronic monitoring program was Palm Beach County, Florida, in 1984.

SOURCE: J. R. Lilly and R. A. Ball, "A Brief History of House Arrest and Electronic Monitoring." *Northern Kentucky Law Review* 13, no. 3 (1987), pp. 343–74.

against self-incrimination, and protection against unreasonable search and seizure. Critics maintain that not only the offender's rights are threatened, but also the rights of persons who share the offender's residence. However, it seems unlikely that the use of those sanctions will be severely restricted on constitutional grounds in the foreseeable future. As criminologists Rolando del Carmen and Joseph Vaughn observe, "A review of decided cases in probation and parole indicates that while the use of electronic devices raises constitutional issues, its constitutionality will most likely be upheld by the courts, primarily based on the concept of diminished rights [for offenders]."[41]

Some people worry that home confinement and electronic monitoring may discriminate against economically disadvantaged persons, who are less likely to have homes and telephone systems for the installation of monitoring devices. Others are concerned that offenders and manufacturers of monitoring equipment have become locked in a perpetual and costly battle to outwit one another. Manufacturers continually work to devise monitors that will resist offender tampering. Meanwhile, offenders seek ways to manipulate the latest monitoring innovations on the market. This situation, of course, is potentially lucrative for equipment vendors, but it is potentially costly for taxpayers and for offenders who must pay monitoring fees. A broader criticism is that a profit incentive is being created to subject more and more persons to government surveillance.

Some people object to monitoring on the grounds that it is impersonal, thus removing the human and helping elements from community corrections. Those critics suggest that by reducing the need for skill and professionalism on the part of probation and parole officers, monitoring may undermine rehabilitation. As criminologist John Conrad writes:

> Probation and parole were once intended to help men and women in the worst kind of trouble to find ways to lead law abiding lives. No more. Official services to

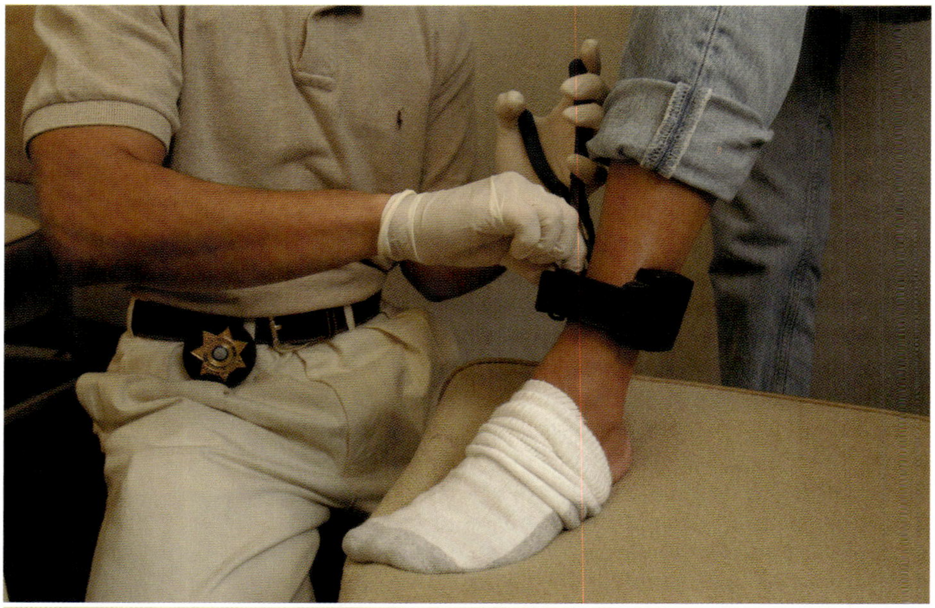

Some electronic monitoring devices use global positioning systems (GPS). *In what ways are GPS-equipped monitoring devices superior to conventional phone or radio signal devices?*

offenders in the community have been transformed into a cat-and-mouse game in which surveillance, not service, has become the primary, if not the exclusive requisite . . . . Electronic surveillance is a recent and welcomed contribution of high technology to the community control of convicted offenders. We settle for temporary control in place of a serious program for changes in attitude, behavior and style of life.[42]

A recent investigation of Florida's house-arrest program provides empirical support for these criticisms. It also reveals some problems heretofore overlooked by house-arrest critics.[43] Florida's house-arrest program, which the Florida Department of Corrections manages and calls "community control," is the largest such program in the United States. In 2002, the state supervised about 10,000 active program participants a day—6 percent of whom were electronically monitored. Since its inception in 1983 and through 2002, more than 215,000 offenders have served time in the program.

A principal reason for the program's creation was the prospect of saving money by reducing the prison population. Whether the program has achieved that goal is a difficult question to answer. On the one hand, participation in house arrest is significantly cheaper than the costs of incarceration. In 2002, house-arrest program participants cost the state as little as $11.16 a day, while state prison inmates cost the state $49.75 a day. By that measure, the program has saved the state of Florida millions of dollars. On the other hand, if in the absence of the program, offenders would have been placed on regular probation, for which the average cost per probationer per day in 2000 was $3.85, then the program produced no cost savings and was just a more expensive alternative to regular probation.

The house-arrest program may have reduced the prison population, but that is not entirely clear, either. From June 1983 through June 2003, Florida's prison population increased each year except from June 1983 to June 1984. During that period, it increased a total of 196 percent. Still, the program may have reduced the prison population by approximately 10,000 inmates per year—the number participating in the house-arrest program. However, if the program participants would have been sentenced to regular probation instead of prison in the absence of the program, then the program has not reduced the prison population.

In any event, Florida's house-arrest program has about a 40 percent success rate. That is, about two of every five program participants (each year between 1996 and 2001) completed a year in the program without being removed for committing new crimes or violating other program rules. The other "unsuccessful" 60 percent of Florida's house-arrest participants were removed from the program and usually incarcerated during the first year for committing crimes or violating rules. About 45 percent of the participants removed from the program violated program rules such as testing positive for drugs, leaving home without authorization, failing to pay restitution, or possessing a firearm.

In addition, during the past two decades, program participants killed at least 234 people and committed at least 538 sex crimes. Approximately 2,000 to 3,000 violent offenders are sentenced to house arrest each year. Of that number, about 400 are placed in the program even though state law prohibits it. In Florida, offenders are not to be placed on house arrest if (1) they have been convicted of a crime that appears on a specific list of violent felonies, including robbery, kidnapping, and assault; and (2) they have a prior conviction from that same list. Judges who sentence such offenders to house arrest either don't know the law or ignore the law. Some judges claim that the law makes no sense. They argue that the law allows some violent offenders

FYI

Costs of Electronic Monitoring

In 2000, the average costs per day for electronic monitoring of probationers and parolees were $4.99 and $23.02, respectively. This compares with average daily costs of $9.94 and $12.42 for intensive probation and parole supervision, $2.16 and $4.76 for regular probation and parole supervision, and $61.04 for prison incarceration.

SOURCE: Camille Graham Camp and George M. Camp, *The 2001 Corrections Yearbook: Adult Systems* (Middletown, CT: Criminal Justice Institute, 2002), pp. 106 and 206.

barred from house arrest to be placed on probation, where they get even less supervision.

Another problem is that between 2,500 and 3,000 house-arrest participants each year flee the program. Although most of them are caught, nearly 5,000 program participants—including 14 killers and 115 people convicted of sex crimes—have not been recaptured. The program is also understaffed. In 2002, for example, the average caseload was 39 even though the state legislature set a limit at 25 cases per officer. By law, officers are supposed to check on program participants three times a week. In practice, however, most participants are checked on only twice a week. For one of those checks, the participant reports to a Department of Corrections office.

House-arrest participants who wear electronic monitors are 5 times more likely to successfully complete their sentences and half as likely to flee the program. However, as noted previously, only about 6 percent of house-arrest participants are electronically monitored. The problem is money. In 2002, it cost \$20.33 a day to monitor an offender by satellite and \$13.91 a day to monitor an offender by radio frequency. By comparison, it cost \$11.16 to supervise a house-arrest participant without electronic monitoring. Florida uses two types of electronic monitoring tracking systems. The newer and more expensive technology utilizes Global Positioning System satellites that track an offender's whereabouts 24 hours a day. The other, older and less expensive technology sends signals over telephone lines. It is called "RF" monitoring for radio frequency. It cannot tell the agency where an offender is, but it can tell when the offender is home or not and alert the department. Both types of monitoring have their problems. For example, the GPS system generates numerous false alarms—a monthly average of 29 false alarms each in 2001. The GPS system's signal also will not penetrate most buildings. Even so, it would seem that electronic monitoring of house-arrest participants would be a good investment, but the Department of Corrections prefers to use the bulk of its resources on prisons.

HALFWAY HOUSES

halfway houses Community-based residential facilities that are less secure and restrictive than prison or jail but provide a more controlled environment than other community correctional programs.

Halfway houses (sometimes referred to as community correctional centers) are community-based residential facilities that are an alternative to confinement in jail or prison. Although those facilities are an alternative to more secure and restrictive placements, they provide a much more controlled environment than is possible with traditional probation and parole, or even with ISP and home confinement. As the term *halfway* implies, the offender is midway between jail or prison and the free community.

The goal of halfway houses is to provide offenders with a temporary (for instance, 6-month) period of highly structured and supportive living so that they will be better prepared to function independently in the community upon discharge. To this end, most programs place a heavy emphasis on addressing offenders' educational and employment deficits. For example, persons who have not completed high school are encouraged to obtain the GED, individuals who have few marketable job skills are encouraged to complete vocational training, and those who lack employment are assisted in finding and keeping jobs.

Halfway houses have existed in the United States since the mid-1800s and, prior to the 1960s, were used primarily for persons coming out of prison and making the transition back into the community. During the 1960s, the number and functions of halfway house programs in the nation expanded. In addition to providing services for parolees and prereleasees (prisoners nearing their release dates), houses began to service probationers, pretrial detainees, and persons on furlough from prison. More recently, in the 1980s, halfway houses became an integral part of the intermediate-sanction movement. They are now sometimes used in conjunction with other intermediate sanctions. For example, as part of a probation sentence, an offender may complete a stay in a halfway house before being discharged to ISP, or a person who has violated a home confinement order may be placed in a halfway house program to give authorities added control.

Halfway houses are quite diverse. Not all houses are for offenders; some facilities serve other populations, such as those with mental disorders or drug addictions. Programs for offenders may serve a specific category of offenders, such as all probationers or all parolees, or some combination of offender groups. In addition, a halfway house's population may be all male, all female, or both male and female. Some houses rely heavily on referrals to other local agencies to ensure that offenders' treatment needs are met, whereas others provide extensive in-house treatment. Programs can be administered publicly or privately, but private administration is more common. Public programs may be administered at the federal, state, or local level of government.

Halfway houses may be operated by private-for-profit or not-for-profit contractors or by public agencies. Some provide room, board, and help with employment. Others provide remedial education, individual or group counseling, and other types of life skills training. *Should halfway houses be restricted in the type of offender that is accepted? If yes, what types of offenders should be barred?*

PROCEDURES Halfway house programming involves five basic procedures:

1. Referral.
2. Administrative screening.
3. Intake and orientation.
4. Program participation.
5. Termination of the stay.

Referral of clients to a halfway house may be done by a correctional institution (as in the case of prereleasees), a court, or a probation or parole agency. The fundamental issue referral sources must confront is whether the offender will benefit from halfway house placement without compromising community safety. Thus, such factors as the offender's propensity for violence and degree of employment and educational deficits are generally given great weight in determining whether to make a referral.

When a referral is made, the next step is *administrative screening*, in which halfway house administrators examine the case and decide whether to accept the offender into the program. Some house administrators have more authority to reject referrals than others. Administrators of private houses often have more discretion to decline referrals than do administrators of public programs. An important point to note is that referral sources and house administrators are sometimes motivated by differing objectives. For instance, correctional institution staff may be motivated by the desire to reduce crowding in their facilities, whereas house administrators may wish to maximize the rate of successful discharge from their programs.

If administrative screening results in a decision to accept the referral, the focus shifts to *intake and orientation*. This entails assessing the new resident's risks and needs as well as orienting him or her to the rules, expectations, and routines of the program. An important aspect of intake and orientation is determining exactly what the resident should accomplish during the stay to improve his or her life and reduce the likelihood of recidivism. That determination is usually written as a treatment plan with specific goals and objectives.

CJ ONLINE

ICCA

To learn more about halfway houses, visit the website of the International Community Corrections Association (ICCA), formerly the International Halfway House Association, at **www.iccaweb.org/** *Does working in a halfway house appeal to you? Why or why not?*

With respect to *program participation*, many halfway houses have a series of levels, or phases, through which residents must pass to receive a successful discharge. Typically, each level is associated with progressively more demanding goals and responsibilities for the resident to meet and also with more privileges and freedoms. For example, a requirement for an offender to move from the entry level to the second level may be the successful completion of a job skills class. Upon promotion to level two, the offender may receive one weekend furlough per month to spend with family and friends. Promotion to level three may carry additional furlough time and require that the offender obtain a job and complete a class on job retention skills.

As noted previously, halfway houses usually provide a variety of treatment services, such as employment counseling and training, life skills training, substance abuse intervention, and remedial education. Those services are provided either directly by house staff or indirectly through referrals to community agencies. To allow control and supervision, houses have a number of rules that govern both the in-house behavior of residents and residents' activities away from the facility. Those rules cover such matters as interaction between residents, care of facility property, curfews, and the use of alcohol. Progress through program levels requires completion of the goals and responsibilities associated with a particular level, participation in relevant treatment components, and compliance with house rules. Failure to achieve goals, to complete treatment components, or to abide by rules can result in the resident's staying at a given level or being demoted to a lower level.

A resident's behavior must be monitored and periodically reviewed throughout the term of program participation because, ultimately, the house administration must decide the resident's *termination,* or discharge, status. Residents who have satisfactorily completed all of the required levels are discharged into the community, frequently under probation or parole supervision. If a resident fails to make satisfactory progress through levels in a reasonable time, compiles an excessive number of less serious rule violations, or commits a serious rule infraction (such as another felony), the resident can also be discharged from the facility. An unsuccessful discharge can be granted at any point in a resident's stay and is frequently followed by incarceration.

Issues Several issues surround the use of halfway houses. Two of the most critical issues are (1) the relations between a halfway house and the local community of which it is a part and (2) recidivism among persons who have been discharged from the house.

For a halfway house to be established in a community and to operate effectively, cooperative relations between the staff of the house and members of the community are essential. Halfway house staff often depend on the surrounding community for such things as resident health care, counseling services, educational programming, and job placements. Furthermore, unfavorable reactions from community members toward residents will simply reinforce the sense of marginalization and alienation that many offenders already experience. To the extent that community members feel threatened by residents or have poor relations with staff, the halfway house program is in jeopardy.

Virtually all halfway houses must confront the issue of community resistance, and some must confront outright hostility from community members. There are at least two keys to doing this effectively. First, halfway house officials must actively cultivate support and assistance from community members by engaging in open, honest communication with them from the earliest possible stage of the halfway house's existence. Many fears that community members have of residents are founded on inaccurate, media-fueled stereotypes and can be reduced with realistic, factual information. Second, it is very

FYI

Halfway Houses for White-Collar Offenders

The Justice Department is no longer allowing the U.S. Bureau of Prisons to assign first-time nonviolent white-collar offenders to federal halfway houses instead of prisons. Advocates of the nearly two-decade-old practice argue that it reduced prison crowding and encouraged rehabilitation of low-risk offenders. Critics claim that the practice allowed wealthy white-collar offenders to circumvent sentencing guidelines and escape prison.

Source: Dan Eggen, "Wealthy Criminals Will Head for Prison," *The Orlando Sentinel*, January 7, 2003, p. A5.

helpful if community members can see that the halfway house is contributing something of value to the community, rather than simply consuming resources. For example, house residents can be involved in well-publicized and highly visible community service projects that save tax dollars. Also, in houses where a high proportion of residents are employed, community residents should be frequently reminded that residents are contributing to the tax base instead of consuming public revenue as jail or prison inmates. If community members can be convinced that the halfway house has a positive, contributing side, they are likely to be more accepting of the house.

Just as there are ways to facilitate cooperative community relations, there also are ways to create unfavorable relations. One way to almost ensure poor relations is for the halfway house to be sprung on the community without any notice of the desire of officials to establish the house and without community input in the early planning process. Another common mistake is for halfway house officials to be content with a low-profile image once the house is established. Believing that adequate community relations will exist as long as offenders are controlled and unfavorable media exposure is avoided, officials may try to minimize exposure of house operations to the public. The typical result is an atmosphere of secrecy, suspicion, and distrust. When the inevitable negative incident occurs, such as a crime by a resident against a community member, public outcry against the house is likely.

Myth	Fact
When an offender halfway house is established in a neighborhood, crime rates increase and property values fall.	Research on this subject has confirmed neither of those assumptions. Crime rates and property values tend to remain the same.

How many persons placed in halfway houses successfully complete their stays, and how high is recidivism among former residents after discharge? Those questions were addressed in a recent study of 156 probationers admitted to a halfway house in Michigan.[44] The study found that nearly 60 percent of all probationers received unsuccessful discharges. However, other studies have discovered successful discharge figures as high as 60 percent.[45] The Michigan study tracked former halfway house residents for 7 years after their discharges. The researchers found that approximately 67 percent of the former residents were arrested at least once during the 7-year period for some type of criminal activity; about 60 percent were arrested at least once for felonies. However, persons who had successfully completed the halfway house program were significantly less likely to incur new arrests than the persons who had not done so. For instance, 44 percent of the persons who had received successful discharges were arrested for new felonies, compared with 68.8 percent of those who had received unsuccessful discharges.

In another study, the recidivism of offenders who had been placed in halfway house programs was compared with the recidivism of those placed on regular probation supervision. Using a 3-year follow-up period, the researchers found that 29.5 percent of the former halfway house residents and 30.7 percent of the regular probationers experienced new criminal convictions. Slightly more than 40 percent of the halfway house residents had failed to complete their programs successfully.[46]

Research clearly suggests that a large number of offenders placed in halfway houses do not successfully complete their programs. However, those who do receive successful discharges seem less likely to commit new crimes than those who do not. Yet, there is little reason to believe that halfway houses are associated with less recidivism than other types of community corrections programs.

THINKING CRITICALLY

1. Do you think people should have the right to reject the placement of a halfway house in their neighborhood? *Why or why not?*
2. What could be done to bring about good relations between a community and the halfway house located within the community?

Temporary-Release Programs

temporary-release programs Programs that allow jail or prison inmates to leave the facility for short periods to participate in approved community activities.

Temporary-release programs allow inmates in jail or prison to leave the facility for short periods to participate in approved community activities. Those programs are designed to permit inmates to establish or maintain community ties, thereby gradually preparing them for reentry into society. The programs also give institutional authorities a means of testing the readiness of inmates for release as well as a means of controlling institutional behavior. Not surprisingly, opportunities for temporary release create a major incentive for inmates to engage in the conduct desired by officials.

Three common temporary-release programs are work release, study release, and furloughs. The persons involved in such programs may be prison or jail inmates, or halfway house residents. As should be apparent from the previous section of this chapter, temporary release is an integral aspect of halfway houses. In prisons and jails, temporary release is reserved for inmates who have demonstrated that they are appropriate candidates to participate in community-based activities.

Organized temporary-release programs are not new in American corrections. Although the programs date to the early 1900s, they did not gain widespread popularity until the 1960s, when the emphasis on community corrections began to grow. Today, almost all states offer temporary release.[47]

In work-release programs, inmates leave the facility for certain hours each day to work for employers in the free community. Work-release inmates are paid prevailing wages, but they are usually required to submit their paychecks to corrections officials to deduct for such things as dependent support and restitution orders before placing the balance in inmates' accounts. Inmates may withdraw some money while in the facility but are usually required to save a certain amount for their ultimate release from incarceration. A limitation of such programs is that most inmates must settle for low-skilled and low-paying jobs. This limitation exists because

1. A large proportion of inmates lack the educational and vocational backgrounds needed to secure higher-paying employment.
2. There is more competition for higher-paying jobs.
3. Many employers are reluctant to hire work-release inmates, especially for jobs that pay well and require skill and responsibility.

Study-release inmates can leave prison for high school equivalency classes, vocational training, or college coursework. A limitation of study release is that, unlike work release, it does not generate financial resources. If inmates cannot pay for their own educational programs or obtain financial aid, study release must be funded by the jurisdiction. Even in the unlikely event that a jurisdiction has resources to fund study release, there may still be reluctance to do so because of the argument that inmates are getting free education at taxpayers' expense.

In furlough programs, inmates are granted leaves of absence for brief periods (for example, 48 hours) to accomplish specific things. Inmates may be granted furloughs to spend time with family members, to attend funerals, or to search for employment and housing before release.

One commonly voiced fear about temporary-release programs is that inmates will flee or commit serious crimes while away from the facility. In fact, research shows that most inmates neither flee nor commit serious offenses. The most frequent problems are late returns and the use of alcohol and illegal drugs.

Temporary-release programs became a significant issue in the U.S. presidential election campaign of 1988. Massachusetts Governor Michael Dukakis, the Democratic presidential nominee, was heavily criticized by Vice President

Temporary release programs allow inmates in jail or prison to leave the facility for short periods to participate in approved community activities. *Should temporary release from jail or prison be allowed? Why or why not?*

George Bush, the Republican nominee, for allowing temporary release of inmates with records of violence. Willie Horton, a black man who had been serving a first-degree murder sentence at a Massachusetts institution, committed violent crimes against a white couple during his tenth furlough from the institution. Bush made much of the "liberal" prison release policies of Massachusetts in an attempt to discredit Dukakis.

Around the same time, an evaluation of temporary release in Massachusetts was being conducted. The evaluation was published in 1991.[48] The researchers studied persons released from Massachusetts facilities between 1973 and 1983. Offenders were tracked for 1 year after release, and recidivism was defined as return to prison. The recidivism of persons who participated in furloughs, prerelease-center (halfway house) programs, and both furloughs and prerelease centers was compared with the recidivism of persons who participated in neither. Using statistical controls for differences in offenders' backgrounds, researchers concluded that "prerelease programs following prison furloughs, and prison furloughs alone, appear to reduce dramatically the risks to public safety after release." This study implies that eliminating or significantly curtailing temporary-release programs is likely to result in a long-term decline in community safety and an increase in recidivism.

THINKING CRITICALLY

1. Do you think offenders should be allowed to take college courses, at taxpayers' expense, through study-release programs? *Why or why not?*
2. Do you think temporary-release programs help rehabilitate offenders? *Why or why not?*

SUMMARY

1. Define community corrections and identify the goals and responsibilities of community corrections agencies and their staffs

   Although community corrections programs are very diverse across the nation, the common feature of those programs is that they provide supervision and treatment services for offenders outside jails and prisons. The dual emphasis on supervision and treatment creates a potential role conflict for community corrections staff. There is some indication, however, that the traditional focus on treatment has been declining relative to the growing emphasis on supervision.

2. Define probation and summarize the research findings on recidivism rates

   The most commonly used type of community sentence is probation. Offenders placed on probation are supervised and provided with various services in the community instead of being incarcerated. In return, they are required to abide by the rules of the probation sentence. Overall, studies indicate that probation is about as effective as incarceration in controlling recidivism. Available data indicate that recidivism is quite high among felons sentenced to probation. Furthermore, research has not found a strong association between probation officers' caseloads and the likelihood of probationer recidivism. If anything, reduced caseloads seem to increase the probability that instances of recidivism will be detected.

3. Distinguish parole from probation

   Unlike probation, parole is not a court-imposed sentence. Parole is a mechanism of releasing persons from prison and a means of supervising them after release, instead of an alternative to an incarceration sentence. Parole supervision is often confused with probation because the two share many similarities. Four major objectives of parole agencies are to: (1) preserve community safety by supervising the behavior of parolees; (2) promote the betterment of parolees by responding to their treatment needs; (3) control prison crowding; and (4) control the behavior of prison inmates by providing early release opportunities in exchange for good prison conduct.

4. Explain the functions of a parole board

   In general, a parole board directs a jurisdiction's parole policies and manages the parole release and termination processes. Parole board members (or their representatives) conduct parole-grant hearings to determine which inmates should receive early release from prison. Boards also determine whether to revoke the parole of persons who have violated parole conditions. In most states, field service agencies are administratively independent of parole boards. A field service agency provides community supervision and treatment services for persons who have been granted parole release by the board and makes recommendations to the board concerning termination of parole.

5. Describe how intermediate sanctions differ from traditional community corrections programs

   Compared with traditional programs in community corrections, intermediate sanctions are oriented less toward rehabilitation and more toward retribution, deterrence, and incapacitation. They are more punitive and more restrictive. The recent popularity of intermediate sanctions is attributable largely to the record high levels of prison crowding that plague many jurisdictions and a corresponding need to devise acceptable alternatives to imprisonment.

6. Explain two major concerns about intensive-supervision probation and parole (ISP)

   Two major concerns about ISP are (1) the potential for net-widening, and (2) the lack of demonstrated reduction of recidivism. Net-widening occurs when offenders placed in a novel program such as ISP are not the offenders for whom the program was intended. The consequence is that those in the program receive more severe sanctions than they would have received had the new program been unavailable. Studies show that ISP is associated with a substantially higher percentage of technical violations than alternative sanctions such as regular probation, prison, or regular parole.

7. Explain what day reporting centers and structured fines are

   Day reporting centers allow offenders to live at home but require them to report to the center regularly to confer with center staff about supervision and treatment matters. Program components commonly focus on work, education, counseling, and community service. Structured fines, or day fines, differ fundamentally from the fines (called tariff fines*) more typically imposed by American criminal courts. Whereas tariff fines require a single fixed amount of money, or an amount within a narrow range, to be paid by all defendants convicted of a particular crime, without regard to their financial circumstances, structured fines, or day fines, are based on defendants' ability to pay. The basic premise of structured fines is that punishment by a fine should be proportionate to the seriousness of the offense and should have a roughly similar economic impact on persons with differing financial resources who are convicted of the same offense.*

8. Explain what home confinement and electronic monitoring are

In home confinement programs (also known as home incarceration, home detention, and house arrest), offenders are required by the court to remain in their homes except for preapproved periods of absence. Electronic monitoring, which is generally coupled with home confinement, allows an offender's whereabouts to be gauged through the use of computer technology.

9. Identify the goal of halfway houses and compare them with other community corrections programs

The goal of halfway houses is to provide offenders with a temporary (for instance, 6-month) period of highly structured and supportive living so that they will be better prepared to function independently in the community upon discharge. To this end, most programs place a heavy emphasis on addressing offenders' educational and employment deficits. Research clearly suggests that a large number of offenders placed in halfway houses do not successfully complete their programs. However, those who do receive successful discharges seem less likely to commit new crimes than those who do not. Yet, there is little reason to believe that halfway houses are associated with less recidivism than other community corrections programs.

10. Summarize the purposes and outcomes of temporary-release programs

By allowing incarcerated persons to temporarily leave their facilities to participate in approved activities in the community, temporary-release programs are intended to foster ties between inmates and their communities, thus gradually preparing inmates for return to society. These programs also give officials a way to judge the readiness of inmates for release, and since most inmates want to participate in temporary release, the programs give inmates an incentive to maintain good institutional behavior. Although fear and other forms of resistance from community members often plague the programs, there is evidence that participation in temporary release is associated with a decreased likelihood of recidivism upon release from incarceration. Some common types of temporary release include work release, study release, and furlough.

KEY TERMS

community corrections, p. 425
probation, p. 428
diversion, p. 430
presentence investigation (PSI), p. 432
probation conditions, p. 435
restitution, p. 435
revocation, p. 436
technical violations, p. 436
recidivism, p. 439
parole, p. 440
parole guidelines, p. 443
reintegration, p. 449
intermediate sanctions, p. 452
intensive-supervision probation and parole (ISP), p. 453
net widening, p. 454
day reporting centers, p. 456
structured fines, or day fines, p. 457
home confinement, p. 458
electronic monitoring, p. 459
halfway houses, p. 462
temporary-release programs, p. 466

REVIEW QUESTIONS

1. What are David Duffee's three varieties of community corrections, and how do they differ?
2. What are three aspects of the helping role of community corrections staff?
3. Why is community corrections important?
4. What are five types of probation?
5. What are three fundamental objectives of probation agencies?
6. What is a probation subsidy, and what is its goal?
7. What is the main task of the PSI?
8. What are two types of probation conditions, and how do they differ?
9. For what general types of violations can probation be revoked?
10. What two landmark Supreme Court cases define the procedural guidelines for revoking probation or parole?
11. What are two general types of parole, and what is their function?
12. According to a recent study, what are the four most important factors parole authorities consider before granting release on parole?
13. What are some criticisms of parole release?
14. What are two ways that halfway house officials might effectively confront community resistance?

IN THE FIELD

1. **Tour a Probation Agency** Take a guided tour of the probation or parole agency in your community. (1) Ask the guide to explain the various activities of the agency. Also ask to speak with various officers about their work. (2) Request sample copies of agency documents, such as risk-and-needs-assessment instruments. (3) Write a short essay describing what the agency documents reveal about the work of the agency.

2. **Evaluate Halfway House Rules** Obtain a copy of the rules of behavior for a halfway house. (1) Evaluate the rules, and decide whether you think they are too strict, not strict enough, or on target. (2) Rewrite any rules that you think need changing.

ON THE NET

1. **Local Community Corrections** Visit the Sedgwick County, Kansas, Department of Corrections, Community Corrections website (www.sedgwick.ks.us/corrections/index.html) or the North Carolina Department of Correction, Division of Community Corrections website (www.doc.state.nc.us/dcomcor). Choose from the topics provided, and write a brief summary of the information you find and how it is related to community corrections.
2. **U.S. Parole Commission** Visit the website of the United States Parole Commission at www.usdoj.gov/uspc and click on "Our History" to read a contextual history of the federal parole system. Then click on "Answering Your Questions" for the answers to many commonly asked questions about federal parole. Write a short essay explaining why you support or oppose the 1987 abolition of federal parole.

CRITICAL THINKING EXERCISES

1. **Probation/Parole Officer** You are a probation or parole officer. Your caseload averages 100 clients.
   a. A client tells you that her boss is treating her unfairly at work because of her criminal record and probation or parole status. Your client is afraid of being fired and having her probation or parole revoked. What do you do?
   b. You discover that a client is using marijuana. You like the client, and other than the marijuana use, he has been doing well on probation or parole. What do you do?
   c. You have a problem client who is using drugs (marijuana and cocaine), hanging out with a "bad" group of people, and probably (though you have no hard evidence) committing petty thefts to support her drug habit. You have warned the client to stop this behavior, but she has ignored your warnings. Furthermore, the client has threatened to harm you and your family should you revoke her probation or parole. What do you do?
   d. You have a client who, as a condition of his probation or parole, is required to earn his GED. Although the client has been attending classes regularly and seems to be trying very hard, his teacher informs you that the client just does not have the intellectual capacity to earn the GED. What do you do?
2. **Halfway House** As an employee of your state department of corrections, you have been asked to establish a halfway house for parolees, all of whom are former substance abuse offenders, in the nice, middle-class community where you live. Assuming that you take the job, how would you address the following questions?
   a. Would you communicate to the community your intention of establishing the halfway house? Why or why not?
   b. How would you address community resistance to the halfway house should it arise?
   c. Would you ask community residents to aid you in your efforts? Why or why not?
   d. Besides community resistance, what other problems might arise in your effort to establish the halfway house? How would you handle them?
   e. Would you be willing to remain a resident of the community after the halfway house is established (especially if you have a family with small children)? Why or why not?

PART FIVE

Additional Issues in Criminal Justice

CHAPTER THIRTEEN

Juvenile Justice

CHAPTER FOURTEEN

The Future of Criminal Justice in the United States

JUVENILE JUSTICE

CHAPTER THIRTEEN

Chapter Outline

Chapter Objectives

After completing this chapter, you should be able to:

1. Describe some of the early institutions used to respond to wayward and criminal youths.
2. Explain the effects of some landmark U.S. Supreme Court cases on the juvenile justice system.
3. Identify and describe factors that influence the ways that police process juvenile cases.
4. Summarize the rationale for the use of diversion in juvenile justice.
5. Describe the adjudication hearing in juvenile justice.
6. Describe the disposition hearing and the types of dispositions available to the juvenile court.
7. Identify the types and describe the effectiveness of community-based correctional programs for juveniles.
8. Summarize recent trends in juvenile incarceration.
9. Identify the types and describe the effectiveness of institutional programs for juveniles.

Crime Story

On January 25, 2001, a jury unanimously convicted Lionel Tate of first-degree murder. The judge stunned the court when he ordered Tate to serve the rest of his life in prison, which is a mandatory sentence in the state of Florida. Tate was 12-years old when he killed family friend and occasional playmate, 6-year-old Tiffany Eunick. He became what is believed to be the youngest person in America ever sentenced to life in prison without parole.

Tate's trial raised questions about the manner in which juveniles are prosecuted in the United States. On the night of Tiffany's death, Lionel and Tiffany were allegedly play-wrestling downstairs in his home while Lionel's mother was taking a nap upstairs before her scheduled work shift as a Florida State Trooper. Tate's mother recalled hearing a noise coming from downstairs and asking Lionel what it was. He replied to her that it was "Tiff." Shortly after 11 P.M. Lionel entered his mother's room where she was still napping and told her Tiffany was not breathing. Lionel admitted to accidentally throwing Tiffany against a stairway post. He later revealed in an ABC News telephone interview with Barbara Walters that he playfully jumped on the girl from the stairs. The autopsy results showed Tiffany suffered a crushed skull, broken ribs, and a shredded liver. Lionel was nearly 6 feet tall and 166 pounds at age 12. At trial, his defense attorneys argued unsuccessfully that he was only playing and did not intend to kill his friend.

On September 2, 2003, Tate's lawyers argued before Florida's Fourth District Court of Appeals to have his life sentence for murder commuted because of his inability to understand the severity of his punishment at time of sentencing. On December 10, 2003, the appeals court ordered a new trial for Tate ruling that his competency should have been evaluated prior to trial. Before his new trial, however, on January 30, 2004, Tate pleaded guilty to second-degree murder, accepting the same plea bargain that his lawyers and mother had rejected prior to his original trial. The plea deal required him to serve 3 years in a juvenile detention facility, which he had already done; to spend the next year on house arrest, only allowed to leave for school, church, or other approved outings; and to follow the year of house arrest with 10 years of probation, 1,000 hours of community service, and psychological testing and counseling. Tate could be sentenced to life in prison without parole again if he violates any conditions of the deal.

Chapter 13 discusses the processing of juvenile offenders. Society has a long history of struggling over how to process and treat juvenile offenders, and how to determine at what age a person is able to form criminal intent for the commission of a crime. Some observers suggest children are too immature to form the "evilness" required to commit certain acts of violence and therefore deserve compassion. Others suggest the retributive notion that if juvenile offenders are going to commit adult-style crimes, then juveniles should suffer the same consequences. Has the appropriate justice been served in the case of Lionel Tate? The unique circumstances surrounding the Tate case undoubtedly polarize the view of observers and compel us to analyze the juvenile justice system in America.

Historical Development of Juvenile Justice

From a historical perspective, juvenile delinquency and a separate justice process for juveniles are recent concepts. So, too, are the ideas of childhood and adolescence. **Juvenile delinquency,** as you may recall from Chapter 2, is a special category of offense created for youths—that is, in most U.S. jurisdictions, persons between the ages of 7 and 18. Through most of recorded history, the young have not enjoyed the statuses of childhood and adolescence as special times during which the young need nurturing and guidance for their healthy development.

juvenile delinquency A special category of offense created for youths who, in most U.S. jurisdictions, are persons between the ages of 7 and 18.

Before the sixteenth century, the young were viewed either as property or as miniature adults who, by the age of 5 or 6, were expected to assume the responsibilities of adults. They were also subject to the same criminal sanctions as adults. However, in the sixteenth and seventeenth centuries, a different view of the young emerged that recognized childhood as a distinct period of life, and children as corruptible but worth correcting.[1] Youths began to be viewed, not as miniature adults or as property, but rather as persons who required molding and guidance to become moral and productive members of the community. American colonists brought with them those new ideas about childhood as well as European mechanisms for responding to violators of social and legal rules.

During the colonial period, the family was the basic unit of economic production and the primary mechanism through which social control was exerted. Survival depended on the family's ability to produce what it needed, rather than relying on the production of others. Consequently, a primary responsibility of the family was overseeing the moral training and discipline of the young. During this period, two age-old mechanisms were employed to teach children who were difficult to handle or needed supervision a trade to allow them an opportunity to earn a livelihood. One of those mechanisms was the **apprenticeship system,** which served as a primary means for teaching skilled trades to the children of the middle and upper classes. The other tradition was the binding-out system, which was reserved for poor children. Under the **binding-out system,** children were bound over to masters for care.

apprenticeship system The method by which middle- and upper-class children were taught skilled trades by a master.

binding-out system Practice in which children were "bound over" to masters for care. However, under the binding-out system, masters were not required to teach youths a trade.

Description when liberated.
Age (on discharge) 11
Height .... 4 ft 1 3/4
Hair .... Brown
Eyes .... Brown
Complexion .... Fresh
Where born .... Middlesex
Married or single .... Single
Trade or occupation .... None
Any other distinguishing mark .... Scar on forehead and on right shoulder

Photograph of Prisoner.

Until the early 1900s, children were subject to the same punishments as adults. *Should children be punished in the same way as adults? Why or why not?*

However, under this system, masters were not required to teach the youths a trade. As a result, boys were often given farming tasks, while girls were assigned to domestic duties.[2]

Religion, particularly in New England, was another powerful force that shaped social life in the colonies. Regular church attendance was expected, and religious beliefs dominated ideas about appropriate behavior. Present-day concerns about the separation of church and state were nonexistent. What was believed to be immoral was also unlawful and subject to punishment by the authorities. Punishments such as fines, whipping, branding, and the use of stocks and the pillory served as reminders to both young and old that violations of community norms would not go unpunished.[3]

By the early 1800s, the social organization of colonial life began to change as a result of economic and social developments. The family-based production unit that had characterized colonial social life was giving way to a factory-based system in the growing towns. As parents—particularly fathers—and children began to leave the home for work in a factory, fundamental changes occurred in the relationships between family members and in the role of the family in controlling the behavior of children. Further, as industry developed and as towns grew, communities became more diverse and experienced problems on a scale unheard of during earlier periods.

THE DEVELOPMENT OF INSTITUTIONS FOR YOUTHS

FYI

Juvenile Crime Wave

Each generation of Americans seems to believe that the country is experiencing a "juvenile crime wave."

SOURCE: Thomas J. Bernard, *The Cycle of Juvenile Justice* (New York: Oxford University Press, 1992).

At the time of the American Revolution, Philadelphia had fewer than 20,000 residents, and other large towns, such as New York, Boston, Newport, and Charleston, had fewer than 15,000 inhabitants each. However, by 1820, the population of New York City was about 120,000 and was growing rapidly as a result of immigration. Immigration, in turn, was changing the composition of communities, which had been more homogeneous during colonial times.

houses of refuge The first specialized correctional institutions for youths in the United States.

THE HOUSES OF REFUGE Accompanying those changes in the social and economic life of the growing cities were a host of social problems, such as poverty, vagrancy, drunkenness, and crime, including crimes committed by children. In response to those conditions, the first correctional institutions specifically for youths developed. Those institutions were called **houses of refuge.** The first was established in New York City in 1825, and houses of refuge soon spread to other cities such as Boston and Philadelphia.[4]

A primary goal of the houses of refuge was to prevent pauperism and to respond to youths who were ignored by the courts. Houses of refuge were meant to be institutions where children could be reformed and turned into hard-working members of the community. To accomplish this mission, youths were placed in houses of refuge for indeterminate periods or until their 18th or 21st birthdays. Placement, moreover, did not require a court hearing. A child could be committed to a house of refuge by a constable, by a parent, or on the order of a city alderman.[5]

While there, children engaged in a daily regimen of hard work, military drills, and enforced silence, as well as religious and academic training. It was also common practice for outside contractors to operate shops within the houses of refuge. In those shops, children produced goods such as shoes or furniture, and in return, the houses of refuge were paid 10 to 15 cents per youth each day. This arrangement allowed houses of refuge to pay a substantial percentage of their daily operating expenses.[6] When the youthful inmates failed to meet production quotas, they were often punished. After "reformation," boys were frequently indentured to masters on farms or to tradesmen, and girls were placed in domestic service.[7]

Houses of refuge were the first correctional institutions specifically for youths. *Should houses of refuge be used again for delinquent youths? Why or why not?*

Placing Out Soon after the establishment of houses of refuge, reformers began to recognize the inability of those institutions to accommodate the large numbers of children needing placement and to either reform or control youths. One early response to those problems was the development of placing out. **Placing out,** which involved the placing of children on farms in the West and Midwest, was believed to have several advantages over the houses of refuge. First, placing out was seen as a way of removing children from the supposedly corrupting influences of their parents, who frequently were immigrants, and especially of the cities, which reformers viewed as breeding grounds for idleness and crime. Second, many reformers recognized that the conditions in the houses of refuge were counterproductive to the goal of reform. Third, rural areas were assumed to be an ideal environment for instilling in children the values the reformers cherished—values that stressed discipline, hard work, and piety.

placing out The practice of placing children on farms in the Midwest and West to remove them from the supposedly corrupting influences of their parents and the cities.

Agents hired by charitable organizations would take children west by train and place them with farm families. Although some children were placed in caring homes and were treated as members of the family, others were not so lucky. Many of the children who were placed out were required to work hard for their keep, were abused, were not accepted as members of the family, and never saw their own families again.

Probation Another effort to deal with troubled children was initiated by a Boston shoemaker, John Augustus. As described in Chapter 12, Augustus spent considerable time observing the court and became convinced that many minor offenders could be salvaged. As a result of his concern and his willingness to work with offenders, Augustus was permitted to provide bail for his first probation client in 1841.

Augustus's first client was a drunkard who showed remarkable improvement during the period in which he was supervised. The court was impressed with Augustus's work and permitted him to stand bail for other minor offenders, including children.

After Augustus died, the Boston Children's Aid Society and other volunteers carried on his work. Then, in 1869, the state of Massachusetts formalized the existing volunteer probation system by authorizing visiting probation agents, who were to work with both adult and child offenders who showed promise. Under this arrangement, youths were allowed to return home to their parents, provided they obeyed the law.[8] In 1878, an additional law was passed in Boston that provided for paid probation officers.[9] Subsequently, several other states authorized the appointment of probation officers. However, it was not until after the turn of the twentieth century and the development of the first juvenile court that probation gained widespread acceptance.[10]

reform, industrial, or **training schools** Correctional facilities for youths, first developed in the late 1800s, that focused on custody. Today, those institutions are often called training schools and although they may place more emphasis on treatment, they still rely on custody and control.

cottage reformatories Correctional facilities for youths, first developed in the late 1800s, that were intended to closely parallel family life and remove children from the negative influences of the urban environment. Children in those facilities lived with surrogate parents, who were responsible for the youths' training and education.

Reform Schools, Industrial Schools, and Training Schools By the late 1800s, the failure of houses of refuge was well known. Dislocations produced by the Civil War placed tremendous strain on houses of refuge and the placing out system. Perhaps most disappointing, the number of problem youths was growing. In response, state and city governments took over the administration of institutions for juvenile delinquents. Another response was the establishment of **reform, industrial,** or **training schools,** correctional facilities that focused on custody.[11] Those institutions were of two types: cottage reformatories and institutional reformatories.

Cottage reformatories were usually located in rural areas to avoid the negative influences of the urban environment. They were intended to closely

Juveniles incarcerated at the turn of the twentieth century were put into job training programs that would help them when they were released. Typically, male offenders learned industrial trades; female offenders learned ironing, laundry work, and cooking. *Should these practices be revived? Why or why not?*

parallel family life. Each cottage contained 20–40 youths, who were supervised by cottage parents charged with the task of overseeing residents' training and education.[12]

In addition to cottage reformatories, larger, more institutional reformatories were developed in many states. Like the cottage reformatories, the institutional reformatories were usually located in rural areas in an effort to remove youths from the negative influences of city life. However, the institutions were frequently large and overcrowded.

Another development, in the late 1800s, was the establishment of separate institutions for females. Previously, girls had been committed to the same institutions as boys, although there was strict gender segregation in those institutions. Moreover, girls were often committed by parents or relatives for moral, as opposed to criminal, offenses. Those moral offenses consisted of such actions as "vagrancy, beggary, stubbornness, deceitfulness, idle and vicious behavior, wanton and lewd conduct, and running away."[13] The expressed goal of those institutions was to prepare girls to be good housewives and mothers. Yet, the institutions, like those for boys, were little different from the prisons of that era.

The reform, industrial, and training schools placed more emphasis on formal education than did the houses of refuge, but in many other respects there was little difference. Indeed, those institutions confronted many of the same problems as the houses of refuge had. Moreover, the conditions in the reformatories were certainly no better than those in the houses of refuge, and in many cases they were worse.

THE DEVELOPMENT OF THE JUVENILE COURT

By the end of the 1800s, a variety of institutions and mechanisms had been developed in response to problem children. Still, the problems presented by children who were believed to be in need of correctional treatment—problems such as homelessness, neglect, abuse, waywardness, and criminal behavior—proved difficult to solve. Consequently, during the late 1800s a new group of reformers, the *child savers,* began to advocate a new institution to deal with youth problems. This new institution was the juvenile court.

The Social Context of the Juvenile Court The period from 1880 to 1920, a period historians refer to as the Progressive Era, was a time of major change in the United States. Although industrialization and urbanization were well underway, and previous waves of immigrants had added to the population of the country, the pace of industrialization, urbanization, and immigration quickened.

In an effort to respond to the problem of youth crime and waywardness, reformers again sought to save children from the crime-inducing conditions of the cities. Supported by important philanthropic and civic organizations, the child savers worked to improve jail and reformatory conditions. However, the primary outcome of the child-saving movement was the extension of governmental control over children's lives. The child savers argued for stricter supervision of children, and they improved legal mechanisms designed to regulate children's activities.[14] In short, the child savers felt that children needed to be protected and that the best institutions for protecting them were government agencies such as the police and the courts, as well as local charitable organizations.

FYI — The Progressive Era

The city of Chicago provides a good example of the changes experienced during the Progressive Era. Between 1890 and 1910, Chicago's population grew from one million to two million. Between 1880 and 1890, the number of factories nearly tripled. By 1889, nearly 70 percent of the inhabitants of the city were immigrants.

Source: Harold Finestone, *Victims of Change* (Westport, CT: Greenwood Press, 1976).

The Legal Context of the Juvenile Court By the late 1800s, legal mechanisms for treating children differently and separately from adults had existed for some time. For example, jurisdictions had set the minimum age at which a child could be considered legally responsible for criminal behavior. Minimum ages for placement in adult penitentiaries were also enacted during the first half of the 1800s.[15] Moreover, special institutions for dealing with youths had been in existence since 1825, when the first house of refuge was established in New York City. Yet, cases involving juveniles were still heard in criminal courts. Many of the child savers believed that criminal courts failed to respond adequately to many of the transgressions of the young.

parens patriae The legal philosophy justifying state intervention in the lives of children when their parents are unable or unwilling to protect them.

The legal philosophy justifying state intervention in the lives of children, the doctrine of ***parens patriae*** (the state as parent), was given judicial endorsement in the case *Ex parte Crouse* (1838). Mary Ann Crouse had been committed to the Philadelphia House of Refuge by her mother against her father's wishes. Mary Ann's father contested his daughter's placement, arguing that she was being punished even though she had committed no criminal offense. However, the Pennsylvania Supreme Court ruled that Mary Ann's placement was legal because (1) the purpose of the Philadelphia House of Refuge was to reform youths, not to punish them, (2) formal due process protections provided to adults in criminal trials were unnecessary because Mary Ann was not being punished, and (3) when parents were unwilling or unable to protect their children, the state had a legal obligation to do so.[16]

[FYI] Daniel O'Connell

Like Mary Ann Crouse, who was committed by her mother against her father's wishes, Daniel O'Connell was institutionalized even though he had committed no criminal offense. He was placed in the house of refuge because he was perceived to be in danger of becoming a pauper or a criminal. However, Daniel's case differed from Mary Ann's because both his parents objected to his placement and, even more important, because the court ruled that Daniel's placement was harmful, not helpful.

However, the right of the state to intervene in the lives of children did not go unchallenged. In *People* v. *Turner* (1870), for example, the Illinois Supreme Court ruled that Daniel O'Connell, who was committed to the Chicago House of Refuge against both his parents' wishes, was being punished and not helped by his placement. The court also decided that because placement in the house of refuge actually was punishment, due process protections were necessary.[17] The ruling, together with increasing concern over the willingness or ability of the criminal courts to protect or control youths, led reformers in Chicago to consider other mechanisms by which their aims might be achieved. The mechanism they created was the first juvenile court, which was established in Chicago in 1899 by passage of the Juvenile Court Act in Illinois.[18] Some scholars argue that the Juvenile Court Act was a means for the child savers, intent on salvaging poor children—especially poor immigrant children—to get around the *Turner* decision's requirement of due process protections for youths.

The Operation of Early Juvenile Courts The Juvenile Court Act of 1899 gave the Chicago juvenile court broad jurisdiction over persons under the age of 16 who were delinquent, dependent, or neglected. In addition, the act required:

1. The court to be overseen by a special judge.
2. Hearings to be held in a separate courtroom.
3. Separate records to be kept of juvenile hearings.[19]

It also made probation a major component of the juvenile court's response to offenders and emphasized the use of informal procedures at each stage of the juvenile court process. Indeed, this informality has been a hallmark of the juvenile court since its beginning, a key feature distinguishing it from criminal court proceedings. The major reason for this informality is that the juvenile court has traditionally focused not on the act, but on the *whole child.*

In practice, the informality of the juvenile court allowed complaints against children to be made by almost anyone in the community. It also allowed juvenile court hearings to be held in offices, instead of in traditional courtrooms, and to be closed to the public, unlike criminal trials, which were open to the public. In the typical juvenile court hearing, the only persons present were the judge, the parents, the child, and the probation officer, who met and discussed the case. Also, few (if any) records were kept of hearings, proof of guilt was not necessary for the court to intervene in children's lives, and little or no concern for due process existed. Finally, judges exercised wide discretion in how they dealt with children, ranging from a warning to placement in an institution.[20]

The idea of a juvenile court spread rapidly after the passage of the Juvenile Court Act. Within a decade, 10 states had established special courts for children, and by 1925 all but two states had juvenile courts.[21] Moreover, those juvenile courts followed closely the model developed in Chicago of an informal court intended to "serve the best interests of children."

Despite the growing popularity of the new courts, they did not go completely unchallenged. In the case *Commonwealth of Pennsylvania* v. *Fisher* (1905), for example, the Pennsylvania Supreme Court again examined the juvenile court's mission, the right to intervene, and the due process protections owed to children. In this case, Frank Fisher, a 14-year-old male, was indicted for larceny and committed to the house of refuge until his 21st birthday. Frank's father objected to his placement, claiming that Frank's 7-year sentence for a minor offense was more severe than he would have received in criminal court.[22]

The use of informal procedures is characteristic of the juvenile court system. *Are the juvenile court's informal procedures desirable? Why or why not?*

In its ruling, the Pennsylvania Supreme Court upheld the idea of the juvenile court, and in many respects repeated the arguments it had made in the *Crouse* decision. The court found that the state may intervene in families when parents are unable or unwilling to prevent their children from engaging in crime and that Frank was being helped by his placement in the house of refuge. It further ruled that due process protections were unnecessary when the state acted under its *parens patriae* powers.[23]

The *Fisher* case set the legal tone for the juvenile court from its beginnings until the mid-1960s, when new legal challenges began to be mounted. Those legal challenges attempted primarily to expand juveniles' due process protections. Critics of the juvenile courts recognized that despite their expressed goal of "serving the best interests of children," the established institutions of juvenile justice often did the opposite.

THE LEGAL REFORM YEARS: THE JUVENILE COURT AFTER *GAULT* The 1960s and 1970s provided the social context for a more critical assessment of American institutions, including juvenile justice. Beginning in the mid-1960s and continuing though the mid-1970s, a number of cases decided by the U.S. Supreme Court altered the operation of the juvenile court. The most important of those cases was *In re Gault,* which expanded the number of due process protections afforded juveniles within the juvenile court. However, a number of other cases also helped define juveniles' rights within juvenile justice and contributed to the legal structure found in juvenile courts today. The first of those cases was *Kent* v. *United States* (1966).

Morris Kent was a 16-year-old juvenile on probation who was transferred to criminal court to stand trial on charges of robbery and rape. Although the juvenile court judge received several motions from Kent's attorney opposing the transfer, he made no ruling on them. Further, after indicating that a "full investigation" had been completed, the juvenile court judge transferred Kent to criminal court for trial.[24] Thus, an important decision had been made, the decision to try Kent as an adult, even though no hearing had been held. Kent's

FYI *In re*

The Latin phrase *in re* in the description of court cases (for example, *In re Gault*) means, literally, "in the matter of" or "concerning." It is used when a case does not involve adversarial parties.

CJ ONLINE

Juvenile Justice by State
Go to **www.acf.dhhs.gov/programs/cb/laws/pi/pi9902a7.htm** to access the website for the National Center for Juvenile Justice to find descriptive information and analyses of the various juvenile justice systems in the United States. Compare your state's juvenile justice system to that of another state. *How are the two states similar? Different?*

attorney had no opportunity to see or to question material that had been used to make the decision to transfer jurisdiction, and no reasons for the court's decision were given.

The *Kent* case is important for several reasons. It was the first major ruling by the U.S. Supreme Court that closely examined the operation of the juvenile courts. It also made clear the need for due process protections for juveniles who were being transferred to criminal court for trial. The Court noted that even though a hearing to consider transfer to criminal court is far less formal than a trial, juveniles are still entitled to some due process protections. Specifically, the Court ruled that before a juvenile court could transfer a case to criminal court, there must be a hearing to consider the transfer, the defendant must have the assistance of defense counsel if requested, defense counsel must have access to social records kept by the juvenile court, and the reasons for the juvenile court's decision to transfer must be stated.[25]

Having given notice that it would review the operations of the juvenile court, the Supreme Court, within a year of the *Kent* decision, heard another landmark case. This case, *In re Gault* (1967), went far beyond the ruling in *Kent* in its examination of juvenile court practices. The *Gault* case is important because it extended a variety of due process protections to juveniles. In addition, the facts of the case clearly demonstrate the potential for abuse in the informal practices of the traditional juvenile court.

Gerald Gault was 15 years old when he, along with a friend, was taken into custody by the Gila County, Arizona, sheriff's department for allegedly making an obscene phone call to a neighbor, Ms. Cook. At the time of his arrest, Gerald was on 6-months' probation as a result of his presence when another friend had stolen a wallet from a woman's purse. Without notifying his mother, a deputy took Gerald into custody on the oral complaint of Ms. Cook and transported him to the local detention unit.

When Ms. Gault heard Gerald was in custody, she went to the detention facility. The superintendent of the facility told her that a juvenile court hearing would be held the next day. On the following day, Gerald, his mother, and the deputy who had taken Gerald into custody appeared before the juvenile court judge in chambers. The deputy had filed a petition alleging that Gerald was delinquent. Ms. Cook, the complainant, was not present. Without being informed that he did not have to testify, Gerald was questioned by the judge about the telephone call and was sent back to detention. No record was made of this hearing, no one was sworn, and no specific charge was made, other than an allegation that Gerald was delinquent. At the end of the hearing, the judge said he would "think about it." Gerald was released a few days later, although no reasons were given for his detention or release.

On the day of Gerald's release, Ms. Gault received a letter indicating that another hearing would be held a few days later about Gerald's delinquency. The hearing was held and, again, the complainant was not present. Again, there was no transcript or recording of the proceedings, and what was said was later disputed by the parties. Neither Gerald nor his parent was advised of a right to remain silent, a right to be represented by counsel, or any other constitutional rights. At the conclusion of the hearing, Gerald was found delinquent and was committed to the state industrial school until he was 21 years old, unless released earlier by the court. This meant that Gerald received a sentence of up to 6 years for an offense that if committed by an adult, would have been punished by a maximum sentence of 2 months in jail and a $50 fine.

When the case finally reached the Supreme Court, the Court held that a youth has procedural rights in delinquency hearings where there is the

FYI

Due Process

Many states have required more due process protections for juveniles than have been mandated by the Supreme Court. For example, many state laws specify that juveniles have a right to trial (adjudication) by a jury. In fact, Texas requires that all adjudications be heard by a jury. Nevertheless, jury trials are rare in states that have this right, including Texas. This is because the right must be exercised or, as in Texas, the automatic right to a trial by jury can be waived. In practice, jury trials are often discouraged because they are time-consuming and costly.

possibility of confinement in a state institution. Specifically, the Court ruled that juveniles have a right against self-incrimination, a right to adequate notice of charges against them, a right to confront and to cross-examine their accusers, and a right to assistance of counsel. In addition, the Court's ruling implied that juveniles also have the rights to sworn testimony and appeal.

The landmark *Gault* decision was not the last Supreme Court decision to influence juvenile court procedures. The Supreme Court further expanded protections for juveniles 3 years after *Gault*. In a 1970 case, *In re Winship,* the Court ruled that delinquency charges must be proven beyond a reasonable doubt where there was a possibility that a youth could be confined in a locked facility. Until the *Winship* ruling, the standard of proof typically employed at the adjudication stage of the juvenile justice process was a preponderance of the evidence, the level of proof employed in civil proceedings. **Adjudication** is the juvenile court equivalent of a trial in criminal court, or the process of rendering a judicial decision regarding the truth of the facts alleged in a petition. Under the preponderance-of-the-evidence standard of proof, juveniles could be adjudicated delinquent (found guilty) if the weight of the evidence was slightly against them, a much lower standard of proof than the standard required in criminal courts.

In the 1967 landmark case of *In re Gault,* Supreme Court Justice Abe Fortas wrote, "Due process of law is the primary and indispensable foundation of individual freedom." *Do you agree with Justice Fortas? Why or why not?*

adjudication The juvenile court equivalent of a trial in criminal court, or the process of rendering a judicial decision regarding the truth of the facts alleged in a petition.

It is important to note that both the *Gault* and *Winship* decisions not only increased procedural formality in juvenile court cases but also shifted the traditional focus from the "whole child" to the child's act. Once this shift occurred, it was only a short step to offense-based sentencing and the more punitive orientation that is characteristic of the juvenile justice system today.

The Supreme Court's extension of due process protections to juveniles slowed in the year following the *Winship* decision. In a 1971 ruling, *McKeiver v. Pennsylvania,* the Court held that juveniles were not entitled to a trial by jury. The Court cited several reasons for the decision:

1. The Court did not want to turn the juvenile court into a fully adversarial process.
2. The Court determined that bench trials could produce accurate determinations.
3. The Court felt that it was too early to completely abandon the philosophy of the juvenile court and its treatment mission.

To grant juveniles all of the protections accorded adults, the Court surmised, would make the juvenile court indistinguishable from the criminal court.

The continued informality of the juvenile court may explain why very few youths contest charges against them and why a surprising number of youths who are not adjudicated delinquent (found guilty) are placed on probation. Indeed, most youths who appear before the juvenile court admit to the charges against them.[26] Moreover, data collected by the National Center for Juvenile Justice indicate that in 1998 (the latest year for which data were available), about 15 percent of youths who were not adjudicated delinquent in juvenile courts were still placed on some form of probation (see also Figure 13.3 on page 493).[27]

Today, juveniles have been granted many, but not all, of the due process protections given adults in criminal trials. However, the daily operation of

FYI Juvenile Courts

Each state has at least one court with juvenile jurisdiction, but only in a few states is it called juvenile court. Other names include district, superior, circuit, county, family, or probate court. Regardless of the name, courts with juvenile jurisdiction are generally referred to as juvenile courts.

SOURCE: Melissa Sickmund, "Juveniles in Court," U.S. Department of Justice, Office of Juvenile Justice and Delinquency Prevention, *Juvenile Offenders and Victims National Report Series Bulletin* (Washington, DC: GPO, June 2003), p. 4.

THINKING CRITICALLY

1. Should youths in juvenile court proceedings be granted the same due process protections as adults in criminal trials? Why or why not?
2. Historically, what do you think was the most significant change in the treatment of juvenile offenders? How did the change occur?

juvenile courts calls into question the extent to which court-mandated changes in juvenile justice procedures have influenced the traditional informality of the juvenile court. Juvenile court procedures are still characterized by an informality that most people would find unacceptable if it were applied to adults in criminal court.

FYI: Illegal Behavior

Although few juveniles commit serious violent crimes, self-report studies show that most juveniles have engaged in some type of illegal behavior. For example, a 2001 national survey of high school seniors revealed that nearly 80 percent of them had consumed alcohol illegally during the last 12 months, and nearly 50 percent of them had consumed alcohol illegally within the previous 30 days.

SOURCE: Kathleen Maguire and Ann L. Pastore (eds.), *Sourcebook of Criminal Justice Statistics 2001*, U.S. Department of Justice, Bureau of Justice Statistics (Washington, DC: GPO, 2002), p. 249, Table 3.70.

informal juvenile justice The actions taken by citizens to respond to juvenile offenders without involving the official agencies of juvenile justice.

The Processing of Juvenile Offenders

Juvenile delinquency in the United States is widespread, and people respond to it both formally and informally. Informal responses consist of actions taken by members of the public that do not rely on official agencies of juvenile justice. Formal responses, on the other hand, rely on official agencies of juvenile justice such as the police and juvenile court. Figure 13.1 depicts the stages in the formal juvenile justice process. Before providing a detailed examination of the formal juvenile justice process, however, we take a brief look at the informal juvenile justice process.

THE INFORMAL JUVENILE JUSTICE PROCESS

An examination of the juvenile justice process usually begins with the police, and the police do play a critical role in juvenile justice. However, any discussion of the juvenile justice process should really begin with the public, because police involvement with juveniles is typically the result of citizen complaints.

The informal actions taken by citizens to respond to delinquency constitute an **informal juvenile justice** process that operates outside the official agencies of juvenile justice. Many illegal behaviors by juveniles are handled informally by neighbors, business owners, teachers, and others who are not part of the formal juvenile justice apparatus. The informal processing of juveniles is important because it is one of the mechanisms that operates to control youths' behavior. The more citizens rely on informal control and the more effective it is, the less necessary the formal processing of juveniles becomes.

Although many delinquent actions are handled informally, in other instances members of the public decide to call the police or the juvenile court and to request action from the formal agencies of juvenile justice. Thus, most youths become involved in the formal juvenile justice process when the people who make up the informal process decide, in their discretion, to involve the police or the juvenile court. This means that some combination of the public and the police plays a major role in determining who the clientele of juvenile justice will be.

THE FORMAL JUVENILE JUSTICE PROCESS

The police represent the primary gatekeepers to the formal juvenile justice process. For example, in 1998 (the latest year for which data are available), 84 percent of delinquency cases referred to the juvenile courts came from police agencies.[28] This percentage has remained about the same for more than a decade. In the case of status offenses, however, the percentage of cases referred from police agencies varies greatly by offense. Between 1989 and 1999, for example, 92 percent of status liquor law violation cases were referred by police agencies to the juvenile courts, while only 40 percent of cases of running away, 11 percent of ungovernability (being beyond the control of parents or guardians) cases, and 10 percent of truancy cases were referred from police

FIGURE 13.1 The Formal Juvenile Justice Process

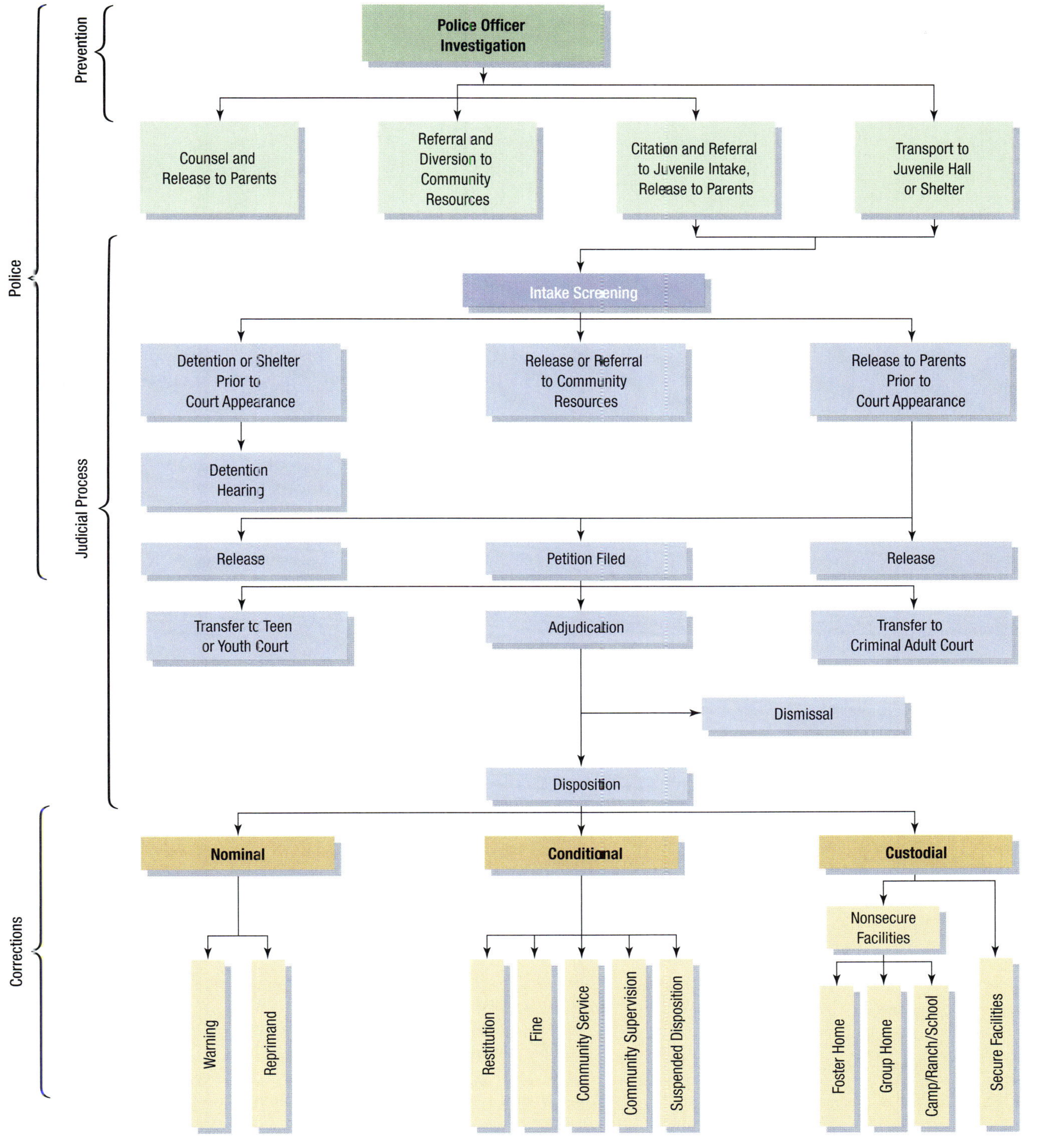

Teachers are an important part of the informal juvenile justice process. *What can teachers do to keep students from becoming delinquent?*

agencies.[29] **Status offenses,** as you may recall, are acts that are not crimes when committed by adults but are illegal for minors.

status offenses Acts that are not crimes when committed by adults but are illegal for minors (for example, truancy or running away from home).

THE POLICE RESPONSE TO JUVENILES Like citizens, the police exercise discretion in handling juvenile cases. Typical responses that police officers may employ are to

1. Warn and release.
2. Refer to parents.
3. Refer to a diversionary program operated by the police or another community agency.
4. Refer to court.

In some communities, an officer may have a variety of options, while in other communities available options are more limited.

Describing the typical police response to juveniles in trouble is difficult because there is considerable variation in the ways individual officers approach juvenile offenders. A number of factors influence the ways police officers handle juvenile suspects. Among those factors are:

1. The seriousness of the offense.
2. The police organization.
3. The community.
4. The wishes of the complainant.
5. The demeanor of the youth.
6. The gender of the offender.
7. The race and social class of the offender.

Offense Seriousness The most important factor in the decision to arrest is the seriousness of the offense. Regardless of the subject's demeanor or other factors, as the seriousness of the offense increases, so does the likelihood of arrest. Most police-juvenile encounters involving felony offenses result in an arrest. However, most police-juvenile encounters involve minor offenses. When offenses are minor, a number of other factors have been found to influence police decision making.

The Police Organization As described in Chapter 6, police departments develop their own particular styles of operation. Those styles, in turn, help structure the way officers respond to juvenile offenders. For example, in one study that categorized police departments by the extent to which they employed a legalistic style of policing, characterized by a high degree of professionalism and bureaucratic structure, it was discovered that officers in most legalistic departments were more likely to arrest juvenile suspects than were officers in less legalistic departments.[30] Thus, the ways that police department personnel respond to juvenile offenders is to some extent a product of the organizational characteristics and policies developed by their individual departments. However, police departments do not operate in a political and social vacuum. They are also influenced by the communities in which they operate.

The Community Communities influence policing in a variety of ways. Through their interactions with residents of a community, police develop assumptions about the communities they police, the people who live in those communities,

FYI

Juveniles and Curfew

Juvenile arrests for curfew and loitering violations increased 81percent between 1991 and 2000. In 2000, 28 percent of curfew arrests involved juveniles under the age of 15 and 31 percent involved females.

SOURCE: Howard N. Snyder, "Juvenile Arrests 2000," U.S. Department of Justice, Office of Juvenile Justice and Delinquency Prevention, *Juvenile Justice Bulletin* (Washington, DC: GPO, November 2002), p. 1.

and the ability and willingness of community residents to respond to crime and delinquency. Research suggests that police operate differently in lower-class communities than in wealthier communities. Police expect lower-class communities to have higher levels of crime and delinquency because more arrests are made in those communities and because they know that lower-class communities have fewer resources with which to respond informally to the array of problems experienced there. Consequently, when police have contact with juveniles in lower-class communities, formal responses become more likely because informal responses are believed to be ineffective in most cases. Indeed, research that has examined the effect of neighborhood socioeconomic status has found that as the socioeconomic status of the neighborhood increases, the likelihood that a police-juvenile encounter will end in arrest declines.[31]

Myth | **Fact**

Myth: The commission of serious, violent crime by juveniles is widespread.

Fact: In 2000, there were 309 arrests for every 100,000 juveniles 10 to 17 years of age for murder and nonnegligent manslaughter, forcible rape, robbery, and aggravated assault. If each of those arrests involved a different juvenile (which is very unlikely), then fewer than one-half of 1 percent of all persons aged 10 to 17 in the United States were arrested for one of those four crimes in 2000.

SOURCE: Howard N. Snyder, "Juvenile Arrests 2000," U.S. Department of Justice, Office of Juvenile Justice and Delinquency Prevention, *Juvenile Justice Bulletin* (Washington, DC: GPO, November 2002), p. 14.

The Wishes of the Complainant As noted earlier, many police-juvenile interactions occur because of a citizen complaint to the police. What police do in those situations often depends on whether the complainant is present, what the complainant would like the police to do, and, sometimes, who the complainant is.

The Demeanor of the Youth As one might expect, how youths behave toward the police can influence whether an arrest is made. Interestingly, youths who

FYI

"Child Delinquents"

In 1999, the police arrested about one-quarter of a million (230,800) youths age 12 and younger. Such very young offenders represented about 9 percent of the total number of juvenile arrestees. Nearly one in four was a girl. These numbers may underestimate the number of child delinquents because in many jurisdictions it is unusual for delinquents under age 12 to be arrested or referred to juvenile court.

SOURCE: *OJJDP Research 2000*, U.S. Department of Justice, Office of Juvenile Justice and Delinquency Prevention (Washington, DC: GPO, May 2001), p. 3.

A juvenile's demeanor can influence arrest decisions. *How would you advise a juvenile to act if he or she is stopped by a police officer?*

FYI

Gang Stereotypes

Youth gang members, contrary to popular stereotypes, are not typically male, urban, poor, minority, or from single-parent households. Although they are more likely to live in socially disorganized and marginalized communities, youth gang members come from a variety of backgrounds. One thing they do have in common, however, is that once they join a gang, juveniles engage in high levels of criminal activity.

SOURCE: Finn-Aage Esbensen, "Preventing Adolescent Gang Involvement," U.S. Department of Justice, *Juvenile Justice Bulletin* (Washington, DC: GPO, September 2000), p. 9.

are either unusually antagonistic or unusually polite are more likely to be arrested. In contrast, youths who are moderately respectful to the police are less likely to be arrested—as long as the offense is not serious.[32]

The Gender of the Offender Gender also appears to influence the decision to arrest, particularly when status offenses are involved. A number of studies have found that female status offenders are more likely to be formally processed than male status offenders.[33]

When it comes to criminal offenses, however, research results are mixed. Some of the research shows that girls are less likely than boys to be arrested for criminal offenses, even when prior record and seriousness of offense are taken into account.[34] Other research suggests that any gender bias that existed in the past has diminished or disappeared.[35]

The Race and Social Class of the Offender There is strong evidence that a juvenile's race and social class influence police decision making. The evidence is clear that minority and poor youths are represented disproportionately in arrest statistics. For example, according to 2001 UCR data, white youths accounted for 71 percent of all arrests of persons under 18 years of age. They accounted for 68.5 percent of arrests for index property offenses and about 55 percent of arrests for index violent offenses. In contrast, African-American youths accounted for about 26 percent of all arrests of persons under 18 years of age, 28 percent of index property-crime arrests, and approximately 42.5 percent of index violent-crime arrests. Other racial groups accounted for the remainder of arrests of persons under 18 years of age.[36] Thus, although white youths account for the majority of juvenile arrests, African-American youths are arrested in disproportionate numbers, since they comprise only 15.5 percent of the U.S. population under 18 years of age.[37]

The UCR does not report arrests by social class. However, self-report data reveal that the prevalence of delinquency (that is, the proportion of the youth population involved in delinquency) does not differ significantly between social classes when all types of offenses are considered. In other words, the proportions of middle-class and lower-class youths who engage in delinquency are similar. However, when different types of offenses are examined, significant social class differences appear. Middle-class youths have higher rates of involvement in such offenses as stealing from their families, cheating on tests, cutting classes, disorderly conduct, and drunkenness. Lower-class youths, on the other hand, have higher rates of involvement in more serious offenses, such as felony assault and robbery.[38]

POLICE PROCESSING OF JUVENILE OFFENDERS When a police officer encounters a juvenile who has committed an illegal act, the officer must decide what to do. One option is to make an arrest. (In some jurisdictions, this is referred to as "taking into custody.") For practical purposes, an arrest takes place whenever a youth is not free to walk away.

As a general rule, the basis for arresting a juvenile is the same as for arresting an adult. An officer needs to have probable cause. There are, however, several differences between arrests of adults and juveniles. First, the police can arrest juveniles for a wider range of behaviors. For example, juveniles, but not adults, can be arrested for status offenses. (Technically, juveniles are not "arrested" for status offenses, because such offenses are not crimes. Also, because status offenses are not crimes, the apprehension of juveniles for status offenses does not require probable cause.) Second, at least in some jurisdictions, juveniles are given the *Miranda* warnings in the presence of a parent, guardian, or attorney. This is not necessary, however, because the Supreme Court, in *Fare* v. *Michael C.* (1979), ruled that parents or attorneys do not have to be present for juveniles to waive their rights. Third, in many jurisdictions, juveniles are more likely than adults who have committed similar offenses to be detained pending adjudication. In *Schall* v. *Martin* (1984), the Supreme Court ruled that preventive detention of juveniles is acceptable.

Concern about the detention of juveniles generally focuses on the use of preventive detention. Some critics argue that it amounts to punishment before a youth has been found guilty of an offense. The conditions juveniles are sometimes exposed to in detention units and adult jails raise additional concerns.

The exact procedures that the police must follow when taking a juvenile into custody vary from state to state and are specified in state juvenile codes. However, those codes typically require officers to notify a juvenile's parents that the juvenile is in custody. Police often ask parents to come to the police station. Sometimes, an officer transports a youth home prior to any questioning. When an officer feels that detention of a juvenile is appropriate, the juvenile is transported to a juvenile detention facility. If such facilities are not available, the youth may be taken to an adult jail in some jurisdictions. In cases where a juvenile is released to his or her parents, the juvenile and the parents are informed that they will be contacted by the court at a later date about the case. After a juvenile is released, an officer completes the complaint, collecting any additional information needed, and then forwards it to the next stage of the juvenile justice process for further action. When a juvenile is detained in a juvenile detention facility or an adult jail, the processing of the complaint is expedited because juvenile codes require a detention hearing (and therefore, a specific complaint) to determine the appropriateness of detention.

Trends in Police Processing of Juveniles In 2001, approximately 72 percent of all juveniles taken into police custody were referred to juvenile court, 19 percent were handled within the police department and released, and 6.5 percent were referred to adult or criminal courts.[39] However, an examination of such data over time reveals a trend toward increased formal processing of cases (referral to court) by police agencies. For example, in 1972, approximately 51 percent of youths taken into custody by the police were referred to the juvenile court, 45 percent were handled within the police department and released, and only about 1 percent were referred to criminal courts. Table 13.1 shows that there has been a trend toward

1. Referring more youths to juvenile court.
2. Handling fewer cases within police departments.
3. Referring more cases to criminal courts.

Diversion The goal of juvenile diversion programs is to respond to youths in ways that avoid formal juvenile justice processing. Diversion can occur at any stage of the juvenile justice process, but it is most often employed before adjudication.

Diversion programs are based on the understanding that formal responses to youths who violate the law, such as arrest and adjudication, do not always protect the best interests of the youths or the community. Consequently, efforts to divert youths *from* the juvenile justice process by warning and releasing them, as well as efforts to divert youths *to* specific diversionary programs, such as counseling, have long been a part of juvenile justice practice. This is especially true for status offenders. Since the enactment of the Juvenile Justice and Delinquency Act of 1974, which stipulated that status offenders not be placed in secure detention facilities or secure correctional facilities, the number of

FYI

Juveniles and Jail

On a typical day in 2002, 7,248 juveniles were confined in adult jails in the United States—a 30 percent decrease from 1999 and an 8 percent decrease from 1995. Of the 7,248 juveniles confined in adult jails on a typical day in 2002, 84 percent were tried or awaiting trial as adults. In states that allow the jailing of juveniles, statutes usually prevent youths from being placed in cells with adults. This means that jail administrators must provide separate rooms and supervision for juveniles within their facilities. For juveniles, separation often means isolation, which is in turn related to an increased risk of self-destructive behavior. A national study found that the suicide rate for juveniles in adult jails was almost 5 times the suicide rate for juveniles in the general population, and nearly 8 times the suicide rate of juveniles in juvenile detention facilities.

Source: Paige M. Harrison and Jennifer C. Karberg, "Prison and Jail Inmates at Midyear, 2002," U.S. Department of Justice, *Bureau of Justice Statistics Bulletin* (Washington, DC: GPO, April 2003), p. 8, Table 9; Community Research Center, *An Assessment of the National Incidence of Juvenile Suicide in Adult Jails, Lockups, and Juvenile Detention Centers.* (Champaign, IL: Community Research Center, 1980).

TABLE 13.1 Percentage Distribution of Juveniles Taken Into Police Custody, by Method of Disposition

	Referred to Juvenile Court Jurisdiction	Handled Within Department and Released	Referred to Criminal or Adult Court	Referred to Other Police Agency	Referred to Welfare Agency
1972	50.8%	45.0%	1.3%	1.6%	1.3%
1973	49.5	45.2	1.5	2.3	1.4
1974	47.0	44.4	3.7	2.4	2.5
1975	52.7	41.6	2.3	1.9	1.4
1976	53.4	39.0	4.4	1.7	1.6
1977	53.2	38.1	3.9	1.8	3.0
1978	55.9	36.6	3.8	1.8	1.9
1979	57.3	34.6	4.8	1.7	1.6
1980	58.1	33.8	4.8	1.7	1.6
1981	58.0	33.8	5.1	1.6	1.5
1982	58.9	32.5	5.4	1.5	1.6
1983	57.5	32.8	4.8	1.7	3.1
1984	60.0	31.5	5.2	1.3	2.0
1985	61.8	30.7	4.4	1.2	1.9
1986	61.7	29.9	5.5	1.1	1.8
1987	62.0	30.3	5.2	1.0	1.4
1988	63.1	29.1	4.7	1.1	1.9
1989	63.9	28.7	4.5	1.2	1.7
1990	64.5	28.3	4.5	1.1	1.6
1991	64.2	28.1	5.0	1.0	1.7
1992	62.5	30.1	4.7	1.1	1.7
1993	67.3	25.6	4.8	0.9	1.5
1994	63.2	29.5	4.7	1.0	1.7
1995	65.7	28.4	3.3	0.9	1.7
1996	68.6	23.3	6.2	0.9	0.9
1997	66.9	24.6	6.6	0.8	1.1
1998	69.2	22.2	6.8	0.9	1.0
1999	69.2	22.5	6.4	1.0	0.8
2000	70.8	20.3	7.0	1.1	0.8
2001	72.4	19.0	6.5	1.4	0.7

Note: Because of rounding, percentages may not add to 100.

Source: *Sourcebook of Criminal Justice Statistics Online,* Table 4.26 at www.albany.edu/sourcebook/1995/pdf/t426.pdf.

status offenders diverted from formal juvenile justice processing has increased dramatically.

radical nonintervention A practice based on the idea that youths should be left alone if at all possible, instead of being formally processed.

Today, diversion strategies are of two basic types. Some diversion strategies are based on the idea of radical nonintervention. Other strategies are designed to involve youths, and possibly parents, in a diversionary program. **Radical nonintervention** is based on the idea that youths should be left alone if at all possible, instead of being formally processed. The police practice of warning and releasing some juvenile offenders is an example of radical nonintervention. The practice of referring juveniles to community agencies for services such as individual or family counseling is an example of a strategy that involves youths in a diversionary program.

Contemporary diversion programs are operated by both juvenile justice and community agencies. Interventions employed in those programs include providing basic casework services to youths; providing individual, family, and group counseling; requiring restitution; and imposing community service.

Recently, a relatively small number of juvenile offenders (estimates suggest more than 100,000 cases a year) have been adjudicated in teen courts or youth courts instead of juvenile courts or adult courts.[40] Teen courts or youth courts are a new way of dealing with relatively young and usually first-time offenders charged with offenses such as theft, misdemeanor assault, disorderly conduct, and possession of alcohol. As of July 2003, there were more than 890 teen court programs in the United States, up from about 50 in 1991.

Teen courts are based on one of four models:

1. Adult judge—An adult serves as judge and rules on legal matters and courtroom procedure. Youths serve as attorneys, jurors, clerks, bailiffs, etc.
2. Youth judge—Similar to the adult judge model, but a youth serves as judge.
3. Tribunal—Youth attorneys present the case to a panel of three youth judges, who decide the appropriate disposition for the defendant. A jury is not used.
4. Peer jury—This model does not use youth attorneys; the case is presented to a youth jury by a youth or adult. The youth jury then questions the defendant directly.

Nearly half of all teen courts use the adult judge model.

Most teen courts do not determine guilt or innocence. Rather they serve as diversion alternatives and youths must admit to the charges against them to qualify for teen court. Figure 13.2 shows the state laws governing the use of teen courts. The most common disposition used in teen court cases is

CJ ONLINE

Teen Courts

To learn more about teen courts, visit the website of the National Youth Court Center at **www.youthcourt.net.** *Do you think teen courts are a good idea? Why or why not?*

FIGURE 13.2 State Laws Governing the Use of Teen Courts

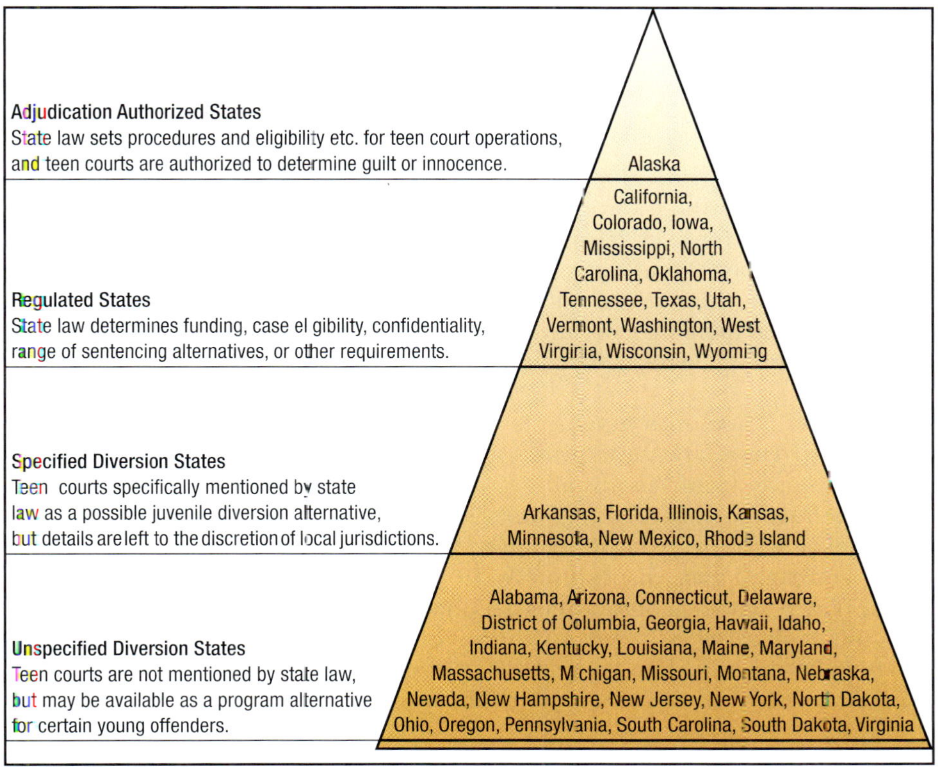

SOURCE: Jeffrey A. Butts, Janeen Buck, and Mark B. Coggeshall, *The Impact of Teen Court on Young Offenders,* U.S. Department of Justice, Office of Juvenile Justice and Delinquency Prevention (Washington, DC: The Urban Institute, April 2002) p. 3.

community service. Other frequently used dispositions included victim apology letters, apology essays, teen court jury duty, drug/alcohol classes, and monetary restitution.

Another new juvenile diversion program is restorative justice conferences or family group conferences.[41] Commonly used in Australia and New Zealand and increasingly being used throughout the world, restorative justice conferences bring together juvenile offenders, their victims, and other relevant parties (such as parents or guardians) with trained facilitators to discuss the offense and the harm done to victims and the other relevant parties. As is the case with teen courts, juvenile offenders who have been screened to participate in restorative justice conferences are generally nonviolent offenders who commit less-serious offenses and have not had a previous referral.

At the conferences, victims and the other relevant parties have an opportunity to explain how they have been affected by the offense and to question the offending juveniles. At the end of the conference, the participants determine how the offending juveniles can make amends to the victims for the wrong done and then sign a reparation agreement. These agreements typically include an apology and some type of restitution to the victims. They may also require the offenders to perform community service or complete other requirements such as improving school attendance, finishing homework, or doing chores at home or school. If an agreement cannot be reached or a juvenile challenges the allegations, then the matter proceeds to juvenile court.

Advocates of restorative justice conferences and teen courts maintain that the programs provide greater benefits to all parties involved than does the traditional juvenile court system. Advocates argue that restorative justice conferences and teen courts hold juveniles more accountable for their offenses, better enable offending juveniles to appreciate how their actions negatively affected others, better involve and meet the needs of victims, and create a more supportive community for offending juveniles. Additional benefits include the timelier handling of cases, cost savings because of the heavy reliance on volunteers, and higher levels of victim satisfaction. Because of the lack of rigorous studies, it is not possible at this time to determine whether restorative justice conferences and teen courts are more effective at reducing recidivism than is the traditional juvenile court system or other juvenile diversion programs. However, based on the research available, as well as anecdotal evidence, it appears that both restorative justice conferences and teen courts may be positive alternatives to the traditional juvenile court process, especially in jurisdictions that do not have a wide variety of intervention options for young, first-time juvenile offenders.

> **FYI — Net widening**
>
> Even though diversion programs are frequently touted as a way to reduce the number of youths involved in juvenile justice, some diversionary strategies contribute to net widening. Net widening occurs when a program handles youths who would have been left alone in the absence of the new program.

Detention Sometimes a youth is held in a secure detention facility during processing. There are three primary reasons for this practice: (1) to protect the community from the juvenile, (2) to ensure that the juvenile appears at a subsequent stage of processing, and (3) to secure the juvenile's own safety. In 1998, juveniles were held in detention facilities at some point between referral to court and case disposition in 19 percent of all delinquency cases disposed. The percentage of juveniles detained during processing has not changed very much since 1988.[42] Federal rules require that a juvenile who is detained in an adult jail or lockup be held for no more than 6 hours and in a separate area out of sight or sound of adult inmates.[43]

intake screening The process by which decisions are made about the continued processing of juvenile cases. Decisions might include dismissing the case, referring the youth to a diversion program, or filing a petition.

Intake Screening When the decision to arrest a youth is made, or a social agency such as a school alleges that an offense has occurred, the next step in the juvenile justice process is **intake screening.** The purpose of intake screening is to make decisions about the continued processing of cases. Those decisions and others made during juvenile court processing of delinquency cases in 1998 are shown in Figure 13.3. The location of the intake screening and the educational background and training of the person who conducts it vary from jurisdiction to jurisdiction. Traditionally, intake screening has been performed by probation officers. However, in recent years there has been a move toward involving the prosecuting attorney in the intake process. In fact, in some jurisdictions, such as Colorado and Washington, intake screening is now the

FIGURE 13.3 **Juvenile Court Processing of Delinquency Cases, 1998, National Estimates**

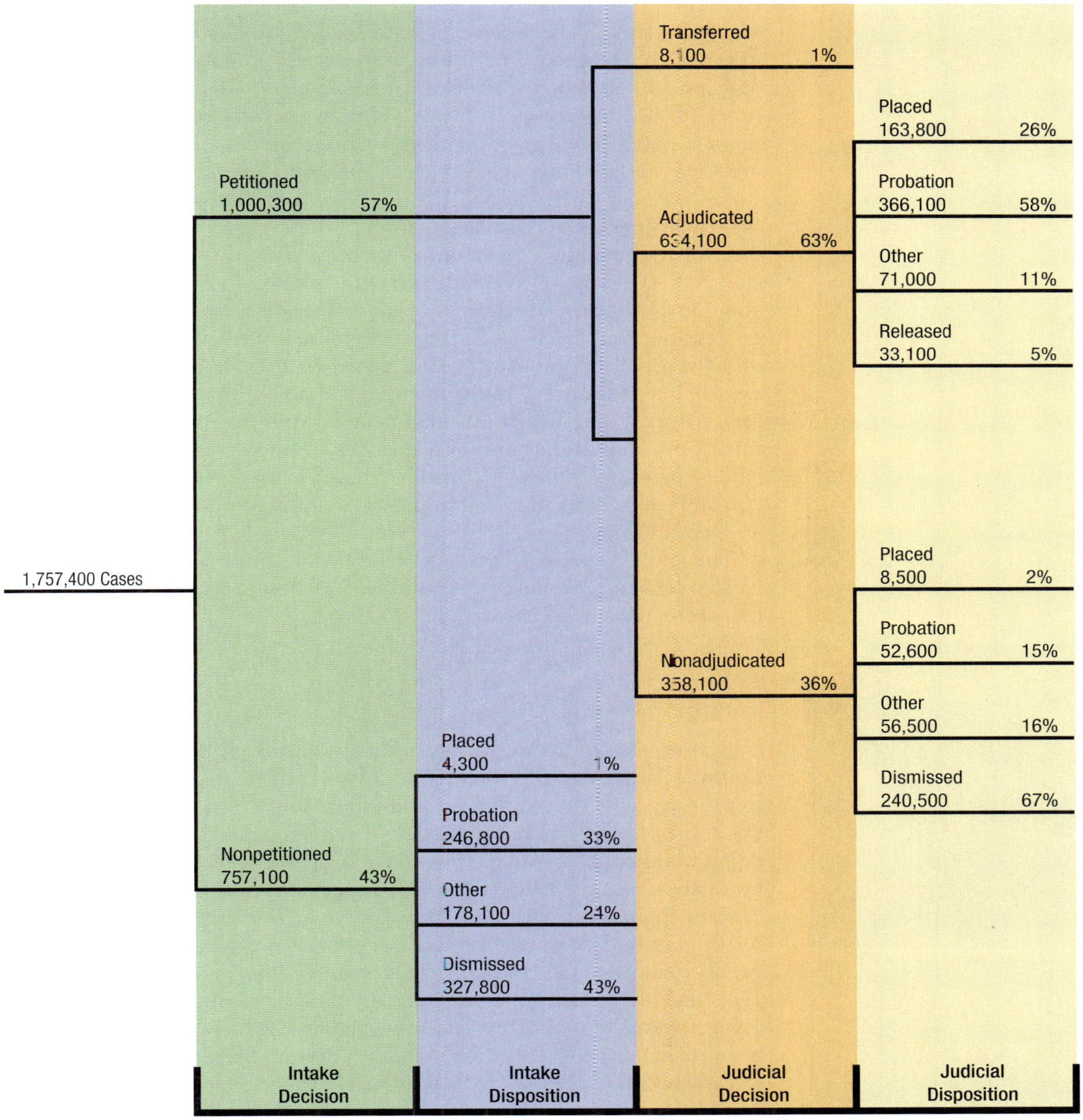

Note: Detail may not add to totals because of rounding.

SOURCE: Charles Puzzanchera, Anne L. Stahl, Terrence A. Finnegan, Nancy Tierney, and Howard N. Snyder, "Juvenile Court Statistics 1998," U.S. Department of Justice, Office of Juvenile Justice and Delinquency Prevention (Pittsburgh, PA: National Center for Juvenile Justice, June 2003), p. 38.

responsibility of the prosecuting attorney's office.[44] In other states, such as Michigan, intake screening is done by an intake officer (probation officer) who works for the juvenile court, although the prosecuting attorney's office reviews most complaints for legal sufficiency.

Possible intake decisions might include dismissing the case or having youths and parents in for a conference or an informal hearing to collect additional information for making the intake decision. Other decisions include referral of the youth to a diversion program (for example, informal probation or counseling at a community agency), filing a **petition** (a legal form of the police complaint that specifies the charges to be heard at the adjudication), and waiver or transfer of the case to criminal court.

petition A legal form of the police complaint that specifies the charges to be heard at the adjudication.

As in police decision making, a number of factors have been found to influence intake screening decisions. For example, youths who have committed serious offenses, those with prior records, and those who are uncooperative are more likely to have petitions filed. In addition, lower-class minority males, at least in some jurisdictions, are more likely than other groups to receive more formal responses at intake. Finally, there is considerable evidence that female status offenders are likely to be treated more harshly at intake than are their male counterparts, at least in some jurisdictions.[45]

TRANSFER, WAIVER, OR CERTIFICATION TO CRIMINAL COURT Since the early days of the juvenile court, state legislatures have given juvenile court judges statutory authority to transfer certain juvenile offenders to criminal court. In some jurisdictions, transfer is called waiver or certification. **Transfer, waiver,** or **certification** may occur in cases where youths meet certain age, offense, and (in some jurisdictions) prior-record criteria. For example, in Mississippi, waiver may occur if a youth has reached 13 years of age and has committed any criminal offense. In Michigan, a juvenile must be 14 years of age and must have committed one of a number of felonies specified by law. In many states, before a youth is transferred to an adult criminal court, a separate transfer or waiver hearing must be conducted to determine the waiver's appropriateness.

transfer, waiver, or **certification** The act or process by which juveniles who meet specific age, offense, and (in some jurisdictions) prior-record criteria are transferred to criminal court for trial.

Nathaniel Abraham was 11 when he was charged with first-degree murder for shooting an 18-year-old stranger outside a convenience store in Pontiac, Michigan. *Should youths such as Abraham be transferred to criminal courts for trials? Why or why not?*

The judicial waiver process varies from state to state, but at the typical waiver hearing, probable cause must be shown. In addition, in many states the prosecutor must show that

1. The youth presents a threat to the community.
2. Existing juvenile treatment programs would not be appropriate.
3. Programs within the adult system would be more appropriate.

Historically, judicial transfer authority has been exercised infrequently. For example, between 1988 and 2000, the percentage of petition cases transferred to criminal court remained around 1 percent. However, because of changes in the total number of petition cases between 1988 and 2000, the number of delinquency cases waived by juvenile court judges rose about 81 percent between 1988 and 1994 (from 6,700 cases to 12,100 cases), then dropped 61 percent between 1994 and 2000 (from 12,100 cases to 7,500 cases). The net result was that the number of cases judicially waived was 12 percent higher in 1999 than in 1988. The greatest relative change in waived cases between 1988 and 1998 was for drug and person offense cases (78 percent and 74 percent, respectively). In the 8,100 cases waived in 1998, 93 percent of the juveniles were male, 87 percent were 16 or older, and 55 percent were white (42 percent were black).[46]

The number of juvenile cases transferred to criminal court in recent years is actually much larger than the aforementioned data suggest. This is because there are no national statistics available on the number of prosecutorial transfers. Prosecutorial transfers occur in states that have passed legislation giving prosecutors concurrent jurisdiction. In the 15 concurrent jurisdiction states (as of 1999), both the juvenile court and the criminal court have original jurisdiction in cases that meet certain age, offense, and (in some jurisdictions) prior-record criteria. In those states, prosecutors have discretion to file eligible cases in either court. In Florida alone, more than 4,000 juvenile cases were transferred to criminal court in fiscal year 1998–1999 through prosecutorial transfer. Today, because of the availability of prosecutorial transfer, judicial waiver is almost never used in Florida.[47]

Additional developments in this area include (1) an expansion of the number of transfer mechanisms, (2) simplification of the transfer process in some states, including the *exclusion* of offenders charged with certain offenses from juvenile court jurisdiction, or their *mandatory* or *automatic waiver* to criminal court, and (3) the lowering by some states of the maximum age for juvenile court jurisdiction. Statutory exclusion ("legislature transfers") accounts for the largest number of transfers.[48] As for lowering the maximum age, since 1995, all 17-year olds in at least 10 states (Georgia, Illinois, Louisiana, Massachusetts, Michigan, Missouri, New Hampshire, South Carolina, Texas, and Wisconsin) and all 16- and 17-year olds in at least three states (Connecticut, New York, and North Carolina) have been subject only to criminal court jurisdiction. Additionally, in many states, juveniles who have been convicted as adults must be prosecuted in criminal court for any subsequent offenses (the "Once an adult, always an adult" provision). Those developments reflect a shift in many jurisdictions toward a more punitive orientation toward juvenile offenders.[49]

FYI: Incompetent to Stand Trial

A recent study suggests that thousands of juveniles tried as adults in the United States are incompetent to stand trial because they are emotionally or intellectually unable to contribute to their own defense. When compared with young adults, children ages 11 to 13 were more than 3 times as likely to be found "seriously impaired" in understanding the judicial process and aiding their own defense. Children 14 or 15 years old were twice as likely to be "seriously impaired" in such awareness and reasoning. Youths age 16 and 17 did not differ from those at least 18 years of age.

SOURCE: Greg Krikorian, "Study: Many Kids Tried as Adults Don't Grasp System," *The Orlando Sentinel*, March 3, 2003, p. A3.

THE ADJUDICATION HEARING When a petition is filed at intake and the case is not transferred to criminal court, the next step is adjudication. As noted previously, adjudication is the juvenile court equivalent of a trial in criminal court. In some states, such as Michigan, adjudication is now called a trial. It is at adjudication, moreover, that a juvenile begins to develop an official court record.

Before adjudication can take place, several preliminary actions are necessary. A petition must be filed, a hearing date must be set, and the necessary parties (such as the youth, the parents, and witnesses) must be given notice of the hearing. Notice is typically given through a summons or subpoena. A summons, which is an order to appear in court, is issued to the youth; copies are also given to the parents or guardians. The summons specifies the charges and the date, time, and location of the hearing, and it may list the youth's rights, such as a right to an attorney. Subpoenas are issued to witnesses, instructing them to appear on a certain day, time, and place to provide testimony or records.

When charges specified in the petition are contested by a juvenile and the juvenile is represented by an attorney, another critical event often takes place before adjudication—a plea bargain. Plea bargaining, including its problems, was discussed in detail in Chapter 8. Although the extent of plea bargaining in juvenile justice is unknown, it is believed to be a common practice in many juvenile courts.

There are two types of adjudications: contested ones (in which juveniles dispute the charges) and uncontested

Myth	Fact
Greater use of transfer or expansion of transfer criteria will reduce crime because of the adult sanctions that will be applied.	Youths transferred to criminal court are more likely to commit further crimes than others retained in the juvenile justice system. There is no evidence that transfer has any deterrent effect.

SOURCE: Donna M. Bishop, Charles E. Frazier, Lonn Lanza-Kaduce, and Lawrence Winner, "The Transfer of Juveniles to Criminal Court: Does It Make a Difference?" *Crime and Delinquency* 42 (1996), pp. 171–91; Jeffrey Fagan, "Separating the Men from the Boys: The Comparative Advantage of Juvenile versus Criminal Court Sanctions on Recidivism Among Adolescent Felony Offenders," in James C. Howell, Barry Krisberg, J. David Hawkins, and John Wilson, eds., *A Sourcebook: Serious, Violent, and Chronic Juvenile Offenders* (Thousand Oaks, CA: Sage, 1995), pp. 213–37; Eric Jensen and Linda Metsger, "A Test of the Deterrent Effect of Legislative Waiver on Violent Juvenile Crime," *Crime and Delinquency* 40 (1994), pp. 96–104.

Uncontested adjudications are generally brief. At the end, the youth or the youth's attorney admits the charges. *Why do you suppose most adjudications are uncontested?*

ones. Contested adjudications are similar to trials in criminal courts, which were described in Chapter 8. They typically employ the same rules of evidence and procedure. Most contested adjudications are bench adjudications, in which the hearing officer—a judge, referee, court master, or commissioner—makes a finding of fact based on the evidence presented. A **hearing officer** is a lawyer empowered by the juvenile court to hear juvenile cases. In some jurisdictions, contested adjudications are jury trials. However, as noted earlier in this chapter, juveniles do not have a constitutional right to a jury trial, and even in states that give juveniles the right to a jury trial, jury trials are rare.

hearing officer A lawyer empowered by the juvenile court to hear juvenile cases.

Like their criminal court counterparts, the vast majority of juvenile court adjudications are uncontested. Uncontested adjudications are generally brief and consist of a reading of the charges, advice of rights, and possibly brief testimony by the youth or other parties, such as a probation officer. After this, the youth, or frequently the youth's attorney, admits the charges. In some states, an uncontested adjudication is called an arraignment.

The majority of cases that are not adjudicated are dismissed. Surprisingly, however, many juveniles whose cases are neither adjudicated nor dismissed are still placed on informal probation or treated in some other way. For example, of the estimated 358,100 delinquency cases filed but not adjudicated in 1998, 67 percent were dismissed. In 15 percent, the juvenile was placed on informal probation, and the remaining 18 percent were disposed of in other ways (see Figure 13.3). However, the majority of cases in which petitions are filed are adjudicated. In 1998, for example, 63 percent of the delinquency cases in juvenile courts were adjudicated (see Figure 13.3). Although 63 percent may not seem like a large percentage, keep in mind that many cases not adjudicated still receive some court supervision, such as informal probation.

FYI: Plea Bargaining

In a nationwide study of plea bargaining in juvenile courts, it was found that "much of the country has either not addressed at all or has not fully developed standards regarding the guilty plea process in juvenile court." It was also discovered that there was considerable variability in the ways that plea bargaining was carried out in various courts. For example, urban courts were more likely to institute formal procedures to regulate plea bargaining than were suburban or rural courts.

SOURCE: Joseph B. Sanborn, Jr., "Pleading Guilty in Juvenile Court," *Justice Quarterly* 9 (1992), pp. 127–50.

DISPOSITION **Disposition** is the juvenile court equivalent of sentencing in criminal court. At the disposition hearing, the court makes its final determination of what to do with the juvenile officially labeled delinquent. Some of the options available to juvenile courts are probation, placement in a diversion program, restitution, community service, detention, placement in foster care, placement in a long-term or short-term residential treatment program, placement with a relative, and placement with the state for commitment to a state facility. In addition, the court may order some combination of those

disposition The juvenile court equivalent of sentencing in criminal court. At the disposition hearing, the court makes its final determination of what to do with the juvenile officially labeled delinquent.

dispositions, such as placement on probation, restitution, and a short stay in detention. However, disposition possibilities are limited by the available options in a particular jurisdiction. In a few jurisdictions, they are also limited by statutory sentencing guidelines. In practice, the disposition options available to most juvenile courts are quite narrow, consisting of probation or incarceration. When incarceration is used, an indeterminate period of commitment or incarceration is the norm.[50]

As part of the disposition, the court also enters various orders regarding the youth's behavior. Those orders consist of rules the youth must follow. Also, the court may enter orders regarding parents, relatives, or other people who live in the home. For example, the court may order parents to attend counseling or a substance abuse treatment program, a boyfriend to move out of the house, or parents to clean up their house and pay for court costs or services provided, such as counseling caseworker services. If parents fail to follow those orders, at least in some jurisdictions, they may be held in contempt of court and placed in jail.

In making the disposition, the hearing officer usually relies heavily on a presentence investigation report (sometimes called a predisposition report), which is completed by a probation officer or an investigator before the disposition. Presentence investigation reports for criminal courts were described in detail in Chapter 9.

The most frequently used disposition in juvenile courts is probation, followed by placement. In 1998, for example, approximately 58 percent of the

FYI: Juvenile Court Cases

The number of juvenile court cases increased 27 percent between 1990 and 2000, to nearly 1.7 million cases. Between 1990 and 2000, the percent of homicides decreased 21 percent (1,800 cases in 1999), the percent of forcible rapes decreased 19 percent (4,200 cases in 1999,) the percent of aggravated assaults decreased 5 percent (55,800 cases in 1999), and the percent of robberies decreased 9 percent (25,100 cases in 1999). The percent of property offenses also decreased 9 percent, but the percent of drug law violations increased 169 percent and the percent of public order offenses increased 74 percent.

SOURCE: *OJJDP Statistical Briefing Book*, Online at www.ojjdp.ncjrs.org/ojstatbb/html/qa179.html (May 3, 2002, revised September 4, 2002).

CAREERS IN CRIMINAL JUSTICE

Juvenile Probation Officer

My name is Kelly Webster. I am a deputy probation officer (P.O.) with Los Angeles County Probation Department. I work at Camp Scott, a boot camp housing females ages 12–19. Camp Scott is the only female boot camp in L.A. County. Minors sentenced to camp are wards of the court and spend from 4 months to a year incarcerated. They are sentenced to camp for any crime leading up to attempted murder, so their sentences vary.

To become a P.O., a 4-year degree is required, in any subject. I have a B.A. in social welfare from the University of California, Berkeley. However, I never intended on becoming a social worker. My interest has always been in the criminal justice system. I became a P.O. by looking into county job openings upon completing my undergraduate degree. The Probation Department had an opening as a detention services officer in juvenile hall. I worked there for a year before promoting to a P.O. The only difference in the two jobs is the degree required, because of the court report writing.

I work a 56-hour shift, meaning that I work two days and then I have four and a half days off; I sleep at work for two nights. My routine consists of supervising approximately 115 minors at all times. Because camp is structured like the military, I wear fatigues, as do the minors. Minors must ask permission to speak, salute me when walking by, and march around the facility calling cadences.

During the week, the minors are in school. On the weekends, they are cleaning, receiving visits on Sunday, or writing letters in the dormitory. They do physical training every day and twice on the weekend.

When I am not with the whole group, I have time assigned to counsel my own caseload. I am responsible for about five minors at a time. I write court reports when the minor is scheduled for release, informing the judge of the minor's behavior in camp. I recommend release or more time, depending on how they have progressed. Camp's philosophy is family reunification, so I have as much contact with the minor's family as possible.

What I like most about being a juvenile P.O. is the ability to affect some minors. What I like least about the job is that some of these "hardened" children cannot be helped. It is difficult to hear about what some of these children have endured.

Which aspects of this job would you find most difficult? Why?

FIGURE 13.4 **Blended Sentencing Options Create a "Middle Ground" between Traditional Juvenile Sanctions and Adult Sanctions**

Blended sentencing option	State
Juvenile-exclusive blend: The juvenile court may impose a sanction involving either the juvenile or adult correctional systems. Juvenile court — or — Juvenile / Adult	New Mexico
Juvenile-inclusive blend: The juvenile court may impose both juvenile and adult correctional sanctions. The adult sanction is suspended pending a violation and revocation. Juvenile court — and — Juvenile / Adult	Connecticut Kansas Minnesota Montana
Juvenile-contiguous blend: The Juvenile court may impose a juvenile correctional sanction that may remain in force after the offender is beyond the age of the court's extended jurisdiction, at which point the offender may be transferred to the adult correctional system. Juvenile court —— Juvenile —— Adult	Colorado[1] Massachusetts Rhode Island South Carolina Texas
Criminal-exclusive blend: The criminal court may impose a sanction involving either the juvenile or adult correctional systems. Criminal court — or — Juvenile / Adult	California Colorado[2] Florida Idaho Michigan Oklahoma Virginia West Virginia
Criminal-inclusive blend: The criminal court may impose both juvenile and adult correctional sanctions. The adult sanction is suspended, but is reinstated if the terms of the juvenile sanction are violated and revoked. Criminal court — and — Juvenile / Adult	Arkansas Iowa Missouri Virginia[3]

Note: Blends apply to a subset of juveniles specified by state statute.

[1]Applies to those designated as "aggravated juvenile offenders."
[2]Applies to those designated as "youthful offenders."
[3]Applies to those designated as "violent juvenile felony offenders."

SOURCE: "New Laws Have Had a Dramatic Impact on Sentencing for Serious or Violent Juvenile Offenders," U.S. Department of Justice, Office of Juvenile Justice and Delinquency Prevention, *1999 National Report Series, Juvenile Justice Bulletin* (Washington DC: GPO, December 1999).

FYI: Disposition and Extralegal Factors

Although some research has failed to find evidence that extralegal factors, such as race or social class, influence disposition, the bulk of the research indicates that extralegal factors often play a role in disposition. For example, a number of studies have found that minority and lower-class youths are more likely to receive the most severe dispositions, even when seriousness of offense and prior record are taken into account.

SOURCE: Jeffrey Fagan, Ellen Slaughter, and Richard Hartstone, "Blind Justice: The Impact of Race on the Juvenile Justice Process," *Crime and Delinquency,* 33 (1987), pp. 244–58; Belinda R. McCarthy and Brent L. Smith, "The Conceptualization of Discrimination in the Juvenile Justice Process," *Criminology* 24 (1986), pp. 41–64.

youths adjudicated delinquent were placed on probation; 26 percent received some type of commitment. Relatively few delinquency cases received other dispositions or were released after adjudication (see Figure 13.3).

Because of recent heightened concerns about violent juvenile offenders, many states have legislatively redefined the juvenile court's mission by deemphasizing the goal of rehabilitation and stressing the need for public safety, punishment, and accountability in the juvenile justice system. Along with this change in purpose has been a fundamental philosophical change in the focus of juvenile justice, from offender-based dispositions to offense-based dispositions, which emphasize punishment or incapacitation instead of rehabilitation. These changes are reflected in new disposition or sentencing practices, including (1) the use of *blended sentences,* which combine both juvenile and adult sanctions (see Figure 13.4), (2) the use of mandatory minimum sentences for specific types of offenders or offense categories, and (3) the extension of juvenile court dispositions beyond the offender's age of majority, that is, lengthening the time an offender is held accountable in juvenile court.[51]

THINKING CRITICALLY

Which do you think is a better way to handle juvenile crime—the informal or formal process? Why?

Correctional Programs for Juveniles

As noted, when youths are adjudicated, a number of disposition options are available to juvenile courts, although the options typically used in any one jurisdiction are fairly narrow. Three general types of dispositions are

1. Dismissal of the case, which is used in a small percentage of cases.
2. The use of a community-based program.
3. The use of an institutional program.

Because both community-based and institutional correctional programs for adults were the subjects of previous chapters of this book, only the features of those programs that are unique to juveniles will be discussed in the following sections.

COMMUNITY-BASED CORRECTIONAL PROGRAMS FOR JUVENILES

Among the community-based correctional programs for juvenile offenders are diversion, pretrial release, probation, foster care, group home placement, and parole. Some of those programs are designed to provide services to youths in their own homes, while others provide services to youths who have been removed from their homes, at least for short periods of time. Moreover, although all community-based programs are intended to control offenders and provide sanctions for their behavior, they are also designed to accomplish a variety of additional objectives. Those objectives include allowing youths to maintain existing ties with the community, helping them restore ties and develop new and positive ones with the community (reintegration), avoiding the negative consequences of institutional placement, providing a more cost-effective response to offenders, and reducing the likelihood of recidivism. Some of the community-based correctional programs for juveniles are examined in the following sections.

FYI: Nathanial Abraham

On January 13, 2000, 13-year-old Nathaniel Abraham, the youngest American ever convicted of murder as an adult, was sentenced by a family court judge in Pontiac, Michigan, to a 7-year term at a maximum-security juvenile facility. The sentence allows Abraham to be released when he turns 21. In sentencing Abraham, who at age 11 shot and killed a stranger, the judge criticized the growing tendency of the U.S. judicial system to treat children as adults. He believed that the boy had a chance of being rehabilitated.

SOURCE: *Facts on File: World News Digest with Index,* 60 no. 3094 (March 23, 2000), p. 196; "Young Killer Gets Another Chance," *The Orlando Sentinel,* January 14, 2000, p. A3.

PROBATION Probation is the most frequently used correctional response for youths who are adjudicated delinquent in juvenile courts. Juvenile probation officers are referred to as "the workhorses of the juvenile justice system." In 1998 (the latest year for which data were available), juvenile probation officers processed about 1.75 million cases.[52] Although the actual practice of juvenile probation varies from one jurisdiction to the next, probation officers usually perform four important roles in the juvenile justice process:

1. They perform intake screening.
2. They conduct presentence investigations.
3. They supervise offenders.
4. They provide assistance to youths placed on probation.

In some jurisdictions, all of those roles are performed by the same individual. In other jurisdictions, each probation officer specializes in only one of the roles.

A recent trend in juvenile probation is the development of intensive-supervision (probation) programs, which in some jurisdictions involve home confinement. Intensive-supervision programs are intended to ensure regular contact between probationers and probation officers. They are also intended to serve as an intermediate response that is more restrictive than standard probation but less restrictive than incarceration. However, like standard probation programs, the frequency of contact between probation officers and probationers varies considerably.[53]

Although there is wide variation in the meaning of intensive supervision, there is some indication that programs that provide frequent supervision of offenders, as well as services, are as effective as incarceration at reducing recidivism.[54] The same research also suggests that intensive-supervision programs are more cost-effective than incarceration, provided they actually divert a sizable number of youths from institutions.

A recent trend in intensive supervision of juveniles is the use of home confinement, which began to be used with juvenile offenders in the 1970s[55] and has grown in popularity since that time. Today, home confinement programs use two mechanisms to monitor youths: frequent probation officer contacts and electronic monitoring. Electronic monitoring requires an offender to wear a tamper-resistant electronic device that automatically notifies the probation department if the juvenile leaves home or another designated location.

The use of home confinement employing electronic monitoring of juvenile offenders began in the 1980s and has grown substantially.[56] However, because electronic monitoring technology is diverse, rapidly developing, and relatively new, little evidence of its effectiveness exists. Still, there are good reasons that some jurisdictions find electronic monitoring attractive:

1. It eases the problem of detention overcrowding.
2. It allows youths to participate in counseling, education, and vocational programs without endangering public safety.
3. It allows youths to live with supervision in a more natural environment than an institution.
4. It allows court workers to better assess the ability of youths to live in the community under standard probation after they leave the program.[57]

Besides probation, juvenile courts in some jurisdictions employ several other types of community-based interventions with juvenile offenders, such as restitution or community service programs, wilderness probation programs, and day treatment programs. In practice, probation is often combined with one of those other community-based interventions.

CJ ONLINE

OJJDP
Visit the Office of Juvenile Justice and Delinquency Prevention website at **www.ojjdp.ncjrs.org** to review the various programs offered by the organization. *Which programs do you think would help deter juvenile crime?*

Restitution Restitution programs, as you may recall, require offenders to compensate victims for damages to property or for physical injuries. The primary goal of restitution programs is to hold youths accountable for their actions. In practice, there are three types of restitution:

1. *Monetary restitution,* a cash payment to the victim for harm done.
2. *Victim-service restitution,* in which the youth provides some service to the victim.

3. *Community-service restitution,* in which the youth provides assistance to a community organization.

Despite the growing popularity of juvenile restitution programs, as well as some programs' effective reduction of recidivism, there are potential problems with some of those programs. Problems include poorly managed, informal programs with low compliance rates; high recidivism rates in some programs; and hearing officers' ordering restitution that is unrealistic to expect juveniles to complete. There is also a potential for net-widening, and restitution requirements can be subject to discretionary abuse; some jurisdictions, however, have established restitution guidelines to remedy this problem. Thus, rather than achieving the goals of accountability, offender treatment, and victim compensation, restitution programs may fail to protect community safety. Moreover, they are likely to produce negative perceptions of juvenile justice by both offenders and victims.

Wilderness Probation (Outdoor Adventure) Programs Wilderness probation or outdoor adventure programs for juvenile offenders are based, in part, on ideas derived from programs such as Outward Bound. (Outward Bound is a company that sells outdoor experiences such as mountain climbing, backpacking, and mountain biking.) A basic assumption of those programs is that learning is best accomplished by acting in an environment where there are consequences for one's actions. Consequently, the programs involve youths in a physically and sometimes emotionally challenging outdoor experience intended to help them develop confidence in themselves, learn to accept responsibility for themselves and others, and develop a relationship of trust with program staff. This is done by engaging youths in a variety of activities, such as camping, backpacking, rock climbing, canoeing, sailing, negotiating rope courses, and a solo experience (spending one or more nights alone in the wilderness).[58]

Evaluations of several wilderness probation programs have shown that they can produce positive effects, such as increases in self-esteem and a decrease in criminal activity both during and after the program.[59] However, research also indicates that the positive effects of the programs may diminish over time

CJ ONLINE

Wilderness Probation
You can learn more about wilderness probation programs by accessing The Hope for Youth website at **www.hfyny.org.** *What do you think are some of the benefits and drawbacks of wilderness probation?*

Some juvenile treatment programs strive to provide physically and emotionally challenging experiences to help youthful offenders gain confidence and learn responsibility for their actions. *What are the benefits and drawbacks of these kinds of programs?*

or may be no greater than the effects produced by probation programs that provide regular and meaningful contacts between probation officers and probationers.[60]

Day Treatment Programs Day treatment programs for juvenile offenders operate in a number of jurisdictions around the United States. The programs often target serious offenders who would otherwise be candidates for institutionalization. They provide treatment or services to youths during the day and allow them to return home at night. Because they are viewed as alternatives to incarceration, they are believed to be cost-effective. Because they provide highly structured programs for youths during the day, it is assumed that they protect community safety as well. The range of services or treatments can be quite varied and may include academic remediation, individual and group counseling, job skills training, job placement, and social-skills training. Although some evidence suggests that day treatment programs are as effective as, or more effective than, institutional placement, some programs may be no more effective at reducing recidivism than standard probation.[61]

Foster Homes Foster homes are out-of-home placements intended to resemble, as much as possible, a family setting. Foster parents are licensed to provide care for one or more youths (usually one to three) and are paid a daily rate for the costs of care. Foster placement is often used by a court when a youth's home life has been particularly chaotic or harmful. In such a case, foster care is used to temporarily separate the youth from the parents or guardian in an effort to resolve the problems that resulted in the youth's removal. Foster homes are also used to remove youths from particular neighborhoods and for some nonviolent offenders instead of more restrictive placements, such as institutionalization. When used in those ways, they are considered "halfway-in programs." In other instances, foster homes are used as transitions to home and are considered "halfway-out programs."

Group homes for delinquent youths are generally less impersonal than institutions and are less expensive than institutional placements. *What are some other advantages of group homes? What are some disadvantages?*

Although foster homes are widely used by juvenile courts in some jurisdictions, there are few sound evaluations of their effectiveness. The limited research that exists indicates that foster care is generally not effective and may even be counterproductive.

Group Homes Similar to foster homes, group homes are open, nonsecure community-based facilities used in both "halfway-in programs" and "halfway-out programs." However, they are somewhat larger and frequently less familylike than foster homes. The purpose of many group homes is to avoid requiring youths to accept "substitute parents," because many youths are in the process of developing emotional independence from parental figures. Nevertheless, group homes are generally less impersonal than institutions and are less expensive than institutional placements. In addition, their location allows residents to take advantage of community services. Youths who live in group homes usually go to school in the home or in the community or work in the community. Treatment typically consists of group or individual counseling provided by group-home staff or outside counselors.

FYI

Group Homes

Although group homes are used extensively in juvenile justice, relatively little sound recent research has examined their effectiveness. One well-known, but older, study of a group home program, the Silverlake Experiment, found that youths placed in the program for approximately 6 months were no more likely to commit further crimes than similar youths who were randomly assigned to an institutional placement. In other words, placement in the program was neither more nor less effective than institutionalization at reducing recidivism.

INSTITUTIONAL PROGRAMS FOR JUVENILES

A variety of correctional institutions house juveniles within the United States, including detention centers, adult jails, shelter facilities (some of them are more community based), reception and diagnostic centers, ranches, forestry camps, farms, and training schools. These institutions hold a variety of youths, including those who are status offenders as well as those who have committed violent offenses against others. They are administered by either state or local governments or by private agencies.

Juvenile Correctional Institutions What distinguishes institutional programs from their community-based counterparts is that institutional programs typically restrict youths' access to the community more than community-based programs do. Indeed, institutional programs are the most restrictive placements available to juvenile courts. However, juvenile institutions vary in the extent to which they focus on custody and control.

For example, some juvenile institutions employ a variety of security hardware: perimeter fencing or walls, barbed or razor wire, and surveillance and detection devices, such as motion detectors, sound monitors, and security cameras. Those juvenile institutions, classified as secure facilities, closely monitor residents' movement within the facility and restrict residents' access to the community. Most public and private detention centers, reception and diagnostic centers, and state training schools are secure facilities. In contrast, other juvenile institutions rely much less on security devices. Those facilities have no perimeter fencing, and some do not lock entrances or exits at night. Classified as open institutions, they rely more heavily on staff than on physical security. Most private facilities, as well as most public shelters, ranches, forestry camps, and farms, are open institutions.[62]

In addition to differences in the use of security hardware, juvenile correctional institutions also differ in a number of other ways. Some of the institutions are

Myth	Fact
Most of the youths housed in juvenile correctional institutions pose an immediate threat to public safety.	As Jerome Miller notes in his book, *Last One Over the Wall: The Massachusetts Experiment in Closing Reform Schools* (1991), in Massachusetts only about 25 percent of youths committed to state correctional facilities had committed offenses against persons. Many of those offenses against persons did not actually involve physical violence or the threat of physical violence. Consequently, many youths placed in correctional facilities, including many of those placed for violent offenses, do not pose a grave threat to public safety.

Historically, large juvenile institutions have proven ineffective at preventing youths from offending again. *What do you think could be done to make these institutions more effective?*

privately operated institutions, although the majority are public institutions. The majority of both private and public institutions are small, housing 40 or fewer residents, although some large, state-operated institutions have a legal capacity of 800 or more. Some institutions are coed; others are single-gender institutions.

Institutions also differ in the average length of time that residents stay in the facility. Typically, youths stay longer in private facilities than in public facilities. However, some private and public facilities are for short-term placements, while others are for long-term placements. Institutions such as detention centers and diagnostic and reception centers are typically for short-term placements. Detention centers usually house youths awaiting adjudication or those who have been adjudicated and are awaiting disposition. In some cases, youths are placed in those institutions for a period of time as a disposition. Other institutions, such as ranches, forestry camps, farms, and training schools, are generally for long-term placements. Youths are placed in them as a result of disposition or possibly assessment at a reception and diagnostic center.

Juvenile institutions also differ in types of programming and quality of care. Almost all juvenile correctional institutions offer basic educational and counseling programs for their residents. Moreover, more than half of all institutions offer family counseling, employment counseling, peer group meetings, a point system, or behavioral contracts. However, there is considerable variability in the extent to which institutions offer more specialized educational or counseling programs for clients and the extent to which residents participate in the programs. For example, research shows that many institutions do not offer vocational training, GED courses, tutoring, suicide prevention, or programs for special offender types, such as violent offenders, sex offenders, or drug offenders.[63]

An examination of the history of juvenile institutions reveals that children have often been subjected to abuse and inhumane treatment in juvenile correctional institutions. Certainly, the overall quality of institutional life in

FYI: Boot Camps

In response to the significant increase in juvenile arrests and repeat offenses from the mid-1980s to the mid-1990s, a few states and many localities have established juvenile boot camps, modeled after adult boot camps. Evaluations of three juvenile boot camp pilot projects found that program completion rates were high, academic skills improved, and many participants found jobs during aftercare. However, none of the projects reduced recidivism. For one of them, recidivism among participants was greater than among juvenile offenders confined in traditional juvenile correctional facilities.

SOURCE: Eric Peterson, "Juvenile Boot Camps: Lessons Learned," U.S. Department of Justice, Office of Juvenile Justice and Delinquency Prevention, Fact Sheet #36 (Washington, DC: GPO, June 1996).

correctional facilities today is vastly improved over that experienced by most youths placed in houses of refuge and early reform and training schools. Many juvenile institutions are administered by competent, caring, and professional administrators, who oversee skilled and caring staff in delivering a variety of high-quality services to their residents. Yet, many of the problems that have historically plagued juvenile correctional institutions are still evident. In a recent study of juvenile correctional institutions, for example, researchers learned that approximately 40 percent of the institutions were overcrowded (that is, they did not have enough beds for all of their residents and exceeded standards based on square footage, utility use, or fire codes).[64] Facilities with fewer standard beds were more likely to have transported residents to emergency rooms for treatment of injuries sustained at the institution. Another, older study of the conditions of confinement in American juvenile correctional facilities found overcrowding that resulted in the following substantial deficiencies: a lack of adequate living space, security practices that resulted in escapes or injuries to residents, inadequate health care for residents, and inadequate mechanisms for controlling suicidal behavior. In addition, the study discovered that such "deficiencies were distributed widely across facilities."[65]

Despite the long history of juvenile correctional institutions, there is surprisingly little information on the effectiveness of this response to juvenile offenders. Moreover, what is known is not encouraging. Although there is some indication that effective institutional programs for juveniles exist,[66] the bulk of the evidence indicates that many juvenile institutions have little effect on recidivism. For example, a review of the re-arrest rates of youths released in states that rely heavily on institutions found that the percentage of youths re-arrested ranged from 51 percent to more than 70 percent.[67] The results may not be surprising, considering the quality of life in many juvenile institutions.

Recent Trends in Juvenile Incarceration

Among recent trends in juvenile incarceration are (1) its increased use (at least until recently), (2) the use of both public and private facilities, (3) the disproportionately large percentage of males and racial or ethnic minorities that are incarcerated, and (4) the increasing number of juveniles being incarcerated in local adult jails and state prisons. Incarceration has become an increasingly popular response to delinquency, though that trend may be moderating somewhat. For example, at year-end 1999 (the latest year for which data were available), nearly 109,000 juvenile offenders were held in residential placement facilities, about the same number as was held in 1995.[68] The District of Columbia had the highest juvenile incarceration rate in 1997 (662 per every 100,000

Juvenile boot camps are popular in some jurisdictions. *What are some of the advantages and disadvantages of juvenile boot camps?*

Myth / Fact

Myth: The increasing use of incarceration for juvenile offenders during the past 15 to 20 years is a response to the growing juvenile crime rate, particularly the growing rate of violent juvenile crime.

Fact: The overall juvenile crime rate has been quite stable over time, and the violent juvenile crime rate, as measured by index arrest rates (see Figure 13.5), did not show a significant increase for 15 years, until 1989, well after the trend toward increased incarceration began. Moreover, between 1994 and 2001, arrests for serious violent crimes by juveniles dropped 41 percent. This suggests that the increase in juvenile incarceration is not simply a product of the extent or the seriousness of juvenile crime.

Source: Howard N. Snyder, "Juvenile Arrests 2000," U.S. Department of Justice, Office of Juvenile Justice and Delinquency Prevention, *Juvenile Justice Bulletin* (Washington, DC: GPO, November 2002), p. 4.

FYI: Correctional Facility Conditions

A survey of 984 detention centers, training schools, ranches, farms, and camps holding 65,000 juveniles found that only 20 to 26 percent had adequate bed space, health care, security, or suicide control. The survey discovered that more than 11,000 juveniles committed 18,000 acts of attempted suicide, suicidal gestures, or self-mutilation, and that institutions frequently failed to provide appropriate housing for suicidal juveniles. Nearly half the facilities exceeded their design capacity, and only 24 percent of detained youths were in places that met all living-space standards.

SOURCE: Dale J. Parent, Valerie Leiter, Stephen Kennedy, Lisa Livens, Daniel Wentworth, and Sarah Wilcox, *Conditions of Confinement: Juvenile Detention and Corrections Facilities Research Summary* (Washington, DC: OJJDP, 1994) p. 5.

FIGURE 13.5 Violent Crime Index Arrest Rates of Juveniles, 1980–2000

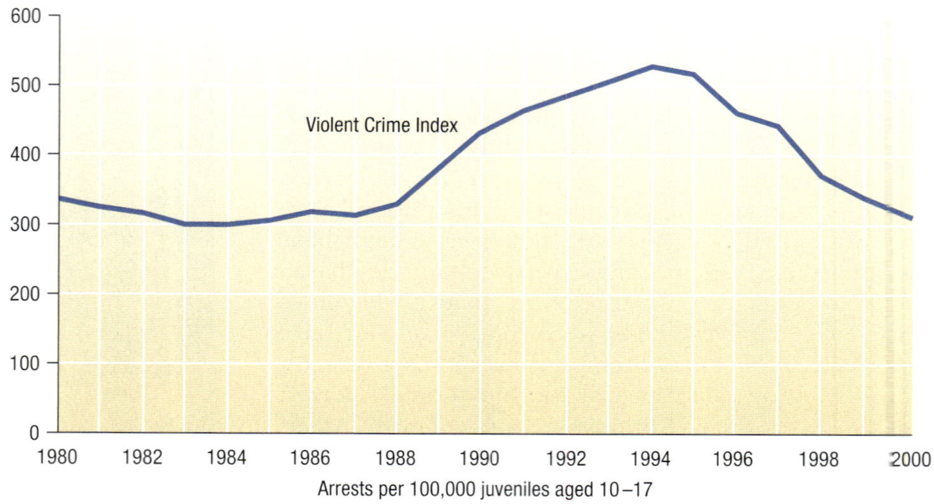

Note: The juvenile violent crime index arrest rate in 2000 was at its lowest level since 1985—41% below the peak year of 1994. All the growth in the juvenile violent crime arrest rate that began in the latter part of the 1980s was erased by 2000.

SOURCE: Howard N. Snyder, "Juvenile Arrests 2000," U.S. Department of Justice, Office of Juvenile Justice and Delinquency Prevention, *Juvenile Justice Bulletin* (Washington, DC: GPO, November 2002), p. 4.

Myth / Fact

Myth: A new type of violent juvenile offender, one for whom violence is a way of life—a "superpredator"—emerged in the late 1980s and early 1990s.

Fact: Although evidence shows that in the early 1990s, juvenile arrest rates for violent crimes broke out of their historic range and increased to a level greater than in previous generations, the evidence also shows that by 1995 arrest rates for juvenile violence had returned to a level comparable to that of a generation ago. Ironically, because of the myth of the "superpredator," nearly every state legislature made it easier to handle juveniles as adult offenders.

SOURCE: "Challenging the Myths," U.S. Department of Justice, Office of Juvenile Justice and Delinquency Prevention, *1999 National Report Series: Juvenile Justice Bulletin* (Washington, DC: GPO, February 2000).

juveniles in the population), while Vermont had the lowest (70).

Ninety-six percent of juveniles placed in residential facilities in 1999 committed delinquency offenses; only 4 percent committed status offenses. The delinquency offenses included violent person offenses (36 percent of all offenses for which juveniles were incarcerated), property offenses (30.5 percent), drug offenses (9 percent), and public order offenses (10 percent). Another 14.5 percent of juveniles were confined for technical violations. Furthermore, whether a juvenile was placed in a public or private facility depended primarily on whether a delinquency or status offense was committed. Of the juveniles who were placed for delinquency offenses, 72 percent were placed in public facilities and 27 percent were placed in private facilities. Conversely, of the juveniles placed for status offenses, 35 percent were placed in public facilities and 65 percent were placed in private facilities. However, states varied greatly in the extent to which they used public or private residential facilities. At one extreme, Mississippi placed 99 percent of its juvenile offenders in public facilities; at the other extreme, Massachusetts placed 64 percent of its juvenile offenders in private facilities.

A disproportionately large percentage of males and racial or ethnic minorities are incarcerated in juvenile facilities. Although juvenile males comprised half of the U.S. juvenile population aged 10–17 in 1999, 85 percent of all juveniles incarcerated in 1999 were males. However, a larger proportion of females was incarcerated

FIGURE 13.6 Racial and Ethnic Composition of Inmate Population of Public and Private Juvenile Incarceration Facilities, 1997

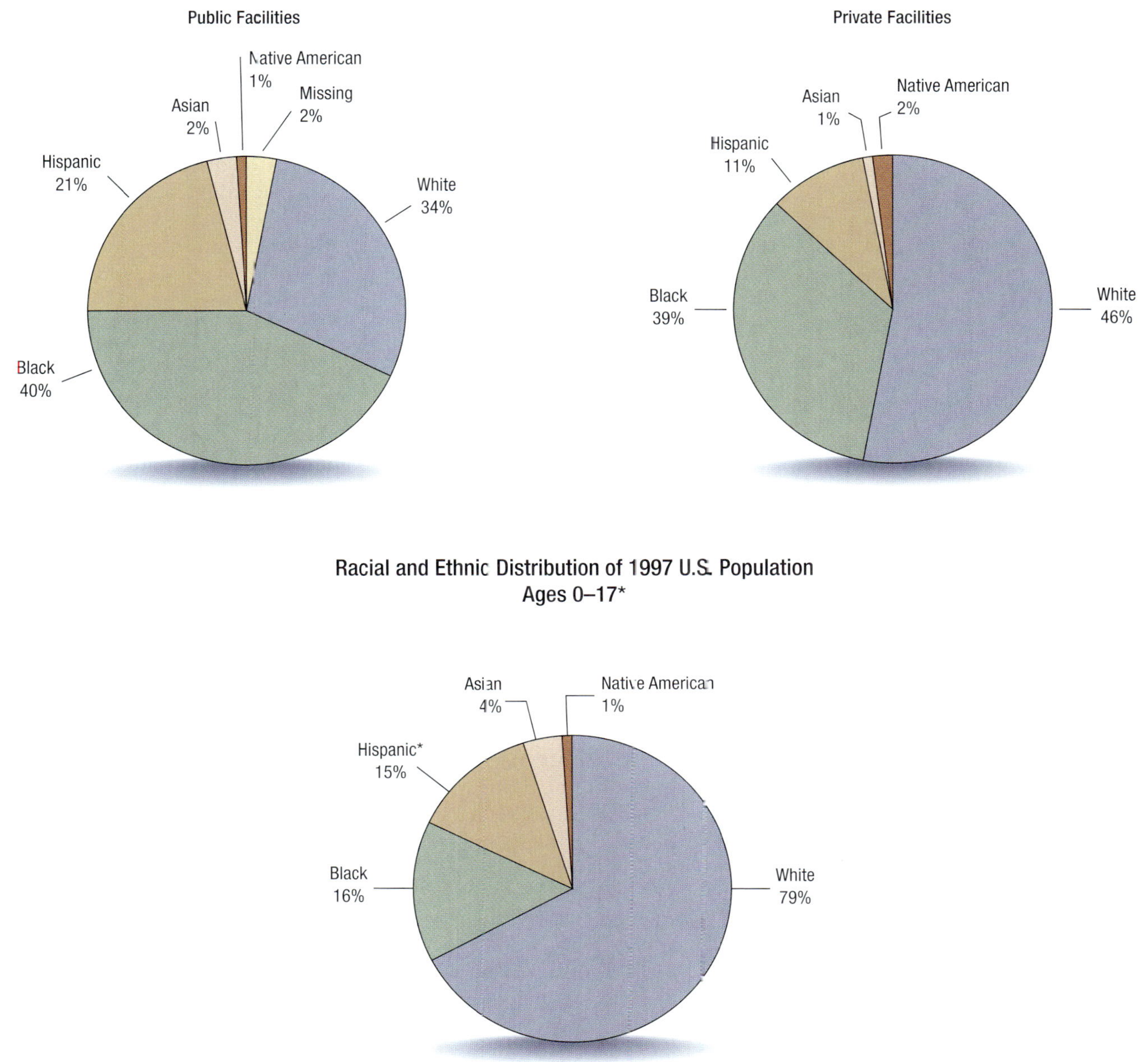

*Note: Adds to more than 100 percent because race proportions include persons of Hispanic ethnicity. Persons of Hispanic ethnicity can be of any race; however, most are white.

SOURCE: Howard N. Snyder and Melissa Sickmund, *Juvenile Offenders and Victims: 1999 National Report.* U.S. Department of Justice, National Center for Juvenile Justice, Office of Juvenile Justice and Delinquency Prevention (Washington, DC: GPO, September 1999), pp. 4, 195.

for status offenses (39 percent of females compared to 61 percent of males). Nearly half of all females incarcerated for status offenses were placed in private as opposed to public facilities.

As for racial and ethnic minorities, in 1999, minorities (that is, nonwhites) comprised about 35 percent of the American population aged 10–17. Yet, minorities accounted for more than 60 percent of all juveniles in custody in 1999. About two-thirds of all juveniles in public facilities and more than half of all juveniles in private facilities in 1997 were members of minority groups. Figure 13.6 illustrates the racial and ethnic composition of public and private juvenile incarceration facilities in 1997. Whites are underrepresented in both public and private facilities, blacks are overrepresented in both, Hispanics are overrepresented in public facilities and are underrepresented in private facilities, Asians and Pacific Islanders are underrepresented in both, and Native Americans are overrepresented in private facilities and represented proportionally in public facilities. The Juvenile Justice and Delinquency Prevention Act of 1974, as amended, requires states to determine whether minorities are disproportionately represented in confinement. If overrepresentation is found, the state must reduce it.

Juveniles have also been increasingly held in local adult jails and state prisons. Those juveniles are not included in the aforementioned total of approximately 109,000 juveniles who were incarcerated. At midyear 2002, local adult jails held 7,248 juveniles, a decrease of about 8 percent from 1995. Eighty-four percent of the juveniles were being held as adults, and 16 percent were being held as juveniles. Another 3,055 juveniles were being held in adult prisons at midyear 2002.[69]

FYI: New Prison for Females

In 2000, Florida opened its first maximum-security prison devoted to women ages 13 to 21. The prison, surrounded by razor wire and concrete walls, houses about 50 females who have committed crimes such as murder, armed robbery, drug dealing, and prostitution, as well as some women who have suffered physical and sexual abuse. The goal is to rehabilitate girls. The girls must attend school and therapy sessions during their 18-month to 3-year stays. Previously, 1 year was the longest sentence that could be imposed on a girl committed to a juvenile justice program.

Source: "Girls get a prison of their own," *The Orlando Sentinel*, March 21, 2000, p. D-3.

Aftercare Programs Aftercare involves the provision of services to assist youths in successfully making the transition from juvenile institutions to life back in the community. The services are the same as those provided by other types of community-based programs and may include foster care, shelter or group-home placement, home placement, or efforts to help youths live on their own. Parole, too, is one form of aftercare.

Unfortunately, the quality of many aftercare programs is questionable, and in some cases, youths fail to receive any services after institutional release. As in probation, parole supervision, in practice, may involve very little contact between parole officers and parolees. Moreover, large caseloads carried by aftercare workers may prevent the provision of meaningful services.

For those reasons and others (at the time, increasing juvenile crime rates, increasing numbers of juveniles requiring secure care, increasing costs, and the general failure to control or reduce the delinquent behavior of many juveniles in aftercare), the Office of Juvenile Justice and Delinquency Prevention in the late 1980s initiated an intensive community-based aftercare pilot project called the Intensive Aftercare Program (IAP).[70] The goal of IAP is to reduce recidivism among high-risk juvenile parolees. The creators of IAP describe it in this way:

> [IAP is a] correctional continuum consisting of three distinct, yet overlapping, segments: pre-release and preparatory planning during incarceration; structured transition that requires the participation of institutional and aftercare staff prior to and following community re-entry; and long-term, reintegrative activities that ensure adequate service delivery and the necessary level of social control.[71]

Table 13.2 shows the specific components of IAP as they are being implemented at three of the pilot project sites. To date, the program has not been evaluated to determine whether it is achieving its goal.

In conclusion, as juvenile justice in the United States enters the twenty-first century, several important problems remain unresolved. Many of the problems are the same ones that have plagued juvenile justice since the first specialized institutions for children were established in the early 1800s. The problems include:

1. Providing adequate due process protections to youths at all stages of the juvenile justice process.
2. Continuing to build on knowledge of effective correctional interventions and developing a range of effective and humane correctional responses, from diversion to institutional aftercare programs.

TABLE 13.2 Transition Components of IAP Programming

Transition Component	IAP Site: Colorado	Nevada	Virginia
Early parole planning	Initial plan complete at 30 days after institutional placement; final plan complete at 60 days prior to release.	Initial plan complete at 30 days after institutional placement; final plan complete 30 days prior to furlough.	Initial plan complete 30 days after institutional placement; final plan complete 30 days prior to release.
Multiple perspectives incorporated in plan	Case manager, Institutional staff, youth, parents, and community providers all routinely involved.	Parole officer, institutional community liaison, institutional staff, and youth; parent participation limited.	Parole officer, institutional case manager, youth, interagency "Community Assessment Team," and parent.
Parole officer visits to institution	One to two times per week; routine.	Once per month; routine since spring 1997.	One to two times per month; routine.
Treatment begun in institution and continued in community	Via community providers. Includes multifamily counseling, life skills training, individual counseling, and vocational skills training, done routinely.	Via an institutional-community liaison and parole officers. Includes life skills and drug/alcohol curriculums; done routinely until liaison vacancy.	Via one provider at Hanover only. Drug/alcohol treatment; sporadic use. State policy discourages contract services by community providers for institutionalized youth.
Youth prerelease visits to community	Supervised day trips to community programs, beginning 60 days prior to release.	Not allowed.	Not allowed.
Preparole furlough	Overnight/weekend home passes, beginning 30 days prior to release.	Thirty-day conditional release to community, prior to official parole.	Not allowed.
Transitional residence	Not part of the design, but occurs for some youth.	Not part of the design.	Two group homes in Norfolk; 30- to 60-day length of stay; used for most youth.
Transitional day programming	Two-day-treatment programs in Denver; used for almost all youth during the first few months after release.	One-day-supervision/treatment program; used for most youth.	Day treatment used for youth who do not go to group homes.
Phased supervision levels on parole	Informal system: contact once per week during the first few months, down to once per month later.	Four-phase system: contact four times per week during furlough; three times per week next 90 days; two times per week next 60–90 days; once per week next 30–60 days.	Four-phase system: group home; contact five to seven times per week next 60 days; three to five times per week next 60 days; three times per week last 30 days.

SOURCE: Richard G. Wiebush, Betsy McNulty, and Thao Le, "Implementation of the Intensive Community-Based Aftercare Program, "U.S. Department of Justice, Office of Juvenile Justice and Delinquency Prevention, *Juvenile Justice Bulletin* (Washington, DC: GPO, July 2000), p. 9, Table 3.

3. Eliminating the abusive treatment of youths placed in correctional programs.
4. Working out the appropriate balance between community-based and institutional correctional programs.
5. Conducting rigorous evaluations of juvenile justice agencies and programs.
6. Recognizing the limits of correctional responses in solving the juvenile crime problem.
7. Working out an appropriate balance between preventing and correcting delinquency.

THINKING CRITICALLY

1. Which of the community-based correctional programs described in the chapter (e.g., restitution, wilderness probation, and day treatment) do you think would be most effective at rehabilitating youths? Why?
2. What do you think are the pros and cons of institutional programs for juveniles?

SUMMARY

1. Describe some of the early institutions used to respond to wayward and criminal youths

Among the early institutions used to respond to wayward and criminal youths were houses of refuge, placing out, reform schools, industrial schools, and training schools.

2. Explain the effects of some landmark U.S. Supreme Court Cases on the juvenile justice system

Landmark Supreme Court cases on juvenile justice include Ex parte Crouse, People *v.* Turner, Commonwealth *v.* Fisher, Kent *v.* United States, In re Gault, In re Winship, *and* McKeiver *v.* Pennsylvania. *Some of the effects of those cases on juvenile justice are the right to adequate notice of charges, protection against compelled self-incrimination, the right to confront and to cross-examine accusers, and the right to the assistance of counsel.*

3. Identify and describe factors that influence the ways that police process juvenile cases

Among the factors that influence the ways that police process juvenile cases are (1) the seriousness of the offense, (2) the community, (3) the wishes of the complainant, (4) the demeanor of the youth, (5) the gender of the offender, (6) the race and social class of the offender, and (7) the police organization.

4. Summarize the rationale for the use of diversion in juvenile justice

Diversion programs in juvenile justice are based on the understanding that formal responses to youths who violate the law, such as arrest and adjudication, do not always protect the best interests of children or the community. Indeed, some formal responses may be harmful to many youths and may increase the likelihood of future delinquent behavior. This is because formal processing may cause youths to develop negative or delinquent self-images, may stigmatize youths in the eyes of significant others, or may subject youths to inhumane treatment.

5. Describe the adjudication hearing in juvenile justice

There are two types of adjudication: contested ones (in which juveniles dispute the charges) and uncontested ones. Contested adjudications are similar to trials in criminal courts. Most contested adjudications are bench adjudications, in which the hearing officer makes a finding of fact based on the evidence presented. In some jurisdictions, contested adjudications are jury trials. At an uncontested adjudication hearing, the youth, or frequently the youth's attorney, admits to the charges. The vast majority of juvenile court adjudications are uncontested.

6. Describe the disposition hearing and the types of dispositions available to the juvenile court

The disposition is the juvenile court equivalent of sentencing in criminal court. At the disposition hearing, the court makes its final determination of what to do with the youth who is officially labeled delinquent. At the disposition, the court also enters various orders regarding the youth's behavior. Those orders consist of various rules the youth must follow. Also, the court may enter orders regarding parents, relatives, or other people who live in the home. Dispositions available to the juvenile court include probation, placement in a diversion program, restitution, community service, detention, placement in foster care, placement in a long-term or short-term residential treatment program, placement with a relative, and placement with the state for commitment to a state facility. Not all disposition alternatives are available in all jurisdictions.

7. Identify the types and describe the effectiveness of community-based correctional programs for juveniles

Community-based correctional programs include diversion, pretrial release, probation, foster care, group home placements, and parole. Evaluations of some programs indicate that they are effective at reducing recidivism or that they are as effective as institutional placement. In contrast, evaluations of other community-based programs indicate that they have little effect on subsequent offenses.

8. Summarize recent trends in juvenile incarceration

Among recent trends in juvenile incarceration are (1) its increased use (at least until recently), (2) the use of both public and private facilities, (3) the disproportionately large percentage of males and racial or ethnic minorities that are incarcerated, and (4) the increasing number of juveniles being incarcerated in local adult jails and state prisons.

9. Identify the types and describe the effectiveness of institutional programs for juveniles

In the United States, a variety of correctional institutions house juveniles, including detention centers, adult jails, shelter facilities, reception and diagnostic centers, ranches, forestry camps, farms, and training schools. There is some evidence that small, secure treatment facilities for violent or chronic offenders are effective at reducing recidivism. However, many institutions, particularly large state institutions, have often been found to have little positive effect on youths' subsequent delinquent behaviors. In fact, they may increase the likelihood that youths will commit further offenses.

KEY TERMS

juvenile delinquency, p. 475
apprenticeship system, p. 475
binding-out system, p. 475
houses of refuge, p. 476
placing out, p. 477
reform, industrial, or training schools, p. 478
cottage reformatories, p. 478
parens patriae, p. 480
adjudication, p. 483
informal juvenile justice, p. 484
status offenses, p. 486
radical nonintervention, p. 490
intake screening, p. 492
petition, p. 494
transfer, waiver, or certification, p. 494
hearing officer, p. 496
disposition, p. 496

REVIEW QUESTIONS

1. What changes occurred in the sixteenth and seventeenth centuries in the ways the young were viewed?
2. What were the purposes of houses of refuge?
3. What is *parens patriae,* and what was the legal context in which it arose?
4. What was the social and historical context in which the juvenile court was created?
5. Historically, what has been the fundamental difference between the procedures used in juvenile courts and those employed in criminal courts?
6. What is the informal juvenile justice process, and why is it important?
7. What are four typical responses that police officers employ when handling juvenile cases?
8. What are three recent trends in police processing of juveniles?
9. What are two relatively new juvenile diversion alternatives?
10. What are five possible intake decisions that might be made in the juvenile justice process?
11. What are five recent trends in the practice of transferring juvenile cases to criminal court, and what do they suggest about the current orientation of juvenile justice?
12. In practice, what two dispositions are typically available to juvenile court judges in most jurisdictions, and which one is most frequently used?
13. What are three new dispositional or sentencing practices employed by juvenile court judges?
14. What are six objectives of community-based correctional programs for juveniles?
15. What are four problems commonly found in juvenile correctional facilities?
16. What are some important problems that remain unresolved as juvenile justice in the United States enters the twenty-first century?

IN THE FIELD

1. **Debate Juvenile Justice** With fellow students, family members, or friends, debate whether the juvenile justice system ought to be abolished and juvenile offenders treated as adults.
2. **Compare Correctional Facilities** Visit different juvenile correctional facilities in your community, both community-based facilities and institutional facilities. Compare what you observe at these facilities based on the following criteria:
   a. How do terms for similar offenses compare at each facility?
   b. How are juveniles treated?
   c. Are there educational or rehabilitation opportunities?
   d. How does the way of life compare?

ON THE NET

1. **Juvenile Information Center** Go to the Justice Information Center website at www.ncjrs.org. Click on Juvenile Justice and then choose one of the documents listed. Read the document and then write a brief summary of it.
2. **Research Parenting Issues** Go to the *Parenting Resources for the 21st Century* online guide at www.parentingresources.ncjrs.org. Select one or more of the major subject headings and then choose one or more of the specific topics to read. Write a report on the delinquency implications of the various parenting issues. (It may be helpful to review theories of delinquency in Chapter 3.)

CRITICAL THINKING EXERCISES

1. **The Case of Paul** Paul, a 15-year-old, sexually assaulted, robbed, and killed Billy, an 11-year-old. Billy was missing for 2 days. Paul hid Billy's body for those 2 days in his family's garage before dumping it in a wooded area near the house. Neighbors describe Paul as quiet and introverted. His parents state that he grew increasingly violent after they kept him from a 43-year-old man named Smith who Paul had met in a chat room. Smith was subsequently charged with sexually assaulting Paul. The two apparently had sex in motels five times during the previous 4 months.
   a. Should Paul be handled by the justice system (either juvenile or adult) or be diverted, perhaps to a mental health facility? Why?
   b. Should he be charged with first-degree murder (as well as the other crimes)? Why or why not?
   c. Should he be transferred to criminal court and tried as an adult?
   d. If tried as an adult, should he enter a plea of not guilty by reason of insanity? A plea of guilty but insane? Why or why not?
   e. If Paul is convicted of any of the charges, what sentence should be imposed? Why?
2. **The Case of James** Seventeen-year-old James lives in a nice lower-middle-class neighborhood in central Florida. A few years ago, James began running with a bad crowd. His parents tried a variety of punishments, to no avail. James was eventually arrested for burglary, theft, and other crimes. A juvenile court judge placed him on probation and ordered him to receive counseling. James violated probation, stopped going to counseling sessions, and began committing crimes again. After a subsequent arrest, James was ordered into a residential rehabilitation program for several months. After finishing the program, he was placed in a special school, from which he soon ran away. He was next placed in another residential program, one designed for youths "needing more structure." He ran away. After he was caught, a juvenile court judge returned him to the residential program for about 6 months.

   James's father states that the rehabilitation programs are a waste of time and money, because they are disorganized and ineffectual. He fears James will kill or be killed, and he wants James to be locked up until the age of 19. However, space is limited in the most secure juvenile institutions. In Florida, youths must commit an average of 12 crimes before they are placed in such institutions.
   a. Should James be handled by the justice system (either juvenile or adult) or be diverted? Why?
   b. If he is diverted, what type of program would benefit him most? Why?
   c. If James is retained in the juvenile justice system, what disposition would be most appropriate and beneficial for him?

THE FUTURE OF CRIMINAL JUSTICE IN THE UNITED STATES

CHAPTER FOURTEEN

Chapter Outline

Chapter Objectives

After completing this chapter, you should be able to:

1. Describe the possible future of law enforcement if the crime control model dominates, and the possible future if the due process model dominates.
2. Describe the possible future of the administration of justice if the crime control model dominates, and the possible future if the due process model dominates.
3. Identify perhaps the most divisive issue that will confront correctional policy makers in the future.
4. Describe the possible future of corrections.
5. List some of the cost-reduction strategies likely to be advocated in corrections in the future.
6. Explain what identity theft is and describe the extent of the problem in the United States.
7. Summarize the reasons why transnational organized crime poses special problems for law enforcement.
8. Describe some of the challenges faced by criminal justice in the Age of Terror.

Crime Story

In July of 2003, law enforcement authorities arrested 23 members of an identity theft ring that stole more than $2 million from hundreds of people in 12 states. With more than 40 members, the ring is based in an area in Orange County, California, known as Little Saigon. Members were arrested in Oregon, Washington, Idaho, and Georgia. The ages of the suspects ranged from 19 to 53.

Thuong Mong Nguyen, the alleged ringleader, was arrested for suspicion of bank fraud and identity theft. He was also named in an arrest warrant in Virginia after being detected on a surveillance camera while trying to withdraw money from a bank. Additionally, the 31-year-old Nguyen is facing charges for carjacking and robbery in an unrelated incident. Authorities allege that Nguyen and his associates assumed the identities of Orange County residents and withdrew large sums of cash from out-of-state banks or applied for instant credit to purchase jewelry and electronics. The items were later resold by the suspects and converted to cash.

Authorities contend that the theft ring has operated for more than $1\frac{1}{2}$ years under the direction of Nguyen and four others. Nguyen's wife, Mai Le, 28, was arrested for a subsequent identity theft case following a grand jury indictment in Kansas. Mai Le's latest arrest follows recent arrests for identity theft in Newport Beach, California; Georgia; and Kansas. She skipped bond in each case. Thuong Mong Nguyen and his associates are believed to have obtained bank account records from connections in the banks and used the information to create fake driver's licenses and credit cards in the victims' names. Once the identity had been assumed, Nguyen would allegedly send small teams of his associates to other states where they would withdraw large sums of cash from banks or apply for instant credit at shopping malls. Reportedly, the theft-ring members posed as manicurists as a cover for their alleged stealing.

Chapter 14 discusses the nature and extent of identity theft in the United States. Identity theft is an increasing problem for law enforcement agencies. Frequently the crime is completed before victims are aware that their identities have been stolen. Besides the difficulties in arresting and prosecuting offenders are the hardships experienced by victims who attempt to reestablish new credit and reclaim their former credit identities. Another concern is the growing transnational aspect of identity theft, which often involves the use of computer and Internet services that easily transcend national borders. Is law enforcement adequately equipped to deal with the problem of identity theft, particularly its transnational component? What new tools does law enforcement need to address the problem? Each of us must be vigilant in a public effort to thwart identity theft.

The Future of Criminal Justice

In the preceding chapters of this book, you have learned about the nature of crime and its consequences in the United States, theories of crime and delinquency causation, criminal law and its application, and the historical development of criminal and juvenile justice. You have also examined in detail the current operation of criminal and juvenile justice and have analyzed problems associated with each. In this last chapter, you will explore the directions that American criminal and juvenile justice might take in the future and consider some predictions. Excluded from this chapter are predictions about future trends in the most common types of crime and delinquency, because that subject is too far afield. However, we do examine two crimes that are likely to pose special problems for law enforcement and criminal justice in the twenty-first century: identity theft and transnational organized crime. We conclude the chapter with a summary of the criminal justice response to terrorism, the defining crime of the early twenty-first century.

The principal guide that informs predictions of the future directions of criminal and juvenile justice is Herbert Packer's model of the U.S. criminal justice process, which was introduced in Chapter 1.[1] For us, Packer's model has had considerable explanatory power for more than 30 years, and it seems that its explanatory power will remain strong in the future. However, in making predictions, this text will not limit itself to Packer's vision of possible futures for criminal and juvenile justice, but will instead peer into its own crystal ball—and those of others—to venture some predictions in areas where Packer's model is silent.

THE FUTURE OF LAW ENFORCEMENT

The manner in which law is enforced in the future will vary substantially depending on whether it is driven by crime control model principles or due process model principles (see the discussion of these models in Chapter 1). Either way, advances in technology will play a huge role in law enforcement's future. This section addresses those issues.

Law Enforcement Under Crime Control If the future of law enforcement increasingly reflects the principles and policies of the crime control model, then you might expect fewer limitations on how the police attempt to combat crime. For example, the practice of detaining and arresting suspects for investigation without probable cause is likely to increase, as is the length of time a suspect may be held before being charged. The Supreme Court may augment those practices by granting good-faith exceptions to the Fifth Amendment protection against compelled self-incrimination. If the crime control model is fully embraced, it is possible that the Court's decision in *Miranda* v. *Arizona* could be overturned and that coerced confessions would be admissible at trial.

The investigative abilities of the police should be improved and made easier by the expansion of community policing. Although the current meaning of community policing remains vague (see Chapter 6), it will ultimately be defined by the way it is actually employed. If it is employed according to crime control principles, American citizens can expect greater intrusion into their lives. Privacy will be sacrificed for efficiency in crime control.

Greater intrusion into people's lives will be facilitated by advances in electronic surveillance. For example, advances in **bionics** (the replacing of human body parts with mechanical parts) may someday produce bionic eyes powerful enough for law enforcement officers to see for miles or through walls, and bionic ears sensitive enough to enable law enforcement officers, from a

bionics The replacing of human body parts with mechanical parts.

CJ ONLINE

Bionics

Visit *Scientific American*'s website at **www.sciam.com** to learn more about scientific research in bionics. *Do you think the use of bionics could have a significant impact on law enforcement in the future? Why?*

FYI

Carnivore

The FBI has implemented a new surveillance system, called *Carnivore*. The system, when placed at an Internet service provider such as America Online, will allow law enforcement agents to intercept and analyze huge amounts of incoming and outgoing e-mail in connection with the target of a criminal investigation.

SOURCE: Federal Bureau of Investigation at www.fbi.gov/hq/lab/carnivore/carnivore2.htm.

considerable distance, to clearly hear conversations held behind closed doors.[2] Already, computer-controlled supersensitive listening and video devices are able to accomplish the same things.[3] Miniaturization and remote-control technology will allow the creation of tiny eavesdropping aerial drones equipped with a camera and microphone that can fly into open spaces to record what is happening.[4] To the extent that the crime control model is followed, there may be fewer or, perhaps, no limitations on the future uses of electronic surveillance. According to this scenario, George Orwell's vision of a society monitored totally by Big Brother (the state and its agents) may become a reality in the United States, as it did to varying degrees in the totalitarian nations of Eastern Europe, Communist China, and the former Soviet Union. In other words, to facilitate efficient crime control, according to the logic of the crime control model, it is conceivable that every move you make, every word you say, and, possibly, every thought you think will be recorded for future incrimination, if the need arises.

New software is being developed that allows law enforcement agencies nationwide to share data in a timely manner.[5] The new software combines several public, private, and criminal databases and allows them to be searched simultaneously. An advanced feature of the software is the ability to take vague bits of information, such as a partial license tag number, and get lists of possible suspects or vehicles in seconds. The software is intended primarily for terrorism investigations, but it may also be used to help solve child abductions or other time-sensitive crimes. Another feature of the software is the ability to use digital driver's license photos to quickly generate a photo lineup that can be shown to witnesses. Critics of the new software contend that it infringes on civil liberties and privacy rights and could lead to racial profiling. It may even be possible, as depicted in Steven Spielberg's recent movie, *The Minority Report*, that certain people or devices will be able to see into the future to identify criminals before they could do any harm. In any event, advanced electronic surveillance devices and other new technologies in law enforcement (to be discussed in more detail later in this chapter) should be available sooner than might normally be expected because of the war on terrorism.

LAW ENFORCEMENT UNDER DUE PROCESS On the other hand, if Americans see a shift to the principles and policies of the due process model, they should expect existing limitations on how the police combat crime to remain intact or even be expanded. Certainly, the practice of detaining and arresting suspects for investigation without probable cause will end or, at least, be decreased substantially. The present 48-hour limitation—with certain exceptions—on the length of time a suspect may be held before being charged will be standard operating procedure. Good-faith exceptions to protections against compelled self-incrimination will not be allowed, and current good-faith exceptions to the exclusionary rule may be eliminated. Adherence to the *Miranda* requirements will become even more routine among police officers than it is currently. Perhaps suspects will no longer be allowed to waive their rights.

To the extent that the due process model shapes future law enforcement practice, electronic surveillance will not be allowed under any circumstances or will at least be strictly limited to a few types of crimes (for example, crimes that threaten national security, such as treason and espionage).

Regardless of which of Packer's two models dominates in the future, community policing is likely to become standard practice throughout the country, as police officers become known as *public service officers*.[6] Community policing will at least make citizens feel much safer in their homes and communities (and, perhaps, reduce the likelihood of victimization by predatory criminal behavior) than did previous forms of policing. However, if community

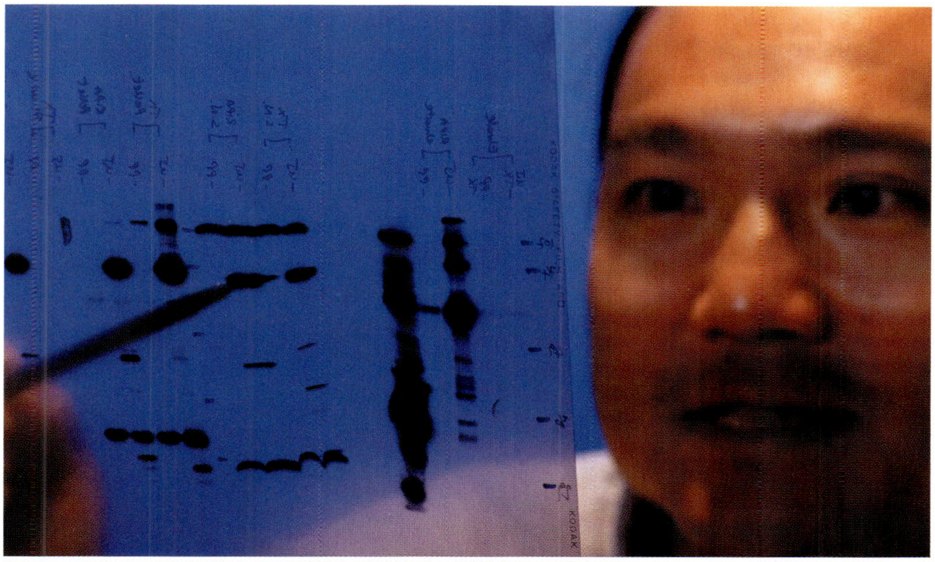

DNA profiling will be used increasingly in the future. *How should the DNA database be collected and used?*

policing adheres to principles of the due process model, it will not in any way violate the privacy of citizens unless there is probable cause (strictly defined) to do so. Instead, for citizens and communities that seek help, community policing will help reduce the incidence of criminal victimization and, by doing so, improve the conditions of life—while respecting the privacy of citizens who do not want help.

As described more fully in Chapter 6, a recent development in criminal investigation is DNA profiling. Although this new technology is still controversial, it will probably become a routine law enforcement tool in the near future. Perhaps the most thorny issue with this new technology is how the DNA database will be collected and used. If the principles of the due process model prevail in the future, then the DNA database will probably comprise DNA samples taken only from booked suspects (and criminal justice personnel upon hiring), as is the current practice with fingerprints. Such a policy is unlikely to be very controversial or to attract much public resistance. On the other hand, if policy reflects the principles of the crime control model, then the DNA database may comprise DNA samples taken shortly after birth from all infants born in the United States. This latter strategy would clearly make the DNA database more complete and, therefore, a more efficient tool in the effort to solve crimes. It would also be much more controversial and would probably be resisted by a large segment of the population as a violation of privacy rights.

CJ ONLINE

DNA

You can learn more about DNA profiling by visiting the National Institute of Justice's National Commission on the Future of DNA Evidence website at **www.ojp.usdoj.gov/nij/dna/welcome.html.** *Do you think that DNA profiling will play an important role in the future of law enforcement? Why?*

Advances in law enforcement technology are inevitable, but technology employed according to due process principles will be used to protect citizens and law enforcement personnel. For example, robots will be employed with greater frequency to perform a variety of law enforcement duties. Robots have been used by law enforcement personnel since the mid-1970s for handling bombs, and they are currently being used in other law enforcement situations, usually in SWAT or other dangerous circumstances.[7] In the future, they may be used routinely in hostage situations and in the arrest of dangerous suspects.

Some police departments are beginning to install digital video systems in their patrol cars to record and store pictures of every encounter their officers

FYI Robot Security

The Los Angeles Art Museum currently uses a cybermotion robot sentry to patrol at night. The robot checks for intruders, leaky pipes, or fire. If it finds a door open that should be closed, it calls security and takes a video picture of the scene.

SOURCE: Gene Stephens, "Drugs and Crime in the Twenty-First Century," *The Futurist*, May–June 1992, pp. 19–22.

have.[8] Although many police departments already have camera systems in their cars to provide evidence in arrests and to protect themselves from lawsuits, the new systems record and store the data in computers. Also, unlike analog video systems, which usually are not activated until after a violation has occurred, the new digital systems allow the police to record the events preceding the infraction and the infraction, itself, while it is taking place. The new systems also come with small microphones that officers wear on their belts so they can record what is said outside their cars.

When officers begin their shifts, they plug a portable hard drive into a computer mounted between the front seats of their patrol cars. They then activate a microphone and bi-directional camera that is mounted on the car's visor. The microphone and camera record continuously but only save 3 to 4 minutes at a time. When officers turn on their pursuit lights, the system automatically saves and stores the last few minutes and whatever comes next, until the system is turned off. Once their shifts are completed, officers take the portable hard drive to police headquarters and upload all the stored data to a central server.[9]

Some police departments have plans to put small wireless video cameras on police officers' lapels and to install equipment in patrol cars that will allow officers to remotely monitor video feeds from banks.[10]

New Law Enforcement Technology Some other ideas currently on drawing boards are

- A pocket-sized, voice-activated voice-stress analyzer that police officers could use to determine whether suspects or witnesses experienced stress during questioning, indicating possible dishonest answers (used like current polygraph machines).
- An ultrasmall, two-way cellular phone (like a Dick Tracy wrist communicator), possibly implanted in officers' larynxes, that would allow police officers to be in constant contact with headquarters, fellow officers, or anyone around the world.
- A universal translator (that is, an ultrasmall computer) that could instantly translate speech from one language to another, allowing police officers to question suspects, witnesses, or crime victims without the language barrier they frequently confront today.[11]
- An ultra-wideband device that will allow police officers to detect motions through surfaces such as walls (for example, to determine whether there are people inside a room before they knock down a door).[12]
- A "smart" gun that would electronically disable itself if taken away from a police officer during a struggle.
- A microwave device to shut off a car's ignition, stopping fleeing suspects without the risk of a high-speed chase.
- A supersticky foam that could be sprayed on armed suspects, neutralizing them by temporarily gluing their arms to their bodies.
- Spikes embedded in retractable panels beneath roads that could be raised by remote control to blow out a getaway car's tires.[13]
- Jet packs that officers could wear on their backs so that they could patrol by air.[14]
- A hand-held scanner that will allow remote body-cavity searches.[15]

Some law enforcement agencies use robots to handle bombs and other dangerous assignments. *Should all law enforcement agencies have access to robots? If so, how should they be financed and distributed?*

- Nanosized computer chips that can be placed in the neural networks (such as the human brain) of police officers to give them access to billions of gigabytes of instantly accessible data (such as criminal records of suspects).[16]

The future of law enforcement in the United States is likely to be very different from law enforcement today. New styles of policing, such as community policing, will be embraced and new technologies employed. The form that the change ultimately takes, however, will depend substantially on whether there is a dramatic shift toward the principles and policies of the crime control model or toward the principles and policies of its due process counterpart. In the next section, possible future developments in the administration of justice are considered.

FYI

Smart Houses

Future technology will enhance crime prevention. It is likely that houses and vehicles will be made "smarter" in an effort to foil criminals. For example, smart houses and vehicles will be equipped to deny access and even to take defensive action against unauthorized intruders by calling police and releasing knockout gas into the home or vehicle.

SOURCE: "Forensics Revolution Not Far Off," *The Orlando Sentinel*, October 9, 1997, p. A13.

THE FUTURE OF THE ADMINISTRATION OF JUSTICE

Depending on whether the crime control model or the due process model dominates the future of criminal justice, there are likely to be many changes in the ways that justice is administered. Some of those changes may involve the right to counsel at various stages of the criminal justice process, the preliminary hearing, the grand jury, pretrial detention, plea bargaining, sentencing, appeals, and juvenile justice. The criminal courts will also have to adapt to the changing demographics of the population. Most of the conflicts currently processed by the criminal courts are likely to be handled by alternative dispute resolution programs that utilize mediation and arbitration. Restorative justice may play a greater role in the future. Finally, advances in technology will undoubtedly change the administration of justice.

RIGHT TO COUNSEL If, in the future, the administration of justice in the United States is more in line with the crime control model, then the right to legal counsel (both court-appointed and privately retained) at critical pre- and posttrial stages may be scaled back significantly. Advocates of the crime control model consider legal representation at any stage, other than perhaps at trial, a luxury and an unnecessary impediment to the efficient operation of the process. Advocates of the crime control model argue that prior to trial (for example, during interrogation), providing counsel to a suspect only hampers the ability of police to investigate a case. After trial, during the appellate process, the availability of legal counsel further reduces the speed with which a case can be brought to closure. Crime control model supporters maintain that in both situations, a crafty lawyer may be able to win the freedom of a factually guilty client by means of a legal technicality.

If the principles and policies of the due process model dominate the future of the administration of justice, however, then it is likely that the current right to counsel at a variety of critical stages in the process will be retained and, perhaps, even extended somewhat (for example, to appeals beyond the first one). Advocates of the due process model believe that legal counsel is crucial throughout the process and must be made available immediately after arrest. Otherwise, the likelihood that innocent people will be subject to harassment, or worse, by agents of the state (police officers and prosecutors) is increased to an intolerable level.

PRELIMINARY HEARING Along with a greatly reduced role for legal counsel in the administration of justice, crime control model enthusiasts advocate the abolition of the preliminary hearing. They argue that it is a waste of time and money to conduct a preliminary testing of the evidence and the charges imposed, because prosecutors have no reason to pursue cases that are unlikely

Los Angeles Lakers' star Kobe Bryant arrives for his preliminary hearing. *Should the preliminary hearing be abolished, as crime control model proponents advocate? Why or why not?*

to lead to conviction. Recall from the discussion in Chapter 8 that prosecutors' reputations and chances of achieving higher political office depend at least partially on the proportion of convictions they are able to obtain. Besides, for several reasons, including the sheer volume of cases that must be handled in the lower courts, the evidence against a suspect is rarely tested at the preliminary hearing anyway. Today, the preliminary hearing is used mostly for making decisions about bail.

Due process model advocates, however, believe that the preliminary hearing is a critical stage in the administration of justice. Although they concede that this hearing is not currently being used as it is supposed to be, they argue that it needs reform instead of abandonment. As described previously, due process model advocates are skeptical about the motivations of prosecutors in criminal cases. History has certainly recorded numerous incidences of prosecutorial misbehavior. Because most criminal cases are resolved through plea bargaining rather than criminal trial, the preliminary hearing may be the only opportunity for a judicial officer to scrutinize the prosecutor's work. Elimination of the preliminary hearing (as it is supposed to operate in theory) would substantially reduce the effectiveness of the entire adversary process of justice.

Grand Jury Instead of elimination of the preliminary hearing, due process model enthusiasts are more inclined to argue for elimination of the grand jury. As described in Chapter 8, the grand jury is another vehicle by which the evidence and charges brought by a prosecutor against a suspect are examined by an impartial body. However, in practice, the grand jury is even more of a sham than the preliminary hearing, having become nothing more than a tool or a rubber stamp for the prosecutor. Invariably, a grand jury will indict or not indict a suspect if that is what the prosecutor wants. Moreover, abuses of the process are more likely to occur in grand jury proceedings, which are conducted in private—away from the watchful eyes of defense attorneys and the public—than in preliminary hearings, which allow the presence of defense attorneys and are open to the public.

Pretrial Detention If the crime control model dominates the administration of justice in the future, it is likely that the use of pretrial detention will be expanded. Advocates of the crime control model maintain that expanded use of pretrial detention will encourage more factually guilty offenders to plead guilty—they would have nothing to gain by not doing so—and will better protect society from the crimes those people are likely to commit if not confined. As for the protection of society, perhaps in the future the pretrial detention of potentially dangerous suspects will be unnecessary because of technical advances in electronic monitoring. For example, the use of electronically monitored house arrest, in which suspects are connected to monitors by electrodes (perhaps surgically implanted in their bodies) that shock them intermittently when they are outside designated areas, may be sufficient to ensure that suspects do not pose a threat to society while awaiting trial.[17] If this type of monitoring is employed, it is likely that suspects would be given a choice between it and jail. Most suspects would probably choose electronic monitoring.

Due process model supporters argue that pretrial detention should be used sparingly if at all. They believe that people accused of crimes should be entitled to remain free until they are found guilty, unless they are unlikely to appear when required or they pose a significant threat to society. Regarding those two exceptions to pretrial release, due process model advocates believe that nonappearance problems can be handled adequately through the existing bail system. They do admit, however, that the present bail system discriminates against the poor. That discrimination is another problem that must be rectified. As for the pretrial detention of defendants who presumably pose a significant threat to society, due process model advocates doubt that prosecutors and judges can predict accurately which defendants actually pose a significant threat and which do not. The result is that many defendants who do not need to be jailed prior to trial will be jailed—or electronically monitored—because of inevitable false predictions. Due process model enthusiasts also suggest that both exceptions to pretrial release—nonappearance and potential threat to society—could be handled by methods other than pretrial detention—for example, by a prompt trial, as required by the Sixth Amendment.

Plea Bargaining As mentioned earlier in this chapter, a key to the crime control model's efficiency in the administration of justice is heavy reliance on plea bargaining. Thus, if the crime control model dominates the administration of justice in the future, Americans should expect even fewer criminal trials than today. If there is instead a dramatic shift to the principles and policies of the due process model, plea bargaining will probably be discouraged, and the number of criminal cases that go to trial will increase substantially. For due process model supporters, a principal problem with plea bargaining is that after a guilty plea has been accepted, the possibility of any further judicial examination of earlier stages of the process is eliminated. In other words, with the acceptance of a guilty plea, there is no longer any chance that police or prosecutorial errors before trial will be detected. Plea bargaining will probably not be eliminated entirely, however, even in a legal atmosphere dominated by due process model principles and policies, because eliminating it would be impractical. The time and expense involved in subjecting every criminal case to a trial would be prohibitive.

Sentencing As discussed in Chapter 9 ("Sentencing, Appeals, and the Death Penalty"), more jurisdictions are eliminating or significantly reducing judicial discretion in sentencing by enacting mandatory sentencing statutes and using sentencing guidelines. This policy seems to reflect crime control model principles, although a due process model argument could be made that the restriction of judicial discretion in sentencing will reduce unwarranted judicial disparity in sentencing. In any event, if the trend continues, it is likely that in the area of sentencing, judges in the future will function simply as automatons, empowered only to apply the specific sentence dictated by law.

Appeals If the crime control model dominates the future of the administration of justice, it is likely that appeals—following the few trials that occur—will be strongly discouraged and limited. Crime control model advocates consider appeals a remote and marginal part of the process. They do recognize that the appellate process can correct errors in procedure or in the determination of factual guilt, and they endorse that role. They believe, however, that such errors occur only occasionally. For crime control model supporters, the appellate process can impede the efficient operation of the administration of justice.

If the due process model dominates the administration of justice in the future, there will probably be no limitations on the right to appeal. Due process model advocates, in contrast to their crime control model counterparts, believe that the right to appeal is a significant and indispensable part of the process, one where earlier errors and infringements of rights can be corrected. Perhaps even more important, due process model enthusiasts maintain that the prospect, if not the actual act, of appellate review can deter the commission of similar errors and other forms of misbehavior in subsequent cases. Due process model proponents argue that without the real prospect of appellate review, there would be no effective deterrent of police, prosecutorial, or judicial misbehavior or error.

CHANGING DEMOGRAPHICS OF THE POPULATION Because the population of the United States in the future will have greater cultural and racial diversity, criminal courts may be forced to adapt their routines and personnel to those changing demographics. Among the changes that may be required in the future are

1. A greater sensitivity of court personnel to cultural diversity issues.
2. An increased ability of court personnel to communicate effectively with non-English-speaking people (this will require the employment of interpreters and multilingual staff, as well as the provision of other language services, to ensure that due process rights are protected).
3. A more culturally and racially diverse workforce that better reflects the demographic characteristics of the population it serves.[18]

FYI: The Aging Population

According to U.S. Bureau of Census forecasts, the percentage of the U.S. population 65 or older, which was 8.1 percent in 1950 and 12.7 percent in 1998, will reach 16.5 percent in 2020 and 20.4 percent by the middle of the twenty-first century.

As the number of people aged 65 and over increases, the operation of criminal courts will probably have to change in other ways as well. In the first place, the types of cases routinely heard in criminal courts are likely to change somewhat and to reflect more and more the problems confronted by the elderly. For example, crimes committed by and against the elderly will probably increase, as will consideration of such issues as the right to die and the appropriate use of new medical technologies.[19] An older population will also put new demands on the way criminal courts conduct business. At the very least, courts will have to better accommodate people with physical disabilities, such as hearing and visual impairments. For example, to serve hearing-impaired

Courts are already adapting to the future by employing signers for hearing-impaired persons. *In what other ways will courts of the future have to change?*

clients, a text telephone (telecommunications device for the deaf, or TDD) or an interpreter will probably become a standard fixture in courtrooms of the future. Likewise, court personnel might be trained to establish eye contact when addressing people with hearing impairments, to provide verbal prompts to people with visual impairments, and to sit down when talking to people who are confined to wheelchairs.[20]

JUVENILE JUSTICE If the crime control model dominates the future, criminal courts will probably have to handle an increasing number of juvenile offenders, too, as the practice of transferring juvenile offenders to criminal court for trial increases (see the discussion in Chapter 13). Moreover, to the extent that crime control model principles guide the practice, Americans should expect younger and younger juvenile offenders to be transferred. If this trend becomes the norm, it is conceivable that sometime in the future the juvenile court, and possibly the entire juvenile justice system, could be eliminated entirely, in which case juvenile offenders would be treated similarly to adult criminal offenders.

Ironically, even if due process model principles guide the future, juvenile justice might be eliminated anyway. Juvenile courts are currently providing juvenile offenders with a greater number of procedural rights and are adopting more adversarial procedures (reflecting due process model principles). They are also increasingly replacing paternalistic, treatment-oriented correctional strategies with more punitive ones. As a result of those changes, there may be no practical need for a separate juvenile justice process in the future. In other words, if juvenile offenders are going to be treated exactly the same as adult criminal offenders, why have a separate juvenile justice process?

ALTERNATIVE DISPUTE RESOLUTION PROGRAMS AND RESTORATIVE JUSTICE Regardless of which model of criminal justice dominates the future, it is likely that most conflicts—with the possible exception of the more serious

FYI Bilingual Courts

On January 19, 2000, the New Mexico Supreme Court ruled that people cannot be disqualified from serving as jurors simply because they do not speak English. The decision will require the use of translators in New Mexico courtrooms.

SOURCE: "Court: Jurors Don't Have to Speak English to Serve," *The Orlando Sentinel*, January 20, 2000, p. A10.

Montana state Representative Karl Ohs helps mediate the end to the 81-day standoff between the Montana Freemen and the FBI. *Should mediation be used more often in criminal justice? Why or why not?*

ones—that today are dealt with through the adversary process of justice will be handled differently through alternative dispute resolution programs. In other words, criminal courts will become the arenas of last resort for most conflicts, used only when all other methods of resolving disputes have been exhausted. The two alternative methods of dispute resolution that will probably be used most widely in the future are mediation and arbitration.

mediation A dispute resolution process that brings disputants together with a third party (a mediator) who is trained in the art of helping people resolve disputes to everyone's satisfaction. The agreed-upon resolution is then formalized into a binding consent agreement.

arbitration A dispute resolution process that brings disputants together with a third party (an arbitrator) who has the skills to listen objectively to evidence presented by both sides of a conflict, to ask probing and relevant questions of each side, and to arrive at an equitable solution to the dispute.

Gene Stephens, a criminologist who specializes in the future of crime and criminal justice, proposes a model, based on current neighborhood justice centers, that integrates mediation and arbitration into a process he calls "participatory justice."[21] **Mediation** brings disputants together with a third party (a mediator) who is trained in the art of helping people resolve disputes. The job of the mediator is to help the disputants talk out their problems, to offer suggestions about possible resolutions, and, if possible, to achieve consensus about how the dispute can be resolved to everyone's satisfaction. The agreed-upon resolution is then formalized into a binding consent agreement. **Arbitration,** on the other hand, brings disputants together with a third party (an arbitrator) who has the skills to listen dispassionately to evidence presented by both sides of a conflict. The arbitrator asks probing and relevant questions of each side and arrives at an equitable solution to the dispute. The process is concluded when the arbitrator imposes a resolution of the dispute, which is binding on all parties.

CAREERS IN CRIMINAL JUSTICE

BARJ Coordinator

My name is Donald J. Haldemann. I am the balanced and restorative justice (BARJ) coordinator for the Delaware County Juvenile Court in Southeastern Pennsylvania. I also supervise our Victim Services Unit with a staff of six. I have a bachelor's in history, a master's in administration of justice, and a juris doctor from Widener Law School in Delaware.

I worked with 1,300 juveniles as a juvenile probation officer for 21 years before embarking on the quest for restorative justice. In 1995, Pennsylvania's Juvenile Act was amended to include the concept of restorative justice. Slowly, with grant money from the Pennsylvania Commission on Crime and Delinquency, individual counties hired restorative justice specialists and I jumped at the opportunity to join this elite fraternity. So what is restorative justice and how can you join the movement?

A crime is considered to be an offense against the "State" under the traditional model but restorative justice views crime as a harm against individual victims and the community. Offenders need to accept responsibility for the harm they have caused and participate in victim and community restoration.

On a daily basis my job consists largely of educating my staff, criminal justice professionals, social agencies, schools, and communities on restorative justice and how it can be a win/win proposition for all stakeholders in the process.

I can't possibly list all the positives about my job. I get to promote a philosophy of justice which is based on practices used in cultures all over the world for hundreds of years. What I find most difficult about my job is the reluctance of many criminal justice "players" to welcome a new way of looking at crime, opting instead to hang on to a process which has served no one's best interest. Offenders have not been helped to accept responsibility, victims have been ignored, and communities have been trained to believe that crime is a government problem and not their concern.

If you are thinking about becoming a restorative justice coordinator, I recommend you take a restorative justice training like the one sponsored by Florida Atlantic University in partnership with the National Institute of Corrections. The more exposure you have to restorative justice philosophy and practitioners, the better.

Do you share this BARJ coordinator's enthusiasm for this philosophy of justice? Why or why not?

For Stephens, the goal of both methods is to resolve any conflicts through a consent agreement completed by all parties involved in the dispute. Mediation is the primary method of resolution. Arbitration is a backup procedure used only when mediation fails or is inappropriate (for example, in contract murder cases). In Stephens's model, appeals from mediation would be unnecessary because of the consent agreement, while appeals from arbitration would be limited to a single appeal to a three-member board of arbitrators. A variety of resolutions, whether by consent agreement or imposed arbitration, would be available. They include monetary restitution, community service, therapy, and even incarceration. Violations of consent agreements would be handled through arbitration, and violations of imposed arbitration resolutions would be dealt with through increasingly coercive measures—probably ending with incarceration. Stephens maintains that participatory justice would be cheaper, faster, and more equitable than the current adversary process of justice.[22] As of 2001, 29 states had victim-offender mediation (VOM) or VOM-type statutory authority in criminal cases (see Table 14.1). Table 14.2 shows the types of criminal offenses for which states authorize VOM.

Participatory justice is a form of restorative justice, an alternative to the punitive justice currently used in the United States and many other countries. The primary goals of **restorative justice** are to restore the health of the community, meet victims' needs, repair the harm done, and require the offender

restorative justice A process whereby an offender is required to contribute to restoring the health of the community, repairing the harm done, and meeting victims' needs.

TABLE 14.1 Statutory Authority for Victim-Offender Mediation in Criminal Cases

Little/No Mention of VOM	Codes Detail Programs That May Involve Victim Offender Dialogue	Basic Statutory Provision for VOM	Specific Statutory Provision for VOM	Comprehensive VOM Program
Connecticut	Alaska	Alabama	Arkansas	Delaware
District of Columbia	Florida	Arizona	Louisiana	Indiana
Georgia	Illinois	California	Minnesota	Kansas
Hawaii	Maine	Colorado	Ohio	Montana
Idaho	New York	Iowa	Oklahoma	Nebraska
Kentucky	Vermont	Missouri	Texas	Oregon
Maryland		North Carolina	Virginia	Tennessee
Massachusetts		Washington		
Michigan		Wisconsin		
Mississippi				
Nevada				
New Hampshire				
New Jersey				
New Mexico				
North Dakota				
Pennsylvania				
Rhode Island				
South Carolina				
South Dakota				
Utah				
West Virginia				
Wyoming				
22 States & DC	6 States	9 States	7 States	7 States

Source: Mark S. Umbreit, Elizabeth Lightfoot, and Johnathan Fier, "Legislative Statutes on Victim Offender Mediation: A National Review," Center for Restorative Justice and Peacemaking, School of Social Work, University of Minnesota (May 1, 2001), p. 4, at http://ssw.che.umn.edu/rjp.

TABLE 14.2 Types of Criminal Offenses for Which States Authorize Victim-Offender Mediation

Felonies & Aggravated Misdemeanors	Felonies If No Death Sentence Imposed	Felonies with No Mandatory Prison Sentence (or Fourth-Degree Vehicular Felonies with Mandatory Sentencing)	Formula Based on Seriousness and Criminal History	Nonviolent Offenses Only	Not for Violent or Serious Offenses	First-Time Nonviolent Offenses Only	Only for Persons with a Low Risk of Violence	Unspecified or Left to Discretion of Authorities
Delaware	Minnesota	Ohio	North Carolina	Nebraska	Alabama	Florida	Montana	Arizona
Iowa	Oklahoma			New York	Alaska	Kansas		Arkansas
Tennessee				Oregon				California
Texas								Colorado
Wisconsin								Illinois
								Indiana
								Louisiana
								Maine
								Missouri
								Vermont
								Virginia
								Washington

SOURCE: Mark S. Umbreit, Elizabeth Lightfoot, and Johnathan Fier, "Legislative Statutes on Victim Offender Mediation: A National Review," Center for Restorative Justice and Peacemaking, School of Social Work, University of Minnesota (May 1, 2001), p. 13, at http://ssw.che.umn.edu/rjp.

reintegrative shaming A strategy in which disappointment is expressed for the offender's actions, the offender is shamed and punished, and, more importantly, following the expression of disappointment and shame is a concerted effort on the part of the community to forgive the offender and reintegrate him or her back into society.

to contribute to those repairs. Another form of restorative justice that may be adopted in the United States in the future is Australian criminologist John Braithwaite's "reintegrative shaming."[23] **Reintegrative shaming** is a strategy in which disappointment is expressed for the offender's actions, the offender is shamed and punished, but, what is more important, following the expression of disappointment and shame is a concerted effort on the part of the community to forgive the offender and reintegrate him or her back into society. Braithwaite contends that the practice of reintegrative shaming is one of the primary reasons for Japan's relatively low crime rate.

Clearly, the future of the administration of justice in the United States should be quite different from what it is today. The exact differences will depend on which model's principles and policies dominate. Areas in which differences and changes are likely to be most pronounced include the availability of legal counsel at various stages in the process; retention or abolition of the preliminary hearing, the grand jury, and juvenile justice; and the extent of pretrial detention, plea bargaining, alternative dispute resolution procedures, judicial sentencing flexibility, and the appellate process. Courts of the future will also have to adapt to the needs of an increasingly older and more racially and culturally diverse population.

TECHNOLOGY AND THE ADMINISTRATION OF JUSTICE Before considering the future of corrections in the United States, it is important to emphasize that advances in technology are likely to influence the administration of justice in the future, just as they will affect the future of law enforcement. The possible substitution of electronically monitored house arrest for pretrial detention has already been examined. Additionally, in many jurisdictions in the United States today it is no longer necessary for defendants to physically appear in court for the initial appearance, preliminary hearing, arraignment, or even trial. Interactive television can be used to administer justice to defendants without incurring the risks involved in physically transporting them to a courtroom. This development has allowed jails to be built in more remote areas of municipalities, affording greater protection to the citizens of a community and reducing the costs of constructing jails because they need not be built in expensive urban locations. Courts are also allowing witnesses to provide videotaped depositions when they are physically unable to be present in court and allowing children to testify via interactive television in some child sex abuse cases.[24] Those practices are likely to continue and be expanded.

Perhaps, someday, determination of guilt or innocence, as well as the truthfulness of testimony, will become a routine matter of simply employing mind-reading technology. For example, the transfer to the public domain, via computer or some other device, of ribonucleic acid (RNA) structures that form memories will make deception and privacy of thoughts nearly impossible.[25] Sometime in the future, it may even be possible to retrieve memories of the events of a crime from the stored RNA memory chains (or "memory banks") of deceased victims and witnesses.[26] Imagine the constitutional questions raised by such technological abilities.

Among other technological advances that people should expect in the administration of justice in the future (some are available today) are the following:

1 More efficient processing and recording of information by computer (thus eliminating the need for paper files).
2 Instantaneous long-distance communication between integrated court systems.
3 Use of artificial intelligence to assist in legal research and various decision-making duties, such as sentencing.
4 Use of computer-generated graphics to reconstruct crime incidents.

The use of interactive television in the administration of justice is likely to be expanded in the future. *Besides those mentioned, what are some of the other benefits of having interactive television in the courtroom?*

5. Use of computers to create a virtual reality in which court participants can experience an interactive three-dimensional re-creation of a crime scene.
6. Use of a computer that can extract the events of a crime from the conscious and unconscious memory of a witness.
7. Kiosk jurisprudence, that is, court information stations located throughout the community, where 24 hours a day, citizens can conduct court business such as filing complaints or paying fines, or receive court information such as the court's daily calendar, the estimated time of an arraignment, and the outcomes of cases that have already been heard.[27]

FYI: Prisons of the Future

Prisoners in the future may be incarcerated in self-supporting undersea or space prisons, as the old practice of transporting prisoners is revived.

SOURCE: Gene Stephens, "Prisons," in G. T. Kurian and G. T. T. Molitor (eds.), *Encyclopedia of the Future* (New York: Simon & Schuster, Macmillan, 1996), p. 751.

THE FUTURE OF CORRECTIONS

The crime control and due process models used in the previous sections do not lend themselves as well to a consideration of the future of corrections. The primary reason is that in the area of corrections, crime control is, and probably will remain, the paramount goal. This does not mean that due process concerns are unimportant, however. Whatever new strategies are employed in corrections in the future will have to conform to constitutional restrictions. Specifically, the Eighth Amendment protection against cruel and unusual punishment—however that phrase is interpreted in the future—will have to be respected and will no doubt set the outer limits of what corrections in the future might be.

The federal supermaximum-security prison in Florence, Colorado, was one of the first of the "new penology" institutions that has abandoned rehabilitation in favor of efficiently managing a large population of violent offenders. *What are some of the problems of abandoning rehabilitation as a goal of punishment?*

THE "NEW PENOLOGY" Perhaps the most divisive issue that will confront correctional policy makers in the future is whether increasingly scarce resources should be devoted more to punishment (to achieve the goals of retribution and incapacitation) or to rehabilitation (to achieve the goals of specific deterrence and successful reintegration). If the current trend continues, the answer is easy: scarce correctional dollars will be devoted primarily to punishment. In fact, it has recently been argued that a "new penology" has already emerged—a penology that has abandoned rehabilitation in favor of efficiently managing large numbers of prisoners.[28] Success for this new penology is not measured by reductions in recidivism (a standard measure of correctional success used in the past), but rather by how efficiently correctional systems manage prisoners within budgetary constraints.[29]

ALTERNATIVES TO INCARCERATION Most people knowledgeable about corrections in the United States paint a rather bleak picture of its future. They believe that the number of citizens under correctional custody—in jail, in prison, on probation, or on parole—will continue to increase. Increasing numbers of offenders under correctional supervision, in turn, are likely to consume increasingly larger proportions of city, county, state, and federal budgets.

To make matters worse, scholars knowledgeable about corrections predict that alternatives to incarceration will not prevent the need to fund hundreds of costly new jails and prisons in the immediate future. In the first place, they contend, recent history demonstrates that increases in the use of alternatives to incarceration do not necessarily lead to decreases in the use of incarceration. Instead, increases in the use of alternatives coincide with increases in the use of incarceration, through net-widening, for example. This phenomenon occurred in the 1980s, when the use of community-based supervision nearly tripled and the use of incarceration almost doubled.[30]

A second reason that alternatives to incarceration will probably not reduce the need for more jails and prisons is that only a small percentage of future prisoners are likely to be good candidates for alternative programs. According to one authority, more than 95 percent of current prisoners are either violent offenders or repeat offenders with two or more felony convictions. Only 5 percent of prisoners can be considered low-risk offenders and thus good candidates for alternatives to incarceration.[31] This ratio of high-risk prisoners to low-risk prisoners is not likely to change dramatically in the future.

Cost-Reduction Strategies Future expenditures of tax dollars on corrections by governments at all levels will be made grudgingly, after much wrangling and debate. Every attempt will be made to carry out corrections functions as inexpensively as possible. Because the vast majority of correctional clientele will be members of the underclass, as is the case today, there will be little public resistance to low-cost management strategies. Indeed, corrections in the future is likely to take on "a kind of waste management function."[32]

Among the cost-reduction strategies likely to be advocated in the future are various alternatives to incarceration. For example, most persons convicted of minor offenses may be required to perform community service such as litter control and maintenance and construction of government buildings and grounds.[33] However, as described earlier, the cost savings of alternatives to incarceration tend to be illusory. In any case, most offenders who otherwise would be sent to prison will be considered poor candidates for the available alternatives.

Another cost-reduction strategy likely to receive increasing support in the future is the privatization of corrections. As described in Chapter 10 ("Institutional Corrections"), the private sector has been involved in corrections in various ways for a long time. Recently, private companies have entered the business of operating entire jails and prisons, and this practice, no doubt, will increase dramatically in the future.

However, a problem with the operation of jails and prisons by private companies—and a reason that cost savings from this strategy may prove minimal at best—is that private companies are in business to make a profit. If the companies are publicly owned, there is tremendous pressure on management to maximize shareholder value. As a result, it can be expected that private or public correctional companies will do all in their power to protect and enhance their interests by lobbying government officials for more favorable terms of operation and by using marketing to produce a greater demand for their products (that is, more offenders jailed or imprisoned).[34]

A third cost-reduction strategy—potentially the most effective one—is the use of new technology. For example, the use of cameras to watch prisoners and robots to service them, as well as the use of sensing devices on an institution's perimeter, would reduce the need for most correctional officers. The use of ultrasound may be the solution to costly prison riots. "Piping high-pitched sound over improved intercom systems would momentarily render everyone in the affected area unconscious and allow staff to enter, disarm, and regain custody."[35] If the death penalty continues to be employed in the United States, ultrasound may provide a more humane and cost-effective method of execution. In the near future, ultrasound could be provided at levels that would literally dematerialize the offender (eliminating the costs of disposing of the body).[36]

FYI

Privatization

At year-end 2001, about 13 private companies owned or managed about 150 correctional institutions in 30 states, the District of Columbia, and Puerto Rico. Two companies, Corrections Corporation of America (with a 52 percent market share) and Wackenhut Corrections Corporation (with a 22 percent market share), dominated the industry.

Source: From Charles W. Thomas, "Private Adult Correctional Facility Census: A 'Real-Time' Statistical Profile," http://web.crim.ufl.edu/PCP, (September 4, 2001), Table 1 and Chart 3.

Prison overcrowding could someday lead to the use of cryonics and other forms of human hibernation. *What problems might arise if cryonics were used to deal with prison overcrowding?*

Another possibility is instant death by laser ray.[37] The costs of building or enlarging more jails and prisons because of overcrowding would be reduced significantly in the future through the use of **cryonics** (freezing) and other forms of human hibernation.[38] Many prisoners could be "stored" in a small amount of space with the use of such technologies. In fact, they could literally be stacked on top of each other in coffinlike containers.

You have already learned about the use of electronically monitored house arrest for pretrial detainees (using electrodes connected to a monitor, perhaps surgically implanted, that would intermittently shock clients while they were outside a designated area). The same technology could be used for probationers and parolees, reducing the number of probation and parole officers needed. In addition, a subliminal-message player might be implanted in probationers, parolees, and prisoners that would provide 24-hour anticrime messages, such as "Obey the law" or "Do what is required of you," or synthesized body chemicals could be implanted that would keep offenders under constant control.[39] The costs related to future violations could be reduced dramatically through such methods.

However, it is important to keep in mind that several possible factors might significantly reduce or negate the tremendous cost savings anticipated from new correctional technologies. For example, the success of the strategy may create incentives for net-widening, which will reduce or eliminate any anticipated cost savings.[40] In addition, technology has its own costs: Experts must be employed, staff must be trained, equipment must be serviced, and systems must be upgraded as new technologies are introduced.[41]

cryonics A process of human hibernation that involves freezing the body.

You may have noticed that this discussion did not cover an important subject: crime and delinquency prevention—the effort to prevent criminal and delinquent acts from being committed in the first place. Although crime and delinquency prevention will probably be a priority in the future, it will be mostly the responsibility of government agencies and philanthropic organizations outside the criminal justice process (for example, social, health, and welfare agencies). Because the focus of this book is criminal justice in the United States, we will not speculate here about future crime and delinquency prevention strategies.

THINKING CRITICALLY

1. What impact do you think DNA profiling will have on the future of law enforcement?
2. Review the FYI on Bilingual Courts presented on page 525. Do you think that people who don't speak English should be allowed to serve as jurors? Why or why not?
3. When it comes to corrections, to what do you think more money should be devoted: punishment or rehabilitation? Why?

Special Crime Problems of the Twenty-First Century

At the dawn of the twenty-first century, five interrelated crimes are likely to pose special problems for law enforcement agencies and criminal justice. The first three are drug crime, cybercrime, and terrorism—all of which have been examined in previous chapters. Terrorism is considered again in the final section of this chapter. The two other crimes are identity theft and transnational organized crime, which are considered below.

IDENTITY THEFT: WHEN BAD THINGS HAPPEN TO YOUR GOOD NAME

Tania Collins of Apopka, Florida, had her purse snatched.[42] Among the items lost were her driver's license, Social Security card, and about $25 in cash. Although the incident scared her and the loss of her personal belongings was an inconvenience, the theft of her purse and its contents was only the beginning of what would become a much bigger problem. Not long after the purse snatching, Tania discovered that someone else had been using her identity to accumulate more than $20,000 in credit card charges, bogus checks, grocery bills, phone bills, and other unpaid debt. Tania Collins had become a victim of identity theft.

EXTENT, DEFINITION, AND TYPES OF IDENTITY THEFT Tania Collins is not alone. Identity theft is a much larger problem than even the experts suspected. A recent survey by the federal government's General Accounting Office, for example, pegged the number of identity theft victims at between 500,000 and 700,000 a year.[43] However, according to a more recent survey commissioned by the Federal Trade Commission (FTC), nearly 10 million Americans may have been victims of some type of identity theft in 2002, and as many as 27 million Americans may have been victims of identity theft during the 5 years between 1998 and 2002.[44] Figure 14.1 displays identity theft victimization rates (per 100,000 population) by state in 2002.

FIGURE 14.1 **Identity Theft Victims by State (per 100,000 population)* January 1–December 31, 2002**

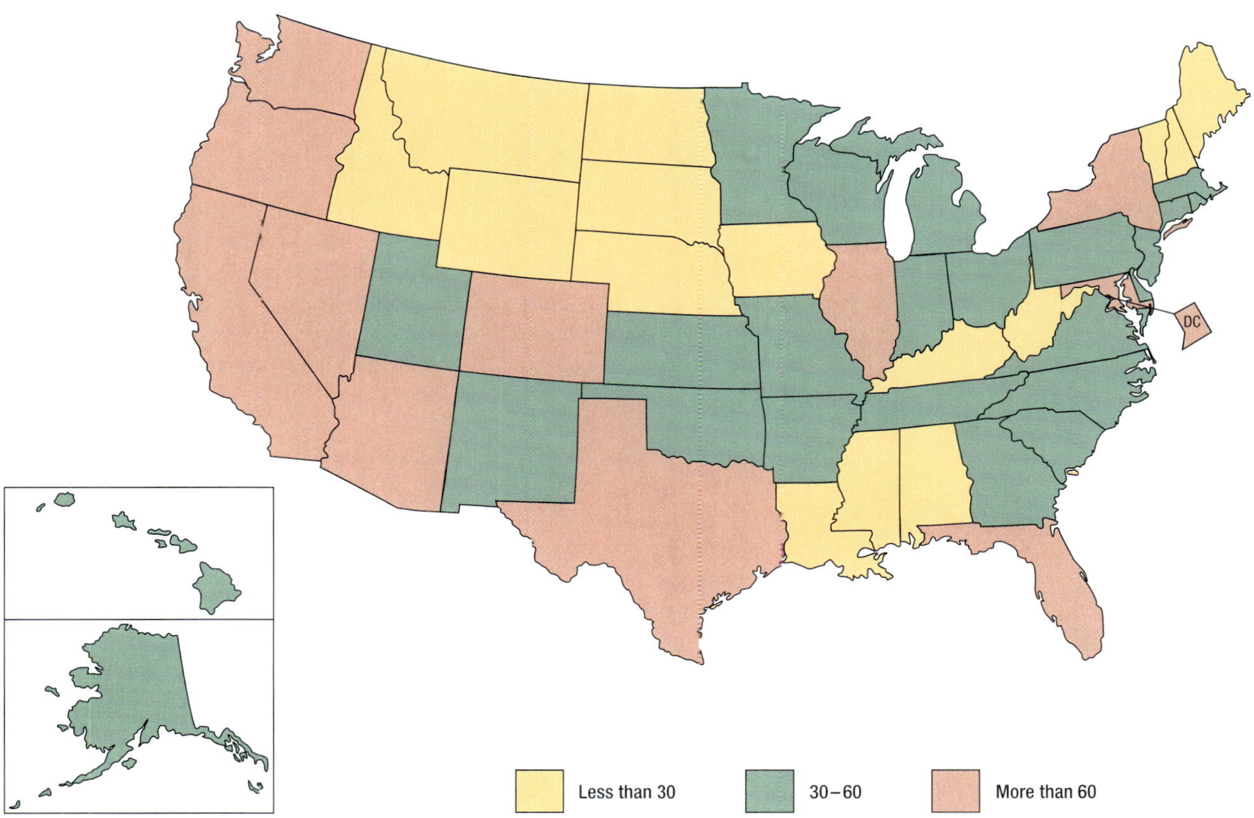

*Figured using the Census 2000 state population estimates from the U.S. Census Bureau. Ninety-six percent of the 161,819 total victims reporting indicated their state of residence.
SOURCE: "Identity Theft Victim Complaint Data," Identity Theft Data Clearinghouse, Federal Trade Commission at www.consumer.gov/idtheft/stats.html.

FIGURE 14.2 How Victims' Information Is Misused[a], January 1–December 31, 2002

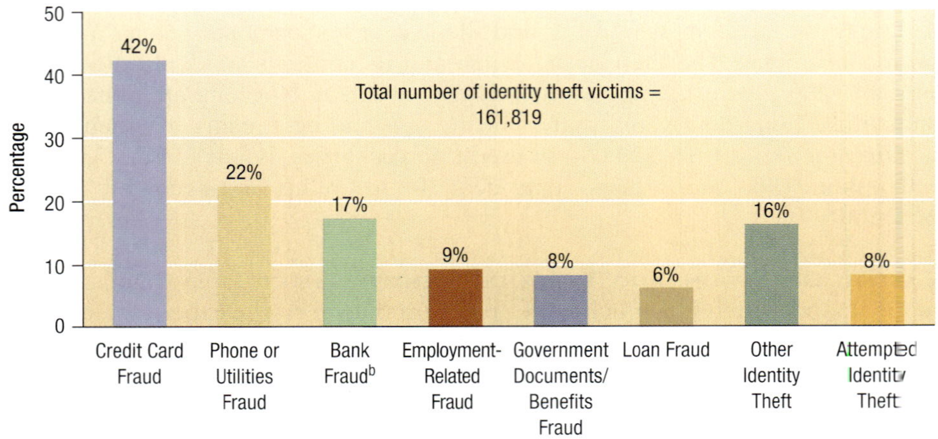

[a]Percentages are based on the 161,819 total victims reporting. Percentages add to more than 100 because approximately 22% of victims reported experiencing more than one type of identity theft. All victims reported experiencing at least one type of identity theft.

[b]Includes fraud involving checking and savings accounts and electronic fund transfers.

SOURCE: "Identity Theft Victim Complaint Data," Identity Theft Data Clearinghouse, Federal Trade Commission, at www.consumer.gov/idtheft/stats.html.

identity theft The transfer or use without legal authority of the identification documentation of another person with the intent to commit, aid, or abet any unlawful activity that constitutes a felony.

Identity theft became a federal crime in 1998, when Congress passed The Identity Theft and Assumption Deterrence Act. The law stipulates that **identity theft** is committed "when anyone knowingly transfers or uses without legal authority the identification documentation of another person with the intent to commit, aid, or abet any unlawful activity that constitutes a felony."[45]

There are three general types of identity theft that vary in seriousness of victimization. From the most serious to least serious, identity theft may involve (1) *the misuse of personal information* to open new credit accounts, take out new loans, or engage in other types of fraud, such as misuse of the victim's name and identifying information when the thief is charged with a crime by law enforcement officers, when renting an apartment or home, when obtaining medical care, or when applying for a job; (2) *the misuse of existing accounts other than credit cards,* such as checking or savings accounts or telephone accounts; and (3) *the misuse of one or more existing credit cards or credit card account numbers.* Figure 14.2 shows how victims' information was misused in 2002.

IDENTITY THEFT VICTIMIZATION Identity theft cost its victims about $50 billion in 2002 (see Table 14.3). The bulk of that loss, $33 billion, was from the misuse of a victim's personal information ("New Accounts & Other Frauds" in Table 14.3). The average annual loss per victim for all types of identity theft was approximately $4,800, but the per capita loss from the misuse of personal information was $10,200. Businesses and financial institutions and not individuals incur most of the losses from identity theft because a variety of laws protect individuals from the fraudulent actions of identity thieves. Thus, of the approximately $50 billion lost to identity theft in 2002, only about 10 percent of the loss was borne by individuals. The average loss per individual was about $500 (it was $1,180 per individual in cases of personal information misuse) and most of that amount was spent trying to resolve the problem.

In 2002, victims of all three types of identity theft spent 30 hours, on average, attempting to resolve their problems (see Table 14.3). Victims of personal information misuse spent 60 hours, on average, dealing with their problems.

TABLE 14.3 Costs of ID Theft in 2002[a]

	New Accounts & Other Frauds	Misuse of Existing Accounts (Both Credit Card & Non-Credit Card)	All ID Theft
Victims in 2002			
Percent of population	1.5%	Credit Card, 2.4% Non–Credit Card, 0.7%	4.6%
Number of persons[b]	3.23 million	6.68 million	9.91 million
Loss to Businesses & Financial Institutions			
Average per victim[c]	$10,200	$2,100	$4,800
Total	$32.9 billion	$14.0 billion	$47.6 billion
Loss to Victims			
Average per victim	$1,180	$160	$500
Total	$3.8 billion	$1.1 billion	$5.0 billion
Hours Victims Spent Resolving Their Problems			
Average per victim	60 hours	15 hours	30 hours
Total	194 million hours	100 million hours	297 million hours

[a]Totals by type of ID theft may not sum to the amount shown in the totals column due to rounding.

[b]Based on U.S. population age 18 and over of 215.47 million as of July 1, 2002, from http://eire.census.gov/popest/data/national/tables/asro/NA-EST2002-ASRO-01.php (visited July 14, 2003).

[c]"Average per victim" figures in the "All ID Theft" column are a weighted average of the values for the different types of ID theft with the incidence in the past year used as weights.

SOURCE: *Federal Trade Commission—Identity Theft Survey Report* (McLean, VA: Synovate, September 2003), p. 7, at www.ftc.gov/reports/index.htm.

As a group, Americans spent almost 300 million hours resolving problems related to identity theft in 2002. Almost two-thirds of that time was spent clearing up problems from the misuse of personal information.

When a victim's identity was stolen, it was sometimes misused for a relatively long period of time. For example, 13 percent of survey respondents reported that information was misused for 6 months or more, and 27 percent of the personal information stolen was misused for at least 6 months. On the other hand, more than a quarter of the information from identity theft in general and 36 percent of cases involving existing credit cards and card numbers were misused for only 1 day. The survey also found that the more quickly an identity theft was discovered, the smaller the loss incurred.

About a quarter of the survey respondents reported that the identity thief got their personal information from a lost or stolen wallet or pocketbook or theft of mail. About half the respondents did not know how the thief stole their identities. Among common techniques used in identity theft are "dumpster diving," "shoulder surfing," and "spamming."[46] Thieves who "dumpster dive" go through dumpsters or trash cans to get copies of checks, credit card and bank statements, credit card applications, or other records with identifying information. "Shoulder surfers" look over victims' shoulders as they enter personal information into phones, computers, and ATMs. "Spammers" send unsolicited e-mail messages to victims, usually advertising a product, service, or get-rich-quick scheme, and ask the victim to provide identifying information in order to receive whatever is being advertised. Identifying information can also be found on the Internet by accessing public record sites and fee-based information broker sites. Other ways of obtaining personal information are by getting credit reports fraudulently by posing as an employer, loan officer, or landlord or by obtaining names and social security numbers from personnel or customer files in the workplace.[47]

The FTC survey revealed that only about 20 percent of all victims and 35 percent of personal information misuse victims notified one or more credit

FYI
A New Scam: "Phishing"

The Federal Trade Commission recently reported a new identity theft scam called "phishing." It worked like this: the thief sent consumers e-mail messages claiming that there was a problem with their AOL account. The messages warned consumers to update their billing information or risk losing their accounts and Internet access. The message directed consumers to click on a hyperlink to connect to the "AOL Billing Center." When consumers clicked on the link, they went to a look-alike AOL Web page. The thief had stolen AOL's identity and was using it to steal consumers' identities. Consumers were asked to enter the numbers from the credit card they used to open the account and the numbers from a new credit card to correct the problem. They were also asked for additional identifying information.

SOURCE: "Identity Thief Goes 'Phishing' for Consumers' Credit Information," Federal Trade Commission, July 21, 2003, at www.ftc.gov/opa/2003/07/phishing.htm.

bureaus about the theft. Of those who contacted credit bureaus, 62 percent requested that a "fraud alert" be attached to their credit reports.

Only about 25 percent of identity theft victims in general and 40 percent of personal information theft victims reported the crime to the police. Many victims of identity theft are too embarrassed to report the crime to the police. The higher the amount lost, the more likely that the theft was reported. In approximately 75 percent of the identity thefts reported to the police, the local agency filed a formal report (about 80 percent in personal information misuse cases). The more quickly a theft was reported, the more likely the police filed a report. More than half of the victims who reported thefts to the police were "somewhat satisfied" (17 percent) or "very satisfied" (36 percent) with the law enforcement response, but more than a third of them were "somewhat dissatisfied" (9 percent) or "very dissatisfied" (28 percent).

For many victims, identity theft can be a traumatic experience. It can provoke a host of emotions such as feelings of loss, helplessness, hopelessness, vulnerability, fear, denial, anger, isolation, betrayal, rage, and embarrassment.[48] A particularly common emotion felt by identity theft victims is frustration with the very people to whom the victims turn for help, especially law enforcement and criminal justice personnel. Identity theft can be life altering. Many victims never see the world in the same way again. They lose their innocence. For other victims, the experience is life altering in another way: they are empowered; they develop an assertiveness that they did not have before; they become bolder; and they discover who their true friends are.

DEALING WITH IDENTITY THEFT When asked what could be done to improve their victimization experience, identity theft victims who had spent at least 10 hours trying to resolve their problems responded that law enforcement officers could improve the way they investigate the crime. Law enforcement officials counter that identity theft cases are hard to investigate because they

In an effort to thwart identity theft, the Mississippi Department of Public Safety is using special software that allows its driver's-license examiners to program computers to compare a driver's previous photograph with a newly taken one. *How effective do you think this system will be?*

often involve multiple jurisdictions, evidence problems, and complex financial matters. Law enforcement officials also complain of having too few investigators.[49] Still, victims wanted the police to (1) make a greater commitment to catch the thief or thieves, (2) follow up and communicate better with the victim, and (3) increase the assistance they provide victims. Victims also wanted offenders to receive stiffer penalties.

Many victims noted that people needed to be more aware of identity theft and better prepared to prevent and respond to it when it occurred. They recommended that people (1) use greater security precautions when handling personal information (for example, they should destroy materials containing personal information instead of putting them in the trash); (2) should not place personal information on the Internet, (3) should secure personal information in homes and at work, (4) should more carefully monitor their mail, billing cycles, and credit reports, and (5) should know who to contact and notify the affected companies and credit reporting agencies more quickly when something wrong is detected.

Some victims wanted financial institutions to do a better job of preventing and detecting the crime. They listed (1) improving authentication measures (for example, photos on credit cards), (2) more thorough identification procedures by employees during credit transactions, (3) better monitoring of account activity and notification of irregularities, and (4) better follow-up and assistance while repairing financial records (for example, fewer documents for victims to sign, just listening to victims, and treating victims with understanding instead of suspicion).

Few things in life are worse than losing your good name. However, with the inevitable increase of financial transactions over the Internet, the continual bombardment of people with preapproved credit card applications, and new, yet unknown ways of obtaining personal identifying information by thieves, identity theft is likely to become an even greater problem and headache for victims and law enforcement agencies than it currently is.

CJ ONLINE

Survey of Identify Theft Victims
To learn more about identity theft, read the results of the FTC survey of victims. It can be accessed at **www.consumer.gov/idtheft/stats.html.** Click on Synovate Report of ID Theft Survey (September 2003). *What did you learn from the report that surprised you?*

TRANSNATIONAL ORGANIZED CRIME: CRIME IN A GLOBAL CONTEXT

Transnational organized crime is a growing concern among law enforcement officials worldwide. As one leading authority on the subject puts it:

> Transnational organized crime will be one of the major problems facing policy makers in the 21st century. It will be a defining issue of the 21st century as the Cold War was for the 20th century and Colonialism was for the 19th. No area of international affairs will remain untouched as political and economic systems and the social fabric of many countries will deteriorate under the increasing financial power of international organized crime groups.[50]

Former FBI Director Louis Freeh and former CIA Director R. James Woolsey have both maintained that "transnational organized crime threatens the national security interests of the United States and other nations" and jeopardizes "the very fabric of democratic society" everywhere.[51]

A Definition of Transnational Organized Crime Unfortunately, there is no universally agreed-upon definition of "transnational organized crime." So following the lead of the framers of the United Nations Convention Against Transnational Organized Crime, we will define the key concept by combining the definitions of "organized crime group" and "transnational crime." "An organized crime group" is a "structured group of three or more persons existing for a period of time and acting in concert with the aim of committing one or more serious crimes or offenses in order to obtain, directly or indirectly, a financial or other material benefit."[52] A "serious crime" is defined as "an offense punishable by a maximum deprivation of liberty of at least four years or a more serious penalty."[53] A "transnational crime" is a crime that (a) "is committed in more than one State" [nation]; (b) "is committed in one State but a substantial part of its preparation, planning, direction or control takes place in another State"; (c) "is committed in one State but involves an organized criminal group that engages in criminal activities in more than one State"; or (d) "is committed in one State but has substantial effects in another State."[54]

Characteristics of Transnational Organized Crime Groups Until the last quarter of the twentieth century, organized crime, except for some cross-border smuggling, was primarily a local—or at worst, a national—problem. Organized crime became transnational with the expansion of multinational corporations, the opening of national borders to trade, and growing economic interdependence. However, unlike multinational corporations, transnational organized crime groups are not constrained by domestic and host country laws and regulations. They are able to exploit economic opportunities by using corruption, blackmail, and intimidation.[55]

Transnational organized crime groups vary widely in their structure, size, use of violence, scope of activities, level of transborder operations, corruption, level of political influence, extent of activity in the legitimate economy, and degree of cooperation with other organized crime groups.[56] Nevertheless, a recent survey of 40 selected transnational organized crime groups in 16 countries and one region by the United Nation's Centre for International Crime Prevention reveals some common characteristics:

- Two-thirds of the groups have a classical hierarchical type of structure [with a single leader, relatively clearly defined hierarchy, and strict systems of internal discipline] while one-third are more loosely organized
- The majority of the groups are of moderate size, with between 20 and 50 participants.
- Violence is essential to the undertaking of their activities for the majority of the groups.
- Under half of the groups do not have a strong social or ethnic identity, while ethnic-based organizations represent less than a third of the organized crime groups.
- The largest number of groups engaged in only one primary criminal activity.
- In the majority of cases groups are engaged in criminal activities in multiple countries.
- The vast majority of the groups make use of corruption, either extensively or occasionally.
- Just under half of the groups are said to have no political influence, while one-third of the groups have an influence at the local/regional level.
- Under half of the groups have extensively penetrated the legitimate economy.
- The largest number of groups cooperates with other organized criminal groups, largely as a source of illicit commodities.[57]

Table 14.4 lists some of the "named" transnational organized crime groups, their base countries, and their criminal activities.

Criminal Activities of Transnational Organized Crime Groups Like most organized crime groups, transnational organized crime groups

TABLE 14.4 Named Transnational Organized Crime Groups, Base Country, and Criminal Activities*

Transnational Organized Crime Group (Base Country)	Criminal Activities (Primary Activity Listed First)
Italian Group (Germany; controlled by La Cosa Nostra)	Large-scale tax evasion primarily through employment in construction industry; large-scale fraud; money laundering; illegal immigration; smuggling; loan sharking
Verhagen Group (The Netherlands)	Hashish trafficking; large-scale fraud/embezzlement; theft of electronic goods; fraud involving precious materials; trafficking in expensive jewelry; fraudulent real estate transactions
Outlaw Motorcycle Gangs (Australia)	Drug production and distribution (mainly amphetamines and cannabis); prostitution; trafficking of stolen vehicles; many other crimes
The McLean Syndicate (Australia)	Drug trafficking (mainly cannabis, but also cocaine); money laundering; illegal immigration/smuggling; armed robbery; theft of antiques; trafficking in women; prostitution; extortion; gambling; debt collection; murder; tax evasion
Japanese Yakuza (Australia)	Investment of the proceeds of crime from elsewhere; money laundering
The Orange Case (Caribbean)	Drug smuggling (mainly cannabis and cocaine)
Dream House Case (Caribbean)	Smuggling cocaine
The Meij Case (Caribbean)	Political corruption resulting in extensive penetration into the legal economy
The Fuk Ching (United States)	Extortion; smuggling of illegal immigrants; human trafficking; kidnapping; drug trafficking; armed robberies; money laundering; organized prostitution; environmental crimes
La Cosa Nostra (United States)	Gambling; loan sharking; extortion; drug trafficking (heroin, cocaine, and synthetic drugs); prostitution; murder; fraud; insurance scams; air cargo theft; environmental crimes; racketeering in labor unions, the construction, music, and garbage industries
Clan Paviglianiti (Italy)	Drug trafficking (mainly cocaine); forgery; large-scale fraud and embezzlement; armed robbery; vehicle theft and trafficking; manufacturing of firearms and ammunition; illegal trafficking in explosives
Syzranskaya Groopirovka (Russia)	Drug trafficking (heroin, cannabis, and opium)
Ziberman Group (Russia)	Smuggling of cigarettes and alcohol; theft of vehicles; illegal gambling; large-scale fraud and embezzlement; money laundering; armed robbery; extortion; murder
Vasi Iliev Security-2 (Bulgaria)	Insurance scams; illegal gambling; illegal import and export of food, equipment, alcohol, and cigarettes; many other crimes
The Cock Group (Lithuania)	Extortion; trafficking in heroin; vehicle theft; organized prostitution; many other crimes
Savlokhov Group (Ukraine)	Extortion; gambling; money laundering; forgery; fraud; loan sharking; usury; trafficking in illicit goods; prostitution; kidnapping; armed robbery
Juvenal Group (Colombia)	Drug trafficking; smuggling of migrants; money laundering
Hells Angels (Canada)	Drug manufacturing and trafficking (synthetic drugs, heroin, cannabis, and cocaine); prostitution; money laundering; insurance scams; vehicle theft and trafficking; extortion; gun running
The 28s Prison Gang (South Africa)	Drug trafficking (heroin, cannabis, cocaine, and synthetic drugs); illegal trading in firearms; organized prostitution; burglary; money laundering; gambling; vehicle theft and trafficking; armed robbery; extortion; trafficking in women and children for the sex industry
The Trapani Cosa Nostra (Italy)	Extortion; money laundering; trafficking in firearms; drug manufacturing and trafficking
The Licciardi Clan (Italy)	International drug trafficking; extortion; cigarette smuggling; loan sharking; counterfeiting; forgery; insurance scams; money laundering; armed robbery; organized prostitution; smuggling of firearms; trafficking of explosives; illegal gambling
Yamaguchi-Gumi (Japan)	Drug trafficking; extortion; gambling; organized prostitution; insurance scams; money laundering; armed robbery; trafficking in stolen goods; kidnapping; trafficking in firearms
The Liu Yong Syndicate (China)	Trafficking in illicit goods and services; racketeering; smuggling of human beings; organized prostitution; armed robbery; gambling; extortion
The Zhang Wei Syndicate (China)	Trafficking in illicit goods and services; racketeering; smuggling of human beings; prostitution; gambling; extortion; armed robbery
The Liang Xiao Min Syndicate (China)	Gambling; kidnapping; extortion; organized prostitution; armed robbery; racketeering; trafficking in illicit goods and services
Amezcua Contreras Organization (Mexico)	Producing and trafficking methamphetamine; supplying various chemicals to other trafficking organizations
Mocha Orejas Organization (Mexico)	Kidnapping; blackmail
Carillo Fuentes Organization (Mexico)	Transporting cocaine; trafficking in heroin and marijuana
Arellano-Felix Organization (Mexico)	Drug trafficking (cocaine, heroin, cannabis, and methamphetamine)

*Many transnational organized crime groups are not named, and not all named groups are included in this list. Also, some of the listed groups are no longer in operation, having been successfully dismantled by law enforcement efforts.

SOURCE: *Results of a Pilot Survey of Forty Selected Organized Criminal Groups in Sixteen Countries,* Global Programme Against Transnational Organized Crime, United Nations Office on Drugs and Crime (September 2002), Appendix B, at www.unodc.org/unodc/organized_crime.html.

FYI

Transnational Organized Crime Is Profitable

The United Nations estimates that transnational organized crime groups bring in about $1.5 trillion a year, more than the GNP of many small countries. The criminal proceeds from money laundering worldwide are estimated to be between $600 billion and $1 trillion a year. An estimated $2 billion to $4 billion is earned annually from illegally dumping trash and hazardous waste.

SOURCE: Wendy Chamberlin, "Intensifying the Fight Against Transnational Organized Crime," U.S. Department of State, 2001, p. 1, at www.state.gov/g/inl/rls/rm/2001/jan_apr/1078pf.htm.

provide illegal goods and services for which there is public demand. The following is a list of some of the more significant criminal activities of transnational organized crime groups:

- Smuggling
  - Commodities (such as weapons and human beings)
  - Drugs
  - Protected species
- Contraband (goods subject to tariffs or quotas)
  - Stolen cars
  - Tobacco products
- Services
  - Immigrants
  - Prostitution
  - Indentured servitude
  - Money laundering
  - Fraud (such as bank or insurance fraud)[58]

Transnational organized crime groups smuggle human beings into the United States. *How can this be prevented? Should it be prevented? Why?*

Transnational organized crime groups have also been involved in hijackings, terrorism, and civil wars. In approximately 30 countries, insurgent or terrorist groups, in league with transnational organized crime groups, have financed all or part of their activities with income generated from taxes imposed on illegal drug production or from trafficking in illegal drugs themselves. Illegal trade in diamonds and oil has also financed civil wars and terrorist activities.[59]

Civil wars create refugees eager to escape to safer countries. This, too, provides a financial opportunity for transnational organized crime groups that smuggle people, especially women and children, across national borders. Poor women are also lured from their native countries by promises of good jobs in another country. Estimates of the number of women and children involved in these activities vary widely from 27 million to 200 million a year worldwide. Many of the women and children are enslaved in the countries to which they are smuggled or brought, often forced into prostitution to pay off the trafficker.[60]

Trying to Control Transnational Organized Crime Transnational organized crime poses special problems for law enforcement. Many transnational organized crime groups use legitimate import-export companies, service industries, or multinational financial institutions as fronts for their illegal activities. Sometimes organized crime groups nest themselves inside legitimate businesses; other times they control them. Many groups employ experts in the use of global technology, such as the Internet and advanced wireless communications, and conduct market research to determine where to operate. They look for jurisdictions with weak law enforcement and criminal justice institutions. Transnational organized crime groups can also hide behind national borders and take advantage of the jurisdictional limitations or confusion of law enforcement.[61]

In addition, many transnational organized crime groups can claim among their members present and former state officials and military and state intelligence agency personnel. This is especially true of former communist nations, but it is not confined to them. The professional intelligence, police, and military skills provided by these members often give the crime groups an advantage over local law enforcement officials.[62]

Another problem is that some countries have no statutory or popular basis for preventing transnational organized crime. For example, in Russia as late as the 1990s no laws against organized crime existed; there were no criminal penalties for phony businesses or fictitious bankruptcies; and there was little financial or social support for law enforcement itself.[63]

Law enforcement agencies around the world are increasingly cooperating with each other to fight transnational organized crime. The legal bases for this cooperation are high-level bilateral and multilateral assistance treaties. The treaties provide rules for intelligence and evidence sharing and for determining jurisdiction in individual cases. The treaties also set standards for investigation techniques, the extradition of offenders, and the imposition of sanctions. Frequently, the treaties allow the exchanging of subject-matter experts and investigative expertise, the stationing of another nation's law enforcement officers in embassies, or the opening of a law enforcement headquarters or training facility in a foreign capital. The U.S. Departments of State, Justice, and Treasury, for example, have established international law enforcement academies in Budapest, Bangkok, and Gaborone (the capital of Botswana in Africa).[64]

A particularly promising development in this cooperative effort was the signing of the United Nations Convention Against Transnational Organized Crime by the United States and 123 other countries at a conference in Palermo, Italy, in December 2000. The convention was the first international instrument

FYI

Interpol

Interpol is the world's largest international police organization with 181 member countries. It was created to enhance and facilitate international police cooperation and will undoubtedly play a major role in the fight against transnational organized crime. Every member country has an Interpol office called a National Central Bureau, which is staffed by the country's own police. The bureau is the point of contact for foreign governments needing assistance with overseas investigations. Contrary to popular belief, Interpol officers do not travel around the world to investigate cases in different countries. Rather each member country employs its own officers to operate on its own territory and in accordance with its own national laws. The organization's General Secretariat is located in Lyon, France.

Source: "Interpol—An Overview," Interpol at www.interpol.int/Public/Icpo/FactSheets/FS200101.asp.

against this type of crime. It requires member countries to criminalize some of the major offenses committed by transnational organized crime groups, such as obstruction of justice, money laundering, corruption of public officials, and conspiracy.[65] The convention also encourages cooperation among member countries in the investigation, apprehension, and prosecution of transnational organized crime group members involved in serious crimes. This applies to countries with which the United States currently does not have a mutual legal assistance treaty. Cooperation can include exchanging information on organized crime groups, conducting joint investigations, employing special investigative methods (such as electronic or other forms of surveillance and undercover operations), the seizure and confiscation of the proceeds of illegal activities, the extradition of fugitives, and the protection of witnesses. However, at no time do member countries relinquish their sovereignty or jurisdictional integrity to another country. The convention also has three protocols that require member states to criminalize the trafficking in human beings, the smuggling of migrants, and the illicit manufacturing and trafficking in firearms. Additionally, the United States and other donor countries are to contribute funds to a special UN account to support developing countries that need technical assistance to implement the convention and its protocols. The convention and protocols have received the requisite number of signatures and are in force.

Currently, transnational organized crime is mainly addressed at the national level, when it is dealt with at all. Local law enforcement is ill-equipped to handle or even recognize it. Local law enforcement officers have neither the training nor the expertise to investigate sophisticated computer crimes or securities frauds, for example. When they work street-level drug sales, smuggling cases, and homicides, they rarely recognize that those crimes may be transnational organized crimes. Experts are divided on what the most promising strategy might be. Some of them believe that local law enforcement officers must be taught to recognize and respond to transnational organized crimes, especially since such crimes first surface at the local level. Others believe that transnational organized crime should be left to federal law enforcement agencies that are better able to deal with the technological, cultural, political, legal, and language complexities often involved in such crimes. Still others advocate greater cooperation among different levels of law enforcement through multiagency task forces, but they have problems as well. Some experts are dubious about the ability of any level of law enforcement to significantly reduce the illegal markets that sustain transnational organized crime groups. Those experts believe that significant reductions in illegal markets depend not on law enforcement, but primarily on social and economic changes, changes in public attitudes, advances in science, or shifts in profitability.[66] One thing is clear: while experts debate and law enforcement agencies fight over jurisdiction, transnational organized crime groups operate with relative impunity.

THINKING CRITICALLY

1. What do you think is the most effective way to deal with identity theft?
2. What do you think is the most effective way to deal with transnational organized crime?

Criminal Justice in the Age of Terror

The tragic events of September 11, 2001, have transformed the United States in many ways. A new kind of fear has gripped the American people, who no longer feel as safe as they did before that infamous day. The most notable change to occur is the war on terrorism—a financially costly war conceivably with no end. The war on terrorism, in turn, has altered criminal justice in the United States, as the fear of terrorism has joined the fear of crime in the nation's collective nightmares.

However, terrorism and crime are not separate phenomena. Although they may think of themselves as "freedom fighters," according to the FBI's counterterrorism policy, terrorists are criminals. Furthermore, as the U.S. government and its allies have increasingly succeeded in freezing their financial assets, al-Qaeda and other terrorist groups have turned to different types of crime to support their operations. Many of those crimes are the same ones committed by transnational organized crime groups: bootlegging of cigarettes; the counterfeiting of compact discs, movies and other products; drug trafficking; and smuggling human beings for profit to name a few.[67]

LEGISLATIVE RESPONSES TO TERRORISM

As for the response to terrorism, one of the more controversial developments in this new Age of Terror was the passage of the USA PATRIOT Act less than 2 months after the planes slammed into the World Trade Center and the Pentagon. As described in Chapter 4, the law gave the government broad new powers to address the menacing threat. For example, in terrorism-related matters, it expanded the government's search and surveillance powers and eliminated safeguards such as judicial oversight, the need for a warrant and probable cause, the ability to challenge certain searches in court, and public accountability. The law also created the new crime of "domestic terrorism," which is defined so broadly that it could include members of controversial activist groups such as Operation Rescue, the Earth Liberation Front, Greenpeace, or the World Trade Organization protesters, as long as they committed acts "dangerous to human life" to "influence the policy of a government by intimidation or coercion." Another provision of the law allows the Attorney General to detain noncitizens in the United States indefinitely without trial if there is reason to believe that the noncitizens endanger national security and a foreign country will not accept them for deportation. Critics contend that in removing traditional checks on law enforcement the PATRIOT Act and other similar legislation threaten the very rights and freedoms that the war on terrorism is trying to preserve.

Another legislative response to 9/11 was passage of the Homeland Security Act of 2002. As described in Chapter 5, the Act established the new Department of Homeland Security, the institutional apparatus whose mission in large part is to prevent terrorist attacks in the United States and to minimize the damage, and assist in the recovery, from terrorist acts that do occur. The creation of the Department of Homeland Security, which is ongoing, involves a massive reorganization of the federal law enforcement bureaucracy. Federal law enforcement agencies have been moved from their traditional departments, such as Justice or Treasury, to the new Department of Homeland Security. Other agencies have been combined or reconfigured. For example, the border and agency functions of the U.S. Customs Service, the Federal Protective Service, and the former Immigration and Naturalization Service have been reorganized into the Bureau of Immigration and Customs Enforcement under the Department of Homeland Security. New agencies have also been created, such as the Bureau of Citizenship and Immigration Services, the Office of State and Local Government Coordination, and the Office of Private Sector Liaison. Each of these new agencies is part of the Department of Homeland Security.

TERRORISM AND LAW ENFORCEMENT

As also discussed in Chapter 5, the FBI was *not* moved to the Department of Homeland Security (it remains in the Justice Department), but it has undergone some fundamental changes in response to 9/11. For example, its top priority has shifted from being a federal police agency to being an intelligence and counterterrorism agency. The management hierarchy at the FBI's headquarters in Washington has been restructured to support counterterrorism efforts. A quarter of the FBI's 11,000 agents have been reassigned to work on counterterrorism. A National Joint Terrorism Task Force has been established at FBI headquarters to coordinate the flow of information with task forces in each of the bureau's 56 field offices, and new FBI offices are being opened in foreign countries where al-Qaeda and other terrorist groups have a presence.

Local law enforcement officers have also become soldiers in the war on terrorism, as explained in Chapter 6. As "first responders" and the "front line of defense," local police officers and sheriffs' deputies not only must be able to respond to terrorist acts, but they also must be proactive in preventing them as well. Their job is especially difficult because they must be ever vigilant without engaging in racial or ethnic profiling. Local law enforcement agencies are increasingly trying to train their personnel for their new roles but, according to recent reports, are drastically underfunded and dangerously unprepared.

TERRORISM AND THE ADMINISTRATION OF JUSTICE

The war on terrorism has revealed the existence of a secretive federal court, previously unknown to most Americans. The Foreign Intelligence Surveillance Court, or FISA court, which is described in Chapter 8, has been in operation since the late 1970s. The court has approved thousands of Justice Department requests to conduct secret searches and surveillance of people in the United States who are suspected of having links to foreign agents or powers, often involving terrorism and espionage. American citizens who have been suspected of being terrorists or having ties to terrorist groups in the wake of 9/11 have been arrested and detained without being charged with any crimes and have been denied legal representation and access to the criminal courts to challenge their detention. Non-U.S. citizens accused of terrorism by the U.S. government may be tried by military tribunals instead of federal courts, if they are charged and tried at all. Military tribunals provide fewer procedural rights than do civilian courts. At this writing, hundreds of noncitizen detainees are being held in legal limbo at a federal prison in Cuba. When detained terrorist suspects are allowed to consult with attorneys, the federal government has determined that it has the right to eavesdrop on their conversations, ignoring the traditional attorney/client privilege.

The United States is hated by people all over the world. *Why?*

TERRORISM AND CORRECTIONS

As noted above and described in Chapter 10, the U.S. government has established a new supermaximum-security prison at the Guantanamo Bay Naval Base in Cuba. Named Camp Delta, the purpose of the new prison is to hold what Pentagon officials call the "worst of the worst enemies in the war on terror." The prisoners, from 42 different countries, are being held until they no longer have useful intelligence to provide, are cleared of criminal wrongdoing, and no longer pose a threat to the

United States. They may be held until the war on terror is over, whenever that might be. The U.S. government has not filed criminal charges against them or assigned them prisoner-of-war status, leaving them in legal limbo. They do not routinely have access to lawyers and are not allowed visits from family. The federal courts have determined that they do not have jurisdiction over the prisoners.

FINAL REMARKS

Few people question the threat to U.S. citizens' lives and well-being posed by twenty-first century terrorism. The tragic events of September 11, 2001, provided a frightening wake-up call for most Americans. Unfortunately, there is no established roadmap to follow in fighting the war on terror. There are few precedents to guide decision makers in the difficult task of preserving domestic security. Critics contend that some government officials have been overzealous in their efforts. Some critics question the motives of particular government officials. Perhaps the most often made criticism of the war on terror is that some of the legislation enacted and tactics allowed threaten the very rights and freedoms that the war on terrorism is trying to preserve. Some people worry that provisions of the PATRIOT Act and other similar legislation designed for the war on terror—provisions that override or set aside traditional procedural safeguards—will become a permanent part of the way criminal justice is administered in the United States. Some people are concerned that law enforcement strategies implemented to fight the war on terror—strategies that remove traditional constraints on law enforcement activity—will become commonplace in the ways law enforcement officers carry out their duties. There is no doubt that the collapse of the World Trade Center's twin towers changed the United States in unanticipated ways. The challenge faced by the United States in this Age of Terror is to defend domestic security without sacrificing the rights and freedoms of American citizens.

THINKING CRITICALLY

1. Do you think there should be legal limits on the ways the United States fights the war on terrorism? If so, what should they be? If not, why not?
2. Do you think it is acceptable to suspend traditional legal rights and freedoms in the war on terrorism? Why or why not? If your answer is in the affirmative, which legal rights and freedoms should be suspended and which ones should not? Defend your choices.

SUMMARY

1. Describe the possible future of law enforcement if the crime control model dominates, and the possible future if the due process model dominates

If law enforcement in the future increasingly reflects the principles and policies of the crime control model, then Americans might expect fewer limitations on how the police attempt to combat crime. However, if there is a shift to the principles and policies of the due process model, Americans should expect existing limitations on how the police combat crime to remain intact or even to be expanded.

2. Describe the possible future of the administration of justice if the crime control model dominates, and the possible future if the due process model dominates

If the crime control model dominates the administration of justice in the future, then the right to legal counsel at critical pre- and posttrial stages may be scaled back significantly, the preliminary hearing may be abolished, and the use of pretrial detention may be expanded; there may be fewer criminal trials and more plea bargaining, and appeals may be strongly discouraged and limited. If the due process model dominates, then the current right to counsel at a variety of critical stages in the process is likely to be maintained or, perhaps, extended somewhat (for example, to appeals beyond the first one); the grand jury may be eliminated; plea bargaining probably will be discouraged, and the number of criminal cases that go to trial is therefore likely to increase substantially; and there will probably be no limitations on the right to appeal.

3. Identify perhaps the most divisive issue that will confront correctional policy makers in the future

Perhaps the most divisive issue that will confront correctional policy makers in the future is whether increasingly scarce resources will be devoted more to punishment (to achieve the goals of retribution and incapacitation) or to rehabilitation (to achieve the goals of specific deterrence and successful reintegration).

4. Describe the possible future of corrections

Most people knowledgeable about corrections in the United States paint a rather bleak picture of its future: an increasing number of offenders under correctional supervision, consuming larger and larger proportions of state and federal budgets. Future expenditures of tax dollars on corrections by governments at all levels will be made grudgingly, after much wrangling and debate. Every attempt will be made to carry out corrections functions as inexpensively as possible.

5. List some of the cost-reduction strategies likely to be advocated in corrections in the future

Among the cost-reduction strategies likely to be advocated in corrections in the future are various alternatives to incarceration. However, cost savings from those alternatives may be illusory. Another cost reduction strategy likely to receive increasing support in the future is the privatization of corrections. A third cost reduction strategy, and potentially the most effective one, is the use of new technology.

6. Explain what identity theft is and describe the extent of the problem in the United States

Identity theft is the transfer or use without legal authority the identification documentation of another person with the intent to commit, aid, or abet any unlawful activity that constitutes a felony. Identity theft is widespread. According to a recent survey commissioned by the Federal Trade Commission, nearly 10 million Americans may have been victims of some type of identity theft in 2002, and as many as 27 million Americans may have been victims of identity theft during the 5 years between 1998 and 2002.

7. Summarize the reasons why transnational organized crime poses special problems for law enforcement

One reason transnational organized crime poses special problems for law enforcement is that many transnational organized crime groups use legitimate import-export companies, service industries, or multinational financial institutions as fronts for their illegal activities. Sometimes organized crime groups nest themselves inside legitimate businesses; other times they control them. Many groups employ experts in the use of global technology and conduct market research to determine where to operate. They can also hide behind national borders and take advantage of the jurisdictional limitations or confusion of law enforcement. In addition, many transnational organized crime groups can claim among their members present and former state officials and military and state intelligence agency personnel whose expertise often gives the crime groups an advantage over local law enforcement officials. Another problem is that some countries have no statutory or popular basis for preventing transnational organized crime.

8. Describe some of the challenges faced by criminal justice in the age of terror

A major challenge for criminal justice is to fight the war on terrorism without threatening the very rights and freedoms that the war on terrorism is trying to preserve. Another challenge is to create the institutions, such as the Department of Homeland Security, to fight the war on terrorism. The FBI has the challenge of shifting its priorities from being a federal police agency to being an intelligence and counterterrorism agency. Local law enforcement agencies have the challenge of preventing terrorist acts and responding to them when they occur, without engaging in racial or ethnic profiling.

KEY TERMS

bionics, p. 517
mediation, p. 526
arbitration, p. 526
restorative justice, p. 527
reintegrative shaming, p. 528
cryonics, p. 532
identity theft p. 533

REVIEW QUESTIONS

1. How might community policing based on the crime control model of criminal justice differ from community policing based on the due process model?
2. How might bionics affect law enforcement in the future?
3. What is perhaps the thorniest issue regarding the use of DNA technology as a law enforcement tool?
4. What is a principal problem with plea bargaining for due process model supporters?
5. How might the changing demographics of the U.S. population affect the operation of criminal courts?
6. What is the principal difference between mediation and arbitration?
7. What are restorative justice and reintegrative shaming, and how do they differ from punitive justice?
8. What is the *new penology,* and how is its measurement of success different from the measurement of correctional success in the past?
9. What is cryonics, and how might it be used in corrections in the future?
10. What are three general types of identity theft, and which one is considered the most serious for victims?
11. What are some of the ways that identity thieves obtain personal information?
12. What are some of the common characteristics of transnational organized crime groups?
13. What are some of the criminal activities of transnational organized crime groups?

IN THE FIELD

1. **Criminal Justice in the Movies** There are numerous science fiction movies or videos that depict criminal justice in the future. Examples are *Blue Thunder, Escape from New York, Demolition Man, Blade Runner, Minority Report* and the *RoboCop* series. Watch one or more of those movies or videos, and consider how plausible they seem in light of what you have read in this chapter. Have any of the innovations of these futuristic justice systems become a part of the current American justice system? Are any of these innovations discussed in this chapter?

2. **Identity Theft Vulnerability** Test how vulnerable family members or friends are to identity theft. If you live at home, go "dumpster diving" through trash cans looking for your family members' personal information, such as copies of checks, credit card and bank statements, credit card applications, or other records with identifying information. If you live in a dormitory or apartment, do the same with your roommate or roommates. Present what you find to the "victims." Discuss with them the problems that befall identity theft victims and how identity theft can be prevented.

ON THE NET

1. **Explore New Technologies** Go to the Justice Technology Information Network at www.nlectc.org/frontpage.html. Click on Technology Assistance or Equipment Needs. Survey the new technologies available and write a three-page scenario of how criminal justice will change when the new technology is implemented.

2. **Evaluate Programs** Access "Creating a New Criminal Justice System for the 21st Century: Findings and Results from State and Local Program Evaluations" at www.ncjrs.org/txtfilesl/bja/178936.txt. Read some of the program evaluations. Write a short essay on why the programs may or may not be important in the twenty-first century.

CRITICAL THINKING EXERCISES

1. **Corrections in the Future** It is the year 2028, and you have been asked to serve on a citizens' committee charged with providing input about the creation of a new supermaximum-security federal prison. The prison will be built either several hundred feet beneath the ocean's surface off the east coast of the United States or on the moon. The rationale for these locations is to better isolate prisoners from the law-abiding population and to take advantage of prison labor for the high-risk jobs of either marine farming or the mining of new and useful materials in space. The technology and the resources to build the prison, though expensive, are available.
   a. Which location would be preferable? Why?
   b. Should public tax dollars be used to fund the project, or should a private corporation be allowed to build and operate the facility at its own expense and keep any profits from the farming or mining business?
   c. What special problems might arise because of the location of the prison?

2. **Law Enforcement in the Future** It is the year 2028 in Washington, DC, and public service officers, formerly called police officers, are flying routine patrol with the aid of their new jet packs. While flying over a condo near the city's center, two of the officers, using their bionic eyes and ears, detect what appear to be a half-dozen men plotting to bomb the White House. Surveying the condo from their sky perch, the officers see, stored in a bedroom closet, enough of a new, illegal, and largely undetectable hydrogen-based explosive to do the job. The officers, using the ultrasmall two-way communication devices implanted in their larynxes, communicate to headquarters what they have seen. They await further orders.
   a. Do the officers have probable cause to obtain a search warrant from a magistrate or to make an arrest? If you were a proponent of Packer's crime control model, what would your answer be? If you were a proponent of Packer's due process model, what would your answer be?
   b. How might the legal issues of the right to privacy, the admissibility of evidence, the exclusionary rule, and the plain-view doctrine affect the use of this new technology by law enforcement officers?
   c. What restraints, if any, should be imposed on the use of this new technology by law enforcement officers? If you were a proponent of Packer's crime control model, what would your answer be? If you were a proponent of Packer's due process model, what would your answer be?

ENDNOTES

Chapter 1

1. The top crime news stories for 2002 and 2003 are taken from *Facts on File World News Digest,* "Top News Stories of 2002"; no. 3240, January 16, 2003, p. 52; no. 3245, February 20, 2003, p. 108; no. 3247, March 6, 2003, p. 147; no. 3248, March 13, 2003, p. 170; no. 3249, March 20, 2003, p. 191.
2. Our thanks to Chicago Police Officer Monica Chester of the Research and Development Division and Tom Dugan of the Office of Emergency Communications, for their help in securing and explaining these data.
3. Herbert Packer, *The Limits of the Criminal Sanction* (Stanford, CA: Stanford University Press, 1968).
4. See, for example, Walter B. Miller, "Ideology and Criminal Justice Policy: Some Current Issues," *Journal of Criminal Law and Criminology* 64 (1973), pp. 141–62.
5. Unless otherwise indicated, the data in this section are from Sidra Lea Gifford, "Justice Expenditure and Employment in the United States, 1999," *Bureau of Justice Statistics Bulletin,* U.S. Department of Justice (Washington, DC: GPO, February 2002).
6. Ibid.
7. Sourcebook of Criminal Justice Statistics 2001, p. 131, Table 2.51 at www.albany.edu/sourcebook/1995/pdf/t251.pdf.
8. Robert M. Bohm, *Deathquest II: An Introduction to the Theory and Practice of Capital Punishment in the United States* (Cincinnati, OH: Anderson, 2003), p. 135.
9. Laurie A. Gould, "A Case Study of the Monetary Costs of Criminal Justice in a Local Jurisdiction" (unpublished manuscript, 2000).
10. D. Nimmo and J. E. Combs, *Subliminal Politics: Myths and Mythmakers in America* (Englewood Cliffs, NJ: Prentice Hall, 1980), p. 6.
11. Ibid., p. 16.
12. Many of the myths presented in this book were taken from the following sources: Jeffrey H. Reiman, *The Rich Get Richer and the Poor Get Prison: Ideology, Class, and Criminal Justice,* 7th ed. (Boston: Allyn & Bacon, 2004); Harold E. Pepinsky and Paul Jesilow, *Myths That Cause Crime,* 2nd ed. (Cabin John, MD: Seven Locks, 1985); Kevin N. Wright, *The Great American Crime Myth* (Westport, CT: Greenwood, 1987); also see Robert M. Bohm, "Myths About Criminology and Criminal Justice: A Review Essay," *Justice Quarterly* 4 (1987), pp. 631–42.; William Wilbanks, *The Myth of a Racist Criminal Justice System* (Belmont, CA: Wadsworth, 1987); Victor E. Kappeler, Mark Blumberg, and Gary W. Potter, *The Mythology of Crime and Criminal Justice,* 3rd ed. (Prospect Heights, IL: Waveland, 2000); Samuel Walker, *Sense and Nonsense About Crime, and Drugs: A Policy Guide,* 5th ed. (Belmont, CA: Wadsworth, 2000). For a discussion of why these myths exist, see Robert M. Bohm, "Crime, Criminal and Crime Control Policy Myths," *Justice Quarterly* 3 (1986), pp. 193–214.

Chapter 2

1. For additional examples and further discussion of this issue, see Robert M. Bohm, "Some Relationships That Arguably Should Be Criminal Although They Are Not: On the Political Economy of Crime," pp. 3–29 in K. D. Tunnell (ed.), *Political Crime in Contemporary America: A Critical Approach* (New York: Garland, 1993); Gregg Barak (ed.), *Crimes by the Capitalist State: An Introduction to State Criminality* (New York: State University of New York Press, 1991); Gregg Barak and Robert M. Bohm, "The Crimes of the Homeless or the Crime of Homelessness? On the Dialectics of Criminalization, Decriminalization, and Victimization," *Contemporary Crises* 13 (1989), pp. 275–88; James W. Coleman, *The Criminal Elite: Understanding White Collar Crime,* 4th ed. (New York: St. Martin's, 1998); David O. Friedrichs, *Trusted Criminals: White Collar Crime in Contemporary Society* (Belmont, CA: Wadsworth, 1995); Gary S. Green, *Occupational Crime,* 2nd ed. (Chicago: Nelson-Hall, 1996); David R. Simon, *Elite Deviance,* 6th ed. (Boston: Allyn and Bacon, 1999).
2. These elements and the discussion that follows are based on material from Edwin H. Sutherland and Donald R. Cressey, *Criminology,* 9th ed. (Philadelphia: J. B. Lippincott, 1974), pp. 13–15.
3. *M'Naghten's Case,* 8 Eng. Rep. 718 (1843).
4. Sutherland and Cressey, op. cit., p. 25.
5. Ibid. The remainder of the discussion in this section is based on material from the aforementioned source, pp. 25–30.
6. Ibid.
7. Ibid., pp. 27–28.
8. D. Seidman and M. Couzens, "Getting the Crime Rate Down: Political Pressure and Crime Reporting," *Law and Human Behavior* 8 (1974), pp. 327–42. See also L. DeFleur, "Biasing Influences on Drug Arrest

Records: Implications for Deviance Research," *American Sociological Review* 40 (1975), pp. 88–103; W. L. Selke and H. E. Pepinsky, "The Politics of Police Reporting in Indianapolis, 1948–1978," *Law and Human Behavior* 6 (1982), pp. 327–42.

9. Federal Bureau of Investigation, *Crime in the United States 2001,* U.S. Department of Justice (Washington, DC: GPO, 2002).
10. Ibid.
11. Ibid., p. 60.
12. Ibid., p. 61.
13. Ibid.
14. Ibid., p. 232.
15. Ibid., p. 233.
16. Ibid.
17. Ibid., p. 232.
18. Ibid., p. 251, Table 42.
19. Ibid., p. 220.
20. Ibid.
21. Ibid.
22. Ibid., pp. 302–313.
23. Unless indicated otherwise, all information in this section is from Brian A. Reaves, "Using NIBRS Data to Analyze Violent Crime," U.S. Department of Justice, Bureau of Justice Statistics Technical Report (Washington, DC: GPO, October 1993).
24. U.S. Department of Justice, Office of Justice Programs, Bureau of Justice Statistics, www.ojp.usdoj.gov/bjs/nibrsstatus.htm.
25. U.S. Department of Justice, "Implementing the National Incident-Based Reporting System: A Project Status Report," (Washington, DC: GPO, July 1997).
26. U.S. Department of Justice, Office of Justice Programs, Bureau of Justice Statistics, *Criminal Victimization in the United States, 1994* (Annapolis, MD: Bureau of Justice Statistics Clearinghouse, 1997).
27. See, for example, J. S. Wallerstein and C. J. Wylie, "Our Law-Abiding Lawbreakers," *Probation* 25 (1947), pp. 107–12; I. Silver, Introduction to *The Challenge of Crime in a Free Society* (New York: Avon, 1968). See also C. Tittle, W. Villemez, and D. Smith, "The Myth of Social Class and Criminality," *American Sociological Review* 43 (1978), pp. 643–56. Juvenile delinquency is also widespread. See, for example, Jerald Bachman, Lloyd Johnston, and Patrick O'Malley, *Monitoring the Future* (Ann Arbor: University of Michigan, Institute for Social Research, 1992); Martin Gold, "Undetected Delinquent Behavior," *Journal of Research in Crime and Delinquency* 3 (1966), pp. 27–46; Martin Gold, *Delinquent Behavior in an American City* (Belmont, CA: Brooks/Cole, 1970); Maynard Erickson and LaMar Empey, "Court Records, Undetected Delinquency, and Decision-Making," *Journal of Criminal Law, Criminology, and Police Science* 54 (1963), pp. 446–69; James Short and F. Ivan Nye, "Extent of Unrecorded Delinquency," *Journal of Criminal Law, Criminology, and Police Science* 49 (1958), pp. 296–302.
28. *Criminal Victimization in the United States 2001,* Statistical Tables, Table 82, www.ojp.usdoj.gov/bjs/pub/pdf/cvus0104pdf.
29. U.S. Department of Justice, Office of Justice Programs, Bureau of Justice Statistics, *Criminal Victimization in the United States, 1992* (Annapolis, MD: Bureau of Justice Statistics Clearinghouse, 1994), p. 148.
30. Simon, op. cit., p. 93
31. Ted R. Miller, Mark A. Cohen, and Brian Wiersema, "Victim Costs and Consequences: A New Look," U.S. Department of Justice, National Institute of Justice Report (Washington, DC: GPO, February 1996).
32. Wesley Skogan, "Fear of Crime and Neighborhood Change," in Albert J. Reiss, Jr., and Michael Tonry (eds.), *Communities and Crime,* Vol. 8 of *Crime and Justice: A Review of Research* (Chicago: The University of Chicago Press, 1986).
33. Sourcebook of Criminal Justice Statistics Online, June 1997, p. 156, Table 2.37 (1995 data).
34. Kathleen Maguire and Ann L. Pastore (eds.), *Sourcebook of Criminal Justice Statistics 1993,* U.S. Department of Justice, Bureau of Justice Statistics (Washington, DC: GPO, 1994), p. 182, Table 2.30; Bahram Haghighi and Jon Sorensen, "America's Fear of Crime," in Timothy J. Flanagan and Dennis R. Longmire (eds.), *Americans View Crime and Justice: A National Public Opinion Survey* (Thousand Oaks, CA: Sage, 1996), p. 22, Table 2.1.
35. Ann L. Pastore and Kathleen Maguire (eds.), *Sourcebook of Criminal Justice Statistics 2001,* U.S. Department of Justice, Bureau of Justice Statistics (Washington, DC: GPO, 2002), p. 125, Table 2.41.
36. Ibid.
37. Kathleen Maguire and Ann L. Pastore (eds.), *Sourcebook of Criminal Justice Statistics 2001,* U.S. Department of Justice, Bureau of Justice Statistics (Washington, DC: GPO, 2002), pp. 126–127, Table 2.42; Kathleen Maguire and Ann L. Pastore (eds.), *Sourcebook of Criminal Justice Statistics 1994,* U.S. Department of Justice, Bureau of Justice Statistics (Washington, DC: GPO, 1995) (from draft data); Haghighi and Sorensen, op. cit., p. 19.
38. Haghighi and Sorensen, op. cit., pp. 26–27.
39. Wesley Skogan and Michael G. Maxwell, *Coping with Crime: Individual and Neighborhood Reactions* (Beverly Hills, CA: Sage, 1981).
40. Haghighi and Sorensen, op. cit., p. 19.
41. Skogan, "Fear of Crime and Neighborhood Change," op. cit., p. 215.
42. Callie Marie Rennison, "Criminal Victimization 2001: Changes 2000–2001 with Trends 1993–2001," U.S. Department of Justice, Bureau of Justice Statistics, National Crime Victimization Survey (Washington, DC: GPO, September 2002), p. 3, Table 1.
43. Ibid.
44. Ibid.
45. Ibid.
46. Ibid., p. 1
47. Ibid
48. Ibid.
49. Ibid., pp. 6–7, Tables 2 and 3.
50. Ibid. pp. 5–6.
51. Ibid., p. 8, Table 4.
52. Ibid., p. 8, Table 5.

Chapter 3

1. Cesare Beccaria, *An Essay on Crimes and Punishments,* trans., with introduction, by Harry Paolucci (Indianapolis: Bobbs-Merrill, 1975), p. ix.
2. Ibid., p. 8.
3. Ibid., p. 42.
4. Ibid., p. 99.
5. Beccaria, op. cit.
6. See Irving M. Zeitlin, *Ideology and the Development of Sociological Theory,* 3rd ed. (Englewood Cliffs, NJ: Prentice Hall, 1987).
7. See Ian Taylor, Paul Walton, and Jock Young, *The New Criminology: For a Social Theory of Deviance* (New York: Harper and Row, 1974), pp. 24–32.
8. George B. Vold and Thomas J. Bernard, *Theoretical Criminology,* 3rd ed. (New York: Oxford, 1986), p. 48.
9. See William H. Sheldon, *Varieties of Delinquent Youth* (New York: Harper, 1949).
10. Diana H. Fishbein, *The Science, Treatment, and Prevention of Antisocial Behaviors: Application to the Criminal Justice System* (Kingston, NJ: Civic Research Institute, 2000).
11. See Diana H. Fishbein, "Biological Perspectives in Criminology." *Criminology* 28 (1990), pp. 27–72; Vold and Bernard, op. cit., pp. 87–92; Daniel J. Curran and Claire M. Renzetti, *Theories of Crime* (Boston: Ally and Bacon, 1994), pp. 54–63; James Q. Wilson and Richard J. Herrnstein, *Crime and Human Nature* (New York: Simon & Schuster, 1985), pp. 75–81, 90–100.
12. See Curran and Renzetti, op. cit., p. 78; Fishbein, op. cit., pp. 38, 47.
13. See National Institute for Juvenile Justice and Delinquency Prevention, *Preventing Delinquency,* Vol. 1 (Washington, DC: GPO, 1977), pp. 120–122; Vold and Bernard, op. cit., pp. 101–103.
14. See Fishbein, op. cit., pp. 48, 53; National Institute, op. cit.; Curran and Renzetti, op. cit., pp. 73–77, 80–81.
15. Edwin H. Sutherland and Donald R. Cressey, *Criminology,* 9th ed. (Philadelphia: J. B. Lippincott, 1974), p. 152.
16. Robert Gordon, "Prevalence: The Rare Datum in Delinquency Measurement and Its Implications for the Theory of Delinquency," in Malcolm W. Klein (ed.), *The Juvenile Justice System* (Beverly Hills, CA: Sage, 1976), pp. 201–84; Travis Hirschi and Michael J. Hindelang, "Intelligence and Delinquency: A Revisionist Review," *American Sociological Review* 42 (1977), pp. 572–87.
17. See Robert S. Woodworth and Mary R. Sheehan, *Contemporary Schools of Psychology,* 3rd ed. (New York: The Ronald Press Co., 1964).
18. Walter Bromberg and Charles B. Thompson, "The Relation of Psychosis, Mental Defect, and Personality Types to Crime," *Journal of Criminal Law and Criminology* 28 (1937), pp. 70–89; Karl F. Schuessler and Donald R. Cressey, "Personality Characteristics of Criminals," *American Journal of Sociology* 55 (1950), pp. 476–84; Gordon P. Waldo and Simon Dinitz, "Personality Attributes of the Criminal: An Analysis of Research Studies, 1950–1965," *Journal of Research in Crime and Delinquency* (1967), pp. 185–202; John Monahan and Henry J. Steadman, "Crime and Mental Disorder: An Epidemiological Approach," in Michael Tonry and Norval Morris (eds.), *Crime and Justice,* Vol. 4 (Chicago: University of Chicago Press, 1983).
19. Abraham H. Maslow, *Motivation and Personality,* 2nd ed. (New York: Harper and Row, 1970).
20. Seymour L. Halleck, *Psychiatry and the Dilemmas of Crime* (New York: Harper and Row, 1967).
21. Émile Durkheim, *Rules of Sociological Method* (New York: Free Press, 1964).
22. Vold and Bernard, op. cit., p. 160.
23. Robert E. Park, Ernest Burgess, and Roderick D. McKenzie, *The City* (Chicago: University of Chicago Press, 1928).
24. Clifford R. Shaw, *Delinquency Areas* (Chicago: University of Chicago Press, 1929); Clifford R. Shaw and Henry D. McKay, *Social Factors in Juvenile Delinquency* (Chicago: University of Chicago Press, 1931); Clifford R. Shaw and Henry D. McKay, *Juvenile Delinquency and Urban Areas* (Chicago: University of Chicago Press, 1942).
25. Clifford R. Shaw, *The Jackroller* (Chicago: University of Chicago Press, 1930); Clifford R. Shaw, *The National History of Delinquent Career* (Chicago: University of Chicago Press, 1931); Clifford R. Shaw, *Brothers in Crime* (Chicago: University of Chicago Press, 1938).
26. Robert K. Merton, "Social Structure and Anomie," *American Sociological Review* 3 (1938), pp. 672–82.
27. Albert K. Cohen, *Delinquent Boys: The Culture of the Gang* (New York: Free Press, 1955).
28. Richard A. Cloward and Lloyd E. Ohlin, *Delinquency and Opportunity: A Theory of Delinquent Gangs* (New York: Free Press, 1960).
29. See, for example, Albert Bandura, *Social Learning Theory* (Englewood Cliffs, NJ: Prentice Hall, 1977).
30. See, for example, Edwin H. Sutherland and Donald R. Cressey, *Criminology,* 9th ed. (Philadelphia: J. B. Lippincott, 1974).
31. Daniel Glaser, "Criminality Theories and Behavioral Images," *American Journal of Sociology* 61 (1956), pp. 433–44.
32. Definitions of learning theory concepts are from Howard Rachlin, *Introduction to Modern Behaviorism,* 2nd ed. (San Francisco: W. H. Freeman, 1976).
33. Michael R. Gottfredson and Travis Hirschi, *A General Theory of Crime* (Stanford, CA: Stanford University Press, 1990).
34. Edwin Lemert, *Social Pathology: A Systematic Approach to the Theory of Sociopathic Behavior* (New York: McGraw-Hill, 1951).
35. See Edwin M. Schur, *Radical Nonintervention* (Englewood Cliffs, NJ: Prentice Hall, 1973).
36. Robert J. Lilly, Francis T. Cullen, and Richard A. Ball, *Criminological Theory: Context and Consequences* (Newbury Park, CA: Sage, 1989), pp. 131–35.
37. John Braithwaite, *Crime, Shame and Reintegration* (Cambridge: Cambridge University Press, 1989).

38. Vold and Bernard, op. cit., p. 256.
39. George B. Vold, *Theoretical Criminology* (New York: Oxford, 1958).
40. William J. Chambliss, "Functional and Conflict Theories of Crime: The Heritage of Emile Durkheim and Karl Marx," in W. J. Chambliss and M. Mankoff (eds.), *Whose Law, What Order?* (New York: Wiley, 1976), p. 9.
41. Tony Platt, "Prospects for a Radical Criminology in the USA," in I. Taylor et al. (eds.), *Critical Criminology* (Boston: Routledge & Kegan Paul, 1975), p. 103.
42. Ibid.; for a similar definition, see also Herman Schwendinger and Julia Schwendinger, "Defenders of Order or Guardians of Human Rights?" in I. Taylor et al. (eds.), *Critical Criminology,* pp. 113–46.
43. See, for example, Richard Kinsey, John Lea, and Jock Young, *Losing the Fight Against Crime* (London: Basil Blackwell, 1976); Roger Matthews and Jock Young (eds.), *Confronting Crime* (London: Sage, 1986).
44. Jock Young, "Left Realism: The Basics," in B. D. MacLean and D. Milovanovic (eds.), *Thinking Critically About Crime* (Vancouver, BC: Collective Press, 1997), pp. 28–36.
45. Werner Einstadter and Stuart Henry, *Criminological Theory: An Analysis of Its Underlying Assumptions* (Fort Worth, TX: Harcourt Brace, 1995), p. 256.
46. Ibid., p. 257.
47. See Harold E. Pepinsky and Richard Quinney (eds.), *Criminology as Peacemaking* (Bloomington: Indiana University Press, 1991).
48. For two excellent reviews, see Kathleen Daly and Meda Chesney–Lind, "Feminism and Criminology," *Justice Quarterly* 5 (1988), pp. 497–538; Sally S. Simpson, "Feminist Theory, Crime, and Justice," *Criminology* 27 (1989), pp. 605–31.
49. See Einstadter and Henry, op. cit., p. 275.
50. Ibid.
51. Ibid., p. 278.
52. Ibid., p. 287.
53. Bruce Arrigo and T. R. Young, "Chaos, Complexity, and Crime: Working Tools for a Postmodern Criminology," in MacLean and Milovanovic, op. cit., p. 77. For an interesting postmodern analysis of the William Kennedy Smith rape trial, see Gregory M. Matoesian, *Law and the Language of Identity: Discourse in the William Kennedy Smith Rape Trial* (New York: Oxford University Press, 2001).
54. Einstadter and Henry, op. cit., p. 291.
55. Arrigo and Young, op. cit., pp. 81–2; Stuart Henry and Dragan Milovanovic, *Constitutive Criminology: Beyond Postmodernism* (London: Sage, 1996).
56. Einstadter and Henry, op. cit., p. 294.
57. Ibid., p. 280.

Chapter 4

1. Jay A. Sigler, *Understanding Criminal Law* (Boston: Little, Brown, 1981), p. 3.
2. The discussion in the remainder of this section is based on material from Edwin H. Sutherland and Donald R. Cressey, *Criminology,* 9th ed. (Philadelphia: J. B. Lippincott, 1974), p. 8.
3. Most of the material in this section comes from Will Durant, *Our Oriental Heritage,* Part 1 of *The Story of Civilization* (New York: Simon & Schuster, 1954).
4. Most of the material in this section comes from Raymond J. Michalowski, *Order, Law, and Crime: An Introduction to Criminology* (New York: Random House, 1985).
5. See Archibald Cox, *The Court and the Constitution* (Boston: Houghton Mifflin, 1987), pp. 239–49.
6. For an examination of the influence of the Burger and Rehnquist Courts on criminal procedure, see Mary Margaret Weddington and W. Richard Janikowski, "The Rehnquist Court: The Counter-Revolution That Wasn't: Part II, The Counter-Revolution That Is," *Criminal Justice Review* 21 (1997), pp. 231–50.
7. In addition to the Supreme Court cases themselves, much of the information in the remainder of this chapter is from the following sources: John Ferdico, *Criminal Procedure for the Law Enforcement Officer* (St. Paul, MN: West, 1975); Yale Kamisar, Wayne R. LaFave, and Jerold H. Israel, *Modern Criminal Procedure,* 7th ed. (St. Paul, MN: West, 1990); Sanford H. Kadish and Monrad G. Paulsen, *Criminal Law and Its Processes,* 3rd ed. (Boston: Little, Brown, 1975); Wayne R. LaFave and Jerold H. Israel, *Criminal Procedure* (St. Paul, MN: West, 1984, Supp. 1991); Jerold H. Israel and Wayne R. LaFave, *Criminal Procedure in a Nutshell* (St. Paul, MN: West, 1975); John M. Scheb and John M. Scheb II, *Criminal Law and Procedure,* 2nd ed. (St. Paul, MN: West, 1994).
8. *Katz* v. *United States,* 389 U.S. 347 (1967).
9. *United States* v. *Jacobsen,* 466 U.S. 109 (1984).
10. Ibid.
11. *Florida* v. *J. L.,* 529 U.S. 266 (2000).
12. *Illinois* v. *Wardlow,* 528 U.S. 119 (2000).
13. Unless indicated otherwise, information in this section is from www.epic.org/privacy/terrorism/hr3162.html, which provides the full text of the USA PATRIOT Act; American Civil Liberties Union, "Surveillance Under the USA PATRIOT Act," www.aclu.org/SafeandFree/SafeandFree.cfm?ID=12263&c=206, April 3, 2003; Electronic Frontier Foundation, "EFF Analysis of the Provisions of the USA PATRIOT Act," www.eff.org/Privacy/Surveillance/Terrorism_militias/20011031_eff_usa_patriot_analysis.htm, October 31, 2001.
14. American Civil Liberties Union Legislative Update, "ACLU Fact Sheet on PATRIOT Act II," www.aclu.org/SafeandFree/SafeandFree.cfm?ID=12234&c=205, March 28, 2003.
15. *Dickerson* v. *United States,* 530 U.S. 428 (2000).
16. See Raymond Paternoster, *Capital Punishment in America* (New York: Lexington, 1991), p. 51.
17. Barry Scheck, Peter Neufeld, and Jim Dwyer, *Actual Innocence: When Justice Goes Wrong and How to Make It Right* (New York: Signet, 2001), p. xx.

18 C. Ronald Huff, Arye Rattner, and Edward Sagarin, "Guilty Until Proven Innocent: Wrongful Conviction and Public Policy," *Crime and Delinquency* 32 (1986), pp. 518–44.
19 U.S. Department of Justice, Federal Bureau of Investigation, *Crime in the United States, 2001* (Washington: GPO, 2002), p. 232.
20 See Huff et al., op. cit., p. 523.
21 Scheck et al., op. cit., p. 95.
22 Ibid., p. 226.
23 Marcia Coyle, Fred Strasser, and Marianne Lavelle, "Fatal Defense," *The National Law Journal* 12 (1990), pp. 30–44.
24. Scheck et al., op. cit., p. 242.
25. Huff et al., op. cit., pp. 530–33; Scheck et al. op. cit.
26. The National Institute of Justice, "The Effects of the Exclusionary Rule: A Study in California" (Washington, DC: U.S. Department of Justice, 1983).
27. American Bar Association Special Committee on Criminal Justice in a Free Society, "Criminal Justice in Crisis" (1988), at www.druglibrary.org/special/king/cjic.htm; F. Feeney, F. Dill, and A. Weir, *Arrests Without Conviction: How Often They Occur and Why* (Washington, DC: U.S. Department of Justice, National Institute of Justice, 1983); P. Nardulli, "The Societal Cost of the Exclusionary Rule: An Empirical Assessment," *American Bar Foundation Research Journal* (1983), pp. 585–609; *Report of the Comptroller General of the United States, Impact of the Exclusionary Rule on Federal Criminal Prosecutions* (Washington, DC: U.S. General Accounting Office, 1979); K. Brosi, *A Cross City Comparison of Felony Case Processing* (Washington, DC: U.S. Department of Justice, Law Enforcement Assistance Administration, 1979); B. Forst, J. Lucianovic, and S. Cox, *What Happens After Arrest: A Court Perspective of Police Operations in the District of Columbia* (Washington, DC: U.S. Department of Justice, Law Enforcement Assistance Administration, 1978).
28. *Report of the Comptroller General of the United States*, op. cit.
29. Cited in Tamar Jacoby, "Fighting Crime by the Rules: Why Cops Like Miranda," *Newsweek*, July 18, 1988, p. 53.
30. Karen L. Guy and Robert G. Huckabee, "Going Free on a Technicality: Another Look at the Effect of the *Miranda* Decision on the Criminal Justice Process," *Criminal Justice Research Bulletin* 4 (1988), pp. 1–3.
31. Jacoby, op. cit.; Scheck et al., op. cit., p. 117.
32. Guy and Huckabee, op. cit.
33. See, for example, George C. Thomas, III, and Richard Leo, "The Effects of *Miranda* v. *Arizona:* 'Embedded' in Our National Culture?" in Michael Tonry (ed.), *Crime and Justice: A Review of Research* (2002), pp. 203–271.
34. For a different view, see Paul G. Cassell and Bret S. Hayman, "Police Interrogation in the 1990s: An Empirical Study of the Effects of *Miranda,*" *UCLA Law Review* 43 (1996), pp. 839–931; and George C. Thomas, III, "Is *Miranda* a Real-World Failure? A Plea for More and Better Empirical Evidence," *UCLA Law Review* 43 (1996), pp. 821–37.

Chapter 5

1. Material in this section was taken from T. A. Critchley, *A History of Police in England and Wales,* 2nd ed. rev. (Montclair, NJ: Patterson Smith, 1972).
2. Ibid.
3. Patrick Pringle, *Hue and Cry: The Story of Henry and John Fielding and Their Bow Street Runners* (New York: William Morrow, 1965).
4. Material in this section was taken from A. C. Germann, F. Day, and R. Gallati, *Introduction to Law Enforcement and Criminal Justice* (Springfield, IL: Charles C. Thomas, 1962), pp. 54–55.
5. Edward Savage, *Police Records and Recollections, or Boston by Daylight and Gaslights for Two Hundred and Forty Years* (Boston: John P. Dale, 1873).
6. This material came from Carl Sifakis, *The Encyclopedia of American Crime* (New York: Smithmark, 1992), pp. 579–80.
7. Information in this section is from W. Marvin Dulaney, *Black Police in America* (Bloomington: Indiana University Press, 1996).
8. Center for Research on Criminal Justice, *The Iron Fist and the Velvet Glove: An Analysis of the U.S. Police* (Berkeley, CA: Center for Research on Criminal Justice, 1975); Hubert Williams and Patrick V. Murphy, "The Evolving Strategy of Police: A Minority View," *Perspectives on Policing, No. 13* (Washington, DC: U.S. Department of Justice, January 1990).
9. Dulaney, op. cit., p. 2.
10. Thad Sitton, *Texas High Sheriffs* (Austin: Texas Monthly Press, 1988).
11. Adrian N. Anderson, Ralph A. Wooster, David G. Armstrong, and Jeanie R. Stanley, *Texas and Texans* (New York: Glencoe/McGraw-Hill, 1993).
12. Bruce Smith, *Police Systems in the United States* (New York: Harper & Row, 1960), pp. 178–205.
13. *Our Police* (Cincinnati Police Division, 1984).
14. Gene Carte and Elaine Carte, *Police Reform in the United States: The Era of August Vollmer* (Berkeley: University of California Press, 1975).
15. Malcolm K. Sparrow, Mark H. Moore, and David M. Kennedy, *Beyond 911* (New York: Basic Books, 1990).
16. U.S. Department of Justice, *Response Time Analysis: Executive Summary* (Washington, DC: GPO, 1978).
17. Samuel Walker, *The Police in America: An Introduction,* 2nd ed. (New York: McGraw-Hill, 1992).
18. Robert C. Trojanowicz and Bonnie Bucqueroux, *Community Policing: A Contemporary Perspective* (Cincinnati: Anderson, 1989); Robert C. Trojanowicz and Bonnie Bucqueroux, *Community Policing: How to Get Started* (Cincinnati: Anderson, 1994).
19. Federal Bureau of Investigation, *Crime in the United States, 2001* (Washington, DC: GPO, 2002), www.fbi.gov.
20. Brian A. Reaves and Timothy C. Hart, *Federal Law Enforcement Officers, 2000,* U.S. Department of Justice. Bureau of Justice Statistics (Washington, DC, July 2001).
21. Matthew J. Hickman and Brian A. Reaves, *Local Police Departments, 2000* (Washington, DC: Bureau of Justice Statistics, 2003).

22. V. A. Leonard, *Police Organization and Management* (New York: Foundation Press, 1964).
23. Matthew J. Hickman and Brian A. Reaves, *Sheriffs' Officers 2000* (Washington, DC: Bureau of Justice Statistics, 2003).
24. Ibid.
25. Brian A. Reaves and Matthew J. Hickman, *Census of state and Local Law Enforcement Agencies, 2000* (Washington, DC: Bureau of Justice Statistics, 2002).
26. Reaves and Hart, *Federal Law Enforcement Officers, 2000,* op. cit.
27. Ibid.
28. Ibid
29. Reaves and Bauer, *Federal Law Enforcement Officers, 2002,* op. cit., pp. 7 and 10.
30. Ibid.
31. Material on FLETC is from Reaves and Bauer, *Federal Law Enforcement Officers, 2002,* ibid., p. 11; the Federal Law Enforcement Training Center at www.fletc.gov; "FLETC History" at www.fas.org/irp/agency/ustreas/fletc/history.htm.
32. Material on the Department of Homeland Security is from the U.S. Department of Homeland Security website at www.dhs.gov/dhspublic.
33. *Terrorism in the United States, 1999,* op. cit., p. 10.
34. Material on Homeland Security and the FBI is from the following sources: Rebecca Carr, "FBI Chief: My Agency Can Handle Spying Job," *The Orlando Sentinel,* December 20, 2002, p. A11; Eric Lichtblau, "Pressure on FBI Grows from Within," *The Orlando Sentinel,* December 2, 2002, p. A9; Curt Anderson, "FBI Seeks to Expand Presence Overseas," *The Orlando Sentinel,* March 29, 2003, p. A3; "Senate Confirms Ridge as Head of Homeland Dept," *USA Today,* January 23, 2003, p. 12A.
35. *Patterns of Global Terrorism 2002,* op. cit., p. iv.
36. Ibid., p. iii.
37. Ibid., p. v.
38. Ibid., p. viii.
39. Ibid., p. xi.
40. Kim Bolan, "Canada a Haven for Terrorists," *Vancouver Sun,* June 30, 2003.
41. Michelle Malkin, *Invasion: How America Still Welcomes Terrorists, Criminals, and Other Foreign Menaces to Our Shores* (Washington, DC: Regnery Publishing, Inc., 2001).
42. William Cunningham, John Strauchs, and Clifford Van Meter, *The Hallcrest Report II: Private Security Trends 1970–2000* (McLean, VA: Hallcrest Systems, 1990).
43. Unless indicated otherwise, most of the information in this section is from the *Occupational Outlook Handbook* at www.bls.gov/oco/pdf/ocos159.pdf (accessed May 2003).

Chapter 6

1. Keith Haley, "Training," in Gary Cordner and Donna Hale (eds.), *What Works in Policing? Operations and Administration Examined* (Cincinnati: Anderson, 1992).
2. Lee Rainwater, "The Revolt of the Dirty Workers," *Transaction* (November 1967), p. 2.
3. Jerome Skolnick, *Justice Without Trial* (New York Wiley, 1966).
4. U.S. Department of Justice, Federal Bureau of Investigation, "Law Enforcement Officers Killed and Assaulted in 2002," www.fbi.gov/pressrel/pressrel03/leoka051203.htm; U.S. Department of Justice, Federal Bureau of Investigation, *Uniform Crimes Reports, 2001, 2000, 1999,* www.fbi.gov/ucr/ucr.htm, May 10, 2003.
5. "Law Enforcement Officers Killed and Assaulted in 2002," ibid.
6. "Law Enforcement Officers Killed and Assaulted in 2002," ibid.; *Uniform Crimes Reports, 2001, 2000, 1999,* op. cit.
7. Ibid.; *Sourcebook of Criminal Justice Statistics, 2001,* www.albany.edu/sourcebook/1995/tost_3.html#3_av, p. 328, Table 3.164.
8. James Q. Wilson, *Varieties of Police Behavior* (Cambridge, MA: Harvard University Press, 1968) pp. 140–227.
9. John Broderick, *Police in a Time of Change* (Morristown, NJ: General Learning Press, 1977), pp. 9–88.
10. William Muir, Jr., *Police: Streetcorner Politicians* (Chicago: University of Chicago Press, 1977).
11. Ellen Hochstedler, "Testing Types: A Review and Test of Police Types," *Journal of Criminal Justice* 9 (1981), pp. 451–66.
12. G. Kelling, T. Pate, D. Dieckman, and C. Brown, *The Kansas City Preventive Patrol Experiment: A Summary Report* (Washington, DC: Police Foundation, 1974).
13. Gary Cordner, "Patrol," in Gary Cordner and Donna Hale (eds.), op. cit.
14. Daniel Mabrey, "Crime Mapping: Tracking the Hotspots," *Crime & Justice International* 18, no. 67 (2002), pp. 31–32.
15. Ibid.
16. James Q. Wilson and Barbara Boland, "The Effect of Police on Crime," *Law and Society Review* 12 (1978), pp. 367–84.
17. George Kelling, *The Newark Foot Patrol Experiment* (Washington, DC: Police Foundation, 1981).
18. Robert C. Trojanowicz, *The Neighborhood Foot Patrol Program in Flint, Michigan* (East Lansing, MI: National Neighborhood Foot Patrol Center, n.d.).
19. Bruce L. Berg and John J. Horgan, *Criminal Investigation,* 3rd ed. (Westerville: Glencoe/McGraw-Hill, 1998).
20. Christine Wicker, "Death Beat," in Keith N. Haley and Mark A. Stallo, *Texas Crime, Texas Justice* (New York: McGraw-Hill, 1996).
21. U.S. Department of Justice, Federal Bureau of Investigations, *Crime in the United States, 2001* (Washington, DC: GPO, 2002), p. 220.
22. Mark Willman and John Snortum, "Detective Work: The Criminal Investigation Process in a Medium-Size Police Department," *Criminal Justice Review* 9 (1984), pp. 33–39; V. Williams and R. Sumrall, "Productivity Measures in the Criminal Investigation

Function," *Journal of Criminal Justice* 10 (1982), pp. 111–22; I. Greenberg and R. Wasserman, *Managing Criminal Investigations* (Washington, DC: U.S. Department of Justice, 1979); P. Greenwood and J. Petersilia, *The Criminal Investigation Process, Vol. I, Summary and Policy Implications* (Washington, DC: U.S. Department of Justice, 1975); B. Greenberg, C. Elliot, L. Kraft, and H. Procter, *Felony Investigation Decision Model: An Analysis of Investigative Elements of Information* (Washington, DC: GPO, 1975).

23. John Conklin, *Robbery and the Criminal Justice System* (New York: J. B. Lippincott, 1972), p. 149.
24. Mike Berry, "Cop's Best Clue—a Fingerprint," *The Orlando Sentinel*, November 8, 2002, p. B1.
25. Hollis Stambaugh, David Beaupre, David Icove, Richard Baker, Waynes Cassady, and Wayne P. Williams, *State and Local Law Enforcement Needs to Combat Local Crime*, National Institute of Justice, August 2000.
26. Ronald T. Holmes, Richard Tewksberry, and Stephen T. Holmes, "Pornography on the Internet," *Law and Order* 45, no. 9 (September 1997).
27. Stambaugh, et al., op. cit.
28. Unless indicated otherwise, information in this section on drug enforcement is from the following sources: Matthew J. Hickman and Brian A. Reaves, *Local Police Departments, 2000*, U.S. Department of Justice, Bureau of Justice Statistics (Washington, DC: GPO, January 2003), pp. 11–12; H. Williams, "Drug Control Strategies of United States Law Enforcement," United Nations, Office on Drugs and Crime at www.unodc.org/unodc/en/bulletin/bulletin_1990-01-01_1_page004.html#s005; Scott Ehlers, *Policy Briefing: Asset Forfeiture*, The Drug Policy Foundation (Washington, DC: GPO, 1999); Samuel Walker, *Sense and Nonsense about Crime and Drugs: A Policy Guide*, 5th ed. (Belmont, CA: Wadsworth, 2001), chap. 13; Victor E. Kappeler, Mark Blumberg, and Gary W. Potter, *The Mythology of Crime and Criminal Justice*, 3rd ed. (Prospect Heights, IL: Waveland Press, 2000), chap. 8; "Long-Term Trends in Illicit Drug Use," U.S. Department of Health and Human Services, Office of Applied Studies at www.samhsa.gov/oas/nhsda/2k1nhsda/vol1/chapter9.htm#9.2.
29. Material on research studies based on information in Alfred Blumstein and Joan Petersilia, "NIJ and Its Research Program," *25 Years of Criminal Justice Research* (Washington, DC: The National Institute of Justice, 1994), pp. 10–14.
30. James Q. Wilson and George L. Kelling, "Broken Windows: The Police and Neighborhood Safety," *Atlantic Monthly* 256 (1982), pp. 29–38.
31. Material in this subsection is based on information in the following sources: Community Policing Consortium, *Understanding Community Policing: A Framework for Action*, monograph, www.communitypolicing.org/conpubs.html, January 1998; U.S. Department of Justice, National Institute of Corrections, *Community Justice: Striving for Safe, Secure, and Just Communities* (Louisville, KY: LIS, 1996).
32. Federal Bureau of Investigation, *Terrorism in the United States, 1999*, p. 15, at www.fbi.gov/publications/terror/terroris.htm.
33. Ibid.
34. Ibid., p. 16.
35. U.S. State Department, *Patterns of Global Terrorism, 2001*, May 2002, p. v, at www.state.gov/s/ct/rls/pgtrpt/2000/pdf.
36. Ibid., p. 1.
37. *Terrorism in the United States, 1999*, op. cit., p. 15.
38. Ibid., p. i.
39. Ibid.
40. U.S. State Department, *Patterns of Global Terrorism, 2002*, April 2003, p. xiii, at www.state.gov/s/ct/rls/pgtrpt/2002.
41. *Terrorism in the United States, 1999*, op. cit. p. ii.
42. Ibid.
43. Ibid., p. 18.
44. Ibid., p. 19.
45. Ibid., p. 20.
46. Ibid., pp. 25–26.
47. Ibid., p. 16.
48. Ibid., p. 23.
49. Ibid. p. xi.
50. *Terrorism in the United States, 1999*, op. cit., p. 23.
51. Ibid.
52. Ibid., pp. 38–40.
53. Ibid., p. i.
54. See Howard Zinn, *A People's History of the United States* (New York: Harper Colophon, 1980), chap. 4.
55. Kathleen Maguire and Ann L. Pastore (eds), *Sourcebook of Criminial Justice Statistics, 2001*, U.S. Department of Justice, Bureau of Justice Statistics (Washington, DC: GPO, 2002), p. 339, Table 3.184.
56. *Patterns of Global Terrorism, 2002*, op. cit., p. xi.
57. Eric Lichtblau, "Bush Issues Federal Ban on Racial Profiling," *The New York Times*, June 18, 2003.
58. Deborah Orin and David Kadison, "Government Still Knapping as New 9/11 Looms," *New York Post Online Edition*, June 30, 2003.
59. David Johnston, "Report Calls U.S. Agencies Understaffed for Bioterror," *The New York Times*, July 6, 2003.

Chapter 7

1. W. S. Wilson Huang and Michael S. Vaughn, "Support and Confidence: Public Attitudes Toward the Police," in Timothy J. Flanagan and Dennis R. Longmire (eds.), *Americans View Crime and Justice: A National Public Opinion Survey* (Thousand Oaks, CA: Sage, 1996), pp. 31–45.
2. Humphrey Taylor, "Love Affair with NYPD Has Not Changed Nationwide Attitudes Toward Police," *The Harris Poll* #13, March 20, 2002, at www.harrisinteractive.com/harris_poll/printerfriend/index.asp?PID=290; also see Kathleen Maguire and Ann L. Pastore (eds.), *Sourcebook of Criminal Justice Statistics, 2001*, p. 115, Tables 2.28, 2.17, at www.albany.edu/sourcebook.
3. Maguire and Pastore, op. cit., p. 112, Table 2.21.
4. Larry Gaines and Victor Kappeler, "Police Selection," in Gary Cordner and Donna Hale (eds.), *What Works*

in Policing: Operations and Administration Examined (Cincinnati: Anderson, 1992).
5. Robert B. Mills, “Psychological, Psychiatric, Polygraph, and Stress Evaluation,” in Calvin Swank and James Conser (eds.), *The Police Personnel System* (New York: Wiley, 1981).
6. O. W. Wilson and Roy McLaren, *Police Administration* (New York: McGraw-Hill, 1972), p. 261.
7. Albert Reiss, *The Police and the Public* (New Haven, CT: Yale University Press, 1971).
8. Matthew J. Hickman and Brian A. Reaves, *Local Police Departments, 2000,* U.S. Department of Justice, Bureau of Justice Statistics (Washington, DC: GPO, 2003), and U.S. Census Bureau.
9. David Carter, Allen Sapp, and Darrel Stephens, *The State of Police Education: Policy Direction for the 21st Century* (Washington, DC: Police Executive Research Forum, 1989).
10. Information on the Police Corps is from The Police Corps Act, 42 U.S.C., sections 14091 et seq. as amended through November 2, 2002 (Title XX, Subtitle A, of the Violent Crime Control and Law Enforcement Act of 1994); U.S. Department of Justice, Office of the Police Corps at www.ojp.usdoj.gov/opclee/about.html.
11. *Hild* v. *Bruner,* 1980; *Bonsignore* v. *City of New York,* 1981.
12. Jack Gregory, “The Background Investigation and Oral Interview,” in Calvin Swank and James Conser (eds.), op. cit.
13. Jerome Skolnick, *Justice Without Trial* (New York: Wiley, 1996).
14. Lawrence W. Sherman and Richard A. Berk, *The Minneapolis Domestic Violence Experiment* (Washington, DC: The Police Foundation, 1984).
15. Steve Lackmeyer and Ken Raymond, “City Leaders Balk at Ban on Police Profiling,” *The Oklahoman,* June 3, 2000.
16. Alex Johnson, “Fear and Loathing on the Job,” MSNBC, September 4, 2000.
17. NIOSH, “Stress at Work,” www.cdc.gov/niosh/stresswk.html.
18. The Word Spy at www.LOGOPHILIA.com/WordSpy/c.html.
19. “10% of Police Shootings Found to Be ‘Suicide by Cop,’” *Criminal Justice Newsletter* 29, no. 17 (September 1, 1998), pp. 1–2.
20. Alan Feuer, “Drawing a Bead on a Baffling Endgame: Suicide by Cop,” *The New York Times,* June 25, 1998.
21. NIOSH, op. cit.
22. John Dugan and Daniel Breda, “Complaints About Police Officers: A Comparison Among Types and Agencies,” *Journal of Criminal Justice* 19 (1991), pp. 165–71.
23. Knapp Commission, *Report on Police Corruption* (New York: George Braziller, 1972).
24. Ellwyn R. Stoddard, “The Informal ‘Code’ of Police Deviancy: A Group Approach to Blue-Coat Crime,” *Journal of Criminal Law, Criminology, and Police Science* 59 (1968), p. 204.
25. Candace McCloy, “Lawsuits Against Police: What Impact Do They Have?” *Criminal Law Bulletin* 20 (1984), pp. 49–56.

Chapter 8

1. Administrative Office of the U.S. Courts, Federal Judiciary website, “History of Federal Judgeships” at www.uscourts.gov/history/district.html.
2. Administrative Office of the U.S. Courts, Federal Judiciary website, “Federal Judicial Caseload Statistics, March 31, 2002” at www.uscourts.gov/caseload2002/contents.html. (Tables C and D-2).
3. Administrative Office of the U.S. Courts, Federal Judiciary website, “About the U.S. Courts,” at www.uscourts.gov.
4. Ibid. at www.uscourts.gov/cgi-bin/cmsa2002.pl.
5. Administrative Office of the U.S. Courts, Federal Judiciary website, “About the U.S. Courts,” op. cit.; also “History of Federal Judgeships,” op. cit.
6. Ibid., “History of Federal Judgeships” at www.uscourts.gov/history/appeal.html.
7. Kathleen Maguire and Ann L. Pastore (eds.), *Sourcebook of Criminal Justice Statistics 2001* at www.albany.edu/sourcebook/1995/tost_5.html, p. 454, Table 5.70 (calculated from data in tables).
8. Ibid.
9. Material on the state courts is based on information from the following sources: David B. Rottman, Carol R. Flango, Melissa T. Cantrell, Randall Hansen, Neil LaFountain, *State Court Organization 1998,* U.S. Department of Justice, Bureau of Justice Statistics (Washington, DC: GPO, June 2000); David W. Neubauer, *America's Courts and the Criminal Justice System,* 4th ed. (Pacific Grove, CA: Brooks/Cole, 1992); Christopher Smith, *Courts, Politics, and the Judicial Process* (Chicago: Nelson-Hall, 1993); N. Gary Holten and Lawson L. Lamar, *The Criminal Courts: Structures, Personnel, and Processes* (New York: McGraw-Hill, 1991); Lawrence Baum, *American Courts,* 3rd ed. (Boston: Houghton Mifflin, 1994). U.S. Department of Justice, Bureau of Justice Statistics, *Report to the Nation on Crime and Justice,* 2nd ed. (Washington, DC: GPO, 1988); H. Ted Rubin, *The Courts: Fulcrum of the Justice System* (Santa Monica, CA: Goodyear, 1976); James Eisenstein, Roy Flemming, and Peter Nadulli, *The Contours of Justice: Communities and Their Courts* (Boston: Little, Brown, 1988); Malcolm Feeley, *The Process Is the Punishment: Handling Cases in Lower Criminal Court* (New York: Russell Sage, 1979); Harry P. Stumpf and John H. Culver, *The Politics of State Courts* (New York: Longman, 1992); Paul Wice, *Chaos in the Courthouse: The Inner Workings of the Urban Criminal Courts* (New York: Praeger, 1985).
10. Material in this section about drug courts is from “Drug Courts: Overview of Growth, Characteristics, and Results,” GAO/GGD-97-106, www.ncjrs.org/txtfiles/dcourts.txt, July 31, 1997; Rottman et al., op. cit., p. 207.
11. Maya Bell, “Mentally Ill Get Court of Their Own—and Help,” *The Orlando Sentinel,* July 13, 1997, p. A-1.
12. John Wolfson and Sherri M. Owens, “Few Pay Back What They Took from Crime Victims,” *The Orlando Sentinel,* February 23, 2003, p. B1.

13. Judith S. Kaye, "Making the Case for Hands-On Courts," *Newsweek,* October 11, 1999, p. 13.
14. "American Court Systems Flow Chart" at www.judicial.state.ia.us/students/6.
15. Rottman et al., op. cit., p. 7.
16. Ibid.
17. Rubin, op. cit.
18. In addition to the other sources cited, material on the key actors in the court process is from Neubauer, op. cit.; David W. Neubauer, *Judicial Process: Law, Courts and Politics in the United States* (Pacific Grove, CA: Brooks/Cole, 1991); Smith, op. cit.; Holten and Lamar, op. cit.; Baum, op. cit.
19. Material about prosecutors is also taken from David Heilbroner, *Rough Justice: Days and Nights of a Young D.A.* (New York: Pantheon, 1990).
20. Data in this section are from Carol J. DeFrances, "Prosecutors in State Courts, 2001," U.S. Department of Justice, Bureau of Justice Statistics *Bulletin* (Washington, DC: GPO, May 2002).
21. In addition to the other sources cited, material on defense attorneys is from Elizabeth Loftus and E. Ketcham, *For the Defense* (New York: St. Martin's, 1991); Paul Wice, *Judges and Lawyers: The Human Side of Justice* (New York: Harper-Collins, 1991); Paul Wice, *Criminal Lawyers: An Endangered Species* (Newbury Park, CA: Sage, 1978); Seymour Wishman, *Confessions of a Criminal Lawyer* (New York: Penguin, 1982); Lisa J. McIntyre, *The Public Defender: The Practice of Law in the Shadows of Repute* (Chicago: Univ. of Chicago Press, 1987).
22. Data about indigent defense are from Bureau of Justice Statistics, "Indigent Defense Statistics," at www.ojp.usdoj.gov/bjs/id.htm.
23. In addition to the other sources cited, material on judges is from Paul Ryan, Allan Ashman, Bruce D. Sales, and Sandra Shane-DuBow, *American Trial Judges* (New York: Free Press, 1980); Robert Satter, *Doing Justice: A Trial Judge at Work* (New York: Simon & Schuster, 1990); Wice (1991), op. cit.; Wice (1985), op. cit.
24. *Sourcebook of Criminal Justice Statistics,* Online, Tables 1.70 and 1.72.
25. In addition to the other sources cited, material on pretrial stages is from Neubauer (1992), op. cit.; Holten and Lamar, op. cit.
26. David C. Steelman, James E. McMillan, and John A. Goerdt, *Caseflow Management: The Heart of Court Management in the New Millennium* (Williamsburg, VA: National Center for State Courts, 2000).
27. G. Thomas Munsterman, Paula L. Hannaford, and G. Marc Whitehead (eds.), *Jury Trial Innovations* (Williamsburg, VA: National Center for State Courts, 1997).
28. Timothy R. Murphy, Paula L. Hannaford, Genevra Kay Loveland, and G. Thomas Munsterman, *Managing Notorious Cases* (Williamsburg, VA: National Center for State Courts, 1998).
29. Debbie Salamone Wickhan, "On the Run," *The Orlando Sentinel,* January 7, 2001, p. A-1.
30. Ibid.
31. In addition to the other sources cited, material on plea bargaining is from Neubauer (1992), op. cit.; Neubauer (1991), op. cit.; Holten and Lamar, op. cit.; Baum, op. cit.
32. In addition to the other sources cited, material on criminal trials is from Neubauer (1992), op. cit.; Neubauer (1991), op. cit.; Smith, op. cit.; Holten and Lamar, op. cit.
33. In addition to the other sources cited, material on juries is from Rottman et al., op. cit.; Holten and Lamar, op. cit.; Valerie P. Hans and Neil Vidmar, *Judging the Jury* (New York: Plenum, 1986); Harry Kalvan, Jr., and Hans Zeisel, *The American Jury* (Boston: Little, Brown, 1996); James P. Levine, *Juries and Politics* (Pacific Grove, CA: Brooks/Cole, 1992).
34. *Sourcebook of Criminal Justice Statistics* (Online), p. 80, Table 1.76.
35. In addition to the other sources cited, material on the trial process is from Satter (1990), op. cit.
36. Brian J. Ostrom, Neal B. Kauder, and Robert C. LaFountain, *Examining the Work of State Courts, 2001* (Williamsburg, VA: National Center for State Courts, 2003), chap. 2, at www.ncsconline.org; Jeffrey Rosen, "One Angry Woman: Why Are Hung Juries on the Rise?" *The New Yorker,* February 24 & March 3, 1997, p. 55.

Chapter 9

1. In addition to the other sources cited, material on sentencing and appeals is from David W. Neubauer, *America's Courts and the Criminal Justice System,* 7th ed. (Belmont, CA: Wadsworth, 2002); Christopher Smith, *Courts, Politics, and the Judicial Process* (Chicago: Nelson-Hall, 1993); N. Gary Holten and Lawson L. Lamar, *The Criminal Courts: Structures, Personnel, and Processes* (New York: McGraw-Hill, 1991); Lawrence Baum, *American Courts,* 3rd ed. (Boston: Houghton Mifflin, 1994); David Garland, *Punishment and Modern Society: A Study in Social Theory* (Chicago: Univ. of Chicago Press, 1990); Paul Wice, *Chaos in the Courthouse: The Inner Workings of the Urban Criminal Courts* (New York: Praeger, 1985); John Paul Ryan, Allan Ashman, Bruce D. Sales, and Sandra Shane-DuBow, *American Trial Judges* (New York: Free Press, 1980); Robert Satter, *Doing Justice: A Trial Judge at Work* (New York: Simon & Schuster, 1990); Herbert Packer, *The Limits of the Criminal Sanction* (Stanford, CA: Stanford Univ. Press, 1968).
2. Matthew R. Durose and Patrick A. Langan, *Felony Sentences in State Courts, 2000,* U.S. Department of Justice, Bureau of Justice Statistics *Bulletin* (Washington, DC: GPO, 2003), p. 5.
3. *American Correctional Association 2002 Directory: Juvenile and Adult Correctional Departments, Institutions, Agencies and Paroling Authorities* (Lanham, MD: American Correctional Association, 2002), p. 16.
4. "Sentence Disparity in New York: The Response of Forty-One Judges," *New York Times,* March 30, 1979, p. B3.

5. See Robert M. Bohm, "Retribution and Capital Punishment: Toward a Better Understanding of Death Penalty Opinion," *Journal of Criminal Justice* 20 (1992), pp. 227–35.
6. "New Directions from the Field: Victims' Rights and Services for the 21st Century," U.S. Department of Justice, Office for Victims of Crime, *OVC Bulletin* (Washington, DC: GPO, August 1998).
7. *Report to the Nation 2001: Fiscal Years 1999 and 2000,* U.S. Department of Justice, Office for Victims of Crime (Washington, DC: GPO, December 2001).
8. *1996 Victims' Rights Sourcebook: A Compilation and Comparison of Victims' Rights Laws,* The National Center for Victims of Crime at www.ncvc.org/resources/reports/sourcebook.
9. "New Directions from the Field: Victims' Rights and Services for the 21st Century," op. cit.
10. "Restorative Justice: An Interview with Visiting Fellow Thomas Quinn," *National Institute of Justice Journal,* No. 235 (March 1998), p. 10.
11. "Ordering Restitution to the Crime Victim," U.S. Department of Justice, Office for Victims of Crime, *Legal Series Bulletin #6* (Washington, DC: GPO, November 2002).
12. Unless indicated otherwise, material about the death penalty is from Robert M. Bohm, *Deathquest II: An Introduction to the Theory and Practice of Capital Punishment in the United States,* 2nd ed. (Cincinnati, OH: Anderson, 2003); James R. Acker, Robert M. Bohm, and Charles S. Lanier (eds.), *America's Experiment with Capital Punishment: Reflections on the Past, Present, and Future of the Ultimate Penal Sanction,* 2nd ed. (Durham, NC: Carolina Academic Press, 2003); Hugo Alan Bedau, *The Death Penalty in America; Current Controversies* (New York: Oxford University Press, 1997); Hugo Adam Bedau (ed.), *The Death Penalty in America,* 3rd ed. (London: Oxford Univ. Press, 1982); William J. Bowers, with Glenn L. Pierce and John McDevitt, *Legal Homicide: Death as Punishment in America, 1864–1982* (Boston: Northeastern Univ. Press, 1984); Raymond Paternoster, *Capital Punishment in America* (New York: Lexington, 1991); Robert M. Bohm, "Humanism and the Death Penalty, with Special Emphasis on the Post-*Furman* Experience," *Justice Quarterly* 6 (1989), pp. 173–95; Victoria Schneider and John Ortiz Smykla, "A Summary Analysis of Executions in the United States, 1608–1987: The Espy File," in R. M. Bohm (ed.), *The Death Penalty in America: Current Research* (Cincinnati: Anderson, 1991), pp. 1–19.
13. Death Penalty Information Center at www.deathpenaltyinfo.org; Amnesty International at web.amnesty.org/library/Index/ENGACT500072002? open&of=ENG-392.
14. Death Penalty Information Center, op. cit.
15. Bohm, op. cit., p. 35.
16. Tracy L. Snell, *Capital Punishment 2001,* U.S. Department of Justice, Bureau of Justice Statistics *Bulletin* (Washington: GPO, 2002), p. 15, appendix table 3.
17. Ibid., Paternoster, op. cit., pp. 208–9; Barry Scheck, Peter Neufeld, and Jim Dwyer, *Actual Innocence: When Justice Goes Wrong and How to Make It Right* (New York: Penguin Putnam, 2001); James S. Liebman, Jeffrey Fagan, and Valerie West, "A Broken System: Error Rates in Capital Cases, 1973–1995," The Justice Project at www.justice.policy.net/jpreport.html.
18. The Death Penalty Information Center, op. cit.
19. Snell, op. cit.
20. Death Penalty Information Center, op. cit.
21. Ibid.
22. Jeffrey M. Jones, "Support for the Death Penalty Remains High at 74%," The Gallup Organization at www.deathpenaltyinfo.org/article.php?scid=23&dis=592; www.deathpenaltyinfo.org/article.php?scid=23&did=210#Harris1/17/03.
23. Jones, op. cit.
24. Death Penalty Information Center, op. cit.
25. Robert M. Bohm, *Deathquest II,* op. cit., pp. 242 and 249.
26. "The Shadow over America," *Newsweek,* May 29, 2000, p. 27.
27. Death Penalty Information Center, op. cit.
28. Bohm, *Deathquest II,* op. cit.
29. Survey cited in Edmund F. McGarrell and Marla Sandys, "The Misperception of Public Opinion Toward Capital Punishment: Examining the Spuriousness Explanation of Death Penalty Support," *American Behavioral Scientist* 39 (1996), pp. 500–13, p. 509.
30. Robert M. Bohm, Louise J. Clark, and Adrian F. Aveni, "Knowledge and Death Penalty Opinion: A Test of the Marshall Hypotheses," *Journal of Research in Crime and Delinquency* 28 (1991), pp. 360–87; Robert M. Bohm and Ronald E. Vogel, "A Comparison of Factors Associated with Uninformed and Informed Death Penalty Opinions," *Journal of Criminal Justice* 23 (1994), pp. 125–43; Robert M. Bohm, Ronald E. Vogel, and Albert A. Maisto, "Knowledge and Death Penalty Opinion: A Panel Study," *Journal of Criminal Justice* 21 (1993), pp. 29–45.
31. Jeffrey M. Jones, "Understanding Americans' Support for the Death Penalty," The Gallup Organization, Gallup Poll Tuesday *Briefing,* June 3, 2003.
32. Bohm, "Retribution and Capital Punishment," op. cit.; see also Bohm and Vogel, "A Comparison of Factors Associated with Uninformed and Informed Death Penalty Opinions," op. cit.

Chapter 10

1. See Robert Johnson, *Hard Time: Understanding and Reforming the Prison* (Monterey, CA: Brooks/Cole, 1987).
2. Michel Foucault, *Discipline and Punish: The Birth of the Prison* (New York: Pantheon, 1978).
3. See Graeme Newman, *The Punishment Response* (Albany, NY: Harrow and Heston, 1985).
4. Todd R. Clear and George F. Cole, *American Corrections,* 3rd ed. (Belmont, CA: Wadsworth, 1994).
5. Graeme Newman and Pietro Marongiu, "Penological Reform and the Myth of Beccaria," *Criminology* 28 (1990), pp. 325–46.
6. Ibid.

7. Clear and Cole, op. cit.
8. David J. Rothman, *The Discovery of the Asylum: Social Order and Disorder in the New Republic* (Boston: Little, Brown, 1971).
9. See Paul Takagi, "The Walnut Street Jail: A Penal Reform to Centralize the Powers of the State," *Federal Probation* (December 1975), pp. 18–26.
10 Rothman, op. cit.
11 Clear and Cole, op. cit.
12 Nicole Hahn Rafter, "Gender and Justice: The Equal Protection Issue," in L. Goodstein and D. L. MacKenzie (eds.), *The American Prison: Issues in Research and Policy* (New York: Plenum, 1989), pp. 89–109; and see Nicole Hahn Rafter, *Partial Justice: Women in State Prisons, 1800–1935* (Boston: Northeastern University Press, 1985).
13 John Irwin, *Prisons in Turmoil* (Boston: Little, Brown, 1980).
14 Ibid., p. 3.
15 See Robert Martinson, "What Works? Questions and Answers About Prison Reform," *The Public Interest* 42 (1974), pp. 22–54; see also The American Friends Service Committee, *Struggle for Justice: A Report on Crime and Justice in America* (New York: Hill & Wang, 1971).
16. From Charles W. Thomas, "Private Adult Correctional Facility Census: A 'Real-Time' Statistical Profile," www.crim.ufl.edu/pcp, September 4, 2001, Table 1 and Chart 3.
17. Ibid.
18. Ibid.
19. Ibid.
20. Ibid.
21. Doris Layton MacKenzie and James W. Shaw, "The Impact of Shock Incarceration on Technical Violations and New Criminal Activities," *Justice Quarterly* 10 (1993), pp. 463–87; also see Doris Layton MacKenzie and Claire Souryal, *Multisite Evaluation of Shock Incarceration*, National Institute of Justice, November 1994.
22. "Poor Evaluation Brings End to California's Boot Camp," *Criminal Justice Newsletter* 28, no. 15 (August 1, 1997), pp. 1–2.
23. United States Department of Justice, Bureau of Justice Statistics *Bulletin, Prisoners in 1992,* May 1993.
24. Paige M. Harrison and Allen J. Beck, "Prisoners in 2002," U.S. Department of Justice, Bureau of Justice Statistics *Bulletin,* July 2003.
25. Ibid.
26. Ibid.
27. Paige M. Harrison and Jennifer C. Karberg, "Prison and Jail Inmates at Midyear 2002," U.S. Department of Justice, Bureau of Justice Statistics *Bulletin,* April 2003.
28. Ibid.
29. Harrison and Beck, "Prisoners in 2002," op. cit.
30. Harrison and Karberg, "Prison and Jail Inmates at Midyear 2002," op. cit.
31. James P. Lynch, "A Cross National Comparison of the Length of Custodial Sentences for Serious Crimes," *Justice Quarterly* 10 (1993), pp. 639–60.
32. Camille Graham Camp and George M. Camp, *The 2001 Corrections Yearbook: Adult Systems* (Middletown, CT: Criminal Justice Institute, 2002), pp. 98–102.
33. Ibid., pp. 105–106.
34. The Corrections Yearbook: Download Jails at www.cji-inc.com/cyb/jails01.html.
35. Nils Christie, *Crime Control as Industry: Toward Gulags Western Style?* (New York: Routledge, 1993).
36. Franklin E. Zimring, "The Great American Lockup," *Washington Post* National Weekly Edition, March 1991, pp. 4–10.
37. Harrison and Beck, "Prisoners in 2002," op. cit.
38. See, for example, John Kramer and Darrell Steffensmeir, "Race and Imprisonment Decisions," *Sociological Quarterly* 34 (1993), pp. 357–76; Ronald L. Akers, *Criminological Theories: Introduction and Evaluation,* 2nd ed. (Los Angeles: Roxbury, 1997). For different views, see Edmund F. McGarrell, "Institutional Theory and the Stability of a Conflict Model of the Incarceration Rate," *Justice Quarterly* 10 (1993), pp. 7–28; Cassia Spohn and Jerry Cederblom, "Race and Disparities in Sentencing: A Test of the Liberation Hypothesis," *Justice Quarterly* 8 (1991), pp. 305–27.
39. Harrison and Beck, "Prisoners in 2002," op. cit.; Harrison and Karberg, "Prison and Jail Inmates at Midyear 2002," op. cit.; published and unpublished data from 1997 surveys of state and federal inmates that were graciously provided by Allen Beck and Christopher Mumola, U.S. Department of Justice, Bureau of Justice Statistics, November 9, 2000.
40. The Federal Bureau of Prisons, "Mission Statement," at www.bop.gov.
41. The Federal Bureau of Prisons, "The Bureau in Brief," at www.bop.gov/pubinfo.html.
42. Camp and Camp, *Adult Systems,* op. cit., p. 80.
43. Francis X. Clines, "A Futuristic Prison Awaits the Hard Core 400." *The New York Times,* national ed., October 17, 1994, p. 1A.
44. Chase Riveland, "Supermax Prisons: Overview and General Considerations," U.S. Department of Justice, *National Institute of Corrections*, January 1999.
45. Material on Camp Delta is from Matthew Hay Brown, "Detainees Await an Unkown Fate," *The Orlando Sentinel*, July 20, 2003, p. A1.
46. Harrison and Beck, "Prisoners in 2002," op. cit., p. 5.
47. Ibid.
48. *2002 Directory: Juvenile and Adult Correctional Departments, Institutions, Agencies and Paroling Authorities,* The American Correctional Association, 2002, p. 28.
49. Ibid.
50. John Ortiz Smykla and Jimmy J. Williams, "Co-Corrections in the United States, 1970–1990: Two Decades of Disadvantages for Women Prisoners," *Women and Criminal Justice* 8 (1996), pp. 61–76.
51. Harrison and Karberg, "Prison and Jail Inmates at Midyear 2002," op. cit., p. 7.
52. Ibid., p. 8.

53. Ibid.
54. John Irwin, *The Jail: Managing the Underclass in American Society* (Berkeley: University of California Press, 1985).
55. John A. Backstrand, Don C. Gibbons, and Joseph F. Jones, "Who Is in Jail: An Examination of the Rabble Hypothesis," *Crime and Delinquency* 38 (1992), pp. 219–29.
56. See Dale K. Sechrest and William C. Collins, *Jail Management and Liability Issues* (Miami: Coral Gables Publishing, 1989).
57. Unless indicated otherwise, information in this section on jail design is from Frank Schmalleger and John Ortiz Smykla, *Corrections in the 21st Century* (Columbus, OH: Glencoe/McGraw-Hill, 2001), pp. 94–98; *Podular, Direct Supervision Jails: Information Packet*, U.S. Department of Justice, National Institute of Corrections, Jails Division (January 1993) at www.nicic.org/resources/topics/DirectSupervisionJails.aspx; Steve Fishback, "The Design of the New Anchorage Jail," *Alaska Justice Forum* 18, no. 3 (Fall 2001) at www.uaa.alaska.edu/just/forum/f183fa01/c_anchjail.html.
58. Mary Stohr-Gillman, Linda Zupan, Craig Curtis, Ben Menke, and Nicholas Lourich, "The Development of a Behavioral-Based Performance Appraisal System," *American Jails* 5 (1992), pp. 10–16.
59. Jeffrey D. Senese, "Evaluating Jail Reform: A Comparative Analysis of Popular/Direct and Linear Jail Inmate Infractions," *Journal of Criminal Justice* 25 (1997), pp. 61–73; Linda L. Zupan, *Jails: Reform and the New Generation Philosophy* (Cincinnati: Anderson, 1991); Schmalleger and Smykla, op. cit., p. 98; Fishback, op. cit.
60. *2001 Directory of Direct Supervision Jails*, U.S. Department of Justice, National Institute of Corrections, at www.nicic.org/resources/topics/DirectSupervisionJails.aspx.
61. James W. Marquart and Ben M. Crouch, "Coopting the Kept: Using Inmates for Social Control in a Southern Prison," in M. K. Carlie and K. I. Minor (eds.), *Prisons Around the World: Studies in International Penology* (Dubuque, IA: Wm. C. Brown, 1992), pp. 124–38.
62. United States Department of Justice, Bureau of Justice Statistics Special Report, Prison Rule Violators, December 1989.
63. From Camp and Camp, *Adult Systems*, op. cit., p. 35; "Longer Sentences Mean Older Prisoners and New Set of Problems," *The Orlando Sentinel*, September 1, 1996, p. A-15.
64. Most of the information on the mentally ill is from "Fact Sheet: Criminalization of Americans with Severe Mental Illnesses," Treatment Advocacy Center at www.psychlaws.org/GeneralResources/Fact3.htm.
65. Allen J. Beck and Laura M. Maruschak, "Mental Health Treatment in State Prisons, 2000," U.S. Department of Justice, Bureau of Justice Statistics *Special Report* (Washington, DC: GPO, July 2001.
66. Information in this section about HIV and AIDS is from Laura Maruschak, *HIV in Prisons, 2000,* U.S. Department of Justice, Bureau of Justice Statistics *Bulletin,* October 2002.
67. Camp and Camp, *Adult Systems,* op. cit., pp. 130–131; Camille Graham Camp and George M. Camp, *The Corrections Yearbook 1999* (Middletown, CT: Criminal Justice Institute), pp. 39–42.
68. National Institute for Literacy, "FACT SHEET: Corrections Education," January 2001, at www.nifl.gov.
69. For reference, see Anthony Walsh, *Understanding, Assessing, and Counseling the Criminal Justice Client* (Pacific Grove, CA: Brooks/Cole, 1988); also see Patricia van Voorhis, Michael Braswell, and David Lester, *Correctional Counseling and Rehabilitation,* 4th ed. (Cincinnati: Anderson, 2000).
70. Ted Palmer, *A Profile of Correctional Effectiveness and New Directions for Research* (Albany, NY: State University of New York Press, 1994).
71. Johnson, op. cit.

Chapter 11

1. Erving Goffman, *Asylums* (New York: Doubleday, 1961), p. xiii.
2. James B. Jacobs, *Stateville: The Penitentiary in Mass Society* (Chicago: University of Chicago Press, 1977).
3. See Donald Clemmer, *The Prison Community* (New York: Holt, Rinehart & Winston, 1940); Gresham M. Sykes, *The Society of Captives: A Study of a Maximum Security Prison* (Princeton, NJ: Princeton University Press, 1958).
4. Clemmer, op. cit.
5. John Irwin and Donald R. Cressey, "Thieves, Convicts, and the Inmate Culture," *Social Problems* 10 (1962), pp. 142–55. Also see Clarence Schrag, "Some Foundations for a Theory of Corrections," in D. R. Cressey (ed.), *The Prison: Studies in Institutional Organization and Change* (New York: Holt, Rinehart & Winston, 1961), pp. 30–35.
6. See Richard Hawkins and Geoffrey P. Alpert, *American Prison Systems: Punishment and Justice* (Englewood Cliffs, NJ: Prentice Hall, 1989); John Irwin, *Prisons in Turmoil* (Boston: Little, Brown, 1980). Also see Leo Carroll, *Hacks, Blacks, and Cons: Race Relations in a Maximum Security Prison* (Lexington, MA: Heath, 1974); Geoffrey Hunt, Stephanie Riegel, Tomas Morales, and Dan Waldorf, "Changes in Prison Culture: Prison Gangs and the Case of the 'Pepsi Generation,'" *Social Problems* 40 (1993), pp. 398–409; James B. Jacobs, *New Perspectives on Prisons and Imprisonment* (Ithaca, NY: Cornell University Press, 1983).
7. Camille Graham Camp and George M. Camp, *The Corrections Yearbook 2001: Adult Systems* (Middletown, CT: Criminal Justice Institute, 2002), pp. 42 and 173.
8. Lee Bowker, *Prison Victimization* (New York: Elsevier, 1980).
9. Ann Cordilia, *The Making of an Inmate: Prison as a Way of Life* (Cambridge, MA: Schenkman, 1983).
10. Goffman, op. cit., p. 14.
11. Hans Toch, *Living in Prison: The Ecology of Survival* (New York: Free Press, 1977).

12. Robert Johnson, *Hard Time: Understanding and Reforming the Prison* (Monterey, CA: Brooks/Cole, 1987).
13. Irwin, op. cit.
14. David Ward and Gene Kassebaum, "Homosexuality: A Model of Adaptation in a Prison for Women," *Social Problems* 12 (1964), pp. 159–77.
15. Joycelyn Pollock-Byrne, *Women, Prison, and Crime* (Pacific Grove, CA: Brooks/Cole, 1990).
16. Christopher J. Mumola, "Incarcerated Parents and Their Children," U.S. Department of Justice, Bureau of Justice Statistics Special Report (Washington, DC: GPO, August 2000), p. 2, Table 1 and p. 3, Table 4.
17. Phyllis Jo Baunach, *Mothers in Prison* (New Brunswick, NJ: Transaction Books, 1985).
18. Rose Giallombardo, *Society of Women: A Study of a Women's Prison* (New York: Wiley, 1966); Esther Heffernan, *Making It in Prison: The Square, the Cool, and the Life* (New York: Wiley, 1972); Alice M. Propper, *Prison Homosexuality* (Lexington, MA: Heath, 1981).
19. Propper, op. cit.
20. Giallombardo, op. cit.
21. David Ward and Gene Kassebaum, *Women's Prison: Sex and Social Structure* (Chicago: Aldine, 1965).
22. Heffernan, op. cit.; Schrag, op. cit.
23. Gordon Hawkins, *The Prison: Policy and Practice* (Chicago: University of Chicago Press, 1976), p. 85.
24. Camp and Camp, op. cit., pp. 150–176.
25. Hawkins and Alpert, op. cit.
26. Ibid.
27. Sykes, op. cit.
28. John D. Hewitt, Eric D. Poole, and Robert M. Regoli, "Self-Reported and Observed Rule-Breaking in Prison: A Look at Disciplinary Response," *Justice Quarterly* 3 (1984), pp. 437–47.
29. Hawkins and Alpert, op. cit.
30. Lucien X. Lombardo, *Guards Imprisoned: Correctional Officers at Work*, 2nd ed. (Cincinnati: Anderson, 1989). And see Johnson, op. cit.
31. Barbara A. Owen, "Race and Gender Relations Among Prison Workers," *Crime and Delinquency* 31 (1985), pp. 147–59.
32. American Correctional Association, *Corrections Compendium*, February 2003, p. 11.
33. American Correctional Association, *Corrections Compendium*, January 2003, p. 9.
34. Jacobs, op. cit., pp. 36–37.
35. *Wilson* v. *Seiter*, 111 S.Ct. 2321 (1991).
36. Hawkins and Alpert, op. cit.
37. Lauren E. Glaze, "Probation and Parole in the United States, 2001," U.S. Department of Justice, Bureau of Justice Statistics *Bulletin* (Washington, DC: GPO, August 2002), p. 6.
38. Unless indicated otherwise, information about recidivism is from Patrick A. Langan and David J. Levin, "Recidivism of Prisoners Released in 1994," U.S. Department of Justice, Bureau of Justice Statistics *Special Report* (Washington, DC: GPO, June 2002). Also see Miles D. Harer, *Recidivism Among Federal Prison Releasees in 1987: A Preliminary Report*, Federal Bureau of Prisons, Office of Research and Evaluation, December 9, 1993; United States Department of Justice, Bureau of Justice Statistics *Special Report, Recidivism of Prisoners Released in 1983*, April 1989; United States Department of Justice, Bureau of Justice Statistics Special Report, *Recidivism of Young Parolees*, May 1987.
39. *Recidivisn of Prisoners Released in 1983*, op. cit.
40. Ben M. Crouch, "Is Incarceration Really Worse? Analysis of Offenders' Preferences for Prison over Probation," *Justice Quarterly* 10 (1993), pp. 67–88.
41. Kenneth D. Tunnell, "Choosing Crime: Close Your Eyes and Take Your Chances," *Justice Quarterly* 7 (1990), pp. 673–90.
42. Robert Martinson, "What Works? Questions and Answers About Prison Reform," *The Public Interest* 42 (1974), pp. 22–54.
43. Lynne Goodstein, "Inmate Adjustment to Prison and the Transition to Community Life," in R. M. Carter, D. Glaser, and L. T. Wilkins (eds.), *Correctional Institutions*, 3rd ed. (New York: Harper & Row, 1985), pp. 285–302.
44. Francis T. Cullen and Paul Gendreau, "Assessing Correctional Rehabilitation: Policy, Practice, and Prospects," in U.S. Department of Justice, Office of Justice Programs, *Criminal Justice 2000*, vol. 3, at www.ojp.usdoj.gov/nij/criminal_justice2000/vol3_2000.html.

Chapter 12

1. David E. Duffee, "Community Corrections: Its Presumed Characteristics and an Argument for a New Approach," in D. E. Duffee and E. F. McGarrell (eds.), *Community Corrections: A Community Field Approach* (Cincinnati: Anderson, 1990), pp. 1–41.
2. Patricia M. Harris, Todd R. Clear, and S. Christopher Baird, "Have Community Supervision Officers Changed Their Attitudes Toward Their Work?" *Justice Quarterly* 6 (1989), pp. 233–46. And see Robert T. Sigler, "Role Conflict for Adult Probation and Parole Officers: Fact or Myth," *Journal of Criminal Justice* 16 (1988), pp. 121–29.
3. Lauren E. Glaze, "Probation and Parole in the United States, 2002," U.S. Department of Justice, Bureau of Justice Statistics *Bulletin* (Washington, DC: GPO, August 2003), p. 4, Table 4.
4. David J. Rothman, *Conscience and Convenience: The Asylum and Its Alternatives in Progressive America* (Boston: Little, Brown, 1980), p. 44; www.ohnd.uscourts.gov/U_S_Probation/U_S_Probation_Employment/u_s_probation_employment.html.
5. Tom Condon, "Prison Experiment: Sentenced to Read" at www.ctnow.com/templates/misc/printstory.jsp?slug=hc%2Dcondon1010%2Eartoct10
6. Rolando V. del Carmen, "Legal Issues and Liabilities in Community Corrections," in T. Ellsworth (ed.), *Contemporary Community Corrections* (Prospect Heights, IL: Waveland Press, 1992), pp. 383–407.

7. Jay S. Albanese, Bernadette A. Fiore, Jerie H. Powell, and Janet R. Storti, *Is Probation Working? A Guide for Managers and Methodologists* (New York: University Press of America, 1981), p. 65.
8. Ibid.
9. Joan Petersilia, Susan Turner, James Kahan, and Joyce Peterson, *Granting Felons Probation: Public Risks and Alternatives* (Santa Monica, CA: Rand, 1985).
10. United States Department of Justice, Bureau of Justice Statistics *Special Report, Recidivism of Felons on Probation, 1986–89* (Washington, DC: GPO, February 1992).
11. Rothman, op. cit.
12. John C. Runda, Edward E. Rhine, and Robert E. Wetter, *The Practice of Parole Boards* (Lexington, KY: Host Communications Printing, 1994).
13. Ibid.
14. Ibid.
15. Ibid.
16. Ibid.
17. Ibid.
18. Ibid.
19. Ibid.
20. Ibid.
21. Ibid.
22. Ibid.
23. Richard McCleary, *Dangerous Men: The Sociology of Parole* (Beverly Hills, CA: Sage, 1978).
24. Peggy B. Burke, *Abolishing Parole: Why the Emperor Has No Clothes* (Lexington, KY: American Probation and Parole Association, 1995); Peggy B. Burke, "Issues in Parole Release Decision Making," in C. A. Hartjen and E. E. Rhine (eds.), *Correctional Theory and Practice* (Chicago: Nelson-Hall, 1992), pp. 213–32.
25. Timothy A. Hughes, Doris James Wilson, and Allen J. Beck, "Trends in State Parole, 1990–2000," U.S. Department of Justice, Bureau of Justice Statistics *Special Report* (Washington, DC: GPO, October 2001), p. 2.
26. Paula M. Ditton and Doris James Wilson, "Truth in Sentencing in State Prisons," U.S. Department of Justice, Bureau of Justice *Special Report* (Washington, DC: GPO, January 1999), p. 3.
27. Burke, *Abolishing Parole,* op. cit.
28. John C. Watkins, Jr., "Probation and Parole Malpractice in a Noninstitutional Setting: A Contemporary Analysis," *Federal Probation* 53 (1989), pp. 29–34 (quotations from p. 30). Also see Rolando V. del Carmen, op. cit.
29. Calculated from Lauren E. Glaze, "Probation and Parole in the United States, 2002," op. cit., p. 1. Lauren E. Glaze, "Probation and Parole in the United States, 2001," U.S. Department of Justice, Bureau of Justice Statistics *Bulletin* (Washington, DC: GPO, August 2002), p. 1.
30. Jeffrey K. Liker, "Wage and Status Effects of Employment on Affective Well-Being Among Ex-Felons," *American Sociological Review* 47 (1982), pp. 264–83 (quotation from p. 282).
31. Richard A. Berk and David Rauma, "Capitalizing on Nonrandom Assignment to Treatments: A Regression-Discontinuity Evaluation of a Crime-Control Program," *Journal of the American Statistical Association* 78 (1983), pp. 21–27. And see Peter H. Rossi, Richard A. Berk, and K. J. Lenihan, *Money, Work, and Crime: Experimental Evidence* (New York: Academic Press, 1980).
32. Information evaluating parole is from Timothy A. Hughes, Doris James Wilson, and Allen J. Beck, "Trends in State Parole, 1990–2000," U.S. Department of Justice, Bureau of Justice Statistics *Special Report* (Washington, DC: GPO, October 2001), pp. 10–14; Lauren E. Glaze, "Probation and Parole in the United States, 2002," op. cit., p. 6, Table 7; "U.S. Correctional Population Reaches 6.3 Million Men and Women Represents 3.1 Percent of the Adult U. S. Population," U.S. Department of Justice, Bureau of Justice Statistics Press Release, July 23, 2000, at www.ojp.usdoj.gov/bjs/pub/pdf/pp99pr.pdf; "Recidivism of Young Parolees," U.S. Department of Justice, Bureau of Justice Statistics *Special Report* (Washington, DC: GPO, May 1987).
33. Runda et al., op. cit. Also see United States G.A.C., *Intermediate Sanctions: Their Impacts on Prison Crowding, Costs, and Recidivism Are Still Unclear* (Washington, DC: General Accounting Office, 1990).
34. Billie S. Erwin and Lawrence A. Bennett, *New Dimensions in Probation: Georgia's Experience with Intensive Probation Supervision,* United States Department of Justice, National Institute of Justice, Research in Brief (Washington, DC: GPO, 1987), p. 4.
35. Joan Petersilia and Susan Turner, "Comparing Intensive and Regular Supervision for High-Risk Probationers: Early Results from an Experiment in California," *Crime and Delinquency* 36 (1990), pp. 87–111.
36. Joan Petersilia and Susan Turner, *Evaluating Intensive Supervision Probation/Parole: Results of a Nationwide Experiment,* U.S. Department of Justice, National Institute of Justice, Research in Brief (Washington, DC: GPO, 1993). For further detail see Joan Petersilia and Susan Turner, "Intensive Probation and Parole," in M. Tonry and A. J. Reiss (eds.), *Crime and Justice: A Review of Research,* Vol. 17 (Chicago: University of Chicago Press, 1993), pp. 281–335.
37. Dale G. Parent, *Day Reporting Centers for Criminal Offenders: A Descriptive Analysis of Existing Programs,* U.S. Department of Justice, National Institute of Justice, Issues and Practices (Washington, DC: GPO 1990).
38. Paige M. Harrison and Jennifer C. Karberg, "Prison and Jail Inmates at Midyear 2002," U.S. Department of Justice, Bureau of Justice Statistics *Bulletin* (Washington, DC: GPO, April 2003), p. 7, Table 8.
39. Material in this section is from *How to Use Structured Fines (Day Fines) as an Intermediate Sanction,* U.S. Department of Justice, Bureau of Justice Assistance, November 1996.

40. Harrison and Karberg, "Prison and Jail Inmates at Midyear 2002, " op. cit.
41. Rolando V. del Carmen and Joseph B. Vaughn, "Legal Issues in the Use of Electronic Surveillance in Probation," in T. Ellsworth (ed.), *Contemporary Community Corrections* (Prospect Heights, IL: Waveland Press, 1992), p. 426.
42. John P. Conrad, "Concluding Comments: VORP and the Correctional Future," in B. Galaway and J. Hudson (eds.), *Criminal Justice, Restitution, and Reconciliation* (Monsey, NY: Criminal Justice Press, 1990), p. 229.
43. Rene Stutzman, "State Takes Eyes Off Inmates," *The Orlando Sentinel,* December 29, 2002, p. A1; Rene Stutzman, "Ankle Monitors Show a Higher Rate of Success, " *The Orlando Sentinel,* December 29, 2002, p. A15; Florida Department of Corrections at www.dc.state.fl.us; Camille Graham Camp and George M. Camp, *The 2001 Corrections Yearbook: Adult Systems* (Middletown, CT: Criminal Justice Institute, 2002), p. 206.
44. David J. Hartmann, Paul C. Friday, and Kevin I. Minor, "Residential Probation: A Seven-Year Follow-Up Study of Halfway House Discharges," *Journal of Criminal Justice* 22 (1994), pp. 503–15.
45. Patrick G. Donnelly and Brian E. Forschner, "Client Success or Failure in a Halfway House," *Federal Probation* 48 (1984), pp. 38–44. Also see R. E. Seiter, H. Bowman Carlson, J. Grandfield, and N. Bernam, *Halfway Houses: National Evaluation Program: Phase I, Summary Report,* U.S. Department of Justice (Washington, DC: GPO, 1977).
46. Edward J. Latessa and Lawrence F. Travis, "Halfway House or Probation: A Comparison of Alternative Dispositions," *Journal of Crime and Justice* 14 (1991), pp. 53–75.
47. Belinda Rodgers McCarthy, Bernard J. McCarthy, Jr., and Matthew C. Leone, *Community-Based Corrections,* 4th ed. (Belmont, CA: Wadsworth, 2001). Unless otherwise noted, the material in the remainder of this section draws on pp. 148–156 of this source.
48. Daniel P. LeClair and Susan Guarino-Ghezzi, "Does Incapacitation Guarantee Public Safety? Lessons from the Massachusetts Furlough and Prerelease Programs," *Justice Quarterly* 8 (1991), pp. 9–36 (quotation from p. 26).

Chapter 13

1. Philippe Aries, *Centuries of Childhood: A Social History of Family Life,* translated by Robert Baldick (New York: Random House, 1962).
2. Barry Krisberg and James F. Austin, *Reinventing Juvenile Justice* (Newbury Park, CA: Sage, 1993), p. 9.
3. Harry Elmer Barnes, *The Story of Punishment,* 2nd ed. (Montclair, NJ: Patterson Smith, 1972).
4. David J. Rothman, *The Discovery of the Asylum* (Boston: Little, Brown, 1971).
5. Thomas J. Bernard, *The Cycle of Juvenile Justice* (New York: Oxford University Press, 1992), p. 63; Rothman, op. cit., p. 207.
6. Robert M. Mennel, *Thorns and Thistles* (Hanover, NH: University Press of New England, 1973); Steven L. Schlossman, *Love and the American Delinquent* (Chicago: University of Chicago Press, 1977).
7. Alexander Pisciotta, "Treatment on Trial: The Rhetoric and Reality of the New York House of Refuge, 1857–1935," *The American Journal of Legal History* 29 (1985), pp. 151–81; Rothman, op. cit., p. 231.
8. Clemens Bartollas and Stuart J. Miller, *Juvenile Justice in America* (Englewood Cliffs, NJ: Regents/Prentice Hall, 1994), p. 136.
9. LaMar T. Empey and Mark C. Stafford, *American Delinquency: Its Meaning and Construction,* 3rd ed. (Belmont, CA: Wadsworth, 1991), p. 368.
10. Belinda R. McCarthy and Bernard J. McCarthy, *Community-Based Corrections,* 2nd ed. (Pacific Grove, CA: Brooks/Cole, 1991), p. 98.
11. Krisberg and Austin, op. cit., pp. 23–24; Hastings Hart, *Preventive Treatment of Neglected Children* (New York: Russell Sage, 1910), p. 70.
12. Bartollas and Miller, op. cit., p. 209; John T. Whitehead and Steven P. Lab, *Juvenile Justice: An Introduction* (Cincinnati: Anderson, 1990), p. 47.
13. Cited in Meda Chesney-Lind and Randall G. Shelden, *Girls, Delinquency, and Juvenile Justice* (Pacific Grove, CA: Brooks/Cole, 1992), p. 111.
14. Anthony M. Platt, *The Child Savers: The Invention of Delinquency* (Chicago: University of Chicago Press, 1969), p. 99.
15. Ibid., pp. 101–102.
16. Bernard, op. cit., pp. 68–69.
17. Ibid., pp. 70–71.
18. Platt, op. cit., pp. 134–36; Bernard, op. cit., p. 73.
19. Empey and Stafford, op. cit, pp. 58–59.
20. Bartollas and Miller, op. cit., p. 92; Empey and Stafford, op. cit., p. 59.
21. Krisberg and Austin, op. cit., p. 30.
22. Bernard, op. cit., p. 96.
23. Ibid., pp. 96–97.
24. Walter Wadlington, Charles H. Whitebread, and Samuel M. Davis, *Cases and Materials on Children in the Legal System* (Mineola, NY: Foundation Press, 1983), p. 202; Bernard, op. cit., p. 110.
25. M. A. Bortner, *Delinquency and Justice: An Age of Crisis* (New York: McGraw-Hill, 1988), p. 60.
26. Bernard, op. cit., p. 141.
27. Charles Puzzanchera, Anne L. Stahl, Terrence A. Finnegan, Nancy Tierney, and Howard N. Snyder, "Juvenile Court Statistics 1998," U.S. Department of Justice, Office of Juvenile Justice and Delinquency Prevention (Pittsburgh, PA: National Center for Juvenile Justice, June 2003), p. 38.
28. Ibid., p. 19.
29. Ibid., p. 52.
30. Douglas A. Smith, "The Organizational Context of Legal Control," *Criminology* 22 (1984), pp. 19–38.
31. Robert J. Sampson, "Effects of Socioeconomic Context on Official Reaction to Juvenile Delinquency," *American Sociological Review* 51 (1986), pp. 876–85; also see A. Cicourel, *The Social Organization of Juvenile Justice* (New York: Wiley, 1968).

32. Donald Black and Albert J. Reiss, "Police Control of Juveniles," *American Sociological Review* 35 (1970), pp. 63–77; Richard J. Lundman, Richard E. Sykes, and John P. Clark, "Police Control of Juveniles: A Replication," in Ralph Weisheit and Robert G. Culbertson (eds.), *Juvenile Delinquency: A Justice Perspective* (Prospect Heights, IL: Waveland Press, 1978), pp. 107–15; Irving Piliavan and Scott Briar, "Police Encounters with Juveniles," *American Journal of Sociology* 70 (1964), pp. 206–14.
33. Marvin D. Krohn, James P. Curry, and Shirley Nelson-Kilger, "Is Chivalry Dead? An Analysis of Changes in Police Dispositions of Males and Females," *Criminology* 21 (1983), pp. 417–37; Katherine Teilmann and Pierre H. Landry, "Gender Bias in Juvenile Justice," *Journal of Research in Crime and Delinquency* 18 (1981), pp. 47–80; see also William G. Staples, "Law and Social Control in Juvenile Justice Dispositions," *Journal of Research in Crime and Delinquency* 24 (1987), pp. 7–22; Meda Chesney-Lind, "Judicial Paternalism and the Female Status Offender: Training Women to Know Their Place," *Crime and Delinquency* 23 (1977), pp. 121–30.
34. Robert J. Sampson, "Sex Differences in Self-Reported Delinquency and Official Records: A Multiple-Group Structural Modeling Approach," *Journal of Quantitative Criminology* 1 (1985), pp. 345–67; Dale Dannefer and Russell K. Schutt, "Race and Juvenile Justice Processing in Court and Police Agencies," *American Journal of Sociology* 87 (1982), pp. 1113–32.
35. Merry Morash, "Establishment of a Juvenile Police Record: The Influence of Individual and Peer Group Characteristics," *Criminology* 22 (1984), pp. 97–111; Krohn et al., op. cit.; D. Elliott and H. L. Voss, *Delinquency and Dropout* (Lexington, MA: Lexington Books, 1974).
36. Federal Bureau of Investigation, *Crime in the United States 2001,* U.S. Department of Justice (Washington, DC: GPO, 2002), p. 253, Table 43.
37. *Statistical Abstract of the United States* (1999), p. 22, Table No. 22.
38. Delbert S. Elliott and David Huizinga, "Social Class and Delinquent Behavior in a National Youth Panel," *Criminology* 21 (1983), pp. 149–77.
39. *Sourcebook of Criminal Justice Statistics Online,* Table 4.26 at www.albany.edu/sourcebook/1995/pdf/t426.pdf.
40. Information about teen courts or youth courts is from Jeffrey Butts, Dean Hoffman, and Janeen Buck, "Teen Courts in the United States: A Profile of Current Programs," U.S. Department of Justice, Office of Juvenile Justice and Delinquency Prevention, Office of Juvenile Justice and Delinquency Prevention Fact Sheet #118 (Washington, DC: GPO, October 1999); Jeffrey A. Butts and Janeen Buck, "Teen Courts: A Focus on Research," U.S. Department of Justice, Office of Juvenile Justice and Delinquency Prevention, *Juvenile Justice Bulletin* (Washington, DC: GPO, October 2000); Jeffrey A. Butts, Janeen Buck, and Mark B. Coggeshall, *The Impact of Teen Court on Young Offenders,* U.S. Department of Justice, Office of Juvenile Justice and Delinquency Prevention (Washington, DC: The Urban Institute, April 2002); National Youth Court Center at www.youthcourt.net.
41. Information on restorative justice conferences or family group conferences is from Edmund F. McGarrell, "Restorative Justice Conferences as an Early Response to Young Offenders," U.S. Department of Justice, Office of Juvenile Justice and Delinquency Prevention, *Juvenile Justice Bulletin* (Washington, DC: GPO, August 2001); *OJJDP Research 2000,* U.S. Department of Justice, Office of Juvenile Justice and Delinquency Prevention (Washington, DC: GPO, May 2001).
42. Puzzanchera et al., op. cit., p. 22.
43. Howard N. Snyder and Melissa Sickmund, *Juvenile Offenders and Victims: 1999 National Report,* U.S. Department of Justice, National Center for Juvenile Justice, Office of Juvenile Justice and Delinquency Prevention (Washington, DC: GPO, September 1999), p. 97.
44. Ted Rubin, "The Emerging Prosecutor Dominance of the Juvenile Court Intake Process," *Crime and Delinquency* 26 (1980), pp. 299–318.
45. For a review of this literature, see Chesney-Lind and Shelden, op. cit., pp. 137–39.
46. From Excel file in *OJJDP Statistical Briefing Book,* Online at http://ojjdp.ncjrs.org/ajstatbb/qa191.html (May 3, 2002, revised September 4, 2002); Charles M. Puzzanchera, "Delinquency Cases Waived to Criminal Court, 1988–1997," U.S. Department of Justice, Office of Juvenile Justice and Delinquency Prevention, Fact Sheet #02 (Washington, DC: GPO, February 2000); Charles M. Puzzanchera, "Delinquency Cases Waived to Criminal Court, 1989–1998, " U.S. Department of Justice, Office of Juvenile Justice and Delinquency Prevention, Fact Sheet #35 (Washington, DC: GPO, September 2001).
47. Melissa Sickmund, "Juveniles in Court," U.S. Department of Justice, Office of Juvenile Justice and Delinquency Prevention, *Juvenile Offenders and Victims National Report Series Bulletin* (Washington, DC: GPO, June 2003), p. 9.
48. Sickmund, "Juveniles in Court," op. cit., p. 10.
49. Unless indicated otherwise, material in this section is from the following sources: Barry C. Feld, "Criminalizing the American Juvenile Court," in Michael Tonry (ed.), *Crime and Justice: A Review of Research,* Vol. 17 (Chicago: University of Chicago Press, 1993), pp. 197–280; Joseph B. Sanborn, Jr., "Policies Regarding the Prosecution of Juvenile Murderers: Which System and Who Should Decide," *Law & Policy* 18 (1996), pp. 151–78; Joseph B. Sanborn, Jr., "Certification to Criminal Court: The Important Policy Questions of How, When, and Why," *Crime and Delinquency* 40 (1994), pp. 262–81; Howard N. Snyder, *Juvenile Arrests 1995,* U.S. Department of Justice, Office of Juvenile Justice and Delinquency Prevention, *Juvenile Justice Bulletin* (Washington, DC: GPO, February 1997), p. 12; Barry C. Feld, "The Juvenile Court Meets the Principle of the Offense: Legislative Changes in Juvenile Waiver Statutes," *Journal of Criminal Law and Criminology* 78 (1987), pp. 471–533; Barry Krisberg, Ira M. Schwartz, Paul Litsky, and James Austin, "The Watershed of Juvenile Justice Reform," *Crime and Delinquency* 32

(1986), pp. 5–38; Donna Hamparian, Linda Estep, Susan M. Muntean, Ramon R. Prestino, Robert G. Swisher, Paul L. Wallace, and Joseph L. White, *Youth in Adult Court: Between Two Worlds* (Washington, DC: OJJDP, 1982); Sickmund, "Juveniles in Court," op. cit., p. 5; and personal communications from Donna M. Bishop and Joseph B. Sanborn, Jr.

50. Martin L. Forst, Bruce A. Fisher, and Robert B. Coates, "Indeterminate and Determinate Sentencing of Juvenile Delinquents: A National Survey of Approaches to Commitment and Release Decision-Making," *Juvenile and Family Court Journal,* Summer 1985, pp. 1–12.
51. Patricia Torbert, Richard Gable, Hunter Hurst IV, Imogene Montgomery, Linda Szymanski, and Douglas Thomas, *State Responses to Serious and Violent Juvenile Crime,* U.S. Department of Justice, Office of Juvenile Justice and Delinquency Prevention (Washington, DC: GPO, July 1996), chap. 3.
52. Patricia McFall Torbet, "Juvenile Probation: The Workhorse of the Juvenile Justice System," U.S. Department of Justice, Office of Juvenile Justice and Delinquency Prevention, *Juvenile Justice Bulletin* (Washington, DC: GPO, March 1996); Puzzanchera et al., *Juvenile Court Statistics 1998,* op. cit., p. 38.
53. Troy L. Armstrong, "National Survey of Juvenile Intensive Supervision" (Parts I and II), *Criminal Justice Abstracts* 20 (1988), pp. 342–48 (Part I) and 497–523 (Part II).
54. Richard G. Wiebush, "Juvenile Intensive Supervision: The Impact on Felony Offenders Diverted from Institutional Placement," *Crime and Delinquency* 39 (1993), pp. 68–89; William H. Barton and Jeffrey A. Butts, "Viable Options: Intensive Supervision Programs for Juvenile Delinquents," *Crime and Delinquency* 36 (1990), pp. 238–56.
55. Richard A. Ball, Ronald Huff, and Robert Lilly, *House Arrest and Correctional Policy: Doing Time at Home* (Newbury Park, CA: Sage, 1988).
56. See Marc Renzema and David T. Skelton, "Use of Electronic Monitoring in the United States: 1989 Update," National Institute of Justice, Research in Brief (Washington, DC: National Institute of Justice, 1990); Daniel Ford and Annesley K. Schmidt, "Electronically Monitored Home Confinement," National Institute of Justice, Research in Action (Washington, DC: National Institute of Justice, 1985).
57. Joseph B. Vaughn, "A Survey of Juvenile Electronic Monitoring and Home Confinement Programs," *Juvenile and Family Court Journal* 40 (1989), pp. 1–36.
58. Kevin I. Minor and Preston Elrod, "The Effects of a Probation Intervention on Juvenile Offenders' Self-Concepts, Loci of Control, and Perceptions of Juvenile Justice," *Youth and Society* 25 (1994), pp. 490–511; Gerald L. Golins, *Utilizing Adventure Education to Rehabilitate Juvenile Delinquents* (Las Cruces, NM: Educational Resources Information Center, Clearinghouse on Rural Education and Small Schools, 1980).
59. See, for example, R. Callahan, "Wilderness Probation: A Decade Later," *Juvenile and Family Court Journal* 36 (1985), pp. 31–51; John Winterdyk and Ronald Roesch, "A Wilderness Experiential Program as an Alternative for Probationers: An Evaluation," *Canadian Journal of Criminology* 24 (1982), pp. 39–49.
60. H. Preston Elrod and Kevin I. Minor, "Second Wave Evaluation of a Multi-Faceted Intervention for Juvenile Court Probationers," *International Journal of Offender Therapy and Comparative Criminology* 36 (1992), pp. 247–62; John Winterdyk and Curt Griffiths, "Wilderness Experience Programs: Reforming Delinquents or Beating Around the Bush?" *Juvenile and Family Court Journal* 35 (1984), pp. 35–44; Winterdyk and Roesch, op. cit.
61. Ted Palmer, *The Re-Emergence of Correctional Intervention* (Newbury Park, CA: Sage, 1992); Office of Juvenile Justice and Delinquency Prevention, *Project New Pride: Replication* (Washington: OJJDP, 1979); LaMar T. Empey and Maynard L. Erickson, *The Provo Experiment: Evaluating Community Control of Delinquency* (Lexington, MA: Lexington Books, 1972).
62. Terrence P. Thornberry, Stewart E. Tolnay, Timothy J. Flanagan, and Patty Glynn, *Office of Juvenile Justice and Delinquency Prevention Report on Children in Custody 1987: A Comparison of Public and Private Juvenile Custody Facilities* (Washington, DC: OJJDP, 1991).
63. Thornberry et al. (1991), op. cit.
64. Melissa Sickmund, "Juvenile Residential Facility Census, 2000: Selected Findings, " U.S. Department of Justice, Office of Juvenile Justice and Delinquency Prevention, *Juvenile Offenders and Victims National Report Series Bulletin* (Washington, DC: GPO, December 2002), p. 3.
65. Dale G. Parent, Valerie Leiter, Stephen Kennedy, Lisa Livens, Daniel Wentworth, and Sarah Wilcox, *Conditions of Confinement: Juvenile Detention and Corrections Facilities Research Summary* (Washington: OJJDP, 1994), p. 5.
66. See, for example, Barry Krisberg, "Juvenile Justice: Improving the Quality of Care," *National Council on Crime and Delinquency* (San Francisco: NCCD, 1992); Carol J. Garrett, "Effects of Residential Treatment on Adjudicated Delinquents," *Journal of Research in Crime and Delinquency* 22 (1985), pp. 287–308.
67. Barry Krisberg, Robert DeComo, and Norma C. Herrera, *National Juvenile Custody Trends 1978–1989* (Washington: OJJDP, 1992), p. 2; also see Steven Lab and John T. Whitehead, "A Meta-Analysis of Juvenile Correctional Treatment," *Journal of Research in Crime and Delinquency* 26 (1989), pp. 276–95; Norman G. Hoffmann, Ana M. Abrantes, and Ronald Anton, "Criminals, Troubled Youth, or a Bit of Both," *Addiction Professional* 1, no. 4 (July 2003).
68. Unless indicated otherwise, data in this section are from National Center for Juvenile Justice, "Census of Juveniles in Residential Placement Databook" at http://ojjdp.ncjrs.org/ojstatbb/cjrp/asp/selection.asp; Snyder and Sickmund, op. cit., chap. 7.
69. Harrison and Karberg, "Prison and Jail Inmates at Midyear 2002," op. cit., p. 8, Table 9, and p. 5, Table 5.
70. Richard G. Wiebush, Betsy McNulty, and Thao Le, "Implementation of the Intensive Community-Based

Aftercare Program," U.S. Department of Justice, Office of Juvenile Justice and Delinquency Prevention, *Juvenile Justice Bulletin* (Washington, DC: GPO, July 2000).
71. Ibid., p. 2.

Chapter 14

1. Herbert Packer, *The Limits of the Criminal Sanction* (Stanford, CA: Stanford University Press, 1968).
2. Gene Stephens, "High-Tech Crime: The Threat to Civil Liberties," *The Futurist*, July–August 1990, pp. 20–25.
3. Gene Stephens, "Law Enforcement," in G. T. Kurian and G. T. T. Molitor (eds.), *Encyclopedia of the Future* (New York: Simon & Schuster, Macmillan, 1996), p. 538; Jeff Kunerth, "You Have No Right to Privacy You Seek," *The Orlando Sentinel*, August 8, 1999, p. A1.
4. Scott Parks, "High-Tech's Time Is on Horizon in Security Business," *The Orlando Sentinel*, October 7, 2001, p. A10.
5. Etan Horowitz, "Speedy Database Helps Cops Put Pieces Together," *The Orlando Sentinel*, August 24, 2003, p. B1.
6. Jack Cheevers, "Beyond '*RoboCop*': Concern for Officer Safety Fuels Innovation," *The Charlotte Observer*, August 26, 1994, p. 14A.
7. Gene Stephens, "Drugs and Crime in the Twenty-First Century," *The Futurist*, May–June 1992, pp. 19–22.
8. "Police to Use IBM's Digital Video System," *The Orlando Sentinel*, May 18, 2003, p. H3.
9. Ibid.
10. Ibid.
11. Stephens (1996), op. cit., p. 539; "Police Test Voice Translator Box," *The Orlando Sentinel*, December 5, 1999, p. A17.
12. "New Ultra-Wideband Could Make Walls See-through," *The Orlando Sentinel*, June 15, 2000, p. A3.
13. Cheevers, op. cit.
14. Stephens (1996), op. cit., p. 539.
15. Terry D. Anderson, Kenneth D. Gisborne, Marilyn Hamilton, Pat Holiday, John C. LeDoux, Gene Stephens, and John Welter, *Every Officer Is a Leader: Transforming Leadership in Police, Justice, and Public Safety* (Boca Raton, FL: St. Lucie Press, 2000), p. 368.
16. Ibid.
17. Stephens (1990), op. cit.
18. Anita Neuberger Blowers, "The Future of American Courts," in B. Maguire and P. Radosh (eds.), *The Past, Present, and Future of American Criminal Justice* (New York: General Hall, 1995).
19. Ibid.
20. Ibid.
21. Gene Stephens, "Crime and Punishment: Forces Shaping the Future," *The Futurist*, January–February 1987, pp. 18–26.
22. Ibid.
23. John Braithwaite, *Crime, Shame and Reintegration* (Cambridge: Cambridge University Press, 1989).
24. Blowers, op. cit.
25. Stephens (1990), op. cit.
26. Ibid.
27. Blowers, op. cit.
28. Malcolm M. Feeley and Jonathan Simon, "The New Penology: Notes on the Emerging Strategy of Corrections and Its Implications," *Criminology* 30 (1992), pp. 449–74.
29. Ibid.
30. John J. DiIulio, Jr., *No Escape: The Future of American Corrections* (New York: Basic Books, 1991), p. 4.
31. Ibid.
32. Feeley and Simon, op. cit., p. 470.
33. Stephens, "Prisons," op. cit.
34. See Francis T. Cullen and John P. Wright, "The Future of Corrections," in B. Maguire and P. Radosh (eds.), *The Past, Present, and Future of American Criminal Justice* (New York: General Hall, 1995).
35. Stephens (1990), op. cit.
36. Ibid.
37. Stephens, "Prisons," op. cit., p. 751.
38. Stephens (1990), op. cit.
39. Ibid.
40. Cullen and Wright, op. cit.
41. Ibid.
42. Richard Burnett, "Putting Pieces Back Together," *The Orlando Sentinel*, August 20, 2003, p. C1.
43. Richard Burnett, "Identity Theft Hits 'Epidemic' Levels," *The Orlando Sentinel*, September 4, 2003, p. A1.
44. *Federal Trade Commission—Identity Theft Survey Report* (McLean, VA: Synovate, September 2003), at www.ftc.gov/reports/index.htm. Unless indicated otherwise, survey material is from this source.
45. Pub. L. No. 105–318, 112 Stat. 3007 (Oct. 30, 1998).
46. "Identity Theft," The National White Collar Crime Center at www.nw3c.org/research_topics.html.
47. "Coping with Identity Theft: Reducing the Risk of Fraud," Privacy Rights Clearinghouse, Fact Sheet No. 17 (May 1995, revised February 2003), at www.privacyrights.org/fs/fs17-it.htm.
48. Linda Goldman-Foley, "Identity Theft—Overcoming the Emotional Impact," The Identity Theft Resource Center, Fact Sheet 17e (2000, revised November 25, 2001), at www.idtheftcenter.org/html/fs109.htm. Material about the identity theft victimization experience is from this source.
49. Burnett, "Identity Theft Hits 'Epidemic' Levels," op. cit.
50. Louise Shelley, Director, Transnational Crime and Corruption Center at www.american.edu/traccc.
51. *Transnational Organized Crime: Summary of a Workshop*, The National Academy of Sciences, 2000, p. 28, at www.nap.edu/books/0309065755/html.
52. United Nations Convention Against Transnational Organized Crime, 2000, Article 2(a) at www.unodc.org/palermo/convmain.html.
53. Ibid., Article 2(b).
54. Ibid., Article 3(2).
55. Pino Ariacchi, "Nations Build Alliances to Stop Organized Crime," *Global Issues: Arresting Transnational Crime*, U.S. Department of State, p. 1, at http://usinfo.state.gov/journals/itgic/0801/gj08.htm.

56. *Results of a Pilot Survey of Forty Selected Organized Criminal Groups in Sixteen Countries*, Global Programme Against Transnational Organized Crime, United Nations Office on Drugs and Crime, September 2002, p. 20, at www.unodc.org/unodc/organized_crime.html.
57. Ibid., p. 28.
58. *Transnational Organized Crime: Summary of a Workshop*, op. cit., pp. 11–12.
59. Ariacchi, op. cit., p. 20.
60. Ibid.
61. Ariacchi, op. cit., pp. 1–2; Chamberlin, op. cit., p. 1.
62. Ariacchi, op. cit., p. 2.
63. *Transnational Organized Crime: Summary of a Workshop*, op. cit., p. 32.
64. Ibid., p. 29; Chamberlin, op. cit., p. 2.
65. *Convention Against Transnational Organized Crime,* United Nations Crime and Justice Network, Centre for International Crime Prevention, Office for Drug Control and Crime Prevention at www.uncjin.org/Documents/Conventions/conventions.html; Elizabeth Verville, "U.S. Joins Global Convention Against Transnational Organized Crime," *Global Issues: Arresting Transnational Crime*, U.S. Department of State, pp. 1–2, at http://usinfo.state.gov/journals/itgic/0801/ijge/gj02.htm; Ariacchi, op. cit., pp. 3–5. Information about the convention is from these sources.
66. *Transnational Organized Crime: Summary of a Workshop*, op. cit., pp. 34–39.
67. Josh Meyer, "Diminished al-Qaeda Remains a Threat to U.S.," *The Orlando Sentinel*, September 11, 2003, p. A8.

GLOSSARY

actus reus Criminal conduct—specifically, intentional or criminally negligent (reckless) action or inaction that causes harm. (2)

adjudication The juvenile court equivalent of a trial in criminal court or the process of rendering a judicial decision regarding the truth of the facts alleged in a petition. (13)

administrative segregation The keeping of inmates in secure isolation so that they cannot harm others. (10)

aggravating factors In death sentencing, circumstances that make a crime worse. (9)

aggressive patrol The practice of having an entire patrol section make numerous traffic stops and field interrogations. (6)

allocution The procedure at a sentencing hearing in which the convicted defendant has the right to address the court before the sentence is imposed. During allocution, a defendant is identified as the person found guilty and has a right to deny or explain information contained in the PSI if his or her sentence is based on it. (9)

anomie For Durkheim, the dissociation of the individual from the collective conscience. For Merton, the contradiction between the cultural goal of achieving wealth and the social structure's inability to provide legitimate institutional means for achieving the goal. For Cohen, it is caused by the inability of juveniles to achieve status among peers by socially acceptable means. (3)

appellate jurisdiction The power of a court to review a case for errors of law. (8)

apprenticeship system The method by which middle- and upper-class children were taught skilled trades by a master. (13)

arbitration A dispute resolution process that brings disputants together with a third party (an arbitrator) who has the skills to listen objectively to evidence presented by both sides regarding a conflict, to ask probing and relevant questions of each side, and to arrive at an equitable solution to the dispute. (14)

arraignment A pretrial stage to hear the formal information or indictment and to allow the defendant to enter a plea. (8)

arrest The seizure of a person or the taking of a person into custody, either actual physical custody, as when a suspect is handcuffed by a police officer, or constructive custody, as when a person peacefully submits to a police officer's control. (4)

arrest warrant A written order directing law enforcement officers to arrest a person. The charge or charges against a suspect are specified on the warrant. (1)

atavist A person who reverts to a savage type. (3)

Auburn system An early system of penology, originating at Auburn Penitentiary in New York, under which inmates worked and ate together in silence during the day and were placed in solitary cells for the evening. (10)

bail bond/bail Usually a monetary guarantee deposited with the court that is supposed to ensure that the suspect or defendant will appear at a later stage in the criminal justice process. (8)

banishment A punishment, originating in ancient times, that required offenders to leave the community and live elsewhere, commonly in the wilderness. (10)

bench trial A trial before a judge without a jury. (8)

bench warrant or *capias* A document that authorizes a suspect's or defendant's arrest for not appearing in court as required. (8)

beyond a reasonable doubt The standard of proof necessary to find a defendant guilty in a criminal trial. (4)

bifurcated trial A two-stage trial (unlike the one-stage trial in other felony cases) consisting of a guilt phase and a separate penalty phase. (9)

binding-out system Practice in which children were "bound over" to masters for care. However, under the binding-out system, masters were not required to teach youths a trade. (13)

biological inferiority According to biological theories, a criminal's innate physiological makeup produces certain physical or genetic characteristics that distinguish criminals from noncriminals. (3)

bionics The replacing of human body parts with mechanical parts. (14)

booking The administrative recording of an arrest. Typically, the suspect's name, the charge, and perhaps the suspect's fingerprints or photograph are entered into the police blotter. (1)

Chicago School A group of sociologists at the University of Chicago who assumed in their research that delinquent behavior was a product of social disorganization. (3)

civil law One of two types of law practiced in the United States (other is criminal law); a means of resolving conflicts between individuals. It includes personal injury claims (torts), the law of contracts and property, and subjects such as administrative law and the regulation of public utilities. (4)

class struggle For radical criminologists, the competition among wealthy people and among poor people and between rich people and poor people, which causes crime.

classical theory A product of the Enlightenment, based on the assumption that people exercise free will and are thus completely responsible for their actions. In classical theory, human behavior, including criminal behavior, is motivated by a hedonistic rationality in which actors weigh the potential pleasure of an action against the possible pain associated with it. (3)

classification facility A facility to which newly sentenced offenders are taken so that their security risks and needs can be assessed and they can be assigned to a permanent institution. (10)

clear and convincing evidence The standard of proof required in some civil cases and, in federal courts, the standard of proof necessary for a defendant to make a successful claim of insanity. (4)

cocorrectional facilities Usually small, minimum-security institutions that house both men and women with the goal of normalizing the prison environment by integrating the daytime activities of the sexes. (10)

collective conscience The general sense of morality of the times. (3)

college academies Schools where students pursue a program that integrates an associate's degree curriculum in law enforcement or criminal justice with the state's required peace officer training. (7)

community corrections The subfield of corrections in which offenders are supervised and provided services outside jail or prison. (12)

community policing A contemporary approach to policing that actively involves the community in a working partnership to control and reduce crime. (5)

commutation Reduction of the original sentence given by executive authority, usually a state's governor. (8)

complaint A charging document specifying that an offense has been committed by a person or persons named or described. It is usually used for misdemeanors and ordinance violations. (8)

conditional release A form of release that requires a suspect/defendant to maintain contact with a pretrial release program or undergo regular drug monitoring or treatment. (8)

confession An admission by a person accused of a crime that he or she committed the offense charged. (4)

conflict theory A theory that assumes society is based primarily on conflict between competing interest groups and that criminal law and the criminal justice system are used to control subordinate groups. Crime is caused by relative powerlessness. (3)

conjugal visits An arrangement whereby inmates are permitted to visit in private with their spouses or significant others to maintain their personal relationship. (10)

constable The peacekeeper in charge of protection in early English towns. (5)

constable-watch system A system of protection in early England in which citizens, under the direction of a constable, or chief peacekeeper, were required to guard the city and to pursue criminals. (5)

contraband An illegal substance or object. (4)

contract security Protective services that a private security firm provides to people, agencies, and companies that do not employ their own security personnel or that need extra protection. (5)

convict code A constellation of values, norms, and roles that regulate the way inmates interact with one another and with prison staff. (8)

copicide A form of suicide in which a person gets fatally shot after intentionally provoking police officers. (7)

cottage reformatories Correctional facilities for youths, first developed in the late 1800s, that were intended to closely parallel family life and remove children from negative influences of the urban environment. Children in those facilities lived with surrogate parents, who were responsible for the youths' training and education. (13)

crime control model One of Packer's two models of the criminal justice process. Politically, it reflects traditional conservative values. In this model, the control of criminal behavior is the most important function of criminal justice. (1)

crime index An estimate of crimes committed. (2)

crime index offenses cleared The number of offenses for which at least one person has been arrested, charged with the commission of the offense, and turned over to the court for prosecution. (2)

crime rate A measure of the incidence of crime expressed as the number of crimes per unit of population or some other base. (2)

criminal anthropology The study of "criminal" human beings. (3)

criminal law One of two general types of law practiced in the United States (the other is civil law); "a formal means of social control [that uses] rules . . . interpreted [and enforced] by the courts . . . to set limits to the conduct of the citizens, to guide the officials, and to define . . . unacceptable behavior." (4)

criminal sanctions or criminal punishment Penalties that are imposed for violating criminal law. (9)

criminalization process The way people and actions are defined as criminal. (3)

criminological theory The explanation of criminal behavior, as well as the behavior of police, attorneys, prosecutors, judges, correctional personnel, victims, and other actors in the criminal justice system. (3)

crisis intervention A counselor's efforts to address some crisis in an inmate's life and to calm the inmate. (10)

cryonics A process of human hibernation that involves freezing the body. (14)

custody level The classification assigned to an inmate to indicate the degree of precaution that needs to be taken when working with that inmate. (10)

cybercrime The use of computer technology to commit crime. (6)

dark figure of crime The number of crimes not officially recorded by the police. (2)

day reporting centers Facilities that are designed for offenders who would otherwise be in prison or jail. Offenders are required to report regularly to confer with staff about supervision and treatment matters. (12)

defendant A person against whom a legal action is brought, a warrant is issued, or an indictment is found. (1)

deprivation model A theory that the inmate society arises as a response to the prison environment and the painful conditions of confinement. (8)

determinate sentence A sentence with a fixed period of incarceration, which eliminates the decision-making responsibility of parole boards. (9)

differential association Sutherland's theory that persons who become criminal do so because of contacts with criminal patterns and isolation from anticriminal patterns. (3)

directed patrol Patrolling under guidance or orders on how to use patrol time. (6)

discretion The exercise of individual judgment, instead of formal rules, in making decisions. (7)

disposition An order of the court specifying what is to be done with a juvenile who has been adjudicated delinquent. A disposition hearing is similar to a sentencing hearing in criminal court. (13)

diversion Organized, systematic efforts to remove individuals from further processing in criminal justice by placing them in alternative programs; diversions may be pretrial or post-trial. (12)

doctrine of fundamental fairness The rule that makes confessions inadmissible in criminal trials if they were obtained by means of either psychological manipulation or "third-degree" methods. (4)

doctrine of legal guilt The principle that people are not to be held guilty of crime merely on a showing, based on reliable evidence, that in all probability they did in fact commit the crime they are accused of committing. Legal guilt results only when factual guilt is determined in a procedurally regular fashion, as in a criminal trial, and when the procedural rules designed to protect suspects and defendants and to safeguard the integrity of the process are employed. (1)

domestic terrorism The unlawful use, or threatened use, of force or violence by a group or individual based and operating entirely within the United States or its territories without foreign direction committed against persons or property to intimidate or coerce a government, the civilian population, or any segment thereof, in furtherance of political or social objectives. (6)

double jeopardy The trying of a defendant a second time for the same offense when jeopardy attached in the first trial and a mistrial was not declared. (4)

dual court system The court system in the United States, consisting of one system of state and local courts and another system of federal courts. (8)

due process The rights of people suspected of or charged with crimes. The procedures followed by courts to ensure that a defendant's constitutional rights are not violated. (8)

due process model One of Packer's two models of the criminal justice process. Politically, it embodies traditional liberal values. In this model, the principal goal of criminal justice is at least as much to protect the innocent as it is to convict the guilty. (1)

duress Force or coercion as an excuse for committing a crime. (2)

eight index crimes The Part I offenses in the FBI's Uniform Crime Reports. They are (1) murder and nonnegligent manslaughter, (2) forcible rape, (3) robbery, (4) aggravated assault, (5) burglary, (6) larceny/theft, (7) motor vehicle theft, and (8) arson, which was added in 1979. (2)

electronic monitoring An arrangement that allows an offender's whereabouts to be gauged through the use of computer technology. (12)

entrapment A legal defense against criminal responsibility when a person, who was not already predisposed to it, is induced into committing a crime by a law enforcement officer or by his or her agent. (2)

***ex post facto* law** A law that (1) declares criminal an act that was not illegal when it was committed, (2) increases the punishment for a crime after it is committed, or (3) alters the rules of evidence in a particular case after the crime is committed. (2)

excessive force A measure of coercion beyond that necessary to control participants in a conflict. (7)

exclusionary rule The rule that illegally seized evidence must be excluded from trials in federal courts. (4)

extinction A process in which behavior that previously was positively reinforced is no longer reinforced. (3)

felony A relatively serious offense punishable by death or by confinement in prison for more than 1 year. (1)

feminist theory A perspective on criminality that focuses on women's experiences and seeks to abolish men's control over women's labor and sexuality. (3)

field interrogation A temporary detention in which officers stop and question pedestrians and motorists they find in suspicious circumstances. (6)

flat-time sentencing Sentencing in which judges may choose between probation and imprisonment but have little discretion in setting the length of a prison sentence. (9)

frisking Conducting a search for weapons by patting the outside of a suspect's clothing, feeling for hard objects that might be weapons. (4)

full enforcement A practice in which the police make an arrest for every violation of law that comes to their attention. (7)

general deterrence The attempt to prevent people in general from engaging in crime by punishing specific individuals and making examples of them. (8)

general jurisdiction The power of a court to hear any type of case. (8)

GIS crime mapping A technique that involves the charting of crime patterns within a geographic area. (6)

good time The number of days deducted from a sentence by prison authorities for good behavior or for other reasons. (9)

grand jury Generally a group of 12 to 23 citizens who meet in closed sessions to investigate charges coming from preliminary hearings or to engage in other responsibilities. A primary purpose of the grand jury is to determine whether there is probable cause to believe that the accused committed the crime or crimes. (8)

grand jury indictment A written accusation by a grand jury charging that one or more persons have committed a crime. (8)

grass eaters Officers who occasionally engage in illegal and unethical activities, such as accepting small favors, gifts, or money for ignoring violations of the law during the course of their duties. (7)

habeas corpus A court order requiring that a confined person be brought to court so that his or her claims can be heard. (8)

halfway houses Community-based residential facilities that are less secure and restrictive than prison or jail but provide a more controlled environment than other community correctional programs. (12)

hands-off philosophy A philosophy under which courts are reluctant to hear prisoners' claims regarding their rights while incarcerated. (8)

harm The external consequence required to make an action a crime. (2)

hearing officer A lawyer empowered by the juvenile court to hear juvenile cases. (13)

highway patrol model A model of state law enforcement services in which officers focus on highway traffic safety, enforcement of the state's traffic laws, and the investigation of accidents on the state's roads, highways, and property. (5)

home confinement A program that requires offenders to remain in their homes except for approved periods of absence; commonly used in combination with electronic monitoring. (12)

houses of refuge The first specialized correctional institutions for youths in the United States. (13)

hung jury The result when jurors cannot agree on a verdict. The judge declares a mistrial. The prosecutor must decide whether to retry the case. (8)

identity theft The transfer or use without legal authority of the identification documentation of another person with the intent to commit, aid, or abet any unlawful activity that constitutes a felony. (14)

imitation or modeling A means by which a person can learn new responses by observing others without performing any overt act or receiving direct reinforcement or reward. (3)

importation model A theory that the inmate society is shaped by the attributes inmates bring with them when they enter prison. (8)

incapacitation The removal or restriction of the freedom of those found to have violated criminal laws. (9)

incarceration rate A figure derived by dividing the number of people incarcerated by the population of the area and multiplying the result by 100,000; used to compare incarceration levels of units with different population sizes. (10)

indeterminate sentence A sentence with a fixed minimum and maximum term of incarceration, rather than a set period. (9)

indictment A document that outlines the charge or charges against a defendant. (8)

informal juvenile justice The actions taken by citizens to respond to juvenile offenders without involving the official agencies of juvenile justice. (13)

information A document that outlines the formal charge or charges, the law or laws that have been violated, and the evidence to support the charge or charges. (8)

initial appearance A pretrial stage in which a defendant is brought before a lower court to be given notice of the charge(s) and advised of her or his constitutional rights. (1)

insanity Mental or psychological impairment or retardation as a defense against a criminal charge. (2)

institution of social control An organization that persuades people, through subtle and not-so-subtle means, to abide by the dominant values of society. (1)

intake screening The process by which decisions are made about the continued processing of juvenile cases. Decisions might include dismissing the case, referring the youth to a diversion program, or filing a petition. (13)

Intensive-Supervision Probation and Parole (ISP) An alternative to incarceration that provides stricter conditions, closer supervision, and more treatment services than traditional probation and parole. (12)

intermediate sanctions Sanctions that, in restrictiveness and punitiveness, lie between traditional probation and traditional imprisonment or, alternatively, between imprisonment and traditional parole. (12)

internal affairs investigations units The police unit that ferrets out illegal and unethical activity engaged in by the police. (7)

international terrorism Involves violent acts dangerous to human life that are a violation of the criminal laws of the United States or any State, or that would be a criminal violation if committed within the jurisdiction of the

United States or any State. These acts appear to be intended to intimidate or coerce a civilian population, influence the policy of a government by intimidation or coercion, or affect the conduct of a government by assassination or kidnapping. International terrorist acts occur outside the United States or transcend national boundaries in terms of the means by which they are accomplished, the persons they appear intended to coerce or intimidate, or the locale in which the perpetrators operate or seek asylum. (6)

jail A facility, usually operated at the local level, that holds convicted offenders and unconvicted persons for relatively short periods. (10)

jailhouse lawyer An inmate skilled in legal matters. (8)

job stress The harmful physical and emotional outcomes that occur when the requirements of a job do not match the capabilities, resources, or needs of the worker.

jurisdiction The right or authority of a justice agency to act in regard to a particular subject matter, territory, or person. (5)

just deserts The punishment rationale based on the idea that offenders should be punished automatically, simply because they have committed a crime—they "deserve" it—and the idea that the punishment should fit the crime. (9)

juvenile delinquency A special category of offense created for young offenders, usually those between 7 and 18 years of age. (2)

labeling theory A theory that emphasizes the criminalization process as the cause of some crime. (3)

learning theory A theory that explains criminal behavior and its prevention with the concepts of positive reinforcement, negative reinforcement, extinction, punishment, and modeling or imitation. (3)

left realists A group of social scientists who argue that critical criminologists need to redirect their attention to the fear and the very real victimization experienced by working-class people. (3)

legal definition of crime An intentional violation of the criminal law or penal code, committed without defense or excuse and penalized by the state. (2)

legality The requirement (1) that a harm must be legally forbidden for the behavior to be a crime and (2) that the law must not be retroactive. (2)

less-eligibility principle The position that prisoners should receive no service or program superior to the services and programs available to free citizen without charge. (10)

limbic system A structure surrounding the brain stem that, in part, controls the life functions of heartbeats, breathing, and sleep. (3)

lockup A very short-term holding facility that is frequently located in or very near an urban police agency so that suspects can be held pending further inquiry. (10)

mala in se Wrong in themselves. A description applied to crimes that are characterized by universality and timelessness. (2)

mala prohibita Offenses that are illegal because laws define them as such. They lack universality and timelessness. (2)

mandatory release A method of prison release under which an inmate is released after servicing a legally required portion of his or her sentence, minus good-time credits. (8)

mandatory sentencing Sentencing in which a specified number of years of imprisonment (usually within a range) are provided for particular crimes. (9)

meat eaters Officers who actively seek ways to make money illegally while on duty.

mediation A dispute resolution process that brings disputants together with a third party (a mediator) who is trained in the art of helping people resolve disputes to everyone's satisfaction. The agreed-upon resolution is then formalized into a binding consent agreement. (14)

medical model A theory of institutional corrections, popular during the 1940s and 1950s, in which crime was seen as symptomatic of personal illness in need of treatment. (10)

mens rea Criminal intent; a guilty state of mind.

mere suspicion The standard of proof with the least certainty; a "gut feeling." With mere suspicion, a law enforcement officer cannot legally even stop a suspect. (4)

merit system A system of employment whereby an independent civil service commission, in cooperation with the city personnel section and the police department, sets employment qualifications, performance standards, and discipline procedures. (7)

milieu therapy A variant of group therapy that encompasses the total living environment so that the environment continually encourages positive behavioral change. (10)

misdemeanor A less serious crime generally punishable by a fine or by incarceration in jail for not more than 1 year. (1)

mitigating factors In death sentencing, circumstances that make a crime less severe than usual. (9)

myths Beliefs based on emotion rather than analysis. (1)

National Crime Victimization Surveys (NCVS) A source of crime statistics based on interviews in which respondents are asked whether they have been victims of any of the FBI's index offenses (except murder, nonnegligent manslaughter, and arson) or other crimes during the past 6 months. If they have, they are asked to provide information about the experience. (2)

necessity defense A legal defense against criminal responsibility used when a crime has been committed to prevent a more serious crime. (2)

negative reinforcement The removal or reduction of a stimulus whose removal or reduction increases or maintains a response. (3)

negligence The failure to take reasonable precautions to prevent harm. (2)

neoclassical theory A modification of classical theory in which it was conceded that certain factors, such as insanity, might inhibit the exercise of free will. (3)

net widening A phenomenon that occurs when the offenders placed in a novel program are not the offenders for whom the program was designed. The consequence is that those in the program receive more severe sanctions than they would have received had the new program remained unavailable. (12)

nolle prosequi (nol. pros.) The notation placed on the official record of a case when prosecutors elect not to prosecute. (8)

nolo contendere Latin for "no contest." When defendants plead *nolo,* they do not admit guilt but are willing to accept punishment. (8)

non-enforcement The failure to routinely enforce prohibitions against certain behaviors. (2)

norm Any standard or rule regarding what human beings should or should not think, say, or do under given circumstances. (2)

offenses known to the police A crime index, reported in the FBI's Uniform Crime Reports, composed of crimes that are both reported to and recorded by the police. (2)

operational styles The different overall approaches to the police job. (6)

ordinance violation Usually the violation of a law of a city or town. (1)

original jurisdiction The authority of a court to hear a case when it is first brought to court. (8)

overcriminalization The prohibition by the criminal law of some behaviors that arguably should not be prohibited. (2)

panopticon A prison design consisting of a round building with tiers of cells lining their inner circumference and facing a central inspection tower. (10)

pardon A "forgiveness" for the crime committed that stops further criminal processing. (9)

parens patriae The legal philosophy justifying state intervention in the lives of children when their parents are unable or unwilling to protect them. (13)

parole A method of prison release whereby inmates are released at the discretion of a board or other authority before having completed their entire sentences; can also refer to the community supervision received upon release. (12)

parole guidelines Structured instruments used to estimate the probability of parole recidivism and to direct the release decisions of parole boards. (12)

patriarchy Men's control over women's labor and sexuality. (3)

peacemaking criminology An approach that suggests the solutions to all social problems, including crime, are the transformation of human beings, mutual dependence, reduction of class structures, the creation of communities of caring people, and universal social justice. (3)

Peel's Principles of Policing A dozen standards proposed by Robert Peel, the author of the legislation resulting in the formation of the London Metropolitan Police Department The standards are still applicable to today's law enforcement. (5)

penal code The criminal law of a political jurisdiction. (4)

penal sanction An ideal characteristic of criminal law; the principle that violators will be punished or at least threatened with punishment by the state. (4)

Pennsylvania system An early system of U.S. penology in which inmates were kept in solitary cells so that they could study religious writings, reflect on their misdeeds, and perform handicraft work. (10)

penology The study of prison management and the treatment of offenders. (10)

personal jurisdiction A court's authority over the parties to a lawsuit. (8)

petition A legal form of the police complaint that specifies the charges to be heard at the adjudication. (13)

placing out The practice of placing children on farms in the Midwest and West to remove them from the supposedly corrupting influences of their parents and the cities. (13)

plea bargaining or plea negotiating The practice whereby the prosecutor, the defense attorney, the defendant, and—in many jurisdictions—the judge agree on a specific sentence to be imposed if the accused pleads guilty to an agreed-upon charge or charges instead of going to trial. (8)

police cadet program A program that combines a college education with agency work experience and academy training. Upon graduation, a cadet is promoted to police officer. (7)

politicality An ideal characteristic of criminal law, referring to its legitimate source. Only violations of rules made by the state, the political jurisdiction that enacted the laws, are crimes. (4)

positive reinforcement The presentation of a stimulus that increases or maintains a response. (3)

posses Groups of able-bodied citizens of a community, called into service by a sheriff or constable to chase and apprehend offenders. (5)

postmodernism An area of critical thought that, among other things, attempts to understand the creation of knowledge, and how knowledge and language create hierarchy and domination. (3)

power differentials The ability of some groups to dominate other groups in a society. (3)

precedent A decision that forms a potential basis for deciding the outcomes of similar cases in the future; a by-product of decisions made by trial and appellate court judges, who produce case law whenever they render a decision in a particular case. (4)

preliminary hearing A pretrial stage used in about one-half of all states and only in felony cases. Its purpose is for a judge to determine whether there is probable cause to support the charge or charges imposed by the prosecutor. (8)

preponderance of evidence Evidence that more likely than not outweighs the opposing evidence, or sufficient evidence to overcome doubt or speculation. (4)

Presentence Investigation (PSI) An investigation conducted by a probation agency or other designated authority at the request of a court into the past behavior, family circumstances, and personality of an adult who has been convicted of a crime, to assist the court in determining the most appropriate sentence. (12)

Presentence Investigative Reports (PSIs or PSIRs) Reports that are used in the federal system and the majority of states to help judges determine the appropriate sentence. They are also used in classifying probationers, parolees, and prisoners according to their treatment needs and security risks. (9)

presumptive sentencing Sentencing that allows a judge to retain some sentencing discretion, subject to appellate review. The legislature determines a sentence range for each crime. The judge is expected to impose the typical sentence, specified by statute, unless mitigating or aggravating circumstances justify a sentence below or above the range set by the legislature. (9)

preventive detention Holding suspects or defendants in jail without giving them an opportunity to post bail, because of the threat they pose to society. (8)

preventive patrol Patrolling the streets with little direction. Between responses to radio calls, officers are "systematically unsystematic" and observant in an attempt to both prevent and ferret out crime. Also known as random patrol. (6)

prisonization The process by which an inmate becomes socialized into the customs and principles of the inmate society. (8)

privatization The involvement of the private sector in the construction and the operation of confinement facilities. (10)

probable cause The amount of proof necessary for a reasonably intelligent person to suspect that a crime has been committed or that items connected with criminal activity can be found in a particular place. It is the standard of proof needed to conduct a search or to make an arrest. (4)

probation A sentence in which the offender, rather than being incarcerated, is retained in the community under the supervision of a probation agency and required to abide by certain rules and conditions to avoid incarceration. (12)

probation conditions Rules that specify what an offender is and is not to do during the course of a probation sentence. (12)

procedural law The body of law that governs the ways substantive laws are administered; sometimes called *adjective* or *remedial* law. (4)

proportionality review A review in which the appellate court compares the sentence in the case it is reviewing with penalties imposed in similar cases in the state. The object is to reduce, as much as possible, disparity in death penalty sentencing. (9)

proprietary security In-house protective services that a security staff, not classified as sworn peace officers, provide for the entity that employs them. (5)

protective custody The segregation of inmates for their own safety. (10)

psychopaths, sociopaths, or antisocial personalities Persons characterized by no sense of guilt, no subjective conscience, and no sense of right and wrong. They have difficulty in forming relationships with other people; they cannot empathize with other people. (3)

public safety officers Police department employees who perform many police services but do not have arrest powers. (7)

punishment The imposition of a penalty for criminal wrongdoing. (8)

racial profiling The stopping and/or detaining of individuals by law enforcement officers based solely on race. (7)

radical nonintervention A practice based on the idea that youths should be left alone if at all possible, instead of being formally processed. (13)

radical theories Theories of crime causation that are generally based on a Marxist theory of class struggle. (3)

reasonable suspicion A standard of proof that is more than a gut feeling. It includes the ability to articulate reasons for the suspicion. With reasonable suspicion, a law enforcement officer is legally permitted to stop and frisk a suspect. (4)

recidivism The return to illegal activity after release from incarceration. (8)

reform, industrial, or training schools Correctional facilities for youths, first developed in the late 1800s, that focused on custody. Today, these institutions are often called training schools and although they may place more emphasis on treatment, they still rely on custody and control. (13)

regularity An ideal characteristic of criminal law: the applicability of the law to all persons, regardless of social status. (4)

rehabilitation The attempt to "correct" the personality and behavior of convicted offenders through educational, vocational, or therapeutic treatment and to return them to society as law-abiding citizens. (8)

reintegration The process of rebuilding former ties to the community and establishing new ties after release from prison. (12)

reintegrative shaming A strategy in which disappointment is expressed for the offender's actions, the offender is shamed and punished, and, more importantly, following the expression of disappointment and shame is a concerted effort on the part of the community to forgive the offender and reintegrate him or her back into society. (14)

relative powerlessness In conflict theory, the inability to dominate other groups in society. (3)

release on own recognizance (ROR) A release secured by a suspect's written promise to appear in court. (8)

restitution Money paid or services provided by a convicted offender to victims, their survivors, or the community to make up for the injury inflicted. (9)

restorative justice A process whereby an offender is required to contribute to restoring the health of the community, repairing the harm done, and meeting victims' needs. (14)

retribution A justification for punishment that implies the payment of a debt to society and the atonement for one's crime. (9)

revenge The punishment rationale expressed by the biblical phrase, "An eye for an eye, and a tooth for a tooth." People who seek revenge want to pay back offenders by making them suffer for what they have done. (9)

revocation The repeal of a probation sentence or parole, and substitution of a more restrictive sentence, because of violation of probation or parole conditions. (12)

role The rights and responsibilities associated with a particular position in society. (6)

role conflict The psychological stress and frustration that result from trying to perform two or more incompatible responsibilities. (6)

role expectation The behavior and actions that people expect from a person in a particular role. (6)

rules of discovery Rules that mandate that a prosecutor provide defense counsel with any exculpatory evidence (evidence favorable to the accused that affects the guilt or punishment) in the prosecutor's possession. (8)

searches Exploration or inspections, by law enforcement officers, of homes, premises, vehicles, or persons, for the purpose of discovering evidence of crimes or persons who are accused of crimes. (4)

security level A designation applied to a facility to describe the measures taken, both inside and outside, to preserve security and custody. (10)

seizures The taking of persons or property into custody in response to violations of the criminal law. (4)

selective enforcement The practice of relying on the judgment of the police leadership and rank-and-file officers to decide which laws to enforce. (7)

self-incrimination Being a witness against oneself. If forced, it is a violation of the Fifth Amendment. (4)

Self-Report Crime Surveys Surveys in which subjects are asked whether they have committed crimes. (2)

shire reeve In medieval England, the chief law enforcement officer in a territorial area called a shire; later called the sheriff. (5)

shock incarceration The placement of offenders in facilities patterned after military boot camps. (10)

slave patrols The earliest form of policing in the South. They were a product of the slave codes. (5)

snitch system A system in which staff learn from inmate informants about the presence of contraband, the potential for disruptions, and other threats to security. (10)

social contract An imaginary agreement to sacrifice the minimum amount of liberty necessary to prevent anarchy and chaos. (3)

social control theory A view in which people are expected to commit crime and delinquency unless they are prevented from doing so. (3)

social disorganization The condition in which the usual controls over delinquents are largely absent, delinquent behavior is often approved of by parents and neighbors, there are many opportunities for delinquent behavior, and there is little encouragement, training, or opportunity for legitimate employment. (3)

special jurisdiction The power of a court to hear only certain kinds of cases. (8)

special or specific deterrence The prevention of individuals from committing crime again by punishing them. (3)

specificity An ideal characteristic of criminal law, referring to its scope. Although civil law may be general in scope, criminal law should provide strict definitions of specific acts. (4)

stare decisis The principle of using precedents to guide future decisions in court cases; Latin for "to stand by decided cases." (4)

state police model A model of state law enforcement services in which the agency and its officers have the same law enforcement powers as local police but can exercise them anywhere within the state. (5)

status offenses Acts that are not crimes when committed by adults but are illegal for chidren (for example, truancy or running away from home). (2)

structured fines or day fines Fines that are based on defendants' ability to pay. (12)

subject matter jurisdiction The power of a court to hear a particular type of case. (8)

subpoena A written order issued by a court that requires a person to appear at a certain time and place to give testimony. It can also require that documents and objects be made available for examination by the court. (4)

sub-rosa economy The secret exchange of goods and services that, though often illicit, are in high demand among inmates; the black market of the prison. (8)

substantive law The body of law that defines criminal offenses and their penalties. (4)

summary (or bench) trial An immediate trial without a jury. (1)

system A smoothly operating set of arrangements and institutions directed toward the achievement of common goals. (1)

tech prep (technical preparation) A program in which area community colleges and high schools team up to offer 6 to 9 hours of college law enforcement courses in the 11th and 12th grades, as well as one or two training certifications, such as police dispatcher or local corrections officer. Students who graduate are eligible for police employment at age 18. (7)

technical violations Failure to abide by the technical rules or conditions of probation or parole (for example, not reporting regularly to the probation officer), as distinct from commission of a new criminal act. (12)

temporary-release programs Programs that allow jail or prison inmates to leave the facility for short periods to participate in approved community activities. (12)

terrorism The systematic use of terror or unpredictable violence against governments, publics, or individuals to attain a political objective; the unlawful use of force and violence against persons or property to intimidate or coerce a government, the civilian population, or any segment thereof, in furtherance of political or social objectives; or premeditated, politically motivated violence perpetrated against noncombatant targets by subnational groups or clandestine agents, usually intended to influence an audience. (6)

theory An assumption (or set of assumptions) that attempts to explain why or how things are related to each other. (3)

three I's of police selection Three qualities of the American police officer that seem to be of paramount importance: intelligence, integrity, and interaction skills. (7)

tithing system A private self-help protection system in early medieval England in which a group of 10 families, or a tithing, agreed to follow the law, keep the peace in their areas, and bring law violators to justice. (5)

tort A violation of the civil law. (4)

total institution An institutional setting in which persons sharing some characteristics are cut off from the wider society and expected to live according to institutional rules and procedures. (8)

traffic accident investigation crews In some agencies, the special units assigned to all traffic accident investigations. (6)

transfer, waiver, or certification The act or process by which juveniles who meet specific age, offense, and (in some jurisdictions) prior-record criteria are transferred to criminal court for trial. (13)

transportation A punishment in which offenders were transported from their home nation to one of that nation's colonies to work. (10)

trial *de novo* A trial in which an entire case is reheard by a trial court of general jurisdiction because there is an appeal and there is no written transcript of the earlier proceeding. (8)

undercriminalization The failure to prohibit some behaviors that arguably should be prohibited. (2)

Uniform Crime Reports (UCR) A collection of crime statistics and other law enforcement information gathered under a voluntary national program administered by the FBI. (2)

uniformity An ideal characteristic of criminal law; the enforcement of the laws against anyone who violates them, regardless of social status. (4)

unsecured bond An arrangement in which bail is set but no money is paid to the court. (8)

utility The principle that a policy should provide "the greatest happiness shared by the greatest number." (3)

venire The pool from which jurors are selected. (8)

venue The place of the trial. It must be geographically appropriate. (4)

victim-impact statements Descriptions of the harm and suffering that a crime has caused victims and their survivors. (9)

voir dire The process in which potential jurors who might be biased or unable to render a fair verdict are screened out. (8)

warrant A written order from a court directing law enforcement officers to conduct a search or to arrest a person. (4)

workhouses European forerunners of the modern U.S. prison, where offenders were sent to learn discipline and regular work habits. (10)

writ of *certiorari* A written order, from the U.S. Supreme Court to a lower court whose decision is being appealed, to send the records of the case forward for review. (8)

writ of *habeas corpus* An order from a court to an officer of the law to produce a prisoner in court to determine whether the prisoner is being legally detained or imprisoned. (8)

Photo Credits

Table of Contents

p. viiiT: © Stephen Chernin/Getty Images; p. viiiM: © AFP Photo/Seth McAllister/Corbis; p. viiiB: © Tony Savino/Corbis Sygma; p. ixT: © Henry Barrios/Corbis; p. ixM: © D. Boone/Corbis; p. ixE: © Bob Daemmrich/PhotoEdit; p. xT: © Corbis; p. xM: © Rich Meyer/Corbis; p. xB: © Mark M. Lawrence/Corbis; p. xiT: © Al Seib-Pool/Getty Images; p. xiM: © John Neubauer/PhotoEdit; p. xiB: © Darren McCollester/Getty Images; p. xiiT: © Pat Sullivan/AP Photo/Wide World; p. xiiM: © Corbis; p. xiiB: © Ed Kashi/Corbis; p. xiiiT: © Jeff Greenberg/The Image Works; p. xiiiM: © Mike Fiala/Getty Images; p. xiiiB: © Joel Gordon; p. xiv: © The Kobal Collection.

Chapter 1

p. 1TL: © AFP Photo/Seth McAllister/Corbis; p. 1TR: © Tony Savino/Corbis Sygma; p. 1BL: © Henry Barrios/Corbis; p. 1BR: © D. Boone/Corbis; p. 2: © AFP Photo/Seth McAllister/Corbis; p. 6L: © AFP Photo/ Tariq MAHMOOD/Corbis; p. 6M: © AFP Photo/POOL/Jahi Chikwendiu/Corbis; p. 6R: © REUTERS/Mike Blake/Corbis; p. 7: © Richard Lord/The Image Works; p. 13: © Joel Gordon; p. 15: © A. Ramey/PhotoEdit; p. 18: © Elaine Thompson/AP Photo/Wide World; p. 21L: © Bettmann/Corbis; p. 21R: © REUTERS/Jim Bourg-Files/Corbis; p. 23: © Giraudon/Bridgeman Art Library; p. 25: © Stephen Chernin/Getty Images.

Chapter 2

p. 28: © Tony Savino/Corbis Sygma; p. 32: © Getty Images; p. 33: © Kim Kulish/Corbis; p. 35L: © Jeffrey Markowitz/Corbis Sygma; p. 35R: © Jeffrey Markowitz/Corbis Sygma; p. 39: © Michael Macor/Corbis; p. 41: © AP Photo/Mike Meadows/Wide World; p. 47: © Jose Luis Pelaez, Inc./Corbisp. 49: © AP Photo/Pablo Marteniz Monsivais/Wide World; p. 52: ©Syracuse Newspapers/The Image Works; p. 54: © Greg Smith/Corbis; p. 57: Courtesy of Dori de Jong; p. 60: © Bob Daemmrich.

Chapter 3

p. 62: © Henry Barrios/Corbis; p. 68: © Bettmann/Corbis; p. 69: © U.S. Attorney's Office/Wide World; p. 71: Courtesy of Alida Merlo; p. 73BL: © Elizabeth Barrett/Taxi/Getty Images; p. 73BM: © PhotoDisc/Getty Images; p. 73R: © Image Source Limited/Index Stock Imagery; p. 77: © Bettmann/Corbis; p. 78: © Reuters NewMedia Inc./Corbis; p. 81: © Art Archive; p. 82: © Marc Asnin/Corbis Saba; p. 84: © A. Ramey/PhotoEdit; p. 87: © Jonathan Drake/Reuters NewMedia Inc./Corbis; p. 91L: © The Image Works; p. 91R: © A. Ramey/PhotoEdit; p. 93: © Vince Mannino/Corbis; p. w96: © AFP Photo/Bert Maprangala/Corbis; p. 100: © James Marshall/The Image Works.

Chapter 4

p. 102: © D. Boone/Corbis; p. 108: © Charles Walker/Topfoto/The Image Works; p. 109: © Bettmann/Corbis; p. 110: © CSPAN via APTN/AP Photo/Wide World; p. 111: © Syracuse Newspapers/Kevin Jacobus/The Image Works; p. 114L: © Diana Walker/Liaison/Getty Images; p. 114M: © Bruce Hoertel/Liaison/Getty Images; p. 114R: © AP Photos/Wide World; p. 115: © Charles Bennett/Wide World; p. 123L: © Mark Richards/PhotoEdit; p. 123M: © Bettmann/Corbis; p. 123R: © Daniel Sheehan/Liaison Agency/Newsmakers/Getty Images; p. 127: © Stephen Jaffe/AFP Photo/Corbis; p. 129: Courtesy of Junior A. Barrett; p. 133: © Bettmann/Corbis; p. 134: Courtesy of Renee Daniel; p. 136 © David Leeson/Dallas Morning News/The Image Works; p. 141: © Corbis.

Chapter 5

p. 143TL: © Corbis; p. 143TR: © Rich Meyer/Corbis; p. 143B: © Mark M. Lawrence/Corbis; p. 144: © Corbis; p. 147: © Bill Bachmann/The Image Works; p. 149: © Topham/Fotomas/The Image Work; p. 152: © Corbis; p. 153: © Bettmann/Corbis; p. 154: © ANA/The Image Works; p. 155: Texas Rangers Hall of Fame; p. 157: © AP Photo/Bill Hudson/Wide World; p. 160: © Hussein Akhtar/Sygma/Corbis; p. 163: © David Young-Wolff/PhotoEdit; p. 168: © Chet Gordon/The Image Works; p. 170: © Evy Mages/Reuters NewMedia Inc./Corbis; p. 175: © A. Ramey/PhotoEdit; p. 175: © Mike Segar/Reuters NewMedia/Corbis; p. 179: © Corbis; p. 180: © David McNew/Getty Images; p. 182: Courtesy of Jose Pagan; p. 186: © Bob Daemmrich/PhotoEdit.

Chapter 6

p. 188: © Rich Meyer/Corbis; p. 191: © Spencer Ainsley/The Image Works; p. 197: © Joseph Sohm; ChromoSohm Inc./Corbis; p. 200: © Spencer Grant/Photo Researchers; p. 203: © Bettmann/Corbis; p. 206: © Corbis; p. 208: © Corbis; p. 210: © Syracuse Newspapers/The Image Works; p. 213: © Tony Savino/The Image Works; p. 214: © Tom Carter/PhotoEdit; p. 216: © Bernd Obermann/Corbis; p. 217: © Bob Daemmrich; p. 218: © Courtesy of Brenda Sue Collins; p. 219: © AFP/Corbis; p. 226: © Johnny Crawford/The Image Works.

Chapter 7

p. 228: © Mark M. Lawrence/Corbis; p. 231: © David McNew/Getty Images; p. 232: © Bob Daemmrich; p. 235: Courtesy of Robert Bour; p. 236: © Bob Daemmrich; p. 237: © Bob Daemmrich/The Image Works; p. 240: © Sandy Felsenthal/Corbis; p. 241: © Reuters/Brendan McDermid/Corbis; p. 243: © Michael Newman/PhotoEdit; p. 245: © Doug Martin; p. 248: © Spencer Grant/PhotoEdit; p. 250: © Joel Gordon; p. 252: © Ralf-Finn Hestoft/Corbis; p. 253: © Mitchell Crooks/Getty Images; p. 257: © Melanie Einzig /Getty Images; p. 261: © Philadelphia Daily News/Jim MacMillan/The Image Works.

Chapter 8

p. 263T: © John Neubauer/PhotoEdit; p. 263B: © Darren McCollester/Getty Images; p. 264: © John Neubauer/PhotoEdit;

p. 269: © John Gaps III/AP Photo/Wide World; p. 270: © Paul Sakuma/Pool/Reuters NewMedia Inc./Corbis; p. 272: Courtesy of The Supreme Court Historical Society; p. 274: Courtesy of Todd Nuccio; p. 275: © Reuters NewMedia Inc./Corbis; p. 277: © Bettmann/Corbis; p. 279: Courtesy of Wilson Green; p. 280: © Ed Andrieski/AP Photo/Wide World; p. 281: © REUTERS/Jim Ruymen/Corbis; p. 285L: © Joe Skipper/ Reuters NewMedia Inc./Corbis; p. 285M: © Garth Dowling/Liaison/Getty Images; p. 285R: © Dan Groshong/Reuters NewMedia Inc./Corbis; p. 287: © Shelley Gazin/Corbis; p. 289: © Syracuse Newspapers/ The Image Works; p. 294: © Mary Kate Denny/PhotoEdit; p. 303: © Lawrence Jackson/AP Photo/Wide World; p. 307: © Al Seib-Pool/Getty Images.

Chapter 9

p. 308: © Darren McCollester/Getty Images; p. 312: © Damian Dovarganes/AP Photo/ Wide World; p. 319: © David Woo/Stock Boston; p. 321: © Bettmann/Corbis; p. 323: © Reuters NewMedia Inc./Corbis; p. 324: © Bob Daemmrich/The Image Works; p. 325: Courtesy of Debora Randolph; p. 326: © Dee Marvin/AP Photo/ Wide World; p. 329: © Jon Freeman/Getty Images; p. 330: © Greg Smith/Corbis SABA; p. 331: © Douglas C. Pizac/AP Photo/Wide World; p. 336: © Shepard Sherbell/Corbis SABA; p. 341: © REUTERS/Jim Bourg/Corbis; p. 344: © Steve Grayson-Pool/ Getty Images.

Chapter 10

p. 347TL: © Corbis; p. 347TR: © Ed Kashi/Corbis; p. 347B: © James Nuble/The Image Works; p. 348: © Corbis; p. 352: © Bettmann/Corbis; p. 354: © Chicago Sun-Times, Richard A. Chapman/AP Photo/Wide World; p. 355: © Bettmann/Corbis; p. 356: © The News Tribune, Julie Smith/AP Photo/Wide World; p. 357: © Lennox McLendon/AP Photo/Wide World; p. 366: © Mark Peterson/Corbis; p. 367: © AFP Photo/Tannen Maury/ Corbis; p. 371: © Phil Degginger/H. Armstrong Roberts; p. 372: © Petty Officer 1st class Shane T. McCoy/U.S. Navy/Getty Images; p. 378: © Andrew Lichenstein/Corbis Sygma; p. 379: © Marilyn Humphries; p. 380: Courtesy of Federal Bureau of Prisons; p. 383: Courtesy of Pat Bryant; p. 383: © Mathew McVay/Stock Boston; p. 384: © Joel Gordon; p. 389: © Bob Daemmrich/The Image Works; p. 393: © Pat Sullivan/AP Photo/Wide World.

Chapter 11

p. 394: © Ed Kashi/Corbis; p. 398: © P. F. Bently/Black Star; p. 399: © The Wheeling News Register, Scott McCloskey/AP Photo/Wide World; p. 400: © Arthur Grace/Stock Boston; p. 401: © Patti Longmire/AP Photo/Wide World; p. 402: © Bill Gentile/Corbis; p. 403: © Sean Cayton/The Image Works; p. 405: © A. Ramey/PhotoEdit; p. 406: Courtesy of Pietro DeSantis II; p. 409: © Bob Daemmrich/Corbis Sygma; p. 410: Courtesy of Commissioner Epps; p. 412: © Joe Raedle/Getty Images; p. 413: © David Woo/Stock Boston; p. 415: © Jim Cole/AP Photo/Wide World; p. 420: © The Kobal Collection.

Chapter 12

p. 422: © James Nuble/The Image Works; p. 426: © Janet Hostetter/AP Photo/Wide World; p. 427: Courtesy of Steve E. Whisenant; p. 429: © Mary Kate Denny/PhotoEdit; p. 432: © Joel Gordon; p. 438: © A. Ramey/Woodfin Camp & Associates; p. 441: Courtesy of Arthur J. Ramirez; p. 442: © Spencer Tirey/ AP Photo/Wide World; p. 446: © Bob Daemmrich; p. 454: © Bob Daemmrich; p. 456: © John Boykin/PhotoEdit; p. 459: © A.Ramey/PhotoEdit; p. 460: © Bob Daemmrich; p. 463: © Rick Weber; p. 467: © Jeff Greenberg/The Image Works; p. 470: © Bob Daemmrich.

Chapter 13

p. 471T: © Joel Gordon; p. 471B: © The Kobal Collection; p. 472: © Joel Gordon; p. 475: © Public Record Office/Topham-HIP/The Image Works; p. 477: © Bettmann/Corbis; p. 478L: Photo by Indiana Department of Corrections/Courtesy of ACA; p. 478R: Courtesy of ACA; p. 481: © Joel Gordon; p. 483: © Bettmann/ Corbis; p. 486: © Dorothy Littel Greco/The Image Works; p. 487: © Daniel Wray/The Image Works; p. 494: © Richard Sheinwald/ AP Photo/Wide World; p. 496: © Bob Daemmrich/Stock Boston; p. 497: Courtesy of Kelly Webster; p. 501: © Kenneth Murray/ Photo Researchers; p. 502: © Richard Lord/The Image Works; p. 504: © Will Shilling/AP Photo/Wide World; p. 505: © Joel Gordon; p. 511: © Mike Fiala/Getty Images.

Chapter 14

p. 514: © The Kobal Collection; p. 519: © Richard T. Nowitz/ Corbis; p. 520: © Bob Self/AP Photo/Wide World Photo; p. 522: © Ed Andrieski-Pool/Getty Images; p. 524: © Bob Daemmrich/ The Image Works; p. 525: © Jeff Robbins/AP Photo/Wide World; p. 526: Courtesy of Donald J.Haldemann; p. 529: © Douglas C.Pizac/Getty Images; p. 530: © Lizzie Himmel/Corbis; p. 532: © Jeff Topping/Getty Images; p. 536: © Rogelio Solis/AP Photo/Wide World; p. 544: © Lenny Ignelzi/AP Photo/Wide World; p. 547: © The Kobal Collection

Case Index

Subject Index